Marketing Scales Handbook

A Compilation of Multi-Item Measures

Marketing Scales Handbook

A Compilation of Multi-Item Measures

Gordon C. Bruner II   •   Paul J. Hensel

American Marketing Association
Chicago, Illinois USA

Library of Congress Cataloging-in-Publication Data
Bruner, Gordon C., 1954-
    Marketing scales handbook: a compilation of multi-item measures /
Gordon C. Bruner II and Paul J. Hensel.
        p.   cm
    Includes index.
    ISBN 0-87757-226-7
    1. Marketing research—Statistical methods—Handbooks, manuals,
etc. 2 Scaling (Social sciences)—Handbooks, manuals, etc.
    I. Hensel, Paul J. II. Title
    HF5415.3.B785   1992
    658.8'3028—dc20   92-18858
                                                         CIP

Published by American Marketing Association
250 S Wacker Drive
Chicago, Illinois 60606, U S A
Jeffrey Heilbrunn, President
Rick Kean, Publisher
Francesca Van Gorp, Editor
Emily McNamara, Copy editor

Contents

· · · · · · · · · · ·

115723

Acknowledgments

· ·

Work on this book began in the fall of 1987 and continued until the summer of 1992 and, as awkward as it may be to admit, in many ways it was a "labor of love." By that we mean that the book was neither written under the delusion of obtaining a large economic return nor because we were carrying out the mandate of a professional association. In fact, most publishers were not interested in this book at all and, except for the limited funding we found within our university, our requests for grants went unheeded. That is why it is important now to express in writing our gratitude to the individuals and organizations that did support us in some way in accomplishing this task.

First, we thank the researchers who developed and/or reported using the scales that are included here. Without their research and publication activity this book would not have been possible. Extra appreciation is expressed to those who responded to our request for more information.

Many organizations and individuals spoke well about this project but were unwilling to help bring it to market. Our thanks are extended to those that stepped forward and lent a helping hand. The greatest financial support came from the **Office of Research and Development Administration** at **SIU**, which funded a doctoral candidate to work with us on this project for a three-year period. We acknowledge the **College of Business and Administration** at **SIU** as well as the **Pontikes Center for Management of Information** for providing financial support and counseling, the latter of which will be most useful as the computer-addressable version of this database is developed.

We are grateful to Jeffrey Heilbrunn of AMA for providing words of encouragement during the early stages of our work. His assurance to us in the summer of 1990 that AMA would publish and market the book came at just the right time. It would have been very difficult to engage in the incredible amount of work we did in late 1990 and the first half of 1991 if we had not known that publication was likely. Our gratitude is also extended to Francesca Van Gorp and her assistants at AMA who have been intimately involved this past year in getting the manuscript into publishable form.

We would certainly be remiss if we overlooked the support we received from the Marketing Department at SIU. We appreciate the help routinely received form the department's secretaries: Sharon Harward, Janice Fry, and Tammy Broida. Dr. Clifton Andersen was quite helpful and saw to it that we had plenty of graduate assistants. Among the graduate assistants, Linda Puryear Stout and Scott Thorne deserve special mention, as do several doctoral candidates who worked on the project, namely Cal Berkey, Mark Hill, Shelly Verma, John Drea, and Tanuja Srivastava. Finally, Hemant (Rusty) Rustogi and Letty Workman were the two doctoral candidates who successively ran the **Office of Scale Research** during the last four years and were intimately involved in the day-to-day operations. We were quite dependent on them and extend our thanks for their hard work and dedication.

Last but not least, we thank our families for putting up with the drain on our time and attention, particularly during the last year of manuscript preparation. We trust that our efforts on the project were not too demanding given that each of our families has grown by one in the past year.

Gordon C. Bruner II
Southern Illinois University

Paul J. Hensel
University of New Orleans

July 1992

Introduction

. . . .

During the course of our academic careers we, like so many others, have wanted to engage in research using multi-item, summated ratings scales to measure marketing-related constructs. More recently we have recognized the need for some central source for these measures to aid doctoral students in their dissertation research. Up until now the conscientious researcher would either perform a tedious literature review in search of appropriate scales or would instead have to engage in the equally tedious job of scale development.

Others in the past decade have been sensing the time was right for something like what has been produced here. For example, 21 of the country's largest advertising agencies addressed inadequacies in the present state of copy testing (Yuspeh 1982). Among the problems they noted was the use of single versus multiple measures to assess the performance of ads and the failure to empirically validate the measures being used. Another problem was identified by the AMA Task Force on the Development of Marketing Thought (1988). It indicated that one reason for the insufficient communication between the developers and the users of marketing information is that the research conducted in academia is reported in scholarly journals that are largely unread by practitioners.

Therefore, this sort of handbook has been needed in our field for some time, but appears to be particularly welcomed in the 1990s. Scale development and use in marketing research though somewhat limited during the 1970s, increased dramatically in the 1980s. Therefore, after a decade of heavy scale use, the job of compiling those uses did appear to be overwhelming. In fact, some organizations approached for support thought it was a worthwhile goal but one that could not be accomplished. Luckily, we were not overly discouraged by their lack of support and set our minds on seeing the project through, as discussed elsewhere (Bruner and Hensel 1990; Hensel, Bruner, and Berkey 1990).

However, we did have to set limits on what we would attempt to do in a first edition. The two major limits had to do with the domain of published literature we would review: time frame and number of journals. We decided to cover the 10-year period from 1980 to 1989 for seven marketing-related journals: **Journal of Marketing, Journal of Marketing Research, Journal of Consumer Research, Journal of the Academy of Marketing Science, Journal of Advertising, Journal of Advertising**

Research, and **Industrial Marketing Management.** Our logic was that if scales were of reasonable quality and relevance they would have been reported in one of these journals. Ultimately, **Industrial Marketing Management** was dropped from the domain because so few articles reported the use of scales and most of the scales were already being reported in another journal in the domain. Admittedly, there are two or three other journals that we would have liked to cover. We plan to include them in future revisions.

Not every scale that was used and discussed in the domain was written up. Scales were included only if sufficient information was available from known published sources or we were able to get necessary information from authors. The most critical information we required for including scales was the items themselves and an indication of reliability. We focused our efforts on simple multi-item scales, typically of the Likert or semantic differential variety. Also, preference was given to measures with three or more items. Though some two-item scales are included here, they are primarily from articles that used other, longer scales as well. So, if some scales appear to be missing it may be because they were too short or we were not able to secure enough critical information.

Of course, there may be some innocent oversights as well. We suspect that errors and misstatements are present and will be found by users. We encourage people to let us know about them because we will make corrections for future printings and editions. For example, reverse coding of items where necessary is a very important process and one to which we have been sensitive. However, indications of reverse coding were not always presented in the articles, books, or correspondence consulted to get the items. Therefore, we had to use some judgment. **We urge users of any scale presented in this handbook to examine the items and independently determine through logical if not statistical means whether or not reverse coding is necessary.**

What to call scales was a problem. Our guiding goals were consistency and clarity. Researchers have not been consistent in referring to the same constructs with the same names and in many cases the names appeared to us to be very awkward if not misleading. So, we took it upon ourselves to look at every use of the scale, examine its items, compare it with names of measures of similar constructs, and then give it a name. We tried to make the names short and to have the first word or two provide the general idea of the construct being measured. In many cases descriptors were put at the end of scale names to indicate their specific applications; e.g., Opinion Leadership (Clothing).

The majority of the write-ups are at the "scale" level rather than the "use" or "construct" level. Consequently, for many constructs we report multiple scales and for many scales we report multiple uses. Where there were multiple uses of the same scale, they were written up together so the reader can easily determine most of what is known about the scale's psychometric characteristics and use in research. Because in many cases similar though not exactly the same versions of scales were used in more than one study, our rule of thumb was to write up scale uses together if the measures shared half or more of the items in common.

The major exception to this rule is for attitude toward the ad, brand, and product scales. These write-ups include discussions of a variety of different scales that appear to measure the same construct but may not have items in common. This approach seemed to be the most parsimonious way to present these commonly assessed constructs that have been measured numerous ways.

We attempted in many cases to contact authors when the information available in known published sources was insufficient to fully describe a scale. We wrote to some authors two or three times, urging them to share the information with us so their work could be included and accurately reported. Though many were eager to comply, others chose not to. If possible, we still included the nonresponding authors' work, but in many cases critical information was lacking and we reluctantly decided to eliminate discussion of scale usage by those authors.

The write-ups are mostly descriptive, but we made some evaluation of quality as well. Though we tried not to be too critical of a scale's quality, it would have been inappropriate for us not to provide some word of caution to novice users about a scale with poor psychometric characteristics. If anything, we held back from making more negative comments that are probably justified. **So, readers are urged to not rely exclusively on what we say about a scale, but to judge the quality of a measure by using whatever criteria are relevant to them.**

The format of the write-ups is, to the extent possible, constant. With two authors and numerous assistants, however, some variation may be noted. The write-ups take the general form illustrated in the table.

We provide several means to assist users in finding scales of interest. First, the Table of Contents lists every scale included in the book alphabetically by section. Also, there are two indexes. One consists of key words and synonyms related to the discussion of particular scales. The other is an author index listing names of researchers who are linked with the development and use of specific scales.

There was no one way to lay out this manual. Certainly major divisions could be made in the types of scales reported in the domain, but smaller subdivisions were more difficult to justify because many scales could relate to more than one area. Ultimately, we decided on three major groupings: consumer behavior-related scales, salesforce and organizational scales, and advertising-related scales. Measures within each major section are alphabetized for easy usage.

Finally, with the publication of this compilation, the time for developing or using "quick and dirty" scales out of ignorance or convenience should be past. Previously researchers commonly used whatever scales were convenient to use and not necessarily the ones most appropriate and psychometrically sound for a situation. Too many times yet another scale was developed when several "good" ones were already available. Our intent is to make it considerably easier for researchers to determine whether a measure exists and, if more than one exists, to provide the information from which a logical selection can be made.

By funneling the efforts of academia into industry, we hope to make the practical applications of the former more obvious to the latter. We trust that it is not too naive to hope that as researchers make better use of scales, the quality of market research will ultimately improve.

REFERENCES

AMA Task Force on the Development of Marketing Thought (1988), "Developing, Disseminating, and Utilizing Marketing Knowledge," *Journal of Marketing*, 52 (October), 1-25.

Bruner, Gordon C., II, and Paul J. Hensel (1990), "University Develops Data Base of Psychometric Scales," *Marketing News*, 24 (July 23), 10.

Hensel, Paul J., Gordon C. Bruner II, and Calvin J. Berkey (1990), "Towards the Compilation and Critical Assessment of Psychometric Scales Reported in Marketing Research," in *Proceedings of the Southern Marketing Association*, 33-334.

Yuspeh, Sonia (1982), "PACT," *Journal of Advertising*, 11 (4), 3-29.

Table
Description of Scale Write-Up Format

SCALE NAME: A short, descriptive name of the construct being measured.

SCALE DESCRIPTION: A sentence or two describing the physical structure of the measure(s) and the psychological construct apparently being assessed. The number of items, the number of points on the scale, and its Likert or semantic differential type are typically specified. If significantly different names were used by authors of articles, they are usually noted here.

SCALE ORIGIN: Some limited information is given about the creation of the scale if developed prior to 1980 or if its origination was first published in a source not covered in the handbook's domain. Most of the scales originated in one article in the domain and were not known to have been used again. If so, that is stated here. If prior use is known, it is discussed.

SAMPLES: For all known uses of the scale in the domain, separate descriptions are provided of their samples, limited in most cases to what was available in the journal articles. Sample size is provided in almost every case and some information about subject characteristics and study designs is given in many cases.

RELIABILITY: For the most part, reliability is described in terms of Chronbach's alpha, a measure of internal consistency. If available, other issues related to reliability are mentioned as well, such as item-total correlations and test-retest correlations.

VALIDITY: The validity section was among the most difficult to write. For vast majority of scale uses in the domain, the authors did not report examining validity at all. Some simply performed factor analyses, which may offer some limited evidence of discriminant or convergent validity for scale items. In rare cases, scale authors made greater effort to assess convergent or construct validity through use of correlation matrices. In some instances the nomological or face validity of scales could be commented upon even if scale authors provided little or no other information.

ADMINISTRATION: This section describes the manner in which a scale was administered to a sample. In the overwhelming majority of cases, scales were of the paper-and-pencil variety and were part of self-administered questionnaires. In many instances the meaning of scale scores is described as well.

MAJOR FINDINGS: A brief discussion of the results associated with a scale, study by study, is given in this section. Though the information offers the reader an idea of previous research findings related to a specific scale, it is not intended to replace a thorough review of the relevant literature.

COMMENTS: This field is not always used. Occasionally something significant was observed in writing up a scale that we felt should be pointed out to readers. If the psychometric characteristics of a scale were judged to be poor, that observation is mentioned. Also, when insufficient information was available for fully describing some scale uses, they are cited here as "see also."

REFERENCES: Every source other than personal correspondence that is noted in the write-up is cited here in the *Journal of Marketing* style. Also, we use the following abbreviations for the six primary journals from which scales were taken.

Journal of Marketing = JM
Journal of Marketing Research = JMR
Journal of Consumer Research = JCR
Journal of the Academy of Marketing Science = JAMS
Journal of Advertising = JA
Journal of Advertising Research = JAR

Titles of other journals and sources noted in the write-up of scales are cited less frequently and are written out in full.

SCALE ITEMS: The scale items used in published research are listed here, as are the directions for administering the scale, if known. Also, in most cases we indicate the graphic scale used to record responses to items. Where an item is marked **(r)**, the numerical response to the item should be reverse coded in calculating scale scores. Other idiosyncrasies may be noted as well. For example, when different versions of the same scale are discussed in the same write-up, we indicate which items were used in particular studies.

About the Authors

Dr. Gordon C. Bruner II is an Associate Professor and Director of the office of Scale Research in the Marketing Department at Southern Illinois University. He received his B.B.A. and M.S. degrees in Marketing from Texas A&M University and graduated in 1983 from the University of North Texas with a Ph.D. in Marketing. Prior to his focus on scales research, consumer decisionmaking was his main area of study. Bruner's articles have been published in the *Journal of Marketing, Journal of Marketing Education, Journal of Consumer Marketing, Journal of Retailing, Journal of the Academy of Marketing Science, Journal of Personal Selling and Sales Management* as well as several other journals and conference proceedings.

Dr. Paul J. Hensel is an Associate Dean in the College of Business at the University of New Orleans. He received his Bachelor's degree in Communications from the University of Illinois, his MBA from Southern Illinois University, and his Ph.D. from the University of Houston. Prior to his present position, he taught marketing courses at the University of Kentucky and Southern Illinois University. His interest in scaling and measurement began during his years in the military where he taught statistical process control for the U.S.A.F. His research interests beyond scaling and measurement include advertising, particularly, political and negative messages and various ethical issues in marketing and business. Hensel has authored or co-authored over 30 articles in academic and practitioner based publications.

Part I

Consumer Behavior Scales

Table of Contents
· · · · · · · · · · · · · · · · ·

SCALE NAME: Activity (Stimulus)

SCALE DESCRIPTION:

A three-item, seven-point semantic differential summated ratings scale measuring the perceived "activity" of a stimulus.

SCALE ORIGIN:

These or similar items were used and reported by Holbrook in several articles published in the early 1980s. They bear similarity to items found in the classic work of Osgood, Suci, and Tannenbaum (1957). After examining a wide variety of judgmental situations, the latter authors reported that the same three major factors were found repeatedly: evaluation, potency, and activity. The activity dimension was most associated with the "quickness, excitement, warmth, agitation" and related aspects of a stimulus (pp. 72, 73). The activity factor also was rather consistently found to account for half as much variance as the evaluation factor. Though the validity of the activity factor was discussed in the book, the psychometric properties of a particular scale were not tested.

SAMPLES:

Analysis by Holbrook (1981) was based on **16** subjects chosen from volunteers with an interest in classical piano music. Half had never played an instrument but enjoyed listening to such music ("nonexperts") and the other half were highly trained musicians ("experts").

RELIABILITY:

An alpha of **.59** was reported for the scale.

VALIDITY:

Beyond the observation that the items loaded together in a factor analysis, no specific examination of scale validity was reported.

ADMINISTRATION:

In both studies, subjects self-administered the scale along with several other measures. Higher summated scores suggest that respondents perceive a lot of activity in an object whereas lower scores mean that they do not perceive the object to be active.

MAJOR FINDINGS:

Holbrook (1981) illustrated a two-stage integrative model of evaluative judgment in which objective product features influenced perceptions, which in turn shaped affect. Specifically, he found that the direct effects of objective music characteristics on affect were not nearly as large or as significant as the indirect effects of those features through intervening perceptions. Perceived expressiveness, **activity**, and complexity had significant positive influences on affect, perceived novelty had a significant negative impact, and perceived potency did not make a salient contribution. Of the musical features examined, tempo was the largest determinant of perceived **activity.**

COMMENTS:

Though the items apparently loaded together in a factor analysis, the low internal consistency suggests that the scale is not very stable. Also, two of the items (heavy/light, serious/humorous) were most associated with the potency factor in the work of Osgood, Suci, and Tannenbaum (1957, pp. 37, 69). It is not clear why they were identified here as measuring the activity factor. Development and testing are certainly needed before this scale is used in anything other than exploratory research.

REFERENCES:

Holbrook, Morris B. (1981), "Integrating Compositional and Decompositional Analyses to Represent the Intervening Role of Perceptions in Evaluative Judgments," *JMR*, 18 (February), 13-28.

Osgood, Charles E., George J. Suci, and Percy H. Tannenbaum (1957), *The Measurement of Meaning*. Urbana, Ill.: University of Illinois Press.

SCALE ITEMS: ACTIVITY (STIMULUS)

serious	___ : ___ : ___ : ___ : ___ : ___ : ___	humorous
	1 2 3 4 5 6 7	

slow	___ : ___ : ___ : ___ : ___ : ___ : ___	fast
	1 2 3 4 5 6 7	

heavy	___ : ___ : ___ : ___ : ___ : ___ : ___	light
	1 2 3 4 5 6 7	

SCALE NAME: Affect (General)

SCALE DESCRIPTION:

> A four-item, seven-point, bipolar adjective, summated ratings scale measuring the degree to which one likes some stimulus and perceives it to be "good." Leigh (1984) used these items and four more of his own in a modified Likert-like format.

SCALE ORIGIN:

> These or similar items were used and reported by Holbrook in several articles published in the early 1980s. They bear similarity to items found in the classic work of Osgood, Suci, and Tannenbaum (1957) to measure the "evaluative" dimension of a stimulus. After examining a wide variety of judgmental situations, the latter authors reported that the same three major factors were found repeatedly: evaluation, potency, and activity. They also rather consistently found that the evaluation factor appeared first and accounted for half or more of the extractable variance. Though the validity of the factor was discussed in the book, the psychometric properties of a particular scale were not tested.

SAMPLES:

> Analysis by Holbrook (1981) was based on **16** subjects chosen from volunteers with an interest in classical piano music. Half had never played an instrument but enjoyed listening to such music ("nonexperts") and the other half were highly trained musicians ("experts"). The study by Leigh (1984) was based on data from **240** college students taking an introductory marketing course but not in a section taught by the researcher. Participation in the experiment was compensated by partial course credit. The experimental sessions were conducted with 10 to 30 subjects in a nonclassroom location. Holbrook's (1986) subjects were **42** male and **22** female MBA candidates in a marketing course who were required to respond to the questionnaire.

RELIABILITY:

> Alpha values of **.94** and **.95** were reported for the scale by Holbrook (1981 and 1986, respectively). Leigh's (1984) modified version of the scale was reported to have an alpha of **.83**.

VALIDITY:

> Beyond the observation that the items loaded together in a factor analysis (Holbrook 1981), no specific examination of scale validity was reported in the studies. Leigh (1984) reported no examination of scale validity.

ADMINISTRATION:

> In each of the studies, subjects self-administered the scale along with several other measures. If a scale is used with numbers 1 to 7, lower summated scores suggest that respondents have a positive affect toward some specific object whereas higher scores mean that they do not like it or do not feel it is good.

MAJOR FINDINGS:

Holbrook (1981) illustrated a two-stage integrative model of evaluative judgment in which objective product features influenced perceptions, which in turn shaped **affect**. Specifically, he found that the direct effects of objective music characteristics on **affect** were not nearly as large or as significant as the indirect effects of those features through intervening perceptions. Perceived expressiveness, activity, and complexity had significant positive influences on **affect**, perceived novelty had a significant negative impact, and perceived potency did not make a salient contribution.

The purpose of Leigh's (1984) study was to examine the influence of family branding and number of products included on the effectiveness of "umbrella" advertising (referring in an ad to several products that are linked together in some way). Ads with 11 products in them were found to be evaluated more positively (**affect**) than those with either five or eight products in them.

The roles of certain personality variables and gender were studied by Holbrook (1986). He illustrated a method using canonical correlation analysis to examine individual differences in **affect** for clothing design features. In general, the canonical correlation analysis indicated different **affective** responses for visualizing and verbalizing men and women. (See the article for more specific findings.)

COMMENTS:

See also Holbrook and Moore (1981), who measured this construct with similar items but used factor scores rather than a simple sum.

REFERENCES:

Holbrook, Morris B. (1981), "Integrating Compositional and Decompositional Analyses to Represent the Intervening Role of Perceptions in Evaluative Judgments, *JMR*, 18 (February), 13-28.

———— (1986), "Aims, Concepts, and Methods for the Representation of Individual Differences in Esthetic Responses to Design Features," *JCR*, 13 (December), 337-347.

———— and William L. Moore (1981), "Feature Interactions in Consumer Judgments of Verbal Versus Pictorial Presentations," *JCR*, 8 (June), 103-113.

Leigh, James H. (1984), "Recall and Recognition Performance for Umbrella Print Advertisements," *JA*, 13 (4), 5-18, 30.

Osgood, Charles E., George J. Suci, and Percy H. Tannenbaum (1957), *The Measurement of Meaning*. Urbana, Ill.: University of Illinois Press.

SCALE ITEMS: AFFECT (GENERAL) +

1. I like it ____ : ____ : ____ : ____ : ____ : ____ : ____ I dislike it
          1   2   3   4   5   6   7

2. Good ____ : ____ : ____ : ____ : ____ : ____ : ____ Bad*
          1   2   3   4   5   6   7

3. Beautiful ____ : ____ : ____ : ____ : ____ : ____ : ____ Ugly*
          1   2   3   4   5   6   7

4. Pleasing* ____ : ____ : ____ : ____ : ____ : ____ : ____ Displeasing
               1   2   3   4   5   6   7

5. Enjoyable* ____ : ____ : ____ : ____ : ____ : ____ : ____ Not enjoyable
               1   2   3   4   5   6   7

+ Holbrook used items 1 through 4 (1986) and items 2 through 5 (1981).

* Leigh (1984) used these four terms (not the pairs) as well as the following terms: meaningful, informative, interesting, and valuable. The scale ranged from "does not describe at all" to "describes very well."

SCALE NAME: Affect (Music)

SCALE DESCRIPTION:

A nine-item, six-point, bipolar adjective, summated ratings scale measuring the degree to which one likes some stimulus and perceives it to be "good." Obermiller (1985) used a three-item subset of this scale. All of the studies reported here used the scale with musical stimuli, but it could be used for other stimuli as well.

SCALE ORIGIN:

The items were among a group of 93 generated by Holbrook and Huber (1979). The stimuli in their study were jazz recordings and the purpose was to examine different methods of extracting affective bias from perceptions and attitudes, particularly in the area of consumer aesthetics. Data were collected from 16 subjects responding to bulletin board ads at Columbia University. Each subject expressed a strong interest in jazz and was paid $5 for participating. Eight of the 93 items were found to have high correlations ($-.70 < r > +.70$) with the bad/good item. Scores of these nine items were summed to create a global measure of affective evaluation. An alpha of **.95** was reported for the scale. An indication of the scale's validity was given by the high average intra-individual correlation between scale scores and preference rankings of the jazz recordings ($r = .80$).

SAMPLES:

Dillon, Mulani, and Frederick (1984) reanalyzed the data used by Holbrook and Huber (1979) described above. Obermiller (1985) used **155** undergraduates at the University of Washington. They were randomly grouped and assigned to experimental treatments.

RELIABILITY:

Dillon, Mulani, and Frederick (1984) reanalyzed the data used by Holbrook and Huber (1979) described above. Obermiller (1985) calculated alpha for 16 short tone sequences and it ranged from **.70** to **.85**.

VALIDITY:

Dillon, Mulani, and Frederick (1984) reanalyzed the data used by Holbrook and Huber (1979) described above. No examination of scale validity was reported by Obermiller (1985).

ADMINISTRATION:

The scale was self-administered along with other measures in both datasets. High scores on the scale suggest that respondents like a particular musical stimulus (e.g., jazz recording) and low scores imply that respondents do not like a stimulus or do not feel that it is good.

MAJOR FINDINGS:

Building on the work of Holbrook and Huber (1979) and using the same data, Dillon, Mulani, and Frederick (1984) illustrated another means of removing distortion in perceptual judgments. The method they proposed involved a two-step double-centering transformation. In essence this procedure shifts the means of the observations as well as the variables to the same value. The authors imply that their method is superior because it does not require data to be ignored, nor is it as arbitrary in transforming the data.

Obermiller (1985) tested two competing models of exposure effects by examining the impact of processing style on affect formation under repetition. The results failed to strongly support either theory. Though the results generally showed a significant association between **affective evaluation** and both the number of exposures and processing style, the mediating roles of confidence and familiarity suggested a more complex relationship between learning and liking than was expected.

COMMENTS:

Because the scale has been used only with music stimuli, some adjustment may be necessary if it is used with different stimuli.

REFERENCES:

Dillon, William R., Narendra Mulani, and Donald G. Frederick (1984), ''Removing Perceptual Distortion in Product Space Analysis,'' *JMR*, 11 (May), 184-193.

Holbrook, Morris B. and Joel Huber (1979), ''Separating Perceptual Dimensions from Affective Overtones: An Application to Consumer Aesthetics,'' *JCR*, 5 (March), 272-282.

Obermiller, Carl (1985), ''Varieties of Mere Exposure: The Effects of Processing Style and Repetition on Affective Response,'' *JCR*, 12 (June), 17-30.

SCALE ITEMS: AFFECT (MUSIC)

	1	2	3	4	5	6	
bad	___ :	___ :	___ :	___ :	___ :	___	good +
distasteful	___ :	___ :	___ :	___ :	___ :	___	tasty
untalented	___ :	___ :	___ :	___ :	___ :	___	talented
tasteless	___ :	___ :	___ :	___ :	___ :	___	tasteful
unimaginative	___ :	___ :	___ :	___ :	___ :	___	imaginative
dull	___ :	___ :	___ :	___ :	___ :	___	exciting
pleasant	___ :	___ :	___ :	___ :	___ :	___	unpleasant (r) +

memorable	___ : ___ : ___ : ___ : ___ : ___	forgetable **(r)**
	1 2 3 4 5 6	
interesting	___ : ___ : ___ : ___ : ___ : ___	boring **(r)**+
	1 2 3 4 5 6	

+ Items used by Obermiller (1985).

SCALE NAME: Age-Related Responsibility (Child)

SCALE DESCRIPTION:

A two-item, five-point Likert-type summated ratings scale measuring the degree to which a person (a parent) believes that a child should be "older" before being allowed to take on certain responsibilities alone. It was referred to as Fostering Responsibility by Carlson and Grossbart (1988).

SCALE ORIGIN:

Carlson and Grossbart (1988) indicate that they adapted a scale from previous work by Crosby and Grossbart (1984).

SAMPLES:

The survey instrument used by Carlson and Grossbart (1988) was distributed to mothers via students at three elementary schools in an unidentified U.S. city. The schools were chosen on a convenience basis but appeared to represent a variety of socioeconomic areas of the city. A $1 contribution to the PTO was offered for each completed questionnaire returned by the children. Analysis was based on **451** completed questionnaires. Ninety-three percent of the responding mothers indicated that they were the primary person in the child's socialization.

RELIABILITY:

Carlson and Grossbart (1988) reported an alpha of **.66** and a beta of .66 for the scale.

VALIDITY:

No examination of scale validity was reported by Carlson and Grossbart (1988).

ADMINISTRATION:

The scale was self-administered along with many other measures in the questionnaire used by Carlson and Grossbart (1988). Higher scores on the scale mean that parents strongly believe that children should be "older" before being allowed to take on certain responsibilities.

MAJOR FINDINGS:

The authors investigated the relationship between general parental socialization styles and children's consumer socialization. Of the five parental socialization style clusters examined, Rigid Controlling and Neglecting mothers expressed significantly greater willingness to allow younger children to take on **responsibility** than did the other three parental style clusters.

COMMENTS:

The low reliability of the scale is justification for cautious use. The addition of a few more appropriate items might improve its psychometric quality substantially.

REFERENCES:

Carlson, Les and Sanford Grossbart (1988), ''Parental Style and Consumer Socialization of Children,'' *JCR*, 15 (June), 77-94.

Crosby, Lawrence A. and Sanford L. Grossbart (1984), ''Parental Style Tendencies and Concern About Children's Advertising,'' in *Current Issues in Research in Advertising*, James H. Leigh and Claude R. Martin, Jr., eds. Ann Arbor, Mich.: Division of Research, Graduate School of Business Administration, University of Michigan, 43-63.

SCALE ITEMS: AGE-RELATED RESPONSIBILITY (CHILD) +

Strongly Disagree	Disagree	Neither	Agree	Strongly Agree
1————————	2————————	3————————	4————————	5

1. A child should be older before being allowed to go to a familiar grocery store alone.
2. A child should be older before being allowed to choose his or her own meal in the school cafeteria.
3. A child should be older before being allowed to cross a street with traffic lights alone.

+ The final version of the scale apparently had only two items. The copy of the instrument supplied by the author did not indicate which item was eventually eliminated or why.

SCALE NAME: Aggressiveness (Consumer)

SCALE DESCRIPTION:

A six-item, five-point Likert-type summated ratings scale purported to measure a consumer's tendency to express and/or exhibit hostility toward a marketer, especially salespeople. An 11-item version of the scale translated into Dutch was used by Richins (1987).

SCALE ORIGIN:

The scale was constructed by Richins (1983). After examination of the literature and some depth interviews, 79 items reflecting either assertive or aggressive behavior were generated. Initial screening reduced the list to 59 by eliminating redundant or ambiguous items as well as those with a high probability for social desirability. Further details of the scale's development and psychometric quality follow.

SAMPLES:

Several samples were used in the development and testing of the scale. The preliminary samples are mentioned below in the discussion of reliability and validity. The final and largest sample was composed of respondents from one of three groups: 400 questionnaires were mailed to a random sample of residents of a western SMSA, 212 were mailed to members of a consumer protection group residing in the same area, and 198 were sent to people who had in the past year registered a complaint with either the government or a private consumer protection group. After this mailing and a reminder postcard, **356** usable forms were returned for analysis.

RELIABILITY:

Fifty-nine assertiveness and aggressiveness items were administered to **118** students at a western urban university and **59** adult consumers in the same area. Items were eliminated if they had item-total correlations less than .35. Six items were retained for use in the aggressiveness scale. Each item's correlation with total scale scores was over .40. The scale had an alpha of **.73**. A t-retest correlation **.82 was calculated with 112** students and a two-week interval. For the sample of **356** adults, an alpha of **.76** was calculated (.89, corrected for few items).

VALIDITY:

Several tests of validity were made. The results of a factor analysis on a sample of **117** students indicated that the six aggressiveness items all loaded together, having loadings greater than .60 on that factor but less than .35 on the other factors, which represented three different assertiveness domains. This factor structure was generally replicated with the sample of **356** adults.

As evidence of convergent validity, the aggressiveness scale had a correlation of .42 ($p < .01$) with a psychological measure of irritability, assault, and verbal hostility (Buss and Durkee 1957). The aggressiveness scale had correlations of .16 (insignificant) and .34 ($p < .05$) with the consumer assertiveness scale and a psychological assertiveness scale (Rathus 1973), respectively. For a student sample of **93**, the correlation between the aggressiveness scale and the Marlowe-Crowne Social Desirability Scale (1960) was -.28

(p.01). All of these tests indicate that there is evidence for the discriminant and convergent validity of the aggressiveness scale, but it is not very strong.

ADMINISTRATION:

The scale was self-administered in both a classroom setting and by mail along with several other measures. Higher scores on the scale suggest that consumers express willingness to act hostile toward a marketer or salespeople whereas lower scores imply that respondents are not likely to express such aggressive behavior.

MAJOR FINDINGS:

Richins (1983) reported on the construction of consumer assertiveness and **aggressiveness** scales. Further, the findings indicated that consumers can be divided into four categories depending on the strategies they use to interact with marketers and their representatives: Some consumers are high on both traits, some are low on both traits, and some are low on one trait and high on the other. Those who scored high on **aggressiveness** had more negative attitudes about business, enjoyed complaining more, and perceived complaining to be more socially acceptable.

REFERENCES:

Buss, Arnold H. and Ann Durkee (1957), "An Inventory for Assessing Different Kinds of Hostility," *Journal of Consulting Psychology*, 21 (August), 343-349.

Crowne, Douglas P. and David Marlowe (1960), "A New Scale of Social Desirality Independent of Psychopathology," *Jounal of Consulting Psychology*, 24 (August), 349-354.

Rathus, Spencer A. (1973), "A 30-Item Schedule for Assessing Assertive Behavior," *Behavior Therapy*, 4 (May), 398-406.

Richins, Marsha L. (1983), "An Analysis of Consumer Interaction Styles in the Market-place, *JCR*, 10 (June), 73-82.

_____ (1987), "A Multivariate Analysis of Responses to Dissatisfaction," *JAMS*, 15 (Fall), 24-31.

SCALE ITEMS: ASSERTIVENESS (CONSUMER)

Strongly Disagree	Disagree	Neither	Agree	Strongly Agree
1	2	3	4	5

1. I have on occasion told salespeople I thought they were too rude.
2. On occasion, I have tried to get a complaint taken care of by causing a stir which attracts the attention of their customers.
3. I get a certain amount of satisfaction from putting a discourteous salesperson in his place.
4. Sometimes being nasty is the best way to get a complaint taken care of.
5. I'll make a scene at the store if necessary to get a complaint handled to my satisfaction.
6. Salespeople need to be told off when they are rude.

SCALE NAME: Aggressiveness (General)

SCALE DESCRIPTION:

A 34-item summated ratings scale measuring a person's expressed tendency to experience three dimensions of psychological hostility: assault, irritability, and verbal hostility.

SCALE ORIGIN:

The items used by Richins (1983) were taken from the three subscales of the Buss-Durkee Hostility-Guilt Inventory (1957). Most related to aggression: assault, irritability, and verbal hostility. Testing was done with several sets of college students. In developing the scale, a minimum item-total correlation was set at .40. No item was retained that was answered by more than 85% or less than 15% of either men or women. Using the Edwards' procedure for measuring social desirability (1953), Richins determined that it was having a small but significant influence on the direction of responding to their inventory. When summed separately, the three subscales had relatively high correlations in comparison with the other subscales and loaded on the same factor.

SAMPLES:

The scale was administered by Richins (1983) to **83** college students.

RELIABILITY:

An alpha of **.77** was reported for the scale.

VALIDITY:

No examination of scale validity was reported except as noted below in the findings.

ADMINISTRATION:

The scale was self-administered by students along with several other measures. Higher scores on the scale mean that respondents express greater amounts of psychological aggression whereas lower scores imply that respondents are not as hostile.

MAJOR FINDINGS:

Richins (1983) reported on the construction of consumer assertiveness and **aggressiveness** scales. Further, the findings indicated that consumers can be divided into four categories depending on the strategies they use to interact with marketers and their representatives: Some consumers are high on both traits, some are low on both traits, and some are low on one trait and high on the other. The general psychological measure of **aggressiveness** was used to help validate a new scale for consumer **aggressiveness**. The correlation between the two measures was .42 (p < .01). In contrast, the general psychological scale of **aggressiveness** had correlations of only .12 and .24 (p < .05) with a consumer assertiveness scale and a general psychological scale of assertiveness, respectively.

COMMENTS:

Scores could be summed for each subscale or over the three subscales. It is not clear which approach is psychometrically superior.

REFERENCES:

Buss, Arnold H. and Ann Durkee (1957), "An Inventory For Assessing Different Kinds of Hostility," *Journal of Consulting Psychology*, 21 (August), 343-349.

Edwards, A. L. (1953), "The Relationship Between the Judged Desirability of a Trait and the Probability That the Trait Will Be Endorsed," *Journal of Applied Psychology*, 37 (April), 90-93.

Richins, Marsha L. (1983), "An Analysis of Consumer Interaction Styles in the Marketplace," *JCR*, 10 (June), 73-82.

SCALE ITEMS: AGGRESSIVENESS (GENERAL) +

Assault

1. Once in a while I can not control my urge to harm others.
2. I can think of no good reason for ever hitting anyone. (r)
3. If someone hits me first, I let him have it.
4. Whoever insults me or my family is asking for a fight.
5. People who continually pester you are asking for a punch in the nose.
6. I seldom strike back, even if someone hits me first. (r)
7. When I really lose my temper, I am capable of slapping someone.
8. I get into fights about as often as the next person.
9. I have known people who pushed me so far that we came to blows.

Irritability

1. I lose my temper easily but get over it quickly.
2. I am always patient with others. (r)
3. I am irritated a great deal more than people are aware of.
4. It makes my blood boil to have somebody make fun of me.
5. If someone doesn't treat me right, I don't let it annoy me. (r)
6. Sometimes people bother me just by being around.
7. I often feel like a powder keg ready to explode.
8. I sometimes carry a chip on my shoulder.
9. I can't help being a little rude to people I don't like.
10. I don't let a lot of unimportant things irritate me. (r)
11. Lately, I have been kind of grouchy.

Verbal Hostility

1. When I disapprove of my friends' behavior, I let them know it.
2. I often find myself disagreing with people.
3. I can't help getting into arguments when people disagree with me.
4. I demand that people respect my rights.
5. Even when my anger is aroused, I don't use "strong language." (r)
6. If somebody annoys me, I am apt to tell him what I think of him.

7. When people yell at me, I yell back.
8. When I get mad, I say nasty things.
9. I could not put someone in his place, even if he needed it.**(r)**
10. I often make threats I don't really mean to carry out.
11. When arguing, I tend to raise my voice.
12. I generally cover up my poor opinion of others.**(r).**
13. I would rather concede a point than get into argument about it.

+ Buss and Durkee (1957) had subjects respond to these items as either True or False. It is not clear whether Richins (1983) treated them the same way or used a multipoint agree-disagree scale.

SCALE NAME: Appropriateness (Object)

SCALE DESCRIPTION:

A two-item, seven-point semantic differential summated ratings scale measuring the perceived suitability of an object for consumption. The objects studied by Stayman and Deshpande (1989) were all food.

SCALE ORIGIN:

The scale was apparently original to Stayman and Deshpande (1989).

SAMPLES:

A convenience sample of students was used in the study. Some of the students were recruited from a marketing department at a large West Coast university and the others were members of undergraduate business organizations at a large southwestern university. The authors gathered data just from students who identified themselves as Anglo-Americans (n = **195**), Chinese-Americans (n = **54**), or Mexican-Americans (n = **57**).

RELIABILITY:

An alpha of **.86** was reported for the scale.

VALIDITY:

No examination of scale validity was reported except that these items were selected after a pretest factor analysis.

ADMINISTRATION:

The scale was self-administered along with other measures as part of a experiment. The numerical responses to each item were averaged to calculate scale scores. Higher scores on the scale suggest that respondents believe an object, such as some specific food, is very appropriate to consume whereas lower scores imply that they think consuming such an object would be unsuitable.

MAJOR FINDINGS:

Social situation and felt-ethnicity were examined for their influence on food choices. The findings indicated that students had different perceptions of what were **appropriate** food choices depending on the social surroundings. Specifically, the Mexican and Chinese students indicated that choosing their respective ethnically-familiar foods would be less **appropriate** when business associates were present (nonethnic social surroundings) than when their parents were present (ethnic social surroundings).

REFERENCE:

Stayman, Douglas M. and Rohit Deshpande (1989), ''Situational Ethnicity and Consumer Behavior,'' *JCR*, 16 (December), 361-371.

SCALE ITEMS: APPROPRIATENESS (OBJECT)

1. inappropriate ___ : ___ : ___ : ___ : ___ : ___ : ___ appropriate
           1   2   3   4   5   6   7

2. unsuitable ___ : ___ : ___ : ___ : ___ : ___ : ___ suitable
           1   2   3   4   5   6   7

SCALE NAME: Arousal

SCALE DESCRIPTION:

A six-item, seven-point semantic differential summated ratings scale measuring one's arousal-related emotional reaction to an environmental stimulus.

SCALE ORIGIN:

This scale is taken from the work of Mehrabian and Russell (1974). Given previous work by others as well as their own research, they proposed that three factors compose all emotional reactions to environmental stimuli. They referred to the three factors as pleasure, arousal, and dominance. A series of studies were used to develop measures of each factor. In a study of the "final" set of items, 214 University of California undergraduates each used the scales to evaluate a different subset of six situations (hence, the analysis was based on 1284 observations). A principal components factor analysis with oblique rotation was used and the expected three factors emerged. Pleasure, arousal, and dominance explained 27%, 23%, and 14% of the available evidence, respectively. Scores on the pleasure scale had correlations of -.07 and .03 with arousal and dominance, respectively. Dominance had a correlation of .18 with arousal.

SAMPLES:

Holbrook et al. (1984) used **60** MBA students with a mean age of 25.6 years.

RELIABILITY:

An alpha of **.89** was reported for the scale.

VALIDITY:

No examination of the scale's validity was reported.

ADMINISTRATION:

The scale was self-administered along with several other measures in the middle of individual experimental sessions. Lower scores on the scale suggest that respondents are stimulated by some specified stimulus whereas higher scores imply that they are unaroused by the stimulus. Holbrook at al. (1984) noted that scores were normalized for each individual by subtracting the scale mean from the response to each item and then summing the corrected numeric responses.

MAJOR FINDINGS:

Holbrook et al. (1984) examined the role of emotions, performance, and personality in the enjoyment of games. In general, they found that emotions depend on personality-game congruity, perceived complexity, and prior performance. Specifically, the **arousal** expressed with playing a video game was most significantly predicted by the perceived complexity of the game.

COMMENTS:

As noted above, this scale was developed along with two other scales, dominance and pleasure. Though scored separately, they are typically used together in a study. See also Havlena and Holbrook (1986).

REFERENCES:

Havlena, William J. and Morris B. Holbrook (1986), "The Varieties of Consumption Experience: Comparing Two Typologies of Emotion in Consumer Behavior," *JCR*, 13 (December), 394-404.

Holbrook, Morris B., Robert W. Chestnut, Terence A. Oliva, and Eric A. Greenleaf (1984), "Play as a Consumption Experience: The Roles of Emotions, Performance, and Personality in the Enjoyment of Games," *JCR*, 11 (September), 728-739.

Mehrabian, Albert and James A. Russell (1974), *An Approach to Environmental Psychology*, Cambridge, MA: The MIT Press.

SCALE ITEMS: AROUSAL

stimulated	___ : ___ : ___ : ___ : ___ : ___ : ___	relaxed
	1 2 3 4 5 6 7	
excited	___ : ___ : ___ : ___ : ___ : ___ : ___	calm
	1 2 3 4 5 6 7	
frenzied	___ : ___ : ___ : ___ : ___ : ___ : ___	sluggish
	1 2 3 4 5 6 7	
jittery	___ : ___ : ___ : ___ : ___ : ___ : ___	dull
	1 2 3 4 5 6 7	
wide-awake	___ : ___ : ___ : ___ : ___ : ___ : ___	sleppy
	1 2 3 4 5 6 7	
aroused	___ : ___ : ___ : ___ : ___ : ___ : ___	unaroused
	1 2 3 4 5 6 7	

SCALE NAME: Arousal-Seeking Tendency

SCALE DESCRIPTION:

A 40-item, nine-point Likert-type summated ratings scale measuring the level of stimulation and arousal a person prefers.

SCALE ORIGIN:

The scale was constructed by Mehrabian and Russell (1974). Three studies with three separate samples of University of California undergraduates (203, 316, 214) were conducted to arrive at the final 40-item inventory. An initial set of items was generated from similar measures such as curiosity, change-seeking, and sensation-seeking. Some items were written to augment those borrowed from past studies and to tap into dimensions not represented by the other measures.

Among other things, the final scale consisted of items that had the best item-total correlations, the highest factor loadings, and the lowest correlations with social desirability. Scores on the 40-item version had a correlation of .96 with a larger 125-item version. A Kuder-Richardson reliability coefficient of **.87** was reported for the 40-item set. A test-retest correlation of **.88** was calculated for a group of 78 students. A pattern of correlations with measures of other personality constructs provided evidence of construct validity.

SAMPLES:

Analysis by Goodwin and Etgar (1980) was based on data collected from **180** students enrolled in business courses in a northeastern state university. A 2 × 3 × 3 factorial between-subjects design was used (two types of products, three levels of product attributes, and three different message appeals), with 10 subjects per cell. Convenience samples of homemakers and students in undergraduate business courses were used by Raju (1980). The scale was administered to groups of various sizes in an initial study, with the homemaker groups ranging between 30 and 39 and the student groups ranging between 51 and 69. In a larger follow-up study there were **336** homemakers and **105** students.

RELIABILITY:

No examination of scale reliability was reported in the studies.

VALIDITY:

No examination of scale validity was reported by Goodwin and Etgar (1980). Raju (1980) used the scale to construct a related scale that measured consumer exploratory tendencies. The correlation between the two scales was reported to be .53 for homemakers (n = 336) and .51 for students (n = 105). These findings provide some evidence of the scale's convergent validity.

ADMINISTRATION:

Subjects in the Goodwin and Etgar (1980) study completed the scale along with several other self- administered measures one month prior to the experiment. Raju (1980) had subjects self-administer the scale along with other measures. Higher scores on the scale suggest a person prefers a high level of optimal stimulation whereas lower scores imply the person has a low level of optimal arousal.

MAJOR FINDINGS:

The communication effectiveness of three ad appeals was investigated by Goodwin and Etgar (1980). **Arousal-seeking** was one of several personality variables included as a covariate in the analysis to minimize error variation in the findings. None of the personality variables was found to have a significant influence on the relative effectiveness of the three appeals.

Raju (1980) examined optimal stimulation level and numerous personality, demographic, and consumer-related characteristics. Among the many findings was that **arousal-seeking tendency** had significant positive correlations with such consumer behaviors as risk taking, brand switching, and innovativeness; significant negative correlations with age, employment status, rigidity, and intolerance of ambiguity; and no significant correlations with dogmatism and household income.

REFERENCES:

Goodwin, Stephen and Michael Etgar (1980), ''An Experimental Investigation of Comparative Advertising: Impact of Message Appeal, Information Load, and Utility of Product Class,'' *JMR*, 17 (May), 187-202.

Mehrabian, Albert and James A. Russell (1974), *An Approach to Environmental Psychology*. Cambridge, Mass.: MIT Press.

Raju, P. S. (1980), ''Optimum Stimulation Level: Its Relationship to Personality, Demographics, and Exploratory Behavior,'' *JCR*, 7 (December), 272-282.

SCALE ITEMS: AROUSAL-SEEKING TENDENCY

Please use the following scale to indicate the degree of your agreement or disagreement with each of the following statements.

+4 = very strong agreement
+3 = strong agreement
+2 = moderate agreement
+1 = slight agreement
 0 = neither agreement nor disagreement
−1 = slight disagreement
−2 = moderate disagreement
−3 = strong disagreement
−4 = very strong disagreement

1. Designs or patterns should be bold and exciting.
2. I feel best when I am safe and secure. **(r)**
3. I would like the job of a foreign correspondent for a newspaper.
4. I don't pay much attention to my surroundings. **(r)**
5. I don't like the feeling of wind in my hair. **(r)**
6. I prefer an unpredictable life that is full of change to a more routine one.

7. I.wouldn't like to try the new group-therapy techniques involving strange body sensations. **(r)**
8. Sometimes I really stir up excitement.
9. I never notice textures. **(r)**
10. I like surprises.
11. My ideal home would be peaceful and quiet. **(r)**
12. I eat the same kind of food most of the time. **(r)**
13. As a child I often imagined leaving home, just to explore the world.
14. I don't like to have lots of activity around me. **(r)**
15. I am interested in only what I need to know. **(r)**
16. I like meeting people who give me new ideas.
17. I would be content to live in the same town for the rest of my life. **(r)**
18. I like continually changing activities.
19. I like a job that offers change, variety, and travel, even if it involves some danger.
20. I avoid busy, noisy places. **(r)**
21. I like to look at pictures that are puzzling in some way.
22. I wouldn't enjoy dangerous sports such as mountain climbing, airplane flying, or sky diving. **(r)**
23. I like to experience novelty and change in my daily routine.
24. Shops with thousands of exotic herbs and fragrances fascinate me.
25. I much prefer familiar people and places. **(r)**
26. When things get boring, I like to find some new and unfamiliar experience.
27. I like to touch and feel a sculpture.
28. I don't enjoy daring, foolhardy things just for fun. **(r)**
29. I prefer a routine way of life to an unpredictable one full of change. **(r)**
30. I like to go somewhere different nearly every day.
31. I seldom change the decor and furniture arrangement at my place. **(r)**
32. People view me as a quite unpredictable person.
33. I like to run through heaps of fallen leaves.
34. I sometimes like to do things that are a little frightening.
35. I prefer friends who are reliable and predictable to those who are excitingly unpredictable. **(r)**
36. I am interested in new and varied interpretations of different art forms.
37. I seldom change the pictures on my walls. **(r)**
38. I am not interested in poetry. **(r)**
39. It's unpleasant seeing people in strange, weird clothes. **(r)**
40. I am continually seeking new ideas and experiences.

SCALE NAME: Arts Enthusiast

SCALE DESCRIPTION:

A three-item, six-point, Likert-type, summated ratings scale ranging from strongly disagree (1) to strongly agree (6). The scale measures a person's interest in the arts. See also a five-item measure by Dickerson and Gentry (1983) referred to as Aesthetic Enthusiast scale, which combines statements from Wells and Tigert's (1971) Arts Enthusiast and Wide Horizons scales.

SCALE ORIGIN:

These items were part of a classic study of psychographics by Wells and Tigert (1971). One thousand questionnaires were mailed to homemaker members of the Market Facts mail panel. In addition to gathering demographic, product use, and media data, the survey contained 300 statements that have since served as the basis for the construction of many lifestyle-related scales. The three items for this scale are reported in the article, but they were not analyzed as a multi-item scale. The purpose of the article was to explain how psychographics could improve upon mere demographic description of target audiences and product users. No psychometric information was reported.

One of the first uses of the items as a multi-item scale was by Darden and Perreault (1976). Analysis was based on self-administered questionnaires completed by 278 suburban housewives randomly selected in Athens, Georgia. A split-half reliability of .74 was reported for the scale. Arts enthusiasm was *not* found to be significantly related to reported outshopping behavior.

SAMPLES:

Lumpkin and Darden (1982) had **145** usable responses gathered from the consumer research panel of the University of Arkansas. Data were collected from the individuals by mail questionnaire. Lumpkin (1985) collected data from a sample drawn from the Market Facts Consumer Mail Panel. A total of **2854** completed questionnaires were received, but Lumpkin focused on **373** respondents who indicated they were 65 years of age or older.

RELIABILITY:

Alpha values of **.77** and **.7374** were calculated by Lumpkin and Darden (1982) and Lumpkin (1985), respectively.

VALIDITY:

Factor analysis in both studies indicated the items loaded together.

ADMINISTRATION:

Both Lumpkin and Darden (1982) and Lumpkin (1985) gathered data through self-administered mail questionnaires. Scale scores are calculated by averaging numerical responses to individual items. A score of 6 indicates that a person greatly enjoys art galleries, concerts, and ballets whereas a score of 1 suggests that a person strongly dislikes those activities.

MAJOR FINDINGS:

In their study of television program preference groups, Lumpkin and Darden (1982) found a few lifestyle variables that were significantly different among the six groups, but **arts enthusiasm** was *not* one of them. Elderly consumers were cluster analyzed by Lumpkin (1985) and **arts enthusiasm** appeared to provide the greatest discrimination among the three groups (statistical significance not reported). The group with the highest mean on the scale was the most socially active and the most interested in shopping.

COMMENTS:

No reported study has done so, but using all four items appears to be the best thing to do improve the pyschometric quality of the scale.

REFERENCES:

Darden, William R. and William D. Perreault, Jr. (1976), ''Identifying Interurban Shoppers: Multiproduct Purchase Patterns and Segmentation Profiles,'' *JMR*, 13 (Feb.), 51- 60.

Dickerson, Mary D. and James W. Gentry (1983), ''Characteristics of Adopters and Non-Adopters of Home Computers,'' *JCR*, 10 (September), 225-235.

Lumpkin, James R. (1985), ''Shopping Orientation Segmentation of the Elderly Consumer,'' *JAMS*, 13 (Spring), 271-289.

_____ and William R. Darden (1982), ''Relating Television Preference Viewing to Shopping Orientations, Lifestyles, and Demographics,'' *JA*, 11 (4), 56-67.

Wells, William D. and Douglas Tigert (1971), ''Activities, Interests, and Opinions,'' *JAR*, 11 (August), 27-35.

SCALE ITEMS: ARTS ENTHUSIAST +

Strongly Disagree	Disagree	Slightly Disagree	Slightly Agree	Agree	Strongly Agree
1	2	3	4	5	6

1. I enjoy going through an art gallery.
2. I enjoy going to concerts.
3. I like ballet (and opera).
4. I like to browse in museums.

+ Items 1 through 3 were suggested by Wells and Tigert (1971) and apparently used by Darden and Perreault (1976). Lumpkin (1985, and Darden 1982) used items 2, 4, and the longer version of 3.

SCALE NAME: Assertiveness (Consumer)

SCALE DESCRIPTION:

A 15-item, Likert-type summated ratings scale purported to measure a consumer's expressed tendency to stand up for his/her rights with marketers and their representatives. The scale covers three interaction situations: resisting requests for compliance, requesting information or assistance, and seeking redress. An 11-item version of the scale translated into Dutch was used by Richins (1987).

SCALE ORIGIN:

The scale was constructed by Richins (1983). After examination of the literature and some depth interviews, 79 items reflecting either assertive or aggressive behavior were generated. Initial screening reduced the list to 59 by eliminating redundant or ambiguous items as well as those with a high probability for social desirability. Further details of the scale's development and psychometric quality follow.

SAMPLES:

Several samples were used in the development and testing of the scale. The preliminary samples are mentioned below in relation to reliability and validity. The final and largest sample was composed of respondents from one of three groups: 400 questionnaires were mailed to a random sample of residents of a western SMSA, 212 were mailed to members of a consumer protection group residing in the same area, and 198 were sent to people who had in the past year registered a complaint with either the government or a private consumer protection group. After this mailing and a reminder postcard, **356** usable forms were returned for analysis.

RELIABILITY:

Fifty-nine assertiveness and aggressiveness items were administered to **118** students at a western urban university and **59** adult consumers in the same area. Items were eliminated if they had item-total correlations less than .35. Fifteen items were retained for use in the assertiveness scale. Each item's correlation with total scale scores was over .35. The scale had an alpha of **.85.** A test-retest correlation of **.83** was calculated with **112** students and a two-week interval. For the sample of **356** adults, an alpha of **.80** was calculated.

VALIDITY:

Several tests of validity were made. The results of a factor analysis on a sample of **117** students indicated that the 15 assertiveness items loaded on three different factors representing three different interaction situations. This factor structure was generally replicated with the sample of **356** adults.

As evidence of convergent validity, the assertiveness scale had a correlation of .68 (p.01) with a psychological measure of assertiveness (Rathus 1973). The assertiveness scale had correlations of .16 (insignificant) and .12 (insignificant) with the consumer aggressiveness scale and a psychological measure of irritability, assault, and verbal hostility (Buss and Durkee 1957), respectively. For a student sample of **93**, the correlation between the assertiveness scale and the Marlowe-Crowne Social Desirability Scale (1960) was .13 (p > .10).

ADMINISTRATION:

The scale was self-administered in both a classroom setting and by mail along with several other measures. Higher scores on the scale suggest that consumers express willingness to resist requests for compliance, request information or assistance, and seek redress from marketers, whereas lower scores imply that respondents are not likely to assert themselves in the marketplace.

MAJOR FINDINGS:

Richins (1983) reported on the construction of consumer **assertiveness** and aggressiveness scales. Further, the findings indicated that consumers can be divided into four categories depending on the strategies they use to interact with marketers and their representatives: Some consumers are high on both traits, some are low on both traits, and some are low on one trait and high on the other. Those who scored high on **assertiveness** had more positive attitudes about business and business responsiveness to complaints, perceived complaining to be somewhat more socially acceptable, and exhibited more complaining behavior than did those who scored low on **assertiveness**.

REFERENCES:

Buss, Arnold H. and Ann Durkee (1957), ''An Inventory for Assessing Different Kinds of Hostility,'' *Journal of Consulting Psychology*, 21 (August), 343-349.

Crowne, Douglas P. and David Marlowe (1960), ''A New Scale of Social Desirability Independent of Psychopathology,'' *Journal of Consulting Psychology*, 24 (August), 349-354.

Rathus, Spencer A. (1973), ''A 30-Item Schedule for Assessing Assertive Behavior,'' *Behavior Therapy*, 4 (May), 398-406.

Richins, Marsha L. (1983), ''An Analysis of Consumer Interaction Styles in the Market-place,'' *JCR*, 10 (June), 73-82.

———— (1987), ''A Multivariate Analysis of Responses to Dissatisfaction,'' *JAMS*, 15 (Fall), 24-31.

SCALE ITEMS: ASSERTIVENESS (CONSUMER)

Strongly Disagree	Disagree	Neither	Agree	Strongly Agree
1	2	3	4	5

Resisting Requests for Compliance
1. I have no trouble getting off the phone when called by a person selling something I don't want.
2. I really don't know how to deal with aggressive salespeople. **(r)**

3. More often than I would like, I end up buying something I don't want because I have a hard time saying "no" to the salesperson.(r)
4. If a salesperson comes to my door selling something I don't want, I have no trouble ending the conversation.
5. If a salesperson has gone to a lot of trouble to find an item for me, I would be embarrassed not to buy it even if it wasn't exactly right.(r)

Requesting Information or Assistance

6. I sometimes don't get all the information I need about a product because I am uncomfortable bothering salespeople with questions.(r)
7. I am uncomfortable asking store employees where products are located in the store.(r)
8. In signing a sales contract or credit agreement, I am reluctant to ask for an explanation of everything I don't understand.(r)
9. If a store doesn't have the size or color of an item I need, I don't mind asking the salesperson to check for the item at other store locations.
10. If a cashier is talking with friends while I am waiting to be waited upon, it would not bother me to interrupt the conversation and ask for assistance.

Seeking Redress

11. If a defective product is expensive, I usually keep it rather than put up a fuss or complain.(r)
12. I'd rather do almost anything than return a product to the store.(r)
13. I am probably more likely to return an unsatisfactory product than most people I know.
14. I often procrastinate when I know I should return a defective product to the store.(r)
15. I would attempt to notify store management if I thought service in a store was particularly bad.

SCALE NAME: Assertiveness (General)

SCALE DESCRIPTION:

A 30-item, Likert-like summated ratings scale purported to measure a person's expressed tendency to stand up for his/her rights with marketers and their representatives. Rathus (1973) used a six-point response scale in his work, but Richins (1983) did not specify the number of points on the response scale she used or whether the full scale or the abbreviated version was used.

ORIGIN:

The scale was constructed and tested by Rathus (1973). He indicates that the items were borrowed from other scales or were suggested by comments made in diaries kept by students on assertiveness-related attitudes and behaviors. Test-retest reliability of .7782 was calculated by using **68** undergraduate students and an eight-week interval. Split-half reliability of .7723 was found for **67** people ranging in age from 15 to 70 years. Validity was assessed in several ways, one of which was by correlating scores on the scale with impartial judges' ratings of behaviors that subjects said they would exhibit in certain situations. For responses from **47** coeds, a correlation of .7049 was found between the judges' ratings and scale scores. See Rathus (1973) for further tests of the scales reliability and validity.

SAMPLES:

The scale was administered by Richins (1983) to **83** college students.

RELIABILITY:

An alpha of .86 was reported for the scale by Richins (1983).

VALIDITY:

No examination of scale validity was reported except as noted below in the findings.

ADMINISTRATION:

The scale was self-administered by students along with several other measures. Higher scores on the scale suggest that respondents are highly assertive individuals whereas lower scores imply that respondents are not likely to assert themselves in most situations.

MAJOR FINDINGS:

Richins (1983) reported on the construction of consumer assertiveness and aggressiveness scales. Further, the findings indicated that consumers can be divided into four categories depending on the strategies they use to interact with marketers and their representatives: Some consumers are high on both traits, some are low on both traits, and some are low on one trait and high on the other. As evidence of the convergent validity of the consumer assertiveness scale, it had a correlation of .68 (p.01) with the general psychological measure of assertiveness (Rathus 1973). The general assertiveness scale had correlations of .34 (p < .01) and .24 (p < .05) with a consumer aggressiveness scale and a psychological measure of irritability, assault, and verbal hostility (Buss and Durkee 1957), respectively.

COMMENTS:

Though no reliability information is reported, Rathus (1973) notes that results of an item analysis indicate that a 19-item version of the scale appears to be just as valid, if not more so, than the full 30-item version.

REFERENCES:

Buss, Arnold H. and Ann Durkee (1957), "An Inventory for Assessing Different Kinds of Hostility," *Journal of Consulting Psychology*, 21 (August), 343-349.

Rathus, Spencer A. (1973), "A 30-Item Schedule for Assessing Assertive Behavior," *Behavior Therapy*, 4 (May), 398-406.

Richins, Marsha L. (1983), "An Analysis of Consumer Interaction Styles in the Marketplace," *JCR*, 10 (June), 73-82.

SCALE ITEMS: ASSERTIVENESS (GENERAL) +

Directions: Indicate how characteristic or descriptive each of the following statements is of you by using the code given below:

+3 = very characteristic of me, extremely descriptive
+2 = rather characteristic of me, quite descriptive
+1 = somewhat characteristic of me, slightly descriptive
−1 = somewhat uncharacteristic of me, slightly nondescriptive
−2 = rather uncharacteristic of me, quite nondescriptive
−3 = very uncharacteristic of me, extremely nondescriptive

1. Most people seem to be more aggressive and assertive than I am. **(r)**
2. I have hesitated to make or accept dates because of "shyness." **(r)**
3. When the food served at a restaurant is not done to my satisfaction, I complain about it to the waiter or waitress.
4. I am careful to avoid hurting other people's feelings, even when I feel that I have been injured. **(r)**
5. If a salesman has gone to considerable trouble to show me merchandise which is not quite suitable, I have a difficult time in saying "No." **(r)**
6. When I am asked to do something, I insist upon knowing why.
7. There are times when I look for a good, vigorous argument.
8. I strive to get ahead as well as most people in my position.
9. To be honest, people often take advantage of me. **(r)**
10. I enjoy starting conversations with new acquaintances and strangers.
11. I often don't know what to say to attractive persons of the opposite sex. **(r)**
12. I will hesitate to make phone calls to business establishments and institutions. **(r)**
13. I would rather apply for a job or admission to a college by writing letters than by going through with personal interviews. **(r)**
14. I find it embarrassing to return merchandise. **(r)**

15. If a close and respected relative were annoying me, I would smother my feelings rather than express my annoyance. **(r)**
16. I have avoided asking questions for fear of sounding stupid. **(r)**
17. During an argument I am sometimes afraid that I will get so upset that I will shake all over. **(r)**
18. If a famed and respected lecturer makes a statement which I think is incorrect, I will have the audience hear my point of view as well.
19. I avoid arguing over prices with clerks and salesmen. **(r)**
20. When I have done something important or worthwhile, I manage to let others know about it.
21. I am open and frank about my feelings.
22. If someone has been spreading false and bad stories about me, I see him (her) as soon as possible to "have a talk" about it.
23. I often have a hard time saying "No." **(r)**
24. I tend to bottle up my emotions rather than make a scene. **(r)**
25. I complain about poor service in a restaurant and elsewhere.
26. When I am given a compliment, I sometimes just don't know what to say. **(r)**
27. If a couple near me in a theater or at a lecture were conversing rather loudly, I would ask them to be quiet or to take their conversation elsewhere.
28. Anyone attempting to push ahead of me in a line is in for a good battle.
29. I am quick to express an opinion.
30. There are times when I just can't say anything. **(r)**

+ As indicated above in the comments, Rathus (1973) noted that a shortened version of the scale was possible. Items to include are 2-4, 6, 11-14, 16, 17, 19, 22-25, and 28-30.

SCALE NAME: Attitude Toward Branded Products

SCALE DESCRIPTION:

A five-item, five-point Likert-type summated ratings scale measuring a person's opinion of brand name products in general.

SCALE ORIGIN:

The measure originates from a dissertation published by Moschis in 1978. His 1981 study, reported below, is from that same dissertation research.

SAMPLES:

Moschis' (1981) data came from **806** middle school or senior school students: 365 "older" adolescents (15 years and older) and 441 "younger" adolescents (younger than 15 years). The students came from 13 schools and seven towns in Wisconsin representing a wide variety of urban to rural situations. The author indicates that the sample was well balanced in terms of most demographic characteristics except sex, because nearly two-thirds of the respondents were female.

RELIABILITY:

An alpha of **.50** was reported for the scale.

VALIDITY:

No examination of scale validity was reported.

ADMINISTRATION:

The scale was self-administered by students along with several other measures in a 10-page instrument during a regular class session. Lower scores on the scale indicate that respondents have positive opinions about branded products whereas higher scores suggest that they have negative attitudes.

MAJOR FINDINGS:

The study investigated the validity of the cognitive development approach to socialization (e.g., Piaget) to predict a wide variety of consumer-related cognitions learned during adolescence. In general, the findings indicated that the cognitive developmental model did not explain consumer socialization during adolescence very well. Older adolescents had significantly less favorable **attitudes** towards advertising, **brands**, and prices than did younger children.

COMMENTS:

The low internal consistency indicates that the scale is not reliable. This could be due to several different factors being represented in the scale. Redevelopment and testing are needed before the scale is used further.

REFERENCES:

Moschis, George P. (1978), *Acquisition of the Consumer Role by Adolescents*, Research Monograph No. 82. Atlanta, Ga.: Publishing Services Division, College of Business Administration, Georgia State University.

_____ (1981), ''Patterns of Consumer Learning,'' *JAMS*, 9 (2), 110-126.

SCALE ITEMS: ATTITUDE TOWARD BRANDED PRODUCTS

Strongly Disagree	Disagree	Neither	Agree	Strongly Agree
1	2	3	4	5

1. Advertised brands are better than those that are not advertised.
2. Quality products are made by well-known companies.
3. I prefer a certain brand of most products I buy or use.
4. I don't care about the brand of most products I buy.(r)
5. Brand-name products work better than ''off-brands.''

SCALE NAME: Attitude Toward Business

SCALE DESCRIPTION:

A six-item, five-point Likert-type summated ratings scale measuring a consumer's attitude toward business and products in general.

SCALE ORIGIN:

The scale was constructed by Richins (1983) with items taken from Allison (1978) and Lundstrom and Lamont (1976). Allison (1978) constructed a 35-item, Likert-type scale to measure consumer alienation from the marketplace. A scale developed by Lundstrom and Lamont (1976) contained both pro- and antibusiness statements. It consisted of 82 Likert-type items and was called the Consumer Discontent Scale.

SAMPLES:

The sample was composed of respondents from one of three groups: 400 questionnaires were mailed to a random sample of residents of a western SMSA, 212 were mailed to members of a consumer protection group residing in the same area, and 198 were sent to people who in the past year had registered a complaint with either the government or a private consumer protection group. After this mailing and a reminder postcard, **356** usable forms were returned for analysis.

RELIABILITY:

An alpha of **.74** was reported.

VALIDITY:

No examination of scale validity was reported.

ADMINISTRATION:

The scale was self-administered in a mail survey along with several other measures. Higher scores on the scale suggest that consumers express positive attitudes toward business whereas lower scores imply that respondents have low regard for business and products in general.

MAJOR FINDINGS:

Richins (1983) reported on the construction of consumer assertiveness and aggressiveness scales. Further, the findings indicated that consumers can be divided into four categories depending upon the strategies they use to interact with marketers and their representatives: Some consumers are high on both traits, some are low on both traits, and some are low on one trait and high on the other. Consumers scoring low on aggression had more positive **attitudes toward business** than those high on aggression.

REFERENCES:

Allison, Neil K. (1978), ''A Psychometric Development of a Test for Consumer Alienation From the Marketplace,'' *JMR*, 15 (November), 565-575.

Lundstrom, William J. and Lawrence M. Lamont (1976), ''The Development of a Scale to Measure Consumer Discontent,'' *JMR*, 13 (November), 373-381.

Richins, Marsha L. (1983), ''An Analysis of Consumer Interaction Styles in the Marketplace,'' *JCR*, 10 (June), 73-82.

SCALE ITEMS: ATTITUDE TOWARD BUSINESS

Strongly Agree	Agree	Neither	Disagree	Strongly Disagree
1	2	3	4	5

1. Many businesses try to take advantage of customers.
2. Most products are not as durable as they should be.
3. Most companies are concerned about their customers.**(r)**
4. In general, I am satisfied with most of the products I buy.**(r)**
5. What most products claim to do and what they actually do are two different things.
6. The business community has helped raise our country's standard of living.**(r)**

SCALE NAME: Attitude Toward Business Ethics

SCALE DESCRIPTION:

A three-item, five-point Likert-type scale measuring a consumer's sense of the ethical behavior displayed by companies in general. The scale was referred to as Consumer Normlessness by Durand and Lambert (1985).

SCALE ORIGIN:

The scale was originally constructed and used by Lambert (1980). Items were adapted from several previously published empirical and conceptual studies. A mail sample of residents in four southeastern metropolitan areas yielded **200** usable returns. The alpha for this scale was reported as **.673**. The scale was just one of four alienation measures used together in a cluster analysis to group consumers. No individual findings for the scale were reported. In general, dissatisfaction with the marketplace was found to be significantly related to levels of consumer alienation.

SAMPLES:

A systematic sample of 1320 customers of a large, investor-owned electric utility company was made. Questionnaires were mailed to them and **325** were returned after a reminder mailed two weeks later. The average respondent was at least 45 years of age, male, white, married, had at least graduated from high school, and was socioeconomically upscale.

RELIABILITY:

An alpha of **.73** was reported for the scale.

VALIDITY:

No examination of scale validity was reported.

ADMINISTRATION:

The scale was self-administered along with several other measures included in the mail questionnaire. Higher scores on the scale indicate that consumers feel companies take unfair advantage of them whereas lower scores mean that consumers think companies are generally ethical.

MAJOR FINDINGS:

The purpose of the study was to investigate the degree to which criticisms of advertising are positively related to various aspects of consumer and political alienation. Respondents were first grouped according to levels of alienation by cluster analysis. (**Ethical behavior** was one of the alienation variables on which the cluster analysis was based.) Then, differences in advertising criticisms were compared across the groups. The cluster analysis produced four alienation groups and a MANOVA indicated significant differences between the groups when all of the 12 advertising criticisms were considered simultaneously.

REFERENCES:

Durand, Richard M. and Zarrel V. Lambert (1985), ''Alienation and Criticisms of Advertising,'' *JA*, 14 (3), 9-17.

Lambert, Zarrel V. (1980), ''Consumer Alienation, General Dissatisfaction, and Consumerism Issues: Conceptual and Managerial Perspectives,'' *JR*, 56 (Summer), 3-24.

SCALE ITEMS: ATTITUDE TOWARD BUSINESS ETHICS +

Strongly Agree	Agree	Neither	Disagree	Strongly Disagree
1	2	3	4	5

1. Companies are usually out to make a lot of money even if it means violating ethics and taking unfair advantage of consumers.
2. Most durable products . . . could be made to last much longer but . . . are made to wear out quickly . . . to necessitate repurchase.
3. If people really knew . . . what businesses do to deceive . . . and take advantage . . . of consumers, they would be up-in-arms.

+ The authors noted that these items were abbreviated to conserve space as indicated by the dots. They should be contacted to obtain the full items.

SCALE NAME: Attitude Toward Buying American-Made Products

SCALE DESCRIPTION:

A four-item, seven-point Likert-type summated ratings scale measuring American consumers' attitudes about purchasing products, particularly clothing, produced in the United States.

SCALE ORIGIN:

The scale was apparently original to the Shimp and Sharma (1987) study.

SAMPLES:

Many samples having varied characteristics were used in the studies reported by Shimp and Sharma (1987), but the one in which this scale was measured was composed of **145** college students, about 60% of whom were male and with a mean age of 21.5 years.

RELIABILITY:

An alpha of **.81** was reported for the scale.

VALIDITY:

The validity of the scale was not specifically examined in the study. However, as noted below, the scale had a correlation of .50 with Americans' ethnocentrism, which provides some evidence of convergent validity.

ADMINISTRATION:

Shimp and Sharma (1987) had students complete the scale along with other measures after an in-class "experiment." Higher scores on the scale suggest respondents have positive attitudes toward the purchase of American-made products whereas lower scores imply that they have a bias against products made in this country.

MAJOR FINDINGS:

The purpose of the study was to describe the construction and validation of a scale to measure the American consumer's ethnocentrism. Subjects were exposed to three commercials portraying celebrities expressing their preference for American-made products. Ethnocentrism was found to have a significant positive correlation with **attitude toward buying American-made clothing.**

REFERENCE:

Shimp, Terence A. and Subhash Sharma (1987), "Consumer Ethnocentrism: Construction and Validation of the CETSCALE," *JMR*, 24 (August), 280-289.

SCALE ITEMS: ATTITUDE TOWARD BUYING AMERICAN-MADE PRODUCTS

Strongly   Strongly
Agree   Disagree
7————6————5————4————3————2————1

1. I personally favor buying American-made rather than foreign-made apparel items.
2. In general, I prefer purchasing American products (any product, not just apparel) over foreign-made products.
3. Foreign-made products are generally higher quality than American-made products. **(r)**
4. It is important that I purchase American-made products so that jobs are not lost to foreign countries.

SCALE NAME: Attitude Toward Computer Technology

SCALE DESCRIPTION:

A two-item, six-point, Likert-type summated ratings scale from strongly disagree (1) to strongly agree (6). The scale reflects a person's lack of comfort with some aspects of computer technology and was referred to as Computer Attitudes by Dickerson and Gentry 1983).

SCALE ORIGIN:

The items were generated and used first as a summated ratings scale by Dickerson and Gentry (1983).

SAMPLES:

Two mailing lists were used to collect data in the Dickerson and Gentry study (1983). One was a list of *Psychology Today* subscribers and the other was a list of members of computer clubs. The former was used to reach non-adopters of computers and the latter was used to reach PC adopters. Analysis was based on a total of **639** questionnaires. Results from a second mailing to non- respondents indicated that their demographic makeup was not significantly different from that of respondents. On the basis of 1980 Census data, the sample was younger and more upscale than the general population.

RELIABILITY:

An alpha of **.50** was calculated for the scale in the Dickerson and Gentry (1983) study.

VALIDITY:

Factor analysis indicated the items loaded together.

ADMINISTRATION:

Data were gathered through self-administered mail questionnaires. Scale scores are calculated by averaging numerical responses to individual items. A score of 6 indicates that a person is concerned about computer technology whereas a 1 suggests that a person worries little about it.

MAJOR FINDINGS:

Dickerson and Gentry (1983) found that the scale was one of several lifestyle variables that was a significant discriminator between adopters and nonadopters of home computers. In fact, this variable was the best predictor of all the AIOs. This finding indicates that expressing little fear of **computer technology** predicted adoption of a home computer well.

COMMENTS:

The internal validity is extremely low and could be improved through additional items that focus on the construct of interest. The two items could relate to different issues, which might lower reliability.

REFERENCE:

Dickerson, Mary D. and James W. Gentry (1983), "Characteristics of Adopters and Non-Adopters of Home Computers," *JCR*, 10 (Sept.), 225-235.

SCALE ITEMS: ATTITUDE TOWARD COMPUTER TECHNOLOGY

Strongly Disagree	Disagree	Slightly Disagree	Slightly Agree	Agree	Strongly Agree
1	2	3	4	5	6

1. Computer technology is an invasion of my privacy.
2. I like to handle my own financial affairs without using any electronic machines.

SCALE NAME: Attitude Toward Humor

SCALE DESCRIPTION:

A nine-item, six-point semantic differential summated ratings scale measuring one's attitude toward some object with humor potential.

SCALE ORIGIN:

The scale is apparently original to Allen and Madden (1985). It was pretested using a convenience sample of 33 females and found to have an alpha of .90.

SAMPLES:

The main study by Allen and Madden (1985) was based on data collected from **60** women, 15 in each of the humor-stimuli by pen-color cells of the experiment. The subjects were recruited from an eastern university's School of Management and university cafeteria. They were offered $1 to participate in the study and were screened so as not to include the authors' students.

RELIABILITY:

An alpha of **.90** (same as in the pretest) was reported for the scale (Allen and Madden 1985).

VALIDITY:

No specific examination of scale validity was reported (Allen and Madden 1985).

ADMINISTRATION:

The scale was self-administered by subjects in the presence of an experimenter and after being exposed to the humor stimulus (Allen and Madden 1985). Higher scores on the scale indicate that respondents have a very unpleasant feeling after being exposed to some "humorous" object.

MAJOR FINDINGS:

The purpose of the experiment by Allen and Madden (1985) was to replicate and extend Gorn's (1982) study of affective conditioning. Though two pieces of comic material were used successfully to evoke opposite affective reactions in subjects, significant between-group differences predicted by an affective conditioning hypothesis were not produced.

REFERENCES:

Allen, Chris T. and Thomas J. Madden (1985), "A Closer Look at Classical Conditioning," *JCR*, 12 (December), 301-315.

Gorn, Gerald J. (1982), "The Effects of Music in Advertising on Choice Behavior: A Classical Conditioning Approach," *JM*, 46 (Winter), 94-101.

SCALE ITEMS: ATTITUDE TOWARD HUMOR

	1	2	3	4	5	6	
pleasant	__ :	__ :	__ :	__ :	__ :	__	unpleasant
left me with a good feeling	__ :	__ :	__ :	__ :	__ :	__	left me with a bad feeling
refined	__ :	__ :	__ :	__ :	__ :	__	vulgar
likeable	__ :	__ :	__ :	__ :	__ :	__	unlikable
interesting	__ :	__ :	__ :	__ :	__ :	__	boring
tasteful	__ :	__ :	__ :	__ :	__ :	__	tasteless
entertaining	__ :	__ :	__ :	__ :	__ :	__	unentertaining
artful	__ :	__ :	__ :	__ :	__ :	__	artless
good	__ :	__ :	__ :	__ :	__ :	__	bad

SCALE NAME: Attitude Toward Pricing Practices

SCALE DESCRIPTION:

A five-item, five-point Likert-type summated ratings scale measuring consumer attitudes about prices in general. A seven-item version of the scale with similar psychometric properties is also discussed below.

SCALE ORIGIN:

The scale was developed by Gaski and Etgar (1986). Using a formula described in the article, the scale can be combined with data from several other measures to form an index of consumer attitudes toward marketing-related activities. The authors request that the index be referred to as the University of Notre Dame/Market Facts Index of Consumer Sentiment Toward Marketing. Some items were taken or adapted from the literature but the majority were written especially for the index. Pretesting involved 50 members of the Market Facts mail panel completing the index.

SAMPLES:

The sample was taken from the 200,000 household panel maintained by Market Facts. Questionnaires were mailed to 2000 households and **1428** were completed and returned. While the overall panel is nationally balanced and continually updated to reflect the most recent national demographics, the characteristics of the final sample were not given.

RELIABILITY:

A seven-item version of the scale had an alpha of **.772** and the item-total correlations were .33 or higher. Two items with the lowest item-total correlations were eliminated leaving a scale with an alpha of **.776**.

VALIDITY:

A factor analysis of the twenty items composing the entire index was conducted. The five items composing each of the four scales loaded most heavily on their respective factors and had extremely low loadings on the other three factors. This pattern of loadings provides some evidence of convergent and discriminant validity.

ADMINISTRATION:

The scale was self-administered along with several other measures in a mail survey instrument. Higher scores indicate that consumers have positive attitudes about prices in general whereas low scores suggest that they are not satisfied with product prices and think they are too high.

MAJOR FINDINGS:

The purpose of the study was to report on the construction and validation of an index to measure consumers attitudes towards marketing which could be used repeatedly over time as an indicator of the public's general sentiment about the field. Scores on the index were strongly correlated with another general measure of consumer sentiment and consumer satisfaction with the marketing mix elements. As noted above, **pricing** was just one of four subscales composing the index. Its scores had the following significant correlations with the other subscales: .332 (advertising), .443 (product quality), and .254 (retailing).

REFERENCE:

Gaski, John F. and Michael J. Etzel (1986), "The Index of Consumer Sentiment Toward Marketing," *JM*, 50 (July), 71- 81.

SCALE ITEMS: ATTITUDE TOWARD PRICING PRACTICES

Agree Strongly	Agree Somewhat	Neutral	Disagree Somewhat	Disagree Strongly
1————	————2————	————3————	————4————	————5

1. Most products I buy are overpriced.
2. Businesses could charge lower prices and still be profitable.
3. Most prices are reasonable considering the high cost of doing business. **(r)**
4. Competition between companies keeps prices reasonable. **(r)**+
5. Companies are unjustified in charging the prices they charge. +
6. Most prices are fair. **(r)**
7. In general, I am satisfied with the prices I pay. **(r)**

+ These items were eliminated in order to have a five item scale.

SCALE NAME: Attitude Toward Salespeople

SCALE DESCRIPTION:

A five-item, five-point Likert-type summated ratings scale measuring a person's attitude toward salespeople in general.

SCALE ORIGIN:

The measure originates from a dissertation published by Moschis in 1978. His 1981 study, reported below, is from that same dissertation research.

SAMPLES:

Moschis' (1981) data came from **806** middle school or senior high school students. There were 365 "older" adolescents (15 years and older) and 441 "younger" adolescents (younger than 15 years). The students came from 13 schools and seven towns in Wisconsin representing a wide variety of urban to rural situations. The author indicates that the sample was well balanced in terms of most demographic characteristics except sex, because nearly two-thirds of the respondents were female.

RELIABILITY:

An alpha of **.56** was reported for the scale.

VALIDITY:

No examination of scale validity was reported.

ADMINISTRATION:

The scale was self-administered by students along with several other measures in a 10-page instrument during a regular class session. Lower scores on the scale indicate that respondents believe that salespeople in general are friendly and honest whereas higher scores suggest that respondents have negative opinions of salespeople.

MAJOR FINDINGS:

The study investigated the validity of the cognitive development approach to socialization (e.g., Piaget) to predict a wide variety of consumer-related cognitions learned during adolescence. In general, the findings indicated that the cognitive developmental model did not explain consumer socialization during adolescence very well. Though older adolescents had significantly less favorable attitudes toward advertising, brands, and prices than did younger children, the two groups had similar **attitudes toward salespeople**.

COMMENTS:

The low internal consistency indicates that the scale is not reliable. This could be due to several different factors being represented in the scale. Redevelopment and testing are needed before the scale is used further.

REFERENCES:

Moschis, George P. (1978), *Acquisition of the Consumer Role by Adolescents*, Research Monograph No. 82, Atlanta, Ga.: Publishing Services Division, College of Business Administration, Georgia State University.

_____ (1981), ''Patterns of Consumer Learning,'' *JAMS*, 9 (2), 110-126.

SCALE ITEMS: ATTITUDE TOWARD SALESPEOPLE

Strongly Disagree	Disagree	Neither	Agree	Strongly Agree
5	4	3	2	1

1. Most salespeople try to trick you into buying something you don't really need. **(r)**
2. Salespeople are honest.
3. Salespeople are friendly.
4. Most salespeople would take advantage of those who don't know much about buying things. **(r)**
5. Salespeople are polite.

SCALE NAME: Attitude Toward Shampoo

SCALE DESCRIPTION:

A three-item, five-point semantic differential summated ratings scale measuring a person's evaluation of a brand of shampoo.

SCALE ORIGIN:

The scale is original to Kisielius and Sternthal (1984) and appears to have been used only in that one study. In a pilot study with 43 undergraduate and graduate students, a fictitious brand of shampoo was judged on 10 items. After factor analysis, a three-item attitude scale was constructed that had an alpha of .60. The same scale was used in the other three experiments reported in the article.

SAMPLES:

Three experiments were conducted with **90, 58,** and **58** students, respectively. The samples included both undergraduate and graduate students and had approximately equal proportions of men and women. In each experiment participation was motivated by the opportunity to win a prize.

RELIABILITY:

Alpha values for the scale in the three experiments were **.61, .60,** and **.59.**

VALIDITY:

No examination of scale validity was reported apart from the factor analysis described in the pilot study.

ADMINISTRATION:

Though there were differences in the three experimental sessions, in each the scale was self-administered after the subjects were exposed to information about the fictitious brand of shampoo. Higher scores on the scale indicate that respondents have much better attitudes toward the product than those with lower scores.

MAJOR FINDINGS:

In a series of experiments, Kisielius and Sternthal (1984) investigated the degree to which the favorableness of available information determines the persuasive effect of vividness. Among the many findings were that verbal information seemed to produce more favorable **attitudes** when it was used alone than when it was accompanied with pictorial analogs, instructions to image, or extra-communication information about favorable alternatives.

COMMENTS:

The repeated finding of low internal consistency suggests that the scale should be used cautiously until further work can improve its reliability.

REFERENCE:

Kisielius, Jolita and Brian Sternthal (1984), "Detecting and Explaining Vividness Effects in Attitudinal Judgments," *JMR*, 21 (February), 54-64.

SCALE ITEMS: ATTITUDE TOWARDS SHAMPOO

1. gentle   ___ : ___ : ___ : ___ : ___   harsh
               1   2   3   4   5

2. easy to   ___ : ___ : ___ : ___ : ___   difficult to
   handle   1   2   3   4   5   handle

3. good for   ___ : ___ : ___ : ___ : ___   bad for your
   your hair   1   2   3   4   5   hair

SCALE NAME: Attitude Toward Soft Drink Consumption

SCALE DESCRIPTION:

A seven-item, nine-point summated ratings scale measuring the degree to which a person likes consuming soft drinks. It was referred to by Beatty and Kahle (1988) as simply Attitude.

SCALE ORIGIN:

The items were original to Beatty and Kahle (1988), but they note their sentences were modeled after those used in similar types of constructs measured by Fishbein and Ajzen (1975) as well as Ajzen and Fishbein (1980).

SAMPLES:

Data were collected from respondents at two points in time, four weeks apart. The sample was composed of **187** student volunteers enrolled in various undergraduate business courses at three universities in the western United States. The proportions of men and women were unspecified but noted to be approximately equal. The product examined was soft drinks, and college students were thought to be an appropriate convenience sample. The majority (88%) had consumed at least one soft drink in the previous week.

RELIABILITY:

Alpha values of **.74** and **.79** were reported for the scale for times 1 and 2, respectively. Test-retest stability was **.56**.

VALIDITY:

No examination of scale validity was reported.

ADMINISTRATION:

The scale was filled out by students as part of a larger self-administered questionnaire in an unspecified setting. Higher scores on this scale imply that respondents **enjoy drinking soft drinks** whereas lower scores suggest that for some reason they do not like soft drinks.

MAJOR FINDINGS:

The authors investigated the association between **attitudes** and behaviors in the consumption of a frequently purchased product (soft drinks). The theory of reasoned action and the low involvement hierarchy model were specifically tested. **Soft drink attitude** was not found to be significantly associated with drinking intentions for either high or low brand-committed drinkers. Further, for low brand-committed drinkers, **soft drink enjoyment** was not found to be significantly associated with drinking behavior of the previous week.

COMMENTS:

The internal consistency of the scale is acceptable though low, but the stability of scores over time is cause for concern.

REFERENCES:

Ajzen, Icek and Martin Fishbein (1980), *Understanding Attitudes and Predicting Social Behavior*. Engelwood Cliffs, N.J.: Prentice-Hall, Inc.

Beatty, Sharon E. and Lynn R. Kahle (1988), ''Alternative Hierarchies of the Attitude-Behavior Relationship: The Impact of Brand Commitment and Habit,'' *JAMS*, 16 (Summer), 1-10.

Fishbein, Martin and Icek Ajzen (1975), *Belief, Attitude, Intention, and Behavior: An Introduction to Theory and Research*. Reading, Mass.: Addison-Wesley Publishing Company.

SCALE ITEMS: ATTITUDE TOWARD SOFT DRINK CONSUMPTION

1. I like to enjoy soft drinks.
   Disagree ___:___:___:___:___:___:___:___:___ Agree
        1   2   3   4   5   6   7   8   9

2. I enjoy having a soft drink with a meal.
   Never ___:___:___:___:___:___:___:___:___ Often
        1   2   3   4   5   6   7   8   9

3. Drinking a soft drink to keep me alert is _____.
   Bad ___:___:___:___:___:___:___:___:___ Good
        1   2   3   4   5   6   7   8   9

4. I like drinking a soft drink because it helps me to relax.
   Disagree ___:___:___:___:___:___:___:___:___ Agree
        1   2   3   4   5   6   7   8   9

5. I like drinking a soft drink because it quenches my thirst.
   Disagree ___:___:___:___:___:___:___:___:___ Agree
        1   2   3   4   5   6   7   8   9

6. Drinking a soft drink is *not* healthy for me.
   Likely ___:___:___:___:___:___:___:___:___ Unlikely
        1   2   3   4   5   6   7   8   9

7. I enjoy drinking soft drinks because they taste good.
   Disagree ___:___:___:___:___:___:___:___:___ Agree
        1   2   3   4   5   6   7   8   9

SCALE NAME: Attitude Toward The Act (Getting Flu Shot)

SCALE DESCRIPTION:

A nine-item, seven-point semantic differential summated ratings scale measuring a respondent's overall opinion about getting a flu shot.

SCALE ORIGIN:

The scale was apparently constructed for this study.

SAMPLES:

Systematic random sampling was used to select names and addresses from two sources: the telephone directory of a south-central U.S. city and preregistration data from a major university in the same city. Questionnaires were sent to those selected from the two samples. Of those returning usable forms, **291** residents and **162** students reported receiving a flu shot; **65** residents and **86** students reported that they did not get flu shots.

RELIABILITY:

An alpha of **.94** was reported for the scale.

VALIDITY:

No specific examination of scale validity was reported.

ADMINISTRATION:

The scale was self-administered by respondents along with several other measures at two points in time. The scale was first administered before the flu vaccine became available in the community and then later at the officially designated end of flu season. Higher scores on the scale suggest that respondents have a more positive view of getting the flu shot compared to those with low scores who have a negative opinion.

MAJOR FINDINGS:

Oliver (1980; and Berger 1979) tested a model of consumer satisfaction that expresses satisfaction as a function of expectation and expectancy disconfirmation. The model was examined in the context of comparing people's expectations regarding a flu shot with its perceived benefits and their problems after having received the shot. The results indicated that for all samples (residents and students, inoculated and non-inoculated) the primary determinant of postexposure **attitude** was satisfaction with the decision about receiving the shot.

COMMENTS:

With an adjustment to the opening statement (see below), the scale appears to be flexible for measuring attitudes toward other activities, particularly those that are health-related. However, the quality of the scale for other uses is unknown.

REFERENCES:

Oliver, Richard L. (1980), "A Cognitive Model of the Antecedents and Consequences of Satisfaction Decisions," *JMR*, 17 (November), 460-469.

_____ and Philip K. Berger (1979), "A Path Analysis of Preventative Health Care Decision Models," *JCR*, 6 (September), 113-122.

SCALE ITEMS: ATTITUDE TOWARD THE ACT (GETTING FLU SHOT)

Getting a swine flu shot next fall would be:

foolish	___ : ___ : ___ : ___ : ___ : ___ : ___ 1 2 3 4 5 6 7	wise
safe	___ : ___ : ___ : ___ : ___ : ___ : ___ 1 2 3 4 5 6 7	risky **(r)**
harmful	___ : ___ : ___ : ___ : ___ : ___ : ___ 1 2 3 4 5 6 7	beneficial
pleasant	___ : ___ : ___ : ___ : ___ : ___ : ___ 1 2 3 4 5 6 7	unpleasant **(r)**
waste of time	___ : ___ : ___ : ___ : ___ : ___ : ___ 1 2 3 4 5 6 7	wise use of time
good for me	___ : ___ : ___ : ___ : ___ : ___ : ___ 1 2 3 4 5 6 7	bad for me **(r)**
useful	___ : ___ : ___ : ___ : ___ : ___ : ___ 1 2 3 4 5 6 7	useless **(r)**
worthless	___ : ___ : ___ : ___ : ___ : ___ : ___ 1 2 3 4 5 6 7	valuable
ineffective	___ : ___ : ___ : ___ : ___ : ___ : ___ 1 2 3 4 5 6 7	effective

SCALE NAME: Attitude Toward the Act (Likert)

SCALE DESCRIPTION:

A two-item, seven-point Likert-like summated ratings scale measuring a consumer's inclination to look actively for a brand and purchase it for his/her own use or as a gift for another person.

SCALE ORIGIN:

Bello, Pitts, and Etzel (1983) give no indication in their article that the scale was constructed prior to the reported study.

SAMPLES:

The sample was composed of **217** undergraduate students (138 men and 79 women). The sample was considered appropriate because the subjects' age group represented the largest buyers of the product category under examination (jeans). Groups of students were assigned randomly to one of the experimental treatments.

RELIABILITY:

An alpha of **.86** was reported for the scale.

VALIDITY:

No examination of scale validity was reported.

ADMINISTRATION:

Immediately after viewing several bits of TV programming as well as several commercials, subjects were given a self-administered questionnaire pertaining to the last program and ad they viewed. Lower scores on the scale suggest that respondents have a strong purchase intention toward a brand whereas higher scores mean that they do not expect to be buying the brand.

MAJOR FINDINGS:

The purpose of the experiment was to assess the effectiveness of using ads with controversial sexual content. The findings indicated that brand attitude and **purchase intention** where highly correlated. However, though the controversial ad produced greater interest than the noncontroversial ad, it did not generate a significantly stronger **purchase intention.**

COMMENTS:

See also Petroshius and Crocker (1989) for a potentially similar measure.

REFERENCES:

Bello, Daniel C., Robert E. Pitts, and Michael J. Etzel (1983), ''The Communication Effects of Controversial Sexual Content in Television Programs and Commercials,'' *JA*, 12 (3), 32-42.

Petroshius, Susan M. and Kenneth E. Crocker (1989), ''An Empirical Analysis of Spokesperson Characteristics on Advertisement and Product Evaluations,'' *JAMS*, 17 (Summer), 217-225.

SCALE ITEMS: ATTITUDE TOWARD THE ACT (LIKERT) +

Yes,   ___ : ___ : ___ : ___ : ___ : ___ : ___   No, definitely

definitely   1   2   3   4   5   6   7   not

1. I will actively seek out the product.
2. I will buy the product for myself or as a gift.

+ Only phrases were given in the article, but these sentences are assumed to be similar to those used in the study.

SCALE NAME: Attitude Toward the Act (Likert)

SCALE DESCRIPTION:

A four-item, seven-point Likert-like summated ratings scale measuring the degree of interest a consumer expresses toward buying a product. The scale was used to study both calculators and typewriters.

SCALE ORIGIN:

Petroshius and Monroe (1987) provide no information on the origin of the scale; therefore, it is assumed that they constructed it specifically for use in their study.

SAMPLES:

The sample was composed of **456** undergraduate students. Homogeneous subjects were desired because the study's purpose was to test theoretical propositions. The students were randomly assigned to one of 16 experimental conditions to test the hypotheses.

RELIABILITY:

The alpha values reported for the two products examined were **.86** and **.88**.

VALIDITY:

A factor analysis indicated that the items loaded together and not on other related factors, providing some evidence of convergent and discriminant validity.

ADMINISTRATION:

The scale was self-administered by respondents along with other measures in an unspecified experimental setting. Higher scores on the scale indicate that respondents are very willing to buy a product whereas lower scores suggest they are not interested in purchasing it.

MAJOR FINDINGS:

The study's objective was to examine the relationship between the price structure of a product line and consumer assessments of a product model within the line. The results indicated that price had a negative influence on **purchase willingness**. Also, respondents expressed greater **willingness to purchase** a product when there were constant price differences in the line rather than logarithmic differences.

REFERENCE:

Petroshius, Susan M. and Kent B. Monroe (1987), "Effect of Product- Line Pricing Characteristics on Product Evaluations," *JCR*, 13 (March), 511-519.

SCALE ITEMS: ATTITUDE TOWARD THE ACT (LIKERT) +

1. The likelihood that I would not buy this _____ but continue searching for a _____ is:

Very high	Moderately high	Slightly high	Neither high nor low	Slightly low	Moderately low	Very low
1	2	3	4	5	6	7

2. The likelihood that I would buy this _____ is:

Very high	Moderately high	Slightly high	Neither high nor low	Slightly low	Moderately low	Very low
1	2	3	4	5	6	7

3. At the price shown, I would not buy this _____.(r)

Strongly Agree	Moderately Agree	Slightly Agree	Neither Agree nor Disagree	Slightly Disagree	Moderately Disagree	Strongly Disagree
1	2	3	4	5	6	7

4. If I were going to buy a _____, I would consider buying this model at the price shown.(r)

Strongly Agree	Moderately Agree	Slightly Agree	Neither Agree nor Disagree	Slightly Disagree	Moderately Disagree	Strongly Disagree
1	2	3	4	5	6	7

+ Place the name of the generic product in the blank.

SCALE NAME: Attitude Toward the Act (Reuse Salesperson)

SCALE DESCRIPTION:

A four-item, seven-point semantic differential measuring the degree to which a consumer expects to engage in a particular behavior in the future. In Oliver and Swan (1989) the behavior measured was a consumer's intention to deal with the same salesperson again on his/her next car purchase.

SCALE ORIGIN:

The scale was apparently original to Oliver and Swan (1989).

SAMPLES:

Oliver and Swan's (1989) findings were based upon **415** completed questionnaires from two random samples of new car buyers. Because the two samples did not differ significantly on any demographics measured, the data sets were combined. The sample was 63% male, 30% college educated, 22% having incomes between $30,000 and $39,999, an average of 41 years old, and had owned 7.8 cars.

RELIABILITY:

The estimate of reliability provided by LISREL was **.964.**

VALIDITY:

No specific examination of scale validity was reported by Oliver and Swan (1989).

ADMINISTRATION:

The scale was one of many other measures that were self-administered in Oliver and Swan (1989). Lower scores on the scale suggest that respondents are very likely to engage in a certain behavior whereas high scores imply that customers do not expect to engage in the behavior. The behavior of interest in Oliver and Swan (1989) was dealing with the same car salesperson again.

MAJOR FINDINGS:

The general purpose of Oliver and Swan (1989) was to examine customer perceptions of satisfaction in the context of new car purchases. Using LISREL, it was determined that fairness is more important than disconfirmation in producing interpersonal satisfaction and advantageous inequity is unrelated to it (1989a). **Intention** was found to be strongly related to satisfaction.

COMMENTS:

While the scale was developed with respect to reusing a salesperson, it appears to be amenable for use in other contexts where one wants to measure intentions.

REFERENCES:

Oliver, Richard L. and John E. Swan (1989), "Consumer Perceptions of Interpersonal Equity and Satisfaction in Transactions: A Field Survey Approach," *JM*, 53 (April), 21-35.

SCALE ITEMS: ATTITUDE TOWARD THE ACT (REUSE SALESPERSON)

Indicate whether you would want to deal with the same salesperson on your next car purchase *if he were still available*? I would ask for this salesperson again:

likely   ___ : ___ : ___ : ___ : ___ : ___ : ___   unlikely
               1   2   3   4   5   6   7

not very   ___ : ___ : ___ : ___ : ___ : ___ : ___   probable **(r)**
probable   1   2   3   4   5   6   7

very possible   ___ : ___ : ___ : ___ : ___ : ___ : ___   impossible
                1   2   3   4   5   6   7

no chance   ___ : ___ : ___ : ___ : ___ : ___ : ___   certain **(r)**
                1   2   3   4   5   6   7

SCALE NAME: Attitude Toward the Act (Semantic Differential)

SCALE DESCRIPTION:

The scales consist of various bipolar adjectives presumed to measure the subject's overall evaluation of a purchase activity. The various versions of the scale are similar in that they are not specific to the behaviors under investigation, though certain adjectives may or may not be appropriate (face validity issue) for every behavior one may want to assess.

SCALE ORIGIN:

The scales seem to have been developed in the research cited here. Though no references to previous use of these scales are given in the cited work used in this compendium, this common technique for assessing attitude toward the object has a relatively long history in marketing and advertising research. Slight variations are reported here for several attitude toward specific object measures. What all seem to have in common is some semblance of Osgood, Suci, and Tannenbaum's (1957) Semantic Differential. Nevertheless, no reason is generally given to justify the particular sets of adjectives used in particular studies.

SAMPLES:

Gill, Grossbart, and Laczniak (1988) used **109** student subjects recruited from undergraduate classes. Muehling (1987) used **133** student subjects randomly assigned to one of six treatment conditions. Mitchell (1986) used **69** undergraduate student subjects who were each paid $4 for their participation. There were either 17 or 18 subjects in each of the four cells of the design. Grossbart, Muehling, and Kangun (1986) used **111** undergraduate student subjects in a one-way, between-subjects design. Gardner, Mitchell, and Russo (1985) gathered complete data from 25 subjects, mostly male university students.

Perrien, Dussart, and Paul (1985) used a sample of **186** members of The Montreal Advertising Club and had a 26% response rate. All respondents were French speaking. There was some evidence that the sample was not representative of the population. Kilbourne, Painton, and Ridley (1985) used **238** male and **186** female undergraduate students from a southwestern university. Oliver and Bearden (1985) used **353** members of a bistate consumer panel. Panel members were selected to be representative of urban and suburban households with family income greater that $10,000 annually. Subjects were typically white (89%), female (56%), and had at least some education beyond high school (70%).

Raju and Hastak (1983) used **61** undergraduate student subjects ranging in age from 19 to 23 years. Subjects were randomly assigned to one of three groups and each subject was compensated $4 for participating in the study. Baggozi (1982) used a convenience quota sample of **136** students, **7** faculty, and **27** staff members at a university. Both male and female subjects were included. Mitchell and Olson (1981) used **71** junior and senior undergraduate students of both sexes who were recruited from an introductory marketing course. Subjects were paid for participation in the study reported here.

Kilbourne (1986) used a convenience sample of **49** men and **52** women residing in several communities around a large metropolitan area. Median age was 30 years, 44% had graduated college, 35% had attended college, 21% had graduated high school, and median income was $20,700. Okechuku and Wang (1988) used subjects recruited at shopping malls and other public places in Detroit and surrounding suburbs in Michigan and in Windsor, London, Sarnia, Toronto, and Hamilton, Ontario. Sample sizes were 27, 27, and 26 for three Chinese ads for clothes and 29, 30, and 26 for three North American ads for clothes; 26, 26, and 30 for three Chinese ads for shoes and 25, 24, and 26 for three North American ads for shoes.

Shimp and Sharma (1987) used **145** students in their Crafted in Pride portion of the CETSCALE validation. Unfortunately, no validation of the intention to purchase scales was presented.

RELIABILITY:

Cronbach's alpha was reported to be **.85** by Mitchell and Olson (1981); **.87** by Raju and Hastak (1983); **.90** to **.95** in two similar measures in Muehling (1987); **.85** and **.88** in two uses of the measure by Mitchell (1986); **.92** to **.95** by Grossbart, Muehling, and Kangun (1986); **.97** by Gardner, Mitchell, and Russo (1985); **.861** by Gill, Grossbart, and Laczniak; **.91** by Kilbourne, Painton, and Ridley (1985); **.8115** by Perrien, Dussart, and Paul (1985); **.95** by Bagozzi (1982); **.73** by Kilbourne (1986); and **.84** for intentions to purchase American-made products and **.92** and **.90** for two separate administrations of the attitude toward purchasing foreign-made products scale by Shimp and Sharma (1987). Okechuku and Wang (1988) report alpha values of **.82** and **.77** for their conative measures for clothing and shoe ads, respectively. Reliability information was not reported by Oliver and Bearden (1985).

Note that Okechuku and Wang (1988) also combined the cognative with cognive and affective measures to assess overall attitude toward the ad, acheiving alpha values of **.91** and **.92** for clothing and shoe ads, respectively. The cognitive and affective measures are reported elsewhere in this compendium.

VALIDITY:

Little validity information is provided, per se, though Mitchell and Olson (1981) develop the background for using evaluative belief statements as measures of attitude from Fishbein and Ajzen (1975) and Ahtola (1975). Perrien, Dussart, and Paul (1985) used only those items taken from the literature of which 15 marketing experts agreed measured the conative dimension of an attitude. Okechuku and Wang (1988) factor analyzed their data as per the original. They added ''interesting'' to the affective measure and deleted ''try product from the conative component (reported elsewhere in this compendium).

ADMINISTRATION:

Paper-and-pencil administration as a part of a longer instrument appears to be the method of choice. Subjects are asked to evaluate a specific advertisement on the basis of the adjective listing and to mark the scale appropriately. The lead-in instructions for these scales differ substantially from one use to the next. In some instances, the leads are part of each scale item (e.g., Perrien, Dussart, and Paul 1985). Review of the specific research is recommended. Time is of minimal consequence.

MAJOR FINDINGS:

Mitchell and Olson (1981) used this measure to assess attitude toward the act of purchase of specific brands of facial tissue. Attitude toward the act of purchase of a brand of tissue advertised via a picture of an abstract painting was significantly lower than attitude toward the act of purchase of brands that were advertised with a picture of a kitten or of a sunset or without a picture but with an explicit claim of softness. Additional analysis supports theoretical and empirical contentions that attitude toward the act is influenced by attitude toward the brand and attitude toward the advertisement, and in turn is primarily a significant predictor of behavioral intentions.

Raju and Hastak (1983) found that the use of coupons had very little influence on pretrial beliefs about the brand. Significant correlations were found between attitude toward buying the brand, attitude toward the brand, and belief structure. Pairwise comparisons indicate that subjects responding to a $1.20-off coupon had a significantly greater intention to buy than did subjects with either a $.40-off coupon or no coupon (p $>$ .02). In sum, the magnitude of the deal has little influence on belief structure, attitude toward the brand, and attitude toward buying the brand.

Muehling (1987) tested the effect of five different comparative advertising treatment conditions on attitudes toward purchasing the sponsor's brand and attitude toward purchasing the competitor's brand. For each type of comparative advertisement tested, the attitude toward the ad had a significant, positive influence (p $<$ .05) on attitude toward purchasing the sponsor's brand. However, no significant influence was found on attitude toward purchasing the competitor's brand.

Mitchell (1986) found significant main effects due to product for attitude toward purchasing and using the brand (p $<$ .001). In the first set of measures, a marginally significant effect for picture type (p $<$ .1) was found for attitude toward purchasing and using the brand. In the second set of measures used by Mitchell, however, this relationship was not significant (p $>$ .2). In the first set of measures, for attitudes toward purchasing and using the brand, a series of pairwise tests found significant differences (p $<$ .05) between positive and negative picture conditions, negative and neutral picture conditions, and neutral and the copy-only conditions. A second set of measures, however, were found not to be significant (p $>$ .05).

As hypothesized, Grossbart, Muehling, and Kangun (1986) found no significant differences in purchase intentions associated with comparative and noncomparative advertisements (F $>$ 1.00, p $<$ .10).

Gardner, Mitchell, and Russo (1985) conceptualized involvement as having two dimensions, intensity (amount of attention) and direction (type of processing strategy). The purpose of their study was to vary the direction component of involvement and note its effect on attitudes toward purchase and use of a product. In an experimental setting, some subjects were assigned a brand evaluation goal (high involvement) whereas others were told to evaluate the ad's ability to attract and hold attention (low involvement). As hypothesized, those in the low involvement condition retained less correct brand knowledge than those in the high involvement condition, but expressed more positive attitudes toward buying and using the brand.

Oliver and Bearden (1985) found that in endogenous cases, attitude toward the act was a strong predictor of behavioral intention for subjects high in involvement, whereas the subjective norm was a stronger predictor for subjects high in confidence.

Gill, Grossbart, and Laczniak (1988) found that Fishbein's summation of beliefs and evaluations was directly linked to attitude (p $<$ .01), which subsequently affected purchase intention (p $<$ .01). This relationship was found to be consistent whether subjective-only claims were used in a treatment advertisement or a combination of both objective and subjective claims was used.

Kilbourne, Painton, and Ridley (1985) found significantly higher behavioral intentions toward purchase of Scotch whiskey (p $=$ .003) when the print ad contained a sexual embed than when it did not. These results were not replicated for a cigarette product.

Perrien, Dussart, and Paul (1985) report significantly higher (p < .001) attitudinal scores as amounts of factual information increased from one to three factual claims without regard to percieved risk of the product. They found no differences dependent on the respondent's professional category (agency, advertiser, media, service).

Bagozzi (1982), through LISREL analysis, posits attitude (affect) toward the act of giving blood influences behavioral intention but does not directly influence behavior. He also found that the overall expectancy-value judgement directly determines attitude (affect) toward the act.

Kilbourne (1986) found attitude toward the act of purchase of an electronic calculator was significantly higher (p < .03) for subjects who had viewed an ad for the product in which the female model was portrayed as a professional than for those who had viewed an ad in which she was portrayed as a housewife.

Okechuku and Wang (1988) compared North American subjects' attitudes toward ads from China and the U. S. for shoes and clothing. They found a significant difference in affective responses to both the clothes (p = .016) and shoe (p = .006) ads.

Shimp and Sharma report significant correlations (p < .001) between both the attitude toward the purchase of foriegn-made products and intentions to purchase American-made products and the CETSCALE.

COMMENTS:

This scale is a generally recognized method for measuring attitude toward an act. It relies on researcher judgement as to which specific adjective pairs are appropriate for a given attitude and is therefore not usually assessed for validity. The tests of nomologic and predictive validity are, in a sense, necessary to the success of the research in which they are put to use.

REFERENCES:

Ahtola, Olli T. (1975), "The Vector Model of Preferences: An Alternative to the Fishbein Model," *JMR*, 12 (February), 52-59.

Bagozzi, Richard P. (1982), "A Field Investigation of Causal Relations Among Cognitions, Affect, Intentions, and Behavior," *JMR*, 19 (November), 562-584.

Fishbein, Martin and Icek Ajzen (1975), *Belief, Attitude, Intention and Behavior: An Introduction to Theory and Research*. Reading, Mass.: Addison-Wesley Publishing Company.

Gardner, Meryl Paula, Andrew A. Mitchell, and J. Edward Russo (1985), "Low Involvement Strategies for Processing Advertisements," *JA*, 14 (2), 44-56.

Gill, James D., Sanford Grossbart, and Russell N. Laczniak (1988), "Influence of Involvement, Commitment and Familiarity on Brand Beliefs and Attitudes of Viewers Exposed to Alternative Claim Strategies," *JA*, 17 (2), 33-43.

Grossbart, Sanford, Darrel D. Muehling, and Norman Kangun (1986), "Verbal and Visual References to Competition in Comparative Advertising," *JA*, 15 (1), 10-23.

Kilbourne, William E. (1986), "An Exploratory Study of Sex Role Stereotyping on Attitudes Toward Magazine Advertisements," *JAMS*, 14 (4), 43-46.

_____, Scott Painton, and Danny Ridley (1985), "The Effect of Sexual Embedding on Responses to Magazine Advertisements," *JA*, 14 (2), 48-56.

Mitchell, Andrew A. (1986), "The Effect of Verbal and Visual Components of Advertisements on Brand Attitudes and Attitude Toward the Advertisement," *JCR,* 13 (June), 12-24.

———— and Jerry C. Olson (1981), "Are Product Attribute Beliefs the Only Mediator of Advertising Effects on Brand Attitude?" *JMR,* 18 (August), 318-332.

Muehling, Darrel D. (1987), "Comparative Advertising: The Influence of Attitude-Toward-The-Ad on Brand Evaluation," *JA,* 16 (4), 43-49.

Okechuku, Chike and Gongrong Wang (1988), "The Effectiveness of Chinese Print Advertisements in North America," *JAR,* 28 (October/November), 25-34.

Oliver, Richard L. and William O. Bearden (1985), "Crossover Effects in the Theory of Reasoned Action: A Moderating Influence Attempt," *JCR,* 12 (December), 324-340.

Osgood, Charles E., George J. Suci, and Percy H. Tannenbaum (1957), *The Measurement of Meaning.* Urbana, Ill.: University of Illinois Press.

Perrien, Jean, Christian Dussart, and Francoise Paul (1985), "Advertisers and the Factual Content of Advertising," *JA,* 14 (1), 30-35, 53.

Raju, P. S. and Manoj Hastak (1983), "Pre-Trial Cognitive Effects of Cents-Off Coupons," *JA,* 12 (2), 24-33.

Shimp, Terence A. and Subhash Sharma (1987), "Consumer Ethnocentrism: Construction and Validation of The CETSCALE," *JMR,* 24 (August), 280-289.

SCALE ITEMS: ATTITUDE TOWARD THE ACT (SEMANTIC DIFFERENTIAL)

Scale items used in specific studies are listed below with indication whether item sums or means of sums were used in the research analysis. Some researchers have reversed the polarity of items.

Mitchell and Olson (1981): 1,2,3 (mean)
Raju and Hastak (1983): 1,2,3,4 (mean), 7-point
Muehling (1987): 1,2,3 (mean), 7-point
Mitchell (1986): 1,2,3 (mean), 7-point
Grossbart, Muehling, and Kangun (1986): 1,2,3 (mean), 7-point.
Gardner, Mitchell, and Russo (1985): 1,2,3, 7-point
Oliver and Bearden (1985): 1,2,4
Gill, Grossbart, and Laczniak (1988): 5,6,7,8, 7-point
Kilbourne, Painton, and Ridley (1985): 9,10,11 (sum)
Kilbourne (1986): 9,10,11 (mean), 7-point
Perrien, Dussart, and Paul (1985): 9,11,12,13 (sum), 7-point
Bagozzi (1982): 1,2,4,14,15, 7-point
Okechuku and Wang (1988): 10,11 (mean), 9-point
Shimp and Sharma (1987) American products: 5,7,16, 7-point
Shimp and Sharma (1987) Foreign products: 1,2,3, 7-point.

1. good   ___ : ___ : ___ : ___ :   bad

2. foolish   ___ : ___ : ___ : ___ :   wise **(r)**

3. beneficial   ___ : ___ : ___ : ___ :   harmful

4. unpleasant   ___ : ___ : ___ : ___ :   pleasant **(r)**

5. unlikely   ___ : ___ : ___ : ___ :   likely **(r)**

6. non-existent   ____ : ____ : ____ : ____ :   existent **(r)**

7. improbable   ____ : ____ : ____ : ____ :   probable **(r)**

8. impossible   ____ : ____ : ____ : ____ :   possible **(r)**

9. try product   ____ : ____ : ____ : ____ :   not try product

10. seek out product   ____ : ____ : ____ : ____ :   not seek out product

11. buy product   ____ : ____ : ____ : ____ :   not by product

12. influential   ____ : ____ : ____ : ____ :   not influential

13. look actively for   ____ : ____ : ____ : ____ :   not look actively for

14. safe   ____ : ____ : ____ : ____ :   unsafe

15. punishing   ____ : ____ : ____ : ____ :   rewarding **(r)**

16. certain   ____ : ____ : ____ : ____ :   uncertain

SCALE NAME: Attitude Toward the Offer

SCALE DESCRIPTION:

A five-item, summated ratings scale measuring a person's attitude about a certain product offered at a certain price. The scale is composed of four-bipolar adjectives and one agree-disagree item, each measured on a nine point graphic scale.

SCALE ORIGIN:

There is no information to indicate that the scale originated anywhere than in this study reported in both Burton and Lichtenstein (1988) as well as Lichtenstein and Bearden (1989).

SAMPLES:

Analysis by Burton and Lichtenstein (1988) and Lichtenstein and Bearden (1989) were based upon the same data collected from **278** undergraduate business students. The students were randomly assigned to one of twelve treatment conditions in a $2 \times 2 \times 3$ experimental design. There were between 21 and 28 students per cell.

RELIABILITY:

An alpha of **.92** was reported for the scale.

VALIDITY:

No examination of scale validity was reported.

ADMINISTRATION:

The scale was self-administered by students along with several other measures in an experimental setting. Higher scores on the scale imply that respondents hold a positive attitude about some specified deal (price and product) whereas lower scores suggest that respondents have unfavorable attitudes about an offer.

MAJOR FINDINGS:

The study reported by Burton and Lichtenstein (1988) and Lichtenstein and Bearden (1989) examined the influence of merchant-supplied reference prices, ad distinctiveness, and ad message consistency on perception of source credibility, value of the deal, and attitude toward the deal. In Burton and Lichtenstein (1988), the findings indicated that both the cognitive and affective components of attitude toward the ad were significant predictors of **attitude toward the offer** beyond that which could be explained by other components examined. Among many other findings reported in Lichtenstein and Bearden (1989), **attitude toward the offer** was better for plausible-high merchant-supplied prices than for implausible-high merchant-supplied prices.

REFERENCES:

Burton, Scot and Donald R. Lichtenstein (1988), ''The Effect of Ad Claims and Ad Context on Attitude Toward the Advertisement,'' *JA*, 17 (1), 3-11.

Lichtenstein, Donald R. and William O. Bearden (1989), ''Contextual Influences on Perceptions of Merchant-Supplied Reference Prices,'' *JCR*, 16 (June), 55-66.

SCALE ITEMS: ATTITUDE TOWARD THE OFFER

My attitude toward this deal is:

favorable ___ : ___ : ___ : ___ : ___ : ___ : ___ : ___ : ___ unfavorable **(r)**
        1   2   3   4   5   6   7   8   9

bad ___ : ___ : ___ : ___ : ___ : ___ : ___ : ___ : ___ good
        1   2   3   4   5   6   7   8   9

harmful ___ : ___ : ___ : ___ : ___ : ___ : ___ : ___ : ___ beneficial
        1   2   3   4   5   6   7   8   9

attractive ___ : ___ : ___ : ___ : ___ : ___ : ___ : ___ : ___ unattractive **(r)**
        1   2   3   4   5   6   7   8   9

I like this deal:

strongly disagree ___ : ___ : ___ : ___ : ___ : ___ : ___ : ___ : ___ strongly agree
        1   2   3   4   5   6   7   8   9

SCALE NAME: Attitude Toward the Product

SCALE DESCRIPTION:

A 44-item, three-point summated ratings scale measuring a consumer's satisfaction with a specified product.

SCALE ORIGIN:

The scale was original to Maddox (1982) and was developed as part of a doctoral dissertation (Maddox 1976). Only a few details of the scale's development are provided here, but much more can be found by consulting the dissertation.

SAMPLES:

Participants in the study were students enrolled in sociology, home economics, or business courses at the Ohio State University during the summer of 1975. About 700 survey forms were distributed and **373** completed ones were returned. The typical respondent was male (68%), undergraduate (69%), a business major (68%), never married (57%), and worked either full or part-time (50%). Respondents were randomly assigned one of four products to evaluate: bread (n = 94), electric toasters (n = 88), spray deodorant (n = 94), or tennis shoes (n = 97).

RELIABILITY:

Separate alpha values were calculated for each of the four products evaluated in the study and ranged from .83 (tennis shoes) to .91 (spray deodorant). The alpha for the scale across products was reported as **.88**.

VALIDITY:

The multitrait-multimethod technique was used to examine the scales developed in the study. As with the other scales, this one apparently exhibited convergent and discriminant validity.

ADMINISTRATION:

Students were given the survey instrument, asked to complete it outside the classroom, and to return it at another time. The author assigned the following numerical values to the potential item responses: Y = 3, ? = 2, and N = 1. On this sort of scoring system, high scores indicate consumers are very satisfied with a product. Low scores mean that consumers have very negative attitudes about a product.

MAJOR FINDINGS:

The purpose of the study was to develop a standardized instrument that could be used to compare relative consumer **satisfaction** with different products. A 60-item instrument resulted, which was composed of four subscales: satisfaction with the **product**, its advertising, its pricing, and its placement. The subscales showed evidence of convergent validity and limited evidence of discriminant validity.

COMMENTS:

This scale can be treated as one subscale of a larger 60-item instrument. Other subscales measure satisfaction with the product's advertising, its price, and its placement. The 60-item set was reported to have an alpha of .90 calculated across the four products examined.

Also, though not mentioned as a problem by the author, many of the items in the scale appear to be totally inappropriate in a measure intended to be standardized. For example, how is one supposed to respond to "improved my appearance" for a food item with which one is truly satisfied? Or, what does "greasy" mean with respect to clothing or appliances?

REFERENCES:

Maddox, R. Neil (1976), "Measuring Consumer Satisfaction," unpublished doctoral dissertation, The Ohio State University.

_____ (1982), "The Structure of Consumers' Satisfaction: Cross-Product Comparisons," *JAMS*, 10 (Winter), 37-53.

SCALE ITEMS: ATTITUDE TOWARD THE PRODUCT

Y: This item describes the product
?: Undecided
N: This item does *not* describe the product

Y	?	N	Effective
Y	?	N	Practical
Y	?	N	Investment
Y	?	N	Improved my appearance
Y	?	N	Disappointing **(r)**
Y	?	N	Coordinate easily
Y	?	N	Dressy
Y	?	N	Conversation piece
Y	?	N	Too many attachments **(r)**
Y	?	N	Does the job
Y	?	N	Status symbol
Y	?	N	Favorite color
Y	?	N	Sufficient
Y	?	N	Overloaded with extras **(r)**
Y	?	N	Inferior **(r)**
Y	?	N	Greasy **(r)**
Y	?	N	Tiresome **(r)**
Y	?	N	Harsh **(r)**
Y	?	N	Depressing **(r)**
Y	?	N	Supportive
Y	?	N	Good Looking
Y	?	N	Capable

Y	?	N	Fits my needs
Y	?	N	Ugly **(r)**
Y	?	N	Uncomfortable **(r)**
Y	?	N	Decorative
Y	?	N	Unsafe features **(r)**
Y	?	N	Waste **(r)**
Y	?	N	Attractive
Y	?	N	Met expectations
Y	?	N	Sticky **(r)**
Y	?	N	Flexible
Y	?	N	Unpleasant **(r)**
Y	?	N	Irritating **(r)**
Y	?	N	Poor service **(r)**
Y	?	N	Functional
Y	?	N	Fine gift
Y	?	N	Friends admired
Y	?	N	Impressive
Y	?	N	Quality pleases me
Y	?	N	Risky **(r)**
Y	?	N	Tacky **(r)**
Y	?	N	Frustrating **(r)**
Y	?	N	Undependable **(r)**

SCALE NAME: Attitude Toward the Product/Brand (Likert)

SCALE DESCRIPTION:

The scales reported here are similar in that each purports to measure a consumer's attitude toward a specific brand or product using a Likert format.

SCALE ORIGIN:

Likert-type scales have a long history in marketing as well areas of social science research. The scales reported here have been developed to assess the subject's attitude toward some brand of product. What they all have in common is the Likert format consisting of a statement about some attribute of the attitude object to which respondents indicate their level of agreement or disagreement. The intervals are generally assumed to be equal-appearing for analysis purposes. Common variations on this standard format replace "agree/disagree" scale anchors with other bipolar evaluative word pairs such as "appealing/not appealing." Often the anchors have modifiers such as "strongly," "very," or "extremely." In some cases all response possibilities are labeled (e.g., "strongly agree, moderately agree, somewhat agree, neither agree nor disagree, somewhat disagree, moderately disagree, strongly disagree"). In other cases only the scale anchors and the number of intervals between them are indicated. The midpoint can be either neutral or of unknown specification and is a major point of comment on this and similar scales such as the semantic differential.

In this compendium, all Likert-type scales purported to assess attitude toward the ad, brand, and product are treated as though they were developed for the work in which they were first represented in the marketing literature. Scale anchors other than "agree/disagree" are indicated, as are (whenever possible) the number of scale intervals, the labeling of intervals, and whether scale item means or sums are used in analysis.

SAMPLES:

Petroshius and Crocker (1989) used a total of **160** male and **160** female white undergraduate students. Duncan and Nelson (1985) used **149** male undergraduate student subjects; each subject was paid $4 for participating in the study. Stayman and Aaker (1988) used **116** undergraduate student subjects who were paid $8 and given a chance to win $50 or $100 in a lottery for their participation.

RELIABILITY:

Cronbach's alpha was reported to be between **.75** and **.87** by Petroshius and Crocker (1989), **.82** to **.88** in two repetitions of the same scale by Stayman and Aaker (1986), and **.75** for "liking the product" and **.71** for "positive beliefs about a product" by Duncan and Nelson (1985).

VALIDITY:

No specific validation information was provided by Stayman and Aaker (1988) or Duncan and Nelson (1985). Petroshius and Crocker (1989) factor analyzed seven scale items (exact content unreported), finding two distinct factors related to product perceptions: willingness to purchase and perceived product quality.

ADMINISTRATION:

These scales are generally a part of a survey instrument. The subject is told to respond to each item in the scale by checking, circling, or identifying the number that corresponds to the appropriate scale interval for the attitude object. The scales are generally short and ammenable to self-administration.

MAJOR FINDINGS:

Stayman and Aaker (1988) found that for five of the six products they tested, prior brand attitude (PBA) and attitude toward the ad accounted for significantly more variance ($p < .05$) in brand attitude than PBA alone. For four of the six products tested, execution-related feelings, PBA, and attitude toward the ad were found to account for significantly more variance ($p < .1$) than PBA and attitude toward the ad. Adding the construct "nontarget feelings" produced a significant effect ($p < .1$) in only two of the six products tested.

Duncan and Nelson (1985) found that a humorous treatment in a commercial produced positive changes in the mean response for "liking the product," though the humorous treatment produced little change in "positive product beliefs." High perceived humor treatments resulted in greater mean responses to liking the product and to positive product benefits than did moderate or low humor treatments. For the construct "liking the product," significant ($p < .05$) positive correlations were found with perceived humor ($r = .28$), attention paid (.40), positive product beliefs (.56), liking the commercial (.50), intention to buy (.61), and selling points recalled (.14). For the same construct, significant negative ($p < .05$) correlations were reported for counterarguments ($r = -.15$) and irritation experienced (-.39). For the construct "positive beliefs about the product," significant positive ($p < .05$) correlations were reported with attention paid ($r = .34$), liking the commercial (.37), liking the product (.56), and intention to buy (.30). Significant negative correlations were found between the construct and counterarguments ($r = -.18$) and irritation experienced (-.26).

Petroshious and Crocker (1989) found perceptions of product quality were influnced by the sex and race of the communicator.

COMMENTS:

Some of the scale items used by Duncan and Nelson (1985) to measure positive beliefs about a product appear to measure beliefs about the product category instead of beliefs about a specific product (see scale items). Therefore, though the reliability may be acceptable, the validity of the measure used is questionable.

REFERENCES:

Duncan, Calvin P. and James E. Nelson (1985), "Effect of Humor in a Radio Advertising Experiment," *JA*, 14 (2), 33-40+.

Petroshius, Susan B. and Kenneth E. Crocker (1989), "An Empirical Analysis of Spokesperson Characteristics on Advertisement and Product Evaluations," *JAMS*, 17 (Summer) 217-25.

Stayman, Douglas M. and David A. Aaker (1988), ''Are All Effects of Ad-Induced Feelings Mediated by Attitude Toward the Ad?'' *JCR*, 15 (December), 368-73.

SCALE ITEMS: ATTITUDE TOWARD THE PRODUCT/BRAND (LIKERT) +

Strongly   Strongly
Agree   Disagree

1————2————3————4————5————6————7————8————9

Liking the Product*

1. If I used _____, I probably would like it.
2. Men like myself would probably not like _____. **(r)**
3. I would expect that most men using _____ would be satisfied.
4. Overall, I would describe _____ as:

Extremely   Extremely
Appealing   Unappealing

1————2————3————4————5————6————7————8————9

Positive Beliefs About the Product*

1. _____ gives hair body.
2. Most men could use _____ without harmful consequences.
3. Women would find a user of a men's _____ attractive.
4. On me, _____ would look ridiculous. **(r)**
5. Giving oneself _____ is easy.
6. The points made in the _____ commercial were believable.

+ The items were used by Duncan and Nelson (1985). Items were not reported for the measure used by Stayman and Aaker (1988). Petroshius and Crocker (1989) used a seven item measure that was desribed in their article, though the items were not provided.

*The brand name of the product should be put in the blanks.

SCALE NAME: Attitude Toward the Product/Brand (Semantic Differential)

SCALE DESCRIPTION:

The scales consist of various bipolar adjectives presumed to measure a subject's overall evaluation of a product or brand. The various versions of the scale are similar in that they are not specific to the product or brand under investigation, though certain adjectives may or may not be appropriate (face validity issue) for every product or brand one may want to assess.

SCALE ORIGIN:

Most scales used to measure this construct seem to have been developed in the research cited here. The basis for most of these scales is the semantic differential, developed by Osgood, Suci, and Tannenbaum (1957). The underlying concept for the semantic differential is that a stimulus becomes a sign of the significate when it gives rise to the idea or thought of the significate. Measurement is accomplished by the use of a series of semantic differential scales (a combination of controlled word association and scaling procedures). Each semantic differential scale is purported to represent a straight line through the origin of a semantic space. A selected combination of such scales is then believed to represent a multidimensional space. A listing of potential scale items and the dimension of semantic space they are purported to represent is provided by Osgood, Suci, and Tannenbaum (1957, Ch. 2). The technique is believed by the authors to be highly generalizable and adaptable to most research needs. They generally recommend a seven-point scale, though specific circumstances may warrant a different number of scale points.

SAMPLES:

Dröge (1989) used a total of **178** student subjects, 89 in each of two experimental treatment groups. Edell and Keller (1989) used **243** undergradute student subjects. Participation in the study was required to fulfill a course requirement. Subjects were assigned to one of 12 treatment groups. Hastak and Olson (1989) used **160** undergraduate student subjects in a four-way ($2 \times 2 \times 2 \times 2$) mixed design with three between-subjects factors and one repeated-measures factor.

MacKenzie and Lutz (1989) used a sample of **203** student subjects at a major midwestern university. Subject ages ranged from 20 to 25 years, and subjects were balanced for gender. A validation sample was also used, composed of **120** student subjects at a major university in southern California. Subject ages in the validation sample ranged from 20 to 32 years, and 60% of the subjects were male. Stout and Burda (1989) used a total of **163** male and female undergraduate volunteers from undergraduate communication classes. Subjects were offered extra credit for their participation.

Sujan and Bettman (1989) used **46** undergraduate and graduate business student subjects at a large eastern university. Announcements were made in classes to ask for volunteers, with a $100 lottery as an incentive to participate. The sample was divided into two groups and experimental conditions were conducted in two large classrooms. Cox and Cox (1988) used **240** student subjects recruited from MBA classes at a large southwestern university. Most subjects were employed on a full-time basis and attended the MBA program on a part-time basis. The ages of subjects ranged from 21 to 62 years with a median age of 26 years; 45% of the respondents were female.

Gill, Grossbart, and Laczniak (1988) used **109** undergradute students randomly assigned to one of two treatment groups. Iyer (1988) used **200** subjects recruited at a shopping mall, with 25 subjects randomly assigned to each of eight treatments. Subjects' ages ranges from 16 to 70 years, with a mean age of 29 years; 56% of the subjects were male, 40% of the subjects were married, 61% had at least a college degree, and average income was slightly under $26,000. Munch and Swasy (1988) used **240** undergraduate student subjects at a large eastern university. Subjects were paid $3 for their participation in the study.

Sanbonmatsu and Kardes (1988) used **136** undergraduate student subjects (58 male). Participation was voluntary and subjects were each paid $3. All subjects were screened for health problems prior to the study (which required physical exertion by subjects). Assignment of subjects to the eight treatment groups was made on a random basis. Cox and Locander (1987) used **240** part-time graduate business student subjects from a large southwestern urban area. Age of the subjects ranged from 21 to 62 years with a mean of 31 years; 55% of the subjects were male. Subjects were assigned randomly to treatment groups. Holmes and Crocker (1987) used **155** students at a large midwestern university. Subjects volunteered to participate in the study. Twenty-five were used in a pretest and the remaining 130 were used in the main experiment.

Batra and Ray (1986) used **120** female subjects recruited from the Palo Alto, Calif. area. Subjects were assigned randomly to one of 10 treatment groups. Debevec and Iyer (1986) used **104** junior and senior business students as subjects. Gelb and Zinkhan (1986) used **120** employed adult subjects enrolled in graduate or undergradute business classes on a part-time basis. The design appears to be a variation of a pre-post (post) design, with no control group. Ninety-six of the 120 subjects were used in the final analysis. Grossbart, Muehling, and Kangun (1986) used **111** undergraduate student subjects, with approximately 22 subjects per cell in a five-cell design. Mitchell (1986) used **69** undergraduate student subjects who were each paid $4 for their participation. There were either 17 or 18 subjects in each of the four cells of the design.

Zinkhan, Locander, and Leigh (1986) used **420** subjects recruited by an advertisng agency, with 21 subjects assigned to each of 20 cells. Each subject participated in three sessions and was compensated an unspecified amount at the end of the experiment. Macklin, Bruvold, and Shea (1985) used **127** subjects recruited from a festival held at a public elementary magnet school in a large midwestern city. Subjects were given free tickets (value = $1.00) for participating in the study. Gardner, Mitchell, and Russo (1985) used **10** female and **20** male volunteers recruited through direct interrupt on a university campus. Twenty-six of the subjects were either current students or recent graduates and four were university employees.

Bello, Pitts, and Etzel (1983) used **138** male and **79** female undergraduate student subjects randomly assigned to experimental treatment groups. The authors considered the sample appropriate because the subjects' age groups represented the largest groups of buyers of the product category under examination (jeans). Raju and Hastak (1983) used **61** undergradute student subjects ranging in age from 19 to 23 years. Subjects were assigned randomly to one of three groups and each subject was compensated $4 for participating in the study.

Sheffet (1983) used **180** female "heads of household" obtained through an intercept at two shopping centers. Subjects were believed by the author to be diverse and without major derivations from population statistics. Subjects were assigned randomly to one of 18 treatment groups (n = 10). Smith and Swinyard (1983) used **79** undergraduate business students at a major western university; 76% of the subjects had purchased the product category (snack food items) in the previous month. Mitchell and Olson (1981) used **71** junior and senior undergraduate students of both sexes who were recruited from an introductory marketing course. Subjects were paid for participation in the study reported. Rossiter and Percy (1980) used **88** adult subjects (44 female) recruited in intercept interviews at a midwestern shopping center. All subjects were consumers of the product used in the study (beer).

Berger and Mitchell (1989) used **52** male and **52** female students randomly assigned by sex to one of four experimental condition. Subjects were paid $5 each for participation. Kamins and Marks (1987) used **172** undergraduate and graduate students at a major western university. Subjects were assigned randomly to treatment conditions.

RELIABILITY:

Cronbach's alpha was reported to be **.942** and **.941** for comparative and noncomparative treatment groups, respectively, by Droge (1989); **.90** or better for each of two measures used by Hastak and Olson (1989); **.86** by MacKenzie and Lutz (1989); **.75** by Stout and Burda (1989); **.94** by Sujan and Bettman (1989); **.94** by Cox and Cox (1988); **.95** by Gill, Grossbart, and Laczniak (1988); **.698** by Iyer (1988); **.89** by Munch and Swasy (1988); **.98** by Sanbonmatsu and Kardes (1988); **.90** by Cox and Locander (1987); **.80** by Batra and Ray (1986); **.91** by Gelb and Zinkhan (1986); **.96** and **.97** in two repetitions of the same scale by Grossbart, Muehling, and Kangun (1986); **.89** to **.92** by Mitchell (1986); **.93** by Zinkhan, Locander, and Leigh (1986); **.83** by Macklin, Bruvold, and Shea (1985); **.86** by Bello, Pitts, and Etzel (1983); **.90** by Raju and Hastak (1983); **.88** by Mitchell and Olson (1981); **.86** by Rossiter and Percy (1980); **.94** by Berger and Mitchell (1989) for the entire sample and .95, .89, .95, and .91 for each experimental condition.

The correlation between the two scale items used by Edell and Keller (1989) was .97. No alpha information was reported by Debevec and Iyer (1986), Sheffet (1983), or Kamins and Marks (1987).

VALIDITY:

Limited validity information was provided. Munch and Swasy (1988) analyzed validity through statistically significant ($p < .01$) correlations with dependent variable sets, and factor analysis. Iyer (1988) used principal components analysis on the three scale items to determine their appropriateness. He achieved a one-factor solution with three factor loadings of .961, .452, and .902. Mitchell and Olson (1981) developed the background for using evaluative belief statements as measures of attitude from Fishbein and Ajzen (1975) and Ahtola (1975). A manipulation check by Holmes and Crocker (1987) indicated that between 81.3% and 88% of the subjects perceived the appeal treatments as intended. A manipulation check was also performed by Cox and Cox (1988), who determined that materials intended to be perceived by subjects as high in complexity were perceived as such. No reliabilty measure reported by Smith and Swinyard.

ADMINISTRATION:

Paper-and-pencil administration as a part of a longer instrument appears to be the method of choice. Subjects are asked to evaluate a specific brand of product on the basis of the adjective listing and to mark the scale appropriately. Items are scaled on a five- to nine-point scale, with lower scores indicating a lower attitude toward the product/brand. Time is of minimal consequence in completing the instrument.

MAJOR FINDINGS:

Dröge (1989) used structural equation modeling via LISREL to support the dual mediation hypothesis about the causal relationship between attitude toward the ad and attitude toward the brand for noncomparative ads (relatively less central processing) and lack thereof for comparative ads (relatively more central processing). It should be noted that alpha for the noncomparative ad treatment group measure of attitude toward the ad is relatively low (.693) in comparison with that for the comparative group, that no explanation for this difference is offered, and that LISREL is very sensitive to reliability violations. In addition to this finding, attitude toward the brand was found to be significantly linked with conative measures of intention to try and information search intentions. This was true for both the comparative and noncomparative conditions for the former and only for the comparative for the latter, though in the intention to try scenario the comparative ad showed a greater magnitude of relationship.

Edell and Keller (1989) found a significant effect for a media exposure condition (TV and radio) on attitude toward the brand ($p < .05$). They attributed differences in attitude toward the brand to exposure to at least one television advertisement treatment (vs. exposure to only radio advertisements).

Hastak and Olson (1989) found that brand cognitive responses had significant correlations with brand attitudes ($r = .61$, $p < .01$). Subjects with ad evaluation goals (in comparison with subjects with brand evaluation goals) were found to have weaker correlations between target attribute cognitive responses and (a) an overall expectancy value index of beliefs ($r = .29$ and $.56$, respectively) and (b) attitude toward the brand ($r = .40$ and $.56$, respectively).

MacKenzie and Lutz (1989) found that brand attitude is strongly influenced by attitude toward the ad and is not influenced by brand perceptions. The effect of attitude toward the ad was strong for both brand attitudes and brand perceptions. Consistant with the authors' hypotheses, brand attitudes and brand perceptions were found to be relatively independent of each other. Ad credibility was found to have a weak influence on brand attitude (which was unexpected) in both the developmental and validation samples.

Stout and Burda (1989) used brand attitude as a measure of advertising effectiveness for zipped commercials. To assess whether brand-related attitudes were affected by the speed of a commercial, they performed a series of two-factor ANOVAs. The results indicate that the speed of the commercial significantly affected attitude toward the brand ($p = .001$). Viewers in the zip speed conditions had more neutral attitudes than those in normal speed conditions.

Sujan and Bettman (1989) investigated the influence of advertising strongly versus moderately discrepant information on brand positioning, brand perceptions, and category perceptions. Greater correlation was found between focal attribute importance and brand attitude in the strong discrepancy condition than in the moderate discrepancy condition.

Cox and Cox (1988) found that exposures (two exposures vs. one) have a positive and statistically significant ($p < .05$) effect on brand liking. Brand liking was found to increase with an increase in exposures (from one to two) for both simple and complex ads, even though simple ads did not have a significant gain in ad liking with exposure. Thus, a simple transfer of ad liking from the product to the brand does not account for why brand liking should increase with an increase in exposures for brands using simple advertisements.

Gill, Grossbart, and Laczniak (1988) found that brand attitude had a strong, direct effect ($p < .01$) on purchase intention. Commitment was found to be negatively associated ($p < .1$) with brand attitude. Fishbein and Ajzen's (1975) summation of beliefs and their evaluation aspects was found to be significantly related to brand attitude ($p < .01$).

Iyer (1988) found that brand attitude was influenced by verbal content of a message. Purchase intention, however, was not influenced by verbal content. The author speculates that if multiple exposures of the advertising stimulus had taken place, purchase intention might have affected results.

Munch and Swasy (1988) found a significant effect for argument strength on attitude toward the product (message acceptance) ($p < .01$). For all types of strong arguments, attitude toward the product decreased as the frequency of summarizing rhetorical questions in the argument increased. Attitude toward the product declined for strong arguments when there was distraction in the interpretation of rhetorical questions under high involvement. For weak arguments, no significant differences were found for attitude toward the product.

Sanbonmatsu and Kardes (1988) found that brand attitude was related more positively to strong arguments than weak ($p < .001$). Brand attitude was also found to be significantly greater ($p < .03$) when celebrity endorsers were used (vs. noncelebrity endorsers). A significant interaction ($p < .04$) was interpreted to indicate that brand attitude was less affected when subjects were highly aroused.

Cox and Locander (1987) found that for novel products, 40% of the variance in brand attitude was explained by attitude toward the ad. For familiar products, 26% of the variance in brand attitude was explained by attitude toward the ad.

Holmes and Crocker (1987) found that rational appeals evoked a greater positive response in attitude toward the brand advertised and toward intention to buy than either the emotional or discrepant appeal for a high involvement product. The more positive the predisposition toward the product, the more positive the indicated response in attitude toward the brand and intention to purchase. For low involvement products, an emotional appeal evoked a greater positive response for attitude toward the advertisement and attitude toward the brand. Again, the more positive the predisposition, the more positive the response. For the low involvement product, there was no significant appeal effect (rational, emotional, or discrepant) for the intention to purchase.

Batra and Ray (1986) measured both immediate and delayed brand attitudes (one week later). They found that SEVA (surgency, elation, vigor/activation) ($p = .02$) and social affection ($p = .002$) are significant predictors of brand attitude, but that the effect of these two responses drops to a nonsignificant level ($p = .984$ and $.605$, respectively) when attitude toward the ad and support and counter arguments are considered. Attitude toward the brand was also found to mediate the effects of SEVA and social affection on purchase intention. The results obtained through an ANCOVA procedure are consistent with the theory that attitude toward the ad affects attitude toward the brand, which affects purchase intention.

Debevec and Iyer (1986) found that attitudes toward the product, the message, usage intention, and the spokesperson are significantly more positive ($p < .0001$) when the perceived gender of the product and the gender of the spokesperson differ than when the two genders match.

Gelb and Zinkhan (1986) found that humor is positively related to brand attitude (beta weight = .42). The correlation between humor and brand attitude ($r = .35$) was found to be significant ($p < .01$). Brand attitude was also found to have significant correlations with purchase intention probability ($r = .51$, $p < .01$) and choice behavior ($r = .32$, $p < .01$).

Grossbart, Muehling, and Kangun (1986) found that comparative ads containing only verbal cues to the competition generated more positive attitude toward the sponsor's brand than comparative ads with both visual and verbal references to the competition ($p < .1$). Noncomparative ads were found to provoke more positive brand attitudes than comparative ads using both verbal and visual cues to the competition (p < .1). Noncomparative ads, however, were not found to be more effective than ads containing only verbal references to the competition (F < 1.0).

Mitchell (1986) used a repeated-measures ANOVA to analyze two measures of brand attitude and two measures of attitude toward purchasing and using the product. The results indicate that the use of affect-laden photographs in advertisements that also contain copy has an effect on brand attitudes when individuals execute a brand-processing strategy. Negatively evaluated photographs resulted in less favorable attitudes than positively or neutrally evaluated photographs.

Zinkhan, Locander, and Leigh (1986) found that attitude toward the ad and attitude toward the brand are strongly related (p < .0001) to aided brand recall and recognition. Attitude toward the ad was one of several variables found to relate to four memory measures. The authors state that attitude toward the brand appears to be largely cognitive.

Macklin, Bruvold, and Shea (1985) found that when the concreteness of verbal messages was held constant, the readability level of advertisements did not have a significant effect on attitude toward the brand.

Bello, Pitts, and Etzel (1983) examined the effect and interactions of using ads with controversial sexual content within different types of programs. The findings indicate that brand attitude and purchase intention are highly correlated. Though the controversial ad produced greater interest than the noncotroversial ad, it did not produce a significantly better attitude.

Raju and Hastak (1983) found that attitude toward the brand was significantly correlated (p < .01) with attitude toward the act (r = .65), the summation of beliefs and evaluation (r = .73), and behavioral intention (r = .61). However, the authors found that coupons have very little effect on consumers' pretrial beliefs about the brand.

Sheffet (1983) found that attitude toward the brand in (a) high involvement products (b) whose search attribute claims indicate that product results are available was significantly more favorable (p < .01) than that in (a) high involvement products (b) whose experience claims had been so documented. For low involvement products, attitude toward the brand did have a significant relationship with the disclosure of product test results by the Federal Trade Commission (p < .05).

Mitchell and Olson (1981) assessed attitude toward the brand of facial tissue via this measure. Attitude differed significantly depending on the content of the ad and the direction expected. Tissue in an ad with a nonrelated visual and in an ad with explicit claims of softness but no visual elicited significantly lower scores on attitude toward the brand than did similar ads that included a picture of a kitten and a picture of a sunset (p < .001).

Rossiter and Percy (1980) found that ads with a high visual emphasis and explicit verbal claims produced a significantly greater product attribute rating (p < .005) than ads with a low visual emphasis and implicit verbal claims.

Berger and Mitchell (1989) found that attitude toward the product (candy bar)-behavior consistency was significantly lower for single ad exposure than for direct product, three or four ad exposure conditions (p < .05, .06 and .05, respectively). Brand attitude was significantly higher in the four exposure condition than any other condition (p < .01).

COMMENTS:

These scales represent a generally recognized method for measuring attitude toward an object. They rely on researcher judgment about which specific adjective pairs are appropriate for a given attitude object. The tests of nomological and predictive validity are, in a sense, necessary to the success of the research in which these scales are used.

Note that though all of the scales reported here are bipolar adjective scales and all in some way are purpoted to measure the construct of interest or some dimension of it, each is a slightly different conceptualization of the construct. The researcher must ascertain the most appropriate variation for his or her specific research needs.

REFERENCES:

Ahtola, Olli T. (1975), "The Vector Model of Preferences: An Alternative to the Fishbein Model," *JMR*, 12 (February), 52-59.

Batra, Rajeev and Michael L. Ray (1986), "Affective Responses Mediating Acceptance of Advertising," *JCR*, 13 (September), 234-249.

Bello, Daniel C., Robert E. Pitts, and Michael J. Etzel (1983), "The Communication Effects of Controversial Sexual Content in Television Programs and Commercials," *JA*, 12 (3), 32-42.

Berger, Ida E. and Andrew A. Mitchell (1989), "The Effect of Advertising on Attitude Accessibility, Attitude Confidence, and the Attitude-Behavior Relationship," *JCR*, 16 (December), 269-279.

Cox, Dena Saliagas and Anthony D. Cox (1988), "What Does Familiarity Breed? Complexity as a Moderator of Repetition Effects in Advertisement Evaluations," *JCR*, 15 (June), 111-116.

_____ and William B. Locander (1987), "Product Novelty: Does It Moderate the Relationship Between Ad Attitudes and Brand Attitudes?" *JA*, 16 (3), 39-44.

Debevec, Kathleen and Easwar Iyer (1986), "The Influence of Spokespersons in Altering a Product's Gender Image: Implications for Advertising Effectiveness," *JA*, 15 (4), 12-20.

Dröge, Cornelia (1989), "Shaping the Route to Attitude Change: Central Versus Peripheral Processing Through Comparative Versus Noncomparative Advertising," *JMR*, 26 (May), 193-204.

Edell, Julie and Kevin Lane Keller (1989), "The Information Processing of Coordinated Media Campaigns," *JMR*, 26 (May), 149-163.

Fishbein, Martin and Icek Ajzen (1975), *Belief, Attitude, Intention and Behavior: An Introduction to Theory and Research*. Reading, Mass.: Addison-Wesley Publishing Company.

Gardner, Meryl Paula, Andrew A. Mitchell, and J. Edward Russo (1985), "Low Involvement Strategies for Processing Advertisements," *JA*, 14 (2), 4-12, 56.

Gelb, Betsy G. and George M. Zinkhan (1986), "Humor and Advertising Effectiveness After Repeated Exposures to a Radio Commercial," *JA*, 15 (2), 15-20+.

Gill, James D., Sanford Grossbart, and Russel N. Laczniak (1988), "Influence of Involvement, Commitment, and Familiarity on Brand Beliefs and Attitudes of Viewers Exposed to Alternative Advertising Claim Strategies," *JA*, 17 (2), 33-43.

Grossbart, Sanford, Darrel D Muehling, and Norman Kangun (1986), "Verbal and Visual References to Competition in Comparative Advertising," *JA*, 15 (1), 10-23.

Hastak, Manoj and Jerry C. Olson (1989), "Assessing the Role of Brand Related Cognitive Responses as Mediators of Communication Effects," *JCR*, 15 (March), 444-456.

Holmes, John H. and Kenneth E. Crocker (1987), "Predispositions and the Comparative Effectiveness of Rational, Emotional, and Discrepant Appeals for Both High Involvement and Low Involvement Products," *JAMS*, 15 (Spring), 27-35.

Iyer, Easwar S. (1988), ''The Influence of Verbal Content and Relative Newness on the Effectiveness of Comparative Advertising,'' *JA*, 17 (3), 15-21.

Kamins, Micheal A. and Lawarnce J. Marks (1987), ''Advertising Puffery: The Impact of Using Two-Sided Claims on Product Attitude and Purchase Intention,'' *JA*, 16 (4), 6-15.

MacKenzie, Scott B. and Richard J. Lutz (1989), ''An Empirical Examination of the Structural Antecedents of Attitude Toward the Ad in an Advertising Pretesting Context,'' *JM*, 53 (April), 48-65.

Macklin, M. Carole, Norman T. Bruvold, and Carole Lynn Shea (1985), ''Is It Always as Simple as 'Keep It Simple'?'' *JA*, 14 (4), 28-35.

Mitchell, Andrew A. (1986), ''The Effect of Verbal and Visual Components of Advertisements on Brand Attitudes and Attitude Toward the Advertisement,'' *JCR*, 13 (June), 12- 24.

_____ and Jerry C. Olson (1981), ''Are Product Attribute Beliefs the Only Mediator of Advertising Effects on Brand Attitude? '' *JMR*, 18 (August), 318-332.

Munch, James M. and John L. Swasy (1988), ''Rhetorical Question, Summarization Frequency, and Argument Strength Effects on Recall,'' *JCR*, 15 (June), 69-76.

Osgood, Charles E., George J. Suci, and Percy H. Tannenbaum (1957), *The Measurement of Meaning*. Urbana, Ill.: University of Illinois Press.

Raju, P. S. and Manoj Hastak (1983), ''Pre-Trial Cognitive Effects of Cents-Off Coupons,'' *JA*, 12 (2), 24-33.

Rossiter, John R. and Larry Percy (1980), ''Attitude Change Through Visual Imagery in Advertising,'' *JA*, 9 (2), 10-16.

Sanbonmatsu, David and Frank R. Kardes (1988), ''The Effects of Physiological Arousal on Information Processing and Persuasion,'' *JCR*, 15 (December), 379-385.

Sheffet, Mary Jane (1983), ''An Experimental Investigation of the Documentation of Advertising Claims,'' *JA*, 12 (1), 19-29.

Smith, Robert E. and William R. Swinyard (1983), ''Attitude- Behavior Consistancy: The Impact of Product Trial Versus Advertising,'' *JMR*, 20 (August), 257-267.

Stout, Patricia and Benedicta L. Burda (1989), ''Zipped Commericals: Are They Effective?'' *JA*, 18 (4), 23-32.

Sujan, Mita and James R. Bettman (1989), ''The Effects of Brand Positioning Strategies on Consumers' Brand and Category Perceptions: Some Insights From Schema Research,'' *JMR*, 26 (November), 454-467.

Zinkhan, George M., William B. Locander, and James H. Leigh (1986), ''Dimensional Relationships of Aided Recall and Recognition,'' *JA*, 15 (1), 38-46.

SCALE ITEMS: ATTITUDE TOWARD THE PRODUCT/BRAND (SEMANTIC DIFFERENTIAL) +

Scale items used in specific studies are listed below with indication whether item sums or mean of sums were used in the research analysis and number of points used for each scale item. Some of the items may not reflect bipolar opposites, as originally suggested by Osgood, Suci, and Tannenbaum (1957). Bello et al. (1983) provided only positive anchors. Negative anchors are assumed. Debevec and Iyer (1986) indicated a fifth scale item (masculine-feminine), though the item did not appear to be used in most calculations of attitude toward the brand. Some authors have used scale anchors that have essentially the same meaning but minor semantic differences, such as ''very likable-not very likable'' instead of "like very much-dislike very much." For parsimony, only one alternative in each case is reported.

Berger and Mitchell (1989): 1,29 (mean), 7-point
Dröge (1989): 1,2,5,6,7,8 (mean), 7-point
Edell and Keller (1989): 1,2 (mean), 7-point
Hastak and Olson (1989): 1,2,4 (mean), 7-point
MacKenzie and Lutz (1989): 1,3,9 (mean), 7-point
Stout and Burda (1989): 2,9 (mean), 7-point
Sujan and Bettman (1989): 1,9,14, 7-point
Cox and Cox (1988): 1,2,3 (sum), 9-point
Gill, Grossbart, and Laczniak (1988): 1,2,9, 21 (sum), 7-point
Iyer (1988): 1,8,16 (sum), 7-point
Munch and Swasy (1988): 1,3,14 (mean?), 7-point
Sanbonmatsu and Kardes (1988): 1,6,9 (mean), 9-point
Cox and Locander (1987): 1,2,3 (sum), 9-point
Holmes and Crocker (1987): 10,11,12,13 (mean), 7-point
Kamins and Marks (1987): 1,3,27,30 (mean), 7-point
Batra and Ray (1986): 1,3,16,18,19 (mean), 7-point
Debevec and Iyer (1986): 1,8,16,26 (sum), 7-point
Gelb and Zinkhan (1986): 1,6,9 (summated index)
Grossbart, Muehling, and Kangun (1986): 1,9,14 (index), 7- point
Mitchell (1986): 1,2,3 (mean), 7-point
Zinkhan, Locander, and Leigh (1986): 1,3,21 (sum), 8-point
Macklin, Bruvold, and Shea (1985): 1,3,18,21,27,28, 7-point
Bello, Pitts, and Etzel (1983): 1,4,7,8,14,15,16,17,18, 7-point
Raju and Hastak (1983): 1,2,4, 7-point
Sheffet (1983): 1,7,8,16,19,20,21,22,23,24,25, (mean), 7-point
Smith and Swinyard (1983): 1,3,5,6 (mean), 7-point
Mitchell and Olson (1981): 1,2,3,4 (mean), 5-point
Rossiter and Percy (1980): 1,3,27,28, (sum), 7-point

1. good   ____ : ____ : ____ : ____ : ____   bad

2. dislike very much   ____ : ____ : ____ : ____ : ____   like very much (r)

3. pleasant   ____ : ____ : ____ : ____ : ____   unpleasant

4. poor quality   ____ : ____ : ____ : ____ : ____   high quality (r)

5. disagreeable   ____ : ____ : ____ : ____ : ____   agreeable (r)

6. unsatisfactory   ____ : ____ : ____ : ____ : ____   satisfactory (r)

7. foolish   ___ : ___ : ___ : ___ : ___   wise **(r)**

8. harmful   ___ : ___ : ___ : ___ : ___   beneficial **(r)**

9. favorable   ___ : ___ : ___ : ___ : ___   unfavorable

10. very distinctive   ___ : ___ : ___ : ___ : ___   not very distinctive

11. more positive   ___ : ___ : ___ : ___ : ___   more negative

12. positive opinion   ___ : ___ : ___ : ___ : ___   negative opinion

13. Seek more information   ___ : ___ : ___ : ___ : ___   not seek more information

14. negative   ___ : ___ : ___ : ___ : ___   positive **(r)**

15. distinctive   ___ : ___ : ___ : ___ : ___   common

16. useful   ___ : ___ : ___ : ___ : ___   useless

17. desirable   ___ : ___ : ___ : ___ : ___   undesirable

18. nice   ___ : ___ : ___ : ___ : ___   awful

19. important   ___ : ___ : ___ : ___ : ___   unimportant

20. unusual   ___ : ___ : ___ : ___ : ___   usual

21. worthless   ___ : ___ : ___ : ___ : ___   valuable **(r)**

22. pleasing   ___ : ___ : ___ : ___ : ___   annoying

23. likely   ___ : ___ : ___ : ___ : ___   unlikely

24. dangerous   ___ : ___ : ___ : ___ : ___   safe **(r)**

25. intellegent   ___ : ___ : ___ : ___ : ___   unintelligent

26. harmful   ___ : ___ : ___ : ___ : ___   harmless **(r)**

27. inferior   ___ : ___ : ___ : ___ : ___   superior **(r)**

28. interesting   ___ : ___ : ___ : ___ : ___   boring

29. like   ___ : ___ : ___ : ___ : ___   dislike
     extremely   extremely

30. unagreeable   ___ : ___ : ___ : ___ : ___   agreeable **(r)**

+ Scale items 10-13 attempt to incorporate instructions with the scale items. It is reasonable to view the scale items with only the operative semantic opposites, e.g., item 10: very distinctive--not very distinctive.

SCALE NAME: Attitude Toward the Product Price

SCALE DESCRIPTION:

A five-item, three-point summated ratings scale measuring a consumer's satisfaction with the pricing of a specified product.

SCALE ORIGIN:

The scale was original to Maddox (1982) and was developed as part of a doctoral dissertation (Maddox 1976). Only a few details of the scale's development are provided here, but much more can be found by consulting the dissertation.

SAMPLES:

Participants in the study were students enrolled in sociology, home economics, or business courses at the Ohio State University during the summer of 1975. About 700 survey forms were distributed and **373** completed ones were returned. The typical respondent was male (68%), undergraduate (69%), a business major (68%), never married (57%), and worked either full or part time (50%). Respondents were randomly assigned one of four products to evaluate: bread (n = 94), electric toasters (n = 88), spray deodorant (n = 94), or tennis shoes (n = 97).

RELIABILITY:

Separate alpha values were calculated for each of the four products evaluated in the study and ranged from .88 (tennis shoes) to .82 (spray deodorant). The alpha for the scale across products was reported as **.87**.

VALIDITY:

The multitrait-multimethod technique was used to examine the scales developed in the study. As with the other scales, this one apparently had convergent validity for all products and some limited aspects of discriminant validity.

ADMINISTRATION:

Students were given the survey instrument, asked to complete it outside the classroom, and asked to return it at another time. The author assigned the following numerical values to the potential item responses: Y = 3, ? = 2, and N = 1. On this sort of scoring system, high scores indicate consumers are very satisfied with the pricing of a product and low scores mean consumers have very negative attitudes about a product's pricing.

MAJOR FINDINGS:

The purpose of the study was to develop a standardized instrument that could be used to compare relative consumer **satisfaction** with different products. A 60-item instrument resulted, which was composed of four subscales: satisfaction with the product, its advertising, its **pricing**, and its placement. The subscales showed evidence of convergent validity and limited evidence of discriminant validity.

COMMENTS:

This scale can be treated as one subscale of a larger 60-item instrument. Other subscales measure satisfaction with the product, its advertising, and its placement. The 60-item set was reported to have an alpha of .90 calculated across the four products examined.

REFERENCES:

Maddox, R. Neil (1976), "Measuring Consumer Satisfaction," unpublished doctoral dissertation, Ohio State University.

———— (1982), "The Structure of Consumers' Satisfaction: Cross-Product Comparisons," *JAMS*, 10 (Winter), 37-53.

SCALE ITEMS: ATTITUDE TOWARD THE PRODUCT PRICE

Y: This item describes this product's price
?: Undecided
N: This item does *not* describe this product's price

Y	?	N	Good buy
Y	?	N	Happy with the price
Y	?	N	Worth the money
Y	?	N	Too high for the quality **(r)**
Y	?	N	Too high **(r)**

SCALE NAME: Attitude Toward the Product Retail Placement

SCALE DESCRIPTION:

A six-item, three-point summated ratings scale measuring a consumer's satisfaction with the retail placement aspects of a specified product.

SCALE ORIGIN:

The scale was original to Maddox (1982) and was developed as part of a doctoral dissertation (Maddox 1976). Only a few details of the scale's development are provided here, but much more can be found by consulting the dissertation.

SAMPLES:

Participants in the study were students enrolled in sociology, home economics, or business courses at the Ohio State University during the summer of 1975. About 700 survey forms were distributed and **373** completed ones were returned. The typical respondent was male (68%), undergraduate (69%), a business major (68%), never married (57%), and worked either full or part time (50%). Respondents were randomly assigned one of four products to evaluate: bread (n = 94), electric toasters (n = 88), spray deodorant (n = 94), or tennis shoes (n = 97).

RELIABILITY:

Separate alpha values were calculated for each of the four products evaluated in the study and ranged from .71 (tennis shoes) to .50 (spray deodorant). The alpha for the scale across products was reported as **.54**.

VALIDITY:

The multitrait-multimethod technique was used to examine the scales developed in the study. This scale apparently had adequate convergent validity for all products but lacked significant discriminant validity.

ADMINISTRATION:

Students were given the survey instrument, asked to complete it outside the classroom, and asked to return it at another time. The author assigned the following numerical values to the potential item responses: Y = 3, ? = 2, and N = 1. On this sort of scoring system, high scores indicate consumers are very satisfied with the retail placement of a product and low scores mean consumers have very negative attitudes about a product's placement.

MAJOR FINDINGS:

The purpose of the study was to develop a standardized instrument that could be used to compare relative consumer **satisfaction** with different products. A 60-item instrument resulted which was composed of four subscales: satisfaction with the product, its advertising, its pricing, and its **placement**. Though the **placement** subscale showed evidence of convergent validity, it had lower internal consistency and discriminability than the other subscales.

COMMENTS:

The low internal consistency and lack of discriminant validity suggest this scale should not be used further until its psychomteric quality is improved substantially. Further, note that this scale can be treated as one part of a larger 60-item instrument. Other subscales measure satisfaction with the product, its advertising, and its placement. The 60-item set was reported to have an alpha of .90 calculated across the four products examined.

REFERENCES:

Maddox, R. Neil (1976), ''Measuring Consumer Satisfaction,'' unpublished doctoral dissertation, Ohio State University.

———— (1982), ''The Structure of Consumers' Satisfaction: Cross-Product Comparisons,'' *JAMS*, 10 (Winter), 37-53.

SCALE ITEMS: ATTITUDE TOWARD THE PRODUCT RETAIL PLACEMENT

Y: This item describes the places you buy the product
?: Undecided
N: This item does *not* describe the places you buy the product

Y	?	N	Poor selection **(r)**
Y	?	N	Don't fulfill responsibility **(r)**
Y	?	N	Clerks available
Y	?	N	Unfriendly **(r)**
Y	?	N	Inconvenient **(r)**
Y	?	N	Competent

SCALE NAME: Attitude Toward the Purchase (Feeling Dimension)

SCALE DESCRIPTION:

A three-item, seven-point summated semantic differential rating scale measuring the degree to which a purchase decision is influenced by one's feelings versus one's cognitive thinking.

SCALE ORIGIN:

The scale was constructed for the study reported by Ratchford (1987).

SAMPLES:

The version of the scale described here was used in a preliminary study and one final study reported by Ratchford (1987). The preliminary study was based on 50 mall-intercept interviews. The sample for the final study was composed of the **1792** adult members of the Market Facts mail panel who provided responses to the questionnaire.

RELIABILITY:

Alpha values of .66 and **.64** were calculated for the scale in the preliminary and final studies by Ratchford (1987), respectively.

VALIDITY:

Ratchford (1987) did not specifically examine the validity of the scale, but did assess its validity when used as part of the think/feel matrix, as discussed below with the findings. In a factor analysis of involvement, think, and feel items, there was definitely a feeling factor but two of the items had positive loadings on the involvement factor also.

ADMINISTRATION:

The scale was self-administered along with other measures in the final study by Ratchford (1987). Higher scores on the scale indicate that consumers' feelings are highly involved with their decisions to purchase some specified product whereas lower scores suggest that their feelings have little to do with their purchase decisions.

MAJOR FINDINGS:

The purpose of the study by Ratchford (1987) was to publicize research done by the Foote Cone and Belding agency in its development and testing of a thinking/**feeling** grid. Scores on the involvement scale and a composite think/**feel** scale were calculated for 254 products in the main study. The results for 60 products were plotted in a four-cell matrix, presented in the article, that had degree of involvement as one axis and think/**feel** as the other axis. The plot was described by the author as being "generally intuitive" (p. 30) because most products were in a cell of the grid one would expect.

REFERENCE:

Ratchford, Brian T. (1987), ''New Insights About the FCB Grid,'' *JAR*, 27 (August/September), 24-38.

SCALE ITEMS: ATTITUDE TOWARD THE PURCHASE (FEELING DIMENSION)

Please rate the process of choosing a brand of _____ on each of the following scales. Please base your rating on your most recent choice of a brand of_____.

1. decision expresses one's personality

___ : ___ : ___ : ___ : ___ : ___ : ___   decision does not express one's personality
  7   6   5   4   3   2   1

2. decision is based on a lot of feeling

___ : ___ : ___ : ___ : ___ : ___ : ___   decision is based on little feeling
  7   6   5   4   3   2   1

3. decision is not based on looks, taste, touch, smell, or sounds

___ : ___ : ___ : ___ : ___ : ___ : ___   decision is not based on looks, taste, touch, smell or sounds
  7   6   5   4   3   2   1

SCALE NAME: Attitude Toward the Purchase (Thinking Dimension)

SCALE DESCRIPTION:

A two-item, seven-point semantic differential rating scale measuring the degree to which a purchase decision is influenced by one's cognitive thinking rather than feelings.

SCALE ORIGIN:

The scale was constructed for the study reported by Ratchford (1987).

SAMPLES:

The version of the scale described here was used in a preliminary study and one final study reported by Ratchford (1987). The preliminary study was based upon 50 mall- intercept interviews. The sample for the final study was composed of the **1792** adult members of the Market Facts mail panel who provided responses to the questionnaire.

RELIABILITY:

Alpha values of .48 and **.50** were calculated for the scale in the preliminary and final studies by Ratchford (1987), respectively.

VALIDITY:

Ratchford (1987) did not specifically examine the validity of the scale, but did assess its validity when used as part of the think/feel matrix, as discussed below with the findings. In a factor analysis of involvement, think, and feel items, the items for thinking and involvement loaded on the same factor, which diminishes the scale's discriminant validity to some degree.

ADMINISTRATION:

The scale was self-administered along with other measures in the final study by Ratchford (1987). Higher scores on the scale indicate that consumers' fact-based cognitions are highly involved with their decisions to purchase some specified product whereas lower scores suggest that their cognitive thinking has little to do with their purchase decisions.

MAJOR FINDINGS:

The purpose of the study by Ratchford (1987) was to publicize research done by the Foote Cone and Belding agency in its development and testing of a **thinking**/feeling grid. Scores on the involvement scale and a composite **think**/feel scale were calculated for 254 products in the main study. The results for 60 products were plotted in a four-cell matrix, presented in the article, that had degree of involvement as one axis and **think**/feel as the other axis. The plot was described by the author as being "generally intuitive" (p. 30) because most products were in a cell of the grid one would expect.

REFERENCE:

Ratchford, Brian T. (1987), ''New Insights About the FCB Grid,'' *JAR*, 27 (August/ September), 24-38.

SCALE ITEMS: ATTITUDE TOWARD THE PURCHASE (THINKING DIMENSION)

Please rate the process of choosing a brand of _____ on each of the following scales. Please base your rating on your most recent choice of a brand of _____.

1. decision is mainly logical or objective

_____ : _____ : _____ : _____ : _____ : _____ : _____
   7   6   5   4   3   2   1

decision is not mainly logical or objective

2. decision is based mainly on functional facts

_____ : _____ : _____ : _____ : _____ : _____ : _____
   7   6   5   4   3   2   1

decision is not based mainly on functional facts

SCALE NAME: Attribute Importance

SCALE DESCRIPTION:

A three-item, seven-point semantic differential summated ratings scale measuring the importance of a specified product characteristic to a consumer. Sujan and Bettman (1989) used it for attributes of 35mm SLR cameras.

SCALE ORIGIN:

No information about the scale's origin is provided in the article.

SAMPLES:

Data were gathered from **46** undergraduate and graduate business students at a large eastern university. Announcements were made in classes to ask for student volunteers and a $100 lottery was offered as an incentive to participate. The sample was divided into two groups and experimental conditions were run in two large classrooms. The three experiments, debriefing, and lottery took about 40 minutes to administer.

RELIABILITY:

The scale was used with two different camera features by Sujan and Bettman (1989). An alpha of **.93** was reported for use of the scale with reference to the focal attribute ("sturdiness of construction") and **.92** was reported for the control attribute ("compactness of design").

VALIDITY:

No examination of scale validity was reported.

ADMINISTRATION:

The scale was self-administered along with several other measures as described above. Scores were calculated by averaging numerical responses to the items. Lower scores indicate that a product characteristic is not very important to respondents whereas high scores suggest an attribute is quite salient.

MAJOR FINDINGS:

The purpose of the study was to investigate the influence of advertising strongly versus moderately discrepant information on brand positioning, brand perceptions, and category perceptions. Greater correlation was found between **focal attribute importance** and brand attitude in the strong discrepancy condition than in the moderate discrepancy condition. There were no significant differences found in **importance** of the control attribute across any of the experimental conditions.

REFERENCE:

Sujan, Mita and James R. Bettman (1989), "The Effects of Brand Positioning Strategies on Consumers' Brand and Category Perceptions: Some Insights From Schema Research," *JMR*, 26 (November), 454-467.

SCALE ITEMS: ATTRIBUTE IMPORTANCE

1. Not at all important ___ : ___ : ___ : ___ : ___ : ___ : ___ Very important
1   2   3   4   5   6   7

2. A feature I would not consider ___ : ___ : ___ : ___ : ___ : ___ : ___ A feature I definitely consider
1   2   3   4   5   6   7

Irrelevant to my choice ___ : ___ : ___ : ___ : ___ : ___ : ___ Very relevant to my choice
1   2   3   4   5   6   7

+ Some product category and product attribute would have to be specified for respondents.

SCALE NAME: Attribute Variability

SCALE DESCRIPTION:

A two-item, seven-point semantic differential summated ratings scale measuring how much variability a consumer perceives there to be among brands of a specified product on a specified feature. Sujan and Bettman (1989) used it for attributes of 35mm SLR cameras.

SCALE ORIGIN:

No information is provided in the article indicating the scale's origin.

SAMPLES:

Data were gathered from **46** undergraduate and graduate business students at a large eastern university. Announcements were made in classes to ask for student volunteers and a $100 lottery was offered as an incentive to participate. The sample was divided into two groups and experimental conditions were run in two large classrooms. The three experiments, debriefing, and lottery all took about 40 minutes to administer.

RELIABILITY:

The scale was used with two different camera features by Sujan and Bettman (1989). An alpha of **.94** was reported for use of the scale with reference to the focal attribute ("sturdiness of construction") and **.93** was reported for the control attribute ("compactness of design").

VALIDITY:

No examination of scale validity was reported.

ADMINISTRATION:

The scale was self-administered along with several other measures as described above. Scores were calculated by averaging numerical responses to the items. Lower scores indicate that respondents perceive brands to be quite similar on some specified product characteristic whereas high scores suggest they view considerable variability to exist among the brands.

MAJOR FINDINGS:

The purpose of the study was to investigate the influence of advertising strongly versus moderately discrepant information on brand positioning, brand perceptions, and category perceptions. Strong discrepancy led to greater levels of perceived **variability** on the focal attribute than moderate discrepancy. There were no significant differences found in perceived **variability** of the control attribute across any of the experimental conditions.

REFERENCE:

Sujan, Mita and James R. Bettman (1989), ''The Effects of Brand Positioning Strategies on Consumers' Brand and Category Perceptions: Some Insights From Schema Research,'' *JMR*, 26 (November), 454-467.

SCALE ITEMS: ATTRIBUTE VARIABILITY +

Little variabilty	___ : ___ : ___ : ___ : ___ : ___ : ___	A great deal of variability
	1 2 3 4 5 6 7	

Brands are not at all different	___ : ___ : ___ : ___ : ___ : ___ : ___	Brands are very different
	1 2 3 4 5 6 7	

+ Some product category and product attribute would have to be specified for respondents.

SCALE NAME: Brand Differentiation (Cameras)

SCALE DESCRIPTION:

A two-item, seven-point Likert-type summated ratings scale measuring the degree to which a consumer perceives a certain brand to be in a class apart from other brands of a specified product category. Sujan and Bettman (1989) referred to this scale as Brand Subtyping and used it for 35mm SLR cameras.

SCALE ORIGIN:

No information about the scale's origin is provided in the article.

SAMPLES:

Data were gathered from **46** undergraduate and graduate business students at a large eastern university. Announcements were made in classes to ask for student volunteers and a $100 lottery was offered as an incentive to participate. The sample was divided into two groups and experimental conditions were run in two large classrooms. The three experiments, debriefing, and lottery all took about 40 minutes to administer.

RELIABILITY:

An alpha of **.94** was reported for the scale.

VALIDITY:

No direct examination of scale validity was reported.

ADMINISTRATION:

The scale was self-administered along with several other measures as described above. Scores were calculated by averaging numerical responses to the items. Lower scores indicate that respondents perceive a specified brand to be so distinctive that it is in a class by itself whereas higher scores suggest they view a brand to be similar to other brands of the product.

MAJOR FINDINGS:

The purpose of the study was to investigate the influence of advertising strongly versus moderately discrepant information on brand positioning, brand perceptions, and category perceptions. Strongly discrepant information led respondents to perceive **a brand to be more differentiated** than did moderately discrepant information.

COMMENTS:

Though the items as used in the study and provided below refer to cameras, they could be easily modified for use in studying other product categories.

REFERENCE:

> Sujan, Mita and James R. Bettman (1989), "The Effects of Brand Positioning Strategies on Consumers' Brand and Category Perceptions: Some Insights From Schema Research," *JMR*, 26 (November), 454-467.

SCALE ITEMS: BRAND DIFFERENTIATION (CAMERAS)

Strongly Disagree	Disagree	Slightly Disagree	Neutral	Slightly Agree	Agree	Strongly Agree
1	2	3	4	5	6	7

1. The camera is in a class by itself.
2. Compared to other brands of 35mm SLR cameras, the camera is a different type of 35mm SLR camera.

SCALE NAME: Brand Loyalty (Soft Drink)

SCALE DESCRIPTION:

A three-item, nine-point summated ratings scale measuring the degree to which a person expresses loyalty to a brand of soft drink. It was referred to by Beatty and Kahle (1988) as Brand Commitment.

SCALE ORIGIN:

The items were original to Beatty and Kahle (1988), but they note their sentences "evolved from a review of the literature on involvement, commitment, and brand loyalty" (p. 5).

SAMPLES:

Data were collected from respondents at two points in time, four weeks apart. The sample was composed of **187** student volunteers enrolled in various undergraduate business courses at three universities in the western United States. The proportions of men and women were unspecified but noted to be approximately equal. The product examined was soft drinks and college students were thought to be an appropriate convenience sample. The majority (88%) had consumed at least one soft drink in the previous week.

RELIABILITY:

Alpha values of **.75** and **.75** were reported for the scale for times 1 and 2, respectively. Test-retest stability was **.77**.

VALIDITY:

In an effort to see whether the scale captured the hypothesized construct, respondents were divided into two groups by splitting the distribution of scores at the median. Then the two groups were compared in their responses to the following statement: "If I have a choice I generally purchase one brand of soft drink." Eighty-two percent of subjects in the high brand loyalty group agreed with the statement versus only 37.5% of the low loyalty group. This difference was extremely significant ($p < .001$), indicating that the scale showed evidence of concurrent validity.

ADMINISTRATION:

The scale was filled out by students as part of a larger self-administered questionnaire in an unspecified setting. Higher scores on this scale imply that respondents express strong loyalty to a brand of soft drink whereas lower scores suggest they do not have much commitment to any particular brand.

MAJOR FINDINGS:

The authors investigated the association between attitudes and behaviors in the consumption of a frequently purchased product (soft drinks). The theory of reasoned action and the low involvement hierarchy model were specifically tested. Clear differences were found for the two loyalty groups. High **brand loyal** consumers seem to engage in reasoned action that is strongly influenced by intentions and subjective norms. In contrast, low **brand loyal** consumers appear to be using more of a low involvement hierarchy model and engage in little reasoned action.

REFERENCE:

Beatty, Sharon E. and Lynn R. Kahle (1988), "Alternative Hierarchies of the Attitude-Behavior Relationship: The Impact of Brand Commitment and Habit," *JAMS*, 16 (Summer), 1-10.

SCALE ITEMS: BRAND LOYALTY (SOFT DRINK)

Disagree ____ : ____ : ____ : ____ : ____ : ____ : ____ : ____ : ____ Agree
         1   2   3   4   5   6   7   8   9

1. I consider myself to be loyal to one brand of soft drink.
2. If my preferred brand or type of soft drink were not available at the store, it would make little difference to me if I had to choose another brand. **(r)**
3. When another brand is on sale, I generally purchase it rather than my usual brand. **(r)**

SCALE NAME: Brand Name Appropriateness

SCALE DESCRIPTION:

The scale consists of a three-item, seven-point semantic differential purporting to measure a subject's attitudinal evaluation of a specific word.

SCALE ORIGIN:

The scale is original to Allen and Janiszewski (1989).

SAMPLES:

Allen and Janiszewski (1989) used two separate samples in their research. The first consisted of **61** first-year MBA students. The second consisted of **78** second-year MBA students.

RELIABILITY:

The authors reported alpha values of **.86** and **.86** for the two samples, respectively.

VALIDITY:

No validity assessment is reported.

ADMINISTRATION:

This scale appears appropriate for paper-and- pencil administration. Subjects responded to the scale on a computer screen. Time to administer seems inconsequential. Scale sums were used in the analysis reported here.

MAJOR FINDINGS:

Allen and Janiszewski (1989) report that subjects who were contingently or demand-aware of the purpose of their study evaluated words more favorably in general. Those not aware of the purpose of the research did not do so. Therefore no support was found for a classical conditioning explanation of word association for brand names.

REFERENCE:

Allen, Chris T. and Chris A. Janiszewski (1989), ''Assessing the Role of Contingency Awareness in Attitudinal Conditioning With Implications for Advertising Research,'' *JMR*, 26 (February), 30-43.

SCALE ITEMS: BRAND NAME APPROPRIATENESS

1. appropriate ___ : ___ : ___ : ___ : ___ : ___ : ___ inappropriate
                       1   2   3   4   5   6   7

2. undesirable   ___ : ___ : ___ : ___ : ___ : ___ : ___   desirable (r)

                         1   2   3   4   5   6   7

3. fitting   ___ : ___ : ___ : ___ : ___ : ___ : ___   not fitting

                         1   2   3   4   5   6   7

SCALE NAME: Brand Similarity

SCALE DESCRIPTION:

A four-item, seven-point semantic differential summated ratings scale measuring the degree to which a consumer perceives a certain brand to be like other brands typical of a specified product category. Sujan and Bettman (1989) used it for 35mm SLR cameras.

SCALE ORIGIN:

Sujan and Bettman (1989) provide no information indicating the scale's origin.

SAMPLES:

Data were gathered from **46** undergraduate and graduate business students at a large eastern university. Announcements were made in classes to ask for student volunteers and a $100 lottery was offered as an incentive to participate. The sample was divided into two groups and experimental conditions were run in two large classrooms. The three experiments, debriefing, and lottery all took about 40 minutes to administer.

RELIABILITY:

An alpha of **.96** was reported for the scale.

VALIDITY:

No direct examination of scale validity was reported.

ADMINISTRATION:

The scale was self-administered along with several other measures as described above. Scores were calculated by averaging numerical responses to the items. Lower scores indicate that respondents perceive a specified brand to be so distinctive that it is in a class by itself whereas higher scores suggest they view a brand to be similar to other brands of the product.

MAJOR FINDINGS:

The purpose of the study was to investigate the influence of advertising strongly versus moderately discrepant information on brand positioning, brand perceptions, and category perceptions. The scale was used as a manipulation check and, indeed, strongly discrepant information led respondents to perceive a brand to be more **unlike** other brands than did moderately discrepant information, which in turn was perceived as more different than information with no discrepancy.

COMMENTS:

Though the items as used in the study and provided below refer to cameras, they could be easily modified for use in studying other product categories.

REFERENCE:

Sujan, Mita and James R. Bettman (1989), ''The Effects of Brand Positioning Strategies on Consumers' Brand and Category Perceptions: Some Insights From Schema Research,'' *JMR*, 26 (November), 454-467.

SCALE ITEMS: BRAND SIMILARITY

Identical	____ : ____ : ____ : ____ : ____ : ____ : ____ 7 6 5 4 3 2 1	Completely different
Similar	____ : ____ : ____ : ____ : ____ : ____ : ____ 7 6 5 4 3 2 1	Not similar at all
Few features in common with other 35mm SLRs	____ : ____ : ____ : ____ : ____ : ____ : ____ 7 6 5 4 3 2 1	Many features in common with other 35mm SLRs
Typical	____ : ____ : ____ : ____ : ____ : ____ : ____ 7 6 5 4 3 2 1	Atypical

SCALE NAME: Brand Switcher

SCALE DESCRIPTION:

A seven-item, seven-point Likert-type summated ratings scale measuring the degree to which a person reports him/herself liking to try new and/or different brands rather than sticking with the same brand all the time. This is basically the opposite of brand loyalty.

SCALE ORIGIN:

Though the items may have been drawn from previous work, the scale was developed along with six others by Raju (1980). An initial pool of 90 items related to exploratory behavior and lifestyle were compiled and then tested for low social desirability bias and high item-total correlations. Thirty-nine items were found to meet the criteria and were common to two separate samples. Items were grouped into seven categories on the basis of interitem correlations and subjective judgment.

SAMPLES:

Data were collected by Raju (1980) from **336** homemakers and **105** students. The home-makers were contacted through local women's clubs and the students were contacted mostly through junior and senior level college classes.

RELIABILITY:

The scale was reported by Raju (1980) to have reliability (Spearman-Brown) of **.784** and **.832** for the homemaker and student samples, respectively.

VALIDITY:

Though the author notes that a factor analysis was performed, the grouping of items for scale purposes was based more on interitem correlations and a subjective classification process.

ADMINISTRATION:

The manner of scale administration was not specifically addressed for either sample. However, Raju implied that the homemakers received the questionnaire at a club meeting, filled it out at home by themselves, and returned it by mail. The student sample is assumed to have completed the survey instrument in class. Lower scores on the scale suggest that respondents are brand loyal whereas higher scores imply that they like trying different brands from time to time.

MAJOR FINDINGS:

In two studies, the author examined the relationships between optimal stimulation level (OSL) and certain personality traits, demographics, and purchase-related psychographics. For both samples, significant correlations were found between **brand switching** and OSL.

This finding along with others indicated that people with higher OSLs were more likely to exhibit exploratory behaviors in their consumer behavior.

COMMENTS:

The construct validity of the scale is highly suspect given the manner in which the seven scales used in the study were constructed (as noted in the origination information above). Sixteen of the 39 items were used to compose more than one scale, thus making it unclear what construct the items and their respective scales actually measured. Though the reported reliability levels for this scale are reasonable, further validity testing is needed.

REFERENCE:

Raju, P. S. (1980), "Optimum Stimulation Level: Its Relationship to Personality, Demographics, and Exploratory Behavior," *JCR*, 7 (December), 272-282.

SCALE ITEMS: BRAND SWITCHER

Completely   Completely
Disagree   Agree

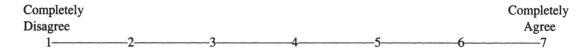

1——————2——————3——————4——————5——————6——————7

1. I enjoy sampling different brands of commonplace products for the sake of comparison.
2. I would rather stick with a brand I usually buy than try something I am not very sure of. **(r)**
3. If I like a brand, I rarely switch from it just to try something different. **(r)**
4. I get bored with buying the same brands even if they are good.
5. A lot of the time I feel the urge to buy something really different from the brands I usually buy.
6. If I did a lot of flying, I would probably like to try all the different airlines, instead of flying one most of the time.
7. I enjoy exploring several different alternatives or brands while shopping.

SCALE NAME: Brand Variability (Cameras)

SCALE DESCRIPTION:

> A two-item, seven-point summated ratings scale measuring the degree to which a consumer perceives a product category to have many different types of brands composing it. Sujan and Bettman (1989) referred to this scale as ''Product category submarkets'' and used it for 35mm SLR cameras.

SCALE ORIGIN:

> Sujan and Bettman (1989) provide no information indicating the scale's origin.

SAMPLES:

> Data were gathered from **46** undergraduate and graduate business students at a large eastern university. Announcements were made in classes to ask for student volunteers and a $100 lottery was offered as an incentive to participate. The sample was divided into two groups and experimental conditions were run in two large classrooms. The three experiments, debriefing, and lottery all took about 40 minutes to administer.

RELIABILITY:

> An alpha of **.79** was reported for the scale.

VALIDITY:

> No direct examination of scale validity was reported.

ADMINISTRATION:

> The scale was self-administered along with several other measures as described above. Scores were calculated by averaging numerical responses to the items. Lower scores indicate that respondents perceive a product category (e.g., 35mm SLR cameras) to have few different types of brands whereas higher scores suggest they view the category as having many (7+) submarkets.

MAJOR FINDINGS:

> The purpose of the study was to investigate the influence of advertising strongly versus moderately discrepant information on brand positioning, brand perceptions, and category perceptions. Strongly discrepant information did not lead respondents to perceive the product category to have significantly more types of brands (**submarkets**) than did moderately discrepant information.

COMMENTS:

> Though the items as used in the study and provided below refer to cameras, they could be easily modified for use in studying other product categories.

REFERENCE:

Sujan, Mita and James R. Bettman (1989), ''The Effects of Brand Positioning Strategies on Consumers' Brand and Category Perceptions: Some Insights From Schema Research,'' *JMR*, 26 (November), 454-467.

SCALE ITEMS: BRAND VARIABILITY (CAMERAS)

Strongly Disagree	Disagree	Slightly Disagree	Neutral	Slightly Agree	Agree	Strongly Agree
1	2	3	4	5	6	7

1. There are many different types of 35mm SLR cameras.
2. The number of types of 35mm SLR cameras is_____.*

* Respondents could indicate a number from 1 to 7.

SCALE NAME: Choice Independence (Child)

SCALE DESCRIPTION:

A five-item, four-point Likert-like summated ratings scale measuring the degree to which a parent reports a child exercises autonomy in the purchase of several products that the child will consume. Referred to by Carlson and Grossbart (1988) as Consumption Independence.

SCALE ORIGIN:

The use of these items as a multi-item measure appears to be original to Carlson and Grossbart (1988). The items themselves and the graphic structure of the measure, however, were taken from the research of Ward, Wackman, and Wartella (1977).

SAMPLES:

The survey instrument used by Carlson and Grossbart (1988) was distributed to mothers via students at three elementary schools in an unidentified U.S. city. The schools were chosen on a convenience basis but appeared to represent a variety of socioeconomic areas of the city. A $1 contribution to the PTO was offered for each completed questionnaire returned by the children. Analysis was based on **451** completed questionnaires. Ninety-three percent of the responding mothers indicated that they were the primary person in the child's socialization.

RELIABILITY:

Carlson and Grossbart (1988) reported an alpha of **.63** and a beta of .51 for the scale.

VALIDITY:

No examination of scale validity was reported by Carlson and Grossbart (1988).

ADMINISTRATION:

The scale was self-administered along with many other measures in the questionnaire used by Carlson and Grossbart (1988). Higher scores on the scale mean that parents choose products for their children and do not consult with them about the choice, whereas lower scores imply that the children are allowed a high degree of freedom in the purchase of the items they consume.

MAJOR FINDINGS:

The authors investigated the relationship between general parental socialization styles and children's consumer socialization. In a factor analysis of scale scores, scores on the **Choice Independence** scale loaded on a factor described as the "child's consumption autonomy." No significant difference was found, however, in the reported degree of child consumption autonomy between any of the five parental socialization styles examined.

COMMENTS:

> The low alpha and beta indicate that the scale is of dubious reliability, most likely because the child's degree of autonomy is product-dependent and is not consistent across product categories.

REFERENCES:

Carlson, Les and Sanford Grossbart (1988), ''Parental Style and Consumer Socialization of Children,'' *JCR*, 15 (June), 77-94.

Ward, Scott, Daniel B. Wackman, and Ellen Wartella (1977), *How Children Learn to Buy*, Beverly Hills, Calif.: Sage Publications, Inc.

SCALE ITEMS: CHOICE INDEPENDENCE (CHILD)

> Place a check to indicate how each of these products is usually purchased, either with your money or with your child's own money. Choose only one answer for each product.

Child chooses for self	Child chooses but talks to parent first	Parent chooses but talks to child first	Parent chooses, doesn't talk to child
1—————	————2—————	————3—————	————4

1. Candy
2. Game or toy
3. Snack food
4. Sports equipment
5. Magazines/comic books

SCALE NAME: Clothing Interest

SCALE DESCRIPTION:

A five-item, six-point, Likert-type summated ratings scale that assesses a person's involvement with and enjoyment of clothes. See also a variation on this scale by Hawes and Lumpkin (1984) in which two items from this scale are combined with two from a shopping interest scale.

SCALE ORIGIN:

It is not clear where the items originated or where the scale was first used as a multi-item summated ratings scale.

SAMPLES:

Lumpkin (1985) analyzed data collected from a sample drawn from the Market Facts Consumer Mail Panel. A total of 2,854 completed questionnaires were received, but Lumpkin focused just on **373** respondents who indicated they were 65 years of age or older.

RELIABILITY:

An alpha of **.8291** was reported by Lumpkin (1985).

VALIDITY:

Factor analysis indicated the items loaded together.

ADMINISTRATION:

Lumpkin (1985) gathered data through self-administered mail questionnaires. Scale scores are calculated by averaging numerical responses to individual items. A score of 6 indicates that a person has a strong interest in clothing whereas a 1 implies that a person is relatively uninvolved with clothing.

MAJOR FINDINGS:

Elderly consumers were cluster analyzed by Lumpkin (1985) and clothing interest discriminated somewhat between the three groups, though the level of statistical significance was not reported. The group with the highest mean on the scale was also the most likely to be clothing opinion leaders and innovators. The group with the lowest mean score appeared to be much less involved with clothing as well as with shopping in general.

REFERENCES:

Hawes, Jon M. and James R. Lumpkin (1984), ''Understanding the Outshopper,'' *JAMS*, 12 (Fall), 200-218.

Lumpkin, James R. (1985), "Shopping Orientation Segmentation of the Elderly Consumer," *JAMS*, 13 (Spring), 271-289.

SCALE ITEMS: CLOTHING INTEREST

Strongly Disagree	Disagree	Slightly Disagree	Slightly Agree	Agree	Strongly Agree
1	2	3	4	5	6

1. I enjoy clothes like some people do such things as books, records, and movies.
2. Clothing is so attractive to me that I am tempted to spend more money than I should.
3. I would like to be considered as one of the best-dressed women/men.
4. Planning and selecting my wardrobe can be included among my favorite activities.
5. I would rather spend my money on clothes than on anything else.

SCALE NAME: Communication Avoidance (Parent/Child)

SCALE DESCRIPTION:

A three-item, five-point Likert-type summated ratings scale measuring the degree to which a person (a parent) believes that it is best to leave children alone and not discuss their worries with them.

SCALE ORIGIN:

The items seem to originate from Schaefer and Bell (1958), but may have been used even earlier. Those authors discuss a considerable amount of testing of the items as part of a larger multiscaled instrument. The three-item version reported here was not tested in their studies, but five- and eight-item versions were. The findings indicated somewhat low internal consistency and test-retest stability.

SAMPLES:

The survey instrument used by Carlson and Grossbart (1988) was distributed to mothers via students at three elementary schools in an unidentified U.S. city. The schools were chosen on a convenience basis but appeared to represent a variety of socioeconomic areas of the city. A $1 contribution to the PTO was offered for each completed questionnaire returned by the children. Analysis was based on **451** completed questionnaires. Ninety-three percent of the responding mothers indicated that they were the primary person in the child's socialization.

RELIABILITY:

Carlson and Grossbart (1988) reported an alpha of **.66** and a beta of .57 for the scale.

VALIDITY:

No examination of scale validity was reported by Carlson and Grossbart (1988).

ADMINISTRATION:

The scale was self-administered along with many other measures in the questionnaire used by Carlson and Grossbart (1988). Higher scores on the scale mean that parents strongly believe that children should be left alone and that openly discussing their problems may only make them worse.

MAJOR FINDINGS:

The authors investigated the relationship between general parental socialization styles and children's consumer socialization. Of the five parental socialization style clusters examined, Authoritarian and Neglecting mothers expressed significantly greater interest in **avoiding communication** with children than did any of the other three parental style clusters, particularly the Permissives and Authoritatives clusters.

COMMENTS:

The low reliability of the scale is justification for cautious use. The addition of a few more appropriate items might improve its psychometric quality substantially. Potential items may be found in the Schaefer and Bell (1958) article.

REFERENCES:

Carlson, Les and Sanford Grossbart (1988), "Parental Style and Consumer Socialization of Children," *JCR*, 15 (June), 77-94.

Schaefer, Earl S. and Richard Q. Bell (1958), "Development of a Parental Attitude Research Instrument," *Child Development*, 29 (September), 339-361.

SCALE ITEMS: COMMUNICATION AVOIDANCE (PARENT/CHILD)

Please indicate your opinion by checking one response (strongly disagree, disagree, neither disagree or agree, agree, strongly agree) for each statement. Check one for each statement.

Strongly Disagree	Disagree	Neither	Agree	Strongly Agree
1	2	3	4	5

1. If you let children talk about their troubles, they end up complaining even more.
2. Parents who start a child talking about his/her worries don't realize that sometimes it' better to leave well enough alone.
3. If a child has upset feelings it is best to leave him/her alone and not make it look serious.

SCALE NAME: Communication Encouragement (Parent/Child)

SCALE DESCRIPTION:

A four-item, five-point Likert-type summated ratings scale measuring the degree to which a person (a parent) believes that children should be free to candidly express their own views and disagree with parents when they feel like it. This scale was called Encouraging Verbalization by Schaefer and Bell (1958) and Carlson and Grossbart (1988).

SCALE ORIGIN:

The items seem to originate from Schaefer and Bell (1958), but may have been used even earlier. Those authors discuss a considerable amount of testing of the items as part of a larger multiscaled instrument. The four-item version reported here was not tested in their studies, but five- and eight-item versions were. The findings indicated rather low internal consistency and test-retest stability.

SAMPLES:

The survey instrument used by Carlson and Grossbart (1988) was distributed to mothers via students at three elementary schools in an unidentified U.S. city. The schools were chosen on a convenience basis but appeared to represent a variety of socioeconomic areas of the city. A $1 contribution to the PTO was offered for each completed questionnaire returned by the children. Analysis was based on **451** completed questionnaires. Ninety-three percent of the responding mothers indicated that they were the primary person in the child's socialization.

RELIABILITY:

Carlson and Grossbart (1988) reported an alpha of **.69** and a beta of .69 for the scale.

VALIDITY:

No examination of scale validity was reported by Carlson and Grossbart (1988).

ADMINISTRATION:

The scale was self-administered along with many other measures in the questionnaire used by Carlson and Grossbart (1988). Higher scores on the scale mean that parents strongly believe children should be encouraged to openly express their opinions even if it means disagreeing with their parents.

MAJOR FINDINGS:

The authors investigated the relationship between general parental socialization styles and children's consumer socialization. Of the five parental socialization styles clusters examined, Permissive mothers expressed significantly greater interest in encouraging **communication** from children than did any of the other four parental style clusters, particularly the Neglecting and Authoritative clusters.

REFERENCES:

Carlson, Les and Sanford Grossbart (1988), "Parental Style and Consumer Socializatio
of Children," *JCR*, 15 (June), 77-94.

Schaefer, Earl S. and Richard Q. Bell (1958), "Development of a Parental Attitud
Research Instrument," *Child Development*, 29 (September), 339-361.

SCALE ITEMS: COMMUNICATION ENCOURAGEMENT (PARENT/CHILD)

Please indicate your opinion by checking one response (strongly disagree, disagree, neithe
disagree or agree, agree, strongly agree) for each statement. Check one for each statement

Strongly Disagree	Disagree	Neither	Agree	Strongl Agree
1————————	—2————————	—3————————	—4————————	—5

1. Children should be allowed to disagree with their parents if they feel their own idea
   are better.
2. Children should be encouraged to tell their parents about it whenever they feel famil
   rules are unreasonable.
3. A child has a right to his/her own point of view and ought to be allowed to express it
4. A child's ideas should be seriously considered before making family decisions.

SCALE NAME: Community Mindedness

SCALE DESCRIPTION:

A six-point, Likert-type summated ratings scale ranging from strongly disagree (1) to strongly agree (6) with varying numbers of items. The scale measures how active one is with social work in the local community. Though not explicitly stated, this is apparently the version of the scale used by Dickerson and Gentry (1983). Modified versions of the scale were used by Lumpkin and Darden (1982), Lumpkin (1985), Hawes and Lumpkin (1984), and Lumpkin and Hunt (1989). See also Schnaars and Schiffman (1984).

SCALE ORIGIN:

These items were part of a classic study of psychographics by Wells and Tigert (1971). One thousand questionnaires were mailed to homemaker members of the Market Facts mail panel. In addition to gathering demographic, product use, and media data, the survey contained 300 statements that have since served as the basis for the construction of many lifestyle-related scales. The four items for this scale are reported in the article, but they were not analyzed as a multi-item scale. The purpose of the article was to explain how psychographics could improve upon mere demographic description of target audiences and product users. No psychometric information was reported.

One of the first uses of the items as a multi-item scale was by Darden and Perreault (1976). Analysis was based on self-administered questionnaires completed by 278 suburban housewives randomly selected in Athens, Georgia. A split-half reliability of .65 was reported for the scale. Community mindedness was *not* found to be significantly related to reported outshopping behavior.

SAMPLES:

Lumpkin and Darden (1982) had **145** usable responses gathered from the consumer research panel of the University of Arkansas. Data were collected from the individuals by mail questionnaire.

Two mailing lists were used to collect data in the Dickerson and Gentry study (1983). One was a list of *Psychology Today* subscribers and the other was a list of members of computer clubs. The former was used to reach non- adopters of computers and the latter was used to reach PC adopters. Analysis was based on a total of **639** questionnaires. Results from a second mailing to nonrespondents indicated that their demographic makeup was not significantly different from that of respondents. On the basis of 1980 Census data, the sample was younger and more upscale than the general population.

Hawes and Lumpkin (1984) collected data from **581** residents of 14 communities near the Ft. Worth-Dallas metroplex. Each of the communities was randomly sampled in proportion to its population by means of the respective telephone directories. The questionnaire was to be filled out by the household member responsible for most of the shopping. The distribution of respondents by community was similar to the actual population distribution.

Lumpkin's (1985) sample was drawn from the Market Facts Consumer Mail Panel. A total of 2854 completed questionnaires were received, but Lumpkin focused on **373** respondents who indicated they were 65 years of age or older. Another large sample from the Market Facts Consumer Mail Panel was used by Lumpkin and Hunt (1989). They focused on a subset of all respondents who indicated they were 65 years of age or older (n = **789**).

RELIABILITY:

The scale was reported to have an alpha of **.68** by Dickerson and Gentry (1983). The modified versions of the scale used by Lumpkin and Darden (1982), Hawes and Lumpkin (1984), Lumpkin (1985), and Lumpkin and Hunt (1989) had alpha values of **.45**, **.65**, **.6555** and **.824**, respectively.

VALIDITY:

Factor analyses performed in the studies indicated that the items loaded together.

ADMINISTRATION:

Data were gathered through self-administered mail questionnaires. Scale scores are typically calculated by averaging numerical responses to individual items. A score of 6 indicates that a person is actively involved in the community whereas a 1 means a person does not get personally involved in community-related activities.

MAJOR FINDINGS:

In their study of television program preference groups, Lumpkin and Darden (1982) found a few lifestyle variables that were significantly different among the six groups, but **community mindedness** was *not* one of them. Dickerson and Gentry (1983) expected to find a negative relationship between adoption of home computers and **community mindedness,** but it was *not* among the lifestyle variables that significantly discriminated between adopters and non-adopters.

The purpose of the study by Hawes and Lumpkin (1984) was to examine demographic and psychographic characteristics of outshoppers. **Community mindedness** did .*not* significantly differentiate between inshoppers and outshoppers. Elderly consumers were cluster analyzed by Lumpkin (1985) and **community mindedness** appeared to discriminate among the three groups (statistical significance not reported). The group with the highest mean on the scale was also the most interested in shopping and the arts. The elderly were broken down into two groups by Lumpkin and Hunt (1989): those who were self-reliant in terms of transportation and those who were dependent on others. The self-reliant were significantly more active in the community than those who were dependent.

COMMENTS:

Care should be taken in deciding which items to use because different configurations have yielded widely varying internal reliability levels.

REFERENCES:

Darden, William R. and William D. Perreault, Jr. (1976), "Identifying Interurban Shoppers: Multiproduct Purchase Patterns and Segmentation Profiles," *JMR*, 13 (February), 51-60.

Dickerson, Mary D. and James W. Gentry (1983), "Characteristics of Adopters and Non-Adopters of Home Computers," *JCR*, 10 (September), 225-235.

Hawes, Jon M. and James R. Lumpkin (1984), "Understanding the Outshopper," *JAMS*, 12 (Fall), 200-218.

Lumpkin, James R. (1985), "Shopping Orientation Segmentation of the Elderly Consumer," *JAMS*, 13 (Spring), 271-289.

_____ and William R. Darden (1982), "Relating Television Preference Viewing to Shopping Orientations, Lifestyles, and Demographics," *JA*, 11 (4), 56-67.

_____ and James B. Hunt (1989), "Mobility as an Influence on Retail Patronage Behavior of the Elderly: Testing Conventional Wisdom," *JAMS*, 17 (Winter), 1-12.

Schnaars, Steven P. and Leon G. Schiffman (1984), "An Application of Segmentation Design Based on a Hybrid of Canonical Correlation and Simple Crosstabulation," *JAMS*, 12 (Fall), 177-189.

Wells, William D. and Douglas Tigert (1971), Activities, Interests, and Opinions," *JAR*, 11 (August), 27-35.

SCALE ITEMS: COMMUNITY MINDEDNESS +

Strongly Disagree	Disagree	Slightly Disagree	Slightly Agree	Agree	Strongly Agree
1	2	3	4	5	6

1. I am an active member of more than one service organization.
2. I do volunteer work for a hospital or service organization on a fairly regular basis.
3. I like to work on community projects.
4. I have personally worked in a political campaign or for a candidate or an issue.
5. I am an active member of more than one social organization or church organization.
6. I do volunteer work on a regular basis.
7. I stay home most evenings. **(r)**

+ Items 1 through 4 were suggested by Wells and Tigert (1971). Lumpkin and Darden (1982) and Lumpkin (1985) used 1, 3, 6, and 7. Lumpkin and Hunt (1989) used 1, 3, 5, and 6 whereas Hawes and Lumpkin (1984) used just 3 and 5.

SCALE NAME: Comparison Shopping

SCALE DESCRIPTION:

A six-point, Likert-type summated ratings scale from strongly disagree (1) to strongly agree (6). The scale measures a person's belief that one should shop around before buying. A three-item version of this scale was called Propensity to Shop by Lumpkin (1985). A four-item version by Hawes and Lumpkin (1984) was referred to as Careful Shopping and bears some similarity to **Sales Advertising Watcher** (*#325*).

SCALE ORIGIN:

It is not clear where the items originated or where the scale was first used as a multi-item summated ratings scale.

SAMPLES:

Hawes and Lumpkin (1984) collected data from **581** residents of 14 communities near the Ft. Worth-Dallas metroplex. Each of the communities was randomly sampled in proportion to its population by means of the respective telephone directories. The questionnaire was to be filled out by the household member responsible for most of the shopping. The distribution of respondents by community was similar to the actual population distribution.

Lumpkin (1985) analyzed data collected from a sample drawn from the Market Facts Consumer Mail Panel. A total of **2,854** completed questionnaires were received but, Lumpkin focused just on **373** respondents who indicated they were 65 years of age or older.

RELIABILITY:

Alpha values of **.728** and **.6108** were calculated by Hawes and Lumpkin (1984) and Lumpkin (1985), respectively.

VALIDITY:

Factor analysis indicated the items loaded together.

ADMINISTRATION:

Data were gathered through self-administered mail questionnaires. Scale scores are calculated by averaging numerical responses to individual items. A score of 6 indicates that a person believes strongly that consumers ought to shop around before buying whereas a 1 implies a person does not think shopping around is very important.

MAJOR FINDINGS:

The purpose of the study by Hawes and Lumpkin (1984) was to examine demographic and psychographic characteristics of outshoppers.

Comparison shopping did **not** differentiate between inshoppers and outshoppers. Elderly consumers were cluster analyzed by Lumpkin (1985) and **comparison shopping**

appeared to be a major discriminator between the three groups, though the level of statistical significance was not reported. The group with the highest mean on the scale was also the most likely to be shopping opinion leaders and expressed the most enjoyment of shopping. The group with the lowest mean score appeared to be much less interested in shopping.

COMMENTS:

Internal consistency may be low because some of the items pertain to shopping whereas others are more advertising oriented.

REFERENCES:

Hawes, Jon M. and James R. Lumpkin (1984), ''Understanding the Outshopper,'' *JAMS*, 12 (Fall), 200-218.

Lumpkin, James R. (1985), ''Shopping Orientation Segmentation of the Elderly Consumer,'' *JAMS*, 13 (Spring), 271-289.

SCALE ITEMS: COMPARISON SHOPPING +

Strongly Disagree	Disagree	Slightly Disagree	Slightly Agree	Agree	Strongly Agree
1	2	3	4	5	6

1. ''Never buy the first one you look at'' is a good motto.
2. I make it a rule to shop at a number of stores before I buy.
3. You can save a lot of money by shopping around.
4. I always check the ads before shopping.
5. I usually watch advertisements.

+ Hawes and Lumpkin (1984) used items 1, 2, 4, and 5 whereas Lumpkin (1985) used items 1, 2, and 3.

SCALE NAME: Complaining Acceptability

SCALE DESCRIPTION:

A four-item, Likert-type summated ratings scale measuring a consumer's perception of the appropriateness of complaining.

SCALE ORIGIN:

Detail of the scale's origin is provided by Richins (1982). The same data were used in her 1983 study. Thirty-one items were generated from depth interviews with 16 consumers and tested with a convenience sample of 43 student and 14 adult consumers. A final group of 15 items was factor analyzed, which resulted in three complaint-related factors, one of which is the four-item scale discussed here.

SAMPLES:

The sample was composed of respondents from one of three groups: 400 questionnaires were mailed to a random sample of residents of a western SMSA, 212 were mailed to members of a consumer protection group residing in the same area, and 198 were sent to people who in the past year had registered a complaint with either the government or a private consumer protection group. After this mailing and a reminder postcard, **356** usable forms were returned for analysis.

RELIABILITY:

An alpha of **.62** was reported.

VALIDITY:

A factor analysis indicated that the items loaded together.

ADMINISTRATION:

The scale was self-administered in a mail survey along with several other measures. Lower scores on the scale suggest that respondents perceive complaining to be justified behavior and socially acceptable whereas higher scores imply that respondents think complaining is inappropriate.

MAJOR FINDINGS:

Richins reported on the construction of consumer assertiveness and aggressiveness scales. Further, the findings indicated that consumers can be divided into four categories depending on the strategies they use to interact with marketers and their representatives: some consumers are high on both traits, some are low on both traits, and some are low on one trait and high on the other. Consumers who perceived **complaining to be the most acceptable** were also the most aggressive whereas those who thought it was **the least appropriate** were low on aggressiveness and assertiveness.

REFERENCES:

Richins, Marsha L. (1982), ''An Investigation of Consumers' Attitudes Toward Complaining,'' in *Advances in Consumer Research*, Vol. 9, Andrew Mitchell, ed. Ann Arbor, Mich.: Association for Consumer Research, 502-506.

———— (1983), ''An Analysis of Consumer Interaction Styles in the Marketplace,'' *JCR*, 10 (June), 73-82.

SCALE ITEMS: COMPLAINING ACCEPTABILITY

Strongly Disagree	Agree	Neutral	Disagree	Strongly Agree
1—————————	2—————————	3—————————	4—————————	5

1. Most people don't make enough complaints to businesses about unsatisfactory products.
2. I feel a sense of accomplishment when I have managed to get a complaint to a store taken care of satisfactorily.
3. People are bound to end up with unsatisfactory products once in a while so they shouldn't complain about them. **(r)**
4. It bothers me quite a bit if I don't complain about an unsatisfactory product when I know I should.

SCALE NAME: Complaint Responsiveness

SCALE DESCRIPTION:

A seven-item, Likert-type summated ratings scale measuring a person's perception of the responsiveness of business to consumer complaints.

SCALE ORIGIN:

Detail of the scale's origin is provided by Richins (1982). The same data were used in her 1983 study. Thirty-one items were generated from depth interviews with 16 consumers and tested with a convenience sample of 43 student and 14 adult consumers. A final group of 15 items was factor analyzed, which resulted in three complaint-related factors, one of which is the seven-item scale discussed here.

SAMPLES:

The sample was composed of respondents from one of three groups: 400 questionnaires were mailed to a random sample of residents of a western SMSA, 212 were mailed to members of a consumer protection group residing in the same area, and 198 were sent to people who in the past year had registered a complaint with either the government or a private consumer protection group. After this mailing and a reminder postcard, **356** usable forms were returned for analysis.

RELIABILITY:

An alpha of **.72** was reported.

VALIDITY:

No examination of scale validity was reported.

ADMINISTRATION:

The scale was self-administered in a mail survey along with several other measures. Higher scores on the scale suggest that respondents perceive business to be responsive to consumer complaints whereas lower scores imply that respondents do not think business is generally responsive to complaints.

MAJOR FINDINGS:

Richins reported on the construction of consumer assertiveness and aggressiveness scales. Further, the findings indicated that consumers can be divided into four categories depending on the strategies they use to interact with marketers and their representatives: some consumers are high on both traits, some are low on both traits, and some are low on one trait and high on the other. Consumers scoring low on aggression perceived **business to be more responsive to consumer complaints** than those high on aggression.

REFERENCES:

Richins, Marsha L. (1982), "An Investigation of Consumers' Attitudes Toward Complaining," in *Advances in Consumer Research*, Vol. 9, Andrew Mitchell, ed. Ann Arbor, Mich.: Association for Consumer Research, 502-506.

_____ (1983), "An Analysis of Consumer Interaction Styles in the Marketplace," *JCR*, 10 (June), 73-82.

SCALE ITEMS: COMPLAINT RESPONSIVENESS

Strongly Agree	Agree	Neutral	Disagree	Strongly Disagree
1————————	—2————————	—3————————	—4————————	—5

1. Most stores are willing to adjust reasonable complaints. **(r)**
2. Many stores say they want their customers satisfied but they aren't willing to stand behind their word.
3. Store employees are often quite unpleasant to customers who return unsatisfactory products.
4. I often find it embarrassing to return or exchange products I am dissatisfied with.
5. Many people think ill of those who make complaints to stores, even when the complaint is reasonable.
6. When a customer returns a defective product, he usually has to go through a lot of annoying paperwork.
7. Making a complaint about a defective product usually takes a lot of time.

SCALE NAME: Complexity (Stimulus)

SCALE DESCRIPTION:

A three-item, seven-point semantic differential summated ratings scale measuring how dynamic or difficult a stimulus is perceived to be.

SCALE ORIGIN:

The scale bears some similarity with items found by Osgood, Suci, and Tannenbaum (1957) to measure the activity dimension and Berlyne (1974) to measure the uncertainty factor. Neither of these previous efforts, however, offered these three items per se as a measure of complexity.

SAMPLES:

Analysis in Holbrook (1981) was based upon **16** subjects chosen from volunteers with an interest in classical piano music. Half had never played an instrument but enjoyed listening to it (''nonexperts'') while the other half were highly trained musicians (''experts'').

RELIABILITY:

An alpha of .**82** was reported for the scale.

VALIDITY:

Beyond noting that the items loaded together in a factor analysis, no specific examination of scale validity was reported.

ADMINISTRATION:

In both studies, subjects self-administered the scale along with several other measures. Higher summated scores suggest that respondents perceive a lot of complexity in an object whereas lower scores mean that they perceive the object to be simple and/or constant.

MAJOR FINDINGS:

Holbrook (1981) illustrated a two-stage integrative model of evaluative judgment where objective product features influenced perceptions which in turn shaped affect. Specifically, it was found that the direct effects of objective music characteristics on affect were not nearly as large or as significant as the indirect effects of those features through intervening perceptions. Perceived expressiveness, activity, and **complexity** had significant positive influences on affect, perceived novelty had a significant negative impact, and perceived potency did not make a salient contribution. Of the musical features examined, dynamics (volume) was the strongest determinant of perceived **complexity.**

REFERENCES:

Berlyne, D.E. (1974), *Studies in the New Experimental Aesthetics*, New York, N.Y.: John Wiley and Sons.

Holbrook, Morris B. (1981), "Integrating Compositional and Decompositional Analyses to Represent the Intervening Role of Perceptions in Evaluative Judgments," *JMR*, 18 (February), 13-28.

Osgood, Charles E., George J. Suci, and Percy H. Tannenbaum (1957), *The Measurement of Meaning*, Urbana, Ill.: University of Illinois Press.

SCALE ITEMS: COMPLEXITY (STIMULUS)

simple	___ :	___ :	___ :	___ :	___ :	___ :	___	complex
	1	2	3	4	5	6	7	

constant	___ :	___ :	___ :	___ :	___ :	___ :	___	changing
	1	2	3	4	5	6	7	

repetitive	___ :	___ :	___ :	___ :	___ :	___ :	___	varied
	1	2	3	4	5	6	7	

SCALE NAME: Compliance (Physician's Advice)

SCALE DESCRIPTION:

A four-item, Likert-type summated ratings scale measuring a person's willingness to follow a physician's advice.

SCALE ORIGIN:

The items and scale appear to be original to the study by Friedman and Churchill (1987).

SAMPLES:

Female graduate students were used as subjects in an experimental setting. A total of **396** students cooperated in the study. Female subjects were used because they were expected to relate better to the female patients on the tape recordings to which they would listen. Graduate students were used because they were assumed to be experienced enough to make the required judgments about physicians.

RELIABILITY:

An alpha of **.64** was reported.

VALIDITY:

The correlation of the scale with a one-item measure of the same construct was .69, providing evidence of convergent validity. The scale had a correlation of .06 with social desirability, providing evidence of discriminant validity. There were indications of nomological validity as well.

ADMINISTRATION:

The scale was presented to subjects as part of a larger self-administered questionnaire to be filled out in an experimental setting. The higher the score on the scale, the greater the subject's expressed willingness to comply with a physician's requests. Lower scores suggest a physician's advice will not be followed.

MAJOR FINDINGS:

The purpose of the experiment was to examine how a physician's social power behaviors can be used to achieve maximum effectiveness, as judged by patients. Subjects listened to recorded conversations between a physician and a patient and were asked to imagine they were the latter. They were then asked to respond to the physician's behavior on a questionnaire. **Compliance** was influenced little by the power behavior used by the physician, but was affected greatly by the riskiness of the ailment. **Willingness to comply** was always greater for the nonrisky ailment (common cold) than for the risky ailment (breast cancer).

REFERENCE:

> Friedman, Margaret L. and Gilbert A. Churchill, Jr. (1987), "Using Consumer Percep-
> tions and a Contingency Approach to Improve Health Care Delivery," *JCR*, 13
> (March), 492-510.

SCALE ITEMS: COMPLIANCE (PHYSICIAN'S ADVICE) +

1. I would probably seek an outside opinion from another physician before doing anything.
   (r)
2. I would follow the preventive health measures the physician suggested.
3. I would report back to the physician as he requested.
4. I would follow through with the treatment advice the physician gave.

+ The number of points on the Likert-type response scale was not specified in the article.

SCALE NAME: Compliance Motivation

SCALE DESCRIPTION:

A three-item, summated ratings scale measuring the degree to which a person expresses the desire to conform to a friend's expectations about a purchase decision. Two of the items had seven-point scales and one had a five-point vertical scale. Bearden, Netemeyer, and Teel (1989) did not explain why they constructed the scale this way.

SCALE ORIGIN:

This measure was constructed by Bearden, Netemeyer, and Teel (1989), but is in the form of scales described by Ajzen and Fishbein (1980).

SAMPLES:

Bearden and his coauthors provide little description of the sample except that it was composed of **143** subjects. On the basis of other samples reported in the same article, it is likely to have been a convenience sample of undergraduate students.

RELIABILITY:

An alpha of **.81** was reported for the scale.

VALIDITY:

This scale was developed and used to help validate two other scales constructed by Bearden, Netemeyer, and Teel (1989). Therefore, beyond the findings discussed below, no other examination of its validity was reported.

ADMINISTRATION:

The scale was self-administered in each of the studies reported by Bearden and his coauthors. Higher scores on the scale indicate that respondents are strongly motivated to comply with what close friends suggest when making purchase decisions.

MAJOR FINDINGS:

The purpose of the study by Bearden, Netemeyer, and Teel (1989) was to develop scales for measuring the dimensions of consumer susceptibility to interpersonal influence. A series of studies provided support for a two-factor model (normative and informational factors). Among the many findings were that the normative factor had a significantly stronger positive correlation than did the informational factor with a measure of **compliance motivation**.

COMMENTS:

Before being administered this scale, subjects were given the following shopping scenario: "While in the process of considering the purchase of a brand of jeans in a store, a close friend (or classmate) approaches you and recommends the jeans you are thinking about."

REFERENCES:

Ajzen, Icek and Martin Fishbein (1980), *Understanding Attitudes and Predicting Social Behavior*. Englewood Cliffs, N.J.: Prentice-Hall, Inc.

Bearden, William O., Richard G. Netemeyer, and Jesse E. Teel (1989), ''Measurement of Consumer Susceptibility to Interpersonal Influence,'' *JCR*, 15 (March), 473-481.

SCALE ITEMS: COMPLIANCE MOTIVATION

1. With respect to this purchase, I would _____ like to do what my close friend (class-mate) thinks I ought to do.

very much   ____ : ____ : ____ : ____ : ____ : ____ : ____   very much not
                           1   2   3   4   5   6   7

2. Regarding this purchase, I want to do what my friend thinks I should do.

unlikely   ____ : ____ : ____ : ____ : ____ : ____ : ____   likely
                     1   2   3   4   5   6   7

3. How much do you want to do what your close friend (classmate) thinks you should do?

    not at all   1
                       2
                       3
                       4
    very strongly   5

SCALE NAME: Compulsivity (General)

SCALE DESCRIPTION:

A five-item, five-point Likert-type summated ratings scale measuring the degree to which a person is characterized by an abnormal amount of fear, worry, and self-debasing feelings and attitudes.

SCALE ORIGIN:

The scale represents a subset of items from scale 7 of the Minnesota Multiphasic Personality Inventory (Dahlstrom, Welsh, and Dahlstrom 1982a). That scale is purported to measure the obsessive-compulsive syndrome and has a long history of development and use. In a variety of studies using a variety of measures, internal consistency has always been above .80 (Dahlstrom, Welsh, and Dahlstrom 1982b, p. 260). Test-retest correlations have been estimated in numerous studies as well and seem to have been influenced by several factors, the main one being the time between administrations. For example, .93 was calculated for male college students when there was a one day interval but .37 was reported for male adolescents with a three-year interval (Dahlstrom, Welsh, and Dahlstrom 1982b, pp. 253-259). The items used by O'Guinn and Faber (1989) were ones that were reported to have the highest item-total correlation (Dahlstrom, Welsh, and Dahlstrom 1982a, p. 213).

SAMPLES:

Two samples were employed by O'Guinn and Faber (1989). One consisted of **386** completed responses (out of 808 questionnaires sent) from people who had written an organization that aided compulsive buyers. A second group was used for comparison and was intended to represent the general population. Eight hundred questionnaires were mailed to people in three Illinois areas: Chicago, Springfield, and Bloomington-Normal. Two mailings produced a total of **250** completed survey forms.

RELIABILITY:

An alpha of .92 was reported for the version of the scale used by O'Guinn and Faber (1989).

VALIDITY:

No specific examination of scale validity was made by O'Guinn and Faber (1989), but some evidence of criterion validity was found as two known groups had significantly different mean scores on the scale and the differences were in the hypothesized directions. (See discussion of study findings below.)

ADMINISTRATION:

The scale was one of several self-administered measures used in a mail survey instrument. Higher scores on the scale indicate that respondents have a tendency to engage in compulsive behaviors whereas lower scores indicate that they are not likely to have abnormal obsessions.

MAJOR FINDINGS:

O'Guinn and Faber (1989) studied compulsive shopping. Their results showed that a sample of compulsive shoppers scored significantly higher on the **compulsivity** scale than a general sample of consumers.

REFERENCES:

Dahlstrom, W. Grant, George Schlager Welsh, and Leona E. Dahlstrom (1982a), *An MMPI Handbook: (V. I) Clinical Interpretation.* Minneapolis, Minn.: University of Minnesota Press.

———, ———, and ——— (1982b), *An MMPI Handbook: (V. II) Research Applications.* Minneapolis, Minn.: University of Minnesota Press.

O'Guinn, Thomas C. and Ronald J. Faber (1989), ''Compulsive Buying: A Phenomenological Exploration,'' *JCR*, 16 (September), 147-157.

SCALE ITEMS: COMPULSIVITY (GENERAL)

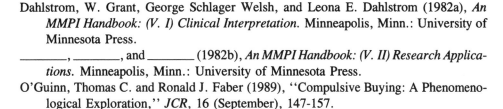

Strongly Disagree	Agree	Neutral	Disagree	Strongly Agree
1	2	3	4	5

1. I frequently find myself worrying about something.
2. Almost everyday something happens to frighten me.
3. Even when I am with people I feel lonely much of the time.
4. Much of the time I feel as if I have done something wrong or evil.
5. I am certainly lacking in self confidence.

SCALE NAME: Compulsivity (Purchase)

SCALE DESCRIPTION:

A three-item, five-point Likert-type summated ratings scale measuring the frequency with which a consumer buys something not so much because of a desire for the product itself but because of a desire to engage in purchase activity.

SCALE ORIGIN:

The scale was apparently original to O'Guinn and Faber (1989).

SAMPLES:

Two samples were employed by O'Guinn and Faber (1989). One consisted of **386** completed responses (out of 808 questionnaires sent) from people who had written an organization that aided compulsive buyers. A second group was used for comparison and was intended to represent the general population. Eight hundred questionnaires were mailed to people in three Illinois areas: Chicago, Springfield, and Bloomington-Normal. Two mailings produced a total of **250** completed survey forms.

RELIABILITY:

An alpha of .**75** was reported for the scale.

VALIDITY:

Beyond a factor analysis indicating that the items loaded together, no specific examination of scale validity was reported.

ADMINISTRATION:

The scale was one of several self-administered measures used in a mail survey instrument. Higher scores on the scale indicate that respondents frequently purchase items that they do not need out of a compulsion to just buy something, whereas lower scores suggest either that they do not purchase a lot or that what they do buy they feel they use and need.

MAJOR FINDINGS:

O'Guinn and Faber (1989) studied compulsive shopping. Their results showed that a sample of shoppers who were generally more compulsive also exhibited significantly more **purchase compulsion** than a general sample of consumers. This finding supports the position that compulsive buyers are less motivated by the desire to own the object of the purchase and more motivated by the activity of purchasing itself.

REFERENCE:

O'Guinn, Thomas C. and Ronald J. Faber (1989), "Compulsive Buying: A Phenomenological Exploration," *JCR*, 16 (September), 147-157.

SCALE ITEMS: COMPULSIVITY (PURCHASE) +

Very Infrequent	Infrequent	Sometimes	Frequent	Very Frequent
1———————	—2———————	—3———————	—4———————	—5

How frequently have you experienced each of the following?

1. Bought something and when I got home wasn't sure why I had bought it.
2. Just wanted to buy things and didn't care what I bought.
3. My closets are full of unopened items.

+ Except for the items themselves, this is the assumed structure of the rest of the scale since it was not described in the article.

SCALE NAME: Conformity (Dress)

SCALE DESCRIPTION:

A six-item, six-point, Likert-type summated ratings scale ranging from strongly disagree (1) to strongly agree (6). The scale measures the importance to a consumer of dressing similarly to one's friends.

SCALE ORIGIN:

It is not clear where the items originated or where the scale was first used as a multi-item summated ratings scale.

SAMPLES:

Lumpkin (1985) analyzed data collected from a sample drawn from the Market Facts Consumer Mail Panel. A total of **2854** completed questionnaires were received, but Lumpkin focused just on **373** respondents who indicated they were 65 years of age or older.

RELIABILITY:

An alpha of **.6812** was reported by Lumpkin (1985).

VALIDITY:

Factor analysis indicated the items loaded together.

ADMINISTRATION:

Lumpkin (1985) gathered data through self-administered mail questionnaires. Scale scores are calculated by averaging numerical responses to individual items. A score of 6 indicates that a person has a strong desire to dress similarly to persons in his or her reference group whereas a 1 means a person expresses little interest in conforming to group dress norms.

MAJOR FINDINGS:

Elderly consumers were cluster analyzed by Lumpkin (1985) and **conformity** discriminated somewhat between the three groups, though the level of statistical significance was not reported. The group with the highest mean on the scale also scored highest of the three groups on fashion innovativeness and opinion leadership. The group with the lowest mean score appeared to have little interest in shopping or fashion.

COMMENTS:

Factor scores for this scale in the Lumpkin study indicate that higher internal consistency might be achieved by dropping item 5 and possibly item 6.

REFERENCE:

Lumpkin, James R. (1985), "Shopping Orientation Segmentation of the Elderly Consumer," *JAMS*, 13 (Spring), 271-289.

SCALE ITEMS: CONFORMITY (DRESS)

Strongly Disagree	Disagree	Slightly Disagree	Slightly Agree	Agree	Strongly Agree
1	2	3	4	5	6

1. It is important to be dressed similarly to those in one's group.
2. Wearing the right clothes is important to acceptance in a group.
3. Friends who dress similarly strengthen the friendship ties.
4. One should be careful not to dress too differently from one's friends.
5. It is not worthwhile to make an effort to conform to the clothing standards of one's social group. **(r)**
6. Dressing similarly to others in my group means little to me. **(r)**

SCALE NAME: Conformity Motivation

SCALE DESCRIPTION:

A 13-item, six-point summated ratings scale measuring the degree to which a person looks to others to determine how to behave and desires to act in accordance with group norms. This measure was called Attention to Social Comparison Information by Lennox and Wolfe (1984) as well as Bearden, Netemeyer, and Teel (1989).

SCALE ORIGIN:

The scale was constructed by Lennox and Wolfe (1984) in the process of refining an index of self-monitoring measures presented by Snyder (1974). The scale was developed in several stages and the final version was tested on **224** introductory psychology students at SUNY Genesco who were required to participate as part of a course. Testing was done in small groups. The scale had an alpha of .**83** and item-total correlations between .34 and .60. The conclusion was that this should not be considered a component of the self-monitoring construct, though it does seem to measure tendency to conform.

SAMPLES:

The sample was just one of many used in a series of studies by Bearden, Netemeyer, and Teel (1989). All that is known about the sample is that it was composed of **47** undergraduate business students.

RELIABILITY:

An alpha of .**82** was reported for the scale by Bearden, Netemeyer, and Teel (1989).

VALIDITY:

This scale was used by Bearden and his coauthors to help validate two other scales constructed in their study. Therefore, beyond the findings discussed below, no other examination of its validity was reported.

ADMINISTRATION:

The scale was self-administered in each of the studies reported by Bearden, and his coauthors. Higher scores on the scale indicate that respondents are strongly motivated to seek information from others about appropriate behavior and desire to conform to group norms.

MAJOR FINDINGS:

The purpose of the study by Bearden, Netemeyer, and Teel (1989) was to develop scales for measuring the dimensions of consumer susceptibility to interpersonal influence. A series of studies provided support for a two-factor model (normative and informational factors). Among the many findings were that the normative factor had a significantly stronger positive correlation than the informational factor with **conformity motivation.**

REFERENCES:

Bearden, William O., Richard G. Netemeyer, and Jesse E. Teel (1989), ''Measurement of Consumer Susceptibility to Interpersonal Influence,'' *JCR*, 15 (March), 473-481.

Lennox, Richard D. and Raymond N. Wolfe (1984), ''Revision of the Self-Monitoring Scale,'' *Journal of Personality and Social Psychology*, 46 (6), 1349-1364.

Snyder, Mark (1974), ''The Self-Monitoring of Expressive Behavior,'' *Journal of Personality and Social Psychology*, 30 (October), 526-537.

SCALE ITEMS: CONFORMITY MOTIVATION

Respond to the statements below using the following scale:

0 = Certainly, always false
1 = Generally false
2 = Somewhat false, but with exception
3 = Somewhat true, but with exception
4 = Generally true
5 = Certainly, always true

1. It is my feeling that if everyone else in a group is behaving in a certain manner, this must be the way to behave.
2. I actively avoid wearing clothes that are not in style.
3. At parties I usually try to behave in a manner that makes me fit in.
4. When I am uncertain how to act in a social situation, I look to the behavior of others for cues.
5. I try to pay attention to the reaction of others to my behavior in order to avoid being out of place.
6. I find that I tend to pick up slang expressions from others and use them as part of my own vocabulary.
7. I tend to pay attention to what others are wearing.
8. The slightest look of disapproval in the eyes of a person with whom I am interacting is enough to make me change my approach.
9. It's important to me to fit in with the group I'm with.
10. My behavior often depends on how I feel others wish me to behave.
11. If I am the least bit uncertain as to how to act in a social situation, I look to the behavior of others for cues.
12. I usually keep up with clothing style changes by watching what others wear.
13. When in a social situation, I tend not to follow the crowd, but instead behave in a manner that suits my particular mood at the time. **(r)**

SCALE NAME: Consequences (Physician's Treatment)

SCALE DESCRIPTION:

A six-item, Likert-type summated ratings scale measuring the severity of the action a person might take if his or her condition worsened after being treated by a physician.

SCALE ORIGIN:

The items and scale appear to be original to the study by Friedman and Churchill (1987).

SAMPLES:

Female graduate students were used as subjects in an experimental setting. A total of **396** students cooperated in the study. Female subjects were used because they were expected to relate better to the female patients on the tape recordings to which they would listen. Graduate students were used because they were assumed to be experienced enough to make the required judgments about physicians.

RELIABILITY:

The internal consistency for this specific scale was not reported by the authors, but they did say that it was among the measures with alpha of **.8** or greater.

VALIDITY:

The pattern of correlations provided evidence of nomological validity. For example, the scale had a correlation of .0 with social desirability, providing evidence of discriminant validity.

ADMINISTRATION:

The scale was presented to subjects as part of a larger self-administered questionnaire to be filled out in an experimental setting. The higher the score on the scale, the more severe the negative consequences of a physician's behavior. Lower scores suggest a patient's response to a worsening condition would **not** involve blaming the physician.

MAJOR FINDINGS:

The purpose of the experiment was to examine how a physician's social power behaviors can be used to achieve maximum effectiveness, as judged by patients. Subjects listened to recorded conversations between a physician and a patient and were asked to imagine they were the latter. They were then asked to respond to the physician's behavior on a questionnaire. The findings involving **consequence** were not clearly reported, but it appears that when referent as well as coercive power behaviors were used there were main effects for power levels and riskiness on **consequences**.

REFERENCE:

Friedman, Margaret L. and Gilbert A. Churchill, Jr. (1987), "Using Consumer Perceptions and a Contingency Approach to Improve Health Care Delivery," *JCR*, 13 (March), 492-510.

SCALE ITEMS: CONSEQUENCES (PHYSICIAN'S TREATMENT)+

1. I would complain to the physician that I didn't like the treatment I received if my health deteriorated.
2. I would still recommend this physician to a friend, even if my condition worsened. **(r)**
3. I would give the physician the "benefit of the doubt" and not complain if my condition worsened. **(r)**
4. I would complain to the local chapter of the AMA about this physician if my health deteriorated.
5. I would bring a legal suit against this physician if my health deteriorated.
6. I would still choose this physician to be my personal physician even if my condition worsened. **(r)**

+ The number of points on the Likert-type response scale was not specified in the article.

SCALE NAME: Conservatism (Politicoeconomic)

SCALE DESCRIPTION:

A six-item, seven-point Likert-type summated ratings scale measuring the degree to which a person holds views about political and economic issues that are considered to be conservative and tend to preserve the status quo.

SCALE ORIGIN:

The items in the scale are taken from the Politico-Economic Conservatism Scale (Form 60) (Levinson 1950, p. 163). That scale had 14 items whereas the version used by Shimp and Sharma (1987) had just six. Further, several of the items have been rephrased slightly to update the scale. Information about the reliability of the scale and mean scores of different groups are given by Levinson (1950, p. 165), but are not particularly relevant because several items are out-of-date and hence that version of the scale should not be used now.

SAMPLES:

Shimp and Sharma (1987) administered the scale in three different samples. One sample consisted of names and addresses obtained from a list broker. One thousand questionnaires were mailed to each of three deliberately chosen cities: Detroit, Denver, and Los Angeles. The response rate was just less than one third for each area. At the same time, 950 questionnaires were sent to former panel members in the Carolinas. The response rate was nearly 60%. The total sample size in this "four-areas study" was **1535**.

The "Carolinas study" involved a group of **417** people who were a part of the "four-areas study." Data for the former study were collected two years prior to data for the latter. A third study examined data from **145** college students. Though having varying proportions, each of the samples except the student group had respondents representing most age and income groups.

RELIABILITY:

Alpha values of .**64** to .**80** were reported for the short version of this scale by Shimp and Sharma (1987), depending on the various geographic areas and studies.

VALIDITY:

The validity of the scale was not specifically examined in the study.

ADMINISTRATION:

The scale was self-administered along with other measures as part of a larger survey instrument in each of the four samples. All except the student sample received questionnaires in the mail. Higher scores imply that respondents express views about politics and economics that are typically considered to be conservative, whereas lower scores imply that respondents are very liberal.

MAJOR FINDINGS:

The purpose of the study was to describe the construction and validation of a scale to measure the American consumer's ethnocentrism. In each of the samples, ethnocentrism was found to have a significant positive correlation with **politicoeconomic conservatism.**

REFERENCES:

Levinson, Daniel J. (1950), "Politico-Economic Ideology and Group Memberships in Relation to Ethnocentrism," in *The Authoritarian Personality*, T. W. Adorno, Else Frenkel-Brunswik, Daniel J. Levinson, and R. Nevitt Sanford, eds. New York, N.Y.: Harper & Row Publishers, Inc.

Shimp, Terence A. and Subhash Sharma (1987), "Consumer Ethnocentrism: Construction and Validation of the CETSCALE," *JMR*, 24 (August), 280-289.

SCALE ITEMS: CONSERVATISM (POLITICOECONOMIC)

Strongly Disagree	Moderately Disagree	Slightly Disagree	Neither Agree Nor Disagree	Slightly Agree	Moderately Agree	Strongly Agree
1	2	3	4	5	6	7

1. Labor unions should become stronger and have more influence generally.**(r)**
2. It is up to the government to make sure that everyone has a secure job and a good standard of living.**(r)**
3. Poverty could be almost entirely done away with if we made certain basic changes in our social and economic system.**(r)**
4. Depressions can be prevented by proper government planning.**(r)**
5. No one should be allowed to earn more than $200,000 a year.**(r)**
6. More government controls over business are needed.**(r)**

SCALE NAME: Consumer Affairs Knowledge

SCALE DESCRIPTION:

An 11-item, true/false summated ratings scale measuring a person's awareness of common pieces of information the educated consumer should know.

SCALE ORIGIN:

The measure originates from a dissertation published by Moschis in 1978. His 1981 study, reported below, is from that same dissertation research. Another version is reported by Moschis and Moore (1978). It was called Legal Knowledge, contained only six items, and had an alpha of only .44. In that study, older children were found to have greater legal knowledge than younger children.

SAMPLES:

Moschis' (1981) data came from **806** middle school or senior high school students. There were 365 "older" adolescents (15 years and older) and 441 "younger" adolescents (younger than 15 years). The students came from 13 schools and seven towns in Wisconsin representing a wide variety of urban to rural situations. The author indicates that the sample was well balanced in terms of most demographic characteristics except sex, as nearly two-thirds of the respondents were female.

RELIABILITY:

An alpha of **.57** was reported for the scale.

VALIDITY:

No examination of scale validity was reported.

ADMINISTRATION:

The scale was self-administered by students along with several other measures in a 10-page instrument during a regular class session. Scores are calculated by totaling the number of items for which a respondent gives the correct answer. Higher scores on the scale indicate that respondents have better understanding of some basic consumer laws, rights, and issues whereas lower scores suggest either that they do not know much about these sorts of things or that what they do "know" is incorrect.

MAJOR FINDINGS:

The study investigated the validity of the cognitive development approach to socialization (e.g., Piaget) to predict a wide variety of consumer-related cognitions learned during adolescence. In general, the findings indicated that the cognitive developmental model did not explain consumer socialization during adolescence very well. Older adolescents had significantly less favorable attitudes toward advertising, brands, and prices than did younger children, but significantly greater **consumer affairs knowledge**.

COMMENTS:

The low internal consistency indicates that the scale is not very reliable. This could be due to several different factors being represented in the scale. Redevelopment and testing should be conducted before the scale is used further, particularly because legislation has changed since the scale was developed.

REFERENCES:

Moschis, George P. (1978), *Acquisition of the Consumer Role by Adolescents*, Research Monograph No. 82. Atlanta, Ga.: Publishing Services Division, College of Business Administration, Georgia State University.

_____(1981), "Patterns of Consumer Learning," *JAMS*, 9 (2), 110-126.

_____ and Roy L. Moore (1978), "An Analysis of the Acquisition of Some Consumer Competencies Among Adolescents," *Journal of Consumer Affairs*, 12 (Winter), 277-291.

SCALE ITEMS: CONSUMER AFFAIRS KNOWLEDGE +

1. When you buy stock you own part of a company.
2. Milk sold in the store must show the last date it can be sold.
3. A "shortage economy" is when the country is short of money.
4. The mortgage is the down payment on a house.
5. When you have liability insurance you don't have to pay for wrecking someone else's car.
6. The Better Business Bureau helps consumers, not merchants.
7. A credit union is a group of people who agree to save their money together and make loans to each other.
8. Ground beef sold at the store must have two prices; one that shows how much the whole package costs and another that says how much one pound costs.
9. All products show the name of the company that makes them.
10. It is legal for a store to advertise a product at $20.00 and sell it for $21.00 on the same day.
11. The Office of Consumer Protection helps people who have been tricked by merchants.

+ Items 1, 2, 7, 8, 10, and 11 were scored as true and the rest were counted as false.

SCALE NAME: Consumer Role Expectations (Adolescents')

SCALE DESCRIPTION:

An 11-item, five-point summated ratings scale measuring adolescents' expectations about their consumer roles once they start to work and raise a family. The roles reflect things "good" consumers are supposed either to do or not do.

SCALE ORIGIN:

A similar scale is described by Moschis and Moore (1978), but it is a 10-item, three-point scale and at least some of the items are different. That version of the scale was reported to have an alpha of **.50**. The results of that study indicated older adolescents had better knowledge of socially desirable consumer roles than younger ones, and upper class children had better knowledge than lower class ones. No difference was found in consumer role perceptions based on sex, however. See also Moschis (1978, p. 44) for a scale with some of the same items.

SAMPLES:

The study by Moschis and Moore (1984) was based on data collected from **784** adolescents from six counties in Georgia that varied widely in rural/urban nature. The surveys were administered to middle school or high school students in a regular class session. The sample was reported to be very representative given that, among other demographic variables, it was 48% male and 88% white.

RELIABILITY:

The alpha for the scale was not specifically reported, but the scale was among those for which alpha was indicated to be between .48 and .87.

VALIDITY:

No examination of scale validity was reported.

ADMINISTRATION:

The scale was self-administered by students in a regular class session along with other measures as part of a larger questionnaire. Higher scores indicate that adolescents intend to engage in socially desirable consumer activities whereas lower scores suggest that they do not expect to engage in such activities.

MAJOR FINDINGS:

The purpose of the study was to examine the development of consumption-related cognitions and behaviors among adolescents. Stronger intentions of socially desirable **consumer roles** were found to be significantly correlated with the degree of parent-child purchasing-related communication, but not significantly associated with the amount of formal consumer education or socioeconomic background.

COMMENTS:

The internal consistency of the scale is low enough that caution should be exercised in its use until further refinement can improve its psychometric quality.

REFERENCES:

Moschis, George P. (1978), *Acquisition of the Consumer Role by Adolescents*, Research Monograph No. 82. Atlanta, Ga.: Publishing Services Division, College of Business Administration, Georgia State University.

_____ and Roy L. Moore (1978), ''An Analysis of the Acquisition of Some Consumer Competencies Among Adolescents,'' *Journal of Consumer Affairs*, 12 (Winter), 277-290.

_____ and _____ (1984), ''Anticipatory Consumer Socialization,'' *JAMS*, 12 (Fall), 109-123.

SCALE ITEMS: CONSUMER ROLE EXPECTATIONS (ADOLESCENTS')

1 = Definitely would do it
2 = Probably would do it
3 = Don't Know
4 = Probably wouldn't do it
5 = Definitely wouldn't do it

1. Call or write the Consumer Protection Agency if you think you have been tricked by a store. **(r)**
2. Carefully read directions before using things you buy. **(r)**
3. Try to buy throwaway bottles instead of returnable ones.
4. Return things for refund when you are not happy with them. **(r)**
5. Check warranties and guarantees before buying. **(r)**
6. Buy things to impress others.
7. Shop around before buying things that cost a lot of money. **(r)**
8. Keep a record of the money you spend and save. **(r)**
9. Buy some things to feel like those people you wish you were.
10. Plan out how to spend your money. **(r)**
11. Read packages and labels before buying. **(r)**

SCALE NAME: Consumption Motivation (Objective)

SCALE DESCRIPTION:

>A five-item, five-point summated ratings scale measuring the importance a consumer places on objective, functional, and economic issues before buying five common products. It was referred to as Economic Motivations for Consumption by Moschis (1978, 1981) and Carlson and Grossbart (1988).

SCALE ORIGIN:

>The measure originates from a dissertation published by Moschis in 1978. His 1981 study, reported below, is from that same dissertation research.

SAMPLES:

>Moschis' (1981) data came from **806** middle school or senior high school students. There were 365 ''older'' adolescents (15 years and older) and 441 ''younger'' adolescents (younger than 15 years). The students came from 13 schools and seven towns in Wisconsin representing a wide variety of urban to rural situations. The author indicates that the sample was well balanced in terms of most demographic characteristics except sex, as nearly two-thirds of the respondents were female.
>
>The survey instrument used by Carlson and Grossbart (1988) was distributed to mothers via students at three elementary schools in an unidentified U.S. city. The schools were chosen on a convenience basis but appeared to represent a variety of socioeconomic areas of the city. A $1 contribution to the PTO was offered for each completed questionnaire returned by the children. Analysis was based on **451** completed questionnaires. Ninety-three percent of the responding mothers indicated that they were the primary person in the child's socialization.

RELIABILITY:

>Alpha values of **.69** and **.73** were reported for the scale by Moschis (1981) and Carlson and Grossbart (1988), respectively.

VALIDITY:

>No examination of scale validity was reported.

ADMINISTRATION:

>The scale was self-administered along with other measures in the studies reported by Moschis (1981) and Carlson and Grossbart (1988). Scores are calculated by adding for the five products the total number of ''objective'' issues a person says he/she would consider before purchasing. Higher scores on the scale indicate that respondents are concerned about ''objective'' issues before making purchases whereas lower scores suggest that they are not very much motivated by functional or economic considerations.

MAJOR FINDINGS:

Moschis (1981) investigated the validity of the cognitive development approach to social-ization (e.g., Piaget) to predict a wide variety of consumer-related cognitions learned during adolescence. In general, the findings indicated that the cognitive developmental model did not explain consumer socialization during adolescence very well. Older adoles-cents had significantly less favorable attitudes toward advertising, brands, and prices than did younger children, but had significantly greater **"objective" consumptive motiva-tions.**

Carlson and Grossbart (1988) investigated the relationship between general parental socialization styles and children's consumer socialization. **Objective motivations for consumption** significantly differentiated between several of the parental socialization style clusters examined. Specifically, Authoritative mothers scored highest on the scale and Neglecting mothers scored lowest.

REFERENCES:

Carlson, Les and Sanford Grossbart (1988), ''Parental Style and Consumer Socialization of Children,'' *JCR*, 15 (June), 77-94.

Moschis, George P. (1978), *Acquisition of the Consumer Role by Adolescents*, Research Monograph No. 82. Atlanta, Ga.: Publishing Services Division, College of Business Administration, Georgia State University.

_____ (1981), ''Patterns of Consumer Learning,'' *JAMS*, 9 (2), 110-126.

SCALE ITEMS: CONSUMPTION MOTIVATION (OBJECTIVE)

Strongly Disagree	Disagree	Neutral	Agree	Strongly Agree
1	2	3	4	5

Before purchasing a product it is important to know:
1. Guarantees on different brands.
2. Name of the company that makes the product.
3. Whether any brands are on sale.
4. Kinds of materials different brands are made of.
5. Quality of store selling a particular brand.

SCALE NAME: Consumption Motivation (Social)

SCALE DESCRIPTION:

A four-item, five-point Likert-type summated ratings scale measuring the importance a consumer places on what others think or are doing before buying five common products. This was referred to as Social Motivations for Consumption by Moschis (1981, 1978) and Carlson and Grossbart (1988).

SCALE ORIGIN:

The measure originates from a dissertation published by Moschis in 1978. His 1981 study, reported below, is from that same dissertation research.

SAMPLES:

Moschis' (1981) data came from **806** middle school or senior high school students. There were 365 "older" adolescents (15 years and older) and 441 "younger" adolescents (younger than 15 years). The students came from 13 schools and seven towns in Wisconsin representing a wide variety of urban to rural situations. The author indicates that the sample was well balanced in terms of most demographic characteristics except sex, as nearly two-thirds of the respondents were female.

The survey instrument used by Carlson and Grossbart (1988) was distributed to mothers via students at three elementary schools in an unidentified U.S. city. The schools were chosen on a convenience basis but appeared to represent a variety of socioeconomic areas of the city. A $1 contribution to the PTO was offered for each completed questionnaire returned by the children. Analysis was based on **451** completed questionnaires. Ninety-three percent of the responding mothers indicated that they were the primary person in the child's socialization.

RELIABILITY:

Alpha values of .**85** and .**74** were reported for the scale by Moschis (1981) and Carlson and Grossbart (1988), respectively.

VALIDITY:

No examination of scale validity has been reported.

ADMINISTRATION:

The scale was self-administered along with other measures in the studies reported by Moschis (1981) and Carlson and Grossbart (1988). Scores are calculated by adding for the five products the total number of social issues a person says he/she would consider before purchasing. Higher scores on the scale indicate that respondents have a high sensitivity about the social visibility of their consumption whereas lower scores suggest that they are not very much motivated by social visibility considerations.

MAJOR FINDINGS:

Moschis (1981) investigated the validity of the cognitive development approach to socialization (e.g., Piaget) to predict a wide variety of consumer-related cognitions learned during adolescence. In general, the findings indicated that the cognitive developmental model did not explain consumer socialization during adolescence very well. Older adolescents had significantly less favorable attitudes toward advertising, brands, and prices than did younger children, but a significantly greater prepurchase information source usage. No significant difference was found between the two groups of adolescents on the basis of their **social visibility consumption motivation**.

Carlson and Grossbart (1988) investigated the relationship between general parental socialization styles and children's consumer socialization. Neglecting mothers exhibited more **social motivation for consumption** than any of the other four parental socialization style clusters examined. However, the difference was only significant in comparison with Permissive mothers, who scored lowest on the scale.

REFERENCES:

Carlson, Les and Sanford Grossbart (1988), ''Parental Style and Consumer Socialization of Children,'' *JCR*, 15 (June), 77-94.

Moschis, George P. (1978), *Acquisition of the Consumer Role by Adolescents*, Research Monograph No. 82. Atlanta, Ga.: Publishing Services Division, College of Business Administration, Georgia State University.

_____ (1981), ''Patterns of Consumer Learning,'' *JAMS*, 9 (2), 110-126.

SCALE ITEMS: CONSUMPTION MOTIVATION (SOCIAL)

Strongly Disagree	Disagree	Neutral	Agree	Strongly Agree
1	2	3	4	5

Before purchasing a product it is important to know:

1. What friends think of different brands or products.
2. What kinds of people buy certain brands or products.
3. What others think of people who use certain brands or products.
4. What brands or products to buy to make good impressions on others.

SCALE NAME: Contact Frequency (Sales Agent)

SCALE DESCRIPTION:

An eight-item, five-point Likert- type summated ratings scale measuring the number of times a customer indicates having been contacted by his/her agent in the previous two years. Crosby and Stephens (1987) used the scale with policy owners and asked them to respond about insurance agents.

SCALE ORIGIN:

There is no indication that the scale was constructed elsewhere than in the Crosby and Stephens (1987) study.

SAMPLES:

The sample was selected from a nationally representative consumer panel and screened for ownership of life insurance. Analysis of the first wave of the survey was based on **1362** responses. The sample was slightly better educated and more upscale than the population at large, but the authors considered the differences to be minor and unrelated to the studied relationships. A year later, respondents to the first wave of the survey (or from a holdout sample) were contacted. Analysis was based on **447** responses. Comparison of main sample and holdout sample data did not indicate any bias due to wave 1 premeasurement.

RELIABILITY:

Alpha values for the scale were **.91** for both waves of the study.

VALIDITY:

Factor analyses in the two waves of the study produced nearly identical factor solutions.

ADMINISTRATION:

The scales were self-administered as part of a larger mail questionnaire. High scores indicate that customers have been contacted by their agent many times in the past two years whereas low scores suggest that customers have rarely if ever been contacted their agent.

MAJOR FINDINGS:

The purpose of the study was to compare two proposed models of buyer satisfaction with life insurance, the relationship generalization model (RGM) and a rational evaluation model (REM). The RGM assumes that consumers generalize positive feelings about the provider to the core service whereas the REM views consumers as most concerned about core service quality, with the relationship merely adding value to it. In general, the results supported the REM over the RGM. This means that though the agent's performance affects satisfaction, it is balanced against the perceived performance of the core service. **Personal contact** was found to have a significant and positive relationship with the **satisfaction** customers felt toward their **core policy** as well as their **agents**.

REFERENCE:

Crosby, Lawrence A. and Nancy Stephens (1987), "Effects of Relationship Marketing on Satisfaction, Retention, and Prices in the Life Insurance Industry," *JMR*, 24 (November), 404-411.

SCALE ITEMS: CONTACT FREQUENCY (SALES AGENT)

Never	Once	Twice	Three or Four Times	Five Times or More
1——————2——————3——————4——————5				

How often in the last one or two years did you recall experiencing the following:
1. Was contacted by my agent who wanted to stay "in touch" and make sure I was still satisfied.
2. Was contacted by my agent who wanted to keep abreast of changes in my family and insurance needs.
3. Was contacted by my agent who wanted to make changes in this policy to better serve my needs.
4. Was contacted by my agent who wanted to restructure my insurance program to better serve my needs.
5. My agent explained why it was a good idea to keep this whole life policy in force.
6. Received something of a personal nature from my agent (e.g., birthday card, holiday gift, etc.)
7. Was contacted by my agent who wanted to sell me more life insurance.
8. Was contacted by my agent who wanted to describe new types of policies that had become available.

SCALE NAME: **Convenience (Locating Products Within Store)**

SCALE DESCRIPTION:

A five-item, five-point summated ratings scale ranging from not important to very important. The scale measures the degree of importance a consumer places on ease of finding products in a store. The measure was called Ease of Finding Items in Store by Lumpkin and Hunt (1989).

SCALE ORIGIN:

The measure was apparently developed by Lumpkin and Hunt (1989) for use in their study, though the items may have come from previous studies reviewed in the article.

SAMPLES:

Lumpkin and Hunt's sample was drawn from the Market Facts Consumer Mail Panel and focused on **789** respondents who indicated they were 65 years of age or older. The proportions of men and women were similar to those in the national population, but fewer of the men and more of the women in the sample were married. The sample was better educated and had a greater percentage still employed than was true nationally. The sample was composed of more people in lower income levels, but reasonably matched the elderly geographic distribution.

RELIABILITY:

An alpha of **.723** was calculated for the scale.

VALIDITY:

Factor analysis indicated that the items loaded together.

ADMINISTRATION:

Data were gathered through self-administered mail questionnaires. Scale scores were calculated by averaging numerical responses to individual items. A score of 5 indicates that a person feels ease of finding products in stores is very important whereas a 1 suggests that such convenience in shopping is not important.

MAJOR FINDINGS:

The elderly were broken down into two groups by Lumpkin and Hunt (1989): those who were self-reliant in terms of transportation and those who were dependent on others. In general, the two groups did not differ significantly on the importance placed on ease of **finding products** in a store. It is noteworthy that three of the items in this scale (1, 2, 3) were among the most important store attributes for both groups.

REFERENCE:

Lumpkin, James R. and James B. Hunt (1989), "Mobility as an Influence on Retail Patronage Behavior of the Elderly: Testing Conventional Wisdom," *JAMS*, 17 (Winter), 1-12.

SCALE ITEMS: CONVENIENCE (LOCATING PRODUCTS WITHIN STORE)

Not Important	Below Average Importance	Average Importance	Above Average Importance	Very Important
1	2	3	4	5

1. Knowledgeable salespersons
2. Help in finding items in store
3. Ease of finding items
4. Small store so items can be found easily
5. Limited variety so items can be found easily

SCALE NAME: Convenience (Movement in Store)

SCALE DESCRIPTION:

> A four-item, five-point summated ratings scale ranging from not important (1) to very important (5). The scale measures the degree of importance a consumer places on ease of movement within a store. The measure was called Ease of Movement Within Store by Lumpkin and Hunt (1989).

SCALE ORIGIN:

> The measure was apparently developed by Lumpkin and Hunt (1989) for use in their study, though the items may have come from previous studies reviewed in the article.

SAMPLES:

> Lumpkin and Hunt's sample was drawn from the Market Facts Consumer Mail Panel and focused on **789** respondents who indicated they were 65 years of age or older. The proportions of men and women were similar to those in the national population, but fewer of the men and more of the women in the sample were married. The sample was better educated and had a greater percentage still employed than was true nationally. The sample was composed of more people in lower income levels, but reasonably matched the elderly geographic distribution.

RELIABILITY:

> An alpha of **.771** was calculated for the scale.

VALIDITY:

> Factor analysis indicated that the items loaded together.

ADMINISTRATION:

> Data were gathered through self-administered mail questionnaires. Scale scores were calculated by averaging numerical responses to individual items. A score of 5 indicates that a person feels ease of movement within stores is very important whereas a 1 suggests that such convenience in shopping is not important.

MAJOR FINDINGS:

> The elderly were broken down into two groups by Lumpkin and Hunt (1989): those who were self-reliant in terms of transportation and those who were dependent on others. In general the two groups did not differ significantly on the importance placed on **convenience of movement within the store**. However, though convenient entrances and exits were important to both groups, they were significantly more important to the dependent elderly than to the self-reliant.

REFERENCE:

Lumpkin, James R. and James B. Hunt (1989), ''Mobility as an Influence on Retail Patronage Behavior of the Elderly: Testing Conventional Wisdom,'' *JAMS*, 17 (Winter), 1-12.

SCALE ITEMS: CONVENIENCE (MOVEMENT IN STORE)

Not Important	Below Average Importance	Average Importance	Above Average Importance	Very Important
1	2	3	4	5

1. Convenient/fast checkout
2. Convenient entrance/exit
3. Wide aisles
4. Uncrowded store

SCALE NAME: Convenience (Shopping)

SCALE DESCRIPTION:

A six-item, five-point summated ratings scale assessing the degree of importance a consumer places on a variety of aspects related to getting to a store or ordering from it. The measure was called Convenience Getting to Store by Lumpkin and Hunt (1989).

SCALE ORIGIN:

The measure was apparently developed by Lumpkin and Hunt (1989) for use in their study, though the items may have come from previous studies reviewed in the article.

SAMPLES:

Lumpkin and Hunt's (1989) sample was drawn from the Market Facts Consumer Mail Panel and focused on **789** respondents who indicated they were 65 years of age or older. The proportions of men and women were similar to those in the national population, but fewer of the men and more of the women in the sample were married. The sample was better educated and had a greater percentage still employed than was true nationally. The sample was composed of more people in lower income levels, but reasonably matched the elderly geographic distribution.

RELIABILITY:

An alpha of **.624** was reported for this scale.

VALIDITY:

Factor analysis indicated that the items loaded together.

ADMINISTRATION:

Data were gathered through self-administered mail questionnaires. Scale scores were calculated by averaging numerical responses to individual items. A score of 5 indicates that a person feels issues involved with getting to stores are very important whereas a 1 suggests that such aspects of shopping are not important.

MAJOR FINDINGS:

The elderly were broken down into two groups by Lumpkin and Hunt (1989): those who were self-reliant in terms of transportation and those who were dependent on others. The self-reliant perceived the **convenience aspects of getting to a store** to be significantly less important than did the dependent elderly.

COMMENTS:

The low alpha for this measure suggests that further work is necessary to refine its stability. Possibly the problem is not that it has too few items, but that the items are tapping into related but slightly different issues.

REFERENCE:

Lumpkin, James R. and James B. Hunt (1989), ''Mobility as an Influence on Retail Patronage Behavior of the Elderly: Testing Conventional Wisdom,'' *JAMS*, 17 (Winter), 1-12.

SCALE ITEMS: CONVENIENCE (SHOPPING)

Not Important	Below Average Importance	Average Importance	Above Average Importance	Very Important
1—————	——2—————	—3—————	—4—————	—5

1. Delivery to home
2. Phone in order
3. Transportation to store
4. Convenient parking
5. Location close to home
6. Variety of stores close together

SCALE NAME: Convenience (Shopping Ease)

SCALE DESCRIPTION:

A seven-item, five-point Likert-type summated ratings scale measuring the degree to which a consumer considers several specific conveniences associated with a store to be important.

SCALE ORIGIN:

As a summated scale, the measure is original to Saegert, Hoover, and Hilger (1985). The authors note that the items were adapted from some used by Kelly and Stephenson (1967). The items in that study were used in the form of bipolar descriptors and do not appear to have been summated.

SAMPLES:

Saegert, Hoover, and Hilger (1985) reported on four surveys, only two of which utilized the scale of interest. One of those studies involved a random selection of 1000 Spanish names and 1000 non-Spanish names and mailing questionnaires to those individuals. A total of **299** questionnaires were returned. The response rates for both groups were very low (9% for Hispanics and 21% for others), indicating a need to confirm the findings with personal interviews from another sample. The second survey of interest was conducted in a small Texas town with **195** women (95 Hispanic and 100 non-Hispanic) who were selected randomly from blocks in the town and houses within the blocks.

RELIABILITY:

An alpha of **.84** was calculated for the scale by Saegert, Hoover, and Hilger (1985).

VALIDITY:

A factor analysis of 25 shopping-related items indicated that the items in this scale loaded together. (Information in the article as well as some provided by Saegert in personal correspondence suggests that the factor analysis and the alpha reported above were based on data collected just in the mail survey. The article specifically states, however, that analyses of the separate ethnic groups as well as the data from the personal interviews produced almost identical factor interpretations.)

ADMINISTRATION:

In one survey by Saegert and his coauthors, the scale was self-administered as part of a mail questionnaire, whereas in the other survey it was administered by bilingual interviewers. Higher scores on the scale indicate that consumers think ease of getting to a store, into a store, and out of a store is very important.

MAJOR FINDINGS:

Saegert, Hoover, and Hilger used the results of four surveys to examine differences between Anglo-Americans and Mexican-Americans in shopping-related attitudes and behaviors. In both samples described above, **ease of shopping** was significantly more important to Hispanics than to non-Hispanics.

REFERENCES:

Kelly, Robert F. and Ronald Stephenson (1967), ''The Semantic Differential: An Information Source for Designing Retail Patronage Appeals,'' *JM*, 31 (October), 43-47.

Saegert, Joel, Robert J. Hoover, and Marye Tharp Hilger (1985), ''Characteristics of Mexican American Consumers,'' *JCR*, 12 (June), 104-109.

SCALE ITEMS: CONVENIENCE (SHOPPING EASE) +

Not important at all   ____ : ____ : ____ : ____ : ____   Very important
                                  1   2   3   4   5

1. The store has fast check-out.
2. It is easy to move through the store.
3. It is easy to park at the store.
4. The store is nice inside.
5. It is easy to find products.
6. The store is close to my home.
7. The store has well-known brands.

+ These items were reconstructed from phrases supplied in personal correspondence from Saegert.

SCALE NAME: Convenience (Store Features)

SCALE DESCRIPTION:

A six-item, five-point Likert-type summated ratings scale measuring the degree to which a consumer considers several store-related convenience features to be important.

SCALE ORIGIN:

The measure appears to be original to Saegert, Hoover, and Hilger (1985) and was used only in their study.

SAMPLES:

The authors reported on four surveys, only two of which utilized the scale of interest. One of those studies involved a random selection of 1000 Spanish names and 1000 non-Spanish names and mailing questionnaires to those individuals. A total of **299** questionnaires were returned. The response rates for both groups were very low (9% for Hispanics and 21% for others), indicating a need to confirm the findings with personal interviews of another sample. The second survey of interest was conducted in a small Texas town with **195** women (95 Hispanic and 100 non-Hispanic) who were selected randomly from blocks in the town and houses within the blocks.

RELIABILITY:

An alpha of **.73** was calculated for the scale.

VALIDITY:

A factor analysis of 25 shopping-related items indicated that the items in this scale loaded together. (Information in the article as well as some provided by Saegert in personal correspondence suggests that the factor analysis and the alpha reported above were based on data collected just in the mail survey. The article specifically states, however, that analyses of the separate ethnic groups as well as the data from the personal interviews produced almost identical factor interpretations.)

ADMINISTRATION:

In one survey the scale was self-administered as part of a mail questionnaire, whereas in the other survey it was administered by bilingual interviewers. Higher scores on the scale indicate that consumers think shopping at a store that has several convenience-related characteristics is very important.

MAJOR FINDINGS:

The authors used the results of four surveys to examine differences between Anglo-Americans and Mexican- Americans in shopping-related attitudes and behaviors. In both samples described above, convenience-related **store features** were significantly more important to Hispanics than to non-Hispanics, but for both groups it was among the least important of the shopping factors studied.

REFERENCE:

Saegert, Joel, Robert J. Hoover, and Marye Tharp Hilger (1985), "Characteristics of Mexican American Consumers," *JCR*, 12 (June), 104-109.

SCALE ITEMS: CONVENIENCE (STORE FEATURES) +

Not important at all   ____ : ____ : ____ : ____ : ____   Very important
  1 2 3 4 5

1. I can cash a check there.
2. The store is open on Sunday.
3. The store is open hours when others are closed.
4. The store lets me buy on credit.
5. I can buy beer there.
6. The store has lots of beverages.

+ These items were reconstructed from phrases supplied in personal correspondence from Saegert.

SCALE NAME: Convenience (Within Store)

SCALE DESCRIPTION:

A four-item, five-point summated ratings scale ranging from not important (1) to very important (5). The scale measures the degree of importance a consumer places on several physical aspects within a store that can affect the ease of shopping. The measure was called Physical Aspects in Store by Lumpkin and Hunt (1989).

SCALE ORIGIN:

The measure was apparently developed by Lumpkin and Hunt (1989) for use in their study, though the items may have come from previous studies reviewed in the article.

SAMPLES:

Lumpkin and Hunt's sample was drawn from the Market Facts Consumer Mail Panel and focused on **789** respondents who indicated they were 65 years of age or older. The proportions of men and women were similar to those in the national population, but fewer of the men and more of the women in the sample were married. The sample was better educated and had a greater percentage still employed than was true nationally. The sample was composed of more people in lower income levels, but reasonably matched the elderly geographic distribution.

RELIABILITY:

An alpha of **.673** was calculated for the scale.

VALIDITY:

Factor analysis indicated that the items loaded together.

ADMINISTRATION:

Data were gathered through self-administered mail questionnaires. Scale scores were calculated by averaging numerical responses to individual items. A score of 5 indicates that a person feels particular conveniences within stores are very important whereas a 1 suggests that such conveniences in shopping are not important.

MAJOR FINDINGS:

The elderly were broken down into two groups by Lumpkin and Hunt (1989): those who were self-reliant in terms of transportation and those who were dependent on others. In general, the two groups were significantly different in the overall importance they placed on these characteristics of a store. Though the two groups did not differ significantly on items 1 and 4, they both placed much more importance on those items than they did on items 2 and 3, on which they differed. In the case of the latter, the dependent elderly placed more importance on the **conveniences** than did the self-reliant.

COMMENTS:

The low alpha suggests more effort is needed to refine the scale. The items appear to tap into related but slightly different issues, which could lower its stability.

REFERENCE:

Lumpkin, James R. and James B. Hunt (1989), ''Mobility as an Influence on Retail Patronage Behavior of the Elderly: Testing Conventional Wisdom,'' *JAMS*, 17 (Winter), 1-12.

SCALE ITEMS: CONVENIENCE (WITHIN STORE)

Not Important	Below Average Importance	Average Importance	Above Average Importance	Very Important
1	2	3	4	5

1. Readable labels/logos on product
2. Rest area in store
3. Package carryout
4. Comfortable physical environment in store

SCALE NAME: Cooking Enjoyment

SCALE DESCRIPTION:

A four-item, six-point, Likert-type summated ratings scale assessing a person's enjoyment of and interest in cooking. It appears to be the scale used by Dickerson and Gentry (1983) and called Culinary Enthusiast. It may also be similar to the scale called Attitude Toward Cooking used by Burnett and Bush (1986).

SCALE ORIGIN:

These items were part of a classic study of psychographics by Wells and Tigert (1971). One thousand questionnaires were mailed to homemaker members of the Market Facts mail panel. In addition to gathering demographic, product use, and media data, the survey contained 300 statements that have since served as the basis for the construction of many lifestyle-related scales. The four items for this scale are reported in the article, but they were not analyzed as a multi-item scale. The purpose of the article was to explain how psychographics could improve upon mere demographic description of target audiences and product users. No psychometric information was reported.

SAMPLES:

Two mailing lists were used to collect data in the Dickerson and Gentry study (1983). One was a list of *Psychology Today* subscribers and the other was a list of members of computer clubs. The former was used to reach non- adopters of computers and the latter was used to reach PC adopters. Analysis was based on a total of **639** questionnaires. Results from a second mailing to non- respondents indicated that their demographic makeup was not significantly different from that of respondents. On the basis of 1980 Census data, the sample was younger and more up upscale than the general population.

RELIABILITY:

An alpha of **.81** (Dickerson and Gentry 1983) has been reported.

VALIDITY:

A factor analysis indicated the items loaded together.

ADMINISTRATION:

Data were gathered through self-administered mail questionnaires. Scale scores are calculated by averaging numerical responses to individual items. A score of 6 indicates that a person greatly enjoys cooking whereas a 1 suggest that a person does not like to cook.

MAJOR FINDINGS:

Dickerson and Gentry (1983) found that cooking orientation was one of the most significant lifestyle variables that discriminated between adopters and non- adopters of home computers. Specifically, though adopters appeared to be homebodies in other characteristics, they were *not* interested in cooking.

REFERENCES:

Burnett, John J. and Alan J. Bush (1986), "Profiling the Yuppies," *JAR*, 26 (April/May), 27-35.

Dickerson, Mary D. and James W. Gentry (1983), "Characteristics of Adopters and Non-Adopters of Home Computers," *JCR*, 10 (September), 225-235.

Wells, William D. and Douglas Tigert (1971), "Activities, Interests, and Opinions," *JAR*, 11 (August), 27-35.

SCALE ITEMS: COOKING ENJOYMENT

Strongly Disagree	Disagree	Slightly Disagree	Slightly Agree	Agree	Strongly Agree
1	2	3	4	5	6

1. I love to cook.
2. I am a good cook.
3. I love to bake and frequently do.
4. I am interested in spices and seasonings.

SCALE NAME: Coping (Life)

SCALE DESCRIPTION:

A four-item, five-point Likert- type summated ratings scale ranging from strongly disagree (1) to strongly agree (5). The scale measures the degree to which a person feels that he/ she is not coping with changes occurring in society. Lumpkin and Hunt (1989) referred to this scale as Not Coping.

SCALE ORIGIN:

The measure was apparently developed by Lumpkin and Hunt (1989) for use in their study, though the items may have come from previous studies reviewed in the article.

SAMPLES:

Lumpkin and Hunt's sample was drawn from the Market Facts Consumer Mail Panel and focused on **789** respondents who indicated they were 65 years of age or older. The proportions of men and women were similar to those in the national population, but fewer of the men and more of the women in the sample were married. The sample was better educated and had a greater percentage still employed than was true nationally. The sample was composed of more people in lower income levels, but reasonably matched the elderly geographic distribution.

RELIABILITY:

An alpha of **.727** was reported by Lumpkin and Hunt (1989).

VALIDITY:

Factor analysis indicated that the items loaded together.

ADMINISTRATION:

Data were gathered through self-administered mail questionnaires. Scale scores were calculated by averaging numerical responses to individual items. A score of 5 indicates that a person feels life is too complicated and things are changing too fast whereas a 1 suggests that one is coping with life relatively well.

MAJOR FINDINGS:

The elderly were broken down into two groups by Lumpkin and Hunt (1989): those who were self-reliant in terms of transportation and those who were dependent on others. The self-reliant perceived themselves to be **coping** with life significantly better than did the dependent elderly.

REFERENCE:

Lumpkin, James R. and James B. Hunt (1989), ''Mobility as an Influence on Retail Patronage Behavior of the Elderly: Testing Conventional Wisdom,'' *JAMS*, 17 (Winter), 1-12.

SCALE ITEMS: COPING (LIFE)

Strongly Disagree	Disagree	Neutral	Agree	Strongly Agree
1	2	3	4	5

1. In general, things are just too complicated today.
2. Products are too complicated today.
3. Society is changing too fast for me.
4. I can't keep up with all the new products being offered.

SCALE NAME: Coviewing TV (Parent/Child)

SCALE DESCRIPTION:

A four-item, five-point Likert-type summated rating scale measuring the degree to which a parent reports watching TV with a child and the importance of doing that in order to monitor what is watched.

SCALE ORIGIN:

The scale is indicated as being original to Carlson and Grossbart (1988).

SAMPLES:

The survey instrument used by Carlson and Grossbart (1988) was distributed to mothers via students at three elementary schools in an unidentified U.S. city. The schools were chosen on a convenience basis but appeared to represent a variety of socioeconomic areas of the city. A $1 contribution to the PTO was offered for each completed questionnaire returned by the children. Analysis was based on **451** completed questionnaires. Ninety-three percent of the responding mothers indicated that they were the primary person in the child's socialization.

RELIABILITY:

Carlson and Grossbart (1988) reported an alpha of .**90** and a beta of .85 for the scale.

VALIDITY:

No examination of scale validity was reported by Carlson and Grossbart (1988).

ADMINISTRATION:

The scale was self-administered along with many other measures in the questionnaire used by Carlson and Grossbart (1988). Higher scores on the scale mean that respondents report they often watch TV with their children whereas lower scores suggest that they do not think doing so is very important and do not do so often.

MAJOR FINDINGS:

The authors investigated the relationship between general parental socialization styles and children's consumer socialization. In a factor analysis of scale scores, scores on the **Coviewing** scale loaded on a separate factor from the other scales. A significant difference was found in the degree of parent-child communication between one of the parental socialization styles and several of the others. Especially, Authoritative mothers reported significantly more **coviewing** than did three of the other four parental style clusters examined.

REFERENCE:

Carlson, Les and Sanford Grossbart (1988), ''Parental Style and Consumer Socialization of Children,'' *JCR*, 15 (June), 77-94.

SCALE ITEMS: COVIEWING TV (PARENT/CHILD) +

Very Seldom	Seldom	Sometimes	Often	Very Often
1—————	—2—————	—3—————	—4—————	—5

I watch TV with my children on:
1. . . . weekdays.
2. . . . Saturdays.
3. . . . Sundays.
4. It is important for my child and I to watch TV together so I know what kind of programs he/she is watching.

Strongly Disagree	Disagree	Neither	Agree	Strongly Agree
1—————	—2—————	—3—————	—4—————	—5

+ Items 1 through 3 are scaled from very seldom to very often. Item 4 is scaled strongly disagree to strongly agree.

SCALE NAME: Creativity (Product Usage)

SCALE DESCRIPTION:

A six-item, Likert-type summated ratings scale. The scale measures a person's tendency to use a product to its fullest and in numerous ways. The scale was referred to as Multiple Use Potential by both Price and Ridgway (1983) and Childers (1986).

SCALE ORIGIN:

A seven-item version of the scale was first constructed by Price and Ridgway (1983). It was part of a larger five-component, 44-item Use Innovativeness index. Multiple Use Potential had an alpha of .56. The subscale was constructed along with the other parts of the index to measure the use of a previously adopted product in a novel way or a variety of ways. Data were collected from student subjects in undergraduate classes representing a variety of courses. Analysis was based on 358 usable questionnaires. A couple of rounds of factor analysis, with examination of internal consistency and item-total correlations, reduced the original collection of 60 items to 44 items among five factors. The correlation between scores on the Multiple Use Potential subscale and scores on the Use Innovativeness index was .51. Validity of the overall index rather than the individual subscales was assessed. This was done by noting that students with the highest scores on the Use Innovativeness index engaged in significantly more innovative behaviors (toward calculators) than those scoring lower on the index. The authors urge that further testing of the psychometric properties be done.

SAMPLES:

Childers' (1986) samples were taken from the files of a cable television franchise in a large metro area. One sample was of people who subscribed to cable and another sample was of people who had been contacted but refused to subscribe. Questionnaires were dropped off by an employee of the franchise, but responses were mailed in. **One hundred and seventy six** questionnaires were returned within the three-week period before the cutoff date.

RELIABILITY:

An alpha of **.74** was calculated for the scale.

VALIDITY:

Validity was not examined except in the sense that it was used as part of the assessment of an opinion leadership scale.

ADMINISTRATION:

The scale was self-administered in a survey instrument format. Higher scores on the scale indicate a person reports him/herself as desiring to use products to their fullest whereas lower scores suggest a person has little creativity in using products in numerous ways.

MAJOR FINDINGS:

The purpose of the study by Childers (1986) was to compare the psychometric properties of two versions of an opinion leadership scale. In most respects the modified version of the scale was superior to the previous version. The Creativity (Product Usage) scale had significant though low correlations with both versions of the opinion leadership scale.

COMMENTS:

On the basis of information reported by Price and Ridgway (1983), none of the items in the scale have both strong item-total correlations and factor loadings. Because those authors admit that the construct "was not measured very well" (p. 683), further development should be performed on this scale before it is used.

REFERENCES:

Childers, Terry L. (1986), "Assessment of the Psychometric Properties of an Opinion Leadership Scale," *JMR*, 23 (May), 184-188.

Price, Linda L. and Nancy M. Ridgway (1983), "Development of a Scale to Measure Use Innovativeness," in *Advances in Consumer Research*, Vol. 10, Richard P. Bagozzi and Alice M. Tybout, eds. Ann Arbor, Mich.: Association for Consumer Research, 679-684.

SCALE ITEMS: CREATIVITY (PRODUCT USAGE) +

Strongly Disagree	Disagree	Slightly Disagree	Neutral	Slightly Agree	Agree	Strongly Agree
1	2	3	4	5	6	7

1. I do not enjoy a product unless I can use it to its fullest capacity.
2. I use products in more ways than most people.
3. I often buy a food item for a particular recipe but end up using it for something else.
4. A product's value is directly related to the ways it can be used.
5. It's always possible to improve upon a project by adding new features.
6. After purchase of a product like a stereo or camera, I try to keep track of new accessories that come out onto the market.
7. I enjoy expanding and adding onto projects that I'm involved in on a continuing basis.

+ This is the form of the scale offered by Price and Ridgway (1983). Childers (1986) did not specify which six items he used or the exact nature of the graphic scale and its verbal anchors.

SCALE NAME: Credit Usage

SCALE DESCRIPTION:

A four-item, six-point, Likert-type summated ratings scale ranging from strongly disagree (1) to strongly agree (6). The scale measures a person's willingness to use credit. The items in this scale were used by Wilkes, Burnett, and Howell (1986) though not in simple summated form, nor was reliability information provided. Abbreviated two-item versions have been used by Hawes and Lumpkin (1984), Lumpkin (1985), and Davis and Rubin (1983).

SCALE ORIGIN:

The items were part of a classic study of psychographics by Wells and Tigert (1971). One thousand questionnaires were mailed to homemaker members of the Market Facts mail panel. In addition to gathering demographic, product use, and media data, the survey contained 300 statements that have since served as the basis for the construction of many lifestyle-related scales. The four items for this scale are reported in the article, but were not analyzed as a multi-item scale. The purpose of the article was to explain how psychographics could improve upon mere demographic description of target audiences and product users. No psychometric information was reported.

One of the first uses of the items as a multi-item scale was by Darden and Ashton (1974-1975). Analysis was based on self-administered questionnaires completed by 116 middle-class suburban housewives selected from the telephone directory of a medium-sized southern city. A split-half reliability of .73 was reported for the scale. Respondents were grouped on the basis of their supermarket attribute preferences. Credit usage was *not* found to be significantly different between groups.

SAMPLES:

Two mailing lists were used to collect data in the Dickerson and Gentry study (1983). One was a list of *Psychology Today* subscribers and the other was a list of members of computer clubs. The former was used to reach non-adopters of computers and the latter was used to reach PC adopters. Analysis was based on a total of **639** questionnaires. Results from a second mailing to non-respondents indicated that their demographic makeup was not significantly different from that of respondents. On the basis of 1980 Census data, the sample was younger and more upscale than the general population.

Davis and Rubin (1983) mailed questionnaires to a sample of two groups in Florida: known adopters of solar energy devices and the general population over the age of 18 years. Analysis was based on **817** usable questionnaires, of which 488 were from solar energy adopters.

Hawes and Lumpkin (1984) collected data from **581** residents of 14 communities near the Ft. Worth-Dallas metroplex. Each of the communities was randomly sampled in proportion to its population by means of the respective telephone directories. The questionnaire was to be filled out by the household member responsible for most of the shopping. The distribution of respondents by community was similar to the actual population distribution.

Lumpkin (1985) collected data from a sample drawn from the Market Facts Consumer

Mail Panel. A total of 2854 completed questionnaires were received, but Lumpkin focused on **373** respondents who indicated they were 65 years of age or older.

RELIABILITY:

Chronbach's alpha values of **.77** (Dickerson and Gentry 1983), **.71** (Davis and Rubin 1983), **.655** (Hawes and Lumpkin 1984), and **.7638** (Lumpkin 1985) were reported.

VALIDITY:

Factor analyses in the studies indicated the items loaded together. More effort was made by Davis and Rubin (1983), who randomly split their data in half and factor analyzed the two subsamples. Identical factor solutions were found in the two subsamples. The factors found within the full data set were consistent with the subsample solutions.

ADMINISTRATION:

Data were gathered in the studies through self-administered mail questionnaires. Scale scores are calculated by averaging numerical responses to individual items. A score of 6 indicates that a person has a strong propensity to use credit and a score of 1 implies that a consumer does not use credit.

MAJOR FINDINGS:

Dickerson and Gentry (1983) found **credit usage** to be one of several lifestyle variables that was a significant discriminator between adopters and non-adopters of home computers. Davis and Rubin (1983) determined that person's who expressed a high degree of energy conservation opinion leadership were significantly more conservative in their **use of credit** but were more financially optimistic than those with less leadership.

The purpose of the study by Hawes and Lumpkin (1984) was to examine demographic and psychographic characteristics of outshoppers. **Credit usage** significantly differentiated between inshoppers and outshoppers. Persons who engaged in outshopping the most expressed the greatest inclination to **use credit**.

Elderly consumers were cluster analyzed by Lumpkin (1985) and **credit usage** appeared to discriminate between two of the three groups (statistical significance not reported). The group with the highest mean on the scale was the most conscious of inflation and the least optimistic about their future finances. The group with the lowest mean on the scale tended to score low on most of the shopping orientation measures and was characterized as "uninvolved" or "apathetic."

REFERENCES:

Darden, William R. and Dub Ashton (1974-1975), "Psychographic Profiles of Patronage Preference Groups," *JR*, 50 (Winter), 99-112.

Davis, Duane L. and Ronald S. Rubin (1983), "Identifying the Energy Conscious Consumer: The Case of the Opinion Leader," *JAMS*, 11 (Spring), 169-190.

Dickerson, Mary D. and James W. Gentry (1983), "Characteristics of Adopters and Non-Adopters of Home Computers," *JCR*, 10 (September), 225-235.

Hawes, Jon M. and James R. Lumpkin (1984), "Understanding the Outshopper," *JAMS*, 12 (Fall), 200-218.

Lumpkin, James R. (1985), "Shopping Orientation Segmentation of the Elderly Consumer," *JAMS*, 13 (Spring), 271-289.

Wells, William D. and Douglas Tigert (1971), "Activities, Interests, and Opinions," *JAR*, 11 (August), 27-35.

Wilkes, Robert E., John J. Burnett, and Roy D. Howell (1986), "On the Meaning and Measurement of Religiosity in Consumer Research," *JAMS*, 14 (Spring), 47-56.

SCALE ITEMS: CREDIT USAGE +

Strongly Disagree	Disagree	Slightly Disagree	Slightly Agree	Agree	Strongly Agree
1	2	3	4	5	6

1. I buy many things with a credit card or a charge card.
2. I like to pay cash for everything I buy. **(r)**
3. It is good to have charge accounts.
4. To buy anything, other than a house or a car, on credit is unwise. **(r)**

+ Hawes and Lumpkin (1984) and Lumpkin (1985) used items 1 and 3. Davis and Rubin used item 2 and one other unspecified item.

SCALE NAME: Curiosity (Product Operation)

SCALE DESCRIPTION:

A seven-item, Likert-type summated ratings scale. The scale measures a person's desire to understand how a product works. It was referred to as the Creativity/Curiosity component of the Use Innovativeness Index by Childers (1986) as well as Price and Ridgway (1983).

SCALE ORIGIN:

A 13-item version of the scale was first constructed by Price and Ridgway (1983). It was part of a larger five-component, 44-item Use Innovativeness index. The Creativity/ Curiosity subscale had an alpha of .86. The subscale was constructed along with the other parts of the index to measure the use of a previously adopted product in a novel way or a variety of ways. Data were collected from student subjects in undergraduate classes representing a variety of courses. Analysis was based on 358 usable questionnaires. A couple of rounds of factor analysis with examination of internal consistency and item-total correlations reduced the original collection of 60 items to 44 items among five factors. The Creativity/Curiosity subscale was considered to be the strongest of the five factors. The correlation between scores on the Creativity/Curiosity subscale and scores on the Use Innovativeness index was .82. Validity of the overall index rather than that of the individual subscales was assessed. This was done by noting that students with the highest scores on the Use Innovativeness index engaged in significantly more innovative behaviors (toward calculators) than those scoring lower on the index. The authors urge that further testing of the psychometric properties be done.

SAMPLES:

Childers' (1986) samples were taken from the files of a cable television franchise in a large metro area. One sample was of people who subscribed to cable and another sample was of people who had been contacted but refused to subscribe. Questionnaires were dropped off by an employee of the franchise, but responses were mailed in. **One hundred and seventy six** questionnaires were returned within the three-week period before the cutoff date.

RELIABILITY:

An alpha of **.86** was calculated for the scale.

VALIDITY:

Validity was not examined except in the sense that it was used as part of the assessment of an opinion leadership scale.

ADMINISTRATION:

The scale was self-administered in a survey instrument format. Higher scores on the scale indicate a person reports him/herself as being very curious about how things work whereas lower scores suggest a person has very little interest in fixing things or knowing how they work.

MAJOR FINDINGS:

The purpose of the study by Childers (1986) was to compare the psychometric properties of two versions of an opinion leadership scale. In most respects the modified version of the scale was superior to the previous version. The **Creativity/Curiosity** scale had a low and insignificant correlation with the initial version of the opinion leadership scale ($r = .04$) and a significant though low correlation ($r = .18$) with the modified version.

REFERENCES:

Childers, Terry L. (1986), "Assessment of the Psychometric Properties of an Opinion Leadership Scale," *JMR*, 23 (May), 184-188.

Price, Linda L. and Nancy M. Ridgway (1983), "Development of a Scale to Measure Use Innovativeness," in *Advances in Consumer Research*, Vol. 10, Richard P. Bagozzi and Alice M. Tybout, eds. Ann Arbor, Mich.: Association for Consumer Research, 679-684.

SCALE ITEMS: CURIOSITY (PRODUCT OPERATION) +

Strongly Disagree	Disagree	Slightly Disagree	Neutral	Slightly Agree	Agree	Strongly Agree
1	2	3	4	5	6	7

1. Knowing how a product works offers almost as much pleasure as knowing that the product works well.
2. I am very creative when using products.
3. I'm less interested in the appearance of an item than in what makes it tick.
4. As a child, I really enjoyed taking things apart and putting them back together again.
5. As long as a product works well, I don't really care how it works. **(r)**
6. Curiosity is one of the permanent and certain characteristics of a vigorous intellect.
7. I am very curious about how things work.
8. I like to build things for my home.
9. If I can't figure out how something works, I would rather tinker with it than ask for help.
10. I never take anything apart because I know I'll never be able to put it back together again.
11. I like to fix things around the house.
12. I have gotten instruction in self-reliance skills (e.g., carpentry, car tune-up, etc.)
13. I would rather fix something myself than take it to someone else to fix.

+ This is the form of the scale offered by Price and Ridgway (1983). Childers (1986) did not specify which seven items he used or the exact nature of the graphic scale and its verbal anchors. On the basis of factor loadings and item-total correlations reported by Price and Ridgway (1983), items 3, 4, 7 through 11, and 13 appear to be the strongest of the set.

SCALE NAME: Cynicism (Political)

SCALE DESCRIPTION:

A four-item, five-point Likert-type scale measuring a person's belief about the ability and/or desire of government to handle what one perceives to be important matters. This scale was referred to as Political Trust by Durand and Lambert (1985).

SCALE ORIGIN:

The scale was originally constructed and used by Olsen (1969), though he appears to have drawn heavily on previous work. His sample was drawn from two census tracts in Ann Arbor, one a "lower middle class" neighborhood and the other very much "upper middle class." The analysis was based on successful interviews of **154** people . The coefficient of reproducibility was .**921**. Political cynicism appeared to be most prevalent in the following groups: the elderly, the poorly educated, persons with small businesses, and Republicans.

SAMPLES:

The study be Durand and Lambert (1985) was based on a systematic sample of 1320 customers of a large, investor-owned electric utility company. Questionnaires were mailed to them and **325** were returned following a reminder mailed after two weeks. The average respondent was at least 45 years of age, male, white, married, had at least graduated from high school, and was socioeconomically upscale.

RELIABILITY:

An alpha of **.59** was reported for the scale.

VALIDITY:

No examination of scale validity was reported.

ADMINISTRATION:

The scale was self-administered along with several other measures included in the mail questionnaire. Higher scores on the scale indicate that respondents feel government is incapable of coping with important problems whereas lower scores suggest that respondents trust government to be concerned and responsive.

MAJOR FINDINGS:

The purpose of the study was to investigate the degree to which criticisms of advertising are positively related to various aspects of consumer and political alienation. Respondents were first grouped according to levels of alienation by cluster analysis. (**Cynicism** was one of the alienation variables on which the cluster analysis was based.) Then differences in advertising criticisms were compared across the groups. The cluster analysis produced four alienation groups and a MANOVA indicated significant differences between the groups with all of the 12 advertising criticisms considered simultaneously.

COMMENTS:

The low reliability estimate in the consumer study suggests that the scale may have stability only with certain samples. Caution is urged until some refinement and improvement is done.

REFERENCES:

Durand, Richard M. and Zarrel V. Lambert (1985), "Alienation and Criticisms of Advertising," *JA*, 14 (3), 9-17.

Olsen, Marvin E. (1969), "Two Categories of Political Alienation," *Social Forces*, 47 (March), 288-299.

SCALE ITEMS: CYNICISM (POLITICAL)

Strongly Agree	Agree	Neutral	Disagree	Strongly Disagree
1	2	3	4	5

1. These days the government is trying to do too many things, including some activities that I don't think it has the right to do.
2. For the most part the government serves the interests of a few organized groups, such as business or labor, and isn't very concerned about the needs of people like myself.
3. It seems to me that government often fails to take necessary actions on important matters, even when people favor such actions.
4. As the government is now organized and operated, I think it is hopelessly incapable of dealing with all of the crucial problems facing the country today.

SCALE NAME: Dieter

SCALE DESCRIPTION:

A three-item, six-point, Likert-type summated ratings scale that assesses a person's interest in dieting.

SCALE ORIGIN:

These items were part of a classic study of psychographics by Wells and Tigert (1971). One thousand questionnaires were mailed to homemaker members of the Market Facts mail panel. In addition to gathering demographic, product use, and media data, the survey contained 300 statements that have since served as the basis for the construction of many lifestyle-related scales. The three items for this scale are reported in the article, but they were not analyzed as a multi-item scale. The purpose of the article was to explain how psychographics could improve upon mere demographic description of target audiences and product users. No psychometric information was reported.

One of the first uses of the items as a multi-item scale was by Darden and Perreault (1976). Analysis was based on self-administered questionnaires completed by 278 suburban housewives randomly selected in Athens, Georgia. A split- half reliability of .69 was reported for the scale. Dieting was one of a few lifestyle variables that differentiated between outshopping groups. The group with the greatest tendency to diet showed little outshopping behavior except that they were the heaviest outbuyers of home entertainment products. The group with the least tendency to diet were the inshoppers (those who predominantly shopped in the home trading area for the 13 product categories studied.)

SAMPLES:

Lumpkin and Darden (1982) had **145** usable responses gathered from the consumer research panel of the University of Arkansas. Data were collected from the individuals by mail questionnaire.

RELIABILITY:

An alpha of **.66** was calculated by Lumpkin and Darden (1982).

VALIDITY:

A factor analysis indicated that the items loaded together.

ADMINISTRATION:

Data were gathered through self-administered mail questionnaires. Scale scores are calculated by averaging numerical responses to individual items. A score of 6 indicates that a person is very interested in dieting whereas a 1 means that dieting is not of interest at all.

MAJOR FINDINGS:

In their study of television program preference groups, Lumpkin and Darden (1982) found a few lifestyle variables that were significantly different among the six groups, but tendency to diet was *not* one of them.

COMMENTS:

The phrase ''during the warm weather'' in item 1 (below) may influence responses, and validity may be increased by eliminating it. The reference to ''housewife'' in item 2 may need to be changed to make it relevant to the sample being surveyed. Also, the reference to Metracal in item 3 should either be deleted or updated with a more current brand name.

See also the scale used by Burnett and Bush (1986), which may be the same as or similar to this one.

REFERENCES:

Burnett, John J. and Alan J. Bush (1986), ''Profiling the Yuppies,'' *JAR*, 26 (April/May), 27-35.

Darden, William R. and William D. Perreault, Jr. (1976), ''Identifying Interurban Shoppers: Multiproduct Purchase Patterns and Segmentation Profiles,'' *JMR*, 13 (February), 51-60.

Lumpkin, James R. and William R. Darden (1982), ''Relating Television Preference Viewing to Shopping Orientations, Lifestyles, and Demographics,'' *JA*, 11 (4), 56-67.

Wells, William D. and Douglas Tigert (1971), ''Activities, Interests, and Opinions,'' *JAR*, 11 (August), 27-35.

SCALE ITEMS: DIETER

Strongly Disagree	Disagree	Slightly Disagree	Slightly Agree	Agree	Strongly Agree
1	2	3	4	5	6

1. During the warm weather I drink low calorie soft drinks several times a week.
2. I buy more low calorie foods than the average housewife.
3. I have used Metracal or other diet foods at least one meal a day.

SCALE NAME: Disconfirmation

SCALE DESCRIPTION:

A three-item, five-point Likert-type scale measuring the degree to which a consumer's expectations about a decision are not met. The three-item version of the scale was used by Oliver and Swan (1989a, b) and Westbrook (1987). A two-item, seven-point version was used by Oliver (1980).

SCALE ORIGIN:

The three-item version of the scale was based on the two-item version developed and used originally by Oliver (1980). See further details below.

SAMPLES:

Systematic random sampling was used by Oliver (1980) to select names and addresses from two sources: the telephone directory of a south-central U.S. city and preregistration data from a major university in the same city. Questionnaires were sent to persons selected from the two samples. Of those returning useable forms, **291** residents and **162** students reported receiving a flu shot; **65** residents and 86 students reported that they did not get flu shots.

The study by Westbrook (1987) was based on two independent survey samples. One survey focused on CATV services, used area probability sampling of households in a U.S. metropolitan area, and successfully and professionally interviewed **154** adults heads of households. The other survey obtained responses from **200** vehicle owners in the same metro area using personally delivered and picked up self-administered questionnaires. The samples were said to match their respective populations on selected demographic and product usage characteristics.

Oliver and Swan's (1989a) findings were based on **415** completed questionnaires from two random samples of new car buyers. Because the two samples did not differ significantly on any demographic characteristics measured, the datasets were combined. The sample was 63% male and 30% college educated; 22% had income between $30,000 and $39,999, average age was 41 years, and respondents had owned 7.8 cars.

Subsequent analysis by Oliver and Swan (1989b) was based on just one of the initial samples mentioned above. Completed surveys were obtained from **184** people who had bought new cars within six months prior to the survey. The average respondent was male (67%), college educated (32%), had an income between $20,000 and $29,999, was 43 years of age, had owned 7.8 cars in his lifetime, and had purchased his latest car 4.5 months previously.

RELIABILITY:

The version of the scale used by Westbrook (1987) was reported to have an alpha of **.84**. Three LISREL estimates of the scale's reliability were made by Oliver and Swan (1989b). The consumers' disconfirmation perceptions about the dealer, the salesperson, and the car produced alpha values of **.86**, **.87**, and **.84**, respectively. For disconfirmation with a salesperson, Oliver and Swan (1989a) reported a LISREL estimate of **.856**. No reliability information was reported by Oliver (1980).

VALIDITY:

No specific examination of scale validity has been reported.

ADMINISTRATION:

The scale was one of many measures that were self-administered in each of the studies. Lower scores on the scale suggest that results of a decision have turned out much worse than expected whereas higher scores imply that the results of a decision have turned out much better than expected.

MAJOR FINDINGS:

Oliver (1980) tested a model of consumer satisfaction that expresses satisfaction as a function of expectation and **disconfirmation**. The model was examined in the context of comparing people's expectations about a flu shot with their perceived benefits and problems after they had received the shot. The results indicated that **disconfirmation** was not significantly related to any pre-exposure measure, but had the greatest impact on satisfaction of the variables studied.

Affective responses to consumption experiences and their influence on postpurchase processes were studied by Westbrook (1987). **Disconfirmation** is a significant positive predictor of satisfaction and a significant negative predictor of complaint behavior. However, the latter relationship is fully mediated by satisfaction.

The general purpose of both studies by Oliver and Swan (1989a, b) was to examine customer perceptions of satisfaction in the context of new car purchases. Using LISREL, the authors determined that fairness was more important than **disconfirmation** in producing interpersonal satisfaction and that advantageous inequity was unrelated to it (1989a).

The findings were the same in their subsequent study (1989b) with the added insight that customer satisfaction with the dealer was primarily related to the former's perception of fairness, followed by satisfaction with the salesperson, and then somewhat influenced by **disconfirmation**.

COMMENTS:

Though there are similarities between the versions of the scales used, the object of the expectations does make a difference in the phrasing of the items (as can be noted below). However, with minimal adjustment the scale might be usable for other decisions.

REFERENCES:

Oliver, Richard L. (1980), ''A Cognitive Model of the Antecedents and Consequences of Satisfaction Decisions,'' *JMR*, 17 (November), 460-469.

_____ and John E. Swan (1989a), ''Consumer Perceptions of Interpersonal Equity and Satisfaction in Transactions: A Field Survey Approach,'' *JM*, 53 (April), 21-35.

_____ and _____ (1989b), ''Equity and Disconfirmation Perceptions as Influences on Merchant and Product Satisfaction,'' *JCR*, 16 (December), 372-383.

Westbrook, Robert A. (1987), ''Product/Consumption-Based Affective Responses and Postpurchase Processes,'' *JMR*, 24 (August), 258-270.

SCALE ITEMS: DISCONFIRMATION +

Reflecting on your recent shot, respond to the following statements.

1. The problems you have encountered have been:

Much less serious than expected		Pretty much as expected		Much more serious than expected
1————2————3————4————5————6————7				

2. The benefits you have experienced have been:

Much more than expected		Pretty much as expected		Much less than expected
1————2————3————4————5————6————7				

+ The actual items were not provided by Oliver (1980) but, on the basis of their description, this is their assumed form. Similarly, Westbrook (1987) did not give the items, but they appear to be similar to those above except that they referred to the purchase of a car and the scale had a third item similar to those below.

Much worse than expected	Worse than expected	As expected	Better than expected	Much better than expected
1————2————3————4————5				

Compared to what I expected the salesperson to be like:*
1. The problems I had with him were. . . .
2. His good points were. . . .
3. Overall, my salesman was. . . .

Compared to what I expected the dealership to be like:**
1. The problems I had were. . . .
2. The benefits I expected were. . . .
3. Overall, the dealer was. . . .

Compared to what I expected:**
1. The car's strength's were. . . .
2. The car's weaknesses were. . . .
3. All things about the car were. . . .

*Used by Oliver and Swan (1989a and 1989b).
**Used by Oliver and Swan (1989b).

SCALE NAME: Dogmatism

SCALE DESCRIPTION:

A five-item, Likert-type summated ratings scale measuring the degree to which a person asserts his/her opinion in an unyielding manner.

SCALE ORIGIN:

No information is provided in the article that indicates the scale was not original to Bruning, Kovacic, and Oberdick (1985).

SAMPLES:

Questionnaires were distributed at five airports in the U.S. that offered major/national and regional/commuter service. To provide an adequate representation of various types of flyers the sample was stratified by time of day and day of week. Questionnaires were distributed on a ''random'' basis to passengers waiting for flights to leave at departure gates. Self-addressed, stamped envelopes were provided with the survey forms and **591** usable forms were returned.

RELIABILITY:

An alpha of **.64** was reported for the scale.

VALIDITY:

A factor analysis indicated that the items loaded together.

ADMINISTRATION:

The scale was self-administered with other parts of the questionnaire while passengers were waiting at departure gates at airports. The questionnaires were returned by mail. Higher scores on this scale indicate that respondents are very **dogmatic** whereas lower scores imply respondents are more open minded and willing to admit error.

MAJOR FINDINGS:

Bruning, Kovacic, and Oberdick (1985) were studying the reasons why air travelers choose a certain form of airline and how such information could be used to segment carriers into distinct markets. Discriminant analysis was used to identify personality factors, demographic variables, and airline-related perceptions that would significantly discriminate between commuter and noncommuter travelers. **Dogmatism** was not statistically significant in separating passenger respondents into one of the two markets.

COMMENTS:

The internal consistency of the scale is low enough that some effort should be spent on further development and testing.

REFERENCE:

Bruning, Edward R., Mary L. Kovacic, and Larry E. Oberdick (1985), "Segmentation Analysis of Domestic Airline Passenger Markets," *JAMS*, 13 (Winter), 17-31.

SCALE ITEMS: DOGMATISM +

Strongly Disagree	Disagree	Somewhat Disagree	Somewhat Agree	Agree	Strongly Agree
1	2	3	4	5	6

1. I do everything in my power not to have to admit defeat.
2. I try to convince others to accept my political principles.
3. People find it difficult to convince me that I am wrong on a point no matter how hard they try.
4. I would get into a long discussion rather than admit that I am wrong.
5. When someone opposes me on an issue, I usually find myself taking an even stronger stand than I did at first.

+ The graphic scale was not specified in the article but was likely to be similar to the above and have between five and seven points on it.

SCALE NAME: Dogmatism

SCALE DESCRIPTION:

A forty-item, six-point Likert-type summated ratings scale measuring the degree of openness and closedness in a person's belief systems. A 20-item version of the scale was used by Shimp and Sharma (1987).

SCALE ORIGIN:

Construction of the scale is reported in detail by Rokeach (1960). Most of the items were generated by Rokeach but a few were borrowed from the work of others. The scale went through several revisions that led to the final 40-item version as of 1960.

Split-half reliability was calculated for several samples (mostly college students) and ranged from **.68** to **.93**. Test-retest reliability for a college student sample (n=58) with about five months between tests was **.71**. Validity was examined by noting how known groups with open or closed belief systems scored on the scale. One study found differences between groups in scale scores but another did not. A possible reason for the conflicting findings is that the person who selects people and puts them in the two groups may not be an accurate judge. (Graduate students in psychology judging their peers appeared to do better than nonpsychology professors judging their students.)

SAMPLES:

Analysis by Goodwin and Etgar (1980) was based on data collected from **180** students enrolled in business courses in a northeastern state university. A 2 × 3 × 3 factorial between-subjects design was used, with 10 subjects per cell. (There were two types of products, three levels of product attributes, and three different message appeals.)

Convenience samples of homemakers and students in undergraduate business courses were used by Raju (1980). The scale was administered to **30** homemakers and **65** students.

Many samples of varying characteristics were used in the studies reported by Shimp and Sharma (1987), but the one in which dogmatism was measured was composed of **145** college students, about 60% of whom were men and with a mean age of 21.5 years.

RELIABILITY:

No examination of scale reliability was reported by Goodwin and Etgar (1980) or Raju (1980). The short version used by Shimp and Sharma (1987) was reported to have an alpha of **.74**.

VALIDITY:

No examination of scale validity was reported in any of the studies.

ADMINISTRATION:

Raju (1980) had subjects self-administer the scale along with other measures. Goodwin and Etgar (1980), had subjects complete the scale along with several other self-administered measures one month prior to the experiment. Similarly, Shimp and Sharma (1987) had students complete the scale along with other measures in a class setting and this was followed five weeks later by other treatments and measures. Higher scores on the scale suggest a person is very dogmatic whereas lower scores imply the person is open-minded. For the 40-item scale, if a constant of 4 is added to the responses to each item, the range of possible scale scores is from 40 to 280. For each item, agreement implies close-mindedness and disagreement suggests open-mindedness.

MAJOR FINDINGS:

The communication effectiveness of three ad appeals was investigated by Goodwin and Etgar (1980). **Dogmatism** was one of several personality variables included as a covariate in the analysis to minimize error variation in the findings. None of the personality variables was found to have a significant influence on the relative effectiveness of the three appeals.

Raju (1980) examined optimal stimulation level and numerous personality, demographic, and consumer-related characteristics. **Dogmatism** was not found to have a significant correlation with arousal-seeking tendency for either homemakers or students. The purpose of the study by Shimp and Sharma (1987) was to describe the construction and validation of a scale to measure the American consumer's ethnocentrism. It was found to have a significant positive correlation with **dogmatism.**

COMMENTS:

Scores on the 20-item version have been found to have extremely high correlations with those on the 40-item version (Robinson and Shaver 1973). The former therefore can be used in place of the latter with little reluctance. However, the scale is more than 30 years old now and may require some rechecking and adjustment before it is assumed to be as valid and reliable as it once was. For example, item 1 below may not differentiate between open- and close-minded people as it once did given the significant political changes that have occurred in what was the Soviet Union.

REFERENCES:

Goodwin, Stephen and Michael Etgar (1980), ''An Experimental Investigation of Comparative Advertising: Impact of Message Appeal, Information Load, and Utility of Product Class,'' *JMR*, 17 (May), 187-202.

Raju, P. S. (1980), ''Optimum Stimulation Level: Its Relationship to Personality, Demographics, and Exploratory Behavior,'' *JCR*, 7 (December), 272-282.

Robinson, John B. and Philip R. Shaver (1973), *Measures of Social Psychological Attitudes*. Ann Arbor, Mich.: Survey Research Center, Institute for Social Research.

Rokeach, Milton (1960), *The Open and Closed Mind*. New York, N.Y.: Basic Books, Inc.

Shimp, Terence A. and Subhash Sharma (1987), ''Consumer Ethnocentrism: Construction and Validation of the CETSCALE,'' *JMR*, 24 (August), 280-289.

SCALE ITEMS: DOGMATISM

The following is a study of what the general public thinks and feels about a number of important social and personal questions. The best answer to each statement below is your personal opinion. We have tried to cover many different and opposing points of view; you may find yourself agreeing strongly with some of the statements, disagreeing just as strongly with others, and perhaps uncertain about others; whether you agree or disagree with any statement, you can be sure that many people feel the same as you do. Mark each statement according to how much you agree or disagree with it.

Please mark every one using the following scale:

+1 = I agree a little
+2 = I agree on the whole
+3 = I agree very much
−1 = I disagree a little
−2 = I disagree on the whole
−3 = I disagree very much

1. The United States and Russia have just about nothing in common. +
2. The highest form of government is a democracy and the highest form of democracy is a government run by those who are most intelligent. +
3. Even though freedom of speech for all groups is a worthwhile goal, it is unfortunately necessary to restrict the freedom of certain political groups. +
4. It is only natural that a person would have a much better acquaintance with ideas he believes in than with ideas he opposes.
5. Man on his own is a helpless and miserable creature. +
6. Fundamentally, the world we live in is a pretty lonesome place.
7. Most people just don't give a "damn" for others. +
8. I'd like it if I could find someone who could tell me how to solve my personal problems. +
9. It is only natural for a person to be rather fearful of the future.
10. There is so much to be done and so little time to do it.
11. Once I get wound up in a heated discussion I just can't stop.
12. In a discussion I often find it necessary to repeat myself several times to make sure I am being understood. +
13. In a heated discussion I generally become so absorbed in what I am going to say that I forget to listen to what others are saying.
14. It is better to be a dead hero than a live coward. +
15. While I don't like to admit this even to myself, my secret ambition is to become a great man, like Einstein, or Beethoven, or Shakespeare. +
16. The main thing in life is for a person to want to do something important. +
17. If given the chance I would do something of great benefit to the world
18. In the history of mankind there have probably been just a handful of great thinkers.
19. There are a number of people I have come to hate because of the things they stand for.
20. A man who does not believe in some great cause has not really lived.
21. It is only when a person devotes himself to an ideal or cause that life becomes meaningful. +
22. Of all the different philosophies which exist in this world there is probably only one which is correct. +
23. A person who gets enthusiastic about too many causes is likely to be a pretty "wishy-washy" sort of person.
24. To compromise with our political opponents is dangerous because it usually leads to the betrayal of our own side. +

25. When it comes to differences in opinion in religion we must be careful not to compromise with those who believe differently from the way we do.
26. In times like these, a person must be pretty selfish if he considers primarily his own happiness.
27. The worst crime a person could commit is to attack publicly the people who believe in the same thing he does.
28. In times like these it is often necessary to be more on guard against ideas put out by people or groups in one's own camp than by those in the opposing camp.
29. A group which tolerates too many differences of opinion among its own members cannot exist for long.
30. There are two kinds of people in this world: those who are for the truth and those who are against the truth. +
31. My blood boils whenever a person stubbornly refuses to admit that he is wrong. +
32. A person who thinks of primarily his own happiness is beneath contempt.
33. Most of the ideas that get printed nowadays aren't worth the paper they are printed on. +
34. In this complicated world of ours the only way we can know what's going on is to rely on leaders or experts who can be trusted. +
35. It is often desirable to reserve judgment about what's going on until one has had a chance to hear the opinions of those one respects. +
36. In the long run the best way to live is to pick friends and associates whose tastes and beliefs are the same as one's own.
37. The present is all too often full of unhappiness. It is only the future that counts. +
38. If a man is to accomplish his mission in life it is sometimes necessary to gamble "all or nothing at all."
39. Unfortunately a good many people with whom I have discussed important social and moral problems don't really understand what's going on.
40. Most people just don't know what's good for them. +

+ These 20 items have the highest item-total correlations and compose the short-version used by Shimp and Sharma (1987).

SCALE NAME: Dominance

SCALE DESCRIPTION:

A six-item, seven-point semantic differential summated ratings scale measuring one's dominance-related emotional reaction to an environmental stimulus.

SCALE ORIGIN:

This scale is taken from the work of Mehrabian and Russell (1974). Given previous work by others as well as their own research, they proposed that three factors compose all emotional reactions to environmental stimuli. They referred to the three factors as pleasure, arousal, and dominance. A series of studies were used to develop measures of each factor. In a study of the "final" set of items, 214 University of California undergraduates each used the scales to evaluate a different subset of six situations (hence the analysis was based on 1284 observations). A principal components factor analysis with oblique rotation was used and the expected three factors emerged. Pleasure, arousal, and dominance explained 27%, 23%, and 14% of the available evidence, respectively. Scores on the pleasure scale had correlations of -.07 and .03 with arousal and dominance, respectively. Dominance had a correlation of .18 with arousal.

SAMPLES:

Holbrook et al. (1984) used **60** MBA students with a mean age of 25.6 years.

RELIABILITY:

An alpha of **.88** was reported for the scale.

VALIDITY:

No examination of the scale's validity was reported.

ADMINISTRATION:

The scale was self-administered along with several other measures in the middle of individual experimental sessions. Lower scores on the scale suggest that respondents feel in control of some specified stimulus whereas higher scores imply that they are instead heavily influenced by the stimulus. Holbrook at al. (1984) noted that scores were normalized for each individual by subtracting the scale mean from the response to each item and then summing the corrected numeric responses.

MAJOR FINDINGS:

Holbrook et al. (1984) examined the role of emotions, performance, and personality in the enjoyment of games. In general, they found that emotions depend on personality-game congruity, perceived complexity, and prior performance. Specifically, the **dominance** expressed in playing a video game was most significantly predicted by a match between cognitive style (visualizing/verbalizing) and game format (visual/verbal) as well as the number of successful performances in four immediately preceding plays.

COMMENTS:

As noted above, this scale was developed along with two other scales, arousal and pleasure. Though scored separately, they are typically used together in a study. See also Havlena and Holbrook (1986).

REFERENCES:

Havlena, William J. and Morris B. Holbrook (1986), "The Varieties of Consumption Experience: Comparing Two Typologies of Emotion in Consumer Behavior," *JCR*, 13 (December), 394-404.

Holbrook, Morris B., Robert W. Chestnut, Terence A. Oliva, and Eric A. Greenleaf (1984), "Play as a Consumption Experience: The Roles of Emotions, Performance, and Personality in the Enjoyment of Games," *JCR*, 11 (September), 728-739.

Mehrabian, Albert and James A. Russell (1974), *An Approach to Environmental Psychology*. Cambridge, Mass.: The MIT Press.

SCALE ITEMS: DOMINANCE

controlling	____ :	____ :	____ :	____ :	____ :	____ :	____	controlled
	1	2	3	4	5	6	7	
influential	____ :	____ :	____ :	____ :	____ :	____ :	____	influenced
	1	2	3	4	5	6	7	
in control	____ :	____ :	____ :	____ :	____ :	____ :	____	cared for
	1	2	3	4	5	6	7	
important	____ :	____ :	____ :	____ :	____ :	____ :	____	awed
	1	2	3	4	5	6	7	
dominant	____ :	____ :	____ :	____ :	____ :	____ :	____	submissive
	1	2	3	4	5	6	7	
autonomous	____ :	____ :	____ :	____ :	____ :	____ :	____	guided
	1	2	3	4	5	6	7	

SCALE NAME: Energy Consciousness

SCALE DESCRIPTION:

A three-item, six-point, Likert-type summated ratings scale ranging from strongly disagree (1) to strongly agree (6). The scale measures the degree to which a sensitivity toward the use of energy has influenced a person's lifestyle. See also Heslop, Moran, and Cousineau (1981).

SCALE ORIGIN:

It is not clear where the items originated or where the scale was first used as a multi-item summated ratings scale.

SAMPLES:

Lumpkin (1985) analyzed data collected from a sample drawn from the Market Facts Consumer Mail Panel. A total of **2854** completed questionnaires were received but Lumpkin focused just on **373** respondents who indicated they were 65 years of age or older.

RELIABILITY:

An alpha of **.6513** was reported by Lumpkin (1985).

VALIDITY:

Factor analysis indicated the items loaded together.

ADMINISTRATION:

Lumpkin (1985) gathered data through self-administered mail questionnaires. Scale scores are calculated by averaging numerical responses to individual items. A score of 6 indicates that a person has a strong awareness of his/her energy use and that it influences his/her lifestyle whereas a 1 implies the person is not very sensitive about saving energy.

MAJOR FINDINGS:

Elderly consumers were cluster analyzed by Lumpkin (1985) and **energy consciousness** discriminated somewhat between the three groups, though the level of statistical significance was not reported. All three groups seem to reflect rather high levels of sensitivity, but the group with the highest mean on the scale was also the most socially active and had the most interest in shopping and the arts. The group with the lowest mean score appeared to be much less active and involved all around.

COMMENTS:

Several more items should be tested and added to this measure to improve its reliability. Further, the items seem to be most appropriate for use when there is an energy crisis and may not be the best measure of general desire for conserving energy apart from a crisis situation.

REFERENCES:

Heslop, Louise A., Lori Moran, and Amy Cousineau (1981), "'Consciousness' in Energy Conservation Behavior: An Exploratory Study," *JCR*, 8 (December), 299-305.
Lumpkin, James R. (1985), "Shopping Orientation Segmentation of the Elderly Consumer," *JAMS*, 13 (Spring), 271-289.

SCALE ITEMS: ENERGY CONSCIOUSNESS

Strongly Disagree	Disagree	Slightly Disagree	Slightly Agree	Agree	Strongly Agree
1	2	3	4	5	6

1. I find that I am making fewer shopping trips to save on gas.
2. I am conscious of the amount of energy I use.
3. The energy crisis has changed my "lifestyle."

SCALE NAME: Envy

SCALE DESCRIPTION:

An eight-item, five-point Likert- type summated ratings scale measuring the degree to which a person desires another person's possessions and resents others who have the desired possessions. A shorter version of the scale was used by O'Guinn and Faber (1989).

SCALE ORIGIN:

The origin of the scale is reported by Belk (1984). The measure of envy was one of three scales constructed for examining aspects of materialism. Initial pools of 30 or more items were tested for each of the three measures with **237** business school students. By means of factor analysis, item-total correlations, and measures of internal consistency, seven or more items were chosen from each pool to measure the three materialism-related constructs. The eight items retained for measuring envy were reported to have an alpha of **.80**.

SAMPLES:

Belk (1984, 1985) examined the scale in various ways with three more samples. One was composed of **48** business students. Another sample had **338** subjects, 213 of whom were business students. (These two samples were reported to be about two-thirds male.) A third sample was composed of 33 families representing **99** people who ranged in age from 13 to 92 years.

Two samples were employed by O'Guinn and Faber (1989). One consisted of **386** completed responses (out of 808 questionnaires sent) from people who had written an organization that aided compulsive buyers. A second group was used for comparison and was intended to represent the general population. Eight hundred questionnaires were mailed to people in three Illinois areas: Chicago, Springfield, and Bloomington-Normal. Two mailings produced a total of **250** completed survey forms.

RELIABILITY:

An alpha of **.64** was reported for one of the Belk (1984) samples (n = 338). A two week interval, test-retest correlation of **.70** (n = 48) was reported for another Belk (1984, 1985) sample. O'Guinn and Faber (1989) calculated an alpha of **.72**.

VALIDITY:

Belk (1984) compared scale scores with other measures in a multitrait-multimethod matrix. As evidence of convergent validity, scores on the envy scale were significantly correlated with two other measures used to assess the same construct. Only partial support for discriminant validity was found. Evidence of criterion validity was found by noting that two known groups had significantly different mean scores on the scale and the differences were in the hypothesized directions.

No examination of scale validity was made by O'Guinn and Faber (1989) beyond factor analysis. Items pertaining to envy and two other materialism-related constructs were factor analyzed and three factors clearly emerged. The authors did indicate that the scales were slightly modified on the basis of the factor analysis, however.

ADMINISTRATION:

The scale was one of several self-administered measures in each of the studies. Higher scores on the scale indicate that respondents have a tendency to desire others' possessions and hold resentment toward persons who own the possessions whereas lower scores indicate that respondents do not tend to be as envious.

MAJOR FINDINGS:

Belk's (1984) purpose was to discuss the construction and characteristics of three materialism-related constructs: **envy**, possessiveness, and nongenerosity. Many of the findings are reported above. In addition, there was evidence that women were significantly less **envious** than men, that older people were less **envious** than younger people, and that the most **envious** individuals tended to be the least happy.

Belk (1985) examined other aspects of the three subscales and also the psychometric characteristics of the materialism scale as a whole. In particular, he studied generational differences in materialism. Among the many findings was that the youngest and middle generations were similar in their **envy** but were both significantly more **envious** than the oldest generation.

O'Guinn and Faber (1989) studied compulsive shopping. Their results showed that a sample of compulsive shoppers were significantly more **envious** than a general sample of consumers.

COMMENTS:

The three materialism-related measures mentioned above have been used summed separately and also together. Two alpha values for the combined scale were reported by Belk (1985): .66 (n = 338) and .73 (n = 48). Belk (1985) also reported a test-retest correlation of .68 (n = 48). O'Guinn and Faber (1989) calculated an alpha of .71 for the combined scale.

REFERENCES:

Belk, Russell W. (1984), "Three Scales to Measure Constructs Related to Materialism: Reliability, Validity, and Relationships to Measures of Happiness," in *Advances in Consumer Research*, Vol. 11, Thomas Kinnear, ed. Provo, Utah: Association for Consumer Research, 291-297.

———— (1985), "Materialism: Trait Aspects of Living in the Material World," *JCR*, 12 (December), 265-280.

O'Guinn, Thomas C. and Ronald J. Faber (1989), "Compulsive Buying: A Phenomenological Exploration," *JCR*, 16 (September), 147-157.

SCALE ITEMS: ENVY +

Strongly Disagree	Disagree	Neutral	Agree	Strongly Agree
1—————	—2—————	—3—————	—4—————	—5

1. I am bothered when I see people who buy anything they want.
2. I don't know anyone whose spouse or steady date I would like to have as my own. **(r)**
3. When friends do better than me in competition it usually makes me feel happy for them. **(r)**
4. People who are very wealthy often feel they are too good to talk to average people.
5. There are certain people I would like to trade places with.
6. When friends have things I cannot afford it bothers me.
7. I don't seem to get what is coming to me.
8. When Hollywood stars or prominent politicians have things stolen I really feel sorry for them. **(r)**

+ The short version of the scale used by O'Guinn and Faber (1989) employed just items 1, 5, 6, and 7.

SCALE NAME: Ethnocentrism (CETSCALE)

SCALE DESCRIPTION:

A 17-item, seven-point Likert-type summated ratings scale measuring a respondent's attitude toward the appropriateness of purchasing American-made products versus those manufactured in other countries. The scale was called CETSCALE (consumers' ethnocentric tendencies) by its originators (Shimp and Sharma 1987).

SCALE ORIGIN:

The scale is original to the studies reported by Shimp and Sharma (1987). Development of the scale passed through several stages with numerous different samples. The information provided below is based primarily on the final 17-item version of the scale rather than larger preliminary sets.

SAMPLES:

Four separate samples were used to assess the psychomteric properties of the CETSCALE. One sample consisted of names and addresses obtained from a list broker. One thousand questionnaires were mailed to each of three deliberately chosen cities: Detroit, Denver, and Los Angeles. The response rate was just less than one third for each area. At the same time, 950 questionnaires were sent to former panel members in the Carolinas. The response rate was nearly 60%. The total sample size in this "four-areas study" was **1535**.

The "Carolinas study" involved a group of **417** people who were a part of the "four-areas study." Data for the former study were collected two years prior to data for the latter. A smaller, 10-item version of the scale was tested in national consumer good study. A total of more than **2000** completed responses were received. A fourth study examined data from **145** college students.

Though having varying proportions, each of the samples except the student group had respondents representing most age and income groups.

RELIABILITY:

Alpha values of between .**94** and .**96** were found for the scale in the four samples. Test-retest reliability was estimated with the student sample only. With a five-week interval between administrations, a correlation of .**77** was reported.

VALIDITY:

Convergent, discriminant, and nomological validity were addressed and provided evidence of the scale's quality. Some of the specific evidence is discussed with the findings below.

ADMINISTRATION:

The scale was self-administered along with other measures as part of a larger survey instrument in each of the four studies. All except the student sample received questionnaires in the mail. Scores can range from 17 to 119. Higher scores imply that respondents strongly believe in buying American-made products whereas lower scores suggest that respondents do not think buying domestically produced goods is particularly important.

MAJOR FINDINGS:

The purpose of the study was to describe the construction and validation of the CETSCALE. In one or more samples, **ethnocentrism** was found to have a significant positive correlation with the following variables: patriotism, politicoeconomic conservatism, dogmatism, domestic car ownership, intent to purchase a domestic car, and country-of-origin importance. **Ethnocentrism** had a significant negative correlation with attitude toward foreign made products.

COMMENTS:

The absence of negatively stated items makes the scale vulnerable to response bias.

REFERENCE:

Shimp, Terence A. and Subhash Sharma (1987), "Consumer Ethnocentrism: Construction and Validation of the CETSCALE," *JMR*, 24 (August), 280-289.

SCALE ITEMS: ETHNOCENTRISM (CETSCALE)

Respond to the following statements on a scale between 1 (strongly disagree) to 7 (strongly agree).

1. American people should always buy American-made products instead of imports.
2. Only those products that are unavailable in the U.S. should be imported. +
3. Buy American-made products. Keep America working.
4. American products first, last, and foremost. +
5. Purchasing foreign-made products is un-American. +
6. It is not right to purchase foreign products, because it puts Americans out of jobs. +
7. A real American should always buy American-made products. +
8. We should purchase products manufactured in America instead of letting other countries get rich off us. +
9. It is always best to purchase American products.
10. There should be very little trading or purchasing of goods from other countries unless out of necessity.
11. Americans should not buy foreign products, because this hurts American business and causes unemployment. +
12. Curbs should be put on all imports.
13. It may cost me in the long-run but I prefer to support American products. +
14. Foreigners should not be allowed to put their products on our markets.
15. Foreign products should be taxed heavily to reduce their entry into the U.S.
16. We should buy from foreign countries only those products that we cannot obtain within our own country. +
17. American consumers who purchase products made in other countries are responsible for putting their fellow Americans out of work. +

+ These are the 10 items used in the national consumer good study.

SCALE NAME: Exchange Equity (Customer's With Dealer)

SCALE DESCRIPTION:

A three-item, seven-point scale measuring the degree to which a consumer perceives that he or she benefited more from a transaction than the other party. Oliver and Swan (1989b) refer to this as a ''Preference'' scale but admit that ''advantageous inequity'' is a more accurate term for the construct being measured (1989a, p. 25).

SCALE ORIGIN:

The scale was apparently original to Oliver and Swan (1989b). The information here refers to that study although related information can be found in Oliver and Swan (1989a).

SAMPLES:

Analysis was based on completed forms obtained from **184** people who had bought new cars within six months prior to the survey. The average respondent was male (67%), college educated (32%), had an income between $20,000 and $29,999, was 43 years of age, had owned 7.8 cars in his lifetime, and had purchased his latest car 4.5 months previously.

RELIABILITY:

A LISREL estimate of **.78** was reported for the scale.

VALIDITY:

No specific examination of scale validity was reported.

ADMINISTRATION:

The scale was one of many self-administered measures. Low scores on the scale suggest that respondents feel they got more out of the deal than the dealer. High scores imply that customers feel the dealer came out ahead.

MAJOR FINDINGS:

The general purpose of the study was to examine customer perceptions of satisfaction in the context of new car purchases. Using LISREL, the authors determined that fairness was more important than disconfirmation in producing interpersonal satisfaction and **advantageous inequity** was unrelated to it. Also, the findings indicated that customer satisfaction with the dealer was primarily related to the former's perception of fairness, followed by satisfaction with the salesperson, and then somewhat influenced by disconfirmation.

REFERENCES:

Oliver, Richard L. and John E. Swan (1989a), ''Consumer Perceptions of Interpersonal Equity and Satisfaction in Transactions: A Field Survey Approach,'' *JM*, 53 (April), 21-35.

_____ and _____ (1989b), "Equity and Disconfirmation Perceptions as Influences on Merchant and Product Satisfaction," *JCR*, 16 (December), 372-383.

SCALE ITEMS: EXCHANGE EQUITY (CUSTOMER'S WITH DEALER)

Strongly Agree			Neither			Strongly Disagree
1————	—2————	—3————	—4————	—5————	—6————	—7

1. I think the dealer got more out of the sale than I did. (r)
2. I think I got more out of the sale than my dealer.
3. Please circle the number below that best expresses your feelings:

I came out ahead			We both benefitted equally			The dealer came out ahead
1————	—2————	—3————	—4————	—5————	—6————	—7

SCALE NAME: Exchange Equity (Customer's With Salesperson)

SCALE DESCRIPTION:

A three-item, seven-point scale measuring the degree to which a consumer perceives that he/she benefited more from a transaction than the salesperson. Oliver and Swan (1989a) refer to this as the "Preference" scale but admit that "advantageous inequity" is a more accurate term for the construct being measured (p. 25).

SCALE ORIGIN:

The scale was apparently original to Oliver and Swan (1989a, b).

SAMPLES:

Oliver and Swan's (1989a) findings were based on **415** completed questionnaires from two random samples of new car buyers. Because the two samples did not differ significantly on any demographic characteristics measured, the datasets were combined. The sample was 63% male and 30% college educated; 22% had income between $30,000 and $39,999, average age was 41 years, and respondents had owned 7.8 cars.

Subsequent analysis (1989b) was based on just one of the initial samples mentioned above. Completed surveys were obtained from **184** people who had bought new cars within six months prior to the survey. The average respondent was male (67%), college educated (32%), had an income between $20,000 and $29,999, was 43 years of age, had owned 7.8 cars in his lifetime, and had purchased his latest car 4.5 months previously.

RELIABILITY:

The estimates of reliability provided by LISREL were **.754** and **.75** (1989a and 1989b, respectively).

VALIDITY:

No specific examinations of scale validity were reported by Oliver and Swan (1989a, b).

ADMINISTRATION:

The scale was one of many measures that were self-administered in both studies by Oliver and Swan (1989a, b). Low scores on the scale suggest that respondents feel they got more out of the deal than the salesperson. High scores imply that respondents feel the salesperson came out ahead.

MAJOR FINDINGS:

The general purpose of both studies was to examine customer perceptions of satisfaction in the context of new car purchases. Using LISREL, the authors determined that **fairness** was more important than disconfirmation in producing interpersonal satisfaction and that **advantageous inequity** was unrelated to it (1989a). The findings were the same in their subsequent study (1989b) with the added insight that customer satisfaction with the dealer was primarily related to the former's perception of **fairness**, followed by satisfaction with the salesperson, and then somewhat influenced by disconfirmation.

REFERENCES:

Oliver, Richard L. and John E. Swan (1989a), ''Consumer Perceptions of Interpersonal Equity and Satisfaction in Transactions: A Field Survey Approach,'' *JM*, 53 (April), 21-35.

_____ and _____ (1989b), ''Equity and Disconfirmation Perceptions as Influences on Merchant and Product Satisfaction,'' *JCR*, 16 (December), 372-383.

SCALE ITEMS: EXCHANGE EQUITY (CUSTOMER'S WITH SALESPERSON)

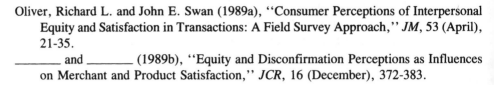

```
Strongly                         Neither                        Strongly
Agree                                                           Disagree
  1————2————3————4————5————6————7
```

1. I think my salesperson got more out of the deal than I. **(r)**
2. I think I got more out of the deal than my salesperson.
3. Please circle the number below that best expresses your feelings:

```
I came                      We both benefitted              He/she came
out ahead                        equally                     out ahead
  1————2————3————4————5————6————7
```

SCALE NAME: Exchange Inputs (Customer's With Dealer)

SCALE DESCRIPTION:

A six-item, seven-point Likert-type scale measuring the amount of time, effort, and/or money a consumer perceives were put into making a transaction with a car dealer.

SCALE ORIGIN:

The scale was apparently original to Oliver and Swan (1989).

SAMPLES:

Analysis was based on completed forms obtained from **184** people who had bought new cars within six months prior to the survey. The average respondent was male (67%), college educated (32%), had an income between $20,000 and $29,999, was 43 years of age, had owned 7.8 cars in his lifetime, and had purchased his latest car 4.5 months previously.

RELIABILITY:

A LISREL estimate of **.72** was reported for the scale.

VALIDITY:

No specific examination of scale validity was reported.

ADMINISTRATION:

The scale was one of many self-administered measures. Lower scores on the scale suggest that respondents feel they put a lot into a transaction whereas higher scores imply that customers feel they did not provide much to the dealer in a transaction.

MAJOR FINDINGS:

The general purpose of the study was to examine customer perceptions of satisfaction in the context of new car purchases. **Customer inputs** was not examined separately but was part of a measure of equity (see Comments below). The findings indicated that perceived fairness increased as the equity score increased. In other words, consumers perceived a transaction to be more fair when the difference in buyer and seller outcome-to-input scores favored the buyer.

COMMENTS:

This scale can be used with other scales to construct an exchange equity formula (Oliver and Swan 1989, p. 377). Though the scale was developed for exchanges involving a car dealer, with some adjustment and retesting it might be suitable for use with other retailers.

REFERENCE:

Oliver, Richard L. and John E. Swan (1989), "Equity and Disconfirmation Perceptions as Influences on Merchant and Product Satisfaction," *JCR*, 16 (December), 372-383.

SCALE ITEMS: EXCHANGE INPUTS (CUSTOMER'S WITH DEALER)

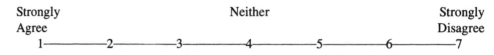

In buying from the dealership, I:
1. Went to a great deal of trouble to shop at this dealer.
2. Gave the dealer a high profit sale.
3. Traded in a good, easy to sell, used car.
4. Did not provide much to the dealership. **(r)**
5. My car purchase should have helped the dealer's business.
6. My inputs were very profitable to the dealership.

SCALE NAME: Exchange Inputs (Customer's With Salesperson)

SCALE DESCRIPTION:

A seven-item, seven-point Likert- type scale measuring the amount of time and effort a consumer perceives that he/she put into dealing with a salesperson. Oliver and Swan (1989b) report using the full seven item version of this scale whereas previously (1989a) they had used an abbreviated version in their analyses (see below).

SCALE ORIGIN:

The scale was apparently original to Oliver and Swan (1989a, b).

SAMPLES:

Oliver and Swan's (1989a) findings were based on **415** completed questionnaires from two random samples of new car buyers. Because the two samples did not differ significantly on any demographic characteristics measured, the datasets were combined. The sample was 63% male and 30% college educated; 22% had income between $30,000 and $39,999, average age was 41 years, and respondents had owned 7.8 cars. Subsequent analysis (1989b) was based on just one of the initial samples mentioned above. Completed surveys were obtained from **184** people who had bought new cars within six months prior to the survey. The average respondent was male (67%), college educated (32%), had an income between $20,000 and $29,999, was 43 years of age, had owned 7.8 cars in his lifetime, and had purchased his latest car 4.5 months previously.

RELIABILITY:

The estimate of reliability provided by LISREL (Oliver and Swan 1989a) was **.79** for the full scale and **.802** for the abbreviated version. Subsequently, a LISREL estimate of **.81** was reported for the full scale (Oliver and Swan 1989b).

VALIDITY:

No specific examinations of scale validity were reported by Oliver and Swan (1989a, b).

ADMINISTRATION:

The scale was one of many measures that were self-administered in both studies by Oliver and Swan (1989a, b). Lower scores on the scale suggest that respondents feel they put a lot into the deal whereas higher scores imply that respondents feel they put little energy or thought into dealing with the salesperson.

MAJOR FINDINGS:

The general purpose of both studies was to examine customer perceptions of satisfaction in the context of new car purchases. **Customer inputs** were not found to be related to the perceived equity or fairness of the exchange.

#90 *Exchange Inputs (Customer's With Salesperson)*

COMMENTS:

Use of the term "salesperson" in the items may be more appropriate for situations in which customers may interact with either a salesman or saleswoman. Also, this scale can be used with other scales to construct an **exchange** equity formula (Oliver and Swan 1989b, p. 377).

REFERENCES:

Oliver, Richard L. and John E. Swan (1989a), "Consumer Perceptions of Interpersonal Equity and Satisfaction in Transactions: A Field Survey Approach," *JM*, 53 (April), 21-35.

_____ and _____ (1989b), "Equity and Disconfirmation Perceptions as Influences on Merchant and Product Satisfaction," *JCR*, 16 (December), 372-383.

SCALE ITEMS: + EXCHANGE INPUTS (CUSTOMER'S WITH SALESPERSON)

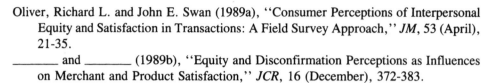

```
Strongly                        Neither                    Strongly
Agree                                                      Disagree
1———————2———————3———————4———————5———————6———————7
```

In dealing with the salesman, I:
1. Put in a lot of attention to what the salesman said.
2. Made a large number of visits to see the salesman.
3. Did a lot of bargaining with the salesman.
4. Put up with a lot of frustration in dealing with the salesman.
5. Put in a lot of time and effort.
6. Put in very *little* energy or thought. **(r)**
7. Overall, I put quite a lot into this deal.

+ Oliver and Swan (1989b) used all of these items whereas previously (1989a) they used just items 3, 5, and 7.

SCALE NAME: Exchange Inputs (Dealer's With Customer)

SCALE DESCRIPTION:

A seven-item, seven-point Likert- type scale measuring the amount of money, time, and/ or effort a consumer perceives that a car dealer invested in a transaction.

SCALE ORIGIN:

The scale was apparently original to Oliver and Swan (1989).

SAMPLES:

Analysis was based on completed forms obtained from **184** people who had bought new cars within six months prior to the survey. The average respondent was male (67%), college educated (32%), had an income between $20,000 and $29,999, was 43 years of age, had owned 7.8 cars in his lifetime, and had purchased his latest car 4.5 months previously.

RELIABILITY:

A LISREL estimate of **.84** was reported for the scale.

VALIDITY:

No specific examination of scale validity was reported.

ADMINISTRATION:

The scale was one of many self-administered measures. Lower scores on the scale suggest that respondents feel the dealer invested a lot in the transaction whereas higher scores imply that respondents feel the dealer did not put much into the making the exchange.

MAJOR FINDINGS:

The general purpose of the study was to examine customer perceptions of satisfaction in the context of new car purchases. **Dealer inputs** was not examined separately but was part of a measure of equity (see Comments below). The findings indicated that perceived fairness increased as the equity score increased. In other words, consumers perceived a transaction to be more fair when the difference in buyer and seller outcome-to-input scores favored the buyer.

COMMENTS:

This scale can be used with other scales to construct an exchange equity formula (Oliver and Swan 1989, p. 377). Though the scale was developed for exchanges involving a car dealer, with some adjustment and retesting it might be suitable for use with other retailers.

REFERENCE:

> Oliver, Richard L. and John E. Swan (1989), "Equity and Disconfirmation Perceptions as Influences on Merchant and Product Satisfaction," *JCR*, 16 (December), 372-383.

SCALE ITEMS: EXCHANGE INPUTS (DEALER'S WITH CUSTOMER)

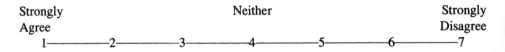

```
Strongly                        Neither                     Strongly
Agree                                                       Disagree
    1————2————3————4————5————6————7
```

In selling me my car, the dealership put in:
1. A large investment in service and repair facilities.
2. Honesty and fair dealings.
3. A good selection of cars in stock.
4. A comfortable, attractive showroom.
5. The dealer went out of his way to provide customers with the best facilities.
6. The dealer provided little in the way of inputs to customers. **(r)**
7. The dealer spent a great deal of money to please customers.

SCALE NAME: Exchange Inputs (Salesperson's With Customer)

SCALE DESCRIPTION:

A seven-item, seven-point Likert-type scale measuring the amount of time and effort a consumer perceives that a salesperson put into a deal. Oliver and Swan (1989b) report using the full seven-item version of this scale whereas previously (1989a) they had used an abbreviated version in their analyses (see below).

SCALE ORIGIN:

The scale was apparently original to Oliver and Swan (1989a and 1989b).

SAMPLES:

Oliver and Swan's (1989a) findings were based on **415** completed questionnaires from two random samples of new car buyers. Because the two samples did not differ significantly on any demographic characteristics measured, the datasets were combined. The sample was 63% male and 30% college educated; 22% had income between $30,000 and $39,999, average age was 41 years, and respondents had owned 7.8 cars.

Subsequent analysis (1989b) was based on just one of the initial samples mentioned above. Completed surveys were obtained from **184** people who had bought new cars within six months prior to the survey. The average respondent was male (67%), college educated (32%), had an income between $20,000 and $29,999, was 43 years of age, had owned 7.8 cars in his lifetime, and had purchased his latest car 4.5 months previously.

RELIABILITY:

The estimate of reliability provided by LISREL (Oliver and Swan 1989a) was **.899** for the full scale and **.9** for the abbreviated version. Subsequently, a LISREL estimate of **.89** was reported for the full scale (Oliver and Swan 1989b).

VALIDITY:

No specific examinations of scale validity were reported by Oliver and Swan (1989a, b).

ADMINISTRATION:

The scale was one of many measures that were self-administered in both studies by Oliver and Swan (1989a, b). Lower scores on the scale suggest that respondents feel the salesperson put a lot into the deal whereas higher scores imply that respondents feel the salesperson did not **invest much time or energy in making the deal.**

MAJOR FINDINGS:

The general purpose of both studies was to examine customer perceptions of satisfaction in the context of new car purchases. **Salesperson inputs** were found to have a positive association with perceived fairness of the deal but no significant role in the explanation of **exchange equity.**

COMMENTS:

Use of the term "salesperson" in the items may be more appropriate for situations in which customers may interact with either a salesman or saleswoman. Also, this scale can be used with other scales to construct an exchange equity formula (Oliver and Swan 1989b, p. 377).

REFERENCES:

Oliver, Richard L. and John E. Swan (1989a), "Consumer Perceptions of Interpersonal Equity and Satisfaction in Transactions: A Field Survey Approach," *JM*, 53 (April), 21-35.

_____ and _____ (1989b), "Equity and Disconfirmation Perceptions as Influences on Merchant and Product Satisfaction," *JCR*, 16 (December), 372-383.

SCALE ITEMS: + EXCHANGE INPUTS (SALESPERSON'S WITH CUSTOMER)

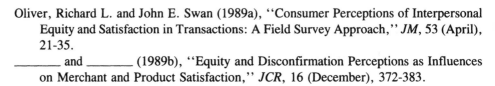

In dealing with me, the salesman:
1. Put in a great deal of time and effort.
2. Had a lot of knowledge about _____.
3. Took time away from other customers to deal with me.
4. Tried to answer my questions carefully.
5. Put a lot into dealing with me.
6. Made a high quality and professional effort.
7. Worked as hard as possible with me.

+ Oliver and Swan (1989b) used all of these items whereas previously (1989a) they had used just items 4, 6, and 7. In both studies the product examined was cars.

SCALE NAME: Exchange Outcomes (Customer's With Dealer)

SCALE DESCRIPTION:

A seven-item, seven-point Likert- type scale measuring the degree of benefit a consumer perceives was received from a car dealer in a transaction.

SCALE ORIGIN:

The scale was apparently original to Oliver and Swan (1989).

SAMPLES:

Analysis was based on completed forms obtained from **184** people who had bought new cars within six months prior to the survey. The average respondent was male (67%), college educated (32%), had an income between $20,000 and $29,999, was 43 years of age, had owned 7.8 cars in his lifetime, and had purchased his latest car 4.5 months previously.

RELIABILITY:

A LISREL estimate of **.76** was reported for the scale.

VALIDITY:

No specific examination of scale validity was reported.

ADMINISTRATION:

The scale was one of many self-administered measures. Lower scores on the scale suggest that respondents feel they **received a lot of benefits** from the transaction whereas higher scores imply that customers feel they did not get much out of their purchase from the dealer.

MAJOR FINDINGS:

The general purpose of the study was to examine customer perceptions of satisfaction in the context of new car purchases. **Customer outcomes** was not examined separately but was part of a measure of equity (see Comments below). The findings indicated that perceived fairness increased as the equity score increased. In other words, consumers perceived **a transaction to be more fair** when the difference in buyer and seller outcome-to-input scores favored the buyer.

COMMENTS:

This scale can be used with other scales to construct an exchange equity formula (Oliver and Swan 1989, p. 377). Though the scale was developed for **exchanges** involving a car dealer, with some adjustment and retesting it might be suitable for use with other retailers.

REFERENCE:

Oliver, Richard L. and John E. Swan (1989), "Equity and Disconfirmation Perceptions as Influences on Merchant and Product Satisfaction," *JCR*, 16 (December), 372-383.

SCALE ITEMS: EXCHANGE OUTCOMES (CUSTOMER'S WITH DEALER)

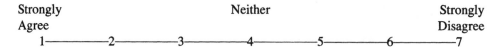

Strongly   Neither   Strongly
Agree   Disagree
1————2————3————4————5————6————7

The Dealer provided me with:
1. Excellent quality warranty and repair service.
2. A poor selection of cars to choose from. **(r)**
3. Help in financing my car purchase.
4. A good trade-in value for my old car.
5. Excellent service.
6. The dealer had little concern for me.
7. I received many benefits from this dealer.

SCALE NAME: Exchange Outcomes (Customer's With Salesperson)

SCALE DESCRIPTION:

A seven-item, seven-point Likert-type scale measuring the degree of benefits a consumer perceives that he or she received from dealing with a salesperson. Oliver and Swan (1989b) report using the full seven-item version of this scale whereas previously (1989a) they had used an abbreviated version in their analyses (see below).

SCALE ORIGIN:

The scale was apparently original to Oliver and Swan (1989a, b).

SAMPLES:

Oliver and Swan's (1989a) findings were based on **415** completed questionnaires from two random samples of new car buyers. Because the two samples did not differ significantly on any demographic characteristics measured, the datasets were combined. The sample was 63% male and 30% college educated; 22% had income between $30,000 and $39,999, average age was 41 years, and respondents had owned 7.8 cars.

Subsequent analysis (1989b) was based on just one of the initial samples mentioned above. Completed surveys were obtained from **184** people who had bought new cars within six months prior to the survey. The average respondent was male (67%), college educated (32%), had an income between $20,000 and $29,999, was 43 years of age, had owned 7.8 cars in his lifetime, and had purchased his latest car 4.5 months previously.

RELIABILITY:

The estimate of reliability provided by LISREL (Oliver and Swan 1989a) was **.811** for the full scale and **.814** for the abbreviated version. Subsequently, a LISREL estimate of **.76** was reported for the full scale (Oliver and Swan 1989b).

VALIDITY:

No specific examinations of scale validity were reported by Oliver and Swan (1989a, b).

ADMINISTRATION:

The scale was one of many measures that were self-administered in both studies by Oliver and Swan (1989a, b). Lower scores on the scale suggest that respondents feel they received a lot from the deal with the salesperson whereas higher scores imply that respondents feel they received little help or understanding from the salesperson.

MAJOR FINDINGS:

The general purpose of both studies was to examine customer perceptions of satisfaction in the context of new car purchases. **Customer outcomes** were found to have a positive association with perceived equity and fairness of the exchange.

COMMENTS:

Use of the term "salesperson" in the items may be more appropriate for situations in which customers may interact with either a salesman or saleswoman. Also, this scale can be used with other scales to construct an exchange equity formula (Oliver and Swan 1989b, p. 377).

REFERENCES:

Oliver, Richard L. and John E. Swan (1989a), "Consumer Perceptions of Interpersonal Equity and Satisfaction in Transactions: A Field Survey Approach," *JM*, 53 (April), 21-35.

_____ and _____ (1989b), "Equity and Disconfirmation Perceptions as Influences on Merchant and Product Satisfaction," *JCR*, 16 (December), 372-383.

SCALE ITEMS: EXCHANGE OUTCOMES (CUSTOMER'S WITH SALESPERSON) +

Strongly Agree			Neither			Strongly Disagree
1————	—2————	—3————	—4————	—5————	—6————	—7

In dealing with the salesman:
1. I received a good explanation of the _____'s features.
2. I received a good deal on the _____ he sold me.
3. I received very little personal attention. **(r)**
4. I felt he/she had a good understanding of my needs.
5. I received a lot of help from the salesman.
6. He/she gave me poor service and understanding. **(r)**
7. Overall, I got a good deal from the salesman.

+ Oliver and Swan (1989b) used all of these items whereas previously (1989a) they had used just items 4, 5, and 7. In both studies the product examined was cars.

SCALE NAME: Exchange Outcomes (Dealer's With Customer)

SCALE DESCRIPTION:

A six-item, seven-point Likert-type scale measuring the degree of benefit a consumer perceives that a car dealer received from him/her in a transaction.

SCALE ORIGIN:

The scale was apparently original to Oliver and Swan (1989).

SAMPLES:

Analysis was based on completed forms obtained from **184** people who had bought new cars within six months prior to the survey. The average respondent was male (67%), college educated (32%), had an income between $20,000 and $29,999, was 43 years of age, had owned 7.8 cars in his lifetime, and had purchased his latest car 4.5 months previously.

RELIABILITY:

A LISREL estimate of **.64** was reported for the scale.

VALIDITY:

No specific examination of scale validity was reported.

ADMINISTRATION:

The scale was one of many self-administered measures. Lower scores on the scale suggest that respondents feel the dealer received a lot from the transaction whereas higher scores imply that customers feel the dealer did not get much out of their purchase.

MAJOR FINDINGS:

The general purpose of the study was to examine customer perceptions of satisfaction in the context of new car purchases. **Dealer outcomes** was not examined separately but was part of a measure of equity (see Comments below). The findings indicated that perceived fairness increased as the equity score increased. In other words, consumers perceived a transaction to be more fair when the difference in buyer and seller outcome-to-input scores favored the buyer.

COMMENTS:

Further work is needed to improve the reliability of this measure. Also, this scale can be used with other scales to construct an exchange equity formula (Oliver and Swan 1989, p. 377). Though the scale was developed for exchanges involving a car dealer, with some adjustment and retesting it might be suitable for use with other retailers.

REFERENCE:

Oliver, Richard L. and John E. Swan (1989), ''Equity and Disconfirmation Perceptions as Influences on Merchant and Product Satisfaction,'' *JCR*, 16 (December), 372-383.

SCALE ITEMS: EXCHANGE OUTCOMES (DEALER'S WITH CUSTOMER)

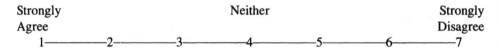

Strongly   Neither   Strongly
Agree   Disagree
1————————2————————3————————4————————5————————6————————7

In selling me my car, the dealership got:
1. A high profit from the car they sold me.
2. Visits from people I recommended to the dealership.
3. A high price when they resold my trade-in.
4. Very positive outcomes from me.
5. On balance, the dealer took a financial loss in dealing with me. **(r)**
6. My purchase from the dealer will keep his business going strong.

SCALE NAME: Exchange Outcomes (Salesperson's With Customer)

SCALE DESCRIPTION:

A seven-item, seven-point Likert-type scale measuring the degree of benefits a consumer perceives that a salesperson received from him/her in a deal. Oliver and Swan (1989b) report using the full seven-item version of this scale whereas previously (1989a) they had used an abbreviated version in their analyses (see below).

SCALE ORIGIN:

The scale was apparently original to Oliver and Swan (1989a, b).

SAMPLES:

Oliver and Swan's (1989a) findings were based on **415** completed questionnaires from two random samples of new car buyers. Because the two samples did not differ significantly on any demographic characteristics measured, the datasets were combined. The sample was 63% male and 30% college educated; 22% had income between $30,000 and $39,999, average age was 41 years, and respondents had owned 7.8 cars.

Subsequent analysis (1989b) was based on just one of the initial samples mentioned above. Completed surveys were obtained from **184** people who had bought new cars within six months prior to the survey. The average respondent was male (67%), college educated (32%), had an income between $20,000 and $29,999, was 43 years of age, had owned 7.8 cars in his lifetime, and had purchased his latest car 4.5 months previously.

RELIABILITY:

The estimates of reliability provided by LISREL (Oliver and Swan 1989a) was **.595** for the full scale and **.651** for the abbreviated version. Subsequently, a LISREL estimate of **.76** was reported for the full scale (Oliver and Swan 1989b).

VALIDITY:

No specific examinations of scale validity were reported by Oliver and Swan (1989a, b).

ADMINISTRATION:

The scale was one of many measures that were self-administered in both studies by Oliver and Swan (1989a, b). Lower scores on the scale suggest that respondents feel the salesperson received a lot from a deal whereas higher scores imply that respondents feel the salesperson did not get much out of making the deal.

MAJOR FINDINGS:

The general purpose of both studies was to examine customer perceptions of satisfaction in the context of new car purchases. **Salesperson outcomes** were found to have a negative association with the perceived equity of the **exchange** but appear to be unrelated to the perceived fairness of the deal.

COMMENTS:

Use of the term "salesperson" in the items may be more appropriate for situations in which customers may interact with either a salesman or saleswoman. Further work is called for to improve the reliability of this measure. Also, this scale can be used with other scales to construct an **exchange** equity formula (Oliver and Swan 1989b, p. 377).

REFERENCES:

Oliver, Richard L. and John E. Swan (1989a), "Consumer Perceptions of Interpersonal Equity and Satisfaction in Transactions: A Field Survey Approach," *JM*, 53 (April), 21-35.

_____ and _____ (1989b), "Equity and Disconfirmation Perceptions as Influences on Merchant and Product Satisfaction," *JCR*, 16 (December), 372-383.

SCALE ITEMS: EXCHANGE OUTCOMES (SALESPERSON'S WITH CUSTOMER) +

Strongly Agree			Neither			Strongly Disagree
1	2	3	4	5	6	7

In dealing with me, the salesman received:
1. A high commission on the sale.
2. A sale that would help him get ahead on the job.
3. A satisfied customer that would likely buy another _____ from him.
4. Other interested _____ shoppers that I referred to him.
5. A lot from me.
6. Very few benefits as a result of dealing with me. **(r)**
7. Dealing with me was certainly worthwhile for him.

+ Oliver and Swan (1989b) used all of these items whereas previously (1989a) they had used just items 2, 5, and 7. In both studies the product examined was cars.

SCALE NAME: Exploratory Shopper

SCALE DESCRIPTION:

A seven-item, seven-point Likert-type summated ratings scale measuring the degree to which a person reports him/herself to like shopping around and gathering product information even if not immediately needing to buy anything. Raju (1980) referred to the measure as Exploration Through Shopping.

SCALE ORIGIN:

Though some of the items may be similar to those used in other scales, this group of items was put into scale form along with six other scales by Raju (1980). An initial pool of 90 items related to exploratory behavior and lifestyle were compiled and then tested for low social desirability bias and high item-total correlations. Thirty-nine items were found to meet the criteria and were common to two separate samples. Items were grouped into seven categories on the basis of inter-item correlations and subjective judgment.

SAMPLES:

Raju (1980) collected data from **336** homemakers and **105** students. The homemakers were contacted through local women's clubs and the students were contacted through mostly junior and senior level college classes.

RELIABILITY:

The scale was reported by Raju (1980) to have reliability (Spearman-Brown) of **.759** and **.866** for the homemaker and student samples, respectively.

VALIDITY:

Though Raju notes that a factor analysis was performed, the grouping of items for scale purposes was based more on inter-item correlations and a subjective classification process.

ADMINISTRATION:

The manner of scale administration was not specifically addressed for either sample by Raju (1980). However, he implied that the homemakers received the questionnaire at a club meeting, filled it out at home by themselves, and returned it by mail. The student sample is assumed to have completed the survey instrument in class. Lower scores on the scale suggest that respondents are uninterested in shopping around whereas higher scores suggest that respondents enjoy exploratory shopping.

MAJOR FINDINGS:

In two studies, Raju (1980) examined the relationships between optimum stimulation level (OSL) and certain personality traits, demographics, and purchase-related psychographics. For both samples, low but significant correlations were found between **exploratory shop-**

ping and OSL. This along with other findings indicated that people with higher OSLs were more likely to exhibit a variety of exploratory behaviors in their consumer behavior.

COMMENTS:

The construct validity of the scale is highly suspect given the manner in which the seven scales used in the study were constructed (as noted in the origination information above). Sixteen of the 39 items were used to compose more than one scale, thus making it unclear what construct the items and their respective scales actually measured. Though the reported reliability levels for this scale are reasonable, further validity testing is needed.

REFERENCE:

Raju, P. S. (1980), ''Optimum Stimulation Level: Its Relationship to Personality, Demographics, and Exploratory Behavior,'' *JCR*, 7 (December), 272-282.

SCALE ITEMS: EXPLORATORY SHOPPER

```
Completely                                                        Completely
Disagree                                                             Agree
    1————————2————————3————————4————————5————————6————————7
```

1. I have little interest in fads or fashion. **(r)**
2. I like to shop around and look at displays.
3. I like to browse through mail order catalogs even when I don't plan to buy anything.
4. I shop around a lot for my clothes just to find out more about the latest styles.
5. I hate window shopping. **(r)**
6. When I see a new brand somewhat different from the usual, I investigate it.
7. I enjoy exploring several different alternatives or brands while shopping.

SCALE NAME: Expressiveness (Stimulus)

SCALE DESCRIPTION:

A three-item, seven-point semantic differential summated ratings scale measuring the degree of emotion perceived to be expressed by a stimulus.

SCALE ORIGIN:

Though Holbrook (1981) may have drawn on the work of Osgood, Suci, and Tannenbaum (1957) and Berlyne (1974) in composing this scale, neither of the latter articles offered these three items per se as a measure of expressivness.

SAMPLES:

Holbrook's (1981) analysis was based on **16** subjects chosen from volunteers with an interest in classical piano music. Half had never played an instrument but enjoyed listening to such music ("nonexperts") and the other half were highly trained musicians ("experts").

RELIABILITY:

An alpha of **.68** was reported for the scale.

VALIDITY:

The first item below loaded highest on this factor; the other two items loaded higher on another factor but were included with this scale in order to have three items.

ADMINISTRATION:

In both studies (Holbrook 1981), subjects self-administered the scale along with several other measures. Higher summated scores suggest that respondents perceive a lot of emotional expression in an object whereas lower scores mean that they perceive the object to be cold and unemotional.

MAJOR FINDINGS:

Holbrook (1981) illustrated a two-stage integrative model of evaluative judgment in which objective product features influenced perceptions, which in turn shaped affect. Specifically, he found that the direct effects of objective music characteristics on affect were not nearly as large or as significant as the indirect effects of those features through intervening perceptions. Perceived **expressiveness,** activity, and complexity had significant positive influences on affect, perceived novelty had a significant negative impact, and perceived potency did not make a salient contribution. Of the musical features examined, phrasing (the degree of connectedness in the musical notes) was the strongest determinant of perceived **expressiveness.**

COMMENTS:

Improvement in the psychometric qualities of this scale is necessary for before it is used in anything other than exploratory research.

REFERENCES:

Berlyne, D. E., ed. (1974), *Studies in the New Experimental Aesthetics.* New York, N.Y.: John Wiley & Sons, Inc.

Holbrook, Morris B. (1981), "Integrating Compositional and Decompositional Analyses to Represent the Intervening Role of Perceptions in Evaluative Judgments," *JMR*, 18 (February), 13-28.

Osgood, Charles E., George J. Suci, and Percy H. Tannenbaum (1957), *The Measurement of Meaning.* Urbana, Ill.: University of Illinois Press.

SCALE ITEMS: EXPRESSIVENESS (STIMULUS)

intellectual	___ : ___ : ___ : ___ : ___ : ___ : ___	emotional
	1 2 3 4 5 6 7	

jagged	___ : ___ : ___ : ___ : ___ : ___ : ___	smooth
	1 2 3 4 5 6 7	

cold	___ : ___ : ___ : ___ : ___ : ___ : ___	warm
	1 2 3 4 5 6 7	

SCALE NAME: Fairness (Dealer's Treatment of Customer)

SCALE DESCRIPTION:

A three-item, seven-point Likert-type scale measuring the degree to which a consumer perceives a transaction was fair, particularly in relation to treatment by a car dealer.

SCALE ORIGIN:

The scale was apparently original to Oliver and Swan (1989).

SAMPLES:

Analysis was based on completed forms obtained from **184** people who had bought new cars within six months prior to the survey. The average respondent was male (67%), college educated (32%), had an income between $20,000 and $29,999, was 43 years of age, had owned 7.8 cars in his lifetime, and had purchased his latest car 4.5 months previously.

RELIABILITY:

A LISREL estimate of **.87** was reported for the scale.

VALIDITY:

No specific examination of scale validity was reported.

ADMINISTRATION:

The scale was one of many self-administered measures. Lower scores on the scale suggest that respondents feel the dealer was very evenhanded in the transaction whereas higher scores imply that customers feel strongly that they were not **treated fairly.**

MAJOR FINDINGS:

The general purpose of the study was to examine customer perceptions of satisfaction in the context of new car purchases. Using LISREL, the authors determined that **fairness** was more important than disconfirmation in producing interpersonal satisfaction and that advantageous inequity was unrelated to it. Also, customer satisfaction with the dealer appeared to be primarily related to the former's perception of **fairness**, followed by satisfaction with the salesperson, and then somewhat influenced by disconfirmation.

COMMENTS:

Though the scale was developed for exchanges involving a car dealer, with some adjustment it might be suitable for use with other retailers.

REFERENCE:

Oliver, Richard L. and John E. Swan (1989), "Equity and Disconfirmation Perceptions as Influences on Merchant and Product Satisfaction," *JCR*, 16 (December), 372-383.

SCALE ITEMS: FAIRNESS (DEALER'S TREATMENT OF CUSTOMERS)

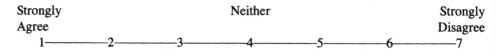

1. The dealer was fair to me.
2. Generally my dealer is an ethical company.
3. The dealer always tried to treat me right.

SCALE NAME: Fairness (Salesperson's Treatment of Customer)

SCALE DESCRIPTION:

A three-item, seven-point Likert-type scale measuring the degree to which a consumer perceives a transaction was fair, particularly in relation to treatment by a salesperson.

SCALE ORIGIN:

The scale was apparently original to Oliver and Swan (1989a, b).

SAMPLES:

Oliver and Swan's (1989a) findings were based on **415** completed questionnaires from two random samples of new car buyers. Because the two samples did not differ significantly on any demographic characteristics measured, the datasets were combined. The sample was 63% male and 30% college educated; 22% had income between $30,000 and $39,999, average age was 41 years, and respondents had owned 7.8 cars.

Analysis by Oliver and Swan (1989b) was based on just one of the initial samples mentioned above. Completed surveys were obtained from **184** people who had bought new cars within six months prior to the survey. The average respondent was male (67%), college educated (32%), had an income between $20,000 and $29,999, was 43 years of age, had owned 7.8 cars in his lifetime, and had purchased his latest car 4.5 months previously.

RELIABILITY:

The estimates of reliability provided by LISREL (Oliver and Swan 1989a, b) were **.832** and **.85**, respectively.

VALIDITY:

No specific examinations of scale validity were reported by Oliver and Swan (1989a, b).

ADMINISTRATION:

The scale was one of many measures that were self-administered in both studies by Oliver and Swan (1989a, b). Lower scores on the scale suggest that respondents feel the salesperson was very evenhanded in the transaction whereas higher scores imply that respondents feel they were not treated fairly.

MAJOR FINDINGS:

The general purpose of both studies was to examine customer perceptions of satisfaction in the context of new car purchases. Using LISREL, the authors determined that **fairness** was more important than disconfirmation in producing interpersonal satisfaction and that advantageous inequity was unrelated to it (1989a). The findings were the same in their subsequent study (1989b) with the added insight that customer satisfaction with the dealer was primarily related to the former's perception of **fairness**, followed by satisfaction with the salesperson, and then somewhat influenced by disconfirmation.

REFERENCES:

Oliver, Richard L. and John E. Swan (1989a), "Consumer Perceptions of Interpersonal Equity and Satisfaction in Transactions: A Field Survey Approach," *JM*, 53 (April), 21-35.

_____ and _____ (1989b), "Equity and Disconfirmation Perceptions as Influences on Merchant and Product Satisfaction," *JCR*, 16 (December), 372-383.

SCALE ITEMS: FAIRNESS (SALESPERSON'S TREATMENT OF CUSTOMER)

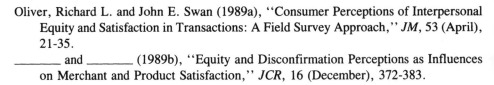

```
Strongly                              Neither                          Strongly
Agree                                                                  Disagree
    1————————2————————3————————4————————5————————6————————7
```

1. I was treated fairly by my salesperson.
2. I did *not* get treated fairly by the salesperson. **(r)**
3. The deal I agreed upon with the salesperson was fair.

SCALE NAME: Familiarity (Generalized)

SCALE DESCRIPTION:

A two-item, seven-point semantic differential summated ratings scale measuring the degree to which an object is perceived as being familiar. The objects evaluated by subjects in Hirschman's (1986) study were print advertisements.

SCALE ORIGIN:

This scale appears to have been used first in this form by Hirschman and Solomon (1984). In that study the authors explored consumers' perceptions of visual versus verbal ads on three dimensions: functional utility, aesthetic value, and familiarity. Data were gathered from college students who were asked to fill out a questionnaire themselves and to have four more completed by others. Satisfactory forms were received from **162** respondents. Seventy-nine subjects received all verbal ads and 83 received all visual ads. The mean age of the sample was 29 years and 53.7% were women. Respondents were each exposed to two ads in their questionnaires and filled out the dimension scales twice. The two alpha values reported for this scale were .**76** and .**84**. As hypothesized, visual ads were found to be more familiar than verbal ads.

SAMPLES:

A total of **154** social science college students participated in the study as part of their course requirements. Students were randomly assigned to treatment groups and no difference in any demographic or control variables was noted. The all-verbal-ads group had 78 subjects and the all-visual-ads group had 76.

RELIABILITY:

The alpha for this scale was not specifically reported, but the author reports the scale to be among those for which alpha values were between .**82** and .**96**.

VALIDITY:

The validity of this scale was not specifically examined or discussed by Hirschman (1986).

ADMINISTRATION:

The scale was self-administered by subjects along with other measures after viewing ads. The items are scored such that extreme positive responses are coded as sevens and extreme negative responses are coded as ones. Higher scores on the scale suggest that respondents view an object (such as a product) to be very familiar whereas lower scores imply that they think an object is not known to them at all.

MAJOR FINDINGS:

The purpose of the study was to examine the differences in perceptions of products portrayed in both all- verbal versus all-visual ads. For all 14 products examined, all-visual ads were perceived to be significantly more **familiar** than all-verbal ads.

REFERENCES:

Hirschman, Elizabeth C. (1986), "The Effect of Verbal and Pictorial Advertising Stimuli on Aesthetic, Utilitarian and Familiarity Perceptions," *JA*, 15 (2), 27-34.

_____ and Michael R. Solomon (1984), "Utilitarian, Aesthetic, and Familiarity Responses to Verbal Versus Visual Advertisements," in *Advances in Consumer Research,* Vol. 11, Thomas C. Kinnear, ed. Ann Arbor, Mich.: Association for Consumer Research.

SCALE ITEMS: FAMILIARITY (GENERALIZED)

1. known to me   ____ : ____ : ____ : ____ : ____ : ____ : ____   not known to me
                   7   6   5   4   3   2   1

2. familiar   ____ : ____ : ____ : ____ : ____ : ____ : ____   not familiar
                   7   6   5   4   3   2   1

SCALE NAME: Familiarity (Object)

SCALE DESCRIPTION:

A three-item, seven-point semantic differential scale measuring a person's reported knowledge about an object. The object studied by Oliver and Bearden (1965) was a branded appetite suppressant.

SCALE ORIGIN:

The measure was developed for the Oliver and Bearden (1965) study.

SAMPLES:

Analysis was based on **353** completed questionnaires from members of a bistate consumer panel. Subjects were selected to be representative of urban and suburban households with family income greater than $10,000. Ninety-one triers and 262 nontriers of a new, heavily promoted time-release diet suppressant responded. The average respondent was female (56%), white (89%), with some education beyond high school (70%), and in the $20,000 to $29,999 income category (25.5%).

RELIABILITY:

A reliability of **.85** was reported.

VALIDITY:

A confirmatory factor analysis was performed once, weak items were deleted, and the analysis was run again, resulting in higher overall factor loadings.

ADMINISTRATION:

Data were gathered through use of self-administered mail questionnaires. The method for calculating scale scores was not specified, but it is likely that higher scores on this scale suggest a person is very familiar with a specified object whereas lower scores imply that a person knows very little about an object.

MAJOR FINDINGS:

The purpose of the study was to examine the presence and operation of "crossover effects" in the Fishbein behavioral intention model under various moderating conditions. Evidence generally supporting the normative structure attitude crossover path was found; that is, a person's attitude toward a behavior is strengthened to the extent that relevant others are believed to agree with it. The moderator variable analysis provided little insight into the mechanisms people use to process normative information. However, the crossover model predicted worst for persons low in **familiarity**.

#102 *Familiarity (Object)*

COMMENTS:

Though the scale had reasonably good internal consistency, the authors admitted that it might lack stability over time, samples, or product categories.

REFERENCE:

Oliver, Richard L. and William O. Bearden (1985), "Crossover Effects in the Theory of Reasoned Action: A Moderating Influence Attempt," *JCR*, 12 (December), 324-340.

SCALE ITEMS: FAMILIARITY (OBJECT)

1. In general, would you consider yourself familiar or unfamiliar with _____?

Very Familiar	____ : ____ : ____ : ____ : ____ : ____ : ____	Very Unfamiliar
	7 6 5 4 3 2 1	

2. Would you consider yourself informed or uninformed about _____?

Not at all informed	____ : ____ : ____ : ____ : ____ : ____ : ____	Highly informed
	7 6 5 4 3 2 1	

3. Would you consider yourself knowledgeable about _____?

Know a great deal	____ : ____ : ____ : ____ : ____ : ____ : ____	Know nothing at all
	7 6 5 4 3 2 1	

SCALE NAME: Fantasizing

SCALE DESCRIPTION:

A three-item, five-point Likert-type summated ratings scale measuring the degree to which a person has a vivid imagination and fantasizes.

SCALE ORIGIN:

The scale was apparently original to O'Guinn and Faber (1989).

SAMPLES:

Two samples were employed by O'Guinn and Faber (1989). One consisted of **386** completed responses (out of 808 questionnaires sent) from people who had written an organization that aided compulsive buyers. A second group was used for comparison and was intended to represent the general population. Eight hundred questionnaires were mailed to people in three Illinois areas: Chicago, Springfield, and Bloomington-Normal. Two mailings produced a total of **250** completed survey forms.

RELIABILITY:

An alpha of **.75** was reported for this scale.

VALIDITY:

No examination of scale validity was reported.

ADMINISTRATION:

The scale was one of several self-administered measures used in a mail survey instrument. Higher scores on the scale indicate that respondents have a strong tendency to fantasize whereas lower scores indicate that respondents do not have vivid imaginations.

MAJOR FINDINGS:

O'Guinn and Faber (1989) studied compulsive shopping. Their results showed that a sample of compulsive shoppers scored significantly higher on the **fantasizing** scale than did a general sample of consumers.

REFERENCE:

O'Guinn, Thomas C. and Ronald J. Faber (1989), "Compulsive Buying: A Phenomenological Exploration," *JCR*, 16 (September), 147-157.

SCALE ITEMS: FANTASIZING

Strongly Disagree	Disagree	Neutral	Disagree	Strongly Agree
1————————2————————3————————4————————5				

1. I daydream a lot.
2. When I go to the movies I find it easy to lose myself in the film.
3. I often think of what might have been.

SCALE NAME: Fashion Consciousness

SCALE DESCRIPTION:

A six-point, Likert-type summated ratings scale ranging from strongly disagree (1) to strongly agree (6). The scale measures the importance of being in fashion, particularly in terms of dress. A four-item version was suggested by Wells and Tigert (1971) and apparently used by Darden and Perreault (1976). A two-item version was used by Lumpkin and Darden (1982). See also the scale used by Schinaars and Schiffman (1984).

SCALE ORIGIN:

These items were part of a classic study of psychographics by Wells and Tigert (1971). One thousand questionnaires were mailed to homemaker members of the Market Facts mail panel. In addition to gathering demographic, product use, and media data, the survey contained 300 statements that have since served as the basis for the construction of many lifestyle-related scales. The four items for this scale are reported in the article, but they were not analyzed as a multi-item scale. The purpose of the article was to explain how psychographics could improve upon mere demographic description of target audiences and product users. No psychometric information was reported.

One of the first uses of the items as a multi-item scale was by Darden and Perreault (1976). Analysis was based on self-administered questionnaires completed by 278 suburban housewives randomly selected in Athens, Georgia. A split-half reliability of .61 was reported for the scale. Fashion consciousness was significantly lower for inshoppers than for any of the four outshopping groups. It was highest for the group that primarily outshopped for home entertainment products, not clothing.

SAMPLES:

Lumpkin and Darden (1982) had **145** usable responses gathered from the consumer research panel of the University of Arkansas. Data were collected from the individuals by mail questionnaire.

RELIABILITY:

An alpha of **.71** was calculated by Lumpkin and Darden (1982).

VALIDITY:

Factor analysis indicated that the items loaded together.

ADMINISTRATION:

Data were gathered through self-administered mail questionnaires. Scale scores are typically calculated by averaging numerical responses to individual items. A score of 6 indicates that a person is very concerned about being in fashion whereas a 1 means a person has little interest in his/her fashionability.

MAJOR FINDINGS:

In their study of television program preference groups, Lumpkin and Darden (1982) found **fashion consciousness** to be one of only a few lifestyle variables that were significantly different between the six groups. Specifically, respondents in the most **fashion conscious** group were the youngest, with the least education, and who seemed to prefer female-oriented comedies or dramas, *not* football.

COMMENTS:

All of the items below refer to clothes except item 4. If one is studying clothing alone, it might be best to drop the hair-related item.

REFERENCES:

Darden, William R. and William D. Perreault, Jr. (1976), "Identifying Interurban Shoppers: Multiproduct Purchase Patterns and Segmentation Profiles," *JMR*, 13 (February), 51- 60.

Lumpkin, James R. and William R. Darden (1982), "Relating Television Preference Viewing to Shopping Orientations, Lifestyles, and Demographics," *JA*, 11 (4), 56-67.

Schnaars, Steven P. and Leon G. Schiffman (1984), "An Application of Segmentation Design Based on a Hybrid of Canonical Correlation and Simple Crosstabulation," *JAMS*, 12 (Fall), 177-189.

Wells, William D. and Douglas Tigert (1971), "Activities, Interests, and Opinions," *JAR*, 11 (August), 27-35.

SCALE ITEMS: FASHION CONSCIOUSNESS +

Strongly Disagree	Disagree	Slightly Disagree	Slightly Agree	Agree	Strongly Agree
1	2	3	4	5	6

1. I usually have one or more outfits that are of the very latest style.
2. When I must choose between the two I usually dress for fashion, not for comfort.
3. An important part of my life and activities is dressing smartly.
4. I often try the latest hairdo styles when they change.
5. It is important to me that my clothes be of the latest style.
6. A person should try to dress in style.

+ Items 1 through 4 were suggested by Wells and Tigert (1971) and apparently used by Darden and Perreault (1976). Items 5 and 6 were used by Lumpkin and Darden (1982).

SCALE NAME: Femininity

SCALE DESCRIPTION:

A 10-item, seven-point, summated ratings scale measuring the degree to which a person indicates having feminine personality characteristics.

SCALE ORIGIN:

The items for the scale used by Barak and Stern (1985/86) were taken from the Bem (1974) Sex-Role Inventory (BSRI). The inventory went through several rounds of development and testing. The initial development involved 40 undergraduate students judging 400 personality characteristics for their appropriateness for each sex. The list was narrowed to the 20 characteristics for each sex that were considered to be most the most desirable for them to have in American society. The measure then asked respondents to rate themselves on all of the characteristics so that both masculinity and **femininity** scale scores could be computed. (An androgyny score could also be calculated by determining the difference between the other two scores.)

Internal consistency was estimated with two samples: 444 male and 279 female students in introductory psychology at Stanford University and an additional 117 male and 77 female paid volunteers at Foothill Junior College. From the two samples, an alpha of .86 was calculated both times for the masculinity scale and alpha values of .8 and .82 were calculated for the **femininity** scale. Test-retest stability was estimated with 28 male and 28 female subjects. The students took the BSRI once and again four weeks later. For both scales the correlation of the scores was reported to be .90. Scores on the scales were correlated with two other measures of sex roles. The low correlations led Bem to conclude that her scales were tapping constructs not directly measured by the others.

SAMPLES:

The survey form used by Barak and Stern (1985/1986) was personally distributed to and collected from an age-quota sample of women living in the greater New York metropolitan area. The study focused on the **567** responding women who categorized themselves as either ''young'' or ''middle-aged'' and stated an age in years between 25 and 69.

RELIABILITY:

Barak and Stern (1985/1986) say only that the scale's alpha was above **.85**.

VALIDITY:

Factor analysis was performed on the BSRI inventory offered by Bem (1974). Though not expressly stated, the items used by Barak and Stern (1985/1986) were probably the ones that loaded highest on the factor related to femininity.

ADMINISTRATION:

The scale used by Barak and Stern (1985/1986) was self-administered by respondents in their homes as part of a larger survey form. Higher scores indicate greater **femininity** whereas lower scores suggest little **femininity** though not necessarily strong masculinity.

MAJOR FINDINGS:

Barak and Stern (1985/1986) examined the differences in profiles between the baby-boomer and pre-boomer generations as well as between women who characterized themselves as young and those who categorized themselves as middle-aged. No significant difference was found in **femininity** between either pair of groups.

COMMENTS:

Though presented here by itself, the scale is most properly used along with the **masculinity** scale of the BSRI. The lack of stronger evidence of scale validity should cause scores to be viewed cautiously.

REFERENCES:

Barak, Benny and Barbara Stern (1985/1986), ''Women's Age in Advertising: An Examination of Two Consumer Age Profiles,'' *JAR*, 25 (December/January), 38-47.

Bem, Sandra L. (1974), ''The Measurement of Psychological Androgyny,'' *Journal of Consulting and Clinical Psychology*, 42 (2), 155-162.

SCALE ITEMS: FEMININITY +

Indicate on the following scale how well each of the following traits describes you:

Never or almost never true ____ : ____ : ____ : ____ : ____ : ____ : ____ Always or almost always true

1   2   3   4   5   6   7

1. Affectionate
2. Cheerful
3. Childlike
4. Compassionate
5. Does not use harsh language
6. Eager to soothe hurt feelings
7. Feminine
8. Flatterable
9. Gentle
10. Gullible
11. Love Children
12. Loyal
13. Sensitive to the needs of others
14. Shy
15. Soft spoken
16. Sympathetic
17. Tender

18. Understanding
19. Warm
20. Yielding

+ Barak and Stern (1985/1986) calculated scale scores on just 10 of these items based on the results of a factor analysis. Those 10 items were not specified in their article.

SCALE NAME: Financial Concern

SCALE DESCRIPTION:

A two-item, six-point Likert-type summated ratings scale from strongly disagree (1) to strongly agree (6). The scale measures the degree of concern one expresses about his or her financial situation.

SCALE ORIGIN:

Though Rahtz, Sirgy, and Meadow (1989) may have developed items for the scale by examining previous research, the specific items and scales are original to their study.

SAMPLES:

Two independent samples were drawn from the same population one year apart by systematic random sampling of a mailing list. The mailing list was from a government-sponsored regional agency on aging. People's names were added to the list when social security records indicated they had reached the age of 60. The respondents in the two samples were all living in a three-county area of Virginia. The number of usable questionnaires returned from the first and second samples was **788** and **752**, respectively.

RELIABILITY:

The items in the first and second samples had inter-item correlations of **.3684** and **.4027**, respectively.

VALIDITY:

No analysis of scale validity was reported.

ADMINISTRATION:

The scales were administered to both samples as part of larger mail questionnaires. Scale scores are calculated by averaging numerical responses to items. Higher scores indicate respondents are very concerned about their finances whereas low scores suggest respondents are not very worried about spending money or financial security.

MAJOR FINDINGS:

The purpose of the study was to examine the relationships between elderly people's television usage and a variety of demographic and psychographic variables. The two samples provided mixed evidence about the relationship between **financial concern** and TV usage. The correlations were low in both studies, but one was at least high enough to be statistically significant (p < .0001). Hence, there may be some small association between the two behaviors but it is not likely to be strong.

COMMENTS:

Given the low inter-item correlations as well as the lack of evidence about validity, some caution should be exercised in use of this scale as it is.

REFERENCE:

Rahtz, Don R., M. Joseph Sirgy, and H. Lee Meadow (1989), "The Elderly Audience: Correlates of Television Orientation," *JA* (3), 9-20.

SCALE ITEMS: FINANCIAL CONCERN

Strongly Disagree	Disagree	Slightly Disagree	Slightly Agree	Agree	Strongly Agree
1—————	—2—————	—3—————	—4—————	—5—————	—6

1. I am very cautious when spending my money.
2. I often worry about financial security.

SCALE NAME: Freedom

SCALE DESCRIPTION:

A five-item, six-point Likert-type summated ratings scale measuring the degree to which a person would willingly engage in an activity without coercion or obligation. The activity investigated by Unger (1981; Unger and Kernan 1983) was subjective leisure.

SCALE ORIGIN:

Relevant literature was surveyed prior to scale construction, but the items themselves and certainly the scale as a whole are original to Unger (1981).

SAMPLES:

The scale was developed in one stage of the overall study and then used to test hypotheses in another stage. In the first stage, the scale was administered by three different people to a total of **169** undergraduate business students at Miami University and the University of Cincinnati (Unger 1981). In the second stage, the questionnaires were delivered and picked up by members of a Girl Scout troop. A quota sample of **160** adults living in the Cincinnati SMSA was used that balanced eight equal age-by-sex groups. However, the sample was representative of neither the Cincinnati SMSA nor the U.S. population as a whole, being composed mostly of white people (98%) of middle to upper socioeconomic status (84%).

RELIABILITY:

The final scale consists of items that remained after several tests of reliability. The tests were conducted for the scale in six different situations. Alpha values for the scale ranged from **.79** to **.88**. See Unger (1981) for more detailed information.

VALIDITY:

Factor analysis provided general support that the items tend to load together; however, the results seem to have some sensitivity to the sample and situation being evaluated. When not loading separately, the items in this scale loaded with those of an intrinsic satisfaction scale, which indicates the two are psychologically related for some samples and situations. As evidence of construct validity, perceived freedom was found to be positively and significantly related to three subjective leisure measures.

ADMINISTRATION:

The scale was self-administered by respondents in both stages of the survey described above. Higher scores on the scale indicate that respondents express their willingness to engage freely in some specified activity whereas lower scores imply that respondents would not voluntarily engage an activity.

MAJOR FINDINGS:

The study by Unger (1981; Unger and Kernan 1983) examined dimensions of the subjective leisure experience across six different situations. **Perceived freedom** was found to be one of the primary determinants of subjective leisure across situations.

REFERENCES:

Unger, Lynette S. (1981), *Measure Validation in the Leisure Domain*, unpublished doctoral dissertation, University of Cincinnati.

_____ and Jerome B. Kernan (1983), ''On the Meaning of Leisure: An Investigation of Some Determinants of the Subjective Experience,'' *JCR*, 9 (March), 381-391.

SCALE ITEMS: FREEDOM +

Strongly Disagree	Disagree	Somewhat Disagree	Somewhat Agree	Agree	Strongly Agree
1	2	3	4	5	6

1. I do not feel forced.
2. It is completely voluntary.
3. I do not feel obligated.
4. Others would not have to talk me into it.
5. ''Not because I have to but because I want to'' would characterize it.

+ The questionnaire would describe a situation for respondents and they would be asked to respond to the statements as they feel about the situation.

SCALE NAME: Futility (Political)

SCALE DESCRIPTION:

A four-item, five-point Likert-type scale measuring a person's perceived inability to influence the political system. This scale was referred to as Political Efficacy by Durand and Lambert (1985).

SCALE ORIGIN:

The scale was originally constructed and used by Olsen (1969), though he appears to have drawn heavily on previous work. His sample was drawn from two census tracts in Ann Arbor, one a "lower middle class" neighborhood and the other very much "upper middle class." The analysis was based on successful interviews of **154** people. The coefficient of reproducibility was **.893**. Political futility appeared to be most prevalent in the following groups: the elderly, the poorly educated, persons with small businesses, and Republicans.

SAMPLES:

A systematic sample of 1320 customers of a large, investor-owned electric utility company was made. Questionnaires were mailed to them and **325** were returned following a reminder mailed after two weeks. The average respondent was at least 45 years of age, male, white, married, had at least graduated high school, and was socioeconomically upscale.

RELIABILITY:

An alpha of **.57** was reported for the scale.

VALIDITY:

No examination of scale validity was reported.

ADMINISTRATION:

The scale was self-administered along with several other measures included in the mail questionnaire. Higher scores on the scale indicate that respondents feel they are unable to influence the political system whereas lower scores suggest that respondents think they have the ability to influence the government.

MAJOR FINDINGS:

The purpose of the study was to investigate the degree to which criticisms of advertising are positively related to various aspects of consumer and political alienation. Respondents were first grouped according to levels of alienation by cluster analysis. (Cluster analysis used **futility** and five other related measures as inputs.) Then differences in advertising criticisms were compared across the groups. The cluster analysis produced four alienation groups and a MANOVA indicated significant differences between the groups when all of the 12 advertising criticisms were considered simultaneously.

COMMENTS:

The low reliability estimate in the consumer study suggests that the scale may have stability only with certain samples. Caution is urged until some refinement and improvement is done.

REFERENCES:

Durand, Richard M. and Zarrel V. Lambert (1985), ''Alienation and Criticisms of Advertising,'' *JA*, 14 (3), 9-17.

Olsen, Marvin E. (1969), ''Two Categories of Political Alienation,'' *Social Forces*, 47 (March), 288-299.

SCALE ITEMS: FUTILITY (POLITICAL)

Strongly Disagree	Disagree	Neutral	Agree	Strongly Agree
1	2	3	4	5

1. I believe public officials don't care much what people like me think.
2. There is no way other than voting that people like me can influence the action of the government.
3. Sometimes politics and government seem so complicated that I can't really understand what's going on.
4. People like me don't have any say about what the government does.

SCALE NAME: Generosity

SCALE DESCRIPTION:

A seven-item, five-point Likert-type summmated ratings scale measuring the degree to which a person likes to share his/her possessions. As used by Belk (1985) as well as O'Guinn and Faber (1989), the scoring of the items was done in such a way as to measure "nongenerosity." A five-item version of the scale was used by O'Guinn and Faber (1989).

SCALE ORIGIN:

The origin of the scale is reported by Belk (1984). The measure of generosity was one of three scales constructed for examining aspects of materialism. Initial pools of 30 or more items were tested for each of the three measures with **237** business school students. On the basis of factor analysis, item-total correlations, and measures of internal consistency, seven or more items were chosen from each pool to measure the three materialism-related constructs. The eight items retained for measuring generosity were reported to have an alpha of **.72**.

SAMPLES:

Belk (1984, 1985) examined the scale in various ways with three more samples. One was composed of **48** business students. Another sample had **338** subjects, 213 of whom were business students. (These two samples were reported to be about two-thirds male.) A third sample was composed of 33 families representing **99** people who ranged in age from 13 to 92 years.

Two samples were employed by O'Guinn and Faber (1989). One consisted of **386** completed responses (out of 808 questionnaires sent) from people who had written an organization that aided compulsive buyers. A second group was used for comparison and was intended to represent the general population. Eight hundred questionnaires were mailed to people in three Illinois areas: Chicago, Springfield, and Bloomington-Normal. Two mailings produced a total of **250** completed survey forms.

RELIABILITY:

An alpha of **.58** was reported for one of the Belk (1984) samples (n = 338). A two-week-interval test-retest correlation of **.64** (n = 48) was reported for another Belk (1984, 1985) sample. O'Guinn and Faber (1989) calculated an alpha of **.63**.

VALIDITY:

Belk (1984) compared scale scores with other measures in a multitrait-multimethod matrix. As evidence of convergent validity, scores on the generosity scale were significantly correlated with two other measures used to assess the same construct. Only partial support for discriminant validity was found. Evidence of criterion validity was found, as two known groups had significantly different mean scores on the scale and the differences were in the hypothesized directions.

No examination of scale validity was made by O'Guinn and Faber (1989) beyond factor analysis. Items pertaining to generosity and two other materialism-related constructs were factor analyzed and three factors clearly emerged. The authors did indicate that the scales were slightly modified on the basis of the factor analysis, however.

ADMINISTRATION:

The scale was one of several self-administered measures in each of the studies. Higher scores on the scale indicate that respondents do not want to share their possessions with others whereas lower scores indicate that respondents are more generous.

MAJOR FINDINGS:

The purpose of Belk's (1984) article was to discuss the construction and characteristics of three materialism-related constructs: envy, possessiveness, and **nongenerosity**. Many of the findings are reported above. In addition, there was evidence that older people were less **generous** than younger people and that the most **generous** individuals tended to be the happiest with their lives.

Belk (1985) examined further aspects of the three subscales, and also the psychometric characteristics of the materialism scale as a whole. In particular, he studied generational differences in materialism. Among the many findings was that each of the three generational groups was significantly different from the others in terms of **generosity.** Specifically, the oldest generation was the most **generous** and the middle generation was the least **generous**.

O'Guinn and Faber (1989) studied compulsive shopping. Their results showed that a sample of compulsive shoppers were significantly less **generous** than a general sample of consumers.

COMMENTS:

The three materialism-related measures mentioned above have been used summed separately as well as together. Two alpha values for the combined scale were reported by Belk (1985): .66 (n = 338) and .73 (n = 48). Belk (1985) also reported a test-retest correlation of .68 (n = 48). O'Guinn and Faber (1989) calculated an alpha of .71 for the combined scale. Given the low reliability of the combined scale and the generosity subscale, further work is needed before they are used extensively.

REFERENCES:

Belk, Russell W. (1984), "Three Scales to Measure Constructs Related to Materialism: Reliability, Validity, and Relationships to Measures of Happiness," in *Advances in Consumer Research*, Vol. 11, Thomas Kinnear, ed. Provo, Utah: Association for Consumer Research, 291-297.

———— (1985), "Materialism: Trait Aspects of Living in the Material World," *JCR*, 12 (December), 265-280.

O'Guinn, Thomas C. and Ronald J. Faber (1989), "Compulsive Buying: A Phenomenological Exploration," *JCR*, 16 (September), 147-157.

SCALE ITEMS: GENEROSITY +

Strongly Disagree	Disagree	Neutral	Agree	Strongly Agree
1————————2————————3————————4————————5				

1. I enjoy having guests stay at my home. **(r)**
2. I enjoy sharing what I have. **(r)**
3. I don't like to lend things, even to good friends.
4. It makes sense to buy a lawnmower with a neighbor and share it. **(r)**
5. I don't mind giving rides to those who don't have a car. **(r)**
6. I don't like to have anyone in my home when I'm not there.
7. I enjoy donating things to charities. **(r)**

\+ Items similar to or exactly the same as 1, 2, 3, 5, and 7 were used by O'Guinn and Faber (1989).

SCALE NAME: Healthiness

SCALE DESCRIPTION:

A three-item, five-point Likert-type summated ratings scale ranging from strongly disagree (1) to strongly agree (5). The scale measures a person's feeling of healthiness in comparison with others of similar age. Lumpkin and Hunt (1989) referred to this scale as Good Health.

SCALE ORIGIN:

The measure was apparently developed by Lumpkin and Hunt (1989) for use in their study, though the items may have come from previous studies reviewed in the article.

SAMPLES:

Lumpkin and Hunt's (1989) sample was drawn from the Market Facts Consumer Mail Panel and focused on **789** respondents who indicated they were 65 years of age or older. The proportions of men and women were similar to those in the national population, but fewer of the men and more of the women in the sample were married. The sample was better educated and had a greater percentage still employed than was true nationally. The sample was composed of more people in lower income levels, but reasonably matched the elderly geographic distribution.

RELIABILITY:

An alpha of **.730** was reported by Lumpkin and Hunt (1989).

VALIDITY:

Factor analysis indicated that the items loaded together.

ADMINISTRATION:

Data were gathered through self-administered mail questionnaires. Scale scores were calculated by averaging numerical responses to individual items. A score of 5 indicates that a person feels very healthy in comparison with others of similar age whereas a 1 means that a person is likely to have physical problems and take a lot of medicine.

MAJOR FINDINGS:

The elderly were broken down into two groups by Lumpkin and Hunt (1989): those who were self-reliant in terms of transportation and those who were dependent on others. The self-reliant group perceived themselves to be significantly more **healthy** than the dependent elderly.

REFERENCE:

Lumpkin, James R. and James B. Hunt (1989), ''Mobility as an Influence on Retail Patronage Behavior of the Elderly: Testing Conventional Wisdom,'' *JAMS*, 17 (Winter), 1-12.

#110 *Healthiness*

SCALE ITEMS: HEALTHINESS

Strongly Disagree	Disagree	Neutral	Agree	Strongly Agree
1—————————	2—————————	3—————————	4—————————	5

1. Compared to others my age, I take less medicine.
2. Compared to others my age, I think I'm in better health.
3. I really don't have any physical problems.

SCALE NAME: Heathiness

SCALE DESCRIPTION:

A four-item, six-point Likert-type summated ratings scale from strongly disagree to strongly agree. The scale appears to measure one's lack of self esteem due to poor health, old age, loneliness, and/or immobility.

SCALE ORIGIN:

Though Rahtz, Sirgy, and Meadow (1989) may have developed items for the scale by examining previous research, the specific items and scales are original to their study.

SAMPLES:

Two independent samples were drawn from the same population one year apart by systematic random sampling of a mailing list. The mailing list was from a government-sponsored regional agency on aging. People's names were added to the list when social security records indicated they had reached the age of 60. The respondents in the two samples were all living in a three-county area of Virginia. The number of usable questionnaires returned from the first and second samples was **788** and **752**, respectively.

RELIABILITY:

The first and second samples had alpha values of **.7067** and **.6769**, respectively.

VALIDITY:

No analysis of scale validity was reported.

ADMINISTRATION:

The scales were administered to both samples as part of larger mail questionnaires. Scale scores are calculated by averaging numerical responses to items. Higher scores indicate a respondent has low morale for one or more reasons whereas low scores suggest respondents have a positive physical and psychological condition.

MAJOR FINDINGS:

The purpose of the study was to examine the relationships between elderly people's television usage and a variety of demographic and psychographic variables. In both samples, low but significant correlations were found between **healthiness** and TV usage. Specifically, lower morale was associated with greater viewing of television.

REFERENCE:

Rahtz, Don R., M. Joseph Sirgy, and H. Lee Meadow (1989), ''The Elderly Audience: Correlates of Television Orientation,'' *JA* (3), 9-20.

SCALE ITEMS: HEALTHINESS

Strongly Disagree	Disagree	Slightly Disagree	Slightly Agree	Agree	Strongly Agree
1	2	3	4	5	6

1. I feel old.
2. I often find myself feeling lonely.
3. I am in good physical condition. **(r)**
4. Getting around town is difficult for me.

SCALE NAME: Health/Safety Concern

SCALE DESCRIPTION:

> A two-item, six-point Likert-type summated ratings scale from strongly disagree (1) to strongly agree (6). The scale appears to measure the amount of thought one gives to his or her health and safety.

SCALE ORIGIN:

> Though Rahtz, Sirgy, and Meadow (1989) may have developed items for the scale by examining previous research, the specific items and scales are original to their study.

SAMPLES:

> Two independent samples were drawn from the same population one year apart by systematic random sampling of a mailing list. The mailing list was from a government-sponsored regional agency on aging. People's names were added to the list when social security records indicated they had reached the age of 60. The respondents in the two samples were all living in a three-county area of Virginia. The number of usable questionnaires returned from the first and second samples was **788** and **752**, respectively.

RELIABILITY:

> The items in the first and second samples had inter-item correlations of **.3652** and **.4462**, respectively.

VALIDITY:

> No analysis of scale validity was reported.

ADMINISTRATION:

> The scales were administered to both samples as part of larger mail questionnaires. Scale scores are calculated by averaging numerical responses to items. Higher scores indicate respondents think a lot about their **health and safety** whereas low scores suggest respondents rarely dwell on such issues.

MAJOR FINDINGS:

> The purpose of the study was to examine the relationships between elderly people's television usage and a variety of demographic and psychographic variables. In both samples, low but significant correlations were found between morale and TV usage. Specifically, personal concern was associated with greater viewing of television.

COMMENTS:

> Given the low inter-item correlations as well as the lack of evidence about validity, some caution should be exercised in use of this scale as it is.

REFERENCE:

Rahtz, Don R., M. Joseph Sirgy, and H. Lee Meadow (1989), "The Elderly Audience: Correlates of Television Orientation," *JA* (3), 9-20.

SCALE ITEMS: HEALTH/SAFETY CONCERN

Strongly Disagree	Disagree	Slightly Disagree	Slightly Agree	Agree	Strongly Agree
1	2	3	4	5	6

1. I frequently think about my health.
2. I often think about my personal safety.

SCALE NAME: Hemispheric Orientation

SCALE DESCRIPTION:

A seven-item, seven-point semantic differential summated ratings scale measuring a person's tendency to rely more on the functions associated with one brain hemisphere than on those associated with the other. The construct was referred to by Hirschman (1986) as cognitive function asymmetry.

SCALE ORIGIN:

The scale was constructed for a study reported by Hirschman (1983) that explored gender and psychological sexual identity as influencers of hemispheric orientation. Data were gathered by college students who were asked to fill out a questionnaire themselves and to have four more completed by others. Satisfactory forms were received from **440** respondents (219 men and 221 women). The internal consistency of the measure was reported as .82. Evidence indicated a significant relationship between gender and hemispheric orientation, though the pattern was not perfect.

SAMPLES:

A total of **154** social science college students participated in the study by Hirschman (1986) as part of their course requirements. Students were assigned randomly to treatment groups and no difference in any demographic or control variables was noted. The all-verbal-ads group had 78 subjects and the all-visual ads group had 76.

RELIABILITY:

The alpha was reported by Hirschman (1986) to be **.72**.

VALIDITY:

The validity of this scale was not specifically examined or discussed by Hirschman (1986).

ADMINISTRATION:

The scale was self-administered by subjects along with at least two other measures one week before they viewed the advertising stimuli (Hirschman 1986). Higher scores on the scale suggest that respondents place greater reliance on right-brain hemispheric functions whereas lower scores imply that they have a left hemispheric orientation.

MAJOR FINDINGS:

The purpose of the study by Hirschman (1986) was to compare the differences in perceptions of products portrayed in all-verbal versus all-visual ads. For five of 14 products examined, **hemispheric orientation** had a significant positive relationship with preference for visual ads. However, the scale did not have a significant influence on the main effects and the author suggests the correlations might have been spurious.

REFERENCES:

Hirschman, Elizabeth C. (1983), "Psychological Sexual Identity and Hemispheric Orientation," *Journal of General Psychology*, 108, (April) 153-168.

_____ (1986), "The Effect of Verbal and Pictorial Advertising Stimuli on Aesthetic, Utilitarian and Familiarity Perceptions," *JA*, 15 (2), 27-34.

SCALE ITEMS: HEMISPHERIC ORIENTATION

1. I prefer to think in pictures
   ___ : ___ : ___ : ___ : ___ : ___ : ___
     1   2   3   4   5   6   7
   I prefer to think in words **(r)**

2. I am very conscious of time passing
   ___ : ___ : ___ : ___ : ___ : ___ : ___
     1   2   3   4   5   6   7
   I am not usually conscious of time passing

3. I try to exclude emotional feelings from my decisions
   ___ : ___ : ___ : ___ : ___ : ___ : ___
     1   2   3   4   5   6   7
   The best way to make decisions is to follow your feelings and emotions

4. I like to make decisions by thinking about the pluses and minuses of each alternative
   ___ : ___ : ___ : ___ : ___ : ___ : ___
     1   2   3   4   5   6   7
   I prefer to think about alternatives as wholes, in their entirety.

5. I am basically emotional and sensual
   ___ : ___ : ___ : ___ : ___ : ___ : ___
     1   2   3   4   5   6   7
   I am basically logical and rational **(r)**

6. I like to plan and carefully organize my activities
   ___ : ___ : ___ : ___ : ___ : ___ : ___
     1   2   3   4   5   6   7
   I prefer to act on impulse

7. I am like a computer programmer
   ___ : ___ : ___ : ___ : ___ : ___ : ___
     1   2   3   4   5   6   7
   I am like an artist

SCALE NAME: Homebody

SCALE DESCRIPTION:

A two-item, six-point Likert-type summated ratings scale from strongly disagree (1) to strongly agree (6). The scale measures the strength of one's motivation to stay at home rather than go out. The scale was referred to as Limited Activity by Rahtz, Sirgy, and Meadow (1989).

SCALE ORIGIN:

Though the authors may have developed items for the scale by examining previous research, the specific items and scales are original to their study.

SAMPLES:

Two independent samples were drawn from the same population one year apart by systematic random sampling of a mailing list. The mailing list was from a government-sponsored regional agency on aging. People's names were added to the list when social security records indicated they had reached the age of 60. The respondents in the two samples were all living in a three-county area of Virginia. The number of usable questionnaires returned from the first and second samples was **788** and **752**, respectively.

RELIABILITY:

The items in the first and second samples had inter-item correlations of **.4201** and **.3426**, respectively.

VALIDITY:

No analysis of scale validity was reported.

ADMINISTRATION:

The scales were administered to both samples as part of larger mail questionnaires. Scale scores are calculated by averaging numerical responses to items. Higher scores indicate respondents have a strong home orientation whereas low scores suggest respondents have less motivation to stay home and would rather go out with friends.

MAJOR FINDINGS:

The purpose of the study was to examine the relationships between elderly people's television usage and a variety of demographic and psychographic variables. In both samples, significant correlations were found between **home orientation** and TV usage. Specifically, homebodies watched more television.

COMMENTS:

Given the low inter-item correlations as well as the lack of evidence about validity, some caution should be exercised in use of this scale as it is.

REFERENCE:

Rahtz, Don R., M. Joseph Sirgy, and H. Lee Meadow (1989), ''The Elderly Audience: Correlates of Television Orientation,'' *JA* (3), 9-20.

SCALE ITEMS: HOMEBODY

Strongly Disagree	Disagree	Slightly Disagree	Slightly Agree	Agree	Strongly Agree
1	2	3	4	5	6

1. I stay home mostly.
2. I would rather stay at home than go with friends.

SCALE NAME: Homebody

SCALE DESCRIPTION:

This three-item, six-point, Likert-type summated ratings scale ranges from strongly disagree (1) to strongly agree (6). The scale measures a person's enjoyment of staying at home rather than going out. See also scales used by Schnaars and Schiffman (1984).

SCALE ORIGIN:

These items were part of a classic study of psychographics by Wells and Tigert (1971). One thousand questionnaires were mailed to homemaker members of the Market Facts mail panel. In addition to gathering demographic, product use, and media data, the survey contained 300 statements that have since served as the basis for the construction of many lifestyle-related scales. The four items for this scale are reported in the article, but they were not analyzed as a multi-item scale. The purpose of the article was to explain how psychographics could improve upon mere demographic description of target audiences and product users. No psychometric information was reported.

SAMPLES:

Two mailing lists were used to collect data in the Dickerson and Gentry study (1983). One was a list of *Psychology Today* subscribers and the other was a list of members of computer clubs. The former was used to reach non-adopters of computers and the latter was used to reach PC adopters. Analysis was based on a total of **639** questionnaires. Results from a second mailing to non-respondents indicated that their demographic makeup was not significantly different from that of respondents. On the basis of 1980 Census data, the sample was younger and more upscale than the general population.

RELIABILITY:

An alpha of **.55** was calculated for the scale in the Dickerson and Gentry (1983) study.

VALIDITY:

Factor analysis indicated the items loaded together.

ADMINISTRATION:

Data were gathered through self-administered mail questionnaires. Scale scores are calculated by averaging numerical responses to individual items. A score of 6 indicates that a person greatly enjoys being at home whereas a 1 suggests that a person would rather be elsewhere than at home.

MAJOR FINDINGS:

Dickerson and Gentry (1983) found that being a "**homebody**" was one of several lifestyle variables that was a significant discriminator between adopters and nonadopters of home computers.

COMMENTS:

The low reported reliability of this scale indicates that modification should be made before it is used further. One simple possibility is to add a few more items, which may increase the internal consistency to an acceptable level.

REFERENCES:

Dickerson, Mary D. and James W. Gentry (1983), "Characteristics of Adopters and Non-Adopters of Home Computers," *JCR*, 10 (September), 225-235.

Schnaars, Steven P. and Leon G. Schiffman (1984), "An Application of Segmentation Design Based on a Hybrid of Canonical Correlation and Simple Crosstabulation," *JAMS*, 12 (Fall), 177-189.

Wells, William D. and Douglas Tigert (1971), "Activities, Interests, and Opinions," *JAR*, 11 (August), 27-35.

SCALE ITEMS: HOMEBODY

Strongly Disagree	Disagree	Slightly Disagree	Slightly Agree	Agree	Strongly Agree
1	2	3	4	5	6

1. I would rather spend a quiet evening at home than go out to a party.
2. I like parties where there is lots of music and talk. **(r)**
3. I am a homebody.

SCALE NAME: Household Chore Expectations (Parent/Child)

SCALE DESCRIPTION:

A four-item, forced-choice summated ratings scale measuring the degree to which a parent believes a preschool child should take on some household responsibilities. It was referred to by Carlson and Grossbart (1988) as Early Maturity Demands.

SCALE ORIGIN:

Though this scale bears similarity to a construct described by Baumrind (1971), correspondence with Carlson indicates that the Baumrind article did not highlight data collected with the scale but via observation. Carlson obtained the scale items in personal correspondence with Baumrind.

SAMPLES:

The survey instrument used by Carlson and Grossbart (1988) was distributed to mothers via students at three elementary schools in an unidentified U.S. city. The schools were chosen on a convenience basis but appeared to represent a variety of socioeconomic areas of the city. A $1 contribution to the PTO was offered for each completed questionnaire returned by the children. Analysis was based on **451** completed questionnaires. Ninety-three percent of the responding mothers indicated that they were the primary person in the child's socialization.

RELIABILITY:

Carlson and Grossbart (1988) reported an alpha of **.59** and a beta of .54 for the scale.

VALIDITY:

No examination of scale validity was reported by Carlson and Grossbart (1988).

ADMINISTRATION:

The scale was self-administered along with many other measures in the questionnaire used by Carlson and Grossbart (1988). Answer A of a pair should be scored as 1 and answer B should be scored as 2, with reverse scoring where indicated. Higher scores on the scale mean that parents expect their preschool children to take on some household responsibilities whereas lower scores imply that they do not expect their young children to help much at all.

MAJOR FINDINGS:

The authors investigated the relationship between general parental socialization styles and children's consumer socialization. Of the five parental socialization style clusters examined, Rigid Controlling and Authoritative mothers expressed significantly higher **household chore expectations** than did the other parental style clusters.

COMMENTS:

The low alpha indicates that the scale does not have good internal consistency and should be used cautiously until its reliability can be substantially improved.

REFERENCES:

Baumrind, Diana (1971), "Current Patterns of Parental Authority," *Developmental Psychology Monograph*, 4 (January), 1-103.

Carlson, Les and Sanford Grossbart (1988), "Parental Style and Consumer Socialization of Children," *JCR*, 15 (June), 77-94.

SCALE ITEMS: HOUSEHOLD CHORE EXPECTATIONS (PARENT/CHILD)

Please indicate your opinion by checking one response (A or B) for each statement. There are no right or wrong answers, so answer according to your opinion. It is important to answer all questions even if you are not completely sure of your answer. Just check the response (A or B) that comes *closest* to your opinion. Some statements may seem alike but are necessary to show slight differences of opinion. *All questions refer to your youngest child who attends this school.*

A. It is best for a three-year-old to be permitted to play and not be asked to help with chores.
B. It is best for a three-year-old to be given his/her share of the household chores.

A. A four-year-old cannot be expected to take care of a younger child.
B. A four-year-old can be expected to be of some help in the care of a younger child.

I would expect my child to help make his/her bed and tidy up his/her room:
A. by age five or younger.
B. by age five and a half or older. **(r)**

A. Most preschool children cannot be of any real help around the house.
B. Most preschool children can be trained to be of real help around the house.

SCALE NAME: Housework Hater

SCALE DESCRIPTION:

A four-item, six-point, Likert-type summated ratings scale ranging from strongly disagree (1) to strongly agree (6). The scale measures a person's dislike of housekeeping. A two-item version of the scale has been used by Lumpkin and Darden (1982) as well as Hawes and Lumpkin (1984).

SCALE ORIGIN:

These items were part of a classic study of psychographics by Wells and Tigert (1971). One thousand questionnaires were mailed to homemaker members of the Market Facts mail panel. In addition to gathering demographic, product use, and media data, the survey contained 300 statements that have since served as the basis for the construction of many lifestyle-related scales. The four items for this scale are reported in the article, but they were not analyzed as a multi-item scale. The purpose of the article was to explain how psychographics could improve upon mere demographic description of target audiences and product users. No psychometric information was reported.

One of the first uses of the items as a multi-item scale was by Darden and Perreault (1976). Analysis was based on self-administered questionnaires completed by 278 suburban housewives randomly selected in Athens, Georgia. A split-half reliability of .74 was reported for the scale. Dislike of housework was one of a few lifestyle variables that differentiated between outshopping groups. The group with the most dislike for it were heavy outbuyers of jewelry and clothing whereas the group indicating the least dislike of it showed little outshopping behavior except that they were the heaviest outbuyers of home entertainment products.

SAMPLES:

Lumpkin and Darden (1982) had **145** usable responses gathered from the consumer research panel of the University of Arkansas. Data were collected from the individuals by mail questionnaire. Hawes and Lumpkin (1984) collected data from **581** residents of 14 communities near the Ft. Worth-Dallas metroplex. Each of the communities was randomly sampled in proportion to its population by means of the respective telephone directories. The questionnaire was to be filled out by the household member responsible for most of the shopping. The distribution of respondents by community was similar to the actual population distribution.

RELIABILITY:

Lumpkin and Darden (1982) and Hawes and Lumpkin (1984) calculated alpha values of **.66** and **.829**, respectively, for a two-item version of the scale.

VALIDITY:

Factor analysis indicated the items loaded together.

ADMINISTRATION:

Data were gathered through self-administered mail questionnaires. Scale scores are calculated by averaging numerical responses to individual items. A score of 6 indicates that a person strongly dislikes housekeeping whereas a 1 means a person does not perceive housework to be particularly distasteful.

MAJOR FINDINGS:

In their study of television program preference groups, Lumpkin and Darden (1982) found a few lifestyle variables that were significantly different among the six groups, but dislike of housework was *not* one of them. The purpose of the study by Hawes and Lumpkin (1984) was to examine demographic and psychographic characteristics of outshoppers. Attitude toward **housework** did **not** significantly differentiate between inshoppers and outshoppers.

COMMENTS:

Use should be made of as many of the items below as possible to keep the scale's reliability in the acceptable range.

REFERENCES:

Darden, William R. and William D. Perreault, Jr. (1976), "Identifying Interurban Shoppers: Multiproduct Purchase Patterns and Segmentation Profiles," *JMR*, 13 (February), 51- 60.

Hawes, Jon M. and James R. Lumpkin (1984), "Understanding the Outshopper," *JAMS*, 12 (Fall), 200-218.

Lumpkin, James R. and William R. Darden (1982), "Relating Television Preference Viewing to Shopping Orientations, Lifestyles, and Demographics," *JA*, 11 (4), 56-67.

Wells, William D. and Douglas Tigert (1971), "Activities, Interests, and Opinions," *JAR*, 11 (August), 27-35.

SCALE ITEMS: HOUSEWORK HATER +

Strongly Disagree	Disagree	Slightly Disagree	Slightly Agree	Agree	Strongly Agree
1	2	3	4	5	6

1. I must admit I really don't like household chores.
2. I find cleaning my house an unpleasant task.
3. I enjoy most forms of housework. **(r)**
4. My idea of housekeeping is "once over lightly."
5. The less I have to do around the house, the better I like it.

+ Items 1 through 4 were suggested by Wells and Tigert (1971) and apparently were the ones used by Darden and Perreault (1974). Items 1 and 5 were used by Lumpkin and Darden (1982) as well as Hawes and Lumpkin (1984).

SCALE NAME: Imagery Vividness

SCALE DESCRIPTION:

A 16-item, five-point Likert-type summated ratings scale measuring the clarity of mental images a person evokes. It was referred to by several users as the Vividness of Visual Imagery Questionnaire (e.g., Childers and Houston 1984; Childers, Houston, and Heckler 1985; Marks 1973).

SCALE ORIGIN:

Marks (1973) originated this particular scale. Eleven of the items in the scale are original but five items were taken from a 35-item measure reported by Sheehan (1967), which was itself a shortened form of the 150-item measure of mental imagery developed by Betts (1909). Marks (1973) reported that his scale had a test-retest correlation of .74 (n = 68) and a split-half reliability coefficient of .85 (n = 150). The results of three experiments indicated that visual image vividness was an accurate predictor of the recall of information contained in pictures. Unexpectedly, two of the three experiments also showed that women were more accurate in their recall.

SAMPLES:

The scale was administered in two studies reported by Childers, Houston, and Heckler (1985). The first study involved **263** undergraduate college student volunteers. The second study collected data from 106 subjects who were described as being undergraduate students at a major midwestern university. The subjects in the second study were divided into two groups, one with **54** subjects and the other with **52**.

RELIABILITY:

An alpha of .85 was reported for the scale in the first study and alpha values of .84 and .85 were found in the second study. For item-total correlations, the authors reported that "each item was relatively equivalent in tapping the domain of interest" Childers, Houston, and Heckler (1985, p. 127).

VALIDITY:

A factor analysis in the first study indicated that the items all loaded together. All of the loadings were above .30 but six were below .50. Evidence of the scale's discriminant validity came from its insignificant correlation with a measure of social desirability.

ADMINISTRATION:

The scale was self-administered by students along with other measures in both studies reported by Childers, Houston, and Heckler (1985). Higher scores on the scale indicate that respondents are able to evoke clear mental images whereas lower scores suggest that they do not have vivid imagery.

MAJOR FINDINGS:

Childers, Houston, and Heckler (1985) compared several measures of visual/verbal mental imagery. The measure of **imagery vividness** was *not* found to be significantly correlated with measures of imagery control, imagery style, aided recall or recognition.

COMMENTS:

See also an adaptation of a portion of this scale by Hirschman (1986).

REFERENCES:

Betts, G. H. (1909), "The Distributions and Functions of Mental Imagery," *Columbia University Contributions to Education*, 26, 1-99.

Childers, Terry L. and Michael J. Houston (1984), "Conditions for a Picture-Superiority Effect on Consumer Memory," *JCR*, 11 (September), 643-654.

————, ————, and Susan E. Heckler (1985), "Measurement of Individual Differences in Visual Versus Verbal Information Processing," *JCR*, 12 (September), 125-134.

Hirschman, Elizabeth C. (1986), "The Effect of Verbal and Pictorial Advertising Stimuli on Aesthetic, Utilitarian and Familiarity Perceptions," *JA*, 15 (2), 27-34.

Marks, David F. (1973), "Visual Imagery Differences in the Recall of Pictures," *British Journal of Psychology*, 64 (1), 17-24.

Sheehan, Peter Winston (1967), "A Shortened Form of Betts Questionnaire Upon Mental Imagery," *Journal of Clinical Psychology*, 23 (3), 386-389.

SCALE ITEMS: IMAGERY VIVIDNESS

Rating	Description
1	Perfectly clear and as vivid as normal vision
2	Clear and reasonably vivid
3	Moderately clear and vivid
4	Vague and dim
5	No image at all, you only "know" that you are thinking of the object

INSTRUCTIONS:

For items 1-4, think of some relative or friend whom you frequently see (but who is not with you at present) and consider carefully the picture that comes before your mind's eye.
1. The exact contour of face, head, shoulders, and body.
2. Characteristic poses of head, attitudes of body, etc.
3. The precise carriage, length of step, etc., in walking.
4. The different colors worn in some familiar clothes.

Visualize a rising sun. Consider carefully the picture that comes before your mind's eye.
5. The sun is rising above the horizon into a hazy sky.
6. The sky clears and surrounds the sun with blueness.
7. Clouds. A storm blows up, with flashes of lightning.
8. A rainbow appears.

Think of the front of a shop which you often go to. Consider the picture that comes before your mind's eye.

9. The overall appearance of the shop from the opposite side of the road.
10. A window display, including colors, shapes and details of individual items for sale.
11. You are near the entrance. The color, shape and details of the door.
12. You enter the shop and go to the counter. The counter assistant serves you. Money changes hands.

Finally, think of a country scene which involves trees, mountains, and a lake. Consider the picture that comes before your mind's eye.

13. The contours of the landscape.
14. The color and shape of the trees.
15. The color and shape of the lake.
16. A strong wind blows on the trees and on the lake causing waves.

SCALE NAME: Inflation Consciousness

SCALE DESCRIPTION:

A two-item, six-point, Likert-type summated ratings scale ranging from strongly disagree (1) to strongly agree (6). The scale measures a person's belief that inflation will continue and probably be worse.

SCALE ORIGIN:

It is not clear where the items originated or where the scale was first used as a multi-item summated ratings scale.

SAMPLES:

Lumpkin (1985) analyzed data collected from a sample drawn from the Market Facts Consumer Mail Panel. A total of **2854** completed questionnaires were received, but Lumpkin focused just on **373** respondents who indicated they were 65 years of age or older.

RELIABILITY:

An alpha of **.5778** was reported by Lumpkin (1985).

VALIDITY:

Factor analysis indicated the items loaded together.

ADMINISTRATION:

Data were gathered through self-administered mail questionnaires. Scale scores are calculated by averaging numerical responses to individual items. A score of 6 indicates that a person strongly believes inflation will continue whereas 1 implies that a person thinks inflation will be less of a problem in the future.

MAJOR FINDINGS:

Elderly consumers were cluster analyzed by Lumpkin (1985) and it is not clear whether **inflation consciousness** significantly discriminated between the three groups because the level of statistical significance was not reported. However, the group with the highest mean on the scale were the least optimistic about their finances and appeared to be the most favorable about using credit.

COMMENTS:

Internal consistency is seriously low and should be raised to improve the scale's reliability and validity. A few more items should generated, tested, and included in the measure.

REFERENCE:

Lumpkin, James R. (1985), ''Shopping Orientation Segmentation of the Elderly Consumer,'' *JAMS*, 13 (Spring), 271-289.

SCALE ITEMS: INFLATION CONSCIOUSNESS

Strongly Disagree	Disagree	Slightly Disagree	Slightly Agree	Agree	Strongly Agree
1	2	3	4	5	6

1. Inflation is here to stay.
2. I think there will be less inflation than there is today. **(r)**

SCALE NAME: Information Seeker (Interpersonal)

SCALE DESCRIPTION:

A three-item, six-point, Likert-type summated ratings scale with responses ranging from strongly disagree (1) to strongly agree (6). The scale measures a person's interest in talking about products as well as seeking information from others. See also Moschis (1981).

SCALE ORIGIN:

These items were part of a classic study of psychographics by Wells and Tigert (1971). One thousand questionnaires were mailed to homemaker members of the Market Facts mail panel. In addition to gathering demographic, product use, and media data, the survey contained 300 statements that have since served as the basis for the construction of many lifestyle-related scales. The three items for this scale are reported in the article, but they were not analyzed as a multi-item scale. The purpose of the article was to explain how psychographics could improve upon mere demographic description of target audiences and product users. No psychometric information was reported. One of the first uses of the items as a multi-item scale was by Darden and Perreault (1976). Analysis was based on self-administered questionnaires completed by 278 suburban housewives randomly selected in Athens, Georgia. A split-half reliability of .53 was reported for the scale. Though several lifestyle variables differentiated between the groups of outshoppers, information seeking was **not** one of them.

SAMPLES:

Two mailing lists were used to collect data in the Dickerson and Gentry study (1983). One was a list of *Psychology Today* subscribers and the other was a list of members of computer clubs. The former was used to reach non-adopters of computers and the latter was used to reach PC adopters. Analysis was based on a total of **639** questionnaires. Results from a second mailing to non- respondents indicated that their demographic makeup was not significantly different from that of respondents. On the basis of 1980 Census data, the sample was younger and more upscale than the general population.

RELIABILITY:

An alpha of **.55** was reported by Dickerson and Gentry (1983).

VALIDITY:

Factor analysis indicated the items loaded together.

ADMINISTRATION:

Data were gathered through self-administered mail questionnaires. Scale scores are calculated by averaging numerical responses to individual items. A score of 6 indicates that a person actively pursues information about products from others whereas a 1 suggests that a person rarely engages in such activity.

MAJOR FINDINGS:

Dickerson and Gentry (1983) found a significant relationship between **information seeking** and adoption of home computers. Specifically, adopters were more likely than nonadopters to gather **information** from others.

COMMENTS:

The one reported alpha value indicates that the scale currently has low internal consistency. Several additional similar items should be generated and tested to improve the quality of the measure.

REFERENCES:

Darden, William R. and William D. Perreault, Jr. (1976), ''Identifying Interurban Shoppers: Multiproduct Purchase Patterns and Segmentation Profiles,'' *JMR*, 13 (February), 51- 60.

Dickerson, Mary D. and James W. Gentry (1983), ''Characteristics of Adopters and Non-Adopters of Home Computers,'' *JCR*, 10 (September), 225-235.

Moschis, George P. (1981), ''Patterns of Consumer Learning,'' *JAMS*, 9 (Spring), 110-126.

Wells, William D. and Douglas Tigert (1971), ''Activities, Interests, and Opinions,'' *JAR*, 11 (August), 27-35.

SCALE ITEMS: INFORMATION SEEKER (INTERPERSONAL)

Strongly Disagree	Disagree	Slightly Disagree	Slightly Agree	Agree	Strongly Agree
1	2	3	4	5	6

1. I often seek out the advice of my friends regarding which brand to buy.
2. I spend a lot of time talking with my friends about products and brands.
3. My neighbors or friends usually give me good advice on what brands to buy in the grocery store.

SCALE NAME: Information Seeker (Interpersonal)

SCALE DESCRIPTION:

A four-item, seven-point Likert-type summated ratings scale measuring the degree to which a person expresses the tendency to seek information about products by observing others' behavior or asking for their opinions.

SCALE ORIGIN:

This measure was constructed by Bearden, Netemeyer, and Teel (1989) and is only known to have been used in their study. A series of studies were conducted by the authors to determine the reliability and validity of the scale, only a portion of which are discussed here. From a review of previous research, 166 items were generated that were suspected to measure one of the three hypothesized dimensions of interpersonal influence susceptibility: informational, normative, and value expressiveness. After ambiguous and essentially identical items were dropped, the content validity of the remaining items was evaluated by five judges. Then the remaining items were rated again for their clarity in representing one of the dimensions of the construct by four more judges. Some other aspects of the analysis are described below.

SAMPLES:

Sixty-two items were administered initially to a convenience sample of **220**. Fifteen items were reevaluated by a convenience sample of **141** undergraduate students.

RELIABILITY:

Alpha values for the eight-item normative dimension were reported as being **.83** and **.82** in the first and second administrations, respectively. The estimates of construct reliability based on LISREL results were also **.83** and **.82** for the initial and followup administrations, respectively. Thirty-five students from the second administration group participated in a retest session three weeks later and a correlation of **.75** was found between their scores on the scale.

VALIDITY:

After an initial effort to develop separate scales to measure the three hypothesized dimensions of the construct, strong evidence of discriminant and convergent validity was found for the informational dimension but not for the utilitarian and value expressive dimensions. The latter two sets of items were combined to form one scale. Confirmatory factor analysis indicated a stable two-factor correlated structure (the normative and informational factors). Some further analyses that provided evidence of construct validity are discussed below under Findings.

ADMINISTRATION:

The scale was self-administered in each of the studies reported by the authors. Higher scores on the scale indicate that respondents are very likely to seek information about products from others by observing their behavior and/or asking them directly.

MAJOR FINDINGS:

The purpose of the study by Bearden, Netemeyer, and Teel (1989) was to develop scales for measuring the dimensions of consumer susceptibility to interpersonal influence. A series of studies provided support for a two-factor model. Among the many findings were that the normative factor positively correlated much more strongly than the **informational** factor with a measure of attention to social comparison information; the normative factor had a significantly stronger positive correlation than the **informational** factor with a measure of compliance motivation; and both factors had similar negative correlations with a measure of self-esteem.

COMMENTS:

To measure more fully the interpersonal influence susceptibility construct, this measure ought to be used along with the eight-item measure of the normative dimension.

REFERENCE:

Bearden, William O., Richard G. Netemeyer, and Jesse E. Teel (1989), "Measurement of Consumer Susceptibility to Interpersonal Influence," *JCR*, 15 (March), 473-481.

SCALE ITEMS: INFORMATION SEEKER (INTERPERSONAL)

strongly disagree	___ :	___ :	___ ·	___ :	___ :	___ :	___	strongly agree
	1	2	3	4	5	6	7	

1. To make sure I buy the right product or brand, I often observe what others are buying and using.
2. If I have little experience with a product, I often ask my friends about the product.
3. I often consult other people to help choose the best alternative available from a product class.
4. I frequently gather information from friends or family about a product before I buy.

SCALE NAME: Information Usage (Company Sources)

SCALE DESCRIPTION:

A five-item, five-point Likert-type summated ratings scale measuring the number of times in the previous two years a customer recalls receiving information from his/her insurance company about policies or other products.

SCALE ORIGIN:

There is no indication that the scale was constructed elsewhere than in the Crosby and Stephens (1987) study.

SAMPLES:

The sample was selected from a nationally representative consumer panel and screened for ownership of life insurance. Analysis of the first wave of the survey was based on **1362** responses. The sample was slightly better educated and more upscale than the population at large, but the authors considered the differences to be minor and unrelated to the studied relationships. A year later, respondents to the first wave of the survey (or from a holdout sample) were contacted. Analysis was based on **447** responses. Comparison of main sample and holdout sample data did not indicate any bias due to wave 1 premeasurement.

RELIABILITY:

Alpha values for the scale were **.81** and **.84** for the two waves of the study.

VALIDITY:

Factor analyses in the two waves of the study produced nearly identical factor solutions.

ADMINISTRATION:

The scales were self-administered as part of a larger mail questionnaire. High scores indicate that customers have received information from their insurance company many times in the past two years about policies or other services whereas low scores suggest that customers have rarely if ever received such information from their company.

MAJOR FINDINGS:

The purpose of the study was to compare two proposed models of buyer satisfaction with life insurance, the relationship generalization model (RGM) and a rational evaluation model (REM). The RGM assumes that consumers generalize positive feelings about the provider to the core service whereas the REM views consumers as most concerned about core service quality, with the relationship merely adding value to it. In general, the results supported the REM over the RGM. This means that though the agent's performance affects satisfaction, it is balanced against the perceived performance of the core service. Use of **information** directly from the insurance company was not found to have a significant impact on the satisfaction customers felt toward their core policy or toward their company.

REFERENCE:

Crosby, Lawrence A. and Nancy Stephens (1987), ''Effects of Relationship Marketing on Satisfaction, Retention, and Prices in the Life Insurance Industry,'' *JMR*, 24 (November), 404-411.

SCALE ITEMS: INFORMATION USAGE (COMPANY SOURCES)

Never	Once	Twice	Three or Four Times	Five Times or More
1————	——2——	——3——	——4——	——5

How often in the last one or two years did you recall experiencing the following:

1. Received information from my company explaining why it is a good idea to keep this policy in force.
2. Received information from my company suggesting I buy additional life insurance.
3. Received information from my company describing new types of policies it was introducing.
4. Received information from my company explaining its other financial or insurance services.
5. Received information from my company that discussed the company's financial performance.

SCALE NAME: Information Usage (Personal Sources)

SCALE DESCRIPTION:

A four-item, five-point Likert-type summated ratings scale measuring the number of times in the previous two years that a customer recalls a personal source providing information that led to questioning the value of his/her insurance policy. The personal sources were individuals other than those working for the insurance company. (See items below.)

SCALE ORIGIN:

There is no indication that the scale was constructed elsewhere than in the Crosby and Stephens (1987) study.

SAMPLES:

The sample was selected from a nationally representative consumer panel and screened for ownership of life insurance. Analysis of the first wave of the survey was based on **1362** responses. The sample was slightly better educated and more upscale than the population at large, but the authors considered the differences to be minor and unrelated to the studied relationships. A year later, respondents to the first wave of the survey (or from a holdout sample) were contacted. Analysis was based on **447** responses. Comparison of main sample and holdout sample data did not indicate any bias due to wave 1 premeasurement.

RELIABILITY:

Alpha values for the scale were **.62** and **.61** for the two waves of the study.

VALIDITY:

Factor analyses in the two waves of the study produced nearly identical factor solutions.

ADMINISTRATION:

The scales were self-administered as part of a larger mail questionnaire. High scores indicate that customers have received information from personal sources other than the company's employees many times in the past two years that led them to question the value of their insurance policies, whereas low scores suggest that customers have rarely if ever received such information from personal sources.

MAJOR FINDINGS:

The purpose of the study was to compare two proposed models of buyer satisfaction with life insurance, the relationship generalization model (RGM) and a rational evaluation model (REM). The RGM assumes that consumers generalize positive feelings about the provider to the core service whereas the REM views consumers as most concerned about core service quality, with the relationship merely adding value to it. In general, the results supported the REM over the RGM. This means that though the agent's performance affects satisfaction, it is balanced against the perceived performance of the core service. **Personal**

source usage was found to have a significant but small negative impact on the satisfaction customers felt toward their core policy. This finding may mean that buyers are recalling negative information disseminated by people such as competitors' agents or customers that leads them to ''question the value'' of their policies.

COMMENTS:

The internal consistency should be increased before further use is made of the scale.

REFERENCE:

Crosby, Lawrence A. and Nancy Stephens (1987), ''Effects of Relationship Marketing on Satisfaction, Retention, and Prices in the Life Insurance Industry,'' *JMR*, 24 (November), 404-411.

SCALE ITEMS: INFORMATION USAGE (PERSONAL SOURCES)

Never	Once	Twice	Three or Four Times	Five Times or More
1	2	3	4	5

How often in the last one or two years did you recall experiencing the following:

1. A different agent recommended that I should replace the policy.
2. Attended a financial planning seminar that made me question the value of this policy.
3. Other financial advisors recommended I should replace or stop making payments on this policy.
4. Other consumers recommended I should replace or stop making payments on this policy.

SCALE NAME: In-Home Shopper

SCALE DESCRIPTION:

A seven-item, six-point, Likert-type summated ratings scale from strongly disagree (1) to strongly agree (6). The scale measures a person's interest in shopping at home through phone or mail order.

SCALE ORIGIN:

The scale appears to be original to Hawes and Lumpkin (1984).

SAMPLES:

Hawes and Lumpkin (1984) collected data from **581** residents of 14 communities near the Ft. Worth-Dallas metroplex. Each of the communities was randomly sampled in proportion to its population by means of their respective telephone directories. The questionnaire was to be filled out by the household member responsible for most of the shopping. The distribution of respondents by community was similar to the actual population distribution.

RELIABILITY:

An alpha of **.755** was calculated for the scale.

VALIDITY:

Factor analysis indicated that items loaded together and that their loadings were all higher than **.5**. Content validity was deemed adequate given that the construct included items similar to those used in other (unspecified) studies.

ADMINISTRATION:

Data were gathered through self-administered mail questionnaires. Scale scores are calculated by averaging numerical responses to individual items. A score of 6 indicates that a person is actively involved in **shopping out of the home** whereas a 1 implies a person has little interest in **in-home shopping** and probably prefers conventional shopping.

MAJOR FINDINGS:

The purpose of the study by Hawes and Lumpkin (1984) was to examine demographic and psychographic characteristics of outshoppers. **In-home shopping** significantly differentiated between inshoppers and outshoppers. Persons who engaged in outshopping the most expressed the least interest in in-home shopping.

REFERENCE:

Hawes, Jon M. and James R. Lumpkin (1984), "Understanding the Outshopper," *JAMS*, 12 (Fall), 200-218.

SCALE ITEMS: IN HOME SHOPPER

Strongly Disagree	Disagree	Slightly Disagree	Slightly Agree	Agree	Strongly Agree
1———————2———————3———————4———————5———————6					

1. I love to browse through catalogs.
2. I am ordering more things from my home in order to save energy.
3. By shopping at home through mail/phone order, I save a lot of time.
4. I don't like to shop at home through mail or phone order. **(r)**
5. I use mail/phone order from home because I can't find what I want in the local stores.
6. Mail or phone ordering at home is more convenient than going to the store.
7. In-home shopping via mail/phone costs too much for what you get. **(r)**

SCALE NAME: Innovativeness (Brand)

SCALE DESCRIPTION:

This three-item, six-point, Likert-type summated ratings scale ranges from strongly disagree to strongly agree. The scale measures a person's perceived tendency to try new brands. These items as a set have been called New Brand Tryer in several studies.

SCALE ORIGIN:

These items were part of a classic study of psychographics by Wells and Tigert (1971). One thousand questionnaires were mailed to homemaker members of the Market Facts mail panel. In addition to gathering demographic, product use, and media data, the survey contained 300 statements that have since served as the basis for the construction of many lifestyle-related scales. The three items for this scale are reported in the article, but they were not analyzed as a multi-item scale. The purpose of the article was to explain how psychographics could improve upon mere demographic description of target audiences and product users. No psychometric information was reported.

One of the first uses of the items as a multi-item scale was by Darden and Perreault (1976). Analysis was based on self-administered questionnaires completed by 278 suburban housewives randomly selected in Athens, Georgia. A split-half reliability of .52 was reported for the scale. Though a few lifestyle variables differentiated between outshopping groups, brand innovativeness was **not** one of them.

SAMPLES:

Two mailing lists were used to collect data in the Dickerson and Gentry study (1983). One was a list of *Psychology Today* subscribers and the other was a list of members of computer clubs. The former was used to reach non-adopters of computers and the latter was used to reach PC adopters. Analysis was based on a total of **639** questionnaires. Results from a second mailing to non-respondents indicated that their demographic makeup was not significantly different from that of respondents. On the basis of 1980 Census data, the sample was younger and more upscale than the general population.

RELIABILITY:

An alpha of **.28** was reported by Dickerson and Gentry (1983).

VALIDITY:

Factor analysis indicated that the items loaded together.

ADMINISTRATION:

Data were gathered through self-administered mail questionnaires. Scale scores are typically calculated by averaging numerical responses to individual items. A score of 6 indicates that a person frequently purchases new brands whereas a 1 means a person rarely exhibits brand **innovativeness**.

MAJOR FINDINGS:

Dickerson and Gentry (1983) apparently dropped this scale from the analysis because of its low internal consistency.

COMMENTS:

It is not clear from the items themselves why the scale had such a low alpha in the Dickerson and Gentry (1983) study. However, extra care should be exercised if these items are used alone and it would be better to generate and test a few more relevant items.

REFERENCES:

Darden, William R. and William D. Perreault, Jr. (1976), ''Identifying Interurban Shoppers: Multiproduct Purchase Patterns and Segmentation Profiles,'' *JMR*, 13 (February), 51-60.

Dickerson, Mary D. and James W. Gentry (1983), ''Characteristics of Adopters and Non-Adopters of Home Computers,'' *JCR*, 10 (September), 225-235.

Wells, William D. and Douglas Tigert (1971), ''Activities, Interests, and Opinions,'' *JAR*, 11 (August), 27-35.

SCALE ITEMS: INNOVATIVENESS (BRAND)

Strongly Disagree	Disagree	Slightly Disagree	Slightly Agree	Agree	Strongly Agree
1	2	3	4	5	6

1. When I see a new brand on the shelf I often buy it just to see what it's like.
2. I often try new brands before my friends and neighbors do.
3. I like to try new and different things.

SCALE NAME: Innovativeness (Fashion)

SCALE DESCRIPTION:

A three-item, five-point, Likert-type summated ratings scale ranging from don't know (0) to often (4). The scale measures a person's desire to be among the first to own clothing of the latest style.

SCALE ORIGIN:

The items are original to Hirschman (1980), though they are adapted from prior self-report studies of this general construct reported by Rogers and Shoemaker (1971).

SAMPLES:

Data were gathered through a telephone survey in Atlanta. Weeknight calling, random digit dialing, and five callbacks per number were used to maximize the sample's representativeness. The survey focused on women and obtained **599** usable interviews (**125** black and **474** white respondents).

RELIABILITY:

No test of reliability was reported.

VALIDITY:

No test of validity was reported.

ADMINISTRATION:

Hirschman (1980) used telephone interviews to gather data for the study. Scale scores were calculated by adding numerical responses to the first two items and subtracting the numerical response to the last item. Higher scores indicate that a person often buys new fashions whereas lower scores mean that a person rarely if ever purchases the newest fashions.

MAJOR FINDINGS:

Hirschman's (1980) focus was not on **innovators** per se but on the differences between black and white **fashion innovative** communicators (those who are both opinion leaders and **innovators**). Fewer significant differences were found than expected. Black innovative communicators were found to subscribe to fewer newspapers than their white counterparts and to have different radio station preferences. Also, different patterns of group membership were found between the two groups such that white subjects participated more in formal groups and organized social activities.

COMMENTS:

Some pretesting ought to be performed to determine the scale's psychometric properties and improve them if necessary before it is used in a large survey.

REFERENCES:

Hirschman, Elizabeth C. (1980), ''Black Ethnicity and Innovative Communication,'' *JAMS*, 8 (Spring), 100-119.

Rogers, Everett M. and Floyd Shoemaker (1971), *Communication of Innovations*. New York, N.Y.: Free Press.

SCALE ITEMS: INNOVATIVENESS (FASHION)

Often	Sometimes	Seldom	Never	Don't Know
4————	——3———	——2———	—1———	———0

1. Are you willing to try new ideas about clothing fashions? How often?
2. Do you try something new in the next season's fashions? How often?
3. Are you usually among the last to try new clothing fashions? How often?

SCALE NAME: Innovativeness (Fashion)

SCALE DESCRIPTION:

A three-item, six-point, Likert-type summated ratings scale from strongly disagree (1) to strongly agree (6). The scale measures a person's desire to own clothing of the latest style. See also Hawes and Lumpkin (1984) for a combination of items from this scale used with items from a fashion opinion leadership scale.

SCALE ORIGIN:

It is not clear where the items originated or where the scale was first used as a multi-item summated ratings scale.

SAMPLES:

Lumpkin (1985) analyzed data collected from a sample drawn from the Market Facts Consumer Mail Panel. A total of 2854 completed questionnaires were received, but Lumpkin focused just on **373** respondents who indicated they were 65 years of age or older.

RELIABILITY:

An alpha of **.7106** was reported by Lumpkin (1985).

VALIDITY:

Factor analysis indicated the items loaded together.

ADMINISTRATION:

Data were gathered through self-administered mail questionnaires. Scale scores are calculated by averaging numerical responses to individual items. A score of 6 indicates that a person has a strong tendency to buy new fashions whereas 1 implies that a person is relatively uninterested in wearing the newest fashions.

MAJOR FINDINGS:

Elderly consumers were cluster analyzed by Lumpkin (1985) and **fashion innovativeness** appeared to discriminate between the three groups, though the level of statistical significance was not reported. The group with the highest mean on the scale also scored highest on fashion opinion leadership and had the most interest in shopping. The group with the lowest mean score appeared to be much less involved all around.

COMMENTS:

Internal consistency might be improved somewhat by the addition of related items.

REFERENCES:

Hawes, Jon M. and James R. Lumpkin (1984), ''Understanding the Outshopper,'' *JAMS*, 12 (Fall), 200-218.

Lumpkin, James R. (1985), ''Shopping Orientation Segmentation of the Elderly Consumer,'' *JAMS*, 13 (Spring), 271-289.

SCALE ITEMS: INNOVATIVENESS (FASHION)

Strongly Disagree	Disagree	Slightly Disagree	Slightly Agree	Agree	Strongly Agree
1	2	3	4	5	6

1. I often try new fashion ideas.
2. It is important that my clothes be of the latest style.
3. I am among the first to try a new fashion.

SCALE NAME: Innovativeness (Open Processing)

SCALE DESCRIPTION:

The measure consists of two 12-item, five-point scales, for which the difference in scores assesses the degree to which a person is open to new and different experiences. This scale was originally referred to as Innovativeness by Leavitt and Walton (1975), but later they and other authors called it a measure of Open Processing (Joseph and Vyas 1984).

SCALE ORIGIN:

The two parts of the innovativeness measure were constructed by Leavitt and Walton (1975), who report that three "experts" generated 144 positive items that were administered to **300** female respondents. The group was narrowed down to 29. Thirty-three negative items were generated and tested along with the 29 positive items on **299** women. By examining item-to-total correlations, the authors narrowed both sets down to 20 a piece. The internal consistency (KR 20) of the full 40-item scale was reported to be .**88**. To establish construct validity, the scale was correlated with 14 psychological measures. The expected pattern of correlations was generally found. The measure used by Joseph and Vyas (1984) was an unpublished version of the scale (Form A) that had a total of 24 items, 12 for the openness dimension and 12 for the cautiousness dimension.

SAMPLES:

Joseph and Vyas (1984) selected women for inclusion in the study by use of systematic sampling in a large suburban shopping mall. During busy weekend shopping hours, a female interviewer stopped every third female adult and asked whether she was primarily responsible for the shopping in her household. If so, she was briefed on the purpose of the study, asked to fill out a questionnaire later, and asked to return it by mail. Of the 350 questionnaires distributed, **139** usable forms were returned. The majority of the sample were under 40 years of age, married, employed either full- or part-time, high school graduates, and were from households of 2 to 4 individuals. Half had annual household income between $15,000 and $30,000, and one fourth of the sample had income over that amount.

RELIABILITY:

Joseph and Vyas (1984) report alpha values of .**77**, .**67**, and .**61** for the open subscale, the cautious subscale, and the combined items, respectively.

VALIDITY:

No specific examination of scale validity was made beyond that involved in the test of hypotheses described below.

ADMINISTRATION:

The scale was filled out by respondents along with several other measures as part of a self-administered questionnaire. Scale scores are calculated by subtracting the sum of the numerical responses to the 12 cautiousness items from the sum of the numerical responses to the 12 openness items. Higher final scores imply that people have an open processing style and are interested in new experiences. Lower scores suggest that people are cautious and not willing to try new things.

MAJOR FINDINGS:

Joseph and Vyas (1984) were interested in determining whether women with high open processing scores were more innovative than those with low scores. They found that though **high open processors** were significantly more innovative than **low open processors,** they were not significantly different from the **medium open processors**. The findings also indicated that **open processing** was a more powerful predictor of innovativeness than any of the demographic variables examined.

COMMENTS:

The internal consistency for the combined scale was very low and not as high as that reported for the version of the measure used by Leavitt and Walton (1975). Some concern is necessary to determine whether this somewhat abbreviated version is as sound as the longer one.

REFERENCES:

Joseph, Benoy and Shailesh J. Vyas (1984), ''Concurrent Validity of a Measure of Innovative Cognitive Style,'' *JAMS*, 12 (Spring), 159-175.

Leavitt, Clark and John Walton (1975), ''Development of a Scale for Innovativeness,'' in *Advances in Consumer Research*, Vol. 2, Mary Jane Slinger, ed. Ann Arbor, Mich.: Association for Consumer Research, 545-554.

SCALE ITEMS: INNOVATIVENESS (OPEN PROCESSING)

Not well at all	Not well	Fairly well	Very well	Extremely well
1—————	—2—————	—3—————	—4—————	—5

Items Comprising the Open Dimension:
1. I like to take a chance.
2. I enjoy looking at new styles as soon as they come out.
3. Often the most interesting and stimulating people are those who don't mind being original and different.
4. I would like a job that required frequent changes from one kind of task to another.
5. I like to try new and different things.
6. I like people who are a little shocking.
7. When I see a new brand on the shelf, I often buy it just to see what it is like.
8. I often try new brands before my friends and neighbors do.
9. I like to experiment with new ways of doing things.
10. Some modern art is stimulating.

11. I like to fool around with new ideas even if they turn out later to be a total waste of time.
12. Today is a good day to start a new project.

Items Comprising the Cautious Dimension:
1. I don't like to talk to strangers.
2. The unusual gift is often a waste of money.
3. Buying a new product that has not yet been proven is usually a waste of time and money.
4. If people would quit wasting their time experimenting, we would get more accomplished.
5. If I got an idea, I would give a lot of weight to what others think of it.
6. In hunting for the best way to do something, it is usually a good idea to try the obvious way first.
7. I like to wait until something has been proven before I try it.
8. When it comes to taking chances, I would rather be safe than sorry.
9. I feel that too much money is wasted on new styles.
10. I enjoy being with people who think like I do.
11. At work, I think that everyone should work on only one thing thereby becoming more of an expert.
12. In the long run the usual ways of doing things are best.

SCALE NAME: Innovativeness (Product)

SCALE DESCRIPTION:

A three-item, seven-point Likert-type scale measuring a person's reported desire to be among the first to buy new things.

SCALE ORIGIN:

The measure did not originate with Oliver and Bearden (1985, p. 329, 338), but was supplied by a sponsoring institution.

SAMPLES:

Analysis was based on **353** completed questionnaires from members of a bistate consumer panel. Subjects were selected to be representative of urban and suburban households with family income greater than $10,000. Ninety-one triers and 262 nontriers of a new, heavily promoted time-release diet suppressant responded. The average respondent was female (56%), white (89%), with some education beyond high school (70%), and in the $20,000 to $29,999 income category (25.5%).

RELIABILITY:

A reliability of **.72** was reported.

VALIDITY:

Confirmatory factor analysis was performed once, weak items were deleted, and the analysis was run again, resulting in higher overall factor loadings.

ADMINISTRATION:

Data were gathered through use of self-administered mail questionnaires. The method for calculating scale scores was not specified, but it is likely that higher scores on this scale suggest that a person greatly likes being among the first to buy new products whereas lower scores imply that a person does not like taking such chances.

MAJOR FINDINGS:

The purpose of the study was to examine the presence and operation of "crossover effects" in the Fishbein behavioral intention model under various moderating conditions. Evidence generally supporting the normative structure attitude crossover path was found; that is, a person's attitude toward a behavior is strengthened to the extent that relevant others are believed to agree with it. The moderator variable analysis provided little insight into the mechanisms people use to process normative information. However, the crossover model predicted best for persons high in **innovativeness** and worst for persons low in **innovativeness**.

COMMENTS:

Though the scale had adequate internal consistency, the authors admitted that it might lack stability over time, samples, or product categories.

REFERENCE:

Oliver, Richard L. and William O. Bearden (1985), ''Crossover Effects in the Theory of Reasoned Action: A Moderating Influence Attempt,'' *JCR*, 12 (December), 324-340.

SCALE ITEMS: INNOVATIVENESS (PRODUCT)

Disagree _____ : _____ : _____ : _____ : _____ : _____ : _____ Agree
          1   2   3   4   5   6   7

1. I like to buy new and different things.
2. I am usually among the first to try new products.
3. I don't like to take chances. **(r)**

SCALE NAME: Innovativeness (Shopping)

SCALE DESCRIPTION:

A four-item, six-point, Likert-type summated ratings scale ranging from strongly disagree (1) to strongly agree (6). The scale measures a shopper's innovativeness, particularly in relation to stores and brands. It was referred to as Shopping Innovation by Hawes and Lumpkin (1984).

SCALE ORIGIN:

Though one item of this scale comes from the New Brand Tryer measure offered by Wells and Tigert (1971), as a construct it bears more similarity to the Patronage Innovator scale used by Darden and Perreault (1976). Analysis in the latter study was based on self-administered questionnaires completed by 278 suburban housewives randomly selected in Athens, Georgia. A split-half reliability of .83 was reported for a two-item version of the scale. Shopping innovativeness was one of a few lifestyle variables that differentiated between outshopping groups. All outshopper groups expressed more innovativeness than did inshoppers. The outshopper group expressing the most innovativeness was characterized by its members being heavy outbuyers of jewelry and clothing.

SAMPLES:

Hawes and Lumpkin (1984) collected data from **581** residents of 14 communities near the Ft. Worth-Dallas metroplex. Each of the communities was randomly sampled in proportion to its population by means of the respective telephone directories. The questionnaire was to be filled out by the household member responsible for most of the shopping. The distribution of respondents by community was similar to the actual population distribution.

RELIABILITY:

An alpha of **.609** was calculated for the scale.

VALIDITY:

Factor analysis indicated that items loaded together and that their loadings were all higher than .5. Content validity was deemed adequate given that the construct included items similar to those used in other (unspecified) studies.

ADMINISTRATION:

Hawes and Lumpkin (1984) gathered data through self-administered mail questionnaires. Scale scores are calculated by averaging numerical responses to individual items. A score of 6 indicates that a person is very innovative in his/her shopping activities whereas 1 implies that a person is unlikely to be interested in trying new stores or brands.

MAJOR FINDINGS:

The purpose of the study by Hawes and Lumpkin (1984) was to examine demographic and psychographic characteristics of outshoppers. Of all the psychographic variables examined, **shopping innovativeness** was among the most salient in differentiating between inshoppers and outshoppers. Persons who engaged in outshopping the most expressed the most **innovativeness**.

COMMENTS:

The internal consistency for the measure is very low and may be improved somewhat by separating items that measure innovativeness toward stores from those measuring innovativeness toward brands. In any case, further work on the scale appears to be necessary.

REFERENCES:

Darden, William R. and William D. Perreault, Jr. (1976), "Identifying Interurban Shoppers: Multiproduct Purchase Patterns and Segmentation Profiles," *JMR*, 13 (Feb.), 51- 60.

Hawes, Jon M. and James R. Lumpkin (1984), "Understanding the Outshopper," *JAMS*, 12 (Fall), 200-218.

Wells, William D. and Douglas Tigert (1971), "Activities, Interests, and Opinions," *JAR*, 11 (August), 27-35.

SCALE ITEMS: INNOVATIVENESS (SHOPPING)

Strongly Disagree	Disagree	Slightly Disagree	Slightly Agree	Agree	Strongly Agree
1	2	3	4	5	6

1. I like to try new and different things.
2. I like to try new and different places to shop.
3. When I see a new brand on the shelf, I often buy it just to see what it is like.
4. When a new store opens, I am among the first to try it.

SCALE NAME: Innovativeness (Shopping)

SCALE DESCRIPTION:

A ten-item, seven-point Likert-type summated ratings scale measuring the degree to which a person reports him/herself to be interested in trying new stores, restaurants, products, and brands.

SCALE ORIGIN:

Though some of the items are similar to those used in other innovativeness scales, this group of items was put into scale form along with six other scales by Raju (1980). An initial pool of 90 items related to exploratory behavior and lifestyle were compiled and then tested for low social desirability bias and high item-total correlations. Thirty-nine items were found to meet the criteria and were common to two separate samples. Items were grouped into seven categories on the basis of inter-item correlations and subjective judgement.

SAMPLES:

Raju (1980) collected data from **336** homemakers and **105** students. The homemakers were contacted through local women's clubs and the students were contacted through mostly junior and senior level college classes.

RELIABILITY:

The scale was reported by Raju (1980) to have reliability (Spearman-Brown) of **.804** and **.845** for the homemaker and student samples, respectively.

VALIDITY:

Though Raju (1980) notes that a factor analysis was performed, the grouping of items for scale purposes was based more on inter-item correlations and a subjective classification process.

ADMINISTRATION:

The manner of scale administration by Raju (1980) was not specifically addressed for either sample. However, he implied that the homemakers received the questionnaire at a club meeting, filled it out at home by themselves, and returned it by mail. The student sample is assumed to have completed the survey instrument in class. Respondents with lower scores on the scale are much less innovative in their consumer behavior than those with higher scores.

MAJOR FINDINGS:

In two studies, Raju (1980) examined the relationships between optimal stimulation level (OSL) and certain personality traits, demographics, and purchase-related psychographics. For both samples, significant correlations were found between **innovativeness** and OSL.

This finding along with others indicated that people with higher OSLs are more likely to exhibit exploratory behaviors in their consumer behavior.

COMMENTS:

The construct validity of the scale is highly suspect given the manner in which the seven scales used in the study were constructed (as noted in the origination information above). Sixteen of the 39 items were used to compose more than one scale, thus making it unclear what construct the items and their respective scales actually measured. Though the reported reliability levels for this scale are reasonable, further validity testing is needed.

REFERENCE:

Raju, P. S. (1980), ''Optimum Stimulation Level: Its Relationship to Personality, Demographics, and Exploratory Behavior,'' *JCR*, 7 (December), 272-282.

SCALE ITEMS: INNOVATIVENESS (SHOPPING)

```
Completely                                                    Completely
Disagree                                                          Agree
    1————————2————————3————————4————————5————————6————————7
```

1. When I see a new or different brand on the shelf, I often pick it up just to see what it is like.
2. I am the kind of person who would try any new product once.
3. A new store or restaurant is not something I would be eager to find out about. **(r)**
4. I am very cautious in trying new/different products. **(r)**
5. Even for an important date or dinner, I wouldn't be wary of trying a new or unfamiliar restaurant.
6. I would rather wait for others to try a new store or restaurant than try it myself. **(r)**
7. When I see a new brand somewhat different from the usual, I investigate it.
8. Investigating new brands of grocery and other similar products is generally a waste of time. **(r)**
9. When I hear about a new store or restaurant, I take advantage of the first opportunity to find out more about it.
10. I enjoy taking chances in buying unfamiliar brands just to get some variety in my purchases.

SCALE NAME: In-Shopping Preference

SCALE DESCRIPTION:

A three-item, six-point, Likert-type summated ratings scale that assesses a consumer's degree of loyalty toward local retailers. It was referred to as Loyalty to Local Merchants by Hawes and Lumpkin (1984).

SCALE ORIGIN:

These items were apparently first used and reported as a multi-item scale by Hawes and Lumpkin (1984).

SAMPLES:

Hawes and Lumpkin (1984) collected data from **581** residents of 14 communities near the Ft. Worth-Dallas metroplex. Each of the communities was randomly sampled in proportion to its population by means of the respective telephone directories. The questionnaire was to be filled out by the household member responsible for most of the shopping. The distribution of respondents by community was similar to the actual population distribution.

RELIABILITY:

An alpha of **.764** was calculated for the scale.

VALIDITY:

Factor analysis indicated that items loaded together and that their loadings were all higher than .6. Content validity was deemed adequate given that the construct included items similar to those used in other (unspecified) studies.

ADMINISTRATION:

Data were gathered through self-administered mail questionnaires. Scale scores are calculated by averaging numerical responses to individual items. A score of 6 indicates that a person strongly prefers to shop at local stores whereas a 1 implies a person has little loyalty toward local retailers.

MAJOR FINDINGS:

The purpose of the study by Hawes and Lumpkin (1984) was to examine demographic and psychographic characteristics of outshoppers. **Inshopping preference** was one of the most salient psychographic variables in differentiating between inshoppers and outshoppers. Persons who engaged in outshopping the most expressed the least **preference** for local shopping.

REFERENCE:

Hawes, Jon M. and James R. Lumpkin (1984), ''Understanding the Outshopper,'' *JAMS*, 12 (Fall), 200-218.

SCALE ITEMS: IN-SHOPPING PREFERENCE

Strongly Disagree	Disagree	Slightly Disagree	Slightly Agree	Agree	Strongly Agree
1	2	3	4	5	6

1. I owe it to my community to shop at local stores.
2. Shopping at local stores helps build my community.
3. I would rather shop at local stores to keep the money "at home."

SCALE NAME: In-Shopping Preference

SCALE DESCRIPTION:

A 10-item, four-point Likert-type summated ratings scale ranging from never (1) to always (4). The scale measures a consumer's reported desire to shop loyally in the local community. The measure was called General Retail Patronage Loyalty Scale by Hozier and Stem (1985).

SCALE ORIGIN:

Though the items may have been borrowed from previous unspecified studies, the scale itself was constructed by Hozier and Stem (1985).

SAMPLES:

Questionnaires were mailed to respondents drawn by means of a systematic sampling plan from the telephone directories of four small towns in eastern Washington and western Idaho. The first and followup questionnaires produced a total of **705** usable responses.

RELIABILITY:

Test-retest reliability was estimated to be **.87**.

VALIDITY:

An idea of the scale's validity comes from a variety of findings. First, the items composing the scale were selected from a larger list based on the results of a factor analysis. Second, the correlation between scale scores and scores on a single-item measure of the same construct was .51. Finally, as an indicator of actual in-shopping behavior, respondents were asked to state where they had most recently purchased each of 12 different products. The scale had a .37 correlation with that behavioral measure.

ADMINISTRATION:

The scale was self-administered in a mail survey format. Scores were calculated by summing the coded responses to each of the 10 items. The closer a score was to 40, the more it indicated a consumer was expressing loyalty to local retailers, whereas a score closer to 10 meant that a consumer preferred out-shopping.

MAJOR FINDINGS:

The purpose of the Hozier and Stem (1985) study was to examine the strength of **in-shopping preference** as a factor predicting **in-shopping behavior**. Most of the explanatory power in the regression models came from the in-shopping scale. Direct attitudinal ratings of local retailers appeared to explain little. None of the demographic variables were significantly correlated with in-shopping behavior or the scale. There was an indication that results were not town-specific and could be geographically generalizable.

REFERENCE:

Hozier, George C., Jr. and Donald E. Stem, Jr. (1985), "General Retail Patronage Loyalty as a Determinant of Consumer Outshopping Behavior," *JAMS*, 13 (Winter), 32-46.

SCALE ITEMS: IN-SHOPPING PREFERENCE

Never	Occasionally	Frequently	Always
1————————————	————2————————	————3————————	————4

1. I will pay slightly more for products if I can buy them locally.
2. I shop outside my local retail area before looking to see what is offered locally. **(r)**
3. I shop at local stores because it is important to help my community.
4. I shop locally because the convenience outweighs the other advantages of shopping outside the community.
5. I shop locally to support the local merchants and business district.
6. Shopping at local stores is an enjoyable experience.
7. I will increase my interest in local stores when more goods/services are available through them.
8. Because I am more familiar with local stores, I prefer shopping locally rather than out of town.
9. I shop locally even when the selection/variety of goods is poor.
10. I am loyal to my local shopping area.

SCALE NAME: Interaction-Orientation of Salesperson (Customer's Perception)

SCALE DESCRIPTION:

A seven-item, five-point Likert-type summated ratings scale measuring the degree to which a customer perceived a salesperson to have been friendly and helpful. Williams and Spiro (1985) viewed this scale as measuring the interaction-oriented dimension of customer communication style, which stresses enjoyment and maintenance of personal relationships to the possible extent of ignoring the task at hand.

SCALE ORIGIN:

The items were developed from work performed by Bass (1960) on orientation motivation. Based on earlier work by others, he suggested that members of groups are motivated to remain in the groups for different reasons. He developed measures of three motivations: the task orientation, the interaction orientation, and the self orientation (Bass 1977). Williams and Spiro (1985) adapted these measures for their studies in two ways: they were more specific to the sales context and they were perceptions of other's behaviors, not self-perceptions.

SAMPLES:

Williams and Spiro (1985) data were collected from all 13 sporting goods stores in a major southeastern U.S. city. Customers were approached just after leaving the stores. If they agreed to fill out a questionnaire, their respective sales people were asked to fill out a survey instrument as well. A total of **251** dyadic interactions were captured, with the responses coming from 64 different sales people and 251 different customers. All sales people in the stores participated as did 90% of the customers who were approached.

RELIABILITY:

An alpha of **.85** was reported for the scale by Williams and Spiro (1985) and item-total correlations were all above .65.

VALIDITY:

A factor analysis indicated that the items loaded higher on this factor than any other (Williams and Spiro 1985).

ADMINISTRATION:

As implied above, the customer completed a self-administered survey form that included several measures (Williams and Spiro (1985). The authors computed scale scores by averaging numerical responses to the items. High scores on the scale suggest that customers perceive the sales people with whom they have just interacted as very friendly and helpful whereas low scores imply that they felt their respective sales people were not interested in them personally or concerned about their needs.

MAJOR FINDINGS:

Williams and Spiro's (1985) study examined the use of communication styles in dyadic sales situations and their effect on sales outcomes. The findings indicated that though the communication style of the two parties of the transaction plays a role in the outcome, it is the customer's orientation that has the greatest impact. With respect to **salesperson's interaction-orientation**, it did not appear to have a significant positive effect on sales. However, there was some evidence that the direction and degree of the influence depended to some extent on the customer's communication style.

REFERENCES:

Bass, Bernard M. (1960), *Leadership, Psychology, and Organizational Behavior*. New York, N.Y.: Harper Brothers.

_____ (1977), *ORI-Manual for the Orientation Inventory*. Palo Alto, Calif.: Consulting Psychologists Press, Inc.

Williams, Kaylene C. and Rosann L. Spiro (1985), "Communication Style in the Salesperson-Customer Dyad," *JMR*, 12 (November), 434-442.

SCALE ITEMS: INTERACTION ORIENTATION OF SALESPERSON (CUSTOMER'S PERCEPTION)

Strongly Disagree	Disagree	Neutral	Agree	Strongly Agree
1	2	3	4	5

1. This salesperson genuinely enjoyed helping me.
2. This salesperson was easy to talk with.
3. This salesperson likes to help customers.
4. This salesperson was a cooperative person.
5. This salesperson tried to establish a personal relationship.
6. This salesperson seemed interested in me not only as a customer, but also as a person.
7. This salesperson was friendly.

SCALE NAME: Interpersonal Influence Susceptibility (Normative)

SCALE DESCRIPTION:

An eight-item, seven-point Likert-type summated ratings scale measuring the degree to which a person expresses the need to identify with others and a willingness to conform to their expectations about purchase decisions.

SCALE ORIGIN:

This measure was constructed by Bearden, Netemeyer, and Teel (1989) and is only known to have been used in their study. A series of studies were conducted by the authors to determine the reliability and validity of the scale, only a portion of which are discussed here. From a review of previous research, 166 items were generated that were suspected to measure one of the three hypothesized dimensions of interpersonal influence susceptibility: informational, normative, and value expressiveness. After ambiguous and essentially identical items were dropped, the content validity of the remaining items was evaluated by five judges. Then the remaining items were rated again for their clarity in representing one of the dimensions of the construct by four more judges. Some other aspects of the analysis are described below.

SAMPLES:

Sixty-two items were initially administered to a convenience sample of **220**. Fifteen items were reevaluated by a convenience sample of **141** undergraduate students.

RELIABILITY:

Alpha values for the eight-item normative dimension were reported as being **.87** and **.88** in the first and second administrations, respectively. The estimates of construct reliability based on LISREL results were **.90** and **.89** for the initial and followup administrations, respectively. Thirty-five students from the second administration group participated in a retest session three weeks later and a correlation of **.79** was found between their scores on the scale.

VALIDITY:

After an initial effort to develop separate scales to measure the three hypothesized dimensions of the construct, strong evidence of discriminant and convergent validity was found for the informational dimension but not for the utilitarian and value expressive dimensions. The latter two sets of items were combined to form one scale. Confirmatory factor analysis indicated a stable two-factor correlated structure (the normative and informational factors). Some further analyses that provided evidence of construct validity are discussed below under Findings.

ADMINISTRATION:

The scale was self-administered in each of the studies reported by the authors. Higher scores on the scale indicate that respondents are very sensitive to what others think about purchase decisions and want to conform to group norms.

MAJOR FINDINGS:

The purpose of the study by Bearden, Netemeyer, and Teel (1989) was to develop scales for measuring the dimensions of consumer susceptibility to interpersonal influence. A series of studies provided support for a two-factor model. Among the many findings were that the **normative** factor positively correlated much more strongly than the information factor with a measure of attention to social comparison information; the **normative** factor had a significantly stronger positive correlation than the informational factor with a measure of compliance motivation; and, both factors had similar negative correlations with a measure of self-esteem.

COMMENTS:

To measure more fully the interpersonal influence susceptibility construct, this measure ought to be used along with the four-item measure of the informational dimension.

REFERENCE:

Bearden, William O., Richard G. Netemeyer, and Jesse E. Teel (1989), "Measurement of Consumer Susceptibility to Interpersonal Influence," *JCR*, 15 (March), 473-481.

SCALE ITEMS: INTERPERSONAL INFLUENCE SUSCEPTIBILITY (NORMATIVE)

strongly disagree	____ : ____ : ____ : ____ : ____ : ____ : ____	strongly agree
	1 2 3 4 5 6 7	

1. I rarely purchase the latest fashions until I am sure my friends approve of them.
2. It is important that others like the products and brands I buy.
3. When buying products, I generally purchase those brands that I think others will approve of.
4. If other people can see me using a product, I often purchase the brand they expect me to buy.
5. I like to know what brands and products make good impressions on others.
6. I achieve a sense of belonging by purchasing the same products and brands that others purchase.
7. If I want to be like someone, I often try to buy the same brands that they buy.
8. I often identify with other people by purchasing the same products and brands they purchase.

SCALE NAME: Involvement (Activity)

SCALE DESCRIPTION:

A five-item, six-point Likert-type summated ratings scale that is supposed to measure the degree to which a person would willingly engage in an activity, without coercion or obligation. This scale was called Involvement by Unger (1981; Unger and Kernan 1983) and the activity investigated was subjective leisure.

SCALE ORIGIN:

Though relevant literature was surveyed prior to scale construction, the items themselves and certainly the scale as a whole are original to Unger (1981).

SAMPLES:

The scale was developed in one stage of the overall study and then used to test hypotheses in another stage. In the first stage the scale was administered by three different people to a total of **169** undergraduate business students at Miami University and the University of Cincinnati (Unger 1981). In the second stage the questionnaires were delivered and picked up by members of a Girl Scout troop. A quota sample of **160** adults living in the Cincinnati SMSA was used that balanced eight equal age by sex groups. However, the sample was representative of neither the Cincinnati SMSA nor the U.S. population as a whole, being composed mostly of white people (98%) of middle to upper socioeconomic status (84%).

RELIABILITY:

The final scale consists of items that remained after several tests of reliability. The tests were conducted for the scale in six different situations. Alpha values for the scale ranged from **.77** to **.86.** See Unger (1981) for more detailed information.

VALIDITY:

Factor analyses provided general support that the items tend to load together across samples and situations.

ADMINISTRATION:

The scale was self-administered by respondents in both stages of the survey described above. High scores on the scale indicate that respondents view some specified activity as so involving that seems like an escape from reality whereas low scores imply that respondents do not view an activity as being **absorbing**.

MAJOR FINDINGS:

The study by Unger (1981; Unger and Kernan 1983) examined dimensions of the subjective leisure experience across six different situations. **Perceived absorption** was found to be one of the primary determinants of subjective leisure across situations.

REFERENCES:

Unger, Lynette S. (1981), *Measure Validation in the Leisure Domain*, unpublished doctoral dissertation, University of Cincinnati.

———— and Jerome B. Kernan (1983), ''On the Meaning of Leisure: An Investigation of Some Determinants of the Subjective Experience,'' *JCR*, 9 (March), 381-391.

SCALE ITEMS: INVOLVEMENT (ACTIVITY)+

Strongly Agree	Agree	Somewhat Agree	Somewhat Disagree	Disagree	Strongly Disagree
6	5	4	3	2	1

1. It helps me to forget about the day's problems.
2. It totally absorbs me.
3. It is like ''getting away from it all.''
4. It makes me feel like I'm in another world.
5. I could get so involved that I would forget everything else.

+ The questionnaire described a situation for respondents and they were asked to respond to the statements as they felt about the situation.

SCALE NAME: Involvement (Body Weight)

SCALE DESCRIPTION:

A six-item, seven-point Likert-type scale measuring person's reported concern about his or her body weight.

SCALE ORIGIN:

The measure was developed by Oliver and Bearden (1985).

SAMPLES:

Analysis was based on **353** completed questionnaires from members of a bistate consumer panel. Subjects were selected to be representative of urban and suburban households with family income greater than $10,000. Ninety-one triers and 262 nontriers of a new, heavily promoted time-release diet suppressant responded. The average respondent was female (56%), white (89%), with some education beyond high school (70%), and in the $20,000 to $29,999 income category (25.5%).

RELIABILITY:

A reliability of **.85** was reported.

VALIDITY:

Confirmatory factor analysis was performed once, weak items were deleted, and the analysis was run again, resulting in higher overall factor loadings.

ADMINISTRATION:

Data were gathered through use of self- administered mail questionnaires. The method for calculating scale scores was not specified, but it is likely that higher scores on this scale suggest that a person worries a lot about his/her weight whereas lower scores imply that a person thinks very little about weight control.

MAJOR FINDINGS:

The purpose of the study was to examine the presence and operation of "crossover effects" in the Fishbein behavioral intention model under various moderating conditions. Evidence generally supporting the normative structure attitude crossover path was found; that is, a person's attitude toward a behavior is strengthened to the extent that relevant others are believed to agree with it. The moderator variable analysis provided little insight into the mechanisms people use to process normative information. However, attitude was found to be a stronger predictor of intention for persons high in **involvement**. This finding suggests a greater reliance on personal preference by highly involved persons.

#137 *Involvement (Body Weight)*

COMMENTS:

Though the scale had reasonably good internal consistency, the authors admitted that it might lack stability over time, samples, or product categories.

REFERENCE:

Oliver, Richard L. and William O. Bearden (1985), "Crossover Effects in the Theory of Reasoned Action: A Moderating Influence Attempt," *JCR*, 12 (December), 324-340.

SCALE ITEMS: INVOLVEMENT (BODY WEIGHT)

Agree   ____ : ____ : ____ : ____ : ____ : ____ : ____   Disagree
         7   6   5   4   3   2   1

1. I never worry about my weight. **(r)**
2. My weight is a concern in my life.
3. I worry about my weight more than most other people worry about their weight.
4. I never think about my weight. **(r)**
5. Others seem more concerned about their weight than I am about mine. **(r)**
6. I am always seeking information on weight control ideas.

SCALE NAME: Involvement (Enduring)

SCALE DESCRIPTION:

A four-item, summated ratings scale measuring the enduring and intrinsic (rather than situational) relevance of an object to a person. The object in the Slama and Tashchian (1987) study was shampoo. Stapel, Likert, and semantic differential versions of the scale were developed and tested.

SCALE ORIGIN:

The scale was original to Slama and Tashchian (1987), though they referred to the work of Houston and Rothschild (1977) to help generate the items.

SAMPLES:

Systematic area sampling was used to gather data from a sample of 98 people in a southeastern city. The questionnaires were personally delivered and picked up. Attempts were made to have the sample be as representative of the city's population as possible. Comparison of the sample and census data indicated that the former was representative in sex and age but was biased upward in income and had a greater proportion of white people.

RELIABILITY:

Alpha values of .501, .567, and .633 were reported by Slama and Tashchian (1987) for the Likert, semantic differential, and Stapel versions of the scale, respectively.

VALIDITY:

Convergent and discriminant validity was estimated by both the multitrait and multimethod matrix approaches, as well as the linear structural equations analysis approach. The authors interpret the evidence as indicating that the scales were reasonably valid. For example, the Stapel version of the enduring involvement scale had correlations of .735 and .725 with the Likert and semantic differential versions, respectively. The semantic differential and Likert versions had a correlation of .697.

ADMINISTRATION:

The questionnaires were self-administered by respondents in their homes. Numerical responses to the items are summed. High scores indicate that respondents have a strong personal involvement with the object (shampoo). Low scores suggest that the object has little importance to respondents.

MAJOR FINDINGS:

The purpose of the Slama and Tashchian (1987) study was to assess the validity of the tripartite classification of involvement. That is, it examined whether there are three types of involvement: one internal to the individual (enduring), one external (situational), and one that is a combination of the other two (response). The findings appear to support the model but indicate that, at least for shampoo purchases, situational involvement has the most influence on response involvement and **enduring involvement** has little impact. Specifically for **enduring involvement**, the structural equations analysis indicated that it was measured best by the Likert, followed closely by the Stapel, and then the semantic differential scale.

COMMENTS:

Each version of the scale had low internal consistency, which implies that more work is needed on the items themselves rather than the method of scaling used.

REFERENCES:

Houston, Michael J. and Michael L. Rothschild (1977), ''A Paradigm for Research on Consumer Involvement,'' unpublished paper, Graduate School of Business, University of Wisconsin, Madison.

Slama, Mark E. and Armen Tashchian (1987), ''Validating the S-O-R Paradigm for Consumer Involvement with a Convenience Good,'' *JAMS*, 15 (Spring), 36-45.

SCALE ITEMS: INVOLVEMENT (ENDURING) +

Likert Scale Items:
1. I do not know much about _____ . **(r)**
2. I am not familiar with many brands of _____ . **(r)**
3. My choice of _____ is relevant to my self image.
4. _____ is relevant to my values or goals in life.

+ The graphic scales for each of the three versions of the measure were not specified in the article. The items used in the semantic differential and Stapel scale versions are assumed to be phrases based on the sentences above. The generic name of the product should be placed in the blanks.

SCALE NAME: Involvement (Enduring)

SCALE DESCRIPTION:

A 20-item, seven-point semantic differential scale measuring the enduring and intrinsic (rather than situational) relevance of an object to a person. The scale is easily customized to measure involvement with a product category, a particular brand, an ad for a particular brand, or a particular purchase decision. The scale was referred to as Personal Involvement Inventory (PII) by the originator (Zaichkowsky 1985). A nine-item version of the scale was used by Lichtenstein, Bloch, and Black (1988) with reference to running shoes.

SCALE ORIGIN:

Though previous research was reviewed and may have provided ideas for scale items, the scale as a unit was generated and tested first by Zaichkowsky (1985). Construction of the scale was based on four datasets with 286 undergraduate psychology students, two datasets with 49 MBA students, and two datasets with 57 clerical and administrative staff members.

The stability of the measure was checked over two subject groups for four products, producing test-retest correlations from .88 to .93. Internal consistency calculated with the same data ranged from .95 to .97 (Chronbach's alpha).

Content validity was demonstrated through use of expert judges at two points, first by reducing the list of word pairs to those most appropriate for measuring the construct and second by successful classification of open-ended statements from subjects.

Criterion validity was examined by demonstrating the similarity between subjects' average involvement levels with products and the expected degree of involvement based on previous studies. Construct validity was checked for three products by noting the association between subjects' scale scores and their statements of behavior expected to reflect involvement. For each of the three products, there was a positive relationship between scale scores and responses to statements.

SAMPLES:

Subjects for the experiment by Celsi and Olson (1988) were **91** undergraduate students, **10** graduate students, **20** adult residents of the local community, and **15** present or former members of university tennis teams. Subjects' ages ranged from 17 to 79 years, with a mean of 23 years. Fifty-one percent of the sample were female.

Lichtenstein, Bloch, and Black (1988) mailed questionnaires to 1800 participants in a regional running event. Analysis was based on the **452** responses that were received within five weeks. In comparison with the area's general population, the respondents were more likely to be younger and male, with higher education and income.

RELIABILITY:

No test of reliability was reported by Celsi and Olson (1988). The reliability (LISREL estimate?) of the condensed version of the scale used by Lichtenstein, Bloch, and Black (1988) was calculated to be **.93**.

VALIDITY:

No test of validity was reported by Celsi and Olson (1988) or Lichtenstein, Bloch, and Black (1988).

ADMINISTRATION:

The scale was given by Celsi and Olson (1988) as a screening instrument to 400 college students and adults in unspecified settings, whereas Lichtenstein, Bloch, and Black (1988) administered it in a mail survey along with many other measures. Scores were calculated by summing numerical responses to items, with reverse coding where necessary. The closer a score was to 20 (the full version), the more it suggested that a person had little involvement with the object. The closer a score was to 140, the more it implied that a person was very interested and personally involved with the object. The object in the Celsi and Olson (1988) study was playing tennis, whereas in the study by Lichtenstein, Bloch, and Black (1988) it was running shoes.

MAJOR FINDINGS:

The purpose of the Celsi and Olson (1988) study was to examine the effects of enduring and situational **involvement** on felt **involvement** as well as on information processing of print advertising. The authors found that subjects' knowledge of tennis was significantly correlated with their **enduring involvement** with the sport. Both enduring and situational **involvement** affected felt **involvement,** with the former having a substantially larger impact. **Enduring involvement** was also significantly related to time spent processing ads and cognitive effort exerted during the processing of ads.

Lichtenstein, Bloch, and Black (1988) examined the cognitive tradeoffs consumers make between price and product quality. The findings indicated a positive relationship between product **involvement** and price-quality inferences as well as price acceptability level, but involvement was inversely correlated with price consciousness.

COMMENTS:

Zaichkowsky (1985) admitted that a smaller number of items might be almost as reliable as the 20-item version, but warned against haphazardly reducing the number of items. She also pointed out that though the scale could be used for various purposes, her work had focused mainly on demonstrating its quality for product involvement. More research was called for to verify its quality for other objects such as ads and purchase decisions. Lichtenstein, Bloch, and Black (1988) do not say how they determined which items of the full scale to use in their condensed version.

REFERENCES:

Celsi, Richard L. and Jerry C. Olson (1988), ''The Role of Involvement in Attention and Comprehension Processes,'' *JCR*, 15 (September), 210-224.

Lichtenstein, Donald R., Peter H. Bloch, and William C. Black (1988), ''Correlates of Price Acceptability,'' *JCR*, 15 (September), 243-252.

Zaichkowsky, Judith L. (1985), ''Measuring the Involvement Construct,'' *JCR*, 12 (December), 341-352.

SCALE ITEMS: INVOLVEMENT (ENDURING)

(name of object)

	1 : 2 : 3 : 4 : 5 : 6 : 7	
important	1 : 2 : 3 : 4 : 5 : 6 : 7	unimportant (r)*
of no concern to me	1 : 2 : 3 : 4 : 5 : 6 : 7	of concern to me*
irrelevant	1 : 2 : 3 : 4 : 5 : 6 : 7	relevant*
means a lot to me	1 : 2 : 3 : 4 : 5 : 6 : 7	means nothing to me (r)*
useless	1 : 2 : 3 : 4 : 5 : 6 : 7	useful*
valuable	1 : 2 : 3 : 4 : 5 : 6 : 7	worthless(r)*
trivial	1 : 2 : 3 : 4 : 5 : 6 : 7	fundamental
beneficial	1 : 2 : 3 : 4 : 5 : 6 : 7	not beneficial(r)*
matters to me	1 : 2 : 3 : 4 : 5 : 6 : 7	doesn't matter(r)
uninterested	1 : 2 : 3 : 4 : 5 : 6 : 7	interested
significant	1 : 2 : 3 : 4 : 5 : 6 : 7	insignificant(r)
vital	1 : 2 : 3 : 4 : 5 : 6 : 7	superfluous(r)
boring	1 : 2 : 3 : 4 : 5 : 6 : 7	interesting
unexciting	1 : 2 : 3 : 4 : 5 : 6 : 7	exciting
appealing	1 : 2 : 3 : 4 : 5 : 6 : 7	unappealing(r)
mundane	1 : 2 : 3 : 4 : 5 : 6 : 7	fascinating
essential	1 : 2 : 3 : 4 : 5 : 6 : 7	nonessential(r)*

undesirable   ____ : ____ : ____ : ____ : ____ : ____ : ____   desirable
                   1   2   3   4   5   6   7

wanted   ____ : ____ : ____ : ____ : ____ : ____ : ____   unwanted**(r)**
                   1   2   3   4   5   6   7

not needed   ____ : ____ : ____ : ____ : ____ : ____ : ____   needed*****
                   1   2   3   4   5   6   7

* Items used in condensed version of scale by Lichtenstein, Bloch, and Black (1988).

SCALE NAME: Involvement (Product)

SCALE DESCRIPTION:

A four-item, eight-point Likert-type summated ratings scale measuring the degree of involvement a consumer has with calculators. Zinkhan and Locander (1988) referred to this measure as Product Interest. The scale used by Zinkhan, Locander, and Leigh (1986) had only three items.

SCALE ORIGIN:

The scales used to measure product involvement by Zinkhan, Locander, and Leigh (1986) and by Zinkhan and Locander (1988) appear to be very similar though the actual items are not specifically reported in either article. The items appear to be have been developed by those authors as no other origination information is provided.

SAMPLES:

A total of **420** people were used in the study by Zinkhan, Locander, and Leigh (1986) and were recruited as part of ongoing copytesting activities by an advertising agency. The subjects were divided into 20 equal groups and paid for their services after the last of three sessions. No more is reported about the sample used by Zinkhan and Locander (1988) except that it was composed of **260** students.

RELIABILITY:

Alpha values of **.90** and **.873** were reported for the scale by Zinkhan, Locander, and Leigh (1986) and Zinkhan and Locander (1988), respectively.

VALIDITY:

No examination of scale validity was reported in either article.

ADMINISTRATION:

The scale was administered similarly in both studies in that they both involved multiple sessions over several weeks and the scale was self-administered along with other measures in a session before the stimulus ad was shown. Higher scores on the scale suggest that respondents have much stronger interest and involvement with some specified product than respondents with lower scores.

MAJOR FINDINGS:

Both studies made use of a new multi- dimensional analysis technique: ESSCA (External Single-Set Component Analysis). Zinkhan, Locander, and Leigh (1986) used it to examine the dimensionality of several predictors of ad recall and recognition measures. Two dimensions were found, one more affective and the other more cognitive. **Product involvement** loaded with the former but not with the latter.

Zinkhan and Locander (1988) used the technique to investigate four advertising recall measures and found that two dimensions were actually being measured: favorable recall of ad features and brand name recall. **Involvement** with the product category (calculators) was split in its loading on the two dimensions, but appeared to be more related to recall of the ad than to recall of the brand name itself.

REFERENCES:

Zinkhan, George M. and William B. Locander (1988), "ESSCA: A Multi-dimensional Analysis Tool for Marketing Research," *JAMS*, 16 (Spring), 36-46.

_____, _____, and James H. Leigh (1986), "Dimensional Relations of Aided Recall and Recognition," *JA*, 15 (1), 38- 46.

SCALE ITEMS: INVOLVEMENT (PRODUCT) +

Very Little ____ : ____ : ____ : ____ : ____ : ____ : ____ : ____ Very Much

1   2   3   4   5   6   7   8

Using the above scale, please indicate how much you:
1. use _____.
2. are involved with _____.
3. are a _____ expert.
4. are interested in _____, relative to other people.

+ Items like 1, 2, and 4 were apparently used by Zinkhan, Locander, and Leigh (1986). The exact phrasing of the items as well as the scales' verbal anchors were not provided in either article but are reconstructed here on the basis of the descriptions given.

SCALE NAME: Involvement (Product)

SCALE DESCRIPTION:

A nine-item, five-point Likert-type summated ratings scale measuring a consumer's degree of differentiation, familiarity, importance, and commitment for a specified product category, **not** brand. Though not clearly stated by Korgaonkar and Moschis (1982), there were apparently differences in the verbal anchors depending on the item, as noted below.

SCALE ORIGIN:

The scale is similar to one described by Bowen and Chaffee (1974). The latter was a seven-item, five-point Likert-type scale that purportedly measured one's degree of **product involvement**. No assessment of reliability was reported for the scale. Evidence for face validity was found in a pretest and replicated in the main study. Using the scale, the authors found a small but significant difference between high- and low-involvement group evaluation means for ads that do not use pertinent (objective) appeals. In contrast, the difference was substantial when pertinent ads were being evaluated. The authors concluded that pertinent ads are more effective than nonpertinent ads, especially when consumer involvement with the product is high.

SAMPLES:

In a series of pretests and a main experiment, data were collected from students enrolled in a large section of an introductory marketing course at a large urban university. **Eighty-four** students participated in the main experiment.

RELIABILITY:

Alpha values were calculated for 10 product categories and were reported as ranging from **.43** to **.65** (n=75). The study specifically focused on two categories, radios (high involvement) and soft drinks (low involvement), for which alpha values of **.55** and **.53**, respectively, were calculated.

VALIDITY:

The authors concluded that the scale had face validity and that the results of the factor analysis were similar to those in the Bowen and Chaffee (1974) study.

ADMINISTRATION:

The scale was given to subjects on paper in a classroom setting. Scores were calculated by summing numerical responses to the nine items. High scores suggest subjects are very involved with the product category whereas low scores imply that the product is unfamiliar and/or unimportant to them.

MAJOR FINDINGS:

Korgaonkar and Moschis (1982) investigated the effects of cognitive dissonance, expectations, and product performance on product evaluations. The results indicate that **product**

involvement acts as a moderator in the post- decision product evaluation process. Specifically, there is a positive relationship between expectations and product evaluations for high involvement products but a negative relationship for low involvement products.

COMMENTS:

The internal consistency of the scale is unacceptably low, most likely because the factor analysis indicates that it taps into not one, but four, constructs. The scale should not be used in its present form without modification and retesting.

REFERENCES:

Bowen, Lawrence and Steven H. Chaffee (1974), ''Product Involvement and Pertinent Advertising Appeals,'' *Journalism Quarterly*, 51 (Winter), 613-621, 644.

Korgaonkar, Pradeep K. and George P. Moschis (1982), ''An Experimental Study of Cognitive Dissonance, Product Involvement, Expectations, Performance and Consumer Judgement of Product Performance,'' *JA*, 11 (3), 32-44.

SCALE ITEMS: INVOLVEMENT (PRODUCT)+

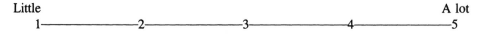

Little   A lot

1————————2————————3————————4————————5

1. Degree of substitution within brands
2. Degree of similarity of brands
3. Number of brands available
4. Differences in prices within brands
5. Differences in performances within brands
6. Importance of getting the brand I want
7. Number of store/dealer brands available
8. Willingness to discard the chosen brand after receiving discrepant information
9. Willingness to buy another brand if the preferred brand is not available

+ Korgaonkar and Moschis (1982) did not report the verbal anchors for any of these items. In addition to these items, subjects must be told which specific product category they are to evaluate.

SCALE NAME: Involvement (Purchase Decision)

SCALE DESCRIPTION:

A three-item, seven-point summated semantic differential rating scale measuring the degree of importance a person places on a purchase decision for some product and the amount of attention devoted to it.

SCALE ORIGIN:

The scale was constructed for the study reported by Ratchford (1987).

SAMPLES:

The version of the scale provided here was used in three preliminary studies and one final study reported by Ratchford (1987). The preliminary studies were mall- intercept interviews. The sample for the final study was composed of the **1792** adult members of the Market Facts mail panel who provided responses to the questionnaire.

RELIABILITY:

Alpha values of .81 (n = 30), .74 (n = 249), and .75 (n = 50) were calculated for the scale in the preliminary studies by Ratchford (1987). The scale was reported to have an alpha of **.77** in the final study.

VALIDITY:

Among the variety of evidence provided by Ratchford (1987) for the validity of the scale was that of criterion validity. Ten products in the Ratchford study had also been a examined by Zaichkowsky (1985). The correlation of the average involvement scores for the two studies was .76 (p < .01). Discriminant validity was not quite as strong, however, because in a factor analysis of involvement, think, and feel items, most of the think and two of the feel items loaded on the involvement factor also.

ADMINISTRATION:

The scale was self-administered in the final study by Ratchford (1987) along with other measures. Higher scores on the scale indicate that consumers are highly involved with their decisions to purchase some specified product whereas lower scores suggest that they are not interested or paying much attention to some purchase decision.

MAJOR FINDINGS:

The purpose of the study by Ratchford (1987) was to publicize research done by the Foote Cone and Belding agency in its development and testing of a thinking/feeling grid. Scores on the **involvement** scale and a think/feel scale were calculated for 254 products in the main study. In the article, the results for 60 products were plotted in a four-cell matrix that had degree of involvement as one axis and think/feel as the other axis. The plot was described by the author as being "generally intuitive" (p. 30) as most products were in a cell of the grid one would expect.

REFERENCES:

Ratchford, Brian T. (1987), "New Insights About the FCB Grid," *JAR*, 27 (August/September), 24-38.

Zaichkowsky, Judith L. (1985), "Measuring the Involvement Construct," *JCR*, 12 (December), 341-352.

SCALE ITEMS: INVOLVEMENT (PURCHASE DECISION)

Please rate the process of choosing a brand of _____ on each of the following scales. Please base your rating on your most recent choice of a brand of _____.

1. very important decision   ____ : ____ : ____ : ____ : ____ : ____ : ____   very unimportant decision
         7   6   5   4   3   2   1

2. decision requires a lot of thought   ____ : ____ : ____ : ____ : ____ : ____ : ____   decision requires little thought
         7   6   5   4   3   2   1

3. a lot to lose if you choose the wrong brand   ____ : ____ : ____ : ____ : ____ : ____ : ____   little to lose if you choose the wrong brand
         7   6   5   4   3   2   1

SCALE NAME: Involvement (Response)

SCALE DESCRIPTION:

A five-item, summated ratings scale measuring the relevance of an object to a person due to the combined influences of enduring and situational **involvement**. The object in the Slama and Tashchian (1987) study was shampoo. Stapel, Likert, and semantic differential versions of the scale were developed and tested.

SCALE ORIGIN:

The scale was original to Slama and Tashchian (1987), though they referred to the work of Houston and Rothschild (1977) to help generate the items.

SAMPLES:

Systematic area sampling was used to gather data from a sample of **98** people in a southeastern city. The questionnaires were personally delivered and picked up. Attempts were made to have the sample be as representative of the city's population as possible. Comparison of the sample and census data indicated that the former was representative in sex and age but was biased upward in income and had a greater proportion of white people.

RELIABILITY:

Alpha values of **.651**, **.681**, and **.813** were reported by Slama and Tashchian (1987) for the Likert, semantic differential, and Stapel versions of the scale, respectively.

VALIDITY:

Convergent and discriminant validity was estimated by both the multitrait and multimethod matrix approaches as well as the linear structural equations analysis approach. The authors interpret the evidence as indicating that the scales were reasonably valid. For example, the Stapel version of the situational **involvement** scale had correlations of **.772** and **.664** with the Likert and semantic differential versions, respectively. The semantic differential and Likert versions had a correlation of **.673**.

ADMINISTRATION:

The questionnaires were self-administered by respondents in their homes. Numerical responses to the items are summed. High scores indicate that respondents have strong **involvement** with the object (shampoo). Low scores suggest that the object has little importance to respondents.

MAJOR FINDINGS:

The purpose of the Slama and Tashchian (1987) study was to assess the validity of the tripartite classification of **involvement**. That is, it examined whether there are three types of **involvement**: one internal to the individual (enduring), one external (situational), and one that is a combination of the other two (response). The findings appear to support the model but indicate that, at least for shampoo purchases, situational **involvement** has the most influence on **response involvement** and enduring **involvement** has little impact. Specifically for **response involvement,** the structural equations analysis indicated that it was measured best by the Likert scale, followed by the Stapel scale, with the semantic differential being the weakest alternative.

REFERENCES:

Houston, Michael J. and Michael L. Rothschild (1977), ''A Paradigm for Research on Consumer Involvement,'' unpublished paper, Graduate School of Business, University of Wisconsin, Madison.

Slama, Mark E. and Armen Tashchian (1987), ''Validating the S-O-R Paradigm for Consumer Involvement with a Convenience Good,'' *JAMS*, 15 (Spring), 36-45.

SCALE ITEMS: INVOLVEMENT (RESPONSE) +

1. In purchasing shampoo I feel that ingredients which give my hair body are highly important.
2. In purchasing shampoo I feel that how well it cleans is highly important.
3. In purchasing shampoo I feel that how it smells is not important. **(r)**
4. In purchasing shampoo I feel that proper pH balance is highly important.
5. In purchasing shampoo I feel that how well it conditions is not highly important. **(r)**

+ The graphic scales for each of the three versions of the measure were not specified in the article. The items used in the semantic differential and Stapel scale versions are assumed to be phrases based on the sentences above that were used in the Likert scale version.

SCALE NAME: Involvement (Shopping)

SCALE DESCRIPTION:

A nine-item, six-point, Likert-type summated ratings scale from strongly disagree (1) to strongly agree (6). The scale measures a person's degree of interest in a variety of shopping-related activities. Referred to as Shopping Enjoyment by Lumpkin (1985). See also Hawes and Lumpkin (1984) for a scale that combines two items from this measure with two from a clothing interest scale.

SCALE ORIGIN:

It is not clear where the items originated or where the scale was first used as a multi-item summated ratings scale.

SAMPLES:

Lumpkin (1985) analyzed data collected from a sample drawn from the Market Facts Consumer Mail Panel. A total of 2854 completed questionnaires were received, but Lumpkin focused just on **373** respondents who indicated they were 65 years of age or older.

RELIABILITY:

An alpha of **.8303** was reported by Lumpkin (1985).

VALIDITY:

Factor analysis indicated the items loaded together.

ADMINISTRATION:

Lumpkin (1985) gathered data through self-administered mail questionnaires. Scale scores are calculated by averaging numerical responses to individual items. A score of 6 means that a person enjoys shopping whereas a 1 suggests the consumer does not want to be any more involved in shopping than necessary.

MAJOR FINDINGS:

Elderly consumers were cluster analyzed by Lumpkin (1985) and **shopping involvement** discriminated somewhat between the three groups, though the level of statistical significance was not reported. The group with the highest mean on the scale was the most socially active and the most likely to be fashion opinion leaders and innovators. The group with the lowest mean score appeared to be much less active and involved all around.

COMMENTS:

Though the reported internal consistency is acceptable, low factor scores of several of the items and findings in others studies suggest that the nine items may not always load together as one construct. For example, items 5 and 6 could easily be constructed as shopping innovativeness measures. If a shorter or "purer" measure of shopping involvement is desired, items 7 through 9 are the best subset.

REFERENCES:

Hawes, Jon M. and James R. Lumpkin (1984), "Understanding the Outshopper," *JAMS*, 12 (Fall), 200-218.

Lumpkin, James R. (1985), "Shopping Orientation Segmentation of the Elderly Consumer," *JAMS*, 13 (Spring), 271-289.

SCALE ITEMS: INVOLVMENT (SHOPPING)

Strongly Disagree	Disagree	Slightly Disagree	Slightly Agree	Agree	Strongly Agree
1	2	3	4	5	6

1. I like to go shopping with a friend.
2. When I talk to my friends, shopping is a topic of conversation.
3. I enjoy going to regional shopping centers.
4. I often combine shopping with lunch or dinner at a restaurant.
5. When a new store opens, I among the first to try it.
6. I like to try new and different places to shop.
7. I get a psychological lift from shopping.
8. Shopping gives me a chance to get out and do something.
9. I am interested in shopping.

SCALE NAME: Involvement (Situational)

SCALE DESCRIPTION:

A four-item, summated ratings scale measuring the situation-specific (not enduring) relevance of an object to a person. The object in the Slama and Tashchian (1987) study was shampoo. Stapel, Likert, and semantic differential versions of the scale were developed and tested.

SCALE ORIGIN:

The scale was original to Slama and Tashchian (1987), though they referred to the work of Houston and Rothschild (1977) to help generate the items.

SAMPLES:

Systematic area sampling was used to gather data from a sample of **98** people in a southeastern city. The questionnaires were personally delivered and picked up. Attempts were made to have the sample be as representative of the city's population as possible. Comparison of the sample and census data indicated that the former was representative in sex and age but was biased upward in income and had a greater proportion of white people.

RELIABILITY:

Alpha values of **.428**, **.442**, and **.406** were reported by Slama and Tashchian (1987) for the Likert, semantic differential, and Stapel versions of the scale, respectively.

VALIDITY:

Convergent and discriminant validity was estimated by both the multitrait and multimethod matrix approaches as well as the linear structural equations analysis approach. The authors interpret the evidence as indicating that the scales were reasonably valid. For example, the Stapel version of the situational involvement scale had correlations of **.61** and **.628** with the Likert and semantic differential versions, respectively. The semantic differential and Likert versions had a correlation of **.624**.

ADMINISTRATION:

The questionnaires were self-administered by respondents in their homes. Numerical responses to the items are summed. High scores indicate that a particular situation evokes a strong **involvement** with the object (shampoo). Low scores suggest that the object has little importance to respondents despite the situation.

MAJOR FINDINGS:

The purpose of the Slama and Tashchian (1987) study was to assess the validity of the tripartite classification of involvement. That is, it examined whether there are three types of **involvement:** one internal to the individual (enduring), one external (situational), and one that is a combination of the other two (response). The findings appear to support the model but indicate that, at least for shampoo purchases, **situational involvement** has the most influence on response involvement and enduring **involvement** has little impact. Specifically for **situational involvement**, the structural equations analysis indicated that it was measured best by the semantic differential scale, though none of the measures was particularly strong.

COMMENTS:

Each version of the scale had extremely low internal consistency, which implies that more work is needed on the items themselves rather than the method of scaling used. In fact, with such low reliability, the validity of the measures is in serious question.

REFERENCES:

Houston, Michael J. and Michael L. Rothschild (1977), ''A Paradigm for Research on Consumer Involvement,'' unpublished paper, Graduate School of Business, University of Wisconsin, Madison.

Slama, Mark E. and Armen Tashchian (1987), ''Validating the S-O-R Paradigm for Consumer Involvement with a Convenience Good,'' *JAMS*, 15 (Spring), 36-45.

SCALE ITEMS: INVOLVEMENT (SITUATIONAL) +

1. In purchasing a _____ I am very concerned with what others might think of my choice.
2. In purchasing a _____ I am not very concerned with getting the type of product performance and features I want.
3. In purchasing _____ I feel most brands are equally acceptable.
4. The cost of _____ as compared to other products is low.

+ The graphic scales for each of the three versions of the measure were not specified in the article. The items used in the semantic differential and Stapel scale versions are assumed to be phrases based on the sentences above. Also, the authors did not indicate whether any of the items should be reverse coded before calculation of scale scores. The generic name of the product should be placed in the blanks.

SCALE NAME: Involvement (Store)

SCALE DESCRIPTION:

The scale measures the degree of importance a person places on a variety of department store attributes. Arora (1982) used a 14-item, nine-point scale and subsequently a 15-item, seven-point version denoted IMP (Arora 1985).

SCALE ORIGIN:

The items for the scale represent store attributes offered by Hansen and Deutscher (1977-78) and King and Ring (1980). The scale itself appears to have been reported first by Arora (1982).

SAMPLES:

Arora (1982) systematically sampled adult men and women at a mall. Different days and times were used to gather data to ensure a representative sample, but no attempt was made to make the sample representative of particular population characteristics. Analysis was based on **190** usable questionnaires (51 from men and 139 from women). In the second study (Arora 1985), a similar sample was gathered, resulting in **273** completed questionnaires. Interviews were conducted at two shopping malls in a medium-sized midwestern city. Both men and women (21 years of age and older) were contacted in approximate proportion to their presence during interviewing days.

RELIABILITY:

An alpha of .**68** was reported by Arora (1985). No mention of reliability was made in the second article (Arora 1982).

VALIDITY:

It is not clear how or if Arora (1982) made a check of validity. He estimated nomological validity in the second study (1985) by noting the pattern of correlations between scores on the Involvement scale and price consciousness, shopping proneness, frequency of shopping, purchase satisfaction, and confidence. Though the correlations were low, they were positive and significant in each case as hypothesized.

ADMINISTRATION:

Data were collected in both studies through personal interviews. Calculation of scale scores was based on the total of the numerical responses made to individual scale items. Higher scores indicate that consumers are very involved with retail stores whereas lower scores indicate that consumers place little importance on a variety of store attributes.

MAJOR FINDINGS:

On the basis of pairwise comparisons as well as preference rankings, Arora (1982) used MDS to analyze data about eight department stores. He found weak support for the notion of significant differences in the cognitive structures of **involved** versus **uninvolved shoppers**. Subsequently (1985), he found low though significant and positive correlations between retail **store involvement** and price consciousness, shopping proneness, frequency of shopping, purchase satisfaction, and confidence.

COMMENTS:

Factor analysis should be performed to confirm that the items are, indeed, loading on a single factor.

REFERENCES:

Arora, Raj (1982), "Consumer Involvement in Retail Store Positioning," *JAMS*, 10 (Spring), 109-124.

_____ (1985), "Involvement: Its Measurement for Retail Store Research," *JAMS*, 13 (Spring), 229-241.

Hansen, Robert A. and Terry Deutscher (1977-78), "An Empirical Investigation of Attribute Importance in Retail Store Selection," *Journal of Retailing*, 53 (Winter), 59-72, 95.

King, Charles W. and Lawernce J. Ring (1980), Market Positioning Across Retail Fashion Institutions: A Comparative Analysis of Store Types," *Journal of Retailing*, 56 (Spring), 37-55.

SCALE ITEMS: INVOLVEMENT (STORE)+

Not Important at All						Extremely Important
1————	—2————	—3————	—4————	—5————	—6————	—7

1. Nationally known brands
2. High quality
3. Low prices
4. Helpful sales people
5. Attractive decor/displays
6. Fast checkout
7. Easy to return/exchange merchandise
8. Large overall assortment/selection
9. Convenient to get to/from home
10. Convenient charge/credit account
11. Good parking facilities
12. Lay away
13. Friends shop there
14. Clean store
15. Best value for money
16. Latest, fashionable products
17. Availability of refreshments/lunch
18. Knowledgeable sales people

+ The other verbal anchors were not identified in the articles. Also, a nine-point graphic scale was used in the first study (Arora 1982). The two studies had the first 11 items in common (or essentially the same items.) Items 11 to 14 were used just in the first study whereas items 15 to 18 were used just in the second study.

SCALE NAME: Involvement (Television)

SCALE DESCRIPTION:

A three-item, six-point Likert-type summated ratings scale from strongly disagree (1) to strongly agree (6). The scale measures the degree of importance television has for a person.

SCALE ORIGIN:

Though Rahtz, Sirgy and Meadow (1989) may have developed items for the scale by examining previous research, the specific items and scales are original to their study.

SAMPLES:

The sample was drawn by systematic random sampling of a mailing list maintained by a government-sponsored regional agency on aging. People's names were added to the list when social security records indicated they had reached the age of 60. The respondents in the sample were all living in a three county area of Virginia. Analysis was based on the **752** usable questionnaires returned.

RELIABILITY:

An alpha of **.66** was reported for the scale.

VALIDITY:

Factor analysis indicated the items loaded together.

ADMINISTRATION:

The scale was administered as part of larger mail questionnaire. Scale scores are calculated by averaging numerical responses to items. Higher scores indicate respondents are highly **involved with television** whereas lower scores suggest that television is not very important to them as a source of entertainment.

MAJOR FINDINGS:

The purpose of the study was to examine the relationships between elderly people's television usage and a variety of demographic and psychographic variables. Greater **television involvement** was most associated with low education levels, a home orientation, and a low sense of morale.

COMMENTS:

Because of the low internal consistency, some caution should be exercised in use of this scale as it is. The addition of a few relevant items might improve it somewhat.

REFERENCE:

Rahtz, Don R., M. Joseph Sirgy, and H. Lee Meadow (1989), ''The Elderly Audience: Correlates of Television Orientation,'' *JA* (3), 9-20.

SCALE ITEMS: INVOLVEMENT (TELEVISION)

Strongly Disagree	Disagree	Slightly Disagree	Slightly Agree	Agree	Strongly Agree
1	2	3	4	5	6

1. Television is my primary form of entertainment.
2. Magazines are more interesting than television. **(r)**
3. I frequently watch daytime television.

SCALE NAME: Involvement With Education (Enduring)

SCALE DESCRIPTION:

A five-item, six-point summated ratings scale measuring the enduring and intrinsic (rather than situational) relevance of college to a person. The object in the Arora (1982) study was a university and he developed and tested Stapel, Likert, and semantic differential versions of the scale.

SCALE ORIGIN:

The scale was original to Arora (1982), though he referred to the work of Scott (1965) as well as that of Houston and Rothschild (1977) to help develop the concept and specific items.

SAMPLES:

Subjects were **96** upperclassmen enrolled in business courses at a midsized private university. The questionnaire was administered to groups ranging in size from 20 to 40 persons.

RELIABILITY:

Alpha values of **.79**, **.69**, and **.74** were reported by Arora (1982) for the Stapel, Likert, and semantic differential versions of the scale, respectively.

VALIDITY:

Convergent and discriminant validity was estimated by both the multitrait and multimethod matrix approaches as well as the linear structural equations analysis approach. Though not completely supportive and consistent, most evidence indicated that the scales were reasonably valid. For example, the semantic differential version of the enduring involvement scale had correlations of **.84** and **.8** with the Stapel and Likert versions, respectively. The Stapel and Likert versions had a correlation of **.77**.

ADMINISTRATION:

The scale was given to students as part of a self-report questionnaire and apparently was filled out in an classroom setting. Numerical responses to the items are summed. High scores indicate that respondents have a strong **personal involvement with the object (a university)**. Low scores suggest that the object has little importance to respondents.

MAJOR FINDINGS:

The purpose of the Arora (1982) study was to assess the validity of the tripartite classification of involvement. That is, the study examined whether there are three types of involvement: one internal to the individual (enduring), one external (situational), and one that is a combination of the other two (response). The findings appear to support the model except that no direct relationship was found between situational and response involvement. Situational involvement appeared to work through **enduring involvement** to indirectly influence response involvement. Specifically for **enduring involvement**, the evidence indicated that it was measured best by the semantic differential, followed by the Stapel and then the Likert scales.

REFERENCES:

Arora, Raj (1982), ''Validation of an S-O-R Model for Situation, Enduring, and Response Components of Involvement,'' *JMR*, 19 (November), 505-516.

Houston, Michael J. and Michael L. Rothschild (1977), ''A Paradigm for Research on Consumer Involvement,'' unpublished paper, Graduate School of Business, University of Wisconsin, Madison.

Scott, William A. (1965), ''Personal Values Scales,'' in *Values and Organizations*. Chicago: Rand McNally and Company, 245-257.

SCALE ITEMS: INVOLVEMENT WITH EDUCATION (ENDURING) +

Strongly Disagree	Disagree	Slightly Disagree	Slightly Agree	Agree	Strongly Agree
1	2	3	4	5	6

1. I belive in studying hard to get good grades.
2. I am not the one to be contented with a ''gentlemanly C'' grade.
3. I am constantly involved in studying to become a well educated person.
4. I have an active interest in all scholarly things.
5. I like to keep abreast of current events.

+ These items were provided by Arora in personal correspondence, and he indicated that corresponding items were phrased for the semantic differential and Stapel scale versions.

SCALE NAME: Involvement With Education (Response)

SCALE DESCRIPTION:

A four-item, six-point summated ratings scale measuring the importance of college to a person due to the combined influences of enduring and situational involvement. The object in the Arora (1982) study was a university and he developed and tested Stapel, Likert, and semantic differential versions of the scale.

SCALE ORIGIN:

The scale was original to Arora (1982), though he referred to the work of Houston and Rothschild (1977) to help construct a classification system for attitude statements.

SAMPLES:

Subjects were **96** upperclassmen enrolled in business courses at a midsized private university. The questionnaire was administered to groups ranging in size from 20 to 40 persons.

RELIABILITY:

Alpha values of **.79**, **.86**, and **.7** were reported by Arora (1982) for the Stapel, Likert, and semantic differential versions of the scale, respectively.

VALIDITY:

Convergent and discriminant validity was estimated by both the multitrait and multimethod matrix approaches as well as the linear structural equations analysis approach. Though not completely supportive and consistent, most evidence indicated that the scales were reasonably valid. For example, the semantic differential version of the response involvement scale had correlations of .6 and .59 with the Stapel and Likert versions, respectively. The Stapel and Likert versions had a correlation of .49.

ADMINISTRATION:

The scale was given to students as part of a self-report questionnaire and apparently was filled out in an classroom setting. Numerical responses to the items are summed. High scores indicate that respondents have a strong involvement with the object (a university). Low scores suggest that the object has little importance to respondents.

MAJOR FINDINGS:

The purpose of the Arora (1982) study was to assess the validity of the tripartite classification of involvement. That is, the study examined whether there are three types of involvement: one internal to the individual (enduring), one external (situational), and one that is a combination of the other two (response). The findings appear to support the model except that no direct relationship was found between situational and **response involvement**. Situational involvement appeared to work through enduring involvement to indirectly influence **response involvement**. Specifically for **response involvement**, the evidence indicated that it was measured best by the semantic differential, followed by the Likert and then the Stapel scales.

REFERENCES:

Arora, Raj (1982), "Validation of an S-O-R Model for Situation, Enduring, and Response Components of Involvement," *JMR*, 19 (November), 505-516.

Houston, Michael J. and Michael L. Rothschild (1977), "A Paradign for Research on Consumer Involvement," unpublished paper, Graduate School of Business, University of Wisconsin, Madison.

SCALE ITEMS: INVOLVEMENT WITH EDUCATION (RESPONSE) +

Strongly Disagree	Disagree	Slightly Disagree	Slightly Agree	Agree	Strongly Agree
1	2	3	4	5	6

1. The quality of faculty is of great importance in selecting a school to attend.
2. The variety of courses offered by a school are important in the choice of a school to attend.
3. The small class size is quite important in the choice of a school.
4. The amount of individual assistance is of great importance in the selection of a school.

+ These items were provided by Arora in personal correspondence, and he indicated that corresponding items were phrased for the semantic differential and Stapel scale versions.

SCALE NAME: Involvement With Education (Situational)

SCALE DESCRIPTION:

> A four-item, six-point summated ratings scale measuring the situation-specific (rather than enduring) importance of a college to a person. The object in the Arora (1982) study was a university and he developed and tested Stapel, Likert, and semantic differential versions of the scale.

SCALE ORIGIN:

> The scale was original to Arora (1982), though he referred to the work of Houston and Rothschild (1977) to help construct a classification system for attitude statements.

SAMPLES:

> Subjects were **96** upperclassmen enrolled in business courses at a midsized private university. The questionnaire was administered to groups ranging in size from 20 to 40 persons.

RELIABILITY:

> Alpha values of **.7**, **.8**, and **.78** were reported by Arora (1982) for the Stapel, Likert, and semantic differential versions of the scale, respectively.

VALIDITY:

> Convergent and discriminant validity was estimated by both the multitrait and multimethod matrix approaches as well as the linear structural equations analysis approach. Though not completely supportive and consistent, most evidence indicated that the scales were reasonably valid. For example, the semantic differential version of the situational involvement scale had correlations of **.73** and **.55** with the Stapel and Likert versions, respectively. The Stapel and Likert versions had a correlation of **.65**.

ADMINISTRATION:

> The scale was given to students as part of a self-report questionnaire and apparently was filled out in a classroom setting. Numerical responses to the items are summed. High scores indicate that a particular situation evokes a strong involvement with the object (a university). Low scores suggest that the object has little importance to respondents despite the situation.

MAJOR FINDINGS:

> The purpose of the Arora (1982) study was to assess the validity of the tripartite classification of involvement. That is, the study examined whether there are three types of involvement: one internal to the individual (enduring), one external (situational), and one that is a combination of the other two (response). The findings appear to support the model except that no direct relationship was found between **situational** and response **involvement**. **Situational involvement** appeared to work through enduring involvement to indirectly

influence response involvement. Specifically for **situational involvement**, the evidence indicated that it was measured best by the Stapel scale, followed by the semantic differential and then the Likert scales.

REFERENCES:

Arora, Raj (1982), "Validation of an S-O-R Model for Situation, Enduring, and Response Components of Involvement," *JMR*, 19 (November), 505-516.

Houston, Michael J. and Michael L. Rothschild (1977), "A Paradigm for Research on Consumer Involvement," unpublished paper, Graduate School of Business, University of Wisconsin, Madison.

SCALE ITEMS: INVOLVEMENT WITH EDUCATION (SITUATIONAL) +

Strongly Disagree	Disagree	Slightly Disagree	Slightly Agree	Agree	Strongly Agree
1	2	3	4	5	6

1. _____ has a fine academic reputation.
2. Although expensive, the benefits of education at _____ are long lasting.
3. It is an honor to be a graduate from _____.
4. _____ takes personal interest in its student body.

+ These items were provided by Arora in personal correspondence, and he indicated that corresponding items were phrased for the semantic differential and Stapel scale versions. Further, the blanks were filled in by the name of the specific university studied.

SCALE NAME: Likelihood of Eating (Specified Food)

SCALE DESCRIPTION:

A two-item, seven-point semantic differential summated ratings scale measuring the perceived probability of eating some specified food.

SCALE ORIGIN:

The scale was apparently original to Stayman and Deshpande (1989).

SAMPLES:

A convenience sample of students was used in the study. Part of the students were recruited from a marketing department at a large West Coast university and the other part were members of undergraduate business organizations at a large southwestern university. The study gathered data just from students who identified themselves as Anglo-Americans (n = **195**), Chinese-Americans (n = **54**), or Mexican-Americans (n = **57**).

RELIABILITY:

An alpha of **.94** was reported for the scale.

VALIDITY:

No examination of scale validity was reported except that the items were selected after a pretest factor analysis.

ADMINISTRATION:

The scale was self-administered along with other measures as part of an experiment. The numerical responses to each item were averaged to calculate scale scores. Higher scores on the scale suggest that respondents find some specified food desirable and are likely to eat it whereas lower scores imply that they are unlikely to eat it.

MAJOR FINDINGS:

Social situation and felt-ethnicity were examined for their influence on food choices. The findings indicated that students had different perceptions of what were **likely** food choices depending on the social surroundings. Specifically, the Mexican and Chinese students indicated that choosing their respective ethnically familiar foods would be less **likely** when business associates were present (non-ethnic social surroundings) than when their parents were present (ethnic social surroundings).

REFERENCE:

Stayman, Douglas M. and Rohit Deshpande (1989), "Situational Ethnicity and Consumer Behavior," *JCR*, 16 (December), 361-371.

SCALE ITEMS: LIKELIHOOD OF EATING (SPECIFIED FOOD)

1. unlikely to eat   ___ : ___ : ___ : ___ : ___ : ___ : ___   likely to eat
                             1   2   3   4   5   6   7

2. undesirable   ___ : ___ : ___ : ___ : ___ : ___ : ___   desirable
                             1   2   3   4   5   6   7

SCALE NAME: Locus of Control

SCALE DESCRIPTION:

A three-item, five-point Likert-type summated ratings scale ranging from strongly disagree to strongly agree. The scale measures the degree to which a person attributes success to his or her own efforts versus fate or other forces.

SCALE ORIGIN:

The items for this scale were taken from Rotter (1966). His scale consisted of 23 pairs of opposing statements in a forced-choice format. Correlations between each set of items and the total scale score (minus that item) are reported for a sample composed of 200 men and 200 women, apparently psychology majors at Ohio State University. However, Rotter reports on several tests of the scale's reliability and validity being conducted with numerous samples. Internal consistency (Kuder-Richardson) was calculated to be .7 with the 400 Ohio State students and ranged from .65 to .79 with other samples. Factor analyses indicate there is one general factor. The author presents evidence supporting the scale's validity but it is not consistently strong, making assessment difficult.

SAMPLES:

Lumpkin and Hunt's (1989) sample was drawn from the Market Facts Consumer Mail Panel and focused on **789** respondents who indicated they were 65 years of age or older. The proportions of men and women were similar to those in the national population, but fewer of the men and more of the women in the sample were married. The sample was better educated and had a greater percentage still employed than was true nationally. The sample was composed of more people in lower income levels, but reasonably matched the elderly geographic distribution.

RELIABILITY:

An alpha of **.617** was reported by Lumpkin and Hunt (1989).

VALIDITY:

Factor analysis indicated that the items loaded together.

ADMINISTRATION:

Data was gathered through self-administered mail questionnaires. Scale scores were calculated by averaging numerical responses to individual items. A score of 5 indicates that a person has a strong internal locus of control whereas a 1 suggests that a person believes what happens is strongly determined by fate, luck, others' actions, etc. (external locus of control).

MAJOR FINDINGS:

The elderly were broken down into two groups by Lumpkin and Hunt (1989): those who were self-reliant in terms of transportation and those who were dependent on others. The self-reliant group exhibited a significantly stronger **internal locus of control** than the dependent group.

COMMENTS:

The low alpha suggests that further work should be done to improve the measure's stability, possibly by adding a few more pertinent items. Refer to Rotter (1966) for many other items that have been previously tested and used.

REFERENCES:

Lumpkin, James R. and James B. Hunt (1989), "Mobility as an Influence on Retail Patronage Behavior of the Elderly: Testing Conventional Wisdom," *JAMS*, 17 (Winter), 1-12.

Rotter, J. B. (1966), "Generalized Expectancies for Internal and External Control of Reinforcement," *Psychological Monographs: General and Applied*, 80 (1), Whole No. 609.

SCALE ITEMS: LOCUS OF CONTROL

Strongly Disagree	Disagree	Neutral	Agree	Strongly Agree
1	2	3	4	5

1. What happens is my own doing.
2. Getting people to do the right things depends upon ability not luck.
3. When I make plans, I am certain I can make them work.

SCALE NAME: Loyalty Proneness (Product)

SCALE DESCRIPTION:

A seven-item, seven-point Likert-type summated ratings scale measuring the degree to which a person reports being loyal to what he or she has been using rather than trying something new and/or different. This construct does not appear to be as specific as brand loyalty. It was referred to by Raju (1980) as Repetitive Behavior Proneness.

SCALE ORIGIN:

Though the items may have been drawn from previous work, the scale was developed along with six others by Raju (1980). An initial pool of 90 items related to exploratory behavior and lifestyle were compiled and then tested for low social desirability bias and high item-total correlations. Thirty-nine items were found to meet the criteria and were common to two separate samples. Items were grouped into seven categories on the basis of interitem correlations and subjective judgment.

SAMPLES:

Data were collected by Raju (1980) from **336** homemakers and **105** students. The homemakers were contacted through local women's clubs and the students were contacted through mostly junior and senior level college classes.

RELIABILITY:

The scale was reported by Raju (1980) to have reliability (Spearman-Brown) of **.697** and **.700** for the homemaker and student samples, respectively.

VALIDITY:

Raju (1980) notes that a factor analysis was performed, but the grouping of items for scale purposes was based more on interitem correlations and a subjective classification process.

ADMINISTRATION:

The manner of scale administration was not specifically addressed for either sample by Raju (1980). However, he implied that the homemakers received the questionnaire at a club meeting, filled it out at home by themselves, and returned it by mail. The student sample is assumed to have completed the survey instrument in class. Higher scores on the scale suggest that respondents prefer to try different things whereas lower scores imply that they have a high degree of loyalty to one brand, company, flavor, etc.

MAJOR FINDINGS:

In two studies, Raju (1980) examined the relationships between optimal stimulation level (OSL) and certain personality traits, demographics, and purchase-related psychographics. For both samples significant correlations were found between **loyalty proneness** and OSL.

This finding along with others indicated that people with higher OSLs were more likely to exhibit exploratory behaviors in their consumer behavior.

COMMENTS:

The construct validity of the scale is highly suspect given the manner in which the seven scales used in the study were constructed (as noted in the origination information above). Sixteen of the 39 items were used to compose more than one scale, thus making it unclear what construct the items and their respective scales actually measured. Though the reported reliability levels for this scale are reasonable, further validity testing is needed.

REFERENCE:

Raju, P. S. (1980), "Optimum Stimulation Level: Its Relationship to Personality, Demographics, and Exploratory Behavior," *JCR*, 7 (December), 272-282.

SCALE ITEMS: LOYALTY PRONENESS (PRODUCT)

Completely Disagree 1————2————3————4————5————6————7 Completely Agree

1. Even though certain food products are available in a number of different flavors, I always tend to buy the same flavor. **(r)**
2. If I like a brand, I rarely switch from it just to try something different. **(r)**
3. I get bored with buying the same brands even if they are good.
4. I would get tired of flying the same airline every time.
5. I would prefer to keep using old appliances and gadgets even if it means having to get them fixed, rather than buying new ones every few years. **(r)**
6. A lot of the time I feel the urge to buy something really different from the brands I usually buy.
7. If I did a lot of flying, I would probably like to try all the different airlines, instead of flying one most of the time.

SCALE NAME: Market Maven

SCALE DESCRIPTION:

A six-item, seven-point Likert-type summated ratings scale measuring the degree to which a person has a wide range of knowledge about products to buy, places to shop, and other consumption-related activities and influences others by passing on this information.

SCALE ORIGIN:

The scale is original to Feick and Price (1987). A set of 40 items was originally generated and was reduced to 19 by a group of marketing academicians and practitioners. The reduced set was administered to 265 part- time MBA students at a major northeastern university. Because a short scale was needed for a telephone survey, factor analysis, item-total correlations, and Chronbach's alpha were used to reduce the list to the final set of six. This final set had an alpha of .84 and item-total correlations from .51 to .67. Details of the scale's use in the main study are discussed below.

SAMPLES:

A survey was conducted by random digit dialing of the telephone numbers of people living in one of the 48 contiguous states. A total of **1531** successful interviews were conducted. Though 64% of the sample was female, the authors reported the other demographic characteristics to be similar to those in the 1980 census as well as the 1984 update. The survey form was the same for all interviewees except that one group (n = **771**) was asked some questions about common food and household items and an other (n = **760**) was asked about nonprescription drugs and health and beauty items.

RELIABILITY:

An alpha of **.82** was reported for the scale and item-total correlations ranged from **.48** to **.65**.

VALIDITY:

A factor analysis conducted in a pilot study, mentioned above, indicated that the items loaded together, as did another pilot study. A telephone survey was made of 303 male and female heads of household in a large northeastern metropolitan area. Evidence of discriminant validity was provided by the pattern of loadings in the factor analysis. Two factors were produced: the Market Maven items loaded on one factor and items from a seven-item opinion leadership scale (King and Summers 1970) as well as a one-item opinion leadership scale loaded on the other factor.

ADMINISTRATION:

The scale was administered to interviewees along with other measures in a telephone survey. Scores on the scale can range from 6 to 42. Higher scores suggest that consumers are very likely to have a lot of shopping knowledge and influence others whereas lower scores imply that they are not market mavens.

MAJOR FINDINGS:

The authors identified and examined a type of consumer they referred to as the **Market Maven**. Support was found for all hypotheses advanced. Persons scoring high on the **Market Maven** scale were aware of new products earlier, engaged in more information seeking, disseminated information about a variety of products to others, and showed greater market interest and attentiveness. The findings indicated that **Market Mavens** were distinct as a group from opinion leaders and early adopters.

REFERENCES:

Feick, Lawrence F. and Linda L. Price (1987), ''The Market Maven: A Diffuser of Marketplace Information,'' *JM*, 51 (January), 83-97.

King, Charles W. and John O. Summers (1970), ''Overlap of Opinion Leadership Across Consumer Product Categories,'' *JMR,* 7 (February), 43-50.

SCALE ITEMS: MARKET MAVEN

Strongly Disagree	Disagree	Slightly Disagree	Neutral	Slightly Agree	Agree	Strongly Agree
1	2	3	4	5	6	7

1. I like introducing new brands and products to my friends.
2. I like helping people by providing them with information about many kinds of products.
3. People ask me for information about products, places to shop, or sales.
4. If someone asked where to get the best buy on several types of products, I could tell him or her where to shop.
5. My friends think of me as a good source of information when it comes to new products or sales.
6. Think about a person who has information about a variety of products and likes to share this information with others. This person knows about new products, sales, stores, and so on, but does not necessarily feel he or she is an expert on one particular product. How well would you say that this description fits you?

SCALE NAME: Masculinity

SCALE DESCRIPTION:

A 10-item, seven-point, summated ratings scale measuring the degree to which a person indicates having masculine personality characteristics.

SCALE ORIGIN:

The items for the scale used by Barak and Stern (1985/1986) were taken from the Bem (1974) Sex-Role Inventory (BSRI). The inventory went through several rounds of development and testing. The initial development involved 40 undergraduate students judging 400 personality characteristics for their appropriateness for each sex. The list was narrowed to the 20 characteristics for each sex that were considered to be the most desirable for them to have in American society. The measure then asked respondents to rate themselves on all of the characteristics so that both masculinity and femininity scale scores could be computed. (An androgyny score could also be calculated by determining the difference between the other two scores.)

Internal consistency was estimated with two samples: 444 male and 279 female students in introductory psychology at Stanford University and an additional 117 male and 77 female paid volunteers at Foothill Junior College. From the two samples, an alpha of .86 was calculated both times for the masculinity scale and alpha values of .8 and .82 were calculated for the femininity scale. Test-retest stability was estimated with 28 male and 28 female subjects. The students took the BSRI once and then four weeks later. For both scales the correlation of the scores was reported to be .90. Scores on the scales were correlated with two other measures of sex roles. The low correlations led Bem to conclude that her scales were tapping constructs not directly measured by the others.

SAMPLES:

The survey form used by Barak and Stern (1985/1986) was personally distributed to and collected from an age-quota sample of women living in the greater New York metropolitan area. The study focused on the **567** responding women who categorized themselves as either "young" or "middle-aged" and stated an age in years between 25 and 69.

RELIABILITY:

Barak and Stern (1985/1986) say only that the scale's alpha was above **.85**.

VALIDITY:

Factor analysis was performed on the BSRI inventory offered by Bem (1974). Though not expressly stated, the items used by Barak and Stern (1985/1986) were probably the ones that loaded highest on the factor related to masculinity.

ADMINISTRATION:

The scale used by Barak and Stern (1985/1986) was self-administered by respondents in their homes as part of a larger survey form. Higher scores indicate greater masculinity whereas lower scores suggest little masculinity though not necessarily strong femininity.

MAJOR FINDINGS:

Barak and Stern (1985/1986) examined the differences in profiles between the baby-boomer and pre-boomer generations as well as between women who characterized themselves as young and those who characterized themselves as middle-aged. The only significant difference found in **masculinity** was between women who identified themselves as either young or middle-aged. Specifically, those identifying themselves as young expressed more **masculine** characteristics than those identifying themselves as middle-aged.

COMMENTS:

Though presented here by itself, the scale is most properly used along with the femininity scale of the BSRI. The lack of stronger evidence of scale validity should cause scores to be viewed cautiously.

REFERENCES:

Barak, Benny and Barbara Stern (1985/1986), ''Women's Age in Advertising: An Examination of Two Consumer Age Profiles,'' *JAR,* 25 (December/January), 38-47.
Bem, Sandra L. (1974), ''The Measurement of Psychological Androgyny,'' *Journal of Consulting and Clinical Psychology*, 42 (2), 155-162.

SCALE ITEMS: MASCULINITY +

Indicate on the following scale how well each of the following traits describes you:

Never or almost never true ____ : ____ : ____ : ____ : ____ : ____ : ____ Always or almost always true

    1   2   3   4   5   6   7

1. Acts as a leader
2. Aggressive
3. Ambitious
4. Analytical
5. Assertive
6. Athletic
7. Competitive
8. Defends own beliefs
9. Dominant
10. Forceful
11. Has leadership abilities
12. Independent
13. Individualistic
14. Makes decisions easily
15. Masculine
16. Self-reliant
17. Self-sufficient
18. Strong personality

19. Willing to take a stand
20. Willing to take risks

+ Barak and Stern (1985/1986) calculated scale scores on just 10 of these items based on the results of a factor analysis. Those 10 items were not specified in their article.

SCALE NAME: Mastery (Situation)

SCALE DESCRIPTION:

A four-item, six-point Likert-type summated ratings scale that is supposed to measure the degree to which a person feels he/she has been challenged but prevailed in a situation. The activity investigated by Unger (1981; Unger and Kernan 1983) was subjective leisure.

SCALE ORIGIN:

Though relevant literature was surveyed prior to scale construction, the items themselves and certainly the scale as a whole are original to Unger (1981).

SAMPLES:

The scale was developed in one stage of the overall study and then used to test hypotheses in another stage. In the first stage, the scale was administered by three different people to a total of **169** undergraduate business students at Miami University and the University of Cincinnati (Unger 1981). In the second stage, the questionnaires were delivered and picked up by members of a Girl Scout troop. A quota sample of **160** adults living in the Cincinnati SMSA was used that balanced eight equal age-by-sex groups. However, the sample was representative of neither the Cincinnati SMSA nor the U.S. population as a whole, being composed mostly of white people (98%) of middle to upper socioeconomic status (84%).

RELIABILITY:

The final scale consists of items that remained after several tests of reliability. The tests were conducted for the scale in six different situations. Alpha values for the scale ranged from **.79** to **.86**. See Unger (1981) for more detailed information.

VALIDITY:

Several rounds of factor analysis provided general support that the items tend to load together. However, the results seem to have some sensitivity to the sample and situation being evaluated. When not loading separately, the items in this scale loaded with those of the Novelty (Activity) scale, which indicates the two are psychologically related for some samples and situations.

ADMINISTRATION:

The scale was self-administered by respondents in both stages of the survey described above. Higher scores on the scale indicate that respondents are expressing their curiosity and interest in a stimulus whereas a low score implies respondents do not perceive it to be novel.

MAJOR FINDINGS:

The study by Unger (1981; Unger and Kernan 1983) examined dimensions of the subjective leisure experience across six different situations. **Perceived mastery** was not found to be one of the primary determinants of subjective leisure across situations. Instead, it appeared to be linked to just some kinds of leisure activity.

REFERENCES:

Unger, Lynette S. (1981), *Measure Validation in the Leisure Domain*, unpublished doctoral dissertation, University of Cincinnati.
_____ and Jerome B. Kernan (1983), "On the Meaning of Leisure: An Investigation of Some Determinants of the Subjective Experience," *JCR*, 9 (March), 381-391.

SCALE ITEMS: MASTERY (SITUATION)+

Strongly Disagree	Disagree	Somewhat Disagree	Somewhat Agree	Agree	Strongly Agree
1	2	3	4	5	6

1. I feel like I'm conquering the world.
2. I get a sense of adventure or risk.
3. I feel like a real champion.
4. I feel I have been thoroughly tested.

+ The questionnaire described a situation for the respondents and they were asked to respond to the statements as they felt about the situation.

SCALE NAME: Materialism

SCALE DESCRIPTION:

A six-item, five-point Likert-type summated ratings scale measuring the degree to which a person is oriented toward possessing goods and money as a means of personal happiness and social progress.

SCALE ORIGIN:

The measure originates from a dissertation published by Moschis in 1978. His 1981 study, reported below, is from that same dissertation research. Some of the items for the scale were apparently derived from items used by Ward and Wackman (1971). The psychometric properties of the latter are unknown. Ward and Wackman (1971) found no significant difference between the mean scores of 537 eighth and ninth graders and the mean scores of 557 tenth, eleventh, and twelfth graders on the materialism scale.

SAMPLES:

Moschis' (1981) data came from **806** middle school or senior high school students. There were 365 "older" adolescents (15 years and older) and 441 "younger" adolescents (younger than 15 years). The students came from 13 schools and seven towns in Wisconsin representing a wide variety of urban to rural situations. The author indicates that the sample was well balanced in terms of most demographic characteristics except sex, as nearly two-thirds of the respondents were female.

The survey instrument used by Carlson and Grossbart (1988) was distributed to mothers via students at three elementary schools in an unidentified U.S. city. The schools were chosen on a convenience basis but appeared to represent a variety of socioeconomic areas of the city. A $1 contribution to the PTO was offered for each completed questionnaire returned by the children. Analysis was based on **451** completed questionnaires. Ninety-three percent of the responding mothers indicated that they were the primary person in the child's socialization.

RELIABILITY:

Alpha values of **.60** and **.68** have been reported for the scale by Moschis (1981) and Carlson and Grossbart (1988), respectively.

VALIDITY:

No examination of scale validity has been reported. However, Carlson and Grossbart (1988) note that social desirability was a significant covariate with the scale.

ADMINISTRATION:

The scale was self-administered along with other measures in the studies reported by Moschis (1981) and Carlson and Grossbart (1988). Higher scores on the scale indicate that respondents do not tend to be materialistic whereas lower scores suggest that they are very oriented toward accumulating material things as a means of achieving happiness.

MAJOR FINDINGS:

Moschis (1981) investigated the validity of the cognitive development approach to social-ization (e.g., Piaget) to predict a wide variety of consumer-related cognitions learned during adolescence. In general, the findings indicated that the cognitive developmental model did not explain consumer socialization during adolescence very well. Older adoles-cents had significantly less favorable attitudes toward advertising, brands, and prices than did younger children, but had significantly greater prepurchase information source usage. No significant difference was found between the two groups of adolescents on the basis of **materialism.**

Carlson and Grossbart (1988) investigated the relationship between general parental socialization styles and children's consumer socialization. Neglecting mothers exhibited more **materialism** than any of the other four parental socialization style clusters examined. However, the difference was only significant in comparison with Authoritative mothers, who scored lowest on **materialism.**

COMMENTS:

The level of internal consistency indicates that the scale is not very reliable. This could be due to several different factors being represented in the scale. Redevelopment and testing should be conducted before the scale is used further.

REFERENCES:

Carlson, Les and Sanford Grossbart (1988), ''Parental Style and Consumer Socialization of Children,'' *JCR*, 15 (June), 77-94.

Moschis, George P. (1978), *Acquisition of the Consumer Role by Adolescents*, Research Monograph No. 82. Atlanta, Ga.: Publishing Services Division, College of Business Administration, Georgia State University.

_____ (1981), ''Patterns of Consumer Learning,'' *JAMS*, 9 (2), 110-126.

Ward, Scott and Daniel Wackman (1971), ''Family and Media Influences on Adolescent Consumer Learning,'' *American Behavioral Scientist*, 14 (January/February), 415-427.

SCALE ITEMS: MATERIALISM

Strongly Disagree	Disagree	Neutral	Agree	Strongly Agree
1—————————	—2—————————	—3—————————	—4—————————	—5

1. It is really true that money can buy happiness.
2. My dream in life is to be able to own expensive things.
3. People judge others by the things they own.
4. I buy some things that I secretly hope will impress other people.
5. Money is the most important thing to consider in choosing a job.
6. I think others judge me as a person by the kinds of products and brands I use.

SCALE NAME: Materialism

SCALE DESCRIPTION:

A six-item, five-point Likert-type scale measuring a consumer's own sense of materialism as well as that of society in general. The scale was referred to as Cultural Estrangement by Durand and Lambert (1985).

SCALE ORIGIN:

The scale was originally constructed and used by Lambert (1980). Items were adapted from several previously published empirical and conceptual studies. A mail sample of residents of four southeastern metropolitan areas yielded **200** usable returns. The alpha for the powerlessness scale was reported as **.42**. Powerlessness was just one of four alienation scales used together in a cluster analysis to group consumers. In general, dissatisfaction with the marketplace was found to be significantly related to levels of consumer alienation. Materialism (cultural estrangement) seemed to vary in impact depending on the issue.

SAMPLES:

The study of Durand and Lambert (1985) was based on a systematic sample of 1320 customers of a large, investor-owned electric utility company was made by Durand and Lambert (1985). Questionnaires were mailed to them and **325** were returned following a reminder mailed after two weeks. The average respondent was at least 45 years of age, male, white, married, had at least graduated high school, and was socioeconomically upscale.

RELIABILITY:

An alpha of **.42** was reported for the scale.

VALIDITY:

No examination of scale validity was reported.

ADMINISTRATION:

The scale was self-administered along with several other measures included in the mail questionnaire. Higher scores on the scale indicate that consumers feel society would be better off if it were less materialistic whereas lower scores mean that consumers think there is nothing particularly wrong with buying products and enjoying them.

MAJOR FINDINGS:

The purpose of the study was to investigate the degree to which criticisms of advertising are positively related to various aspects of consumer and political alienation. Respondents were first grouped according to levels of alienation by cluster analysis. (**Materialism** was one of the alienation variables on which the cluster analysis was based.) Then, differences in advertising criticisms were compared across the groups. The cluster analysis produced four alienation groups and a MANOVA indicated significant differences between the groups when all of the 12 advertising criticisms were considered simultaneously.

COMMENTS:

The internal consistency of the scale is unacceptably low and caution is necessary until some refinement and improvement is done. A problem with the scale is that it appears to tap several different though related constructs, as admitted by one of the authors (Lambert 1980, p. 12). A better focus would probably improve its reliability.

REFERENCES:

Durand, Richard M. and Zarrel V. Lambert (1985), ''Alienation and Criticisms of Advertising,'' *JA*, 14 (3), 9-17.

Lambert, Zarrel V. (1980), ''Consumer Alienation, General Dissatisfaction, and Consumerism Issues: Conceptual and Managerial Perspectives,'' *Journal of Retailing*, 56 (Summer), 3-24.

SCALE ITEMS: MATERIALISM +

Strongly Disagree	Disagree	Neutral	Agree	Strongly Agree
1	2	3	4	5

1. The variety . . . in the market enables a consumer like myself to express my own . . . personality and tastes. **(r)**
2. Our society would be a lot better if people were less concerned with . . . money and more interested in others' welfare.
3. Any . . . enjoyment I get from buying new products disappears . . . quickly even when they work as advertised.
4. For the most part, advertising is insulting to good taste and judgement.
5. I enjoy buying something new . . . that I have not owned before. **(r)**
6. Materialism is one of the things wrong with our society.

+ The authors noted that these items were abbreviated to conserve space as indicated by the dots. They should be contacted if the full items are desired.

SCALE NAME: Mood

SCALE DESCRIPTION:

A four-item, seven-point semantic differential purporting to measure a subject's affective mood state at a particular point in time.

SCALE ORIGIN:

The scale is original to Allen and Janiszewski (1989).

SAMPLES:

Allen and Janiszewski (1989) used two separate samples in their research. The first consisted of **61** first-year MBA students. The second consisted of **76** second-year MBA students.

RELIABILITY:

The authors (1989) reported an alpha of **.72**.

VALIDITY:

No validity assessment was reported.

ADMINISTRATION:

This scale appears appropriate for paper-and-pencil administration. In Allen and Janiszewski's study, subjects responded to the scale on a computer screen. Time to administer seems inconsequential. Scale sums were used in the analysis reported here.

MAJOR FINDINGS:

Allen and Janiszewski (1989) reported that subjects in both control and experimental conditions were not significantly different in mood at the time of the study.

REFERENCE:

Allen, Chris T. and Chris A. Janiszewski (1989), "Assessing the Role of Contingency Awareness in Attitudinal Conditioning with Implications for Advertising Research," *JMR*, 26 (February), 30-43.

SCALE ITEMS: MOOD

Subjects are prompted to respond by the phrase, "at this moment I am feeling":

1. good   ____ : ____ : ____ : ____ : ____ : ____ : ____   bad
                         1   2   3   4   5   6   7

2. unpleasant   ____ : ____ : ____ : ____ : ____ : ____ : ____   pleasant **(r)**

                                  1   2   3   4   5   6   7

3. happy   ____ : ____ : ____ : ____ : ____ : ____ : ____   sad

                                    1   2   3   4   5   6   7

4. negative   ____ : ____ : ____ : ____ : ____ : ____ : ____   positive

                                    1   2   3   4   5   6   7

SCALE NAME: Motivation to Engage in Activities (Intrinsic/Extrinsic)

SCALE DESCRIPTION:

A 16-item, seven-point Likert-type summated ratings scale measuring a person's tendency to engage in a variety of activities because of their intrinsic value (i.e., for their own sake rather than as a means to an end). The scale is composed of items referring to eight activities. Half of the statements suggests the activities are pursued for intrinsic reasons and the others imply they are pursued for extrinsic reasons.

SCALE ORIGIN:

The scale was apparently original to Holbrook (1986).

SAMPLES:

Subjects used in the study were **42** male and **22** female MBA candidates in a marketing course who were required to respond to the questionnaire.

RELIABILITY:

An alpha of **.68** was reported for the scale.

VALIDITY:

Though the validity of the scale was not intensively examined, some evidence of its concurrent and nomological validity was reported.

ADMINISTRATION:

Subjects self-administered the scale along with several other measures. If the scale is used with numbers 1 through 7, lower summated scores suggest that respondents have a tendency to engage in activities as a means to an end (extrinsic motivation) whereas higher scores mean that they usually engage in activities for their intrinsic value.

MAJOR FINDINGS:

The role of certain personality variables and gender was studied by Holbrook (1986). He illustrated a method using canonical correlation analysis to examine individual differences in affect toward clothing design features. In general, **intrinsic/extrinsic** motivation appeared to have a significant but weak influence on affect.

REFERENCE:

Holbrook, Morris B. (1986), ''Aims, Concepts, and Methods for the Representation of Individual Differences in Esthetic Responses to Design Features,'' *JCR*, 13 (December), 337- 347.

SCALE ITEMS: MOTIVATION TO ENGAGE IN ACTIVITIES (INTRINSIC/EXTRINSIC)

Strongly   Strongly
Disagree   Agree
1————2————3————4————5————6————7

1. When I engage in a noncompetitive sport like skiing, jogging, or body-building, I tend to view the activity as an end in itself.
2. I would not throw a party or take someone out to dinner unless I expected to gain some benefit from it. **(r)**
3. When I perform some creative activity such as writing, drawing, or playing a musical instrument, I am aware that the process is inherently its own reward.
4. When I read a magazine, listen to the radio, or watch television, I always know what I expect to get out of it. **(r)**
5. When I play a competitive sport such as tennis, golf, or ping pong, my primary motivation is to enjoy the game for its own sake.
6. When I perform some creative activity such as writing, drawing, or playing a musical instrument, I set a goal for myself to try to achieve. **(r)**
7. When I attend an artistic event like a play, a concert, or an art exhibit, I usually have some specific purpose in mind. **(r)**
8. When I read a magazine, listen to the radio, or watch television, I just appreciate the experience on its own terms.
9. I would not throw a party or take someone out to dinner unless I expected to enjoy the companionship of the people involved.
10. When I play a competitive sport such as tennis, golf, or ping pong, my primary motivation is to win. **(r)**
11. In playing cards, board games, or video games, winning is everything. **(r)**
12. When I fix something or do chores around the house, I am filled with a sense of purpose. **(r)**
13. In playing cards, board games, or video games, winning matters less than how you play the game.
14. When I engage in a noncompetitive sport like skiing, jogging, or body-building, I tend to view the activity as a contest between myself and the environment. **(r)**
15. When I fix something or do chores around the house, sometimes I am just puttering around for the fun of it.
16. When I attend an artistic event like a play, a concert, or an art exhibit, my only purpose is to gain aesthetic satisfaction.

SCALE NAME: Multi-Store Shopper

SCALE DESCRIPTION:

A three-item, five-point Likert-type summated ratings scale measuring the degree to which a respondent reports shopping for groceries, clothes, and household items at more than one store.

SCALE ORIGIN:

The use of these items as a multi-item measure appears to be original to Carlson and Grossbart (1988). The idea for the items was reported to come from the research of Ward, Wackman, and Wartella (1977).

SAMPLES:

The survey instrument used by Carlson and Grossbart (1988) was distributed to mothers via students at three elementary schools in an unidentified U.S. city. The schools were chosen on a convenience basis but appeared to represent a variety of socioeconomic areas of the city. A $1 contribution to the PTO was offered for each completed questionnaire returned by the children. Analysis was based on **451** completed questionnaires. Ninety-three percent of the responding mothers indicated that they were the primary person in the child's socialization.

RELIABILITY:

Carlson and Grossbart (1988) reported an alpha of **.66** and a beta of .63 for the scale.

VALIDITY:

No examination of scale validity was reported. However, the authors do report that social desirability was a significant covariate with this scale.

ADMINISTRATION:

The scale was self-administered along with many other measures in the questionnaire used by Carlson and Grossbart (1988). Higher scores on the scale mean that respondents report a high degree of multi-store shopping whereas lower scores suggest that they are limit their shopping to just a few stores.

MAJOR FINDINGS:

The authors investigated the relationship between general parental socialization styles and children's consumer socialization. No significant differences were found in the degree of **multi- store shopping** between any of the five parental socialization styles examined.

COMMENTS:

The low reliability suggests that caution should be exercised in using this scale and further work is needed to improve its psychometric quality.

REFERENCES:

Carlson, Les and Sanford Grossbart (1988), ''Parental Style and Consumer Socialization of Children,'' *JCR*, 15 (June), 77-94.

Ward, Scott, Daniel B. Wackman, and Ellen Wartella (1977), *How Children Learn to Buy*. Beverly Hills, Calif.: Sage Publications, Inc.

SCALE ITEMS: MULTI-STORE SHOPPER

Very Seldom	Seldom	Sometimes	Often	Very Often
1————————	2—————————	3————————	4————————	5

1. I shop for groceries at more than one store.
2. I shop for clothes at more than one store.
3. I shop for household furnishings and appliances at more than one store.

SCALE NAME: Novelty (Activity)

SCALE DESCRIPTION:

A four-item, six-point Likert-type summated ratings scale that is supposed to measure the degree to which a person views a specified activity as being novel and curious. This scale was called Arousal by Unger (1981; Unger and Kernan 1983) and the activity investigated was subjective leisure.

SCALE ORIGIN:

Though relevant literature was surveyed prior to scale construction, the items themselves and certainly the scale as a whole are original to Unger (1981).

SAMPLES:

The scale was developed in one stage of the overall study and then used to test hypotheses in another stage. In the first stage, the scale was administered by three different people to a total of **169** undergraduate business students at Miami University and the University of Cincinnati (Unger 1981). In the second stage, the questionnaires were delivered and picked up by members of a Girl Scout troop. A quota sample of **160** adults living in the Cincinnati SMSA was used that balanced eight equal age-by-sex groups. However, the sample was representative of neither the Cincinnati SMSA nor the U.S. population as a whole, being composed mostly of white people (98%) of middle to upper socioeconomic status (84%).

RELIABILITY:

The final scale consists of items that remained after several tests of reliability. The tests were conducted for the scale in six different situations. Alpha values for the scale ranged from **.73** to **.79**. See Unger (1981) for more detailed information.

VALIDITY:

Factor analysis provided general support that the items tend to load together. However, the results seem to have some sensitivity to the sample and situation being evaluated. When not loading separately, the items in this scale loaded with those of the mastery scale, which indicates the two are psychologically related for some samples and situations.

ADMINISTRATION:

The scale was self-administered by respondents in both stages of the survey described above. Higher scores on the scale indicate that respondents are expressing their curiosity and interest in a stimulus whereas a low score implies that respondents do not perceive the stimulus to be novel.

MAJOR FINDINGS:

The study by Unger (1981; Unger and Kernan 1983) examined dimensions of the subjective leisure experience across six different situations. **Perceived novelty** was not found to be one of the primary determinants of subjective leisure across situations. Instead, it appeared to be linked to just some kinds of leisure activity.

REFERENCES:

Unger, Lynette S. (1981), ''Measure Validation in the Leisure Domain,'' unpublished doctoral dissertation, University of Cincinnati.

_____ and Jerome B. Kernan (1983), ''On the Meaning of Leisure: An Investigation of Some Determinants of the Subjective Experience,'' *JCR*, 9 (March), 381-391.

SCALE ITEMS: NOVELTY (ACTIVITY) +

Strongly Agree	Agree	Somewhat Agree	Somewhat Disagree	Disagree	Strongly Disagree
1	2	3	4	5	6

1. There is novelty in it.
2. It satisfies my sense of curiosity.
3. It offers novel experiences.
4. I feel like I'm exploring new worlds.

+ The questionnaire described a situation for respondents and they were asked to respond to the statements as they felt about the situation.

SCALE NAME: Novelty (Stimulus)

SCALE DESCRIPTION:

A three-item, seven-point semantic differential summated ratings scale measuring how new or different a stimulus is perceived to be.

SCALE ORIGIN:

Though Holbrook (1981) may have drawn on the work of Osgood, Suci, and Tannenbaum (1957) and Berlyne (1974) in composing this scale, neither of the latter articles offered these three items per se as a measure of perceived novelty.

SAMPLES:

Holbrook's (1981) analysis was based on **16** subjects chosen from volunteers with an interest in classical piano music. Half had never played an instrument but enjoyed listening to such music ("nonexperts") and the other half were highly trained musicians ("experts").

RELIABILITY:

An alpha of **.59** was reported for the scale.

VALIDITY:

The first two items below had loadings greater than .5 on the same factor, but the third item had a loading of only .39, had its highest loading on another factor, and was included with this scale in order to have three items.

ADMINISTRATION:

In both studies (Holbrook 1981), subjects self-administered the scale along with several other measures. Higher summated scores suggest that respondents perceive a lot of novelty in an object whereas lower scores mean that they perceive the object to be familiar or old.

MAJOR FINDINGS:

Holbrook (1981) illustrated a two-stage integrative model of evaluative judgment in which objective product features influenced perceptions, which in turn shaped affect. Specifically, he found that the direct effects of objective music characteristics on affect were not nearly as large or as significant as the indirect effects of those features through intervening perceptions. Perceived expressiveness, activity, and complexity had significant positive influences on affect, perceived **novelty** had a significant negative impact, and perceived potency did not make a salient contribution. Of the musical features examined, the degree of fluctuation in rhythm was the strongest determinant of perceived novelty.

COMMENTS:

The low internal consistency suggests that the scale is not very stable. Development and testing are certainly called for before this scale is used in anything other than exploratory research.

REFERENCES:

Berlyne, D. E., ed. (1974), *Studies in the New Experimental Aesthetics*. New York, N.Y.: John Wiley & Sons, Inc.

Holbrook, Morris B. (1981), "Integrating Compositional and Decompositional Analyses to Represent the Intervening Role of Perceptions in Evaluative Judgments," *JMR*, 18 (February), 13-28.

Osgood, Charles E., George J. Suci, and Percy H. Tannenbaum (1957), *The Measurement of Meaning*. Urbana, Ill.: University of Illinois Press.

SCALE ITEMS: NOVELTY (STIMULUS)

familiar ___ : ___ : ___ : ___ : ___ : ___ : ___ unusual
         1   2   3   4   5   6   7

old ___ : ___ : ___ : ___ : ___ : ___ : ___ new
         1   2   3   4   5   6   7

regular ___ : ___ : ___ : ___ : ___ : ___ : ___ irregular
         1   2   3   4   5   6   7

SCALE NAME: Nurturance (Parental)

SCALE DESCRIPTION:

A nine-item, five-point Likert-type summated ratings scale measuring the degree to which a person (a parent) describes the interaction with his/her children as being warm, affectionate, and encouraging.

SCALE ORIGIN:

The items in the scale are from the Child Rearing Practices Report (Block 1965) as tested and modified by Rickel and Biasatti (1982). Using three samples representing a broad range of socioeconomic factors, Rickel and Biasatti (1982) offered an 18-item scale of nurturance in which all items loaded on the same factor with loadings of .40 or higher. The alpha values for this 18-item version of the scale were found to be .84, .82, and .73 for the three samples tested.

SAMPLES:

The survey instrument used by Carlson and Grossbart (1988) was distributed to mothers via students at three elementary schools in an unidentified U.S. city. The schools were chosen on a convenience basis but appeared to represent a variety of socioeconomic areas of the city. A $1 contribution to the PTO was offered for each completed questionnaire returned by the children. Analysis was based on **451** completed questionnaires. Ninety-three percent of the responding mothers indicated that they were the primary person in the child's socialization.

RELIABILITY:

Carlson and Grossbart (1988) reported an alpha of **.90** and a beta of .81 for the scale.

VALIDITY:

No examination of scale validity was reported by Carlson and Grossbart (1988).

ADMINISTRATION:

The scale was self-administered along with many other measures in the questionnaire used by Carlson and Grossbart (1988). Higher scores on the scale mean that parents indicate having a very warm, affectionate, and encouraging relationship with their children.

MAJOR FINDINGS:

The authors investigated the relationship between general parental socialization styles and children's consumer socialization. Of the five parental socialization style clusters examined, Permissive and Authoritative mothers described themselves as being significantly more **nurturing** than did the other three parental style clusters.

REFERENCES:

Block, Jeanne H. (1965), *The Child Rearing Practices Report*. Berkeley, Calif.: University of California, Institute of Human Development.

Carlson, Les and Sanford Grossbart (1988), ''Parental Style and Consumer Socialization of Children,'' *JCR*, 15 (June), 77-94.

Rickel, Annette U. and Lawrence L. Biasatti (1982), ''Modification of the Child Rearing Practices Report,'' *Journal of Clinical Psychology*, 38 (January), 129-134.

SCALE ITEMS: NUTURING (PARENTAL)

Please indicate your opinion by checking one response (strongly disagree, disagree, neither disagree or agree, agree, strongly agree) for each statement. Check one for each statement.

Strongly Disagree	Disagree	Neither	Agree	Strongly Agree
1————	—2————	—3————	—4————	—5

1. My child and I have warm intimate moments together. +
2. I encourage my child to talk about his troubles. +
3. I joke and play with my child. +
4. I make sure my child knows that I appreciate what he tries to accomplish. +
5. I encourage my child to wonder and think about life. +
6. I feel that a child should have time to daydream, think, and even loaf sometimes.
7. I express my affection by hugging, kissing, and holding my child. +
8. I talk it over and reason with my child when he misbehaves. +
9. I find it interesting and educational to be with my child for long periods.
10. I encourage my child to be curious, to explore, and question things.
11. I find some of my greatest satisfactions in my child.
12. When I am angry with my child, I let him know about it.
13. I respect my child's opinion and encourage him to express it. +
14. I feel that a child should be given comfort and understanding when he is scared and upset. +
15. I am easygoing and relaxed with my child.
16. I trust my child to behave as he should, even when I am not with him.
17. I believe in praising a child when he is good and think it gets better results that punishing him when he is bad.
18. I usually take into account my child's preference when making plans for the family.

+ These nine items were the subset used by Carlson and Grossbart (1988) and are listed here in order of factor loading strength as reported by Rickel and Biasatti (1982).

SCALE NAME: Nutritional Knowledge

SCALE DESCRIPTION:

A six-item, true-false, summated ratings scale measuring a child's general level of knowledge about nutrition and diet.

SCALE ORIGIN:

The scale was original to Wiman and Newman (1989). Questions for the scale were selected from teachers' manuals for elementary school health textbooks. Between one and three questions were taken from each of seven manuals for a total of 13 items. The results of a factor analysis led the authors to reduce the scale to six items.

SAMPLES:

Data were collected from all students in grades three through six in two elementary schools serving three central New Jersey communities. A total of **327** students participated and all questionnaires were usable.

RELIABILITY:

An alpha of **.56** was reported for the scale.

VALIDITY:

The items in this scale and those in one measuring understanding of nutritional phraseology were reported to have loaded on separate factors in a factor analysis.

ADMINISTRATION:

The scale was administered to students in their classrooms during a normal school day and with the "interviewer" instructing them on what to do. Teachers introduced the interviewer and remained in their rooms as observers but did not participate in the administration. Scores on the scale are calculated by adding the number of correct responses. The higher the score, the greater the apparent knowledge a student has of nutrition- and diet-related issues.

MAJOR FINDINGS:

The study examined the relationship between children's exposure to television and their levels of nutritional awareness. **Nutritional knowledge** was found to have a low though significant negative correlation with Saturday morning TV exposure, a low but significant positive correlation with weekday evening TV exposure, and no significant correlation with weekday afternoon TV exposure.

COMMENTS:

The low internal consistency and lack of evidence of validity suggest that this scale be used cautiously until improved further.

REFERENCE:

Wiman, Alan R. and Larry M. Newman (1989), ''Television Advertising Exposure and Children's Nutritional Awareness,'' *JAMS*, 17 (Spring), 179-188.

SCALE ITEMS: NUTRITIONAL KNOWLEDGE +

What do you think? Are these sentences true or not? Read each one carefully before you make up your mind.

_____ 1. Food that is not needed at once can be stored in the body.

_____ 2. Milk contains all the vitamins you need each day.

_____ 3. You need just one kind of food to take care of all your body's needs.

_____ 4. A very useful food guide is this: ''Eat lots and lots of food daily.''

_____ 5. Milk should always be taken in liquid form.

_____ 6. Your body does not need sugar at any time.

+ Item 1 is true and all the rest are false.

SCALE NAME: Nutritional Phraseology Understanding

SCALE DESCRIPTION:

A seven-item, multiple-choice summated ratings scale measuring a child's understanding of common nutrition-related phrases.

SCALE ORIGIN:

The scale was original to Wiman and Newman (1989). The authors report that phrases were collected by watching ads broadcast during about five hours of children's programming. Multiple choice questions written with these phrases were used to test children's understanding.

SAMPLES:

Wiman and Newman (1989) collected data from all students in grades three through six in two elementary schools serving three central New Jersey communities. A total of **327** students participated and all questionnaires were usable.

RELIABILITY:

An alpha of **.69** was reported for the scale by Wiman and Newman (1989).

VALIDITY:

The items in this scale and those in one measuring understanding of nutritional knowledge were reported to have loaded on separate factors in a factor analysis.

ADMINISTRATION:

The scale was administered to students in their classrooms during a normal school day and with the "interviewer" instructing them on what to do. Teachers introduced the interviewer and remained in their rooms as observers but did not participate in the administration. Scores on the scale are calculated by adding the number of correct responses. The higher the score, the greater the apparent understanding of nutritional phraseology common to ads run during children's shows.

MAJOR FINDINGS:

Wiman and Newman (1989) examined the relationship between children's exposure to television and their levels of nutritional awareness. **Understanding nutritional phraseology** was found to have a low though significant negative correlation with Saturday morning TV exposure but no significant correlation with weekday afternoon or evening TV exposure.

REFERENCE:

Wiman, Alan R. and Larry M. Newman (1989), "Television Advertising Exposure and Children's Nutritional Awareness," *JAMS*, 17 (Spring), 179-188.

SCALE ITEMS: NUTRITIONAL PHRASEOLOGY UNDERSTANDING +

1. If a commercial for Capt. Crunch cereal says that it is "part of a good breakfast," this means:
   a. a bowl of Capt. Crunch is all you should eat for breakfast.
   b. you should eat Capt. Crunch *only* in the morning.
   c. you should have more than just a bowl of Capt. Crunch for breakfast.

2. If a commercial for Cocoa Crispies says that it is "fortified with vitamins" this means:
   a. Cocoa Crispies has things in it that are good for you.
   b. if you eat Cocoa Crispies, you don't need to take vitamin pills.
   c. you can eat as much Cocoa Crispies as you want.

3. A "nutritious breakfast" is:
   a. one that only tastes good.
   b. a healthy meal you should start your day with.
   c. always a very big meal.

4. If a commercial for Cheerios says that it has "10 essential vitamins and minerals," this means:
   a. you will probably get sick if you don't eat Cheerios.
   b. Cheerios is the only kind of cereal you should eat.
   c. Cheerios has certain things in it that are very important for your body.

5. If a commercial for Trix says, "Trix tastes like fruit and looks like fruit too," this means:
   a. if you eat Trix you don't need to eat fruit.
   b. Trix is made of fruit.
   c. Trix has the color or flavor that an apple or pear might have.

6. A "balanced diet" is:
   a. a group of foods that give your body everything it needs.
   b. a group of foods that weigh the right amount.
   c. a meal that has only one kind of food.

7. Which one of the following is the best example of a "nutritious breakfast?"
   a. a glass of orange juice and a bowl of cereal with milk.
   b. three pancakes and three pieces of toast.
   c. a glass of tomato juice and two pieces of toast.

+ The bold-faced answer in each group is the one the authors counted as correct.

SCALE NAME: Obedience Expectations for Kids at School

SCALE DESCRIPTION:

A three-item, forced-choice summated ratings scale measuring the degree to which a parent believes a child should obey school teachers and rules. It was referred to by Carlson and Grossbart (1988) as Values Conformity.

SCALE ORIGIN:

Though this scale bears similarity to a construct described by Baumrind (1971), correspondence with Carlson indicates that the Baumrind article did not highlight data collected with the scale but via observation. Carlson obtained the scale items in personal correspondence with Baumrind.

SAMPLES:

The survey instrument used by Carlson and Grossbart (1988) was distributed to mothers via students at three elementary schools in an unidentified U.S. city. The schools were chosen on a convenience basis but appeared to represent a variety of socioeconomic areas of the city. A $1 contribution to the PTO was offered for each completed questionnaire returned by the children. Analysis was based on **451** completed questionnaires. Ninety-three percent of the responding mothers indicated that they were the primary person in the child's socialization.

RELIABILITY:

Carlson and Grossbart (1988) reported an alpha of **.69** and a beta of .69 for the scale.

VALIDITY:

No examination of scale validity was reported by Carlson and Grossbart (1988).

ADMINISTRATION:

The scale was self-administered along with many other measures in the questionnaire used by Carlson and Grossbart (1988). Answer A of a pair should be scored as 1 and answer B should be scored as 2, with reverse scoring where indicated. Higher scores on the scale mean that parents expect their children to obey rules and authority figures, with particular emphasis on the school context.

MAJOR FINDINGS:

The authors investigated the relationship between general parental socialization styles and children's consumer socialization. Of the five parental socialization style clusters examined, Permissive mothers expressed significantly less **obedience expectations** than did all of the other parental style clusters.

REFERENCES:

Baumrind, Diana (1971), ''Current Patterns of Parental Authority,'' *Developmental Psychology Monograph*, 4 (January), 1-103.

Carlson, Les and Sanford Grossbart (1988), ''Parental Style and Consumer Socialization of Children,'' *JCR*, 15 (June), 77-94.

SCALE ITEMS: OBEDIENCE EXPECTATIONS FOR KIDS AT SCHOOL

Please indicate your opinion by checking one response (A or B) for each statement. There are no right or wrong answers, so answer according to your opinion. It is important to answer all questions even if you are not completely sure of your answer. Just check the response (A or B) that comes *closest* to your opinion. Some statements may seem alike but are necessary to show slight differences of opinion. *All questions refer to your youngest child who attends this school.*

A. A child must learn to conform to all school rules and regulations.
B. A child should not have to conform to all school rules. **(r)**

A. Some public school rules are so arbitrary or foolish that I would not insist that they be obeyed by my child.
B. I would expect my school-age child to obey all school rules.

A. A child should not have to obey all demands of his/her teachers.
B. A child should be taught to obey all his/her teachers' demands.

SCALE NAME: Opinion Leadership (Fashion)

SCALE DESCRIPTION:

A three-item, five-point, Likert-type summated ratings scale ranging from don't know (0) to often (4). One item has different verbal anchors (see below). The scale measures a person's tendency to influence the fashion purchase decisions of others.

SCALE ORIGIN:

The items are original to Hirschman (1980), though they are adapted from prior self-report studies of this general construct reported by Rogers and Shoemaker ((1971).

SAMPLES:

Data were gathered through a telephone survey in Atlanta. Weeknight calling, random digit dialing, and five callbacks per number were used to maximize the sample's representativeness. The survey focused on women and obtained **599** usable interviews (**125** black and **474** white respondents).

RELIABILITY:

No test of reliability was reported.

VALIDITY:

No test of validity was reported.

ADMINISTRATION:

Hirschman (1980) used telephone interviews to gather data for the study. Scale scores were calculated by adding numerical responses to the first two items and subtracting the numerical response to the last item. Higher scores indicate that a person often buys new fashions whereas lower scores mean that a person rarely if ever purchases the newest fashions.

MAJOR FINDINGS:

The focus was not on **opinion leaders** per se but on the differences between black and white fashion innovative communicators (persons who are both **opinion leaders** and innovators). Fewer significant differences were found than expected. Black innovative communicators were found to subscribe to fewer newspapers than their white counterparts and to have different radio station preferences. Also, different patterns of group membership were found between the two groups such that white subjects participated more in formal groups and organized social activities.

COMMENTS:

Some pretesting ought to be performed to determine the scale's psychometric properties and to improve them if necessary before it is used in a large survey.

REFERENCES:

Hirschman, Elizabeth C. (1980), "Black Ethnicity and Innovative Communication," *JAMS*, 8 (Spring), 100-119.

Rogers, Everett M. and Floyd Shoemaker (1971), *Communication of Innovations*. New York, N.Y.: Free Press.

SCALE ITEMS: OPINION LEADERSHIP (FASHION)

1. How often do you influence the types of clothing fashions your friends buy?

Often	Sometimes	Seldom	Never	Don't Know
4	3	2	1	0

2. How often do others turn to you for advice on fashion and clothing?

Often	Sometimes	Seldom	Never	Don't Know
4	3	2	1	0

3. How many of your friends and neighbors regard you as a good source of advice on clothing fashions?

Almost everyone I know	More than half	Less than half	Almost no one
4	3	2	1

SCALE NAME: Opinion Leadership (Fashion)

SCALE DESCRIPTION:

An eight-item, six-point, Likert-type summated ratings scale ranging from strongly disagree (1) to strongly agree (6). The scale measures a person's tendency to inform and persuade others' fashion-related views. See also Hawes and Lumpkin (1984) for use of a few items from this scale with a few items from a fashion innovativeness scale.

SCALE ORIGIN:

It is not clear where the items originated or where the scale was first used as a multi-item summated ratings scale.

SAMPLES:

Lumpkin (1985) analyzed data collected from a sample drawn from the Market Facts Consumer Mail Panel. A total of **2854** completed questionnaires were received, but Lumpkin focused just on **373** respondents who indicated they were **65** years of age or older.

RELIABILITY:

An alpha of **.8619** was reported by Lumpkin (1985).

VALIDITY:

Factor analysis indicated the items loaded together.

ADMINISTRATION:

Lumpkin (1985) gathered data through self-administered mail questionnaires. Scale scores are calculated by averaging numerical responses to individual items. A score of 6 indicates that a person believes strongly in his/her tendency to influence others' fashion ideas whereas a 1 implies a person has little or no influence on others.

MAJOR FINDINGS:

Elderly consumers were cluster analyzed by Lumpkin (1985) and **fashion opinion leadership** appeared to discriminate between the three groups, though the level of statistical significance was not reported. The group with the highest mean on the scale also scored highest on fashion innovativeness and had the most interest in shopping. The group with the lowest mean score appeared to be much less involved all around.

COMMENTS:

One or two items might be eliminated without seriously decreasing internal consistency. Item 6 has a significantly lower factor loading and might be an initial candidate for elimination.

REFERENCES:

Hawes, Jon M. and James R. Lumpkin (1984), "Understanding the Outshopper," *JAMS*, 12 (Fall), 200-218.

Lumpkin, James R. (1985), "Shopping Orientation Segmentation of the Elderly Consumer," *JAMS*, 13 (Spring), 271-289.

SCALE ITEMS: OPINION LEADERSHIP (FASHION)

Strongly Disagree	Disagree	Slightly Disagree	Slightly Agree	Agree	Strongly Agree
1	2	3	4	5	6

1. I believe in sharing with others what I know about trends in fashion.
2. I enjoy being asked about fashion trends.
3. It is important to share one's opinion about the new styles with others.
4. I enjoy discussing fashion.
5. I like to help others make fashion decisions.
6. My friends don't think of me as a knowledgeable source of information about fashion trends. **(r)**
7. I dislike discussing fashion and clothing. **(r)**
8. My friends ask for my opinion about new styles.

SCALE NAME: Opinion Leadership (Generalized)

SCALE DESCRIPTION:

A three-item, seven-point Likert-type summated ratings scale measuring the degree to which a person reports liking to talk to friends about products.

SCALE ORIGIN:

Though some of the items are similar to ones used in other scales, this group of items was put into scale form along with six other scales by Raju (1980). An initial pool of 90 items related to exploratory behavior and lifestyle were compiled and then tested for low social desirability bias and high item-total correlations. Thirty- nine items were found to meet the criteria and were common to two separate samples. Items were grouped into seven categories on the basis of interitem correlations and subjective judgement.

SAMPLES:

Raju (1980) collected data from **336** homemakers and **105** students. The homemakers were contacted through local women's clubs and the students were contacted through mostly junior and senior level college classes.

RELIABILITY:

The scale was reported to have reliability (Spearman-Brown) of **.725** and **.738** for the homemaker and student samples, respectively.

VALIDITY:

Though Raju (1980) notes that a factor analysis was performed, the grouping of items for scale purposes was based more on interitem correlations and a subjective classification process.

ADMINISTRATION:

The manner of scale administration was not specifically addressed for either sample by Raju (1980). However, he implied that the homemakers received the questionnaire at a club meeting, filled it out at home by themselves, and returned it by mail. The student sample is assumed to have completed the survey instrument in class. Lower scores on the scale suggest that respondents do not engage in much interpersonal communication about products whereas higher scores imply that they like talking about products and purchases with friends.

MAJOR FINDINGS:

In two studies, Raju (1980) examined the relationships between optimal stimulation level (OSL) and certain personality traits, demographics, and purchase-related psychographics. For both samples, low but significant correlations were found between **interpersonal**

communication and OSL. This finding along with others indicated that people with higher OSLs were more likely to exhibit exploratory behaviors in their consumer behavior.

COMMENTS:

The construct validity of the scale is highly suspect given the manner in which the seven scales used in the study were constructed (as noted in the origination information above). Sixteen of the 39 items were used to compose more than one scale, thus making it unclear what construct the items and their respective scales actually measured. Though the reported reliability levels for this scale are reasonable, further validity testing is needed.

REFERENCE:

Raju, P. S. (1980), "Optimum Stimulation Level: Its Relationship to Personality, Demographics, and Exploratory Behavior," *JCR*, 7 (December), 272-282.

SCALE ITEMS: OPINION LEADERSHIP (GENERALIZED)

Completely Disagree 1————2————3————4————5————6————7 Completely Agree

1. I don't like to talk with my friends about my purchases. **(r)**
2. I like introducing new brands or products to my friends.
3. My friends or neighbors often come to me for advice.

SCALE NAME: Opinion Leadership (Generalized)

SCALE DESCRIPTION:

A six-item, five-point summated ratings scale with varying verbal anchors (see below). The scale measures a person's degree of opinion leadership for a specific product category or topic.

SCALE ORIGIN:

A seven-item version of this scale was first used by King and Summers (1970). Their version was a slight modification of the six-item measure originally developed by Rogers (1961) and discussed by Rogers and Cartano (1962). The six-item scale was used in a 1957 study of the diffusion of new farm ideas among Ohio farmers. Personal interviews were completed with a statewide random area sample of 104 farm operators. A split-half reliability of .703 was calculated for the scale. In that study, a crude version of the sociometric technique of measuring opinion leadership produced scores with a correlation of .225 with the scale scores (Rogers 1961; Rogers and Cartano 1962). The validity of the scale was examined in several studies by correlating scale scores with scores from the key informant method as well as the sociometric technique. Though positive correlations were found, they were not high.

In a series of studies with the King and Summers (1970) version of the scale, reported alpha values ranged from .5 to .87. Childers (1986) reports an alpha of .66 that was raised to a .68 when one of the seven items was removed from the summated scale. Childers also found low nomological validity for the scale. The information below is related to his use of the scale.

SAMPLES:

Samples were taken from the files of a cable television franchise in a large metro area. One sample consisted of people who subscribed to cable and another consisted of people who had been contacted but refused to subscribe. Questionnaires were dropped off by an employee of the franchise but responses were mailed in. **One hundred and seventy six** questionnaires were returned within a three-week period before the cutoff date.

RELIABILITY:

The final version of the scale (shown below) had an alpha of **.83**.

VALIDITY:

Nomological validity was assessed by examining the pattern of correlations between the modified opinion leadership scale and scales measuring other constructs with which it should correlate, according to theory. As expected, the scale had significant though low correlations with several related variables: curiosity about product operation, product usage creativity, perceived risk of adopting cable TV, and ownership of technically oriented products. It did not have a significant correlation with risk preferences. Validity was also examined by comparing known groups' scores on the scale for predictable differences. Subscribers to cable TV had significantly higher scores than non-subscribers, but no significant difference was found between scores of people who subscribed to premium cable and of people who just bought the basic service.

ADMINISTRATION:

The scale was self-administered in a survey instrument format. Lower scores on the scale indicate a person reports him/herself as informing and persuading others whereas higher scores suggest a person has very little opinion leadership.

MAJOR FINDINGS:

The purpose of the study by Childers (1986) was to compare the psychometric properties of the King and Summers (1970) scale with those of a modified version. The main changes were elimination of an item and use of a five-point response scale for each item. In most respects the modified version of the scale was superior to the previous version. The context in which the scale was studied was cable TV adoption.

REFERENCES:

Childers, Terry L. (1986), "Assessment of the Psychometric Properties of an Opinion Leadership Scale," *JMR*, 23 (May), 184-188.

King, Charles W. and John O. Summers (1970), "Overlap of Opinion Leadership Across Consumer Product Categories," *JMR*, 7 (February), 43-50.

Rogers, Everett M. (1961), *Characteristics of Innovators and Other Adopter Categories*. Wooster, Ohio: Ohio Agricultural Experiment Station Research Bulletin #882.

_____ and David G. Cartano (1962), "Methods of Measuring Opinion Leadership," *Public Opinion Quarterly*, 26 (Fall), 435-441.

SCALE ITEMS: OPINION LEADERSHIP (GENERALIZED)

1. In general, do you talk to your friends and neighbors about _____.

Very   Never
Often
   1————————2————————3————————4————————5

2. When you talk to you friends and neighbors about cable television do you:

give a great   give very little
deal of information   information
   1————————2————————3————————4————————5

3. During the past six months, how many people have you told about _____?

told a number   told
of people   no one
   1————————2————————3————————4————————5

4. Compared with your circle of friends, how likely are you to be asked about _____?

| very likely | | | | not at all |
| to be asked | | | | likely to be asked |

1————————2————————3————————4————————5

5. In discussions of _____, which of the following happens most often: (r)

| you tell your | | | | your friends tell |
| friends about ____ | | | | you about ____ |

1————————2————————3————————4————————5

6. *Overall* in all of your discussions with friends and neighbors are you:

| often used as a | | | | not used as a |
| source of advice | | | | source of advice |

1————————2————————3————————4————————5

SCALE NAME: Opinion Leadership (Generalized)

SCALE DESCRIPTION:

A seven-item, summated ratings scale. The scale measures a person's tendency to provide information to and influence others. The topic or product of concern is specified in the items by the user.

SCALE ORIGIN:

The seven-item generalized version of this scale (presented below) was first used by King and Summers (1970). Their version of the scale was a slight modification of the six-item measure originally developed by Rogers (1961) and discussed by Rogers and Cartano (1962). The six-item scale was used in a 1957 study of the diffusion of new farm ideas among Ohio farmers. Personal interviews were completed with a statewide random area sample of 104 farm operators. A split-half reliability of .703 was calculated for the scale. In that study, a crude version of the sociometric technique of measuring opinion leadership produced scores with a correlation of .225 with the scale scores (Rogers 11961; Rogers and Cartano 1962). The validity of the scale was examined in several studies by correlating scale scores with scores from the key informant method as well as the sociometric technique. Though positive correlations were found, they were not high.

SAMPLES:

Davis and Rubin (1983) mailed questionnaires to a sample of two groups in Florida: known adopters of solar energy devices and the general population over the age of 18 years. Analysis was based on **817** usable questionnaires, of which **488** were from solar energy adopters.

RELIABILITY:

An alpha of **.82** was reported by Davis and Rubin (1983).

VALIDITY:

Davis and Rubin (1983) compared scores on their energy-related version of the scale with whether or not a person had purchased a solar energy device in the past. This procedure produced a highly significant Kendall's Tau (.47).

ADMINISTRATION:

Davis and Rubin (1983) gathered data through self-administered mail questionnaires. The higher the score, the more a person expresses a tendency to provide information to others about energy conservation. The lower the score, the less a person appears to inform and influence others.

MAJOR FINDINGS:

Davis and Rubin (1983) examined a few psychographic variables that might distinguish between energy conscious opinion leader groups. Persons with a high amount of **opinion**

leadership expressed more energy consciousness, had a higher degree of self-confidence and leadership traits, were more conservative with the use of credit, and had a greater degree of financial optimism.

COMMENTS:

Though not used in the main study reported by Feick and Price (1987), this scale was used in one of their pilot studies to examine the discriminant validity of a one-item generalized opinion leadership scale and a six-item Market Maven scale.

REFERENCES:

Davis, Duane L. and Ronald S. Rubin (1983), "Identifying the Energy Conscious Consumer: The Case of the Opinion Leader," *JAMS*, 11 (Spring), 169-190.

Feick, Lawrence F. and Linda L. Price (1987), "The Market Maven: A Diffuser of Marketplace Information," *JM*, 51 (January), 83-97.

King, Charles W. and John O. Summers (1970), "Overlap of Opinion Leadership Across Consumer Product Categories," *JMR*, 7 (February), 43-50.

Rogers, Everett M. (1961), *Characteristics of Innovators and Other Adopter Categories*. Wooster, Ohio: Ohio Agricultural Experiment Station Research Bulletin #882.

_____ and David G. Cartano (1962), "Methods of Measuring Opinion Leadership," *Public Opinion Quarterly*, 26 (Fall), 435-441.

SCALE ITEMS: OPINION LEADERSHIP (GENERALIZED)

1. In general, do you like to talk about _____ with your friends? **(r)**
   Yes _____ (1)   No _____ (2)
2. Would you say *you give very little information, an average amount of information, or a great deal of information* about _____ to your friends?
   You give very little information _____ (1)
   You give an average amount of information _____ (2)
   You give a great deal of information _____ (3)
3. During the past six months, have you told anyone about some _____? **(r)**
   Yes _____ (1)   No _____ (2)
4. Compared with your circle of friends, are you *less likely, about as likely, or more likely* to be asked for advice about _____?
   Less likely to be asked _____ (1)
   About as likely to be asked _____ (2)
   More likely to be asked _____ (3)
5. If you and your friends were to discuss _____, what part would you be most likely to play? Would you mainly listen to your friends' ideas or would you try to convince them of your ideas?
   You mainly listen to your friends' ideas _____ (1)
   You try to convince them of your ideas _____ (2)
6. Which of these happens more often? Do you tell your friends about some _____, or do they tell you about some _____? **(r)**

       You tell them about_____.   _____ (1)

       They tell you about _____.   _____ (2)

7. Do you have the feeling that you are generally regarded by your friends and neighbors as a good source of advice about _____? **(r)**

       Yes _____ (1)

       No _____ (2)

SCALE NAME: Opinion Leadership (Purchase)

SCALE DESCRIPTION:

As offered by Wells and Tigert (1971), this is a three-item, six-point, Likert-type summated ratings scale from strongly disagree (1) to strongly agree (6). The scale measures a person's perceived influence on others' purchase decisions. The items in this scale were also used by Wilkes, Burnett, and Howell (1986) but not as a simple summated scale, nor was any reliability information provided. See variations of this scale by Schnaars and Schiffman (1984) as well as Hawes and Lumpkin (1984).

SCALE ORIGIN:

These items were part of a classic study of psychographics by Wells and Tigert (1971). One thousand questionnaires were mailed to homemaker members of the Market Facts mail panel. In addition to gathering demographic, product use, and media data, the survey contained 300 statements that have since served as the basis for the construction of many lifestyle-related scales. The three items for this scale are reported in the article, but they were not analyzed as a multi-item scale. The purpose of the article was to explain how psychographics could improve upon mere demographic description of target audiences and product users. No psychometric information was reported.

One of the first uses of the items as a multi-item scale was by Darden and Perreault (1976). Analysis was based on self-administered questionnaires completed by 278 suburban housewives randomly selected in Athens, Georgia. A split-half reliability of .62 was reported for a four-item version of the scale. Opinion leadership was /not/ one of the lifestyle variables that significantly discriminated between the outshopper groups.

SAMPLES:

Two mailing lists were used to collect data in the Dickerson and Gentry study (1983). One was a list of *Psychology Today* subscribers and the other was a list of members of computer clubs. The former was used to reach non-adopters of computers and the latter was used to reach PC adopters. Analysis was based on a total of **639** questionnaires. Results from a second mailing to non- respondents indicated that their demographic makeup was not significantly different from that of respondents. On the basis of 1980 Census data, the sample was younger and more upscale than the general population.

Lumpkin's (1985) sample was drawn from the Market Facts Consumer Mail Panel. A total of **2854** completed questionnaires were received, but Lumpkin focused on **373** respondents who indicated they were 65 years of age or older.

RELIABILITY:

Alpha values of **.60** and **.7312** were reported by Dickerson and Gentry (1983) and Lumpkin (1985), respectively.

VALIDITY:

Factor analyses performed in the studies indicated that the items loaded together.

ADMINISTRATION:

Data were gathered through self-administered mail questionnaires. Scale scores are typically calculated by averaging numerical responses to individual items. A score of 6 indicates that a person frequently influences others' purchase decisions whereas a 1 means a person rarely provides information that others use to guide their purchase decisions.

MAJOR FINDINGS:

Dickerson and Gentry (1983) found that **opinion leadership** was an especially significant lifestyle variable for discriminating between adopters and nonadopters of home computers. Elderly consumers were cluster analyzed by Lumpkin (1985) and **opinion leadership** appeared to discriminate between the three groups (statistical significance not reported). The group with the highest mean on the scale was also the most interested in shopping and fashion.

COMMENTS:

For such an important construct as this, the reliability should be much higher. Several similar items should be developed, tested, and added to the summated scale.

REFERENCES:

Darden, William R. and William D. Perreault, Jr. (1976), ''Identifying Interurban Shoppers: Multiproduct Purchase Patterns and Segmentation Profiles,'' *JMR*, 13 (February), 51-60.

Dickerson, Mary D. and James W. Gentry (1983), ''Characteristics of Adopters and Non-Adopters of Home Computers,'' *JCR*, 10 (September), 225-235.

Hawes, Jon M. and James R. Lumpkin (1984), ''Understanding the Outshopper,'' *JAMS*, 12 (Fall), 200-218.

Lumpkin, James R. (1985), ''Shopping Orientation Segmentation of the Elderly Consumer,'' *JAMS*, 13 (Spring), 271-289.

Schnaars, Steven P. and Leon G. Schiffman (1984), ''An Application of Segmentation Design Based on a Hybrid of Canonical Correlation and Simple Crosstabulation,'' *JAMS*, 12 (Fall), 177-189.

Wells, William D. and Douglas Tigert (1971), ''Activities, Interests, and Opinions,'' *JAR*, 11 (August), 27-35.

Wilkes, Robert E., John J. Burnett, and Roy D. Howell (1986), ''On the Meaning and Measurement of Religiosity in Consumer Research,'' *JAMS*, 14 (Spring), 47-56.

SCALE ITEMS: OPINION LEADERSHIP (PURCHASE)

Strongly Disagree	Disagree	Slightly Disagree	Slightly Agree	Agree	Strongly Agree
1	2	3	4	5	6

1. My friends or neighbors often come to me for advice.
2. I sometimes influence what my friends buy.
3. People come to me more often than I go to them for information about brands.

SCALE NAME: Opinion Leadership (Shopping)

SCALE DESCRIPTION:

A two-item, six-point, Likert-type summated ratings scale ranging from strongly disagree (1) to strongly agree (6). The scale measures a person's perceived influence on others' store choice decisions. See also a variation on the scale by Hawes and Lumpkin (1984).

SCALE ORIGIN:

It is not clear where these items originated, though the scale bears some similarity to a two-item scale used by Darden and Perreault (1976).

SAMPLES:

Lumpkin's (1985) sample was drawn from the Market Facts Consumer Mail Panel. A total of **2854** completed questionnaires were received, but Lumpkin focused on **373** respondents who indicated they were 65 years of age or older.

RELIABILITY:

An alpha of **.5233** was reported by Lumpkin (1985).

VALIDITY:

Factor analysis indicated that the items loaded together.

ADMINISTRATION:

Data were gathered through self-administered mail questionnaires. Scale scores are typically calculated by averaging numerical responses to individual items. A score of 6 indicates that a person frequently provides others with information that influences their store choices, whereas a score of 1 means a person rarely influences others' store choice decisions.

MAJOR FINDINGS:

Elderly consumers were cluster analyzed by Lumpkin (1985) and **shopping opinion leadership** appeared to be one of the most discriminating of the variables examined (statistical significance not reported). The group with the highest mean on the scale was also the most interested in fashion and the most socially active. The group scoring lowest on the scale seemed to be uninvolved all around.

COMMENTS:

The internal consistency of this scale should be higher. If a few more items were developed, tested, and added to the summated scale, the reliability would be expected to increase.

REFERENCES:

Darden, William R. and William D. Perreault, Jr. (1976), ''Identifying Interurban Shoppers: Multiproduct Purchase Patterns and Segmentation Profiles,'' *JMR*, 13 (February), 51- 60.

Hawes, Jon M. and James R. Lumpkin (1984), ''Understanding the Outshopper,'' *JAMS*, 12 (Fall), 200-218.

Lumpkin, James R. (1985), ''Shopping Orientation Segmentation of the Elderly Consumer,'' *JAMS*, 13 (Spring), 271-289.

SCALE ITEMS: OPINION LEADERSHIP (SHOPPING)

Strongly Disagree	Disagree	Slightly Disagree	Slightly Agree	Agree	Strongly Agree
1	2	3	4	5	6

1. I sometimes influence where my friends shop.
2. When I find a good store, I often tell my friends about it.

SCALE NAME: Optimism (Financial)

SCALE DESCRIPTION:

A two-item, six-point, Likert-type summated ratings scale ranging from strongly disagree (1) to strongly agree (6). The scale measures a person's belief that the family's future income will be higher. See also the Income Optimism scale used by Burnett and Bush (1986).

SCALE ORIGIN:

These items were part of a classic study of psychographics by Wells and Tigert (1971). One thousand questionnaires were mailed to homemaker members of the Market Facts mail panel. In addition to gathering demographic, product use, and media data, the survey contained 300 statements that have since served as the basis for the construction of many lifestyle-related scales. The two items for this scale are reported in the article, but they were not analyzed as a multi-item scale. The purpose of the article was to explain how psychographics could improve upon mere demographic description of target audiences and product users. No psychometric information was reported.

One of the first uses of the items as a multi-item scale was by Darden and Perreault (1976). Analysis was based on self-administered questionnaires completed by 278 suburban housewives randomly selected in Athens, Georgia. A split-half reliability of .63 was reported for the scale. Financial optimism was one of a few lifestyle variables that differentiated between outshopping groups. The group with the most financial optimism was distinguished by heavy outbuying of furniture. Inshoppers and persons who mostly outshopped for clothing and jewelry scored the lowest on this scale.

SAMPLES:

Two mailing lists were used to collect data in the Dickerson and Gentry study (1983). One was a list of *Psychology Today* subscribers and the other was a list of members of computer clubs. The former was used to reach non-adopters of computers and the latter was used to reach PC adopters. Analysis was based on a total of **639** questionnaires. Results from a second mailing to non-respondents indicated that their demographic makeup was not significantly different from that of respondents. On the basis of 1980 Census data, the sample was younger and more upscale than the general population.

Lumpkin and Darden (1982) had **145** usable responses gathered from the consumer research panel of the University of Arkansas. Data were collected from the individuals by mail questionnaire. Lumpkin (1985) collected data from a sample drawn from the Market Facts Consumer Mail Panel. A total of 2854 completed questionnaires were received, but Lumpkin focused on **373** respondents who indicated they were 65 years of or older.

Davis and Rubin (1983) mailed questionnaires to a sample of two groups in Florida: known adopters of solar energy devices and the general population over the age of 18 years. Analysis was based on **817** usable questionnaires, of which 488 were from solar energy adopters.

RELIABILITY:

Alpha values of **.59**, **.72**, **.64**, and **.6862** were calculated by Lumpkin and Darden (1982), Davis and Rubin (1983), Dickerson and Gentry (1983), and Lumpkin (1985), respectively.

VALIDITY:

Factor analysis in the studies indicated the items loaded together. See Davis and Rubin (1983) for the most detailed discussion of the factor analysis test of the scale's validity.

ADMINISTRATION:

Data were gathered in all studies through self-administered mail questionnaires. Scale scores are calculated by averaging numerical responses to individual items. A score of 6 indicates that a person strongly believes that his/her income will be higher in the future whereas a score of 1 means the person expresses extreme pessimism about his/her future income.

MAJOR FINDINGS:

In their study of television program preference groups, Lumpkin and Darden (1982) found a few lifestyle variables that were significantly different among the six groups, but **financial optimism** was *not* one of them. Dickerson and Gentry (1983) also failed to find a significant relationship between **financial optimism** and adoption of home computers though a related construct, financial satisfaction, was significant.

Elderly consumers were cluster analyzed by Lumpkin (1985) and **financial optimism** appeared to discriminate somewhat between two of the three groups (statistical significance not reported). The group with the highest mean on the scale was also the most socially active and the most interested in shopping.

Davis and Rubin (1983) determined that persons who expressed a high degree of energy conservation opinion leadership were significantly more **optimistic** about their future financial condition than persons with less leadership.

COMMENTS:

The low alpha values reported for this two-item measure suggest that the psychomteric quality of the scale would probably be improved by the addition of a few more items.

REFERENCES:

Burnett, John J. and Alan J. Bush (1986), "Profiling the Yuppies," *JAR*, 26 (April/May), 27-35.

Darden, William R. and William D. Perreault, Jr. (1976), "Identifying Interurban Shoppers: Multiproduct Purchase Patterns and Segmentation Profiles," *JMR*, 13 (February), 51- 60.

Davis, Duane L. and Ronald S. Rubin (1983), "Identifying the Energy Conscious Consumer: The Case of the Opinion Leader," *JAMS*, 11 (Spring), 169-190.

Dickerson, Mary D. and James W. Gentry (1983), "Characteristics of Adopters and Non-Adopters of Home Computers," *JCR*, 10 (September), 225-235.

Lumpkin, James R. (1985), "Shopping Orientation Segmentation of the Elderly Consumer," *JAMS*, 13 (Spring), 271-289.

_____ and William R. Darden (1982), "Relating Television Preference Viewing to Shopping Orientations, Lifestyles, and Demographics," *JA*, 11 (4), 56-67.

Wells, William D. and Douglas Tigert (1971), "Activities, Interests, and Opinions," *JAR*, 11 (August), 27-35.

SCALE ITEMS: OPTIMISM (FINANCIAL)

Strongly Disagree	Disagree	Slightly Disagree	Slightly Agree	Agree	Strongly Agree
1	2	3	4	5	6

1. I will probably have more money to spend next year than I have now.
2. Five years from now the family income will probably be a lot higher than it is now.

SCALE NAME: Parental Ethnocentrism

SCALE DESCRIPTION:

A three-item, five-point Likert-type summated ratings scale measuring the degree to which a person (a parent) believes that a child should not learn to doubt his/her parents' views. This scale was called Excluding Outside Forces by Schaefer and Bell (1958) and Carlson and Grossbart (1988).

SCALE ORIGIN:

The items seem to originate from Schaefer and Bell (1958), but may have been used previously. These authors discuss a considerable amount of testing of the items as part of a larger multiscaled instrument. The three-item version reported here was not tested in their studies, but five- and eight-item versions were. The findings indicated that the scales had reasonable though not high internal consistency and test-retest stability.

SAMPLES:

The survey instrument used by Carlson and Grossbart (1988) was distributed to mothers via students at three elementary schools in an unidentified U.S. city. The schools were chosen on a convenience basis but appeared to represent a variety of socioeconomic areas of the city. A $1 contribution to the PTO was offered for each completed questionnaire returned by the children. Analysis was based on **451** completed questionnaires. Ninety-three percent of the responding mothers indicated that they were the primary person in the child's socialization.

RELIABILITY:

Carlson and Grossbart (1988) reported an alpha of .**74** and a beta of .68 for the scale.

VALIDITY:

No examination of scale validity was reported by Carlson and Grossbart (1988).

ADMINISTRATION:

The scale was self-administered along with many other measures in the questionnaire used by Carlson and Grossbart (1988). Higher scores on the scale mean that parents strongly believe it is best if children never learn to question their parent's ideas.

MAJOR FINDINGS:

The authors investigated the relationship between general parental socialization styles and children's consumer socialization. Of the five parental socialization style clusters examined, Authoritarian mothers expressed significantly greater **family ethnocentrism** than did any of the other parental style clusters. Permissive mothers expressed significantly less **ethnocentrism** than the other clusters.

REFERENCES:

Carlson, Les and Sanford Grossbart (1988), ''Parental Style and Consumer Socialization of Children,'' *JCR*, 15 (June), 77-94.

Schaefer, Earl S. and Richard Q. Bell (1958), ''Development of a Parental Attitude Research Instrument,'' *Child Development*, 29 (September), 339-361.

SCALE ITEMS: PARENTAL ETHNOCENTRISM

Please indicate your opinion by checking one response (strongly disagree, disagree, neither disagree or agree, agree, strongly agree) for each statement. Check one for each statement.

Strongly Disagree	Disagree	Neither	Agree	Strongly Agree
1	2	3	4	5

1. A parent should never be made to look wrong in their children's eyes.
2. It's best for a child if he/she never gets started wondering whether their parent's views are right.
3. Children should never learn things outside the home which make them doubt their parent's ideas.

SCALE NAME: Parental Style (Authoritarian)

SCALE DESCRIPTION:

A seven-item, forced-choice summated ratings scale measuring the degree to which a parent expects unquestioning obedience and respect from his/her children.

SCALE ORIGIN:

Though this scale bears similarity to a construct described by Baumrind (1971), correspondence with Carlson indicates that the Baumrind article did not highlight data collected with the scale but via observation. Carlson obtained the scale items in personal correspondence with Baumrind.

SAMPLES:

The survey instrument used by Carlson and Grossbart (1988) was distributed to mothers via students at three elementary schools in an unidentified U.S. city. The schools were chosen on a convenience basis but appeared to represent a variety of socioeconomic areas of the city. A $1 contribution to the PTO was offered for each completed questionnaire returned by the children. Analysis was based on **451** completed questionnaires. Ninety-three percent of the responding mothers indicated that they were the primary person in the child's socialization.

RELIABILITY:

Carlson and Grossbart (1988) reported an alpha of **.60** and a beta of .54 for the scale.

VALIDITY:

No examination of scale validity was reported by Carlson and Grossbart (1988).

ADMINISTRATION:

The scale was self-administered along with many other measures in the questionnaire used by Carlson and Grossbart (1988). Answer A of a pair should be scored as 1 and answer B should be scored as 2, with reverse scoring where indicated. Higher scores on the scale mean that parents expect their children to respect and obey them with little or no back-talking.

MAJOR FINDINGS:

The authors investigated the relationship between general parental socialization styles and children's consumer socialization. Of the five parental socialization style clusters examined, Permissive mothers expressed significantly less **authoritarianism** than did all of the other parental style clusters.

COMMENTS:

The low alpha indicates that the scale does not have good internal consistency and should be used cautiously until its reliability can be substantially improved.

REFERENCES:

Baumrind, Diana (1971), ''Current Patterns of Parental Authority,'' *Developmental Psychology Monograph*, 4 (January), 1-103.
Carlson, Les and Sanford Grossbart (1988), ''Parental Style and Consumer Socialization of Children,'' *JCR*, 15 (June), 77-94.

SCALE ITEMS: PARENTAL STYLE (AUTHORITARIAN)

Please indicate your opinion by checking one response (A or B) for each statement. There are no right or wrong answers, so answer according to your opinion. It is important to answer all questions even if you are not completely sure of your answer. Just check the response (A or B) that comes *closest* to your opinion. Some statements may seem alike but are necessary to show slight differences of opinion. *All questions refer to your youngest child who attends this school.*

A. A child should be able to question the authority of his/her parents.
B. A child should honor his/her mother and father and accept their authority.

A. The preservation of order and tradition should be highly valued.
B. There is no reason for the younger generation to preserve the order and traditions set by the older generation. **(r)**

A. When a child is called, he/she should come immediately.
B. A child should not have to come immediately when he/she is called. **(r)**

A. Not all parents deserve the respect of their children.
B. A child should respect his/her parents because they are his/her parents.

A. I don't mind it particularly when my child argues with me.
B. I don't particularly like my child to argue with me.

Children would be less likely to get into trouble with the law:
A. if parents taught their children respect for authority.
B. if parents listened more to what their children had to say. **(r)**

A. Parents should take seriously the opinions of young children.
B. Most young children change their minds so frequently that it is hard to take their opinions seriously.

SCALE NAME: Parental Style (Concept-Orientation)

SCALE DESCRIPTION:

A seven-item, five-point Likert-type summated ratings scale measuring the degree to which a parent reports taking an interest in his/her child's ideas about the use of money and purchasing products. The tone suggested in the items is of positive communication, indicating that the child's role, assistance, and opinion are respected rather than that the child's purchases are being dictated.

SCALE ORIGIN:

Some of the items in this scale are similar to ones used in a scale by Moschis (1978, p. 45). However, items in that measure were written from the child's point of view.

SAMPLES:

The survey instrument used by Carlson and Grossbart (1988) was distributed to mothers via students at three elementary schools in an unidentified U.S. city. The schools were chosen on a convenience basis but appeared to represent a variety of socioeconomic areas of the city. A $1 contribution to the PTO was offered for each completed questionnaire returned by the children. Analysis was based on **451** completed questionnaires. Ninety-three percent of the responding mothers indicated that they were the primary person in the child's socialization.

RELIABILITY:

Carlson and Grossbart (1988) reported an alpha of **.71** and a beta of .61 for the scale.

VALIDITY:

No examination of scale validity was reported by Carlson and Grossbart (1988).

ADMINISTRATION:

The scale was self-administered along with many other measures in the questionnaire used by Carlson and Grossbart (1988). Higher scores on the scale mean that respondents report a high frequency of positive communication with their children whereas lower scores imply either a dictatorial mode of communication from the parents or little communication of any kind.

MAJOR FINDINGS:

The authors investigated the relationship between general parental socialization styles and children's consumer socialization. In a factor analysis of scale scores, scores on the **Concept-Orientation** scale loaded on a factor described as the "parent-child communication about consumption." A significant difference was found in the degree of parent-child communication between several of the parental socialization style clusters examined.

REFERENCES:

Carlson, Les and Sanford Grossbart (1988), ''Parental Style and Consumer Socialization of Children,'' *JCR*, 15 (June), 77-94.

Moschis, George P. (1978), *Acquisition of the Consumer Role by Adolescents*, Research Monograph No. 82. Atlanta, Ga.: Publishing Services Division, College of Business Administration, Georgia State University.

SCALE ITEMS: PARENTAL STYLE (CONCEPT-ORIENTATION)

Very Seldom	Seldom	Sometimes	Often	Very Often
1————	——2————	——3————	——4————	——5

1. I ask my child to help me buy things for the family.
2. I tell my child to decide how to spend his/her money.
3. I tell my child to decide about things he/she should or shouldn't buy.
4. I tell my child buying things he/she likes is important even if others don't like them.
5. I ask my child what he/she thinks about things he/she buys for him/herself.
6. I ask my child for advice about buying things.
7. To teach my child to become a consumer I allow my child to learn from his/her own experience.

SCALE NAME: Parental Style (Firm)

SCALE DESCRIPTION:

A two-item, forced-choice summated ratings scale measuring the degree to which a parent believes that he/she is firm rather than permissive with his/her children. This measure was referred to by Carlson and Grossbart (1988) as Firm Enforcement.

SCALE ORIGIN:

Though this scale bears similarity to a construct described by Baumrind (1971), correspondence with Carlson indicates that the Baumrind article did not highlight data collected with the scale but via observation. Carlson obtained the scale items in personal correspondence with Baumrind.

SAMPLES:

The survey instrument used by Carlson and Grossbart (1988) was distributed to mothers via students at three elementary schools in an unidentified U.S. city. The schools were chosen on a convenience basis but appeared to represent a variety of socioeconomic areas of the city. A $1 contribution to the PTO was offered for each completed questionnaire returned by the children. Analysis was based on **451** completed questionnaires. Ninety-three percent of the responding mothers indicated that they were the primary person in the child's socialization.

RELIABILITY:

Carlson and Grossbart (1988) reported an alpha of **.78** and a beta of .78 for the scale.

VALIDITY:

No examination of scale validity was reported by Carlson and Grossbart (1988).

ADMINISTRATION:

The scale was self-administered along with many other measures in the questionnaire used by Carlson and Grossbart (1988). Answer A of a pair should be scored as 1 and answer B should be scored as 2, with reverse scoring where indicated. Higher scores on the scale mean that parents view themselves as being firm with their children and expect them to obey.

MAJOR FINDINGS:

The authors investigated the relationship between general parental socialization styles and children's consumer socialization. Of the five parental socialization style clusters examined, Authoritarian, Rigid Controlling, and Authoritative mothers expressed significantly greater **firm parenting style** than did the Permissive and Neglecting parental style clusters.

REFERENCES:

Baumrind, Diana (1971), ''Current Patterns of Parental Authority,'' *Developmental Psychology Monograph*, 4 (January), 1-103.

Carlson, Les and Sanford Grossbart (1988), ''Parental Style and Consumer Socialization of Children,'' *JCR*, 15 (June), 77-94.

SCALE ITEMS: PARENTAL STYLE (FIRM)

Please indicate your opinion by checking one response (A or B) for each statement. There are no right or wrong answers, so answer according to your opinion. It is important to answer all questions even if you are not completely sure of your answer. Just check the response (A or B) that comes *closest* to your opinion. Some statements may seem alike but are necessary to show slight differences of opinion. *All questions refer to your youngest child who attends this school.*

A. Other parents probably see me as rather firm with my child.
B. Other parents probably see me as rather permissive with my child. **(r)**

With regard to my children, I would characterize my discipline as:

A. quite firm.
B. fairly permissive. **(r)**

SCALE NAME: Parental Style (Protective)

SCALE DESCRIPTION:

A two-item, five-point Likert-type summated ratings scale measuring the degree to which a person (a parent) believes that a child should be shielded from discouraging and difficult situations. This scale was called Fostering Dependency by Schaefer and Bell (1958) and Carlson and Grossbart (1988).

SCALE ORIGIN:

The items seem to originate from Schaefer and Bell (1958), but may have been used previously. These authors discuss a considerable amount of testing of the items as part of a larger multiscaled instrument. The two-item version reported here was not tested in their studies, but five- and eight-item versions were. The findings indicated that the scales had reasonable though not high internal consistency and test-retest stability.

SAMPLES:

The survey instrument used by Carlson and Grossbart (1988) was distributed to mothers via students at three elementary schools in an unidentified U.S. city. The schools were chosen on a convenience basis but appeared to represent a variety of socioeconomic areas of the city. A $1 contribution to the PTO was offered for each completed questionnaire returned by the children. Analysis was based on **451** completed questionnaires. Ninety-three percent of the responding mothers indicated that they were the primary person in the child's socialization.

RELIABILITY:

Carlson and Grossbart (1988) reported an alpha of **.60** and a beta of .60 for the scale.

VALIDITY:

No examination of scale validity was reported.

ADMINISTRATION:

The scale was self-administered along with many other measures in the questionnaire. Higher scores on the scale mean that parents strongly believe children should be protected from disappointment.

MAJOR FINDINGS:

The authors investigated the relationship between general parental socialization styles and children's consumer socialization. Of the five parental socialization style clusters examined, Authoritarian mothers expressed significantly greater concern for **protecting** children than did any of the other parental style clusters.

COMMENTS:

The low reliability of the scale is justification for cautious use. The addition of a few more appropriate items might improve its psychometric quality substantially. Potential items can be found in Schaefer and Bell's (1958) article.

REFERENCES:

Carlson, Les and Sanford Grossbart (1988), ''Parental Style and Consumer Socialization of Children,'' *JCR*, 15 (June), 77-94.

Schaefer, Earl S. and Richard Q. Bell (1958), ''Development of a Parental Attitude Research Instrument,'' *Child Development*, 29 (September), 339-361.

SCALE ITEMS: PARENTAL STYLE (PROTECTIVE)

Please indicate your opinion by checking one response (strongly disagree, disagree, neither disagree or agree, agree, strongly agree) for each statement. Check one for each statement.

Strongly Disagree	Disagree	Neither	Agree	Strongly Agree
1	2	3	4	5

1. Parents should know better than allow their children to be exposed to difficult situations.
2. Children should be kept away from all hard jobs which might be discouraging.

SCALE NAME: Parental Style (Socio-Orientation)

SCALE DESCRIPTION:

A six-item, five-point Likert-type summated ratings scale measuring the degree to which a parent reports communicating to a child what he/she wants the child to do, in contrast to taking an interest in what the child him/herself wants to do.

SCALE ORIGIN:

The use of these items as a multi-item measure appears to be original to Carlson and Grossbart (1988). However, ideas for some of the items came from the research of Moschis (1978, p. 45) and Ward, Wackman, and Wartella (1977).

SAMPLES:

The survey instrument used by Carlson and Grossbart (1988) was distributed to mothers via students at three elementary schools in an unidentified U.S. city. The schools were chosen on a convenience basis but appeared to represent a variety of socioeconomic areas of the city. A $1 contribution to the PTO was offered for each completed questionnaire returned by the children. Analysis was based on **451** completed questionnaires. Ninety-three percent of the responding mothers indicated that they were the primary person in the child's socialization.

RELIABILITY:

Carlson and Grossbart (1988) reported an alpha of **.56** and a beta of .51 for the scale.

VALIDITY:

No examination of scale validity was reported by Carlson and Grossbart (1988).

ADMINISTRATION:

The scale was self-administered along with many other measures in the questionnaire used by Carlson and Grossbart (1988). Higher scores on the scale mean that the parents often tell their children what to buy/not buy whereas lower scores imply that the parents let their children have more freedom in the use of their money.

MAJOR FINDINGS:

The authors investigated the relationship between general parental socialization styles and children's consumer socialization. In a factor analysis of scale scores, scores on the **Socio-Orientation** scale loaded on a factor described as "restriction of consumption." Some but not many significant differences were found in the degree of consumption restriction among the five parental socialization styles examined.

COMMENTS:

The low alpha and beta indicate that the scale is of dubious reliability, possibly because the child's degree of autonomy is product-dependent and is not consistent across product categories.

REFERENCES:

Carlson, Les and Sanford Grossbart (1988), ''Parental Style and Consumer Socialization of Children,'' *JCR*, 15 (June), 77-94.

Moschis, George P. (1978), *Acquisition of the Consumer Role by Adolescents*, Research Monograph No. 82. Atlanta, Ga.: Publishing Services Division, College of Business Administration, Georgia State University.

Ward, Scott, Daniel B. Wackman, and Ellen Wartella (1977), *How Children Learn to Buy*. Beverly Hills, Calif.: Sage Publications, Inc.

SCALE ITEMS: PARENTAL STYLE (SOCIO-ORIENTATION)

Very Seldom	Seldom	Sometimes	Often	Very Often
1———————	—2———————	——3———————	—4———————	—5

1. I tell my child he/she shouldn't ask questions about things children do not usually buy.
2. I tell my child he/she is not allowed to buy certain things.
3. I tell my child what things he/she should or shouldn't buy.
4. I want to know what my child does with his/her money.
5. I complain when I do not like something my child bought for him/herself.
6. To teach my child to become a consumer I stop him/her from doing certain things.

SCALE NAME: Parental Style (Strict)

SCALE DESCRIPTION:

A three-item, five-point Likert-type summated ratings scale measuring the degree to which a parent believes that being strict with children is appropriate.

SCALE ORIGIN:

The items seem to originate from Schaefer and Bell (1958), but may have been used previously. These authors discuss a considerable amount of testing of the items as part of a larger multiscaled instrument. The three-item version reported here was not tested in their studies, but five- and eight-item versions were. The findings indicated that the scales had reasonable though not high internal consistency and test-retest stability.

SAMPLES:

The survey instrument used by Carlson and Grossbart (1988) was distributed to mothers via students at three elementary schools in an unidentified U.S. city. The schools were chosen on a convenience basis but appeared to represent a variety of socioeconomic areas of the city. A $1 contribution to the PTO was offered for each completed questionnaire returned by the children. Analysis was based on **451** completed questionnaires. Ninety-three percent of the responding mothers indicated that they were the primary person in the child's socialization.

RELIABILITY:

Carlson and Grossbart (1988) reported an alpha of **.81** and a beta of .78 for the scale.

VALIDITY:

No examination of scale validity was reported by Carlson and Grossbart (1988).

ADMINISTRATION:

The scale was self-administered along with many other measures in the questionnaire used by Carlson and Grossbart (1988). Higher scores on the scale mean that parents strongly believe that being strict with children is the best way to raise them.

MAJOR FINDINGS:

The authors investigated the relationship between general parental socialization styles and children's consumer socialization. Of the five parental socialization style clusters examined, Authoritarian, Rigid Controlling, and (especially) Authoritative mothers expressed significantly greater **strict parenting styles** than did the Permissive and Neglecting parental style clusters.

REFERENCES:

Carlson, Les and Sanford Grossbart (1988), ''Parental Style and Consumer Socialization of Children,'' *JCR*, 15 (June), 77-94.

Schaefer, Earl S. and Richard Q. Bell (1958), ''Development of a Parental Attitude Research Instrument,'' *Child Development*, 29 (September), 339-361.

SCALE ITEMS: PARENTAL STYLE (STRICT)

Please indicate your opinion by checking one response (strongly disagree, disagree, neither disagree or agree, agree, strongly agree) for each statement. Check one for each statement.

Strongly Disagree	Disagree	Neither	Agree	Strongly Agree
1———————	—2———————	—3———————	—4———————	—5

1. A child will be grateful later on for strict training.
2. Strict discipline develops a fine, strong character.
3. Children who are held to strong rules grow up to be the best adults.

SCALE NAME: Patriotism

SCALE DESCRIPTION:

A five-item, seven-point Likert-type summated ratings scale measuring the degree to which a person holds views about the U.S. that could be considered patriotic. However, this scale may measure a sort of ''psuedopatriotism'' that is related less to love of country and more to blind loyalty and ethnocentrism.

SCALE ORIGIN:

The items in the scale are taken from the Patriotism subscale of the Ethnocentrism scale (Levinson 1950, p. 108). That scale had 10 items whereas the version used by Shimp and Sharma (1987) employed four of those items and one from the Politico-Economic Conservatism Scale (Form 60) (Levinson 1950, p. 163). Further, to update the scale, several of the items were rephrased slightly. Information about the reliability of the scale and mean scores of different groups are given by Levinson (1950, p. 112, 113), but are not particularly relevant because several items are out of date in that version of the scale and it should not be used now.

SAMPLES:

The scale was administered in three different samples. One sample consisted of names and addresses obtained from a list broker. One thousand questionnaires were mailed to each of three deliberately chosen cities: Detroit, Denver, and Los Angeles. The response rate was just less than one third for each area. At the same time, 950 questionnaires were sent to former panel members in the Carolinas. The response rate was nearly 60%. The total sample size in this ''four-areas study'' was **1535**.

The ''Carolinas study'' was conducted with a group of **417** people who were a part of the ''four-areas study.'' Data for the former study were collected two years prior to the latter. A third study examined data from **145** college students. Though the proportions varied, each of the samples except the student group had respondents representing most age and income groups.

RELIABILITY:

Alpha values of **.58** to **.69** were reported for the short version of this scale by Shimp and Sharma (1987), depending on the various geographic areas and studies.

VALIDITY:

The validity of the scale was not specifically examined in the study.

ADMINISTRATION:

The scale was self-administered along with other measures as part of a larger survey instrument in each of the four samples. All except the student sample received question- naires in the mail. Higher scores imply that respondents are strongly ''patriotic'' whereas lower scores suggest that they are very open to the values of other countries and not blindly loyal and supportive of America.

MAJOR FINDINGS:

The purpose of the study was to describe the construction and validation of a scale to measure the American consumer's ethnocentrism. In each of the samples, ethnocentrism was found to have a significant and relatively high (.39 to .66) positive correlations with **patriotism**.

COMMENTS:

The range of alpha values indicates that reliability is consistently low. Only cautious use should be made of this short scale until its psychometric quality is improved.

REFERENCES:

Levinson, Daniel J. (1950), "The Study of Ethnocentric Ideology," in *The Authoritarian Personality*, T. W. Adorno, Else Frenkel-Brunswik, Daniel J. Levinson, and R. Nevitt Sanford, eds. New York, N.Y.: Harper & Row Publishers, Inc.

Shimp, Terence A. and Subhash Sharma (1987), "Consumer Ethnocentrism: Construction and Validation of the CETSCALE," *JMR*, 24 (August), 280-289.

SCALE ITEMS: PATRIOTISM

Strongly Disagree	Moderately Disagree	Slightly Disagree	Neither Agree Nor Disagree	Slightly Agree	Moderately Agree	Strongly Agree
1	2	3	4	5	6	7

1. If a person won't fight for his country, he deserves a lot worse than just prison or work camp.
2. People throughout the world may be in need, but it would be a mistake to lower our immigration quotas and allow them to flood into the country.
3. Patriotism and loyalty are the first and most important requirements of a good citizen.
4. America may not be perfect, but the American Way has brought us about as close as human beings can get to a perfect society.
5. The main threat to basic American institutions during this century has come from the infiltration of foreign ideas, doctrines, and agitators.

SCALE NAME: Personalizing Shopper

SCALE DESCRIPTION:

A three-item, six-point, Likert-type summated ratings scale from strongly disagree (1) to strongly agree (6). The scale measures a consumer's interest in shopping in stores where he or she is known.

SCALE ORIGIN:

It is not clear where the items originated or where they were first used as a multi-item summated ratings scale, though they bear some similarity to items used in a couple of scales by Darden and Reynolds (1971).

SAMPLES:

Lumpkin (1985) analyzed data collected from a sample drawn from the Market Facts Consumer Mail Panel. A total of **2854** completed questionnaires were received, but Lumpkin focused just on **373** respondents who indicated they were 65 years of age or older.

Hawes and Lumpkin (1984) collected data from **581** residents of 14 communities near the Ft. Worth-Dallas metroplex. Each of the communities was randomly sampled in proportion to its population by means of the respective telephone directories. The questionnaire was to be filled out by the household member responsible for most of the shopping. The distribution of respondents by community was similar to the actual population distribution.

RELIABILITY:

Alpha values of **.8492** and **.826** were calculated by Lumpkin (1985) and Hawes and Lumpkin (1984), respectively.

VALIDITY:

Factor analysis indicated the items loaded together.

ADMINISTRATION:

Data were gathered in the studies through self-administered mail questionnaires. Scale scores are calculated by averaging numerical responses to individual items. A score of 6 indicates that a consumer has a strong tendency to shop where he or she is known by the store's employees whereas a 1 implies a person has little concern about that social aspect of shopping.

MAJOR FINDINGS:

Elderly consumers were cluster analyzed by Lumpkin (1985) and **personalizing shopping** discriminated between the three groups, though the level of statistical significance was not reported. The group with the highest mean on the scale was also the most socially active and had the most interest in shopping and fashion. The group with the lowest mean score appeared to be much less involved all around. The purpose of the study by Hawes and Lumpkin (1984) was to examine demographic and psychographic characteristics of outshoppers. **Personalizing shopping** tendencies did **not** significantly differentiate between inshoppers and outshoppers.

REFERENCES:

Darden, William R. and Fred D. Reynolds (1971), ''Shopping Orientations and Product Usage Rates,'' *JMR*, 8 (November), 505-508.

Hawes, Jon M. and James R. Lumpkin (1984), ''Understanding the Outshopper,'' *JAMS*, 12 (Fall), 200-218.

Lumpkin, James R. (1985), ''Shopping Orientation Segmentation of the Elderly Consumer,'' *JAMS*, 13 (Spring), 271-289.

SCALE ITEMS: PERSONALIZING SHOPPER +

Strongly Disagree	Disagree	Slightly Disagree	Slightly Agree	Agree	Strongly Agree
1	2	3	4	5	6

1. I like to shop where people know me.
2. I like to shop where the clerks know my name.
3. I try to get to know the clerks in the stores where I shop.

+ Lumpkin (1985) used all three items but Hawes and Lumpkin (1984) used only items 1 and 2.

SCALE NAME: Personalizing Shopper

SCALE DESCRIPTION:

A four-item, five-point Likert-type summated ratings scale measuring the degree to which a consumer considers it important to shop at a local store where he or she is known. The measure was called Familiarity by Saegert, Hoover, and Hilger (1985).

SCALE ORIGIN:

As a summated scale, the measure is original to Saegert, Hoover, and Hilger (1985). The authors note that the items were adapted from some used by Kelly and Stephenson (1967). The items in that study were used in the form of bipolar descriptors and do not appear to have been summated.

SAMPLES:

Saegert and his coauthors reported on four surveys, only two of which used the scale of interest. One of those studies involved random selection of 1000 Spanish names and 1000 non-Spanish names and mailing questionnaires to those individuals. A total of **299** questionnaires were returned and the response rates for both groups were very low (9% for Hispanics and 21% for others), indicating a need to confirm the findings with personal interviews in another sample. The second survey of interest was conducted in a small Texas town with **195** women (95 Hispanic and 100 non-Hispanic) who were selected randomly from blocks in the town and houses within the blocks.

RELIABILITY:

An alpha of **.82** was calculated for the scale.

VALIDITY:

A factor analysis by Saegert, Hoover, and Hilger (1985) of 25 shopping-related items indicated that the items in this scale loaded together. (Information in the article as well as some provided by Saegert in personal correspondence suggests that the factor analysis and the alpha reported above were based on data collected just in the mail survey. The article specifically states, however, that analyses of the separate ethnic groups as well as the data from the personal interviews produced almost identical factor interpretations.)

ADMINISTRATION:

In one survey by Saegert and his coauthors, the scale was self-administered as part of a mail questionnaire, whereas in the other survey it was administered by bilingual interviewers. Higher scores on the scale indicate that consumers think shopping at a store that is local and where they are known is very important.

MAJOR FINDINGS:

The authors used the results of four surveys to examine differences between Anglo-Americans and Mexican-Americans in shopping-related attitudes and behaviors. In both samples described above, being **personalizing shoppers** was significantly more important to Hispanic than to non-Hispanic respondents, but for both groups it was the least important shopping factor among those studied.

REFERENCES:

Kelly, Robert F. and Ronald Stephenson (1967), ''The Semantic Differential: An Information Source for Designing Retail Patronage Appeals,'' *JA*, 31 (October), 43-47.

Saegert, Joel, Robert J. Hoover, and Marye Tharp Hilger (1985), ''Characteristics of Mexican American Consumers,'' *JCR*, 12 (June), 104-109.

SCALE ITEMS: PERSONALIZING SHOPPER +

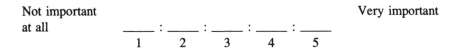

Not important
at all   _____ : _____ : _____ : _____ : _____   Very important
                            1   2   3   4   5

1. My friends and neighbors shop there.
2. I know the owner/manager.
3. The store is locally owned.
4. The store has been in town a long time.

+ These items were reconstructed from phrases supplied in personal correspondence by Saegert.

SCALE NAME: Pleasure

SCALE DESCRIPTION:

A six-item, seven-point semantic differential summated ratings scale measuring one's pleasure-related emotional reaction to an environmental stimulus.

SCALE ORIGIN:

This scale is taken from the work of Mehrabian and Russell (1974). Given previous work by others as well as their own research, they proposed that three factors compose all emotional reactions to environmental stimuli. They referred to the three factors as pleasure, arousal, and dominance. A series of studies were used to develop measures of each factor. In a study of the ''final'' set of items, 214 University of California undergraduates each used the scales to evaluate a different subset of six situations (hence the analysis was based on 1284 observations). A principal components factor analysis with oblique rotation was used and the expected three factors emerged. Pleasure, arousal, and dominance explained 27%, 23%, and 14% of the available evidence, respectively. Scores on the pleasure scale had correlations of -.07 and .03 with arousal and dominance, respectively. Dominance had a correlation of .18 with arousal.

SAMPLES:

Holbrook et al. (1984) used **60** MBA students with a mean age of 25.6 years.

RELIABILITY:

An alpha of **.89** was reported for the scale.

VALIDITY:

No examination of the scale's validity was reported.

ADMINISTRATION:

The scale was self-administered along with several other measures in the middle of individual experimental sessions. Lower scores on the scale suggest that respondents enjoy some specified stimulus whereas higher scores imply that they are bored and/or displeased with the stimulus. Holbrook at al. (1984) noted that scores were normalized for each individual by subtracting the scale mean from the response to each item and then summing the corrected numeric responses.

MAJOR FINDINGS:

Holbrook et al. (1984) examined the role of emotions, performance, and personality in the enjoyment of games. In general, they found that emotions depend on personality-game congruity, perceived complexity, and prior performance. Specifically, **pleasure** expressed with playing a video game was most significantly predicted by a match between cognitive style (visualizing/verbalizing) and game format (visual/verbal), perceived complexity of the game, and number of successful performances out of four immediately preceding plays.

COMMENTS:

As noted above, this scale was developed along with two other scales, arousal and dominance. Though scored separately, they are typically used together in a study. See also Havlena and Holbrook (1986).

REFERENCES:

Havlena, William J. and Morris B. Holbrook (1986), "The Varieties of Consumption Experience: Comparing Two Typologies of Emotion in Consumer Behavior," *JCR*, 13 (December), 394-404.

Holbrook, Morris B., Robert W. Chestnut, Terence A. Oliva, and Eric A. Greenleaf (1984), "Play as a Consumption Experience: The Roles of Emotions, Performance, and Personality in the Enjoyment of Games," *JCR*, 11 (September), 728-739.

Mehrabian, Albert and James A. Russell (1974), *An Approach to Environmental Psychology*. Cambridge, Mass.: The MIT Press.

SCALE ITEMS: PLEASURE

happy	___ : ___ : ___ : ___ : ___ : ___ : ___	unhappy
	1 2 3 4 5 6 7	
pleased	___ : ___ : ___ : ___ : ___ : ___ : ___	annoyed
	1 2 3 4 5 6 7	
satisfied	___ : ___ : ___ : ___ : ___ : ___ : ___	unsatisfied
	1 2 3 4 5 6 7	
contented	___ : ___ : ___ : ___ : ___ : ___ : ___	melancholic
	1 2 3 4 5 6 7	
hopeful	___ : ___ : ___ : ___ : ___ : ___ : ___	despairing
	1 2 3 4 5 6 7	
relaxed	___ : ___ : ___ : ___ : ___ : ___ : ___	bored
	1 2 3 4 5 6 7	

SCALE NAME: Possessiveness

SCALE DESCRIPTION:

A nine-item, five-point Likert-type summated ratings scale measuring the degree to which a person desires to maintain control over his/her possessions. A four-item version of the scale was used by O'Guinn and Faber (1989).

SCALE ORIGIN:

The origin of the scale is reported by Belk (1984). The measure of possessiveness was one of three scales constructed for examining aspects of materialism. Initial pools of 30 or more items were tested for each of the three measures with **237** business school students. On the basis of factor analysis, item-total correlations, and measures of internal consistency, seven or more items were chosen from each pool to measure the three materialism-related constructs. The eight items retained for measuring possessiveness were reported to have an alpha of **.68**.

SAMPLES:

Belk (1984, 1985) examined the scale in various ways with three more samples. One was composed of **48** business students. Another sample had **338** subjects, 213 of whom were business students. (These two samples were reported to be about two-thirds male.) A third sample was composed of 33 families representing **99** people who ranged in age from 13 to 92 years.

Two samples were employed by O'Guinn and Faber (1989). One yielded **386** completed responses (out of 808 questionnaires sent) from people who had written an organization that aided compulsive buyers. A second group was used for comparison and was intended to represent the general population. Eight hundred questionnaires were mailed to people in three Illinois areas: Chicago, Springfield, and Bloomington-Normal. Two mailings produced a total of **250** completed survey forms.

RELIABILITY:

An alpha of **.57** was reported for one of the Belk (1984) samples (n = 338). A two-week-interval test-retest correlation of **.87** (n = 48) was reported for another Belk (1984, 1985) sample. O'Guinn and Faber (1989) calculated an alpha of **.61**.

VALIDITY:

Belk (1984) compared scale scores with other measures in a multitrait-multimethod matrix. As evidence of convergent validity, scores on the possessiveness scale were significantly correlated with two other measures used to assess the same construct. Only partial support for discriminant validity was found. Evidence of criterion validity was found, as two known groups had significantly different mean scores on the scale and the differences were in the hypothesized directions.

No examination of scale validity was made by O'Guinn and Faber (1989) beyond factor analysis. Items pertaining to possessiveness and two other materialism-related constructs were factor analyzed and three factors clearly emerged. The authors did indicate that the scales were slightly modified on the basis of the factor analysis, however.

ADMINISTRATION:

The scale was one of several self-administered measures in each of the studies. Higher scores on the scale indicate that respondents have a strong tendency to buy and save objects whereas lower scores indicate that respondents are more willing to rent, borrow, and discard items.

MAJOR FINDINGS:

The purpose of Belk's (1984) article was to discuss the construction and characteristics of three materialism-related constructs: envy, **possessiveness**, and nongenerosity. Many of the findings are reported above. In addition, possessiveness had a low but significant negative correlation with life satisfaction.

Belk (1985) examined further aspects of the three subscales, but also the psychometric characteristics of the materialism scale as a whole. In particular, he studied generational differences in materialism. Among the many findings was that the youngest and middle generations were similar in their **possessiveness,** but were both significantly more **possessive** than the oldest generation.

O'Guinn and Faber (1989) studied compulsive shopping. Their results showed that a sample of compulsive shoppers were not significantly more **possessive** than a general sample of consumers.

COMMENTS:

The three materialism-related measures mentioned above have been used summed separately and also together. Belk (1985) reported two alpha values for the combined scale, .66 (n = 338) and .73 (n = 48), and a test-retest correlation of .68 (n = 48). O'Guinn and Faber (1989) calculated an alpha of .71 for the combined scale.

REFERENCES:

Belk, Russell W. (1984), "Three Scales to Measure Constructs Related to Materialism: Reliability, Validity, and Relationships to Measures of Happiness," in *Advances in Consumer Research*, Vol. 11, Thomas Kinnear, ed. Provo, Utah: Association for Consumer Research, 291-297.

_____ (1985), "Materialism: Trait Aspects of Living in the Material World," *JCR*, 12 (December), 265-280.

O'Guinn, Thomas C. and Ronald J. Faber (1989), "Compulsive Buying: A Phenomenological Exploration," *JCR*, 16 (September), 147-157.

SCALE ITEMS: POSSESSIVENESS +

Strongly Disagree	Agree	Neutral	Disagree	Strongly Agree
1—————————	2—————————	3—————————	4—————————	5

1. Renting or leasing a car is more appealing to me than owning one. **(r)**
2. I tend to hang on to things I should probably throw out.
3. I get very upset if something is stolen from me even if it has little monetary value.
4. I don't get particularly upset when I lose things. **(r)**
5. I am less likely than most people to lock things up. **(r)**
6. I would rather buy something I need than borrow it from someone else.
7. I worry about people taking my possessions.
8. When I travel I like to take a lot of photographs.
9. I never discard old pictures or snapshots.

+ O'Guinn and Faber (1989) used items similar to or exactly the same as items 2, 3, 7, and 9.

SCALE NAME: Potency (Stimulus)

SCALE DESCRIPTION:

A three-item, seven-point semantic differential summated ratings scale measuring the perceived strength or power of a stimulus.

SCALE ORIGIN:

These or similar items were used and reported by Holbrook in several articles published in the early 1980s. The items are drawn from the classic work of Osgood, Suci, and Tannenbaum (1957). After examining a wide variety of judgmental situations, the latter authors reported that the same three major factors were found repeatedly: evaluation, potency, and activity. The potency dimension was most associated with power and aspects such as size, weight, and toughness (p. 72, 73). The potency factor also was rather consistently found to account for half as much variance as the evaluation factor. Though the validity of the potency factor was discussed in the book, the psychometric properties of a particular scale were not tested.

SAMPLES:

Holbrook's (1981) analysis was based on **16** subjects chosen from volunteers with an interest in classical piano music. Half had never played an instrument but enjoyed listening to such music (''nonexperts') and the other half were highly trained musicians (''experts'').

RELIABILITY:

An alpha of **.81** was reported for the scale.

VALIDITY:

Beyond the observation that the items loaded together in a factor analysis, no specific examination of scale validity was reported.

ADMINISTRATION:

In both studies (Holbrook 1981), subjects self-administered the scale along with several other measures. Higher summated scores suggest that respondents perceive a stimulus to be very strong and powerful whereas lower scores mean that they do not perceive the object to be ''potent.

MAJOR FINDINGS:

Holbrook (1981) illustrated a two-stage integrative model of evaluative judgment in which objective product features influenced perceptions, which in turn shaped affect. Specifically, he found that the direct effects of objective music characteristics on affect were not nearly as large or as significant as the indirect effects of those features through intervening perceptions. Perceived expressiveness, activity, and complexity had significant positive influences on affect, perceived novelty had a significant negative impact, and perceived **potency** did not make a salient contribution.

COMMENTS:

See also Holbrook and Moore (1981), who measured this construct with similar items but used factor scores rather than a simple sum.

REFERENCES:

Holbrook, Morris B. (1981), "Integrating Compositional and Decompositional Analyses to Represent the Intervening Role of Perceptions in Evaluative Judgments," *JMR*, 18 (February), 13-28.

———— and William L. Moore (1981), "Feature Interactions in Consumer Judgments of Verbal Versus Pictorial Presentations," *JCR*, 8 (June), 103-113.

Osgood, Charles E., George J. Suci, and Percy H. Tannenbaum (1957), *The Measurement of Meaning*. Urbana, Ill.: University of Illinois Press.

SCALE ITEMS: POTENCY (STIMULUS)

quiet	____ : ____ : ____ : ____ : ____ : ____ : ____	loud
	1 2 3 4 5 6 7	

soft	____ : ____ : ____ : ____ : ____ : ____ : ____	hard
	1 2 3 4 5 6 7	

feminine	____ : ____ : ____ : ____ : ____ : ____ : ____	masculine
	1 2 3 4 5 6 7	

SCALE NAME: Powerlessness (Consumer)

SCALE DESCRIPTION:

A seven-item, five-point Likert-type scale measuring a consumer's sense of ineffectiveness in getting a company to respond to his or her needs.

SCALE ORIGIN:

The scale was originally constructed and used by Lambert (1980). Items were adapted from several previously published empirical and conceptual studies. A mail sample of residents of four southeastern metropolitan areas yielded **200** usable returns. The alpha for the powerlessness scale was reported as **.763**. Powerlessness was just one of four alienation scales used together in a cluster analysis to group consumers. No individual findings for the scale were reported. In general, dissatisfaction with the marketplace was found to be significantly related to levels of consumer alienation.

SAMPLES:

A systematic sample of 1320 customers of a large, investor-owned electric utility company was made by Durand and Lambert (1985). Questionnaires were mailed to them and **325** were returned following a reminder mailed after two weeks. The average respondent was at least 45 years of age, male, white, married, had at least graduated high school, and was socioeconomically upscale.

RELIABILITY:

An alpha of **.70** was reported for the scale.

VALIDITY:

No examination of scale validity was reported.

ADMINISTRATION:

The scale was self-administered along with several other measures included in the mail questionnaire. Higher scores on the scale indicate that consumers feel incapable of getting companies to respond to their needs whereas lower scores suggest that respondents express an ability to work with companies to have problems solved.

MAJOR FINDINGS:

The purpose of the study was to investigate the degree to which criticisms of advertising are positively related to various aspects of consumer and political alienation. Respondents were first grouped according to levels of alienation by means of cluster analysis. (**Powerlessness** was one of the alienation variables on which the cluster analysis was based.) Then, differences in advertising criticisms were compared across the groups. The cluster analysis produced four alienation groups and a MANOVA indicated significant differences between the groups when all of the 12 advertising criticisms were considered simultaneously.

#189 *Powerlessness (Consumer)*

REFERENCES:

Durand, Richard M. and Zarrel V. Lambert (1985), "Alienation and Criticisms of Advertising," *JA*, 14 (3), 9-17.

Lambert, Zarrel V. (1980), "Consumer Alienation, General Dissatisfaction, and Consumerism Issues: Conceptual and Managerial Perspectives," *Journal of Retailing*, 56 (Summer), 3-24.

SCALE ITEMS: POWERLESSNESS (CONSUMER) +

Strongly Agree	Disagree	Neutral	Agree	Strongly Disagree
1—————	—2—————	—3—————	—4—————	—5

1. If something unordinary occurs in dealing with a company, the firm generally handles it quickly as a special situation to satisfy and please me. **(r)**
2. Consumers like myself generally can get companies…to make changes…to better serve our needs and desires. **(r)**
3. When dealing with a company, consumers like myself generally…can pressure it into doing what…is right and fair. **(r)**
4. Most company employees…won't go out of their way…to help or satisfy a consumer.
5. As an average consumer there is little use in writing complaint letters to company officials.
6. When a product is defective or shoddy, usually there is not much a consumer like myself can do…if the company refuses to make it "right."
7. When dealing with a company, I am often treated…as just another body rather than a person with specific needs and desires.

+ The authors noted that these items were abbreviated to conserve space as indicated by the dots. They should be contacted if the full items are desired.

SCALE NAME: Price Consciousness

SCALE DESCRIPTION:

A four-item, six-point, Likert-type summated ratings scale going from strongly disagree (1) to strongly agree (6). The scale measures a person's interest in sales and sensitivity to pricing. This may be the scale used by Burnett and Bush (1986) as well as Barak and Stern (1985/1986), though the latter used a simpler three-point response scale. See also Arora (1985), Heslop, Moran, and Cousineau (1981), Korgaonkar (1984), and Schnaars and Schiffman (1984) for variations on the measure.

SCALE ORIGIN:

These items were part of a classic study of psychographics by Wells and Tigert (1971). One thousand questionnaires were mailed to homemaker members of the Market Facts mail panel. In addition to gathering demographic, product use, and media data, the survey contained 300 statements that have since served as the basis for the construction of many lifestyle-related scales. The four items for this scale are reported in the article, but they were not analyzed as a multi-item scale. The purpose of the article was to explain how psychographics could improve upon mere demographic description of target audiences and product users. No psychometric information was reported.

One of the first uses of the items as a multi-item scale was by Darden and Perreault (1976). Analysis was based on self-administered questionnaires completed by 278 suburban housewives randomly selected in Athens, Georgia. A split-half reliability of .70 was reported for the scale. Price consciousness did *not* significantly differentiate between the outshopping groups.

SAMPLES:

Two mailing lists were used to collect data in the Dickerson and Gentry (1983) study. One was a list of *Psychology Today* subscribers and the other was a list of members of computer clubs. The former was used to reach non-adopters of computers and the latter was used to reach PC adopters. Analysis was based on a total of **639** questionnaires. Results from a second mailing to non-respondents indicated that their demographic makeup was not significantly different from that of respondents.

On the basis of 1980 Census data, the sample was younger and more upscale than the general population.

The survey form used by Barak and Stern (1985/1986) was personally distributed to and collected from an age-quota sample of women living in the greater New York metropolitan area. The study focused on the **567** responding women who categorized themselves as either "young" or "middle-aged" and stated an age in years between 25 and 69.

RELIABILITY:

An alpha of **.67** (Dickerson and Gentry 1983) has been reported. Barak and Stern (1985/1986) say only that the scale's alpha was above **.5**.

VALIDITY:

Factor analysis was performed in most of the studies and indicated that the items loaded together.

ADMINISTRATION:

Except in the Barak and Stern study, as noted above, data in all of the studies were gathered through self-administered mail questionnaires. Scale scores are calculated by averaging numerical responses to individual items. A score of 6 indicates that a person actively watches for sales information and checks prices whereas 1 suggests that a person is not very price sensitive.

MAJOR FINDINGS:

Dickerson and Gentry (1983) failed to find significant evidence that **price consciousness** discriminated between adopters and nonadopters of home computers. **Price consciousness** was also found to significantly discriminate between the female baby-boomer and pre-boomer generations (Barak and Stern 1985/1986).

COMMENTS:

A possible reason for the low internal consistency of this scale could be that three slightly different subconstructs are measured by the items as noted below: bargain hunting, inspection of prices on products at the store, and watching ads for sales. The last has been treated as a separate construct in some studies (see Sales Advertising Watcher).

REFERENCES:

Arora, Raj (1985), "Involvement: Its Measurement for Retail Store Research," *JAMS*, 13 (Spring), 229-241.

Barak, Benny and Barbara Stern (1985/1986), "Women's Age in Advertising: An Examination of Two Consumer Age Profiles," *JAR*, 25 (December/January), 38-47.

Burnett, John J. and Alan J. Bush (1986), "Profiling the Yuppies," *JAR*, 26 (April/May), 27-35.

Darden, William R. and William D. Perreault, Jr. (1976), "Identifying Interurban Shoppers: Multiproduct Purchase Patterns and Segmentation Profiles," *JMR*, 13 (February), 51- 60.

Dickerson, Mary D. and James W. Gentry (1983), "Characteristics of Adopters and Non-Adopters of Home Computers," *JCR*, 10 (September), 225-235.

Heslop, Louise A., Lori Moran, and Amy Cousineau (1981), "'Consciousness' in Energy Conservation Behavior: An Exploratory Study," *JCR*, 8 (December), 299-305.

Korgaonkar, Pradeep K. (1984), "Consumer Shopping Orientations, Non-Store Retailers, and Consumers' Patronage Intentions: A Multivariate Investigation," *JAMS*, 12 (Winter), 11-22.

Schnaars, Steven P. and Leon G. Schiffman (1984), "An Application of a Segmentation Design Based on the Hybrid of Canonical Correlation and Simple Crosstabulation," *JAMS*, 12 (Fall), 177-189.

Wells, William D. and Douglas Tigert (1971), "Activities, Interests, and Opinions," *JAR*, 11 (August), 27-35.

SCALE ITEMS: PRICE CONSCIOUSNESS

Strongly Disagree	Disagree	Slightly Disagree	Slightly Agree	Agree	Strongly Agree
1	2	3	4	5	6

1. I shop a lot for "specials."
2. I find myself checking the prices in the grocery store even for small items.
3. I usually watch the advertisements for announcements of sales.
4. A person can save a lot of money by shopping around for bargains.

SCALE NAME: Price Consciousness

SCALE DESCRIPTION:

A three-item, five-point, Likert-type summated ratings scale measuring a person's price sensitivity as it relates to the purchase of a specified product. Lichtenstein, Bloch, and Black (1988) used it with respect to running shoes.

SCALE ORIGIN:

The scale was apparently original to Lichtenstein, Bloch, and Black (1988).

SAMPLES:

Lichtenstein, Bloch, and Black (1988) mailed questionnaires to 1800 participants in a regional running event. Analysis was based on the **452** responses received within five weeks. In comparison with the area's general population, the respondents were more likely to be younger and male and to have higher education and income.

RELIABILITY:

The reliability (LISREL estimate?) of the scale used was calculated to be **.66**.

VALIDITY:

No examination of scale validity was reported.

ADMINISTRATION:

The scale was administered along with several other measures in a mail survey instrument. Higher scores indicate that respondents are price sensitive and buy the product when it is on sale, whereas lower scores suggest that respondents are not very concerned about price for that particular product category.

MAJOR FINDINGS:

Lichtenstein and his coauthors examined the cognitive tradeoffs consumers make between price and product quality. The findings indicated an inverse relationship between **price consciousness** and price-quality inferences, price acceptability level, product involvement.

COMMENTS:

The low reliability suggests that caution should be exercised in use of the scale until further work can be done to improve its quality.

REFERENCE:

Lichtenstein, Donald R., Peter H. Bloch, and William C. Black (1988), "Correlates of Price Acceptability," *JCR*, 15 (September), 243-252.

SCALE ITEMS: PRICE CONSCIOUSNESS +

Strongly Disagree	Disagree	Neutral	Agree	Strongly Agree
1—————————	—2—————————	—3—————————	—4—————————	—5

1. I usually buy _____ when they are on sale.
2. I buy the lowest priced _____ that will suit my needs.
3. When it comes to choosing _____ for me, I rely heavily on price.

+ The graphic scale and verbal anchors are not described in the article, but are likely to have been similar to those shown here. The generic name of the product should go in the blanks.

SCALE NAME: Price-Quality Inference (Running Shoes)

SCALE DESCRIPTION:

A four-item, five-point, summated ratings scale measuring a person's perception of the difference between two pairs of running shoes.

SCALE ORIGIN:

The scale was apparently original to Lichtenstein, Bloch, and Black (1988).

SAMPLES:

Lichtenstein, Bloch, and Black (1988) mailed questionnaires to 1800 participants in a regional running event. Analysis was based on the **452** responses received within five weeks. In comparison with the area's general population, the respondents were more likely to be younger and male and to have higher education and income.

RELIABILITY:

The reliability (LISREL estimate?) of the scale used was calculated to be **.83**. The measure had eight items, but after assessment of reliability only four items were retained for calculating scale scores.

VALIDITY:

No examination of scale validity was reported.

ADMINISTRATION:

The scale was administered along with several other measures in a mail survey instrument. Higher scores indicate that respondents perceive a large difference in quality between two pairs of running shoes whereas lower scores suggest that respondents do not perceive much difference in the shoes except for their prices.

MAJOR FINDINGS:

Lichtenstein and his coauthors examined the cognitive tradeoffs consumers make between price and product quality. The findings indicated an inverse relationship between **price-quality inferences** and price consciousness, but a positive correlation with price acceptability level and product involvement.

REFERENCE:

Lichtenstein, Donald R., Peter H. Bloch, and William C. Black (1988), "Correlates of Price Acceptability," *JCR*, 15 (September), 243-252.

SCALE ITEMS: PRICE QUALITY INFERENCE (RUNNING SHOES) +

No difference
at all

_____ : _____ : _____ : _____ : _____

   1   2   3   4   5

A great deal
of difference

Using the above scale, indicate how much difference there is between $75 running shoes and $35 running shoes for each of the following product attributes:

1. Comfort
2. Durability
3. Protection
4. Workmanship

+ The graphic scale was not described in the article but is likely to have been similar to the one shown here.

SCALE NAME: Pricing Issues (Air Travel)

SCALE DESCRIPTION:

A three-item, Likert-type summated ratings scale measuring the degree of interest a person expresses in things involved with lower airline ticket prices. The scale was referred to as Economy by Bruning, Kovacic, and Oberdick (1985).

SCALE ORIGIN:

There is no information provided in the article that indicates the scale was not original to Bruning, Kovacic, and Oberdick (1985).

SAMPLES:

Questionnaires were distributed at five airports in the U.S. that offered major/national and regional/commuter service. To provide an adequate representation of various types of flyers, the sample was stratified by time of day and day of week. Questionnaires were distributed on a ''random'' basis to passengers waiting for flights to leave at departure gates. Self-addressed, stamped envelopes were provided with the survey forms and **591** usable forms were returned.

RELIABILITY:

An alpha of **.78** was reported for the scale.

VALIDITY:

A factor analysis indicated that the items loaded together.

ADMINISTRATION:

The scale was self-administered with other parts of the questionnaire while passengers were waiting at departure gates at airports. The questionnaires were returned by mail. Higher scores on this scale indicate that respondents are very interested in things that can lower airline ticket prices whereas lower scores imply that respondents are not very concerned about ticket prices.

MAJOR FINDINGS:

Bruning and his coauthors were studying the reasons why air travelers choose a certain form of airline and how such information could be used to segment carriers into distinct markets. Discriminant analysis was used to identify personality factors, demographic variables, and airline-related perceptions that would significantly discriminate between commuter and noncommuter travelers. **Price** was a significant predictor such that regional/commuter passengers had greater interest in lower airline ticket **prices** than major/national passengers.

REFERENCE:

> Bruning, Edward R., Mary L. Kovacic, and Larry E. Oberdick (1985), "Segmentation Analysis of Domestic Airline Passenger Markets," *JAMS*, 13 (Winter), 17-31.

SCALE ITEMS: PRICING ISSUES (AIR TRAVEL) +

Strongly Disagree	Disagree	Somewhat Disagree	Somewhat Agree	Agree	Strongly Agree
1	2	3	4	5	6

1. From my experience, I have found that the larger the airline company the lower the actual cost of travel has been.
2. I generally call several airlines or agents to get price quotes and routing before I decide on a particular airline.
3. The price I pay for my ticket is more important to me than the service I receive prior to and during the flight.

+ The graphic scale was not specified in the article but is likely to have been similar to the one shown here, with between five and seven points.

SCALE NAME: Problem Recognition Style (Clothing)

SCALE DESCRIPTION:

An eight-item, seven-point, Likert-type summated ratings scale measuring a consumer's pattern of acknowledging and defining needs/wants for clothing, with particular emphasis on sportswear.

SCALE ORIGIN:

The scale Bruner used in his 1987 study (as well as several others) was adapted from an 18-item scale developed in his dissertation research (Bruner 1983). That original scale was constructed to measure the initial "trigger" of the decision process that might lead to the purchase of clothing. Data in a pretest were gathered from personal interviews with 38 women. The main study used mail survey questionnaires to collect data from 499 women in six communities surrounding the Dallas-Ft. Worth metroplex. The scale had high internal consistency (Chronbach's alpha = .93). Predictive validity (r = .70) was found between pretest subjects' scale scores and estimates of their problem recognition styles made by two judges on the basis of audio recordings of the personal interviews.

SAMPLES:

The sample of **439** used by Bruner (1987) consisted of upperclass students at large midwestern university, the majority being single, white, American citizens, and younger than 25 years of age.

RELIABILITY:

A Chronbach's alpha of **.88** was reported by Bruner (1987).

VALIDITY:

In addition to a factor analysis that confirmed the unidimensional structure of the eight items, a predictive validity of r = .54 (Bruner 1987) was calculated between scale scores and subjects' responses to a single global question about their perceived Problem Recognition Type.

ADMINISTRATION:

In previous uses, scores have been calculated by dividing the sum of the numeric responses by the number of nonzero answers, resulting in scores between 1 and 7. The closer a score is to 7, the more a consumer is considered a Desired State Type, i.e., one who frequently wants new and/or different things despite the status of presently owned clothing. Scores approaching 1 suggest a consumer is an Actual State Type, i.e., one who tends to not become aware of needs until presently owned clothes fail to perform satisfactorily. The instrument appears to be amenable for survey situations in which respondents can read items and fill out the scale themselves. Whether any difficulties would be encountered if items were read to respondents is not known.

MAJOR FINDINGS:

The purpose of the study by Bruner (1987) was to determine any differences between the search behavior of Desired State Type Problem Recognizers and that of Actual State Types. Desired State Types were found to make more clothing-related shopping trips and place greater importance on most information sources (including marketer-dominated). The only source more important to Actual State Types was past dress behavior (internal search).

COMMENTS:

See another use of this same scale by Bruner (1986). Though similar scales have been constructed for measurement of problem recognition style for several other product categories (Bruner 1989, 1990), no generalized version of the scale using a semantic differential or Likert format has been developed.

REFERENCES:

Bruner, Gordon C., II (1983), *Problem Recognition in the Homeostatic Process of Consumer Decision Making: Its Definition, Measurement, and Use*, unpublished doctoral dissertation, University of North Texas.

_____ (1986), "Problem Recognition Styles and Search Patterns: An Empirical Investigation," *Journal of Retailing*, 62 (Fall), 281-297.

_____ (1987), "The Effect of Problem Recognition Style on Information Seeking," *JAMS*, 15 (Winter), 33-41.

_____ (1989), "Profiling Desired State Type Problem Recognizers," *Journal of Business & Psychology*, 4 (Winter), 167-182.

_____ (1990), "Problem Recognition Style: Is It Need Specific or a Generalized Personality Trait?" *Journal of Consumer Studies and Home Economics*, 14 (March), 29-40.

SCALE ITEMS: PROBLEM RECOGNITION STYLE (CLOTHING)

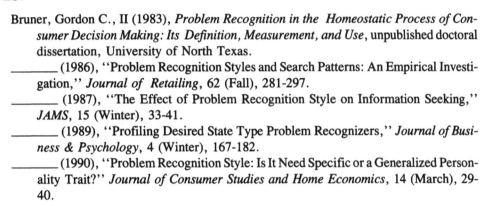

Strongly Disagree	Disagree	Slightly Disagree	Neutral	Slightly Agree	Agree	Strongly Agree
1	2	3	4	5	6	7

1. I go out shopping for clothes long before what I have is worn out.
2. I often feel I need new clothes even though I could "make do" with what I have.
3. I get a lot of wear out of my clothes and am not always looking to buy more.(r)
4. I buy new clothes even when my old ones are still okay to wear.
5. My clothes are still in good condition when I replace them.
6. When I am shopping and see new fashions displayed, it's not unusual for me to feel I need something new.
7. I tend to buy clothes long before my other ones wear out.
8. It's not unusual for me to buy clothes simply because I want something new.

SCALE NAME: Product Aesthetics

SCALE DESCRIPTION:

A five-item, seven-point semantic differential summated ratings scale measuring the degree to which an object arouses one's emotions and is perceived as being attractive and desirable. The objects evaluated by subjects in Hirschman's (1986) study were print advertisements.

SCALE ORIGIN:

The scale appears to have been used first in this form by Hirschman and Solomon (1984). In that study the authors explored consumers' perceptions of visual versus verbal ads on three dimensions: functional utility, aesthetic value, and familiarity. Data were gathered from college students who were asked to fill out a questionnaire themselves and to have four more completed by others. Satisfactory forms were received from **162** respondents. Seventy-nine subjects received all verbal ads and 83 received all visual ads. The mean age of the sample was 29 years and 53.7% were women. Respondents were each exposed to two ads in their questionnaires and filled out the dimension scales twice. The two alpha values reported for this scale were **.85** and **.91**. Only mixed support was found for the hypothesis that visual ads would be perceived as more aesthetic than verbal ads.

SAMPLES:

A total of **154** social science college students participated in Hirschman's (1986) study as part of their course requirements. Students were randomly assigned to treatment groups and no difference in any demographic or control variables was noted. The all-verbal-ads group had 78 subjects and the all-visual-ads group had 76.

RELIABILITY:

The alpha for this scale was not specifically reported, but the author reports the scale to be among those for which alpha was between **.82** and **.96**.

VALIDITY:

The validity of this scale was not specifically examined or discussed by Hirschman (1986).

ADMINISTRATION:

The scale was self-administered by subjects along with other measures after viewing ads. The items are scored such that the extreme positive responses are coded 7 and extreme negative responses are coded 1. Higher scores on the scale suggest that respondents view an object (such as an ad) to be very attractive and desirable whereas lower scores imply that they think an object is ugly and undesirable.

MAJOR FINDINGS:

The purpose of the study was to examine the differences in perceptions of products portrayed in all-verbal versus all-visual ads. For half of the 14 products examined, all-visual ads were perceived to be significantly more **aesthetic** than the all-verbal ads. However, for the other half of the products this relationship was either not significant or was reversed.

REFERENCES:

Hirschman, Elizabeth C. (1986), "The Effect of Verbal and Pictorial Advertising Stimuli on Aesthetic, Utilitarian and Familiarity Perceptions," *JA*, 15 (2), 27-34.

_____ and Michael R. Solomon (1984), "Utilitarian, Aesthetic, and Familiarity Responses to Verbal Versus Visual Advertisements," in *Advances in Consumer Research*, Thomas C. Kinnear, ed. Ann Arbor, Mich.: Association for Consumer Research.

SCALE ITEMS: PRODUCT AESTHETICS

1. attractive   ____ : ____ : ____ : ____ : ____ : ____ : ____   not attractive
         1   2   3   4   5   6   7

2. desirable   ____ : ____ : ____ : ____ : ____ : ____ : ____   not desirable
         1   2   3   4   5   6   7

3. arousing   ____ : ____ : ____ : ____ : ____ : ____ : ____   not arousing
         1   2   3   4   5   6   7

4. beautiful   ____ : ____ : ____ : ____ : ____ : ____ : ____   not beautiful
         1   2   3   4   5   6   7

5. makes me like this product   ____ : ____ : ____ : ____ : ____ : ____ : ____   does not make me like this product
         1   2   3   4   5   6   7

SCALE NAME: Product Knowledge

SCALE DESCRIPTION:

A two-item, five-point Likert-type summated scale ranging from little or no knowledge to a great deal of knowledge. The scale measures a consumer's knowledge of a product in comparison with that of others.

SCALE ORIGIN:

The measure was apparently constructed for the study by Bloch, Ridgway, and Sherrell (1989).

SAMPLES:

Data were collected via probability samples from three groups: a Sunbelt MSA, customer lists of men's and women's clothing stores, and local computer stores' mailing lists. An initial mailing of the survey was followed in 10 days by a second mailing to nonrespondents. Analysis was based on **585** instruments that met certain criteria of interest (244 from the general population sample, 122 from the clothing store sample, 219 from the computer store sample).

RELIABILITY:

Interitem correlations for the two item scale were **.76** (clothing) and **.86** (PCs).

VALIDITY:

No examination of scale validity was reported.

ADMINISTRATION:

The scale was self-administered by respondents along with other parts of a questionnaire sent in a mail survey. Higher scores on the scale indicate that respondents perceive themselves as having a lot of information and **understanding of a product** in comparison with others whereas low scores suggest they have little **knowledge about the product**.

MAJOR FINDINGS:

The purpose of the study was to examine browsing and its relationship with several aspects of consumer behavior. For both product categories studied (clothing and PCs), heavy browsers had more **knowledge about the product** than light browsers, who were more knowledgeable than nonbrowsers. Product involvement was a more significant predictor of **product knowledge** than browsing alone.

REFERENCE:

Bloch, Peter H., Nancy M. Ridgway, and Daniel L. Sherrell (1989), "Extending the Concept of Shopping: An Investigation of Browsing Activity," *JAMS*, 17 (Winter), 13-21.

SCALE ITEMS: PRODUCT KNOWLEDGE +

Little or   A greal deal
no knowledge   of knowledge
1————————2————————3————————4————————5

1. How do you rate your knowledge of _____ relative to other people?
2. How do you rate your knowledge of _____ relative to most of your friends?

+ The graphic scale and items were not fully specified in the article, but are assumed to
  be similar to the ones shown here.

SCALE NAME: Product Performance Evaluation (Radio)

SCALE DESCRIPTION:

> A five-item, eight-point summated ratings scale measuring a person's assessment of the performance of a radio in comparison with that of a most preferred radio brand.

SCALE ORIGIN:

> The scale was apparently developed for use in the study by Korgaonkar and Maschis (1982).

SAMPLES:

> In a series of pretests and a main experiment, data were collected from students enrolled in a large section of an introductory marketing course at a large urban university. **Twenty-five** students were in the pretest in which the scale was used and **84** participated in the main experiment.

RELIABILITY:

> An alpha of **.81** was calculated.

VALIDITY:

> No assessment of scale validity was reported.

ADMINISTRATION:

> The scale was given to subjects on paper in a classroom setting. The students listened to two radios for three minutes and were then asked to evaluate their performance. Though the scoring procedure was not specified, scores were probably calculated by summing numerical responses to the five items. Higher scores suggest subjects were very pleased with the performance of the radio in comparison with that of their most preferred brand whereas low scores imply that they perceived the radio to have performed poorly.

MAJOR FINDINGS:

> Korgaonkar and Mochis (1982) investigated the effects of cognitive dissonance, expectations, and product performance on product evaluations. The **performance evaluation** scale was used to determine whether test products were viewed as significantly different in their performance quality. The results of the main experiment indicated that product involvement acts as a moderator in the post-decision product evaluation process.

COMMENTS:

> The internal consistency is reasonably good for this version of the scale. However, adjustment in the items would be necessary for use with other product categories and the reliability in those cases could be very different.

REFERENCE:

Korgaonkar, Pradeep K. and George P. Mochis (1982), ''An Experimental Study of Cognitive Dissonance, Product Involvement, Expectations, Performance and Consumer Judgement of Product Performance,'' *JA*, 11 (3), 32-44.

SCALE ITEMS: PRODUCT PERFORMANCE EVALUATION (RADIO)

The following questions relate to the performance of the radio you just listened to. Please indicate how you feel about *this* radio, compared to your most preferred brand by circling the appropriate number.

```
Worst                                                           Best
Possible                                                    Possible
    0————1————2————3————4————5————6————7
```

1. Volume control
2. Background noise level
3. Fidelity for voice
4. Fidelity for music
5. Your satisfaction with performance

SCALE NAME: Product Performance Evaluation (Soft Drink)

SCALE DESCRIPTION:

A five-item, eight-point summated ratings scale measuring a person's assessment of the performance of a soft drink in comparison with that of a most preferred soft drink brand.

SCALE ORIGIN:

The scale was apparently developed for use in the study by Korgaonkar and Maschis (1982).

SAMPLES:

In a series of pretests and a main experiment, data were collected from students enrolled in a large section of an introductory marketing course at a large urban university. **Thirty** students were in the pretest in which the scale was used and **84** participated in the main experiment.

RELIABILITY:

An alpha of **.90** was calculated.

VALIDITY:

No assessment of scale validity was reported.

ADMINISTRATION:

The scale was given to subjects on paper in a classroom setting. The students were given about three minutes to drink the two soft drinks and evaluate them. Though the scoring procedure was not specified, scores were probably calculated by summing numerical responses to the five items. Higher scores suggest subjects were very pleased with the taste of a drink whereas low scores imply that they perceived the drink to be much worse than their preferred brand.

MAJOR FINDINGS:

Korgaonkar and Mochis (1982) investigated the effects of cognitive dissonance, expectations, and product performance on product evaluations. The **performance evaluation** scale was used to determine whether test products were viewed as significantly different in their performance quality. The results of the main experiment indicated that product involvement acts as a moderator in the post-decision product evaluation process.

COMMENTS:

The internal consistency is good for this version of the scale. However, adjustment in the items would be necessary for use with other product categories and the reliabilities in those cases could be very different.

REFERENCE:

> Korgaonkar, Pradeep K. and George P. Mochis (1982), "An Experimental Study of Cognitive Dissonance, Product Involvement, Expectations, Performance and Consumer Judgement of Product Performance," *JA*, 11 (3), 32-44.

SCALE ITEMS: PRODUCT PERFORMANCE EVALUATION (SOFT DRINK)

The following questions relate to the performance of the soft drink you just tasted. Please indicate how you feel about *this* soft drink, compared to your most preferred brand by circling the appropriate number.

Worst   Best
Possible   Possible
0————1————2————3————4————5————6————7

1. Taste
2. Body (smoothness)
3. Flavor
4. Nutritional value (calorie content)
5. Your satisfaction

SCALE NAME: Product-Price Relationship

SCALE DESCRIPTION:

A four-item, five-point Likert-type summated ratings scale measuring a person's opinion of product pricing, with emphasis on the reason why products are sold at reduced prices. Moschis (1978, 1981) referred to this scale as Attitudes Toward Prices.

SCALE ORIGIN:

The measure originates from a dissertation published by Moschis in 1978. His 1981 study, reported below, is from that same dissertation research.

SAMPLES:

Moschis' (1981) data came from **806** middle school or senior high school students. There were 365 "older" adolescents (15 years and older) and 441 "younger" adolescents (younger than 15 years). The students came from 13 schools and seven towns in Wisconsin representing a wide variety of urban to rural situations. The author indicates that the sample was well balanced in terms of most demographic characteristics except sex, as nearly two-thirds of the respondents were female.

RELIABILITY:

An alpha of .**28** was reported for the scale.

VALIDITY:

No examination of scale validity was reported.

ADMINISTRATION:

The scale was self-administered by students along with several other measures in a 10-page instrument during a regular class session. Higher scores on the scale indicate that respondents have strong price-product quality perceptions whereas lower scores suggest that they have more critical and cynical attitudes of product pricing.

MAJOR FINDINGS:

The study investigated the validity of the cognitive development approach to socialization (e.g., Piaget) to predict a wide variety of consumer-related cognitions learned during adolescence. In general, the findings indicated that the cognitive developmental model did not explain consumer socialization during adolescence very well. Older adolescents had significantly less favorable attitudes toward advertising, brands, and **prices** than did younger children.

COMMENTS:

The extremely low internal consistency indicates that the scale is unreliable. This could be due to several different factors being represented in the scale. Redevelopment and testing must be conducted before the scale is used further.

REFERENCES:

Moschis, George P. (1978), *Acquisition of the Consumer Role by Adolescents*, Research Monograph No. 82. Atlanta, Ga.: Publishing Services Division, College of Business Administration, Georgia State University.
_____ (1981), "Patterns of Consumer Learning," *JAMS*, 9 (2), 110-126.

SCALE ITEMS: PRODUCT-PRICE RELATIONSHIP

Strongly Agree	Disagree	Neutral	Agree	Strongly Disagree
1	2	3	4	5

1. Many products are not worth the price you pay for them.
2. Most products sold at reduced price are of poor quality.
3. Most products sold at reduced price are never really on sale at all.
4. Most products are sold at reduced prices because they are too old.

SCALE NAME: Product Purchase Influence (Child's)

SCALE DESCRIPTION:

A seven-item, five-point Likert-type summated ratings scale that measures the degree to which a parent believes a child's opinion should be consulted when purchase decisions are made for a variety of specific goods and services.

SCALE ORIGIN:

The idea for the scale comes from a study reported by Jenkins (1979). However, he does not appear to have used the items in summated scale form; that aspect seems to be original to Carlson and Grossbart (1988).

SAMPLES:

The survey instrument used by Carlson and Grossbart (1988) was distributed to mothers via students at three elementary schools in an unidentified U.S. city. The schools were chosen on a convenience basis but appeared to represent a variety of socioeconomic areas of the city. A $1 contribution to the PTO was offered for each completed questionnaire returned by the children. Analysis was based on **451** completed questionnaires. Ninety-three percent of the responding mothers indicated that they were the primary person in the child's socialization.

RELIABILITY:

Carlson and Grossbart (1988) reported an alpha of **.84** and a beta of .63 for the scale.

VALIDITY:

No examination of scale validity was reported by Carlson and Grossbart (1988).

ADMINISTRATION:

The scale was self-administered along with many other measures in the questionnaire used by Carlson and Grossbart (1988). Higher scores on the scale suggest that parents believe their children's opinions should be considered when making purchase decisions whereas lower scores imply that they do not think their children's opinions should be included.

MAJOR FINDINGS:

The authors investigated the relationship between general parental socialization styles and children's consumer socialization. In a factor analysis of scale scores, scores on the **Child's Influence** scale loaded on a factor described as "parent-child communication about consumption." A significant difference was found in the degree of parent-child communication between several of the parental socialization styles examined.

REFERENCES:

Carlson, Les and Sanford Grossbart (1988), ''Parental Style and Consumer Socialization of Children,'' *JCR*, 15 (June), 77-94.

Jenkins, Roger L. (1979), ''The Influence of Children in Family Decision Making: Parents' Perceptions,'' in *Advances in Consumer Research*, Vol. 6, William L. Wilkie, ed. Ann Arbor, Mich.: Association for Consumer Research, 413-418.

SCALE ITEMS: PRODUCT PURCHASE INFLUENCE (CHILD'S)

Strongly Disagree	Disagree	Neither	Agree	Strongly Agree
1—————————	—2—————————	—3—————————	—4—————————	—5

My child's opinions should be included when we make purchase decisions for:
1. Major appliances
2. Automobiles
3. Furniture
4. Groceries
5. Life insurance
6. Vacations
7. General purchases

SCALE NAME: Purchase Expectations (Adolescents')

SCALE DESCRIPTION:

An eight-item, four-point summated ratings scale measuring the general degree to which an adolescent anticipates deferring the purchase of certain specified products until later in life.

SCALE ORIGIN:

Though origin is not specified, the scale was apparently original to Moschis and Moore (1984).

SAMPLES:

The study was based on data collected from **784** adolescents from six counties in Georgia that varied widely in rural/urban nature. The surveys were administered to middle school or high school students in a regular class session. The sample was reported to be very representative given that, among other demographic variables, it was 48% male and 88% white.

RELIABILITY:

The alpha for the scale was not specified, but the scale was apparently among those with alpha between **.48** and **.87**.

VALIDITY:

No examination of scale validity was reported.

ADMINISTRATION:

The scale was self-administered along with other measures as part of a larger questionnaire. Numerical responses to the items are summed to form an 8 to 24 point index. Higher scores indicate that adolescents expect generally to defer purchase of the specified products until after having children whereas lower scores suggest that they plan to buy the products sooner in life, before they get married.

MAJOR FINDINGS:

The purpose of the study was to examine the development of consumption-related cognitions and behaviors among adolescents. Few significant associations were found between deferred purchase expectations and the other variables investigated. However, black respondents appeared to be less likely to defer purchases than white respondents as did respondents of low socioeconomic status.

COMMENTS:

The authors also used this scale to measure the extent to which adolescents expected to purchase the specified products at all. If a respondent answered the eight items with anything but a 0 the response counted as a 1, producing summated scores between 0 and 8. Findings indicated that though no significant association was found between this measure and TV viewing, there was a very significant relationship with the degree to which adolescents reported their families interacted about purchasing products, budgeting money, prudent spending, etc.

REFERENCE:

Moschis, George P. and Roy L. Moore (1984), "Anticipatory Consumer Socialization, *JAMS*, 12 (Fall), 109-123.

SCALE ITEMS: PURCHASE EXPECTATIONS (ADOLESCENTS') +

Indicate the time you plan to anticipate first buying each of the items below using the following scale:

I Don't Know	Before I Get Married	After I Get Married	After I have Children
1—————————	——2————————	——3————————	——4

1. life insurance
2. encyclopedias
3. new car
4. house
5. stocks and bonds
6. trip to Europe
7. stereo
8. new furniture

+ Though not specifically indicated in the article, the scale format is assumed to have been similar to that shown here.

SCALE NAME: Purchase Independence (Child)

SCALE DESCRIPTION:

A 10-item, five-point Likert-type summated ratings scale measuring the degree to which a parent reports a child being free to purchase any of several products as long as the child is in some way involved in the payment. Referred to by Carlson and Grossbart (1988) as Child's Payment.

SCALE ORIGIN:

The use of these items as a multi-item measure appears to be original to Carlson and Grossbart (1988). However, they got ideas for some of the items from the research of Ward, Wackman, and Wartella (1977).

SAMPLES:

The survey instrument used by Carlson and Grossbart (1988) was distributed to mothers via students at three elementary schools in an unidentified U.S. city. The schools were chosen on a convenience basis but appeared to represent a variety of socioeconomic areas of the city. A $1 contribution to the PTO was offered for each completed questionnaire returned by the children. Analysis was based on **451** completed questionnaires. Ninety-three percent of the responding mothers indicated that they were the primary person in the child's socialization.

RELIABILITY:

Carlson and Grossbart (1988) reported an alpha of **.90** and a beta of .78 for the scale.

VALIDITY:

No examination of scale validity was reported by Carlson and Grossbart (1988).

ADMINISTRATION:

The scale was self-administered along with many other measures in the questionnaire used by Carlson and Grossbart (1988). Higher scores on the scale mean that parents often agree to let their children buy any of several products if the children are involved somehow in the payment. Lower scores imply that parents rarely let children buy what they ask for, even if they are willing to use their own money.

MAJOR FINDINGS:

The authors investigated the relationship between general parental socialization styles and children's consumer socialization. In a factor analysis of scale scores, scores on the **Purchase Independence** scale loaded on a factor described as the "child's consumption autonomy." However, no significant difference was found in the reported degree of child consumption autonomy between any of the five parental socialization style clusters examined.

REFERENCES:

Carlson, Les and Sanford Grossbart (1988), ''Parental Style and Consumer Socialization of Children,'' *JCR*, 15 (June), 77-94.

Ward, Scott, Daniel B. Wackman, and Ellen Wartella (1977), *How Children Learn to Buy*. Beverly Hills, Calif.: Sage Publications, Inc.

SCALE ITEMS: PURCHASE INDEPENDENCE (CHILD)

Very Seldom	Seldom	Sometimes	Often	Very Often
1	2	3	4	5

If my child asks for candy:
1. I pay for it if he/she will do his/her share, pay part of the cost, do chores, etc.
2. I'll agree if he/she use his/her own money.

If my child asks for a game or toy:
1. I pay for it if he/she will do his/her share, pay part of the cost, do chores, etc.
2. I'll agree if he/she use his/her own money.

If my child asks for a magazine/comic book:
1. I pay for it if he/she will do his/her share, pay part of the cost, do chores, etc.
2. I'll agree if he/she use his/her own money.

If my child asks for a snack food:
1. I pay for it if he/she will do his/her share, pay part of the cost, do chores, etc.
2. I'll agree if he/she use his/her own money.

If my child asks for sports equipment:
1. I pay for it if he/she will do his/her share, pay part of the cost, do chores, etc.
2. I'll agree if he/she use his/her own money.

SCALE NAME: Purchase-Related Communication (Child's View)

SCALE DESCRIPTION:

A six-item, five-point summated ratings scale measuring an adolescent's perceived degree of overt interaction with parents about issues such as advertising and purchasing products.

SCALE ORIGIN:

The scale used by Moschis and Moore (1984) is similar to, if not the same as, the scales used to measure the same construct by both Ward and Wackman (1971) and Moore and Stephens (1975). The items were used as a summated scale in the latter two studies, but no reliability or validity information was reported. The measure also has some items in common with a scale used by Moschis (1978, p. 45).

SAMPLES:

The study by Moschis and Moore (1984) was based on data collected from **784** adolescents from six counties in Georgia that varied widely in rural/urban nature. The surveys were administered to middle school or high school students in a regular class session. The sample was reported to be very representative given that, among other demographic variables, it was 48% male and 88% white.

RELIABILITY:

An alpha of .**62** was reported for the scale.

VALIDITY:

No examination of scale validity was reported.

ADMINISTRATION:

The scale was self-administered by students in a regular class session along with other measures as part of a larger questionnaire. Higher scores indicate that adolescents rarely discuss purchase-related activities with their parents whereas lower scores suggest that they often talk with their parents about shopping and things they have seen in advertising.

MAJOR FINDINGS:

The purpose of the study was to examine the development of consumption-related cognitions and behaviors among adolescents. Degree of **family communication** was found to be significantly related to adolescents' career decisions, major product purchase expectations, and consumer behavior role perceptions.

COMMENTS:

The internal consistency of the scale is low enough that caution should be exercised in its use until further refinement can improve its psychometric quality.

REFERENCES:

Moschis, George P. (1978), *Acquisition of the Consumer Role by Adolescents*, Research Monograph No. 82. Atlanta, Ga.: Publishing Services Division, College of Business Administration, Georgia State University.

_____ and Roy L. Moore (1984), ''Anticipatory Consumer Socialization,'' *JAMS*, 12 (Fall), 109-123.

Moore, Roy L. and Lowndes F. Stephens (1975), ''Some Communication and Demographic Determinants of Adolescent Consumer Learning,'' *JCR*, 2 (September), 80-92.

Ward, Scott and Daniel Wackman (1971), ''Family and Media Influences on Adolescent Consumer Learning,'' *American Behavioral Scientist*, 14 (January/February), 415-427.

SCALE ITEMS: PURCHASE RELATED COMMUNICATION (CHILD'S VIEW)

Very	Often	Sometimes	Rarely	Never
1————	——2——	——3——	——4——	——5

1. My parents and I talk about things we see or hear advertised.
2. I try to get my parents to buy things I see advertised.
3. I get my parents to buy things that are advertised.
4. I ask my parents for advice about buying things.
5. I go shopping with my parents.
6. My parents and I don't agree on what things I should or shouldn't buy.

SCALE NAME: Purchase-Related Communication (Parent's View)

SCALE DESCRIPTION:

> A seven-item, five-point Likert-type summated ratings scale measuring the degree to which a parent reports communicating about products and purchases with a child.

SCALE ORIGIN:

> The use of these items as a multi-item measure appears to be original to Carlson and Grossbart (1988). However, ideas for some of the items came from the research of Moschis (1978, p. 45) as well as Ward, Wackman, and Wartella (1977).

SAMPLES:

> The survey instrument used by Carlson and Grossbart (1988) was distributed to mothers via students at three elementary schools in an unidentified U.S. city. The schools were chosen on a convenience basis but appeared to represent a variety of socioeconomic areas of the city. A $1 contribution to the PTO was offered for each completed questionnaire returned by the children. Analysis was based on **451** completed questionnaires. Ninety-three percent of the responding mothers indicated that they were the primary person in the child's socialization.

RELIABILITY:

> Carlson and Grossbart (1988) reported an alpha of .**76** and a beta of .65 for the scale.

VALIDITY:

> No examination of scale validity was reported by Carlson and Grossbart (1988).

ADMINISTRATION:

> The scale was self-administered along with many other measures in the questionnaire used by Carlson and Grossbart (1988). Higher scores on the scale mean that respondents report a high degree of purchase-related communication with their children whereas lower scores imply that they do not talk with their children much at all about such things.

MAJOR FINDINGS:

> The authors investigated the relationship between general parental socialization styles and children's consumer socialization. In a factor analysis of scale scores, scores on the **Purchase-Related Communication** scale loaded on a factor described as the "parent-child communication about consumption." A significant difference was found in the degree of parent-child communication between several of the parental socialization style clusters examined.

REFERENCES:

Carlson, Les and Sanford Grossbart (1988), ''Parental Style and Consumer Socialization of Children,'' *JCR*, 15 (June), 77-94.

Moschis, George P. (1978), *Acquisition of the Consumer Role by Adolescents*, Research Monograph No. 82. Atlanta, Ga.: Publishing Services Division, College of Business Administration, Georgia State University.

Ward, Scott, Daniel B. Wackman, and Ellen Wartella (1977), *How Children Learn to Buy*. Beverly Hills, Calif.: Sage Publications, Inc.

SCALE ITEMS: PURCHASE RELATED COMMUNICATION (PARENT'S VIEW)

Very Often	Disagree	Neither	Agree	Never
1	2	3	4	5

1. My children and I talk about buying things.
2. I ask my child his/her preference when I buy something for him/her.
3. I talk to him/her about how much products cost.
4. I talk to him/her about where different products can be bought.
5. To teach my child to become a consumer I lecture him/her on consumer activities.
6. To teach my child to become a consumer we discuss consumer decisions.
7. To teach my child to become a consumer I act as an example.

SCALE NAME: Quality (Product)

SCALE DESCRIPTION:

A five-item, five-point Likert-type summated ratings scale measuring consumer attitudes about product quality in general. A seven-item version of the scale with similar psychometric properties is also discussed below.

SCALE ORIGIN:

The scale was developed by Gaski and Etgar (1986). By a formula described in the article, the scale can be combined with data from several other measures to form an index of consumer attitudes toward marketing-related activities. The authors request that the index be referred to as the University of Notre Dame/Market Facts Index of Consumer Sentiment Toward Marketing. Some items were taken or adapted from the literature, but the majority were written especially for the index. Pretesting involved 50 members of the Market Facts mail panel completing the index.

SAMPLES:

The sample was taken from the 200,000 household panel maintained by Market Facts. Questionnaires were mailed to 2000 households and **1428** were completed and returned. Though the overall panel is nationally balanced and continually updated to reflect the most recent national demographic changes, the characteristics of the final sample were not given.

RELIABILITY:

A seven-item version of the scale had an alpha of **.817** and the item-total correlations were .49 or higher. Two items with the lowest item-total correlations were eliminated, leaving a scale with an alpha of **.781**.

VALIDITY:

A factor analysis of the 20 items composing the entire index was conducted. The five items composing each of the four scales loaded most heavily on their respective factors and had extremely low loadings on the other three factors. This pattern of loadings provides some evidence of convergent and discriminant validity.

ADMINISTRATION:

The scale was self-administered along with several other measures in a mail survey instrument. Higher scores indicate that consumers have positive attitudes about general product quality whereas low scores suggest that they think product quality is poor.

MAJOR FINDINGS:

The purpose of the study was to report the construction and validation of an index to measure consumers' attitudes toward marketing that could be used repeatedly over time as an indicator of the public's general sentiment about the field. Scores on the index were strongly correlated with those of another general measure of consumer sentiment and consumer satisfaction with the marketing mix elements.

As noted above, **product quality** was just one of four subscales composing the index. Its scores had the following significant correlations with those of the other subscales: .443 (price), .377 (advertising), and .366 (retailing).

REFERENCE:

Gaski, John F. and Michael J. Etzel (1986), "The Index of Consumer Sentiment Toward Marketing," *JM*, 50 (July), 71- 81.

SCALE ITEMS: QUALITY (PRODUCT)

Agree Strongly	Agree Somewhat	Neutral	Disagree Somewhat	Disagree Strongly
1	2	3	4	5

1. The quality of most products I buy today is as good as can be expected. **(r)***
2. I am satisfied with most of the products I buy. **(r)**
3. Most products I buy wear out too quickly.
4. Products are not made as well as they used to be.*
5. Too many of the products I buy are defective in some way.
6. The companies that make the products I buy don't care enough about how well they perform.
7. The quality of products I buy has consistently improved over the years. **(r)**

* These items were eliminated in order to have a five-item scale.

SCALE NAME: Quality (Product)

SCALE DESCRIPTION:

A six-item, seven-point semantic differential summated ratings scale measuring the degree of quality a consumer perceives a product to have. The scale was used to study both calculators and typewriters.

SCALE ORIGIN:

Petroshius and Monroe (1987) provide no information about the origin of the scale. Therefore, it is assumed that they constructed it specifically for use in their study.

SAMPLES:

The sample was composed of **456** undergraduate students. Homogeneous subjects were desired because the study's purpose was to test theoretical propositions. The students were randomly assigned to one of 16 experimental conditions to test the hypotheses.

RELIABILITY:

The alpha values reported for the two products examined were **.88** and **.84**.

VALIDITY:

A factor analysis indicated that the items loaded together and not on other related factors, providing some evidence of convergent and discriminant validity.

ADMINISTRATION:

The scale was self-administered by respondents along with other measures in an unspecified experimental setting. Lower scores on the scale indicate that respondents perceive a product to be of high quality whereas higher scores suggest they view a product to be of poor quality.

MAJOR FINDINGS:

The study's objective was to examine the relationship between the price structure of a product line and consumer assessments of a product model within the line. A positive association was found between price and perceived **quality.** Further, the price range of a line had some, though not much, influence on perceptions of product **quality**.

REFERENCE:

Petroshius, Susan M. and Kent B. Monroe (1987), "Effect of Product- Line Pricing Characteristics on Product Evaluations," *JCR*, 13 (March), 511-519.

SCALE ITEMS: QUALITY (PRODUCT) +

1. The likelihood that the _____ will be reliable is:**(r)**

Very low	Moderately low	Slightly low	Neither high nor low	Slightly high	Moderately High	Very High
1————	——2————	——3————	——4————	——5————	——6————	——7

2. The workmanship of the _____ appears to be:

Very High	Moderately high	Slightly high	Neither high nor low	Slightly low	Moderately low	Very low
1————	——2————	——3————	——4————	——5————	——6————	——7

3. This _____ appears to be of:

Very Good Quality	Moderately Good Quality	Slightly Good Quality	Neither Good nor Poor Quality	Slightly Poor Quality	Moderately Poor Quality	Very Poor Quality
1————	——2————	——3————	——4————	——5————	——6————	——7

4. I would consider this _____ to be very functional.**(r)**

Strongly Disagree	Moderately Disagree	Slightly Disagree	Neither Agree Nor Disagree	Slightly Agree	Moderately Agree	Strongly Agree
1————	——2————	——3————	——4————	——5————	——6————	——7

5. The likelihood that this _____ is dependable is:

Very High	Moderately high	Slightly high	Neither high nor low	Slightly low	Moderately low	Very low
1————	——2————	——3————	——4————	——5————	——6————	——7

6. This _____ would seem to be durable.

Strongly Disagree	Moderately Disagree	Slightly Disagree	Neither Agree Nor Disagree	Slightly Agree	Moderately Agree	Strongly Agree
1————	——2————	——3————	——4————	——5————	——6————	——7

+ Place the name of the generic product in the blank.

SCALE NAME: Quality (Store's Products)

SCALE DESCRIPTION:

A five-item, five-point Likert-type summated ratings scale measuring the degree to which a consumer considers the quality of products carried by a grocer to be important. The measure was called Product Quality by Saegert, Hoover, and Hilger (1985).

SCALE ORIGIN:

As a summated scale, the measure is original to Saegert, Hoover, and Hilger (1985). The authors note that some of the items were adapted from ones used by Kelly and Stephenson (1967). The items in that study were used in the form of bipolar descriptors and do not appear to have been summated.

SAMPLES:

Saegert and his coauthors reported on four surveys, only two of which utilized the scale of interest. One of those studies involved a random selection of 1000 Spanish names and 1000 non-Spanish names and mailing questionnaires to those individuals. A total of **299** questionnaires were returned. The response rates for both groups were very low (9% for Hispanics and 21% for others), indicating a need to confirm the findings with personal interviews in another sample. The second survey of interest was conducted in a small Texas town with **195** women (95 Hispanic and 100 non-Hispanic) who were selected randomly from blocks in the town and houses within the blocks.

RELIABILITY:

An alpha of **.76** was calculated for the scale.

VALIDITY:

A factor analysis by Saegert and his coauthors of 25 shopping-related items indicated that the items in this scale loaded together. (Information in the article as well as some provided by Saegert in personal correspondence suggest that the factor analysis and the alpha reported above were based on data collected just in the mail survey. The article specifically states, however, that analyses of the separate ethnic groups as well as the data from the personal interviews produced almost identical factor interpretations.)

ADMINISTRATION:

In one survey the scale was self-administered as part of a mail questionnaire and in the other survey it was administered by bilingual interviewers. Higher scores on the scale indicate consumers think that quality of the products carried by a store is very important.

MAJOR FINDINGS:

The authors used the results of four surveys to examine differences between Anglo-Americans and Mexican-Americans in shopping-related attitudes and behaviors. In the mail survey described above, the quality of products carried by a grocery store was significantly more important to Hispanics than to non-Hispanics. A significant difference was not found in the personal interviews, however. In both surveys and for both ethnic groups, **quality of the store's products** was the most important shopping factor among those studied.

COMMENTS:

Information supplied by Saegert in personal correspondence indicates that item 5 (below) had an extremely low factor loading (.32), had a similar loading on another factor (.30), and is conceptually distinct from the other items in the scale. Hence, strong consideration should be given to dropping the item from the scale.

REFERENCES:

Kelly, Robert F. and Ronald Stephenson (1967), "The Semantic Differential: An Information Source for Designing Retail Patronage Appeals," *JM*, 31 (October), 43-47.
Saegert, Joel, Robert J. Hoover, and Marye Tharp Hilger (1985), "Characteristics of Mexican American Consumers," *JCR*, 12 (June), 104-109.

SCALE ITEMS: QUALITY (STORE'S PRODUCTS) +

```
Not important                                              Very important
at all          ____ : ____ : ____ : ____ : ____
                  1     2     3     4     5
```

1. The store has high product quality.
2. The store carries a large variety of products.
3. The store has fresh products.
4. The store sells good meats.
5. The employees are helpful.

+ These items were reconstructed from phrases supplied in personal correspondence by Saegert.

SCALE NAME: Quantity of Consumption (Soft Drink)

SCALE DESCRIPTION:

A three-item, Likert-like summated ratings scale measuring the quantity of soft drinks a person believes he/she will consume in the next week. Two of the items are answered on a nine-point scale and one asks for ratio-level data.

SCALE ORIGIN:

The items and scale were original to Beatty and Kahle (1988).

SAMPLES:

Data were collected from respondents at two points in time, four weeks apart. The sample was composed of **187** student volunteers enrolled in various undergraduate business courses at three universities in the western United States. The proportions of men and women were unspecified, but noted to be approximately equal. The product examined was soft drinks, and college students were thought to be an appropriate convenience sample. The majority (88%) had consumed at least one soft drink in the previous week.

RELIABILITY:

Alpha values of **.74** and **.75** were reported for the scale for Time 1 and 2, respectively. Test-retest stability was **.75**.

VALIDITY:

No examination of scale validity was reported.

ADMINISTRATION:

The scale was filled out by students as part of a larger self-administered questionnaire in an unspecified setting. Higher scores on this scale imply that respondents plan to consume many (7+) soft drinks in the next week whereas lower scores suggest that they do not plan to drink more than one in the next week.

MAJOR FINDINGS:

The authors investigated the association between attitudes and behaviors in the consumption of a frequently purchased product (soft drinks). The theory of reasoned action and the low involvement hierarchy model were specifically tested. **Intention to drink** was found to be significantly associated with reported drinking behavior of the previous week as well as drinking habits in general.

COMMENTS:

The authors report that the mean and standard deviation for the open-ended item (see item 3 below) were similar enough to the means and standard deviations of the other two items that there was no need to adjust the scales, and simple summation was considered appropriate.

REFERENCE:

Beatty, Sharon E. and Lynn R. Kahle (1988), "Alternative Hierarchies of the Attitude-Behavior Relationship: The Impact of Brand Commitment and Habit," *JAMS*, 16 (Summer), 1-10.

SCALE ITEMS: QUANTITY OF CONSUMPTION (SOFT DRINK)

1. I plan to drink at least one soft drink each day over the next week.

unlikely   ___ : ___ : ___ : ___ : ___ : ___ : ___ : ___ : ___   likely
                 1   2   3   4   5   6   7   8   9

2. I intend to drink at least several soft drinks in the next week.

unlikely   ___ : ___ : ___ : ___ : ___ : ___ : ___ : ___ : ___   likely
                 1   2   3   4   5   6   7   8   9

3. How many soft drinks do you intend to drink in the next week? _____.

SCALE NAME: Rationality (Object)

SCALE DESCRIPTION:

A five-item, seven-point semantic differential summated ratings scale measuring the degree to which an object is perceived as being logical and factual. The objects evaluated by subjects in Hirschman's (1986) study were print advertisements.

SCALE ORIGIN:

The scale used by Hirschman (1986) appears to have been developed in this form by Hirschman and Solomon (1984). In that study the authors explored consumers' perceptions of visual versus verbal ads on three dimensions: functional utility, aesthetic value, and familiarity. Data were gathered from college students who were asked to fill out a questionnaire themselves and to have four more completed by others. Satisfactory forms were received from 162 respondents. Seventy-nine subjects received all verbal ads and 83 received all visual ads. The mean age of the sample was 29 years and 53.7% were women. Respondents were each exposed to two ads in their questionnaires and filled out the dimension scales twice. The two alpha values reported for this scale were .80 and .82. As hypothesized, verbal ads were consistently found to be more rational than visual ads.

SAMPLES:

A total of **154** social science college students participated in Hirschman's (1986) study as part of their course requirements. Students were randomly assigned to treatment groups and no difference in any demographic or control variables was noted. The all-verbal-ads group had 78 subjects and the all-visual-ads group had 76.

RELIABILITY:

The alpha for this scale was not specifically reported but the author reports the scale to be among those for which alpha was between .82 and .96 (Hirschman 1986).

VALIDITY:

The validity of this scale was not specifically examined or discussed by Hirschman (1986).

ADMINISTRATION:

The scale was self-administered by subjects along with other measures after viewing ads (Hirschman 1986). The items are scored such that the extreme positive responses are coded 7 and extreme negative responses are coded 1. Higher scores on the scale suggest that respondents view an object (such as an ad) to be very factual and/or logical whereas lower scores imply that they think an object is irrational.

MAJOR FINDINGS:

The purpose of the study by Hirschman (1986) was to examine the differences in perceptions of products portrayed in all-verbal versus all-visual ads. For 13 of 14 products examined, all-verbal ads were perceived to be significantly more **rational** than the all-visual ads.

REFERENCES:

Hirschman, Elizabeth C. (1986), ''The Effect of Verbal and Pictorial Advertising Stimuli on Aesthetic, Utilitarian and Familiarity Perceptions,'' *JA*, 15 (2), 27-34.

_____ and Michael R. Solomon (1984), ''Utilitarian, Aesthetic, and Familiarity Responses to Verbal Versus Visual Advertisements,'' in *Advances in Consumer Research*, Vol. 11, Thomas C. Kinnear, ed. Ann Arbor, Mich.: Association for Consumer Research.

SCALE ITEMS: RATIONALITY (OBJECT)

1. logical   ____ : ____ : ____ : ____ : ____ : ____ : ____   not logical
             1   2   3   4   5   6   7

2. educational   ____ : ____ : ____ : ____ : ____ : ____ : ____   not educational
             1   2   3   4   5   6   7

3. informative   ____ : ____ : ____ : ____ : ____ : ____ : ____   not imformative
             1   2   3   4   5   6   7

4. factual   ____ : ____ : ____ : ____ : ____ : ____ : ____   not factual
             1   2   3   4   5   6   7

5. useful   ____ : ____ : ____ : ____ : ____ : ____ : ____   not useful
             1   2   3   4   5   6   7

SCALE NAME: Reader

SCALE DESCRIPTION:

A three-item, six-point, Likert-type summated ratings scale from strongly disagree (1) to strongly agree (6). The scale measures a person's tendency to engage in reading activities.

SCALE ORIGIN:

The items used by Davis and Rubin (1983) were cited in an book chapter by Tigert (1974, p. 183). As Tigert did not use the items as a summated ratings scale, no psychometric information was reported.

SAMPLES:

Davis and Rubin (1983) mailed questionnaires to a sample of two groups in Florida: known adopters of solar energy devices and the general population over the age of 18 years. Analysis was based on **817** usable questionnaires, of which **488** were from solar energy adopters.

RELIABILITY:

Davis and Rubin (1983) reported an alpha of **.51**.

VALIDITY:

The authors randomly split their data in half and factor analyzed the two subsamples. Identical factor solutions were found in the two subsamples. The factors found within the full dataset were consistent with the subsample solutions.

ADMINISTRATION:

Data were gathered in the studies through self-administered mail questionnaires. Scale scores are calculated by averaging numerical responses to individual items. A score of 6 indicates a person has a strong tendency to engage in **reading**-related activities whereas a score of 1 implies a person does not like to **read**.

MAJOR FINDINGS:

Davis and Rubin (1983) examined a few psychographic variables that might distinguish between energy-conscious opinion leader groups. Persons with a high amount of opinion leadership expressed more interest in **reading** than those with less leadership.

COMMENTS:

The internal consistency of the three-item scale is extremely low and might be improved by the addition of a few more items. Care should be taken to select items that reflect an interest in reading in general and not just interest in the particular material mentioned in the items.

REFERENCES:

Davis, Duane L. and Ronald S. Rubin (1983), ''Identifying the Energy Conscious Consumer: The Case of the Opinion Leader,'' *JAMS*, 11 (Spring), 169-190.

Tigert, Douglas J. (1974), ''Life Style Analysis as a Basis for Media Selection,'' in *Life Style and Psychographics*, William D. Wells, ed. Chicago, Ill.: American Marketing Association.

SCALE ITEMS: READER

Strongly Disagree	Disagree	Slightly Disagree	Slightly Agree	Agree	Strongly Agree
1	2	3	4	5	6

1. I like to read war stories. +
2. I like to read comic strips.
3. I like science fiction.

+ Davis and Rubin (1983) only specified this item of the ones they used.

SCALE NAME: Rebates (Negative Role)

SCALE DESCRIPTION:

A three-item, six-point Likert-type summated ratings scale that appears to measure consumer pessimism about manufacturer motivation for offering rebates.

SCALE ORIGIN:

Tat, Cunningham, and Babakus (1988) indicate that the items were based on their personal experience and extensive review of unspecified literature.

SAMPLES:

A stratified sample of Memphis area telephone numbers was used. The stratification was based on the first three digits and a random number generator provided the last four digits. Interviews were conducted with the adult member of the household who did most of the shopping. Analysis was based on **303** usable interviews. The typical respondent was a married woman, under 45 years of age, with at least a high school education, in a household with two wage earners making at least $20,000 a year. A variety of occupations were represented, but over half of the respondents were homemakers, students, retired, or self-employed.

RELIABILITY:

An alpha of **.542** was reported for the scale.

VALIDITY:

A factor analysis indicated the items loaded together.

ADMINISTRATION:

The scale was administered by telephone as part of a larger structured but nondisguised questionnaire. It should be amenable for use in mail surveys and other situations in which it can be self-administered. Lower scores on the scale indicate respondents perceive manufacturers to use rebates for self-serving reasons whereas higher scores suggest respondents do not see manufacturers' motives as being so negative.

MAJOR FINDINGS:

The purpose of the study was to examine consumer perceptions of **rebates**. A significant association was found between **rebate** usage and the perceived reasons for their being offered. That is, nonusers seemed to take a dim view of manufacturers' motives for using **rebates**. Nonusers of **rebates** also perceived significantly **more trouble** in using **rebates** than did regular users.

COMMENTS:

The internal consistency is so low that no use should be made of the scale until its psychometric quality can be improved.

REFERENCE:

Tat, Peter, William A. Cunningham III, and Emin Babakus (1988), ''Consumer Perceptions of Rebates,'' *JAR*, 28 (August- September), 45-50.

SCALE ITEMS: REBATES (NEGATIVE ROLE) +

Strongly Agree	Agree	Neither Agree Nor Disagree	Disagree	Strongly Disagree	Don't Know
1————————	—2————————	—3————————	—4————————	—5————————	—6

1. Manufacturers offer rebates to get consumers to buy something they don't really need.
2. Manufacturers use rebate offers to induce consumers to buy slow-moving items.
3. Rebate offers require you to buy more of a product than you need.

+ Though six points were offered on the graphic scale, the don't know responses were excluded from the analyses.

SCALE NAME: Rebates (Negative Role)

SCALE DESCRIPTION:

A four-item, six-point Likert-type summated ratings scale that appears to measure how troublesome a consumer perceives rebates to be.

SCALE ORIGIN:

Tat, Cunningham, and Babakus (1988) indicate that the items were based upon their personal experience and extensive review of unspecified literature.

SAMPLES:

A stratified sample of Memphis area telephone numbers was used. The stratification was based on the first three digits and a random number generator provided the last four digits. Interviews were conducted with the adult member of the household who did most of the shopping. Analysis was based on **303** usable interviews. The typical respondent was a married woman, under 45 years of age, with at least a high school education, in a household with two wage earners making at least $20,000 a year. A variety of occupations were represented, but over half of the respondents were homemakers, students, retired, or self-employed.

RELIABILITY:

An alpha of **.643** was reported for the scale.

VALIDITY:

A factor analysis indicated the items loaded together.

ADMINISTRATION:

The scale was administered by telephone as part of a larger structured but nondisguised questionnaire. It should be amenable for use in mail surveys and other situations in which it can be self-administered. Lower scores on the scale indicate respondents perceive a great deal of trouble in using rebates whereas higher scores suggest that rebates are not viewed as being particularly complicated or troublesome.

MAJOR FINDINGS:

The purpose of the study was to examine consumer perceptions of rebates. A negative association was found between rebate usage and the **perceived hassles** involved. That is, nonusers of rebates perceived significantly more trouble in using rebates than did regular users. Nonusers also seemed to take a dim view of manufacturers' motives for using rebates.

COMMENTS:

The internal consistency is low enough to warrant further development if the scale is to be used in other studies.

REFERENCES:

Tat, Peter, William A. Cunningham III, and Emin Babakus (1988), ''Consumer Perceptions of Rebates,'' *JAR*, 28 (August- September), 45-50.

SCALE ITEMS: REBATES (NEGATIVE ROLE) +

Strongly Agree	Agree	Neither Agree Nor Disagree	Disagree	Strongly Disagree	Don't Know
1—————	—2———	——3———	——4———	——5———	——6

1. Manufacturers make the rebate process too complicated.
2. Mail-in rebates are not worth the trouble involved.
3. It takes too long to receive the rebate check from the manufacturer.
4. Manufacturers could do more to make rebates easier to use.

+ Though six points were offered on the graphic scale, the don't know responses were excluded from the analyses.

SCALE NAME: Rebates (Positive Role)

SCALE DESCRIPTION:

A four-item, six-point Likert-type summated ratings scale that appears to measure a consumer's optimistic view of manufacturers' reasons for using rebates.

SCALE ORIGIN:

Tat, Cunningham, and Babakus (1988) indicate that the items were based upon their personal experience and extensive review of unspecified literature.

SAMPLES:

A stratified sample of Memphis area telephone numbers was used. The stratification was based on the first three digits and a random number generator provided the last four digits. Interviews were conducted with the adult member of the household who did most of the shopping. Analysis was based on **303** usable interviews. The typical respondent was a married woman, under 45 years of age, with at least a high school education, in a household with two wage earners making at least $20,000 a year. A variety of occupations were represented, but over half of the respondents were homemakers, students, retired, or self-employed.

RELIABILITY:

An alpha of **.652** was reported for the scale.

VALIDITY:

A factor analysis indicated the items loaded together.

ADMINISTRATION:

The scale was administered by telephone as part of a larger structured but nondisguised questionnaire. It should be amenable for use in mail surveys and other situations in which it can be self-administered. Lower scores on the scale indicate respondents perceive that manufacturers offer rebates because of the positive benefits they have for consumers whereas higher scores suggest respondents do not perceive that manufacturers use rebates out of concern for the consumer's welfare.

MAJOR FINDINGS:

The purpose of the study was to examine consumer perceptions of **rebates**. No significant difference was found between users and nonusers of rebates in their perception of the **positive role rebates** could play. However, nonusers of **rebates** perceived significantly more trouble in using **rebates** than did regular users. Nonusers also seemed to take a dim view of manufacturers' motives for using **rebates**.

COMMENTS:

The internal consistency is low enough to warrant further development if the scale is to be used in other studies.

REFERENCE:

Tat, Peter, William A. Cunningham III, Emin Babakus (1988), ''Consumer Perceptions of Rebates,'' *JAR*, 28 (August- September), 45-50.

SCALE ITEMS: REBATES (POSITIVE ROLE) +

Strongly Agree	Agree	Neither Agree Nor Disagree	Disagree	Strongly Disagree	Don't Know
1—————	——2————	——3————	——4————	——5———	—6

1. Manufacturers offer rebates because consumers want them.
2. Today's manufacturers take real interest in consumer welfare.
3. Consumer benefit is usually the primary consideration in rebate offers.
4. In general, manufacturers are sincere in their rebate offers to consumers.

+ Though six points were offered on the graphic scale, the don't know responses were excluded from the analyses. Further, all of the items in this scale were reverse coded in the study so scale scores would be more consistent with the direction of the other constructs measured. None of the items has to be reverse coded, however.

SCALE NAME: Refusal of Child's Purchase Requests (With Explanation)

SCALE DESCRIPTION:

A five-item, five-point Likert-type summated ratings scale measuring the degree to which a parent reports refusing to buy any of several specified products for his/her child when the child asks for them, but provides explanations for denying the requests.

SCALE ORIGIN:

The use of these items as a multi-item measure appears to be original to Carlson and Grossbart (1988). However, they got ideas for some of the items from the research of Ward, Wackman, and Wartella (1977).

SAMPLES:

The survey instrument used by Carlson and Grossbart (1988) was distributed to mothers via students at three elementary schools in an unidentified U.S. city. The schools were chosen on a convenience basis but appeared to represent a variety of socioeconomic areas of the city. A $1 contribution to the PTO was offered for each completed questionnaire returned by the children. Analysis was based on **451** completed questionnaires. Ninety-three percent of the responding mothers indicated that they were the primary person in the child's socialization.

RELIABILITY:

Carlson and Grossbart (1988) reported an alpha of **.84** and a beta of .77 for the scale.

VALIDITY:

No examination of scale validity was reported by Carlson and Grossbart (1988).

ADMINISTRATION:

The scale was self-administered along with many other measures in the questionnaire used by Carlson and Grossbart (1988). Higher scores on the scale mean that parents tend to refuse to buy their children any of several products when asked but do give them a reason for denying their requests. Lower scores could imply either that parents are more likely to yield to their children's requests or that they deny requests and do not provide explanations.

MAJOR FINDINGS:

The authors investigated the relationship between general parental socialization styles and children's consumer socialization. In a factor analysis of scale scores, scores on the **Refusal** scale loaded on a factor described as "restriction of consumption." Some but not many significant differences were found in the degree of consumption restriction among the five parental socialization style clusters examined.

REFERENCES:

Carlson, Les and Sanford Grossbart (1988), "Parental Style and Consumer Socialization of Children," *JCR*, 15 (June), 77-94.

Ward, Scott, Daniel B. Wackman, and Ellen Wartella (1977), *How Children Learn to Buy.* Beverly Hills, Calif.: Sage Publications, Inc.

SCALE ITEMS: REFUSAL OF CHILD'S PURCHASE REQUESTS (WITH EXPLANATION)

Very Seldom	Seldom	Sometimes	Often	Very Often
1	2	3	4	5

1. If my child asks for candy I refuse to buy it but give an explanation why.
2. If my child asks for a game or toy I refuse to buy it but give an explanation why.
3. If my child asks for a magazine/comic book I refuse to buy it but give an explanation why.
4. If my child asks for a snack food I refuse to buy it but give an explanation why.
5. If my child asks for sports equipment I refuse to buy it but give an explanation why.

SCALE NAME: Refusal of Child's Purchase Requests (Without Explanation)

SCALE DESCRIPTION:

A five-item, five-point Likert-type summated ratings scale measuring the degree to which a parent reports refusing to buy any of several products for his/her child when the child asks for it, but gives no explanation for the denial.

SCALE ORIGIN:

The use of these items as a multi-item measure appears to be original to Carlson and Grossbart (1988). However, they got ideas for some of the items from the research of Ward, Wackman, and Wartella (1977).

SAMPLES:

The survey instrument used by Carlson and Grossbart (1988) was distributed to mothers via students at three elementary schools in an unidentified U.S. city. The schools were chosen on a convenience basis but appeared to represent a variety of socioeconomic areas of the city. A $1 contribution to the PTO was offered for each completed questionnaire returned by the children. Analysis was based on **451** completed questionnaires. Ninety-three percent of the responding mothers indicated that they were the primary person in the child's socialization.

RELIABILITY:

Carlson and Grossbart (1988) reported an alpha of **.93** and a beta of **.88** for the scale.

VALIDITY:

No examination of scale validity was reported by Carlson and Grossbart (1988).

ADMINISTRATION:

The scale was self-administered along with many other measures in the questionnaire used by Carlson and Grossbart (1988). Higher scores on the scale mean that parents tend to refuse to buy their children any of several products when asked whereas lower scores imply that parents are more likely to purchase items for their children whenever they ask for them.

MAJOR FINDINGS:

The authors investigated the relationship between general parental socialization styles and children's consumer socialization. In a factor analysis of scale scores, scores on the **Refusal** scale loaded on a factor described as "restriction of consumption." Some but not many significant differences were found in the degree of consumption restriction among the five parental socialization style clusters examined.

REFERENCES:

Carlson, Les and Sanford Grossbart (1988), "Parental Style and Consumer Socialization of Children," *JCR*, 15 (June), 77-94.

Ward, Scott, Daniel B. Wackman, and Ellen Wartella (1977), *How Children Learn to Buy.* Beverly Hills, Calif.: Sage Publications, Inc.

SCALE ITEMS: REFUSAL OF CHILD'S PURCHASE REQUESTS (WITHOUT EXPLANATION)

Very Often	Disagree	Neither	Agree	Never
1————————	—2————————	—3————————	—4————————	—5

1. If my child asks for candy I just say no and that's that.
2. If my child asks for a game or toy I just say no and that's that.
3. If my child asks for a magazine/comic book I just say no and that's that.
4. If my child asks for a snack food I just say no and that's that.
5. If my child asks for sports equipment I just say no and that's that.

SCALE NAME: Regulation of Business

SCALE DESCRIPTION:

A four-item, five-point Likert-type summated ratings scale measuring the degree to which a respondent favors greater government control of business practices that can harm consumers rather than depending upon business to regulate itself. The scale was referred to as Favor Governmental Control by Carlson and Grossbart (1988).

SCALE ORIGIN:

The use of these items as a multi-item measure appears to be original to Carlson and Grossbart (1988). However, the items themselves come from the research of Ward, Wackman, and Wartella (1977).

SAMPLES:

The survey instrument used by Carlson and Grossbart (1988) was distributed to mothers via students at three elementary schools in an unidentified U.S. city. The schools were chosen on a convenience basis but appeared to represent a variety of socioeconomic areas of the city. A $1 contribution to the PTO was offered for each completed questionnaire returned by the children. Analysis was based on **451** completed questionnaires. Ninety-three percent of the responding mothers indicated that they were the primary person in the child's socialization.

RELIABILITY:

Carlson and Grossbart (1988) reported an alpha of **.65** and a beta of .51 for the scale.

VALIDITY:

No examination of scale validity was reported by Carlson and Grossbart (1988).

ADMINISTRATION:

The scale was self-administered along with many other measures in the questionnaire used by Carlson and Grossbart (1988). Higher scores on the scale mean that respondents report that the government should increase its control over business whereas lower scores imply that they think business can adequately regulate itself.

MAJOR FINDINGS:

The authors investigated the relationship between general parental socialization styles and children's consumer socialization. Only limited significant differences were found in the desire for greater **business regulation** between the five parental socialization style clusters examined. Specifically, Neglecting and Authoritarian mothers favored **government control** significantly more than Rigid Controlling mothers.

COMMENTS:

The low reliability suggests that caution should be exercised in using this scale and further work is needed to improve its psychometric quality.

REFERENCES:

Carlson, Les and Sanford Grossbart (1988), ''Parental Style and Consumer Socialization of Children,'' *JCR*, 15 (June), 77-94.

Ward, Scott, Daniel B. Wackman, and Ellen Wartella (1977), *How Children Learn to Buy*. Beverly Hills, Calif.: Sage Publications, Inc.

SCALE ITEMS: REGULATION OF BUSINESS

Very Often	Disagree	Neither	Agree	Never
1—————	—2—————	—3—————	—4—————	—5

1. The government should regulate the advertising, sales, and marketing activities of manufacturers.
2. Most business firms make a sincere effort to adjust consumer complaints fairly. **(r)**
3. Generally, business self-regulation can be and is effective. **(r)**
4. The federal government should pass extensive new laws to help consumers get fair deals for their money.

SCALE NAME: Respect Toward the Elderly

SCALE DESCRIPTION:

A two-item, six-point Likert-type summated ratings scale from strongly disagree to strongly agree. The scale appears to measure the pessimism one feels about the respect given to senior citizens in this country.

SCALE ORIGIN:

Rahtz, Sirgy, and Meadow (1989) may have developed items for the scale by examining previous research, but the specific items and scales are original to their study.

SAMPLES:

Two independent samples were drawn from the same population one year apart by systematic random sampling of a mailing list. The mailing list was from a government-sponsored regional agency on aging. People's names were added to the list when social security records indicated they had reached the age of 60. The respondents in the two samples were all living in a three-county area of Virginia. The number of usable questionnaires returned from the first and second samples was **788** and **752**, respectively.

RELIABILITY:

The items in the first and second samples had inter-item correlations of **.2788** and **.1731**, respectively.

VALIDITY:

No analysis of scale validity was reported.

ADMINISTRATION:

The scales were administered to both samples as part of larger mail questionnaires. Scale scores are calculated by averaging numerical responses to items. Higher scores indicate respondents think that they (the elderly) do not receive enough respect from others whereas low scores suggest that they feel adequately respected.

MAJOR FINDINGS:

The purpose of the study was to examine the relationships between elderly people's television usage and a variety of demographic and psychographic variables. In both samples, low but significant correlations were found between **lack of respect** and TV usage. Specifically, concern about **lack of respect** was associated with greater viewing of television.

COMMENTS:

Because of the very low interitem correlations as well as the lack of evidence of validity, this scale should not be used as it is.

REFERENCE:

Rahtz, Don R., M. Joseph Sirgy, and H. Lee Meadow (1989), ''The Elderly Audience: Correlates of Television Orientation,'' *JA* (3), 9-20.

SCALE ITEMS: RESPECT TOWARD THE ELDERLY

Strongly Disagree	Disagree	Slightly Disagree	Slightly Agree	Agree	Strongly Agree
1	2	3	4	5	6

1. My opinion on things doesn't count.
2. Not many people respect senior citizens.

SCALE NAME: Restricted Mobility

SCALE DESCRIPTION:

A three-item, five-point Likert-type summated ratings scale ranging from strongly disagree (1) to strongly agree (5). The scale measures a person's degree of activity with emphasis on interaction with others. Lumpkin and Hunt (1989) referred to this scale as Restriction in Life Space.

SCALE ORIGIN:

The measure was apparently developed by Lumpkin and Hunt (1989) for use in their study, though the items may have come from previous studies reviewed in the article.

SAMPLES:

Lumpkin and Hunt's (1989) sample was drawn from the Market Facts Consumer Mail Panel and focused on **789** respondents who indicated they were 65 years of age or older. The proportions of men and women were similar to those in the national population, but fewer of the men and more of the women in the sample were married. The sample was better educated and had a greater percentage still employed than was true nationally. The sample was composed of more people in lower income levels, but reasonably matched the elderly geographic distribution.

RELIABILITY:

An alpha of **.619** was reported by Lumpkin and Hunt (1989).

VALIDITY:

Factor analysis indicated that the items loaded together.

ADMINISTRATION:

Data were gathered through self-administered mail questionnaires. Scale scores were calculated by averaging numerical responses to individual items. A score of 5 indicates that a person is very restricted in terms of interaction with friends or family whereas 1 suggests that a person gets around well and interacts with others.

MAJOR FINDINGS:

The elderly were broken down into two groups by Lumpkin and Hunt (1989): those who were self-reliant in terms of transportation and those who were dependent on others. The self-reliant group perceived themselves to be significantly less **restricted** than the dependent elderly (which validates the groupings). The reason seems to be that the dependent elderly have fewer friends and relatives and little means of transportation.

COMMENTS:

The reported factor loadings indicate that the low alpha is at least partially due to item 2 (below), which refers to physical mobility whereas the other two items refer more to social mobility. Internal consistency could be increased by the testing and addition of more relevant items and possibly removing item 2.

REFERENCE:

Lumpkin, James R. and James B. Hunt (1989), "Mobility as an Influence on Retail Patronage Behavior of the Elderly: Testing Conventional Wisdom," *JAMS*, 17 (Winter), 1-12.

SCALE ITEMS: RESTRICTED MOBILITY

Strongly Disagree	Disagree	Neutral	Agree	Strongly Agree
1—————————	—2———————	—3———————	—4———————	—5

1. I'm not as active as I used to be because of fewer friends or relatives.
2. I'm not as active as I used to be because I have no transportation.
3. I don't have as many friends or acquaintances as I used to.

SCALE NAME: Restriction of TV Viewing

SCALE DESCRIPTION:

A three-item, five-point Likert-type summated ratings scale measuring the degree to which a parent reports restricting when, what, and how much a child is allowed to watch television.

SCALE ORIGIN:

The use of these items as a multi-item measure appears to be original to Carlson and Grossbart (1988). The items themselves, however, come from the research of Ward, Wackman, and Wartella (1977).

SAMPLES:

The survey instrument used by Carlson and Grossbart (1988) was distributed to mothers via students at three elementary schools in an unidentified U.S. city. The schools were chosen on a convenience basis but appeared to represent a variety of socioeconomic areas of the city. A $1 contribution to the PTO was offered for each completed questionnaire returned by the children. Analysis was based on **451** completed questionnaires. Ninety-three percent of the responding mothers indicated that they were the primary person in the child's socialization.

RELIABILITY:

Carlson and Grossbart (1988) reported an alpha of **.82** and a beta of .76 for the scale.

VALIDITY:

No examination of scale validity was reported by Carlson and Grossbart (1988).

ADMINISTRATION:

The scale was self-administered along with many other measures in the questionnaire used by Carlson and Grossbart (1988). Higher scores on the scale mean that respondents report a high degree of control over the TV viewing of their children whereas lower scores suggest that they impose few restrictions on their children's viewing habits.

MAJOR FINDINGS:

The authors investigated the relationship between general parental socialization styles and children's consumer socialization. In a factor analysis of scale scores, scores on the **Restriction** scale loaded on a factor described as "mediation of the media." Some significant differences were found in the degree of control placed on the type and amount of TV viewing among several of the parental socialization style clusters examined.

REFERENCES:

Carlson, Les and Sanford Grossbart (1988), ''Parental Style and Consumer Socialization of Children,'' *JCR*, 15 (June), 77-94.

Ward, Scott, Daniel B. Wackman, and Ellen Wartella (1977), *How Children Learn to Buy.* Beverly Hills, Calif.: Sage Publications, Inc.

SCALE ITEMS: RESTRICTION OF TV VIEWING

Very Seldom	Seldom	Sometimes	Often	Very Often
1————————	——2————————	——3————————	——4————————	——5

I place restrictions on:
1. ...which programs my child can watch on TV.
2. ...when my child can watch TV.
3. ...how many hours each day my child can watch TV.

SCALE NAME: Risk (Financial)

SCALE DESCRIPTION:

A three-item (Likert-type), nine-point, bipolar-response summated ratings scale measuring the perceived degree of financial risk with a specified product. Financial risk is the uncertainty and the monetary loss one thinks could be incurred if a product does not function at some expected level.

SCALE ORIGIN:

The scale was apparently original to Shimp and Bearden (1982).

SAMPLES:

Data from three student samples and two nonstudent samples were used in the study by Shimp and Bearden (1982). In a multiscreen TV experiment, 12 students were randomly assigned to each of 18 treatments (n = **216**); in one plastic tire experiment, 11 students were randomly assigned to each of 18 treatments (n = **198**); and in a second plastic tire experiment, from 10 to 13 students were randomly assigned to each of 12 treatments (n = **145**). The nonstudent subjects were contacted from a statewide panel. There were 13 to 20 respondents for each of the 18 treatments in a plastic tire experiment (n = **297**) and a jogging device experiment (n = **293**). The respondents were mostly white, above average in age, and economically upscale.

RELIABILITY:

The following alpha values were reported by Shimp and Bearden (1982) for the five separate samples in the order described above: .**86**, .**79**, .**81**, .**75**, and .**72**. A test-retest correlation of .**57** was calculated with 44 students and a three-week interval.

VALIDITY:

The validity of the scale was not specifically examined by Shimp and Bearden (1982).

ADMINISTRATION:

The scale was apparently given to students along with other materials and measures in classroom experimental settings. The panel subjects were asked to complete the scale along with other measures in a packet of materials mailed to them. Higher scores on the scale indicate that respondents associate a lot of financial risk with a product whereas lower scores suggest that they perceive a product to involve little financial risk.

MAJOR FINDINGS:

A series of experiments were designed by Shimp and Bearden (1982) to examine the influence of certain extrinsic cues (warranty quality, warranty reputation, and price) on the risk perceived with innovative product concepts. In contrast to what was expected, only for warranty quality was there significant evidence that the extrinsic cues could reduce perceptions of **financial risk**.

OMMENTS:

An item was dropped from the scale when it was administered to the two nonstudent samples to help reduce the length of the questionnaire.

EFERENCE:

Shimp, Terence A. and William O. Bearden (1982), "Warranty and Other Extrinsic Cue Effects on Consumers' Risk Perceptions," *JCR*, 9 (June), 38-46.

CALE ITEMS: RISK (FINANCIAL) +

Considering the sizable investment associated with the purchase of a _____, how risky would you say purchasing the _____ would be?

ot risky all	____ : ____ : ____ : ____ : ____ : ____ : ____ : ____ : ____	Very risky
	1 2 3 4 5 6 7 8 9	

Given the expense involved with purchasing _____ today, how much risk would you say would be involved with purchasing the new _____? **(r)**

ubstantial sk	____ : ____ : ____ : ____ : ____ : ____ : ____ : ____ : ____	Very little risk
	1 2 3 4 5 6 7 8 9	

How risky do you feel it would be for you to purchase this new _____?

ot risky t all	____ : ____ : ____ : ____ : ____ : ____ : ____ : ____ : ____	Very risky
	1 2 3 4 5 6 7 8 9	

- The name of the product should be placed in the blanks. Item 3 was not administered to the nonstudent samples.

SCALE NAME: Risk (Performance)

SCALE DESCRIPTION:

A four-item (Likert-type), nine-point, bipolar-response summated ratings scale measuring the perceived degree of performance risk with a specified product. Performance risk is the uncertainty and consequence of a product not functioning at some expected level.

SCALE ORIGIN:

The scale was apparently original to Shimp and Bearden (1982).

SAMPLES:

Data from three student samples and two nonstudent samples were used in the study by Shimp and Bearden (1982). In a multiscreen TV experiment, 12 students were randomly assigned to each of 18 treatments (n = **216**); in one plastic tire experiment, 11 students were randomly assigned to each of 18 treatments (n = **198**); and in a second plastic tire experiment, from 10 to 13 students were randomly assigned to each of 12 treatments = **145**). The nonstudent subjects were contacted from a statewide panel. There were 1 to 20 respondents for each of the 18 treatments in a plastic tire experiment (n = **297**) and a jogging device experiment (n = **293**). The respondents were mostly white, above average in age, and economically upscale.

RELIABILITY:

The following alpha values were reported by Shimp and Bearden (1982) for the five separate samples in the order described above: **.84, .77, .73, .84,** and **.85**. A test-retest correlation of **.74** was calculated with 44 students and a three-week interval.

VALIDITY:

The validity of the scale was not specifically examined by Shimp and Bearden (1982).

ADMINISTRATION:

The scale was apparently given to students along with other materials and measures classroom experimental settings. The panel subjects were asked to complete the scale along with other measures in a packet of materials mailed to them. Higher scores on the scale indicate that respondents associate a lot of performance risk with a product whereas lower scores suggest that they perceive a product to involve little performance risk.

MAJOR FINDINGS:

A series of experiments were designed by Shimp and Bearden (1982) to examine the influence of certain extrinsic cues (warranty quality, warranty reputation, and price) on the risk perceived with innovative product concepts. In contrast to what was expected none of the experiments provided significant evidence that the extrinsic cues could reduce perceptions of **performance risk**.

COMMENTS:

An item was dropped from the scale when it was administered to the two nonstudent samples to help reduce the length of the questionnaire.

REFERENCE:

Shimp, Terence A. and William O. Bearden (1982), "Warranty and Other Extrinsic Cue Effects on Consumers' Risk Perceptions," *JCR*, 9 (June), 38-46.

SCALE ITEMS: RISK PERFORMANCE

1. How sure are you about the _____'s ability to perform satisfactorily? **(r)**

Not sure   ____ : ____ : ____ : ____ : ____ : ____ : ____ : ____ : ____   Very sure
at all   1   2   3   4   5   6   7   8   9

2. Considering the possible problems associated with _____'s performance, how much risk would you say would be involved with purchasing the new _____?

Very little   ____ : ____ : ____ : ____ : ____ : ____ : ____ : ____ : ____   A great
risk   1   2   3   4   5   6   7   8   9   deal of
                                                                             risk

3. In your opinion, do you feel that the new _____ if introduced would perform as well as other _____ now on the market? **(r)**

Would not   ____ : ____ : ____ : ____ : ____ : ____ : ____ : ____ : ____   Would
perform   1   2   3   4   5   6   7   8   9   perform
as well   as well

4. How confident are you of the _____'s ability to perform as expected?

Very   ____ : ____ : ____ : ____ : ____ : ____ : ____ : ____ : ____   Not
confident   1   2   3   4   5   6   7   8   9   confident
                                                                             at all

+ The name of the product should be placed in the blanks. Item 4 was not administered to the nonstudent samples.

SCALE NAME: Risk Aversion (Product Usage)

SCALE DESCRIPTION:

A six-item, Likert-type summated ratings scale. The scale measures a person's fear of doing something with a product that he/she has not tried before. The scale was referred to as Risk Preference by both Price and Ridgway (1983) and Childers (1986).

SCALE ORIGIN:

A nine-item version of the scale was first constructed by Price and Ridgway (1983). It was part of a larger five-component, 44-item Use Innovativeness index. Risk aversion had an alpha of .70. The subscale was constructed along with the other parts of the index to measure the use of a previously adopted product in a novel way or a variety of ways. Data were collected from student subjects in undergraduate classes representing a variety of courses. Analysis was based on 358 usable questionnaires. A couple of rounds of factor analysis, with examination of internal consistency and item-total correlations, reduced the original collection of 60 items to 44 items among five factors. The correlation between scores on the Risk Aversion subscale and scores on the Use Innovativeness index was .58. Validity of the overall index rather than the individual subscales was assessed. Students with the highest scores on the Use Innovativeness index engaged in significantly more innovative behaviors (toward calculators) than those scoring lower on the index. The authors urge that further testing of the psychometric properties be done.

SAMPLES:

Childers' (1986) samples were taken from the files of a cable television franchise in a large metro area. One sample was composed of people who subscribed to cable and another sample was composed of people who had been contacted but refused to subscribe. Questionnaires were dropped off by an employee of the franchise but responses were mailed in. **One hundred and seventy six** questionnaires were returned within the three-week period before the cutoff date.

RELIABILITY:

An alpha of **.60** was calculated for the scale by Childers (1986).

VALIDITY:

Validity was not examined except in the sense that it was used as part of the assessment of an opinion leadership scale.

ADMINISTRATION:

The scale was self-administered in a survey instrument format. Higher scores on the scale indicate a person reports being very uncomfortable buying or using products that he/she is not used to whereas lower scores suggest a person has little fear of tackling projects that are less than clear cut.

MAJOR FINDINGS:

The purpose of the study by Childers (1986) was to compare the psychometric properties of two versions of an opinion leadership scale. In most respects the modified version of the scale was superior to the previous version. The **Risk Aversion** scale had insignificant correlations with both versions of the opinion leadership scale. The author speculates that the lack of correlation and other evidence suggests that opinion leadership does not generalize across product categories.

COMMENTS:

Because of the low alpha values for the scale, further developmental work is needed before the scale is used further. The factor loadings and item-total correlations reported by Price and Ridgway (1983) indicate that most items in the scale are weak and should be eliminated and replaced with stronger items.

REFERENCES:

Childers, Terry L. (1986), "Assessment of the Psychometric Properties of an Opinion Leadership Scale," *JMR*, 23 (May), 184-188.

Price, Linda L. and Nancy M. Ridgway (1983), "Development of a Scale to Measure Use Innovativeness," in *Advances in Consumer Research*, Vol. 10, Richard P. Bagozzi and Alice M. Tybout, eds. Ann Arbor, Mich.: Association for Consumer Research, 679-684.

SCALE ITEMS: RISK AVERSION (PRODUCT USE) +

Strongly Disagree	Moderately Disagree	Slightly Disagree	Neither Agree Nor Disagree	Slightly Agree	Moderately Agree	Strongly Agree
1	2	3	4	5	6	7

1. When I try to do projects on my own, I'm afraid I will make a worse mess of them than if I had just left them alone.
2. I always follow manufacturers' warnings against removing the backplates on products.
3. When I try to do projects on my own, without exact directions, they usually work out really well. **(r)**
4. I find very little instruction is needed to use a product similar to one I'm already familiar with. **(r)**
5. I'm afraid to buy a product I don't know how to use.
6. I'm uncomfortable working on projects different from types I'm accustomed to.
7. I always follow manufacturers' warnings regarding how to use a product.
8. If a product comes in an assembled and unassembled form, I always buy the assembled form, even though it costs a little more.
9. I like to improvise when I cook. **(r)**

+ This is the form of the scale offered by Price and Ridgway (1983). Childers (1986) did not specify which six items he used or the exact nature of the graphic scale and its global anchors. On the basis of factor loadings and item-total correlations reported by Price and Ridgway (1983), items 1, 3, and 6 appear to be the strongest of the set.

SCALE NAME: Risk Taker (Purchase)

SCALE DESCRIPTION:

A nine-item, seven-point Likert-type summated ratings scale measuring the degree to which a person reports being willing, even eager, to take a risk by trying unfamiliar restaurants, products, and brands. Raju (1980) referred to the measure as Risk Taking.

SCALE ORIGIN:

Though some of the items may be similar to ones used in other scales, this group of items was put into scale form along with six other scales by Raju (1980). An initial pool of 90 items related to exploratory behavior and lifestyle were compiled and then tested for low social desirability bias and high item-total correlations. Thirty-nine items were found to meet the criteria and were common to two separate samples. Items were grouped into seven categories on the basis of interitem correlations and subjective judgment.

SAMPLES:

Raju (1980) collected data from **336** homemakers and **105** students. The homemakers were contacted through local women's clubs and the students were contacted through mostly junior and senior level college classes.

RELIABILITY:

The scale was reported by Raju (1980) to have reliability (Spearman-Brown) of **.808** and **.831** for the homemaker and student samples, respectively.

VALIDITY:

Though Raju (1980) notes that a factor analysis was performed, the grouping of items for scale purposes was based more on interitem correlations and a subjective classification process.

ADMINISTRATION:

The manner of scale administration was not specifically addressed for either sample by Raju (1980). However, he implied that the homemakers received the questionnaire at a club meeting, filled it out at home by themselves, and returned it by mail. The student sample is assumed to have completed the survey instrument in class. Lower scores on the scale suggest that respondents are uninterested in taking risks with their purchases whereas higher scores suggest that respondents are eager to purchase unfamiliar things.

MAJOR FINDINGS:

In two studies, Raju (1980) examined the relationships between optimal stimulation level (OSL) and certain personality traits, demographics, and purchase-related psychographics. For both samples, relatively high correlations were found between **risk taking** and OSL.

This finding along with others indicated that people with higher OSLs were more likely to exhibit exploratory behaviors in their consumer behavior.

COMMENTS:

The construct validity of the scale is highly suspect given the manner in which the seven scales used in the study were constructed (as noted in the origination information above). Sixteen of the 39 items were used by Raju (1980) to compose more than one scale, thus making it unclear what construct the items and their respective scales actually measured. Though the reported reliability for this scale is reasonable, further validity testing is needed.

REFERENCE:

Raju, P. S. (1980), "Optimum Stimulation Level: Its Relationship to Personality, Demographics, and Exploratory Behavior," *JCR*, 7 (December), 272-282.

SCALE ITEMS: RISK TAKER (PURCHASE)

Strongly Disagree 1————2————3————4————5————6————7 Completely Agree

1. When I eat out, I like to try the most unusual items the restaurant serves, even if I am not sure I would like them.
2. I am the kind of person who would try any new product once.
3. When I go to a restaurant, I feel it is safer to order dishes I am familiar with. **(r)**
4. I am cautious in trying new/different products. **(r)**
5. Even for an important date or dinner, I wouldn't be wary of trying a new or unfamiliar restaurant.
6. I would rather stick with a brand I usually buy than try something I am not very sure of. **(r)**
7. I never buy something I don't know about at the risk of making a mistake. **(r)**
8. If I buy appliances, I will buy only well-established brands. **(r)**
9. I enjoy taking chances in buying unfamiliar brands just to get some variety in my purchases.

SCALE NAME: Role Overload

SCALE DESCRIPTION:

A 13-item, five-point Likert-type summated ratings scale measuring the degree to which a woman perceives herself to be under pressure due to the number of roles she plays.

SCALE ORIGIN:

The scale was constructed and tested by Reilly (1982). After reviewing scales developed previously for organizational settings, the author and doctoral candidates wrote items more appropriate for female consumers. A number of items were tested on a convenience sample of **106** married women. Items with weak item-total correlations were removed from the scale, leaving 13 items. Other properties of the scale are noted below.

SAMPLES:

Data used by Reilly (1982) were collected by 10 experienced interviewers working for a marketing research organization in Milwaukee. The interviewers were told to use the first 10 dwellings at each of two random starting points in the SMSA. The procedure produced **186** completed survey forms from women.

RELIABILITY:

Reilly (1982) reports an alpha of **.88** and item-total correlations from .544 to .797.

VALIDITY:

The validity of the scale was not specifically examined.

ADMINISTRATION:

Though the data collection reported by Reilly (1982) involved interviews, interviewers' judgments, and questionnaires, the scale was self-administered along with several other measures in a survey instrument left with respondents. Higher scores on the scale imply that respondents are experiencing the stress and pressures of role overload whereas lower scores imply either that respondents do not play as many roles or that they are not reacting negatively to the demands on their time.

MAJOR FINDINGS:

Reilly (1982) used causal modeling to examine the relationship between wife's employment status, **role overload**, and the purchase of time-saving durable goods and convenience foods. **Role overload** was found to be causally related to working and time-saving purchases, but the relationships were rather weak.

COMMENTS:

Until validity is assessed, there is some question whether the scale measures role overload, as purported, or time pressure. The two constructs may indeed be related, but they are not the same thing. For example, some people are likely to be quite busy playing just one role whereas others handle multiple roles without expressing much conflict. Therefore, care must be exercised in assuming too much about what this scale can say in terms of the quantity of roles played, but it does appear to indicate the degree of perceived stress despite the amount of role conflict. For another use of the scale, see Bellizzi and Hite (1986).

REFERENCES:

Bellizzi, Joseph A. and Robert E. Hite (1986), ''Convenience Consumption and Role Overload,'' *JAMS*, 14 (Winter), 1-9.

Reilly, Michael D. (1982), ''Working Wives and Convenience Consumption, *JCR*, 8 (March), 407-418.

SCALE ITEMS: ROLE OVERLOAD

Strongly Disagree	Agree	Neutral	Disagree	Strongly Agree
1————————	2————————	3————————	4————————	5

1. I have to do things I don't really have the time and energy for.
2. There are too many demands on my time.
3. I need more hours in the day to do all the things which are expected of me.
4. I can't ever seem to get caught up.
5. I don't ever seem to have any time for myself.
6. There are times when I can't meet everyone's expectations.
7. Sometimes I feel as if there are not enough hours in the day.
8. Many times I have to cancel commitments.
9. I seem to have to overextend myself in order to be able to finish everything I have to do.
10. I seem to have more commitments to overcome than some of the other wives I know.
11. I find myself having to prepare priority lists (lists which tell me which things I should do first) to get done all the things I have to do. Otherwise I forget because I have so much to do.
12. I feel I have to do things hastily and maybe less carefully in order to get everything done.
13. I just can't find the energy in me to do all the things expected of me.

SCALE NAME: Romanticism/Classicism

SCALE DESCRIPTION:

A 55-item, seven-point Likert-type summated ratings scale measuring a person's tendency to approach life, and particularly consumption experiences, with great passion, emotion, and impulsiveness (romanticism) rather than liking things to be neat, controlled, and orderly (classicism).

SCALE ORIGIN:

A 14-item measure of romanticism/classicism was developed and reported by Holbrook and Corfman (1984). An alpha of .83 was calculated for the scale on the basis of data from 21 MBA students. Holbrook (1986, p. 341) reports that though the scale showed evidence of nomological validity, search bias was suspected. Therefore, in the study described below (Holbrook 1986), the scale was redeveloped. A set of 126 items was analyzed and reduced to a 55-item instrument. The 14 items from the Holbrook and Corfman (1984) study are included and noted in the 55 items below.

SAMPLES:

Subjects used in the study (Holbrook 1986) were 42 male and 22 female MBA candidates in a marketing course who were required to respond to the questionnaire.

RELIABILITY:

An alpha of .87 was reported for the scale.

VALIDITY:

Though the validity of the scale was not intensively examined, some evidence of its concurrent and nomological validity was reported. For example, romanticism was higher for women and for subjects with intrinsic motivation tendencies.

ADMINISTRATION:

Subjects self-administered the scale along with several other measures. If the scale is used with numbers 1 through 7, lower summated scores suggest that respondents have a preference for the rational, ordered, and/or familiar (classicism) whereas higher scores mean that respondents like the emotional, exotic, and/or intuitive (romanticism).

MAJOR FINDINGS:

The roles of certain personality variables and gender were studied by Holbrook (1986). He illustrated a method using canonical correlation analysis to examine individual differences in affect toward clothing design features. In general, **romanticism/classicism** motivation appeared to have a significant but weak influence on affect.

REFERENCES:

Holbrook, Morris B. (1986), "Aims, Concepts, and Methods for the Representation of Individual Differences in Esthetic Responses to Design Features," *JCR*, 13 (December), 337- 347.

_____ and Kim Corfman (1984), "Quality and Value in the Consumption Experience: Phaedrus Rides Again," in *Perceived Quality: How Consumers View Stores and Merchandise*, Jacob Jacoby and Jerry C. Olson, eds. Lexington, Mass.: Lexington Books.

SCALE ITEMS: ROMANTICISM/CLASSICISM

Strongly ____ : ____ : ____ : ____ : ____ : ____ : ____ Strongly
Disagree   1   2   3   4   5   6   7   Agree

1. One should adopt a conservative lifestyle. **(r)**
2. Truth often involves an element of mysticism.
3. I am a practical person. **(r)**+
4. Sensitivity is a valuable trait.
5. In art, color excites me more than form.+
6. A routine way of life is preferable to unpredictability. **(r)**
7. I think that life is an awesome mystery.
8. Uncertainty is exciting.
9. I am a sensitive person.
10. Progress in science, technology, and education continues to insure a brighter tomorrow. **(r)**
11. Rigorous training is the true basis of athletic skill. **(r)**
12. Facts are more important than feelings. **(r)**
13. I enjoy art that expresses the artist's emotions.+
14. A cool head wins every time. **(r)**
15. Sometimes evil is consistent with greatness.
16. Intuition is a valuable tool.
17. Disorganization is a major flaw. **(r)**
18. I believe that first impressions are almost always correct.
19. Paintings should attempt to represent their subjects with maximum realism. **(r)**
20. I am *not* an emotional person. **(r)**
21. It is okay to be eccentric.
22. I am organized. **(r)**+
23. Every decision deserves to be carefully thought out. (r)+
24. I think of myself as eccentric.+
25. The heart, not the brain, should be your guide.
26. I like to touch sculpture.+
27. People should try to be more tender.
28. Feelings are more important than facts.
29. Idealism is a wonderful quality.
30. Logic can solve any problem. **(r)**
31. When I am being taken somewhere in an unfamiliar place, I like to know exactly where I am and where I am going. **(r)**
32. Occasionally, it's okay to be moody.

33. I am impulsive. +
34. In life, unpredictability is preferable to routine.
35. I like to keep my home neat and orderly. **(r)** +
36. One's actions should always be carefully planned. **(r)**
37. I prefer to live in a certain amount of chaos. +
38. One should remain stable at all times. **(r)**
39. I prefer a routine way of life to an unpredictable one. **(r)**
40. A nice home is always neat and orderly. **(r)**
41. I think of myself as a precise person. **(r)** +
42. Absent-mindedness is a lovable characteristic.
43. I think of myself as a natural person.
44. One should always be precise. **(r)**
45. It is fun to be exposed to people with new ideas.
46. I tend to be a serious person. **(r)**
47. It's okay to daydream a lot.
48. Self-control is all-important. **(r)**
49. I am precise about where I keep my possessions. **(r)** +
50. I am easily distracted. +
51. New ideas are exciting.
52. I am a controlled person. **(r)** +
53. Forgetfulness is forgivable.
54. I have a scientific outlook on most problems. **(r)**
55. One should always be rational. **(r)**

+ These items composed the scale used by Holbrook and Corfman (1984).

SCALE NAME: Safety (Air Travel)

SCALE DESCRIPTION:

A three-item, Likert-type summated ratings scale measuring the degree of safety a person perceives in airline travel.

SCALE ORIGIN:

No information provided in the Bruning, Kovacic, and Oberdick (1985) article indicates the scale was not original to those authors.

SAMPLES:

Questionnaires were distributed at five airports in the U.S. that offered major/national and regional/commuter service. To provide an adequate representation of various types of flyers, the sample was stratified by time of day and day of week. Questionnaires were distributed on a ''random'' basis to passengers waiting for flights to leave at departure gates. Self-addressed, stamped envelopes were provided with the survey forms and **591** usable forms were returned.

RELIABILITY:

An alpha of **.68** was reported for the scale.

VALIDITY:

A factor analysis indicated that the items loaded together.

ADMINISTRATION:

The scale was self-administered with other parts of the questionnaire while passengers were waiting at departure gates at airports. The questionnaires were returned by mail. Higher scores on this scale indicate that respondents perceive air travel to be safe, particularly on large jet aircraft. Lower scores imply that respondents do not think that flying is safe.

MAJOR FINDINGS:

Bruning, Kovacic, and Oberdick (1985) were studying the reasons why air travelers choose a certain form of airline and how such information could be used to segment carriers into distinct markets. Discriminant analysis was used to identify personality factors, demographic variables, and airline-related perceptions that would significantly discriminate between commuter and noncommuter travelers. **Perceived safety** was a significant predictor such that regional/commuter passengers had greater confidence in airline **safety** than major/national passengers.

REFERENCE:

Bruning, Edward R., Mary L. Kovacic, and Larry E. Oberdick (1985), "Segmentation Analysis of Domestic Airline Passenger Markets," *JAMS*, 13 (Winter), 17-31.

SCALE ITEMS: SAFETY (AIR TRAVEL) +

Strongly Disagree 1	Disagree 2	Slightly Disagree 3	Slightly Agree 4	Agree 5	Strongly Agree 6

1. I believe that airline travel is safer than other forms of travel for trips over 200 miles.
2. I believe that airline travel is safer than other forms of travel for trips under 200 miles.
3. I feel that propeller driven aircraft are less safe than large jet aircraft.

+ The graphic scale was not specified in the article, but is likely to have been similar to the one shown here, with between five and seven points.

SCALE NAME: Satisfaction (Air Travel)

SCALE DESCRIPTION:

A four-item, Likert-type summated ratings scale measuring the degree to which a person expresses satisfaction with air travel. The scale was referred to as Convenience by Bruning, Kovacic, and Oberdick (1985).

SCALE ORIGIN:

There is no information in the article by Bruning, Kovacic, and Oberdick (1985) that indicates the scale was not original to those authors.

SAMPLES:

Questionnaires were distributed at five airports in the U.S. that offered major/national and regional/ commuter service. To provide an adequate representation of various types of flyers, the sample was stratified by time of day and day of week. Questionnaires were distributed on a ''random'' basis to passengers waiting for flights to leave at departure gates. Self-addressed, stamped envelopes were provided with the survey forms and **591** usable forms were returned.

RELIABILITY:

An alpha of **.73** was reported for the scale.

VALIDITY:

A factor analysis indicated that the items loaded together.

ADMINISTRATION:

The scale was self-administered with other parts of the questionnaire while passengers were waiting at departure gates at airports. The questionnaires were returned by mail. Higher scores on this scale indicate that respondents are not only satisfied with the services received from the airlines they have flown, but may have even developed some loyalty to one company. Lower scores imply respondents do not believe the services they have received from airlines have been good.

MAJOR FINDINGS:

Bruning, Kovacic, and Oberdick (1985) were studying the reasons why air travelers choose a certain form of airline and how such information could be used to segment carriers into distinct markets. Discriminant analysis was used to identify personality factors, demographic variables, and airline-related perceptions that would significantly discriminate between commuter and noncommuter travelers. **Satisfaction** was the most significant predictor of variables examined in the study. Specifically, **level of satisfaction** was higher for passengers of major/national carriers than for passengers of regional/commuter airlines.

REFERENCE:

Bruning, Edward R., Mary L. Kovacic, and Larry E. Oberdick (1985), "Segmentation Analysis of Domestic Airline Passenger Markets," *JAMS*, 13 (Winter), 17-31.

SCALE ITEMS: SATISFACTION (AIR TRAVEL) +

Strongly Disagree	Disagree	Slightly Disagree	Slightly Agree	Agree	Strongly Agree
1—————————	2—————————	3—————————	4—————————	5—————————	6

1. I choose to travel by airline because my time is very valuable to me.
2. I feel the services I receive during the flight are good.
3. I feel that the pre-flight services (i.e., baggage handling, ticket processing, etc.) are good.
4. Normally, I fly with one particular airline company.

+ The graphic scale was not specified in the article, but is likely to have been similar to the one shown here, with between five and seven points.

SCALE NAME: Satisfaction (Car)

SCALE DESCRIPTION:

A 12-item, Likert-type summated ratings scale measuring a consumer's degree of satisfaction with a car.

SCALE ORIGIN:

The scale was originally generated and used by Westbrook and Oliver (1981) to measure consumer satisfaction with cars and with calculators. Four other satisfaction measures were used as well and the results were compared in a multitrait multimethod matrix. Convenience samples of students were used from two different universities (n = **68** + **107**). In terms of internal consistency, the alpha values were **.93** and **.96** as measured for cars in the two samples. For both samples, the scale showed strong evidence of construct validity by converging with like constructs and discriminating between unlike constructs. In comparison with the other measures of satisfaction, this Likert version produced the greatest dispersion of individual scores while maintaining a symmetrical distribution.

SAMPLES:

Oliver and Swan's (1989) findings were based on **184** completed questionnaires from people who had bought new cars within six months prior to the survey. The average respondent was male (67%), college educated (32%), had an income between $20,000 and $29,999, was 43 years of age, had owned 7.8 cars in his lifetime, and had purchased his latest car 4.5 months previously.

RELIABILITY:

An alpha of **.94** was reported for the scale.

VALIDITY:

No specific examinations of scale validity were reported by Oliver and Swan (1989).

ADMINISTRATION:

The scale was one of many self-administered measures in the Oliver and Swan (1989) study. High scores on the scale suggest that respondents are very satisfied with their cars whereas low scores imply that respondents are not pleased with their cars.

MAJOR FINDINGS:

The general purpose of Oliver and Swan's (1989) study was to examine customer perceptions of **satisfaction** in the context of new car purchases. The results indicated that **car satisfaction** was positively influenced by **satisfaction** with the dealer and with car disconfirmation, but was negatively influenced by complaint frequency.

COMMENTS:

The scale appears to have such high internal consistency that some items might be removed if necessary without seriously affecting reliability.

REFERENCES:

Oliver, Richard L. and John E. Swan (1989), ''Equity and Disconfirmation Perceptions as Influences on Merchant and Product Satisfaction,'' *JCR*, 16 (December), 372-383.

Westbrook, Robert A. and Richard L. Oliver (1981), ''Developing Better Measures of Consumer Satisfaction: Some Preliminary Results,'' in *Advances in Consumer Research,* Vol. 8, Kent B. Monroe, ed. Ann Arbor, Mich.: Association for Consumer Research, 94-99.

SCALE ITEMS: SATISFACTION (CAR) +

Strongly Agree			Neither			Strongly Disagree
1———	—2———	—3———	—4———	—5———	—6———	—7

1. This is one of the best cars I could have bought.
2. This car is exactly what I need.
3. This car hasn't worked out as well as I thought it would. **(r)**
4. I am satisfied with my decision to buy this car.
5. Sometimes I have mixed feelings about keeping it. (`
6. My choice to buy this car was a wise one.
7. If I could do it over again, I'd buy a different make......el. **(r)**
8. I have truly enjoyed this car.
9. I feel bad about my decision to buy this car. **(r)**
10. I am *not* happy that I bought this car. **(r)**
11. Owning this car has been a good experience.
12. I'm sure it was the right thing to buy this car.

+ Westbrook and Oliver (1981) used a five-point scale whereas Oliver and Swan (1989) used one with seven points.

SCALE NAME: Satisfaction (Coercive Power Behavior)

SCALE DESCRIPTION:

A three-item, Likert-type summated ratings scale measuring a person's degree of satisfaction with a physician's behavior. The particular aspect of behavior evaluated was the physician's use of coercive power.

SCALE ORIGIN:

The items and scale appear to be original to Friedman and Churchill (1987).

SAMPLES:

Female graduate students were used as subjects in an experimental setting. A total of **396** students cooperated in the study. Female subjects were used because they were expected to relate better to the female patients on the tape recordings to which they would listen. Graduate students were used because they were assumed to be experienced enough to make the required judgments about physicians.

RELIABILITY:

The internal consistency for this specific scale was not reported, but the authors did say that this scale was among the measures with alpha of **.8** or greater.

VALIDITY:

The correlation of the scale with a one item measure of the same construct was .72, providing evidence of convergent validity. The scale had a correlation of .0 with social desirability, providing evidence of discriminant validity. There were indications of nomological validity as well.

ADMINISTRATION:

The scale was presented to subjects as part of a larger self-administered questionnaire to be filled out in an experimantal setting. The higher the score on the scale, the greater the subject's satisfaction with a physician's behavior. Lower scores suggest a physician's behavior is considered unsatisfactory.

MAJOR FINDINGS:

The purpose of the experiment was to examine how a physician's social power behaviors can be used to achieve maximum effectiveness, as judged by patients. Subjects listened to recorded conversations between a physician and a patient and were asked to imagine they were the latter. They were then asked to respond to the physician's behavior on a questionnaire. Coercive power had a large impact on **satisfaction** such that low coercion was more effective across all situations studied, despite the level of ailment riskiness and the nature of the patient/physician relationship.

REFERENCE:

> Friedman, Margaret L. and Gilbert A. Churchill, Jr. (1987), "Using Consumer Perceptions and a Contingency Approach to Improve Health Care Delivery," *JCR*, 13 (March), 492-510.

SCALE ITEMS: SATISFACTION (COERCIVE POWER BEHAVIOR) +

I would have felt satisfied/dissatisfied with the:
1. way the physician took charge of the conversation.
2. level of sympathy the physician displayed toward the patient.
3. level of patience the physician displayed toward the patient.

+ The number of points on the Likert-type response scale was not specified in the article.

SCALE NAME: Satisfaction (Expert-Legitimate Power Behavior)

SCALE DESCRIPTION:

A three-item, Likert-type summated ratings scale measuring a person's degree of **satisfaction** with a physician's behavior. The particular aspect of behavior evaluated was the physician's use of expert-legitimate power.

SCALE ORIGIN:

The items and scale appear to be original to Friedman and Churchill (1987).

SAMPLES:

Female graduate students were used as subjects in an experimental setting. A total of **396** students cooperated in the study. Female subjects were used because they were expected to relate better to the female patients on the tape recordings to which they would listen. Graduate students were used because they were assumed to be experienced enough to make the required judgments about physicians.

RELIABILITY:

The internal consistency for this specific scale was not reported, but the authors did say that the scale was among the measures with alpha of **.8** or greater.

VALIDITY:

The correlation of the scale with a one-item measure of the same construct was **.85**, providing evidence of convergent validity. The scale had a correlation of **.06** with social desirability, providing evidence of discriminant validity. There were indications of nomological validity as well.

ADMINISTRATION:

The scale was presented to subjects as part of a larger self-administered questionnaire to be filled out in an experimental setting. The higher the score on the scale, the greater the subject's satisfaction with a physician's behavior. Lower scores suggest a physician's behavior is considered unsatisfactory.

MAJOR FINDINGS:

The purpose of the experiment was to examine how a physician's social power behaviors can be used to achieve maximum effectiveness, as judged by patients. Subjects listened to recorded conversations between a physician and a patient and were asked to imagine they were the latter. They were then asked to respond to the physician's behavior on a questionnaire. High expert-legitimate power was more **satisfying** in the risky situation (breast cancer) than in the nonrisky situation (common cold). Further, high expert-legitimate power was more **satisfying** when the patient and physician had an ongoing relationship than during their first contact.

REFERENCE:

Friedman, Margaret L. and Gilbert A. Churchill, Jr. (1987), ''Using Consumer Perceptions and a Contingency Approach to Improve Health Care Delivery,'' *JCR*, 13 (March), 492-510.

SCALE ITEMS: SATISFACTION (EXPERT-LEGITIMATE POWER BEHAVIOR) +

I would have felt satisfied/dissatisfied with the:
1. credentials of the physician.
2. level of knowledge displayed by the physician.
3. amount of experience the physician possessed regarding the patient's problem.

+ The number of points on the Likert-type response scale was not specified in the article.

SCALE NAME: Satisfaction (Financial)

SCALE DESCRIPTION:

A three-item, six-point, Likert-type summated ratings scale ranging from strongly disagree (1) to strongly agree (6). The scale measures a person's degree of contentment toward his/her income.

SCALE ORIGIN:

These items were part of a classic study of psychographics by Wells and Tigert (1971). One thousand questionnaires were mailed to homemaker members of the Market Facts mail panel. In addition to gathering demographic, product use, and media data, the survey contained 300 statements that have since served as the basis for the construction of many lifestyle-related scales. The four items for this scale are reported in the article, but they were not analyzed as a multi-item scale. The purpose of the article was to explain how psychographics could improve upon mere demographic description of target audiences and product users. No psychometric information was reported.

SAMPLES:

Two mailing lists were used to collect data in the Dickerson and Gentry study (1983). One was a list of *Psychology Today* subscribers and the other was a list of members of computer clubs. The former was used to reach non-adopters of computers and the latter was used to reach PC adopters. Analysis was based on a total of **639** questionnaires. Results from a second mailing to non-respondents indicated that their demographic makeup was not significantly different from that of respondents. On the basis of 1980 Census data, the sample was younger and more upscale than the general population.

RELIABILITY:

An alpha of **.56** was reported by Dickerson and Gentry (1983).

VALIDITY:

Factor analysis indicated the items loaded together.

ADMINISTRATION:

Data were gathered through self-administered mail questionnaires. Scale scores are calculated by averaging numerical responses to individual items. A score of 6 indicates that a person strongly believes that his/her income is adequate for meeting current needs whereas a score of 1 means the person expresses extreme dissatisfaction with his/her level of income.

MAJOR FINDINGS:

Dickerson and Gentry (1983) found a significant relationship between **financial satisfaction** and adoption of home computers such that adopters tended to be more satisfied with their income than nonadopters.

#231 *Satisfaction (Financial)*

COMMENTS:

The level of the one reported alpha indicates that the scale currently has low internal consistency. Several similar items should be generated and tested to improve the quality of the measure.

REFERENCES:

Dickerson, Mary D. and James W. Gentry (1983), "Characteristics of Adopters and Non-Adopters of Home Computers," *JCR*, 10 (September), 225-235.

Wells, William D. and Douglas Tigert (1971), "Activities, Interests, and Opinions," *JAR*, 11 (August), 27-35.

SCALE ITEMS: SATISFACTION (FINANCIAL)

Strongly Disagree	Disagree	Slightly Disagree	Slightly Agree	Agree	Strongly Agree
1———————	—2———————	—3———————	—4———————	—5———————	—6

1. Our family income is high enough to satisfy nearly all our important desires.
2. No matter how fast our income goes up we never seem to get ahead. **(r)**
3. I wish we had a lot more money. **(r)**

SCALE NAME: Satisfaction (Flu Shot Decision)

SCALE DESCRIPTION:

A six-item, Likert-type summated ratings scale measuring the degree to which a respondent is satisfied with a previous decision to receive or not receive a flu shot.

SCALE ORIGIN:

The scale was constructed specifically for the study by Oliver (1980).

SAMPLES:

Systematic random sampling was used to select names and addresses from two sources: the telephone directory of a south-central U.S. city and preregistration data from a major university in the same city. Questionnaires were sent to persons selected from the two samples. Of those returning usable forms, **291** residents and **162** students reported receiving a flu shot; **65** residents and **86** students reported that they did not get flu shots.

RELIABILITY:

An alpha of **.82** was reported for the scale.

VALIDITY:

No specific examination of scale validity was reported.

ADMINISTRATION:

The scale was one of many self-administered measures. Higher scores on the scale suggest that respondents are happy about their inoculation decision whereas low scores imply that respondents are dissatisfied with their decision and would be likely to respond differently if they had it to do over again.

MAJOR FINDINGS:

Oliver (1980) tested a model of consumer **satisfaction** that expresses **satisfaction** as a function of expectation and **disconfirmation**. The model was examined in the context of comparing people's expectations about a flu shot with their perceived benefits and problems after they had received the shot. The results indicated that **disconfirmation** was not significantly related to any preexposure measure but had the greatest impact on **satisfaction** of the variables studied.

REFERENCES:

Oliver, Richard L. (1980), "A Cognitive Model of the Antecedents and Consequences of Satisfaction Decisions," *JMR*, 17 (November), 460-469.

SCALE ITEMS: SATISFACTION (FLU SHOT DECISION) +

Strongly Disagree	Disagree	Slightly Disagree	Slightly Agree	Agree	Strongly Agree
1	2	3	4	5	6

1. I am satisfied with my decision to get or not to get a flu shot.
2. If I had to do it all over again, I would feel differently about the flu shot program. **(r)**
3. My choice to get or not to get a flu shot was a wise one.
4. I feel bad about my decision concerning the flu shot. **(r)**
5. I think that I did the right thing when I decided to get or not get the flu shot.
6. I am not happy that I did what I did about the flu shot. **(r)**

+ The graphic scale was not specified in the article but is likely to have been similar to the one shown here, with between five and seven points.

SCALE NAME: Satisfaction (Generalized)

SCALE DESCRIPTION:

A three-item, seven-point semantic differential summated ratings scale measuring a consumer's degree of satisfaction with some object. Crosby and Stephens (1987) used it with regard to insurance agents, service policies, and insurance agencies.

SCALE ORIGIN:

There is no indication that the scale was constructed elsewhere than in the study by Crosby and Stephens (1987).

SAMPLES:

The sample was selected from a nationally representative consumer panel and screened for ownership of life insurance. Analysis of the first wave of the survey was based on **1362** responses. The sample was slightly better educated and more upscale than the population at large but the authors considered the differences to be minor and unrelated to the studied relationships. A year later, respondents to the first wave of the survey (or from a holdout sample) were contacted. Analysis was based on **447** responses. Comparison of the main sample and the holdout sample data did not indicate any bias due to wave one premeasurement.

RELIABILITY:

Alpha values for the scales in both waves were reported to be over **.96**.

VALIDITY:

An idea of the predictive validity of the scale was gathered by comparing the satisfaction level of four known groups that varied on their policy status. The four groups were: persons who paid the premium and stayed with the same company, persons for whom the policy was still in force but had not paid the next year's premium yet, persons who switched to a different company, and persons whose policy lapsed and had not replaced it with another. The means for each of the groups in wave one on the overall satisfaction scale were 5.94, 5.29, 4.99, and 4.79, respectively. This shows that the scale gave an accurate indication of the policy owners' actual behavior.

ADMINISTRATION:

The scales were self-administered as part of a larger mail questionnaire. Scores were calculated by averaging numerical responses to the three items. High scores indicated greater satisfaction with the object (contact person, core service, or institution) whereas low scores implied that respondents were not pleased or happy.

MAJOR FINDINGS:

The purpose of the study was to compare two proposed models of buyer **satisfaction** with life insurance, the relationship generalization model (RGM) and the rational evaluation model (REM). The RGM assumes that consumers generalize positive feelings about the provider to the core service whereas the REM views consumers as most concerned about core service quality with the relationship merely adding value to it. In general, the results supported the REM over the RGM. This means that while the agent's performance affects **satisfaction**, it is balanced against the perceived performance of the core service.

REFERENCE:

Crosby, Lawrence A. and Nancy Stephens (1987), "Effects of Relationship Marketing on Satisfaction, Retention, and Prices in the Life Insurance Industry," *JMR*, 24 (November), 404-411.

SCALE ITEMS: SATISFACTION (GENERALIZED)

satisfied ____ : ____ : ____ : ____ : ____ : ____ : ____ dissatisfied
        7   6   5   4   3   2   1

pleased ____ : ____ : ____ : ____ : ____ : ____ : ____ displeased
        7   6   5   4   3   2   1

favorable ____ : ____ : ____ : ____ : ____ : ____ : ____ unfavorable
        7   6   5   4   3   2   1

SCALE NAME: Satisfaction (Generalized)

SCALE DESCRIPTION:

A six-item, semantic differential scale measuring a consumer's degree of satisfaction with an object. The scale may be most suited for measuring a consumer's **satisfaction** with the other party involved in a transaction.

SCALE ORIGIN:

The scale used by Oliver and Swan (1989a, b) was adapted from a seven-item version of the scale discussed by Westbrook and Oliver (1981), who generated and used it in measuring consumer **satisfaction** with cars and with calculators. Four other **satisfaction** measures were used as well and their results were compared in a multitrait multimethod matrix. Convenience samples of students were taken from two different universities. In terms of internal consistency, alpha was **.91** or greater as measured for the two products and the two samples. For both products and samples, the scale showed strong evidence of construct validity by converging with like constructs and discriminating between unlike constructs.

SAMPLES:

Oliver and Swan's (1989a) findings were based on **415** completed questionnaires from two random samples of new car buyers. Because the two samples did not differ significantly on any demographic characteristics measured, the datasets were combined. The sample was 63% male and 30% college educated; 22% had income between $30,000 and $39,999, average age was 41 years, and respondents had owned 7.8 cars.

Subsequent analysis by Oliver and Swan (1989b) was based on just one of the initial samples mentioned above. Completed surveys were obtained from **184** people who had bought new cars within six months prior to the survey. The average respondent was male (67%), college educated (32%), had an income between $20,000 and $29,999, was 43 years of age, had owned 7.8 cars in his lifetime, and had purchased his latest car 4.5 months previously.

RELIABILITY:

The estimate of reliability provided by LISREL was **.953** when the scale was used to measure a customer's expressed satisfaction with a car salesperson (1989a). LISREL estimates of **.97** and **.96** were reported for the scale when it was used to measure the consumer's satisfaction with the dealer and the salesperson, respectively (1989b).

VALIDITY:

No specific examinations of scale validity were reported by Oliver and Swan (1989a, b).

ADMINISTRATION:

The scale was one of many measures that were self-administered in both studies by Oliver and Swan. High scores on the scale suggest that respondents are **very satisfied** with an object (e.g., salesperson or dealer as in Oliver and Swan's studies). Low scores imply that respondents are not pleased with a purchase they have made.

MAJOR FINDINGS:

The general purpose of both studies by Oliver and Swan was to examine customer perceptions of **satisfaction** in the context of new car purchases. Using LISREL, the authors determined that fairness was more important than disconfirmation in producing interpersonal **satisfaction** and that advantageous inequity was unrelated to it (1989a). Further, **satisfaction** was very strongly related to intention to deal with same salesperson again. Subsequent findings were the same (1989b), with the added insight that customer **satisfaction** with the dealer was primarily related to the former's perception of fairness, followed by **satisfaction** with the salesperson, and then somewhat influenced by disconfirmation.

REFERENCES:

Oliver, Richard L. and John E. Swan (1989a), ''Consumer Perceptions of Interpersonal Equity and Satisfaction in Transactions: A Field Survey Approach,'' *JM*, 53 (April), 21-35.

_____ and _____ (1989b), ''Equity and Disconfirmation Perceptions as Influences on Merchant and Product Satisfaction,'' *JCR*, 16 (December), 372-383.

Westbrook, Robert A. and Richard L. Oliver (1981), ''Developing Better Measures of Consumer Satisfaction: Some Preliminary Results,'' in *Advances in Consumer Research*, Vol. 8, Kent B. Monroe, ed. Ann Arbor, Mich.: Association for Consumer Research, 94-99.

SCALE ITEMS: SATISFACTION (GENERALIZED)

Please indicate how *satisfied* you were with your * by checking the space that best gives your answer.

	Extremely		Neither one nor the other		Extremely			
* pleased me	___ :	___ :	___ :	___ :	___ :	___ :	___	* displeased me
	7	6	5	4	3	2	1	
contented with	___ :	___ :	___ :	___ :	___ :	___ :	___	disgusted with *
	7	6	5	4	3	2	1	
very stisfied with *	___ :	___ :	___ :	___ :	___ :	___ :	___	very dissatisfied with *
	7	6	5	4	3	2	1	
did a good job for me	___ :	___ :	___ :	___ :	___ :	___ :	___	did a poor job for me
	7	6	5	4	3	2	1	
wise choice in buying from that *	___ :	___ :	___ :	___ :	___ :	___ :	___	poor choice in buying from that *
	7	6	5	4	3	2	1	

happy with *   ____ : ____ : ____ : ____ : ____ : ____ : ____   unhappy with *
                 7   6   5   4   3   2   1

*Insert in these places the object toward which satisfaction is being measured.

SCALE NAME: Satisfaction (Intrinsic)

SCALE DESCRIPTION:

A three-item, six-point Likert-type summated ratings scale that is supposed to measure the degree to which a person expresses enjoyment about engaging in some specified activity. The activity investigated by Unger (1981; Unger and Kernan 1983) was subjective leisure.

SCALE ORIGIN:

Though relevant literature was surveyed prior to scale construction, the items themselves and certainly the scale as a whole are original to Unger (1981).

SAMPLES:

The scale was developed in one stage of the overall study and then used to test hypotheses in another stage. In the first stage the scale was administered by three different people to a total of **169** undergraduate business students at Miami University and the University of Cincinnati (Unger 1981). In the second stage the questionnaires were delivered and picked up by members of a Girl Scout troop. A quota sample of **160** adults living in the Cincinnati SMSA was used that balanced eight equal age-by-sex groups. However, the sample was representative of neither the Cincinnati SMSA nor the U.S. population as a whole, being composed mostly of white people (98%) of middle to upper socioeconomic status (84%).

RELIABILITY:

The final scale consists of items that remained after several tests of reliability. The tests were conducted for the scale in six different situations. Alpha values for the scale ranged from **.42** to **.75**. See Unger (1981) for more detailed information.

VALIDITY:

Factor analysis provided general support that the items tend to load together; however, the results seem to have some sensitivity to the sample and situation being evaluated. When not loading separately, the items in this scale loaded with those of a perceived freedom scale, which indicates the two are psychologically related for some samples and situations. As evidence of construct validity, intrinsic satisfaction was found to be positively and significantly related to three subjective leisure measures.

ADMINISTRATION:

The scale was self-administered by respondents in both stages of the survey described above. High scores on the scale indicate that a person enjoys some specified activity because it is intrinsically motivating whereas a low score implies that the respondent does not like an activity as an end in itself.

MAJOR FINDINGS:

The study by Unger and Kernan (1983) examined dimensions of the subjective leisure experience across six different situations. **Intrinsic satisfaction** was found to be one of the primary determinants of subjective leisure across situations. The findings also support the literature and the authors' intuition that the **intrinsic satisfaction** dimension ''represents the 'essence' of leisure and that the other dimensions are secondary 'causes' of this feeling of happiness'' (p. 390).

REFERENCES:

Unger, Lynette S. (1981), ''Measure Validation in the Leisure Domain,'' unpublished doctoral dissertation, University of Cincinnati.

_____ and Jerome B. Kernan (1983), ''On the Meaning of Leisure: An Investigation of Some Determinants of the Subjective Experience,'' *JCR*, 9 (March), 381-391.

SCALE ITEMS: SATISFACTION (INTRINSIC) +

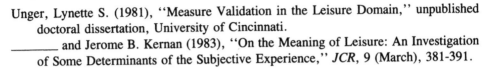

Strongly Disagree	Disagree	Slightly Disagree	Slightly Agree	Agree	Strongly Agree
1	2	3	4	5	6

1. I enjoy it for its own sake, not for what it will get me.
2. Pure enjoyment is the only thing in it for me.
3. It is its own reward.

+ The questionnaire described a situation for respondents and they were asked to respond to the statements as they felt about the situation.

SCALE NAME: Satisfaction (Life)

SCALE DESCRIPTION:

A three-item, five-point Likert-type summated ratings scale ranging from strongly disagree (1) to strongly agree (5). The scale measures a person's degree of satisfaction with his/her life.

SCALE ORIGIN:

The measure was apparently developed by Lumpkin and Hunt (1989) for use in their study, though the items may have come from previous studies reviewed in the article.

SAMPLES:

Lumpkin and Hunt's (1989) sample was drawn from the Market Facts Consumer Mail Panel and focused on **789** respondents who indicated they were 65 years of age or older. The proportions of men and women were similar to those in the national population, but fewer of the men and more of the women in the sample were married. The sample was better educated and had a greater percentage still employed than was true nationally. The sample was composed of more people in lower income levels, but reasonably matched the elderly geographic distribution.

RELIABILITY:

An alpha of **.723** was reported by Lumpkin and Hunt (1989).

VALIDITY:

Factor analysis indicated that the items loaded together.

ADMINISTRATION:

Data were gathered through self-administered mail questionnaires. Scale scores were calculated by averaging numerical responses to individual items. A score of 5 indicates that a person is very happy with his/her past whereas 1 means that a person is very dissatisfied with his/her life.

MAJOR FINDINGS:

The elderly were broken down into two groups by Lumpkin and Hunt (1989): those who were self-reliant in terms of transportation and those who were dependent on others. The self-reliant group perceived things to be better than expected, considered themselves to be in the best years of their lives, and were generally more **satisfied** with their lives than persons who were dependent.

REFERENCE:

Lumpkin, James R. and James B. Hunt (1989), "Mobility as an Influence on Retail Patronage Behavior of the Elderly: Testing Conventional Wisdom," *JAMS*, 17 (Winter), 1-12.

SCALE ITEMS: SATISFACTION (LIFE)

Strongly Disagree	Agree	Neutral	Disagree	Strongly Agree
1—————	—2—————	—3—————	—4—————	—5

1. As I grow older, things seem better than I thought they would be.
2. As I look back on my life I am fairly well satisfied.
3. These are the best years of my life.

SCALE NAME: Satisfaction (Purchases in General)

SCALE DESCRIPTION:

A three-item, seven-point Likert-type summated ratings scale measuring a person's degree of satisfaction with purchases, with an emphasis on department stores.

SCALE ORIGIN:

The scale and its items seem to have originated with Arora (1985), though their origin is not specifically stated in the article.

SAMPLES:

Arora's (1985) analysis was based on **273** completed questionnaires. Interviews were conducted at two shopping malls in a medium-sized midwestern city. Both men and women (21 years of age and older) were contacted in approximate proportion to their presence during interviewing days.

RELIABILITY:

An alpha of **.83** was reported by Arora (1985).

VALIDITY:

It is not clear how or whether Arora checked validity.

ADMINISTRATION:

Data were collected through use of self-administered personal interviews. Higher scores indicate that consumers are very satisfied with their recent purchases made at department stores whereas lower scores indicate that consumers are not happy with their experiences.

MAJOR FINDINGS:

Arora (1985) found that **purchase satisfaction** had a significant though low positive correlation with one measure of retail store involvement but not with another.

REFERENCE:

Arora, Raj (1985), "Involvement: Its Measurement for Retail Store Research," *JAMS*, 13 (Spring), 229-241.

SCALE ITEMS: SATISFACTION (PURCHASES IN GENERAL)

Strongly Disagree	Disagree	Slightly Disagree	Neutral	Slightly Agree	Agree	Strongly Agree
1	2	3	4	5	6	7

1. I am very satisfied with most of my purchases at department stores.
2. I feel very comfortable with my recent purchase decisions.
3. I am confident that I generally make the right decisions.

SCALE NAME: Satisfaction (Referent Power Behavior)

SCALE DESCRIPTION:

A three-item, Likert-type summated ratings scale measuring a person's degree of satisfaction with a physician's behavior. The particular aspect of behavior evaluated was the physician's use of referent power.

SCALE ORIGIN:

The items and scale appear to be original to Friedman and Churchill (1987).

SAMPLES:

Female graduate students were used as subjects in an experimental setting. A total of **396** students cooperated in the study. Female subjects were used because they were expected to relate better to the female patients on the tape recordings to which they would listen. Graduate students were used because they were assumed to be experienced enough to make the required judgments about physicians.

RELIABILITY:

The internal consistency for this specific scale was not reported, but the authors did say that the scale was among the measures with alpha of **.8** or greater.

VALIDITY:

The correlation of the scale with a one item measure of the same construct was .73, providing evidence of convergent validity. The scale had a correlation of .0 with social desirability, providing evidence of discriminant validity. There were indications of nomological validity as well.

ADMINISTRATION:

The scale was presented to subjects as part of a larger self-administered questionnaire to be filled out in an experimental setting. The higher the score on the scale, the greater the subject's satisfaction with a physician's behavior. Lower scores suggest a physician's behavior is considered unsatisfactory.

MAJOR FINDINGS:

The purpose of the experiment was to examine how a physician's social power behaviors can be used to achieve maximum effectiveness, as judged by patients. Subjects listened to recorded conversations between a physician and a patient and were asked to imagine they were the latter. They were then asked to respond to the physician's behavior on a questionnaire. Referent power had a relatively large impact on **satisfaction,** but there was no significant interaction between level of power used and level of riskiness. This finding implies that patients expect some level of friendliness and warmth from the physician regardless of the riskiness of the ailment.

REFERENCE:

Friedman, Margaret L. and Gilbert A. Churchill, Jr. (1987), "Using Consumer Perceptions and a Contingency Approach to Improve Health Care Delivery," *JCR*, 13 (March), 492-510.

SCALE ITEMS: SATISFACTION (REFERENT POWER BEHAVIOR) +

I would have felt satisfied/dissatisfied with the:
1. friendliness of the physician.
2. consideration the physician showed the patient.
3. physician's ability to relate to the patient and her problem.

+ The number of points on the Likert-type response scale was not specified in the article.

SCALE NAME: Satisfaction (With Retailers)

SCALE DESCRIPTION:

A five-item, five-point Likert-type summated ratings scale measuring consumer attitudes about retailers and their salespeople in general. A seven-item version of the scale with similar psychometric properties is also discussed below.

SCALE ORIGIN:

The scale was developed by Gaski and Etgar (1986). By a formula described in the article, the scale can be combined with data from several other measures to form an index of consumer attitudes toward marketing-related activities. The authors request that the index be referred to as the University of Notre Dame/Market Facts Index of Consumer Sentiment Toward Marketing. Some items were taken or adapted from the literature, but the majority were written especially for the index. Pretesting involved 50 members of the Market Facts mail panel completing the index.

SAMPLES:

The sample was taken from the 200,000-household panel maintained by Market Facts. Questionnaires were mailed to 2000 households and **1428** were completed and returned. Though the overall panel is nationally balanced and continually updated to reflect the most recent national demographic changes, the characteristics of the final sample were not given.

RELIABILITY:

A seven-item version of the scale had an alpha of **.783** and, except for one item, the item-total correlations were .41 or higher. Two items with the lowest item-total correlations were eliminated, leaving a scale with an alpha of **.819**.

VALIDITY:

A factor analysis of the 20 items composing the entire index was conducted. The five items composing each of the four scales loaded most heavily on their respective factors and had extremely low loadings on the other three factors. This pattern of loadings provides some evidence of convergent and discriminant validity.

ADMINISTRATION:

The scale was self-administered along with several other measures in a mail survey instrument. High scores indicate that consumers have positive attitudes about retailing whereas low scores suggest that they are not satisfied with retailers in general.

MAJOR FINDINGS:

The purpose of the article was to report on the construction and validation of an index to measure consumers attitudes toward marketing that could be used repeatedly over time as a indicator of the public's general sentiment about the field. Scores on the index were strongly correlated with another general measure of consumer sentiment and consumer satisfaction with the marketing mix elements. As noted above, **retailing** was just one of four subscales composing the index. Its scores had the following significant correlations with those of the other subscales: .254 (price), .301 (advertising), and .366 (product quality).

REFERENCE:

Gaski, John F. and Michael J. Etzel (1986), "The Index of Consumer Sentiment Toward Marketing," *JM*, 50 (July), 71- 81.

SCALE ITEMS: SATISFACTION (WITH RETAILERS)

Strongly Disagree	Agree	Neutral	Disagree	Strongly Agree
1	2	3	4	5

1. Most retail stores serve their customers well. **(r)**
2. Because of the way retailers treat me, most of my shopping is unpleasant.
3. I find most retail salespeople to be very helpful. **(r)**
4. Most retail stores provide an adequate selection of merchandise. **(r)**+
5. In general, most middlemen make excessive profits. +
6. When I need assistance in a store, I am usually not able to get it.
7. Most retailers provide adequate service. **(r)**

+ These items were eliminated to have a five-item scale.

SCALE NAME: Self-Concept

SCALE DESCRIPTION:

A 15-item, semantic differential summated ratings scale that can potentially be used to measure the actual **self-concept**, the ideal **self-concept**, the social **self-concept**, and other similar constructs such as one's concept of another person or one's concept of a product.

SCALE ORIGIN:

Malhotra (1981) generated the items and constructed the scale.

SAMPLES:

Two overlapping samples of college students were used to develop and test the scale. No demographic characteristics of the samples were provided. The first study was based on a sample of **167** students and focused on cars. Four weeks later a sample of **187** students was drawn, 135 of whom had participated in the first survey. The second study focused on perceptions of actors.

RELIABILITY:

The primary method of measuring reliability was through the test-retest method. The 135 respondents common to both surveys had rated their ideal, actual, and social self-concepts both times so it was possible to estimate the four-week test-retest correlation for each of the 15 items as well as the three types of self-concept. All correlations were very significant. The average correlations for the ideal, actual, and social self-concepts were **.80**, **.70**, and **.68**, respectively. Less specific information was provided about internal consistency.

VALIDITY:

Factor analysis, cluster analysis, and regression analysis were used to help reduce a set of 27 items to the final list of 15. Convergent and discriminant validity was assessed through use of the multitrait-multimethod approach. The two traits were cars and actors and the two methods were semantic differential and similarity ratings. The author views the findings as indicating that the scale has reasonable convergent and discriminant validity.

ADMINISTRATION:

The scale was self-administered as part of a larger questionnaire and is amenable for use in person or in mail surveys, though it is likely to be too long and tedious for use in phone surveys. It is not altogether clear what particular scores on the scale mean, as a variety of factors are represented by the scale. However, higher scores appear to suggest a concept is more potent and active whereas low scores could mean a concept is more stable and simple.

MAJOR FINDINGS:

The purpose of the study was to construct a scale that was generalizable enough to measure a variety of constructs related to **self-concept**. A 15-item semantic differential scale was produced. The author suggests that the scale could be used to measure the **self-concept** of a target market and then coordinate it with a product and/or a spokesperson that matches such an image.

COMMENTS:

As noted above, it is not clear what one summated score on this scale would mean. The presence of multiple factors in one measure may be the reason the reliability levels were no higher than they were given the number of items involved. It may be more appropriate to use the items individually to cover a variety of factors related to **self-concept**.

REFERENCE:

Malhotra, Naresh K. (1981), ''A Scale to Measure Self- Concepts, Person Concepts, and Product Concepts,'' *JMR*, 18 (November), 456-464.

SCALE ITEMS: SELF-CONCEPT +

	1	2	3	4	5	6	7	
rugged								delicate
excitable								calm
uncomfortable								comfortable
dominating								submissive
thrifty								indulgent
pleasant								unpleasant
contemporary								noncontemporary
organized								unorganized
rational								emotional
youthful								mature
formal								informal
orthodox								liberal

complex	____ : ____ : ____ : ____ : ____ : ____ : ____	simple
	1 2 3 4 5 6 7	
colorless	____ : ____ : ____ : ____ : ____ : ____ : ____	colorful
	1 2 3 4 5 6 7	
modest	____ : ____ : ____ : ____ : ____ : ____ : ____	vain
	1 2 3 4 5 6 7	

+ Neither the number of points on the scale nor their verbal anchors were specified in the article. Further, the items that must be reverse coded were not specified and must be determined through factor analysis or some other procedure before summated scores can be accurately calculated.

SCALE NAME: Self-Confidence (Generalized)

SCALE DESCRIPTION:

A two-item, seven-point Likert-type summated ratings scale measuring a person's degree of certainty and self-assurance.

SCALE ORIGIN:

The scale and its items may have originated with Arora (1985), though their origin is not specifically stated in the article.

SAMPLES:

Arora's (1985) analysis was based on **273** completed questionaires. Interviews were conducted at two shopping malls in a medium-sized midwestern city. Both men and women (21 years of age and older) were contacted in approximate proportion to their presence during interviewing days.

RELIABILITY:

An alpha of **.59** was reported by Arora (1985).

VALIDITY:

It is not clear how or whether Arora checked validity.

ADMINISTRATION:

Data were collected through use of self-administered personal interviews. Higher scores indicate that consumers are very self-confident whereas lower scores indicate that consumers have much less belief in their abilities.

MAJOR FINDINGS:

Arora (1985) found that **self-confidence** had significant though low positive correlations with two measures of retail store involvement.

COMMENTS:

Internal consistency should be improved by the addition of a few appropriate items before the scale is used.

REFERENCE:

Arora, Raj (1985), ''Involvement: Its Measurement for Retail Store Research,'' *JAMS*, 13 (Spring), 229-241.

SCALE ITEMS: SELF-CONFIDENCE (GENERALIZED)

Strongly Disagree	Disagree	Slightly Disagree	Neutral	Slightly Agree	Agree	Strongly Agree
1	2	3	4	5	6	7

1. I am not at all lacking in self-confidence.
2. I do not spend much time worrying about what people think of me.

SCALE NAME: Self-Confidence (Generalized)

SCALE DESCRIPTION:

A four-item, six-point, Likert-type summated ratings scale ranging from strongly disagree (1) to strongly agree (6). The scale measures the perception of one's self as a leader and having confidence. It may be the scale used by Burnett and Bush (1986). A slightly modified version of this scale used by Davis and Rubin (1983) was referred to as Self-Confidence/ Leadership. A shorter, three-item version was utilized by Lumpkin and Hunt (1989). See also a variation on the scale by Hawes and Lumpkin (1984).

SCALE ORIGIN:

These items were part of a classic study of psychographics by Wells and Tigert (1971). One thousand questionnaires were mailed to homemaker members of the Market Facts mail panel. In addition to gathering demographic, product use, and media data, the survey contained 300 statements that have since served as the basis for the construction of many lifestyle-related scales. The four items for this scale are reported in the article, but they were not analyzed as a multi-item scale. The purpose of the article was to explain how psychographics could improve upon mere demographic description of target audiences and product users. No psychometric information was reported.

One of the first uses of the items as a multi-item scale was by Darden and Ashton (1974-1975). Analysis was based on self-administered questionnaires completed by 116 middle-class suburban housewives selected from the telephone directory of a medium-sized southern city. A split-half reliability of .65 was reported for the scale. Respondents were grouped on the basis of their supermarket attribute preferences. Self-confidence was significantly different between groups and was highest for the group distinguished by a desire for clean stores with a wide variety of brands.

SAMPLES:

Davis and Rubin (1983) mailed questionnaires to a sample of two groups in Florida: known adopters of solar energy devices and the general population over the age of 18 years. Analysis was based on **817** usable questionnaires, of which **488** were from solar energy adopters.

Two mailing lists were used to collect data in the Dickerson and Gentry study (1983). One was a list of *Psychology Today* subscribers and the other was a list of members of computer clubs. The former was used to reach non-adopters of computers and the latter was used to reach PC adopters. Analysis was based on a total of **639** questionnaires. Results from a second mailing to non-respondents indicated that their demographic makeup was not significantly different from that of respondents. On the basis of 1980 Census data, the sample was younger and more upscale than the general population.

A large sample from the Market Facts Consumer Mail Panel was used by Lumpkin and Hunt (1989). Their article focused on a subset of all respondents who indicated they were 65 years of age or older (n = **789**).

RELIABILITY:

Alpha values of **.69**, **.61**, and **.728** were reported by Davis and Rubin (1983), Dickerson and Gentry (1983), and Lumpkin and Hunt (1989), respectively.

VALIDITY:

Assessment was generally through factor analysis. More effort was made by Davis and Rubin (1983), who randomly split their data in half and factor analyzed the two subsamples. Identical factor solutions were found in the two subsamples. The factors found within the full dataset were consistent with the subsample solutions.

ADMINISTRATION:

Data were gathered in all studies through self-administered mail questionnaires. Scale scores are calculated by averaging numerical responses to individual items. A score of 6 indicates that a person strongly expresses confidence in his/her abilities whereas a score of 1 means a person does not see him/herself as the confident/leader type.

MAJOR FINDINGS:

Davis and Rubin (1983) determined that persons who expressed a high degree of energy conservation opinion leadership were significantly more **confident** in their abilities and were more financially optimistic than persons with less leadership. Dickerson and Gentry (1983) expected to find a positive relationship between adoption of home computers and **self-confidence,** but it was *not* among the lifestyle variables that significantly discriminated between adopters and non-adopters. The elderly were broken down into two groups by Lumpkin and Hunt (1989): those who were self-reliant in terms of transportation and those who were dependent on others. The self-reliant group was significantly more **self-confident** than persons who were dependent.

COMMENTS:

The reliability and validity of this measure might be improved by using items that tap into either the confidence trait or the leadership issue, but not both.

REFERENCES:

Burnett, John J. and Alan J. Bush (1986), ''Profiling the Yuppies,'' *JAR*, 26 (April/May), 27-35.

Darden, William R. and Dub Ashton (1974-1975), ''Psychographic Profiles of Patronage Preference Groups,'' *JR*, 50 (Winter), 99-112.

Davis, Duane L. and Ronald S. Rubin (1983), ''Identifying the Energy Conscious Consumer: The Case of the Opinion Leader,'' *JAMS*, 11 (Spring), 169-190.

Dickerson, Mary D. and James W. Gentry (1983), ''Characteristics of Adopters and Non-Adopters of Home Computers,'' *JCR*, 10 (September). 225-235.

Hawes, Jon M. and James R. Lumpkin (1984), ''Understanding the Outshopper,'' *JAMS*, 12 (Fall), 200-218.

Lumpkin, James R. and James B. Hunt (1989), ''Mobility as an Influence on Retail Patronage Behavior of the Elderly: Testing Conventional Wisdom,'' *JAMS*, 17 (Winter), 1-12.

Tigert, Douglas J. (1974), ''Life Style Analysis as a Basis for Media Selection,'' in *Life Style and Psychographics*, William D. Wells, ed. Chicago, Ill.: American Marketing Association.

Wells, William D. and Douglas Tigert (1971), "Activities, Interests, and Opinions," *JAR*, 11 (August), 27-35.

SCALE ITEMS: SELF-CONFIDENCE (GENERALIZED) +

Strongly Disagree	Disagree	Slightly Disagree	Slightly Agree	Agree	Strongly Agree
1	2	3	4	5	6

1. I think I have more self-confidence than most people.
2. I am more independent than most people.
3. I think I have a lot of personal ability.
4. I like to be considered a leader.
5. I have never been really outstanding at anything. **(r)**
6. I often can talk others into doing something.

+ The first four items are those offered by Wells and Tigert (1971). Items 3 through 6 are given by Tigert (1974, p. 181) and are apparently the ones used by Davis and Rubin (1983). Lumpkin and Hunt (1989) used items 1 through 3.

SCALE NAME: Self-Confidence (Nonprescription Drug Purchase)

SCALE DESCRIPTION:

A four-item, seven-point Likert-type scale measuring a person's reported knowledge and confidence about the right over-the-counter drugs to buy to treat an ailment.

SCALE ORIGIN:

The measure did not originate in the Oliver and Bearden (1985) study, but was supplied by a sponsoring institution (p. 329, 338).

SAMPLES:

Analysis was based on **353** completed questionnaires from members of a bistate consumer panel. Subjects were selected to be representative of urban and suburban households with family income greater than $10,000. Ninety-one triers and 262 nontriers of a new, heavily promoted time-release diet suppressant responded. The average respondent was female (56%), white (89%), with some education beyond high school (70%), and in the $20,000 to $29,999 income category (25.5%).

RELIABILITY:

A reliability of **.77** was reported.

VALIDITY:

Confirmatory factor analysis was performed once, weak items were deleted, and the analysis was run again, resulting in higher overall factor loadings.

ADMINISTRATION:

Data were gathered through use of self-administered mail questionnaires. The method for calculating scale scores was not specified, but it is likely that higher scores on this scale suggest a person has great confidence in his/her abilities about which drugs to buy. Lower scores imply that a person perceives him/herself to lack the knowledge and confidence that others appear to have in purchasing home remedies.

MAJOR FINDINGS:

The purpose of the study was to examine the presence and operation of "crossover effects" in the Fishbein behavioral intention model under various moderating conditions. Evidence generally supporting the normative structure—attitude crossover path was found; i.e., a person's attitude toward a behavior is strengthened to the extent that relevant others are believed to agree with it. The moderator variable analysis provided little insight into the mechanisms people use to process normative information. However, contrary to the original hypothesis, persons high in **confidence** were more influenced by the subjective norm than persons low in **confidence**.

COMMENTS:

Though the scale had adequate internal consistency, the authors admitted that it might lack stability over time, samples, or product categories.

REFERENCE:

Oliver, Richard L. and William O. Bearden (1985), ''Crossover Effects in the Theory of Reasoned Action: A Moderating Influence Attempt,'' *JCR*, 12 (December), 324-340.

SCALE ITEMS: SELF-CONFIDENCE (NONPRESCRIPTION DRUG PURCHASES)

Disagree _____ : _____ : _____ : _____ : _____ : _____ : _____ Agree
           1   2   3   4   5   6   7

1. I am very confident about my ability to buy good non-prescription drugs.
2. When I have a minor ailment, I generally know exactly which products I need to buy at the drugstore to cure it.
3. I know as much as the next person about how to use home remedies.
4. I am more confident than the average person when it comes to buying home remedies.

SCALE NAME: Self-Confidence (Shopping)

SCALE DESCRIPTION:

A two-item, six-point, Likert-type summated ratings scale ranging from strongly disagree (1) to strongly agree (6). The scale measures a consumer's belief in his/her own shopping ability. See variation on the scale by Hawes and Lumpkin (1984).

SCALE ORIGIN:

It is not clear where the items originated or where they were first used as a multi-item summated ratings scale.

SAMPLES:

Lumpkin (1985) analyzed data collected from a sample drawn from the Market Facts Consumer Mail Panel. A total of **2854** completed questionnaires were received, but Lumpkin focused just on **373** respondents who indicated they were 65 years of age or older.

RELIABILITY:

An alpha of **.7679** was reported by Lumpkin (1985).

VALIDITY:

Factor analysis indicated the items loaded together.

ADMINISTRATION:

Data were gathered through self-administered mail questionnaires. Scale scores are calculated by averaging numerical responses to individual items. A score of 6 indicates that a consumer strongly believes that he/she is a good shopper whereas 1 implies that a person has little confidence in his/her shopping ability.

MAJOR FINDINGS:

Elderly consumers were cluster analyzed and **shopping confidence** appeared to greatly discriminate between the three groups, though the level of statistical significance was not reported. The group with the highest mean on the scale was also the most interested in **shopping** and expressed the most opinion leadership. The group with the lowest mean score expressed little interest in **shopping**.

COMMENTS:

The internal validity is not bad from one study, but it would be improved by the addition of relevant items.

REFERENCES:

Hawes, Jon M. and James R. Lumpkin (1984), ''Understanding the Outshopper,'' *JAMS*, 12 (Fall), 200-218.

Lumpkin, James R. (1985), ''Shopping Orientation Segmentation of the Elderly Consumer,'' *JAMS*, 13 (Spring), 271-289.

SCALE ITEMS: SELF-CONFIDENCE (SHOPPING)

Strongly Disagree	Disagree	Slightly Disagree	Slightly Agree	Agree	Strongly Agree
1	2	3	4	5	6

1. I think I am a good shopper.
2. I think I am a better shopper than most.

SCALE NAME: Self-Esteem

SCALE DESCRIPTION:

A five-item, five-point Likert-type summated ratings scale measuring the degree of confidence a person has in his/her own abilities.

SCALE ORIGIN:

The scale was apparently original to O'Guinn and Faber (1989).

SAMPLES:

Two samples were employed by O'Guinn and Faber (1989). One consisted of **386** completed responses (out of 808 questionnaires sent) from people who had written an organization that aided compulsive buyers. A second group was used for comparison and was intended to represent the general population. Eight hundred questionnaires were mailed to people in three Illinois areas: Chicago, Springfield, and Bloomington-Normal. Two mailings produced a total of **250** completed survey forms.

RELIABILITY:

An alpha of **.84** was calculated for this scale.

VALIDITY:

No examination of scale validity was reported.

ADMINISTRATION:

The scale was one of several self- administered measures used in a mail survey instrument. Higher scores on the scale indicate that respondents have low self-esteem whereas lower scores indicate that respondents are likely to have greater confidence in their abilities.

MAJOR FINDINGS:

O'Guinn and Faber (1989) studied compulsive shopping. Their results showed that a sample of compulsive shoppers had significantly lower **self-esteem** than a general sample of consumers.

REFERENCE:

O'Guinn, Thomas C. and Ronald J. Faber (1989), ''Compulsive Buying: A Phenomenological Exploration,'' *JCR*, 16 (September), 147-157.

SCALE ITEMS: SELF-ESTEEM

Strongly Disagree	Agree	Neutral	Disagree	Strongly Agree
1—————————	—2—————————	—3—————————	—4—————————	—5

1. I certainly feel useless at times.
2. Life is a strain for me much of the time.
3. I have several times given up doing a thing because I thought too little of my ability.
4. Much of the time I feel as if I have done something wrong or evil.
5. I am certainly lacking in self confidence.

SCALE NAME: Self-Esteem

SCALE DESCRIPTION:

A six-item, Likert-type scale measuring how satisfied a person is with his/her life. Oliver and Bearden (1985) used a seven-point scale but Bown and Richek (1967) used a five point scale ranging from "exactly what I think or feel" to "the opposite of what I think or feel."

SCALE ORIGIN:

The scale used by Oliver and Bearden (1985) is one subscale of a larger inventory constructed by Bown and Richek (1967). That group of 48 items had eight subscales. It was referred to as a Self-Report Inventory and purported to be a quick measure of mental health. The internal consistency of the full inventory was measured with numerous samples of students and teachers and found to be high. Validity of the inventory was not fully explored, but it was used successfully to contrast between groups, which provided some evidence of concurrent validity. The self-esteem subscale was calculated to have an alpha of .7836 when tested with 244 female college students. The item-to-total correlations for the six items ranged from .59 to .81.

SAMPLES:

Oliver and Bearden's analysis was based on **353** completed questionnaires from members of a bistate consumer panel. They were selected to be representative of urban and suburban households with family income greater than $10,000. **Ninety-one** triers and **262** nontriers of a new, heavily promoted time-release diet suppressant responded. The average respondent was female (56%), white (89%), with some education beyond high school (70%), and in the $20,000 to $29,999 income category (25.5%).

RELIABILITY:

A reliability of **.82** was reported.

VALIDITY:

Confirmatory factor analysis was performed once, weak items were deleted, and the analysis was run again, resulting in higher overall factor loadings.

ADMINISTRATION:

Data were gathered through use of self-administered mail questionnaires. The method for calculating scale scores was not specified, but it is likely that persons with higher scores on this scale are very satisfied with themselves and their lives, whereas persons with lower scores are unhappy with who they are and wish to be different.

MAJOR FINDINGS:

The purpose of the study was to examine the presence and operation of "crossover effects" in the Fishbein behavioral intention model under various moderating conditions. Evidence generally supporting the normative structure—attitude crossover path was found; i.e., a person's attitude toward a behavior is strengthened to the extent that relevant others are believed to agree with it. The moderator variable analysis provided little insight into the mechanisms people use to process normative information.

REFERENCES:

Bown, Oliver H. and Herbert G. Richek (1967), "The Bown Self-Report Inventory (SRI): A Quick Screening Instrument for Mental Health Professionals," *Comprehensive Psychiatry*, 8 (February), 45-52.

Oliver, Richard L. and William O. Bearden (1985), "Crossover Effects in the Theory of Reasoned Action: A Moderating Influence Attempt," *JCR*, 12 (December), 324-340.

SCALE ITEMS: SELF-ESTEEM

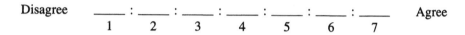

Disagree ____ : ____ : ____ : ____ : ____ : ____ : ____ Agree
   1   2   3   4   5   6   7

1. I seem to have a great deal of self-respect.
2. I feel sour and pessimistic about life in general. **(r)**
3. Thinking back, in a good many ways I don't think I have liked myself very well. **(r)**
4. In almost every respect, I'm very glad to be the person I am.
5. When I think about the kind of person that I have been in the past, it makes me feel very happy or proud.
6. I would give a good deal to be very different than I am. **(r)**

SCALE NAME: Self-Esteem

SCALE DESCRIPTION:

A 20-item, five-point Likert-type summated ratings scale measuring the degree to which a person expresses feelings of self-confidence, self-assurance, and self-esteem.

SCALE ORIGIN:

The scale is a revision by Eagly (1967) of a measure presented previously by Janis and Field (1959). The sample used by Eagly was composed of 144 students enrolled in a introductory psychology course at Michigan State University. Subjects received extra credit and were not required to participate. The split-half reliability for the scale was estimated to be .72 and the Spearman-Brown formula indicated internal consistency to be .84.

SAMPLES:

The sample was just one of many used in a series of studies by Bearden, Netemeyer, and Teel (1989). All that is known about the sample used with this scale is that it was composed of **47** undergraduate business students.

RELIABILITY:

An alpha of **.88** was reported for the scale by Bearden, Netemeyer, and Teel (1989).

VALIDITY:

This scale was used by Bearden and his coauthors to help validate two other scales constructed in the study. Therefore, beyond the findings discussed below, no other examination of its validity was reported.

ADMINISTRATION:

The scale was self-administered in each of the studies reported by Bearden and his coauthors. Higher scores on the scale indicate that respondents are more confident and self-assured.

MAJOR FINDINGS:

The purpose of the study by Bearden and his coauthors was to develop scales for measuring the dimensions of consumer susceptibility to interpersonal influence. A series of studies provided support for a two-factor model (normative and informational factors). Among the many findings were that both of the dimensions had similarly low but significant negative correlations with **self-esteem**.

REFERENCES:

Bearden, William O., Richard G. Netemeyer, and Jesse E. Teel (1989), "Measurement of Consumer Susceptibility to Interpersonal Influence," *JCR*, 15 (March), 473-481.

Eagly, Alice H. (1967), "Involvement as a Determinant of Responses to Favorable and Unfavorable Information," *Journal of Personality and Social Psychology*, 7 (November), 1-15.

Janis, Irving L. and Peter B. Field (1959), "Sex Differences and Personality Factors Related to Persuasibility," in *Personality and Persuasibility*, Carl I. Hovland and Irving L. Janis, eds. New Haven, Conn.: Yale University Press, 55-68.

SCALE ITEMS: SELF-ESTEEM

Very Often	Fairly Often	Sometimes	Once in a Great While	Practically Never
1	2	3	4	5

1. How often do you have the feeling that there is *nothing* you can do well?
2. When you have to talk in front of a class or group of people your own age, how afraid or worried do you usually feel? (e.g., very afraid)
3. How often do you worry about whether other people like to be with you?
4. How often do you feel self-conscious?
5. How often are you troubled with shyness?
6. How often do you feel inferior to most of the people you know?
7. Do you ever think that you are a worthless individual?
8. How much do you worry about how well you get along with other people?
9. How often do you feel that you dislike yourself?
10. Do you ever feel so discouraged with yourself that you wonder whether anything is worthwhile?
11. How often do you feel that you have handled yourself well at a social gathering? **(r)**
12. How often do you have the feeling that you can do everything well? **(r)**
13. When you talk in front of a class or group of people of your own age, how pleased are you with your performance? (e.g., very pleased) **(r)**
14. How comfortable are you when starting a conversation with people whom you don't know? (e.g., very comfortable) **(r)**
15. How often do you feel that you are a successful person? **(r)**
16. How confident are you that your success in your future job or career is assured? (e.g., very confident) **(r)**
17. When you speak in a class discussion, how sure of yourself do you feel? **(r)**
18. How sure of yourself do you feel when among strangers? **(r)**
19. How confident do you feel that some day the people you know will look up to you and respect you? **(r)**
20. In general, how confident do you feel about your abilities? **(r)**

SCALE NAME: Self-Orientation of Salesperson (Customer's Perception)

SCALE DESCRIPTION:

A five-item, five-point Likert-type summated ratings scale measuring the degree to which a customer perceives a salesperson to have greater interest in self than in the customer. Williams and Spiro (1985) viewed this scale as measuring the self-oriented dimension of customer communication style, which stresses interest in self more than others and is unlikely to be empathetic.

SCALE ORIGIN:

The items used by Williams and Spiro (1985) were developed from work performed by Bass (1960) on orientation motivation. On the basis of previous work by others, Bass suggested that members of groups are motivated to remain in the groups for different reasons. He developed measures of three motivations: the task orientation, the interaction orientation, and the self orientation (Bass 1977). Williams and Spiro (1985) adapted these measures for their studies in two ways: their measures were more specific to the sales context and they were perceptions of other's behaviors, not self-perceptions.

SAMPLES:

Williams and Spiro (1985) collected data from all 13 sporting goods stores in a major southeastern U.S. city. Customers were approached just after leaving the stores. If they agreed to fill out a questionnaire, their respective salespeople were asked to fill out a survey instrument as well. A total of **251** dyadic interactions were captured, with responses from 64 different salespeople and 251 different customers. All salespeople in the stores participated, as did 90% of the customers who were approached.

RELIABILITY:

An alpha of **.66** was reported for the scale and item-total correlations were all above .50 (Williams and Spiro 1985).

VALIDITY:

A factor analysis indicated that the items loaded higher on this factor than any other (Williams and Spiro 1985).

ADMINISTRATION:

As implied above, the customer completed a self-administered survey form that included several measures (Williams and Spiro (1985). The authors computed scale scores by averaging numerical responses to the items. Higher scores on the scale suggest that customers perceive the salespeople with whom they have just interacted were much more interested in themselves than in the customers whereas lower scores imply that customers feel their respective salespeople were interested in them and responsive to their needs.

MAJOR FINDINGS:

Williams and Spiro (1985) examined the use of communication styles in dyadic sales situations and their effect on sales outcomes. The findings indicated that though the communication styles of the two parties of the transaction play a role in the outcome, the customer's orientation has the greatest impact. With respect to **salesperson's self-orientation**, it was the greatest hindrance to sales of all the salesperson and customer orientations studied.

REFERENCES:

Bass, Bernard M. (1960), *Leadership, Psychology, and Organizational Behavior*. New York, N.Y.: Harper Brothers.

———— (1977), *ORI-Manual for the Orientation Inventory*. Palo Alto, Calif.: Consulting Psychologists Press, Inc.

Williams, Kaylene C. and Rosann L. Spiro (1985), "Communication Style in the Salesperson-Customer Dyad," *JMR*, 12 (November), 434-442.

SCALE ITEMS: SELF-ORIENTATION OF SALESPERSON (CUSTOMER'S PERCEPTION)

Strongly Disagree	Agree	Neutral	Disagree	Strongly Agree
1—————	—2—————	—3—————	—4—————	—5

1. This salesperson seemed more interested in himself than in me.
2. This salesperson was more interested in what he had to say than in what I had to say.
3. This salesperson talked about his own personal difficulties.
4. This salesperson tried to dominate the conversation.
5. This salesperson really wants to be admired by others.

SCALE NAME: Service Failure by Company

SCALE DESCRIPTION:

A two-item, five-point Likert-type summated ratings scale measuring the number of times a company failed to handle a customer's request efficiently in the previous two years. Crosby and Stephens (1987) used the scale with policy owners and asked them to respond about insurance companies.

SCALE ORIGIN:

There is no indication that the scale was constructed elsewhere than in the Crosby and Stephens (1987) study.

SAMPLES:

The sample was selected from a nationally representative consumer panel and screened for ownership of life insurance. Analysis of the first wave of the survey was based on **1362** responses. The sample was slightly better educated and more upscale than the population at large, but the authors considered the differences to be minor and unrelated to the studied relationships. A year later, respondents to the first wave of the survey (or from a holdout sample) were contacted. Analysis was based on **447** responses. Comparison of main sample and holdout sample data did not indicate any bias due to wave 1 premeasurement.

RELIABILITY:

Alpha values for the scale were **.92** for wave 1 and **.91** for wave 2.

VALIDITY:

Factor analyses in the two waves of the study produced nearly identical factor solutions.

ADMINISTRATION:

The scales were self-administered as part of a larger mail questionnaire. High scores indicate that customers have failed to have their requests handled efficiently by their companies many times in the past two years whereas low scores suggest that customers have rarely failed to receive efficient service from their companies.

MAJOR FINDINGS:

The purpose of the study was to compare two proposed models of buyer satisfaction with life insurance, the relationship generalization model (RGM) and the rational evaluation model (REM). The RGM assumes that consumers generalize positive feelings about the provider to the core service whereas the REM views consumers as most concerned about core service quality, with the relationship merely adding value to it. In general, the results supported the REM over the RGM. This means that though the agent's performance affects satisfaction, it is balanced against the perceived performance of the core service.

Service failure was found to have a significant and negative relationship with the satisfaction customers felt toward their companies.

REFERENCE:

Crosby, Lawrence A. and Nancy Stephens (1987), ''Effects of Relationship Marketing on Satisfaction, Retention, and Prices in the Life Insurance Industry,'' *JMR*, 24 (November), 404-411.

SCALE ITEMS: SERVICE FAILURE BY COMPANY

Never	Once	Twice	Three or Four Times	Five Times or More
1————	——2——	——3——	——4——	——5

How often in the last one or two years did you recall experiencing the following:

1. made a request my company failed to handle properly.
2. made a request my company failed to handle promptly.

SCALE NAME: Service Failure by Sales Agent

SCALE DESCRIPTION:

A two-item, five-point Likert-type summated ratings scale measuring the number of times a sales agent failed to handle a customer's request efficiently in the previous two years. Crosby and Stephens (1987) used the scale with policy owners and asked them to respond about insurance agents.

SCALE ORIGIN:

There is no indication that the scale was constructed elsewhere than in the Crosby and Stephens (1987) study.

SAMPLES:

The sample was selected from a nationally representative consumer panel and screened for ownership of life insurance. Analysis of the first wave of the survey was based on **1362** responses. The sample was slightly better educated and more upscale than the population at large, but the authors considered the differences to be minor and unrelated to the studied relationships. A year later, respondents to the first wave of the survey (or from a holdout sample) were contacted. Analysis was based on **447** responses. Comparison of main sample and holdout sample data did not indicate any bias due to wave 1 premeasurement.

RELIABILITY:

Alpha values for the scale were **.82** for wave 1 and **.87** for wave 2.

VALIDITY:

Factor analyses in the two waves of the study produced nearly identical factor solutions.

ADMINISTRATION:

The scales were self-administered as part of a larger mail questionnaire. High scores indicate that customers have failed to have their requests handled efficiently by their agent many times in the past two years whereas low scores suggest that customers have rarely failed to receive efficient service from their agent.

MAJOR FINDINGS:

The purpose of the study was to compare two proposed models of buyer satisfaction with life insurance, the relationship generalization model (RGM) and the rational evaluation model (REM). The RGM assumes that consumers generalize positive feelings about the provider to the core service whereas the REM views consumers as most concerned about core service quality, with the relationship merely adding value to it. In general, the results supported the REM over the RGM. This means that though the agent's performance affects satisfaction, it is balanced against the perceived performance of the core service. **Service**

failure was found to have a significant and negative relationship with the satisfaction customers felt toward their agents.

REFERENCE:

Crosby, Lawrence A. and Nancy Stephens (1987), "Effects of Relationship Marketing on Satisfaction, Retention, and Prices in the Life Insurance Industry," *JMR*, 24 (November), 404-411.

SCALE ITEMS: SERVICE FAILURE BY SALES AGENT

Never	Once	Twice	Three or Four Times	Five Times or More
1———————2———————3———————4———————5				

How often in the last one or two years did you recall experiencing the following:
1. made a request my agent failed to handle properly.
2. made a request my agent failed to handle promptly.

SCALE NAME: Shop With Children

SCALE DESCRIPTION:

A three-item, five-point Likert-type summated ratings scale measuring the degree to which a parent reports routinely taking a child along on shopping trips. It was referred to as Coshopping by Carlson and Grossbart (1988).

SCALE ORIGIN:

The use of these items as a multi-item measure appears to be original to Carlson and Grossbart (1988). However, they got ideas for some of the items from the research of Ward, Wackman, and Wartella (1977).

SAMPLES:

The survey instrument used by Carlson and Grossbart (1988) was distributed to mothers via students at three elementary schools in an unidentified U.S. city. The schools were chosen on a convenience basis but appeared to represent a variety of socioeconomic areas of the city. A $1 contribution to the PTO was offered for each completed questionnaire returned by the children. Analysis was based on **451** completed questionnaires. Ninety-three percent of the responding mothers indicated that they were the primary person in the child's socialization.

RELIABILITY:

Carlson and Grossbart (1988) reported an alpha of **.95** and a beta of .91 for the scale.

VALIDITY:

No examination of scale validity was reported by Carlson and Grossbart (1988).

ADMINISTRATION:

The scale was self-administered along with many other measures in the questionnaire used by Carlson and Grossbart (1988). Higher scores on the scale mean that respondents report a high frequency of shopping with their children whereas lower scores imply that they do not shop with their children much at all.

MAJOR FINDINGS:

The authors investigated the relationship between general parental socialization styles and children's consumer socialization. In a factor analysis of scale scores, scores on the **Shopping With Child** scale loaded on a factor described as "parent-child communication about consumption." A significant difference was found in the degree of parent-child communication between several of the parental socialization style clusters examined.

REFERENCES:

Carlson, Les and Sanford Grossbart (1988), "Parental Style and Consumer Socialization of Children," *JCR*, 15 (June), 77-94.

Ward, Scott, Daniel B. Wackman, and Ellen Wartella (1977), *How Children Learn to Buy*. Beverly Hills, Calif.: Sage Publications, Inc.

SCALE ITEMS: SHOP WITH CHILDREN

Very Seldom	Seldom	Sometimes	Often	Very Often
1	2	3	4	5

1. When I go grocery shopping, I take my child.
2. When I go general family shopping, I take my child.
3. When I shop for my child, I take him/her along.

SCALE NAME: Shopping Conditions (Local)

SCALE DESCRIPTION:

A five-item, six-point, Likert-type summated ratings scale going from strongly disagree (1) to strongly agree (6). The scale measures a consumer's attitude about shopping at local stores. It was referred to as Negative Attitude Toward Local Shopping by Hawes and Lumpkin (1984).

SCALE ORIGIN:

These items were apparently first used and reported as a multi-item scale by Hawes and Lumpkin (1984).

SAMPLES:

Hawes and Lumpkin (1984) collected data from **581** residents of 14 communities near the Ft. Worth-Dallas metroplex. Each of the communities was randomly sampled in proportion to its population by means of the respective telephone directories. The questionnaire was to be filled out by the household member responsible for most of the shopping. The distribution of respondents by community was similar to the actual population distribution.

RELIABILITY:

An alpha of **.711** was calculated for the scale.

VALIDITY:

Factor analysis indicated that the items loaded together and that their loadings were all higher than .5. Content validity was deemed adequate given that the construct included items similar to those used in other (unspecified) studies.

ADMINISTRATION:

Data were gathered through self-administered mail questionnaires. Scale scores are calculated by averaging numerical responses to individual items. A score of 6 indicates that a person has a strong negative attitude about shopping at local stores whereas 1 implies that a person thinks local merchants offer good quality and variety for the price.

MAJOR FINDINGS:

The purpose of the study by Hawes and Lumpkin (1984) was to examine demographic and psychographic characteristics of outshoppers. **Attitude about local shopping** was the most salient psychographic variable in differentiating between inshopper and outshoppers. Specifically, persons who engaged in outshopping the most expressed the most **negative attitudes** about local **shopping conditions**.

REFERENCE:

Hawes, Jon M. and James R. Lumpkin (1984), "Understanding the Outshopper," *JAMS*, 12 (Fall), 200-218.

SCALE ITEMS: SHOPPING CONDITIONS (LOCAL)

Strongly Disagree	Disagree	Slightly Disagree	Slightly Agree	Agree	Strongly Agree
1	2	3	4	5	6

1. Local stores are never open when you want to shop.
2. Local prices are out of line with other towns.
3. Local stores offer you good quality for the price. **(r)**
4. Local stores just do not meet my shopping needs.
5. Local merchants offer a good variety of merchandise. **(r)**

SCALE NAME: Shopping Enjoyment

SCALE DESCRIPTION:

A three-item, five-point Likert-type summated ratings scale measuring the enjoyment a consumer expresses receiving from the shopping experience. The scale was referred to as Emotional Lift by O'Guinn and Faber (1989).

SCALE ORIGIN:

The scale was apparently original to O'Guinn and Faber (1989).

SAMPLES:

Two samples were employed. One consisted of **386** completed responses (out of 808 questionnaires sent) from people who had written an organization that aided compulsive buyers. A second group was used for comparison and was intended to represent the general population. Eight hundred questionnaires were mailed to people in three Illinois areas: Chicago, Springfield, and Bloomington-Normal. Two mailings produced a total of **250** completed survey forms.

RELIABILITY:

An alpha of **.89** was reported for the scale.

VALIDITY:

Beyond a factor analysis indicating that the items loaded together, no specific examination of scale validity was reported.

ADMINISTRATION:

The scale was one of several self-administered measures used in a mail survey instrument. Higher scores on the scale indicate that respondents feel shopping is a fun activity whereas lower scores suggest that shopping does not bring them happiness or enjoyment.

MAJOR FINDINGS:

O'Guinn and Faber (1989) studied compulsive shopping. Their results showed that a sample of compulsive shoppers expressed a significantly greater amount of **shopping enjoyment** than did a general sample of consumers.

REFERENCE:

O'Guinn, Thomas C. and Ronald J. Faber (1989), ''Compulsive Buying: A Phenomenological Exploration,'' *JCR*, 16 (September), 147-157.

SCALE ITEMS: SHOPPING ENJOYMENT

Strongly Disagree	Agree	Neutral	Disagree	Strongly Agree
1	2	3	4	5

1. I shop because buying things makes me happy.
2. Shopping is fun.
3. I get a real ''high'' from shopping.

SCALE NAME: Shopping Guilt

SCALE DESCRIPTION:

A three-item, five-point Likert-type summated ratings scale measuring the frequency which a consumer reports experiencing shame or remorse after shopping. The scale was referred to as Remorse by O'Guinn and Faber (1989).

SCALE ORIGIN:

The scale was apparently original to O'Guinn and Faber (1989).

SAMPLES:

Two samples were employed. One consisted of **386** completed responses (out of 808 questionnaires sent) from people who had written an organization that aided compulsive buyers. A second group was used for comparison and was intended to represent the general population. Eight hundred questionnaires were mailed to people in three Illinois areas: Chicago, Springfield, and Bloomington-Normal. Two mailings produced a total of **250** completed survey forms.

RELIABILITY:

An alpha of **.71** was reported for the scale.

VALIDITY:

Beyond a factor analysis indicating that the items loaded together, no specific examination of scale validity was reported.

ADMINISTRATION:

The scale was one of several self- administered measures used in a mail survey instrument. Higher scores on the scale indicate that respondents frequently feel shame or remorse after shopping whereas lower scores suggest that shopping rarely makes them feel guilty.

MAJOR FINDINGS:

O'Guinn and Faber (1989) studied compulsive shopping. Their results showed that a sample of compulsive shoppers expressed a significantly greater amount of **shopping guilt** than did a general sample of consumers.

REFERENCE:

O'Guinn, Thomas C. and Ronald J. Faber (1989), ''Compulsive Buying: A Phenomenological Exploration,'' *JCR*, 16 (September), 147-157.

SCALE ITEMS: SHOPPING GUILT +

Very Frequent	Sometimes	Frequent	Infrequent	Very Infrequent
1—————	——2——	——3———	——4———	———5

How frequently have you experienced each of the following?
1. hid new purchases so others wouldn't know about them
2. felt others would be horrified if they knew of my spending habits
3. felt depressed after shopping

+ Except for the items themselves, this is the assumed structure of the rest of the scale as it was not described in the article.

SCALE NAME: Shopping Mall Usage

SCALE DESCRIPTION:

A three-item, six-point, Likert-type summated ratings scale that assesses a person's preference for shopping at malls over other stores and shopping alternatives.

SCALE ORIGIN:

This version of the scale appears to be original to Hawes and Lumpkin (1984), but may have been adapted from a seven-item Shopping Center Enthusiast scale used by Darden and Ashton (1974-1975).

SAMPLES:

Hawes and Lumpkin (1984) collected data from **581** residents of 14 communities near the Ft. Worth-Dallas metroplex. Each of the communities was randomly sampled in proportion to its population by means of the respective telephone directories. The questionnaire was to be filled out by the household member responsible for most of the shopping. The distribution of respondents by community was similar to the actual population distribution.

RELIABILITY:

An alpha of .**759** was calculated for the scale.

VALIDITY:

Factor analysis indicated that items loaded together and that their loadings were all higher than .7. Content validity was deemed adequate given that the construct included items similar to those used in other (unspecified) studies.

ADMINISTRATION:

Data were gathered through self-administered mail questionnaires. Scale scores are calculated by averaging numerical responses to individual items. A score of 6 indicates that a person strongly prefers to shop at malls whereas 1 implies that a person has little preference for malls over other places to shop.

MAJOR FINDINGS:

The purpose of the study by Hawes and Lumpkin (1984) was to examine demographic and psychographic characteristics of outshoppers. Shopping mall usage significantly differentiated between inshoppers and outshoppers. Persons who engaged in outshopping the most expressed the greatest preference for malls.

REFERENCES:

Darden, William R. and Dub Ashton (1974-1975), "Psychographic Profiles of Patronage Preference Groups," *JR*, 50 (Winter), 99-112.

Hawes, Jon M. and James R. Lumpkin (1984), ''Understanding the Outshopper,'' *JAMS*, 12 (Fall), 200-218.

SCALE ITEMS: SHOPPING MALL USAGE

Strongly Disagree	Disagree	Slightly Disagree	Slightly Agree	Agree	Strongly Agree
1	2	3	4	5	6

1. I enjoy going to big shopping malls.
2. Shopping malls are the best places to shop.
3. I prefer shopping malls over downtown or other shopping areas.

SCALE NAME: Shopping Prone

SCALE DESCRIPTION:

A four-item, seven-point Likert-type summated ratings scale measuring a person's tendency to engage in shopping-related activities.

SCALE ORIGIN:

It is not clear that the scale and its items originated elsewhere than in Arora's (1985) study.

SAMPLES:

Arora's (1985) analysis was based on **273** completed questionnaires. Interviews were conducted at two shopping malls in a medium-sized midwestern city. Both men and women (21 years of age and older) were contacted in approximate proportion to their presence during interviewing days.

RELIABILITY:

An alpha of .**53** was reported.

VALIDITY:

It is not clear how or whether Arora checked validity.

ADMINISTRATION:

Data were collected through self-administered personal interviews. Higher scores indicate that consumers are willing to spend a lot of time shopping whereas lower scores indicate that they are not willing to put much effort into shopping.

MAJOR FINDINGS:

Arora (1985) found that **shopping proneness** had very significant and positive correlations with two measures of retail store involvement.

COMMENTS:

The low internal consistency and examination of the scale items suggest that more than one construct is being measured by the scale. Generation and testing of more relevant items should be done before the scale is used further.

REFERENCE:

Arora, Raj (1985), "Involvement: Its Measurement for Retail Store Research, *JAMS*, 13 (Spring), 229-241.

SCALE ITEMS: SHOPPING PRONE

Strongly Disagree	Disagree	Slightly Disagree	Neutral	Slightly Agree	Agree	Strongly Agree
1	2	3	4	5	6	7

1. I do not mind spending a lot of time shopping.
2. I like to have a great deal of information before I buy.
3. I would rather shop at a store of my choice than a store that is convenient in the neighborhood.
4. I like to keep up with changes in styles and fashion.

SCALE NAME: Shopping Responsibility (Wife)

SCALE DESCRIPTION:

A two-item, six-point, Likert-type summated ratings scale ranging from strongly disagree (1) to strongly agree (6). The scale measures the degree to which a person believes shopping is the wife's responsibility. It was referred to as Traditional Sex Role Orientation by Hawes and Lumpkin (1984).

SCALE ORIGIN:

The scale appears to be original to Hawes and Lumpkin (1984).

SAMPLES:

Hawes and Lumpkin (1984) collected data from **581** residents of 14 communities near the Ft. Worth-Dallas metroplex. Each of the communities was randomly sampled in proportion to its population by means of the respective telephone directories. The questionnaire was to be filled out by the household member responsible for most of the shopping. The distribution of respondents by community was similar to the actual population distribution.

RELIABILITY:

An alpha of **.761** was calculated for the scale.

VALIDITY:

Factor analysis indicated that the items loaded together and that their loadings were all higher than **.8**. Content validity was deemed adequate given that the construct included items similar to those used in other (unspecified) studies.

ADMINISTRATION:

Data were gathered through self-administered mail questionnaires. Scale scores are calculated by averaging numerical responses to individual items. A score of 6 indicates that a person strongly believes shopping is the wife's responsibility whereas 1 implies a person strongly disagrees with that traditional role assignment.

MAJOR FINDINGS:

The purpose of the study by Hawes and Lumpkin (1984) was to examine demographic and psychographic characteristics of outshoppers. Attitude about **shopping responsibility** did **not** significantly differentiate between inshoppers and outshoppers.

REFERENCE:

Hawes, Jon M. and James R. Lumpkin (1984), "Understanding the Outshopper," *JAMS*, 12 (Fall), 200-218.

SCALE ITEMS: SHOPPING RESPONSIBILITY (WIFE)

Strongly Disagree	Disagree	Slightly Disagree	Slightly Agree	Agree	Strongly Agree
1	2	3	4	5	6

1. Shopping is one of a wife's major responsibilities to her family.
2. The woman of the house should have responsibility for most shopping activities.

SCALE NAME: Social Desirability Bias (Marlowe-Crowne)

SCALE DESCRIPTION:

A 33-item, true-false summated ratings scale purporting to measure the degree to which people describe themselves in socially acceptable terms to gain the approval of others. See other uses of the scale by Raju (1980), Westbrook (1980, 1987), and Carlson and Grossbart (1988).

SCALE ORIGIN:

The scale was developed by Crowne and Marlowe (1960) by generating items related to behaviors that are culturally sanctioned but are unlikely to occur. Two sets of 10 faculty and graduate student judges helped narrow an original inventory of 50 items down to the final set of 33 items. An internal consistency of .88 (Kuder-Richardson 20) was calculated for the scale for a sample of 10 male and 29 female undergraduates in an abnormal psychology class at Ohio State University. Their mean age was 24.4 years, with a range of 19 to 46 years. Thirty-one of these same people completed the instrument a month later and a test-retest correlation of .89 was calculated. Scores of those 31 students plus 81 others in a course on exceptional children were found to have a correlation of .35 (p < .01) with scores on the Edwards Social Desirability Scale. Considerable work was performed on correlating scale scores with MMPI variables. The authors interpret the findings as being "more in accord with a definition of social desirability" than the Edwards scale (p. 354).

SAMPLES:

The scale was administered by Saxe and Weitz (1982) to salespeople in 48 firms representing a wide variety of sales positions. Usable responses were received from **191** salespeople.

The social desirability scale was used in only one stage of the overall study reported by Unger and Kernan (1983). The scale was administered by three different people to a total of **169** undergraduate business students at Miami University and the University of Cincinnati (Unger 1981).

Several samples were used in the study reported by Richins (1983). All that she reported about the sample in which the Social Desirability Scale was administered was that it was composed of **93** college students.

The scale was administered in one of two studies reported by Childers, Houston, and Heckler (1985). The 106 subjects were described as being undergraduate students at a major midwestern university. The subjects were divided into two groups, one with **54** subjects and the other with **52**.

The study by Moore, Bearden, and Teel (1985) was based on complete responses received over three time periods from **198** members of the University of South Carolina Consumer Panel. Comparison of the known characteristics of the respondents with those of the total 360 members of the panel did not indicate any significant response bias.

Friedman and Churchill (1987) used female graduate students as subjects in an experimental setting. A total of **396** students cooperated in the study. Female subjects were used because they were expected to relate better to the female patients on the tape recordings to which they would listen. Graduate students were used because they were assumed to be experienced enough to make the required judgments about physicians.

RELIABILITY:

The internal consistency was not reported in most of the studies. Childers, Houston, and Heckler (1985) reported alpha values of **.75** and **.76**. Moore, Bearden, and Teel (1985) calculated an internal consistency of **.83** (Kuder-Richardson 20) for the scale.

VALIDITY:

No specific examination of scale validity was conducted in any of the studies. However, as described below in the findings, most of the studies found some evidence of the scale's discriminant validity.

ADMINISTRATION:

The scale was self-administered in all of the studies along with other scales. Scores on the scale can range between 0 and 33. The higher the score on the scale, the more a person appears to respond to questions in a manner he/she deems socially desirable, whereas a low score implies the respondent is less likely to answer questions that way.

MAJOR FINDINGS:

The purpose of the Saxe and Weitz (1982) study was to construct a scale for measuring a salesperson's customer orientation. Scores on the scale were not correlated with scores on the Marlowe-Crowne **Social Desirability** Scale. The lack of correlation provided some evidence of discriminant validity of the customer-orientation scale.

Unger and Kernan (1983) examined dimensions of the subjective leisure experience. The **social desirability** scale was used to help construct scales for measuring those dimensions. Six different dimensions were measured in six different situations. Though there was some evidence that social desirability bias might be present when using the scales, the bias appeared to be situation-specific and not necessarily inherent in the scales themselves.

The construction of two scales, assertiveness and aggressiveness, was the focus of the study by Richins (1983). The correlation between the **social desirability** scale and assertiveness and aggressiveness scales was **.13** (p > .10) and **-.28** (p < .01), respectively. The latter indicates statistical significance, but the author downplays its relevance.

Childers, Houston, and Heckler (1985) examined several measures of visual/verbal mental imagery. The **social desirability** scale was used as one way to test the discriminant validity of the scales. None of them showed any evidence of significant social desirability bias.

The influence of labeling (helpful people like yourself) and dependency (depend upon individual contributions) on potential donor attitudes was examined by Moore, Bearden, and Teel (1985). The **social desirability** scale did not have significant correlations with any of the covariate or dependent measures used in the study.

The purpose of the study by Friedman and Churchill (1987) was to examine how a physician's social power behaviors can be used to achieve maximum effectiveness, as judged by patients. Subjects listened to recorded conversations between a physician and a patient and were asked to imagine they were the latter. They were then asked to respond to the physician's behavior on a questionnaire. The **social desirability** scale was used merely to help validate the other scales constructed for the study. As an indication of discriminant validity, the former had low and insignificant correlations with multi-item scales measuring patient satisfaction with physician behavior, patient compliance with physician's recommendations, and potential consequences of poor treatment.

COMMENTS:

This scale may tap into several constructs, but it is typically used in constructing scales for measuring particular constructs and not by itself. High correlation between scores on the social desirability scale and scores on another measure suggests the latter is measuring respondents' desire to answer in socially acceptable ways. Low correlation is evidence that the scale is relatively free of social desirability bias.

REFERENCES:

Carlson, Les and Sanford Grossbart (1988), "Parental Style and Consumer Socialization of Children," *JCR*, 15 (June), 77-94.

Childers, Terry L., Michael J. Houston, and Susan E. Heckler (1985), "Measurement of Individual Differences in Visual Versus Verbal Information Processing," *JCR*, 12 (September), 125-134.

Crowne, Douglas P. and David Marlowe (1960), "A New Scale of Social Desirability Independent of Psychopathology," *Journal of Consulting Psychology,* 24 (August), 349-354.

Friedman, Margaret L. and Gilbert A. Churchill, Jr. (1987), "Using Consumer Perceptions and a Contingency Approach to Improve Health Care Delivery," *JCR*, 13 (March), 492-510.

Moore, Ellen M., William O. Bearden, and Jesse E. Teel (1985), "Use of Labeling and Assertions of Dependency in Appeals for Consumer Support," *JCR*, 12 (June), 90-96.

Raju, P. S. (1980), "Optimum Stimulation Level: Its Relationship to Personality, Demographics, and Exploratory Behavior," *JCR*, 7 (December), 272-282.

Richins, Marsha L. (1983), "An Analysis of Consumer Interaction Styles in the Marketplace," *JCR*, 10 (June), 73-82.

Saxe, Robert and Barton A. Weitz (1982), "The SOCO Scale: A Measure of the Customer Orientation of Salespeople," *JMR*, 19 (August), 343-351.

Unger, Lynette S. (1981), "Measure Validation in the Leisure Domain," unpublished doctoral dissertation, University of Cincinnati.

_____ and Jerome B. Kernan (1983), "On the Meaning of Leisure: An Investigation of Some Determinants of the Subjective Experience," *JCR*, 9 (March), 381-391.

Westbrook, Robert A. (1980), "Intrapersonal Affective Influences on Consumer Satisfaction with Products," *JCR*, 7 (June), 49-54.

_____ (1987), "Product/Consumption-Based Affective Responses and Postpurchase Processes," *JMR*, 24 (August), 258-270.

SCALE ITEMS: SOCIAL DESIRABILITY BIAS (MARLOWE-CROWNE) +

1. Before voting I thoroughly investigate the qualifications of all the candidates.(T)
2. I never hesitate to go out of my way to help someone in trouble. (T)
3. It is sometimes hard for me to go on with my work if I am not encouraged. (F)
4. I have never intensely disliked anyone. (T)
5. On occasion I have had doubts about my ability to succeed in life. (F)
6. I sometimes feel resentful when I don't get my way. (F)

7. I am always careful about my manner of dress. **(T)**
8. My table manners at home are as good as when I eat out in a restaurant. **(T)**
9. If I could get into a movie without paying and be sure I was not seen I would probably do it. **(F)**
10. On a few occasions, I have given up doing something because I thought too little of my ability. **(F)**
11. I like gossip at times. **(F)**
12. There have been times when I felt like rebelling against people in authority even though I knew they were right. **(F)**
13. No matter who I'm talking to, I'm always a good listener. **(T)**
14. I can remember "playing sick" to get out of something. **(F)**
15. There have been occasions when I took advantage of someone. **(F)**
16. I'm always willing to admit it when I've made a mistake. **(T)**
17. I always try to practice what I preach. **(T)**
18. I don't find it particularly difficult to get along with loud mouthed, obnoxious people. **(T)**
19. I sometimes try to get even rather than forgive and forget. **(F)**
20. When I don't know something I don't at all mind admitting it. **(T)**
21. I am always courteous, even to people who are disagreeable. **(T)**
22. At times I have really insisted on having things my way. **(F)**
23. There have been occasions when I felt like smashing things. **(F)**
24. I would never think of letting someone else be punished for my wrong-doings. **(T)**
25. I never resent being asked to return a favor. **(T)**
26. I have never been irked when people expressed ideas very different from my own. **(T)**
27. I never make a long trip without checking the safety of my car. **(T)**
28. There have been times when I was quite jealous of the good fortune of others. **(F)**
29. I have almost never felt the urge to tell someone off. **(T)**
30. I am sometimes irritated by people who ask favors of me. **(F)**
31. I have never felt that I was punished without cause. **(T)**
32. I sometimes think when people have a misfortune they only got what they deserved. **(F)**
33. I have never deliberately said something that hurt someone's feelings. **(T)**

+ The symbol following each item indicates the socially desirable response. Respondents receive a point each time they answer in a socially desirable manner.

SCALE NAME: Source Pressuring

SCALE DESCRIPTION:

A two-item, semantic differential summated ratings scale designed to measure the degree of pressure a person reports from the source of a message due to the statements made.

SCALE ORIGIN:

Though Swasy and Munch (1985) noted that this construct has been examined in previous studies, this scaled measure appears to be original to their work.

SAMPLES:

Swasy and Munch (1985) collected data from **160** male and female, sophomore and junior business majors who volunteered for the study and were each paid $3 for their participation. A language lab was used for experimental sessions. A $2 \times 2 \times 2$ factorial design was used with 20 students assigned to each cell. The sample in the Munch and Swasy (1988) study was extremely similar. Data were collected from **240** undergraduate students at a large eastern university who were paid $3 each for participating. The experiment was conducted in a language laboratory. A $2 \times 2 \times 3$ factorial design was used with 20 subjects per cell. The few subjects who reported ownership or use of the product under examination were excluded from the study.

RELIABILITY:

Alpha values of **.81** and **.90** were reported for the scale by Swasy and Munch (1985) and Munch and Swasy (1988), respectively.

VALIDITY:

No specific assessment of scale validity was reported in either article.

ADMINISTRATION:

In both studies the scale was self-administered along with other measures after the treatment (message presented by a speaker). Higher scores on the scale indicate that respondents felt a lot of pressure due to the speaker's remarks whereas lower scores suggest that they experienced little pressure.

MAJOR FINDINGS:

Both studies examined the effect of rhetorical questions on message processing. Significant main effects were found in both studies on perceived **pressure** related to argument strength such that subjects expressed feeling more **pressure** when rhetorical (versus declarative) arguments were used.

REFERENCES:

Munch, James M. and John L. Swasy (1988), ''Rhetorical Question, Summarization Frequency, and Argument Strength Effects on Recall,'' *JCR*, 15 (June), 69-76.

Swasy, John L. and James M. Munch (1985), ''Examining the Target of Receiver Elaborations: Rhetorical Question Effects on Source Processing and Persuasion,'' *JCR*, 11 (March), 877-886.

SCALE ITEMS: SOURCE PRESSURING +

To what degree did you feel the speaker was pressuring you?

1. Low pressure   ____ : ____ : ____ : ____ : ____ : ____ : ____   High pressure
            1   2   3   4   5   6   7

2. Not pushy   ____ : ____ : ____ : ____ : ____ : ____ : ____   Pushy
            1   2   3   4   5   6   7

3. Unaggressive   ____ : ____ : ____ : ____ : ____ : ____ : ____   Aggressive
            1   2   3   4   5   6   7

+ Items 2 and 3 were used by Swasy and Munch (1985) whereas items 1 and 2 were used by Munch and Swasy (1988). Also, the exact opening statements were not provided in either article.

SCALE NAME: Spontaneity

SCALE DESCRIPTION:

A five-item, six-point Likert-type summated ratings scale that is supposed to measure the degree to which **a person feels an activity is not routine, planned, or anticipated.** The activity investigated by Unger (1981; Unger and Kernan 1983) was subjective leisure.

SCALE ORIGIN:

Though relevant literature was surveyed prior to scale construction, the items themselves and certainly the scale as a whole are original to Unger (1981).

SAMPLES:

The scale was developed in one stage of the overall study and then used to test hypotheses in another stage. In the first stage, the scale was administered by three different people to a total of **169** undergraduate business students at Miami University and the University of Cincinnati (Unger 1981). In the second stage, the questionnaires were delivered and picked up by members of a Girl Scout troop. A quota sample of **160** adults living in the Cincinnati SMSA was used that balanced eight equal age-by-sex groups. However, the sample was representative of neither the Cincinnati SMSA nor the U.S. population as a whole, being composed mostly of white people (98%) of middle to upper socioeconomic status (84%).

RELIABILITY:

The final scale consists of items that remained after several tests of reliability. The tests were conducted for the scale in six different situations. Alpha values for the scale ranged from **.66** to **.77**. See Unger (1981) for more detailed information.

VALIDITY:

Factor analyses provided support that the items tend to load together.

ADMINISTRATION:

The scale was self-administered by respondents in both stages of the survey described above. High scores on the scale indicate respondents perceive an activity to have a high level of **spontaneity** whereas low scores imply respondents perceive it to be more routine or planned.

MAJOR FINDINGS:

Unger (1981; Unger and Kernan 1983) examined dimensions of the subjective leisure experience across six different situations. **Perceived spontaneity** was not found to be one of the primary determinants of subjective leisure across situations. Instead, it appeared to be linked to just some kinds of leisure activity.

REFERENCES:

Unger, Lynette S. (1981), "Measure Validation in the Leisure Domain," unpublished doctoral dissertation, University of Cincinnati.

_____ and Jerome B. Kernan (1983), "On the Meaning of Leisure: An Investigation of Some Determinants of the Subjective Experience," *JCR*, 9 (March), 381-391.

SCALE ITEMS: SPONTANEITY +

Strongly Disagree	Disagree	Slightly Disagree	Slightly Agree	Agree	Strongly Agree
1	2	3	4	5	6

1. It happens without warning or pre-thought.
2. It is a spontaneous occurrence.
3. It happens "out of the blue."
4. It is a "spur-of-the-moment" thing.
5. I wouldn't know the day before that it was going to happen.

+ The questionnaire described a situation for respondents and they were asked to respond to the statements as they felt about the situation.

SCALE NAME: Sports Activeness

SCALE DESCRIPTION:

A three-item, six-point, Likert-type summated ratings scale going from strongly disagree (1) to strongly agree (6). The scale measures a person's degree of personal involvement in sports activities, *not* just being a spectator. It was referred to as Sports Enthusiast by Lumpkin and Darden (1982) and Physical Fitness by Hawes and Lumpkin (1984).

SCALE ORIGIN:

It is not clear where the items originated nor where they were first used as a multi-item summated ratings scale.

SAMPLES:

Lumpkin and Darden (1982) had **145** usable responses gathered from the consumer research panel of the University of Arkansas. Data were collected from the individuals by mail questionnaire.

Hawes and Lumpkin (1984) collected data from **581** residents of 14 communities near the Ft. Worth-Dallas metroplex. Each of the communities was randomly sampled in proportion to its population by means of the respective telephone directories. The questionnaire was to be filled out by the household member responsible for most of the shopping. The distribution of respondents by community was similar to the actual population distribution.

Lumpkin (1985) analyzed data collected from a sample drawn from the Market Facts Consumer Mail Panel. A total of **2854** completed questionnaires were received, but Lumpkin focused just on **373** respondents who indicated they were 65 years of age or older.

RELIABILITY:

Alpha values of **.6** , **.609**, and **.6918** were reported by Lumpkin and Darden (1982), Hawes and Lumpkin (1984), and Lumpkin (1985), respectively.

VALIDITY:

Factor analysis indicated the items loaded together.

ADMINISTRATION:

Data were gathered in each of the studies through self-administered mail questionnaires. Scale scores are calculated by averaging numerical responses to individual items. A score of 6 indicates that a person has a strong tendency to make exercise and playing sports a major part of his/her life whereas 1 implies that a person is relatively uninvolved in athletic activities.

MAJOR FINDINGS:

In their study of television program preference groups, Lumpkin and Darden (1982) found that sports enthusiasm was one of a few lifestyle variables that differentiated between the six groups. The group with the highest mean score on the scale seemed to prefer male-oriented programs (*Monday Night Football* but also *60 Minutes*); the group with the lowest mean score seemed to like female-oriented comedies and dramas.

The purpose of the study by Hawes and Lumpkin (1984) was to examine demographic and psychographic characteristics of outshoppers. Involvement in sports and exercising significantly differentiated between inshoppers and outshoppers. Persons who engaged in outshopping the most expressed the greatest inclination to be **active in sports**.

Elderly consumers were cluster analyzed by Lumpkin (1985) and **sports activeness** discriminated somewhat between the three groups, though the level of statistical significance was not reported. The group with the highest mean on the scale was the most socially active and had the most interest in shopping and the arts. The group with the lowest mean score appeared to be much less active all around.

COMMENTS:

Reliability and validity might be improved if scale items related to either exercise *or* playing sports, but *not both* in the same measure.

REFERENCES:

Hawes, Jon M. and James R. Lumpkin (1984), "Understanding the Outshopper, *JAMS*, 12 (Fall), 200-218.

Lumpkin, James R. (1985), "Shopping Orientation Segmentation of the Elderly Consumer," *JAMS*, 13 (Spring), 271-289.

_____ and William R. Darden (1982), "Relating Television Preference Viewing to Shopping Orientations, Lifestyles, and Demographics," *JA*, 11 (4), 56-67.

SCALE ITEMS: SPORTS ACTIVENESS +

Strongly Disagree	Disagree	Slightly Disagree	Slightly Agree	Agree	Strongly Agree
1	2	3	4	5	6

1. I bowl, play tennis, golf, or other active sports quite a lot.
2. I exercise regularly to stay physically fit.
3. Sports are a big part of my life.

+ Hawes and Lumpkin (1984) used just items 1 and 2.

SCALE NAME: Sports Enthusiasm

SCALE DESCRIPTION:

A four-item, six-point, Likert-type summated ratings scale from strongly disagree (1) to strongly agree (6). The scale measures a person's interest in watching, talking about, reading about, and attending sporting events, *not* necessarily participating in sports. A five-item scale was used by Dickerson and Gentry (1983).

SCALE ORIGIN:

As a set, these items were referred to as Sports Spectator and were part of a classic study of psychographics by Wells and Tigert (1971). One thousand questionnaires were mailed to homemaker members of the Market Facts mail panel. In addition to gathering demographic, product use, and media data, the survey contained 300 statements that have since served as the basis for the construction of many lifestyle-related scales. The four items for this scale are reported in the article, but they were not analyzed as a multi-item scale. The purpose of the article was to explain how psychographics could improve upon mere demographic description of target audiences and product users. No psychometric information was reported.

SAMPLES:

Two mailing lists were used to collect data in the Dickerson and Gentry study (1983). One was a list of *Psychology Today* subscribers and the other was a list of members of computer clubs. The former was used to reach non-adopters of computers and the latter was used to reach PC adopters. Analysis was based on a total of **639** questionnaires. Results from a second mailing to non-respondents indicated that their demographic makeup was not significantly different from that of respondents. On the basis of 1980 Census data, the sample was younger and more upscale than the general population.

RELIABILITY:

The scale was reported to have an alpha of **.78** by Dickerson and Gentry (1983).

VALIDITY:

Factor analysis performed in the study indicated that the items loaded together.

ADMINISTRATION:

Data were gathered through self-administered mail questionnaires. Scale scores are typically calculated by averaging numerical responses to individual items. A score of 6 indicates a person is very interested in sports whereas 1 means a person has very little interest in most sport-related activities.

MAJOR FINDINGS:

Dickerson and Gentry (1983) examined characteristics of adopters of home computers. No explicit hypothesis involving sports enthusiasm was tested and no evidence was found to indicate a significant association between computer adoption and sports enthusiasm.

REFERENCES:

Dickerson, Mary D. and James W. Gentry (1983), "Characteristics of Adopters and Non-Adopters of Home Computers," *JCR*, 10 (September), 225-235.

Wells, William D. and Douglas Tigert (1971), "Activities, Interests, and Opinions," *JAR*, 11 (August), 27-35.

SCALE ITEMS: SPORTS ENTHUSIASM

Strongly Disagree	Disagree	Slightly Disagree	Slightly Agree	Agree	Strongly Agree
1	2	3	4	5	6

1. I like to watch or listen to baseball or football games.
2. I usually read the sports page in the daily paper.
3. I thoroughly enjoy conversations about sports.
4. I would rather go to a sporting event than a dance.

SCALE NAME: Store Familiarity Importance

SCALE DESCRIPTION:

A four-item, five-point Likert-type summated ratings scale measuring store-related attitudes with an emphasis on the stated tendency to limit shopping to a few stores with which the respondent is familiar.

SCALE ORIGIN:

The measure originates from a dissertation published by Moschis in 1978. His 1981 study, reported below, is from that same dissertation research.

SAMPLES:

Moschis' (1981) data came from **806** middle school or senior high school students. There were 365 "older" adolescents (15 years and older) and 441 "younger" adolescents (younger than 15 years). The students came from 13 schools and seven towns in Wisconsin representing a wide variety of urban to rural situations. The author indicates that the sample was well balanced in terms of most demographic characteristics except sex, as nearly two-thirds of the respondents were female.

RELIABILITY:

An alpha of .52 was reported for the scale.

VALIDITY:

No examination of scale validity was reported.

ADMINISTRATION:

The scale was self-administered by students along with several other measures in a 10-page instrument during a regular class session. Lower scores on the scale indicate that respondents tend to concentrate their shopping in a few well-known stores whereas higher scores suggest that they shop at a variety of stores and do not exhibit as much loyalty.

MAJOR FINDINGS:

The study investigated the validity of the cognitive development approach to socialization (e.g., Piaget) to predict a wide variety of consumer-related cognitions learned during adolescence. In general, the findings indicated that the cognitive developmental model did not explain consumer socialization during adolescence very well. Though older adolescents had significantly less favorable attitudes toward advertising, brands, and prices than younger children, the two groups were not significantly different in their **store attitudes**.

COMMENTS:

The low internal consistency indicates that the scale is not reliable. This could be due to several different factors being represented in the scale. Redevelopment and testing are needed before the scale is used further.

REFERENCES:

Moschis, George P. (1978), *Acquisition of the Consumer Role by Adolescents*, Research Monograph No. 82. Atlanta, Ga.: Publishing Services Division, College of Business Administration, Georgia State University.
_____ (1981), "Patterns of Consumer Learning," *JAMS*, 9 (2), 110-126.

SCALE ITEMS: STORE FAMILIARITY IMPORTANCE

Strongly Disagree	Agree	Neutral	Disagree	Strongly Agree
1	2	3	4	5

1. Once I have made a choice on which store to buy things from, I prefer shopping there without trying other stores.
2. Well-known stores never sell poor quality products.
3. I prefer doing most of my shopping in the same stores I have always shopped in.
4. I judge the value of some products by the name of the store that sells them.

SCALE NAME: Store Image

SCALE DESCRIPTION:

A 13-item, seven-point Likert-type scale measuring a consumer's attitude about a store, especially department or discount retailers.

SCALE ORIGIN:

The scale was developed by Wu and Petroshius (1987), though the items were based on several unspecified previous studies of store image. The latter studies are likely to be the same as those cited in the description of the Involvement (Store) scale.

SAMPLES:

A convenience sample of **86** male and female students attending a large midwestern university was used. The subjects were randomly divided into two groups and a different version of the questionnaire was administered to each group.

RELIABILITY:

The scale was used in the study to measure respondents' attitudes toward 10 different retailers. Alpha was calculated for each of the stores and ranged from **.77** to **.91**.

VALIDITY:

No definite examination of validity was reported. However, the authors did perform some sort of preliminary examination of the items in a pretest. Of the 20 items used in the study, just the 13 that increased the alpha coefficient composed the final scale.

ADMINISTRATION:

Though not specified, data collection by self-administered questionnaires apparently was completed by students in a classroom setting. The exact method of calculating scale scores was not specified, but is likely to have been based on the total or average of the numerical responses to individual scale items. Higher scores indicate that consumers have positive attitudes toward a retailer whereas lower scores indicate that consumers perceive a store to have a poor image.

MAJOR FINDINGS:

The study compared the alternative questionnaire formats on the magnitude of the halo effect in measuring **store image**. The halo effect is the tendency of a respondent to bias ratings of individual scale items in line with his/her overall attitude toward the object being evaluated. The format that was hypothesized to minimize the halo effect produced **store image** scores not significantly better than those obtained with the other format. The authors suggest that selection of a measurement format can be based on issues other than concern about the halo effect.

REFERENCE:

Wu, Bob T. W. and Susan M. Petroshius, (1987), ''The Halo Effect in Store Image Measurement,'' *JAMS*, 15 (Fall), 44- 51.

SCALE ITEMS: STORE IMAGE +

Strongly Disagree	Disagree	Slightly Disagree	Neutral	Slightly Agree	Agree	Strongly Agree
1	2	3	4	5	6	7

1. The store has a pleasant atmosphere.
2. The store has well-known brands.
3. The store has low quality products. **(r)**
4. The store has good service.
5. The store's sales clerks are well-dressed.
6. The store has knowledgeable sales clerks.
7. The store has an unlimited selection of products.
8. The store has helpful sales clerks.
9. The store attracts upper-class customers.
10. The store has an attractive layout.
11. The store is prestigious.
12. The store has informative advertising.
13. The store is pleasant to shop in.

+ The graphic rating scale and verbal anchors were not specified in the article, but are likely to have been similar to those shown here.

SCALE NAME: Store Pricing Importance

SCALE DESCRIPTION:

A three-item, five-point Likert-type summated ratings scale measuring the degree to which a consumer considers the prices charged by a store to be important.

SCALE ORIGIN:

As a summated scale, the measure is original to Saegert, Hoover, and Hilger (1985). Ideas for the items may have come from measures used by Kelly and Stephenson (1967). The items in that study were used in the form of bipolar descriptors and do not appear to have been summated.

SAMPLES:

Saegert, Hoover, and Hilger (1985) reported on four surveys, only two of which used the scale of interest. One of those studies involved a random selection of 1000 Spanish names and 1000 non-Spanish names and mailing questionnaires to those individuals. A total of **299** questionnaires were returned. The response rates for both groups were very low (9% for Hispanics and 21% for others), indicating a need to confirm the findings with personal interviews in another sample. The second survey of interest was conducted in a small Texas town with **195** women (95 Hispanic and 100 non-Hispanic) who were selected randomly from blocks in the town and houses within the blocks.

RELIABILITY:

An alpha of **.66** was calculated for the scale.

VALIDITY:

A factor analysis of 25 shopping-related items indicated that the items in this scale loaded together. (Information in the article as well as some provided by Saegert in personal correspondence suggests that the factor analysis and the alpha reported above were based on data collected just in the mail survey. The article specifically states, however, that analyses of the separate ethnic groups as well as the data from the personal interviews produced almost identical factor interpretations.)

ADMINISTRATION:

In one survey the scale was self-administered as part of a mail questionnaire and in the other survey it was administered by bilingual interviewers. Higher scores on the scale indicate consumers think price-related issues of a store are very important.

MAJOR FINDINGS:

The authors used the results of four surveys to examine differences between Anglo-Americans and Mexican-Americans in shopping-related attitudes and behaviors. In both surveys described above, the **pricing-related issues** were significantly more important to

Hispanics than to non-Hispanics. For both ethnic groups it was among the most important shopping factors of those studied.

COMMENTS:

The low internal consistency is likely to be due to the scale items tapping into slightly different constructs. Some refinement in this measure appears to be necessary before it is used further.

REFERENCES:

Kelly, Robert F. and Ronald Stephenson (1967), "The Semantic Differential: An Information Source for Designing Retail Patronage Appeals," *JM*, 31 (October), 43-47.
Saegert, Joel, Robert J. Hoover, and Marye Tharp Hilger (1985), "Characteristics of Mexican American Consumers," *JCR*, 12 (June), 104-109.

SCALE ITEMS: STORE PRICING IMPORTANCE +

Not important at all   ____ : ____ : ____ : ____ : ____   Very important

                                           1   2   3   4   5

1. The store has low prices.
2. The store has helpful ads.
3. The store has lots of specials.

+ These items were reconstructed from phrases supplied in personal correspondence from Saegert.

SCALE NAME: Subjective Norms (Soft Drink)

SCALE DESCRIPTION:

A three-item, nine-point summated ratings scale measuring the degree to which a person believes consuming soft drinks is acceptable to friends and family. It was referred to by Beatty and Kahle (1988) as Subjective Norm.

SCALE ORIGIN:

The items were original to Beatty and Kahle (1988), but they note their sentences were modeled after those used in similar types of constructs measured by Fishbein and Ajzen (1975) as well as Ajzen and Fishbein (1980).

SAMPLES:

Data were collected from respondents at two points in time, four weeks apart. The sample was composed of **187** student volunteers enrolled in various undergraduate business courses at three universities in the western United States. The proportions of men and women were unspecified, but noted to be approximately equal. The product examined was soft drinks, and college students were thought to be an appropriate convenience sample. The majority (88%) had consumed at least one soft drink in the previous week.

RELIABILITY:

Alpha values of **.59** and **.56** were reported for the scale for times 1 and 2, respectively. Test-retest stability was **.47**.

VALIDITY:

No examination of scale validity was reported.

ADMINISTRATION:

The scale was filled out by students as part of a larger self-administered questionnaire in an unspecified setting. Higher scores on this scale imply that respondents believe their family and friends think consuming soft drinks is acceptable whereas lower scores suggest that they believe such people do not think it is acceptable behavior.

MAJOR FINDINGS:

The authors investigated the association between attitudes and behaviors in the consumption of a frequently purchased product (soft drinks). The theory of reasoned action and the low involvement hierarchy model were specifically tested. **Subjective norms** was **not** found to be significantly associated with drinking intentions for either high or low brand-committed drinkers, but rather was found to be related to drinking behavior of the previous week.

COMMENTS:

Because of evidence of poor reliability and no known evidence of demonstrated validity, the scale should not be used further until its psychometric quality can be improved considerably.

REFERENCES:

Ajzen, Icek and Martin Fishbein (1980), *Understanding Attitudes and Predicting Social Behavior*. Engelwood Cliffs, N.J.: Prentice-Hall, Inc.

Beatty, Sharon E. and Lynn R. Kahle (1988), "Alternative Hierarchies of the Attitude-Behavior Relationship: The Impact of Brand Commitment and Habit," *JAMS*, 16 (Summer), 1-10.

Fishbein, Martin and Icek Ajzen (1975), *Belief, Attitude, Intention, and Behavior: An Introduction to Theory and Research*. Reading, Mass.: Addison-Wesley Publishing Company.

SCALE ITEMS: SUBJECTIVE NORMS (SOFT DRINK)

Unlikely ____ : ____ : ____ : ____ : ____ : ____ : ____ : ____ : ____ Likely
         1   2   3   4   5   6   7   8   9

1. Most people who are important to me think that it is okay to drink soft drinks.
2. My family thinks I should *not* drink soft drinks. **(r)**
3. My friends think that I should drink soft drinks.

SCALE NAME: Task-Orientation of Salesperson (Customer's Perception)

SCALE DESCRIPTION:

A four-item, five-point Likert-type summated ratings scale measuring the degree to which a customer perceived a salesperson to have been interested and diligently attempting to complete a particular sales transaction. Williams and Spiro (1985) viewed this scale as measuring the task-oriented dimension of salesperson communication style, which is goal directed and purposeful.

SCALE ORIGIN:

The items were developed from work by Bass (1960) on orientation motivation. On the basis of previous work by others, he suggested that members of groups are motivated to remain in the groups for different reasons. He developed measures of three motivations: the task orientation, the interaction orientation, and the self orientation (Bass 1977). Williams and Spiro (1985) adapted these measures for their studies in two ways: their measures were more specific to the sales context and they were perceptions of others' behaviors, not self-perceptions.

SAMPLES:

Williams and Spiro (1985) collected data from all 13 sporting goods stores in a major southeastern U.S. city. Customers were approached just after leaving the stores. If they agreed to fill out a questionnaire, their respective salespeople were asked to fill out a survey instrument as well. A total of **251** dyadic interactions were captured, with the responses coming from 64 different salespeople and 251 different customers. All salespeople in the stores participated as did 90% of the customers who were approached.

RELIABILITY:

An alpha of .**76** was reported for the scale and item-total correlations were all above .70.

VALIDITY:

A factor analysis indicated that the items loaded higher on this factor than any other.

ADMINISTRATION:

As implied above, the customer completed a self-administered survey form that included several measures. The authors computed scale scores by averaging numerical responses to the items. Higher scores on the scale suggest that customers perceive the salespeople with whom they have just interacted to be very interested in completing the sale whereas lower scores imply that they feel their respective sales people were not interested, hard-working, and/or persistent enough in completing the sale.

MAJOR FINDINGS:

Williams and Spiro (1985) examined the use of communication styles in dyadic sales situations and their effect on sales outcomes. The findings indicated that though the communication styles of the two parties of the transaction play a role in the outcome, the customer's orientation has the greatest impact. **Salesperson's task orientation** didn't appear to fare well with any of the customer orientations studied.

REFERENCES:

Bass, Bernard M. (1960), *Leadership, Psychology, and Organizational Behavior.* New York, N.Y.: Harper Brothers.

_____ (1977), *ORI-Manual for the Orientation Inventory.* Palo Alto, Calif.: Consulting Psychologists Press, Inc.

Williams, Kaylene C. and Rosann L. Spiro (1985), "Communication Style in the Salesperson-Customer Dyad," *JMR*, 12 (November), 434-442.

SCALE ITEMS: TASK-ORIENTATION OF SALESPERSON (CUSTOMER'S PERCEPTION)

Strongly Disagree	Agree	Neutral	Disagree	Strongly Agree
1	2	3	4	5

1. This salesperson worked hard to complete the sale.
2. This salesperson wanted to complete the sale.
3. This salesperson's primary concern was to help me make a purchase.
4. This salesperson wanted to do the job well.

SCALE NAME: Time Management

SCALE DESCRIPTION:

A three-item, six-point, Likert-type summated ratings scale from strongly disagree (1) to strongly agree (6). The scale measures a person's tendency to schedule activities and organize time.

SCALE ORIGIN:

It is not clear where the items originated or where they were first used as a multi-item summated ratings scale.

SAMPLES:

Lumpkin and Darden (1982) had **145** usable responses gathered from the consumer re-search panel of the University of Arkansas. Data were collected from the individuals by mail questionnaire. Lumpkin (1985) collected data from a sample drawn from the Market Facts Consumer Mail Panel. A total of 2854 completed questionnaires were received, but Lumpkin focused on **373** respondents who indicated they were 65 years of age or older.

Hawes and Lumpkin (1984) collected data from **581** residents of 14 communities near the Ft. Worth-Dallas metroplex. Each of the communities was randomly sampled in proportion to its population by means of the respective telephone directories. The questionnaire was to be filled out by the household member responsible for most of the shopping. The distribution of respondents by community was similar to the actual popula-tion distribution.

RELIABILITY:

Alpha values of **.59**, **.7153**, and **.794** were calculated by Lumpkin and Darden (1982), Lumpkin (1985), and Hawes and Lumpkin (1984), respectively.

VALIDITY:

Factor analysis in the studies indicated the items loaded together.

ADMINISTRATION:

Data were gathered in the studies through self-administered mail questionnaires. Scale scores are calculated by averaging numerical responses to individual items. A score of 6 indicates that a person has a strong tendency to schedule activities and time whereas 1 implies that a person is much less organized according to time.

MAJOR FINDINGS:

In their study of television program preference groups, Lumpkin and Darden (1982) found a few lifestyle variables that were significantly different between the six groups, but **time management** was *not* one of them.

Elderly consumers were cluster analyzed by Lumpkin (1985) and **time management** appeared to discriminate between the three groups (statistical significance not reported). The group with the highest mean on the scale was the most socially active and had the most interest in shopping and the arts. The group with the lowest mean score appeared to be most less active all around and may have had much less need to organize their time to any great degree.

The purpose of the study by Hawes and Lumpkin (1984) was to examine demographic and psychographic characteristics of outshoppers. **Time management** did **not** significantly differentiate between inshoppers and outshoppers.

REFERENCES:

Hawes, Jon M. and James R. Lumpkin (1984), ''Understanding the Outshopper,'' *JAMS*, 12 (Fall), 200-218.

Lumpkin, James R. (1985), ''Shopping Orientation Segmentation of the Elderly Consumer,'' *JAMS*, 13 (Spring), 271-289.

_____ and William R. Darden (1982), ''Relating Television Preference Viewing to Shopping Orientations, Lifestyles, and Demographics,'' *JA*, 11 (4), 56-67.

SCALE ITEMS: TIME MANAGEMENT +

Strongly Disagree	Disagree	Slightly Disagree	Slightly Agree	Agree	Strongly Agree
1	2	3	4	5	6

1. I organize my time better than most people.
2. I like to plan my activities by the clock.
3. Because I schedule my activities by the clock, I am able to get more things done.

+ Lumpkin (1985) used all three items whereas Lumpkin and Darden (1982) used just items 1 and 2 and Hawes and Lumpkin (1984) used items 2 and 3.

SCALE NAME: Time Pressure

SCALE DESCRIPTION:

A five-item, six-point, Likert-type summated ratings scale ranging from strongly disagree (1) to strongly agree (6). The scale measures a person's desire to minimize the time spent on common activities and was referred to as Time Spent In Everyday Activities by Dickerson and Gentry (1983).

SCALE ORIGIN:

The items were generated and first used as a summated ratings scale by Dickerson and Gentry (1983).

SAMPLES:

Two mailing lists were used to collect data in the Dickerson and Gentry study (1983). One was a list of *Psychology Today* subscribers and the other was a list of members of computer clubs. The former was used to reach non-adopters of computers and the latter was used to reach PC adopters. Analysis was based on a total of **639** questionnaires. Results from a second mailing to non- respondents indicated that their demographic makeup was not significantly different from that of respondents. On the basis of 1980 Census data, the sample was younger and more upscale than the general population.

RELIABILITY:

An alpha of **.46** was calculated for the scale in the Dickerson and Gentry (1983) study.

VALIDITY:

Factor analysis indicated the items loaded together.

ADMINISTRATION:

Data were gathered through self-administered mail questionnaires. Scale scores are calculated by averaging numerical responses to individual items. A score of 6 indicates that a person spends a lot of time in many everyday activities whereas 1 suggests that a person tries to spend little time in such activities in order to save energy or have more leisure time.

MAJOR FINDINGS:

Dickerson and Gentry (1983) found that the scale was one of several lifestyle variables that was a significant discriminator between adopters and non-adopters of home computers. Specifically, adopters expressed greater concern about the **time** involved in everyday activities than did the nonadopters.

COMMENTS:

The internal validity is extremely low and could be improved through addition of items that focus better on the construct of interest. As it is, the items could relate to different issues, thus lowering the scale's reliability.

REFERENCE:

Dickerson, Mary D. and James W. Gentry (1983), "Characteristics of Adopters and Non-Adopters of Home Computers," *JCR*, 10 (September), 225-235.

SCALE ITEMS: TIME PRESSURE

Strongly Disagree	Disagree	Slightly Disagree	Slightly Agree	Agree	Strongly Agree
1	2	3	4	5	6

1. If I could spend less time taking care of everyday activities, I would be able to do the things I enjoy the most.
2. Menu planning, food and household shopping take quite a bit of my time.
3. I like to spend as little time as possible taking care of bill paying, shopping for groceries, keeping financial records and running errands.
4. Shopping for gifts, clothes, shoes, and household items has become a real burden on my time.
5. As energy costs go up, I will probably need to do more shopping from my home to conserve energy.

SCALE NAME: Time Pressure

SCALE DESCRIPTION:

A six-item, six-point, Likert-type summated ratings scale ranging from strongly disagree (1) to strongly agree (6). The scale measures a person's lack of free time for him/herself each day. It was referred to as My Time Oriented by Lumpkin (1985). See also Hawes and Lumpkin (1984) for a variation of this scale.

SCALE ORIGIN:

It is not clear where the items originated or where they were first used as a multi-item summated ratings scale.

SAMPLES:

Lumpkin and Darden (1982) had **145** usable responses gathered from the consumer research panel of the University of Arkansas. Data were collected from the individuals by mail questionnaire. Lumpkin (1985) analyzed data collected from a sample drawn from the Market Facts Consumer Mail Panel. A total of 2854 completed questionnaires were received, but Lumpkin focused just on **373** respondents who indicated they were 65 years of age or older.

RELIABILITY:

Alpha values of **.59** and **.6882** were calculated by Lumpkin and Darden (1982) and Lumpkin (1985), respectively.

VALIDITY:

Factor analysis indicated the items loaded together.

ADMINISTRATION:

Data were gathered in the studies through self-administered mail questionnaires. Scale scores are calculated by averaging numerical responses to individual items. A score of 6 indicates that a person is routinely in a hurry and wants more free time each day whereas 1 implies that a person already has sufficient free time.

MAJOR FINDINGS:

In their study of television program preference groups, Lumpkin and Darden (1982) found that **time pressure** was one of a few lifestyle variables that were significantly different between the six groups. The group with the highest score on the scale preferred female-oriented comedies and dramas, had the largest percentage of unmarried persons, and half of the married women were employed. The group with the lowest score on the scale most preferred *Monday Night Football*, had a mixture of other preferences, and had a much higher mean age than the other group.

Elderly consumers were cluster analyzed by Lumpkin (1985) and time for self did not appear to discriminate much between the three groups, though the level of statistical significance was not reported.

COMMENTS:

The internal consistency of the longer version of the scale is higher, but still not high enough for the scale to be considered very reliable. Further development and testing appear to be necessary.

REFERENCES:

Hawes, Jon M. and James R. Lumpkin (1984), "Understanding the Outshopper," *JAMS*, 12 (Fall), 200-218.

Lumpkin, James R. (1985), "Shopping Orientation Segmentation of the Elderly Consumer," *JAMS*, 13 (Spring), 271-289.

_____ and William R. Darden (1982), "Relating Television Preference Viewing to Shopping Orientations, Lifestyles, and Demographics," *JA*, 11 (4), 56-67.

SCALE ITEMS: TIME PRESSURE +

Strongly Disagree	Disagree	Slightly Disagree	Slightly Agree	Agree	Strongly Agree
1	2	3	4	5	6

1. I take time off for leisure activities every day. **(r)**
2. I do things every day that are for "me. **(r)**
3. I set aside time each day for myself. **(r)**
4. I never seem to have enough time to do the things I want to.
5. I always seem to be in a hurry.
6. I have plenty of free time. **(r)**

+ Lumpkin (1985) used all six items whereas Lumpkin and Darden (1982) used just items 4, 5, and 6.

SCALE NAME: Value (Object)

SCALE DESCRIPTION:

A 10-item, six-point Likert-like summated ratings scale purporting to measure the usefulness and/or enjoyment a person perceives in an object such as a good or service.

SCALE ORIGIN:

The scale appears to be original to Deighton, Romer, and McQueen (1989) and is only known to have been used in their study.

SAMPLES:

A total of **1215** persons participated in the study and were recruited at malls in 10 U.S. cities. Between 29 and 31 subjects rated each of the 40 ads examined in the study.

RELIABILITY:

The scale was administered to subjects both before and after they had viewed a commercial. The pre-test alpha was **.91** and the post-test alpha was **.93**.

VALIDITY:

The validity of the scale was not specifically examined. The authors did note that results of a factor analysis indicated respondents differentiated between two kinds of value, one related to "enjoyment" and the other related more to "usefulness."

ADMINISTRATION:

The scale was self-administered via computer before and after the subject viewed a test commercial. Higher scores on the scale suggest a person perceives an object to be valuable whereas lower scores imply that a person views an object as useless and/or unenjoyable.

MAJOR FINDINGS:

The authors examined the extent to which the form (arguments versus dramatization) of a commercial influences viewer processing. The scale was used to measure persuasiveness by determining whether the advertised product increased in **value** after exposure to the commercial. Characteristics of good argument-laden ads were different from those of ads that were more dramatic in form. For example, persuasive drama ads appeared to produce more feeling and empathy but less counterargumentation.

REFERENCE:

Deighton, John, Daniel Romer, and Josh McQueen (1989), "Using Drama to Persuade," *JCR*, 16 (December), 335-343.

SCALE ITEMS: VALUE (OBJECT)

Does not describe ____ : ____ : ____ : ____ : ____ : ____   Describes
at all   1   2   3   4   5   6   extremely well

1. important
2. relevant
3. useful
4. helps get things done
5. necessary
6. enjoyable
7. reflects my personality
8. gives me pleasure
9. exciting
10. desirable

SCALE NAME: Value (Offer)

SCALE DESCRIPTION:

A four-item, nine-point bipolar adjective, summated ratings scale measuring the perceived value of a deal consisting of a certain product offered at a certain price. A very similar scale with three Likert-type items was used by Urbany, Bearden, and Weilbaker (1988).

SCALE ORIGIN:

The bipolar adjectives employed by Burton and Lichtenstein (1988) as well as Lichtenstein and Bearden (1989) were used previously by Berkowitz and Walton (1980). However, the latter did not sum responses to the items.

SAMPLES:

Urbany, Bearden, and Weilbaker (1988) reported two studies. Both used junior and senior level business majors, one with **150** students and the other with **168**. Analyses by Burton and Lichtenstein (1988) as well as Lichtenstein and Bearden (1989) were based on the same data collected from **278** undergraduate business students. The students were randomly assigned to one of 12 treatment conditions in a 2 × 2 × 3 experimental design. There were between 21 and 28 students per cell.

RELIABILITY:

Alpha values of **.79** and **.86** were obtained by Urbany, Bearden, and Weilbaker (1988) in the two uses of their scale. An alpha of **.80** was reported for the scale used by Burton and Lichtenstein (1988) as well as Lichtenstein and Bearden (1989).

VALIDITY:

No examination of scale validity was reported in any of the studies.

ADMINISTRATION:

In the two studies by Urbany and his coauthors, students responded to questions posed to them on a PC in a university computer lab. The scale used by Burton and Lichtenstein (1988) as well as Lichtenstein and Bearden (1989) was self-administered by students along with several other measures in an experimental setting. Higher scores on the scale imply that respondents perceive a deal (price and product) to be a very good value whereas lower scores mean that respondents do not think that the offer is a good buy.

MAJOR FINDINGS:

Urbany and his coauthors studied the effect of price claims on consumer perceptions and price search behavior. Their findings from two experiments indicated that ads with high plausible reference prices for products led to greater perceptions of **value** than ads with no reference prices provided.

Burton and Lichtenstein (1988) as well as Lichtenstein and Bearden (1989) examined the influence of merchant-supplied reference prices, ad distinctiveness, and ad message consistency on perception of source credibility, value of the deal, and attitude toward the deal. Burton and Lichtenstein (1988) found that perceptions of the **value of the offer** were strongly related to several measures of attitude toward the ad. Further, they found a price discount to have a significant effect on attitude toward the ad even after covarying out perceptions of the **value of the offer.** Among many other findings, Lichtenstein and Bearden (1989) reported that perceived **value of the offer** was greatest when the retailers used distinctive ads that did not offer similar deals frequently. Also, the perceived **value of the offer** was greater for plausible high merchant-supplied prices than for implausible merchant-supplied prices.

COMMENTS:

The specific products examined in the studies were a television set (Urbany, Bearden, and Weilbaker 1988) and a desk (Burton and Lichtenstein 1988; Lichtenstein and Bearden 1989), but the items below are general enough for use in studying many other products categories.

REFERENCES:

Berkowitz, Eric N. and John R. Walton (1980), "Contextual Influences on Consumer Price Responses: An Experimental Analysis," *JMR*, 17 (August), 349-358.

Burton, Scot and Donald R. Lichtenstein (1988), "The Effect of Ad Claims and Ad Context on Attitude Toward the Advertisement," *JA*, 17 (1), 3-11.

Lichtenstein, Donald R. and William O. Bearden (1989), "Contextual Influences on Perceptions of Merchant-Supplied Reference Prices," *JCR*, 16 (June), 55-66.

Urbany, Joel E., William O. Bearden, Dan C. Weilbaker (1988), "The Effect of Plausible and Exaggerated Reference Prices on Consumer Perceptions and Price Search," *JCR*, 15 (June), 95-110.

SCALE ITEMS: VALUE (OFFER) +

The semantic differential version of the scale as used by Burton and Lichtenstein (1988) as well as Lichtenstein and Bearden (1989).

1. The _____ is:

an ex-cellent buy									a bad buy
	9	8	7	6	5	4	3	2	1	

2. The prices represent:

an ex-tremely large sav-ings									no sav-ings at all
	9	8	7	6	5	4	3	2	1	

3. The price is:

an ex- tremely fair price	____	:	____	:	____	:	____	:	____	:	____	:	____	:	____	an ex- tremely unfair price
	9		8		7		6		5		4		3		2	1

4. The _____ is:

an ex- tremely good value	____	:	____	:	____	:	____	:	____	:	____	:	____	:	____	not a good value
	9		8		7		6		5		4		3		2	1

The version of the scale used by Urbany, Bearden, and Weilbaker (1988) with Likert-type items.

Strongly Disagree	Moderately Disagree	Slightly Disagree	Neither Agree Nor Disagree	Slightly Agree	Moderately Agree	Strongly Agree
1————	——2————	——3————	——4————	——5————	——6————	—7

1. The advertised _____ is an excellent buy for the money.
2. At the sale price, the _____ is not a very good value for the money. **(r)**
3. The advertised offer represents an extremely fair price.

+ The name of the product should be placed in the blanks.

SCALE NAME: Value (Offer)

SCALE DESCRIPTION:

> A six-item, seven-point Likert-like summated ratings scale measuring the perceived value of an offer consisting of a particular product for a particular price. The scale was used to study both calculators and typewriters.

SCALE ORIGIN:

> Petroshius and Monroe (1987) provide no information about the origin of the scale. Therefore, it is assumed to have been constructed specifically for use in their study.

SAMPLES:

> The sample was composed of **456** undergraduate students. Homogeneous subjects were desired because the study's purpose was to test theoretical propositions. The students were randomly assigned to one of 16 experimental conditions to test the hypotheses.

RELIABILITY:

> The alpha values reported for the two products examined were **.87** and **.92**.

VALIDITY:

> A factor analysis indicated that the items loaded together and not on other related factors (except for one item as noted above), providing some evidence of convergent and discriminant validity.

ADMINISTRATION:

> The scale was self-administered by respondents along with other measures in an unspecified experimental setting. Higher scores on the scale indicate that respondents perceive an offer to be a very good value whereas lower scores suggest that they view a product and price to be a poor value.

MAJOR FINDINGS:

> The study's objective was to examine the relationship between the price structure of a product line and consumer assessments of a product model within the line. The results indicated that price had a negative influence on the **perceived value of the offer**. The lowest **perceived value of an offer** was clearly for price-range treatments in which the ends were both unacceptable (i.e., too high and too low). Also, respondents perceived a product and price to be a better **offer** when there were constant price differences in the line rather than logarithmic differences.

REFERENCES:

> Petroshius, Susan M. and Kent B. Monroe (1987), "Effect of Product- Line Pricing Characteristics on Product Evaluations," *JCR*, 13 (March), 511-519.

SCALE ITEMS: VALUE (OFFER) +

1. This _____ is: (r)

Very Good Value for the Money	Moderately Good Value for the Money	Slightly Good Value for the Money	Neither Good nor Poor Value for the Money	Slightly Poor Value for the Money	Moderately Poor Value for the Money	Very Poor Value for the Money
1	2	3	4	5	6	7

2. At the price shown this_____ is:(r)

Very Economical	Moderately Economical	Slightly Economical	Neither Economical nor Uneconomical	Slightly Uneconomical	Moderately Uneconomical	Very Uneconomical
1	2	3	4	5	6	7

3. I would consider this _____ to be a good buy.

Strongly Disagree	Moderately Disagree	Slightly Disagree	Neither Agree Nor Disagree	Slightly Agree	Moderately Agree	Strongly Agree
1	2	3	4	5	6	7

4. The price shown for this _____ is:(r)

Very Acceptable	Moderately Acceptable	Slightly Acceptable	Neither Acceptable Nor Unacceptable	Slightly Unacceptable	Moderately Unacceptable	Very Unacceptable
1	2	3	4	5	6	7

5. I would consider this _____ to be:

Very Expensive	Moderately Expensive	Slightly Expensive	Neither Expensive nor Inexpensive	Slightly Inexpensive	Moderately Inexpensive	Very Inexpensive
1	2	3	4	5	6	7

6. This _____ appears to be a bargain.

Strongly Disagree	Moderately Disagree	Slightly Disagree	Neither Agree Nor Disagree	Slightly Agree	Moderately Agree	Strongly Agree
1	2	3	4	5	6	7

+ Place the name of the generic product in the blank.

SCALE NAME: Venturesomeness

SCALE DESCRIPTION:

A five-item, Likert-type summated ratings scale measuring the degree to which a person expresses **enjoyment with taking risks.** The scale was referred to as Risk Assessment by Bruning, Kovacic, and Oberdick (1985).

SCALE ORIGIN:

Bruning, Kovacic, and Oberdick (1985) provide no information that indicates the scale was not original to their study.

SAMPLES:

Questionnaires were distributed at five airports in the U.S. that offered major/national and regional/commuter service. To provide an adequate representation of various types of flyers, the sample was stratified by time of day and day of week. Questionnaires were distributed on a ''random'' basis to passengers waiting for flights to leave at departure gates. Self-addressed, stamped envelopes were provided with the survey forms and **591** usable forms were returned.

RELIABILITY:

An alpha of **.7** was reported for the scale.

VALIDITY:

A factor analysis indicated that the items loaded together.

ADMINISTRATION:

The scale was self-administered with other parts of the questionnaire while passengers were waiting at departure gates at airports. The questionnaires were returned by mail. Higher scores on this scale indicate that such persons **enjoy taking chances** even if it involves a bit of danger. Lower scores imply respondents do not like to take risks.

MAJOR FINDINGS:

Bruning and his coauthors were studying the reasons why air travelers choose a certain form of airline and how such information could be used to segment carriers into distinct markets. Discriminant analysis was used to identify personality factors, demographic variables, and airline-related perceptions that would significantly discriminate between the commuter and noncommuter travelers. **Venturesomeness** was not statistically significant in separating passenger respondents into one of the two markets.

REFERENCE:

Bruning, Edward R., Mary L. Kovacic, and Larry E. Oberdick (1985), ''Segmentation Analysis of Domestic Airline Passenger Markets,'' *JAMS*, 13 (Winter), 17-31.

#274 *Venturesomeness*

SCALE ITEMS: VENTURESOMENESS +

Strongly Disagree	Disagree	Slightly Disagree	Slightly Agree	Agree	Strongly Agree
1	2	3	4	5	6

1. I almost always accept a dare.
2. I like to be with people who are unpredictable.
3. Rarely, if ever, do I do anything reckless. **(r)**
4. I would never pass up something that sounded like fun just because it sounded a little bit hazardous.
5. Frequently, I like to take a chance on something that isn't sure; such as gambling.

+ The graphic scale was not specified in the article, but is likely to have been similar to the one shown here, with between five and seven points.

SCALE NAME: Verbal/Visual Processing Style

SCALE DESCRIPTION:

A 22-item, four-point Likert-type summated ratings scale measuring a person's preference for processing information in either a verbal or a visual modality. The measure was referred to as the Style of Processing (SOP) scale by Childers, Houston, and Heckler (1985).

SCALE ORIGIN:

The scale is original to Childers, Houston, and Heckler (1985). The measure was developed after another measure, the Verbal Visualizer Questionnaire (VVQ, Richardson 1977), was found not to have satisfactory reliability or factor structure. Thirty-six items were generated in addition to six from the VVQ. After administration of the 42-item scale to 35 undergraduate students, item-total correlations were used to construct the final 22-item scale. Half of the items tapped the visual component and the other half tapped the verbal component. This final version of the scale included the six items from the VVQ.

SAMPLES:

The scale was administered in two studies reported by Childers, Houston, and Heckler (1985). The first study involved **263** undergraduate college student volunteers. The second study collected data from 106 subjects who were described as being undergraduate students at a major midwestern university. The subjects in the second study were divided into two groups, one with **54** subjects and the other with **52**.

RELIABILITY:

An alpha of .**88** (n = 54) was reported.

VALIDITY:

Evidence of the scale's discriminant validity came from the insignificant correlations with two measures of processing ability (not style) by Childers and his coauthors. The scale also had no correlation with a measure of social desirability. Criterion validity was evident from the scale's significant correlations with measures of recall and recognition.

ADMINISTRATION:

The scale was self-administered by students along with other measures. Higher scores on the scale indicate that respondents tend to process information visually whereas lower scores suggest that they are more likely to process verbally.

MAJOR FINDINGS:

Childers and his coauthors compared several measures of visual/verbal mental imagery. The measure of **verbal/visual processing style** was found to be significantly correlated with measures of aided recall and recognition. Specifically, retention appeared to be best for the verbally oriented processors.

COMMENTS:

Though the authors preferred to compute a single score for the items in this scale, they did point out that some researchers might want to treat the visual and verbal components as separate dimensions. In that context, they note that the 11 items measuring the verbal component had an alpha of .81 and the 11 items measuring the visual component had an alpha of .86.

REFERENCES:

Childers, Terry L., Michael J. Houston, and Susan E. Heckler (1985), "Measurement of Individual Differences in Visual Versus Verbal Information Processing," *JCR*, 12 (September), 125-134.

Richardson, Alan (1977), "Verbalizer-Visualizer: A Cognitive Style Dimension," *Journal of Mental Imagery*, 1 (1), 109- 125.

SCALE ITEMS: VERBAL/VISUAL PROCESSING STYLE +

INSTRUCTIONS: The aim of this exercise is to determine the style or manner you use when carrying out different mental tasks. Your answers to the questions should reflect the manner in which you typically engage in each of the tasks mentioned. There are no right or wrong answers, we only ask that you provide honest and accurate answers. Please answer each question by circling one of the four possible responses. For example, if I provided the statement, "I seldom read books," and this was your typical behavior, even though you might read say one book a year, you would circle the "ALWAYS TRUE" response.

Possible Responses:

ALWAYS TRUE	USUALLY TRUE	USUALLY FALSE	ALWAYS FALSE
1—————————	—2—————————	—3—————————	——4

Items:

1. I enjoy doing work that requires the use of words. (W)
2. There are some special times in my life that I like to relive by mentally "picturing" just how everything looked. (r) (P)
3. I can never seem to find the right word when I need it. (r) (W)
4. I do a lot of reading. (W)
5. When I'm trying to learn something new, I'd rather watch a demonstration than read how to do it. (r) (P)
6. I think I often use words in the wrong way. (r) (W)
7. I enjoy learning new words. (W)
8. I like to picture how I could fix up my apartment or a room if I could buy anything I wanted. (r) (P)
9. I often make written notes to myself. (W)
10. I like to daydream. (r) (P)
11. I generally prefer to use a diagram than a written set of instructions. (r) (P)
12. I like to "doodle. (r) (P)
13. I find it helps to think in terms of mental pictures when doing many things. (r) (P)

14. After I meet someone for the first time, I can usually remember what they look like, but not much about them. **(r)** (P)
15. I like to think of synonyms for words. (W)
16. When I have forgotten something, I frequently try to form a mental picture to remember it. **(r)** (P)
17. I like learning new words. (W)
18. I prefer to read instructions about how to do something rather than have someone show me. (W)
19. I prefer activities that don't require a lot of reading. **(r)** (W)
20. I seldom daydream. (P)
21. I spend very little time attempting to increase my vocabulary. **(r)** (W)
22. My thinking often consists of mental ''pictures'' or images. **(r)** (P)

+ W indicates verbal items; P indicates visual items.

SCALE NAME: Visual Imagery Control

SCALE DESCRIPTION:

A 12-item, three-point summated ratings scale measuring a person's ability to control optical memory images. The full formal title for the scale is the Gordon Test of Visual Imagery Control.

SCALE ORIGIN:

This version of the scale was developed by Richardson (1969) and represents a modification of the measure originally constructed by Gordon (1949). The altered form of the test had 12 items, three response categories, and written instructions whereas the original version had 11 items, yes-or-no responses, and oral instructions. Reviewing several uses of the scale, White, Sheehan, and Ashton (1977) concluded that it was internally consistent, had adequate test-retest stability, and defined a single dimension.

SAMPLES:

The scale was administered in two studies reported by Childers, Houston, and Heckler (1985). The first study involved **263** undergraduate college student volunteers. The second study collected data from 106 subjects who were described as being undergraduate students at a major midwestern university. The subjects in the second study were divided into two groups, one with **54** subjects and the other with **52**.

RELIABILITY:

Alpha values of **.68**, **.75**, and **.77** were reported for the scale by Childers, Houston, and Heckler (1985).

VALIDITY:

A factor analysis indicated that the items each had their highest loadings on this factor. The loadings ranged from .18 to .56, with nine of the items being below .50. Evidence of the scale's discriminant validity came from its insignificant correlation with a measure of social desirability.

ADMINISTRATION:

The scale was self-administered by students along with other measures in both studies reported by Childers and his coauthors (1985). Lower scores on the scale indicate that respondents have mastery over their mental images whereas higher scores suggest that they have difficulty exercising control over optical images evoked in memory.

MAJOR FINDINGS:

Childers and his coauthors (1985) compared several measures of visual/verbal mental imagery. The measure of **visual imagery control** was *not* found to be significantly correlated with aided recall or recognition.

COMMENTS:

Childers and his coauthors (1985) admitted that the scale appeared to have psychometric characteristics that were below acceptable standards. In an effort to increase internal consistency they eliminated three items, but the alpha showed only minor improvement (.683). They kept the items in the scale "for purposes of further analysis (Childers, Houston, and Heckler 1985, p. 127).

REFERENCES:

Childers, Terry L. and Michael J. Houston, and Susan E. Heckler (1985), "Measurement of Individual Differences in Visual Versus Verbal Information Processing," *JCR*, 12 (September), 125-134.

Gordon, Rosemary (1949), "An Investigation Into Some of the Factors That Favor the Formation of Stereotyped Images," *British Journal of Psychology*, 39 (March), 156-167.

Richardson, Alan (1969), *Mental Imagery*. New York, N.Y.: Springer Publishing Company, Inc.

White, K., P. W. Sheehan, and R. Ashton (1977), "Imagery Assessment: A Survey of Self-Report Measures," *Journal of Mental Imagery*, 1 (1), 145-169.

SCALE ITEMS: VISUAL IMAGERY CONTROL

INSTRUCTIONS: This questionnaire will study some aspects of your imagery. The questions are concerned with the ease with which you can control or manipulate visual images. For some people this task is relatively easy and for others relatively hard. One subject who could not manipulate his imagery easily gave this illustration. He visualized a table, one of whose legs began to collapse. He then tried to visualize another table with four solid legs, but found it impossible. The image of the first table with the collapsing leg persisted. Another subject reported that when he visualized a table the image was rather vague and dim. He could visualize it briefly but it was difficult to retain by any voluntary effort. In both these illustrations the subjects had difficulty in controlling or manipulating their visual imagery. It is perhaps important to emphasize that these experiences are in no way abnormal and are as often reported as the controllable type of image. Read each question, then close your eyes while you try to visualize the scene described. Record your answer by underlining 'Yes', 'No', or 'Unsure', whichever is the most appropriate. Remember that your accurate and honest answer to these questions is most important for the validity of this study. If you have any doubts at all regarding the answer to a question, underline 'Unsure'. Please be certain that you answer each of the twelve questions.

Yes	No	Unsure
1————————————	2————————————	3

1. Can you see a car standing in the road in front of a house?
2. Can you see it in color?
3. Can you now see it in a different color?
4. Can you now see that same car lying upside down?
5. Can you now see the same car back on its four wheels again?

6. Can you see the car running along the road?
7. Can you see it climb up a very steep hill?
8. Can you see it climb over the top?
9. Can you see it out of control and crash through a house?
10. Can you now see the same car running along the road with a handsome couple inside?
11. Can you see the car cross a bridge and fall over the side into the stream below?
12. Can you see the car all old and dismantled in a car-cemetery?

SCALE NAME: Volunteerism (Benefits)

SCALE DESCRIPTION:

A three-item, three-point Likert-type summated ratings scale measuring the degree to which one believes that donating time to an organization benefits the community and is appreciated. The measure was referred to as Benefit to the Community by Yavas and Riecken (1985).

SCALE ORIGIN:

The measure appears to be original to Yavas and Riecken (1985).

SAMPLES:

Analysis was based on data collected from **329** men living in Muncie, Indiana. The authors surveyed the sample by telephone, using a ''plus-one'' random digit dialing method to prevent biases due to unlisted numbers. The authors report that the sample was similar to the area's male population in terms of several demographic variables, though they do not state their evidence for that conclusion.

RELIABILITY:

An alpha of **.57** was reported for the scale.

VALIDITY:

No examination of scale validity was reported.

ADMINISTRATION:

The scale was read to respondents along with other measures in a phone survey context. Higher scores on the scale suggest that respondents strongly believe volunteering is valuable and appreciated whereas lower scores imply that they do not think it is beneficial or appreciated.

MAJOR FINDINGS:

The purpose of the study was to examine demographic and attitudinal variables associated with the donation of time to community projects. The variables were used in a discriminant analysis to distinguish between donor and nondonor groups. Though the **perception of community benefits** was the second most important attitudinal discriminator, all of the demographic variables appeared to be stronger discriminators.

COMMENTS:

The internal consistency of the measure is so low that work should be done to improve reliability before it is used further.

REFERENCE:

Yavas, Ugur and Glen Riecken (1985), "Can Volunteers Be Targeted ?" *JAMS*, 13 (Spring), 218-228.

SCALE ITEMS: VOLUNTEERISM (BENEFITS)

Disagree	Neutral	Agree
1————————————————	—2————————————————	——3

1. Volunteering time to an organization does something good for the community.
2. People should be willing to volunteer time to help others who are less fortunate.
3. Volunteer organizations would not appreciate the amount of time donated to them. **(r)**

SCALE NAME: Volunteerism (Family/Job Constraints)

SCALE DESCRIPTION:

A three-item, three-point Likert-type summated ratings scale measuring the perceived effect of one's family- and job-related responsibilities on ability to donate time to a community organization. The measure was referred to as Family/Job Demands on Time by Yavas and Riecken (1985).

SCALE ORIGIN:

The measure appears to be original to Yavas and Riecken (1985).

SAMPLES:

Analysis was based on data collected from **329** men living in Muncie, Indiana. The authors surveyed the sample by telephone, using a "plus-one" random digit dialing method to prevent biases due to unlisted numbers. The authors report that the sample was similar to the area's male population in terms of several demographic variables, though they do not state their evidence for that conclusion.

RELIABILITY:

An alpha of **.60** was reported for the scale.

VALIDITY:

No examination of scale validity was reported.

ADMINISTRATION:

The scale was read to respondents along with other measures in a phone survey context. Higher scores on the scale suggest that respondents feel strongly that donating time would interfere with their family and job responsibilities whereas lower scores imply that there would not be a major conflict in time demands.

MAJOR FINDINGS:

The purpose of the study was to examine demographic and attitudinal variables associated with the donation of time to community projects. The variables were used in a discriminant analysis to distinguish between donor and nondonor groups. Of all the demographic and attitudinal variables examined, the most important discriminator appeared to be the **family/ job time demands** on an individual.

COMMENTS:

The internal consistency of the measure is low, but might be improved satisfactorily with the addition of a few more relevant items.

REFERENCE:

Yavas, Ugur and Glen Riecken (1985), ''Can Volunteers Be Targeted?'' *JAMS*, 13 (Spring), 218-228.

SCALE ITEMS: VOLUNTEERISM (Family/Job Constraints)

Disagree	Neutral	Agree
1———————————————	——2————————————	———3

1. My family/wife would not approve if I donated time to an organization.
2. Volunteering time would interfere too much with my family life.
3. Even if I wanted to donate time, my job responsibilities would not let me.

SCALE NAME: Volunteerism (Willingness)

SCALE DESCRIPTION:

A three-item, three-point Likert-type summated ratings scale measuring one's attitude about donating time to a community organization. The measure was referred to as Willingness to Donate by Yavas and Riecken (1985).

SCALE ORIGIN:

The measure appears to be original to Yavas and Riecken (1985) and their study is the only known use of the scale.

SAMPLES:

Analysis was based on data collected from **329** men living in Muncie, Indiana. The authors surveyed the sample by telephone, using a "plus-one" random digit dialing method to prevent biases due to unlisted numbers. The authors report that the sample was similar to the area's male population in terms of several demographic variables, though they do not state their evidence for that conclusion.

RELIABILITY:

An alpha of **.55** was reported for the scale.

VALIDITY:

No examination of scale validity was reported.

ADMINISTRATION:

The scale was read to respondents along with other measures in a phone survey context. Higher scores on the scale suggest that respondents think they and others should be able to donate time whereas lower scores imply that they do not accept volunteering as being possible and/or worthwhile.

MAJOR FINDINGS:

The purpose of the study was to examine demographic and attitudinal variables associated with the donation of time to community projects. The variables were used in a discriminant analysis to distinguish between donor and nondonor groups. While the attitude toward **volunteering** appeared to be a significant discriminator, all of the other attitudinal and demographic variables were stronger discriminators.

COMMENTS:

The internal consistency of the measure is so low that work should be done to improve reliability before it is used further.

REFERENCE:

> Yavas, Ugur and Glen Riecken (1985), "Can Volunteers Be Targeted?" *JAMS*, 13 (Spring), 218-228.

SCALE ITEMS: ATTITUDE TOWARD VOLUNTEERISM

Disagree	Neutral	Agree
1———————	———2———————	———3

1. People could always find some time to donate if they really wanted to.
2. I should be willing to spend less time with my friends in order to donate time to an organization.
3. Donating time to volunteer organizations would be a waste of my time. **(r)**

SCALE NAME: Weight Control

SCALE DESCRIPTION:

A two-item, seven-point Likert-type scale measuring person's reported ability to control his/her weight. The scale was referred to by Oliver and Bearden (1985) as Personal Control.

SCALE ORIGIN:

The measure did not originate in the Oliver and Bearden (1985) study but was supplied by a sponsoring institution (p. 329, 338).

SAMPLES:

Analysis was based on **353** completed questionnaires from members of a bistate consumer panel. Subjects were selected to be representative of urban and suburban households with family incomes greater than $10,000. Ninety-one triers and 262 nontriers of a new, heavily promoted time-release diet suppressant responded. The average respondent was female (56%), white (89%), with some education beyond high school (70%), and in the $20,000 to $29,999 income category (25.5%).

RELIABILITY:

A reliability of **.65** was reported.

VALIDITY:

Confirmatory factor analysis was performed once, weak items were deleted, and the analysis was run again, resulting in higher overall factor loadings.

ADMINISTRATION:

Data were gathered through use of self-administered mail questionnaires. The method for calculating scale scores was not specified, but it is likely that higher scores on this scale suggest a person has good control over his/her diet and weight whereas lower scores imply that a person lacks such discipline.

MAJOR FINDINGS:

The purpose of the study was to examine the presence and operation of "crossover effects" in the Fishbein behavioral intention model under various moderating conditions. Evidence generally supporting the normative structure—attitude crossover path was found; i.e., a person's attitude toward a behavior is strengthened to the extent that relevant others are believed to agree with it. The moderator variable analysis, in which **weight control** was one moderator variable, provided little insight into the mechanisms people use to process normative information.

COMMENTS:

The scale had low internal consistency and the authors admitted that it might also lack stability over time, samples, or product categories. More items and testing are in order before the scale is used further.

REFERENCE:

Oliver, Richard L. and William O. Bearden (1985), ''Crossover Effects in the Theory of Reasoned Action: A Moderating Influence Attempt,'' *JCR*, 12 (December), 324-340.

SCALE ITEMS: WEIGHT CONTROL

Disagree ____ : ____ : ____ : ____ : ____ : ____ : ____ Agree
            1   2   3   4   5   6   7

1. I am careful about what I eat in order to keep my weight under control.
2. I feel I have fairly good control of my weight.

SCALE NAME: Word Evaluation

SCALE DESCRIPTION:

A four-item, seven-point semantic differential scale purporting to measure a subject's attitudinal evaluation of a specific word. Though not so stated by Allen and Janiszewski (1989), who developed and used this scale, it appears to measure the affective evaluation of a word.

SCALE ORIGIN:

The scale is original to Allen and Janiszewski (1989).

SAMPLES:

The authors used two separate samples in their research. The first consisted of **61** first-year MBA students. The second consisted of **78** second-year MBA students.

RELIABILITY:

Alpha values of **.87** and **.89** were reported for the two samples, respectively.

VALIDITY: No validity assessment was reported.

ADMINISTRATION:

This scale appears appropriate for paper-and-pencil administration. Allen and Janiszewski's subjects responded to scale on a computer screen. Time to administer seems inconsequential. Scale sums were used in the analysis reported here.

MAJOR FINDINGS:

The authors reported that subjects who were contingently or demand-aware of the purpose of their study evaluated words more favorably in general. Subjects not aware of the purpose of the research did not do so. Hence, no support was found for a classical conditioning explanation of word association for brand names.

REFERENCE:

Allen, Chris T. and Chris A. Janiszewski (1989), "Assessing the Role of Contingency Awareness in Attitudinal Conditioning With Implications for Advertising Research," *JMR*, 26 (February), 30-43.

SCALE ITEMS: WORD EVALUATION

1. good ____ : ____ : ____ : ____ : ____ : ____ : ____ bad
        1   2   3   4   5   6   7

2. positive   ____ : ____ : ____ : ____ : ____ : ____ : ____   negative
                   1   2   3   4   5   6   7

3. unpleasant   ____ : ____ : ____ : ____ : ____ : ____ : ____   pleasant
                   1   2   3   4   5   6   7

4. likeable   ____ : ____ : ____ : ____ : ____ : ____ : ____   unlikeable
                   1   2   3   4   5   6   7

SCALE NAME: Workaholic

SCALE DESCRIPTION:

A four-item, Likert-type summated ratings scale measuring the degree to which a person expresses enjoyment of work. The scale was referred to as Lifestyle by Bruning, Kovacic, and Oberdick (1985).

SCALE ORIGIN:

Bruning, Kovacic, and Oberdick (1985) provide no information that indicates the scale was not original to their study.

SAMPLES:

Questionnaires were distributed at five airports in the U.S. that offered major/national and regional/commuter service. To provide an adequate representation of various types of flyers, the sample was stratified by time of day and day of week. Questionnaires were distributed on a ''random'' basis to passengers waiting for flights to leave at departure gates. Self-addressed, stamped envelopes were provided with the survey forms and **591** useable forms were returned.

RELIABILITY:

An alpha of **.53** was reported for the scale.

VALIDITY:

A factor analysis indicated that the items loaded together.

ADMINISTRATION:

The scale was self-administered with other parts of the questionnaire while passengers were waiting at departure gates at airports. The questionnaires were returned by mail. Higher scores on this scale indicate that respondents are **workaholics** whereas lower scores imply that respondents work because they have to and do not enjoy it much.

MAJOR FINDINGS:

Bruning and his coauthors were studying the reasons why air travelers choose a certain form of airline and how such information could be used to segment carriers into distinct markets. Discriminant analysis was used to identify personality factors, demographic variables, and airline-related perceptions that would significantly discriminate between the commuter and noncommuter travelers. The tendency to be a **workaholic** was the only personality variable that significantly discriminated between the two markets. Specifically, regional/commuter passengers were more likely to be **workaholics** than passengers of major/national airlines.

#282 *Workaholic*

COMMENTS:

The internal consistency of this scale is so low that improvements in its psychometric properties are necessary before it is used further.

REFERENCE:

Bruning, Edward R., Mary L. Kovacic, and Larry E. Oberdick (1985), "Segmentation Analysis of Domestic Airline Passenger Markets," *JAMS*, 13 (Winter), 17-31.

SCALE ITEMS: WORKAHOLIC +

Strongly Disagree	Disagree	Slightly Disagree	Slightly Agree	Agree	Strongly Agree
1	2	3	4	5	6

1. I work because I have to and for that reason only. **(r)**
2. When I have a choice between work and enjoying myself, I usually work.
3. Sometimes people say that I neglect other important aspects of my life because I work so hard.
4. I don't mind working while others are having fun.

+ The graphic scale was not specified in the article, but is likely to have been similar to the one shown here, with between five and seven points.

SCALE NAME: Yielding to Child's Requests

SCALE DESCRIPTION:

A five-item, five-point Likert-type summated ratings scale measuring the degree to which a parent reports buying several specific products for his/her child when the child asks for them.

SCALE ORIGIN:

The use of these items as a multi-item measure appears to be original to Carlson and Grossbart (1988). They got ideas for some of the items, however, from the research of Ward, Wackman, and Wartella (1977).

SAMPLES:

The survey instrument used by Carlson and Grossbart (1988) was distributed to mothers via students at three elementary schools in an unidentified U.S. city. The schools were chosen on a convenience basis but appeared to represent a variety of socioeconomic areas of the city. A $1 contribution to the PTO was offered for each completed questionnaire returned by the children. Analysis was based on **451** completed questionnaires. Ninety-three percent of the responding mothers indicated that they were the primary person in the child's socialization.

RELIABILITY:

Carlson and Grossbart (1988) reported an alpha of **.70** and a beta of .57 for the scale.

VALIDITY:

No examination of scale validity was reported by Carlson and Grossbart (1988).

ADMINISTRATION:

The scale was self-administered along with many other measures in the questionnaire used by Carlson and Grossbart (1988). Higher scores on the scale mean that parents often agree to buy their children any of several products when asked whereas lower scores imply that parents rarely purchase items for their children whenever they ask for them.

MAJOR FINDINGS:

The authors investigated the relationship between general parental socialization styles and children's consumer socialization. In a factor analysis of scale scores, scores on the **Yielding** scale loaded on a factor described as the "child's consumption autonomy." No significant difference was found, however, in the reported degree of child consumption autonomy between any of the five parental socialization style clusters examined.

REFERENCES:

Carlson, Les and Sanford Grossbart (1988), ''Parental Style and Consumer Socialization of Children,'' *JCR*, 15 (June), 77-94.

Ward, Scott, Daniel B. Wackman, and Ellen Wartella (1977), *How Children Learn to Buy.* Beverly Hills, Calif.: Sage Publications, Inc.

SCALE ITEMS: YIELDING TO CHILD'S REQUESTS

Very Seldom	Seldom	Sometimes	Often	Very Often
1————————	——2————————	——3————————	——4————————	——5

1. If my child asks for candy I buy it.
2. If my child asks for a game or toy I buy it.
3. If my child asks for a magazine/comic book I buy it.
4. If my child asks for a snack food I buy it.
5. If my child asks for sports equipment I buy it.

Part II

Advertising Scales

Table of Contents

· · · · · · · · · · · · · · · · ·

Table of Contents

SCALE NAME: Ad Distraction

SCALE DESCRIPTION:

A three-item, nine-point Likert-type summated ratings scale measuring the degree to which a person perceives aspects of a commercial to have been distracting, resulting in a less than clear message.

SCALE ORIGIN:

The scale appears to be have been developed by Duncan and Nelson (1985) and is only known to have been used in their study.

SAMPLES:

The sample was composed of **149** male undergraduate students. It was a convenience sample, but was considered appropriate given that 18 to 25 year old men were the target market for the product under study.

RELIABILITY:

An alpha of **.43** was reported for the scale.

VALIDITY:

No examination of scale validity was reported.

ADMINISTRATION:

Subjects were assigned to private listening rooms where they read instructions, heard an ad, and then completed a questionnaire. Higher scores on this scale imply that respondents perceive a particular ad to contain characteristics that are distracting to the process of cognitive comprehension of the message.

MAJOR FINDINGS:

The purpose of the study was to investigate the effects of ad humor on several important consumer responses. **Distraction** had low but significant negative correlations with attention paid to the ad and liking of the commercial. However, there was no significant relationship between degree of perceived humor and perceived **distraction**.

COMMENTS:

The internal consistency is so low that the scale is shown to be unreliable. More items and analysis is necessary before the scale is used further. As used by Duncan and Nelson (1985), the scale items referred specifically to a new (fictitious?) hair care product for men called ''New Wave.'' Blanks have been put in place of the product's name in the statements below to make them amenable for use in other studies. Further minor changes could be made as well.

REFERENCE:

Duncan, Calvin P. and James E. Nelson (1985), "Effects of Humor in a Radio Advertising Experiment," *JA*, 14 (2), 33- 40, 64.

SCALE ITEMS: AD DISTRACTION

Strongly   Strongly
Disagree   ____ : ____ : ____ : ____ : ____ : ____ : ____ : ____ : ____   Agree
           1   2   3   4   5   6   7   8   9

1. Parts of the _____ advertisement were distracting.
2. It was hard to concentrate on major ideas in the _____ advertisement.
3. The _____ advertisement described the product's features clearly. **(r)**

SCALE NAME: Ad Humor

SCALE DESCRIPTION:

A three-item, nine-point Likert-type summated ratings scale measuring the degree to which a person perceives a commercial to have been humorous.

SCALE ORIGIN:

The scale appears to be have been developed by Duncan and Nelson (1985) and was only used in their study.

SAMPLES:

The sample was composed of **149** male undergraduate students. It was a convenience sample, but was considered appropriate given that 18 to 225 year old men were the target market for the product under study.

RELIABILITY:

An alpha of **.61** was reported for the scale.

VALIDITY:

No specific examination of the scale's validity was reported, but some evidence of its predictive validity comes from the fact that the mean score given by subjects to what was supposed to be a humorous ad was higher (i.e., the ad was considered more humorous) than the mean score of the ad designed to be serious. However, the statistical significance of the difference was not reported.

ADMINISTRATION:

Subjects were assigned to private listening rooms where they read instructions, heard an ad, and then completed a questionnaire. Higher scores on this scale imply that people perceive a particular ad to be very humorous.

MAJOR FINDINGS:

The purpose of the study was to investigate the effects of ad humor on several important consumer responses. Perception of **humor** was found to have significant positive correlation with attention to and liking of the ad as well as liking of the product. It had a significant negative correlation with perceived irritation of the ad.

COMMENTS:

The internal consistency of the scale is rather low so cautious use of the measure is necessary until reliability is improved. As used by Duncan and Nelson (1985), the scale items referred specifically to a new (fictitious?) hair care product for men called "New Wave." Blanks have been put in place of the product's name in the statements below to make them amenable for use in other studies. Further minor changes could be made as well.

REFERENCE:

Duncan, Calvin P. and James E. Nelson (1985), "Effects of Humor in a Radio Advertising Experiment," *JA*, 14 (2), 33- 40, 64.

SCALE ITEMS: AD HUMOR

Strongly
Disagree   ____ : ____ : ____ : ____ : ____ : ____ : ____ : ____ : ____   Strongly Agree
     1   2   3   4   5   6   7   8   9

1. The man in the _____ commercial was funny.
2. The _____ commercial was more serious than it was funny. **(r)**
3. Most men would not find the _____ commercial to be humorous. **(r)**

SCALE NAME: Ad Information Usage

SCALE DESCRIPTION:

A three-item, six-point, Likert-type summated ratings scale that assesses the degree to which a consumer reports using magazine and television ads when making purchase decisions.

SCALE ORIGIN:

It is not clear where the items originated or where they were first used as a multi-item summated ratings scale.

SAMPLES:

Lumpkin and Darden (1982) had **145** usable responses gathered from the consumer research panel of the University of Arkansas. Data were collected from the individuals by mail questionnaire.

RELIABILITY:

An alpha of **.69** was calculated.

VALIDITY:

Factor analysis indicated the items loaded together.

ADMINISTRATION:

Lumpkin and Darden gathered data through self-administered mail questionnaires. Scale scores are calculated by averaging numerical responses to individual items. A score of 6 indicates that a person has a strong tendency to use ad information when making a purchase decision whereas 1 implies that a person admits little conscious usage of such information.

MAJOR FINDINGS:

In their study of television program preference groups, Lumpkin and Darden found that ad information usage was one of a few lifestyle variables that differentiated between the six groups. The group with the highest mean score on the scale was the oldest of the groups and had a mixture of program preferences, suggesting it may represent a family viewing group rather than being male or female dominated. The group with the lowest mean score had the lowest age of the groups and seemed to like female- oriented comedies and dramas.

COMMENTS:

The psychometric quality of the scale might be improved by adding a few more items, possibly ones that refer to usage of ad information from other media.

REFERENCE:

Lumpkin, James R. and William R. Darden (1982), "Relating Television Preference Viewing to Shopping Orientations, Lifestyles, and Demographics," *JA*, 11 (4), 56-67.

SCALE ITEMS: AD INFORMATION USAGE

Strongly Disagree	Disagree	Slightly Disagree	Slightly Agree	Agree	Strongly Agree
1	2	3	4	5	6

1. I often read the ads in magazines.
2. Television advertisements are a source of information I use when I am deciding to buy something.
3. Magazine advertisements are a source of information I use when I am deciding to buy something.

SCALE NAME: Ad Irritation

SCALE DESCRIPTION:

A three-item, nine-point Likert-type summated ratings scale measuring the degree to which a person indicates that a commercial was irritating, annoying, and not enjoyable to listen to.

SCALE ORIGIN:

The scale appears to be have been developed by Duncan and Nelson (1985) and was only used in their study.

SAMPLES:

The sample was composed of **149** male undergraduate students. It was a convenience sample, but was considered appropriate given that 18 to 25 year old men were the target market for the product under study.

RELIABILITY:

An alpha of **.75** was reported for the scale.

VALIDITY:

No examination of scale validity was reported.

ADMINISTRATION:

Subjects were assigned to private listening rooms where they read instructions, heard an ad, and then completed a questionnaire. Higher scores on this scale imply that people experienced much greater irritation with an ad than those with lower scores.

MAJOR FINDINGS:

The purpose of the study was to investigate the effects of ad humor on several important consumer responses. Perception of humor was found to have significant positive correlation with attention to and liking of the ad as well as liking of the product. It had a significant negative correlation with perceived **irritation** of the ad.

COMMENTS:

As used by Duncan and Nelson (1985), the scale items referred specifically to a new (fictitious?) hair care product for men called "New Wave." Blanks have been put in place of the product's name in the statements below to make them amenable for use in other studies. Further minor changes could be made as well.

REFERENCE:

Duncan, Calvin P. and James E. Nelson (1985), "Effects of Humor in a Radio Advertising Experiment," *JA*, 14 (2), 33- 40, 64.

SCALE ITEMS: AD IRRITATION

Strongly Disagree										Strongly Agree
	___ :	___ :	___ :	___ :	___ :	___ :	___ :	___ :	___	
	1	2	3	4	5	6	7	8	9	

1. The _____ advertisement was somewhat irritating.
2. The _____ commercial was annoying.
3. The _____ commercial itself was enjoyable. **(r)**

SCALE NAME: Advertising Concerns (Parent)

SCALE DESCRIPTION:

A six-item, five-point Likert-type summated ratings scale measuring the degree to which a parent expresses reservations about the advertising being aimed at children.

SCALE ORIGIN:

Carlson and Grossbart (1988) indicate that they adapted a scale from previous work by Crosby and Grossbart (1984).

SAMPLES:

The survey instrument used by Carlson and Grossbart (1988) was distributed to mothers via students at three elementary schools in an unidentified U.S. city. The schools were chosen on a convenience basis but appeared to represent a variety of socioeconomic areas of the city. A $1 contribution to the PTO was offered for each completed questionnaire returned by the children. Analysis was based on **451** completed questionnaires. Ninety-three percent of the responding mothers indicated that they were the primary person in the child's socialization.

RELIABILITY:

Carlson and Grossbart reported an alpha of **.81** and a beta of .72 for the scale.

VALIDITY:

No examination of scale validity was reported.

ADMINISTRATION:

The scale was self-administered along with many other measures in the questionnaire used by Carlson and Grossbart. Higher scores on the scale mean that respondents express strong reservations about the advertising aimed at children whereas lower scores suggest that they are not concerned about such advertising.

MAJOR FINDINGS:

The authors investigated the relationship between general parental socialization styles and children's consumer socialization. A significant difference was found in the degree **advertising concerns** between one of the parental socialization style clusters and several of the others. Especially, Authoritative mothers reported significantly more **concern about advertising aimed at children** than did three of the other four parental style clusters examined.

REFERENCES:

Carlson, Les and Sanford Grossbart (1988), ''Parental Style and Consumer Socialization of Children,'' *JCR*, 15 (June), 77-94.

Crosby, Lawrence A. and Sanford L. Grossbart (1984), "Parental Style Tendencies and Concern About Children's Advertising," in *Current Issues in Research in Advertising*, James H. Leigh and Claude R. Martin, Jr., eds. Ann Arbor, Mich.: Division of Research, Graduate School of Business Administration, University of Michigan, 43-63.

SCALE ITEMS: ADVERTISING CONCERNS (PARENT)

Strongly Disagree	Disagree	Neither	Agree	Strongly Agree
1———————	—2———————	—3———————	—4———————	—5

1. There is too much food advertising directed at children.
2. Advertisers use tricks and gimmicks to get children to buy their products.
3. Advertising to children makes false claims about the nutrition content of food products.
4. There is too much sugar in the foods advertised to children.
5. Advertising teaches children bad eating habits.
6. Advertising directed at children leads to family conflict.

SCALE NAME: Advertising Expenditures (Bank)

SCALE DESCRIPTION:

A four-item, four-point Likert-type summated ratings scale measuring the amount a bank officer reports that his/her bank spends on media advertising in comparison with its primary competitor. McKee, Varadarajan, and Pride (1989) referred to this measure as Market Scanning.

SCALE ORIGIN:

McKee and his coauthors reported that they constructed the scales, but selected items on the basis of a review of relevant literature and comments by industry executives. Theirs is the only known use of the scale.

SAMPLES:

The study focused on banks operating in 50 SMSAs in seven states that have unit banking laws. CEOs of the 560 banks in the sample frame were sent questionnaires. A total of **333** usable responses were received and an analysis of asset sizes indicated that respondents' banks were not significantly different from nonrespondents' banks.

RELIABILITY:

An alpha of **.88** was reported for the scale.

VALIDITY:

A factor analysis of all items used in the study revealed a pattern such that items belonging to the scale loaded together on one factor and not on other factors.

ADMINISTRATION:

The scale was self-administered along with many other measures in a mail questionnaire format. Higher scores on the scale indicate that respondents' banks spend much more (twice as much) on media advertising than their primary competitors.

MAJOR FINDINGS:

The purpose of the study was to investigate the relationship between strategic orientation and dynamics of the market. Significant differences were found between organization strategy types in terms of several marketing tactics used. **Comparative advertising expenditures** did not differentiate between the organization strategy types as well as some of the other marketing variables, but "prospectors" (those with the highest adaptive capability) did report greater spending than banks with the three other strategic orientations.

COMMENTS:

Though the scale was developed for use with the banking industry, with minor adjustments it apparently can be used in other contexts.

#289 *Advertising Expenditures (Bank)*

REFERENCE:

McKee, Daryl O., P. Rajan Varadarajan, and William M. Pride (1989), ''Strategic Adaptability and Firm Performance: A Market Contingent Perspective,'' *JM*, 53 (July), 21-35.

SCALE ITEMS: ADVERTISING EXPENDITURES (BANK)

Please estimate how much you spend on advertising in the following media, compared to your primary competitor.

Much more = More than twice as much
More = More, but less than twice as much

Much more	More	Same	Less
4———————————3———————————2———————————1			

1. TV
2. Radio
3. Newspaper
4. All media in total

SCALE NAME: Advertising-Related Discussions (Parent/Child)

SCALE DESCRIPTION:

A three-item, five-point Likert-type summated ratings scale measuring the degree to which a parent reports discussing the content of advertising with his/her child.

SCALE ORIGIN:

Carlson and Grossbart (1988) indicate that they adapted a scale from previous work by Crosby and Grossbart (1984).

SAMPLES:

The survey instrument used by Carlson and Grossbart (1988) was distributed to mothers via students at three elementary schools in an unidentified U.S. city. The schools were chosen on a convenience basis but appeared to represent a variety of socioeconomic areas of the city. A $1 contribution to the PTO was offered for each completed questionnaire returned by the children. Analysis was based on **451** completed questionnaires. Ninety-three percent of the responding mothers indicated that they were the primary person in the child's socialization.

RELIABILITY:

Carlson and Grossbart reported an alpha of .**84** and a beta of .80 for the scale.

VALIDITY:

No examination of scale validity was reported.

ADMINISTRATION:

The scale was self-administered along with many other measures in the questionnaire used by Carlson and Grossbart. Higher scores on the scale mean that respondents often discuss advertising content with their children whereas lower scores suggest that they rarely if ever have such discussions with their children.

MAJOR FINDINGS:

The authors investigated the relationship between general parental socialization styles and children's consumer socialization. In a factor analysis of scale scores, scores on the **Advertising-Related Discussions** scale loaded on a factor described as "mediation of the media." A significant difference was found in the degree of parent-child communication between several of the parental socialization style clusters examined.

REFERENCES:

Carlson, Les and Sanford Grossbart (1988), "Parental Style and Consumer Socialization of Children," *JCR*, 15 (June), 77-94.

Crosby, Lawrence A. and Sanford L. Grossbart (1984), "Parental Style Tendencies and Concern About Children's Advertising," in *Current Issues in Research in Advertising,* James H. Leigh and Claude R. Martin, Jr., eds. Ann Arbor, Mich.: Division of Research, Graduate School of Business Administration, University of Michigan, 43-63.

SCALE ITEMS: ADVERTISING-RELATED DISCUSSIONS (PARENT/CHILD)

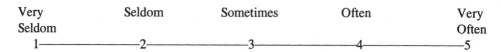

Very Seldom	Seldom	Sometimes	Often	Very Often
1	2	3	4	5

I talk with my child about the content of:

1. . . . TV advertising.
2. . . . magazine and newspaper advertising.
3. . . . radio advertising.

SCALE NAME: Attention to Ad

SCALE DESCRIPTION:

A three-item, nine-point Likert-type summated ratings scale measuring the degree to which a person indicates that a commercial was interesting and got his/her attention.

SCALE ORIGIN:

The scale appears to be have been developed by Duncan and Nelson (1985) and was used only in their study.

SAMPLES:

The sample was composed of **149** male undergraduate students. It was a convenience sample, but was considered appropriate given that 18 to 25 year old men were the target market for the product under study.

RELIABILITY:

An alpha of **.71** was reported for the scale.

VALIDITY:

No examination of scale validity was reported.

ADMINISTRATION:

Subjects were assigned to private listening rooms where they read instructions, heard an ad, and then completed a questionnaire. Higher scores on this scale imply that respondents paid greater attention to an ad whereas lower scores suggest that they considered an ad to be boring and paid little attention to it.

MAJOR FINDINGS:

The purpose of the study was to investigate the effects of ad humor on several important consumer responses. Perception of humor was found to have a significant positive correlation with **attention** paid to an ad.

COMMENTS:

As used by Duncan and Nelson (1985), the scale items referred specifically to a new (fictitious?) hair care product for men called "New Wave." Blanks have been put in place of the product's name in the statements below to make them amenable for use in other studies. Further minor changes could be made as well.

REFERENCE:

Duncan, Calvin P. and James E. Nelson (1985), "Effects of Humor in a Radio Advertising Experiment," *JA*, 14 (2), 33- 40, 64.

SCALE ITEMS: ATTENTION TO AD

Strongly   Strongly
Disagree   ____ : ____ : ____ : ____ : ____ : ____ : ____ : ____ : ____   Agree
           1   2   3   4   5   6   7   8   9

1. The _____ commercial caught my interest.
2. The _____ advertisement was boring. **(r)**
3. I paid close attention to the _____ commercial.

SCALE NAME: Attitude Toward Advertising

SCALE DESCRIPTION:

A five-item, five-point Likert-type summated ratings scale measuring consumer attitudes about advertising in general. A seven-item version of the scale with similar psychometric properties is also discussed below.

SCALE ORIGIN:

The scale was developed by Gaski and Etgar (1986). By a formula described in the article, the scale can be combined with data from several other measures to form an index of consumer attitudes toward marketing-related activities. The authors request that the index be referred to as the University of Notre Dame/Market Facts Index of Consumer Sentiment Toward Marketing. Some items were taken or adapted from the literature but the majority were written especially for the index. Pretesting involved 50 members of the Market Facts mail panel completing the index.

SAMPLES:

The sample was taken from the 200,000-household panel maintained by Market Facts. Questionnaires were mailed to 2000 households and **1428** were completed and returned. Though the overall panel is nationally balanced and continually updated to reflect the most recent national demographic changes, the characteristics of the final sample were not given.

RELIABILITY:

A seven-item version of the scale had an alpha of **.761** and the item-total correlations were .31 or higher. Two items with the lowest item-total correlations were eliminated, leaving a scale with an alpha of **.760**.

VALIDITY:

A factor analysis of the 20 items composing the entire index was conducted. The five items composing each of the four scales loaded most heavily on their respective factors and had extremely low loadings on the other three factors. This pattern of loadings provides some evidence of convergent and discriminant validity.

ADMINISTRATION:

The scale was self-administered along with several other measures in a mail survey instrument. Higher scores indicate that consumers have positive attitudes about advertising in general whereas low scores suggest that they have a poor opinion of advertising and think it is deceptive and annoying.

MAJOR FINDINGS:

The purpose of the study was to report on the construction and validation of an index to measure consumers' attitudes toward marketing that could be used repeatedly over time as an indicator of the public's general sentiment about the field. Scores on the index were strongly correlated with another general measure of consumer sentiment and consumer satisfaction with the marketing mix elements.

As noted above, **advertising** was just one of four subscales composing the index. Its scores had the following significant correlations with the other subscales: .332 (price), .377 (product quality), and .301 (retailing).

REFERENCE:

Gaski, John F. and Michael J. Etzel (1986), "The Index of Consumer Sentiment Toward Marketing," *JM*, 50 (July), 71- 81.

SCALE ITEMS: ATTITUDE TOWARD ADVERTISING

Strongly Disagree	Agree	Neutral	Disagree	Strongly Agree
1	2	3	4	5

1. Most advertising provides consumers with essential information. **(r)**+
2. Most advertising is very annoying.
3. Most advertising makes false claims.
4. If most advertising was eliminated, consumers would be better off.
5. I enjoy most ads. **(r)**
6. Advertising should be more closely regulated. +
7. Most advertising is intended to deceive rather than to inform consumers.

+ These items were eliminated to have a five-item scale.

SCALE NAME: Attitude Toward Advertising

SCALE DESCRIPTION:

A 10-item, five-point Likert-type summated ratings scale measuring a person's belief in advertising and liking of ads in various media.

SCALE ORIGIN:

The measure originates from a dissertation published by Moschis in 1978. His 1981 study, reported below, is from that same dissertation research.

SAMPLES:

Moschis' (1981) data came from **806** middle school or senior high school students. There were 365 "older" adolescents (15 years and older) and 441 "younger" adolescents (younger than 15 years). The students came from 13 schools and seven towns in Wisconsin representing a wide variety of urban to rural situations. The author indicates that the sample was well balanced in terms of most demographic characteristics except sex, as nearly two-thirds of the respondents were female.

RELIABILITY:

An alpha of **.54** was reported for the scale.

VALIDITY:

No examination of scale validity was reported.

ADMINISTRATION:

The scale was self-administered by students along with several other measures in a 10-page instrument during a regular class session. Lower scores on the scale indicate that respondents have positive opinions about advertising whereas higher scores suggest that they have negative attitudes.

MAJOR FINDINGS:

The study investigated the validity of the cognitive development approach to socialization (e.g., Piaget) to predict a wide variety of consumer-related cognitions learned during adolescence. In general, the findings indicated that the cognitive developmental model did not explain consumer socialization during adolescence very well. Older adolescents had significantly less favorable **attitude**s toward **advertising**, brands, and prices than did younger children.

COMMENTS:

The low internal consistency indicates that the scale is not very reliable. This could be due to several different factors being represented in the scale. Redevelopment and testing are needed before the scale is used further.

REFERENCES:

Moschis, George P. (1978), *Acquisition of the Consumer Role by Adolescents*, Research Monograph No. 82. Atlanta, Ga.: Publishing Services Division, College of Business Administration, Georgia State University.

_____ (1981), ''Patterns of Consumer Learning,'' *JAMS*, 9 (2), 110-126.

SCALE ITEMS: ATTITUDE TOWARD ADVERTISING

Strongly Disagree	Agree	Neutral	Disagree	Strongly Agree
5	4	3	2	1

1. Most television commercials are fun to watch.
2. When I see or hear something new advertised, I often want to buy it.
3. Advertisements help people buy things that are best for them.
4. Most radio commercials are annoying. **(r)**
5. I think there should be less advertising than there is now.(r)
6. Most advertising that comes through the mail is junk and not worth looking at. **(r)**
7. Most magazine advertisements are enjoyable to look at.
8. Most advertisements tell the truth.
9. I don't pay much attention to advertising. **(r)**
10. Most newspaper advertisements are enjoyable to look at.

SCALE NAME: Attitude Toward Advertising (Semantic Differential)

SCALE DESCRIPTION:

The scales consist of various bipolar adjectives presumed to measure the subject's overall evaluation of advertising in general. The scales have in common the feature of not being specific to any particular advertisements. Specific scale items and number of scale points are indicated below for the various versions that have been used. Both advertising and comparative advertising measures are reported here for simplicity because they utilize many of the same items.

SCALE ORIGIN:

The scales used to measure this construct seem to have been developed in the research cited herein. The basis for most of these scales is the semantic differential, developed by Osgood, Suci, and Tannenbaum (1957). The underlying concept for the semantic differential is that a stimulus becomes a sign of the significate when it gives rise to the idea or thought of the significate. Measurement is accomplished by use of a series of semantic differential scales (a combination of controlled word association and scaling procedures). Each semantic differential scale is purported to represent a straight line through the origin of a semantic space. A selected combination of such scales is then believed to represent a multidimensional space. A listing of potential scale items and the dimensions of semantic space they are purported to represent is provided by Osgood, Suci, and Tannenbaum (1957, Ch. 2). The technique is believed by the authors to be highly generalizable and adaptable to most research needs.

A seven-point scale is generally recommended by Osgood and his coauthors though specific circumstances may warrant a different number of scale points. A large number of the items used in these scales have been developed over the last 30 years and represent two subconstructs: attitudes toward the institution of advertising and attitudes toward the instruments of advertising (Sandage and Leckenby 1980). The second of these has often been construed as a measure of the general credibility of advertising and/or beliefs about the general credibility of advertising. The scales reported here are identified with such nomenclature where appropriate.

SAMPLES:

Grossbart, Muehling, and Kangun (1986) used **111** graduate students. Muehling (1987) used **88** undergraduate students in a classroom setting. MacKenzie and Lutz (1989) used a developmental sample of **203** students attending a major midwestern university. Age ranged from 20 to 25 years and about half were men. The validation sample consisted of **120** MBA and undergraduate students attending a major university in southern California. Age ranged from 20 to 32 years and approximately 60% were men.

RELIABILITY:

Grossbart, Muelhing, and Kangun (1986) report alpha values of .**75**, .**84**, .**87**, and .**89** for attitude toward advertising, attitude toward comparative advertising, attitude toward advertising claims, and attitude toward comparitive advertising claims, respectively. Muehling (1987) reports alpha values of .**97**, .**73**, and .**79** for global attitude toward advertising, attitute toward the institution of advertising, and attitude toward the instruments of advertising, respectively. MacKenzie and Lutz (1989) report alpha values of **.90** and **.72** for attitude toward advertising and advertising credibility, respectively.

VALIDITY:

The long history of the use of semantic differential scales in advertising and marketing research on attitudes toward ads, products, brands, and institutions such as advertising and advertisers speaks somewhat to the validity of the method. However, only in limited circumstances have the specific measures been subjected to validation procedures. Sandage and Leckenby (1980) reviewed work prior to the inclusion date of this compendium that indicates reasonable construct, nomolgical, and predictive validity for the measures as used by Muehling (1987). Additionally, Muehling subjected his attitude toward the institution and toward the instrument measures to confirmatory factor analysis. The results clearly indicated that the eight items belonged four each to the two distinct dimensions of attitudte toward advertising.

MacKenzie and Lutz (1989) attempted to validate a model of the attitude toward the advertisement process as it develops from the broad constructs of generalized attitudes toward advertising as reported here to the specific attitudes toward the ad and the advertised brand. To the extent that their measures allowed model development and validation, a sense of nomological validity adheres to the measures themselves.

ADMINISTRATION:

Paper-and-pencil administration as a part of a longer instrument appears to be the method of choice. Subjects are asked to evaluate advertising or some component of advertising in general on the basis of the adjective listing and to mark the scale appropriately. All items reported here are on a seven-point scale, with lower scores indicating a lower attitude toward advertising. Time is of minimal consequence in completing the instrument.

MAJOR FINDINGS:

Grossbart, Muehling, and Kangun (1986) assessed global attitude toward advertising measures as possible covariates to the dependent measures of the study. Attitude toward comparative advertising significantly mediated noncomparative recall whereas attitude toward advertising significantly mediated subject's acceptance of advertised claims, attitude toward the sponser, and intention to by the sponser's brand.

Muehling (1987) attempted to assess the dimensionality of the global construct, attitude toward advertising. He found that attitude toward the institution and attitude toward the instrument explained over 57% of the variance in the global measure. Additionally, he found that the two dimension measures were significantly associated with the thought catagories "function" (institution, $p < .05$) and "practices" (instrument, $p < .01$). These thought catagories represent valanced, catagorized cognitive responses from subjects relating to what they thought about advertising. Subjects' attitudes toward the institution of advertising (mean = 5.70) were significantly higher than their attitudes toward the instrument of advertising (mean = 4.32) ($p < .001$). In a separate analysis, Muehling (1987) found five of 20 belief items to be significantly associated with the global attitude toward the ad measure. Beliefs about whether or not advertising insults the intelligence of the consumer, presents a true picture of products advertised, should have legal limits placed on its expenditures, creates desires for unnecessary goods, and has a higher standard than 10 years ago explained 58% of the variance in the attitude toward advertising in general measure's responses. The two scaled dimensions, the two valanced thought catagories, and the five belief statements together explained nearly 75% of the attitude toward advertising in general response.

MacKenzie and Lutz (1989) used their global advertising attitude measures as indicators of the broader latent constructs in a model of the advertising attitude formation process. After fitting their model through a devopmental sample's responses, revising the model on the basis of those results, and then subjecting the model to data from a validation sample, they found advertising credibility causally exogenous to advertiser credibility and advertising attitude, but not directly linked with credibility toward a specific ad. Advertising attitude was found to be causally exogenous to ad perceptions and ad attitude, the latter being significantly stronger than the researchers had hypothesized.

COMMENTS:

Though all of the scales reported here are bipolar adjective scales and all in some way are purported to measure generalized/global or some dimension of generalized/global attitude toward advertising, each is a slightly different conceptualization of the construct. The researcher must ascertain the most appropriate variation for his or her specific research needs.

REFERENCES:

Grossbart, Sanford, Darrel D. Muehling, and Norman Kangun (1986), ''Verbal and Visual References to Competition in Comparative Advertising,'' *JA,* 15 (1), 10-23.

MacKenzie, Scott and Richard J. Lutz (1989), ''An Empirical Examination of the Structural Antecedents of the Ad in an Advertising Pretesting Context,'' *JM,* 53 (April) 48- 65.

Muehling, Darrel D. (1987), ''An Investigation of Factors Underlying Attitude-Toward-Advertising-in-General,'' *JA,* 16 (1), 32-40.

Osgood, Charles E., George J. Suci, and Percy H. Tannenbaum (1957), *The Measurement of Meaning.* Urbana, Ill.: University of Illinois Press.

Sandage, C. H. and John D. Leckenby (1980), ''Student Attitudes Toward Advertising: Institution Vs. Instrument,'' *JA,* 9 (2), 29-32+.

SCALE ITEMS: ATTITUDE TOWARD ADVERTISING (SEMANTIC DIFFERENTIAL)

Scale items used in specific studies are listed below with indication of whether item sums or means of sums were used in the research analysis. All scales reported here had seven points for each scale item. Some of the items may not reflect bi-polar opposites, as originally suggested by Osgood, Suci, and Tannenbaum (1957). Scale name variants or dimensions are indicated.

MacKenzie and Lutz (1989) (credibility): 4,5,6 (mean), 7-point.
MacKenzie and Lutz (1989) (general): 1,2,3 (mean).
Muehling (1987) (global): 1,2,7 (mean).
Muehling (1987) (institution): 1,8,9,10 (mean).
Muehling (1987) (instuments): 11,12,13,14 (mean).

Grossbart, Muehling, and Kangun (1986) (general): 12,15,16,17,18 (mean).
Grossbart, Muehling, and Kangun (1986) (comparative): 12,15,16,17,18 (mean).
Grossbart, Muehling, and Kangun (1986) (advertising claims): 19,20,21,22,23,24 (mean).
Grossbart, Muehling, and Kangun (1986) (comparative claims): 19,20,21,22,23,24. (mean).

1. good   ____ : ____ : ____ : ____ : ____ : ____ : ____   bad
            1   2   3   4   5   6   7

2. pleasant   ____ : ____ : ____ : ____ : ____ : ____ : ____   unpleasant
            1   2   3   4   5   6   7

3. favorable   ____ : ____ : ____ : ____ : ____ : ____ : ____   unfavorable
            1   2   3   4   5   6   7

4. convincing   ____ : ____ : ____ : ____ : ____ : ____ : ____   unconvincing
            1   2   3   4   5   6   7

5. believable   ____ : ____ : ____ : ____ : ____ : ____ : ____   unbelievable
            1   2   3   4   5   6   7

6. biased   ____ : ____ : ____ : ____ : ____ : ____ : ____   unbiased **(r)**
            1   2   3   4   5   6   7

7. negative   ____ : ____ : ____ : ____ : ____ : ____ : ____   positive **(r)**
            1   2   3   4   5   6   7

8. weak   ____ : ____ : ____ : ____ : ____ : ____ : ____   strong **(r)**
            1   2   3   4   5   6   7

9. worthless   ____ : ____ : ____ : ____ : ____ : ____ : ____   valuable **(r)**
            1   2   3   4   5   6   7

10. unnecessary   ____ : ____ : ____ : ____ : ____ : ____ : ____   necessary **(r)**
            1   2   3   4   5   6   7

11. dirty   ____ : ____ : ____ : ____ : ____ : ____ : ____   clean **(r)**
            1   2   3   4   5   6   7

12. dishonest   ____ : ____ : ____ : ____ : ____ : ____ : ____   honest **(r)**
            1   2   3   4   5   6   7

13. insincere   ____ : ____ : ____ : ____ : ____ : ____ : ____   sincere **(r)**
            1   2   3   4   5   6   7

14. dangerous   ____ : ____ : ____ : ____ : ____ : ____ : ____   safe **(r)**
            1   2   3   4   5   6   7

15. attractive   ____ : ____ : ____ : ____ : ____ : ____ : ____   unattractive
            1   2   3   4   5   6   7

16. interesting   ____ : ____ : ____ : ____ : ____ : ____ : ____   dull
            1   2   3   4   5   6   7

17. offensive   ___ : ___ : ___ : ___ : ___ : ___ : ___   unoffensive
   1   2   3   4   5   6   7   **(r)**

18. ethical   ___ : ___ : ___ : ___ : ___ : ___ : ___   unethical
   1   2   3   4   5   6   7

19. clear   ___ : ___ : ___ : ___ : ___ : ___ : ___   unclear
   1   2   3   4   5   6   7

20. confusing   ___ : ___ : ___ : ___ : ___ : ___ : ___   understandable
   1   2   3   4   5   6   7   **(r)**

21. believable   ___ : ___ : ___ : ___ : ___ : ___ : ___   unbelievable
   1   2   3   4   5   6   7

22. truthful   ___ : ___ : ___ : ___ : ___ : ___ : ___   not truthful
   1   2   3   4   5   6   7

23. useful   ___ : ___ : ___ : ___ : ___ : ___ : ___   not useful
   1   2   3   4   5   6   7

24. helpful   ___ : ___ : ___ : ___ : ___ : ___ : ___   not helpful
   1   2   3   4   5   6   7

SCALE NAME: Attitude Toward Advertising by Professionals

SCALE DESCRIPTION:

Hite and Bellizzi (1986) used an eight-item, five-point Likert-type scale measuring overall attitude toward advertising by profesionals (accountants, physicians, and lawyers). Each scale item is constructed so that the name of the profession of interest can be inserted.

SCALE ORIGIN:

The scale used by Hite and Bellizzi originated in their study.

SAMPLES:

The subjects in the Hite and Bellizzi study were **489** (97.8% response rate) members of the Arkansas Household Research Panel.

RELIABILITY:

Cronbach's alpha was **.93, .79,** and **.93** for the accountant, lawyer, and physician versions of the scale, respectively.

VALIDITY:

No validation analysis was reported.

ADMINISTRATION:

Twenty-four items (three eight-item scales) addressing attitude toward professionals' advertising and 28 additional questions of interest were administered to the panel through the mail.

MAJOR FINDINGS:

Subjects were generally positive about professionals' advertising, with more than 80% agreeing that advertising would not lower the image of professionals, could be done tastefully, and useful information could be provided. Subjects were significantly (p=.01) more favorable toward advertising by accountants than toward advertising by either lawyers or physicians.

REFERENCE:

Hite, Robert E. and Joseph A. Bellizzi (1986), "Consumers' Attitudes Toward Accountants, Lawyers, and Physicians With Respect to Advertising Professional Services," *JAR,* 26 (June/July), 45-54.

SCALE ITEMS: ATTITUDE TOWARD ADVERTISING BY PROFESSIONALS

Responses are recorded on a five-point scale where 1 = strongly agree, 3 = no opinion, and 5 = strongly disagree.

1. It is proper for (accountants, lawyers, physicians) to advertise.
2. Advertising would help consumers make more intellegent choices between (accountants, lawyers, physicians).
3. I would use the services, if needed, of a (accountant, lawyer, physician) who advertises.
4. If a (accountant, lawyer, physician) advertises, his credibility is lowered. **(r)**
5. The advertising of fees would lower the public image of (accountants, lawyers, physicians). **(r)**
6. Advertising by (accountants, lawyers, physicians) would tend to lower the dignity of their profession. **(r)**
7. The advertising of services would lower the public's image of (accountants, lawyers, physicians). **(r)**
8. Advertising by (accountants, lawyers, physicians) would tend to lower the credibility of their profession. **(r)**

SCALE NAME: Attitude Toward Advertising by Professionals

SCALE DESCRIPTION:

Snizek and Crocker (1985) used a 10-item, five-point Likert-type scale to measure attitude toward advertising by attorneys.

SCALE ORIGIN:

Snizek and Crocker based their scale on work by Shimp and Dyer (1978) and Darling and Hacket (1978). Items were modified to address attorney advertising.

SAMPLES:

Snizek and Crocker's sample consisted of **109** (after two deletions) practicing attorneys in Virginia (37% response rate).

RELIABILITY:

Cronbach's alpha was reported to be **.834**.

VALIDITY:

No validation analysis was reported.

ADMINISTRATION:

A self-report mail survey included the 10-item attitude toward advertising scale and other attitudinal and demographic measures.

MAJOR FINDINGS:

Overall, attorneys' attitudes toward professionalism accounted for only 5% of the variance in their attitudes toward attorney advertising. The only dimension of professionalism that was significantly negatively related to attitude toward attorney advertising was attitude toward self regulation (p < .05).

COMMENTS:

With minor modifications, the scale items seem to be amenable for use in studying the same construct in other professional fields.

REFERENCES:

Darling, John and Donald Hacket (1978), "The Advertising of Fees and Service: A Study of Contrasts Between and Similarities Among Professional Groups," *JA*, 2 (2), 23-34.
Shimp, Terence and Robert F. Dyer (1978), "How the Legal Profession Views Legal Service Advertising," *JM*, 42 (3), 74-81.

Snizek, William E. and Kenneth E. Crocker (1985), ''Professionalism and Attorney Attitudes Toward Legal Service Advertising,'' *JAMS*, 13 (4), 101-118.

SCALE ITEMS: ATTITUDE TOWARD ADVERTISING BY PROFESSIONALS

Responses are recorded on a five-point Likert scale where 1 = strongly agree and 5 = strongly disagree.

1. Advertising will help the public make more intelligent decisions when choosing a lawyer.
2. Advertising will help increase the public's knowledge of legal services offered.
3. Advertising will serve to increase the competition among lawyers to the benefit of the client.
4. Advertising will diminish the image of lawyers in the eyes of the public. (r)
5. To advertise my qualifications and competence will damage the dignity of my profession. (r)
6. Advertising by attorneys will be beneficial for me personally.
7. If I were to advertise, the reaction on the part of my fellow lawyers would be an adverse one. (r)
8. Advertising of fees and services by lawyers will serve to decrease the degree of skepticism with which the public views the profession.
9. I personally approve of advertising by lawyers.
10. I expect to see an increase in the amount of advertising undertaken by law firms.

SCALE NAME: Attitude Toward the Ad

SCALE DESCRIPTION:

A five-item, three-point summated ratings scale measuring a consumer's satisfaction with the advertisements for a specified product.

SCALE ORIGIN:

The scale was original to the study by Maddox (1982) and was developed as part of a doctoral dissertation (Maddox 1976). Only a few details of the scale's development are provided here, but much more can be found by consulting the dissertation.

SAMPLES:

Participants in the study were students enrolled in sociology, home economics, or business courses at the Ohio State University during the summer of 1975. About 700 survey forms were distributed and **373** completed ones were returned. The typical respondent was male (68%), undergraduate (69%), a business major (68%), never married (57%), and worked either full or part time (50%). Respondents were randomly assigned one of four products to evaluate: bread (n = 94), electric toasters (n = 88), spray deodorant (n = 94), or tennis shoes (n = 97).

RELIABILITY:

Separate alpha values were calculated for each of the four products evaluated in the study and ranged from .73 (tennis shoes) to .79 (spray deodorant). Alpha for the scale across products was reported as **.79**.

VALIDITY:

The multitrait-multimethod technique was used to examine the scales developed in the study. As with the other scales, this one apparently exhibited convergent and discriminant validity.

ADMINISTRATION:

Students were given the survey instrument, asked to complete it outside the classroom, and to return it at another time. The author assigned the following numerical values to the potential item responses: Y = 3, ? = 2, and N = 1. By this sort of scoring system, high scores would indicate consumers are very satisfied with the advertising for a product. Low scores would mean that consumers have very negative attitudes about a product's advertising.

MAJOR FINDINGS:

The purpose of the study was to develop a standardized instrument that could be used to measure relative consumer **satisfaction** with different products. A 60-item instrument resulted that was composed of four subscales: satisfaction with the product, its **advertising**, its pricing, and its placement. The subscales showed evidence of convergent validity and limited evidence of discriminant validity.

COMMENTS:

This scale can be treated as one subscale of a larger 60-item instrument. Other subscales measure satisfaction with the product, its price, and its placement. The 60-item set was reported to have an alpha of .90 calculated across the four products examined.

REFERENCES:

Maddox, R. Neil (1976), "Measuring Consumer Satisfaction," unpublished doctoral dissertation, The Ohio State University.

_____ (1982), "The Structure of Consumers' Satisfaction: Cross-Product Comparisons," *JAMS*, 10 (Winter), 37-53.

SCALE ITEMS: ATTITUDE TOWARD THE AD

Y: This item describes this product's advertising
?: Undecided
N: This item does *not* describe this product's advertising

Y	?	N	Insults people's intelligence **(r)**
Y	?	N	Misleading **(r)**
Y	?	N	False **(r)**
Y	?	N	Accurate
Y	?	N	Deceptive **(r)**

SCALE NAME: Attitude Toward the Ad (Activity Judgments)

SCALE DESCRIPTION:

This is a Likert-like scale purported to measure the activity dimension of semantic judgment of consumers toward advertisements. A 15-item, five-point version of the scale was used by Burke and Edell (1986) and in study 1 of Edell and Burke (1987). A 10-item, five-point version was used by Burke and Edell (1989) and in study 2 of Edell and Burke (1987).

SCALE ORIGIN:

The scale was developed in the studies reported by Burke and Edell (1989) but the items themselves were taken from the Reaction Profile For TV Commercials developed by Wells, Leavitt, and McConville (1971).

SAMPLES:

Subjects were **184** (1986) and **191** (1989) people recruited by newspaper ads and announcements distributed on a university campus. Other than the fact that subjects were deceived about the true purpose of the research and were paid for participation, no other description of the sample was given. It would be reasonable to assume it consisted of university students, however. The scale development subjects were also used for the research reported in the findings section. A similar procedure was used by Edell and Burke (1987) to recruit **29** subjects for study 1 and **32** for study 2.

RELIABILITY:

Cronbach's alpha was reported to be **.93** and **.91** in the 1986 and 1989 studies, respectively. Alpha may be biased upward, however. The authors used repeated measures of the subjects over six different stimuli. Reliability may be biased upward as measurement was based on as many as 1146 observations (six per subject). Because of repeated measurement with the same subjects, the authors claim replicability, though the stimuli were different. Edell and Burke (1987) reported alpha as **.95** for the 15-item version and **.90** for the 10-item version. Again, a concern for the upward bias of these alpha values should be noted because of repeated measurement by 29 subjects for 10 different ads.

The difference in the 10- and 15-word versions was that those items with item-total correlations greater than .9 were eliminated due to redundancy (Edell and Burke 1987, p. 428).

VALIDITY:

Content analysis was demonstrated through principal components factor analysis. Of the original items, only those loading at least .50 on the activity factor alone were retained for the scale. Factors were very similar between studies and virtually identical across repeated measures within studies.

ADMINISTRATION:

The scale is a paper-and-pencil instrument amenable to survey research and experimental studies. Even though measurement requires an object stimulus, it is not necessary that administration be temporally contingent with stimulus presentation. No time period for administration was reported. It is not known if the 10 items in this scale can be administered independently of the five other items in the original pool.

MAJOR FINDINGS:

Burke and Edell (1986) reported two important findings relative to this and two other ad judgment scale measures. First, these scaled measures of ad attitude do not demonstrate decay and subsequent rebound of subjects attitudes over time without exposure. Secondly, over repeated measures, the factor structures from which these scales were developed did not vary. Among the findings in the Edell and Burke studies (1987) was that **activity judgements** had some impact on attitude toward the ad but not as much as evaluation judgments. In Burke and Edell (1989) structural equation analysis indicates **activity judgments** have a significant ($p < .05$) direct effect on attitude toward the ad. They also act as an intermediating variable in channeling significant indirect effects of upbeat and negative feelings to attitudes toward the ad and attitude toward the brand through Attitude toward the ad.

COMMENTS:

Though the authors claim generalizability for their findings, lack of important sample information indicates caution in this respect.

REFERENCES:

Burke, Marian C. and Julie A. Edell (1986), "Ad Reactions Over Time: Capturing Changes in the Real World," *JCR*, 13 (June), 114-118.

_____ and _____ (1989), "The Impact of Feelings on Ad-Based Affect and Cognitions," *JMR*, 26 (February), 69-83.

Edell, Julie E. and Marian C. Burke (1987), "The Power of Feelings in Understanding Advertising Effects," *JCR*, 14 (December), 421-433.

Wells, William D., Clark Leavitt, and Maureen McConville (1971), "A Reaction Profile for TV Commercials," *JAR*, 11 (December), 11-17.

SCALE ITEMS: ATTITUDE TOWARD THE AD (ACTIVITY JUDGMENTS) +

Instructions: Please tell us how well you think each of the words listed below describes the ad you have just seen by putting a number to the right of the word. Here, we are interested in your thoughts about the ad, not the brand or product class. If you think the word describes the ad extremely well, put a 5; very well, put a 4; fairly well, put a 3; not very well, put a 2; not at all well, put a 1.

1. Energetic
2. Exciting
3. Humorous
4. Imaginative
5. Ingenious
6. Merry
7. Novel
8. Playful

9. Unique
10. Vigorous
11. Amusing
12. Enthusiastic
13. Exhilarating
14. Jolly
15. Original

+ The first 10 words compose the shorter version of the scale.

SCALE NAME: Attitude Toward the Ad (Brand Reinforcement)

SCALE DESCRIPTION:

This is a Likert-type scale with two to seven items. Most development has been reported in conjunction with the items Schlinger (1979a) used to measure consumer attitude toward the ad, which relate to the brand in a television advertisement. The items composing each of the scales are changed or modified on a user-determined basis. The items reported here are those available in the published literature used in the development of this compendium.

SCALE ORIGIN:

This scale represents one of seven attitude constructs measured by the Leo Burnett Viewer Response Profile (Schlinger 1979a). An original list of 600 attitudinal statements were culled from verbatim responses of over 400 viewers of 14 different commercials and story boards. These were reduced to 139 items through deletion of duplications and items that were commercial-specific or deemed "theoretically" inappropriate by the researcher. The remaining statements were analyzed empirically to determine factor structure and discriminant characteristics of individual items. After five separate analyses and refinements, the final of which was an analysis of the mean item scores from the first four analyses, a seven-factor solution was achieved. In general, only items with factor loadings of .5 or higher in at least three of the five factor analyses were retained for the scales. These items were then tested through 18 analysis of variance routines to determine their discrimination capabilities. Only items discriminating at $p < .01$ in at least six of 18 trials were retained. The outcome of these analyses produced the seven-factor, 32-item short version of the Leo Burnett Viewer Response Profile.

SAMPLES:

This scale was developed with post-hoc data for the original 600 items. The first factor analysis sample consisted of 20 women assumed to be from the Chicago area for each of 25 tested commercials (n = **500**). The women were selected by age (half older than 35 years, half younger than 35 years) and education level (about one third had two or more years of college). The second factor analysis utilized a sample of 50 respondents similar to those in the first sample for each of 10 of the 25 original commercials (n = **500**). The third analysis used a total of **1504** men and women rating 42 different untested commercials. Though the author reports sample controls remained constant, no indication of the controls is given. As men were included in this sample, it is not clear that reference is to controls used in previous sampling. The fourth sample totaled **1871** men and women rating one of 40 different commercials viewed over a period of four years. No subject statistics are available. The fifth factor analysis sample represented all subjects previously used in the study (n = 4375). No sample information is explicitly stated for ANOVA analysis. During the course of the scale development study, 377 different commercials were used (Schlinger 1979a). Zinkhan and Burton (1989) attempted replication with 26 product class users, each viewing 25 television commercials.

RELIABILITY:

Individual items were tested-retested with a 30-day interval for six different stimuli, resulting in correlations of .87 to .97. Test-retest on a modified version of the scale (only five items, specifics not reported) with the same criteria as used for the individual items yielded r = .86. The sample for reliability tests was 30 respondents per stimulus (n = 180).

As in scale construction, items seem to be added and deleted at the discretion of the researcher. Caution in interpretation is suggested. Schlinger (1979a) claims stability with small samples. The scale generally replicates the factor structure (Schlinger 1979b). Coefficient of congruence was .703 for the entire Schlinger profile and both items of the brand reinforcement scale loaded at less than .20 in the replication by Zinkhan and Burton (1989). Scale stability is questionable.

VALIDITY:

Factor structure was similar to that found in previous research (Wells, Leavitt, and McConville 1971). Some items were developed on the basis of theoretical underpinnings indicating construct validity, face validity is claimed, and predictive validity is demonstrated through case analysis (Schlinger 1979a). Because the scale was developed in a realistic copy-testing setting, the measure should be generalizable to that purpose. However, forced exposure to that condition warrants some caution if the scale is used to assess attitudes in less constrained viewing conditions. When the scale was used in conjunction with the other three scales developed by Schlinger to represent the viewer response profile, Zinkhan and Burton (1989) reported reasonably good nomologic and predictive validity relative to attitude toward the brand (r = .32, p < .01) and choice behavior (r = .30, p < .01). Because this scale did not replicate in their study, its validity is highly questionable.

ADMINISTRATION:

The scale can be administered under typical survey design methodologies in a paper-and-pencil format or responses can be recorded by the researcher in personal or telephone interviews, though no use of the scale has been reported with the latter administrations. No time for administration is noted. Unfortunately, in the scale's development and use, items have been substituted, added, or deleted at the researcher's whim, so the exact items to be used in administration may not be clear.

MAJOR FINDINGS:

Using a six-item version of the scale (items unreported), Olson, Schlinger, and Young (1982) found mean scale scores were significantly higher (p < .001) when consumers rated commercials for existing products than when they rated commercials for new ones. However, two individual items were significantly higher for new products and two were higher for existing ones.

COMMENTS:

The scale appears to be a reliable and valid measure of consumer attitude toward brand reinforcement of an advertisement, but changes in scale items during development cast some suspicion on its validity and reliability. Failure to replicate in Zinkhan and Burton's (1989) study casts serious doubt on this scale as a valid measure.

REFERENCES:

Olson, David, Mary Jane Schlinger, and Charles Young (1982), "How Consumers React to New Product Ads," *JAR*, 22 (3), 24-30.

Schlinger, Mary Jane (1979a), "A Profile of Responses to Commercials," *JAR*, 19 (2), 37-48.

_____ (1979b), "Attitudinal Reactions to Advertisements," in *Attitude Research Under the Sun*, John Eighmey, ed. Chicago, Ill.: American Marketing Association, 171-197.

Wells, William, Clark Leavitt, and Maureen McConville (1971), "A Reaction Profile for TV Commercials," *JAR*, 11 (6), 11-17.

Zinkhan, George and Scot Burton (1989), "An Examination of Three Multidimensional Profiles for Assessing Consumer Reactions to Advertisements," *JA*, 18 (4), 6-14.

SCALE ITEMS: ATTITUDE TOWARD THE AD (BRAND REINFORCEMENT) +

Strongly Disagree	Disagree	Somewhat Disagree	Neutral or no Opinion	Somewhat Agree	Agree	Strongly Agree
1	2	3	4	5	6	7

1. That's a good brand. I wouldn't hesitate recommending it to others.* **abc**
2. I know that the advertised brand is a dependable, reliable one.* **abc**
3. What they said about the product was dishonest. **(r) bc**
4. As I watched, I thought of reasons why I should not buy the product. **(r) bc**
5. The commercial described certain specific product characteristics that are undesirable to me. **(r) c**
6. I found myself disagreing with some things in the commercial. **(r) c**
7. The commercial made exaggerated and untrue claims about the product. **(r) c**

+ Scale items reported here are from Schlinger (1979a), denoted a; Schlinger (1979b), denoted b; and Olson, Schlinger, and Young (1982), denoted c. It is not clear when specific items should be deleted for any particular scale usage. Items identified with an asterisk loaded less than .2 in Zinkhan and Burton's (1989) study.

SCALE NAME: Attitude Toward the Ad (Confusion)

SCALE DESCRIPTION:

A five-item Likert-like scale purporting to measure the cognitive confusion of specific television advertisements to consumers.

SCALE ORIGIN:

The scale was developed in a study by Lastovicka (1983) and was based on items from a more complete list from the Leo Burnett Storyboard Test (1977). Subjects were exposed in small groups to one of six different 60-second television commercials, then answered one open-ended question in which they were asked to list retrospectively the thoughts they had while viewing the commercial. The products advertised were six real branded products (beer, blue jeans, soft drinks, and automobiles). Results of item measurements were factor analyzed, resulting in three factors representing relevance, confusion, and entertainment. Each factor was treated as a scale measuring that respective construct and subjected to multitrait-multimethod testing per Kalleberg and Kluegel (1975).

SAMPLES:

A convenience sample of **634** undergraduate students in 20 class sections of a university business school was utilized. Eighty-three percent of the sample had used or purchased some brand from each of the four product classes in the month prior to the study.

RELIABILITY:

Cronbach's alpha was reported to be **.731**. See validity section for important note on reliability.

VALIDITY:

Construct validity was demonstrated through factor analysis. Of the original 16 items, only those loading at least .30 on the confusion factor alone were retained for the scale. Items expected to load on this factor did so, whereas those expected to load on other factors did not load on this factor. Confirmatory factor analysis of multitrait-multimethod structure indicated convergent and discriminant validity for this scale. However, analysis of the error variance indicated unacceptable levels of random error associated with this scale when paired with the open-ended measure. This finding draws into question the reliability of this measure.

ADMINISTRATION:

The scale is amenable to most survey research techniques. The validation study used a paper-and-pencil questionnaire approach. Time for administration was not given but is assumed to be quite short. The scale is likely to be integrated into a larger measurement study in application.

MAJOR FINDINGS:

Lastovicka (1983) reported no major findings for this scale beyond those pertaining to scale validation (above).

COMMENTS:

Caution should be exercised with use of this scale as the validation study provides no correlates to assess nomologic validity. Face and content validity seem reasonable, but reliability is unsatisfactory and all validation results may be sample-specific. Additionally, subjects were in a forced-exposure condition. Consumers in a realistic environment may choose not to expose themselves to commercials they do not see as relevant.

REFERENCES:

Kalleberg, A. L. and J. R. Kluegel (1975), "Analysis of the Multitrait-Multimethod Matrix: Some Limitations and an Alternative," *Journal of Applied Psychology*, 60 (February), 1-9.

Lastovicka, John L. (1983), "Convergent and Discriminant Validity of Television Rating Scales," *JA*, 12 (2), 14-23, 52.

Leo Burnett Company, Inc. (1977), *Manual for the Leo Burnett Storyboard Test System.* Chicago, Ill.: Leo Burnett Company, Inc.

SCALE ITEMS: ATTITUDE TOWARD THE AD (CONFUSION)

Strongly Disagree					Strongly Agree
1	2	3	4	5	6

1. I clearly understood the commercial. **(r)**
2. The commercial was too complex.
3. I was not sure what was going on in the commercial.
4. I was so busy watching the screen, I did not listen to the talk.
5. The commercial went by so quickly that it just did not make an impression on me.

SCALE NAME: Attitude Toward the Ad (Entertainment)

SCALE DESCRIPTION:

A seven-item Likert scale purported to measure consumer attitude toward the entertainment value of a television advertisement. This scale represents one of seven attitude constructs measured by the Leo Burnett Viewer Response Profile. The items composing each of the scales are changed or modified on a user-determined basis. The items reported here are those available in the published literature used in the development of this compendium.

SCALE ORIGIN:

An original list of 600 attitudinal statements were culled from verbatim responses of over 400 viewers of 14 different commercials and story boards (Schlinger 1979, 1984). These were reduced to 139 items through deletion of dupliations and items that were commercial-specific or deemed "theoretically" inappropriate by the researcher. The remaining statements were analyzed empirically to determine factor structure and discriminant characteristics of individual items. After five separate analyses and refinements, the final of which was an analysis of the mean item scores from the first four analyses, a seven-factor solution was achieved. In general, only items with factor loadings of .5 or higher in at least three of the five factor analyses were retained for the scales. These items were then tested through 18 analysis of variance routines to determine their discrimination capabilities. Only items discriminating at $p < .01$ in at least six of 18 trials were retained. The outcome of these analyses produced the seven-factor, 32-item short version of the Leo Burnett Viewer Response Profile. The entertainment scale reported here includes only one item loading at less than .50 (.49) on only one of the factor analyses.

SAMPLES:

Schlinger (1984) reports that the scale was developed with post-hoc data for the original 600 items. The first factor analysis sample consisted of 20 women assumed to be from the Chicago area for each of 25 tested commercials (n = 500). The women were selected by age (half older than 35 years, half younger than 35 years) and education level (about one third had two or more years of college). The second factor analysis utilized a sample of 50 respondents similar to those in the first sample for each of 10 of the 25 original commercials (n = 500). The third analysis used a total of 1504 men and women rating 42 different untested commercials. Though the author reports sample controls remained constant, no indication of the controls is given. As men were included in this sample, it is not clear that reference is to controls used in previous sampling. The fourth sample totaled 1871 men and women rating one of 40 different commercials viewed over a period of four years. No subject statistics are available. The fifth factor analysis sample represented all subjects previously used in the study (n = 4375). No sample information is explicitly stated for ANOVA analysis. During the course of the scale development study, 377 different commercials were used.

Zinkhan and Burton (1989) attempted replication with **26** product class users, each viewing 25 television commercials. Lastovicka (1983) used **634** undergraduate students in 20 different class sessions in his assessment of convergent and discriminant validity.

RELIABILITY:

Individual items were tested-retested with a 30-day interval by Schlinger (1984) for six different stimuli, resulting in correlations of .87 to .97. Test-retest on a modified version of the scale (only five items, specifics not reported) with the same criteria as used for the individual items yielded r = .86. The sample for reliability tests was 30 respondents per stimulus (n = 180). The author claims the scale has stability with small samples.

Coefficient of congruence was .703 for the entire Schlinger profile, and five of seven items of the entertainment scale loaded at less than .50 in Zinkhan and Burton's (1989) replication. Lastovicka (1983) reported a Cronbach's alpha of **.872**.

VALIDITY:

The factor structure reported by Schlinger (1984) is similar to the structure found in previous research where the entertainment construct emerged as the first factor also (Wells, Leavitt, and McConville 1971). Some items were developed on the basis of theoretical underpinnings indicating construct validity, face validity is claimed, and predictive validity is demonstrated through case analysis. Because the scale was developed in a realistic copy-testing setting, the measure should be generalizable to that purpose. However, forced exposure to that condition warrants some caution if the scale is used to assess attitudes in less constrained viewing conditions.

When the scale was used in conjunction with the other three scales developed by Schlinger to represent the viewer response profile, Zinkhan and Burton (1989) reported reasonably good nomologic and predictive validity relative to attitude toward the brand (r = .32, p < .01) and choice behavior (r = .30, p < .01).

Lastovicka (1983) factor analyzed items related to the constructs of entertainment, relevance, and confusion. Each item in each construct loaded highest and at least at the .30 factor loading on the hypothesized factor. Through path analysis and confirmatory factor analysis, Lastovicka found convergent and discriminant validity for both the entertainment and relevance construct measures with an open-ended, (unstructured) measure of each construct. He warns that method factors were not assessed.

ADMINISTRATION:

The scale can be administered under typical survey design methodologies in a paper-and-pencil format or responses can be recorded by the researcher in personal or telephone interviews, though no use of the scale has been reported with the latter administrations. No time for administration was noted. Unfortunately, in the scale's development, items have been repeatedly substituted, added, or deleted at the researcher's whim, so the exact items to be used in administration are not clear.

MAJOR FINDINGS:

In the domain of marketing literature reviewed, the scale has been used only in validation sorts of studies and no other major findings are available to report.

COMMENTS:

The scale appears to be a reliable and valid measure of consumer attitude toward entertainment quality of an advertisement, but various changes in scale items during development cast some suspicion on its validity and reliability. As four of seven items did not replicate in factor structure at .50 or better in Zinkhan and Burton's (1989) study, caution in use and interpretation should be exercised.

REFERENCES:

Lastovicka, John L. (1983), "Convergent and Discriminant Validiy of Television Commercial Rating Scales," *JA,* 12 *(2),* 14-23,52.

Schlinger, Mary Jane (1979), "Attitudinal Reactions to Advertisements," *Attitude Research Under the Sun,* John Eighmey, ed. Chicago, Ill.: American Marketing Association, 171-197.

_____ (1984), "A Profile of Responses to Commercials," *JAR, Classics,* 2, 26-34. (Note: This article originally appeared in *JAR,* 19 (2), 37-48.)

Wells, William, Clark Leavitt, and Maureen McConville (1971), "A Reaction Profile for TV Commercials," *JAR,* 11 (6), 11-17.

Zinkhan, George, and Scot Burton (1989), "An Examination of Three Multidimensional Profiles for Assessing Consumer Reactions to Advertisements," *JA,* 18 (4), 6-14.

SCALE ITEMS: ATTITUDE TOWARD THE AD (ENTERTAINMENT)+

Strongly Disagree	Disagree	Somewhat Disagree	Neutral or no Opinion	Somewhat Agree	Agree	Strongly Agree
1	2	3	4	5	6	7

1. The commercial was lots of fun to watch and listen to.
2. I thought it was clever and entertaining.
3. The enthusiasm of the commercial is catching—it picks you up.
4. The ad wasn't just selling the product—it was entertaining me. I appreciated that.*
5. The characters (or persons) in the commercial capture your attention. *
6. It's the kind of commercial that keeps running through your mind after you've seen it.*
7. I just laughed at it. I thought it was very funny and good.*
8. I have seen this commercial before. **(r)**
9. I have seen this commercial so many times that I am tired of it. **(r)**

+ Scale items reported here are from Schlinger (1984). It is not clear when specific items should be deleted for any particular scale usage, though on inspection it may be reasonable to separate entertainment items based on humor from others if the commercial being rated does not use a humorous appeal. Lastovicka (1983) validated the scale with items 1, 2, 4, 8, and 9 and, items 8 and 9 were used only in that study with this scale. Items 8 and 9 are similar to items in scale number 302. Items identified with an asterisk loaded less than .5 in the factor analysis by Zinkhan and Burton (1989).

SCALE NAME: Attitude Toward the Ad (Evaluation Judgments)

SCALE DESCRIPTION:

The Likert-like scale has been used with varying numbers of items, mostly single word descriptors, to measure consumers' evaluation of an ad rather than how an ad makes one feel. A 14-item, five-point version was used by Burke and Edell (1986); 11- and 14-item (five point) versions were used in Edell and Burke (1987); and an 11-item, five-point version was used by Burke and Edell (1989). The Whipple and Courtney (1980) version was an eight-item, five-point scale. Zinkhan, Locander, and Leigh (1986) used a three-phrase, eight-point version.

SCALE ORIGIN:

Though the set of items used by the five studies reported here are not exactly the same, they are each similar in that all or most of their items were derived from the Reaction Profile for TV Commercials developed by Wells, Leavitt, and McConville (1971). Four additional adjectives were tested by Burke and Edell (1986): believable, convincing, informative, and interesting. These adjectives were originally used as semantic differential measures in attitude-toward-the-ad research by Holbrook (1978) and Mitchell and Olson (1981). The items used by Zinkhan, Locander, and Leigh (1986) were modified forms of three items in the Reaction profile: likeable, enjoyable, good.

SAMPLES:

Whipple and Courtney (1980) used **144** women grocery shoppers randomly selected from a medium sized city and **68** advertising/marketing practitioners. Each sample was subsequently split into two subsamples matched on significant demographics within samples. In Zinkhan, Locander, and Leigh's study, **420** subjects recruited by an ad agency were divided evenly among 20 treatment groups. Subjects were compensated. Burke and Edell (1986) used **184** subjects recruited by announcements posted on a university campus. Subjects were paid $5 for their participation in the study. Subjects were similarly recruited in their other two studies. Two small samples (**29** and **32**) were utilized by Edell and Burke (1987) and **191** were used in Burke and Edell (1989) with their compensation in this latter study ranging from $7.50 to $40.

RELIABILITY:

Cronbach's alpha was reported to be **.93** by Burke and Edell (1986) and **.93** (n=29) and **.90** (n=32) for the two versions used by Edell and Burke (1987). An alpha of **.89** was reported by Burke and Edell (1989). It may be biased upward however. Authors used repeated measures of the 191 subjects over six different stimuli. Reliability may be biased upward as measurement was based on 1146 observations (six per subject). Because of repeated measurement with the same subjects, the authors claim replicability, though the stimuli were different. The difference in their eleven and fourteen item versions was due to the fact that some items with item-total correlations greater than .9 were eliminated due to redundancy. Whipple and Courtney (1980) report alpha values of .90 to .93 for their evaluative scale. Zinkhan, Locander, and Leigh (1986) report an alpha of **.95** with their three item version of the scale.

VALIDITY:

Principal components factor analysis was used in the three studies by Burke and Edell (1986, 1987, 1989) to determine the underlying factor structure of a large number of descriptors. Virtually identical factors found in each case. Whipple and Courtney (1980) subjected 14 items to principal components factor analysis and determined that there were two factors: a general evaluation factor (described here) and another measuring irritation (described elsewhere).

ADMINISTRATION:

The scale is a paper-and-pencil instrument amenable to survey research and experimental studies. Even though measurement requires an object stimulus, it is not necessary that administration be temporally contingent with stimulus presentation. No time period for administration was reported. In Whipple and Courtney's study, subjects where asked to look at a series of ads and rate each one on the scale items in a self-reported questionnaire.

MAJOR FINDINGS:

In general, Whipple and Courtney (1980) found practitioners and female consumers similar with respect to the **attitudes toward TV commercials** for typical household products. In particular, they found that both groups tended to see commercials that more progressively (sic) represented sex roles as more effective and less irritating than commercials that were more traditional in these portrayals.

Using external single sets components analysis, Zinkham, Locander, and Leigh (1986) found a strong relationship between **Attitude toward the Ad** and aided brand recall and ad recognition.

Burke and Edell (1986) used two different procedures to measure attitude-toward-the-ad: 34 adjective items composing three Likert-type scales and a single seven-point scale intended to measure overall attitude-toward-the-ad. These two approaches were compared with the level of exposure to the ad and a delay condition between exposures as covariates. The results indicated that the significant decrease in attitude-toward-the-ad (single-item global measure) over time could not be explained just by changes in the multi-dimensional evaluation of the ads (three scales).

Edell and Burke (1987) investigated the role of feelings in understanding attitude-toward-the-ad. The finding most relevant to this scale was that feelings generated by an ad (e.g., warmth) contribute uniquely to predictions of attitude-toward-the-ad and brand above that provided by measures of an ad's characteristics (such as the one described here).

In Burke and Edell's (1989) study, structural equation analysis indicated that evaluation judgments have a significant ($p < .05$) direct effect on **attitude toward the ad**. They also act as an intermediating variable in channeling significant indirect effects of upbeat, warm, and negative feelings to **attitudes toward the ad**, Brand attribute evaluations and Attitude toward the brand through **Attitude toward the ad**.

REFERENCES:

Burke, Marian C. and Julie A. Edell (1986), "Ad Reactions Over Time: Capturing Changes in the Real World," *JCR*, 13 (June), 114-118.

_____ and _____ (1989), "The Impact of Feelings on Ad-Based Affect and Cognitions," *JMR*, 26 (February), 69- 83.

Edell, Julie E. and Marian C. Burke (1987), "The Power of Feelings in Understanding Advertising Effects," *JCR,* 14 (December), 421-433.

Holbrook, Morris B. (1978), "Beyond Attitude Structure: Toward the Informational Determinants of Attitude," *JMR,* 15 (November) 546-556.

Mitchell, Andrew A. and Jerry C. Olson (1981), "Are Product Attribute Beliefs the Only Mediator of Advertising Effects on Brand Attitudes?," *JMR,* 18 (August) 318-322.

Wells, William D., Clark Leavitt, and Maureen McConville (1971), "A Reaction Profile for TV Commercials," *JAR,* 11 (December), 11-17.

Whipple, Thomas W. and Alice E. Courtney (1980), "How to Portray Women in TV Commercials," *JAR,* 20 (2) 53-59.

Zinkhan, George M., William B. Locander, and James H. Leigh (1986), "Dimensional Relationships of Aided Recall and Recognition," *JA,* 15 (1), 38-46.

SCALE ITEMS: ATTITUDE TOWARD THE AD (EVALUATION JUDGMENTS) +

Instructions: Please tell us how well you think each of the words listed below describes the ad you have just seen by putting a number to the right of the word. Here, we are interested in your thoughts about the ad, not the brand or product class. If you think the word describes the ad extremely well, put a 5; very well, put a 4; fairly well, put a 3; not very well, put a 2; not at all well, put a 1.

1. Believable
2. For me
3. Informative
4. Interesting
5. Irritating **(r)**
6. Meaningful to me
7. Phoney **(r)**
8. Ridiculous **(r)**
9. Terrible **(r)**
10. Valuable
11. Worth remembering
12. Convincing
13. Important to me
14. Stupid **(r)**
15. Realistic situation
16. Original
17. Intelligent
18. Makes me want to buy

+ Items 1 through 11 composed the 11-item scale referred to above (Burke and Edell 1986; Edell and Burke 1987) and items 1 through 14 composed the 14-item version (Burke and Edell 1989; Edell and Burke 1987). The scale used by Whipple and Courtney (1980) composed of items 2, 6, 11, 12, and 15 through 18.

The following phrases were used by Zinkhan, Locander, and Leigh (1986):
1. Liked the ad
2. Enjoyed the ad
3. Found ad to be good

SCALE NAME: Attitude Toward the Ad (Familiarity)

SCALE DESCRIPTION:

A three-item Likert scale, though some versions have more or fewer items. Most development has been reported in conjunction with the items Schlinger (1979a) used to measure consumer attitude toward the ad, which relate to the familiarity with the advertisement. This scale represents one of seven attitude constructs measured by the Leo Burnett Viewer Response Profile. The items composing each of the scales are changed or modified on a user-determined basis. The items reported here are those available in the published literature used in the development of this compendium.

SCALE ORIGIN:

An original list of 600 attitudinal statements were culled from verbatim responses of over 400 viewers of 14 different commercials and story boards. These were reduced to 139 items through deletion of duplications and items that were commercial-specific or deemed "theoretically" inappropriate by the researcher. The remaining statements were analyzed empirically to determine factor structure and discriminant characteristics of individual items. After five separate analyses and refinements, the final of which was an analysis of the mean item scores from the first four analyses, a seven-factor solution was achieved. In general, only items with factor loadings of .5 or higher in at least three of the five factor analyses were retained for the scales. These items were then tested through 18 analysis of variance routines to determine their discrimination capabilities. Only items discriminating at $p < .01$ in at least six of 18 trials were retained. The outcome of these analyses produced the seven-factor, 32-item short version of the Leo Burnett Viewer Response Profile (Schlinger 1979a).

SAMPLES:

This scale was developed with post-hoc data for the original 600 items. The first factor analysis sample consisted of 20 women assumed to be from the Chicago area for each of 25 tested commercials (n = **500**). The women were selected by age (half older than 35 years, half younger than 35 years) and education level (about one third had two or more years of college). The second factor analysis utilized a sample of 50 respondents similar to those in the first sample for each of 10 of the 25 original commercials (n = **500**). The third analysis used a total of **1504** men and women rating 42 different untested commercials. Though the author reports sample controls remained constant, no indication of the controls is given. As men were included in this sample, it is not clear that reference is to controls used in previous sampling. The fourth sample totaled **1871** men and women rating one of 40 different commercials viewed over a period of four years. No subject statistics are available. The fifth factor analysis sample represented all subjects previously used in the study (n = 4375). No sample information is explicitly stated for ANOVA analysis. During the course of the scale development study, 377 different commercials were used (Schlinger 1979a). Zinkhan and Burton (1989) did not test this scale in their work.

RELIABILITY:

Test-retest was conducted for the individual items with a 30-day interval for six different stimuli, resulting in correlations of .87 to .97. A two-item version test-retest with the same criteria as used for the individual items yielded r = .62. The sample for reliability tests was 30 respondents per stimulus (n = 180). As in scale construction, items seem to be added and deleted at the discretion of the researcher. Caution in use is suggested. Schlinger (1979a) claims stability with small samples. The scale generally replicates the factor structure (Schlinger 1979b).

VALIDITY:

Factor structure was similar to that found in previous research (Wells, Leavitt, and McConville 1971). Some of items were developed on the basis of theoretical underpinnings indicating construct validity, face validity is claimed, and predictive validity is demonstrated through case analysis (Schlinger 1979a). Because the scale was developed in a realistic copy-testing setting, the measure should be generalizable to that purpose. However, forced exposure to that condition warrants some caution if the scale is used to assess attitudes in less constrained viewing conditions.

ADMINISTRATION:

The scale can be administered under typical survey design methodologies in a paper-and-pencil format or responses can be recorded by the researcher in personal or telephone interviews, though no use of the scale has been reported with the latter administrations. No time for administration was noted. Unfortunately, in the scale's development and use, items have been substituted, added, or deleted at the researcher's whim, so the exact items which should be used in administration may not be clear.

MAJOR FINDINGS:

Using a four-item version of the scale (items unreported), Olson, Schlinger, and Young (1982) found mean scale scores were significantly higher (p < .001) when consumers rated commercials for existing products than when they rated commercials for new ones.

COMMENTS:

The scale appears to be a reliable and valid measure of consumer familiarity with an advertisement, but changes in scale items during development cast some suspicion on its validity and reliability.

REFERENCES:

Olson, David, Mary Jane Schlinger, and Charles Young (1982), "How Consumers React to New Product Ads," *JAR,* 22 (3), 24- 30.

Schlinger, Mary Jane (1979a), "A Profile of Responses to Commercials," *JAR,* 19 (2), 37-48.

———— (1979b) "Attitudinal Reactions to Advertisements," *Attitude Research Under the Sun*. John Eighmey, ed. Chicago, Ill.: American Marketing Association, 171-197.

Wells, William, Clark Leavitt, and Maureen McConville (1971), "A Reaction Profile for TV Commercials," *JAR,* 11 (6), 11- 17.

Zinkhan, George and Scot Burton (1989), "An Examination of Three Multidimensional Profiles for Assessing Consumer Reactions to Advertisements," *JA,* 18 (4), 6-14.

SCALE ITEMS: ATTITUDE TOWARD THE AD (FAMILIARITY) +

Strongly Disagree	Disagree	Somewhat Disagree	Neutral or no Opinion	Somewhat Agree	Agree	Strongly Agree
1	2	3	4	5	6	7

1. This kind of commercial has been done many times . . . it's the same old thing. **a**
2. I've seen this commercial so many times—I'm tired of it. **abc**
3. I think that this is an unusual commercial. I'm not sure I've seen another one like it. **(r) a**
4. Familiar. **bc**
5. Saw before. **bc**

+ Scale items reported here are from Schlinger (1979a), denoted by a; Schlinger (1979b), denoted by b; and Olson, Schlinger, and Young (1982), denoted by c. It is not clear when specific items should be deleted for any particular scale usage. Item 2 is also included in the Entertainment scale (#301).

SCALE NAME: Attitude Toward the Ad (Gentleness Judgments)

SCALE DESCRIPTION:

A Likert-like scale purporting to measure the gentleness dimension of consumers' semantic judgment of specific television advertisements. A five-item, five-point version was used by Burke and Edell (1986) as well as in study 1 of Edell and Burke (1987). A four-item, five-point version was used in Burke and Edell (1989) as well as in study 2 of Edell and Burke (1987). The difference in the two scales is that a descriptor with an item-total correlation greater than .9 was eliminated due to redundancy (Edell and Burke 1987, p. 428).

SCALE ORIGIN:

The scale was developed in the studies by Burke and Edell (1989) but the items themselves were all taken from the Reaction Profile For TV Commercials developed by Wells, Leavitt, and McConville (1971). In fact, the five-item version of the scale exactly corresponds to the sensuousness factor reported by Wells, Leavitt, and McConville (1971, p. 134).

SAMPLES:

The subjects were **184** (1986), **29, 32** (1987), and **191** (1989) people recruited by newspaper ads and announcements distributed on a university campus. Other than the fact that subjects were deceived about the true purpose of the research and were paid for participation, no other description of the sample was given. It would be reasonable to assume it consisted of university students, however. The scale development subjects were also used for the research reported in the findings section.

RELIABILITY:

Cronbach's alpha values of **.86**, **.88** (n=29), **.87** (n=32), and **.89** were reported for the Burke and Edell (1986), Edell and Burke (1987), and Burke and Edell (1989) studies, respectively.

VALIDITY:

Of the large group of items factor analyzed in each study, only those loading at least .50 were retained for use in scales. Further, these items always loaded together.

ADMINISTRATION:

The scale is a paper-and-pencil instrument amenable to survey research and experimental studies. Even though measurement requires an object stimulus, it is not necessary that administration be temporally contingent with stimulus presentation. No time period for administration was reported. It is not known if the four items in this scale can be administered independently of the 21 other items in the original pool.

MAJOR FINDINGS:

Burke and Edell (1986) reported two important findings relative to this and two other ad judgment scale measures. First, these scaled measures of ad attitude do not demonstrate decay and subsequent rebound of subjects attitudes over time without exposure. Secondly, over repeated measures, the factor structures from which these scales were developed did not vary.

Among the findings in the Edell and Burke studies (1987) was that **gentleness judgments** had no impact on attitude toward the ad or brand but did seem to be related to brand belief formation.

In Burke and Edell's (1989) study, structural equation analysis indicates that **gentleness judgments** have **no** significant ($p < .05$) direct effect on attitude toward the ad. They also **do not** act as an intermediating variable in channeling significant indirect effects of upbeat, warm, and negative feelings to attitudes toward the ad or brand.

COMMENTS:

Though the authors claim generalizability for their findings, lack of important sample information indicates caution in this respect.

REFERENCES:

Burke, Marian C. and Julie A. Edell (1986), ''Ad Reactions Over Time: Capturing Changes in the Real World,'' *JCR,* 13 (June), 114-118.

_____ and _____ (1989), ''The Impact of Feelings on Ad-Based Affect and Cognitions,'' *JMR,* 26 (February), 69- 83.

Edell, Julie E. and Marian C. Burke (1987), ''The Power of Feelings in Understanding Advertising Effects,'' *JCR,* 14 (December), 421-433.

Wells, William D., Clark Leavitt, and Maureen McConville (1971), ''A Reaction Profile for TV Commercials,'' *JAR,* 11 (December), 11-17.

SCALE ITEMS: ATTITUDE TOWARD THE AD (GENTLENESS JUDGMENTS) +

Instructions: Please tell us how well you think each of the words listed below describes the ad you have just seen by putting a number to the right of the word. Here, we are interested in your thoughts about the ad, not the brand or product class. If you think the word describes the ad extremely well, put a 5; very well, put a 4; fairly well, put a 3; not very well, put a 2; not at all well, put a 1.

1. Gentle
2. Serene
3. Soothing
4. Tender
5. Lovely

+ The first four descriptors above represent the shorter version of the scale.

SCALE NAME: Attitude Toward The Ad (Insulting)

SCALE DESCRIPTION:

The scale used by Whipple and Courtney (1980) measures the degree to which consumers report being insulted or irritated by an ad. Responses were made on a three-item, Likert-like scale where 1 = not at all well, and 5 = extremely well.

SCALE ORIGIN:

The items used by Whipple and Courtney (1980) were modified versions of a couple of items from the Reaction Profile for TV Commercials developed by Wells, Leavitt, and McConville (1971).

SAMPLES:

Whipple and Courtney (1980) used **144** women grocery shoppers randomly selected from a medium sized city and **68** advertising/marketing practitioners. Each sample was subsequently split into two subsamples matched on significant demographics within samples.

RELIABILITY:

Whipple and Courtney (1980) report alpha values of **.70** to **.85** for the six ads they tested.

VALIDITY:

Whipple and Courtney (1980) subjected 14 items to principal components factor analysis to derive the underlying structure. Two factors were found: a general evaluative factor and one measuring ad irritation.

ADMINISTRATION:

In Whipple and Courtney's (1980) study, subjects where asked to look at a series of ads and rate each one on the scale items in a self-report questionnaire.

MAJOR FINDINGS:

In general, Whipple and Courtney (1980) found practitioners and female consumers similar with respect to the attitudes toward TV commercials for typical household products. In particular, they found that both groups tended to see commercials that more progressively represented sex roles as more effective and less **insulting** than commercials that were more traditional in these portrayals.

REFERENCES:

Wells, William D., Clark Leavitt, and Maureen McConville (1971), ''A Reaction Profile for Commercials,'' *JAR*, 11 (December) 11-17.
Whipple, Thomas W. and Alice E. Courtney (1980), ''How to Portray Women in TV Commercials,'' *JAR*, 20 (2) 53-59.

SCALE ITEMS: ATTITUDE TOWARD THE AD (INSULTING)

Not at   Extremely
all well   well
1————————2————————3————————4————————5

Rate the extent to which each of the adjectives below describes the advertisement.

1. Insulting to men
2. Irritating
3. Insulting to women

SCALE NAME: Attitude Toward Advertisement (Negative Feelings)

SCALE DESCRIPTION:

This is a Likert-like scale purporting to measure the degree of negative feelings a consumer reports having toward an ad. The scale has been used with varying numbers of items, mostly single word descriptors, to measure the negative feelings evoked by an ad rather than the evaluation of an ad itself. Fourteen and 20-item (five-point) versions were used in Edell and Burke (1987) and a 14-item, five-point version was used by Burke and Edell (1989). A three-item, six-point scale was used by Madden, Allen, and Twibble (1988).

SCALE ORIGIN:

Each of the scale uses described here are similar in that all or most of their items can be found in the Reaction Profile for TV Commercials developed by Wells, Leavitt, and McConville (1971). Madden, Allen, and Twibble (1988) say, however, that they modeled their initial scales on work by Abelson et al. (1982) with initial adjectives from that source as well as Nowlis (1970) and Madden (1982).

SAMPLES:

The subjects used by Edell and Burke (1987) as well as Burke and Edell (1989) were recruited by newspaper ads and announcements distributed on a university campus. Two small samples (**29** and **32**) were utilized in the former study and **191** was the size of the latter. It would be reasonable to assume it consisted of university students, however. The scale development subjects were also used for the research reported in the findings section.

Madden, Allen, and Twibble (1988) used **143** students recruited from an introductory undergraduate course. Subjects were isolated from each other for data collection.

RELIABILITY:

Cronbach's alpha values were reported to be **.96** (n=29) and **.89** (n=32) by Edell and Burke (1987). Burke and Edell (1989) report an alpha of **.88**. The authors used repeated measures of the 191 subjects over six different stimuli. Reliability may be biased upward as measurement was based on 1146 observations (six per subject). Because of repeated measurement with the same subjects, the authors claim replicability, though stimuli were different. The difference in their 14- and 20-item versions was due to the fact that some items with item-total correlations greater than .9 were eliminated due to redundancy.

Madden, Allen, and Twibble (1988) report composite a reliability of **.75** for their negative affect scale.

VALIDITY:

Principal components factor analysis was used in the two articles by Burke and Edell (1987, 1989) to determine the underlying factor structure of a large number of descriptors. Virtually identical factors were found in each case.

Madden, Allen, and Twibble (1988) reduced an initial set of 15 adjectives to 11 adjectives, seven of which fell into a positive affect factor and four of which fell into the negative affect factor (described here) through principal components analysis. Upon examination of confirmatory factor analysis results via LISREL VI, the five-item positive and three-item negative affect scales were determined to best represent the attitude model. Comparison of the squared structural link between each of these two construct measures and also with a semantic differential measure of ad evaluation resulted in a reasonable claim of discriminant validity for the variable pairs: positive affect/ad evaluation and positive affect/negative affect. A similar claim could not be supported for the variable pair negative affect/ad evaluation.

ADMINISTRATION:

In Edell and Burke (1987) as well as Burke and Edell's (1986) study, subjects were brought to a theater to view the stimulus materials. Scale data was collected through administration of a pencil-and-paper type of method. Madden, Allen, and Twibble (1988) utilized a language lab setting to collect scale data. It is not clear whether data were recorded in paper-and-pencil form or directly input by subjects at computer terminals.

MAJOR FINDINGS:

Edell and Burke (1987) investigated the role of feelings in understanding attitude-toward-the-ad. The finding most relevant to this scale was that feelings generated by an ad (e.g., **negative**) contribute uniquely to predictions of attitude-toward-the-ad and brand above that provided by measures of an ad's characteristics.

In Burke and Edell's (1989) study, structural equation analysis indicated **negative** feelings have a significant ($p < .05$) direct effect on evaluation, activity, and gentleness judgments of ads, attitude-toward-the-ad, and attitude-toward-the-brand. All effects were negative.

Madden, Allen, and Twibble's (1988) findings are particularly interesting in the context of measurement as the entire research is a validation of a three component model of attitude-toward-the-ad. Their findings support this model.

REFERENCES:

Abelson, Robert P., Donald R. Kinder, Mark D. Peters, and Susan T. Fisk (1982), "Affective and Semantic Components in Political Person Perceptions," *Journal of Personality and Social Psychology*, 42 (April) 619-630)

Burke, Marian C. and Julie A. Edell (1989), "The Impact of Feelings on Ad-Based Affect and Cognitions," *JMR*, 26 (February), 69-83.

Edell, Julie E. and Marian C. Burke (1987), "The Power of Feelings in Understanding Advertising Effects," *JCR*, 14 (December), 421-33.

Madden, Thomas J. (1982), *Humor in Advertising: Application of a Hierarchy of Effects Paradigm*, unpublished doctoral dissertation, University of Massachusetts.

Nowlis, Vincent (1970), "Mood, Behavior and Experience," in *Feelings and Emotions*, Magda B. Arnold, ed. New York, N.Y.: Academic Press Inc., 261-277.

Wells, William D., Clark Leavitt, and Maureen McConville (1971), "A Reaction Profile for TV Commercials," *JAR*, 11 (December), 11-17.

SCALE ITEMS: ATTITUDE TOWARD ADVERTISEMENT (NEGATIVE FEELINGS) +

Instructions: We would like you to tell us how the ad you just saw made you feel. We are interested in your reactions to the ad, not how you would describe it. Please tell us how much you felt each of these feelings while you were watching this commercial. If you felt the feeling very strongly put a 5; strongly put a 4; somewhat strongly put a 3; not very strongly put a 2; not at all put a 1.

1. Bored
2. Critical
3. Defiant
4. Depressed
5. Disgusted
6. Disinterested
7. Dubious
8. Dull
9. Lonely
10. Offended
11. Regretful
12. Sad
13. Skeptical
14. Suspicious
15. Angry
16. Annoyed
17. Bad
18. Fed-up
19. Insulted
20. Irritated
21. Repulsed

+ Items 1 through 14 were used by Burke and Edell (1989) and by Edell and Burke (1987) in study 2. Edell and Burke used items 1 through 20 in study 1. Madden, Allen, and Twibble (1988) used items 19 through 21.

SCALE NAME: Attitude Toward the Ad (Relevance)

SCALE DESCRIPTION:

A six-item Likert-like scale purporting to measure the cognitive relevance of specific television advertisements to consumers.

SCALE ORIGIN:

The scale was developed in a study by Lastovicka (1983). The original 16 items for the scale were taken from a more complete list of items used in the **Leo Burnett Storyboard Test** (1977). Subjects were exposed in small groups to one of six different 60-second television commercials, then answered one open-ended question in which they were asked to list retrospectively the thoughts they had while viewing the commercial. The products advertised were six real branded products (beer, blue jeans, soft drinks, and automobiles). Results of item measurements were factor analyzed, resulting in three factors representing relevance, confusion, and entertainment. Each factor was treated as a scale measuring that respective construct and subjected to multitrait-multimethod testing per Kalleberg and Kluegel (1975). The comparison method was a content analysis of verbatim responses to the open-ended question. Written answers to the question were coded to show whether and to what degree they indicated an irritation, entertainment, confusion, comprehension, counterargument, source rejection, or message acceptance response by two different coders, attaining a product moment correlation of .70. The relevance-scaled factor was paired with the rater-summed coded score of verbatim responses for counterargument, source rejection, and message acceptance.

SAMPLES:

A convenience sample of **634** undergraduate students in 20 class sections of a university business school was utilized. Eighty-three percent of the sample had used or purchased some brand from each of the four product classes in the month prior to the study.

RELIABILITY:

Cronbach's alpha was reported to be **.846.**

VALIDITY:

Construct validity was demonstrated through factor analysis. Of the original 16 items, only those loading at least .30 on the relevance factor alone were retained for the scale. Items expected to load on this factor did so, whereas those expected to load on other factors did not load on this factor. Confirmatory factor analysis of multitrait-multimethod structure indicated convergent and discriminant validity for this scale.

ADMINISTRATION:

The scale is amenable to most survey research techniques. The paper-and-pencil questionnaire approach was used by Lastovicka (1983). Time for administration was not given, but is assumed to be quite short. This scale is likely to be integrated into a larger measurement study in application.

MAJOR FINDINGS:

No findings associated with this scale have been reported beyond those pertaining to scale validation (above).

COMMENTS:

Some caution should be exercised with use of this scale as the validation study provides no correlates to assess nomologic validity. Face and content validity seem reasonable and reliability is satisfactory, but all validation results may be sample-specific. Additionally, subjects were in a forced-exposure condition. Consumers in a realistic environment may choose not to expose themselves to commercials they do not see as relevant.

REFERENCES:

Kalleberg, A. L. and J. R. Kluegel (1975), "Analysis of the Multitrait-Multimethod Matrix: Some Limitations and an Alternative," *Journal of Applied Psychology*, 60 (February), 1-9.

Lastovicka, John L. (1983), "Convergent and Discriminant Validity of Television Rating Scales," *JA,* 12 (2), 14- 23, 52.

Leo Burnett Company, Inc. (1977), *Manual for the Leo Burnett Storyboard Test System.* Chicago, Ill.: Leo Burnett Company, Inc.

SCALE ITEMS: ATTITUDE TOWARD THE AD (RELEVANCE)

Strongly Disagree
1————————2————————3————————4————————5————————6
Strongly Agree

1. During the commercial I thought how the product might be useful for me.
2. I felt as though I was right there in the commercial experiencing the same thing.
3. The commercial was meaningful to me.
4. The ad did not have anything to do with my needs. **(r)**
5. The commercial gave me a good idea.
6. As I watched I thought of reasons why I would buy or not buy the product.

SCALE NAME: Attitude Toward The Ad (Relevant News)

SCALE DESCRIPTION:

A five-item Likert scale, though some versions have up to 11 items. Most development has been reported in conjunction with the items Schlinger (1979a) used to measure consumer attitude toward the relevant news value of a television advertisement. The items composing each of the scales are changed or modified on a user-determined basis. The items reported here are those available in the published literature used in the development of this compendium.

SCALE ORIGIN:

This scale represents one of seven attitude constructs measured by the Leo Burnett Viewer Response Profile (Schlinger 1979a). An original list of 600 attitudinal statements were culled from verbatim responses of over 400 veiwers of 14 different commercials and story boards. These were reduced to 139 items through deletion of dupliations and items that were commercial-specific or deemed "theoretically" inappropriate by the researchers. The remaining statements were analyzed empirically to determine factor structure and discriminant characteristics of individual items. After five separate analyses and refinements, the final of which was an analysis of the mean item scores from the first four analyses, a seven-factor solution was achieved. In general, only items with factor loadings of .5 or higher in at least three of the five factor analyses were retained for the scales. These items were then tested through 18 analysis of variance routines to determine their discrimination capabilities. Only items discriminating at $p < .01$ in at least six of 18 trials were retained. The outcome of these analyses produced the seven-factor, 32-item short version of the Leo Burnett Viewer Response Profile.

SAMPLES:

This scale was developed with post-hoc data for the original 600 items. The first factor analysis sample consisted of 20 women assumed to be from the Chicago area for each of 25 tested commercials (n = **500**). The women were selected by age (half older than 35 years, half younger than 35 years) and education level (about one third had two or more years of college). The second factor analysis utilized a sample of 50 respondents similar to those in the first sample for each of 10 of the 25 original commercials (n = **500**). The third analysis used a total of **1504** men and women rating 42 different untested commercials. Though the author reports sample controls remained constant, no indication of the controls is given. As men were included in this sample, it is not clear that reference is to controls used in previous sampling. The fourth sample totaled **1871** men and women rating one of 40 different commercials viewed over a period of four years. No subject statistics are available. The fifth factor analysis sample represented all subjects previously used in the study (n = 4375). No sample information is explicitly stated for ANOVA analysis. During the course of the scale development study, 377 different commercials were used (Schlinger 1979a). Zinkhan and Burton (1989) attempted replication with 26 product class users, each viewing 25 television commercials.

RELIABILITY:

Individual items were tested-retested with a 30-day interval for six different stimuli, resulting in correlations of **.87** to **.97**. Test-retest with the same criteria as used for the individual items yielded r = .87. The sample for reliability tests was 30 respondents per stimulus (n = 180). As in scale construction, items seem to be added and deleted at the discretion of the researcher. Caution in interpretation is suggested. Schlinger (1979a) claims stability with small samples. The scale generally replicates the factor structure (Schlinger 1979b). Coefficient of congruence was .703 for the entire Schlinger profile and two of five items of the relevant news scale loaded at less than .20 in the replication by Zinkhan and Burton (1989). Scale stability is questionable.

VALIDITY:

Factor structure was similar to that found in previous research where the entertainment construct emerged as the first factor also (Wells, Leavitt, and McConville 1971). Some items were developed on the basis of theoretical underpinnings indicating construct validity, face validity is claimed, and predictive validity is demonstrated through case analysis (Schlinger 1979a). Because the scale was developed in a realistic copy-testing setting, the measure should be generalizable to that purpose. However, forced exposure to that condition warrants some caution if the scale is used to assess attitudes in less constrained viewing conditions. When the scale was used in conjunction with the other three scales developed by Schlinger to represent the viewer response profile, Zinkhan and Burton (1989) reported reasonably good nomologic and predictive validity relative to attitude toward the brand (r = .32, p < .01) and choice behavior (r = .30, p < .01).

ADMINISTRATION:

The scale can be administered under typical survey design methodologies in a paper-and-pencil format or responses can be recorded by the researcher in personal or telephone interviews, though no use of the scale has been reported with the latter administrations. No time for administration was noted. Unfortunately, in the scale's development, items have been repeatedly substituted, added, or deleted at the researcher's whim, so the exact items to be used in administration may not be clear.

MAJOR FINDINGS:

Using a nine-item version of the scale (items unreported), Olson, Schlinger, and Young (1982) found mean scale scores were significantly higher (p < .001) when cosumers rated commercials for new products than when they rated commercials for existing ones. Six indvidual items were significantly higher in this test, all at p < .001.

COMMENTS:

The scale appears to be a reliable and valid measure of consumer attitude toward the relevant news value of an advertisement, but changes in scale items during development and use cast some suspicion on its validity and reliability. Lack of replication for two of five items (Zinkhan and Burton 1989) indicates caution should be observed in use and interpretation of results of this measure. Zinkhan and Burton tested only those items reported by Schlinger (1979a).

REFERENCES:

Olson, David, Mary Jane Schlinger, and Charles Young (1982), "How Consumers React to New Product Ads," *JAR*, 22 (3), 24-30.

Schlinger, Mary Jane (1979a), "A Profile of Responses to Commercials," *JAR*, 19 (2), 37-48.

————, (1979b) "Attitudinal Reactions to Advertisements," *Attitude Research Under the Sun*. John Eighmey, ed. Chicago, Ill.: American Marketing Association, 171-197.

Wells, William, Clark Leavitt, and Maureen McConville (1971), "A Reaction Profile for TV Commercials," *JAR*, 11 (6), 11-17.

Zinkhan, George and Scot Burton (1989), "An Examination of Three Multidimensional Profiles for Assessing Consumer Reactions to Advertisements," *JA*, 18 (4), 6-14.

SCALE ITEMS: ATTITUDE TOWARD THE AD (RELEVANT NEWS) +

Strongly Disagree	Disagree	Somewhat Disagree	Neutral or no Opinion	Somewhat Agree	Agree	Strongly Agree
1	2	3	4	5	6	7

1. The commercial gave me a new idea. **abc**
2. The commercial reminded me that I'm dissatisfied with what I'm using now and I'm looking for something better. ***abc**
3. I learned something from the commercial that I didn't know before. **abc**
4. The commercial told about a new product I think I'd like to try. ***ab**
5. During the commercial I thought how that product might be useful to me. **abc**
6. I would be interested in getting more information about the product. **bc**
7. The commercial made me think I might try the brand just to see if it's as good as they say. **bc**
8. The commercial showed me the product has certain advantages. **c**
9. Important for me. **c**
10. The commercial made me feel the product is right for me. **c**
11. The ad didn't have anything to do with me or my needs. **(r) c**

+ Scale items reported here are from Schlinger (1979a), denoted by a; Schlinger (1979b), denoted by b; and Olson, Schlinger, and Young (1982), denoted by c. It is not clear when specific items should be deleted for any particular scale usage. Items identified with an asterisk loaded less than .2 in Zinkhan and Burton's (1989) study.

SCALE NAME: Attitude Toward The Ad (Semantic Differential)

SCALE DESCRIPTION:

The scales consist of various bipolar adjectives presumed to measure the subject's overall evaluation of advertisements. The scales have in common the feature of not being specific to the advertisements under investigation, though certain adjectives may or may not be appropriate (face validity issue) for every advertisement one may want to assess. The scales have five or more points as indicated.

SCALE ORIGIN:

Most scales seem to have been developed in the research cited herein. However, Petroshius and Crocker (1989), cited research by Baker and Churchill (1977) and Kahle and Homer (1985) as the basis for their scales, and Cox and Locander (1987) cited Mitchell and Olson (1981). The basis for most of these scales is the semantic differential, developed by Osgood, Suci, and Tannenbaum (1957). The underlying concept for the semantic differential is that a stimulus becomes a sign of the significate when it gives rise to the idea or thought of the significate. Measurement is accomplished by use of a series of semantic differential scales (a combination of controlled word association and scaling procedures). Each semantic differential scale is purported to represent a straight line through the origin of a semantic space. A selected combination of such scales is then believed to represent a multidimensional space. A listing of potential scale items and the dimensions of semantic space they are purported to represent is provided by Osgood, Suci, and Tannenbaum (1957, Ch. 2). The technique is believed by the authors to be highly generalizable and adaptable to most research needs. A seven-point scale is generally recommended by Osgood and his coauthors, though specific circumstances may warrant a different number of scale points.

SAMPLES:

Dröge (1989) used a total of **178** student subjects, 89 in each of two experimental treatment groups. MacKenzie and Lutz (1989) used **203** student subjects attending a major midwestern university. Subjects ranged in age from 20 to 25 years and approximately 50% were men. A validation sample of **120** student subjects from a major university in southern California was also used. Subjects in the validation sample ranged in age from 20 to 32 years and approximately 60% were men. Petroshius and Crocker (1989) used **320** white undergraduate student subjects (160 female). Each subject was randomly assigned to one of 16 treatment conditions.

Stout and Burda (1989) used **163** student volunteers who were recruited from undergraduate communications classes and offered extra credit for participating. Subjects were randomly assigned to one of four treatment groups (2 × 2 factorial design) ranging in size from 35 to 47 subjects per group. Burton and Lichtenstein (1988) used **278** undergraduate business students who were randomly assigned to one of 12 treatment conditions in a 2 × 2 × 3 between-subjects design. It is not clear whether the design was balanced or not.

Cox and Cox (1988) used **240** student subjects recruited from MBA classes at a large southwestern university. Most subjects worked full time and attended MBA classes on a part-time basis. Ages of subjects ranged from 21 to 62 years, with a median age of 26 years; 45% of the subjects were women. Cox and Locander (1987) used a convenience sample of **240** adult student subjects attending business classes part time at a large southwestern university. Subjects ranged in age from 21 to 62 years with an average age of approximately 31 years; 45% of the subjects were women. Each subject was randomly assigned one of four different ads in each product type.

Holmes and Crocker (1987) used **130** student subjects from a large midwestern university, and an additional 25 student subjects in a pretest. Kilbourne (1986) used **101** adult subjects (49 male) selected from several communities surrounding a large metropolitan area. Each of the four treatment conditions had at least 24 subjects. The median age of subjects was 30 years and 79% had at least attended college. The median income of respondents was $20,700. Macklin, Bruvold, and Shea (1985) used **127** subjects recruited during a festival at a public elementary magnet school in a large midwestern city. Subjects received free tickets to the festival for participation in the study.

Rubin, Mager, and Friedman (1982) used **148** student subjects in 10 graduate business classes at a large New York City graduate school of business; 52% were men, 69% were between 25 and 34 years of age, and 69% earned more than $25,000 annually. Five of these classes (n = 76) were shown a treatment advertisement and five classes (n = 72) were shown a control advertisement. Mitchell and Olson (1981) used **71** junior and senior undergraduate students of both sexes who were recruited from an introductory marketing course. Subjects were paid for participation in the study reported here.

Kilbourne, Painton, and Ridley (1985) used **238** male and **186** female undergraduate students from a southwestern university. Perrien, Dussart, and Paul (1985) used a sample of **186** members of The Montreal Advertising Club. This number represented a 26% response rate. All respondents were French speaking.

There was some evidence that the sample was not representative of the population. Beltramini (1988) used **727** students from two large classes. The average respondent was 23 years of age; 55% were men; 58% were juniors; 38% were seniors; and 86% were business majors. Madden, Allen, and Twible (1988) used **143** undergraduate students recruited from an introductory marketing course.

Hastak and Olson (1989) used **160** undergraduate students. Janiszewski (1988) used **43** graduate students from two marketing management classes in the first experiment reported. These subjects were paid for participation. In the second experiment, **96** undergraduates from two universities were given extra credit for participating. Zinkhan and Zinkhan (1985) used **160** part-time MBA students randomly split into two groups of 80. One hundred thirty-four of the students had full-time jobs; all had bank accounts and their median income was $25,000 a year.

Beltramini (1982) used **584** adult education students at a southwestern university. Beltramini and Evans (1985) mailed 5000 survey booklets to a probabilistically selected sample of recent (last five years) automobile registrants; 1994 were returned for a 40% response rate. Okechuku and Wang (1988) used subjects recruited at shopping malls and other public places in Detroit and surrounding suburbs in Michigan and in Windsor, London, Sarnia, Toronto, and Hamilton, Ontario. Sample sizes were 27, 27, and 26 for three Chinese ads for clothes and 29, 30, and 26 for three North American ads for clothes; 26, 26, and 30 for three Chinese ads for shoes and 25, 24, and 26 for three North American ads for shoes. Muehling (1987) used **123** student subjects.

RELIABILITY:

Kilbourne, Painton, and Ridley (1985) reported alpha values of .57, .77, and .72 for their cognitive, affective, and sexual attitude scales, respectively. Perrien, Dussart, and Paul (1985) reported alpha values of .7832 and .7957 for the cognitive and affective dimensions, respectively. Beltramini (1988) reported alpha of **.90** average across four treatments. Madden, Allen, and Twible (1988) report alpha of **.88**. Hastak and Olson (1989) reported alpha greater than **.90**. Janiszewski (1988) reported alpha values of **.93** and **.91** in experiments 1 and 2, respectively.

Cronbach's alpha was reported to be **.806** and **.693** for a comparative and a noncomparative treatment group, respectively, by Droge (1989); **.89** in the main sample and **.88** in the validation sample by MacKenzie and Lutz (1989); **.89** by Stout and Burda (1989); **.90** by Cox and Cox (1988); **.90** by Cox and Locander (1987); **.65** for the cognitive dimension and **.88** for the affective dimension by Kilbourne (1986); **.85** by Macklin, Bruvold, and Shea (1985); and **.87** by Mitchell and Olson (1981).

Petroshius and Crocker (1989) used two reliability measures. Correlation analysis (only one variable correlated low with its respective group) indicated that each variable set was statistically significant ($p < .01$); Cronbach's alpha was **.52** for the cognitive factor and greater than **.75** for the affective factor. Burton and Lichtenstein (1988) reported Cronbach's alpha to be **.86** and **.73** for the affective and cognitive dimensions, respectively. They also reported a correlation of **.67** between the two dimensions, casting some doubt on the discriminant validity of the two measures.

Beltramini (1982) reported an alpha of **.9485** averaged across three measurements. Okechuku and Wang (1988) reported alpha values of **.61** and **.72** for their cognitive and **.88** and **.86** for their affective measures for clothing and shoe ads, respectively. It should be noted that Okechuku and Wang also combined the cognitive and affective measures with a two-item conative measure to assess overall attitude toward the ad, achieving an alpha of **.91** and **.92** for clothing and shoe ads, respectively. The conative measure (reported elsewhere in this compendium) consisted of "buy/not buy the product" and "seek out/not seek out the product."

Reliability information was not reported by Rubin, Mager, and Friedman (1982), Holmes and Crocker (1987), Beltramini and Evans (1985), Zinkhan and Zinkhan (1985), or Muehling (1987).

VALIDITY:

Little validity information was provided, per se, in most of the studies. Mitchell and Olson (1981) developed the background for using evaluative belief statements as measures of attitude from Fishbein and Ajzen (1975) and Ahtola (1975) and utilized only the four items that loaded together out of seven original ones in their study. Varimax rotation was used to develop factor structure. Stout and Burda (1989) used a manipulation check to assess the manipulation of brand dominance, but not for attitude toward the ad.

Petroshius and Crocker (1989) used factor analysis as a reliability check, noting that the affective and cognitive components in attitude toward the ad comprised 56% of the variance. Burton and Lichtenstein (1988) drew their original items from various previous research, including Wells' (1964) early work in this area. They subjected their original 15 items to a confirmatory factor analysis to arrive at the six affective and five cognitive items reported here. They also used a separate sample (n = 44) to see whether subjects perceived the affective items as more emotional or "feeling-state" desciptive than the cognitive items. The results were highly significant in the expected direction. The authors do not address the point that relative differences do not necessarily indicate measures are valid in the absolute sense.

Perrien, Dussart, and Paul (1985) drew from a list of items extracted from the literature only those 15 items that marketing experts all agreed belonged in the construct dimension. Beltramini (1988) used items developed in previous work (Beltramini 1982) where both convergent and discriminant validity of the 10-item scale was claimed. Madden, Allen, and Twible (1988) reported substantive discriminant validity between ad evaluation and a measure of positive affect. Marginal discriminant validity between ad evaluation and a measure of negative affect was claimed. Both principal components and confirmatory factor analysis support the unidimensionality of the scale measure of the ad evaluation construct.

Janiszewski (1988) reported unidimensionality (ML confirmatory analysis) and support for an assumption of independence of errors in measure. Zinkhan and Zinkhan (1985) attempted to reduce the items in the Response Profile scales (reported elsewhere in this compendium) to four semantic differential scales applicable to print ads for financial services. They factor analyzed data from pretests (sample and items unknown) as an initial validation step. The major findings of their efforts indicated that of the four factors tested, favorable cognitive and favorable affective scales were moderately successful at discriminating for explaining response to a coupon/postcard use/mail-in request in advertising.

Okechuku and Wang (1988) drew their measures from Baker and Churchill (1977), whose principal components factor analysis identified a similar structure for items measuring cognitive, affective, and conative components of attitude toward the ad. Okechuku and Wang factor analyzed their data as per the original. The added "interesting" to the affective measure and deleted "try product" from the conative component (reported elsewhere in this compendium).

ADMINISTRATION:

Kilbourne (1986) used a personal interview procedure to collect data; 39 of the 101 respondents were interviewed at their place of work and the remaining 62 respondents were interviewed in their homes. In general, however, paper-and-pencil administration as a part of a longer instrument appears to be the method of choice. Subjects are asked to evaluate a specific advertisement on the basis of the adjective listing and to mark the scale appropriately. In some instances (Petroshius and Crocker 1989), instructions may also be read aloud by the researchers. Time is of minimal consequence.

MAJOR FINDINGS:

Dröge (1989) used structural equation modeling via LISREL to support the dual mediation hypothesis concerning the causal relationship between attitude toward the ad and attitude toward the brand for noncomparative ads (relatively less central processing) and lack thereof for comparative ads (relatively more central processing). It should be noted that alpha for the noncomparative ad treatment group measure of attitude toward the ad was relatively low (.693) in comparison with that for the comparative group, that no explanation for this difference was offered, and that LISREL is very sensitive to reliability violations.

MacKenzie and Lutz (1989) found that attitude toward the ad is a stronger predictor of brand attitude than ad credibility. Removal of ad attitude from two models predicting brand attitude resulted in a reduction in brand attitude variance of .74 to .58. The removal of ad credibility from these two models resulted in reduction in brand attitude variance of only .13 to .16.

Petroshius and Crocker (1989) found that the physical attractiveness of a spokesperson was significantly related to the subject's affective component of attitude toward the ad (p = .044). None of the other tested sources of variation (sex of communicator, race, product, or sex of subject) were significant as predictors of the affective component, and no significant interactions were found. The only significant source of variation in the cognitive component of attitude toward the ad was the sex of the subject (p = .027), though an examination of mean responses on individual items indicates inconsistent responses between men and women on dependent variables. No significant interactions were found.

Stout and Burda (1989) studied "zipped" television advertisements and their effect on attitudes. They found that the speed of the commercial (i.e., zipped vs. normal) affected attitude toward the ad (p = .001) and brand attitudes (p = .001). Viewers in the zipped speed condition had more neutral attitudes toward the ad than viewers in the normal speed condition.

Burton and Lichtenstein (1988) found that price oriented advertising attitudes were affected by the cognitive component as measured but not by the affective component. They also found after covarying out the effects of the deal in the ads that both affect and cognitions affected attitude toward the deal. They concluded that a two-factor solution to attitude toward the ad is superior to the single-component solution.

Cox and Cox (1988) found that a repeated exposure (two exposures as opposed to one) had a positive and statistically significant (p < .05) effect on the evaluations of complex advertisements (attitude toward the ad), but only a slight and statistically nonsignificant effect on the evaluation of simple ads.

Cox and Locander (1987) tested the impact of attitude toward the ad on brand attitude for novel products versus familiar products. They found that attitude toward the ad accounted for a greater proportion of the variance in brand attitude for novel products (r square = .4) than for familiar products (r square = .26). They did not find support for the hypothesis of a difference by attitude toward the ad in the proportion of variance in purchase intention for novel and familiar products.

Holmes and Crocker (1987) found that for a high involvement product, the rational appeal evoked a greater positive attitude toward the ad than either an emotional or discrepant appeal. Respondents' predispositions toward the product influenced their attitude toward the brand and purchase intention. For the low involvement product, an emotional appeal (as opposed to rational or discrepant) was found to elicit a significantly more affirmative response for attitudes toward the brand (p < .05) and the advertisement (p < .05). There was no significant finding (p < .05) for low involvement brands regarding the use of the three types of appeals and purchase intentions.

Kilbourne (1986) found that the use of a model depicting a professional woman using a calculator had a statistically significant effect (p < .05) on the cognitive dimension of attitude toward the ad in comparison to the use of a model in a similar ad depicting a housewife using the same calculator. The use of the model depicting a professional woman in the test ad also produced a statistically significant effect (p < .001) on the affective dimension of attitude toward the ad in comparison to the use of a model in a similar ad depicting a housewife using the product. Ad content was constant (other than the models) in both test advertisements.

Macklin, Bruvold, and Shea (1985) found when the concreteness of verbal messages was held constant, the readability level of the ads made no significant difference on any of the variables examined, including attitude toward the ad (p = .771). However, the subjects' education and spending on the product category had significant effects on all treatments. The authors found that subjects with higher levels of education uniformly liked ads less (p = .0001). As spending per month on the product category increased, favorable attitudes toward the ad also increased (p = .040).

Rubin, Mager, and Friedman (1982) examined the differences between the use of identified company presidents and the use of nonidentified individuals as spokespersons for their products, and the effect on attitude toward the ad. A Hotelling's T-squared statistic of 20.07 indicated that in general, ads in which the advertising spokesperson was identified as the company president were viewed more favorably than ads in which the spokesperson was not identified (p=.05). From an examination of a univariate t-test and a stepwise discriminant analysis, the authors concluded that the variable "trustworthy" was the most important contributor to the difference in favorability between the ads with identified company presidents as spokespersons and the ads with nonidentified spokespersons.

Mitchell and Olson (1981) assessed attitude toward ads for facial tissue via this measure. It was a significant contributor to attitude toward the brand and attitude toward the act of purchasing the brand (p < .005) in a regression model including brand evaluative beliefs (cf. Fishbein and Ajzen 1975) and attitude toward the picture in the ad. The authors concluded that this finding supported what is now termed the dual routes of brand attitude formation.

Kilbourne, Painton, and Ridley (1985) reported both male and female subjects scored significantly higher on cognitive, affective, and sexual attitudes toward a Scotch whiskey print ad when a sexual embed was present than when it was not. Similar results were not forthcoming when the product was a cigarette. The authors concluded that the product plays an important role in the attitudinal formation process when sexual embeds are present.

Perrien, Dussart, and Paul (1985) reported significantly higher (p < .001) attitudinal scores as amounts of factual information increased from one to three factual claims without regard to percieved risk of the product. They found no differences due to the respondent's professional category (agency, advertiser, media, service).

Beltramini (1988) found significant differences in subjects' perceived believability of five different warning labels on cigarette packages. He also found that perceived believability was related to the "mushiness/firmness" of the respondents' beliefs about the hazards of smoking. No differences were related to whether a subject smoked.

Madden, Allen, and Twible (1988) found processing set to be significantly related to the processing route of ad evaluation. Subjects who were told they were to evaluate ads tended to utilize cognitive response measures and ad evaluation to differentiate between a humorous and a non-humorous treatment. Subjects who were not told the evaluative purpose of the experiment tended to use affective reactions to discriminate between the humorous and non-humorous conditions.

Hastak and Olson (1989) used their three-item measure as a part of a cognitive response/structure study. The results relating to attitude toward the ad supported the contention that it is mediated through processing set cognitive responses.

Janiszewski (1988) performed two experiments to test the hypothesis that right-hemisphere processing of pictoral cues leads to higher ad evaluation than does left-hemisphere processing. In general, the results support this hypothesis. The researcher cautions, however, that this work is somewhat rudimentary.

Zinkhan and Zinkhan (1985) looked at the discriminant and predictive validity of four measures of attitude toward the ad: favorable cognitive response, favorable affective response, energy, and familiarity. Though these construct measures are purported to be developed from various viewer response profiles, they are framed in a semantic differential format and reported here for that reason. Subjects' attitudes toward a financial services ad were measured with the four scales, which were in turn subjected to discriminant analysis as predictors of subject responses to the ads. The response criterion was filling out a post card for information about the financial services. Response was elicited after two exposures over a three-week period. Favorable cognitive and affective measures where both found to be significant predictors of the behavioral response. When the discriminant model developed in the first phase of the research was applied to the responses of a holdout sample, only modest predictive success over chance was acheived (65.0% vs. 53.8%).

Beltramini and Evans (1985) found, contrary to expectations, that ads reporting research results from samples of 100 subjects were less believable ($p < .001$) than ads in which 10 research subjects were claimed to have been used. They also found a contrary non-relationship between ads that stated third-party objective research conduct or that named the third-party reseacher and ads that did neither. The authors also found ads using qualitative research claims to be more believable ($p < .05$) than those using quantitative claims. Finally, they reported a significant curvilinear relationship between the magnitude of the research claim and believability, with ads being increasingly more believable up to claims of 70% favorability and decreasing thereafter.

Okechuku and Wang (1988) compared North American subjects' attitudes toward ads from China and the U.S. for shoes and clothing. They found no difference in subjects' cognitive attitudes toward the ads, but did find a significant ($p < .001$) difference in affective responses to the ads.

In each of five comparative formats, Muehling (1987) found attitude toward the ad to have a significant, positive influence on attitude toward the sponsor and attitude toward purchasing the sponsor while having no influence on attitude toward the competitor or purchasing the competitor.

COMMENTS:

This scale represents a generally recognized method for measuring attitude toward an object. It relies on researcher judgment as to which specific adjective pairs are appropriate for a given attitude object and is not often assessed for validity. The tests of nomologic and predictive validity are, in a sense, necessary to the success of the research in which they are put to use.

REFERENCES:

Ahtola, Olli T. (1975), "The Vector Model of Preferences: An Alternative to the Fishbein Model," *JMR*, 12 (February), 52-59.

Baker, Michael J. and Gilbert A. Churchill, Jr. (1977), "The Impact of Physically Attractive Models on Advertising Evaluations," *JMR*, 14 (November), 538-555.

Beltramini, Richard F. (1982), "Advertising Perceived Believability Scale," in *Proceedings of the Southwest Marketing Association Conference*, Daniel R. Corrigan, Frederic B. Kraft, and Robert H. Ross, eds, 1-3.

_____ (1988), "Perceived Believability of Warning Label Information Presented in Cigarette Advertising," *JA*, 17 (2), 26-32.

_____ and Kenneth R. Evans (1985), "Perceived Believability of Research Results Information in Advertising," *JA*, 14 (3), 18-31.

Burton, Scot and Donald R. Lichtenstein (1988), "The Effect of Ad Claims and Ad Context on Attitude Toward the Advertisement," *JA*, 17 (1), 3-11.

Cox, Dena S. and Anthony D. Cox (1988), "What Does Familiarity Breed? Complexity as a Moderator of Repetition Effects in Advertisement Evaluation," *JCR*, 15 (June), 111-116.

_____ and William B. Locander (1987), "Product Novelty: Does It Moderate the Relationship Between Ad Attitudes and Brand Attitudes?" *JA*, 16 (3), 39-44.

Droge, Cornelia (1989), "Shaping the Route to Attitude Change: Central Versus Peripheral Processing Through Comparative Versus Noncomparative Advertising," *JMR*, 26 (May), 193-204.

Fishbein, Martin and Icek Ajzen (1975), *Belief, Attitude, Intention and Behavior: An Introduction to Theory and Research*. Reading, Mass.: Addison-Wesley Publshing Company.

Hastak, Manoj and Jerry C. Olson (1989), "Assessing the Role of Brand Related Cognitive Responses as Mediators of Communications Effects on Cognitive Structure," *JCR*, 15 (March), 444-456.

Holmes, John H. and Kenneth E. Crocker (1987), "Predispositions and the Comparative Effectiveness of Rational, Emotional, and Discrepant Appeals for Both High Involvement and Low Involvement Products," *JAMS*, 15 (Spring), 27-35.

Janiszewski, Chris (1988), "Preconscious Processing Effects: The Independence of Attitude Formation and Conscious Thought," *JCR*, 15 (September), 199-209.

Kahle, Lynn R. and Pamela M. Homer (1985), "Physical Attractiveness of the Celebrity Endorser: A Social Adaption Perspective," *JCR*, 11 (March), 954-961.

Kilbourne, William E. (1986), "An Exploratory Study of the Effect of Sex Role Stereotyping on Attitudes Toward Magazine Advertisements," *JAMS*, 14 (Winter), 43-46.

_____, Scott Painton, and Danny Ridley (1985), "The Effect of Sexual Embedding on Responses to Magazine Advertisements," *JA*, 14 (2), 48-56.

MacKenzie, Scott B. and Richard J. Lutz (1989), "An Empirical Examination of the Structural Antecedents of Attitude Toward the Ad in an Advertising Pretesting Context," *JM*, 53 (April), 48-65.

Macklin, M. Carole, Norman T. Bruvold, and Carol Lynn Shea (1985), "Is It Always as Simple as 'Keep It Simple!'?" *JA*, 14 (4), 28-35.

Madden, Thomas J., Chris T. Allen, and Jacquelyn L. Twible (1988), "Attitude Toward the Ad: An Assessment of Diverse Measurement Indices Under Different Processing Sets," *JMR*, 25 (August), 242-252.

Mitchell, Andrew A. and Jerry C. Olson (1981), "Are Product Attribute Beliefs the Only Mediator of Advertising Effects on Brand Attitude?" *JMR*, 18 (August), 318-332.

Muehling, Darrel D. (1987), "Comparative Advertising: The Influence of Attitude-Toward-The-Ad on Brand Evaluation," *JA*, 16 (4), 43-49.

Okechuku, Chike and Gongrong Wang (1988), "The Effectiveness of Chinese Print Advertisements in North America," *JAR*, 28 (October/November), 25-34.

Osgood, Charles E., George J. Suci, and Percy H. Tannenbaum (1957) *The Measurement of Meaning*. Urbana, Ill.: University of Illinois Press.

Perrien, Jean, Christian Dussart, and Francoise Paul (1985), "Advertisers and the Factual Content of Advertising," *JA*, 14 (1), 30-35, 53.

Petroshius, Susan M. and Kenneth E. Crocker (1989), "An Empirical Analysis of Spokesperson Characteristics on Advertisement and Product Evaluations," *JAMS*, 17 (Summer), 217-225.

Rubin, Vicky, Carol Mager, and Hershey H. Friedman (1982), "Company President Versus Spokesperson in Television Commercials," *JAR*, 22 (August/September), 31-33.

Stout, Patricia A. and Benedicta L. Burda (1989), "Zipped Commercials: Are They Effective?" *JA*, 18 (4), 23-32.

Wells, William D. (1964), "EQ, Son of EQ, and the Reaction Profile," *JM*, 28 (October), 45-52.

Zinkhan, George M. and Christian F. Zinkhan (1985), "Response Profiles and Choice Behavior: An Application to Financial Services," *JA*, 14 (3), 39-51, 66.

SCALE ITEMS: ATTITUDE TOWARD THE AD (SEMANTIC DIFFERENTIAL) +

Scale items used in specific studies are listed below with indication whether item sums or means of sums were used in the research analysis and the number of response points per scale item.

Droge (1989): 1,3,4,5 (mean), 7-point.
Hastak and Olson (1989): 1,2,18,20 (mean), 7-point.
MacKenzie and Lutz (1989): 1,18,25 (mean), 7-point.
Petroshius and Crocker (1989) (affective): 4,11,12,13,14, 7- point.
Petroshius and Crocker (1989) (cognitive): 8,9,15, 7-point.
Stout and Burda (1989): 2,16 (mean), 7-point.
Cox and Cox (1988): 1,2,18 (sum), 9-point.
Burton and Lichtenstein (1988) (affective): 13,18,26,27,28,29 (mean), 9-point.
Burton and Lichtenstein (1988) (cognitive): 7,8,9,10,22 (mean), 9-point.
Janiszewski (1988): 1,11,13,18,24 (sum), 9- point.
Beltramini (1988): 6,9,21,22,38,39,40,41,42,43 (mean), 5-point.
Madden, Allen, and Twible (1988): 1,18,24,36,44,45.
Okechuku and Wang (1988) (cognitive): 8,9,15 (mean), 9-point.
Okechuku and Wang (1988) (affective): 4,11,12,13,14 (mean), 9- point.
Cox and Locander (1987): 1,2,18, 9-point.
Holmes and Crocker (1987): 8,9,11,12,13,14,15,22,23,24 (mean), 7-point.
Muehling (1987): 1,5,13,25,57,58 (mean), 7-point.
Kilbourne (1986) (affective): 11,12,13, 9-point.
Kilbourne (1986) (cognitive): 6,8,9, 9-point.
Macklin, Bruvold, and Shea (1985): 1,17,18,19,20,21, 7-point.
Perrien, Dussart, and Paul (1985) (cognitive): 8,33,34,35 (sum), 7-point.
Perrien, Dussart, and Paul (1985) (affective): 13,18,36,37 (sum), 7-point.
Kilbourne, Painton, and Ridley (1985) (cognitive): 6,8,9 (sum), 5-point.
Kilbourne, Painton, and Ridley (1985) (affective): 11,12,13 (sum), 5-point.
Kilbourne, Painton, and Ridley (1985) (sexual): 30,31,32 (sum), 5-point.
Zinkhan and Zinkhan (1985) (favorable cognition): 22,46,47,48.
Zinkhan and Zinkhan (1985) (favorable affect): 11,13,18,49.
Zinkhan and Zinkhan (1985) (energy): 32,50,51,52.
Zinkhan and Zinkhan (1985) (familiarity): 53,54,55,56.
Beltramini and Evans (1985): 6,9,21,22,38,39,40,41,42,43, 7-point.
Beltramini (1982): 6,9,21,22,38,39,40,41,42,43 (mean), 7-point.
Rubin, Mager, and Friedman (1982): 1,4,6,7,8,9,10 (mean), 6-point.
Mitchell and Olson (1981): 1,2,3,4 (mean), 5-point.

1. good	___ :	___ :	___ :	___ :	___ :	___ :	___	bad
	1	2	3	4	5	6	7	
2. like	___ :	___ :	___ :	___ :	___ :	___ :	___	dislike
	1	2	3	4	5	6	7	
3. irritating	___ :	___ :	___ :	___ :	___ :	___ :	___	(non) not irritating
	1	2	3	4	5	6	7	(r)

4. interesting   ____ : ____ : ____ : ____ : ____ : ____ : ____   not interesting
              1   2   3   4   5   6   7

5. offensive   ____ : ____ : ____ : ____ : ____ : ____ : ____   (in)nonoffensive **(r)**
            1   2   3   4   5   6   7

6. trustworthy   ____ : ____ : ____ : ____ : ____ : ____ : ____   untrustworthy
            1   2   3   4   5   6   7

7. persuasive   ____ : ____ : ____ : ____ : ____ : ____ : ____   not at all persuasive
            1   2   3   4   5   6   7

8. informative   ____ : ____ : ____ : ____ : ____ : ____ : ____   uninformative
            1   2   3   4   5   6   7

9. believable   ____ : ____ : ____ : ____ : ____ : ____ : ____   unbelievable
            1   2   3   4   5   6   7

10. effective   ____ : ____ : ____ : ____ : ____ : ____ : ____   not at all effective
            1   2   3   4   5   6   7

11. appealing   ____ : ____ : ____ : ____ : ____ : ____ : ____   unappealing
            1   2   3   4   5   6   7

12. impressive   ____ : ____ : ____ : ____ : ____ : ____ : ____   unimpressive
            1   2   3   4   5   6   7

13. attractive   ____ : ____ : ____ : ____ : ____ : ____ : ____   unattractive
            1   2   3   4   5   6   7

14. eye-catching   ____ : ____ : ____ : ____ : ____ : ____ : ____   not eye-catching
            1   2   3   4   5   6   7

15. clear   ____ : ____ : ____ : ____ : ____ : ____ : ____   not clear
            1   2   3   4   5   6   7

16. favorable   ____ : ____ : ____ : ____ : ____ : ____ : ____   unfavorable
            1   2   3   4   5   6   7

17. fair   ____ : ____ : ____ : ____ : ____ : ____ : ____   unfair
            1   2   3   4   5   6   7

18. pleasant   ____ : ____ : ____ : ____ : ____ : ____ : ____   unpleasant
            1   2   3   4   5   6   7

19. stale   ____ : ____ : ____ : ____ : ____ : ____ : ____   fresh **(r)**
            1   2   3   4   5   6   7

20. awful   ____ : ____ : ____ : ____ : ____ : ____ : ____   nice **(r)**
            1   2   3   4   5   6   7

21. honest   ____ : ____ : ____ : ____ : ____ : ____ : ____   dishonest
            1   2   3   4   5   6   7

22. convincing   ____ : ____ : ____ : ____ : ____ : ____ : ____   unconvincing
            1   2   3   4   5   6   7

23. overall liking ____ : ____ : ____ : ____ : ____ : ____ : ____ overall disliking
      1   2   3   4   5   6   7

24. likable ____ : ____ : ____ : ____ : ____ : ____ : ____ unlikable
      1   2   3   4   5   6   7

25. favorable ____ : ____ : ____ : ____ : ____ : ____ : ____ unfavorable
      1   2   3   4   5   6   7

26. soothing ____ : ____ : ____ : ____ : ____ : ____ : ____ not soothing
      1   2   3   4   5   6   7

27. warm hearted ____ : ____ : ____ : ____ : ____ : ____ : ____ cold hearted
      1   2   3   4   5   6   7

28. uplifting ____ : ____ : ____ : ____ : ____ : ____ : ____ depressing
      1   2   3   4   5   6   7

29. affectionate ____ : ____ : ____ : ____ : ____ : ____ : ____ not affectionate
      1   2   3   4   5   6   7

30. sensual ____ : ____ : ____ : ____ : ____ : ____ : ____ not sensual
      1   2   3   4   5   6   7

31. erotic ____ : ____ : ____ : ____ : ____ : ____ : ____ not erotic
      1   2   3   4   5   6   7

32. exciting ____ : ____ : ____ : ____ : ____ : ____ : ____ (un)not exciting
      1   2   3   4   5   6   7

33. clear ____ : ____ : ____ : ____ : ____ : ____ : ____ imprecise
      1   2   3   4   5   6   7

34. complete ____ : ____ : ____ : ____ : ____ : ____ : ____ incomplete
      1   2   3   4   5   6   7

35. well structured ____ : ____ : ____ : ____ : ____ : ____ : ____ badly structured
      1   2   3   4   5   6   7

36. interesting ____ : ____ : ____ : ____ : ____ : ____ : ____ boring
      1   2   3   4   5   6   7

37. agreeable ____ : ____ : ____ : ____ : ____ : ____ : ____ disagreeable
      1   2   3   4   5   6   7

38. not credible ____ : ____ : ____ : ____ : ____ : ____ : ____ credible **(r)**
      1   2   3   4   5   6   7

39. questionable ____ : ____ : ____ : ____ : ____ : ____ : ____ unquestionable
      1   2   3   4   5   6   7

40. inconclusive ____ : ____ : ____ : ____ : ____ : ____ : ____ conclusive **(r)**
      1   2   3   4   5   6   7

41. not authentic   ___ : ___ : ___ : ___ : ___ : ___ : ___   authentic **(r)**
             1   2   3   4   5   6   7

42. unlikely   ___ : ___ : ___ : ___ : ___ : ___ : ___   likely **(r)**
             1   2   3   4   5   6   7

43. reasonable   ___ : ___ : ___ : ___ : ___ : ___ : ___   unreasonable
             1   2   3   4   5   6   7

44. tasteful   ___ : ___ : ___ : ___ : ___ : ___ : ___   tasteless
             1   2   3   4   5   6   7

45. artful   ___ : ___ : ___ : ___ : ___ : ___ : ___   artless
             1   2   3   4   5   6   7

46. meaningful   ___ : ___ : ___ : ___ : ___ : ___ : ___   meaningless
             1   2   3   4   5   6   7

47. valuable   ___ : ___ : ___ : ___ : ___ : ___ : ___   not valuable
             1   2   3   4   5   6   7

48. important to me   ___ : ___ : ___ : ___ : ___ : ___ : ___   not important to me
             1   2   3   4   5   6   7

49. beautiful   ___ : ___ : ___ : ___ : ___ : ___ : ___   ugly
             1   2   3   4   5   6   7

50. lively   ___ : ___ : ___ : ___ : ___ : ___ : ___   lifeless
             1   2   3   4   5   6   7

51. energetic   ___ : ___ : ___ : ___ : ___ : ___ : ___   without energy
             1   2   3   4   5   6   7

52. enthusiastic   ___ : ___ : ___ : ___ : ___ : ___ : ___   unenthusiastic
             1   2   3   4   5   6   7

53. familiar   ___ : ___ : ___ : ___ : ___ : ___ : ___   unfamiliar
             1   2   3   4   5   6   7

54. usual   ___ : ___ : ___ : ___ : ___ : ___ : ___   unusal
             1   2   3   4   5   6   7

55. well known   ___ : ___ : ___ : ___ : ___ : ___ : ___   not well known
             1   2   3   4   5   6   7

56. seen before   ___ : ___ : ___ : ___ : ___ : ___ : ___   not seen before
             1   2   3   4   5   6   7

57. interesting   ___ : ___ : ___ : ___ : ___ : ___ : ___   dull
             1   2   3   4   5   6   7

58. positive   ___ : ___ : ___ : ___ : ___ : ___ : ___   negative
             1   2   3   4   5   6   7

+ All positive items used in the Rubin, Mager, and Friedman (1982) study contained the modifier ''extremely'' on all positive anchors and ''not at all'' on the negative anchors. An example would be ''extremely interesting,'' ''not at all interesting.'' For consistency, the word ''extremely'' has been omitted.

SCALE NAME: Attitude Toward Advertisement (Upbeat Feelings)

SCALE DESCRIPTION:

This is a Likert-like scale (Burke and Edell 1989) purporting to measure the degree of ''upbeat'' feelings a consumer reports having toward an ad. The scale has been used with varying numbers of items, mostly single word descriptors, to measure the positive feelings evoked by an ad rather than evaluation of an ad itself. Thirty-two and 26-item (five-point) versions were used by Edell and Burke (1987) and a 27-item, five-point version was used by Burke and Edell (1989). A five-item, six-point scale was used by Madden, Allen, and Twibble (1988).

SCALE ORIGIN:

Each of the scale uses described here are similar in that all or most of their items can be found in the Reaction Profile for TV Commercials developed by Wells, Leavitt, and McConville (1971). Madden, Allen, and Twible (1988) say, however, that they modeled their initial scales on work by Abelson et al. (1982) with initial adjectives from that source as well as Nowlis (1970) and Madden (1982).

SAMPLES:

The subjects used by Edell and Burke (1987) and Burke and Edell (1989) were recruited by newspaper ads and announcements distributed on a university campus. Two small samples (**29** and **32**) were utilized in the former study and **191** was the size of the latter. It would be reasonable to assume it consisted of university students, however. The scale development subjects were also used for the research reported in the findings section. Madden, Allen, and Twible (1988) used **143** students recruited from an introductory undergraduate course. Subjects were isolated from each other for data collection.

RELIABILITY:

Cronbach's alpha values were reported to be **.98** (n=29) and **.95** (n=32) by Edell and Burke (1987). Burke and Edell (1989) reported an alpha of **.95**. The authors used repeated measures of the 191 subjects over six different stimuli. Reliability may be biased upward as measurement was based on 1146 observations (six per subject). Because of repeated measurement by same subjects, the authors claim replicability, though stimuli were different. The difference in their fourteen- and twenty-item versions was due to the fact that some items with item-total correlations greater than .9 were eliminated due to redundancy.

Madden, Allen, and Twible (1988) report a composite reliability of **.89** their positive affect scale.

VALIDITY:

Principal components factor analysis was used in the two articles by Burke and Edell (1987, 1989) to determine the underlying factor structure of a large number of descriptors. Virtually identical factors were found in each case.

Madden, Allen, and Twible (1988) reduced an initial set of 15 adjectives to 11 adjectives, seven of which fell into a positive affect factor (described here) and four of which fell into the negative affect factor through principal components analysis. Upon examination of confirmatory factor analysis results via LISREL VI, the 5-item positive and 3-item negative affect scales were determined to best represent the attitude model. Comparison of the squared structural link between each of these two construct measures and also with a semantic differential measure of ad evaluation resulted in a reasonable claim of discriminant validity for the variable pairs: positive affect/ad evaluation and positive affect/negative affect.

ADMINISTRATION:

In Edell and Burke (1987) and Burke and Edell's (1986) study, subjects were brought to a theater to view the stimulus materials. Scale data was collected through administration of a pencil-and-paper type of method. Madden, Allen, and Twible (1988) utilized a language lab setting to collect scale data. It is not clear whether data were recorded in paper-and-pencil form or directly input by subjects at computer terminals.

MAJOR FINDINGS:

Edell and Burke (1987) investigated the role of feelings in understanding attitude-toward-the-ad. The finding most relevant to this scale was that feelings generated by an ad (e.g., **upbeat**) contribute uniquely to predictions of attitude-toward-the-ad and brand above that provided by measures of an ad's characteristics.

In Burke and Edell's (1989) study, structural equation analysis indicated **upbeat** feelings have a significant ($p < .05$) effect on evaluation, activity, and gentleness judgments of ads, attitude-toward-the-ad and attitude-toward-the-brand. The conclusion was that brands with ads which evoke positive emotions are evaluauted higher.

Madden, Allen, and Twible's (1988) findings are particularly interesting in the context of measurement as the entire research is a validation of a three component model of attitude-toward-the-ad. Their findings support this model.

REFERENCES:

Abelson, Robert P., Donald R. Kinder, Mark D. Peters and Susan T. Fisk (1982), "Affective and Semantic Components in Political Person Perceptions," *Journal of Personality and Social Psychology*, 42 (April) 619-630)

Burke, Marian C. and Julie A. Edell (1989), "The Impact of Feelings on Ad-Based Affect and Cognitions," *JMR*, 26 (February), 69-83.

Edell, Julie E. and Marian C. Burke (1987), "The Power of Feelings in Understanding Advertising Effects," *JCR*, 14 (December), 421-433.

Madden, Thomas J. (1982), *Humor in Advertising: Application of a Hierarchy of Effects Paradigm*, unpublished doctoral dissertation, University of Massachusetts.

————, Chris T. Allen, and Jacquelyn L. Twibble (1988), "Attitude Toward the Ad: An Assessment of Diverse Measurement Indices Under Differing Processing Sets," *JMR*, 25 (August), 242-252.

Nowlis, Vincent (1970), "Mood, Behavior and Experience," in *Feelings and Emotions*, Magda B. Arnold, ed. New York, N.Y.: Academic Press Inc., 261-277.

Wells, William D., Clark Leavitt, and Maureen McConville (1971), "A Reaction Profile for TV Commercials," *JAR*, 11 (December), 11-17.

SCALE ITEMS: ATTITUDE TOWARD THE AD (UPBEAT FEELINGS) +

Instructions: We would like you to tell us how the ad you just saw made you feel. We are interested in your reactions to the ad, not how you would describe it. Please tell us how much you felt each of these feelings while you were watching this commercial. If you felt the feeling very strongly put a 5; strongly put a 4; somewhat strongly put a 3; not very strongly put a 2; not at all put a 1.

1. Active
2. Alive
3. Amused
4. Attentive
5. Attractive
6. Carefree
7. Cheerful
8. Confident
9. Creative
10. Delighted
11. Elated
12. Energetic
13. Happy
14. Humorous
15. Independent
16. Industrious
17. Inspired
18. Interested
19. Joyous
20. Lighthearted
21. Playful
22. Pleased
23. Proud
24. Satisfied
25. Silly
26. Stimulated
27. Strong
28. Adventurous
29. Enthusiastic
30. Excited
31. Exhilarated
32. Good
33. Lively
34. Soothed

+ Items 1 through 33 (except for item 25) were used by Edell and Burke (1987) in study 1. Items 1 through 27 were used by Burke and Edell (1989) and Edell and Burke (1987) in study 2, except for item 25 in the latter case. Madden, Allen, and Twible (1988) used items 7, 22, 26, 31, and 34.

SCALE NAME: Attitude Toward The Ad (Warm Feelings)

SCALE DESCRIPTION:

A Likert-like scale purporting to measure the degree of "warm" feelings a consumer reports having toward an ad. The scale is composed of single word descriptors that measure feelings evoked by an ad rather than evaluating the ad itself. A 13-item, five-point version was used by Edell and Burke (1987) in study 1. A 12-item, five-point version was used by Burke and Edell (1989) and Edell and Burke (1987) in study 2. The difference in the two scales is that a descriptor with an item-total correlation greater than .9 was eliminated due to redundancy (Edell and Burke 1987, p. 428).

SCALE ORIGIN:

The scale was developed by Edell and Burke in a pilot test described in an appendix to their 1987 article. Sixty people recruited on a college campus viewed 16 TV ads. Afterwards they were asked to write down any feelings the ads evoked. They also were given a checklist of 169 descriptors (gathered from a variety of sources) in which to respond. Sixty of the checklist items and nine more from the open-ended task were used as the feelings inventory, which was factor analyzed by Edell and Burke (1987) in study 1. Three feelings factors were produced: "upbeat," "negative," and "warm."

SAMPLES:

The subjects were **29** (study 1), **32** (study 2), and **191** people recruited by newspaper ads and announcements distributed on a university campus described in the Edell and Burke (1987) and Burke and Edell (1989) articles, respectively. Other than the fact that subjects were deceived about the true purpose of the research and were paid for participation, no other description of the sample was given. It would be reasonable to assume it consisted of university students, however. The scale development subjects were also used for the research reported in the findings section.

RELIABILITY:

Cronbach's alpha values were reported to be .93 (n=29), .90 (n=32), and .89 (n=191) by Edell and Burke (1987) and Burke and Edell (1989), respectively. Alpha may be biased upward however. The authors used repeated measures of the 191 subjects over six different stimuli. Reliability may be biased upward as measurement was based on 1146 observations (six per subject). Because of repeated measurement with the same subjects, the authors claim replicability, though stimuli were different.

VALIDITY:

Of the large group of items factor analyzed in each study, only those loading at least .50 were retained for use in scales. Further, these items always loaded together.

ADMINISTRATION:

The scale is a paper-and-pencil instrument amenable to survey research and experimental studies. Even though measurement requires an object stimulus, it is not necessary that administration be temporally contingent with stimulus presentation. No time period for administration was reported. It is not known if the items in this scale can be administered independently of the other items in the original pool.

MAJOR FINDINGS:

Edell and Burke (1987) investigated the role of feelings in understanding attitude-toward-the-ad. The finding most relevant to this scale was that feelings generated by an ad (e.g., **warm**) contribute uniquely to predictions of attitude-toward-the-ad and brand above that provided by measurements of an ad's characteristics. Structural equation analysis by Burke and Edell (1989) indicated **warm feelings** have a significant ($p < .05$) direct effect on evaluation, activity (negative coefficient), and gentleness judgements of ads. They also demonstrate a significant indirect effect through evaluation judgments on attitude toward the ad, brand attribute evaluations, attitude toward the brand through attitude toward the ad, and attitude toward the brand through attribute evaluations, as well as through activity judgments on attitude toward the ad (negative) and attitude toward the brand through attitude toward the ad (negative). In general, the net effect was that ads that were evaluated as more **warm** were evaluated more positively, as were the brands advertised.

COMMENTS:

Though the authors claim generalizability for their findings, lack of important sample information indicates caution in this respect.

REFERENCES:

Burke, Marian C. and Julie A. Edell (1989), ''The Impact of Feelings on Ad-Based Affect and Cognitions,'' *JMR,* 26 (February), 69-83.
Edell, Julie E. and Marian C. Burke (1987), ''The Power of Feelings in Understanding Advertising Effects,'' *JCR,* 14 (December), 421-433.

SCALE ITEMS: ATTITUDE TOWARD THE AD (WARM FEELINGS) +

Instructions: We would like you to tell us how the ad you just saw made you feel. We are interested in your reactions to the ad, not how you would describe it. Please tell us how much you felt each of these feelings while you were watching this commercial. If you felt the feeling very strongly put a 5; strongly put a 4; somewhat strongly put a 3; not very strongly put a 2; not at all put a 1.

1. Affectionate
2. Calm
3. Concerned
4. Contemplative
5. Emotional
6. Hopeful
7. Kind
8. Moved
9. Peaceful

10. Pensive
11. Sentimental
12. Warmhearted
13. Touched

+ The first 12 items above represent the shorter version of the scale.

SCALE NAME: Attitude Toward the Advertiser (Semantic Differential)

SCALE DESCRIPTION:

The scales consist of various bipolar adjectives presumed to measure the subject's overall evaluation of a specified advertiser. The scales have in common the feature of not being specific to the advertisements under investigation. Specific scale items and number of scale points used in several studies are indicated below.

SCALE ORIGIN:

The scales used to measure this construct seem to be developed in the research cited herein. The basis for most of these scales is the semantic differential, developed by Osgood, Suci, and Tannenbaum (1957). The underlying concept for the semantic differential is that a stimulus becomes a sign of the significate when it gives rise to the idea or thought of the significate. Measurement is accomplished by use of a series of semantic differential scales (a combination of controlled word association and scaling procedures). Each semantic differential scale is purported to represent a straight line through the origin of a semantic space. A selected combination of such scales is then believed to represent a multidimensional space. A listing of potential scale items and the dimensions of semantic space they are purported to represent is provided by Osgood, Suci, and Tannenbaum (1957, Chapter 2). The technique is believed by the authors to be highly generalizable and adaptable to most research needs. A seven-point scale is generally recommended by Osgood and his coauthors, though specific circumstances may warrant a different number of scale points.

SAMPLES:

Muehling (1987) used **133** student subjects. MacKenzie and Lutz (1989) used **203** student subjects from a midwestern university and **120** MBA and undergraduate student subjects from a major university in southern California.

RELIABILITY:

Cronbach's alpha was reported to be **.96** by Muehling (1987) and **.82** (advertiser credibility) and **.90** (advertiser attitude) by MacKenzie and Lutz (1989).

VALIDITY:

Though no specific scale validation is presented in either study reported here, both studies were attempts to validate an attitude toward the ad model. The nomological validity of the measures is somewhat supported by the findings of both research projects, though it is clear that the specific bipolar adjectives used in these scales are not necessarily the only valid descriptors or even possibly the best ones for measuring the given attitudes.

ADMINISTRATION:

The measures are taken in the typical paper- and-pencil self-report format.

MAJOR FINDINGS:

Muehling (1987) found a significant effect of attitude toward the ad on attitude toward the sponsor in each of five different comparative ad format conditions.

Mackenzie and Lutz (1989) essentially substantiated the connection between advertiser credibility, advertiser attitude, and a detailed causal linkage of various consumer perceptions and attitudes culminating in brand perceptions in a causal model. The complexity of their analysis and presentation indicates reference to the original article for a more comprehensive review of their findings.

REFERENCES:

MacKenzie, Scott B. and Richard J. Lutz (1989), "An Empirical Examination of the Structural Antecedents of Attitude Toward the Ad in an Advertising Pretesting Context," *JM*, 53 (April), 48-65.

Muehling, Darrel D. (1987), "Comparative Advertising: The Influence of Attitude-Toward-the-Brand on Brand Evaluation," *JA*, 16 (4), 43-49.

Osgood, Charles E., George J. Suci, and Percy H. Tannenbaum (1957), *The Measurement of Meaning*. Urbana, Ill.: University of Illinois Press.

SCALE ITEMS: ATTITUDE TOWARD THE ADVERTISER (SEMANTIC DIFFERENTIAL)

Scale items used in specific studies are listed below with indication of whether item sums or means were used in the research analysis and the number of points used for each scale item. Some of the items may not reflect bipolar opposites, as originally suggested by Osgood, Suci, and Tannenbaum (1957).

MacKenzie and Lutz (1989) (advertiser credibility): 1,2,3 (mean), 7-point.
MacKenzie and Lutz (1989) (advertiser attitude): 4,5,6 (mean), 7-point.
Muehling (1987) (sponser attitude): 4,6,7 (mean), 7-point.

1. convincing   ____ : ____ : ____ : ____ : ____ : ____ : ____   unconvincing
                   1   2   3   4   5   6   7

2. believable   ____ : ____ : ____ : ____ : ____ : ____ : ____   unbelievable
                   1   2   3   4   5   6   7

3. biased   ____ : ____ : ____ : ____ : ____ : ____ : ____   unbiased (r)
                   1   2   3   4   5   6   7

4. good   ____ : ____ : ____ : ____ : ____ : ____ : ____   bad
                   1   2   3   4   5   6   7

5. pleasant   ____ : ____ : ____ : ____ : ____ : ____ : ____   unpleasant
                   1   2   3   4   5   6   7

6. favorable   ____ : ____ : ____ : ____ : ____ : ____ : ____   unfavorable
                   1   2   3   4   5   6   7

7. negative   ____ : ____ : ____ : ____ : ____ : ____ : ____   positive (r)
                   1   2   3   4   5   6   7

SCALE NAME: Attitude Toward TV Advertising

SCALE DESCRIPTION:

A seven-item, Likert-type summated ratings scale measuring a person's opinion about television commercials. Rossiter (1977) as well as Riecken and Samli (1981) used four response choices whereas Carlson and Grossbart (1988) used five.

SCALE ORIGIN:

The scale was originally constructed and tested by Rossiter (1977). His purpose was to develop a measure of attitude toward television commercials that could be used reliably with children. Twelve initial items were tested on a group of 20 third graders, and some items were either eliminated or reworded. A seven-item version was then tested on a sample of 208 suburban Philadelphia children. The sample was mostly middle class, in grades four through six, and had similar proportions of each gender for each grade level. Item-total correlations ranged from .49 to .67 and the internal consistency (KR-20) was computed to be .69. The scale was administered to the children a month later and the test-retest correlation was .67.

SAMPLES:

Riecken and Samli (1981) gathered data from **152** children in a midwestern school ranging in age from 8 to 12 years. The sample had children from a variety of socioeconomic backgrounds, had slightly more girls than boys, and had six times as many white as black children.

The survey instrument in the Carlson and Grossbart (1988) study was distributed to mothers via students at three elementary schools in an unidentified U.S. city. The schools were chosen on a convenience basis but appeared to represent a variety of socioeconomic areas of the city. A $1 contribution to the PTO was offered for each completed questionnaire returned by the children. Analysis was based on **451** completed questionnaires. Ninety-three percent of the responding mothers indicated that they were the primary person in the child's socialization.

RELIABILITY:

Riecken and Samli reported an alpha of **.60**, a one-week test-rest correlation of .59, and item-total correlations for each item greater than .50. Carlson and Grossbart reported an alpha of **.73** and a beta of .62 for the scale.

VALIDITY:

One factor accounting for 82.7% of the total item variance emerged in a factor analysis by Riecken and Samli. No examination of scale validity was reported by Carlson and Grossbart.

ADMINISTRATION:

In the Riecken and Samli study, the items were read to students in grades two through five but self-administered by those in grades six and seven. Carlson and Grossbart employed the scale as one of many other measures included in a self-administered questionnaire. Higher scores on the scale mean that respondents express much more negative attitudes toward TV advertising than those with lower scores. As noted below, in the studies by Rossiter and by Riecken and Samli, the reversal of items was such that higher scores suggested more positive attitudes toward advertising.

MAJOR FINDINGS:

The purpose of the study by Riecken and Samli was to replicate Rossiter's study as well as to develop three product-specific versions of the scale to measure attitudes toward commercials for breakfast cereals, proprietary medicines, and toys. Reliability was slightly higher for all of the product-specific versions than for the general version reported above.

Carlson and Grossbart investigated the relationship between general parental socialization styles and children's consumer socialization. They found only limited significant differences in **attitudes toward TV advertising** between the five parental socialization style clusters examined. In particular, Authoritative mothers had the most negative attitude, though it was significantly lower than that of only two of the other parental style clusters.

COMMENTS:

See also a use of this scale by Wiman (1983).

REFERENCES:

Carlson, Les and Sanford Grossbart (1988), "Parental Style and Consumer Socialization of Children," *JCR*, 15 (June), 77-94.

Riecken, Glen and A. Coskun Samli (1981), "Measuring Children's Attitudes Toward Television Commercials: Extension and Replication," *JCR*, 8 (June), 57-61.

Rossiter, John R. (1977), "Reliability of a Short Test Measuring Children's Attitudes Toward TV Commercials," *JCR*, 3 (March), 179-184.

Wiman, Alan R. (1983), "Parental Influence and Children's Responses to Television Advertising," *JA*, 12 (1), 12-18.

SCALE ITEMS: ATTITUDE TOWARD TV ADVERTISING +

Strongly Disagree	Agree	Neither	Disagree	Strongly Agree
1—————	—2—————	—3—————	—4—————	—5

1. Television commercials tell the truth. **(r)**
2. Most television commercials are in poor taste and very annoying.
3. Television commercials tell only the good things about a product; they don't tell you the bad things.
4. I like most television commercials. **(r)**
5. Television commercials try to make people buy things they don't really need.
6. You can always believe what the people in commercials say or do. **(r)**
7. The products advertised the most on TV are always the best to buy. **(r)**

+ Rossiter (1977) as well as Riecken and Samli (1981) used four-point scales to eliminate the tendency of children to select a midpoint answer and thus avoid attention to the question. Further, they reversed scores on items 2, 3, and 5, which means high scale scores mean more positive attitudes toward commercials.

SCALE NAME: Complexity (Ad)

SCALE DESCRIPTION:

A two-item, nine-point Likert-type scale measuring the perceived complexity of a specific advertisement to which a person has been exposed.

SCALE ORIGIN:

Inspiration for the scale used by Cox and Cox (1988) came from a review of relevant literature.

SAMPLES:

The study by Cox and Cox was based on data collected from **240** MBA students at a large southwestern U.S. university. The people in the sample had a median age of 26 years, most worked full time, and there were slightly more men than women.

RELIABILITY:

An inter-item correlation of **.86** was reported for the scale by Cox and Cox. It was not based on the study sample, however, but on 34 graduate students in a prestudy exercise.

VALIDITY:

Though the authors' purpose does not appear to have been to specifically validate the scale, some evidence of concurrent validity was offered. Five expert judges identified four complex ads and four simple ads. In a pretest, all of the ads identified as complex scored higher on the scale than did all of the simple ads. Further, the mean score of the complex ads was significantly higher than the mean score of the simple ads. This manipulation check was noted again with the main study sample.

ADMINISTRATION:

In one of the main study sessions, respondents were exposed to the stimulus materials and then completed a self-administered instrument that included the scale and other measures. High scores on the scale suggest that respondents perceive an ad to be much more complex than ads with low scores on the scale.

MAJOR FINDINGS:

The purpose of the study by Cox and Cox was to examine how attitudes toward ads are influenced by previous exposure to them. The findings strongly supported the hypothesis that evaluations of **complex ads** become more positive with greater exposure whereas evaluations of simple ads do not.

REFERENCE:

Cox, Dena S. and Anthony D. Cox (1988), ''What Does Familiarity Breed? Complexity as a Moderator of Repetition Effects in Advertisement Evaluation,'' *JCR*, 15 (June), 111-116.

SCALE ITEMS: COMPLEXITY (AD)

Please tell how well each of these words below *describes* the advertisement. The ad is . . . (check the appropriate number).

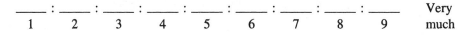

Not at all _____ : _____ : _____ : _____ : _____ : _____ : _____ : _____ : _____ Very
              1   2   3   4   5   6   7   8   9   much

1. Complicated
2. Complex

SCALE NAME: Complexity (Stimulus)

SCALE DESCRIPTION:

A 14-item, seven-point semantic differential summated ratings scale measuring the perceived complexity of some specified stimulus. Holbrook et al. (1984) used a seven-item subset of this scale and Leigh (1984) used nine of the items and three of his own in a modified Likert-like format.

SCALE ORIGIN:

The scale was developed in its original form by Mehrabian and Russell (1974) as a verbal measure of information rate. Factor analysis of data from **214** students helped to reduce a list of 21 pairs down to the final 14 by showing which ones were most related to arousal rather than pleasure or dominance. On the basis of **31** subjects, a reliability of .83 was obtained.

SAMPLES:

Holbrook et al. (1984) used **60** MBA students with a mean age of 25.6 years.

The study by Leigh (1984) was based on data from **240** college students taking an introductory marketing course, but not in a section taught by the researcher. Participation in the experiment was compensated by partial course credit. The experimental sessions were conducted with 10 to 30 subjects in a nonclassroom location.

RELIABILITY:

Holbrook et al. (1984) reported an alpha of **.85** for the short version of the scale used. The modified version of the scale used by Leigh (1984) was reported to have an alpha of **.67**.

VALIDITY:

Data on 14 bipolar adjectives were collected from respondents by Holbrook et al. (1984) for this construct. Their scale was composed of the seven items that loaded highest on the first factor in a principal components analysis of the 14 items. No examination of scale validity was reported by Leigh (1984).

ADMINISTRATION:

The scale was self-administered along with several other measures either in the middle of individual experimental sessions (Holbrook et al. 1984) or as the first of several experimental tasks (Leigh 1984). Lower scores on the scale suggest that respondents perceive some specified stimulus to be rare and/or surprising whereas higher scores imply that they think the stimulus is common and/or simple. Holbrook and his coauthors noted that scores were normalized for each individual by subtracting the scale mean from the response to each item and then summing the corrected numeric responses.

MAJOR FINDINGS:

Holbrook and his coauthors examined the role of emotions, performance, and personality in the enjoyment of games. In general, they found that emotions depend on personality-game congruity, perceived **complexity**, and prior performance. Specifically, the pleasure and arousal expressed with playing a video game were significantly predicted by the perceived **complexity** of the game, and perceived **complexity** was most significantly predicted by the number of unsuccessful performances out of four immediately preceding plays.

The purpose of Leigh's study was to examine the influence of family branding and number of products included on the effectiveness of "umbrella" advertising (referring to several products in an ad that are linked together in some way). The scale was used mainly as control in the study to provide evidence that ads in the treatment groups did not differ significantly in their perceived **complexity**.

REFERENCES:

Holbrook, Morris B., Robert W. Chestnut, Terence A. Oliva, and Eric A. Greenleaf (1984), "Play as a Consumption Experience: The Roles of Emotions, Performance, and Personality in the Enjoyment of Games," *JCR*, 11 (September), 728-739.

Leigh, James H. (1984), "Recall and Recognition Performance for Umbrella Print Advertisements," *JA*, 13 (4), 5-18, 30.

Mehrabian, Albert and James A. Russell (1974), "A Verbal Measure of Information Rate for Studies in Environmental Psychology," *Environment and Behavior*, 6 (June), 233-252.

SCALE ITEMS: COMPLEXITY (STIMULUS) +

varied* ___ : ___ : ___ : ___ : ___ : ___ : ___ redundant
        1   2   3   4   5   6   7

complex* ___ : ___ : ___ : ___ : ___ : ___ : ___ simple
        1   2   3   4   5   6   7

novel ___ : ___ : ___ : ___ : ___ : ___ : ___ familiar*
        1   2   3   4   5   6   7

contrasting ___ : ___ : ___ : ___ : ___ : ___ : ___ similar
        1   2   3   4   5   6   7

surprising* ___ : ___ : ___ : ___ : ___ : ___ : ___ usual
        1   2   3   4   5   6   7

heterogeneous ___ : ___ : ___ : ___ : ___ : ___ : ___ homogeneous
        1   2   3   4   5   6   7

rare ___ : ___ : ___ : ___ : ___ : ___ : ___ common*
        1   2   3   4   5   6   7

small scale ___ : ___ : ___ : ___ : ___ : ___ : ___ large scale (r)
        1   2   3   4   5   6   7

dense* ___ : ___ : ___ : ___ : ___ : ___ : ___ sparse
        1   2   3   4   5   6   7

intermittent   ___ : ___ : ___ : ___ : ___ : ___ : ___   continuous
                 1   2   3   4   5   6   7

uncrowded   ___ : ___ : ___ : ___ : ___ : ___ : ___   crowded*(r)
                1   2   3   4   5   6   7

asymmetrical   ___ : ___ : ___ : ___ : ___ : ___ : ___   symmetrical*
                1   2   3   4   5   6   7

immediate   ___ : ___ : ___ : ___ : ___ : ___ : ___   distant
                1   2   3   4   5   6   7

patterned*   ___ : ___ : ___ : ___ : ___ : ___ : ___   random(r)
                1   2   3   4   5   6   7

+   The first seven items are the ones used by Holbrook et al. (1984).

*   Leigh (1984) used these nine terms (not the pairs) as well as the following terms: cluttered, harmonious (r), and new. The scale ranged from "does not describe at all" to "describes very well."

SCALE NAME: Credibility (Source)

SCALE DESCRIPTION:

A five-item, nine-point bipolar adjective, summated ratings scale measuring the perceived credibility of the source of a message.

SCALE ORIGIN:

There is no information indicating that the scale originated elsewhere than in the study by Lichtenstein and Bearden (1989).

SAMPLES:

Analysis was based on data collected from **278** undergraduate business students. The students were randomly assigned to one of 12 treatment conditions in a 2 X 2 X 3 experimental design. There were between 21 and 28 students per cell.

RELIABILITY:

An alpha of **.78** was reported for the scale.

VALIDITY:

No examination of scale validity was reported.

ADMINISTRATION:

The scale was self-administered by students along with several other measures in an experimental setting. Higher scores on the scale imply that respondents perceive the source of a message to be highly credible whereas lower scores suggest that respondents believe the source to be untrustworthy.

MAJOR FINDINGS:

The study examined the influence of merchant-supplied reference prices, ad distinctiveness, and ad message consistency on perception of **source credibility**, value of the deal, and attitude toward the deal. Among many other findings, the authors reported that perceived **credibility** was higher for plausible-high merchant-supplied prices than for implausible-high merchant-supplied prices.

REFERENCE:

Lichtenstein, Donald R. and William O. Bearden (1989), "Contextual Influences on Perceptions of Merchant-Supplied Reference Prices," *JCR*, 16 (June), 55-66.

SCALE ITEMS: CREDIBILITY (SOURCE)

The *(message source)* is:

insincere	___:___:___:___:___:___:___:___:___ 1 2 3 4 5 6 7 8 9	sincere
honest	___:___:___:___:___:___:___:___:___ 1 2 3 4 5 6 7 8 9	dishonest **(r)**
dependable	___:___:___:___:___:___:___:___:___ 1 2 3 4 5 6 7 8 9	not dependable **(r)**
not trust-worthy	___:___:___:___:___:___:___:___:___ 1 2 3 4 5 6 7 8 9	trustworthy
not credible	___:___:___:___:___:___:___:___:___ 1 2 3 4 5 6 7 8 9	credible

SCALE NAME: Exposure to Company Advertising (Customer)

SCALE DESCRIPTION:

A two-item, five-point Likert-type summated ratings scale measuring the number of times in the previous two years a customer recalls being exposed to mass media advertisements by his/her insurance company.

SCALE ORIGIN:

There is no indication that the scale was constructed elsewhere than in the study by Crosby and Stephens (1987).

SAMPLES:

The sample was selected from a nationally representative consumer panel and screened for ownership of life insurance. Analysis of the first wave of the survey was based on **1362** responses. The sample was slightly better educated and more upscale than the population at large, but the authors considered the differences to be minor and unrelated to the studied relationships. A year later, respondents to the first wave of the survey (or from a holdout sample) were contacted. Analysis was based on **447** responses. Comparison of main sample and holdout sample data did not indicate any bias due to wave 1 premeasurement.

RELIABILITY:

Alpha values for the scale were **.82** and **.83** for the two waves of the study.

VALIDITY:

Factor analyses in the two waves of the study produced nearly identical factor solutions.

ADMINISTRATION:

The scales were self-administered as part of a larger mail questionnaire. High scores indicate that customers recall being exposed to mass media advertising from their insurance company many times in the past two years whereas low scores suggest that customers recall rarely if ever being exposed to such information from their company.

MAJOR FINDINGS:

The purpose of the study was to compare two proposed models of buyer satisfaction with life insurance: the relationship generalization model (RGM) and the rational evaluation model (REM). The RGM assumes that consumers generalize positive feelings about the provider to the core service whereas the REM views consumers as most concerned about core service quality, with the relationship merely adding value to it. In general, the results supported the REM over the RGM. This means that though the agent's performance affects satisfaction, it is balanced against the perceived performance of the core service. **Exposure to advertising** from their insurance companies was not found to have a significant impact on the satisfaction customers felt toward the companies.

REFERENCE:

Crosby, Lawrence A. and Nancy Stephens (1987), ''Effects of Relationship Marketing on Satisfaction, Retention, and Prices in the Life Insurance Industry,'' *JMR*, 24 (November), 404-411.

SCALE ITEMS: EXPOSURE TO COMPANY ADVERTISING (CUSTOMER)

Never	Once	Twice	Three or Four Times	Five Times or More
1—————	—2—————	—3—————	—4—————	—5

How often in the last one or two years do you recall experiencing the following:
1. Saw a magazine/newspaper advertisement sponsored by my company.
2. Saw/heard a TV or radio commercial sponsored by my company.

SCALE NAME: Information Adequacy (Consumer)

SCALE DESCRIPTION:

A three-item, five-point Likert-type scale measuring a consumer's sense of the sufficiency of the information provided by companies for making good purchase decisions. The scale was referred to as Consumer Meaninglessness by Durand and Lambert (1985).

SCALE ORIGIN:

The scale was originally constructed and used by Lambert (1980). Items were adapted from several previously published empirical and conceptual studies. A mail sample of residents of four southeastern metropolitan areas yielded 200 usable returns. Alpha for this scale was reported as **.648**. The scale was just one of four alienation measures used together in a cluster analysis to group consumers. No individual findings for the scale were reported. In general, dissatisfaction with the marketplace was found to be significantly related to levels of consumer alienation.

SAMPLES:

A systematic sample of 1320 customers of a large, investor-owned electric utility company was made. Questionnaires were mailed to them and **325** were returned following a reminder mailed after two weeks. The average respondent was at least 45 years of age, male, white, married, had at least graduated high school, and was socioeconomically upscale.

RELIABILITY:

An alpha of **.50** was reported for the scale.

VALIDITY:

No examination of scale validity was reported.

ADMINISTRATION:

The scale was self-administered along with several other measures included in the mail questionnaire. Higher scores on the scale indicate that consumers feel companies provide **sufficient information** for making purchase decisions whereas lower scores mean that consumers believe they are inadequately informed by companies.

MAJOR FINDINGS:

The purpose of the study was to investigate the degree to which criticisms of advertising are positively related to various aspects of consumer and political alienation. Respondents were first grouped according to levels of alienation by cluster analysis. (**Information adequacy** was one of the alienation variables on which the cluster analysis was based.) Then, differences in advertising criticisms were compared across the groups. The cluster analysis produced four alienation groups and a MANOVA indicated significant differences between the groups when all of the 12 advertising criticisms were considered simultaneously.

COMMENTS:

The internal consistency of the scale is unacceptably low and caution is necessary until refinement and improvement are done.

REFERENCES:

Durand, Richard M. and Zarrel V. Lambert (1985), "Alienation and Criticisms of Advertising," *JA*, 14 (3), 9-17.

Lambert, Zarrel V. (1980), "Consumer Alienation, General Dissatisfaction, and Consumerism Issues: Conceptual and Managerial Perspectives," *Journal of Retailing*, 56 (Summer), 3-24.

SCALE ITEMS: INFORMATION ADEQUACY (CONSUMER) +

Strongly Disagree	Agree	Neutral	Disagree	Strongly Agree
1—————	—2—————	—3—————	—4—————	—5

1. In the face of all the...advertising claims, generally it is hard to know what to believe about . . . different brands. **(r)**
2. When buying most products, I usually have enough information . . . to be confident . . . of choosing a good brand.
3. Generally companies provide enough information . . . so a person like myself can make a wise choice.

+ The authors noted that these items were abbreviated to conserve space as indicated by the dots. They should be contacted to obtain the full items.

SCALE NAME: Information Seeker

SCALE DESCRIPTION:

A 12-item, seven-point Likert-type summated ratings scale measuring the degree to which a person reads ads, shops around, and gathers information apparently out of curiosity. Raju (1980) referred to the measure as Information Seeking.

SCALE ORIGIN:

Though some of the items may be similar to those used in other scales, this group of items was put into scale form along with six other scales by Raju (1980). An initial pool of 90 items related to exploratory behavior and lifestyle were compiled and then tested for low social desirability bias and high item-total correlations. Thirty-nine items were found to meet the criteria and were common to two separate samples. Items were grouped into seven categories using inter-item correlations and subjective judgment.

SAMPLES:

Raju (1980) collected data from **336** homemakers and **105** students. The homemakers were contacted through local women's clubs and the students were contacted through mostly junior and senior level college classes.

RELIABILITY:

The scale was reported by Raju to have reliability (Spearman-Brown) of **.761** and **.842** for the homemaker and student samples, respectively.

VALIDITY:

Though Raju notes that a factor analysis was performed, the grouping of items for scale purposes was based more on inter-item correlations and a subjective classification process.

ADMINISTRATION:

Raju did not specifically address the manner of scale administration for either sample. However, for the homemakers it was implied that they received the questionnaire at a club meeting, filled it out at home by themselves, and returned it by mail. It is assumed that the student sample completed the survey instrument in class. Lower scores on the scale suggest that respondents are unlikely to gather information out of curiosity whereas higher scores suggest that respondents enjoy such exploration.

MAJOR FINDINGS:

In two studies, Raju examined the relationships between optimum stimulation level (OSL) and certain personality traits, demographics, and purchase-related psychographics. For both samples, low but significant correlations were found between **information seeking** and OSL. This along with other findings indicated that people with higher OSLs are more likely to exhibit a variety of exploratory behaviors in their consumer behavior.

COMMENTS:

The construct validity of the scale is highly suspect given the manner in which the seven scales used in the study were constructed (as noted in the origination information above). Sixteen of the 39 items were used to compose more than one scale thus making it unclear what construct the items and their respective scales actually measured. The reported reliability for this scale were reasonable, but further validity testing is needed.

REFERENCE:

Raju, P. S. (1980), "Optimum Stimulation Level: Its Relationship to Personality, Demographics, and Exploratory Behavior," *JCR*, 7 (December), 272-282.

SCALE ITEMS: INFORMATION SEEKER

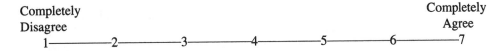

Completely Disagree 1————2————3————4————5————6————7 Completely Agree

1. I get very bored listening to others about their purchases. **(r)**
2. I like to browse through mail order catalogs even when I don't plan to buy anything.
3. I often read the information on the package of products just out of curiosity.
4. I shop around a lot for my clothes just to find out more about the latest styles.
5. A new store or restaurant is not something I would be eager to find out about. **(r)**
6. I generally read even my junk mail just to know what it is about.
7. I enjoy sampling different brands of commonplace products for the sake of comparison.
8. I usually throw away mail advertisements without reading them. **(r)**
9. I don't care to find out about what types of brand names of appliances and gadgets my friends have. **(r)**
10. I often read advertisements just out of curiosity.
11. I rarely read advertisements that just seem to contain a lot of information. **(r)**
12. When I hear about a new store or restaurant, I take advantage of the first opportunity to find out more about it.

SCALE NAME: Information Source Usage

SCALE DESCRIPTION:

The measure is a summated ratings scale assessing a person's typical consultation of six multiple sources of information before purchasing five common items. Moschis (1978, 1981) referred to this as Information Seeking.

SCALE ORIGIN:

The measure originates from a dissertation published by Moschis in 1978. His 1981 study, reported below, is from that same dissertation research.

SAMPLES:

Moschis' (1981) data came from **806** middle school or senior high school students. There were 365 "older" adolescents (15 years and older) and 441 "younger" adolescents (younger than 15 years). The students came from 13 schools and seven towns in Wisconsin representing a wide variety of urban to rural situations. The author indicates that the sample was well balanced in terms of most demographic characteristics except sex, as nearly two-thirds of the respondents were female.

RELIABILITY:

An alpha of **.37** was reported for the scale.

VALIDITY:

No examination of scale validity was reported.

ADMINISTRATION:

The scale was self-administered by students along with several other measures in a 10-page instrument during a regular class session. Scores are calculated by adding up for the five products the total number of sources a person says he/she would consult before purchasing. Higher scores on the scale indicate that respondents tend to consult a large number of sources before purchasing whereas lower scores suggest that they engage in little prepurchase information seeking.

MAJOR FINDINGS:

The study investigated the validity of the cognitive development approach to socialization (e.g., Piaget) to predict a wide variety of consumer-related cognitions learned during adolescence. In general, the findings indicated that the cognitive developmental model did not explain consumer socialization during adolescence very well. Older adolescents had significantly less favorable attitudes toward advertising, brands, and prices that did younger children but significantly greater prepurchase **information source usage**.

COMMENTS:

The extremely low internal consistency indicates that the scale is unreliable. This could be due to several different factors being respresented in the scale. Redevelopment and testing *must* be conducted before the scale is used further.

REFERENCES:

Moschis, George P. (1978), *Acquisition of the Consumer Role by Adolescents*, Research Monograph No. 82. Atlanta, Ga.: Publishing Services Division, College of Business Administration, Georgia State University.
_____ (1981), ''Patterns of Consumer Learning,'' *JAMS*, 9 (2), 110-126.

SCALE ITEMS: INFORMATION SOURCE USAGE

Below are some things people your age may buy. For each one check those people or places you would *rely on* for information and advice *before buying*. (YOU MAY CHECK MORE THAN ONE ANSWER FOR EACH PRODUCT.)

	Friends	TV Ads	Sales-persons	Consumer Reports	One or Both of My Parents	Newspaper or Magazine Ads
1. Camera	___	___	___	___	___	___
2. Hair dryer	___	___	___	___	___	___
3. Pocket calculator	___	___	___	___	___	___
4. Bicycle	___	___	___	___	___	___
5. Wrist watch	___	___	___	___	___	___

SCALE NAME: Interest (Commercial)

SCALE DESCRIPTION:

> A five-item, seven-point semantic differential summated ratings scale measuring a consumer's expressed interest in a commercial he/she has previously viewed.

SCALE ORIGIN:

> Bello, Pitts, and Etzel (1983) give no indication that the scale was constructed prior to the reported study.

SAMPLES:

> The authors used a sample composed of **217** undergraduate students (138 male and 79 female). The sample was considered appropriate given that the subjects' age group represented the largest buyers of the product category under examination (jeans). Groups of students were assigned randomly to one of the experimental treatments.

RELIABILITY:

> An alpha of **.80** was reported for the scale.

VALIDITY:

> No examination of scale validity was reported.

ADMINISTRATION:

> Immediately after viewing several bits of TV programming as well as several commercials, subjects were given a self-administered questionnaire pertaining to the last program and ad they had viewed. Lower scores on the scale suggest that respondents perceive a particular commercial to be interesting whereas higher scores mean that they perceive the advertisement to be dull and uninvolving.

MAJOR FINDINGS:

> The purpose of the experiment reported in the article was to assess the effectiveness of using ads with controversial sexual content. Though subjects viewed the controversial ad as being more **interesting** than the noncontroversial ad, it did not generate a significantly better attitude or purchase intention.

REFERENCE:

> Bello, Daniel C., Robert E. Pitts, and Michael J. Etzel (1983), "The Communication Effects of Controversial Sexual Content in Television Programs and Commercials," *JA*, 12 (3), 32-42.

SCALE ITEMS: INTEREST (COMMERCIAL) +

Eye catching   ___ : ___ : ___ : ___ : ___ : ___ : ___   Boring
                1   2   3   4   5   6   7

Interesting   ___ : ___ : ___ : ___ : ___ : ___ : ___   Uninteresting
                1   2   3   4   5   6   7

Emotional   ___ : ___ : ___ : ___ : ___ : ___ : ___   Unemotional
                1   2   3   4   5   6   7

Memorable   ___ : ___ : ___ : ___ : ___ : ___ : ___   Easily Forgetable
                1   2   3   4   5   6   7

Attention Getting   ___ : ___ : ___ : ___ : ___ : ___ : ___   Dull
                1   2   3   4   5   6   7

+ Only the positive descriptors (on the left) were provided in the article. Terms such as those on the right are assumed to have been used as negative descriptors.

SCALE NAME: Involvement (Ad)

SCALE DESCRIPTION:

A two-item, seven-point semantic differential scale measuring felt involvement toward product information presented in an advertisement. Felt involvement was defined by Celsi and Olson (1988) as the motivation to process information in a particular situation and is caused by two other types of involvement, enduring involvement and situational involvement.

SCALE ORIGIN:

The items used by Celsi and Olson (1988) came from a 10-item measure reported by Wells (1986) that he called the R Scale. The scale is purported to measure the degree to which an ad contains information **relevant** to a consumer's interests. Few specifics are given about the scale except the following: "It is internally consistent and reasonably reliable. It discriminates sharply among ads in ways that are intuitively appealing. And, most important of all, the variable it represents has popped up in study after study—across investigators, across methods and across media" (Wells 1986, p.11).

SAMPLES:

Subjects in the experiment by Celsi and Olson (1988) were **91** undergraduate students, **10** graduate students, **20** adult residents of the local community, and **15** present or former members of university tennis teams. Subjects' age ranged from 17 to 79 years, with a mean of 23 years. Fifty-one percent of the sample were female.

RELIABILITY:

The average interitem correlation for six ads was **.85**.

VALIDITY:

No test of validity was reported by Celsi and Olson.

ADMINISTRATION:

The scale was filled out by subjects in an experimental setting after they had read some print ads and had writen down what they remembered thinking and feeling while looking at the ads. Lower scores suggest that the information in an ad is not considered relevant whereas higher scores mean that the subjects are very interested in the product information.

MAJOR FINDINGS:

The purpose of the Celsi and Olson study was to examine the effects of enduring and situational **involvement** on felt **involvement** as well as on information processing of print advertising. Both enduring and situational **involvement** affected felt **involvement**, with the former having a substantially larger impact. Felt **involvement** appeared to increase as subjects devoted more attention to ads, exerted greater cognitive effort in processing those ads, increasingly focused their attention on the product-related information in the ads, and engaged in more elaboration of the information during comprehension.

COMMENTS:

The internal consistency of the two-item scale reported by Celsi and Olson appears adequate, but the psychometric quality is likely to be improved by the addition of other items. Several more items are already available that have an apparently successful history of use as reported by Wells (1986) and specified below.

REFERENCES:

Celsi, Richard L. and Jerry C. Olson (1988), ''The Role of Involvement in Attention and Comprehension Processes,'' *JCR*, 15 (September), 210-224.

Wells, William D. (1986), ''Three Useful Ideas,'' in *Advances in Consumer Research,* Vol. 13, Richard J. Lutz, ed. Ann Arbor, Mich.: Association for Consumer Research, 9-11.

SCALE ITEMS: INVOLVEMENT (AD) +

Strongly Disagree ____ : ____ : ____ : ____ : ____ : ____ : ____ Strongly Agree

         1   2   3   4   5   6   7

1. The message in the ad was important to me.
2. The ad didn't have anything to do with me or my needs. **(r)**
3. The commercial made me think about buying the brand that was advertised.
4. The commercial made me want the brand that was advertised.
5. During the commercial I thought how the product might be useful for me.
6. The commercial did not show me anything that would make me want to use their product. **(r)**
7. I have a more favorable view of the brand after seeing this commercial.
8. The commercial showed me the product has certain advantages.
9. It was meaningful for me.
10. It was worth remembering.

+ Celsi and Olson (1988) used only items 1 and 2, so totaling responses to the two items produces scores from 2 (very low involvement) to 14 (very high involvement). Wells (1986) reported the other items as having been used in numerous studies (apparently unpublished research by ad agencies).

SCALE NAME: Media Usage (Insurance Customer)

SCALE DESCRIPTION:

A six-item, five-point Likert-type summated ratings scale measuring the number of times in the previous two years a customer recalls the mass media providing information that led to questioning the value of his/her insurance policy. The implication of this measure is that the information originates from sources other than the policy owner's insurance company.

SCALE ORIGIN:

There is no indication that the scale was constructed elsewhere than in the study by Crosby and Stephens (1987).

SAMPLES:

The sample was selected from a nationally representative consumer panel and screened for ownership of life insurance. Analysis of the first wave of the survey was based on **1362** responses. The sample was slightly better educated and more upscale than the population at large but the authors considered the differences to be minor and unrelated to the studied relationships. A year later, respondents to the first wave of the survey (or from a holdout sample) were contacted. Analysis was based on **447** responses. Comparison of main sample and holdout sample data did not indicate any bias due to wave 1 premeasurement.

RELIABILITY:

Alpha values for the scale were **.85** and **.87** for the two waves of the study.

VALIDITY:

Factor analyses in the two waves of the study produced nearly identical factor solutions.

ADMINISTRATION:

The scales were self-administered as part of a larger mail questionnaire. High scores indicate customers have received information from various media many times in the past two years that led them to question the value of their insurance policies, whereas low scores suggest customers have rarely if ever received such information from the media.

MAJOR FINDINGS:

The purpose of the study was to compare two proposed models of buyer satisfaction with life insurance: the relationship generalization model (RGM) and the rational evaluation model (REM). The RGM assumes that consumers generalize positive feelings about the provider to the core service whereas the REM views consumers as most concerned about core service quality, with the relationship merely adding value to it. In general, the results supported the REM over the RGM. This means that though the agent's performance affects satisfaction, it is balanced against the perceived performance of the core service. **Media**

usage was found to have a significant but negative relationship to the satisfaction customers felt toward their core policy. This finding was not clearly explained but may mean that buyers are recalling negative information that was disseminated by the media, leading them to "question the value" of their policies. (See wording of items below.)

REFERENCE:

Crosby, Lawrence A. and Nancy Stephens (1987), "Effects of Relationship Marketing on Satisfaction, Retention, and Prices in the Life Insurance Industry," *JMR*, 24 (November), 404-411.

SCALE ITEMS: MEDIA USAGE (INSURANCE CUSTOMER)

Never	Once	Twice	Three or Four Times	Five Times or More
1	2	3	4	5

How often in the last one or two years do you recall experiencing the following:
1. Read an insurance advertisement in magazine/newspaper that made me question the value of this policy.
2. Read an insurance advertisement sent in the mail that made me question the value of this policy.
3. Saw/heard an insurance commercial that made me question the value of this policy.
4. Read consumer education materials that made me question the value of this policy.
5. Read newspaper/magazine article that made me question the value of this policy.
6. Saw/heard a program on TV or radio that made me question the value of this policy.

SCALE NAME: Novelty (Ad)

SCALE DESCRIPTION:

A three-item, nine-point Likert-type scale measuring the perceived novelty of a specific advertisement to which a person has been exposed.

SCALE ORIGIN:

Inspiration for the scale used by Cox and Cox (1988) came from a review of relevant literature.

SAMPLES:

The study by Cox and Cox (1988) was based on data collected from **240** MBA students at a large southwestern U.S. university. The people in the sample had a median age of 26 years, most worked full time, and there were slightly more men than women.

RELIABILITY:

An alpha of **.77** was reported for the scale.

VALIDITY:

The scale's validity does not appear to have been examined.

ADMINISTRATION:

In one of the main study sessions, respondents were exposed to the stimulus materials and then completed a self-administered instrument that included the scale and other measures. High scores on the scale suggest that respondents perceive an ad to be much more original, new, and or/unusual than ads with low scores on the scale.

MAJOR FINDINGS:

The purpose of the study by Cox and Cox was to examine how attitudes toward ads are influenced by previous exposure to them. The findings strongly supported the hypothesis that evaluations of complex ads become more positive with greater exposure but evaluations of simple ads do not. There was no significant difference in perceived **novelty** between a group of complex ads and a group of simple ads.

REFERENCE:

Cox, Dena S. and Anthony D. Cox (1988), ''What Does Familiarity Breed? Complexity as a Moderator of Repetition Effects in Advertisement Evaluation,'' *JCR*, 15 (June), 111-116.

SCALE ITEMS: NOVELTY (AD)

Please tell how well each of these words below *describes* the _____ advertisement. The ad is . . . (check the appropriate number).

Not at all _____ : _____ : _____ : _____ : _____ : _____ : _____ : _____ : _____ Very much

    1   2   3   4   5   6   7   8   9

1. Unusual
2. Original
3. New

SCALE NAME: Sales Advertising Watcher

SCALE DESCRIPTION:

A four-item, six-point, Likert-type summated ratings scale ranging from strongly disagree (1) to strongly agree (6). The scale measures a person's interest in attending to advertising related to sales. It was referred to as Advertising Special Shopper by Lumpkin (1985).

SCALE ORIGIN:

It is not clear where the items originated or where they were first used as a multi-item summated ratings scale.

SAMPLES:

Lumpkin (1985) analyzed data collected from a sample drawn from the Market Facts Consumer Mail Panel. A total of **2854** completed questionnaires were received, but Lumpkin focused just on **373** respondents who indicated they were 65 years of age or older.

RELIABILITY:

An alpha of **.8360** was reported.

VALIDITY:

Factor analysis indicated the items loaded together.

ADMINISTRATION:

Data were gathered through self-administered mail questionnaires. Scale scores are calculated by averaging numerical responses to individual items. A score of 6 indicates that a person has a strong tendency to watch for sales-related ads, particularly before shopping, whereas 1 implies that a person pays little attention to sales information.

MAJOR FINDINGS:

Elderly consumers were cluster analyzed and the three groups appeared to be discriminated by their degree of interest in **watching ads for sales** (statistical significance was not reported). The group with the highest mean score was the most socially active and had the most interest in shopping. The group with the lowest mean score appeared to be much less active all around.

REFERENCE:

Lumpkin, James R. (1985), "Shopping Orientation Segmentation of the Elderly Consumer," *JAMS*, 13 (Spring), 271-289.

SCALE ITEMS: SALES ADVERTISING WATCHER

Strongly Disagree	Disagree	Slightly Disagree	Slightly Agree	Agree	Strongly Agree
1————	——2————	——3————	——4————	——5————	——6

1. I shop a lot for ''specials.''
2. I always check the ads before shopping.
3. I usually watch advertisements for sales.
4. I read most of the ads in the paper carefully.

Part III

Organizational, Salesforce, and Miscellaneous Scales

Table of Contents

· · · · · · · · · · · · · · · · ·

SCALE NAME: Acceptance by Coworkers

SCALE DESCRIPTION:

The measure is a two-item, seven-point Likert-type scale assessing the degree to which an employee feels accepted and trusted by coworkers. Dubinsky et al. (1986) referred to this measure as Initiation to the Group.

SCALE ORIGIN:

The items for the scale were slightly modified from those developed by Feldman (1976). His study was based on data from **118** hospital employees. Scale scores were calculated not only on responses to questionnaire items, but also with a rating based on interviews with each subject. The Spearman-Brown reliability coefficient (corrected for attenuation) was reported as **.612**. Coworker acceptance was found to have significant positive correlations with work confidence and job suitability.

SAMPLES:

Analysis by Dubinsky et al. (1986) was based on data collected from **189** salespeople. Letters were sent to a national sample of 2000 senior-level executives asking them to have their least experienced salesperson complete the questionnaire. The respondents represented 189 different companies that marketed 50 different product categories. The sample had a median age of 30.5 years, had spent 1.4 years (median) in their present positions, and were mostly male (86%).

RELIABILITY:

A LISREL estimate of reliability was **.45**.

VALIDITY:

No examination of scale validity was reported.

ADMINISTRATION:

The scale was self-administered by respondents along with many other measures in a mail survey format. Higher scores on the scale indicate that respondents have very high sense of coworker acceptance whereas lower scores suggest that they have not been assimilated well into the work group.

MAJOR FINDINGS:

Dubinsky and his coauthors examined a model of salesforce assimilation. Job suitability was found to have a significant positive impact on **coworker acceptance,** which in turn was reported to have a high positive impact on internal work motivation.

COMMENTS:

The reliability of the measure is so low that improvement is necessary before it is used further.

REFERENCES:

Dubinsky, Alan J., Roy D. Howell, Thomas N. Ingram, and Danny Bellenger (1986), "Salesforce Socialization," *JM*, 50 (October), 192-207.

Feldman, Daniel C. (1976), "A Contingency Theory of Socialization," *Administrative Science Quarterly*, 21 (September), 433-452.

SCALE ITEMS: ACCEPTANCE BY COWORKERS

Strongly Disagree	Disagree	Slightly Disagree	Neutral	Slightly Agree	Agree	Strongly Agree
1	2	3	4	5	6	7

1. My coworkers actively try to include me in conversations about things at work.
2. I don't think my coworkers feel relaxed when they are with me. **(r)**

SCALE NAME: Acceptance of Authority

SCALE DESCRIPTION:

A three-item, six-point Likert-like scale purporting to measure a respondent's acceptance of authority and the importance placed on such respect.

SCALE ORIGIN:

The scale was originated by Withey (1965).

SAMPLES:

Ferrell and Skinner (1988) used a systematic sample of market researchers garnered from the membership lists of the Marketing Research Association and the American Marketing Association. **Five hundred and fifty** usable questionnaires were returned from an original mailing of 1500. Thirty percent of the respondents were data subcontractors (86% female), 45% were research firm employees (46% male), and 25% worked in corporate research departments (47% male).

RELIABILITY:

Ferrell and Skinner reported an alpha of **.69**.

VALIDITY:

Measure validation was reported by Ferrell and Skinner. Confirmatory factor analysis was used to assess the construct measure. Only items loading .30 or better and significantly indicating the construct were retained for the scale.

ADMINISTRATION:

The scale was a self-administered paper-and- pencil instrument used as a part of a larger questionnaire. Time to administer seems inconsequential.

MAJOR FINDINGS:

Ferrell and Skinner found no significant effect of acceptance of authority on ethical research behavior for data subcontractors, corporate researchers, or research firm employees.

REFERENCES:

Ferrell, O. C. and Steven J. Skinner (1988), "Ethical Behavior and Bureaucratic Structure in Marketing Research Organizations," *JMR*, 25 (February), 103-109.

Withey, Stephen (1965), "The US and the USSR: A Report of the Public's Perspective on the United States-Russian Relations in Late 1961," in *Components of Defense Policy*, D. Bobrow, ed. Chicago, Ill.: Rand McNally, 164-174.

SCALE ITEMS: ACCEPTANCE OF AUTHORITY

Definitely Agree					Definitely Disagree
1————————2————————3————————4————————5————————6					

1. Young people sometimes get rebellious ideas, but as they grow up they ought to get over them.
2. You have to respect authority and when you stop respecting authority, your situation isn't worth much.
3. Obedience and respect for authority are the most important things in character that children should learn.

SCALE NAME: Account Service Activity (Salesperson)

SCALE DESCRIPTION:

A four-item, seven-point Likert-like summated ratings scale measuring the frequency with which a salesperson provides services that would typically take place at the customer's location, such as inventory control, stocking shelves, and promotion activites.

SCALE ORIGIN:

The scale is original to a study by Moncrief (1986). Several scales were developed for use in the study from a review of the literature and from personal interviews and focus groups with salespeople. A total of 121 selling- related activities were identified and included on the survey questionnaire.

SAMPLES:

Using stratified sampling, Moncrief sent survey forms to 800 firms representing 20 SIC codes (#20-#39). Fifty-one firms ultimately participated and sent copies of the questionnaire to their salespeople. Of the total 2322 sales employees working for these firms, 1393 returned usable forms. The factor analysis was based on responses from **1291**.

RELIABILITY:

An alpha of **.73** was reported for the scale.

VALIDITY:

Though scale validity was not specifically addressed, a factor analysis of 121 items indicated that the items below all had loadings greater than .50 on the same factor and loadings less than .40 other factors. These findings provide some evidence of the convergent and discriminant validity of the scale.

ADMINISTRATION:

The scale was self-administered by respondents along with many other measures in a mail survey format. Higher scores on the scale indicate that respondents frequently engage in service activities at their customers' locations whereas lower scores suggest that they primarily perform activities other than those directly related to servicing their accounts.

MAJOR FINDINGS:

The purpose of the study by Moncrief was to develop a comprehensive list of selling-related activities and the taxonomies created from them. A cluster analysis was performed of the salespeople in the sample and six clusters were found. A group called trade servicer, representing 18% of the sample, had the highest mean on the **account service activity** scale. This cluster had the highest mean of any of the sales groups on seven of 10 sales activity areas examined in the study and it had the second highest mean on the other three activity areas.

#328 *Account Service Activity (Salesperson)*

REFERENCE:

Moncrief, William C, III (1986), "Selling Activity and Sales Position Taxonomies for Industrial Salesforces," *JMR*, 23 (August), 261-270.

SCALE ITEMS: ACCOUNT SERVICE ACTIVITY (SALESPERSON) +

Using the following scale, please indicate how frequently you engage in each of the activities listed below. If you do not perform the activity, please code your response as a zero.

Infrequently   ____ : ____ : ____ : ____ : ____ : ____ : ____   Frequently

                      1   2   3   4   5   6   7

1. Take inventory for the client
2. Setting up point-of-purchase displays
3. Stock shelves with product
4. Handle local advertising

+ The actual directions and items were not stated in the article, but are reconstructed here on the basis of information provided.

SCALE NAME: Achievement-Oriented Supervisory Behavior

SCALE DESCRIPTION:

A three-item, seven-point Likert-type summated ratings scale measuring the degree to which an employee perceives that his/her supervisor emphasizes and encourages performance improvement.

SCALE ORIGIN:

Though the items for this scale apparently were not original to Kohli (1985), he seems to have been the first to publish them. The items themselves are taken from a scale developed by R. J. Stogdill, who passed them on to Fulk and Wendler (1982) in personal correspondence. The latter authors did not report the items themselves, but used them in their study.

SAMPLES:

The analysis by Kohli was based on data from **114** salespeople. The sample was obtained from three companies manufacturing and selling industrial products. An overall response rate of 89.8% was reported.

RELIABILITY:

An alpha of .**70** was reported for the scale.

VALIDITY:

Though Kohli did not report the specific results for this scale, he implied that a factor analysis of this and other scales was used to eliminate items with weak loadings on their hypothesized factors.

ADMINISTRATION:

The scale was self-administered along with many other measures in an unspecified context. Higher scores on this scale indicate that respondents view their supervisors as strongly encouraging achievement whereas lower scores suggest that the employees perceive their supervisors as doing little to emphasize performance improvement.

MAJOR FINDINGS:

Kohli examined several previously unstudied supervisory behaviors toward salespeople. **Achievement-Oriented Supervisory Behavior** was found to be positively related to salespeople's role clarity.

COMMENTS:

Instead of "he", some more neutral descriptor such as "my supervisor" would make the items more generic and applicable to situations involving female supervisors.

REFERENCES:

Kohli, Ajay K. (1985), "Some Unexplored Supervisory Behaviors and Their Influence on Salespeople's Role Clarity, Specific Self-Esteem, Job Satisfaction, and Motivation," *JMR*, 22 (November), 424-433.

Fulk, Janet and Eric R. Wendler (1982), "Dimensionality of Leader-Subordinate Interactions: A Path-Goal Investigation," *Organizational Behavior and Human Performance*, 30, 241-264.

SCALE ITEMS: ACHIEVEMENT-ORIENTED SUPERVISORY BEHAVIOR

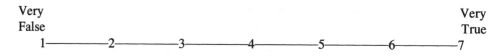

```
Very                                                              Very
False                                                             True
   1———————2———————3———————4———————5———————6———————7
```

1. He lets me know that he expects me to perform at my highest level.
2. He consistently sets challenging goals for me to attain.
3. He encourages continual improvement in my performance.

SCALE NAME: Adoption Costs (Customer)

SCALE DESCRIPTION:

A four-item, six-point Likert-type summated ratings scale measuring the degree to which a person perceives his/her company's last new product introduction to have required considerable planning, learning, and changeover costs. This measure was referred to by Eliashberg and Robertson (1988) as Customer Switching Costs.

SCALE ORIGIN:

The scale appears to be original to Eliashberg and Robertson (1988) and was used only in their study.

SAMPLES:

The sample consisted of **75** business executives who attended a series of executive education seminars at a major university. They were employed by different firms representing a variety of industries. It appeared that the executives either held positions that were connected with preannouncement decisions or made those decisions themselves.

RELIABILITY:

An alpha of .**71** was reported for the scale.

VALIDITY:

No direct examination of scale validity was reported, but results of a factor analysis indicated that the items were part of the same factor.

ADMINISTRATION:

The scale was self-administered by respondents along with other parts of a survey instrument. Higher scores on the scale suggest that respondents perceive customers incurred high switching costs in order to adopt their product; lower scores suggest that respondents perceive lower customer switching costs.

MAJOR FINDINGS:

The purpose of the study was to identify the conditions associated with the preannouncement of new product introductions. **Adoption costs** was found to be a significant predictor of preannouncing behavior such that preannouncing was associated with firms viewed as recently introducing a product with high **adoption costs.**

REFERENCE:

Eliashberg, Jehoshua and Thomas S. Robertson (1988), ''New Product Preannouncing Behavior: A Market Signaling Study,'' *JMR*, 25 (August), 282-292.

#330 *Adoption Costs (Customer)*

SCALE ITEMS: ADOPTION COSTS (CUSTOMER)

Strongly Disagree	Disagree	Slightly Disagree	Slightly Agree	Agree	Strongly Agree
1	2	3	4	5	6

1. The last new product/service we introduced required considerable advance planning on the customer's part.
2. The last new product/service we introduced required a major learning experience by the customer.
3. The last new product/service introduced involved high changeover costs for the customer.
4. Technology in this product/service category changes rapidly.

SCALE NAME: Adoption of the Extended Marketing Concept

SCALE DESCRIPTION:

A six-item, five-point Likert-type summated ratings scale measuring the degree to which a person believes that in some future time period companies will place more emphasis on issues related to the marketing concept as well as on developing good relations with customers, suppliers, and employees (Lusch and Laczniak 1987). This scale is composed of two subscales, Adoption of the Marketing Concept and Adoption of a Stakeholder Orientation. Evidence in the study supported treatment of the subscales together rather than separately.

SCALE ORIGIN:

The scale appears to be original to Lusch and Laczniak and theirs is the only known use of the scale in the published marketing literature reviewed here.

SAMPLES:

All that was reported about the sample was that it was composed of the **103** *Fortune 500* vice presidents of marketing and/or planning who responded to a mail questionnaire.

RELIABILITY:

An alpha of **.71** was reported for the scale. Item-total correlations ranged from .29 to .51.

VALIDITY:

LISREL was used to examine the structural relationships between constructs. The evidence strongly supported a single-factor model (the adoption of the extended marketing concept) rather than two independent factors (adoption of the marketing concept and the stakeholder orientation). Further, a "two-correlated-factors model" was not significantly better than the single-factor model.

ADMINISTRATION:

The scale was self-administered along with several other measures in a mail survey instrument. Higher scores on the scale suggest that respondents expect firms in the future to have adopted the marketing concept and to be more concerned about relations with several stakeholder groups.

MAJOR FINDINGS:

The purpose of the study by Lusch and Laczniak was to investigate the relationship between adoption of the marketing and stakeholder concepts and their perceived impacts on organizational performance. As noted above, the analysis provided greater support for a single-factor model that combined measures of the marketing and stakeholder orientations. Further, evidence from the surveyed executives indicated that increased competitive intensity was positively associated with **adoption of the "extended marketing concept,"** which was in turn positively associated with increased organizational performance.

COMMENTS:

The marketing concept and stakeholder orientation scales had alpha values of .49 and .67, respectively. Though the two scales could be used separately, their psychometric quality appears to be better when they are used together.

REFERENCE:

Lusch, Robert F. and Gene R. Laczniak (1987), "The Evolving Marketing Concept, Competitive Intensity and Organizational Performance," *JAMS*, 15 (Fall), 1-11.

SCALE ITEMS: ADOPTION OF THE EXTENDED MARKETING CONCEPT +

Persons in the sample were asked to state their expectations of the business environment in a future period using the following scale and items:

Strongly Disagree	Disagree	Neither	Agree	Strongly Agree
1————	——2————	——3————	——4————	——5

1. Firms will be more consumer-oriented.
2. Firms will concentrate their efforts more on profits than on sales volume.
3. Marketers will work together more with other functional departments in order to achieve total company objectives.
4. Firms will be more concerned with developing good relations with employees.
5. Firms will be more concerned with developing good relations with their agents and/ or distributors.
6. Firms will be more concerned with developing good relations with suppliers.

+ Items 1 through 3 composed the marketing concept subscale and items 4 through 6 composed the stakeholder orientation subscale.

SCALE NAME: Alienation From Work

SCALE DESCRIPTION:

A five-item, seven-point Likert-type summated ratings scale measuring the degree to which an employee lacks pride in his/her work, feels estranged from it, and works only for external rewards rather than for any inherent value it might have.

SCALE ORIGIN:

The scale used by Michaels et al. (1988) was constructed by Miller (1967). The latter gathered data from 419 scientific and engineering personnel working for a large aerospace company. Analysis of the measure by means of a Guttman scale indicated the following reliability characteristics: coefficient of reproducibility (Goodenough technique) = .91 and coefficient of scalability = .69. Work alienation was most strongly related to type of supervisor and amount of company encouragement among respondents with doctorates rather than those with master's degrees.

SAMPLES:

The analysis by Michaels and his coauthors was based on data from two samples: **215** full-line salespeople of a building materials manufacturer and **330** members of the National Association of Purchasing Management. The average salesperson respondent was 43.9 years of age and had 12.9 years of job tenure, 15.2 years of organizational tenure, and 18.1 years of sales experience. In contrast, the typical respondent in the industrial buyer sample was 42.2 years of age and had 5.7 years of job tenure, 10.6 years of organizational tenure, and 12.5 years of purchasing experience.

RELIABILITY:

Alpha values of **.80** and **.75** were reported for the scale for the salesperson and buyer samples, respectively.

VALIDITY:

No specific examination of scale validity was discussed.

ADMINISTRATION:

The scale was self-administered by respondents along with other measures as part of a larger survey instrument. Higher scores on the scale suggest that employee respondents report great pride and inherent value in their work whereas lower scores indicate that they feel estranged from their work.

MAJOR FINDINGS:

The purpose of the study by Michaels and his coauthors was to examine the impact of organizational formalization on several job-related attitudes. Among the significant findings was that higher levels of **work alienation** were related to higher levels of role ambiguity but lower levels of organizational commitment for both the salesperson and buyer samples.

REFERENCES:

Michaels, Ronald E., William L. Cron, Alan J. Dubinsky, and Eric A. Joachimsthaler (1988), Influence of Formalization on the Organizational Commitment and Work Alienation of Salespeople and Industrial Buyers,'' *JMR*, 25 (November), 376-383.

Miller, George A. (1967), ''Professionals in Bureaucracy: Alienation Among Industrial Scientists and Engineers,'' *American Sociological Review*, 32 (October), 755-768.

SCALE ITEMS: ALIENATION FROM WORK

Strongly disagree = 1
Moderately disagree = 2
Slightly disagree = 3
Neutral = 4
Slightly agree = 5
Moderately agree = 6
Strongly agree = 7

1. I really don't feel a sense of pride or accomplishment as a result of the type of work that I do.
2. My work gives me a feeling of pride in having done the job well. **(r)**
3. I very much like the type of work that I am doing. **(r)**
4. My job gives me a chance to do the things that I do best. **(r)**
5. My work is my most rewarding experience. **(r)**

SCALE NAME: Alternative Offerings (Industrial Sales)

SCALE DESCRIPTION:

A three-item, seven-point summated ratings scale measuring the range of alternative offerings a company's salesforce has and can adjust to meet customer needs. The seven anchors on the graphic scale range from 0% to 100%.

SCALE ORIGIN:

John and Weitz (1989) give no indication that this scale originated elsewhere than in their study.

SAMPLES:

John and Weitz (1989) collected data in a two-stage sampling procedure. Personalized requests were mailed to 750 sales managers or sales vice presidents of manufacturing firms with annual sales of at least $50 million. The 266 respondents were then sent a questionnaire and **161** returned usable survey instruments. The sample appeared to be different from the population in some respects but very similar in others.

RELIABILITY:

An alpha of **.54** was reported for the scale. Item-total correlations were .34, .34, and .35.

VALIDITY:

No specific examination of scale validity was done.

ADMINISTRATION:

The scale was self-administered by respondents along with many other measures in a mail questionnaire format. Higher scores on the scale suggest that respondents believe their salespeople can offer a great range of alternatives to customers whereas lower scores indicate they think their salesforces have limited alternatives for customers.

MAJOR FINDINGS:

The purpose of the study by John and Weitz was to examine the role of salary in sales compensation plans by using a transaction cost analysis framework. The range of **alternative offerings** had its most significant correlations with complexity of the sales task (positive) and salary (negative).

COMMENTS:

The low internal consistency suggests that extreme caution should be exercised in using this scale until further development and testing can be done.

REFERENCE:

John, George and Barton Weitz (1989), ''Salesforce Compensation· An Empirical Investigation of Factors Related to Use of Salary Versus Incentive Compensation,'' *JMR*, 26 (February), 1-14.

SCALE ITEMS: ALTERNATIVE OFFERINGS (INDUSTRIAL SALES) +

The following statements describe circumstances that might exist when one of your salespeople is trying to make a sale. Please indicate how frequently the salesperson would face the situation described in the statement. This can be done by circling the number that most accurately indicates the percentage of sales situations that fit the statement. Each question is independent: your answers do not need to add to 100% or any other number.

Percentage of Situations

0%	10%	30%	50%	70%	90%	100%

1 The salesperson has a wide range of alternatives to offer the customer.
2. The salesperson can tailor his/her offerings to match the customer's needs.
3. The salesperson can be very helpful in terms of assisting the customer in solving his/her problem.

+ The instructions were not included in the article, but are assumed to be similar to those given here.

SCALE NAME: Attitude Toward The Manufacturer (Dealer)

SCALE DESCRIPTION:

A four-item, seven-point Likert-like scale purporting to measure a dealer's attitudes toward a particular manufacturer it represents.

SCALE ORIGIN:

The scale seems to have originated in the study by Frazier and Summers (1986).

SAMPLES:

Frazier and Summers' sample consisted of **435** owners, owner/managers, or general managers of car dealerships in Indiana, Illinois, and Ohio. Response rate was 46.1%.

RELIABILITY:

Frazier and Summers (1986) reported an alpha of **.76**.

VALIDITY:

No validation information is reported.

ADMINISTRATION:

The scale was self-administered by respondents as a section of a mail survey. Time to administer seems inconsequential.

MAJOR FINDINGS:

Frazier and Summers found that in general, dealers' attitude toward manufacturers was related to the dealers' perceptions of the manufacturers' use of coercive influence in the relationship. The more coercive the manufacturer, the less positive was the dealer's attitude toward the manufacturer.

REFERENCE:

Frazier, Gary L. and John O. Summers (1986), "Perceptions of Interfirm Power and Its Use Within a Franchise Channel of Power," *JMR*, 23 (May), 169-176.

SCALE ITEMS: ATTITUDE TOWARD THE MANUFACTURER (DEALER)

Strongly   Strongly
Disagree   Agree
1————2————3————4————5————6————7

1. The manufacturer is very interested in helping me make my dealership profitable. **(r)**

2. My manufacturer tries to push too much inventory on my dealership during slow sales periods.
3. Most of the disagreements I have had with my manufacturer reps in the past year were settled to my satisfaction. **(r)**

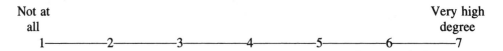

Not at   Very high
 all   degree
1———————2———————3———————4———————5———————6———————7

4. To what degree have the manufacturer and/or the manufacturer reps pressured you into taking actions that you were convinced were not in the best interest of your dealership?

SCALE NAME: Attributional Style (Sales Effort)

SCALE DESCRIPTION:

A two-item, seven-point Likert-like summated ratings scale measuring the degree to which a salesperson reports that his/her failure to make a sale was due to a lack of effort.

SCALE ORIGIN:

The measure was developed by Sujan (1986).

SAMPLES:

Letters were sent by Sujan to 880 sales managers working for large national manufacturing firms representing a wide variety of industries. The 191 who responded indicated a total of 4038 salespeople in their companies who would serve as respondents. Questionnaires were then sent to them and **1283** usable responses were received from salespeople in 123 firms.

RELIABILITY:

An alpha of **.75** was reported for the scale.

VALIDITY:

No specific examination of scale validity was reported.

ADMINISTRATION:

The scale was self-administered by respondents in a mail survey format. Higher scores on the scale indicate that salespeople attribute recent failures to make sales to not working hard enough whereas lower scores suggest that they do not think lost sales were due to a lack of effort.

MAJOR FINDINGS:

The purpose of the study was to use the attributional theory of motivation to understand salespeople's desire to "work smarter." The clearest finding involving this attribution style was that **attributing failure to a lack of effort** had a significant positive impact on salespeople's motivation to work harder.

REFERENCE:

Sujan, Harish (1986), "Smarter Versus Harder: An Exploratory Attributional Analysis of Salespeople's Motivation," *JMR*, 23 (February), 41-49.

SCALE ITEMS: ATTRIBUTIONAL STYLE (SALES EFFORT)

Think about the times in the last twelve months when you failed to obtain an order from a customer. Considering these instances, please indicate on the scale the extent to which each of the following reasons caused you to fail.

Did not contribute   Contributed to
to your failures at   your failures a
all   ____ : ____ : ____ : ____ : ____ : ____ : ____   great deal
                         1   2   3   4   5   6   7

1. Your devoting unusually little effort.
2. Your working less hard than normal.

SCALE NAME: Attributional Style (Sales Strategy)

SCALE DESCRIPTION:

A two-item, seven-point Likert-like summated ratings scale measuring the degree to which a salesperson reports that his/her failure to make a sale was due to a poor sales methods.

SCALE ORIGIN:

The measure was developed by Sujan (1986).

SAMPLES:

Letters were sent to 880 sales managers working for large national manufacturing firms representing a wide variety of industries. The 191 who responded indicated a total of 4038 salespeople in their companies who would serve as respondents. Questionnaires were then sent to them and **1283** usable responses were received from salespeople in 123 firms.

RELIABILITY:

An alpha of .57 was reported for the scale.

VALIDITY:

No specific examination of scale validity was reported.

ADMINISTRATION:

The scale was self-administered by respondents in a mail survey format. Higher scores on the scale indicate that salespeople attribute recent sales failures to poor sales tactics whereas lower scores suggest that they do not think lost sales were due to bad strategy.

MAJOR FINDINGS:

The purpose of the study was to use the attributional theory of motivation to understand salespeople's desire to "work smarter." As expected, **attributing failure to poor strategy** had a significant positive impact on salespeople's motivation to work "smarter." Unexpectedly, however, intrinsic job satisfaction had a significant negative impact on **attributing failure to poor sales strategy**.

REFERENCE:

Sujan, Harish (1986), "Smarter Versus Harder: An Exploratory Attributional Analysis of Salespeople's Motivation," *JMR*, 23 (February), 41-49.

SCALE ITEMS: ATTRIBUTIONAL STYLE (SALES STRATEGY)

Think about the times in the last twelve months when you failed to obtain an order from a customer. Considering these instances, please indicate on the scale the extent to which each of the following reasons caused you to fail.

Did not contribute
to your failures at
all

____ : ____ : ____ : ____ : ____ : ____ : ____
   1   2   3   4   5   6   7

Contributed to
your failures a
great deal

1. Your using unusally poor selling strategies.
2. Your using selling methods different from the ones you normally use.

SCALE NAME: Autocratic Supervisory Behavior

SCALE DESCRIPTION:

> A six-item, seven-point Likert-type summated ratings scale measuring the degree to which an employee perceives arbitrary and punitive behaviors to characterize the leadership style used by a supervisor. The scale has been referred to as Arbitrary and Punitive Behavior by Kohli (1985) as well as others.

SCALE ORIGIN:

> Several of the items in this scale are the same as or similar to those in the Supervisory Behavior Description Questionnaire (Fleishman 1957).

SAMPLES:

> The analysis by Kohli (1985) was based on data from **114** salespeople. The sample was obtained from three companies manufacturing and selling industrial products. An overall response rate of 89.8% was reported.

RELIABILITY:

> An alpha of .83 was reported for the scale.

VALIDITY:

> Though Kohli did not report the specific results for this scale, he implied that a factor analysis of this and other scales was used to eliminate items with weak loadings on their hypothesized factors.

ADMINISTRATION:

> The scale was self-administered along with many other measures in an unspecified context. Higher scores on this scale indicate that respondents view their supervisors as being quite arbitrary and punitive in their management style whereas lower scores suggest that respondents perceive their supervisors to make little use of authoritarian tactics.

MAJOR FINDINGS:

> Kohli examined several previously unstudied supervisory behaviors toward salespeople. The use of **autocratic behavior by a supervisor** was found to be positively related to salespeople's intrinsic, extrinsic, and overall job satisfaction.

COMMENTS:

> Instead of "he," some more neutral descriptor such as "my supervisor" would make the items more generic and applicable to situations involving female supervisors.

REFERENCES:

Fleishman, E. A. (1957), "A Leader Behavior Description for Industry," in *Leader Behavior: Its Description and Measurement*, Ralph M. Stogdill and Alvin E. Coons, eds. Columbus, Ohio: The Bureau of Business Research, The Ohio State University.

Kohli, Ajay K. (1985), "Some Unexplored Supervisory Behaviors and Their Influence on Salespeople's Role Clarity, Specific Self-Esteem, Job Satisfaction, and Motivation," *JMR*, 22 (November), 424-433.

SCALE ITEMS: AUTOCRATIC SUPERVISORY BEHAVIOR

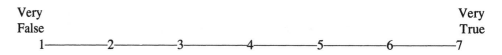

Very
False

Very
True

1————2————3————4————5————6————7

1. He rules with an iron hand.
2. He refuses to give in when I disagree with him.
3. He insists that everything be done his way.
4. He "needles" me for greater effort.
5. He criticizes me in front of others.
6. He rides me if I make a mistake.

SCALE NAME: Autonomy (Job Performance)

SCALE DESCRIPTION:

A six-item, five-point Likert-type scale measuring the degree of freedom an employee expresses having in performing his/her work.

SCALE ORIGIN:

The scale was developed as part of the Job Characteristics Inventory by Sims, Szilagyi, and Keller (1976), though they indicate that they borrowed many items from previous work (Hackman and Lawler 1971). The inventory was tested on a sample of 192 male employees of a large manufacturing firm. The alpha for the job autonomy portion of the inventory was calculated to be .84. A variety of evidence is presented attesting to the scale's convergent and discriminant validity.

SAMPLES:

The analysis by Cummings, Jackson, and Ostrom (1989) was based on data from **201** product managers in firms having annual sales in the range of $8 million to $35 billion.

RELIABILITY:

An alpha of .**791** was reported for the scale by Cummings and his coauthors.

VALIDITY:

No examination of scale validity was reported.

ADMINISTRATION:

The scale was self-administered along with many other measures in a mail survey format. Higher scores on the scale indicate that employees think they have a great amount of autonomy in the jobs they perform whereas lower scores suggest that they feel they have little freedom and independence. Cummings and his coauthors added each respondent's score on this scale with those on three other dimensions of the JCI to obtain an overall "job scope" score.

MAJOR FINDINGS:

The purpose of the study by Cummings and his coauthors was to investigate several aspects of organizational behavior and their impact on the job satisfaction and performance of product managers. **Job autonomy** was not examined per se but was incorporated into the "job scope" measure. Path analysis results indicated that the only variable to have a significant effect (negative) on job scope was centralization of decision making.

COMMENTS:

See also a modification of this scale used by Hunt and Chonko (1984).

REFERENCES:

Cummings, W. Theodore, Donald W. Jackson, and Lonnie L. Ostrom (1989), "Examining Product Managers' Job Satisfaction and Performance Using Selected Organizational Behavior Variables," *JAMS*, 17 (Spring), 147-156.

Hackman, J. R. and E. E. Lawler, III (1971), "Employee Reactions to Job Characteristics," *Journal of Applied Psychology Monographs*, 55, 259-268.

Hunt, Shelby D. and Lawrence B. Chonko (1984), "Marketing and Machiavellianism," *JM*, 48 (Summer), 30-42.

Sims, Henry P., Jr., Andrew D. Szilagyi, and Robert T. Keller (1976), "The Measurement of Job Characteristics," *Academy of Management Journal*, 19 (June), 195-212.

SCALE ITEMS: AUTONOMY IN JOB PERFORMANCE +

1. How much are you left on your own to do your own work?
2. To what extent are you able to act independently of your supervisor in performing your job function?
3. To what extent are you able to do your job independently of others?
4. The freedom to do pretty much what I want on my job.
5. The opportunity for independent thought and action.
6. The control I have over the pace of my work.

+ The following scale was used for the first three items:

Very Little		A Moderate Amount		Very Much
1———————	—2———————	—3———————	—4———————	—5

The following scale was used for the last three items:

A Minimum Amount		A Moderate Amount		A Maximum Amount
1———————	—2———————	—3———————	—4———————	—5

SCALE NAME: Barriers to Entry

SCALE DESCRIPTION:

A five-item, seven-point Likert-type summated ratings scale measuring the degree to which a person describes an industry as having barriers to entry.

SCALE ORIGIN:

The scale was original to Burke (1984), whose study is the only known use of the scale in the published marketing research reviewed here.

SAMPLES:

Data were collected from a total of **86** business units in six of 18 firms personally contacted. The majority of business units were in conglomerate firms. The managers who filled out the survey instruments had bottom-line responsibility for their business units, were highly involved in selecting market share objectives, and were an average of 3.29 levels away from their CEOs.

RELIABILITY:

An alpha of **.85** was reported for the scale.

VALIDITY:

Burke implied that a factor analysis was performed as part of scale development but provided no specific details. No other examination of scale validity was suggested.

ADMINISTRATION:

The sample responded to the scale as part of a self-administered mail questionnaire. Higher scores on the scale suggest that respondents perceive a particular industry to have high entry barriers.

MAJOR FINDINGS:

The study investigated the degree to which business-unit managers of multiproduct firms perceived different variables to influence strategic choices. No significant difference in perception of **entry barriers** was found for three types of strategic thrusts used by business units.

REFERENCE:

Burke, Marian C. (1984), ''Strategic Choice and Marketing Managers: An Examination of Business-Level Marketing Objectives,'' *JMR*, 21 (November), 345-359.

SCALE ITEMS: BARRIERS TO ENTRY

The exact question is not reported in the article, but in general respondents were asked to think back about the most recent strategic market objective for their business units and to describe its nature.

1. The four-firm industry concentration is:

low   ___ : ___ : ___ : ___ : ___ : ___ : ___   high
             1   2   3   4   5   6   7

2. The suitability of competitive products is:

easy   ___ : ___ : ___ : ___ : ___ : ___ : ___   difficult
             1   2   3   4   5   6   7

3. The number of suppliers is:

many   ___ : ___ : ___ : ___ : ___ : ___ : ___   few
             1   2   3   4   5   6   7

4. The number of competitors is:

many   ___ : ___ : ___ : ___ : ___ : ___ : ___   few
             1   2   3   4   5   6   7

5. The number of customers is:

many   ___ : ___ : ___ : ___ : ___ : ___ : ___   few
             1   2   3   4   5   6   7

SCALE NAME: Barriers to Exit

SCALE DESCRIPTION:

A 12-item, seven-point Likert-like summated ratings scale measuring the degree to which a person describes an industry as having barriers to exit.

SCALE ORIGIN:

The scale was original to Burke (1984), whose study is the only known use of the scale in the published marketing research reviewed here.

SAMPLES:

Data were collected from a total of **86** business units in six of 18 firms personally contacted. The majority of business units were in conglomerate firms. The managers who filled out the survey instruments had bottom-line responsibility for their business units, were highly involved in selecting market share objectives, and were an average of 3.29 levels away from their CEOs.

RELIABILITY:

An alpha of **.92** was reported for the scale.

VALIDITY:

Burke implied that a factor analysis was performed as part of scale development, but provided no specific details. No other examination of scale validity was suggested.

ADMINISTRATION:

The sample responded to the scale as part of a self-administered mail questionnaire. Higher scores on the scale suggest that respondents perceive a particular industry to have high exit barriers.

MAJOR FINDINGS:

The study investigated the degree to which business-unit managers of multiproduct firms perceived different variables to influence strategic choices. No significant difference was found in perception of **exit barriers** for three types of strategic thrusts used by business units.

REFERENCE:

Burke, Marian C. (1984), "Strategic Choice and Marketing Managers: An Examination of Business-Level Marketing Objectives," *JMR*, 21 (November), 345-359.

SCALE ITEMS: BARRIERS TO EXIT

If the business unit were eliminated, evaluate the:

1. ability of the firm to absorb production personnel

easy   ____ : ____ : ____ : ____ : ____ : ____ : ____   hard
                 1   2   3   4   5   6   7

2. ability of the firm to absorb management personnel

easy   ____ : ____ : ____ : ____ : ____ : ____ : ____   hard
                  1   2   3   4   5   6   7

3. alternate uses for the facilities within the company

many   ____ : ____ : ____ : ____ : ____ : ____ : ____   few
                  1   2   3   4   5   6   7

4. alternate uses for capital equipment within the company

many   ____ : ____ : ____ : ____ : ____ : ____ : ____   few
                  1   2   3   4   5   6   7

5. impact on costs of other businesses within the company

large decrease   ____ : ____ : ____ : ____ : ____ : ____ : ____   large increase
                  1   2   3   4   5   6   7

6. size of the immediate loss to the company

very small   ____ : ____ : ____ : ____ : ____ : ____ : ____   very large
                  1   2   3   4   5   6   7

Relative to other business units in the firm, rate this one's:

7. size, in terms of sales dollars

much smaller   ____ : ____ : ____ : ____ : ____ : ____ : ____   much larger
                  1   2   3   4   5   6   7

8. contribution to current profits

much smaller   ____ : ____ : ____ : ____ : ____ : ____ : ____   much larger
                  1   2   3   4   5   6   7

9. size of margin

much smaller   ____ : ____ : ____ : ____ : ____ : ____ : ____   much larger
                  1   2   3   4   5   6   7

10. stability of profit margin

more volatile   ___ : ___ : ___ : ___ : ___ : ___ : ___   more stable
       1   2   3   4   5   6   7

11. long-run profit potential

negligible   ___ : ___ : ___ : ___ : ___ : ___ : ___   substantial
       1   2   3   4   5   6   7

12. sales to other parts of the corporation

very low   ___ : ___ : ___ : ___ : ___ : ___ : ___   very high
       1   2   3   4   5   6   7

SCALE NAME: Centralization (Agent/Client Relationship)

SCALE DESCRIPTION:

The scale used by Ferrell and Skinner (1988) indicates the extent to which the employee of one company reports that he/she must seek approval from another company before making decisions. Five six-point Likert-type scale items were used to measure the construct.

SCALE ORIGIN:

The scale used by Ferrell and Skinner to measure centralization was adapted from John (1984). The latter defined centralization as the extent to which marketing-planning-related activities and decisions are concentrated within a few positions. He distinguished between the two dimensions of centralization: locus of authority and participation.

SAMPLES:

In the Ferrell and Skinner study, a self-administered questionnaire was mailed to a sample of 1500 researchers. The frame used was the membership list of the Marketing Research Association. The corporate classification was supplemented by the American Marketing Association membership list. From a single mailing, **550** usable questionnaires were returned. Additionally, 52 undeliverable questionnaires were returned by the post-office, resulting in a 37.9% response rate. Thirty-seven percent of the respondents were data subcontractors. More women (86%) than men (14%) represented this type of organization. Respondents employed by research firms were more balanced (54% women and 46% men). Finally, in corporate research departments, 53% of the respondents were women and 47% were men.

RELIABILITY:

Scale reliability as measured by coefficient alpha was **.82.**

VALIDITY:

The scales were assessed by confirmatory factor analysis. Constructs that did not load in excess of **.30** were deleted. All items were significant indicators of the construct.

ADMINISTRATION:

The scale was self-administered by respondents in a paper-and-pencil format. A value of 1 on the six-point scale implied definitely agree and 6 implied definitely disagree.

MAJOR FINDINGS:

Three models were examined: for data subcontractors, for marketing research firms, and for corporate research departments. The dependent variable was ethical conduct. Centralization was found to be related to higher perceived ethical behavior in research firms, but not related significantly to ethical behavior in the other two models.

COMMENTS:

See also John (1984) and John and Martin (1984).

REFERENCES:

Ferrell, O C , and S J. Skinner (1988), "Ethical Behavior and Bureaucratic Structure in Marketing Research Organizations," *JMR*, 25 (February), 103-109

John, George (1984), "An Empirical Investigation of Some Antecedents of Opportunism in a Marketing Channel," *JMR*, 21 (August), 279-289

_____ and J. Martin (1984), "Effects of Organizational Structure of Marketing Planning on Credibility and Utilization of Plan Output," *JMR*, 21 (May), 17-183.

SCALE ITEMS: CENTRALIZATION (AGENT/CLIENT RELATIONSHIP)

Please indicate the extent to which you agree or disagree with each statement below:

```
Definitely                                              Definitely
Agree                                                   Disagree
    1————————2————————3————————4————————5————————6
```

1. Any major decision that I make have to have this company's approval.
2. In my dealings with this company, even quite small matters have to be referred to someone higher up for a final answer
3 My dealings with this company are subject to a lot of rules and procedures stating how various aspects of my job are to be done.
4. I have to ask company reps before I do almost anything in my business
5. I can take very little action on my own until this company or its reps approves it.

SCALE NAME: Centralization (Buying Group Structure)

SCALE DESCRIPTION:

A five-item, five-point Likert-like summated ratings scale measuring the proportion of time members of a buying group seek approval from higher up in the organization before taking action on source selection decisions. McCabe (1987) referred to this scale as Hierarchy of Authority.

SCALE ORIGIN:

The scale used by McCabe appears to have been inspired by a scale called Hierarchy of Authority developed by Duncan (1971). None of the items are common to both scales, however.

SAMPLES:

The data in McCabe's study came from buying centers in either the airline or the corrugated shipping container industry. In the former, **15** buying centers were involved with the decision to buy aircraft and **13** were involved with the decision to buy jet fuel. In the latter, **14** buying centers were concerned with the purchase of printing inks and **13** were concerned with buying printing presses and other capital equipment. Data were collected just from individuals involved in source selection. There was an average of 1.7 people per buying unit.

RELIABILITY:

An alpha of .**70** was reported for the scale by McCabe.

VALIDITY:

A factor analysis of several items all related to buying group structure indicated that the five items composing this scale all loaded on the same factor.

ADMINISTRATION:

Though interviews of some sort were conducted with buying group members, the measures in the questionnaire are assumed to have been self-administered. Higher scores on the scale indicate that members of a buying group frequently ask for instructions from superiors before taking action on source selection decisions.

MAJOR FINDINGS:

McCabe examined opposing views of the relation between buying group structure and environmental uncertainty. The findings indicated that a higher degree of **centralization** is associated with higher levels of product complexity and task uncertainty.

REFERENCES:

Duncan, Robert Bannerman (1971), ''The Effects of Perceived Environmental Uncertainty on Organizational Decision Unit Structure: A Cybernetic Model,'' unpublished doctoral dissertation, Yale University.

McCabe, Donald L. (1987), ''Buying Group Structure: Constriction at the Top,'' *JM*, 51 (October), 89-98.

SCALE ITEMS: CENTRALIZATION (BUYING GROUP STRUCTURE)

Instructions: The following questions ask about the buying center which makes the source selection decision for printing inks in your organization. They ask what percent of the time members of this group perform various activities in the source selection process. Circle any one of the five numbers for each question. The meaning of these numbers is as follows:

1 = Never or seldom (0 to 20% of the time)
2 = Occasionally (21 to 40% of the time)
3 = Half the time (41 to 60% of the time)
4 = Frequently (61 to 80% of the time)
5 = Usually or always (81 to 100% of the time)

1. When a new type of source selection decision is to be made, how often do you get an approval from someone higher in the organization (including your own boss) before taking action?
2. How frequently do instructions come from someone higher in the organization (including your boss) when existing rules and procedures are not adequate to make a sourcing decision?
3. When problems arise in the source selection process, how often do you go to someone higher in the organization (including your boss) for an answer?
4. When an unusual situation is encountered in the sourcing process, how frequently do you or other members of this buying group go ahead without checking with their boss?
5. When a sourcing decision is made for which rules and procedures do not exist, how often do you act without referring the matter higher up?

SCALE NAME: Centralization (Channel Relationship)

SCALE DESCRIPTION:

Dwyer and Welsh (1985) used a four-item, five-point Likert-like rating scale measuring the degree to which retailers report that decision making is concentrated in their suppliers.

SCALE ORIGIN:

Dwyer and Welsh imply that they developed their scale on the basis of similar measures used in other studies in the marketing literature, the earliest of which was by Spekman and Stern (1979). The authors suggest that the Spekman and Stern scale was condensed and modified for the purposes of their study.

SAMPLES:

Dwyer and Welsh gathered data from retailers in 10 industries that were selected on the basis of their expected environmental and structural diversity. To guard against the use of single informants, environmental perceptions were also obtained from reputed expert observers in the industry. Of the total of 7254 questionnaires mailed, 457 were returned and found uusable for the purposes of the study, resulting in a response rate of 6.3%. The authors contend that an examination of the respondent sample suggests the low response rate is not related to retailer size. Also, no systematic response tendencies were observed. Thus, they used essentially a convenience sample.

RELIABILITY:

An alpha of **.49** was reported for the centralization measure for the four-item scale that was used for the data analysis.

VALIDITY:

The decision structure subscales measuring centralization (along with participation, formalization, and specialization) were item-analyzed in the Dwyer and Welsh study. Next, LISREL was used to test a number of restricted-factor models of the decision structure measures. The authors concluded that the goodness-of-fit index and root mean square residual, combined with marginal reliability coefficients, indicated the tailored measures from Spekman and Stern's interorganizational research sufficed for their exploratory purpose.

ADMINISTRATION:

The scale was self-administered by respondents in a paper-and-pencil format. It appears to be suitable for a telephone interview also. High scores on the scale suggest that channel members experience very little centralization in their relationship with suppliers, whereas low scores represent extensive centralization.

MAJOR FINDINGS:

Dwyer and Welsh had hypothesized that, in comparison with homogeneous environments, heterogeneous channel environments are associated with more decentralized decision making. This hypothesis was partially supported. The other hypothesis, that channels facing variability in the output sector are associated with more centralized decision structures than counterparts in stable settings, was not supported.

COMMENTS:

The reliability is so low that the scale should not be used until significant improvements have been made in internal consistency.

REFERENCES:

Dwyer, F. Robert and M. Ann Welsh (1985), "Environmental Relationship of the Internal Political Economy of Marketing Channels," *JMR*, 22 (November), 397-414.

Spekman, Robert E. and Louis W. Stern (1979), "Environmental Uncertainty and Buying Group Structure: An Empirical Investigation," *JM*, 43 (Spring), 54-64.

SCALE ITEMS: CENTRALIZATION (CHANNEL RELATIONSHIP)

Think about the relationship you have with your supplier(s) of this line. Please use the scale below to describe the different aspects of decision making in that relationship. Thinking about your relationship with suppliers, would you say:

Never	Seldom	Occasionally	Rather Often	Nearly All the Time

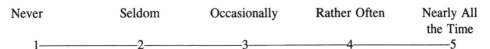

1——————————2——————————3——————————4——————————5

1. You go ahead with actions without checking with your supplier(s). **(r)**
2. You refer marketing matters to your supplier(s).
3. You yield to the recommendations of your supplier(s).
4. You rely on your supplier(s) for an answer.

SCALE NAME: Centralization (Channel Relationship)

SCALE DESCRIPTION:

A four-item, five-point Likert-type summated ratings scale measuring the degree to which a retailer/dealer reports its relationship with another channel member is governed by centralized rules and procedures of decision making.

SCALE ORIGIN:

Dwyer and Oh (1987, 1988) suggest that they based their scale on similar measures used in several other studies in the marketing literature, one of which was by Speckman and Stern (1979), who in turn had adapted items used by Duncan (1972). Dwyer and Oh (1988) stated that their final centralization scale was developed by customizing John's (1984) measure.

SAMPLES:

Dwyer and Oh (1987) gathered data from car dealers in 10 different SMAs: five areas with high growth characteristics and five markets with low growth characteristics. The final sample consisted of **167** dealers, which represented a response rate of 69%. The questionnaire was pretested on 58 dealership managers to evaluate response rates and make a low-power qualitative assessment of the measures. Subsequently, Dwyer and Oh (1988) gathered data from yellow page listings of hardware stores in 10 cities representing a mix of geographic areas across the U.S. A total of 186 questionnaires were mailed, of which **133** were returned with usable data, thus yielding a 71% response rate.

RELIABILITY:

Alpha values of **.68** (1987) and **.72** (1988) were reported by Dwyer and Oh for their four-item versions of the scale, which were finally used in their data analysis.

VALIDITY:

The scale was checked for face validity by four dealers and also by a jury of four faculty colleagues in the 1987 study. If followup discussions did not yield consensus, the discrepant items were deleted. Data from a pretest questionnaire were used to check for item convergence in a restricted one-factor model. Convergence and consistency were checked by item correlation and residual analysis. In their 1988 study, Dwyer and Oh used a LISREL chi-square three-factor measurement model to test the items for this scale along with those for two other scales (formalization and participation). The scale showed convergent and discriminant validity.

ADMINISTRATION:

Respondents self-administered the scale along with many other measures in both studies. Higher scores on the scale suggest that respondents think the decision-making relationship they have with the channel member involves a high need for permission for doing anything, whereas low scores suggest that the need for permission is low.

MAJOR FINDINGS:

The findings (Dwyer and Oh 1987) suggest that environmental munificence has significant negative effects on centralization, which supports the hypothesis that greater levels of environmental munificence in the output environment foster exchange relationships characterized by less centralized supplier authority. The results also support the hypothesis that centralization damages the quality of relationships.

The purpose of the second study by Dwyer and Oh (1988) was to investigate differences between three types of contractually integrated channel systems and decision-making processes within the channel, as well as their competitive strategies. Wholesaler voluntaries had the most centralized and least participative relationships.

REFERENCES:

Duncan, R. B. (1972), "Characteristics of Organizational Environments and Perceived Environmental Uncertainty," *Administrative Sciences Quarterly*, 17 (September), 313- 327.

Dwyer, Robert F. and Sejo Oh (1987), "Output Sector Munificence Effects on Internal Political Economy of Marketing Channels," *JMR*, 24 (November), 347-358.

_____ and _____ (1988), "A Transaction Cost Perspective on Vertical Contractual Structure and Interchannel Competitive Strategies", *JM*, 52 (April), 21-34.

John, George (1984), "An Empirical Investigation of Some Antecedents of Opportunism in a Marketing Channel," *JMR*, 21 (August), 278-289.

Spekman, Robert E. and Louis W. Stern (1979), "Environmental Uncertainty and Buying Group Structure: AN Empirical Investigation," *JM*, Spring, 54-64.

SCALE ITMS: CENTRALIZATION (CHANNEL RELATIONSHIP) +

Please indicate the extent to which you agree or disagree with each statement below:

Strongly Disagree	Disagree	Neutral	Agree	Strongly Agree
1	2	3	4	5

1. I have to ask _____ permission before I do almost anything in my business.
2. I am usually discouraged from making changes in my primary _____ program without checking with his representative first.
3. For many facets of running this store I yield to recommendations of my primary _____.
4. A great many aspects of this store are run according to the strong suggestions of my primary _____.

+ The blanks should be filled with the name of the channel member of interest.

SCALE NAME: Centralization (Retailer With Wholesaler)

SCALE DESCRIPTION:

A three-item, eight-point Likert-like summated ratings scale measuring the degree of influence a retailer reports a specified wholesaler has on several distributive functions involving the retailer.

SCALE ORIGIN:

Though not specified in the article by John and Reve (1982), it is apparent that their data came from the latter's dissertation (Reve 1980). His initial scale had 10 items. The final version had four items and an alpha of .689. The scale used by George and Reve (1982) had one item less than the final version reported by Reve (1980). Because the items used by the former were not reported, it is not known which item below was eliminated.

SAMPLES:

The data analyzed by John and Reve came from the dissertation research by Reve. Initially, 753 wholesalers in Norway were asked to identify their three largest retail customers. One retailer was selected at random from each of those suggested by the 238 responding wholesalers. Those retailers were contacted and 140 provided usable responses. Finally, the 140 wholesalers identified by the retailers were recontacted for further information. Data were ultimately collected from **99** retailer/wholesaler dyads.

RELIABILITY:

The alpha for the version of the scale used by John and Reve was reported to be **.54**. Items with low item-total correlations were said to have been deleted.

VALIDITY:

John and Reve eliminated items with low loadings on a factor. Further, they used the multitrait, multimethod approach as well as a structural equations model, which provided evidence of the convergent and discriminant validity of the scale. When the scale's variance was partitioned into trait and error components, the former was not as high as it was for most of the other scales, which means evidence of its convergent validity was not as great.

ADMINISTRATION:

The scale was self-administered along with many other measures in a mail survey format High scores on the scale indicate that retailers report their wholesalers have a great amount of influence on distribution-related decisions whereas lower scores suggest that retailers think they are highly autonomous.

MAJOR FINDINGS:

The purpose of the study by John and Reve was to examine the validity of several measures of channel relationships with information from wholesaler/retailer dyads The authors concluded that the structural form variables, including **centralization**, generally had convergent and discriminant validity. Further, the correlation between the retailers' and wholesalers' perceptions of the amount of **centralization** in their dyadic relationships was .507.

COMMENTS:

The scale was administered in Norwegian, so it is not known how its psychometric properties might be different if it were used in English as shown below. Further, because the scale has such low internal consistency, improvement is needed before it is used further.

REFERENCES:

John, George and Torger Reve (1982), "The Reliability and Validity of Key Informant Data From Dyadic Relationships in Marketing Channels," *JMR*, 19 (November), 517-524.

Reve, Torger (1980), "Interorganizational Relations in Distribution Channels: An Empirical Study of Norwegian Distribution Channel Dyads," unpublished doctoral dissertation, Northwestern University.

SCALE ITEMS: CENTRALIZATION (RETAILER WITH WHOLESALER)+

Below is listed a number of statements which describe various means of coordination with the supplier level. Please indicate on the following scale to what degree each statement represents a good or poor description of the relationship between your firm and the specified supplier.

Not relevant = 0
Erroneous description = 1
Very poor description = 2
Poor description = 3
Neither poor nor good description = 4
Good description = 5
Very good description = 6
Completely correct description = 7

1. The supplier's prices and discounts are givens that can not be negotiated.
2. The supplier determines the ordering procedures that we follow.
3. We are completely free to buy from any supplier that we want. **(r)**
4. The supplier requires us to use a certain symbol or logo.

+ The scale reported in the article by John and Reve (1982) apparently had only three of these items. According to the information provided by Reve (1980, p. 185), item 1 had the smallest factor loading of the group and appears to be a good candidate for elimination.

SCALE NAME: Centralization (Salesforce Decisions)

SCALE DESCRIPTION:

The two-item, seven-point Likert-type scale used by Phillips (1982) measured centralization of routine salesforce decisions.

SCALE ORIGIN:

Phillips adapted two items used by Dewar and Werbel (1979), but appears to have done the measure development.

SAMPLES:

The data used by Phillips came from a convenience sample of U.S. manufacturers operating sales branch distribution systems. The key informant method was used and no branch was included in the analysis unless responses were received from the headquarters informant, the branch manager informant, and at least two branch personnel other than the manager. Of the 80 branches contacted (two per company), usable information was provided by 70 for a total of **294** individual responses. The average (mean) branch participating in the survey had been in operation for 19 years, had 32 employees, a salesforce of 12, and annual net sales for the previous year of $9.8 million.

RELIABILITY:

A composite alpha of **.70** was reported for the scale.

VALIDITY:

Extensive validation of the constructs was done in the study. The author examined a series of measurement models to ascertain the convergent and discriminant validity of the key informant reports on the constructs under investigation. A series of causal models were tested to ascertain the nomological validity of the theoretical hypotheses. First, informant reports were tested for convergent validity at the monomethod level of analysis. This test examined whether key informants' responses to multiple survey items measuring the same concept achieved convergent validity. A split-half analysis was also performed; split halves of informants were created for each sales branch on each survey item, resulting in two methods per company for each of the items measuring each of the constructs. Tests were also carried out to assess unidimensionality and nomological validity.

ADMINISTRATION:

The scale appears to have been self-administered by the three classes of respondents for each participating sales branch. A higher score on the scale indicates that a greater proportion of routine decisions were referred upward in the hierarchy.

MAJOR FINDINGS:

The results do not support the hypothesis that centralization of routine salesforce decisions increases control loss. However, the author suggests that given the significant measurement errors in the indicators of the centralization concept, the study does not strongly contraindicate this relationship. Also, the centralization variable is positively associated with both control loss dimensions in the overall factor model, as the theory predicts, even though its influence in the causal models is negligible. Consequently, hypotheses maintaining a link between centralization and control loss still warrant investigation.

REFERENCES:

Dewar, Robert, and James Werbel (1979), ''Universalistic and Contingency Predictions of Employee Satisfaction and Conflict,'' *Administrative Sciences Quarterly*, 24, 426-448.

Phillips, Lynn W. (1982), ''Explaining Control Loss in Corporate Marketing Channels: An Organizational Analysis,'' *JMR*, 29 (November), 525-549.

SCALE ITEMS: CENTRALIZATION (SALESFORCE DECISIONS) +

Two seven-point Likert type agreement-disagreement measures were employed by key personnel informants to measure the two items.

Disagree   Agree
1————2————3————4————5————6————7

1. Most of the decisions made by the salesmen in this branch have to have a superior's approval.
2. In their jobs, salesmen have to refer even small matters to someone higher up for a final answer.

+ The Phillips (1988) article does not specifically state the response anchors used, however, those shown here seem reasonable from the information provided.

SCALE NAME: Centralization (Vertical Control)

SCALE DESCRIPTION:

A three-item, seven-point Likert-type summated ratings scale measuring the degree to which a person reports exercising influence over the next stage in the channel on matters such as delivery, promotion, and packaging. The persons responding to the scale in the Klein (1989) study were exporters.

SCALE ORIGIN:

The scale used by Klein (1989) was adpated from a scale constructed in dissertation research by Reve (1980). Two of the three items in Klein's scale (1 and 3) are extremely similar to two that were tested by Reve (1980, p. 69, 181) but not ultimately used in his final version of the scale. Klein's other item (2) is assumed to be original.

SAMPLES:

A mail survey of persons whose names were drawn from a Canadian directory of exporters yielded **477** responses with some usable data. Only the **338** fully completely survey forms were the basis for testing the model in the study. Evaluation of the constructs was based on all cases for which data were available.

RELIABILITY:

An alpha of **.47** was calculated for the scale by Klein (personal correspondence). As evidence of the scale's reliability, the author points out that the items composed a single factor that explained 48% of the variance.

VALIDITY:

No specific analysis of this scale's validity was reported.

ADMINISTRATION:

The scale was self-administered as part of larger mail survey questionnaire. Higher scores on the scale indicate that respondents' firms have great control over some aspects in the next level of the channel for their product line.

MAJOR FINDINGS:

The purpose of the study by Klein (1989) was to use a model based on transaction cost analysis to explain vertical control decisions. A regression analysis provided support for the model. The effects of all independent variables were significant and as hypothesized. Degree of **vertical control** was positively related to channel volume, transaction frequency and specificity, and complexity of the environment. It was negatively related to the rate at which changes occur in the environment.

COMMENTS:

Though this scale and another (Vertical Control Formalization) were separate factors in the study, a linear combination of the two was used in the analysis because of its intuitive appeal to the author. Extreme caution should be exercised in using this measure until its reliability can be improved.

REFERENCES:

Klein, Saul (1989), ''A Transaction Cost Explanation of Vertical Control in International Markets,'' *JAMS*, 17 (Summer), 253-260.

Reve, Torger (1980), ''Interorganizational Relations inDistribution Channels: An Empirical Study of Norwegian Distribution Channel Dyads,'' unpublished doctoral dissertation, Northwestern University.

SCALE ITEMS: CENTRALIZATION (VERTICAL CONTROL)

Strongly Disagree	Disagree	Slightly Disagree	Neutral	Slightly Agree	Agree	Strongly Agree
1	2	3	4	5	6	7

1. We make all the decisions relating to transportation and physical delivery.
2. We have considerable influence on the development of advertising and trade promotion.
3. We require that the product carry a certain symbol or logo.

SCALE NAME: Centralization (Wholesaler With Retailer)

SCALE DESCRIPTION:

A three-item, eight-point Likert-like summated ratings scale measuring the degree of influence a wholesaler reports having over a retailer on several distributive functions. If the numerical responses to items are not reversed, summated scores seem to measure a wholesaler's perception of a retailer's decision-making autonomy.

SCALE ORIGIN:

Though not specified in the article by John and Reve (1982), it is apparent that their data came from the latter's dissertation (Reve 1980). His initial scale had 10 items and the final version had three. Because different alpha values were reported for the scales and the items used by John and Reve (1982) were not reported, it is not known what else is different about the scales.

SAMPLES:

The data analyzed by John and Reve came from the dissertation research by Reve. Initially, 753 wholesalers in Norway were asked to identify their three largest retail customers. One retailer was selected at random from each of those suggested by the 238 responding wholesalers. Those retailers were contacted and 140 provided usable responses. Finally, the 140 wholesalers identified by the retailers were recontacted for further information. Data were ultimately collected from **99** retailer/wholesaler dyads.

RELIABILITY:

The alpha for the version of the scale used by John and Reve was reported to be **.52**. Items with low item-total correlations were said to have been deleted.

VALIDITY:

John and Reve eliminated items with low loadings on a factor. Further, they used the multitrait, multimethod approach as well as a structural equations model, which provided evidence of the convergent and discriminant validity of the scale.

ADMINISTRATION:

The scale was self-administered by respondents along with many other measures in a mail survey format. High scores on the scale indicate that wholesalers report having a great amount of influence on distribution-related decisions involving their retailers whereas lower scores suggest that they think their retailers are highly autonomous.

MAJOR FINDINGS:

The purpose of the study by John and Reve was to examine the validity of several measures of channel relationships with information from wholesaler/retailer dyads. The authors concluded that the structural form variables, including **centralization**, generally had convergent and discriminant validity. Further, the correlation between the retailers' and wholesalers' perceptions of the amount of **centralization** in their dyadic relationships was .507.

COMMENTS:

The scale was administered in Norwegian, so it is not known how its psychometric properties might be different if it were used in English as shown below. Further, because the scale has such low internal consistency and all of the positively stated items were eliminated from the scale during Reve's (1980) testing, the reliability and face validity are suspect. Improvement in the scale's psychometric qualities is needed before it is used further.

REFERENCES:

John, George and Torger Reve (1982), ''The Reliability and Validity of Key Informant Data From Dyadic Relationships in Marketing Channels,'' *JMR*, 19 (November), 517-524.

Reve, Torger (1980), ''Interorganizational Relations in Distribution Channels: An Empirical Study of Norwegian Distribution Channel Dyads,'' unpublished doctoral dissertation, Northwestern University.

SCALE ITEMS: CENTRALIZATION (WHOLESALER WITH RETAILER)

Below is listed a number of statements which describe various means of coordination with the retailing level. Please indicate on the following scale to what degree each statement represents a good or poor description of the relationship between your firm and the specified retail customer.

Not relevant = 0
Erroneous description = 1
Very poor description = 2
Poor description = 3
Neither poor nor good description = 4
Good description = 5
Very good description = 6
Completely correct description = 7

1. Advertising campaigns for our products are determined in detail by the retailer. **(r)**
2. The retailer determines which ordering procedures he is going to use. **(r)**
3. The retailer is completely free to buy from any supplier that he wants. **(r)**

SCALE NAME: Channel Conflict (Administrative)

SCALE DESCRIPTION:

A six-item, four-point Likert-like summated ratings scale measuring the intensity of conflict a channel member reports having with the channel leader on administrative sorts of issues in the past year. In the studies by Schul (1987; Schul, Pride, and Little 1983), the scale specifically related to the conflict between franchisors and franchisees.

SCALE ORIGIN:

This scale and the study reported in the articles by Schul and his coauthors came from the dissertation research by Schul (1980). He reports that a review of the literature and interviews with some franchisees helped to generate 14 items for measuring channel conflict. On the basis of pilot study results, the list was reduced to 14 items that appeared to relate to either administrative issues or problems related to the services franchisees receive.

SAMPLES:

The main study involved an eight-page questionnaire that was mailed to 1052 franchised real estate brokers with six different franchise affiliations. After two waves of mailings, a total of **349** usable survey forms were received. There was no evidence of nonresponse bias.

RELIABILITY:

An alpha of **.78** was calculated for the scale.

VALIDITY:

Evidence of content validity came from the pretest interviews. Using data from the main study, Schul and his coauthors performed a factor analysis with oblique rotation on the scale items generated to measure conflict. With loadings above .60, the adminstrative conflict factor had six items and the service conflict factor had six items; two items did not load high enough on either factor to be retained. The data were reanalyzed by factor analysis with Varimax rotation (Schul 1987). A similar factor structure emerged.

ADMINISTRATION:

The scale was self-administered by respondents along with many other measures in a mail survey format. Higher scores on the scale indicate that channel members report a high amount of administrative conflict with their respective channel leaders in the immediate past year.

MAJOR FINDINGS:

The purpose of the study by Schul and his coauthors was to investigate the influence of different channel leadership types on channel members' perceptions of intrachannel conflict. The data indicated that the three leadership styles examined had significant negative relationships with channel member perceptions of conflict. Participative and supportive leadership styles were most related to **administrative conflict**, but directive leadership was most related to service conflict. An additional insight provided by the path analysis (Schul 1987) is that **administrative conflict** had a significant, direct, and negative effect on channel member satisfaction.

REFERENCES:

Schul, Patrick L. (1980), ''An Empirical Investigation of the Conflict Behavior Process in Franchise Channels of Distribution,'' unpublished doctoral dissertation, Texas A&M University.

———— (1987), ''An Investigation of Path-Goal Leadership Theory and Its Impact on Intrachannel Conflict and Satisfaction,'' *JAMS*, 15 (Winter), 42-52.

————, William M. Pride, and Taylor L. Little (1983), ''The Impact of Channel Leadership Behavior on Intrachannel Conflict,'' *JM*, 47 (Summer), 21-34.

SCALE ITEMS: CHANNEL CONFLICT (ADMINISTRATIVE)

Franchisors and franchisees often disagree over key issues pertaining to franchise policies, operations, rules and regulations. For each of the issues listed below, check the appropriate response to reflect your personal attitude of how intense or serious the overall level of disagreement surrounding each issue has been in the past year.

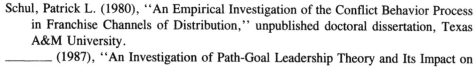

High	Moderate	Low	None
4————————————	—3——————————————	—2————————————	—1

My franchisor and I disagree about:
1. Bureaucratic red tape.
2. Service and/or advertising fees.
3. Contract terms or arrangements promised.
4. Accounting information requirements.
5. Initial franchise fees (or fees on additional new offices).
6. Violation of exclusive territory arrangements (location of too many outlets in your market area).

SCALE NAME: Channel Conflict (Dealer With Manufacturer)

SCALE DESCRIPTION:

A 10-item, five-point Likert-type summated ratings scale measuring the degree to which a retailer/dealer reports experiencing conflict, difficulty, and a lack of fairness in its relationship with a manufacturer.

SCALE ORIGIN:

There was no indication by Gaski and Nevin (1985) that the scale was not original.

SAMPLES:

Data used by Gaski and Nevin were based on a sample of dealers of a manufacturer and distributor of heavy industrial machinery (the Melroe Division of Clarke Equipment). Mail questionnaires were sent to all 634 dealers in the U.S. and Canada. A total of **238** usable responses were eventually received. Several tests failed to provide significant evidence of nonresponse bias.

RELIABILITY:

An alpha of **.892** was reported for the scale.

VALIDITY:

The authors provided some weak evidence of discriminant validity by pointing out that the correlations between the scale and other variables in the study were not nearly as great as the alpha coefficient calculated for the scale.

ADMINISTRATION:

The scale was self-administered along with several other measures in a mail survey format. Higher scores on the scale indicate that dealers experience a high amount of conflict with a manufacturer whereas lower scores suggest that dealers are likely to be reasonably happy in their relationship with a manufacturer.

MAJOR FINDINGS:

The purpose of the study by Gaski and Nevin was to examine the differential effects of exercised versus unexercised power on several variables of interest to channel managers. Coercive power, exercised coercive power, reward power, and exercised reward power were all significantly associated with **conflict between a dealer and a manufacturer**, the first two relationships being positive and the last two being negative. Further, the *exercise* of coercive power did seem to have a significantly greater positive impact on **conflict** than just the *potential use* of coercive power.

REFERENCE:

> Gaski, John F. and John R. Nevin (1985), "The Differential Effects of Exercised and Unexercised Power Sources in a Marketing Channel," *JMR*, 22 (May), 130-142.

SCALE ITEMS: CHANNEL CONFLICT (DEALER WITH MANUFACTURER) +

Strongly Disagree	Disagree	Neutral	Agree	Strongly Agree
1	2	3	4	5

1. My business would be a lot better off if it weren't for _____.
2. I don't like many of the things _____ does.
3. _____'s policies reduce my profits.
4. _____ makes it difficult to do my job.
5. _____ has been very fair with me. **(r)**
6. Sometimes _____ prevents me from doing what I want to do.
7. _____ helps me in getting the job done. **(r)**
8. _____ doesn't seem to have my company's best interests at heart.
9. _____'s policies make things difficult for me.
10. Dealing with _____ benefits my company. **(r)**

+ The blanks should be filled with the name of the channel member (e.g., manufacturer) of interest in the study.

SCALE NAME: Channel Conflict (Service)

SCALE DESCRIPTION:

A six-item, four-point Likert-like summated ratings scale measuring the intensity of conflict a channel member reports having with the channel leader on service-related issues in the past year. In the studies by Schul, Pride, and Little (1983, 1987), the scale specifically related to the conflict between franchisors and franchisees.

SCALE ORIGIN:

This scale and the study reported in the articles by Schul and his coauthors (1983, 1987) came from the dissertation research by Schul (1980). He reported that a review of the literature and interviews with some franchisees helped to generate 14 items for measuring channel conflict. On the basis of pilot study results, the list was reduced to 14 items that appeared to relate to either administrative issues or problems related to the services franchisees receive. His is the only known use of the scale.

SAMPLES:

The main study involved an eight-page questionnaire that was mailed to 1052 franchised real estate brokers with six different franchise affiliations. After two waves of mailings, a total of **349** usable survey forms were received. There was no evidence of nonresponse bias.

RELIABILITY:

An alpha of **.83** was calculated for the scale.

VALIDITY:

Evidence of content validity came from the pretest interviews. Using data from the main study, Schul and his coauthors performed a factor analysis with oblique rotation on the scale items generated to measure conflict. With loadings above .60, the adminstrative conflict factor had six items and the service conflict factor had six items; two items did not load high enough on either factor to be retained. The data were reanalyzed by factor analysis with Varimax rotation (Schul 1987). A similar factor structure emerged.

ADMINISTRATION:

The scale was self-administered by respondents along with many other measures in a mail survey format. Higher scores on the scale indicate that channel members report a high amount of service conflict with their respective channel leaders in the immediate past year.

MAJOR FINDINGS:

The purpose of the study by Schul and his coauthors was to investigate the influence of different channel leadership types on channel members' perceptions of intrachannel conflict. The data indicated that the three leadership styles examined had significant negative relationships with channel member perceptions of conflict. Participative and supportive leadership styles were most related to administrative conflict, but directive leadership was most related to **service conflict**. An additional insight provided by the path analysis (Schul 1987) is that **service conflict** had a significant, direct, and negative effect on channel member satisfaction.

REFERENCES:

Schul, Patrick L. (1980), "An Empirical Investigation of the Conflict Behavior Process in Franchise Channels of Distribution," unpublished doctoral dissertation, Texas A&M University.

_____ (1987), "An Investigation of Path-Goal Leadership Theory and Its Impact on Intrachannel Conflict and Satisfaction," *JAMS*, 15 (Winter), 42-52.

_____, William M. Pride, and Taylor L. Little (1983), "The Impact of Channel Leadership Behavior on Intrachannel Conflict," *JM*, 47 (Summer), 21-34.

SCALE ITEMS: CHANNEL CONFLICT (SERVICE)

Franchisors and franchisees often disagree over key issues pertaining to franchise policies, operations, rules and regulations. For each of the issues listed below, check the appropriate response to reflect your personal attitude of how intense or serious the overall level of disagreement surrounding each issue has been in the past year.

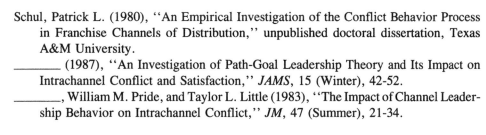

High	Moderate	Low	None
4—————————	———3———————	———2———————	——1

My franchisor and I disagree about:
1. Quality of sales training programs.
2. General responsiveness of the franchisor to your needs.
3. Quality of meetings and conventions.
4. Quality of inter-city referral program.
5. Quality of national advertising program.
6. Quality of management training program.

SCALE NAME: Channel Member Control

SCALE DESCRIPTION:

A 12-item, constant sum, summated ratings scale measuring the degree of control a channel member has over a variety of decision variables in comparison with other channel members. Dwyer and Welsh (1985) only reported the results of the scale as it related to retailer control.

SCALE ORIGIN:

The items come from Etgar (1977), but the use of the constant sum form of the scale is original to Dwyer and Welsh (1985).

SAMPLES:

Dwyer and Welsh mailed questionnaires to 7254 retailers in 10 industries whose addresses had been provided by a list broker. Envelopes were simply addressed to "Manager" in each case. After a second wave to 10% of the original sample, a total of **457** responses were used in the analysis. Because of such a low response rate, the authors provided rather detailed information about response rates and characteristics by industry.

RELIABILITY:

An alpha of **.87** was reported for the scale.

VALIDITY:

Dwyer and Welsh performed a factor analysis of 12 decision variables related to channel control and, unlike Etgar (1977), they reported finding a unidimensional solution.

ADMINISTRATION:

Respondents self-administered the scale along with many other measures in the study by Dwyer and Welsh. Higher scores on the scale suggest that a channel member is perceived to have great amount of influence over decision variables. A score could be calculated for each of the channel members to reflect their relative control over the decision variables.

MAJOR FINDINGS:

Dwyer and Welsh investigated environmental effects on channel structure and processes in a political economy framework. Among their many findings was that strong demand and competitive forces are significantly related to less **retailer control** over marketing decisions.

REFERENCES:

Dwyer, F. Robert and M. Ann Welsh (1985), "Environmental Relationships of the Internal Political Economy of Marketing Channels," *JMR*, 22 (November), 397-414.

Etgar, Michael (1977), ''Channel Environment and Channel Leadership,'' *JMR*, 15 (February), 69-76.

SCALE ITEMS: CHANNEL MEMBER CONTROL

This set of questions pertains to the relative influence of the members of the marketing channel for the marketing of *the same line of merchandise*. Below are a list of decisions that are involved in the selling of your product. Please indicate the relative influence each channel member has on each of those decision areas. To indicate influence, assume you have 10 points to allocate to yourself and the members of the channel. A greater number of points allocated to a member indicates that member's greater influence over a decision area. Be sure each row sums to 10 points.

	Retailer*	Wholesaler*	Producer*	Agent/Broker*	Total*
1. Retail prices	—	—	—	—	10
2. Store location	—	—	—	—	10
3. Minimum order size	—	—	—	—	10
4. Mix of units ordered	—	—	—	—	10
5. Amount and content of retailer advertising	—	—	—	—	10
6. Provision of credit to customers	—	—	—	—	10
7. Ability of retailer to buy from other suppliers	—	—	—	—	10
8. Training of retail salespeople	—	—	—	—	10
9. Hiring of retail salespeople	—	—	—	—	10
10. In-store display of merchandise	—	—	—	—	10
11. Retailer participation in professional and trade associations	—	—	—	—	10
12. Territorial and customer restrictions	—	—	—	—	10

* A series of blanks should be next to each of the 12 items (decision areas) and should have these sorts of headings, one for each member of the channel with potential influence over decision making.

SCALE NAME: Commitment (Organizational)

SCALE DESCRIPTION:

A four-item, three-point Likert-like scale assessing an employee's likelihood of leaving a firm for another job if he/she could receive more pay, status, freedom, etc.

SCALE ORIGIN:

The scale was developed by Hrebiniak and Alutto (1972). The index of 12 items was tested on 318 school teachers and 395 nurses. The four items listed below were found to have the highest item-total correlations. The reliability (Spearman-Brown) for the four-item scale was .79. Though commitment had some relationship with demographic variables, multivariate analyses showed role-related factors were of primary importance in explaining it.

SAMPLES:

Dubinsky and Hartley (1986) based their analysis on completed questionnaires returned by **120** respondents. Questionnaires were sent to 467 agents who sold lines of a large multi-insurance company. No nonresponse bias was apparent. The sample had a mean age of 39.1 years, had spent 6.6 years (mean) in their present positions, were mostly male (91%), and over half were college graduates (56%). The sample used by Hampton, Dubinsky, and Skinner (1986) was based on **116** usable responses from a census of 121 retail salespeople who worked in one of five outlets of a department store chain. The sample had a median age of 23.2 years, had spent 1.4 years (median) in their present positions and 1.1 years (median) with their current supervisors, were mostly female (78%), and 66% had some college education.

RELIABILITY:

Alpha values of .**76** and .**80** were reported by Dubinsky and Hartley (1986) and Hampton, Dubinsky, and Skinner (1986), respectively.

VALIDITY:

No examination of scale validity was reported in any of the marketing studies.

ADMINISTRATION:

The scale was self-administered by respondents along with many other measures in a mail survey format in the study by Dubinsky and Hartley. Hampton and his coauthors distributed the survey instrument to respondents in a conference room in each store, where it was self-administered. Higher scores on the scale indicate that respondents are very sensitive about the quality of the work they perform in their jobs whereas lower scores suggest that their emotions are not significantly influenced by the performance of their jobs.

MAJOR FINDINGS:

The purpose of the study by Dubinsky and Hartley was to investigate several predictors of salesperson performance and the relationships among those predictors. A path analysis indicated that **job performance sensitivity** had a positive effect on job performance (prior year's commissions). In turn, the former was most significantly affected (positively) by job involvement. A causal model of retail sales supervisor leadership behavior was studied by Hampton and his coauthors. The results indicated that job satisfaction had a strong positive effect on **job performance sensitivity**.

REFERENCES:

Dubinsky, Alan J. and Steven W. Hartley (1986), ''A Path- Analytic Study of a Model of Salesperson Performance,'' *JAMS,* 14 (Spring) 36-46.

Hampton, Ron, Alan J. Dubinsky, and Steven J. Skinner (1986), ''A Model of Sales Supervisor Leadership Behavior and Retail Salespeople's Job-Related Outcomes,'' *JAMS*, 14 (Fall), 33-43.

Hrebiniak, Lawrence G. and Joseph A. Alutto (1972), ''Personal and Role-Related Factors in the Development of Organizational Commitment,'' *Administrative Science Quarterly*, 17 (December), 555-573.

SCALE ITEMS: COMMITMENT (ORGANIZATIONAL)

Assume you were offered a position withn another organization. Would you leave your present organization under any of the following conditions? Use the following scale to indicate your response:

3 = yes, definitely would leave
2 = uncertain about leaving
1 = no, definitely would not leave

I would leave my present company:
1. for a slight increase in pay
2. for slightly more freedom to be personally creative
3. for slightly more status
4. to work with people who are a little friendlier

SCALE NAME: Commitment (Organizational)

SCALE DESCRIPTION:

A 15-item, seven-point Likert-type summated ratings scale measuring the degree to which an employee reports being actively involved with a particular organization.

SCALE ORIGIN:

The scale used by Michaels et al. (1988) was constructed by Mowday, Steers, and Porter (1979). The scale was tested on 2563 employees working in a variety of jobs in nine different organizations, though not all tests were performed on all employees. A great amount of information was provided about the scale's reliability and validity. In general, the scale showed evidence of high internal consistency (average alpha of .90), reasonable test-retest correlations, and adequate convergent, discriminant, and predictive validities.

SAMPLES:

The analysis by Michaels and his coauthors was based on data from two samples: **215** full-line salespeople of a building materials manufacturer and **330** members of the National Association of Purchasing Management. The average salesperson respondent was 43.9 years of age, had 12.9 years of job tenure, 15.2 years of organizational tenure, and 18.1 years of sales experience. In contrast, the typical respondent in the industrial buyer sample was 42.2 years of age, had 5.7 years of job tenure, 10.6 years of organizational tenure, and 12.5 years of purchasing experience.

RELIABILITY:

Alpha of **.90** was reported for the scale for both the salesperson and buyer samples.

VALIDITY:

No specific examination of scale validity was discussed.

ADMINISTRATION:

The scale was self-administered by respondents along with other measures as part of a larger survey instrument. Higher scores on the scale suggest that employee respondents report high involvement in their organizations whereas lower scores indicate that they have little loyalty or commitment.

MAJOR FINDINGS:

The purpose of the study by Michaels and his coauthors was to examine the impact of **organizational formalization** on several job-related attitudes. Among the significant findings was that higher levels of **commitment** were related to lower levels of role ambiguity, role conflict, and work alienation for both the salesperson and buyer samples.

REFERENCES:

Michaels, Ronald E., William L. Cron, Alan J. Dubinsky, and Eric A. Joachimsthaler (1988), "Influence of Formalization on the Organizational Commitment and Work Alienation of Salespeople and Industrial Buyers," *JMR*, 25 (November), 376-383.

Mowday, Richard T., Richard M. Steers, and Lyman W. Porter (1979), "The Measurement of Organizational Commitment," *Journal of Vocational Behavior*, 14 (April), 224-247.

SCALE ITEMS: COMMITMENT (ORGANIZATIONAL)

Strongly disagree = 1
Moderately disagree = 2
Slightly disagree = 3
Neutral = 4
Slightly agree = 5
Moderately agree = 6
Strongly agree = 7

1. I am willing to put in a great deal of effort beyond that normally expected in order to help this organization be successful.
2. I talk up this organization to my friends as a great organization to work for.
3. I feel very little loyalty to this organization. **(r)**
4. I would accept almost any type of job assignment in order to keep working for this organization.
5. I find that my values and the organization's values are very similar.
6. I am proud to tell others that I am part of this organization.
7. I could just as well be working for a different organization as long as the type of work was similar. **(r)**
8. This organization really inspires the very best in me in the way of job performance.
9. It would take very little change in my present circumstances to cause me to leave this organization. **(r)**
10. I am extremely glad that I chose this organization to work for over others I was considering at the time I joined.
11. There's not too much to be gained by sticking with this organization indefinitely. **(r)**
12. Often I find it difficult to agree with this organization's policies on important matters relating to its employees. **(r)**
13. I really care about the fate of this organization.
14. For me this is the best of all possible organizations for which to work.
15. Deciding to work for this organization was a definite mistake on my part. **(r)**

SCALE NAME: Company Resource Sharing

SCALE DESCRIPTION:

A seven-item, seven-point Likert-like summated ratings scale measuring the degree to which a person describes the business units in a conglomerate as sharing a variety of resources such as personnel and equipment.

SCALE ORIGIN:

The scale was original to Burke (1984) and her study is the only known use of the scale in the published marketing research reviewed here.

SAMPLES:

Data were collected from a total of **86** business units in six out of 18 firms personally contacted. The majority of business units were in conglomerate firms. The managers who filled out the survey instruments had bottom-line responsibility for their business units, were highly involved in selecting market share objectives, and were an average of 3.29 levels away from their CEOs.

RELIABILITY:

An alpha of **.87** was reported for the scale.

VALIDITY:

Burke implied that a factor analysis was performed as part of scale development, but provided no specific details. No other examination of scale validity was suggested.

ADMINISTRATION:

The sample responded to the scale as part of a self-administered mail questionnaire. Higher scores on the scale suggest that respondents perceive the business units in a firm to share a great amount of resources.

MAJOR FINDINGS:

The study investigated the degree to which business-unit managers of multiproduct firms perceived different variables to influence strategic choices. No significant difference in perception of **company resource sharing** was found for three types of strategic thrusts used by business units.

REFERENCE:

Burke, Marian C. (1984), ''Strategic Choice and Marketing Managers: An Examination of Business-Level Marketing Objectives,'' *JMR*, 21 (November), 345-359.

SCALE ITEMS: COMPANY RESOURCE SHARING

Indicate the extent to which the business unit shares the following with other business units in the company using this scale:

not at all ___ : ___ : ___ : ___ : ___ : ___ : ___ great

             1   2   3   4   5   6   7

1. plant and equipment
2. production personnel
3. salesforce
4. distribution channels
5. management services (e.g., personnel, computer)
6. R&D facilities
7. R&D personnel

SCALE NAME: Competitive Environment

SCALE DESCRIPTION:

A two-item, six-point Likert-type summated ratings scale measuring the degree to which "peaceful coexistence" and nonretaliation are perceived to characterize an industry.

SCALE ORIGIN:

The scale appears to be original to Eliashberg and Robertson (1988) and was only used in their study.

SAMPLES:

The sample consisted of **75** business executives who attended a series of executive education seminars at a major university. They were employed by different firms representing a variety of industries. It appeared that the executives held positions that were either connected with preannouncement decisions or made those decisions themselves.

RELIABILITY:

An alpha of **.45** was reported for the scale.

VALIDITY:

No direct examination of scale validity was reported, but results of a factor analysis indicated that the items were part of the same factor.

ADMINISTRATION:

The scale was self-administered by respondents along with other parts of a survey instrument. Respondents with higher scores on the scale perceive nonretaliation to be more characteristic of their industry than do those with lower scores.

MAJOR FINDINGS:

The purpose of the study was to identify the conditions associated with the preannouncement of new product introductions. **Competitive environment** was found to be a significant predictor of preannoucing behavior such that preannouncing was associated with firms viewed as operating in noncombative competitive environments.

COMMENTS:

The extremely low internal consistency of this scale suggests that it should not be used further until more items can be tested and added to significantly improve its reliability.

REFERENCE:

Eliashberg, Jehoshua and Thomas S. Robertson (1988), ''New Product Preannouncing Behavior: A Market Signaling Study,'' *JMR*, 25 (August), 282-292.

SCALE ITEMS: COMPETITIVE ENVIRONMENT

Strongly Disagree	Disagree	Slightly Disagree	Slightly Agree	Agree	Strongly Agree
1	2	3	4	5	6

1. In our industry, all of us are trying to maintain a peaceful coexistence.
2. Competitive reaction is not an issue.

SCALE NAME: Competitive Retaliation

SCALE DESCRIPTION:

A two-item, six-point Likert-type summated ratings scale measuring the perceived likelihood of a company's competition reacting quickly to a new product introduction.

SCALE ORIGIN:

The scale appears to be original to Eliashberg and Robertson (1988) and was only used in their study.

SAMPLES:

The sample consisted of 75 business executives who attended a series of executive education seminars at a major university. They were employed by different firms representing a variety of industries. It appeared that the executives held positions that were either connected with preannouncement decisions or made those decisions themselves.

RELIABILITY:

An alpha of .67 was reported for the scale.

VALIDITY:

No direct examination of scale validity was reported but results a factor analysis indicated that the items were part of the same factor.

ADMINISTRATION:

The scale was self-administered by respondents along with other parts of a survey instrument. Respondents with higher scores on the scale perceive a greater probability of competitive retaliation if a new product is introduced than do those with lower scores.

MAJOR FINDINGS:

The purpose of the study was to identify the conditions associated with the preannouncement of new product introductions. The perceived likelihood of immediate **competitve retaliation** was not found to be a significant predictor of preannouncing firms.

REFERENCE:

Eliashberg, Jehoshua and Thomas S. Robertson (1988), "New Product Preannouncing Behavior: A Market Signaling Study," *JMR*, 25 (August), 282-292.

SCALE ITEMS: COMPETITIVE RETALIATION

Strongly Disagree	Disagree	Slightly Disagree	Slightly Agree	Agree	Strongly Agree
1	2	3	4	5	6

1. It always takes our competitors a long time to react to our new product/service introductions.
2. Our competitors rarely retaliate with the same weapon.

SCALE NAME: Competence (Task-Specific for Insurance Agent)

SCALE DESCRIPTION:

A 16-item, three-point Likert-like summated ratings scale measuring the sense of competence a salesperson (insurance agent) reports having on several specific activities related to the prospecting, presentation, and postsale phases of the sales process.

SCALE ORIGIN:

The scale appears to be have been developed for the study reported by Lucas et al. (1987), who drew heavily on Korman's (1970) work for inspiration in defining the construct and constructing the items.

SAMPLES:

The dataset used in the study was made available to the researchers by a major national insurance firm. Data had been collected by the company (not the researchers) from its agents in two different time periods: DS1 (1972), DS2 (1976), and DS3 (1976). DS1 consisted of 2357 responses, but only **1412** had employee identification numbers. DS2 was composed of 2314 usable responses, **1045** of which had identification numbers. DS3 was aimed at **282** agents who had provided identification numbers and usable responses to both DS1 and DS2. Evidence indicated that the samples were biased in favor of agents with longer tenure, greater length of service prior to quitting, and higher satisfaction levels than agents not included in the study.

RELIABILITY:

Alpha values of **.875** and **.860** were reported for the scale as used in DS1 and DS2, respectively.

VALIDITY:

No specific examination of scale validity was made.

ADMINISTRATION:

The scale was self-administered by respondents along with other measures. Higher scores on the scale indicate that employees report a high level of competence in their sales activities whereas lower scores suggest that they have low self-confidence in their work.

MAJOR FINDINGS:

The purpose of the study by Lucas et al. (1987) was to make a longitudinal investigation of the effects of demographic and job attitude characteristics on employee turnover. Only in DS1 was a significant relationship found between **task-specific competence** and length of time spent with the company.

COMMENTS:

The wording of the items could be modified slightly to make the scale appropriate for use in contexts other than insurance sales.

REFERENCES:

Korman, A. K. (1970), "Toward a Hypothesis of Work Behavior," *Journal of Applied Psychology*, 54 (February), 31-41.

Lucas, George H., Jr., A. Parasuraman, Robert A. Davis, and Ben M. Enis (1987), "An Empirical Study of Salesforce Turnover," *JM*, 51 (July), 34-59.

SCALE ITEMS: COMPETENCE (TASK-SPECIFIC FOR INSURANCE AGENTS)

Using the following scale, please rate your ability level in performing each of the activities listed below. +

Need Much Help	Need Some Help	Competent
1————————————	—2————————————	————3

1. Prospecting in family market
2. Prospecting in business market
3. Telephone call techniques
4. Face-to-face call techniques
5. Transition to approach to sales interview
6. Fact finding
7. Discussion of prospect needs
8. Presentation
9. Closing
10. Answering objections
11. Delivering a solid case for buying
12. Obtaining referrals
13. Building client base
14. Reselling to policy holders
15. Organizing file records
16. Advising beneficiaries

+ The exact directions were not provided in the article, but appear to have been similar to this statement.

SCALE NAME: Competitive Intensity

SCALE DESCRIPTION:

A three-item, five-point Likert-type summated ratings scale measuring the degree to which a person believes that in some future time period companies will experience greater competition.

SCALE ORIGIN:

The scale appears to be original to Lusch and Laczniak (1987) and theirs is the only known use of the scale in the published marketing literature reviewed here.

SAMPLES:

All that was reported about the sample was that it was composed of the **103** *Fortune 500* vice presidents of marketing and/or planning who responded to a mail questionnaire.

RELIABILITY:

An alpha of **.71** was reported for the scale. Item-total correlations ranged from .49 to .55.

VALIDITY:

No specific examination of scale validity was reported.

ADMINISTRATION:

The scale was self-administered along with several other measures in a mail survey instrument. Higher scores on the scale suggest that respondents expect firms in the future to experience more intense competition.

MAJOR FINDINGS:

The purpose of the study by Lusch and Laczniak was to investigate the relationship between adoption of the marketing and stakeholder concepts and their perceived impacts on organizational performance. The analysis provided greater support for a single-factor model that combined measures of the marketing and stakeholder orientations. Further, evidence from the surveyed executives indicated that increased **competitive intensity** was positively associated with adoption of the "extended marketing concept," which was in turn positively associated with increased organizational performance.

REFERENCE:

Lusch, Robert F. and Gene R. Laczniak (1987), "The Evolving Marketing Concept, Competitive Intensity and Organizational Performance," *JAMS*, 15 (Fall), 1-11.

SCALE ITEMS: COMPETITIVE INTENSITY

Persons in the sample were asked to state their expectations of the business environment in a future period using the following scale and items:

Strongly Disagree	Disagree	Neither	Agree	Strongly Agree
1——————	—2——————	—3——————	—4——————	—5

1. Firms will be spending more of each sales dollar on marketing due to increased competition.
2. Firms in our industry will be aggressively fighting to hold onto their share of the market.
3. Competition will be more intense.

SCALE NAME: Competitive Strength

SCALE DESCRIPTION:

> A 15-item, seven-point Likert-like summated ratings scale measuring the degree to which a person describes a business unit to be strong in relation to its competition.

SCALE ORIGIN:

> The scale was original to Burke (1984), whose study is the only known use of the scale in the published marketing research reviewed here.

SAMPLES:

> Data were collected from a total of **86** business units in six of 18 firms personally contacted. The majority of business units were in conglomerate firms. The managers who filled out the survey instruments had bottom-line responsibility for their business units, were highly involved in selecting market share objectives, and were an average of 3.29 levels away from their CEOs.

RELIABILITY:

> An alpha of **.94** was reported for the scale.

VALIDITY:

> Burke implied that a factor analysis was performed as part of scale development, but provided no specific details. No other examination of scale validity was suggested.

ADMINISTRATION:

> The sample responded to the scale as part of a self-administered mail questionnaire. Higher scores on the scale suggest that respondents perceive a business unit to be very strong in relation to its competition.

MAJOR FINDINGS:

> The study investigated the degree to which business-unit managers of multiproduct firms perceived different variables to influence strategic choices. Business units with either "build" or "hold" strategies described **competitive strength** as being significantly greater than did business units with a "pull back" strategy.

REFERENCE:

> Burke, Marian C. (1984), "Strategic Choice and Marketing Managers: An Examination of Business-Level Marketing Objectives," *JMR*, 21 (November), 345-359.

SCALE ITEMS: COMPETITIVE STRENGTH

Indicate on the following scale the extent to which the business unit is considered the industry leader with respect to:

not at all _____ : _____ : _____ : _____ : _____ : _____ : _____ great
    1   2   3   4   5   6   7

1. product changes
2. price changes
3. service improvements
4. technological innovation
5. marketing methods

Relative to the business unit's major competitors, rate the following:

6. nature of products

very similar _____ : _____ : _____ : _____ : _____ : _____ : _____ unique
    1   2   3   4   5   6   7

7. breadth of product line

narrower _____ : _____ : _____ : _____ : _____ : _____ : _____ broader
    1   2   3   4   5   6   7

8. quality of services

much worse _____ : _____ : _____ : _____ : _____ : _____ : _____ much better
    1   2   3   4   5   6   7

9. salesforce effectiveness

much worse _____ : _____ : _____ : _____ : _____ : _____ : _____ much better
    1   2   3   4   5   6   7

10. image—for quality, etc.

much worse _____ : _____ : _____ : _____ : _____ : _____ : _____ much better
    1   2   3   4   5   6   7

11. The business unit's bargaining position vis-a-vis major customers is:

weak _____ : _____ : _____ : _____ : _____ : _____ : _____ strong
    1   2   3   4   5   6   7

12. The business unit's ability to gain market share is:

weak _____ : _____ : _____ : _____ : _____ : _____ : _____ strong
    1   2   3   4   5   6   7

13. The economies of scale received are:

practically   ____ : ____ : ____ : ____ : ____ : ____ : ____   great
none   1   2   3   4   5   6   7

14. The business unit's pretax profitability is:

low   ____ : ____ : ____ : ____ : ____ : ____ : ____   high
           1   2   3   4   5   6   7

15. The business unit's market share is:

low   ____ : ____ : ____ : ____ : ____ : ____ : ____   high
           1   2   3   4   5   6   7

SCALE NAME: Confidence in Work

SCALE DESCRIPTION:

A three-item, seven-point Likert-type scale assessing the degree to which an employee has confidence in his/her work and is competent in tasks he/she has learned to perform for the job. Dubinsky et al. (1986) referred to this measure as Initiation to the Task.

SCALE ORIGIN:

The items for the scale were slightly modified from those developed by Feldman (1976). His study was based on data from **118** hospital employees. Scale scores were calculated not only on responses to questionnaire items, but also with a rating based on interviews with each subject. The Spearman-Brown reliability coefficient (corrected for attenuation) was reported as **.501**. Work confidence was found to have significant positive correlations with perceived acceptance by coworkers and the degree of control over the way work is carried out.

SAMPLES:

Analysis by Dubinsky et al. (1986) was based on data collected from **189** salespeople. Letters were sent to a national sample of 2000 senior-level executives asking them to have their least experienced salesperson complete the questionnaire. The respondents represented 189 different companies that marketed 50 different product categories. The sample had a median age of 30.5 years, had spent 1.4 years (median) in their present positions, and were mostly male (86%).

RELIABILITY:

A LISREL estimate of reliability was **.59.**

VALIDITY:

No examination of scale validity was reported.

ADMINISTRATION:

The scale was self-administered by respondents along with many other measures in a mail survey format. Higher scores on the scale indicate that respondents have very high confidence about their abilities to perform their jobs whereas lower scores suggest that they have little perceived competence in their work.

MAJOR FINDINGS:

Dubinsky and his coauthors examined a model of salesforce assimilation. **Work confidence** was found to have significant positive impacts on the ability to resolve conflicting demands both at work and outside work and was particularly related to control over the way work is carried out by the salesforce.

COMMENTS:

The reliability of the measure is so low that improvement is necessary before it is used further.

REFERENCES:

Dubinsky, Alan J., Roy D. Howell, Thomas N. Ingram, and Danny Bellenger (1986), "Salesforce Socialization," *JM*, 50 (October), 192-207.

Feldman, Daniel C. (1976), "A Contingency Theory of Socialization," *Administrative Science Quarterly*, 21 (September), 433-452.

SCALE ITEMS: CONFIDENCE IN WORK (SALESPERSON)

Strongly Disagree	Disagree	Slightly Disagree	Neutral	Slightly Agree	Agree	Strongly Agree
1	2	3	4	5	6	7

1. I wonder if people who work with me have confidence in my abilities. **(r)**
2. I am sure that people around me are pleased with my work.
3. I feel confident enough about my abilities to correct other workers' errors.

SCALE NAME: Confirmation of Expectations (Distributor)

SCALE DESCRIPTION:

A 20-item, five-point Likert-like summated ratings scale measuring the degree to which a person (dealer or manager) rates a supplier/manufacturer's performance as being up to expectations.

SCALE ORIGIN:

Drawing on previous work, Cronin and Morris (1989) used a prestudy focus group to select the final 20 items that could be considered appropriate criteria for judging supplier performance. Theirs is the only known use of the scale.

SAMPLES:

The study focused on the distribution channel of a major manufacturer of fluid power products. Data were gathered in a mail survey to 247 distributors, **117** of whom sent back usable responses. All respondents were dealers or managers. The majority of distributors reported annual sales of between $1 million and $7.5 million and at least $75,000 in annual sales with the specific supplier under examination.

RELIABILITY:

An alpha of **.84** was reported for the scale.

VALIDITY:

The scale was highly correlated with two other measures related to confirmation of performance expectations, which provides some evidence of convergent validity. However, no significance levels were provided, so it is not clear whether these correlations were any more statistically relevant than others in the correlation matrix.

ADMINISTRATION:

The scale was self-administered along with other measures in a mail survey format. Higher scores on the scale indicate that respondents report the performance of a supplier to be much better than expected.

MAJOR FINDINGS:

The authors investigated how a supplier's fulfillment of distributors' expectations influences conflict and repurchase intentions. The findings indicated that the **confirmation of distributors' expectations** had a negative relationship with channel conflict and a positive relationship with repurchase intentions.

REFERENCE:

Cronin, J. Joseph, Jr. and Michael H. Morris (1989), ''Satisfying Customer Expectations: The Effect on Conflict and Repurchase Intentions in Industrial Marketing Channels,'' *JAMS*, 17 (Winter), 41-49.

SCALE ITEMS: CONFIRMATION OF EXPECTATIONS (DISTRIBUTOR) +

Below is a list of supplier characteristics which might be important to your operations. Please indicate how well _____ has performed relative to the original level you expected _____ to perform at for each item listed. (Circle the number that most accurately reflects your belief.)

1 = Much worse than expected
2 = Somewhat worse than expected
3 = About as expected
4 = Somewhat better than expected
5 = Much better than expected

1. Product quality
2. Delivery lead time
3. Quality of advertising
4. Pricing
5. Completeness of product line
6. Technical support by engineering
7. Amount of advertising
8. Quantity discount
9. Order processing speed
10. Rate of new product development
11. Returns policy
12. Credit terms
13. Response to emergency orders
14. Clarity of catalogs/price lists
15. Timing of new product development
16. Product application support

Salesforce assistance:
17. Technical support
18. Training
19. Call frequency
20. Responsiveness to field problems

+ The name of the supplier of interest should be placed in the blanks.

SCALE NAME: Conflict Frequency (Channel)

SCALE DESCRIPTION:

A 20-item, five-point Likert-like summated ratings scale measuring the frequency with which a person (dealer or manager) indicates experiencing conflict with a supplier/manufacturer.

SCALE ORIGIN:

Drawing on previous work, Cronin and Morris (1989) used a prestudy focus group to select the final 20 items that could be considered appropriate criteria for judging supplier performance. Theirs is the only known use of the scale.

SAMPLES:

The study focused on the distribution channel of a major manufacturer of fluid power products. Data were gathered in a mail survey to 247 distributors, **117** of whom sent back usable responses. All respondents were dealers or managers. The majority of distributors reported annual sales of between $1 million and $7.5 million and at least $75,000 in annual sales with the specific supplier under examination.

RELIABILITY:

An alpha of **.91** was reported for the scale.

VALIDITY:

The scale had a high correlation with another measure related to channel conflict, which provides some evidence of convergent validity. However, it had a low correlation with another measure of channel conflict. As no significance levels were provided, it is not clear what these correlations or others in the correlation matrix mean.

ADMINISTRATION:

The scale was self-administered along with other measures in a mail survey format. Higher scores on the scale indicate that respondents report they very often experience conflict with a supplier.

MAJOR FINDINGS:

The authors investigated how a supplier's fulfillment of distributors' expectations influences conflict and repurchase intentions. Confirmation of distributors' expectations had a negative relationship with **channel conflict,** but there was a lack of support in the findings for **channel conflict** having a significant impact on repurchase intentions.

REFERENCE:

> Cronin, J. Joseph, Jr. and Michael H. Morris (1989), ''Satisfying Customer Expectations: The Effect on Conflict and Repurchase Intentions in Industrial Marketing Channels,'' *JAMS*, 17 (Winter), 41-49.

SCALE ITEMS: CONFLICT FREQUENCY (CHANNEL) +

> Please indicate how often you experience conflicts with _____ regarding each of these issues. (Circle the number that most accurately reflects your belief.)

Almost never   ____ : ____ : ____ : ____ : ____   Almost always
                  1   2   3   4   5

1. Product quality
2. Delivery lead time
3. Quality of advertising
4. Pricing
5. Completeness of product line
6. Technical support by engineering
7. Amount of advertising
8. Quantity discount
9. Order processing speed
10. Rate of new product development
11. Returns policy
12. Credit terms
13. Response to emergency orders
14. Clarity of catalogs/price lists
15. Timing of new product development
16. Product application support

Salesforce Assistance:
17. Technical support
18. Training
19. Call frequency
20. Responsiveness to field problems

+ Place the name of the supplier of interest in the blank.

SCALE NAME: Conflict Importance (Channel)

SCALE DESCRIPTION:

A 20-item, five-point Likert-like summated ratings scale measuring the significance of the conflict that a person (dealer or manager) indicates experiencing with a supplier/manufacturer.

SCALE ORIGIN:

Drawing on previous work, Cronin and Morris (1989) used a prestudy focus group to select the final 20 items that could be considered appropriate criteria for judging supplier performance. Theirs is the only known use of the scale.

SAMPLES:

The study focused on the distribution channel of a major manufacturer of fluid power products. Data were gathered in a mail survey to 247 distributors, **117** of whom sent back usable responses. All respondents were dealers or managers. The majority of distributors reported annual sales of between $1 million and $7.5 million and at least $75,000 in annual sales with the specific supplier under examination.

RELIABILITY:

An alpha of **.89** was reported for the scale.

VALIDITY:

The scale had low correlations with two other measures related to channel conflict, which provides some limited evidence of convergent validity. However, as no significance levels were provided, it is not clear what these correlations or others in the correlation matrix mean.

ADMINISTRATION:

The scale was self-administered along with other measures in a mail survey format. Higher scores on the scale indicate that respondents report the conflict experienced with a supplier to be very important to them.

MAJOR FINDINGS:

The authors investigated how a supplier's fulfillment of distributors' expectations influences conflict and repurchase intentions. In general, confirmation of distributors' expectations had a negative relationship with **channel conflict,** but there was a lack of support in the findings for **channel conflict** having a significant impact on repurchase intentions. Further, the findings indicated that the fit of the LISREL model was improved by removing the channel conflict importance measure.

COMMENTS:

Some evidence in the study suggests that this measure did not explain much if any variance beyond what was explained by two other channel conflict measures, intensity and frequency. In fact, there may have been a problem with conflict importance (as measured in the study) being perceived as a distinct construct in the minds of respondents. That problem may have been due to the scale instructions which, as noted below, do not appear to guide the respondent to think in terms of conflict.

REFERENCE:

Cronin, J. Joseph, Jr. and Michael H. Morris (1989), "Satisfying Customer Expectations: The Effect on Conflict and Repurchase Intentions in Industrial Marketing Channels," *JAMS*, 17 (Winter), 41-49.

SCALE ITEMS: CONFLICT IMPORTANCE (CHANNEL)

Please indicate how important each characteristic is to you in obtaining your goals. (Circle the number that most accurately reflects your belief.)

No importance   ____ : ____ : ____ : ____ : ____   Great importance
                          1   2   3   4   5

1. Product quality
2. Delivery lead time
3. Quality of advertising
4. Pricing
5. Completeness of product line
6. Technical support by engineering
7. Amount of advertising
8. Quantity discount
9. Order processing speed
10. Rate of new product development
11. Returns policy
12. Credit terms
13. Response to emergency orders
14. Clarity of catalogs/price lists
15. Timing of new product development
16. Product application support

Salesforce Assistance:
17. Technical support
18. Training
19. Call frequency
20. Responsiveness to field problems

SCALE NAME: Conflict Intensity (Channel)

SCALE DESCRIPTION:

A 20-item, five-point Likert-like summated ratings scale measuring the degree to which a person (dealer or manager) rates the intensity of the conflict experienced with a supplier/manufacturer.

SCALE ORIGIN:

Drawing on previous work, Cronin and Morris (1989) used a prestudy focus group to select the final 20 items that could be considered appropriate criteria for judging supplier performance. Theirs is the only known use of the scale.

SAMPLES:

The study focused on the distribution channel of a major manufacturer of fluid power products. Data were gathered in a mail survey to 247 distributors, **117** of whom sent back usable responses. All respondents were dealers or managers. The majority of distributors reported annual sales of between $1 million and $7.5 million and at least $75,000 in annual sales with the specific supplier under examination.

RELIABILITY:

An alpha of **.92** was reported for the scale.

VALIDITY:

The scale had a high correlation with another measure related to channel conflict, which provides some evidence of convergent validity. However, it had a low correlation with another measure of channel conflict. As no significance levels were provided, it is not clear what these correlations or others in the correlation matrix mean.

ADMINISTRATION:

The scale was self-administered along with other measures in a mail survey format. Higher scores on the scale indicate that respondents report the conflict they have experienced with a supplier to be very intense.

MAJOR FINDINGS:

The authors investigated how a supplier's fulfillment of distributors' expectations influences conflict and repurchase intentions. Confirmation of distributors' expectations had a negative relationship with **channel conflict,** but there was a lack of support in the findings for **channel conflict** having a significant impact on repurchase intentions.

REFERENCE:

Cronin, J. Joseph, Jr. and Michael H. Morris (1989), "Satisfying Customer Expectations: The Effect on Conflict and Repurchase Intentions in Industrial Marketing Channels," *JAMS*, 17 (Winter), 41-49.

SCALE ITEMS: CONFLICT INTENSITY (CHANNEL) +

Please describe how intense the conflicts were with _____ regarding each of these issues. (Circle the number that most accurately reflects your belief.)

Not intense at all   ____ : ____ : ____ : ____ : ____   Very intense
                       1   2   3   4   5

1. Product quality
2. Delivery lead time
3. Quality of advertising
4. Pricing
5. Completeness of product line
6. Technical support by engineering
7. Amount of advertising
8. Quantity discount
9. Order processing speed
10. Rate of new product development
11. Returns policy
12. Credit terms
13. Response to emergency orders
14. Clarity of catalogs/price lists
15. Timing of new product development
16. Product application support

Salesforce Assistance:
17. Technical support
18. Training
19. Call frequency
20. Responsiveness to field problems

+ Place the name of the supplier of interest in the blank.

SCALE NAME: Conflict Intensity (Generalized)

SCALE DESCRIPTION:

> A five-item, seven-point semantic differential summated ratings scale measuring the degree to which a person perceives conflict in a process, decision, or activity. Lambert, Boughton, and Banville (1986) used it to measure the level of conflict perceived in a buying center at the following three stages of a particular recent purchase decision: initiation of the purchase process, specification of the product, and selection of the supplier.

SCALE ORIGIN:

> Though the adjectives were drawn from previous research, the scale itself appears to be original to Lambert and his coauthors. Theirs is the only known use of the scale.

SAMPLES:

> Data were collected in personal interviews with **60** respondents in 22 firms located in four U.S. cities. An average of 2.7 persons per firm were interviewed, each of whom was involved to some extent with the purchase decision for a particular product.

RELIABILITY:

> Alpha values of **.834**, **.864**, and **.952** were reported for the scale in the measurement of the purchase initiation stage, the product specification stage, and the supplier selection stage, respectively.

VALIDITY:

> No specific examination of scale validity was reported.

ADMINISTRATION:

> Though not specifically stated in the article, the scale appears to have been self-administered by respondents in a paper-and-pencil format. It seems to be amenable for use in a telephone survey format as well. Respondents with higher scores on the scale perceive much greater conflict in the buying center's decision process than do those with lower scores.

MAJOR FINDINGS:

> The study examined the association between the style of conflict resolution and both the decision process stage and **conflict intensity**. The findings indicated that as **conflict** increases, resolution style changes from a concern for others to confrontation.

REFERENCE:

> Lambert, David R., Paul D. Boughton, and Guy R. Banville (1986), "Conflict Resolution in Organizational Buying Centers," *JAMS*, 14 (Spring), 57-62.

SCALE ITEMS: CONFLICT INTENSITY (GENERALIZED)

1. agreement   ___ : ___ : ___ : ___ : ___ : ___ : ___   disagreement
                   1   2   3   4   5   6   7

2. cooperative   ___ : ___ : ___ : ___ : ___ : ___ : ___   uncooperative
                   1   2   3   4   5   6   7

3. unity   ___ : ___ : ___ : ___ : ___ : ___ : ___   disunity
                   1   2   3   4   5   6   7

4. supportive   ___ : ___ : ___ : ___ : ___ : ___ : ___   obstructive
                   1   2   3   4   5   6   7

5. positive   ___ : ___ : ___ : ___ : ___ : ___ : ___   negative
                   1   2   3   4   5   6   7

SCALE NAME: Conflicts at Work

SCALE DESCRIPTION:

A two-item, seven-point Likert-type scale assessing the degree to which a salesperson reports dealing with conflicts that occur with others at work and not being bothered by them. Dubinsky et al. (1986) referred to this measure as Resolution of Conflicting Demands at Work.

SCALE ORIGIN:

The items for the scale were slightly modified from those developed by Feldman (1976). His study was based on data from **118** hospital employees. Scale scores were calculated not only on responses to questionnaire items, but also with a rating based on interviews with each subject. The Spearman-Brown reliability coefficient (corrected for attenuation) was reported as **.667**. **Work conflict** was found to have significant positive correlations with resolution of work/nonwork conflicts, internal work motivation, and general job satisfaction.

SAMPLES:

Analysis by Dubinsky et al. (1986) was based on data collected from **189** salespeople. Letters were sent to a national sample of 2000 senior-level executives asking them to have their least experienced salesperson complete the questionnaire. The respondents represented 189 different companies that marketed 50 different product categories. The sample had a median age of 30.5 years, had spent 1.4 years (median) in their present positions, and were mostly male (86%).

RELIABILITY:

A LISREL estimate of reliability was **.64.**

VALIDITY:

No examination of scale validity was reported.

ADMINISTRATION:

The scale was self-administered by respondents along with many other measures in a mail survey format. Respondents with higher scores on the scale feel quite capable of handling conflicts that occur at work, whereas those with lower scores are more likely to be greatly bothered by the problems they have with coworkers.

MAJOR FINDINGS:

Dubinsky and his coauthors examined a model of salesforce assimilation. Having realistic job expectations as a recruit had a significant positive impact on **conflicts at work,** which in turn was found to be have a significant positive impact on general job satisfaction.

REFERENCES:

Dubinsky, Alan J., Roy D. Howell, Thomas N. Ingram, and Danny Bellenger (1986), "Salesforce Socialization," *JM*, 50 (October), 192-207.

Feldman, Daniel C. (1976), "A Contingency Theory of Socialization," *Administrative Science Quarterly*, 21 (September), 433-452.

SCALE ITEMS: CONFLICTS AT WORK

Strongly Disagree	Disagree	Slightly Disagree	Neutral	Slightly Agree	Agree	Strongly Agree
1	2	3	4	5	6	7

1. I am not sure what to do when people in another department give me a rough time. **(r)**
2. I'm upset we have to spend so much time dealing with the critics in other departments. **(r)**

SCALE NAME: Consideration (Channel Relationship)

SCALE DESCRIPTION:

> A nine-item, five-point Likert-type summated ratings scale measuring the degree to which a channel member reports a channel leader as exhibiting a concern for the welfare of channel members and creating a cooperative channel environment. In the study by Schul (1987), the scale specifically related to the relationship between franchisors and franchisees.

SCALE ORIGIN:

> This scale and the study reported in the article by Schul (1987) came from the dissertation research by Schul (1980). He reported in a previous article (Schul, Pride, and Little 1983) that a review of the literature and interviews with franchisees helped to generate items for measuring channel leadership. This is the only known use of the scale.

SAMPLES:

> The main study involved an eight-page questionnaire that was mailed to 1052 franchised real estate brokers with six different franchise affiliations. After two waves of mailings, a total of **349** usable survey forms were received. There was no evidence of nonresponse bias.

RELIABILITY:

> An alpha of **.81** was reported for the scale.

VALIDITY:

> Evidence of content validity came from the pretest interviews. With data from the main study, a factor analysis was performed on 12 items involving leadership behavior. The items composing this scale loaded together, with all loadings greater than .50.

ADMINISTRATION:

> The scale was self-administered by respondents along with many other measures in a mail survey format. Higher scores on the scale indicate that channel members report that their respective channel leaders are very concerned about their welfare and create a cooperative channel environment.

MAJOR FINDINGS:

> The purpose of the study by Schul (1987) was to investigate the influence of different channel leadership behaviors on channel members' conflict and satisfaction. A path analysis indicated that **considerate leadership** behavior had a significant, direct, and negative effect on two types of channel conflict and a significant, direct, and positive effect on channel member satisfaction.

#368 *Consideration (Channel Relationship)*

COMMENTS:

In a previous article with a different analysis (Schul, Pride, and Little 1983), most of the items in this scale were divided into one of two scales, Channel Leadership (Participative) or Channel Leadership (Supportive).

REFERENCES:

Schul, Patrick L. (1980), "An Empirical Investigation of the Conflict Behavior Process in Franchise Channels of Distribution," unpublished doctoral dissertation, Texas A&M University.

_____ (1987), "An Investigation of Path-Goal Leadership Theory and Its Impact on Intrachannel Conflict and Satisfaction," *JAMS*, 15 (Winter), 42-52.

_____, William M. Pride, and Taylor L. Little (1983), "The Impact of Channel Leadership Behavior on Intrachannel Conflict," *JM*, 47 (Summer), 21-34.

SCALE ITEMS: CONSIDERATION (CHANNEL RELATIONSHIP)

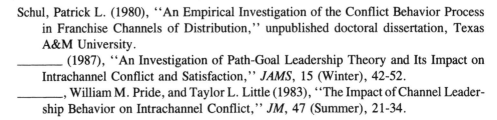

Strongly Disagree	Disagree	Neutral	Agree	Strongly Agree
1—————————	—2—————————	—3—————————	—4—————————	—5

In my franchise agreement:

1. Franchisees have no influence in the determination of policies and standards for this franchise organization. **(r)**
2. Good ideas from franchisees often do not get passed along to franchise management. **(r)**
3. Franchisees are not allowed to provide input into the determination of standards and promotional allowances, or in establishing other key franchise-related criteria (fees, services to be added, etc.). **(r)**
4. There is a definite lack of support, coaching, feedback, and confidence. **(r)**
5. Once they've sold you the franchise, they forget all about you…except when your fees are due again. **(r)**
6. This franchise organization is highly interested in the welfare of its franchisees.
7. I often find myself frustrated and exasperated due to the conflict and ambiguity I experience in dealing with various representatives of my franchise organization. **(r)**
8. I am uncertain about how my agency's performance is actually evaluated by my franchise organization. **(r)**
9. Communication from various franchise offices (regional, national, etc.) is often ambiguous, inconsistent, and/or duplicative in nature. **(r)**

SCALE NAME: Consideration (Leadership Style)

SCALE DESCRIPTION:

A two-item, five-point Likert-type summated ratings scale measuring the degree to which a considerate leadership style is used by a supervisor as viewed by a subordinate. A considerate style implies that there is a good working relationship between the manger and the employee, characterized by respect, trust, and friendliness. As used by Lucas et al. (1987), the scale items are written for insurance agents.

SCALE ORIGIN:

This version of the scale has been used only in a study reported by Lucas et al. (1987). The scale was developed on the basis of similar items in the Supervisory Behavior Description Scale (Fleishman 1957).

SAMPLES:

The dataset used in the study was made available to the researchers by a major national insurance firm. Data had been collected by the company (not the researchers) from its agents in two different time periods: DS1 (1972), DS2 (1976), and DS3 (1976). DS1 consisted of 2357 responses, but only **1412** had employee identification numbers. DS2 was composed of 2314 usable responses, **1045** of which had identification numbers. DS3 was aimed at **282** agents who had provided identification numbers and usable responses to both DS1 and DS2. Evidence indicated that the samples were biased in favor of agents with longer tenure, greater length of service prior to quitting, and higher satisfaction levels than agents not included in the study.

RELIABILITY:

Alpha values of **.774** and **.603** were reported for the scale as used in DS1 and DS2, respectively.

VALIDITY:

No specific examination of scale validity was made.

ADMINISTRATION:

The scale was self-administered by respondents along with other measures. Lower scores on the scale indicate that employees report that their supervisors have a considerate leadership style whereas higher scores suggest that they have a poor working relationship with their managers.

MAJOR FINDINGS:

The purpose of the study by Lucas et al. (1987) was to make a longitudinal investigation of the effects of demographic and job attitude characteristics on employee turnover. Only in DS1 was a significant relationship found between **considerate leadership style** and length of time spent with the company; however, the relationship was negative, in contrast to what was hypothesized.

COMMENTS:

The wording of the items will have to be modified slightly for use in contexts other than insurance sales.

REFERENCES:

Fleishman, Edwin A. (1957), "A Leader Behavior Description for Industry," in *Leader Behavior: Its Description and Measurement*, Ralph M. Stogdill and Alvin E. Coons, eds. Columbus, Ohio: The Bureau of Business Research, The Ohio State University.

Lucas, George H., Jr., A. Parasuraman, Robert A. Davis, and Ben M. Enis (1987), "An Empirical Study of Salesforce Turnover," *JM*, 51 (July), 34-59.

SCALE ITEMS: CONSIDERATION (LEADERSHIP STYLE)

Strongly Agree	Agree	Not Sure	Disagree	Strongly Disagree
1	2	3	4	5

1. There is a good working relationship between the agents in this agency and the manager.
2. Our manager does a good job of providing help with difficult or complex life insurance problems.

SCALE NAME: Consideration (Leadership Style)

SCALE DESCRIPTION:

A 10-item, five-point Likert-like summated ratings scale measuring the degree to which a salesperson reports a supervisor as being supportive, friendly, and considerate of his/ her subordinates. The version used by Teas (1981, 1983) had six items and was in a slightly different form.

SCALE ORIGIN:

The 10-item version of the scale used by Hampton, Dubinsky, and Skinner (1986) is a slightly modified version of the scale developed by Stogdill (1963). In contrast, the six-item version used by Teas (1981, 1983) is more like the version reported by House and Dessler (1974) in that those authors deliberately did not include statements related to a supervisor's tendency to allow subordinates to participate in the decision process. However, the two versions are still very similar.

SAMPLES:

The data used by Teas (1981) were collected from **171** salespeople in group interviews during sales meetings. The salespeople represented 74% of the industrial salesforces of three midwestern companies. The typical salesperson was 36 years of age and had spent 6.5 years with his company. Teas based his 1983 analysis on data collected from two midwestern U.S. firms' salesforces. In both cases, the salespeople were sent survey forms via intracompany mail and were asked to return the completed forms by mail to the researcher at his university address. Usable questionnaires were returned by **116** salespeople, which was described as representing a 55% response rate.

The sample used by Hampton, Dubinsky, and Skinner (1986) was based on **116** usable responses from a census of 121 retail salespeople who worked in one of five outlets of a department store chain. The sample had a median age of 23.2 years, had spent 1.4 years (median) in their present positions and 1.1 years (median) with their current supervisors, were mostly female (78%), and 66% had some college education.

RELIABILITY:

Alpha values of **.837**, **.811**, and **.88** were reported for their respective versions of the scale by Teas (1981, 1983) and Hampton, Dubinsky, and Skinner (1986).

VALIDITY:

Teas (1981) performed factor analyses on six items. All of the items for the scale had loadings greater than .40 on the same factor. No examination of scale validity was reported subsequently by Teas (1983) or by Hampton and his coauthors (1986).

ADMINISTRATION:

In Teas' 1981 study the scale was apparently self-administered by salespeople in "group interviews" during sales meetings, whereas in Teas' 1983 study the scale was apparently self-administered at the salesperson's convenience in a more private setting, as described above. Hampton and his coauthors distributed the survey instrument to respondents in a conference room in each store, where they were self-administered. Higher scores on the scale indicate that salespeople report their respective supervisors as being very considerate in their style of salesforce management whereas lower scores mean that they perceive their supervisors as not being friendly or supportive.

MAJOR FINDINGS:

Teas (1981) investigated the impact of several personality characteristics and job-related perceptions on work motivation. The results indicated that a supervisor's perceived **considerate leadership style** was a significant predictor of job instrumentalities for salespeople, but was not a significant predictor of job performance expectations. Teas (1983) used causal modeling to investigate the relationship between style of sales supervision and salesperson role stress. A supervisor's perceived **considerate leadership style** was found to be a significant positive predictor of job satisfaction, but a negative predictor of role conflict and ambiguity.

A causal model of retail sales supervisor leadership behavior was studied by Hampton, Dubinksy, and Skinner (1986). A **considerate leadership style** by a supervisor was found to have an inverse effect on salesperson role conflict and ambiguity, but it had a stronger positive impact on satisfaction with a supervisor.

COMMENTS:

The actual items used by Teas in 1983 were not specified, but were implied to be the same as those he used in 1981. See another use of the scale by Teas and Horrell (1981).

REFERENCES:

Hampton, Ron, Alan J. Dubinsky, and Steven J. Skinner (1986), "A Model of Sales Supervisor Leadership Behavior and Retail Salespeople's Job-Related Outcomes," *JAMS*, 14 (Fall), 33-43.

House, Robert J. and Gary Dessler (1974), "The Path-Goal Theory of Leadership: Some Post-Hoc and A Priori Tests," in *Contingency Approaches to Leadership*, James G. Hunt and Lars L. Larson, eds. Carbondale, Ill.: Southern Illinois University Press.

Stogdill, Ralph M. (1963), *Manual for Leadership Behavior Description: Questionnaire Form XII*, Columbus, Ohio: Bureau of Business Research, The Ohio State University.

Teas, R. Kenneth (1981), "An Empirical Test of Models of Salespersons' Job Expectancy and Instrumentality Perceptions," *JMR*, 18 (May), 209-226.

_____ (1983), "Supervisory Behavior, Role Stress, and the Job Satisfaction of Industrial Salespeople," *JMR*, 20 (February), 84-91.

_____ and James F. Horrell (1981), "Salespeople's Satisfaction and Performance Feedback," *Industrial Marketing Management*, 10 (February), 49-57.

SCALE ITEMS: CONSIDERATION (LEADERSHIP STYLE)

The version used by Hampton, Dubinksy, and Skinner (1986).

Always	Often	Occasionally	Seldom	Never
5————	——4——	———3———	——2——	———1

My immediate supervisor:
 1. Is friendly and approachable.
 2. Does little things to make it pleasant to be a salesperson in the department.
 3. Puts suggestions made by the department into operation.
 4. Treats all department salespeople as his/her equals.
 5. Gives advance notice of changes.
 6. Keeps to himself/herself. **(r)**
 7. Looks out for the personal welfare of department salespeople.
 8. Is willing to make changes.
 9. Refuses to explain his/her actions. **(r)**
10. Acts without consulting department salespeople. **(r)**

The version used by Teas (1981, 1983).

Very False				Very True
1————	——2———	———3———	——4———	———5

 1. My supervisor gives advance notice of changes.
 2. My supervisor is friendly and approachable.
 3. My supervisor helps make my job pleasant.
 4. My supervisor does little things to make it pleasant to be a member of the salesforce.
 5. My supervisor treats all the salesmen he supervises as his equal.
 6. My supervisor looks out for the personal welfare of group members.

SCALE NAME: Consideration (Leadership Style)

SCALE DESCRIPTION:

An 11-item, five-point Likert-like summated ratings scale measuring the degree to which an employee reports a supervisor as being supportive, friendly, and considerate of the employee's feelings.

SCALE ORIGIN:

The scale was developed in dissertation research by Schriesheim (1978).

SAMPLES:

Data were obtained for the study by Fry et al. (1986) from a survey of 347 salesmen working for a national pharmaceutical manufacturer. A few women responded to the survey, but the analysis was limited to the **216** men who returned usable questionnaires. An analysis indicated that no significant response bias was apparent.

RELIABILITY:

An alpha of **.84** was reported for the scale by Fry et al. (1986).

VALIDITY:

No examination of scale validity was reported.

ADMINISTRATION:

The scale was self-administered along with many other measures in a mail survey format. Higher scores on the scale indicate that employees report their respective supervisors as being very considerate in their style of management whereas lower scores mean that they perceive their supervisors as not being friendly or supportive.

MAJOR FINDINGS:

The purpose of the study by Fry and his coauthors was to test two alternative causal models of leadership, role perceptions, job anxiety, and satisfaction. The findings showed that a supervisor's **considerate leadership style** had a significant negative effect on role conflict and significant positive effects on many facets of job satisfaction.

REFERENCES:

Fry, Louis W., Charles M. Futrell, A. Parasuraman, and Margaret A. Chmielewski (1986), "An Analysis of Alternative Causal Models of Salesperson Role Perceptions and Work-Related Attitudes," *JMR*, 23 (May), 153-163.

Schriesheim, Chester A. (1978), "Development, Validation and Application of New Leadership Behavior and Expectancy Research Instruments," unpublished doctoral dissertation, The Ohio State University.

SCALE ITEMS: CONSIDERATION (LEADERSHIP STYLE)

Below is a list of items which may be used to describe the behavior of your immediate supervisor (the person you report to) towards you as an individual. Each item describes a specific kind of behavior, but does not ask you to judge whether the behavior is desirable or undesirable.

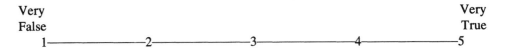

My immediate supervisor:
1. Helps make working on my job more pleasant.
2. Says things to hurt my feelings. **(r)**
3. Considers my personal feelings before acting.
4. Maintains a friendly working relationship with me.
5. Behaves in a manner which is thoughtful of my personal needs.
6. Looks out for my personal welfare.
7. Acts rudely towards me. **(r)**
8. Does things to make my job less pleasant. **(r)**
9. Treats me without considering my feelings. **(r)**
10. Shows respect for my personal feelings.
11. Acts without considering my feelings. **(r)**

SCALE NAME: Consideration of Alternatives (Industrial Buying)

SCALE DESCRIPTION:

One version is a five-item, seven-point Likert-like scale measuring the percentage of situations a sales manager estimates his salespeople face in which accounts are considering new product and/or supplier alternatives. A three-item modification of the scale was also reported in the same article (Anderson, Chu, and Weitz 1987).

SCALE ORIGIN:

Items were generated on the basis of a review of academic and trade literature. Pretesting was performed sequentially with 12 sales managers over several months, allowing the questionnaire to be revised after each stage.

SAMPLES:

The five-item scale was analyzed with data collected from **169** sales managers representing 16 electronic component manufacturers. The three-item version of the scale was used in a survey aimed at sales managers of a broad range of manufacturing firms with sales over $50 million a year. Usable survey instruments were returned by **158** respondents.

RELIABILITY:

Alpha for the five-item and three-item versions of the scale was **.57** and **.54**, respectively.

VALIDITY:

The authors report that they consider the two versions of the scale to show evidence of face validity. In a factor analysis, however, the five-item version had three items with loadings below .40 and/or loadings above .30 with another factor, which raises some doubt about its construct validity. The loading of one item in the three-item version was well below .40.

ADMINISTRATION:

In both studies the scales were filled out by respondents as part of a self-administered mail survey. Higher scores on the scale suggest that respondents (sales managers) report their sales people as frequently encountering sales situations in which the accounts are open and willing to consider different products and/or suppliers rather than sticking with a current product and/or supplier.

MAJOR FINDINGS:

The purpose of the study was to validate the Robinson, Faris, and Wind (1967) framework of industrial buying behavior with particular focus on straight rebuy and new task situations. The only consistent finding of the two studies for this measure was that salesforces that frequently encounter buying centers willing to **consider new alternatives** were reported to have more people involved in the purchase decision.

COMMENTS:

Both versions of the scale have poor psychometric properties. Modification and testing are needed before they are used further.

REFERENCES:

Anderson, Erin, Wujin Chu, and Barton Weitz (1987), ''Industrial Purchasing: An Empirical Exploration of the Buyclass Framework,'' *JM*, 51 (July), 71-86.

Robinson, Patrick J., Charles W. Faris, Yoram Wind (1967), *Industrial Buying and Creative Marketing*. Boston, Mass.: Allyn and Bacon.

SCALE ITEMS: CONSIDERATION OF ALTERNATIVES (INDUSTRIAL BUYING) +

The following statements describe circumstances which might exist when one of your salespeople is trying to make a sale. Please indicate how frequently the salesperson would face the situation described in the statement. This can be indicated by circling the number that most accurately indicates the percentage of sales situations that fit the statement. Each question is independent: your answers do not need to add to 100% or any other number.

EXAMPLE: It is hard to get an appointment to see the account.

Percentage of Situations

0%	10%	**30%**	50%	70%	90%	100%

This manager indicates that in 30% of selling situations, the salesperson has difficulty getting an appointment. Notice that ''account'' means customer or prospect. Those 30% of selling situations that are difficult could be cold calls, followups with a regular customer, or some combination of prospects and customers.

Items:
1. The account is seriously interested in alternatives to the present supplier.
2. The account wants to consider all the alternatives carefully.
3. The account is interested if salespeople call to propose changing suppliers.
4. The account is open for suggestions for change in the current purchase pattern.
5. The account has considerable experience with the product class but is considering new options, new suppliers, or new products.
6. The customer is not interested in new suggestions on ways of meeting his requirements. **(r)**

+ Items 1 through 5 were used in the five-item scale but only items 1, 5, and 6 were used in the shorter version. Also, items in the shorter version of the scale used the word ''customer'' rather than ''account.''

SCALE NAME: Contingent Approving Supervisory Behavior

SCALE DESCRIPTION:

A four-item, seven-point Likert-like summated ratings scale measuring the degree to which an employee perceives that praise, recognition, and complimentary behaviors characterize the leadership style used by a supervisor.

SCALE ORIGIN:

Though the items for this scale were apparently not original to Kohli (1985), he appears to have been the first to publish them. The items themselves were developed by R. J. House, who passed them on to Fulk and Wendler (1982) in personal correspondence. The latter did not report the items themselves but used them in their study.

SAMPLES:

The analysis by Kohli (1985) was based on data from **114** salespeople. The sample was obtained from three companies manufacturing and selling industrial products. An overall response rate of 89.8% was reported.

RELIABILITY:

An alpha of **.95** was reported for the scale.

VALIDITY:

Though Kohli did not report the specific results for this scale, he implied that a factor analysis of this and other scales was used to eliminate items with weak loadings on their hypothesized factors.

ADMINISTRATION:

The scale was self-administered along with many other measures in an unspecified context. Higher scores on this scale indicate that respondents view their supervisors as being quite complimentary in their management style whereas lower scores suggest that the employees perceive their supervisors to voice little praise, recognition, or approval.

MAJOR FINDINGS:

Kohli examined several previously unstudied supervisory behaviors toward salespeople. **Contingent approving supervisory behavior** was found to be positively related to salespeople's role clarity and intrinsic, extrinsic, and overall job satisfaction, as well as overall and extrinsic instrumentalities.

COMMENTS:

Instead of "he", some more neutral descriptor such as "my supervisor" would make the items more generic and applicable to situations involving female supervisors.

REFERENCES:

Fulk, Janet and Eric R. Wendler (1982), ''Dimensionality of Leader-Subordinate Interactions: A Path-Goal Investigation,'' *Organizational Behavior and Human Performance*, 30, 241-64.

Kohli, Ajay K. (1985), ''Some Unexplored Supervisory Behaviors and Their Influence on Salespeople's Role Clarity, Specific Self-Esteem, Job Satisfaction, and Motivation,'' *JMR*, 22 (November), 424-433.

SCALE ITEMS: CONTINGENT APPROVING SUPERVISORY BEHAVIOR

Very
False

Very
True

1————2————3————4————5————6————7

1. He gives clear recognition for outstanding work.
2. He praises me whem my performance is especially good.
3. He shows approval of me when I put forth my best efforts.
4. He gives me recognition for improvement in my performance.

SCALE NAME: Cooperation (Buying Center Members)

SCALE DESCRIPTION:

A six-item, five-point Likert-like summated ratings scale measuring the degree to which a member of a buying center reports that the members worked together as a team with little hostility or infighting. The scale was referred to as Viscidity by Kohli (1989).

SCALE ORIGIN:

The items used by Kohli (1989) for this scale were adapted from work by Hemphill and Westie (1950).

SAMPLES:

A survey instrument was mailed to 500 members of the National Association of Purchasing Management. Usable responses were received from **251** members. No response bias was evident for theoretical variables germane to the study. Respondents provided information about purchases of products in a range of $1000 to $150 million, with an average purchase value of $3.5 million.

RELIABILITY:

An alpha of **.82** was reported for this scale by Kohli (1989).

VALIDITY:

Though some assessment of validity was made for other scales used in the study by Kohli, no evaluation of this scale's validity was discussed.

ADMINISTRATION:

The scale was self-administered by respondents along with many other scales in a mail survey format. Higher scores on the scale indicate that members of specific buying centers are reported by respondents (themselves members of the buying centers) as working together as a team whereas lower scores suggest that respondents are describing their respective buying centers as being tense and hostile.

MAJOR FINDINGS:

The purpose of the study by Kohli was to examine some factors that affect a person's influence in a buying center. When **cooperation** was high among buying center members, information power had a significant impact on the manifest influence of a member; when **cooperation** was low, reinforcement and departmental powers had significant effects. Expert power had significant effects on manifest influence when **cooperation** was both high and low, but had the greater effect in the former situation.

COMMENTS:

Items should be modified for situations in which objects of the questions could be female.

REFERENCES:

Hemphill, John K. and Charles M. Westie (1950), ''The Measurement of Group Dimensions,'' *Journal of Psychology*, 29 (April), 325-342.

Kohli, Ajay (1989), ''Determinants of Influence in Organizational Buying: A Contingency Approach,'' *JM*, 53 (July), 50-65.

SCALE ITEMS: COOPERATION (BUYING CENTER MEMBERS) +

Strongly Disagree	Disagree	Neutral	Agree	Strongly Agree
1	2	3	4	5

1. Certain members were hostile to each other. **(r)**
2. There were certain members of the group who generally took the same side on all issues. **(r)**
3. There was infighting among members of the group. **(r)**
4. There was a tendency toward conniving against one another among members of the group. **(r)**
5. Members of the group worked together as a team.
6. There were tensions among subgroups that interfered with the group's activities. **(r)**

+ Though the directions were not provided in the article, the discussion indicated that respondents were instructed to think of a specific joint purchase decision when answering the questions.

SCALE NAME: Customer Orientation (SOCO)

SCALE DESCRIPTION:

A 24-item, nine-point Likert-like summated ratings scale that measures the degree to which a salesperson engages in behaviors aimed at increasing long-term customer satisfaction versus high pressure sales and low concern for the customer's needs. This scale was called SOCO (Selling Orientation-Customer Orientation) by its originators (Saxe and Weitz 1982). The items in the scale were modified by Michaels and Day (1985) to reflect statements of *buyers* evaluating salespeople rather than salespeople describing themselves.

SCALE ORIGIN:

The scale was originally constructed and tested by Saxe and Weitz (1982). After a literature review and interviews with 25 sales managers and salespeople, a pool of 104 items was generated. Then, 11 sales managers and 13 marketing academicians were asked to determine whether each of the items was representative of the customer-orientation construct. The 70 items retained were rated as "clearly representative" by at least half of the judges. Those 70 items were administered to salespeople in 48 firms. Usable responses were received from **191** salespeople. A final version of the scale was developed on the basis of the 12 positive and 12 negative items with the highest corrected item-total correlations. An alpha of **.86** was reported for the scale with this sample. Scores on the scale were correlated with those on the Marlowe-Crowne Social Desirability Scale. The lack of correlation provided some evidence of discriminant validity.

A second sample was used to further examine the psychometric properties of the scale. Four salesforces participated in the second survey and provided **95** usable responses. The scale had an alpha of **.83** with this sample. After a six-week interval, 46 salespeople were retested and a .67 correlation was found between their two scores, indicating a moderate level of stability. A factor analysis produced two factors: all items had moderate positive loadings on the first factor and the second factor seemed to distinguish between the positive and negative items. As evidence of convergent validity, scores on this scale were found to have a negative correlation (-.47, $p < .001$) with a measure of Machiavellianism, which indicated that respondents with a strong customer orientation were less willing to engage in manipulative practices. Other evidence of the scale's validity was offered in the study, but the authors themselves characterize the results as "not strong" (Saxe and Weitz 1982, p. 351).

SAMPLES:

The study by Michaels and Day (1985) was based on **1005** responses. Questionnaires were sent to a sample of 3216 persons whose names were randomly selected from the membership of the National Association of Purchasing Management. The authors reported that the respondent profile corresponded closely to the national membership profile.

Hart, Moncrief, and Parasuraman (1989) mailed questionnaires to 149 salespeople who worked for 25 independent brokers representing a major food producer. After two followup mailings, usable responses were received from **84** sales representatives.

RELIABILITY:

Alpha values of **.91**. and **.84** were reported by Michaels and Day (1985) and Hart, Moncrief, and Parasuraman (1989), respectively.

VALIDITY:

No specific examination of validity was conducted by Michaels and Day or by Hart and her coauthors. Michaels and Day did note that the factor structure based on their data was very similar to that reported by Saxe and Weitz.

ADMINISTRATION:

In both studies (Michaels and Day 1985; Hart, Moncrief, and Parasuraman 1989), the scale was self-administered by respondents in the form of a mail survey questionnaire. High scores on the Saxe and Weitz version of the scale indicate that a salesperson has a strong customer orientation whereas low scores indicate a sales orientation. High scores on the Michaels and Day version of the scale suggest that a buyer views most salespeople as having a customer-orientation whereas low scores mean that they think most salespeople are most interested in the sale itself, not the customer's satisfaction.

MAJOR FINDINGS:

The Michaels and Day study was designed as a modified replication of the Saxe and Weitz study. The difference, as mentioned above, was that the former examined buyers' perceptions and the latter focused on sellers. To the extent that mean scores can be compared across the two studies, it was found that the mean score of customers was much lower than that of salespeople. One potential explanation for the wide gap is that sellers overestimate their **customer orientation** whereas buyers underestimate it. The purpose of the study by Hart and her coauthors was to investigate goal theory as it relates to sales contests. For salespeople with low self-esteem, both goal acceptance and goal acceptance/goal difficulty were related to higher **customer orientations**.

REFERENCES:

Hart, Sandra Hile, William C. Moncrief, and A. Parasuraman (1989), ''An Empirical Investigation of Salespeople's Performance, Effort and Selling Method During a Sales Contest,'' *JAMS*, 17 (Winter), 29-39.

Michaels, Ronald E. and Ralph L. Day (1985), ''Measuring Customer Orientation of Salespeople· A Replication With Industrial Buyers,'' *JMR*, 22 (November), 443-446.

Saxe, Robert and Barton A. Weitz (1982), ''The SOCO Scale: A Measure of the Customer Orientation of Salespeople,'' *JMR*, 19 (August), 343-351.

SCALE ITEMS: CUSTOMER ORIENTATION (SOCO) +

The statements below describe various ways a salesperson might act with customers or prospects (for convenience, the word ''customer'' is used to refer to both customers and prospects). For each statement please indicate the proportion of your customers with whom you act as described in the statement. Do this by circling one of the numbers from 1 to 9. The meanings of the numbers are:

1 - True for none of your customers - NEVER
2 - True for ALMOST NONE
3 - True for A FEW

4 - True for SOMEWHAT LESS THAN HALF
5 - True for ABOUT HALF
6 - True for SOMEWHAT MORE THAN HALF
7 - True for a LARGE MAJORITY
8 - True for ALMOST ALL
9 - True for ALL of your customers - ALWAYS

Statements:
1. I try to help customers achieve their goals.
2. I try to achieve my goals by satisfying customers.
3. A good salesperson has to have the customer's best interest in mind.
4. I try to get customers to discuss their needs with me.
5. I try to influence a customer by information rather than by pressure.
6. I offer the product of mine that is best suited to the customer's problem.
7. I try to find out what kind of product would be most helpful to a customer.
8. I answer a customer's questions about products as correctly as I can.
9. I try to bring a customer with a problem together with a product that helps him solve that problem.
10. I am willing to disagree with a customer in order to help him make a better decision.
11. I try to give customers an accurate expectation of what the product will do for them.
12. I try to figure out what a customer's needs are.
13. I try to sell a customer all I can convince him to buy, even if I think it is more than a wise customer would buy.
14. I try to sell as much as I can rather than to satisfy a customer.
15. I keep alert for weaknesses in a customer's personality so I can use them to put pressure on him to buy.
16. If I am not sure a product is right for a customer, I will still apply pressure to get him to buy.
17. I decide what products to offer on the basis of what I can convince customers to buy, not on the basis of what will satisfy them in the long run.
18. I paint too rosy a picture of my products, to make them sound as good as possible.
19. I spend more time trying to persuade a customer to buy than I do trying to discover his needs.
20. It is necessary to stretch the truth in describing a product to a customer.
21. I pretend to agree with customers to please them.
22. I imply to a customer that something is beyond my control when it is not.
23. I begin the sales talk for a product before exploring a customer's needs with him.
24. I treat a customer as a rival.

+ The first 12 items are stated in the positive direction whereas the last 12 are stated in the negative direction. Numerical responses to items 13 through 24 must be reverse coded. Further, the positive and negative items should be intermixed when put on a survey instrument.

SCALE NAME: Customer Service Support for Employees (Bank)

SCALE DESCRIPTION:

A seven-item, two-point summated ratings scale measuring the amount of customer service support a bank officer reports that his/her bank provides to tellers and customer contact officers. McKee, Varadarajan, and Pride (1989) referred to this measure as Customer Contact Support.

SCALE ORIGIN:

McKee and his coauthors report that they constructed the scales but selected items on the basis of a review of relevant literature and comments by industry executives. Theirs is the only known use of this scale.

SAMPLES:

The study focused on banks operating in 50 SMSAs of seven states that have unit banking laws. CEOs of the 560 banks in the sample frame were sent questionnaires. A total of **333** usable responses were received and an analysis of asset sizes indicated that respondents' banks were not significantly different from nonrespondents' banks.

RELIABILITY:

An alpha of **.62** was reported for the scale.

VALIDITY:

A factor analysis of all items used in the study revealed a pattern such that items belonging to this scale loaded together on one factor and not on other factors.

ADMINISTRATION:

The scale was self-administered along with many other measures in a mail questionnaire format. High scores on the scale indicate that respondents' banks provide a lot of customer service support to tellers and officers.

MAJOR FINDINGS:

The purpose of the study was to investigate the relationship between strategic orientation and dynamics of the market. Significant differences were found between organization strategy types in terms of several marketing tactics used. Specifically, **customer service support** differed between several of the organization strategy types such that the three of them that were highest in adaptive capability provided significantly more support than the type that had the lowest adaptive capability.

COMMENTS:

Alpha was much worse for this scale than the other scales used in the study by McKee and his coauthors. A variety of reasons are possible. One is that, as noted below, questions refer to different activities performed by two different groups of employees. Another reason is that the scale did not require respondents to respond to each item, but just those they thought applied. Yet another possibility is that only two response categories were available per item rather than a range. Making these items more Likert-type and using a multipoint agree/disagree response scale might improve reliability somewhat.

REFERENCE:

McKee, Daryl O., P. Rajan Varadarajan, and William M. Pride (1989), "Strategic Adaptability and Firm Performance: A Market Contingent Perspective," *JM*, 53 (July), 21-35.

SCALE ITEMS: CUSTOMER SERVICE SUPPORT FOR EMPLOYEES (BANK)

Which of the following topics are covered when your tellers are trained (check *any* that apply):
1. Information about all your bank's products
2. Persuasive communications techniques
3. The philosophy/mission of your bank
4. Specific wording to use in handling complaints

When your officers see a customer (who has deposits with your bank), what information will the officer typically have at hand (check *any* that apply):
1. Deposit history on the customer
2. Summary of customer's business/profession
3. Services the customer uses at your bank

SCALE NAME: Decision-Making Uncertainty (Retailer)

SCALE DESCRIPTION:

Achrol and Stern (1988) used three different versions of a four-item, seven-point Likert-like summated ratings scale that differed only in the anchors used. Though slightly different in their meanings, the scales have in common an attempt to measure the level of uncertainty reported by a retailer in making important product- and promotion-related decisions. Depending on their anchors, one version of the scale measures the adequacy of available information, another measures the predictability of decision consequences, and the third measures a person's confidence in his/her decision-making.

SCALE ORIGIN:

Though conceptually similar to measures by Duncan (1971, 1972), these scales appear to have been developed by Achrol and Stern (1988). Five knowledgeable professors evaluated the definitions of the constructs germane to the study. Then seven doctoral candidates used the definitions to sort scale items. Items missclassified by four or more judges were replaced or eliminated. The scales were pretested in a mail survey format with the same sampling plan as described below for the main survey. Analysis was based on 64 usable returns. Whether further modifications in the scales were made on the basis of the pretest data was not specified.

SAMPLES:

The approach to sampling used by Achrol and Stern was a combination of judgmental and random procedures. In the first phase, the yellow pages of an interstate region were screened for retail organizations with environmental and decision-making characteristics of interest to the researchers. From the approximately 3000 listings, retailers were selected at random. Of the 932 that were sent questionnaires, **269** returned usable forms. The average respondent had $7.5 million in sales and 17 employees, dealt with four different suppliers, and identified a "focal supplier" with whom the firm had more than 15 years of trading history and that accounted for 53% of its sales. No response bias related to theoretical variables of interest was evident.

RELIABILITY:

Using confirmatory factor analysis, Achrol and Stern reported reliabilities of .**892**, .**877**, and .**858** for the information adequacy, predictability, and confidence versions of the scale, respectively.

VALIDITY:

The confirmatory factor analysis generally indicated that items loaded as hypothesized.

ADMINISTRATION:

The scale was self-administered by respondents along with many other scales in a mail survey format. Higher scores on the scale indicate that respondents are very sure about the decisions they make about certain product and promotion issues whereas lower scores suggest than they are very uncertain about such decisions.

MAJOR FINDINGS:

The purpose of the study by Achrol and Stern was to investigate the impact of certain external factors on **decision-making uncertainty** in distribution channels. **Decision-making uncertainty** was the dependent variable in the study and nine hypotheses related to it were tested. In general, the authors concluded that the major factors affecting decision-making uncertainty were diversity among consumers, dynamism of market forces, market concentration, and capacity/potential for growth.

REFERENCES:

Achrol, Ravi S. and Louis W. Stern (1988), ''Environmental Determinants of Decision-Making Uncertainty in Marketing Channels,'' *JMR*, 25 (February), 36-50.

Duncan, Robert Bannerman (1971), ''The Effects of Perceived Environmental Uncertainty on Organizational Decision Unit Structure: A Cybernetic Model,'' unpublished doctoral dissertation, Yale University.

_____ (1972), ''Characteristics of Organizational Environments and Perceived Environmental Uncertainty,'' *Administrative Science Quarterly*, 17 (September), 313-327.

SCALE ITEMS: DECISION-MAKING UNCERTAINTY (RETAILER) +

Items used in all three versions of scale:
1. which product models or brands to carry in stock
2. how much inventory to carry
3. which models/brands to ''push'' in sales strategy
4. local sales promotions and advertising decisions

The anchors used in the three different versions of the scale:

Information Is Always Adequate	____ : ____ : ____ : ____ : ____ : ____ : ____ 7 6 5 4 3 2 1	Information Is Never Adequate
Can Always Predict Consequences	____ : ____ : ____ : ____ : ____ : ____ : ____ 7 6 5 4 3 2 1	Can Never Predict Consequences
Total Confidence	____ : ____ : ____ : ____ : ____ : ____ : ____ 7 6 5 4 3 2 1	No Confidence

+ Though the directions were not reproduced in the article, Achrol and Stern did point out that respondents were told to answer in terms of the previous 12 months and with respect to their focal supplier's products.

SCALE NAME: Directive (Channel Relationship)

SCALE DESCRIPTION:

A three-item, five-point Likert-type summated ratings scale measuring the degree to which a channel member reports that the channel leader exhibits instrumental behavior involving communication to channel members about consistent policies and operating procedures. In the studies by Schul (1987; Schul, Pride, and Little 1983), the scale specifically related to the channel relationships between franchisors and franchisees. In the article by Schul (1987), the scale is referred to as Initiating Structure.

SCALE ORIGIN:

This scale and the study reported in the articles by Schul and his coauthors came from the dissertation research by Schul (1980). He reported that a review of the literature and interviews with 50 franchisees helped to generate 19 items for measuring three types of leadership: participative, supportive, and directive. On the basis of results of a pilot study with data from 31 franchisees, the list was reduced to just nine items (three items per leadership type). Schul's studies are the only known uses of the scale.

SAMPLES:

The main study involved an eight-page questionnaire that was mailed to 1052 franchised real estate brokers with six different franchise affiliations. After two waves of mailings, a total of **349** usable survey forms were received. There was no evidence of nonresponse bias.

RELIABILITY:

Alpha values of .**80** and .**72** were calculated for the scale by Schul and his coauthors (1983) and Schul (1987), respectively. (According to Schul, the difference in alpha was apparently due to one of the studies including data from some pretest respondents and the other not.)

VALIDITY:

Evidence of content validity came from the pretest interviews. With data from the main study, a factor analysis with oblique rotation was performed on the nine scale items representing the three leadership styles (Schul, Pride, and Little 1983). The three items for each scale loaded together and had low loadings on the other factors, which provides some evidence of convergent and discriminate validity. A factor analysis with varimax rotation was reported by Schul (1987) and though only two factors emerged, the only high loadings on one of the factors were for the three items composing the Directive Leadership scale.

ADMINISTRATION:

The scale was self-administered by respondents along with many other measures in a mail survey format. Higher scores on the scale indicate that channel members report that their channel leaders engage in planning, organizing, coordinating, and controlling channel-related activities.

MAJOR FINDINGS:

The purpose of the study by Schul and his coauthors (1983) was to investigate the influence of different channel leadership types on channel members' perceptions of intrachannel conflict. The data indicated that **directive leadership** had a significant negative relationship to channel member perception of conflict. The path analysis of the same data (Schul 1987) indicated that **directive leadership** had a significant, negative, and direct effect on administrative conflict but an insignificant direct effect on servive-related conflict. **Directive leadership** had a significant, positive, and direct effect on channel member satisfaction.

REFERENCES:

Schul, Patrick L. (1980), "An Empirical Investigation of the Conflict Behavior Process in Franchise Channels of Distribution," unpublished doctoral dissertation, Texas A&M University.

———— (1987), "An Investigation of Path-Goal Leadership Theory and Its Impact on Intrachannel Conflict and Satisfaction," *JAMS*, 15 (Winter), 42-52.

————, William M. Pride, and Taylor L. Little (1983), "The Impact of Channel Leadership Behavior on Intrachannel Conflict," *JM*, 47 (Summer), 21-34.

SCALE ITEMS: DIRECTIVE (CHANNEL RELATIONSHIP)

Strongly Disagree	Disagree	Neither	Agree	Strongly Agree
1	2	3	4	5

In my franchise agreement:
1. I am provided sufficient guidelines and careful instructions on how to manage my franchise operations.
2. The rights and obligations of all parties concerned are **clearly** spelled out in the franchise contract.
3. I am encouraged to use uniform policies; they require franchisees to follow standard operational rules as outlined in the franchise rules and regulations.

SCALE NAME: Distributor Interaction (Salesperson)

SCALE DESCRIPTION:

A three-item, seven-point Likert-like summated ratings scale measuring the frequency with which a person engages in activities that require interaction with distributors, such as selling to them or collecting on past due accounts.

SCALE ORIGIN:

The scale is original to a study by Moncrief (1986). Several scales were developed for use in the study from a review of the literature and from personal interviews and focus groups with salespeople. A total of 121 selling-related activities were identified and included on the survey questionnaire.

SAMPLES:

Using stratified sampling, Moncrief sent survey forms to 800 firms representing 20 SIC codes (#20-#39). Fifty-one firms ultimately participated and sent copies of the questionnaire to their salespeople. Of the total 2322 sales employees working for these firms, 1393 returned usable forms but the factor analysis was based on responses from **1291**.

RELIABILITY:

An alpha of **.59** was reported for the scale.

VALIDITY:

Though scale validity was not specifically addressed, a factor analysis of 121 items indicated that the items below all had loadings greater than .50 on the same factor and loadings less than .40 other factors. These findings provide some evidence of the convergent and discriminant validity of the scale.

ADMINISTRATION:

The scale was self-administered by respondents along with many other measures in a mail survey format. Higher scores on the scale indicate that respondents frequently work with distributors in some capacity whereas lower scores suggest that they primarily perform activities that do not involve much interaction with distributors.

MAJOR FINDINGS:

The purpose of the study by Moncrief was to develop a comprehensive list of selling-related activities and the taxonomies created from them. A cluster analysis was performed on the salespeople in the sample and six clusters were found. A group called trade seller, representing 12% of the sample, had the highest mean on the **distributor interaction** scale. This cluster ranked below most of the other sales groups in terms of servicing their accounts.

#379 *Distributor Interaction (Salesperson)*

COMMENTS:

The low alpha indicates that the reliability should be improved before further use is made of this scale.

REFERENCE:

Moncrief, William C., III (1986), "Selling Activity and Sales Position Taxonomies for Industrial Salesforces," *JMR*, 23 (August), 261-270.

SCALE ITEMS: DISTRIBUTOR INTERACTION (SALESPERSON) +

Using the following scale, please indicate how frequently you engage in each of the activities listed below. If you do not perform the activity, please code your response as a zero.

Infrequently   ___ : ___ : ___ : ___ : ___ : ___ : ___   Frequently
               1   2   3   4   5   6   7

1. Sell to distributors
2. Establish good relations with distributors
3. Collect past due accounts

+ The actual directions and items were not given in the article, but are reconstructed here on the basis of information provided.

SCALE NAME: Domain Consensus (Retailer With Wholesaler)

SCALE DESCRIPTION:

A four-item, eight-point Likert-type summated ratings scale measuring the level of agreement a retailer reports having with a specified wholesaler about the assignment of certain distribution-related roles, tasks, and functions.

SCALE ORIGIN:

Though not specified in the article by John and Reve (1982), it is apparent that their data came from the latter's dissertation (Reve 1980). His initial scale had eight items and the final version had four. As different alpha values were reported for the scales and the items used by John and Reve (1982) were not reported, it is not known what else is different about the scales.

SAMPLES:

The data analyzed by John and Reve came from the dissertation research by Reve. Initially, 753 wholesalers in Norway were asked to identify their three largest retail customers. One retailer was selected at random from each of those suggested by the 238 responding wholesalers. Those retailers were contacted and 140 provided usable responses. Finally, the 140 wholesalers identified by the retailers were recontacted for further information. Data were ultimately collected from **99** retailer/wholesaler dyads.

RELIABILITY:

The alpha for the version of the scale used by John and Reve was reported to be **.60**. Items with low item-total correlations were said to have been deleted.

VALIDITY:

John and Reve eliminated items with low loadings on a factor. Further, they used the multitrait, multimethod approach as well as a structural equations model to assess convergent and discriminant validity. These methods indicated poor convergent and discriminant validity.

ADMINISTRATION:

The scale was self-administered by respondents along with many other measures in a mail survey format. High scores on the scale indicate that retailers report a great amount of agreement with specified wholesalers about the assignment of distribution-related roles and tasks.

MAJOR FINDINGS:

The purpose of the study by John and Reve was to examine the validity of several measures of channel relationships with information from wholesaler/retailer dyads. The authors concluded that the ''sentiments'' variables, including **domain consensus**, did not show adequate convergent or discriminant validity. For example, the correlation between the retailers' and wholesalers' perceptions of the amount of **domain consensus** in their dyadic relationships was only .051. Given this finding, the authors wondered if it was not possible that "real" differences existed between dyadic members in their perceptions of this variable.

COMMENTS:

The scale was administered in Norwegian, so it is not known how its psychometric properties might be different if it were used in English as shown below. Further, the scale's current psychometric quality is so low that significant modifications are necessary before it is used further, particularly in English.

REFERENCES:

John, George and Torger Reve (1982), "The Reliability and Validity of Key Informant Data From Dyadic Relationships in Marketing Channels," *JMR*, 19 (November), 517-524.

Reve, Torger (1980), "Interorganizational Relations in Distribution Channels: An Empirical Study of Norwegian Distribution Channel Dyads," unpublished doctoral dissertation, Northwestern University.

SCALE ITEMS: DOMAIN CONSENSUS (WHOLESALER WITH RETAILER)

Not relevant = 0
Very strongly disagree = 1
Strongly disagree = 2
Disagree = 3
Neither agree nor disagree = 4
Agree = 5
Strongly agree = 6
Very strongly agree = 7

1. The supplier and our firm each carry their fair share of storage and handling costs.
2. There is complete agreement between the supplier and our firm concerning our current ordering practices.
3. There is complete agreement between the supplier and our firm regarding which customer groups we are going to serve.
4. The present relationship between our firm and the supplier is based on a very clear division of labor.

SCALE NAME: Domain Consensus (Wholesaler With Retailer)

SCALE DESCRIPTION:

A four-item, eight-point Likert-type summated ratings scale measuring the level of agreement a wholesaler reports having with a specified retailer about the assignment of certain distribution-related roles, tasks, and functions.

SCALE ORIGIN:

Though not specified in the article by John and Reve (1982), it is apparent that their data came from the latter's dissertation (Reve 1980). His initial scale had eight items. The final version had six items and an alpha of .736. The scale used by John and Reve (1982) had two items less than the final version reported by Reve (1980). As the items used by the former were not reported, it is not known which items below were eliminated.

SAMPLES:

The data analyzed by John and Reve came from the dissertation research by Reve. Initially, 753 wholesalers in Norway were asked to identify their three largest retail customers. One retailer was selected at random from each of those suggested by the 238 responding wholesalers. Those retailers were contacted and 140 provided usable responses. Finally, the 140 wholesalers identified by the retailers were recontacted for further information. Data were ultimately collected from **99** retailer/wholesaler dyads.

RELIABILITY:

The alpha for the version of the scale used by John and Reve was reported to be **.66**. Items with low item-total correlations were said to have been deleted.

VALIDITY:

John and Reve eliminated items with low loadings on a factor. Further, they used the multitrait, multimethod approach as well as a structural equations model to assess convergent and discriminant validity. These methods indicated poor convergent and discriminant validity.

ADMINISTRATION:

The scale was self-administered by respondents along with many other measures in a mail survey format. High scores on the scale indicate that wholesalers report a great amount of agreement with specified retailers about the assignment of distribution-related roles and tasks.

MAJOR FINDINGS:

The purpose of the study by John and Reve was to examine the validity of several measures of channel relationships with information from wholesaler/retailer dyads. The authors concluded that the ''sentiments'' variables, including **domain consensus**, did not show adequate convergent or discriminant validity. For example, the correlation between the retailers' and wholesalers' perceptions of the amount of **domain consensus** in their dyadic relationships was only .051. Given this finding, the authors wondered if it was not possible that ''real'' differences existed between dyadic members in their perceptions of this variable.

COMMENTS:

The scale was administered in Norwegian, so it is not known how its psychometric properties might be different if it were used in English as shown below. Further, the scale's current psychometric quality is so low that significant modifications are necessary before it is used further, particularly in English.

REFERENCES:

John, George and Torger Reve (1982), ''The Reliability and Validity of Key Informant Data From Dyadic Relationships in Marketing Channels,'' *JMR*, 19 (November), 517-524.

Reve, Torger (1980), ''Interorganizational Relations in Distribution Channels: An Empirical Study of Norwegian Distribution Channel Dyads,'' unpublished doctoral dissertation, Northwestern University.

SCALE ITEMS: DOMAIN CONSENSUS (WHOLESALER WITH RETAILER) +

Not relevant = 0
Very strongly disagree = 1
Strongly disagree = 2
Disagree = 3
Neither agree nor disagree = 4
Agree = 5
Strongly agree = 6
Very strongly agree = 7

1. The retailer and our firm each carry their fair share of storage and handling costs.
2. There are often discussions between our firm and the retailer as to who has the responsibility for inferior or defective products. **(r)**
3. There is complete agreement between our firm and the retailer concerning the current ordering practices.
4. There are sometimes disagreements between our firm and the retailer regarding which of us is responsible for promotional activities. **(r)**
5. There is complete agreement between the retailer and our firm regarding which customer groups we are going to serve.
6. The present relationship between our firm and the retailer is based on a very clear division of labor.

+ The scale reported in the article by John and Reve apparently used only four of these items. According to the information provided by Reve (1980, p. 183), items 1 and 3 had much smaller factor loadings than the rest and appear to be good candidates for elimination.

SCALE NAME: Dysfunctional Behavior (Employee)

SCALE DESCRIPTION:

A six-item, five-point Likert-like summated ratings scale measuring the frequency with which an employee reports engaging in behaviors that though not necessarily against the rules, help the employee at the long-range expense of the organization. Such behaviors are gaming, focusing, smoothing, and invalid reporting.

SCALE ORIGIN:

The scale was apparently developed by Jaworski and MacInnis (1989). The scale and other aspects of the survey instrument were refined through a series of interviews and a pretest with marketing managers.

SAMPLES:

A national sample of marketing managers was drawn randomly from the American Marketing Association's list of members. Of the 479 managers who appear to have received questionnaires, **379** returned usable forms.

RELIABILITY:

An alpha of **.75** was reported for the scale.

VALIDITY:

The validity of the scale was not specifically examined.

ADMINISTRATION:

The scale was self-administered along with many other measures in a mail survey format. Higher scores on the scale indicate that employees engage in a high level of dysfunctional activities whereas lower scores suggest that they rarely do things that benefit themselves at the expense of the organization.

MAJOR FINDINGS:

Among the many purposes of the study by Jaworski and MacInnis was to examine the simultaneous presence of several types of managerial controls in the context of marketing management. Using structural equations, the authors found that the use of work-related self-control had a significant negative effect on **employee dysfunctional behavior**.

REFERENCE:

Jaworski, Bernard J. and Deborah J. MacInnis (1989), "Marketing Jobs and Management Controls: Toward a Framework," *JMR*, 26 (November), 406-419.

SCALE ITEMS: DYSFUNCTIONAL BEHAVIOR (EMPLOYEE)

Never   Always

5————————4————————3————————2————————1

1. I tend to ignore certain job-related activities simply because they are not monitored by the division.
2. I work on unimportant activities simply because they are evaluated by upper management.
3. Even if my productivity is inconsistent, I still try to make it appear consistent.
4. I have adjusted marketing data to make my performance appear more in line with division goals.
5. When presenting data to upper management, I try to emphasize data that reflects favorably upon me.
6. When presenting data to upper management, I try to avoid being the bearer of bad news.

SCALE NAME: Employee Coordination (Sales/Nonsales)

SCALE DESCRIPTION:

A five-item, seven-point Likert-type summated ratings scale measuring the degree to which "team effort" and coordination of sales and nonsales personnel are deemed necessary for effective selling.

SCALE ORIGIN:

John and Weitz (1989) give no indication that this scale originated elsewhere than in their study.

SAMPLES:

John and Weitz collected data in a two-stage sampling procedure. Personalized requests were mailed to 750 sales managers or sales vice presidents of manufacturing firms with annual sales of at least $50 million. The 266 respondents were then sent a questionnaire and **161** returned usable survey instruments. The sample appeared to be different from the population in some respects but very similar in others.

RELIABILITY:

An alpha of **.76** was reported for the scale. Item-total correlations ranged from .29 to .64.

VALIDITY:

No specific examination of scale validity was made.

ADMINISTRATION:

The scale was self-administered by respondents along with many other measures in a mail questionnaire format. Higher scores on the scale suggest that respondents believe their respective companies need a great deal of coordination of their sales and nonsales personnel in order to have effective selling.

MAJOR FINDINGS:

The purpose of the study by John and Weitz was to examine the role of salary in sales compensation plans by using a transaction cost analysis framework. The need for **employee coordination** had its most significant correlations (positive) with environmental uncertainty, difficulty of salesperson replaceability, and particularly the complexity of the sales task.

REFERENCE:

John, George and Barton Weitz (1989), "Salesforce Compensation: An Empirical Investigation of Factors Related to Use of Salary Versus Incentive Compensation," *JMR*, 26 (February), 1-14.

SCALE ITEMS: EMPLOYEE COORDINATION (SALES/NONSALES)

Strongly Disagree	Disagree	Slightly Disagree	Neutral	Slightly Agree	Agree	Strongly Agree
1	2	3	4	5	6	7

1. A considerable amount of our dollar volume comes from team sales (sales made jointly by two or more salespeople).
2. To be effective, a salesperson has to build strong working relationships with other people in our company.
3. Salespeople in this group have to work very closely with non-sales employees to close sales.
4. These salespeople have to coordinate very closely with other company employees to handle post-sales problems and service.
5. Selling strategies used by these salespeople are arrived at through discussions with people from various departments.

SCALE NAME: Employee Screening (Bank)

SCALE DESCRIPTION:

A four-item, four-point Likert-like summated ratings scale measuring the proportion of customer-contact employees (tellers and officers) a bank officer reports were given personality and aptitude tests prior to being hired. McKee, Varadarajan, and Pride (1989) referred to this measure as Customer Contact Personnel Screening.

SCALE ORIGIN:

McKee and his coauthors report that they constructed the scales but selected items on the basis of a review of relevant literature and comments by industry executives. Theirs is the only known use of the scale.

SAMPLES:

The study focused upon banks operating in 50 SMSAs of seven states that have unit banking laws. CEOs of the 560 banks in the sample frame were sent questionnaires. A total of **333** usable responses were received and an analysis of asset sizes indicated that respondents' banks were not significantly different from nonrespondents' banks.

RELIABILITY:

An alpha of **.87** was reported for the scale.

VALIDITY:

A factor analysis of all items used in the study revealed a pattern such that items belonging to this scale loaded together on one factor and not on other factors.

ADMINISTRATION:

The scale was self-administered along with many other measures in a mail questionnaire format. Higher scores on the scale indicate that respondents' banks administer personality and aptitude tests to most customer-contact employees as part of the screening process.

MAJOR FINDINGS:

The purpose of the study was to investigate the relationship between strategic orientation and dynamics of the market. Significant differences were found between organization strategy types in terms of several marketing tactics used. Specifically, the **employee screening** differed between most of the organization strategy types such that "prospectors" (those with the highest adaptive capability) did the most testing and "reactors" (those with the lowest adaptive capability) did the least.

COMMENTS:

Though the scale was developed for use with the banking industry, with minor adjustments it can be used in other contexts.

REFERENCE:

McKee, Daryl O., P. Rajan Varadarajan, and William M. Pride (1989), ''Strategic Adaptability and Firm Performance: A Market Contingent Perspective,'' *JM*, 53 (July), 21-35.

SCALE ITEMS: EMPLOYEE SCREENING (BANK)

For each statement, please check the response that best represents the *percent* of personnel at your bank who receive the testing indicated.

Most = 75% - 100%
Many = 50% - 74%
Some = 25% - 49%
Few or none = Less than 25%

Most	Many	Some	Few or none
4—————————————	———3———————————	———2———————————	———1

1. Tellers who took written personality tests before being hired.
2. Tellers who took written aptitude tests before being hired.
3. Customer-contact officers who took written personality tests before being hired.
4. Customer-contact officers who took written aptitude tests before being hired.

SCALE NAME: Entertaining Clients (Salesperson)

SCALE DESCRIPTION:

A four-item, seven-point Likert-like summated ratings scale measuring the frequency with which a person engages in sales activities that emphasize entertaining clients, such as with dinner, drinks, parties, or ballgames.

SCALE ORIGIN:

The scale is original to a study by Moncrief (1986). Several scales were developed for use in the study from a review of the literature and from personal interviews and focus groups with salespeople. A total of 121 selling-related activities were identified and included on the survey questionnaire. The activities referred to in the final version of this particular scale were indicated to have been derived from information in the article by Churchill, Ford, and Walker (1981).

SAMPLES:

Using stratified sampling, Moncrief sent survey forms to 800 firms representing 20 SIC codes (#20-#39). Fifty-one firms ultimately participated and sent copies of the questionnaire to their salespeople. Of the total 2322 sales employees working for these firms, 1393 returned usable forms but the factor analysis was based on responses from **1291**.

RELIABILITY:

An alpha of **.73** is reported for the scale.

VALIDITY:

Though scale validity was not specifically addressed in the study by Moncrief, a factor analysis of 121 items indicated that the items below all had loadings greater than .50 on the same factor and loadings less than .40 other factors. These findings provide some evidence of the convergent and discriminant validity of the scale.

ADMINISTRATION:

The scale was self-administered by respondents along with many other measures in a mail survey format. Higher scores on the scale indicate that respondents frequently engage in selling activities that emphasize entertaining clients whereas lower scores suggest that they primarily perform other activities.

MAJOR FINDINGS:

The purpose of the study by Moncrief was to develop a comprehensive list of selling-related activities and the taxonomies created from them. A cluster analysis was performed of the salespeople in the sample and six clusters were found. A group called institutional seller, representing 15% of the sample, had the highest mean on the **entertaining clients** scale.

This cluster had the least to do of any of the sales groups in distributing the product and was below average on activities such as inventory control and shelf stocking.

REFERENCES:

Churchill, Gilbert A., Jr., Neal M. Ford, and Orville C. Walker, Jr. (1981), *Salesforce Management*. Homewood, Ill.: Richard D. Irwin, Inc.

Moncrief, William C., III (1986), ''Selling Activity and Sales Position Taxonomies for Industrial Salesforces,'' *JMR*, 23 (August), 261-270.

SCALE ITEMS: ENTERTAINING CLIENTS (SALESPERSON) +

Using the following scale, please indicate how frequently you engage in each of the activities listed below. If you do not perform the activity, please code your response as a zero.

Infrequently   ___ : ___ : ___ : ___ : ___ : ___ : ___   Frequently

       1   2   3   4   5   6   7

1. Entertain clients by taking them golfing or to a ball game
2. Take clients to dinner
3. Take clients out to drink
4. Throw parties for client

+ The actual directions and items were not given in the article, but are reconstructed here on the basis of information provided.

SCALE NAME: Environmental Capacity

SCALE DESCRIPTION:

The scale used by Achrol and Stern (1988) measures a business' growth potential on a four-item, seven-point Likert-like scale anchored by "very favorable" and "very unfavorable."

SCALE ORIGIN:

Achrol and Stern seem to have used Bagozzi's (1984) measure development and cross-validation methodology for the various constructs in their study.

SAMPLES:

Sampling was a combination of judgmental and random procedures and was conducted in two phases. In phase I of the sampling plan, a sampling frame was established by screening the yellow pages of a region's telephone directory to select retail organizations for which the environmental decision-making context of the research was likely to be valid. For example, chain stores or services businesses that would not have local decision-making authority of the type operationalized were excluded.

In phase II, the sampling frames were randomly sampled to provide mailing lists. Respondent samples of **64** and **269,** representing response rates of 22 and 29%, were used for measure development and measure validation.

Samples consisted of all types of businesses, and judgmental screening did not result in any restriction of product-market diversity. Chosen firms sold products ranging from air conditioning equipment to agricultural equipment. Overall the average firm was relatively small (sales $17.5 million and 17 employees). It dealt with four suppliers, but selected one focal supplier that accounted for more than 53% of its sales and with which it had more than 25 years of trading history.

RELIABILITY:

Coefficient of reliability for the construct was reported to be **.827**.

VALIDITY:

For measures on the validation sample, reliability analysis via coefficient alpha was followed by internal consistency analysis using the similarity of coefficient procedure and confirmatory analysis by LISREL. The similarity coefficient matrix showed that all items clustered as hypothesized in terms of construct structure as well as subconstruct structure. The vast majority of coefficients within the construct met the $\geq$ = **.80** criterion and revealed appropriate ordering patterns. The within-construct coefficients were larger than across-construct row and column coefficients. Confirmatory factor analysis also indicated adequate measurement. All loading parameters were large with small standards errors and significant t-values. From the overall evidence on internal consistency, factor structure, and reliability, the authors concluded that levels of measurement were moderate to high.

ADMINISTRATION:

Though not specifically stated by Achrol and Stern, the scale appears to have been self-administered by respondents in a paper-and-pencil format. A high score on the scale means environmental capacity is very unfavorable and a low score means it is very favorable.

MAJOR FINDINGS:

Achrol and Stern's first hypothesis posits a direct negative relationship between the perceived capacity of the environment and decision-making uncertainty. It is supported (parameter value -.210 and $t = -3.117$). The second hypothesis posits a direct negative relationship between perceived capacity of the environment and perceived conflict. The results support this relationship (parameter value -.133 and $t = -2.244$). The third hypothesis posits a negative relationship between perceived capacity and perceived interdependence of environmental actors. The results reject this hypothesis (parameter value -.024 and $t = -.376$).

REFERENCES:

Achrol, Ravi S. and Louis W. Stern (1988), ''Environmental Determinants of Decision Making Uncertainty in Marketing Channels,'' *JMR*, 25 (February), 36-50.

Bagozzi, Richard P. (1984), ''A Prospectus for Theory Construction in Marketing,'' *JM*, 48 (Winter), 11-29.

SCALE ITEMS: ENVIRONMENTAL CAPACITY +

Please indicate the extent to which the following are applicable to your firm:

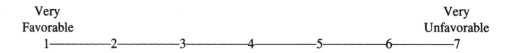

Very
Favorable
1————2————3————4————5————6————7

Very
Unfavorable

1. Potential for economic growth in market area.
2. Demand for products/brands of focal supplier.
3. Demand for focal supplier's product category.
4. General consumer demand conditions for dealership.

+ The specific scale items were not provided in the article, but appear to have been formulated as shown here.

SCALE NAME: Environmental Concentration

SCALE DESCRIPTION:

A three-item, seven-point Likert-like scale measuring the market share of the top four competitors of a business in a local market.

SCALE ORIGIN:

Achrol and Stern (1988) seem to have used Bagozzi's (1984) measure development and cross-validation methodology for the various constructs in their study.

SAMPLES:

Sampling was a combination of judgmental and random procedures and was conducted in two phases. In phase I of the sampling plan, a sampling frame was established by screening the yellow pages of a region's telephone directory to select retail organizations for which the environmental decision-making context of the research was likely to be valid. For example, chain stores or services businesses that would not have local decision-making authority of the type operationalized were excluded.

In phase II, the sampling frames were randomly sampled to provide mailing lists. Respondent samples of **64** and **269**, representing response rates of 22 and 29%, were used for measure development and measure validation.

Samples consisted of all types of businesses, and judgmental screening did not result in any restriction of product-market diversity. Chosen firms sold products ranging from air conditioning equipment to agricultural equipment. Overall the average firm was relatively small (sales $17.5 million and 17 employees). It dealt with four suppliers, but selected one focal supplier that accounted for more than 53% of its sales and with which it had more than 25 years of trading history.

RELIABILITY:

The coefficient of reliability was **.589**.

VALIDITY:

For measures on the validation sample, reliability analysis via coefficient alpha was followed by internal consistency analysis using the similarity of coefficient procedure and confirmatory analysis by LISREL. The similarity coefficient matrix showed that all items clustered as hypothesized in terms of construct structure as well as subconstruct structure. The vast majority of coefficients within the construct met the $\geq$ = **.80** criterion and revealed appropriate ordering patterns. The within-construct coefficients were larger than across-construct row and column coefficients. Confirmatory factor analysis also indicated adequate measurement. All loading parameters were large with small standards errors and significant t-values. From the overall evidence on internal consistency, factor structure, and reliability, the authors concluded that levels of measurement were moderate to high.

ADMINISTRATION:

Though not specifically stated in the study, the questionnaire appears to have been self-administered in a paper-and-pencil format. Environmental Concentration was operationalized by seven-point scales measuring the relative concentration in terms of level of competitor domination, the amount of business resources controlled by the top four dealers in the market. Additionally, a 10-category percentage scale was used to measure market share of the top four leaders.

MAJOR FINDINGS:

The effect of concentration on uncertainty was posited to be nondirectional in the Achrol and Stern study, because there is support in the literature for both positive and negative effects (hence the two-tailed nondirectional hypotheses). Results suggest that in the output environment of marketing channels, concentration is perceived as a moderating factor on competitive behaviors, leading to a reduction in decision uncertainty. The parameter is negative at **-.222** with **t = -2.378**. However, the other hypothesis, that concentration has a negative effect on conflict, is not supported. The authors suggest that the negative result can actually be explained on the basis of the other hypothesis being supported. They state that concentration leads to a reduction in uncertainty because tacit coordination becomes possible or because stable and accurate "conjectural variations" develop. Therefore, because the indicators used to measure conflict represent abnormal competitive behaviors, concentration cannot cause conflict.

REFERENCES:

Achrol, Ravi S. and Louis W. Stern (1988), "Environmental Determinants of Decision Making Uncertainty in Marketing Channels," *JMR*, 25 (February), 36-50.

Bagozzi, Richard P. (1984), "A prospectus for theory construction in marketing," *JM*, 48 (Winter), 11-29.

SCALE ITEMS: ENVIRONMENTAL CONCENTRATION +

Please indicate the relative level of environmental concentration in your industry in terms of the following factors:

Very Low   Very High
1————————2————————3————————4————————5————————6————————7

1. Level of competitor domination.
2. Amount of business resources enjoyed by top four dealers in the market.

In addition, please indicate the percentage market share of the top four dealers.

10%...20%...30%...40%...50%...60%...70%...80%...90%...100%

+ The Achrol and Stern (1988) article does not specifically state the anchors or the items. However, the ones shown here seem reasonable from the information provided.

SCALE NAME: Environmental Conflict (Abnormal Competitive Severity)

SCALE DESCRIPTION:

The scale used by Achrol and Stern (1988) to measure environmental conflict was operationalized through two derived subconstructs, one of which was abnormal competitive severity. It was measured on a five-item, seven-point Likert-like scale.

SCALE ORIGIN:

Achrol and Stern (1988) seem to have used Bagozzi's (1984) measure development and cross-validation methodology for the various constructs in their study.

SAMPLES:

Sampling was a combination of judgmental and random procedures and was conducted in two phases. In phase I of the sampling plan, a sampling frame was established by screening the yellow pages of a region's telephone directory to select retail organizations for which the environmental decision-making context of the research was likely to be valid. For example, chain stores or services businesses that would not have local decision-making authority of the type operationalized were excluded.

In phase II, the sampling frames were randomly sampled to provide mailing lists. Respondent samples of **64** and **269**, representing response rates of 22 and 29%, were used for measure development and measure validation.

Samples consisted of all types of businesses, and judgmental screening did not result in any restriction of product-market diversity. Chosen firms sold products ranging from air conditioning equipment to agricultural equipment. Overall the average firm was relatively small (sales $17.5 million and 17 employees). It dealt with four suppliers, but selected one focal supplier that accounted for more than 53% of its sales and with which it had more than 25 years of trading history.

RELIABILITY:

Coefficient of reliability for abnormal competitive severity was **.878**.

VALIDITY:

For measures on the validation sample, reliability analysis via coefficient alpha was followed by internal consistency analysis using the similarity of coefficient procedure and confirmatory analysis by LISREL. The similarity coefficient matrix showed that all items clustered as hypothesized in terms of construct structure as well as subconstruct structure. The vast majority of coefficients within the construct met the $\geq = .80$ criterion and revealed appropriate ordering patterns. The within-construct coefficients were larger than across-construct row and column coefficients. Confirmatory factor analysis also indicated adequate measurement. All loading parameters were large with small standards errors and significant t-values. From the overall evidence on internal consistency, factor structure, and reliability, the authors concluded that levels of measurement were moderate to high.

ADMINISTRATION:

Though not specifically stated in the study, the scale appears to have been self-administered by respondents in a paper-and-pencil format. A high score on the scale means environmental conflict is very fierce and a low score means it is very normal.

MAJOR FINDINGS:

In Pfeffer and Salancik's (1978) model of interactions among environmental dimensions, uncertainty was viewed as a dependent outcome of a two-tier linkage of environmental dimensions. Conflict and interdependence were the proximal sources of uncertainty, both having positive impacts. Also, it was proposed that conflict is not possible without interdependence. A direct positive relationship was posited between them. The results supported a direct positive linkage between the two mediating endogenous variables. Output market interdependence was seen by channel actors as positively affecting conflict in the environment. It was also proposed that interdependence positively affects decision uncertainties. The corresponding parameter was significant but negative. The authors ascribed this negative value to the conceptual difficulties in distinguishing "interdependence" from other constructs involving competitive factors. The final hypothesis suggesting a positive relationship between uncertainty and perceptions of environmental conflict was rejected.

REFERENCES:

Achrol, Ravi S. and Louis W. Stern (1988), "Environmental Determinants of Decision Making Uncertainty in Marketing Channels," *JMR*, 25 (February), 36-50.

Bagozzi, Richard P. (1984), "A Prospectus for Theory Construction in Marketing," *JM*, 48 (Winter), 11-29.

Pfeffer, J. and R. Salancik (1978), *The External Control of Organizations: A Resource Dependence Perspective*. New York, N.Y.: Harper and Row Publishers, Inc.

SCALE ITEMS: ENVIRONMENTAL CONFLICT (ABNORMAL COMPETITIVE SEVERITY) +

Please describe each of the following as they relate to your firm:

Very Normal   Very Fierce
1————2————3————4————5————6————7

1. Competition in general.
2. Price cutting.
3. Sales promotion.
4. Local advertising.
5. Aggressive selling.

+ The Achrol and Stern (1988) article does not specifically state the anchors and the items used. However, the ones shown here seem reasonable from the information provided.

SCALE NAME: Environmental Conflict (Unfair Trade Practices)

SCALE DESCRIPTION:

A five-item, seven-point Likert-like scale that measures the degree to which an employee reports his/her firm enagages in particular unfair trade activities. The scale used in the Achrol and Stern (1988) study to measure environmental conflict was operationalized through two derived subconstructs, one of which was unfair trade practices.

SCALE ORIGIN:

Achrol and Stern (1988) seem to have used Bagozzi's (1984) measure development and cross-validation methodology for the various constructs in their study.

SAMPLES:

Sampling was a combination of judgmental and random procedures and was conducted in two phases. In phase I of the sampling plan, a sampling frame was established by screening the yellow pages of a region's telephone directory to select retail organizations for which the environmental decision making context of the research was likely to be valid. For example, chain stores or services businesses that would not have local decision-making authority of the type operationalized were excluded.

In phase II, the sampling frames were randomly sampled to provide mailing lists. Respondent samples of **64** and **269**, representing response rates of 22 and 29%, were used for measure development and measure validation.

Samples consisted of all types of businesses, and judgmental screening did not result in any restriction of product-market diversity. Chosen firms sold products ranging from air conditioning equipment to agricultural equipment. Overall the average firm was relatively small (sales $17.5 million and 17 employees). It dealt with four suppliers, but selected one focal supplier that accounted for more than 53% of its sales and with which it had more than 25 years of trading history.

RELIABILITY:

The coefficient of reliability was **.864**.

VALIDITY:

For measures on the validation sample, reliability analysis via coefficient alpha was followed by internal consistency analysis using the similarity of coefficient procedure and confirmatory analysis by LISREL. The similarity coefficient matrix showed that all items clustered as hypothesized in terms of construct structure as well as subconstruct structure. The vast majority of coefficients within the construct met the $\geq$ = **.80** criterion and revealed appropriate ordering patterns. The within-construct coefficients were larger than across-construct row and column coefficients. Confirmatory factor analysis also indicated adequate measurement. All loading parameters were large with small standards errors and significant t-values. From the overall evidence on internal consistency, factor structure, and reliability, the authors concluded that levels of measurement were moderate to high.

ADMINISTRATION:

Though not specifically stated in the study, the scale appears to have been self-administered by respondents in a paper-and-pencil format. A high score on the scale means extensive use of unfair trade practices and a low score means they are never used.

MAJOR FINDINGS:

In Pfeffer and Salancik's (1978) model of interactions among environmental dimensions, uncertainty was viewed as a dependent outcome of a two-tier linkage of environmental dimensions. Conflict and interdependence were the proximal sources of uncertainty, both having positive impacts. Also, it was proposed that conflict is not possible without interdependence. A direct positive relationship was posited between them. The results supported a direct positive linkage between the two mediating endogenous variables. Output market interdependence was seen by channel actors as positively affecting conflict in the environment. It was also proposed that interdependence positively affects decision uncertainties. The corresponding parameter was significant but negative. The authors ascribed this negative value to the conceptual difficulties in distinguishing "interdependence" from other constructs involving competitive factors. The final hypothesis suggesting a positive relationship between uncertainty and perceptions of environmental conflict was rejected.

REFERENCES:

Achrol, Ravi S. and Louis W. Stern (1988), "Environmental Determinants of Decision Making Uncertainty in Marketing Channels," *JMR*, 25 (February), 36-50.

Bagozzi, Richard P. (1984), "A Prospectus for Theory Construction in Marketing," *JM*, 48 (Winter), 11-29.

Pfeffer, J. and R. Salancik (1978), *The External Control of Organizations: A Resource Dependence Perspective*. New York, N.Y.: Harper and Row Publishers, Inc.

SCALE ITEMS: ENVIRONMENTAL CONFLICT (UNFAIR TRADE PRACTICES) +

Please indicate the extent to which your firm uses the following:

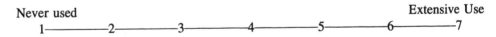

Never used   Extensive Use

1————2————3————4————5————6————7

1. Bait-and-switch tactics
2. Misleading advertising
3. High pressure sales tactics
4. Misleading customers
5. Price promotions on unavailable items

+ The Achrol and Stern (1988) article does not specifically state the anchors and the items used. However, the ones shown here seem reasonable from the information provided.

SCALE NAME: Environmental Diversity (Individual Customers)

SCALE DESCRIPTION:

The four-item scale used by Achrol and Stern (1988) measures environmental diversity among an organization's customers. The seven point Likert-like scale is anchored by ''very similar'' and ''very different.''

SCALE ORIGIN:

Achrol and Stern (1988) seem to have used Bagozzi's (1984) measure development and cross-validation methodology for the various constructs in their study.

SAMPLES:

Sampling was a combination of judgmental and random procedures and was conducted in two phases. In phase I of the sampling plan, a sampling frame was established by screening the yellow pages of a region's telephone directory to select retail organizations for which the environmental decision-making context of the research was likely to be valid. For example, chain stores or services businesses that would not have local decision-making authority of the type operationalized were excluded.

In phase II, the sampling frames were randomly sampled to provide mailing lists. Respondent samples of **64** and **269**, representing response rates of 22 and 29%, were used for measure development and measure validation.

Samples consisted of all types of businesses, and judgmental screening did not result in any restriction of product-market diversity. Chosen firms sold products ranging from air conditioning equipment to agricultural equipment. Overall the average firm was relatively small (sales $17.5 million and 17 employees). It dealt with four suppliers, but selected one focal supplier that accounted for more than 53% of its sales and with which it had more than 25 years of trading history.

RELIABILITY:

The coefficient of reliability was reported to be **.908**.

VALIDITY:

For measures on the validation sample, reliability analysis via coefficient alpha was followed by internal consistency analysis using the similarity of coefficient procedure and confirmatory analysis by LISREL. The similarity coefficient matrix showed that all items clustered as hypothesized in terms of construct structure as well as subconstruct structure. The vast majority of coefficients within the construct met the $\geq$ = **.80** criterion and revealed appropriate ordering patterns. The within-construct coefficients were larger than across-construct row and column coefficients. Confirmatory factor analysis also indicates adequate measurement. All loading parameters were large with small standards errors and significant t-values. From the overall evidence on internal consistency, factor structure, and reliability, the authors concluded that levels of measurement were moderate to high.

ADMINISTRATION:

Though not specifically stated by Achrol and Stern, the scale appears to have been self-administered by respondents in a paper-and-pencil format. A higher score on the scale means that individual customers are very different on the items measured.

MAJOR FINDINGS:

The results in the Achrol and Stern study support the hypothesized positive effect of perceived customer diversity on decision uncertainty (parameter value **.320** and t = **4.702**).

REFERENCES:

Achrol, Ravi S. and Louis W. Stern (1988), "Environmental Determinants of Decision Making Uncertainty in Marketing Channels," *JMR*, 25 (February), 36-50.
Bagozzi, Richard P. (1984), "A Prospectus for Theory Construction in Marketing," *JM*, 48 (Winter), 11-29.

SCALE ITEMS: ENVIRONMENTAL DIVERSITY (INDIVIDUAL CUSTOMERS)

Please indicate the degree of similarity or difference as it pertains to the individual customers of your firm:

Very Similar   Very Different

1————2————3————4————5————6————7

1. Demographic characteristics (income, profession, education, social class).
2. Preferred variety of product brands/features.
3. Product preferences in price/quality.
4. Credit needs.

SCALE NAME: Environmental Diversity (Organizational Customers)

SCALE DESCRIPTION:

A four-item, seven-point Likert-like scale anchored by "very similar" and "very different" for measuring diversity among organizational customers. The scale used by Achrol and Stern (1988) to measure environmental diversity was operationalized through two independent constructs, one which was diversity among organizational customers.

SCALE ORIGIN:

Achrol and Stern (1988) seem to have used Bagozzi's (1984) measure development and cross-validation methodology for the various constructs in their study.

SAMPLES:

Sampling was a combination of judgmental and random procedures and was conducted in two phases. In phase I of the sampling plan, a sampling frame was established by screening the yellow pages of a region's telephone directory to select retail organizations for which the environmental decision-making context of the research was likely to be valid. For example, chain stores or services businesses that would not have local decision-making authority of the type operationalized were excluded.

In phase II, the sampling frames were randomly sampled to provide mailing lists. Respondent samples of **64** and **269**, representing response rates of 22 and 29%, were used for measure development and measure validation.

Samples consisted of all types of businesses, and judgmental screening did not result in any restriction of product-market diversity. Chosen firms sold products ranging from air conditioning equipment to agricultural equipment. Overall the average firm was relatively small (sales $17.5 million and 17 employees). It dealt with four suppliers, but selected one focal supplier that accounted for more than 53% of its sales and with which it had more than 25 years of trading history.

RELIABILITY:

The coefficient of reliability was **.945**.

VALIDITY:

For measures on the validation sample, reliability analysis via coefficient alpha was followed by internal consistency analysis using the similarity of coefficient procedure and confirmatory analysis by LISREL. The similarity coefficient matrix showed that all items clustered as hypothesized in terms of construct structure as well as subconstruct structure. The vast majority of coefficients within the construct met the $\geq = .80$ criterion and revealed appropriate ordering patterns. The within-construct coefficients were larger than across-construct row and column coefficients. Confirmatory factor analysis also indicated adequate measurement. All loading parameters were large with small standards errors and significant t-values. From the overall evidence on internal consistency, factor structure, and reliability, the authors concluded that levels of measurement were moderate to high.

ADMINISTRATION:

Though not specifically stated in the study, the scale appears to have been self-administered by respondents in a paper-and-pencil format. A higher score on the scale means that organizational customers are very different on the items measured.

MAJOR FINDINGS:

The results support the hypothesized positive effect of perceived customer diversity on decision uncertainty (parameter value **.320** and **t = 4.702**). Also, as hypothesized, the results suggest that diversity among organizational consumers does not affect decision uncertainty.

REFERENCES:

Achrol, Ravi S. and Louis W. Stern (1988), "Environmental Determinants of Decision Making Uncertainty in Marketing Channels," *JMR*, 25 (February), 36-50.

Bagozzi, Richard P. (1984), "A Prospectus for Theory Construction in Marketing," *JM*, 48 (Winter), 11-29.

SCALE ITEMS: ENVIRONMENTAL DIVERSITY (ORGANIZATIONAL CUSTOMERS) +

Please indicate the degree of similarity or difference as it pertains to the organizational customers of your firm:

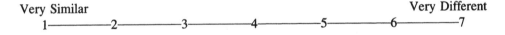

Very Similar   Very Different
1————2————3————4————5————6————7

1. Nature and size of business.
2. Preferred variety of product brand/features.
3. Product preferences in price/quality.
4. Credit needs.

+ The Achrol and Stern (1988) article does not specifically state the anchors and the actual items used. However, the ones shown here seem reasonable from the information provided.

SCALE NAME: Environmental Dynamism (Competitor Dynamism)

SCALE DESCRIPTION:

A three-item, seven-point Likert-like scale measuring the perceived frequency of change and turnover in marketing forces in the output environment. Achrol and Stern (1988) operationalized environmental dynamism through three subconstructs, one of which was competitor dynamism. The scale is anchored by "no change" and "very frequent change."

SCALE ORIGIN:

Achrol and Stern seem to have used Bagozzi's (1984) measure development and cross-validation methodology for the various constructs in their study.

SAMPLES:

Sampling was a combination of judgmental and random procedures and was conducted in two phases. In phase I of the sampling plan, a sampling frame was established by screening the yellow pages of a region's telephone directory to select retail organizations for which the environmental decision-making context of the research was likely to be valid. For example, chain stores or services businesses that would not have local decision-making authority of the type operationalized were excluded.

In phase II, the sampling frames were randomly sampled to provide mailing lists. Respondent samples of **64** and **269**, representing response rates of 22 and 29%, were used for measure development and measure validation.

Samples consisted of all types of businesses, and judgmental screening did not result in any restriction of product-market diversity. Chosen firms sold products ranging from air conditioning equipment to agricultural equipment. Overall the average firm was relatively small (sales $17.5 million and 17 employees). It dealt with four suppliers, but selected one focal supplier that accounted for more than 53% of its sales and with which it had more than 25 years of trading history.

RELIABILITY:

The scale reliability for competitor dynamism was **.794**.

VALIDITY:

For measures on the validation sample, reliability analysis via coefficient alpha was followed by internal consistency analysis using the similarity of coefficient procedure and confirmatory analysis by LISREL. The similarity coefficient matrix showed that all items clustered as hypothesized in terms of construct structure as well as subconstruct structure. The vast majority of coefficients within the construct met the $\geq = $ **.80** criterion and revealed appropriate ordering patterns. The within-construct coefficients were larger than across-construct row and column coefficients. Confirmatory factor analysis also indicated adequate measurement. All loading parameters were large with small standards errors and significant t-values. From the overall evidence on internal consistency, factor structure, and reliability, the authors concluded that levels of measurement were moderate to high.

ADMINISTRATION:

Though not specifically stated in the study, the scale appears to have been self-administered by respondents in a paper-and-pencil format. A high value represents very frequent change and a low value represents no change.

MAJOR FINDINGS:

As hypothesized by Achrol and Stern, perceived dynamism in the environment had a positive impact on decision uncertainty (standard value = .336 and t = 3.274). The findings indicated that environmental dynamism was one of the principal dimensions determining decision-making uncertainty. The authors conceded that the findings were subject to limitations. They assumed that environmental effects on organizations are mediated by uncertainty surrounding key decisions and that the environment should be conceptualized as an enacted phenomenon, and they relied solely on perceptual as opposed to objective measures. These assumptions may not be applicable to all theoretical contexts. The sample also excluded certain kinds of complex channel organizations. Moreover, the model fit was below absolute statistical standards, and hence the evidence was less than conclusive. However, the authors argued that the general evidence was strong enough for their purpose.

REFERENCES:

Achrol, Ravi S. and Louis W. Stern (1988), "Environmental Determinants of Decision Making Uncertainty in Marketing Channels," *JMR*, 25 (February), 36-50.
Bagozzi, Richard P. (1984), "A Prospectus for Theory Construction in Marketing," *JM*, 48 (Winter), 11-29.

SCALE ITEMS: ENVIRONMENTAL DYNAMISM (COMPETITOR DYNAMISM) +

Please indicate the degree of change in competitors' practices as they relate to the your firm with respect to the following items:

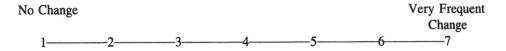

No Change   Very Frequent
Change

1————2————3————4————5————6————7

1. Changes in competitors' mix of products/brands.
2. Changes in competitors' sales strategies.
3. Changes in competitors' sales promotion/advertising.

+ The Achrol and Stern (1988) article does not specifically state the anchors and the items used. However, the ones shown here seem reasonable from the information provided.

#393 *Environmental Dynamism (Customer Dynamism)*

SCALE NAME: Environmental Dynamism (Customer Dynamism)

SCALE DESCRIPTION:

A three-item, seven-point Likert-like scale measuring the perceived frequency of change and turnover in marketing forces in the output environment. Achrol and Stern (1988) operationalized environmental dynamism through three subconstructs, one of which was customer dynamism. The scale is anchored by "no change" and "very frequent change."

SCALE ORIGIN:

Achrol and Stern seem to have used Bagozzi's (1984) measure development and cross-validation methodology for the various constructs in their study.

SAMPLES:

Sampling was a combination of judgmental and random procedures and was conducted in two phases. In phase I of the sampling plan, a sampling frame was established by screening the yellow pages of a region's telephone directory to select retail organizations for which the environmental decision-making context of the research was likely to be valid. For example, chain stores or services businesses that would not have local decision-making authority of the type operationalized were excluded.

In phase II, the sampling frames were randomly sampled to provide mailing lists. Respondent samples of **64** and **269**, representing response rates of 22 and 29%, were used for measure development and measure validation.

Samples consisted of all types of businesses, and judgmental screening did not result in any restriction of product-market diversity. Chosen firms sold products ranging from air conditioning equipment to agricultural equipment. Overall the average firm was relatively small (sales $17.5 million and 17 employees). It dealt with four suppliers, but selected one focal supplier that accounted for more than 53% of its sales and with which it had more than 25 years of trading history.

RELIABILITY:

The scale reliability for customer dynamism was **.799**.

VALIDITY:

For measures on the validation sample, reliability analysis via coefficient alpha was followed by internal consistency analysis using the similarity of coefficient procedure and confirmatory analysis by LISREL. The similarity coefficient matrix showed that all items clustered as hypothesized in terms of construct structure as well as subconstruct structure. The vast majority of coefficients within the construct met the $\geq = .80$ criterion and revealed appropriate ordering patterns. The within-construct coefficients were larger than across-construct row and column coefficients. Confirmatory factor analysis also indicated adequate measurement. All loading parameters were large with small standards errors and significant t-values. From the overall evidence on internal consistency, factor structure, and reliability, the authors concluded that levels of measurement were moderate to high.

ADMINISTRATION:

Though not specifically stated in the study, the scale appears to have been self-administered by respondents in a paper-and-pencil format. A high value represents very frequent change and a low value represents no change.

MAJOR FINDINGS:

As hypothesized by Achrol and Stern, perceived dynamism in the environment had a positive impact on decision uncertainty (standard value = .336 and t = 3.274). The findings indicated that environmental dynamism is one of the principal dimensions determining decision-making uncertainty. The authors conceded that the findings were subject to limitations. They assumed that environmental effects on organizations are mediated by uncertainty surrounding key decisions and that the environment should be conceptualized as an enacted phenomenon, and they relied solely on perceptual as opposed to objective measures. These assumptions may not be applicable to all theoretical contexts. The sample also excluded certain kinds of complex channel organizations. Moreover, the model fit was below absolute statistical standards, and hence the evidence was less than conclusive. However, the general evidence was strong enough for their purpose.

REFERENCES:

Achrol, Ravi S. and Louis W. Stern (1988), "Environmental Determinants of Decision Making Uncertainty in Marketing Channels," *JMR*, 25 (February), 36-50.

Bagozzi, Richard P. (1984), "A Prospectus for Theory Construction in Marketing," *JM*, 48 (Winter), 11-29.

SCALE ITEMS: ENVIRONMENTAL DYNAMISM (CUSTOMER DYNAMISM) +

Please indicate the degree of change in customers' preferences as they relate to the your firm with respect to the following items:

No Change   Very Frequent
                                                                                         Change

1————2————3————4————5————6————7

1. Changes in customer preferences in product features.
2. Changes in customer preference in brands.
3. Changes in customer preference in product quality/price.

+ The Achrol and Stern (1988) article does not specifically state the anchors and the item used. However, the ones shown here seem reasonable from the information provided.

SCALE NAME: Environmental Dynamism (Marketing Practices)

SCALE DESCRIPTION:

A three-item, seven-point Likert-like scale measuring the perceived frequency of change and turnover in marketing forces in the output environment. Achrol and Stern (1988) operationalized environmental dynamism through three subconstructs, one of which was marketing practices. The scale is anchored by ''no change'' and ''very frequent change.''

SCALE ORIGIN:

Achrol and Stern seem to have used Bagozzi's (1984) measure development and cross-validation methodology for the various constructs in their study.

SAMPLES:

Sampling was a combination of judgmental and random procedures and was conducted in two phases. In phase I of the sampling plan, a sampling frame was established by screening the yellow pages of a region's telephone directory to select retail organizations for which the environmental decision-making context of the research was likely to be valid. For example, chain stores or services businesses that would not have local decision-making authority of the type operationalized were excluded.

In phase II, the sampling frames were randomly sampled to provide mailing lists. Respondent samples of **64** and **269**, representing response rates of 22 and 29%, were used for measure development and measure validation.

Samples consisted of all types of businesses, and judgmental screening did not result in any restriction of product-market diversity. Chosen firms sold products ranging from air conditioning equipment to agricultural equipment. Overall the average firm was relatively small (sales $17.5 million and 17 employees). It dealt with four suppliers, but selected one focal supplier that accounted for more than 53% of its sales and with which it had more than 25 years of trading history.

RELIABILITY:

The scale reliability for dynamism in marketing practices was **.763**.

VALIDITY:

For measures on the validation sample, reliability analysis via coefficient alpha was followed by internal consistency analysis using the similarity of coefficient procedure and confirmatory analysis by LISREL. The similarity coefficient matrix showed that all items clustered as hypothesized in terms of construct structure as well as subconstruct structure. The vast majority of coefficients within the construct met the $\geq$ = **.80** criterion and revealed appropriate ordering patterns. The within-construct coefficients were larger than across-construct row and column coefficients. Confirmatory factor analysis also indicates adequate measurement. All loading parameters were large with small standards errors and significant t-values. From the overall evidence on internal consistency, factor structure, and reliability, the authors concluded that levels of measurement were moderate to high.

ADMINISTRATION:

Though not specifically stated in the study, the scale appears to have been self-administered by respondents in a paper-and-pencil format. A higher score on the scale represents very frequent change whereas a lower score represents no change.

MAJOR FINDINGS:

As hypothesized by Achrol and Stern, perceived dynamism in the environment had a positive impact on decision uncertainty (standard value = .336 and t = 3.274). The findings indicated that environmental dynamism is one of the principal dimensions determining decision-making uncertainty. The authors conceded that the findings were subject to limitations. They assumed that environmental effects on organizations are mediated by uncertainty surrounding key decisions and that the environment should be conceptualized as an enacted phenomenon, and they relied solely on perceptual as opposed to objective measures. These assumptions may not be applicable to all theoretical contexts. The sample also excluded certain kinds of complex channel organizations. Moreover, the model fit was below absolute statistical standards, and hence the evidence was less than conclusive. However, Achrol and Stern suggest that the general evidence was strong enough for their purpose.

REFERENCES:

Achrol, Ravi S. and Louis W. Stern (1988), "Environmental Determinants of Decision Making Uncertainty in Marketing Channels," *JMR*, 25 (February), 36-50.
Bagozzi, Richard P. (1984), "A Prospectus for Theory Construction in Marketing," *JM*, 48 (Winter), 11-29.

SCALE ITEMS: ENVIRONMENTAL DYNAMISM (MARKETING PRACTICES) +

Please indicate the degree of change in marketing practices as they relate to the your firm with respect to the following items:

No Change   Very Frequent
                                                                         Change

1————2————3————4————5————6————7

1. Changes in the mix of products/brands carried.
2. Changes in sales strategies.
3. Changes in sales promotion/advertising strategies.

+ The Achrol and Stern (1988) article does not specifically state the anchors and the items used. However, the ones shown here seem reasonable from the information provided.

SCALE NAME: Environmental Forces (Demand & Competition)

SCALE DESCRIPTION:

A ten-item, five-point Likert-like summated ratings scale measuring the impact a channel member perceives demand and competitive forces to have on its decision-making environment. The scale was called Output Sector Variability by Dwyer and Welsh (1985).

SCALE ORIGIN:

The scale is apparently original to Dwyer and Welsh (1985).

SAMPLES:

Questionnaires were mailed to 7254 retailers in 10 industries whose addresses had been provided by a list broker. Envelopes were simply addressed to "Manager" in each case. After a second wave to 10% of the original sample, a total of **457** responses were used in the analysis. Because of such a low response rate, the authors provided rather detailed information about response rates and characteristics by industry.

RELIABILITY:

An alpha of .72 was reported for the scale.

VALIDITY:

Dwyer and Welsh performed a factor analysis of 27 items related to business environments and found multiple factors. The authors considered it to be "methodologically practical and conceptually sound" (p. 404) to consolidate the items into two factors. In a factor analysis constrained to just two factors, the 10 items indicated below had loadings from .30 to .62 on the same factor.

ADMINISTRATION:

Respondents self-administered the scale along with many other measures. Respondents with higher scores on the scale think the demand and competitive forces confronting their industries are great whereas those with lower scores perceive little effect from these sources on their business environments.

MAJOR FINDINGS:

Dwyer and Welsh investigated environmental effects on channel structure and processes in a political economy framework. Among their many findings was that strong **demand and competitive forces** are significantly related to less complex channel configurations and less retailer control over marketing decisions.

REFERENCE:

Dwyer, F. Robert and M. Ann Welsh (1985), "Environmental Relationships of the Internal Political Economy of Marketing Channels," *JMR*, 22 (November), 397-414.

SCALE ITEMS: ENVIRONMENTAL FORCES (DEMAND & COMPETITION)

Immediately below you are asked for your impressions about the business environment confronting your industry. Please consider each of the following features of a business environment as they exist in your industry. Use the following scale to indicate the extent to which each characteristic is present.

Very Great	Considerable	Moderate	Some	None/Only very little
5———————	———4———————	———3———————	——2———————	—1

1. uncertainty regarding overall trend
2. uncertainty regarding business cycle
3. speculative buying
4. declining demand for product
5. price competition
6. competition based upon having prime location—manufacturer
7. competition on merchandise selection and quality—manufacturer
8. competition on service (e.g., delivery, credit, promotion)—manufacturer
9. competition based upon advertising spending—manufacturer
10. periods of resource scarcity

SCALE NAME: Environmental Forces (Regulation & Technology)

SCALE DESCRIPTION:

A 13-item, five-point Likert-like summated ratings scale measuring the impact a channel member perceives regulatory and technological forces to have on its decision-making environment. The scale was called Heterogeneity/Homogeneity by Dwyer and Welsh (1985).

SCALE ORIGIN:

The scale is apparently original to Dwyer and Welsh (1985).

SAMPLES:

Questionnaires were mailed to 7254 retailers in 10 industries whose addresses had been provided by a list broker. Envelopes were simply addressed to "Manager" in each case. After a second wave to 10% of the original sample, a total of **457** responses were used in the analysis. Because of such a low response rate, the authors provided rather detailed information about response rates and characteristics by industry.

RELIABILITY:

An alpha of **.84** was reported for the scale.

VALIDITY:

Dwyer and Welsh performed a factor analysis of 27 items related to business environments and found multiple factors. The authors considered it to be "methodologically practical and conceptually sound" (p. 404) to consolidate the items into two factors. In a factor analysis constrained to just two factors, the 13 items indicated below had loadings from .36 to .66 on the same factor.

ADMINISTRATION:

Respondents self-administered the scale along with many other measures. Respondents with higher scores on the scale think the regulatory and technological forces confronting their industries are great whereas those with lower scores perceive little effect from these sources on their business environments.

MAJOR FINDINGS:

Dwyer and Welsh investigated environmental effects on channel structure and processes in a political economy framework. Among their many findings was that strong **regulatory and technological forces** are significantly related to the use of less formalized decision-making procedures.

REFERENCE:

Dwyer, F. Robert and M. Ann Welsh (1985), "Environmental Relationships of the Internal Political Economy of Marketing Channels," *JMR*, 22 (November), 397-414.

SCALE ITEMS: ENVIRONMENTAL FORCES (REGULATION & TECHNOLOGY)

Immediately below you are asked for your impressions about the business environment confronting your industry. Please consider each of the following features of a business environment as they exist in your industry. Use the following scale to indicate the extent to which each characteristic is present.

Very Great	Considerable	Moderate	Some	None/Only very little
5————	————4————	————3————	————2————	————1

1. government product standards
2. restrictions on seller concentration
3. transportation and handling regulations
4. governmental pricing regulations
5. environmental protection (pollutants, noise, etc.) laws
6. governmental regulation of advertising
7. regulations relating to product resale
8. trade association regulations of business practices
9. rapid rate of product improvement
10. use of elctronic data processing in ordering/selling
11. computerized inventory management
12. containerization in distribution
13. self-service consumer buying

SCALE NAME: Environmental Interconnectedness (Common Input Linkages)

SCALE DESCRIPTION:

A three-item, seven-point Likert-like measure of the degree to which a dealer reports that other dealers and suppliers in a local market are inter-related in their business activities. Interconnectedness in the output environment is expected to increase decision-making uncertainty for channel actors. Achrol and Stern (1988) measured interconnectedness through two **independent** subconstructs, one of which was interconnectedness via common input linkages.

SCALE ORIGIN:

Achrol and Stern seem to have used Bagozzi's (1984) measure development and cross-validation methodology for the various constructs in their study.

SAMPLES:

Sampling was a combination of judgmental and random procedures and was conducted in two phases. In phase I of the sampling plan, a sampling frame was established by screening the yellow pages of a region's telephone directory to select retail organizations for which the environmental decision-making context of the research was likely to be valid. For example, chain stores or service businesses that would not have local decision-making authority of the type operationalized were excluded.

In phase II, the sampling frames were randomly sampled to provide mailing lists. Respondent samples of **64** and **269**, representing response rates of 22 and 29%, were used for measure development and measure validation.

Samples consisted of all types of businesses, and judgmental screening did not result in any restriction of product-market diversity. Chosen firms sold products ranging from air conditioning equipment to agricultural equipment. Overall the average firm was relatively small (sales $17.5 million and 17 employees). It dealt with four suppliers, but selected one focal supplier that accounted for more than 53% of its sales and with which it had more than 25 years of trading history.

RELIABILITY:

The coefficient of reliability for interconnectedness in the input environment was **.695**.

VALIDITY:

For measures on the validation sample, reliability analysis via coefficient alpha was followed by internal consistency analysis using the similarity of coefficient procedure and confirmatory analysis by LISREL. The similarity coefficient matrix showed that all items clustered as hypothesized in terms of construct structure as well as subconstruct structure. The vast majority of coefficients within the construct met the $\geq$ = **.80** criterion and revealed appropriate ordering patterns. The within-construct coefficients were larger than across-construct row and column coefficients. Confirmatory factor analysis also indicated adequate measurement. All loading parameters were large with small standards errors and significant t-values. From the overall evidence on internal consistency, factor structure, and reliability, the authors concluded that levels of measurement were moderate to high.

ADMINISTRATION:

Though not specifically stated in the study, the scale appears to have been self-administered by respondents in a paper-and-pencil format. A high score on the scale means a high degree of interconnectedness and a low score means a low degree of interconnectedness.

MAJOR FINDINGS:

The hypothesis predicting input interconnectedness to have a positive effect on interdependence was rejected. The hypothesis predicting a similar positive effect on decision uncertainty failed the two-tail criteria ($t = 1.722$, and standard value for parameter .131) but met the significance criteria for a one-tailed test and cannot be rejected conclusively.

REFERENCES:

Achrol, Ravi S. and Louis W. Stern (1988), "Environmental Determinants of Decision Making Uncertainty in Marketing Channels," *JMR*, 25 (February), 36-50.

Bagozzi, Richard P. (1984), "A Prospectus for Theory Construction in Marketing," *JM*, 48 (Winter), 11-29.

SCALE ITEMS: ENVIRONMENTAL INTERCONNECTEDNESS (COMMON INPUT LINKAGES) +

Please indicate the degree to which the following practices are common in your industry:

Very Uncommon   Very Common
1————2————3————4————5————6————7

1. Competing suppliers (competing with the focal supplier) deal with common dealers.
2. Competing dealers deal with common suppliers.
3. Other dealers in the local market carry focal supplier's product.

+ The Achrol and Stern (1988) article does not specifically state the anchors and the items used. However, the ones shown here seem reasonable from the information provided.

SCALE NAME: Environmental Interconnectedness (Common Output Linkages)

SCALE DESCRIPTION:

A two-item, seven-point Likert-like scale purported to measure the degree to which the customers of a business are viewed as buying from other dealers (the competition).

SCALE ORIGIN:

Achrol and Stern (1988) seem to have used Bagozzi's (1984) measure development and cross-validation methodology for the various constructs in their study.

SAMPLES:

Sampling was a combination of judgmental and random procedures and was conducted in two phases. In phase I of the sampling plan, a sampling frame was established by screening the yellow pages of a region's telephone directory to select retail organizations for which the environmental decision-making context of the research was likely to be valid. For example, chain stores or services businesses that would not have local decision-making authority of the type operationalized were excluded.

In phase II, the sampling frames were randomly sampled to provide mailing lists. Respondent samples of **64** and **269**, representing response rates of 22 and 29%, were used for measure development and measure validation.

Samples consisted of all types of businesses, and judgmental screening did not result in any restriction of product-market diversity. Chosen firms sold products ranging from air conditioning equipment to agricultural equipment. Overall the average firm was relatively small (sales $17.5 million and 17 employees). It dealt with four suppliers, but selected one focal supplier that accounted for more than 53% of its sales and with which it had more than 25 years of trading history.

RELIABILITY:

The coefficient of reliability for interconnectedness in the output environment was **.694.**

VALIDITY:

For measures on the validation sample, reliability via coefficient alpha was followed by internal consistency analysis using the similarity of coefficient procedure and confirmatory analysis by LISREL. The similarity coefficient matrix showed that all items clustered as hypothesized in terms of construct structure as well as subconstruct structure. The vast majority of coefficients within the construct met the $\geq = .80$ criterion and revealed appropriate ordering patterns. The within-construct coefficients were larger than across-construct row and column coefficients. Confirmatory factor analysis also indicated adequate measurement. All loading parameters were large with small standards errors and significant t-values. From the overall evidence on internal consistency, factor structure, and reliability, the authors concluded that levels of measurement were moderate to high.

ADMINISTRATION:

Though not specifically stated in the study, the scale appears to have been self-administered by respondents in a paper-and-pencil format. A high score on the scale means a higher degree of interconnectedness.

MAJOR FINDINGS:

The hypothesis predicting a positive effect on decision uncertainty failed the two-tail criteria ($t = 1.722$, and standard value for parameter $.131$) but met the significance criteria for a one-tailed test and cannot be rejected conclusively. The other hypothesis predicted positive effects of output interconnectedness on interdependence and decision uncertainty. The effect is supported for interdependence but rejected for decision uncertainty.

REFERENCES:

Achrol, Ravi S. and Louis W. Stern (1988), "Environmental Determinants of Decision Making Uncertainty in Marketing Channels," *JMR*, 25 (February), 36-50.

Bagozzi, Richard P. (1984), "A Prospectus for Theory Construction in Marketing," *JM*, 48 (Winter), 11-29.

SCALE ITEMS: ENVIRONMENTAL INTERCONNECTEDNESS (COMMON OUTPUT LINKAGES)+

Please indicate the degree to which the following practices are common in your industry:

Very Uncommon   Very Common

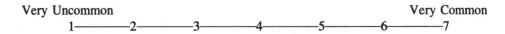
1————2————3————4————5————6————7

1. Customers tend to deal with major competitors.
2. Customers tend to shop around for brands/prices.

+ The Achrol and Stern (1988) article does not specifically state the anchors and the items used. However, the ones shown here seem reasonable from the information provided.

SCALE NAME: Environmental Interdependence

SCALE DESCRIPTION:

A five-item, seven-point Likert-like scale measuring reactivity among dealers to five competitive acts. The study does not describe the anchors but from the information provided, it seems that the anchors could be "very low" to "very high."

SCALE ORIGIN:

Achrol and Stern (1988) seem to have used Bagozzi's (1984) measure development and cross-validation methodology for the various constructs in their study.

SAMPLES:

Sampling was a combination of judgmental and random procedures and was conducted in two phases. In phase I of the sampling plan, a sampling frame was established by screening the yellow pages of a region's telephone directory to select retail organizations for which the environmental decision-making context of the research was likely to be valid. For example, chain stores or services businesses that would not have local decision-making authority of the type operationalized were excluded.

In phase II, the sampling frames were randomly sampled to provide mailing lists. Respondent samples of **64** and **269,** representing response rates of 22 and 29%, were used for measure development and measure validation.

Samples consisted of all types of businesses, and judgmental screening did not result in any restriction of product-market diversity. Chosen firms sold products ranging from air conditioning equipment to agricultural equipment. Overall the average firm was relatively small (sales $17.5 million and 17 employees). It dealt with four suppliers, but selected one focal supplier that accounted for more than 53% of its sales and with which it had more than 25 years of trading history.

RELIABILITY:

The coefficient of reliability was reported to be **.845**.

VALIDITY:

For measures on the validation sample, reliability analysis via coefficient alpha was followed by internal consistency analysis using the similarity of coefficient procedure and confirmatory analysis by LISREL. The similarity coefficient matrix showed that all items clustered as hypothesized in terms of construct structure as well as subconstruct structure. The vast majority of coefficients within the construct met the $\geq = $ **.80** criterion and revealed appropriate ordering patterns. The within-construct coefficients were larger than across-construct row and column coefficients. Confirmatory factor analysis also indicated adequate measurement. All loading parameters were large with small standards errors and significant t-values. From the overall evidence on internal consistency, factor structure, and reliability, the authors concluded that validity levels of measurement were moderate to high.

ADMINISTRATION:

Though not specifically stated in the study, the scale appears to have been self-administered by respondents in a paper-and-pencil format. The seven-point scales measure reactivity among dealers, and though not clearly stated in the study, a high score appears to mean high reactivity.

MAJOR FINDINGS:

Conflict and interdependence were the proximal sources of uncertainty, both having positive impacts. Also, the authors proposed that conflict is not possible without interdependence. A direct positive relationship was posited between them. The results supported a direct positive linkage between the two mediating endogenous variables. Output market interdependence was seen by channel actors as positively affecting conflict in the environment. The authors also proposed that interdependence positively affects decision uncertainties. The results rejected this hypothesis. The authors ascribed this finding to the difficulty involved in distinguishing interdependence from other constructs involving competitive factors.

REFERENCES:

Achrol, Ravi S. and Louis W. Stern (1988), ''Environmental Determinants of Decision Making Uncertainty in Marketing Channels,'' *JMR*, 25 (February), 36-50.
Bagozzi, Richard P. (1984), ''A Prospectus for Theory Construction in Marketing,'' *JM*, 48 (Winter), 11-29.

SCALE ITEMS: ENVIRONMENTAL INTERDEPENDENCE

Please indicate the degree to which your firm reacts to the following competitive acts:

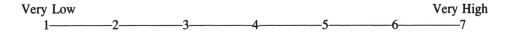

Very Low   Very High
1————2————3————4————5————6————7

1. Price reductions.
2. Sales Promotion Campaigns.
3. Advertising and publicity campaigns.
4. Changes in general marketing practices.
5. Extent of monitoring activity.

SCALE NAME: Environmental Uncertainty (Buying Group Decisions)

SCALE DESCRIPTION:

A 12-item, five-point Likert-like scale (McCabe 1987) measuring a buying group member's perceived uncertainty about decision making.

SCALE ORIGIN:

Most of the scales used to measure the construct were either adapted or derived from other research. McCabe's perceived uncertainty measures were adapted from a scale developed by Duncan (1972). As an improvement over previously developed scales, items were translated into behavioral and individual items.

SAMPLES:

McCabe used 34 organizations, 17 domestic passenger airlines and 17 domestic manufacturers of corrugated shipping containers. He used two buying tasks in each industry to reduce firm-specific differences between the high and low uncertainty buying groups. Initial contact was made either with the office of the president (airline sample) or with the office of the general manager (corrugated shipping container sample).

A total of 68 buying centers, two in each of the 34 firms, were contacted. In the airline sample, a total of **28** centers provided adequate data to be included in the final sample. In the corrugated shipping container sample, a total of **27** centers were included in the final sample. The president or the general manager was asked to identify the individual(s) involved in the initial decision, who in turn were asked to identify other personnel involved in the process. The author points to the one drawback of this method--fewer people are involved in the source selection process.

RELIABILITY:

The alpha coefficient in the McCabe study was **.74.**

VALIDITY:

No validity information was provided by McCabe.

ADMINISTRATION:

McCabe's scale uses numbers 1 through 5 to assess buying group members' experiences in decision making. A score of 1 means never or seldom (0-20% of the time), whereas a score of 5 means usually or always (81-100%). Respondents had to circle any one of the five numbers for each question, remembering to confine their answers to the source selection segment of the overall buying process. Survey interviewees were asked to report on their own perceptions and mental events about the environment.

MAJOR FINDINGS:

McCabe found a positive relationship between hierarchy and perceived task uncertainty. Higher levels of task uncertainty were associated with higher levels of centralization in the buying units. This finding negates the premise of the contingency theory, which states that increased levels of perceived task uncertainty lead to decentralization of decision-making authority. However, the results must be interpreted with caution. The amount of variation explained for hierarchy of authority is a modest 30%. The author also suggests that because only the source-selection phase of the buying process was studied, the findings may not be generalizable to other stages.

COMMENTS:

For a similar discussion of the environmental uncertainty measures, see Lysonski (1985).

REFERENCES:

Duncan, Robert B. (1972), "Characteristics of Organizational Environments and Perceived Environmental Uncertainty," *Administrative Science Quarterly*, 17 (September), 313- 327.

Lysonski S. (1985), "A Boundary Theory Investigation of the Product Manager's Role," *JM*, 49 (Winter), 26-40.

McCabe, D. L. (1987), "Buying Group Structure: Constriction at the Top," *JM*, 51 (October), 89-98.

SCALE ITEMS: ENVIRONMENTAL UNCERTAINTY (BUYING GROUP DECISIONS) +

1 = Never or seldom (0 to 20% of the time)
2 = Occasionally (21 to 40% of the time)
3 = Half the time (41 to 60% of the time)
4 = Frequently (61 to 80% of the time)
5 = Usually always (81 to 100% of the time)

1. How often are you certain about which method would be best for dealing with problems that arise in this buying group?
2. How often does your buying group have all the information it wants in making source selection decisions?
3. How often do changes in social, economic, political, or technological conditions directly affect source selection decisions made in this buying group?
4. How frequently is it difficult to determine whether a source selection you made was a good one?
5. When dealing with others in this organization, how often are you certain about how they want the source selection process carried out?
6. How often are you certain about what factors must be considered to deal with changes in social, economic, political, and technological conditions?
7. How often do you encounter new or unusual sourcing problems in this buying group?
8. How often can you tell whether the buying group's actions in dealing with social, economic, political, or technological conditions were effective?
9. How often are you in doubt about how to obtain the information needed for making sourcing decisions in this buying group?
10. How often can you tell whether you have met the expectations of those you deal with as a member of this buying group?

11. How often is it difficult to determine whether the method you used in dealing with a problem was effective?
12. How often are you certain about how to act to meet the expectations of those you deal with as a member of this buying group?

+ Respondents were asked to circle any one of five responses to each question, remembering to confine their answers to the source selection segment of the overall buying process.

SCALE NAME: Environmental Uncertainty (Complexity)

SCALE DESCRIPTION:

A three-item, seven-point Likert-type summated ratings scale measuring the degree to which a person reports that the market for a product is complex in terms of the number of customers and competitors. Klein (1989) referred to this measure as Uncertainty-Complexity and, as noted below, the persons responding to the scale were exporters.

SCALE ORIGIN:

The scale is original to Klein (1989) and his is the only known use.

SAMPLES:

A mail survey of names from a Canadian directory of exporters yielded **477** responses with some usable data. Only the **338** fully complete surveys were the basis for testing the model in the study. Evaluation of the constructs was based on all cases for which data were available.

RELIABILITY:

An alpha of **.51** was calculated for the scale by Klein (personal correspondence). As evidence of the scale's reliability, the author points out that the items composed a single factor that explained 51% of the variance.

VALIDITY:

No specific analysis of this scale's validity was reported, though the results of a factor analysis provided some evidence of the scale's convergent and discriminant validity.

ADMINISTRATION:

The scale was self-administered as part of larger mail survey questionnaire. Higher scores on the scale indicate that respondents report that the market for their product is very complex because of the great number of customers and competitors.

MAJOR FINDINGS:

The purpose of the study by Klein was to use a model based on transaction cost analysis to explain vertical control decisions. A regression analysis provided support for the model. The effects of all independent variables were significant and as hypothesized. Degree of vertical control was positively related to channel volume, transaction frequency, asset specificity, and **environmental uncertainty.** It was negatively related to the degree of market dynamism.

COMMENTS:

Caution should be exercised in using this measure until its reliability can be improved.

REFERENCE:

Klein, Saul (1989), ''A Transaction Cost Explanation of Vertical Control in International Markets,'' *JAMS*, 17 (Summer), 253-260.

SCALE ITEMS: ENVIRONMENTAL UNCERTAINTY (COMPLEXITY)

Strongly Disagree	Disagree	Slightly Disagree	Neutral	Slightly Agree	Agree	Strongly Agree
1	2	3	4	5	6	7

1. There are many final users of this product.
2. There are many competitors for this product in this market.
3. We have only a few immediate customers for this product in this market. **(r)**

SCALE NAME: Environmental Uncertainty (Dynamism)

SCALE DESCRIPTION:

A four-item, seven-point Likert-type summated ratings scale measuring the degree to which a person reports that the market for a product changes frequently in terms of channel members and/or competitors. Klein (1989) referred to this measure as Uncertainty-Dynamism and, as noted below, the persons responding to the scale were exporters.

SCALE ORIGIN:

The scale is original to Klein (1989) and his is the only known use.

SAMPLES:

A mail survey of names from a Canadian directory of exporters yielded **477** responses with some usable data. Only the **338** fully complete surveys were the basis for testing the model in the study. Evaluation of the constructs was based on all cases for which data were available.

RELIABILITY:

An alpha of **.59** was calculated for the scale by Klein (personal correspondence). As evidence of the scale's reliability, the author points out that the items composed a single factor that explained 48% of the variance.

VALIDITY:

No specific analysis of this scale's validity was reported, though the results of a factor analysis provided some evidence of the scale's convergent and discriminant validity.

ADMINISTRATION:

The scale was self-administered as part of larger mail survey questionnaire. Higher scores on the scale indicate that respondents report that the market for their product is very dynamic because of the rate of changes in customers and competitors.

MAJOR FINDINGS:

The purpose of the study by Klein was to use a model based on transaction cost analysis to explain vertical control decisions. A regression analysis provided support for the model. The effects of all independent variables were significant and as hypothesized. Degree of vertical control was positively related to channel volume, transaction frequency, asset specificity, and market complexity. It was negatively related to the degree of **environmental uncertainty.**

COMMENTS:

Caution should be exercised in using this measure until its reliability can be improved.

REFERENCE:

Klein, Saul (1989), "A Transaction Cost Explanation of Vertical Control in International Markets," *JAMS*, 17 (Summer), 253-260.

SCALE ITEMS: ENVIRONMENTAL UNCERTAINTY (DYNAMISM)

Strongly Disagree	Disagree	Slightly Disagree	Neutral	Slightly Agree	Agree	Strongly Agree
1	2	3	4	5	6	7

1. Our immediate customers change suppliers very frequently.
2. We are often surprised by the actions of retailers and wholesalers.
3. We are often surprised by the actions of our competitors.
4. We are often surprised by customer reaction.

SCALE NAME: Environmental Uncertainty (Market)

SCALE DESCRIPTION:

A three-item, five-point semantic differential summated ratings scale measuring the degree to which the market for the products sold by a company's salesforce is unstable and unpredictable.

SCALE ORIGIN:

John and Weitz (1989) give no indication that this scale originated elsewhere than in their study.

SAMPLES:

Data were collected in a two-stage sampling procedure. Personalized requests were mailed to 750 sales managers or sales vice presidents of manufacturing firms with annual sales of at least $50 million. The 266 respondents were then sent a questionnaire and **161** returned usable survey instruments. The sample appeared to be different from the population in some respects but very similar in others.

RELIABILITY:

An alpha of **.65** was reported for the scale. Item-total correlations ranged from .42 to .52.

VALIDITY:

No specific examination of scale validity was done.

ADMINISTRATION:

The scale was self-administered by respondents along with many other measures in a mail questionnaire format. Higher scores on the scale suggest that respondents believe the markets for the products sold by their respective companies' salesforces are volatile whereas lower scores indicate that they think sales can be accurately forecasted because the markets are relatively stable.

MAJOR FINDINGS:

The purpose of the study by John and Weitz was to examine the role of salary in sales compensation plans by using a transaction cost analysis framework. The degree of **environmental uncertainty** had its most significant correlations (positive) with importance of employee coordination, the transaction asset specificity between the firm and the salesforce, and particularly the complexity of the sales task.

REFERENCE:

John, George and Barton Weitz (1989), "Salesforce Compensation: An Empirical Investigation of Factors Related to Use of Salary Versus Incentive Compensation," *JMR*, 26 (February), 1-14.

SCALE ITEMS: ENVIRONMENTAL UNCERTAINTY (Market)

Describe the market for the products sold by the salesforce:

Stable industry volume	___ : ___ : ___ . ___ : ___ 1 2 3 4 5	Volatile industry volume
Sales forecasts quite accurate	___ : ___ : ___ . ___ . ___ 1 2 3 4 5	Sales forecast quite inaccurate
Unpredictable	___ : ___ : ___ : ___ : ___ 1 2 3 4 5	Predictable **(r)**

SCALE NAME: Ethical Behavior (Management's Emphasis)

SCALE DESCRIPTION:

A three-item, seven-point Likert-like scale purported to measure an employee's perception of top management's actions related to unethical activities undertaken by employees of the company. Akaah and Riordan (1989) modified the scale to a five-point format.

SCALE ORIGIN:

The scale is original to Hunt, Chonko, and Wilcox (1984).

SAMPLES:

Hunt, Chonko, and Wilcox developed the scale and used it to measure ethical problems of researchers. They used a sample of **460** individuals who identified themselves as marketing researchers from a larger sample of practitioners listed in the American Marketing Association directory. The response rate of the larger sample was 28.5%. Low response rates to ethical behavior questions are relatively common. Nevertheless, non- response bias must be of some concern for future researchers using this scale. In general, the respondents were quite homogeneous on most typical demographic comparison criteria and could be presumed to be representative of marketing researchers. Using a similar sampling design, Akaah and Riordan obtained a usable sample of **420** marketing practitioners (response rate = 30.7%).

RELIABILITY:

Hunt and his coauthors reported alpha to be **.74**; Akaah and Riordan reported alpha to be **.75**.

VALIDITY:

Both Hunt and his coauthors and Akaah and Riordan subjected items to a principal components factor analysis, demonstrating one-factor solutions for their respective versions of the scales.

ADMINISTRATION:

The scale was a self-administered paper-and-pencil measure used as a part of larger questionnaire. Time seems of little consequence.

MAJOR FINDINGS:

Hunt, Chonko, and Wilcox found actions of top management to explain 15% of the variance in perceptions of ethical problems of marketing researchers. Akaah and Riordan reported that top managers can influence the behavior of marketing professionals by actions that encourage ethical behavior and discourage unethical behavior.

REFERENCES:

Akaah, Ishmael P. and Edward A. Riordan (1989), ''Judgments of Marketing Professionals About Ethical Issues in Marketing Research: A Replication and Extension,'' *JMR*, 26 (February), 112-120.

Hunt, Shelby D., Lawrence B. Chonko, and James B. Wilcox (1984), ''Ethical Problems of Marketing Researchers,'' *JMR*, 21 (August), 309-324.

SCALE ITEMS: ETHICAL BEHAVIOR (MANAGEMENT'S EMPHASIS)

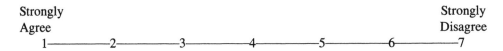

Strongly Agree
1————2————3————4————5————6————7
Strongly Disagree

1. Top management in my company has let it be known in no uncertain terms that unethical behaviors will not be tolerated.
2. If a manager in my company is discovered to have engaged in unethical behavior that results primarily in *personal gain* (rather than corporate gain) he will be promptly reprimanded.
3. If a manager in my company is discovered to have engaged in unethical behavior that results primarily in *corporate gain* (rather than personal gain) he will be promptly reprimanded.

SCALE NAME: Ethical Behavior (Research Activity)

SCALE DESCRIPTION:

A six-item, six-point Likert-like scale purporting to measure a respondent's ethical behavior in research activity by noting the degree to which he/she has engaged in various unethical activities.

SCALE ORIGIN:

The scale was originated in the work by Ferrell and Skinner (1988).

SAMPLES:

Ferrell and Skinner used a systematic sample of market researchers garnered from the membership lists of the Marketing Research Association and the American Marketing Association. **Five hundred and fifty** usable questionnaires were returned from an original mailing of 1500. Thirty-seven percent of the respondents were data subcontractors (86% female), 45% were research firm employees (46% male), and 25% worked in corporate research departments (47% male).

RELIABILITY:

Ferrell and Skinner reported an alpha of .**71**.

VALIDITY:

Measure validation was reported. First, a pool of 70 items was generated in a prestudy interview of marketing researchers in each of the three types of research organization under study. Items were judged for face validity by a panel of 11 market researchers. Only unanimously agreed upon items were retained. Confirmatory factor analysis was used to assess the construct measure. Only items loading .30 or better and significantly indicating the construct were retained for the scale.

ADMINISTRATION:

The scale was a self-administered paper-and-pencil instrument used as a part of a larger questionnaire. Time to administer seems inconsequential.

MAJOR FINDINGS:

Using this measure as the criterion variable, Ferrell and Skinner found existence of an ethical code, formalization, sex of respondent, and enforcement of the ethical code to explain significant variance in subcontractors' ethical behaviors. In the case of the research firm, significant predictors of ethical behavior were formalization, existence of an ethical code, centralization, enforcement of the ethical code, and respondent's sex. For corporate research departments, the significant predictors were existence of an ethical code, formalization, and centralization. The authors found no significant effect of acceptance of authority or controls on ethical research behavior for data subcontractors, corporate researchers, or research firm employees.

REFERENCE:

Ferrell, O. C. and Steven J. Skinner (1988), ''Ethical Behavior and Bureaucratic Structure in Marketing Research Organizations,'' *JMR*, 25 (February), 103-109.

SCALE ITEMS: ETHICAL BEHAVIOR (RESEARCH ACTIVITY)

Definitely Agree
Definitely Disagree

1————2————3————4————5————6

1. Sometimes I compromise the reliability of a study to complete the project. **(r)**
2. Sometimes I report only part of the data because I know my client may not like the results. **(r)**
3. I sometimes have to cover up nonresponse and sampling error to please my clients. **(r)**
4. I have continued a research project after knowing I made errors early. **(r)**
5. Sometimes I have to alter the sampling design in order to obtain enough respondents. **(r)**
6. Sometimes I claim to use the latest research techniques as a selling tool, even though I don't use the techniques. **(r)**

SCALE NAME: Ethical Problems

SCALE DESCRIPTION:

An eight-item, seven-point Likert-type scale that measures managers' beliefs about ethical problems of marketing researchers. Akaah and Riordan (1989) used a five-point version of the scale.

SCALE ORIGIN:

Scale was originated by Hunt, Chonko, and Wilcox (1984).

SAMPLES:

Hunt, Chonko, and Wilcox developed the scale and used it to measure ethical problems of researchers with a sample of **460** individuals who identified themselves as marketing researchers from a larger sample of practitioners listed in the American Marketing Association directory. The response rate of the larger sample was 28.5%. Low response rates to ethical behavior questions are relatively common. Nevertheless, non-response bias must be of some concern for future researchers using this scale. In general, the respondents were quite homogeneous along most typical demographic comparison criteria and could be presumed to be representative of marketing researchers. Using a similar sampling design, Akaah and Riordan obtained a usable sample of **420** marketing practitioners (response rate = 30.7%).

RELIABILITY:

Hunt and his coauthors reported alpha to be **.82**; Akaah and Riordan (1989) reported alpha to be **.87**.

VALIDITY:

Both Hunt and his coauthors and Akaah and Riordan subjected items to a principal components factor analysis, demonstrating one-factor solutions for their respective versions of the scales.

ADMINISTRATION:

The scale was used as a self-administered paper-and-pencil measure as a part of larger questionnaire. Time seems of little consequence.

MAJOR FINDINGS:

Hunt, Chonko, and Wilcox found that presidents and vice-presidents were less likely to see ethical problems than were analysts and junior analysts. Likewise, agency researchers perceived fewer problems than did in-house researchers. The authors also found actions of top management to explain 15% of the variance in perceptions of ethical problems of marketing researchers. The existence of corporate or industry codes of ethics did not significantly affect perceptions of ethical problems. Akaah and Riordan reported that marketing professionals who perceive fewer ethical problems in their organizations tended to disapprove more strongly of unethical/questionable research practices.

REFERENCES:

Akaah, Ishmael P. and Edward A. Riordan (1989), ''Judgments of Marketing Professionals About Ethical Issues in Marketing Research: A Replication and Extension,'' *JMR*, 26 (February), 112-120.

Hunt, Shelby D., Lawrence B. Chonko, and James B. Wilcox (1984), ''Ethical Problems of Marketing Researchers,'' *JMR*, 21 (August), 309-324.

SCALE ITEMS: ETHICAL PROBLEMS

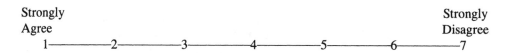

Strongly Agree 1—————2—————3—————4—————5—————6—————7 Strongly Disagree

1. Marketing managers in my company often engage in behaviors that I consider to be unethical.
2. There are many opportunities for marketing managers in my company to engage in unethical behaviors.
3. Successful marketing managers in my company are generally more ethical than unsuccessful managers. **(r)**
4. In order to succeed in my company it is often necessary to compromise one's ethics.
5. Successful managers in my company withhold information that is detrimental to their self-interests.
6. Successful managers in my company make rivals look bad in the eyes of important people in my company.
7. Successful managers in my company look for a ''scapegoat'' when they feel they may be associated with failure.
8. Successful managers in my company take credit for ideas and accomplishments of others.

SCALE NAME: Familiarity With Others (Buying Center Members)

SCALE DESCRIPTION:

A three-item, five-point Likert-like summated ratings scale measuring the degree to which the members of a buying center are perceived by a member to be familiar with each other.

SCALE ORIGIN:

The items used by Kohli (1989) for this scale were adapted from work by Hemphill and Westie (1950).

SAMPLES:

A survey instrument was mailed to 500 members of the National Association of Purchasing Management. Usable responses were received from **251** members. No response bias was evident for theoretical variables germane to the study. Respondents provided information about purchases of products in a range of $1000 to $150 million, with an average purchase value of $3.5 million.

RELIABILITY:

An alpha of .**81** was reported for this scale by Kohli.

VALIDITY:

Though some assessment of validity was made for other scales used in Kohli's study, no evaluation of this scale's validity was discussed.

ADMINISTRATION:

The scale was self-administered by respondents along with many other scales in a mail survey format. Higher scores on the scale indicate that the buying center members for a particular purchase decision are perceived to have a high level of interpersonal familiarity.

MAJOR FINDINGS:

The purpose of the study by Kohli was to examine some factors that affect a person's influence in a buying center. **Familiarity** was *not* found to be a significant moderator of the effect of any power sources on manifest influence.

COMMENTS:

Items should be modified for situations in which objects of the questions could be female.

REFERENCES:

Hemphill, John K. and Charles M. Westie (1950), ''The Measurement of Group Dimensions,'' *Journal of Psychology*, 29 (April), 325-342.

Kohli, Ajay (1989), ''Determinants of Influence in Organizational Buying: A Contingency Approach,'' *JM*, 53 (July), 50-65.

SCALE ITEMS: FAMILIARITY WITH OTHERS (BUYING CENTER MEMBERS) +

None   ____ : ____ : ____ : ____ : ____   All
        1   2   3   4   5

1. They knew each other well.
2. They had known each other for a long time.
3. They were familiar with each other's ways of working.

+ Though the directions were not provided in the article, the discussion indicated that respondents were instructed to think of a specific joint purchase decision when answering the questions.

SCALE NAME: Feedback From Others in Company

SCALE DESCRIPTION:

A three-item, summated ratings scale measuring the degree to which an employee expresses receiving feedback primarily from his/her supervisors and, to a lesser extent, co-workers about how well a job is being performed. Two of the items are evaluated on five-point scales and one has a seven-point scale.

SCALE ORIGIN:

The scale was constructed and tested by Hackman and Oldham (1974). For data collected from approximately 658 employees of seven organizations, the reliability (Spearman-Brown) was reported to be .78.

SAMPLES:

The data used by Teas (1981) were collected from **171** salespeople in group interviews during sales meetings. The salespeople represented 74% of the industrial salesforces of three midwestern companies. The typical salesperson was 36 years of age and had spent 6.5 years with his company.

Teas based his 1983 analysis on data collected from two midwestern U.S. firms' salesforces. In both cases, the salespeople were sent survey forms via intracompany mail and were asked to return the completed forms by mail to the researcher at his university address. Usable questionnaires were returned by **116** salespeople, which was described as representing a 55% response rate.

RELIABILITY:

Alpha values of **.838** (1981) and **.732** (1983) were reported for the scale by Teas.

VALIDITY:

Teas (1981) performed factor analyses of the items composing many of the scales used in his study and found them to have loadings greater than .60 on the same factor. He reported no specific examination of scale validity in 1983.

ADMINISTRATION:

In Teas' 1981 study the scale was apparently self-administered by salespeople in "group interviews" during sales meetings, whereas in Teas' 1983 study the scale was apparently self-administered at the salesperson's convenience in a more private setting, as described above. Higher scores on this scale indicate that salespeople believe their supervisors (and possibly their co-workers as well) let them know how well they are performing their jobs whereas lower scores suggest that they feel they get very little feedback.

MAJOR FINDINGS:

Teas (1981) investigated the impact of several personality characteristics and job-related perceptions on work motivation. The results indicated that though **feedback** was not a significant predictor of job expectancies or job instrumentalities in general, it was a significant negative predictor of company relationships instrumentality and a positive predictor on job status instrumentality.

Teas (1983) used causal modeling to investigate the relationship between style of sales supervision and salesperson role stress. **Feedback** was found to be a significant negative predictor of role ambiguity.

COMMENTS:

The actual items Teas used in 1983 were not specified, but were implied to be the same as those used in 1981. See another use of the scale by Teas and Horrell (1981).

REFERENCES:

Hackman, J. Richard and Greg R. Oldham (1974), *The Job Diagnostic Survey: An Instrument for the Diagnosis of Jobs and the Evaluation of Job Redesign Projects*, Technical Report #4, Department of Administrative Sciences, Yale University.

Teas, R. Kenneth (1981), ''An Empirical Test of Models of Salespersons' Job Expectancy and Instrumentality Perceptions,'' *JMR*, 18 (May), 209-226.

_____ (1983), ''Supervisory Behavior, Role Stress, and the Job Satisfaction of Industrial Salespeople,'' *JMR*, 20 (February), 84-91.

_____ and James F. Horrell (1981), ''Salespeople's Satisfaction and Performance Feedback,'' *Industrial Marketing Management*, 10 (February), 49-57.

SCALE ITEMS: FEEDBACK FROM OTHERS IN COMPANY

Respond to the first two items using the following scale:

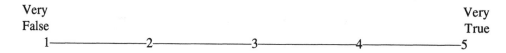

Very
False
1————————2————————3————————4————————5
Very
True

1. The supervisors of this job almost r give me any feedback about how well I am doing in my work. **(r)**
2. Supervisors often let me know how well they think I am performing the job.
3. To what extent do managers or other salesmen let you know how weli you are doing on your job? (Respond using the scale below.)

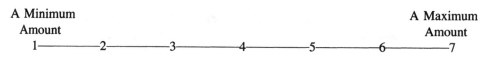

A Minimum
Amount
1————2————3————4————5————6————7
A Maximum
Amount

SCALE NAME: Feedback From Superiors

SCALE DESCRIPTION:

A six-item, five-point Likert-like scale measuring the extent to which an employee receives information from superiors about how well he/she is performing.

SCALE ORIGIN:

The scale was developed as part of the Job Characteristics Inventory by Sims, Szilagyi, and Keller (1976), though they indicate that they borrowed many items from previous work (Hackman and Lawler 1971). The inventory was tested on a sample of 192 male employees of a large manufacturing firm. The alpha for the job feedback portion of the inventory was calculated to be .83. A variety of evidence was presented attesting to the scale's convergent and discriminant validity.

SAMPLES:

The analysis by Cummings, Jackson, and Ostrom (1989) was based on data from **201** product managers in firms that had annual sales in the range of $8 million to $35 billion.

RELIABILITY:

An alpha of **.857** was reported for the scale by Cummings and his coauthors.

VALIDITY:

No examination of scale validity was reported by Cummings and his coauthors.

ADMINISTRATION:

The scale was self-administered along with many other measures in a mail survey format. Higher scores on the scale indicate that employees think they receive a great amount of feedback about their performance whereas lower scores suggest that they feel they have little knowledge of how well they are doing. Cummings and his coauthors added each respondent's score on this scale with those for three other dimensions of the JCI to obtain an overall "job scope" score.

MAJOR FINDINGS:

The purpose of the study by Cummings , Jackson, and Ostrom was to investigate several aspects of organizational behavior and their impact on the job satisfaction and performance of product managers. **Job feedback** was not examined per se, but was incorporated into the "job scope" measure. Path analysis results indicated that the only variable to have a significant effect (negative) on job scope was centralization of decision making.

COMMENTS:

After factor analysis, Sims and his coauthors eliminated one item (item 3 below) and the alpha was recalculated to be .86. As Cummings and his coauthors reported using a six-item scale and the items are not listed, they are assumed to have used the same six items that Sims and his coauthors reported as having an alpha of .83. See also a modification of this scale used by Hunt and Chonko (1984).

REFERENCES:

Cummings, W. Theodore, Donald W. Jackson, Lonnie L. Ostrom (1989), "Examining Product Managers' Job Satisfaction and Performance Using Selected Organizational Behavior Variables," *JAMS*, 17 (Spring), 147-156.

Hackman, J. R. and E. E. Lawler, III (1971), "Employee Reactions to Job Characteristics," *Journal of Applied Psychology*, Monograph 55, 259-268.

Hunt, Shelby D. and Lawrence B. Chonko (1984), "Marketing and Machiavellianism," *JM*, 48 (Summer), 30-42.

Sims, Henry P., Jr., Andrew D. Szilagyi, Robert T. Keller (1976), "The Measurement of Job Characteristics," *Academy of Management Journal*, 19 (June), 195-212.

SCALE ITEMS: FEEDBACK FROM SUPERIORS +

1. To what extent do you find out how well you are doing on the job as you are working?
2. To what extent do you receive information from your superior on your job performance?
3. To what extent are the results of your work clearly evident?
4. The feedback from my supervisor on how well I'm doing.
5. The opportunity to find out how well I am doing on my job.
6. The feeling that I know whether I am performing my job well or poorly.

+ The following scale was used for the first three items:

Very Little		A Moderate Amount		Very Much
1————	——2————	————3————	———4————	——5

The following scale was used for the last three items:

A Minimum Amount		A Moderate Amount		A Maximum Amount
1————	——2————	————3————	———4————	——5

SCALE NAME: Financial Performance (Organizational)

SCALE DESCRIPTION:

A five-item, four-point Likert-type summated ratings scale measuring the degree to which a person believes that in some future time period his/her company will have better financial performance.

SCALE ORIGIN:

The scale appears to be original to Lusch and Laczniak (1987) and theirs is the only known use of the scale in the published marketing literature reveiwed here.

SAMPLES:

All that was reported about the sample was that it was composed of the **103** *Fortune 500* vice presidents of marketing and/or planning who responded to a mail questionnaire.

RELIABILITY:

An alpha of **.90** was reported for the scale. Item-total correlations ranged from .62 to .85.

VALIDITY:

No specific examination of scale validity was reported.

ADMINISTRATION:

The scale was self-administered along with several other measures in a mail survey instrument. Higher scores on the scale suggest that respondents expect their firms to perform better financially in the future.

MAJOR FINDINGS:

The purpose of the study by Lusch and Laczniak was to investigate the relationship between adoption of the marketing and stakeholder concepts and their perceived impacts on organizational performance. The analysis provided greater support for a single-factor model that combined measures of the marketing and stakeholder orientations. Further, evidence from the surveyed executives indicated that increased competitive intensity was positively associated with adoption of the ''extended marketing concept,'' which was in turn positively associated with increased **financial performance**.

REFERENCE:

Lusch, Robert F. and Gene R. Laczniak (1987), ''The Evolving Marketing Concept, Competitive Intensity and Organizational Performance,'' *JAMS*, 15 (Fall), 1-11.

SCALE ITEMS: FINANCIAL PERFORMANCE (ORGANIZATIONAL)

Persons in the sample were asked to state their expectations of the business environment in a future period by using the following scale and items:

Strongly Disagree	Disagree	Neither Agree nor Disagree	Agree
1————————	——2————————	——3————————	——4

1. Our overall financial performance will be less than satisfactory.
2. Our firm will be operating close to its breakeven point.
3. Our return on assets will be less than satisfactory.
4. Corporate liqudity will be less than satisfactory.
5. Our return on stockholders' equity will be less than satisfactory.

SCALE NAME: Formality of Product Elimination Decision

SCALE DESCRIPTION:

A nine-item, five-point Likert-type summated ratings scale measuring the degree of formality characteristic of a company's process for evaluating a product and determining whether it should be eliminated or not.

SCALE ORIGIN:

The scale was original to the study by Avlonitis (1985).

SAMPLES:

The sample was drawn from a population of British engineering companies with more than 100 employees. Questionnaires were mailed to a random sample of the small companies (100 to 499 employees), but to all of the medium (500 to 999 employees) and large (1000+) firms. A total of 300 questionnaires were mailed to someone in top management and **94** usable responses were returned.

RELIABILITY:

An alpha of **.79** was reported for the scale. The item-total correlations ranged from .23 to .74 with a mean of .48.

VALIDITY:

A factor analysis indicated that the items rrepresented three subconstructs as expected: assignment of responsibilities, documentation, and systematic behavior.

ADMINISTRATION:

The scale was self-administered as part of a survey instrument mailed to respondents. Higher scores on the scale suggest that great formality is perceived to characterize the product elimination decision process whereas lower scores indicate that the process is perceived as being very informal.

MAJOR FINDINGS:

Avlonitis examined the role of **formality** in the product elimination process. The only variable that had a significant effect (positive) on decision **formality** was the diversity of products made and sold by a company. However, several other factors influenced at least one component of formality.

COMMENTS:

Given the results, the author suggests (p. 51) that formality might be studied better by its subconstructs than overall.

REFERENCE:

Avlonitis, George (1985), "Product Elimination Decision Making: Does Formality Matter?" *JM*, 49 (Winter), 41-52.

SCALE ITEMS: FORMALITY OF PRODUCT ELIMINATION DECISION

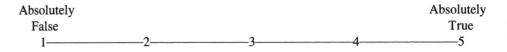

Absolutely False — Absolutely True

1————2————3————4————5

1. The performance of the products is regularly and systematically reviewed.
2. Criteria to evaluate products' performances have been explicitly established.
3. Minimum standards of performance have been explicitly established to serve as warning signals.
4. Elimination activities are initiated only when problems develop with particular products. **(r)**
5. Responsibility for product discontinuance has been clearly and definitely defined.
6. The product elimination decision is guided by a written procedure.
7. No specific responsibilities have been assigned. The elimination decision is materialized as a result of informal conversation and activities. **(r)**
8. A standard form (document) is used to reach the elimination decision.
9. A standard form (document) is used to convey the elimination decision and schedule implementation activities.

SCALE NAME: Formalization (Buying Group Structure)

SCALE DESCRIPTION:

A four-item, five-point Likert-like summated ratings scale measuring the proportion of time members of a buying group use standard procedures to make source selection decisions and handle associated problems.

SCALE ORIGIN:

The scale used by McCabe (1987) appears to have been inspired by a scale called Rules and Procedures developed by Duncan (1971). None of the items are common to both scales, however.

SAMPLES:

The data in McCabe's study came from buying centers in either the airline or corrugated shipping container industry. In the former, **15** buying centers were involved with the decision to buy aircraft and **13** were involved with the decision to buy jet fuel. In the latter, **14** buying centers were concerned with the purchase of printing inks and **13** were concerned with buying printing presses and other capital equipment. Data were collected just from individuals involved in source selection. There was an average of 1.7 people per buying unit.

RELIABILITY:

An alpha of .**55** was reported for the scale.

VALIDITY:

A factor analysis of several items all related to buying group structure indicated that the four items composing this scale all loaded on the same factor.

ADMINISTRATION:

Though interviews of some sort were conducted with buying group members, the measures in the questionnaire are assumed to have been self-administered. Higher scores on the scale indicate that respondents report members of their buying groups frequently follow standard procedures when making source selection decisions.

MAJOR FINDINGS:

McCabe examined opposing views of the relation between buying group structure and environmental uncertainty. The findings indicated that a higher degree of **formalization** was not significantly associated with product complexity or environmental uncertainty.

REFERENCES:

Duncan, Robert Bannerman (1971), "The Effects of Perceived Environmental Uncertainty on Organizational Decision Unit Structure: A Cybernetic Model," unpublished doctoral dissertation, Yale University.

McCabe, Donald L. (1987), "Buying Group Structure: Constriction at the Top," *JM*, 51 (October), 89-98.

SCALE ITEMS: FORMALIZATION (BUYING GROUP STRUCTURE)

Instructions: The following questions ask about the buying center which makes the source selection decision for printing inks in your organization. They ask what percent of the time members of this group perform various activities in the source selection process. Circle any one of the five numbers for each question. The meaning of these numbers is as follows:

1 = Never or seldom (0 to 20% of the time)
2 = Occasionally (21 to 40% of the time)
3 = Half the time (41 to 60% of the time)
4 = Frequently (61 to 80% of the time)
5 = Usually or always (81 to 100% of the time)

1. How often are source selection decisions handled adequately with existing rules and procedures?
2. How often are problems arising in this buying gup handled by following written or verbal instructions previously given to you?
3. Consider source selection problems that cannot be handled with available instructions. How often do you take care of these problems by reporting them in a standard way?
4. How often do you handle problems in this buying group by following a standard procedure?

SCALE NAME: Formalization (Channel Relationship)

SCALE DESCRIPTION:

A four-item, five-point Likert-like summated ratings scale measuring the degree to which a channel member such as a retailer reports that its relationship with suppliers is characterized by formal rules and procedures of decision making.

SCALE ORIGIN:

Dwyer and Welsh (1985) indicate that items for their scale were adapted from the work of Spekman and Stern (1979), who in turn adapted their items from Duncan (1971).

SAMPLES:

Questionnaires were mailed by Dwyer and Welsh to 7254 retailers in 10 industries whose addresses had been provided by a list broker. Envelopes were simply addressed to "Manager" in each case. After a second wave to 10% of the original sample, a total of **457** responses were used in the analysis. Because of such a low response rate, the authors provided rather detailed information about response rates and characteristics by industry.

RELIABILITY:

An alpha of **.72** was reported by Dwyer and Welsh for their four-item version of the scale, which was ultimately used in the data analysis.

VALIDITY:

Five items adapted from Spekman and Stern were originally used by Dwyer and Welsh, but one item was eliminated because of low item-total correlation.

ADMINISTRATION:

Respondents self-administered the scale along with many other measures in the study by Dwyer and Welsh. Higher scores on the scale suggest that respondents think the decision making relationship they have with their suppliers requires a lot of rules and procedures whereas lower scores indicate that they feel decisions are made informally.

MAJOR FINDINGS:

Dwyer and Welsh investigated environmental effects on channel structure and processes in a political economy framework. Among their many findings was that heterogeneous environments were significantly related to less **formalization** in the decision making procedures.

REFERENCES:

Duncan, Robert Bannerman (1971), "The Effects of Perceived Environmental Uncertainty on Organizational Decision Unit Structure: A Cybernetic Model," unpublished doctoral dissertation, Yale University.

Dwyer, F. Robert and M. Ann Welsh (1985), "Environmental Relationships of the Internal Political Economy of Marketing Channels," *JMR*, 22 (November), 397-414.

Spekman, Robert E. and Louis W. Stern (1979), "Environmental Uncertainty and Buying Group Structure: An Empirical Investigation," *JM*, (Spring), 54-64.

SCALE ITEMS: FORMALIZATION (CHANNEL RELATIONSHIP)

Think about the relationship you have with your supplier(s) of this line. There are probably a number of facets involved in marketing the line, e.g., display, mix of assortment, return, etc. Please use the scale below to describe the different aspects of decision making in that relationship.

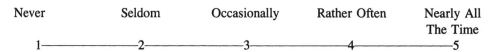

Never	Seldom	Occasionally	Rather Often	Nearly All The Time
1————	——2————	——3————	——4————	——5

Thinking about your relationship with suppliers, would you say . . .

1. you follow strict operating procedures.
2. you have high regard for existing rules and procedures.
3. you follow previously written and verbal instructions.
4. your responsibilities are clearly defined.

SCALE NAME: Formalization (Channel Relationship)

SCALE DESCRIPTION:

A four-item, five-point Likert-type summated ratings scale measuring the degree to which a retailer/dealer reports that its relationship with another channel member is characterized by formal rules and procedures of decision making. As noted below, the two studies by Dwyer and Oh (1987, 1988) had three items in common, and one extra item in each study being different.

SCALE ORIGIN:

Dwyer and Oh (1987, 1988) imply that they developed their scale on the basis of similar measures used in several other studies in marketing, one of which was by Spekman and Stern (1979), who in turn had developed a scale by adapting items used by Duncan (1971).

SAMPLES:

Dwyer and Oh (1987) gathered data from car dealers in 10 different SMSAs: five areas with high growth characteristics and five markets with low growth characteristics. Ultimately, **167** usable responses were received, which represented a 69% response rate.

Subsequently, Dwyer and Oh (1988) gathered data through mail surveys of hardware store managers. Addresses of stores were initially taken from yellow pages for 10 cities representing a variety of geographic areas in the United States. Questionnaires were eventually sent to 186 dealers, of whom **133** responded with usable data.

RELIABILITY:

Alpha values of **.75** (1987)and **.68** (1988) were reported by Dwyer and Oh for their four-item versions of the scale, which were ultimately used in their data analyses.

VALIDITY:

The scale was checked for face validity by four dealers as well as four faculty colleagues. Data from a pretest were used to check for item convergence in a restricted one-factor model. In addition, item correlations and residual analysis were used to check for convergence and consistency.

In their 1988 study, Dwyer and Oh used a LISREL chi-square three-factor measurement model to test the items for this scale along with those for two other scales (participation and centralization). The significance of the measurement model and other data indicated that items for the participation scale showed evidence of discriminant and convergent validity.

ADMINISTRATION:

Respondents self-administered the scale along with many other measures in the studies by Dwyer and Oh. Higher scores on the scale suggest that respondents think the decision-making relationship they have with a channel member requires a lot of rules and procedures whereas lower scores indicate that they feel decisions are informally made.

MAJOR FINDINGS:

Dwyer and Oh (1987) used LISREL to analyze the effects of resource availability on constraints and opportunities in the car dealer's environment. The availability and abundance of critical resources (profit opportunities, growth potential, competition) were found to have a significant negative effect on **formalization,** which in turn, and contrary to expectations, had a significant positive impact on quality of the relationship with the manufacturer.

The purpose of the second study by Dwyer and Oh (1988) was to investigate differences between three types of contractually integrated channel systems and decision-making processes within the channel, as well as their competitive strategies. Retailer cooperatives had a significantly more **formal** decision-making relationship with wholesalers than did wholesaler voluntaries.

REFERENCES:

Duncan, Robert Bannerman (1971), "The Effects of Perceived Environmental Uncertainty on Organizational Decision Unit Structure: A Cybernetic Model," unpublished doctoral dissertation, Yale University.

Dwyer, F. Robert and Sejo Oh (1987), "Output Sector Munificence Effects on the Internal Political Economy of Marketing Channels," *JMR*, 24 (November), 347-358.

_____ and _____ (1988), "A Transaction Cost Perspective on Vertical Contractual Structure and Interchannel Competitive Strategies," *JM*, 52 (April), 21-34.

Spekman, Robert E. and Louis W. Stern (1979), "Environmental Uncertainty and Buying Group Structure: An Empirical Investigation," *JM*, (Spring), 54-64.

SCALE ITEMS: FORMALIZATION (CHANNEL RELATIONSHIP) +

To various degrees, each _____ or dealer depends on the other for: 1) product or market access, 2) promotion or sales support, and 3) distribution or inventory efficiency through coordination. How do you and your _____ coordinate your relationship? Is it characterized by standard routines? Joint problem solving? Authority? Please indicate the extent to which you agree or disagree with each statement below.

Strongly Agree	Agree	Neutral	Disagree	Strongly Disagree
5	4	3	2	1

1. There are standard procedures to be followed in my dealings with _____.
2. In dealing with _____ my responsibilities are clearly defined.
3. My relationship with _____ is governed primarily by written contracts.
4. There are precise ways outlined for ordering, receiving and merchandising the vehicles and parts from _____.
5. My contacts with _____ and his representatives are on a formal, preplanned basis.

+ Items 1 through 3 were used in two studies by Dwyer and Oh (1987, 1988). Item 4 was used just in the former study and item 5 was used just in the latter study. Also, in the former study the blanks were filled with "the manufacturer" whereas in the latter study the items referred to "our primary wholesaler."

SCALE NAME: Formalization (Organizational)

SCALE DESCRIPTION:

> A six-item, six-point Likert-type summated ratings scale measuring the degree to which an employee reports that his/her business is characterized by use of formal rules and procedures.

SCALE ORIGIN:

> The scale is similar to one developed by John (1984).

SAMPLES:

> Using a systematic sample, Ferrell and Skinner (1988) mailed questionnaires to 1500 people who were listed as members of the Marketing Research Association or were categorized as researchers by the American Marketing Association. Ultimately, **550** completed forms were received. Thirty percent of the respondents were data subcontractors, 45% were employees of research firms, and the rest worked in corporate research departments. Similar proportions of men and women responded for the last two groups, whereas the first group was mostly female (86%).

RELIABILITY:

> An alpha of **.75** was reported for the scale.

VALIDITY:

> Though assessment of scale validity was not the purpose of the study, Ferrell and Skinner did perform a confirmatory factor analysis. Results of a t-test showed that all items in the scale were significant indicators. The factor loadings ranged from .44 to .74.

ADMINISTRATION:

> The scale was self-administered by respondents along with other measures in a mail survey format. Lower scores on the scale indicate that employees report rules and procedures are characteristic of their respective businesses whereas higher scores suggest that their organizations are rather informal.

MAJOR FINDINGS:

> The purpose of the study by Ferrell and Skinner was to investigate the association between organizational structure and ethical behavior in firms involved with marketing research activity. **Formalization** had a significant positive relationship with the ethical behavior reported by employees of each of the three different research-related organizations studied.

COMMENTS:

> See also the apparently similar scale used by John (1984).

REFERENCES:

Ferrell, O. C. and Steven J. Skinner (1988), "Ethical Behavior and Bureaucratic Structure in Marketing Research Organizations," *JMR*, 25 (February), 103-109.

John, George (1984), "An Empirical Investigation of Some Antecedents of Opportunism in a Marketing Channel," *JMR*, 21 (August), 278-289.

SCALE ITEMS: FORMALIZATION (ORGANIZATIONAL)

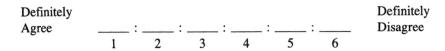

Definitely Agree _____ : _____ : _____ : _____ : _____ : _____ Definitely Disagree
        1   2   3   4   5   6

1. If a written rule does not cover some situation, we make up informal rules for doing things as we go along. **(r)**
2. There are many things in my business that are not covered by some formal procedure for doing it. **(r)**
3. Usually, my contact with my company and its representatives involves doing things "by the rule book."
4. Contacts with my company and its representatives are on a formal preplanned basis.
5. I ignore the rules and reach informal agreements to handle some situations. **(r)**
6. When rules and procedures exist in my company, they are usually written agreements.

SCALE NAME: Formalization (Organizational)

SCALE DESCRIPTION:

> A seven-item, seven-point Likert-type summated ratings scale measuring the degree to which an employee reports that his/her decisions and work behavior as well as those of coworkers are characterized by formal rules and procedures.

SCALE ORIGIN:

> The items composing the scale used by Michaels et al. (1988) were reportedly the same as those used by Aiken and Hage (1966) to measure formalization. The latter authors, in turn, appear to have taken their items from Hall (1961). Interestingly, as measured by Aiken and Hage, the formalization construct had two components that their data indicated were uncorrelated.

SAMPLES:

> The analysis by Michaels and his coauthors was based on data from two samples; **215** full-line salespeople of a building materials manufacturer and **330** members of the National Association of Purchasing Management. The average salesperson respondent was 43.9 years of age and had 12.9 years of job tenure, 15.2 years of organizational tenure, and 18.1 years of sales experience. In contrast, the typical respondent in the industrial buyer sample was 42.2 years of age and had 5.7 years of job tenure, 10.6 years of organizational tenure, and 12.5 years of purchasing experience.

RELIABILITY:

> Alpha values of **.50** and **.69** were reported for the scale for the salesperson and buyer samples, respectively.

VALIDITY:

> No specific examination of scale validity was discussed.

ADMINISTRATION:

> The scale was self-administered by respondents along with other measures as part of a larger survey instrument. Higher scores on the scale suggest that employee respondents report their work behavior is heavily influenced by rules that they are supposed to follow whereas lower scores indicate that they think they can do pretty much as they please and make up their own rules.

MAJOR FINDINGS:

> The purpose of the study by Michaels et al. (1988) was to examine the impact of **organizational formalization** on several job-related attitudes. Among the significant findings was that higher levels of **formalization** were related to lower levels of role ambiguity and role conflict for both the salesperson and buyer samples.

COMMENTS:

The low alpha for the scale may be due to a lack of unidimensionality as evidenced in the factor and correlation analyses reported by Aiken and Hage. As mentioned above, they found the formalization items used by Hall (1961) to be composed of two unrelated dimensions, which they called "job codification" (items 1 through 5 below) and "rule observation" (items 6 and 7).

REFERENCES:

Aiken, Michael and Jerald Hage (1966), "Organizational Alienation: A Comparative Analysis," *American Sociological Review*, 31 (August), 497-507.

Hall, Richard H. (1961), "An Empirical Study of Bureaucratic Dimensions and Their Relation to Other Organizational Characteristics," unpublished doctoral dissertation, Ohio State University.

Michaels, Ronald E., William L. Cron, Alan J. Dubinsky, and Eric A. Joachimsthaler (1988), "Influence of Formalization on the Organizational Commitment and Work Alienation of Salespeople and Industrial Buyers," *JMR*, 25 (November), 376-383.

SCALE ITEMS: FORMALIZATION (ORGANIZATIONAL) +

Strongly Disagree	Disagree	Slightly Disagree	Neutral	Slightly Agree	Agree	Strongly Agree
1	2	3	4	5	6	7

1. I feel that I am my own boss in most matters. **(r)**
2. A person can make his own decisions without checking with somebody else. **(r)**
3. How things are done here is left up to the person doing the work. **(r)**
4. People here are allowed to do almost as they please. **(r)**
5. Most people here make their own rules on the job. **(r)**
6. The employees are constantly being checked on for rule violations.
7. People here feel as though they are constantly being watched, to see that they obey all the rules.

+ The anchors for the graphic scale were not specified, but appear to have been similar to the ones indicated here.

SCALE NAME: Formalization (Retailer With Wholesaler)

SCALE DESCRIPTION:

A four-item, eight-point Likert-like summated ratings scale measuring the degree to which a retailer reports that its relationship with a wholesaler is characterized by formal rules and procedures of decision making.

SCALE ORIGIN:

Though not specified in the article by John and Reve (1982), it is apparent that their data came from the latter's dissertation (Reve 1980). His initial scale had six items. The final version had five items and an alpha of .693. The scale used by George and Reve had one item less than the final version reported by Reve. As the items used by the former were not reported, it is not known which item below was eliminated.

SAMPLES:

The data analyzed by John and Reve came from the dissertation research by Reve. Initially, 753 wholesalers in Norway were asked to identify their three largest retail customers. One retailer was selected at random from each of those suggested by the 238 responding wholesalers. Those retailers were contacted and 140 provided usable responses. Finally, the 140 wholesalers identified by the retailers were recontacted for further information. Data were ultimately collected from **99** retailer/wholesaler dyads.

RELIABILITY:

The alpha for the version of the scale used by John and Reve was reported to be **.75**. Items with low item-total correlations were said to have been deleted.

VALIDITY:

John and Reve eliminated items with low loadings on a factor. Further, they used the multitrait, multimethod approach as well as a structural equations model, which provided evidence of the convergent and discriminant validity of the scale.

ADMINISTRATION:

The scale was self-administered by respondents along with many other measures in a mail survey format. High scores on the scale indicate that retailers report a great amount of rules and procedures in their relationships with their wholesalers.

MAJOR FINDINGS:

The purpose of the study by John and Reve was to examine the validity of several measures of channel relationships by using information from wholesaler/retailer dyads. The authors concluded that the structural form variables, including **formalization**, generally had convergent and discriminant validity. However, the evidence indicated that the **formalization** scale did not have the level of validity exhibited by the other two structural form measures

(Interaction and Centralization). For example, the correlation between the retailers' and wholesalers' perceptions of the amount of **formalization** in their dyadic relationships was only .341 versus the .638 and .507 correlations found for Interaction and Centralization, respectively.

COMMENTS:

The scale was administered in Norwegian, so it is not known how its psychometric properties might be different if it were used in English as shown below.

REFERENCES:

John, George and Torger Reve (1982), "The Reliability and Validity of Key Informant Data From Dyadic Relationships in Marketing Channels," *JMR*, 19 (November), 517-524.

Reve, Torger (1980), "Interorganizational Relations in Distribution Channels: An Empirical Study of Norwegian Distribution Channel Dyads," unpublished doctoral dissertation, Northwestern University, Chicago, Illinois.

SCALE ITEMS: FORMALIZATION (RETAILER WITH WHOLESALER) +

Below is listed a number of statements which describe various means of coordination with the supplier level. Please indicate on the following scale to what degree each statement represents a good or poor description of the relationship between your firm and the specified supplier.

Not relevant = 0
Erroneous description = 1
Very poor description = 2
Poor description = 3
Neither poor nor good description = 4
Good description = 5
Very good description = 6
Completely correct description = 7

1. The relations between the supplier and our firm are governed by written contracts.
2. Our orders to the supplier are made periodically according to formalized routines.
3. Complaints and returns from us to the supplier are handled through standard procedures.
4. The supplier's representatives or consultants visit us according to a fixed time schedule.
5. Deliveries from the supplier are made at fixed days and times.

+ The scale reported in the article by John and Reve (1982) apparently used only four of these items. According to the information provided by Reve (1980, p. 185), items 3 and 4 had much smaller factor loadings than the rest and either would be a good candidate for elimination.

SCALE NAME: Formalization (Vertical Control)

SCALE DESCRIPTION:

A three-item, seven-point Likert-type summated ratings scale measuring the degree to which a person reports formal rules, policies, and procedures as guiding transactions between the company and the next stage in the channel. As noted below, the persons responding to the scale in the Klein (1989) study were exporters.

SCALE ORIGIN:

The scale used by Klein was adpated from a scale constructed in dissertation research by Reve (1980). Two of the three items in Klein's scale (1 and 2) were extremely similar to two that were tested by Reve (pp. 71, 182) but not ultimately used in his final version of the scale. Klein's other item (3) is assumed to be original.

SAMPLES:

A mail survey of names from a Canadian directory of exporters yielded **477** responses with some usable data. Only the **338** fully complete surveys were the basis for testing the model in the study. Evaluation of the constructs was based on all cases for which data were available.

RELIABILITY:

An alpha of **.35** was calculated for the scale by Klein (personal correspondence). As evidence of the scale's reliability, the author points out that the items composed a single factor that explained 45% of the variance.

VALIDITY:

No specific analysis of this scale's validity was reported.

ADMINISTRATION:

The scale was self-administered as part of larger mail survey questionnaire. Higher scores on the scale indicate that respondents' firms have very formal policies for handling communication and transactions with the next level of the channel for their product line.

MAJOR FINDINGS:

The purpose of the study by Klein was to use a model based on transaction cost analysis to explain vertical control decisions. regression analysis provided support for the model. The effects of all independent variables were significant and as hypothesized. Degree of **vertical control** was positively related to channel volume, transaction frequency and specificity, and complexity of the environment. It was negatively related to the rate at which changes occur in the environment.

#418 *Formalization (Vertical Control)*

COMMENTS:

Though this scale and another (Vertical Control Centralization) were separate factors in the study, a linear combination of the two was used in the analysis because of its intuitive appeal to the author. The reliability of this scale is so low that it probably should not be used until further testing and development can improve its psychometric quality.

REFERENCES:

Klein, Saul (1989), "A Transaction Cost Explanation of Vertical Control in International Markets," *JAMS*, 17 (Summer), 253-260.

Reve, Torger (1980), "Interorganizational Relations in Distribution Channels: An Empirical Study of Norwegian Distribution Channel Dyads," unpublished doctoral dissertation, Northwestern University.

SCALE ITEMS: FORMALIZATION (VERTICAL CONTROL)

Strongly Disagree	Disagree	Slightly Disagree	Neutral	Slightly Agree	Agree	Strongly Agree
1	2	3	4	5	6	7

1. Relations between ourselves and outside parties are governed by written contracts, specifying all aspects of performance.
2. Complaints and returns to us are handled through standard procedures.
3. We receive regular and thorough feedback on customer relations.

SCALE NAME: Formalization (Wholesaler With Retailer)

SCALE DESCRIPTION:

A four-item, eight-point Likert-like summated ratings scale measuring the degree to which a wholesaler reports that its relationship with a retailer is characterized by formal rules and procedures of decision making.

SCALE ORIGIN:

Though not specified in the article by John and Reve (1982), it is apparent that their data came from the latter's dissertation (Reve 1980). His initial scale had six items. The final version had five items and an alpha of .635. The scale used by George and Reve had one item less than the final version reported in Reve. As the items used by the former were not reported, it is not known which item below was eliminated.

SAMPLES:

The data analyzed by John and Reve came from the dissertation research by Reve. Initially, 753 wholesalers in Norway were asked to identify their three largest retail customers. One retailer was selected at random from each of those suggested by the 238 responding wholesalers. Those retailers were contacted and 140 provided usable responses. Finally, the 140 wholesalers identified by the retailers were recontacted for further information. Data were ultimately collected from **99** retailer/wholesaler dyads.

RELIABILITY:

The alpha for the version of the cale used by John and Reve was repod to be **.58**. Items with low item-total correlations were said to have been deleted.

VALIDITY:

John and Reve eliminated items with low loadings on a factor. Further, they used the multitrait, multimethod approach as well as a structural equations model to assess convergent and discriminant validity. These methods indicated that the convergent validity of the scale was weaker than that of the other two structural form scales with which it was tested.

ADMINISTRATION:

The scale was self-administered by respondents along with many other measures in a mail survey format. High scores on the scale indicate that wholesalers report a great amount of rules and procedures in their relationships with their retailers.

MAJOR FINDINGS:

The purpose of the study by John and Reve was to examine the validity of several measures of channel relationships by using information from wholesaler/retailer dyads. The authors concluded that the structural form variables, including **formalization**, generally had convergent and discriminant validity. However, as noted above, the evidence indicated that the formalization scale did not have the level of validity exhibited by the other two structural form measures (Interaction and Centralization). For example, the correlation between the retailers' and wholesalers' perceptions of the amount of **formalization** in their dyadic relationships was only .341 versus the .638 and .507 correlations found for Interaction and Centralization, respectively.

COMMENTS:

The scale was administered in Norwegian, so it is not known how its psychometric properties might be different if it were used in English as shown below. Further, the scale's current level of internal consistency is so low that significant modifications are necessary before it is used further, particularly in English.

REFERENCES:

John, George and Torger Reve (1982), "The Reliability and Validity of Key Informant Data From Dyadic Relationships in Marketing Channels," *JMR*, 19 (November), 517-524.

Reve, Torger (1980), "Interorganizational Relations in Distribution Channels: An Empirical Study of Norwegian Distribution Channel Dyads," unpublished doctoral dissertation, Northwestern University.

SCALE ITEMS: FORMALIZATION (WHOLESALER WITH RETAILER) +

Below is listed a number of statements which describe various means of coordination with the retailing level. Please indicate on the following scale to what degree each statement represents a good or poor description of the relationship between your firm and the specified retail customer.

Not relevant = 0
Erroneous description = 1
Very poor description = 2
Poor description = 3
Neither poor nor good description = 4
Good description = 5
Very good description = 6
Completely correct description = 7

1. The orders from the retailer are made periodically according to formalized routines.
2. Complaints and returns from the retailer to us are handled through standard procedures.
3. Our representatives or consultants visit the retailer according to a fixed time schedule.
4. There is an absence of clear standards on our part for product display at the retailer's store(s). **(r)**
5. Deliveries from us to the retailer are made at fixed days and times.

+ The scale reported in the article by John and Reve (1982) apparently used only four of these items. According to the information provided by Reve (1980, p. 182), item 4 had a much smaller factor loading than the rest and appears to be a good candidate for elimination.

SCALE NAME: Goal Acceptance

SCALE DESCRIPTION:

A six-item, seven-point Likert-type summated ratings scale measuring the degree to which the goals set for a person's work are acceptable to him/her.

SCALE ORIGIN:

The items for the scale were adapted from work by Ivancevich and McMahon (1977). Their work was based on data from 141 technicians in a company. The scale had an alpha of .84 and the results of the study indicated that goal acceptance had a very strong influence on effort toward quality, unexcused absenteeism, service complaints, and safety.

SAMPLES:

Hart, Moncrief, and Parasuraman (1989) mailed questionnaires to 149 salespeople who worked for 25 independent brokers representing a major food producer. After two followup mailings, usable responses were received from **84** sales representatives.

RELIABILITY:

An alpha of **.83** was reported for the scale by Hart and her coauthors.

VALIDITY:

No specific examination of validity was conducted.

ADMINISTRATION:

The scale was self-administered by respondents in the form of a mail survey questionnaire. Higher scores on the scale indicate that employees view their work goals as acceptable whereas lower scores suggest that they consider the goals set for them to be unacceptable.

MAJOR FINDINGS:

The purpose of the study by Hart and her coauthors was to investigate goal theory as it relates to sales contests. The results provided evidence that **goal acceptance** was very much related to work effort and performance.

REFERENCES:

Hart, Sandra Hile, William C. Moncrief, and A. Parasuraman (1989), ''An Empirical Investigation of Salespeople's Performance, Effort and Selling Method During a Sales Contest,'' *JAMS*, 17 (Winter), 29-39.

Ivancevich, John M. and J. Timothy McMahon (1977), ''A Study of Task-Goal Attributes, Higher Order Need Strength, and Performance,'' *Academy of Management Journal*, 20 (December), 552-563.

SCALE ITEMS: GOAL ACCEPTANCE

You may have organizational performance goals for the different product lines you represent. Organizational performance goals are those goals assigned to you by your supervisor or set with your input and defined by a representative of your organization. These may flow from the producer to your broker down to you or be established by the broker.

We would like your views on a set of statements that may or may not describe your feelings about your organizational goal(s). Please read each statement carefully and then circle one number from the seven alternatives which best describes your degree of agreement or disagreement with the statement. Please remember that there are no right or best answers. I would like your first impression to each of the following questions:

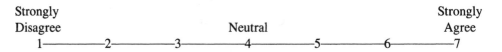

Strongly
Disagree   Neutral   Strongly
Agree

1—————2—————3—————4—————5—————6—————7

1. My performance goals set for this program are quite acceptable.
2. This program is important because it focuses on important goals.
3. I feel uncomfortable about this program. (r)
4. The quality of this program has stimulated my interest in improving my overall performance goal.
5. I would strongly recommend that this type of program be implemented for all products.
6. Each of my goals has been equitably determined through discussions with my supervisor.

SCALE NAME: Goal Clarity

SCALE DESCRIPTION:

A six-item, seven-point Likert-type summated ratings scale measuring the clarity of understanding of the work one is supposed to perform.

SCALE ORIGIN:

The items for the scale were adapted from work by Ivancevich and McMahon (1977). Their work was based on data from 141 technicians in a company. The scale had an alpha of .83 and the results of the study indicated that goal clarity had a significant influence on higher order need fulfillment.

SAMPLES:

Hart, Moncrief, and Parasuraman (1989) mailed questionnaires to 149 salespeople who worked for 25 independent brokers representing a major food producer. After two followup mailings, usable responses were received from **84** sales representatives.

RELIABILITY:

An alpha of **.90** was reported for the scale by Hart and her coauthors.

VALIDITY:

No specific examination of validity was conducted.

ADMINISTRATION:

The scale was self-administered by respondents in the form of a mail survey questionnaire. Higher scores on the scale indicate that employees view their work goals as very clear whereas lower scores suggest that their goals are confusing or ambiguous to them.

MAJOR FINDINGS:

The purpose of the study by Hart and her coauthors was to investigate goal theory as it relates to sales contests. The results *failed* to provide evidence that **clearer goals** were significantly related to either work effort or job performance.

COMMENTS:

Given the results, Hart and her coauthors questioned the validity of the scale.

REFERENCES:

Hart, Sandra Hile, William C. Moncrief, and A. Parasuraman (1989), ''An Empirical Investigation of Salespeople's Performance, Effort and Selling Method During a Sales Contest,'' *JAMS*, 17 (Winter), 29-39.

Ivancevich, John M. and J. Timothy McMahon (1977), ''A Study of Task-Goal Attributes, Higher Order Need Strength, and Performance,'' *Academy of Management Journal*, 20 (December), 552-563.

SCALE ITEMS: GOAL CLARITY

You may have organizational performance goals for the different product lines you represent. Organizational performance goals are those goals assigned to you by your supervisor or set with your input and defined by a representative of your organization. These may flow from the producer to your broker down to you or be established by the broker.

We would like your views on a set of statements that may or may not describe your feelings about your organizational goal(s). Please read each statement carefully and then circle one number from the seven alternatives which best describes your degree of agreement or disagreement with the statement. Please remember that there are no right or best answers. I would like your first impression to each of the following questions:

```
Strongly                                                          Strongly
Disagree                         Neutral                          Agree
  1————2————3————4————5————6————7
```

1. The results expected for my work are extremely clear and help me know exactly what my job is.
2. I feel uncomfortable because the results expected for my work are unclear. **(r)**
3. My performance goals are concise and are not ambiguous.
4. I have no problem understanding my goals.
5. I understand what my supervisor expects me to accomplish with the established goals of this program.
6. I understand the priorities associated with each of my performance goals.

SCALE NAME: Goal Compatibility (Retailer With Wholesaler)

SCALE DESCRIPTION:

A three-item, eight-point Likert-type summated ratings scale measuring the degree to which a retailer reports that it is able to achieve certain distribution-related goals given the actions of a specified wholesaler.

SCALE ORIGIN:

Though not specified in the article by John and Reve (1982), it is apparent that their data came from the latter's dissertation (Reve 1980). His initial scale had seven items. The final version had five items and an alpha of .709. The scale used by John and Reve had two items less than the final version reported by Reve. As the items used by the former were not reported, it is not known which items below were eliminated.

SAMPLES:

The data analyzed by John and Reve came from the dissertation research by Reve (1980). Initially, 753 wholesalers in Norway were asked to identify their three largest retail customers. One retailer was selected at random from each of those suggested by the 238 responding wholesalers. Those retailers were contacted and 140 provided usable responses. Finally, the 140 wholesalers identified by the retailers were recontacted for further information. Data were ultimately collected from **99** retailer/wholesaler dyads.

RELIABILITY:

The alpha for the version of the scale used by John and Reve was reported to be **.60**. Items with low item-total correlations were said to have been deleted.

VALIDITY:

John and Reve eliminated items with low loadings on a factor. Further, they used the multitrait, multimethod approach as well as a structural equations model to assess convergent and discriminant validity. These methods indicated poor convergent and discriminant validity.

ADMINISTRATION:

The scale was self-administered by respondents along with many other measures in a mail survey format. High scores on the scale indicate that retailers report a great amount of compatibility in their goals relating to specified wholesalers.

MAJOR FINDINGS:

The purpose of the study by John and Reve was to examine the validity of several measures of channel relationships by using information from wholesaler/retailer dyads. The authors concluded that the "sentiments" variables, including **goal compatibity**, did not show adequate convergent or discriminant validity. For example, the correlation between the retailers' and wholesalers' perceptions of the amount of **goal compatibility** in their dyadic relationships was only .169. Given this finding, the authors wondered if it was not possible that "real" differences existed between dyadic members in their perceptions of this variable.

COMMENTS:

The scale was administered in Norwegian, so it is not known how its psychometric properties might be different if it were used in English as shown below. Further, the scale's current psychometric quality is so low that significant modifications are necessary before it is used further, particularly in English.

REFERENCES:

John, George and Torger Reve (1982), "The Reliability and Validity of Key Informant Data From Dyadic Relationships Marketing Channels," *JMR*, 19 (November), 517-524.

Reve, Torger (1980), "Interorganizational Relations in Distribution Channels: An Empirical Study of Norwegian Distribution Channel Dyads," unpublished doctoral dissertation, Northwestern University.

SCALE ITEMS: GOAL COMPATIBILITY (RETAILER WITH WHOLESALER) +

Not relevant = 0
Very strongly disagree = 1
Strongly disagree = 2
Disagree = 3
Neither agree nor disagree = 4
Agree = 5
Strongly agree = 6
Very strongly agree = 7

1. The supplier often wants us to buy so many goods that our inventories become too large. **(r)**
2. The supplier is not always able to adjust rapidly to the changing market conditions that we are experiencing. **(r)**
3. The supplier and our firm share a common outlook on how to compete in our local market.
4. High economic profitability at the supplier level is often obtained at the cost of our own profitability. **(r)**
5. The supplier and our firm have different opinions when it comes to the emergence of new, alternative ways of distribution. **(r)**

+ The scale reported by John and Reve (1982) apparently used only three of these items. According to the information provided by Reve (1980, p. 186), items 3 and 5 had much smaller factor loadings than the rest and appear to be good candidates for elimination.

SCALE NAME: Goal Compatibility (Wholesaler With Retailer)

SCALE DESCRIPTION:

A three-item, eight-point Likert-type summated ratings scale measuring the degree to which a wholesaler reports that it is able to achieve certain distribution-related goals given the actions of a specified retailer.

SCALE ORIGIN:

Though not specified in the article by John and Reve (1982), it is apparent that their data came from the latter's dissertation (Reve 1980). His initial scale had seven items. The final version had four items and an alpha of .667. The scale used by John and Reve had one item less than the final version reported by Reve. As the items used by the former were not reported, it is not known which item below was eliminated.

SAMPLES:

The data analyzed by John and Reve came from the dissertation research by Reve. Initially, 753 wholesalers in Norway were asked to identify their three largest retail customers. One retailer was selected at random from each of those suggested by the 238 responding wholesalers. Those retailers were contacted and 140 provided usable responses. Finally, the 140 wholesalers identified by the retailers were recontacted for further information. Data were ultimately collected from **99** retailer/wholesaler dyads.

RELIABILITY:

The alpha for the version of the scale used by John and Reve was reported to be **.55**. Items with low item-total correlations were said to have been deleted.

VALIDITY:

John and Reve eliminated items with low loadings on a factor. Further, they used the multitrait, multimethod approach as well as a structural equations model to assess convergent and discriminant validity. These methods indicated poor convergent and discriminant validity.

ADMINISTRATION:

The scale was self-administered by respondents along with many other measures in a mail survey format. High scores on the scale indicate that wholesalers report a great amount of compatibility in their goals relating to specified retailers.

MAJOR FINDINGS:

The purpose of the study by John and Reve was to examine the validity of several measures of channel relationships by using information from wholesaler/retailer dyads. The authors concluded that the "sentiments" variables, including **goal compatibility**, did not show adequate convergent or discriminant validity. For example, the correlation between the retailers' and wholesalers' perceptions of the amount of **goal compatibility** in their dyadic relationships was only .169. Given this finding, the authors wondered if it was not possible that "real" differences existed between dyadic members in their perceptions of this variable.

COMMENTS:

The scale was administered in Norwegian, so it is not known how its psychometric properties might be different if it were used in English as shown below. Further, the scale's current psychometric quality is so low that significant modifications are necessary before it is used further, particularly in English.

REFERENCES:

John, George and Torger Reve (1982), "The Reliability and Validity of Key Informant Data From Dyadic Relationships in Marketing Channels," *JMR*, 19 (November), 517-524.

Reve, Torger (1980), "Interorganizational Relations in Distribution Channels: An Empirical Study of Norwegian Distribution Channel Dyads," unpublished doctoral dissertation, Northwestern University.

SCALE ITEMS: GOAL COMPATIBILITY (WHOLESALER WITH RETAILER) +

Not relevant = 0
Very strongly disagree = 1
Strongly disagree = 2
Disagree = 3
Neither agree nor disagree = 4
Agree = 5
Strongly agree = 6
Very strongly agree = 7

1. The retailer often wants to order goods in such small quantities that our inventories become too large. **(r)**
2. The retailer and our firm share a common outlook on how to compete in the local market.
3. Our suggestions of new practices are often met with resistance from the retailer due to his strong traditionalism. **(r)**
4. The retailer and our firm have different opinions when it comes to the emergence of new, alternative ways of distribution. **(r)**

+ The scale reported by John and Reve (1982) apparently used only three of these items. According to the information provided by Reve (1980, p. 182), item 1 had a much smaller factor loading than the rest and appears to be a good candidate for elimination.

SCALE NAME: Goal Difficulty

SCALE DESCRIPTION:

A five-item, seven-point Likert-type summated ratings scale measuring the degree of challenge perceived to be inherent in the goals set for a person's work.

SCALE ORIGIN:

The items for the scale were adapted from work by Ivancevich and McMahon (1977). Their work was based on data from 141 technicians in a company. The scale had an alpha of .80 and the results of the study indicated that challenging work (goal difficulty) had a significant influence on higher order need fulfillment.

SAMPLES:

Hart, Moncrief, and Parasuraman (1989) mailed questionnaires to 149 salespeople who worked for 25 independent brokers representing a major food producer. After two followup mailings, usable responses were received from **84** sales representatives.

RELIABILITY:

An alpha of **.67** was reported for the scale by Hart and her coauthors.

VALIDITY:

No specific examination of validity was conducted.

ADMINISTRATION:

The scale was self-administered by respondents in the form of a mail survey questionnaire. Higher scores on the scale indicate that employees view their work as challenging whereas lower scores suggest that they consider their work to not require much effort to reach established goals.

MAJOR FINDINGS:

The purpose of the study by Hart and her coauthors was to investigate goal theory as it relates to sales contests. The results provided evidence that more difficult goals increased effort expended by salespeople but did not improve performance.

REFERENCES:

Hart, Sandra Hile, William C. Moncrief, and A. Parasuraman (1989), "An Empirical Investigation of Salespeople's Performance, Effort and Selling Method During a Sales Contest," *JAMS*, 17 (Winter), 29-39.

Ivancevich, John M. and J. Timothy McMahon (1977), "A Study of Task-Goal Attributes, Higher Order Need Strength, and Performance," *Academy of Management Journal*, 20 (December), 552-563.

SCALE ITEMS: GOAL DIFFICULTY

You may have organizational performance goals for the different product lines you represent. Organizational performance goals are those goals assigned to you by your supervisor or set with your input and defined by a representative of your organization. These may flow from the producer to your broker down to you or be established by the broker.

We would like your views on a set of statements that may or may not describe your feelings about your orgizational goal(s). Please read each statt carefully and then circle one number from the seven alternatives which best describes your degree of agreement or disagreement with the statement. Please remember that there ano right or best answers. I would like your first impression to each of the following questions:

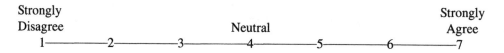

Strongly Disagree ... Neutral ... Strongly Agree
1————2————3————4————5————6————7

1. It takes a high degree of skill on my part to attain the results expected for my work.
2. It takes a lot of effort on my part to attain the results expected for my work.
3. My results expected are very difficult to achieve.
4. I must invest a significant amount of effort to accomplish my performance goals.
5. My performance goals have enabled me to become more interested in my job.

SCALE NAME: Influence (Buying Center Member Self-Perception)

SCALE DESCRIPTION:

A five-item, five-point Likert-like summated ratings scale measuring the degree to which a member of a buying center perceives *him/herself* to have influenced a particular purchase decision made by a buying center.

SCALE ORIGIN:

The measure was developed by Kohli (1989) along with other aspects of the survey instrument by reviewing previous measures and pretesting it in 14 personal interviews.

SAMPLES:

A survey instrument was mailed to 500 members of the National Association of Purchasing Management. Usable responses were received from **251** members. No response bias was evident for theoretical variables germane to the study. Respondents provided information about purchases of products in a range of $1000 to $150 million, with an average purchase value of $3.5 million.

RELIABILITY:

An alpha of **.86** was reported for this scale.

VALIDITY:

Though some assessment of validity was made for other scales used in the study by Kohli, no evaluation of this scale's validity was discussed.

ADMINISTRATION:

The scale was self-administered by respondents along with many other scales in a mail survey format. Higher scores on the scale mean that respondents report having had considerable influence on some specified purchase decisions made by their respective buying centers.

MAJOR FINDINGS:

The purpose of the study by Kohli was to examine some factors that affect a person's influence in a buying center. The findings indicated that a buying center member's perception of his/her own **influence** on a purchase decision was consistently *not* related to the manifest influence of another buying center member.

REFERENCE:

> Kohli, Ajay (1989), ''Determinants of Influence in Organizational Buying: A Contingency Approach,'' *JM*, 53 (July), 50-65.

SCALE ITEMS: INFLUENCE (BUYING CENTER MEMBER'S SELF-PERCEPTION) +

very small   _____ : _____ : _____ : ____ : _____   very large

           1   2   3   4   5

1. How much weight did the committee members give to your opinions?
2. To what extent did you influence the criteria used for making the final decision?
3. How much effect did your involvement in the purchase committee have on how the various options were rated?
4. To what extent did your participation influence the decision eventually reached?
5. To what extent did the final decision reflect your views?

+ Though the directions were not provided in the article, the discussion indicated that respondents were instructed to think of a specific joint purchase decision when answering the questions.

SCALE NAME: Influence Attempts (Buying Center Member)

SCALE DESCRIPTION:

A four-item, five-point Likert-like summated ratings scale measuring the degree to which a member of a buying center is perceived by another member to have exerted considerable effort in comparison with others in *attempting* to influence a purchase decision. The scale does not measure the degree to which others were, in fact, influenced but how much effort was exerted to influence them.

SCALE ORIGIN:

The measure was developed by Kohli (1989) along with other aspects of the survey instrument by reviewing previous measures and pretesting it in 14 personal interviews.

SAMPLES:

A survey instrument was mailed to 500 members of the National Association of Purchasing Management. Usable responses were received from **251** members. No response bias was evident for theoretical variables germane to the study. Respondents provided information about purchases of products in a range of $1000 to $150 million, with an average purchase value of $3.5 million.

RELIABILITY:

An alpha of **.90** was reported for this scale.

VALIDITY:

Though some assessment of validity was made for other scales used in the study by Kohli, no evaluation of this scale's valiy was discussed.

ADMINISTRATION:

The scale was self-administered by respondents along with many other scales in a mail survey format. Higher scores on the scale indicate that specific buying center members (other than the respondents) are perceived to have exerted considerable effort in attempting to influence some specified purchase decisions.

MAJOR FINDINGS:

The purpose of the study by Kohli was to examine some factors that affect a person's influence in a buying center. When informal legitimate and expert powers were accompanied by weak **influence attempts**, they were significantly related to the impact a member was perceived to have ultimately had on the buying center's decision (manifest influence). In contrast, reinforcement power had a significant effect on manifest influence only when **influence attempts** were perceived to have been strong, not weak.

#426 *Influence Attempts (Buying Center Member)*

COMMENTS:

Items should be modified for situations in which objects of the questions could be female.

REFERENCE:

Kohli, Ajay (1989), ''Determinants of Influence in Organizational Buying: A Contingency Approach,'' *JM*, 53 (July), 50-65.

SCALE ITEMS: INFLUENCE ATTEMPTS (BUYING CENTER MEMBER) +

Strongly Disagree	Disagree	Neutral	Agree	Strongly Agree
1	2	3	4	5

Relative to others,
1. . . . he spent time to impress his views on the committee members.
2. . . . he tried harder to shape the thinking of others.
3. . . . he spent more energy to make sure his opinions were taken into account.
4. . . . he exerted more effort to make sure the final decision reflected his views.

+ Though the directions were not provided in the article, the discussion indicated that respondents were instructed to think of a specific joint purchase decision and a specific commie member (excluding themselves) when answering the questions.

SCALE NAME: Influence on Decision-Making Unit

SCALE DESCRIPTION:

A three-item, five-point Likert-like summated ratings scale measuring the degree to which the information offered by a person to others for consideration is perceived to influence the actions of the other members of the decision-making unit.

SCALE ORIGIN:

McQuiston (1989) indicated that he used a measure by Speckman and Stern (1979), but he altered the items enough that even though the two scales may measure the same or similar constructs they are still distinctly different measures.

SAMPLES:

Survey instruments were mailed to customers of a large manufacturer of capital equipment that had purchased one of three different models of a product line within the 18 months preceding the study. A "key informant" in each company was contacted to obtain names of others in the organization who had provided input to the purchase decision. Those others were then contacted and, if willing to participate, were sent questionnaires. Of the 273 forms mailed, **182** usable returns were received from employees of 82 different companies.

RELIABILITY:

An alpha of **.892** was reported for the scale by McQuiston.

VALIDITY:

The validity of the scale was not examined in the study by McQuiston.

ADMINISTRATION:

The scale used by McQuiston was self-administered along with several other measures in a mail questionnaire. Higher scores suggest that respondents perceive another person to have great influence on others in a decision-making unit whereas lower scores imply that they believe another person has little influence.

MAJOR FINDINGS:

The purpose of the study by McQuiston was to examine some attributes of the industrial purchase situation and their influence on the purchase decision. Among other findings, degree of participation was found to have a significant positive relationship with the **influence** a person's communication has on the actions of others in the decision-making unit.

REFERENCES:

McQuiston, Daniel H. (1989), "Novelty, Complexity, and Importance as Causal Determinants of Industrial Buyer Behavior," *JM*, 53 (April), 66-79.

Spekman, Robert and Louis Stern (1979), ''Environmental Uncertainty and Buying Group Structure: An Empirical Investigation,'' *JM*, 43 (Spring), 54-64.

SCALE ITEMS: INFLUENCE ON DECISION MAKING UNIT

Little or none	Some	Quite a lot	A great deal	A very great deal
1—————	—2—————	——3—————	——4—————	——5

1. The perceived influence of the communication offered for consideration at the alternative evaluation stage.
2. The perceived influence of the communication offered for consideration at the choice stage.
3. The total amount of perceived influence of that individual during the entire process.

SCALE NAME: Influence Over Work

SCALE DESCRIPTION:

A two-item, seven-point Likert-type scale assessing the degree to which a salesperson has influence over the way work is carried out by the salesforce. Dubinsky et al. (1986) referred to this measure as Mutual Influence.

SCALE ORIGIN:

The items for the scale were slightly modified from those developed by Feldman (1976). His study was based on data from **118** hospital employees. Scale scores were not only calculated on responses to questionnaire items but also included a rating based on interviews with each subject. The Spearman-Brown reliability coefficient (corrected for attenuation) was reported as **.711**. Influence over work was positively affected by work confidence and even more affected by the similarlity between the work evaluations made by the respondent and those made by his/her superior.

SAMPLES:

Analysis by Dubinsky et al. (1986) was based on data collected from **189** salespeople. Letters were sent to a national sample of 2000 senior-level executives asking them to have their least experienced salesperson complete the questionnaire. The respondents represented 189 different companies that marketed 50 different product categories. The sample had a median age of 30.5 years, had spent 1.4 years (median) in their present positions, and were mostly male (86%).

RELIABILITY:

A LISREL estimate of reliability was **.62.**

VALIDITY:

No examination of scale validity was reported.

ADMINISTRATION:

The scale was self-administered by respondents along with many other measures in a mail survey format. Higher scores on the scale indicate that respondents have a very high sense of influence over the work carried out by the salesforce whereas lower scores suggest that they have little control over what is done.

MAJOR FINDINGS:

Dubinsky and his coauthors examined a model of salesforce assimilation. Work confidence was found to have a high positive impact on the **influence over work**.

REFERENCES:

Dubinsky, Alan J., Roy D. Howell, Thomas N. Ingram, and Danny Bellenger (1986), ''Salesforce Socialization,'' *JM*, 50 (October), 192-207.

Feldman, Daniel C. (1976), ''A Contingency Theory of Socialization,'' *Administrative Science Quarterly*, 21 (September), 433-452.

SCALE ITEMS: INFLUENCE OVER WORK

Strongly Disagree	Disagree	Slightly Disagree	Neutral	Slightly Agree	Agree	Strongly Agree
1	2	3	4	5	6	7

1. I feel I have a lot of influence in my department.
2. If I had any idea about improving the way jobs were done in this department, I doubt I could get action on it. **(r)**

SCALE NAME: Information Management Activity (Salesperson)

SCALE DESCRIPTION:

A four-item, seven-point Likert-like summated ratings scale measuring the frequency with which a person engages in communication activities between customers and management.

SCALE ORIGIN:

The scale is original to a study by Moncrief (1986). Several scales were developed for use in the study from a review of the literature and from personal interviews and focus groups with salespeople. A total of 121 selling- related activities were identified and included on the survey questionnaire.

SAMPLES:

Using stratified sampling, Moncrief sent survey forms to 800 firms representing 20 SIC codes (#20-#39). Fifty-one firms ultimately participated and sent copies of the questionnaire to their salespeople. Of the total 2322 sales employees working for these firms, 1393 returned usable forms but the factor analysis was based on responses from **1291**.

RELIABILITY:

An alpha of **.62** was reported for the scale.

VALIDITY:

Though scale validity was not specifically addressed, a factor analysis of 121 items indicated that the items below all had loadings greater than .50 on the same factor and loadings less than .40 other factors. These findings provide some evidence of the convergent and discriminant validity of the scale.

ADMINISTRATION:

The scale was self-administered by respondents along with many other measures in a mail survey format. Higher scores on the scale indicate that respondents frequently engage in activities involving the communication of information between customers and management whereas lower scores suggest that they primarily perform activities other than those directly related to information management.

MAJOR FINDINGS:

The purpose of the study by Moncrief was to develop a comprehensive list of selling-related activities and the taxonomies created from them. A cluster analysis was performed of the salespeople in the sample and six clusters were found. A group called trade servicer, representing 18% of the sample, had the highest mean on the **information management activity** scale. This cluster had the highest mean of any of the sales groups on seven of 10 sales activity areas examined in the study and it had the second highest mean on other three activity areas.

COMMENTS:

The low alpha indicates that the reliability should be improved before extensive use is made of this scale.

REFERENCE:

Moncrief, William C., III (1986), ''Selling Activity and Sales Position Taxonomies for Industrial Salesforces,'' *JMR*, 23 (August), 261-270.

SCALE ITEMS: INFORMATION MANAGEMENT ACTIVITY (SALESPERSON)+

Using the following scale, please indicate how frequently you engage in each of the activities listed below. If you do not perform the activity, please code your response as a zero.

Infrequently   ____ : ____ : ____ : ____ : ____ : ____ : ____   Frequently
              1   2   3   4   5   6   7

1. Receiving feedback from customers
2. Providing feedback to management
3. Check in with supervisor
4. Provide technical information

+ The actual directions and items were not stated in the article, but are reconstructed here on the basis of information provided.

SCALE NAME: Initiation of Structure (Leadership Style)

SCALE DESCRIPTION:

A three-item, five-point summated ratings scale that measures the degree to which a salesperson perceives that his/her supervisor structures and defines his/her role and those of subordinates in terms of job-related activities.

SCALE ORIGIN:

The scale is a subset of items used by House and Dessler (1974) in their measure of the same construct. In turn, their seven-item scale was similar to one published by Stogdill (1963).

SAMPLES:

The data used by Teas (1981) were collected from **171** salespeople in group interviews during sales meetings. The salespeople represented 74% of the industrial salesforces of three midwestern companies. The typical salesperson was 36 years of age and had spent 6.5 years with his company.

Subsequently, Teas (1983) based his analysis on data collected from two midwestern U.S. firms' salesforces. In both cases, the salespeople were sent survey forms via intracompany mail and were asked to return the completed forms by mail to the researcher at his university address. Usable questionnaires were returned by **116** salespeople, which was described as representing a 55% response rate.

RELIABILITY:

Alpha values of **.513** (1981) and **.682** (1983) were reported for the scale by Teas.

VALIDITY:

Teas (1981) performed a factor analysis on five items thought to measure the construct. Only three items were found to have loadings greater than .40 on the same factor. He reported no specific examination of scale validity in 1983.

ADMINISTRATION:

In the Teas' 1981 study the scale was apparently self-administered by salespeople in "group interviews" during sales meetings, whereas in Teas' 1983 study the scale was apparently self-administered at the salesperson's convenience in a more private setting as described above. High scores on this scale indicate that salespeople believe their respective supervisors have leadership styles that make great use of structuring and defining everyone's roles in terms of job-related activities.

MAJOR FINDINGS:

Teas (1981) investigated the impact of several personality characteristics and job-related perceptions on work motivation. Contrary to expectations, the results failed to indicate that a **supervisor's initiation of structure** was a significant predictor of performance expectations or job instrumentalities.

Teas (1983) used causal modeling to investigate the relationship between style of sales supervision and salesperson role stress. Among the findings was that a supervisor's perceived **initiation of structure** was a significant positive predictor of salesperson role conflict.

COMMENTS:

In its present form, the scale does not appear to be very reliable. Testing and development are needed before it is used further. A simple first step is to test more of the items reported by House and Dessler (1974). See another use of the scale by Teas and Horrell (1981).

REFERENCES:

House, Robert J. and Gary Dessler (1974), "The Path-Goal Theory of Leadership: Some Post-Hoc and A Priori Tests," in *Contingency Approaches to Leadership*, James G. Hunt and Lars L. Larson, eds. Carbondale, Ill.: Southern Illinois University Press.

Stogdill, Ralph M. (1963), *Manual for Leadership Behavior Description Questionnaire Form*, 12, Columbus, Ohio: Bureau of Business Research, The Ohio State University.

Teas, R. Kenneth (1981), "An Empirical Test of Models of Salespersons' Job Expectancy and Instrumentality Perceptions," *JMR*, 18 (May), 209-226.

_____ (1983), "Supervisory Behavior, Role Stress, and the Job Satisfaction of Industrial Salespeople," *JMR*, 20 (February), 84-91.

_____ and James F. Horrell (1981), "Salespeople's Satisfaction and Performance Feedback," *Industrial Marketing Management*, 10 (February), 49-57.

SCALE ITEMS: INITIATION OF STRUCTURE (LEADERSHIP STYLE)+

Very
False
1————————2————————3————————4————————5
Very
True

1. My supervisor decides what shall be done and how it shall be done.
2. My supervisor explains the way tasks should be carried out.
3. My supervisor asks that the salesmen follow standard rules and regulations.

+ The actual items Teas used in 1983 were not specified, but were implied to be the same as those used in 1981.

SCALE NAME: Initiation of Structure (Leadership Style)

SCALE DESCRIPTION:

A six-item, five-point Likert-type summated ratings scale measuring the degree to which a salesperson reports a supervisor as organizing and defining the relationship between him/ herself and the salespeople as well as what is expected of each person. Teas (1980) referred to this measure in parts of his article as Closeness of Supervision.

SCALE ORIGIN:

The items used by Teas were adapted for the sales situation from items developed by Hemphill and others as reported in a series of studies by Stogdill and Coons (1957). The version used by Teas appears to be most similar to one reported in an article by Halpin and Winer (1957, p. 48), where the six items used by Teas are among 15 reported. The six load reasonably well on the same factor; however, several more load just as well or higher so it is not clear why these particular six were chosen. On the basis of a study of 300 air force crew members, the reliability of the 15-item scale was .86 (Spearman-Brown). Halpin and Winer found that initiation of structure was positively related to perceptions of leadership effectiveness.

SAMPLES:

Intracompany mail distribution was used by Teas to reach 184 salesmen of a midwestern company's industrial salesforce. Analysis was based on responses from **127** salespeople.

RELIABILITY:

An alpha of **.694** was reported for the scale by Teas.

VALIDITY:

No specific examination of scale validity was reported by Teas.

ADMINISTRATION:

The scale was self-administered in the Teas study along with several other measures. Higher scores on the scale indicate that salespeople report their respective supervisors as being highly involved in structuring and monitoring the salesforce whereas lower scores mean that they perceive their supervisors as providing only loose definition of roles and supervision.

MAJOR FINDINGS:

Teas used path analysis to examine simultaneously some causes and results of salesperson perceptions of role ambiguity. **Initiation of structure** was found to have a positive direct effect on extrinsic job satisfaction but only a positive indirect effect on intrinsic job satisfaction.

REFERENCES:

Halpin, Andrew W. and B. James Winer (1957), "A Factorial Study of the Leadership Behavior Descriptions," in *Leader Behavior: Its Description and Measurement,* Ralph M. Stogdill and Alvin E. Coons, eds. Columbus, Ohio: The Bureau of Business Research, The Ohio State University.

Stogdill, Ralph M. and Alvin E. Coons, eds. (1957), *Leader Behavior: Its Description and Measurement.* Columbus, Ohio: The Bureau of Business Research, The Ohio State University.

Teas, R. Kenneth (1980), "An Empirical Test of Linkages Proposed in the Walker, Churchill, and Ford Model of Salesforce Motivation and Performance," *JAMS,* 8 (Winter), 58-72.

SCALE ITEMS: INITIATION OF STRUCTURE (LEADERSHIP STYLE)

Strongly Disagree	Disagree	Neither	Agree	Strongly Agree
1—————	——2—————	——3—————	——4—————	——5

1. My supervisor expresses his attitudes, opinions and/or ideas to the group.
2. My supervisor rules with an iron hand.
3. My supervisor emphasizes the use of uniform procedure.
4. My supervisor criticizes poor work or ideas.
5. My supervisor makes certain his job (as sales supervisor) is clearly understood by the sales personnel.
6. My supervisor lets individual salesmen know what is expected of them.

SCALE NAME: Initiation of Structure (Leadership Style)

SCALE DESCRIPTION:

A 10-item, five-point Likert-like summated ratings scale measuring the degree to which a salesperson reports a supervisor as organizing and defining the relationship between him/herself and the salespeople as well as what is expected of each person.

SCALE ORIGIN:

The items are slightly modified versions of part of the LBDQ-XII (Stogdill 1963) that is purported to measure initiation of structure by a supervisor.

SAMPLES:

The sample used by Hampton, Dubinsky, and Skinner (1986) was based on **116** usable responses from a census of 121 retail salespeople who worked in one of five outlets of a department store chain. The sample had a median age of 23.2 years, had spent 1.4 years (median) in their present positions and 1.1 years (median) with their current supervisors, were mostly female (78%), and 66% had some college education.

RELIABILITY:

An alpha of **.85** was reported.

VALIDITY:

No examination of scale validity was reported.

ADMINISTRATION:

Hampton and his coauthors distributed the survey instrument to respondents in a conference room in each store, where they were self-administered. Higher scores on the scale indicate that salespeople report their respective supervisors as being highly involved in structuring and monitoring their salesforces whereas lower scores mean that they perceive their supervisors as providing only loose definition of roles and supervision.

MAJOR FINDINGS:

A causal model of retail sales supervisor leadership behavior was studied by Hampton and his coauthors. **Initiation of structure** by a supervisor was found to have an inverse effect on job performance and role ambiguity. This apparently means that a sales manager may be able to reduce role ambiguity for salespeople by more **explicitly defining what is expected**. However, too much **initiation of structure** appears to reduce job performance.

REFERENCES:

Hampton, Ron, Alan J. Dubinsky, and Steven J. Skinner (1986), ''A Model of Sales Supervisor Leadership Behavior and Retail Salespeople's Job-Related Outcomes,'' *JAMS*, 14 (Fall), 33-43.

Stogdill, Ralph M. (1963), *Manual for Leadership Behavior Description Questionnaire Form*, 12, Columbus, Ohio: Bureau of Business Research, The Ohio State University.

SCALE ITEMS: INITIATION OF STRUCTURE (LEADERSHIP STYLE)

Always	Often	Occasionally	Seldom	Never
5	4	3	2	1

My immediate supervisor:
1. Lets department salespeople know what is expected of them.
2. Encourages the use of uniform procedures.
3. Tries out his/her ideas in the department.
4. Makes his/her attitudes clear to department salespeople.
5. Decides what shall be done and how it will be done.
6. Assigns department salespeople to particular tasks.
7. Makes sure that his/her part in the department is understood by department salespeople.
8. Schedules the work to be done.
9. Maintains definite standards of performance.
10. Asks that department salespeople follow standard rules and regulations.

SCALE NAME: Interaction (Retailer With Wholesaler)

SCALE DESCRIPTION:

A six-item, eight-point Likert-like summated ratings scale measuring the degree to which a retailer reports that its relationship with a wholesaler is characterized by cooperation, support, and joint programs.

SCALE ORIGIN:

Though not specified in the article by John and Reve (1982), it is apparent that their data came from the latter's dissertation (Reve 1980). His initial scale had 12 items. The final version had eight items and an alpha of .854. The scale used by John and Reve had two items less than the final version reported by Reve. As the items used by the former were not reported, it is not known which items below were eliminated.

SAMPLES:

The data analyzed by John and Reve came from the dissertation research by Reve. Initially, 753 wholesalers in Norway were asked to identify their three largest retail customers. One retailer was selected at random from each of those suggested by the 238 responding wholesalers. Those retailers were contacted and 140 provided usable responses. Finally, the 140 wholesalers identified by the retailers were recontacted for further information. Data were ultimately collected from **99** retailer/wholesaler dyads.

RELIABILITY:

The alpha for the version of the scale used by John and Reve was reported to be **.86**. Items with low item-total correlations were said to have been deleted.

VALIDITY:

John and Reve eliminated items with low loadings on a factor. Further, they used the multitrait, multimethod approach as well as a structural equations model, which provided evidence of the convergent and discriminant validity of the scale.

ADMINISTRATION:

The scale was self-administered by respondents along with many other measures in a mail survey format. High scores on the scale indicate that retailers report a great amount of coordination and cooperation in their relationships with their wholesalers.

MAJOR FINDINGS:

The purpose of the study by John and Reve was to examine the validity of several measures of channel relationships by using information from wholesaler/retailer dyads. The authors concluded that the structural form variables, including **interaction**, generally had convergent and discriminant validity. Further, the correlation between the retailers' and wholesalers' perceptions of the amount of **interaction** in their dyadic relationships was .638.

COMMENTS:

The scale was administered in Norwegian, so it is not known how its psychometric properties might be different if it were used in English as shown below.

REFERENCES:

John, George and Torger Reve (1982), "The Reliability and Validity of Key Informant Data From Dyadic Relationships in Marketing Channels," *JMR*, 19 (November), 517-524.

Reve, Torger (1980), "Interorganizational Relations in Distribution Channels: An Empirical Study of Norwegian Distribution Channel Dyads," unpublished doctoral dissertation, Northwestern University.

SCALE ITEMS: INTERACTION (RETAILER WITH WHOLESALER) +

Listed below are a number of different means of coordination between supplier and retailer or dealer. Please indicate to what extent the different means of coordination are currently being used in the relationship between your firm and the specified supplier. Responses can be indicated by use the the following scale.

Not at all = 0
To an extremely low extent = 1
To a very low extent = 2
To a low extent = 3
To a moderate extent = 4
To a high extent = 5
To a very high extent = 6
To an extremely high extent = 7

1. The supplier has established a cooperative advertising program with our firm.
2. The supplier assists us in putting together the appropriate product mixes.
3. The supplier offers us consulting services for store planning, modernizations, and extensions.
4. The supplier offers us various forms of training and courses.
5. The supplier offers us a complete marketing plan for his products.
6. The supplier offers us special trade discounts or bonuses in order to get us to concentrate on his lines of goods.
7. The supplier assists us in direct mail or catalog campaigns directed to our customers.
8. There are close and continuous personal contacts between our firm and the supplier.

+ The scale reported by John and Reve (1982) apparently used only six of these items. According to the information provided by Reve (1980, p. 184), item 6 had a much smaller factor loading than the rest and appears to be a good candidate for elimination. Item 3 had the next smallest loading.

SCALE NAME: Interaction (Wholesaler With Retailer)

SCALE DESCRIPTION:

A six-item, eight-point Likert-like summated ratings scale measuring the degree to which a wholesaler reports that its relationship with a retailer is characterized by cooperation, support, and joint programs.

SCALE ORIGIN:

Though not specified in the article by John and Reve (1982), it is apparent that their data came from the latter's dissertation (Reve 1980). His initial scale had 12 items. The final version had seven items and an alpha of .877. The scale used by John and Reve had one item less than the final version reported by Reve. As the items used by the former were not reported, it is not known which item below was eliminated.

SAMPLES:

The data analyzed by John and Reve came from the dissertation research by Reve. Initially, 753 wholesalers in Norway were asked to identify their three largest retail customers. One retailer was selected at random from each of those suggested by the 238 responding wholesalers. Those retailers were contacted and 140 provided usable responses. Finally, the 140 wholesalers identified by the retailers were recontacted for further information. Data were ultimately collected from **99** retailer/wholesaler dyads.

RELIABILITY:

The alpha for the version of the scale used by John and Reve was reported to be **.85**. Items with low item-total correlations were said to have been deleted.

VALIDITY:

John and Reve eliminated items with low loadings on a factor. Further, they used the multitrait, multimethod approach as well as a structural equations model, which provided evidence of the convergent and discriminant validity of the scale.

ADMINISTRATION:

The scale was self-administered by respondents along with many other measures in a mail survey format. High scores on the scale indicate that wholesalers report a great amount of coordination and cooperation in their relationships with their retailer.

MAJOR FINDINGS:

The purpose of the study by John and Reve was to examine the validity of several measures of channel relationships by using information from wholesaler/retailer dyads. The authors concluded that the structural form variables, including **interaction**, generally had convergent and discriminant validity. Further, the correlation between the retailers' and wholesalers' perceptions of the amount of **interaction** in their dyadic relationships was .638.

COMMENTS:

The scale was administered in Norwegian, so it is not known how its psychometric properties might be different if it were used in English as shown below.

REFERENCES:

John, George and Torger Reve (1982), "The Reliability and Validity of Key Informant Data From Dyadic Relationships in Marketing Channels," *JMR*, 19 (November), 517-524.

Reve, Torger (1980), "Interorganizational Relations in Distribution Channels: An Empirical Study of Norwegian Distribution Channel Dyads," unpublished doctoral dissertation, Northwestern University.

SCALE ITEMS: INTERACTION (WHOLESALER WITH RETAILER) +

Listed below are a number of different means of coordination between supplier and retailer or dealer. Please indicate to what extent the different means of coordination are currently being used in the relationship between your firm and the specified retail customer. Responses can be indicated by using the following scale.

Not at all = 0
To an extremely low extent = 1
To a very low extent = 2
To a low extent = 3
To a moderate extent = 4
To a high extent = 5
To a very high extent = 6
To an extremely high extent = 7

1. We have established a cooperative advertising program with the retailer.
2. We assist the retailer in putting together the appropriate product mixes.
3. We offer the retailer consulting services for store planning, modernizations, and extensions.
4. We offer the retailer various forms of training and courses.
5. We offer the retailer guidelines for store decoration and product display.
6. We offer the retailer a complete marketing plan for his products.
7. There are close and continuous personal contacts between our firm and the retailer.

+ The scale reported by John and Reve (1982) apparently used only six of these items. According to the information provided by Reve (1980, p. 181), item 7 had a much smaller factor loading than the rest and appears to be a good candidate for elimination.

SCALE NAME: Interaction Orientation of Customer (Salesperson's Perception)

SCALE DESCRIPTION:

A seven-item, five-point Likert-type summated ratings scale measuring the degree to which a salesperson perceives a customer to have been friendly and personable. Williams and Spiro (1985) viewed this scale as measuring the interaction-oriented dimension of customer communication style, which stresses enjoyment and maintenance of personal relationships to the possible extent of ignoring tthe task at hand.

SCALE ORIGIN:

The items used by Williams and Spiro were developed from work performed by Bass (1960) on orientation motivation. On the basis of previous work by others, Bass suggested that members of groups are motivated to remain in the groups for different reasons. He developed measures of three motivations: the task orientation, the interaction orientation, and the self orientation (Bass 1977). Williams and Spiro adapted these measures for their studies in two ways: their measures were more specific to the sales context and were perceptions of others' behaviors, not self-perceptions.

SAMPLES:

Williams and Spiro collected data from all 13 sporting goods stores in a major southeastern U.S. city. Customers were approached just after leaving the stores. If they agreed to fill out a questionnaire, their respective salespeople were asked to fill out a survey instrument as well. A total of **251** dyadic interactions were captured, with the responses coming from 64 different salespeople and 251 different customers. All salespeople in the stores participated as did 90% of the customers who were approached.

RELIABILITY:

An alpha of **.89** was reported for the scale and item-total correlations were all above .55.

VALIDITY:

A factor analysis indicated that the items loaded higher on the interaction-orientation factor than any other.

ADMINISTRATION:

As implied above, the customer completed a self-administered survey form that included several measures. The authors computed scale scores by averaging numerical responses to the items. Higher scores on the scale suggest that salespersons perceive that the customers with whom they have just interacted were very friendly and personable whereas lower scores imply that they feel their respective customers were not easy to talk to or interested in the salesperson personally.

MAJOR FINDINGS:

Williams and Spiro examined the use of communication styles in dyadic sales situations and their effect on sales outcomes. The findings indicated that though the communication styles of the two parties of the transaction play a role in the outcome, the customer's orientation has the greatest impact. **Customer's interaction orientation** appeared to have a significant positive impact on sales.

REERENCES:

Bass, Bernard M. (1960), *Leadership, Psychology, and Organizational Behavior*. New York, N.Y.: Harper Brothers

_____ (1977), *ORI-Manual for the Orientation Inventory*. Palo Alto, Calif.: Consulting Psychologists Press, Inc.

Williams, Kaylene C. and Rosann L. Spiro (1985), ''Communication Style in the Salesperson-Customer Dyad,'' *JMR*, 12 (November), 434-442.

SCALE ITEMS: INTERACTION ORIENTATION OF CUSTOMER (SALESPERSON'S PERCEPTION)

Strongly Disagree	Disagree	Neutral	Agree	Strongly Agree
1	2	3	4	5

1. This customer was easy to talk with.
2. This customer genuinely enjoyed my helping him.
3. This customer likes to talk to people.
4. This customer was interested in socializing.
5. This customer was friendly.
6. This customer tried to establish a personal relationship.
7. This customer seemed interested in me not only as an salesperson, but also as a person.

SCALE NAME: Involvement (Job)

SCALE DESCRIPTION:

A seven-point Likert-type scale assessing the degree to which an employee is involved in and committed to the work he/she does. The short form developed by Lodahl and Kejner (1965) had six items, the version used by Dubinsky et al. (1986) had five items, and the version used by Dubinsky and Hartley (1986) had four items.

SCALE ORIGIN:

The scales used by Dubinsky and his coauthors were apparently based on the short version of the job involvement scale developed by Lodahl and Kejner, who began with 110 statements and used the results of a factor analysis, item-total correlations, and other procedures to reduce the list to a 20-item scale. The reliability (Spearman-Brown) of the scale for three different samples ranged from .72 (nurses) to .89 (graduate students). A six-item version had a reliability (Spearman-Brown) of .73 and a correlation of .87 with the longer version (sample unspecified). No examination of the short form's validity was reported, but some evidence of the convergent validity of the longer version came from the scale's significant correlations with several job-satisfaction-related measures.

SAMPLES:

Analysis by Dubinsky et al. (1986) was based on data collected from **189** salespeople. Letters were sent to a national sample of 2000 senior-level executives asking them to have their least experienced salesperson complete the questionnaire. The respondents represented 189 different companies that marketed 50 different product categories. The sample had a median age of 30.5 years, had spent 1.4 years (median) in their present positions, and were mostly male (86%).

Dubinsky and Hartley (1986) based their analysis on completed questionnaires returned by **120** respondents. Questionnaires were sent to 467 agents who sold lines of a large multi-insurance company. No nonresponse bias was apparent. The sample had a mean age of 39.1 years, had spent 6.6 years (mean) in their present positions, were mostly male (91%), and over half were college graduates (56%).

RELIABILITY:

A LISREL estimate of reliability was **.76** (Dubinsky et al. 1986) and an alpha of **.82** was reported (Dubinsky and Hartley 1986).

VALIDITY:

No examination of scale validity was reported.

ADMINISTRATION:

The scale was self-administered by respondents in both studies along with many other measures in a mail survey format. Respondents with higher scores on the scale have a high level of involvement with the work they perform in their jobs whereas those with lower scores are not very committed to their jobs.

MAJOR FINDINGS:

Dubinsky et al. (1986) examined a model of salesforce assimilation. The results indicated that the only significant direct effect on **job involvement** was from job suitability.

The purpose of the study by Dubinsky and Hartley (1986) was to investigate several predictors of salesperson performance and the relationships among those predictors. A path analysis indicated that job involvement had a significant positive effect on ''work motivation'' (a salesperson's concern about the quality of work performed).

COMMENTS:

See also the use of a four-item version of this scale by Cron and Slocum (1986).

REFERENCES:

Cron, William L. and John W. Slocum, Jr. (1986), ''The Influence of Career Stages on Salespeople's Job Attitudes, Work Perceptions, and Performance,'' *JMR*, 23 (May), 119-129.

Dubinsky, Alan J. and Steven W. Hartley (1986), ''A Path-Analytic Study of a Model of Salesperson Performance,'' *JAMS*, 14 (Spring), 36-46.

_____, Roy D. Howell, Thomas N. Ingram, and Danny Bellenger (1986), ''Salesforce Socialization,'' *JM*, 50 (October), 192-207.

Lodahl, Thomas M. and Mathilde Kejner (1965), ''The Definition and Measurement of Involvement,'' *Journal of Applied Psychology*, 49 (1), 24-33.

SCALE ITEMS: INVOLVEMENT (JOB) +

Strongly Disagree	Disagree	Slightly Disagree	Neutral	Slightly Agree	Agree	Strongly Agree
1	2	3	4	5	6	7

1. The major satisfaction in my life comes from my job.
2. The most important things that happen to me involve my work on this job.
3. I'm really a perfectionist about my work.
4. I live, eat, and breathe my job.
5. I am very much personally involved in my work.
6. Most things in life are more important than work. (r)
7. My work on this job is *not* a very central part of my life. (r)
8. Work is *not* very central to the lives of most people in this job in my company. (r)
9. Most people on this job are very personally involved in their work.

+ Items 1 through 6 were those composing the short form of the scale developed by Lodahl and Kejner (1965). Dubinsky et al. (1986) used items 2 and 4, and apparently developed 7 through 9 for their study. Dubinsky and Hartley (1986) used items 1, 2, 4, and 5.

SCALE NAME: Job Challenge (Salesperson)

SCALE DESCRIPTION:

A seven-item, five-point Likert-type summated ratings scale measuring the degree to which a salesperson reports his/her work as being appropriate, challenging, and utilizing his/her skills. Four of the seven items (unspecified) were used by Cron and Slocum (1986).

SCALE ORIGIN:

The scale was developed by Hall and Lawler (1970). Though they used the scale as a summated measure, no psychometric information was reported. Studying professionals employed by research and development firms, they found that being required to work on a wide range of projects having independent budget accounts was associated with low job challenge.

SAMPLES:

The sample used by Cron and Slocum was based on responses from **466** salespeople who worked for one of six manufacturers of industrial equipment and supplies. The salespeople in the companies were similar in that they had entry level positions, were located in the field, were supervised by a field sales manager, and sold multiple product lines. The average respondent was 39 years of age and had job tenure of 8.7 years. Just half had attended college, 72% were married, and 96% were male.

To be included in the study, questionnaires had to be completed not only by salespeople, but also by their respective field managers and CEOs. For three of the companies, survey instruments were filled out at the national meetings. A mail survey was used for salespeople of the other three companies.

RELIABILITY:

An alpha of .**75** was reported for the scale by Cron and Slocum.

VALIDITY:

No specific examination of scale validity was reported.

ADMINISTRATION:

The scale was self-administered in two different settings as noted above. For salespeople filling out the questionnaire at meetings, the scale was completed along with the other parts of the survey instrument at the same time and with one of the researchers present. Salespeople for the other three companies received and returned questionnaires by the mail. Higher scores on the scale indicate that salespeople consider their work to be fulfilling and to offer very good opportunities whereas lower scores suggest that they think their jobs do not challenge them.

MAJOR FINDINGS:

The purpose of the study by Cron and Slocum was to examine salespeople in four career stages: exploration, establishment, maintenance, and disengagement. Among the findings was that older salespeople were more **challenged** by their jobs than younger salespeople and that those in the exploration stage did not feel their jobs were as **challenging** as those in later stages. Further, **job challenge** was found to have a significant negative relationship with job performance for persons in the establishment and maintenance stages.

REERENCES:

Cron, William L. and John W. Slocum, Jr. (1986), "The Influence of Career Stages on Salespeople's Job Attitudes, Work Perceptions, and Performance," *JMR*, 23 (May), 119-129.

Hall, Douglas T. and Edward E. Lawler (1970), "Job Characteristics and Pressures and the Organizational Integration of Professionals," *Administrative Science Quarterly*, 15 (September), 271-281.

SCALE ITEMS: JOB CHALLENGE (SALESPERSON) +

Strongly Disagree	Disagree	Neutral	Agree	Strongly Agree
1————	——2————	——3————	——4————	——5

1. I have challenging work.
2. There is a great deal of incentive for me in my job to try and do better.
3. In light of my training, education, and preparation, my job is very appropriate for my abilities.
4. My job allows me to be creative and use my own ideas if I wish.
5. My job gives me a chance most of the time to do the things I feel that I do best.
6. I have little control and final say about what I do on my job. **(r)**
7. My job gives me the opportunity to learn new skills and techniques.

+ Cron and Slocum (1986) did not specify their four items, but did indicate that the items came from this list of seven by Hall and Lawler (1970).

SCALE NAME: Job Description Index (JDI)

SCALE DESCRIPTION:

A five-subscale, composite measure purporting to evaluate job satisfaction. The five areas are type of work (18 items), opportunities for promotion (9 items), supervision (18 items), pay (9 items), and coworkers (18 items). Each job area measure consists of a list of adjectives or phrases. A summated ratings scale is used, ranging from Y (yes) to N (no) with ? (cannot decide) between for each job area. Teas (1983) modified the scale somewhat as discussed below.

SCALE ORIGIN:

The JDI scales for job satisfaction were originally developed by Smith, Kendall, and Hulin (1969). The research for these scales began in 1959 and a number of studies were done across a wide array of jobs and people. The scales were developed to measure satisfaction on the job within both an "evaluative-general-long-term framework" and a "descriptive-specific-short-term framework," and "to cover the important areas of satisfaction." This wide array of data was used to provide a generally applicable series of measurements of satisfaction (JDI).

SAMPLES:

Busch (1980) obtained data from mail questionnaires sent to the salesforces of three pharmaceutical companies. The analysis was based on **477** usable questionnaires representing an overall response rate of 53.8%. The response rates of the individual companies were 51.5%, 52.5%, and 57.6%. Of the 477 usable questionnaires, 39 were from women and 436 were from men.

Teas (1983) collected data by mail questionnaires sent to two Midwest corporations' salesforces. Included with each questionnaire were cover letters from the researcher and the vice president of sales promising confidentiality and indicating company support for the survey. Usable responses were obtained from **116** salespersons, 49 and 67 salespersons for the two companies, respectively (overall response rate 55%).

Cron and Slocum (1986) obtained data from six companies with national salesforces. A total of **466** usable questionnaires were returned for a response rate of 54.5%. Seventy-two percent of the salespersons were married, 96% were male, and 51% had attended college. Income ranged from $25,000 to $50,000. The average salesperson in the sample was 39 years of age with a tenure of 8.7 years.

Apasu (17) collected data from a U.S.-based mulitnational firm's salesforce. **One hundred fifty-six** usable questionnaires were used for the analysis (the response rate was 60%). The average income of the sample was $30,000, the average sales experience was 7.5 years, and 97% of the respondents were younger than 40 years of age.

RELIABILITY:

Busch reported a Spearman-Brown reliability coefficient of **.87** for the satisfaction with supervision measure of the JDI. Teas reported an alpha reliability coefficient of **.921** for the modified version of the JDI. (See the Scale Items section for a description of his modifications).

Cron and Slocum reported alpha reliability coefficients for each of the JDI measures of job satisfaction: **.76** work, **.84** pay, **.71** opportunities for promotion, **.86** supervision, and **.84** coworkers. Apasu reported a Cronbach alpha of **.81** for the satisfaction with pay measure of the JDI.

VALIDITY:

A literature review conducted by Smith, Kendall, and Hulin supported the multidimensional notion of job satisfaction. This literature review provided the basis for the original construct of the JDI and its five areas: work, pay, promotions, supervision, and coworkers. An item analysis was conducted that included item intercorrelations and item validity. All items within each area were intercorrelated (median item intercorrelations exceeded .24).

Four individual studies were conducted to evaluate the validity of the JDI with very different samples (Cornell undergraduates, employees of a farmers' cooperative, male employees at two plants of a large electronics manufacturer, and male employees of a bank). Validity was assessed for different forms of the JDI (graphic, interview) and for different scorings (triadic, dyadic, direct). The analysis demonstrated that discriminate scores were "obtained from measures directed toward several aspects of the job (discriminate validity for measures and areas), and that several methods of measurement applied to the same aspect show substantial agreement (convergent validity for measures)" (Smith, Kendall, and Hulin 1969, p. 58). These analyses resulted in the final version of **the JDI, which has demonstrated discriminant and convergent validity**. Additionally, the JDI scales have been shown to be predictive in some situations. No other examination of scale validity was reported or available.

ADMINISTRATION:

Busch, Teas, and Apasu collected data by mail and the scale was self-administered along with several other measures included in the questionnaire. Cron and Slocrum collected data by two methods. Questionnaires were administered to salespersons during their national sales meeting for three of the companies used in their sample. For the other three companies, the sample were sent questionnaires by mail thay were subsequently self-administered. The questionnaires used contained the JDI scales along with several other measures.

The scoring of the JDI scale follows:

Response	*Weight*
Yes to a positive item	3
No to a negative item	3
? to any item	1
Yes to a negative item	0
No to a positive item	0

A high score represents a high level of perceived job satisfaction (e.g., a maximum score of 54 for job satisfaction with work indicates high perceived job satisfaction for that area). An overall composite score can be used for overall job satisfaction by summating the five areas' summated scores.

MAJOR FINDINGS:

Busch used only the satisfaction with supervision portion of the JDI. The results indicated that expert ($p \leq .001$) and referent ($p \leq .001$) power were significantly related to satisfaction with supervision for all three firms. Coercive power (p ≤ .01) was significantly related to satisfaction with supervision for two of the three firms. Legitimate and reward power (p ≤ .05) were significantly related to satisfaction with supervision for only one of the three firms. No significant differences due to the power bases were found between men's and women's job satisfaction.

Teas used a modified version of the JDI (see Scale Items section for details). The results indicated that a salesperson's perceivied role conflict (p ≤ .001), consideration (p ≤ .001), participation (p ≤ .001), and selling experience (p ≤ .02) were significantly related to job satisfaction. Role ambiguity was found not to be significantly related to job satisfaction.

Cron and Slocum found that the business strategy of a firm had a significant effect on job satisfaction (p ≤ .01). Age was related to job satisfaction (p ≤ .02), with older persons being more satisfied. Significant main effects of career stages were observed for job satisfaction (p ≤ .01). Statistically significant differences were reported for k (p ≤ .01), supervisio (p ≤ .01), and promotion satisfaction (p ≤ .01). Salespersons in the exploration stage were the least satisfied whereas the salespersons in the established and maintenastages were the most satisfied. The salespersons in the disengagement stage were slightly less satisfied than salespersons in the established and maintenance stages.

Apasu used only the satisfaction with pay measure of the JDI. The results indicated that salespersons with higher achievement-oriented values (p ≤ .05), lower value congruence (p ≤ .01), and higher dissatisfaction with pay (p ≤ .01) perceived pay as an important reward.

COMMENTS:

Also see Teas and Horrell (1981). They appear to have used the scale in a study pertaining to job satisfaction.

REFERENCES:

Apasu, Yao (1987), "The Importance of Value Structures in the Perception of Rewards by Industrial Salespersons," *JAMS*, 15 (Spring), 1-10.

Busch, Paul (1980), "The Sales Manager's Bases of Social Power and Influence Upon the Sales Force," *JM*, 44 (Summer), 91-101.

Cron, William L. and John W. Slocum, Jr. (1986), "The Influence of Career Stages on Salespeople's Job Attitudes, Work Perceptions, and Performance," *JMR*, 23 (May), 119-129.

Smith, Patricia C., Lorne M. Kendall, and Charles L. Hulin (1969). *The Measurement of Satisfaction in Work and Retirement*. Chicago, Ill.: Rand McNally & Company.

Teas, R. Kenneth (1983), "Supervisory Behavior, Role Stress, and the Job Satisfaction of Industrial Salespeople," *JMR*, 20 (February), 84-91.

_____ and James F. Horrell (1981), "Salespeople's Satisfaction and Performance Feedback," *Industrial Marketing Management*, 10, 49-57.

SCALE ITEMS: JOB DESCRIPTION INDEX (JDI)

The instructions for each scale asked the subject to put Y beside an item if the item described the particular aspect of his/her job (work, pay, etc.), N if the item did not describe that aspect, or ? if he/she could not decide. The response beside each item below is the one scored in the "satisfied" direction for each scale.

Work
Y Fascinating
N Routine
Y Satisfying sharing
N Boring
Y Good
Y Creative
Y Respected
N Hot
Y Pleasant
Y Useful
N Tiresome
Y Healthful
Y Challenging
N On your feet
N Frustrating
N Simple
N Endless interests
Y Gives sense of accomplishment
N Hard to meet

Pay
Y Income adequate for normal expenses
Y Satisfactory profit
N Barely live on income
N Bad
Y Income provides luxuries
N Insecure
N Less that I deserve
Y Highly paid
N Underpaid

Coworkers
Y Stimulating
N Boring
N Slow
Y Ambitious
N Stupid
Y Responsible
Y Fast
Y Intelligent
N Easy to make enemies
N Talk too much
Y Smart
N Lazy
N Unpleasant
N No privacy
Y Active
N Narrow interests
Y Loyal

Supervision
Y Asks my advice
N Hard to please
N Impolite
Y Praises good work
Y Tactful
Y Influential
Y Up-to-date
N Doesn't supervise enough
N Quick tempered
Y Tells me where I stand
N Annoying
N Stubborn
Y Knows job well
N Bad
Y Intelligent
Y Leaves me on my own
N Lazy
Y Around when needed

Promotions
Y Good opportunity for advancement
N Opportunity somewhat limited
Y Promotion on ability
N Dead-end job
Y Good chance for promotion
N Unfair promotion policy
N Infrequent promotions
Y Regular promotions
Y Fairly good chance for promotion

Teas' (1983) modified the Satisfaction with Supervision measure and added a satisfaction with customers measure (see below). The coding procedure used was yes = 3, could not decide = 2, and no = 1.

Satisfaction with Supervision
1. Hard to please **(r)**
2. Impolite **(r)**
3. Tactful
4. Up-to-date
5. Quick-tempered **(r)**
6. Annoying **(r)**
7. Knows job well
8. Bad **(r)**
9. Intelligent
10. Around when needed
11. Lazy **(r)**

Satisfaction with Customers
1. Stimulating
2. Unpleasant **(r)**
3. Boring **(r)**
4. Smart
5. Impolite **(r)**
6. Stubborn **(r)**
7. Intelligent
8. Talks too much **(r)**
9. Narrow interests **(r)**
10. Hard to meet **(r)**
11. Honest
12. Quick-tempered **(r)**
13. Tactful
14. Stupid **(r)**
15. Loyal
16. Lazy **(r)**
17. Hard to please **(r)**
18. Annoying **(r)**

SCALE NAME: Job Expectations (Realistic)

SCALE DESCRIPTION:

A three-item, seven-point Likert-type scale assessing the degree to which a salesperson had an accurate and full idea of what to expect about working for a company before starting the job. Dubinsky et al. (1986) referred to this measure as Realism.

SCALE ORIGIN:

The items for the scale were slightly modified from those developed by Feldman (1976). His study was based on data from **118** hospital employees. Scale scores were not only calculated on responses to questionnaire items but also included a rating based on interviews with each subject. The Spearman-Brown reliability coefficient (corrected for attenuation) was reported as **.739**. Realistic job expectations were found to have significant positive correlations with a person's reported suitability for a position and his/her perception that the job description was accurate.

SAMPLES:

Analysis by Dubinsky et al. was based on data collected from **189** salespeople. Letters were sent to a national sample of 2000 senior-level executives asking them to have their least experienced salesperson complete the questionnaire. The respondents represented 189 different companies that marketed 50 different product categories. The sample had a median age of 30.5 years, had spent 1.4 years (median) in their present positions, and were mostly male (86%).

RELIABILITY:

A LISREL estimate of reliability was **.73**.

VALIDITY:

No examination of scale validity was reported.

ADMINISTRATION:

The scale was self-administered by respondents along with many other measures in a mail survey format. Higher scores on the scale indicate that respondents had very accurate perceptions of what life in positions at their respective companies was going to be like whereas lower scores suggest that their expectations were inaccurate.

MAJOR FINDINGS:

Dubinsky and his coauthors examined a model of salesforce assimilation. **Realistic job expectations** were found to have a significant positive impact on perceived accuracy of job descriptions as well as the ability to resolve conflicting work demands.

REFERENCES:

Dubinsky, Alan J., Roy D. Howell, Thomas N. Ingram, and Danny Bellenger (1986), ''Salesforce Socialization,'' *JM*, 50 (October), 192-207.

Feldman, Daniel C. (1976), ''A Contingency Theory of Socialization,'' *Administrative Science Quarterly*, 21 (September), 433-452.

SCALE ITEMS: JOB EXPECTATIONS (REALISTIC)

Strongly Disagree	Disagree	Slightly Disagree	Neutral	Slightly Agree	Agree	Strongly Agree
1	2	3	4	5	6	7

1. I had a pretty good idea of what my particular job would be like.
2. I knew what the good points and bad points of this job were when I was hired.
3. I did not know what to expect when I came to work for this company. **(r)**

SCALE NAME: Job Instrumentality (Salesperson)

SCALE DESCRIPTION:

A 22-item, five-point Likert-like summated ratings scale measuring an employee's perceived probability that achieving a greater level of performance will yield greater rewards. The scale is a composite of the following factors, which can be measured separately if desired: job status, self-fulfillment, company relationships, customer relationships, and performance recognition. See comments below for various versions of the scale.

SCALE ORIGIN:

The scale was constructed by Teas (1981) from a review of the literature and interviews with salespeople. Thirty-one items were developed and factor analysis led to the elimination of nine items as discussed below.

SAMPLES:

Teas collected data from **171** salespeople in group interviews during sales meetings. The salespeople represented 74% of the industrial salesforces of three midwestern companies. The typical salesperson was 36 years of age and had spent 6.5 years with his company.

The analysis by Kohli (1985) was based on data from **114** salespeople. The sample was obtained from three companies manufacturing and selling industrial products. An overall response rate of 89.8% was reported.

RELIABILITY:

Alpha values of **.912** and **.89** were reported for the scale by Teas and Kohli, respectively.

VALIDITY:

Teas performed a factor analysis of the original set of 31 items. Five factors were found and only items with high factor loadings ($\geq$ .40) on only one factor were retained. Nine items were eliminated, leaving the final global measure with 22 items.

Though the specific results were not reported for this scale by Kohli, he implied that a factor analysis of this and other scales was used to eliminate items with weak loadings on their hypothesized factors. This procedure led to one item being dropped from the global version of the measure.

ADMINISTRATION:

The scale was self-administered along with many other measures in the studies by both Teas and Kohli. High scores on this scale indicate that respondents believe there is a high probability that if they improve their level of performance they will be rewarded.

MAJOR FINDINGS:

Teas investigated the impact of several personality characteristics and job-related perceptions on work motivation. The results indicated that having a considerate supervisor, participating in decisions, and having jobs characterized by variety and completeness had positive impacts on **job instrumentality**.

Kohli examined several previously unstudied supervisory behaviors toward salespeople. The only independent variable that had a significant influence on overall **job instrumentality** was a supervisor's contingent approving behavior.

COMMENTS:

Teas used both the 22-item global scale and its five subscales. Alpha values for the subscales were reported as being .619, .988, .893, .590, and .666 for job status, self-fulfillment, company relationships, customer relationships, and performance recognition, respectively.

Kohli also used the global measure, though with one item less than the scale used by Teas. He also divided the global scale into two parts, intrinsic instrumentality (five items) and extrinsic instrumentality (16 items). The two parts had alpha values of .89 and .87, respectively.

REFERENCES:

Kohli, Ajay K. (1985), "Some Unexplored Supervisory Behaviors and Their Influence on Salespeople's Role Clarity, Specific Self-Esteem, Job Satisfaction, and Motivation," *JMR*, 22 (November), 424-433.

Teas, R. Kenneth (1981), "An Empirical Test of Models of Salespersons' Job Expectancy and Instrumentality Perceptions," *JMR*, 18 (May), 209-226.

SCALE ITEMS: JOB INSTRUMENTALITY (SALESPERSON)

Below is a list of potential results of good performance on your job (for example, exceeding your sales quota by 10%). Using the scale provided, indicate the likelihood (probability) that good job performance would lead to the following results for you.

No chance	Low probability	50-50 chance	High probability	Certain to occur
1	2	3	4	5

Self-Fulfillment
1. Increased feeling of self-esteem
2. Increased sense of accomplishment
3. Increased sense of achievement
4. A feeling that I am making good use of my skills and abilities
5. A feeling of self-fulfillment

Company Relationships
6. Increased opportunity to develop close friendships with other employees in this company
7. A better working relationship with my supervisor
8. A better working relationship with other salesmen
9. Being involved in training other salesmen
10. Increased independence from supervision

Customer Relationships

11. Fewer complaints from my customers
12. Receiving recognition for good performance from my customers
13. Increased opportunity to develop close friendships with my customers
14. Better working relationships with my customers

Direct Performance Recognition

15. Increased pay
16. Increased opportunity for influencing my supervisor's decisions
17. Obtaining a job offer from my customer
18. Receiving recognition for good performance from my supervisor

Job Status

19. Increased personal prestige
20. Increased job security
21. Increased responsibility in my job
22. More authority in my job

SCALE NAME: Job Structure

SCALE DESCRIPTION:

A six-item, five-point Likert-like scale measuring the degree of structure an employee reports in his/her job in terms of organizational rules, procedures, and enforcement.

SCALE ORIGIN:

The scale is a modified version of a measure developed as part of the dissertation research conducted by Moorhead (1979). Analysis was based on responses from 87 surgical residents at a hospital. Alpha for the six-item scale was .81. Evidence of convergent and discriminant validity from a factor analysis was strong, but limited testing with the multitrait-multimethod procedure indicated validity was very poor. The results of a path analysis indicated that perceived job structure had direct positive impacts on role conflict but not on job satisfaction or performance.

SAMPLES:

The analysis by Cummings, Jackson, and Ostrom (1989) was based on data from **201** product managers in firms that had annual sales in the range of $8 million to $35 billion.

RELIABILITY:

An alpha of **.775** was reported for the scale by Cummings and his coauthors.

VALIDITY:

No examination of scale validity was reported.

ADMINISTRATION:

The scale was self-administered along with many other measures in a mail survey format. Higher scores on the scale indicate that employees think there is a strong emphasis on following rules and regulations in their companies whereas lower scores suggest that they feel there is little structure in their jobs.

MAJOR FINDINGS:

The purpose of the study by Cummings and his coauthors was to investigate several aspects of organizational behavior and their impact on the job satisfaction and performance of product managers. Path analysis results indicated that, contrary to expectations, **job structure** had a positive impact on role conflict, i.e., greater emphasis on following rules led to increased job tension and anxiety.

REFERENCES:

Cummings, W. Theodore, Donald W. Jackson, Lonnie L. Ostrom (1989), "Examining Product Managers' Job Satisfaction and Performance Using Selected Organizational Behavior Variables," *JAMS*, 17 (Spring), 147-156.

Moorhead, Gregory (1979), "Integrative Analysis of Context, Structure, Jobs and Roles, and Physician Behavior in a General Hospital," unpublished doctoral dissertation, University of Houston.

SCALE ITEMS: JOB STRUCTURE

Definitely False	False	Uncertain	True	Definitely True
1———————	—2———————	—3———————	—4———————	—5

1. Whenever I have a problem, I am supposed to go to the same person for the answer.
2. Going through the proper channels of authority is constantly stressed.
3. Everyone is to follow strict rules and procedures at all times.
4. The employees are constantly being checked on for procedure violations.
5. People here feel as though they are constantly being watched to see that they follow all the procedures.
6. With regard to following written rules and procedures, the supervisor is very strict.

SCALE NAME: Job Suitability

SCALE DESCRIPTION:

A two-item, seven-point Likert-like scale assessing the degree to which an employee's needs and skills are compatible with those for the role the person is expected to play in a company. Dubinsky et al. (1986) referred to this measure as Congruence.

SCALE ORIGIN:

The items for the scale were slightly modified from those developed by Feldman (1976). His study was based on data from **118** hospital employees. Scale scores were not only calculated on responses to questionnaire items, but also included a rating based on interviews with each subject. The Spearman-Brown reliability coefficient (corrected for attenuation) was reported as **.751**. Job suitability was found to have a high and significant positive correlation with a person's reported job satisfaction.

SAMPLES:

Analysis by Dubinsky et al. (1986) was based on data collected from **189** salespeople. Letters were sent to a national sample of 2000 senior-level executives asking them to have their least experienced salesperson complete the questionnaire. The respondents represented 189 different companies that marketed 50 different product categories. The sample had a median age of 30.5 years, had spent 1.4 years (median) in their present positions, and were mostly male (86%).

RELIABILITY:

A LISREL estimate of reliability was **.75**.

VALIDITY:

No examination of scale validity was reported.

ADMINISTRATION:

The scale was self-administered by respondents along with many other measures in a mail survey format. Higher scores on the scale indicate that respondents think they are very suited for their positions at their respective companies whereas lower scores suggest that they perceive low compatibility between what they can do and what the company expects of them.

MAJOR FINDINGS:

Dubinsky and his coauthors examined a model of salesforce assimilation. Among many other salient results, **job suitability** was found to have significant positive impacts on perceived accuracy of job descriptions, job involvement, and job satisfaction.

REFERENCES:

Dubinsky, Alan J., Roy D. Howell, Thomas N. Ingram, and Danny Bellenger (1986), ''Salesforce Socialization,'' *JM*, 50 (October), 192-207.

Feldman, Daniel C. (1976), ''A Contingency Theory of Socialization,'' *Administrative Science Quarterly*, 21 (September), 433-452.

SCALE ITEMS: JOB SUITABILITY

Strongly Disagree	Disagree	Slightly Disagree	Neutral	Slightly Agree	Agree	Strongly Agree
1	2	3	4	5	6	7

1. In some ways, I feel like this is not the right type of work for me, or I'm not the right type of person for this job. **(r)**
2. I'm sure there must be another job in the company for which I am better suited. **(r)**

SCALE NAME: Job Tension

SCALE DESCRIPTION:

>A three-item, five-point Likert-like summated ratings scale measuring the frequency with which an employee reports experiencing stress related to his/her work, the assessment process, and the achievement of performance goals.

SCALE ORIGIN:

>The scale was apparently developed by Jaworski and MacInnis (1989). The scale and other aspects of the survey instrument were refined through a series of interviews and a pretest of marketing managers.

SAMPLES:

>A national sample of marketing managers was drawn randomly from the American Marketing Association's list of members. Of the 479 managers who appear to have received questionnaires, **379** returned usable forms.

RELIABILITY:

>An alpha of **.60** was reported for the scale.

VALIDITY:

>The validity of the scale was not specifically examined.

ADMINISTION:

>The scale was self-administered along with many other measures in a mail survey format. Higher scores on the scale indicate that employees report a high level of job-related stress whereas lower scores suggest that they experience little if any tension related to their work and the evaluation process.

MAJOR FINDINGS:

>Among the many purposes of the study by Jaworski and MacInnis was to examine the simultaneous presence of several types of managerial controls in the context of marketing management. Contrary to expectations, a structural equations analysis did not find **job tension** to be significantly affected by either of the work-related controls studied.

COMMENTS:

>The reliability of the scale is low and should be improved, possibly by adding a few other appropriate items.

REFERENCE:

Jaworski, Bernard J. and Deborah J. MacInnis (1989), "Marketing Jobs and Management Controls: Toward a Framework," *JMR*, 26 (November), 406-419.

SCALE ITEMS: JOB TENSION

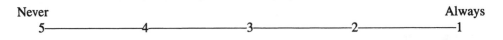

Never   Always

5————————4————————3————————2————————1

1. I experience tension in my job.
2. I experience job tension during performance evaluations.
3. If I don't attain my performance goals, I feel tense.

SCALE NAME: Job Variety

SCALE DESCRIPTION:

A five-item, five-point Likert-like scale measuring the range of duties an employee has the opportunity to perform in his/her work.

SCALE ORIGIN:

The scale was developed as part of the Job Characteristics Inventory by Sims, Szilagyi, and Keller (1976), though they indicate that they borrowed many items from previous work (Hackman and Lawler 1971). The inventory was tested on two diverse samples, one composed of over 1000 hospital employees (mostly female) and the other composed of 192 male employees of a large manufacturing firm. Alpha for the job variety portion of the inventory was calculated to be .80 and .82 for the hospital and manufacturing samples, respectively. A variety of evidence is presented attesting to the scale's convergent and discriminant validity.

SAMPLES:

The analysis by Cummings, Jackson, and Ostrum (1989) was based on data from **201** product managers in firms that had annual sales in the range of $8 million to $35 billion.

RELIABILITY:

An alpha of .**626** was reported for the scale by Cummings and his coauthors.

VALIDITY:

No examination of scale validity was reported.

ADMINISTRATION:

The scale was self-administered along with many other measures in a mail survey format. Higher scores on the scale indicate that employees think there is great variety in the jobs they perform whereas lower scores suggest that they feel their work is repetitious. Cummings and his coauthors (1989) added each respondent's score on this scale with those of three other dimensions of the JCI to obtain an overall "job scope" score.

MAJOR FINDINGS:

The purpose of the study by Cummings and his coauthors was to investigate several aspects of organizational behavior and their impact on the job satisfaction and performance of product managers. **Job variety** was not examined *per se*, but was incorporated into the "job scope" measure. Path analysis results indicated that the only variable to have a significant effect (negative) on job scope was centralization of decision making.

#444 *Job Variety*

COMMENTS:

See also a modification of this scale used by Hunt and Chonko (1984).

REFERENCES:

Cummings, W. Theodore, Donald W. Jackson, and Lonnie L. Ostrom (1989), "Examining Product Managers' Job Satisfaction and Performance Using Selected Organizational Behavior Variables," *JAMS*, 17 (Spring), 147-156.

Hackman, J.R. and E.E. Lawler, III (1971), "Employee Reations to Job Characteristics," *Journal of Applied Psychology*, Monograph 55, 259-268.

Hunt, Shelby D. and Lawrence B. Chonko (1984), "Marketing and Machiavellianism," *JM*, 48 (Summer), 30-42.

Sims, Henry P., Jr., Andrew D. Szilagyi, and Robert T. Keller (1976), "The Measurement of Job Characteristics," *Academy of Management Journal*, 19 (June), 195-212.

SCALE ITEMS: JOB VARIETY +

1. How much variety is there in your job?
2. How repetitious are your duties?
3. How similar are the tasks you perform in a typical work day?
4. The opportunity to do a number of different things.
5. The amount of variety in my job.

+ The following scale was used for the first three items:

Very Little		A Moderate Amount		Very Much
1—————	—2—————	——3—————	—4—————	—5

The following scale was used for the last two items:

A Minimum Amount		A Moderate Amount		A Maximum Amount
1—————	—2—————	——3—————	—4—————	—5

SCALE NAME: Locus of Control

SCALE DESCRIPTION:

A summated ratings scale composed of 11 forced-choice items that measures the degree to which a person attributes success to his/her own efforts versus fate or other forces. The Valecha (1972) version of the scale asks respondents not only to choose between items in each pair, but also to indicate how close the choice is to their own true opinions.

SCALE ORIGIN:

The scale is from the work of Valecha, who developed a measure based on a subset of items from the original Rotter (1966) scale. The scale was tested only on men and no reliability data were reported, but some evidence of the scale's convergent validity was presented.

Rotter's scale consisted of 23 pairs of opposing statements in a forced-choice format. Correlations between each set of items and the total scale score (minus that item) are reported for a sample composed of 200 men and 200 women, apparently psychology majors at The Ohio State University. However, Rotter reports several tests of the scale's reliability and validity being conducted with numerous samples. Internal consistency (Kuder-Richardson) was calculated as .7 with the 400 Ohio State students and ranged from .65 to .79 with other samples. Factor analyses indicated one general factor. The author presents evidence supporting the scale's validity but it is not consistently strong, making assessment difficult.

SAMPLES:

Teas (1981) collected data from **171** salespeople in group interviews during sales meetings. The salespeople represented 74% of the industrial salesforces of three midwestern companies. The typical salesperson was 36 years of age and had spent 6.5 years with his company.

RELIABILITY:

An alpha of **.70** was reported for the scale by Teas.

VALIDITY:

No specific examination of scale validity was reported.

ADMINISTRATION:

The scale was self-administered along with many other measures in the study by Teas. The respondents are asked to make a choice between the two alternatives for each pair. Then, for each choice, they are to indicate how close it is to their true opinions. The following scores are assigned by the researcher for particular responses: a score of 1 means an internal response is much closer, 2 means an internal response is slightly closer, 3 means an external response is slightly closer, and 4 means an external reponse is much closer. Respondents with high scores on this scale believe fate and other forces beyond their control greatly influence what happens to them whereas those with low scores perceive that they have great control over what happens to them in their lives. Teas appears to have scored the scale in the opposite direction.

MAJOR FINDINGS:

Teas investigated the impact of several personality characteristics and job-related perceptions on work motivation. The results indicated that **locus of control** had its most significant influence on the company relationships component of job instrumentalities.

REFERENCES:

Robinson, John P. and Phillip R. Shaver (1975), *Measures of Social Psychological Attitudes*. Ann Arbor, Mich.: Institute For Social Research.

Rotter, J. B. (1966), ''Generalized Expectancies for Internal and External Control of Reinforcement,'' *Psychological Monographs: General and Applied*, 80 (1), Whole No. 609.

Teas, R. Kenneth (1981), ''An Empirical Test of Models of Salespersons' Job Expectancy and Instrumentality Perceptions,'' *JMR*, 18 (May), 209-226.

Valecha, G. K. (1972), ''Construct Validation of Internal-External Locus of Control as Measured by an Abbreviated 11-Item IE Scale,'' unpublished doctoral dissertation, The Ohio State University.

SCALE ITEMS: LOCUS OF CONTROL +

For each pair below, indicate which item is closer to your opinion and then indicate whether it is ''much closer'' or only ''slightly closer'' to your actual opinion.

1. a. Children get into trouble because their parents punish them too much.
   b. The trouble with most children nowadays is that their parents are too easy with them.
2. a. In the long run people get the respect they deserve in this world.
   b. Unfortunately, an individual's worth often passes unrecognized no matter how hard he tries.
3. a. The idea that teachers are unfair to students is nonsense.
   b. Most students don't realize the extent to which their grades are influenced by accidental happenings.
4. a. Becoming a success is a matter of hard work; luck has little or nothing to do with it.
   b. Getting a good job depends mainly on being in the right place at the right time.
5. a. The average citizen can have an influence in government decisions.
   b. This world is run by the few people in power, and there is not much the little guy can do about it.
6. a. In my case, getting what I want has little or nothing to do with luck.
   b. Many times we might just as well decide what to do by flipping a coin.
7. a. Who gets to be the boss often depends on who was lucky enough to be in the right place first.
   b. Getting people to do the right thing depends upon ability; luck has little or nothing to do with it.
8. a. Most people don't realize the extent to which their lives are controlled by accidental happenings.

    b. There really is no such thing as "luck."
9. a. In the long run the bad things that happen to us are balanced by the good things.
    b. Most misfortunes are the result of lack of ability, ignorance, laziness, or all three.
10. a. Many times I feel that I have little influence over the things that happen to me.
    b. It is impossible for me to believe that chance or luck plays an important role in my life.
11. a. What happens to me is my own doing.
    b. Sometimes I feel that I don't have enough control over the direction my life is taking.

+ The external response is alternative **b** for items 2 through 6, and 11, whereas the external response is alternative **a** for items 7 through 10. As indicated by Robinson and Shaver (1975, pp. 232-236), item 1 is a filler item; therefore, responses to it are not used in computing scale scores.

SCALE NAME: Machiavellianism (Mach IV)

SCALE DESCRIPTION:

A 20-item, seven-point Likert-like summated ratings scale measuring the degree to which a person expresses tendencies to control others through manipulative means.

SCALE ORIGIN:

The scale was constructed by Christie and Geis (1970). The final version of the scale had a split-half reliability of .79 and a mean item-total correlation of .38.

SAMPLES:

Hunt and Chonko (1984) mailed a questionnaire to a systematic sample of 4282 members of the American Marketing Association. Usable responses were received from **1076**. Among many other sample characteristics, the typical respondent was male (70%), married (72%), and had a master's degree (53%). A little less than half of the sample worked for firms with over 1000 employees (44%), were in marketing research jobs (41%), and were between the ages of 30 and 39 years (40%).

RELIABILITY:

An alpha of **.76** was reported for the scale.

VALIDITY:

No examination of the scale's validity was reported.

ADMINISTRATION:

The scale was self-administered along with many other measures in a mail survey format. The scale is scored by summing the numerical responses to all items and adding a constant of 20, thus giving the scale a theoretical neutral score of 100 (4.0×20 items + 20). High scores on the scale (over 100) indicate that respondents are expressing strong Machiavellian tendencies whereas low scores (less than 100) suggest that they are low in Machiavellianism.

MAJOR FINDINGS:

The purpose of the study by Hunt and Chonko was to determine whether marketers were more Machiavellian than other members of society. Among the findings was that **Machiavellianism** was higher for younger marketers, single marketers, and female marketers. Further, the sample as a group had a mean score of 85.7 on the scale, which puts it higher than some other groups studied previously but well below several others that have been tested. Finally, though no relationship was found between **Machiavellianism** and success in marketing, it was significantly related to several measures of job satisfaction such that persons high in **Machiavellianism** were less satisfied with their jobs and with marketing as a career.

COMMENTS:

See also a use of the scale by Saxe and Weitz (1982).

REFERENCES:

Christie, Richard and Florence L. Geis (1970), *Studies in Machiavellianism*. New York, N.Y.: Academic Press, Inc.

Hunt, Shelby D. and Lawrence B. Chonko (1984), ''Marketing and Machiavellianism,'' *JM*, 48 (Summer), 30-42.

Saxe, Robert and Barton A. Weitz (1982), ''The SOCO Scale: A Measure of the Customer Orientation of Salespeople,'' *JMR*, 19 (August), 343-351.

SCALE ITEMS: MACHIAVELLIANISM (MACH IV)

Strongly Disagree	Disagree	Slightly Disagree	Neutral	Slightly Agree	Agree	Strongly Agree
1	2	3	4	5	6	7

1. The best way to handle people is to tell them what they want to hear.
2. When you ask someone to do something for you, it is best to give the real reasons for wanting it, rather than giving reasons which might carry more weight. **(r)**
3. Anyone who completely trusts anyone else is asking for trouble.
4. It is hard to get ahead without cutting corners here and there.
5. Honesty is the best policy in all cases. **(r)**
6. It is safest to assume that all people have a vicious streak, and it will come out when they are given a chance.
7. Never tell anyone the real reason you did something unless it is useful to do so.
8. One should take action only when sure it is morally right. **(r)**
9. It is wise to flatter important people.
10. All in all, it is better to be humble and honest than important and dishonest. **(r)**
11. Barnum was very wrong when he said there's a sucker born every minute. **(r)**
12. People suffering from incurable diseases should have the choice of being put painlessly to death.
13. It is possible to be good in all respects. **(r)**
14. Most people are basically good and kind. **(r)**
15. There is no excuse for lying to someone else. **(r)**
16. Most men forget more easily the death of their father than the loss of their property.
17. Most people who get ahead in the world lead clean, moral lives. **(r)**
18. Generally speaking, men won't work hard unless they're forced to do so.
19. The biggest difference between criminals and other people is that criminals are stupid enough to get caught.
20. Most men are brave. **(r)**

SCALE NAME: Manifest Influence of Buying Center Members

SCALE DESCRIPTION:

A nine-item, five-point Likert-like summated ratings scale measuring the degree to which a member of a buying center is perceived by another member to have influenced a particular purchase decision made by the buying center. The emphasis of the scale is on the result rather than the effort expended to achieve it.

SCALE ORIGIN:

Kohli (1989) developed the measure along with other aspects of the survey instrument by reviewing previous measures and pretesting it in 14 personal interviews.

SAMPLES:

A survey instrument was mailed to 500 members of the National Association of Purchasing Management. Usable responses were received from **251** members. No response bias was evident for theoretical variables germane to the study. Respondents provided information about purchases of products in a range of $1000 to $150 million, with an average purchase value of $3.5 million.

RELIABILITY:

An alpha of **.93** was reported for this scale.

VALIDITY:

Though Kohli made some assessment of validity for other scales used in the study, no evaluation of this scale's validity was discussed.

ADMINISTRATION:

The scale was self-administered by respondents along with many other scales in a mail survey format. Higher scores on the scale indicate that specific buying center members (other than the respondents) are perceived to have had considerable influence on some specified purchase decisions made by their respective buying centers.

MAJOR FINDINGS:

The purpose of the study by Kohli was to examine some factors that affect a person's influence in a buying center. **Manifest influence** was the dependent variable of interest in the study. Among the many findings was that expert power was the most important determinant of **manifest influence**, followed by reinforcement power. Other types of power appeared to have little effect on **manifest influence** except under very specific circumstances.

COMMENTS:

Items should be modified for situations in which objects of the questions could be female.

REFERENCE:

Kohli, Ajay (1989), ''Determinants of Influence in Organizational Buying: A Contingency Approach,'' *JM*, 53 (July), 50-65.

SCALE ITEMS: MANIFEST INFLUENCE OF BUYING CENTER MEMBERS +

very small _____ : _____ : _____ : _____ : _____ very large
        1   2   3   4   5

1. How much weight did the committee members give to his opinions?
2. How much impact did he have on the thinking of the other members?
3. To what extent did he influence the criteria used for making the final decision?
4. How much effect did his involvment in the purchase committee have on how the various options were rated?
5. To what extent did he influence others into adopting certain positions about the various options?
6. How much change did he induce in the preferences of other members?
7. To what extent did others go along with his suggestions?
8. To what extent did his participation influence the decision eventually reached?
9. To what extent did the final decision reflect his views?

+ Though the directions were not provided in the article, the discussion indicated that respondents were instructed to think of a specific joint purchase decision and a specific committee member (excluding themselves) when answering the questions.

SCALE NAME: Manifest Influence of Others in Organization

SCALE DESCRIPTION:

A five-item, five-point Likert-like scale purported to measure the degree of perceived influence others have in buying-related decisions in an organizational setting.

SCALE ORIGIN:

This specific measure was developed by Ronchetto, Hutt, and Reingen (1989), but was based on conceptual and empirical developments of the influence construct as reported by Cobb (1980) and Patchen (1963, 1974). See those works for a more detailed presentation of that material.

SAMPLES:

Ronchetto, Hutt, and Reingen used a sample of **171** subjects in a single company who were described by each other as members of a communications network in a workflow relationship. All subjects had duties involving buying-related activities for the company.

RELIABILITY:

Ronchetto, Hutt, and Reingen reported an alpha of **.89**.

VALIDITY:

Nomologic validity was supported in relation to the findings of Cobb and Patchen. Principal components factor analysis suggested unidimensionality as all items fit into a single-factor solution with no loading less than .81 and variance explained of 72%. Convergent validity was demonstrated through significant correlation with number of times an individual was nominated by cowokers as being influential in the buying decision process ($r = .37$, $p \leq .001$).

ADMINISTRATION:

A paper-and-pencil format was used as a part of a survey instrument. Subjects are asked to rate the influence frequency of coworkers. Each individual's score is the averaged sum across coworkers' ratings.

MAJOR FINDINGS:

Ronchetto, Hutt, and Reingen found that individuals' mean influence score was 2.96 (SD = .55). Their results provided strong evidence that structural position of the individual was related to that individual's influence in buying decisions ($p \leq .001$). The greater the centrality of the individual's position, the more influence the person was perceived to have in the buying decision, though this measure of influence did not significantly relate to the individual's distance from the dominant reference group or distance from the organizational boundary. The formal rank and departmental membership of the individual were also significantly related to perceptions of the individual's influence in buying decisions. Finally, the authors contend that network structure variables explain a greater amount of the variance in the influence measure than do formal structure variables.

REFERENCES:

Cobb, Anthony (1980), "Informal Influence in the Formal Organization: Perceived Sources of Power Among Work Unit Peers," *Academy of Management Journal*, 23 (March), 155-161.

Patchen, Martin (1963), "Alternative Questionnaire Approaches to the Measurement of Influence in Organizational Decisions," *American Journal of Sociology*, 69 (1), 41-52.

_____ (1974), "The Locus and Basis of Influence in Organizational Decisions," *Organizational Behavior and Human Performance*, 11 (April), 195-211.

Ronchetto, John R., Jr., Michael D. Hutt, and Peter Reingen (1989), "Embedded Influence Patterns in Organizational Buying Systems," *JM*, 53 (October), 51-62.

SCALE ITEMS: MANIFEST INFLUENCE OF OTHERS IN ORGANIZATION +

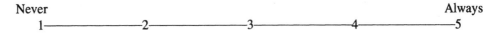

Never   Always

1————————2————————3————————4————————5

1. are sought out for advice about buying-related issues.
2. are included in discussions before a buying-related decision is made.
3. take charge of group discussions about buying-related issues.
4. influence coworkers to stick together in resolving buying-related problems.
5. are active in developing informal agreements in buying-related issues among co-workers.

+ Presumably each individual within the organization who has previously been nominated by the respondent as having influence in the buying decision is listed for rating.

SCALE NAME: Market Attractiveness

SCALE DESCRIPTION:

A six-item, seven-point summated ratings scale measuring the degree to which a person describes a marketing opportunity to be attractive in terms of growth potential and profits.

SCALE ORIGIN:

The scale was original to Burke (1984) and hers is the only known use of the scale in the published marketing research reviewed here.

SAMPLES:

Data were collected from a total of **86** business units in six of 18 firms personally contacted. The majority of business units were in conglomerate firms. The managers who filled out the survey instruments had bottom-line responsibility for their business units, were highly involved in selecting market share objectives, and were an average of 3.29 levels away from their CEOs.

RELIABILITY:

An alpha of **.92** was reported for the scale.

VALIDITY:

Burke implied that a factor analysis was performed as part of scale development, but provided no specific details. No other examination of scale validity was suggested.

ADMINISTRATION:

The sample responded to the scale as part of a self-administered mail questionnaire. Higher scores on the scale suggest that respondents perceive a particular marketing opportunity to be very attractive in terms of profitability and growth potential.

MAJOR FINDINGS:

The study investigated the degree to which business-unit managers of multiproduct firms perceived different variableso influence strategi choices. Managers of business units with ''build'' strategies (to significantly increase market share) described the **market attractiveness** to be significantly greater than did managers of business units with other strategic thrusts.

REFERENCE:

Burke, Marian C. (1984), ''Strategic Choice and Marketing Managers: An Examination of Business-Level Marketing Objectives,'' *JMR*, 21 (November), 345-359.

SCALE ITEMS: MARKET ATTRACTIVENESS

The exact nature of the questions is not reported in the article, but in general respondents were asked to think back about the most recent strategic market objective for their business units and to describe its nature.

1. Short-term (3 years) market growth rate

low   ___ : ___ : ___ : ___ : ___ : ___ : ___   high
            1   2   3   4   5   6   7

2. Stage of product life cycle

decline   ___ : ___ : ___ : ___ : ___ : ___ : ___   introduction
            1   2   3   4   5   6   7

3. Long-term (10 years) market growth rate

low   ___ : ___ : ___ : ___ : ___ : ___ : ___   high
            1   2   3   4   5   6   7

4. Prospects for future profits

possible   ___ : ___ : ___ : ___ : ___ : ___ : ___   high
loss   1   2   3   4   5   6   7   returns

5. Average industry growth margin

low   ___ : ___ : ___ : ___ : ___ : ___ : ___   high
            1   2   3   4   5   6   7

6. Average industry pretax profits

low   ___ : ___ : ___ : ___ : ___ : ___ : ___   high
            1   2   3   4   5   6   7

SCALE NAME: Market Power of Customer (Knowledge)

SCALE DESCRIPTION:

A two-item, five-point Likert-type summated ratings scale measuring the degree to which a distributor informant reports that customers have market power due to the information they have about the market.

SCALE ORIGIN:

The scale is original to the study by Butaney and Wortzel (1988), though some inspiration for the variables came from work by Porter (1980). An original list of 40 items for measuring this and related constructs was reduced by a panel of judges to 21, which were then factor analyzed as discussed below.

SAMPLES:

Data were collected from **83** distributors of electronic components located in six northeastern states. They had sales ranging from less than $500 to more than $25 million. Key informants were identified in each distributorship who had both responsibility for marketing policy and knowledge of their company's relationship with a specified manufacturer. Manufacturer names were selected at random by the researchers from a list supplied by each distributor.

RELIABILITY:

An alpha of **.74** was reported for the scale.

VALIDITY:

Besides the use of judges to eliminate items not appearing to adequately measure the appropriate variables, 12 items generally related to customer market power were factor analyzed. The two items composing this scale had loadings greater than .70 on the same factor and no loadings greater than .20 on other factors.

ADMINISTRATION:

The scale was apparently administered along with other measures in the survey instrument in a personal interview format. Respondents were asked to think of one manufacturer (specified by the researcher) when completing the questionnaire. Higher scores on the scale indicate that respondents view their customers as having a lot of knowledge about the market and distributor costs whereas lower scores suggest that respondents think their customers have little power based on knowledge of the market.

MAJOR FINDINGS:

The purpose of the study by Butaney and Wortzel was to examine the roles of customer and manufacturer power in shaping distributor power. The results indicated that **customer knowledge** did *not* have a significant effect on distributor power.

REFERENCES:

Butaney, Gul and Lawrence H. Wortzel (1988), "Distributor Power Versus Manufacturer Power: The Customer Role," *JM*, 52 (January), 52-63.

Porter, Michael E. (1980), *Competitive Strategy*. New York, N.Y.: The Free Press.

SCALE ITEMS: MARKET POWER OF CUSTOMER (KNOWLEDGE)

Strongly Disagree	Disagree	Neutral	Agree	Strongly Agree
1————————	2————————	3————————	4————————	5

1. The customers possess a great deal of market information.
2. The customers possess a good idea about the costs of the product to the distributor.

SCALE NAME: Market Power of Customer (Size)

SCALE DESCRIPTION:

A three-item, five-point Likert-type summated ratings scale measuring the degree to which a distributor informant reports that customers have market power due to their size and ability to bargain the terms of sales.

SCALE ORIGIN:

The scale is original to the study by Butaney and Wortzel (1988), though some inspiration for the variables came from work by Porter (1980). An original list of 40 items for measuring this and related constructs was reduced by a panel of judges to 21, which were then factor analyzed as discussed below.

SAMPLES:

Data were collected from **83** distributors of electronic components located in six northeastern states. They had sales ranging from less than $500 to more than $25 million. Key informants were identified in each distributorship who had both responsibility for marketing policy and knowledge of their company's relationship with a specified manufacturer. Manufacturer names were selected at random by the researchers from a list supplied by each distributor.

RELIABILITY:

An alpha of .55 was reported for the scale.

VALIDITY:

Besides the use of judges to eliminate items not appto adequately measure the appropriate variables, 12 items generally related to customer market power were factor analyzed. The three items composing this scale had loadings greater than .50 on the same factor.

ADMINISTRATION:

The scale was apparently administered along with other measures in the survey instrument in a personal interview format. Respondents were asked to think of one manufacturer (specified by the researcher) when completing the questionnaire. Higher scores on the scale indicate that respondents view specified customers as being large and/or having the ability to bargain the terms of sales whereas lower scores suggest that they think their customers have llittle market power based on size.

MAJOR FINDINGS:

The purpose of the study by Butaney and Wortzel was to examine the roles of customer and manufacturer power in shaping distributor power. The results indicated that **customer size** did *not* have a significant effect on distributor power.

COMMENTS:

The low level of alpha indicates that scale is not internally consistent in its prsent form. The items may be tapping into different subconstructs of customer market power. In fact, the factor analysis (Butaney and Wortzel 1988, p. 56) indicated that item 3 was seriously split with another factor and therefore diminished the discriminant validity of the scale.

REFERENCES:

Butaney, Gul and Lawrence H. Wortzel (1988), "Distributor Power Versus Manufacturer Power: The Customer Role," *JM*, 52 (January), 52-63.
Porter, Michael E. (1980), *Competitive Strategy*. New York, N.Y.: The Free Press.

SCALE ITEMS: MARKET POWER OF CUSTOMER (SIZE)

Strongly Disagree	Disagree	Neutral	Agree	Strongly Agree
1	2	3	4	5

1. Our customers are able to bargain the terms of sales with us.
2. Twenty percent of my customers account for 80% of my total product sales.
3. Most of my customers can buy the product directly from manufacturers.

SCALE NAME: Market Power of Customer (Switching Costs)

SCALE DESCRIPTION:

A four-item, five-point Likert-like summated ratings scale measuring the degree to which a distributor informant reports that customers have market power due to their choice of suppliers and lack of loyalty to a particular manufacturer or brand.

SCALE ORIGIN:

The scale is original to the study by Butaney and Wortzel (1988), though some inspiration for the variables came from work by Porter (1980). An original list of 40 items for measuring this and related constructs was reduced by a panel of judges to 21, which were then factor analyzed as discussed below.

SAMPLES:

Data were collected from **83** distributors of electronic components located in six northeastern states. They had sales ranging from less than $500 to more than $25 million. Key informants were identified in each distributorship who had both responsibility for marketing policy and knowledge of their company's relationship with a specified manufacturer. Manufacturer names were selected at random by the researchers from a list supplied by each distributor.

RELIABILITY:

An alpha of **.57** was reported for the scale.

VALIDITY:

Besides the use of judges to eliminate items not appearing to adequately measure the appropriate variables, 12 items generally related to customer market power were factor analyzed. The four items composing this scale had loadings greater than .40 on the same factor.

ADMINISTRATION:

The scale was apparely administered along with other measures in the survey instrument in a personal interview format. Respondents were asked to think of one manufacturer (specified by the researcher) when completing the questionnaire. Higher scores on the scale indicate that respondents view specified customers as having a lot of choices and little loyalty whereas lower scores suggest that they think their customers have little market power because switching costs are high.

MAJOR FINDINGS:

The purpose of the study by Butaney and Wortzel (1988) was to examine the roles of customer and manufacturer power in shaping distributor power. The results indicated that perceived **customer switching costs** had a significant effect on distributor channel power such that when **switching costs** were low, the distributor's power was also low.

COMMENTS:

The low level of alpha indicates that the scale is not internally consistent in its present form. The items may be tapping into different subconstructs of customer market power. In fact, the factor analysis (Butaney and Wortzel 1988, p. 56) indicated that item 2 was seriously split with another factor and therefore diminished the discriminant validity of the scale.

REFERENCES:

Butaney, Gul and Lawrence H. Wortzel (1988), "Distributor Power Versus Manufacturer Power: The Customer Role," *JM*, 52 (January), 52-63.
Porter, Michael E. (1980), *Competitive Strategy*. New York, N.Y.: The Free Press.

SCALE ITEMS: MARKET POWER OF CUSTOMER (SWITCHING COSTS)

Strongly Disagree	Disagree	Neutral	Agree	Strongly Agree
1—————	—2—————	—3—————	—4—————	—5

1. The supplier's name and brand are not very important purchasing criteria for our customers.
2. Our customers' costs of finding and qualifying other suppliers is low.
3. Our customers' importance for product quality in their purchasing criteria is low.
4. The customers in the industry do not insist on buying a specific manufacturer's brand.

SCALE NAME: Market Power of Manufacturer (Industry Concentration)

SCALE DESCRIPTION:

A two-item, five-point Likert-like summated ratings scale measuring the degree to which an industry's sales are concentrated among a few manufacturers as reported by a distributor informant.

SCALE ORIGIN:

The scale is original to the study by Butaney and Wortzel (1988), though some inspiration for the variables came from work by Porter (1980). An original list of 40 items for measuring this and related constructs was reduced by a panel of judges to 21, which were then factor analyzed as discussed below.

SAMPLES:

Data were collected from **83** distributors of electronic components located in six northeastern states. They had sales ranging from less than $500 to more than $25 million. Key informants were identified in each distributorship who had both responsibility for marketing policy and knowledge of their company's relationship with a specified manufacturer. Manufacturer names were selected at random by the researchers from a list supplied by each distributor.

RELIABILITY:

An alpha of **.56** was reported for the scale.

VALIDITY:

Besides the use of judges to eliminate items not appearing to adequately measure the appropriate variables, nine items generally related to manufacturer market power were factor analyzed. The two items composing this scale had loadings greater than .75 on the same factor and loadings no greater than .20 on other factors.

ADMINISTRATION:

The scale was apparently administered along with other measures in the survey instrument in a personal interview format. Higher scores on the scale indicate that respondents view a few manufacturers in their industry as having most of the sales volume whereas lower scores suggest that they think sales are rather equally distributed among manufacturers in their industry.

MAJOR FINDINGS:

The purpose of the study by Butaney and Wortzel was to examine the roles of customer and manufacturer power in shaping distributor power. The results indicated that perceived **industry concentration** had a significant effect on distributor channel power such that when sales volume was **concentrated** in a few manufacturers, the distributor's power was low.

REFERENCES:

Butaney, Gul and Lawrence H. Wortzel (1988), "Distributor Power Versus Manufacturer Power: The Customer Role," *JM*, 52 (January), 52-63.
Porter, Michael E. (1980), *Competitive Strategy*. New York, N.Y.: The Free Press.

SCALE ITEMS: MARKET POWER OF MANUFACTURER (INDUSTRY CONCENTRATION)

Strongly Disagree	Disagree	Neutral	Agree	Strongly Agree
1————————	—2————————	——3————————	——4————————	——5

1. Only a few manufacturers produce a large volume of the product in the industry.
2. Industry sales are not equally distributed among the manufacturers.

SCALE NAME: Market Power of Manufacturer (Nature of Competition)

SCALE DESCRIPTION:

A four-item, five-point Likert-like summated ratings scale measuring the degree to which a distributor informant reports that manufacturers have a low concern about the prices or products of their competitors.

SCALE ORIGIN:

The scale is original to the study by Butaney and Wortzel (1988) though some inspiration for the variables came from work by Porter (1980). An original list of 40 items for measuring this and related constructs was reduced by a panel of judges to 21, which were then factor analyzed as discussed below. Theirs is the only known use of the scale in the published marketing research review here.

SAMPLES:

Data were collected from **83** distributors of electronic components located in six northern states. They had sales ranging from less than $500 to more than $25 million. Key informants were identified in each distributorship who had both responsibility for marketing policy and knowledge of their company's relationship with a specified manufacturer. Manufacturer names were selected at random by the researchers from a list supplied by each distributor.

RELIABILITY:

An alpha of **.58** was reported for the scale.

VALIDITY:

Besides the use of judges to eliminate items not appearing to adequately measure the appropriate variables, nine items generally related to manufacturer market power were factor analyzed. The four items composing this scale had loadings greater than .45 on the same factor.

ADMINISTRATION:

The scale was apparently administered along with other measures in the survey instrument in a personal interview format. Higher scores on the scale indicate that respondents view manufacturers in their industry as having great market power due to their apparent insensitivity about products or prices of other manufacturers whereas lower scores suggest that they think their manufacturers have little market power because of competitive concerns.

MAJOR FINDINGS:

The purpose of the study by Butaney and Wortzel was to examine the roles of customer and manufacturer power in shaping distributor power. The results indicated that perceived **manufacturer's competitive concerns** had a significant effect on distributor channel power such that when **manufacturers' competitive concerns** were low, the distributor's power was also low.

COMMENTS:

The low level of alpha indicates that the scale is not internally consistent in its present form. The items may be tapping into different subconstructs of manufacturer market power. In fact, the factor analysis (Butaney and Wortzel 1988, p. 57) indicated that items 1 and 3 were seriously split with other factors and therefore diminished the discriminant validity of the scale.

REFERENCES:

Butaney, Gul and Lawrence H. Wortzel (1988), ''Distributor Power Versus Manufacturer Power: The Customer Role,'' *JM*, 52 (January), 52-63.
Porter, Michael E. (1980), *Competitive Strategy*. New York, N.Y.: The Free Press.

SCALE ITEMS: MARKET POWER OF MANUFACTURER (NATURE OF COMPETITION)

Strongly Disagree	Disagree	Neutral	Agree	Strongly Agree
1	2	3	4	5

1. When one manufacturer reduces the product price, the other manufacturers do not reduce their prices.
2. The industry manufacturers are not very sensitive to customer product requirements.
3. Competition among manufacturers in the industry is not strong.
4. The manufacturer possesses a great deal of industry information (e.g., trends, problems, competitive brands). **(r)**

SCALE NAME: Market Researching Frequency (Bank)

SCALE DESCRIPTION:

A six-item, four-point Likert-like summated ratings scale measuring the frequency with which a bank officer reports that his/her bank researches its own activities as well as those of competitors. McKee, Varadarajan, and Pride (1989) referred to this measure as Market Scanning.

SCALE ORIGIN:

McKee and his coauthors report that they constructed the scales but selected items on the basis of a review of relevant literature and comments by industry executives.

SAMPLES:

The study focused on banks operating in 50 SMSAs of seven states that have unit banking laws. CEOs of the 560 banks in the sample frame were sent questionnaires. A total of **333** usable responses were received and an analysis of asset sizes indicated that respondents' banks were not significantly different from nonrespondents' banks.

RELIABILITY:

An alpha of **.79** was reported for the scale.

VALIDITY:

A factor analysis of all items used in the study revealed that items belonging to this scale loaded together on one factor and not on other factors.

ADMINISTRATION:

The scale was self-administered along with many other measures in a mail questionnaire format. Higher scores on the scale indicate that respondents' banks engage in research activities very frequently.

MAJOR FINDINGS:

The purpose of the study was to investigate the relationship between strategic orientation and dynamics of the market. Significant differences were found between organization strategy types in terms of several marketing tactics used. Specifically, the **frequency of marketing research** activities differed between most of the organization strategy types such that "prospectors" (those with the highest adaptive capability) engaged in it most and "reactors" (those with the lowest adaptive capability) engaged in it least.

COMMENTS:

The scale was developed for use with the banking industry, but with minor adjustments it could be used in other contexts.

REFERENCE:

McKee, Daryl O., P. Rajan Varadarajan, and William M. Pride (1989), "Strategic Adaptability and Firm Performance: A Market Contingent Perspective," *JM*, 53 (July), 21-35.

SCALE ITEMS: MARKET RESEARCHING FREQUENCY (BANK)

For each statement, please check the response that best represents how often your bank conducts these activities.

Very often = two or more times a year
Often = once every year or two
Seldom = less than every two years

Very Often	Often	Seldom	Never
1————————————2————————————3————————————4			

How often does your bank:
1. Conduct surveys of existing customer attitudes toward *your* bank.
2. Hold "focus group" sessions with *your* existing customers.
3. Conduct surveys of bank customers *other than your own*.
4. Pay independent "shoppers" to use a *competing* bank and report on service.
5. Hold "focus group" sessions with bank customers *other than your own*.
6. Collect automobile counts or other traffic measures at *competing* banks.

SCALE NAME: Meeting-Related Activity (Salesperson)

SCALE DESCRIPTION:

A six-item, seven-point Likert-like summated ratings scale measuring the frequency with which a person engages in activities involving conferences and meetings such as attending those events, setting up exhibitions, receiving training, and filling out questionnaires.

SCALE ORIGIN:

The scale is original to a study by Moncrief (1986). Several scales were developed for use in the study from a review of the literature and from personal interviews and focus groups with salespeople. A total of 121 selling-related activities were identified and included on the survey questionnaire.

SAMPLES:

Using stratified sampling, Moncrief sent survey forms to 800 firms representing 20 SIC codes (#20-#39). Fifty-one firms ultimately participated and sent copies of the question-naire to their salespeople. Of the total 2322 sales employees working for these firms, 1393 returned usable forms but the factor analysis was based on responses from **1291**.

RELIABILITY:

An alpha of **.75** is reported for the scale.

VALIDITY:

Though scale validity was not specifically addressed in the study, a factor analysis of 121 items indicated that the items below all had loadings greater than .50 on the same factor and loadings less than .40 other factors. These findings provide some evidence of the convergent and discriminant validity of the scale.

ADMINISTRATION:

The scale was self-administered by respondents along with many other measures in a mail survey format. Higher scores on the scale indicate that respondents frequently engage in activities involving meetings and conferences whereas lower scores suggest that they primarily perform activities other than those.

MAJOR FINDINGS:

The purpose of the study by Moncrief was to develop a comprehensive list of selling-related activities and the taxonomies created from them. A cluster analysis was performed of the salespeople in the sample and six clusters were found. A group called trade servicer, representing 18% of the sample, had the highest mean on the **meeting-related activity** scale. This cluster had the highest mean of any of the sales groups on seven of 10 sales activity areas examined in the study and it had the second highest mean on the other three activity areas.

REFERENCE:

> Moncrief, William C., III (1986), "Selling Activity and Sales Position Taxonomies for Industrial Salesforces," *JMR*, 23 (August), 261-270.

SCALE ITEMS: MEETING-RELATED ACTIVITY (SALESPERSON) +

> Using the following scale, please indicate how frequently you engage in each of the activities listed below. If you do not perform the activity, please code your response as a zero.

Infrequently   ____ : ____ : ____ : ____ : ____ : ____ : ____   Frequently

                  1   2   3   4   5   6   7

1. Attend sales conferences
2. Attend regional sales meetings
3. Attend periodic training
4. Work at client conferences
5. Fill out questionnaires
6. Set up exhibitions and trade shows

+ The actual directions and items were not stated in the article, but are reconstructed here on the basis of information provided.

SCALE NAME: Motivation To Work (Generalized)

SCALE DESCRIPTION:

An eight-item, five-point Likert-like summated ratings scale measuring an employee's enjoyment of his/her work and motivation to engage in it rather than other activities. It is referred to by Duncan (1969) as Commitment to Work and it is called Achievement Motivation by Bagozzi (1980) and Hart, Moncrief, and Parasuraman (1989).

SCALE ORIGIN:

The items composing the scale were apparently used first by Westoff et al. (1961, pp. 385, 386). However, the items were not used together as a summated scale until the research of Duncan (1969). The latter reports a reliability (KR-20) of .7755 based on a sample of 941 men and provides an extended discussion of the scale's validity.

SAMPLES:

The analysis by Bagozzi was based on **122** completed questionnaires from industrial salespeople assigned to exclusive geographic territories.

Hart and her coauthors mailed questionnaires to 149 salespeople who worked for 25 independent brokers representing a major food producer. After two followup mailings, usable responses were received from **84** sales representatives.

RELIABILITY:

Alpha values of **.60** and **.74** were reported for the scale by Bagozzi and by Hart and her coauthors, respectively.

VALIDITY:

No specific examinations of validity were conducted in either study.

ADMINISTRATION:

The scale was self-administered by respondents in the form of a mail survey questionnaire in the study by Hart and her coauthors. The setting of the scale's administration was not specified by Bagozzi. Higher scores on the scale indicate that employees have high motivation toward their work whereas lower scores suggest that they derive little pleasure from their work and would rather be doing other things.

MAJOR FINDINGS:

Bagozzi used causal modeling to investigate the relationship between performance and satisfaction for an industrial salesforce. The results indicated that job satisfaction was influenced to a significant degree by **motivation to work**.

The purpose of the study by Hart and her coauthors was to investigate goal theory as it relates to sales contests. When motivation was used as a moderator variable, the results provided evidence that for persons with low **work motivation**, goal difficulty was positively related to work effort.

COMMENTS:

See also Joreskog and Sorbom (1982) for a reanalysis of Bagozzi's data.

REFERENCES:

Bagozzi, Richard P. (1980), "Performance and Satisfaction in an Industrial Salesforce: An Examination of Their Antecedents and Simultaneity," *JM*, 44 (Spring), 65-77.

Duncan, Otis D. (1969), "Contingencies in Constructing Causal Models," in *Sociological Methodology*, Edgar F. Borgatta and George W. Bohrnstedt, eds. San Francisco, Calif.: Jossey-Bass, Inc.

Hart, Sandra Hile, William C. Moncrief, and A. Parasuraman (1989), "An Empirical Investigation of Salespeople's Performance, Effort and Selling Method During a Sales Contest," *JAMS*, 17 (Winter), 29-39.

Joreskog, Karl G. and Dag Sorbom (1982), "Recent Developments in Structural Equation Modeling," *JMR*, 19 (November), 404-416.

Westoff, Charles F., Robert G. Potter, Jr., Philip C. Sagi, and Elliot G. Mishler (1961), *Family Growth in Metropolitan America*. Princeton, N.J.: Princeton University Press.

SCALE ITEMS: MOTIVATION TO WORK (GENERALIZED)

Salespeople differ in their attitude and preferences toward work, their job, leisure activities, and so on. So that I may learn more about how salespeople feel about things, please indicate for each of the following questions if you strongly agree, agree, are undecided, disagree, or strongly disagree. Since there are really no correct or wrong answers and since some salespeople will agree with a particular question while others may disagree with it, please answer with the first response that comes to mind.

Strongly Disagree	Disagree	Undecided	Agree	Strongly Agree
1	2	3	4	5

1. I would much rather relax around the house all day than go to work. **(r)**
2. My work is more satisfying to me than the time I spend around the house.
3. If I inherited so much money that I didn't have to work, I would still continue to work at the same thing I am doing now.
4. Some of my main interests and pleasures in life are connected with my work.
5. I have sometimes regretted going into the kind of work I am now in. **(r)**
6. The work I do is one of the most satisfying parts of my life.
7. I enjoy my spare-time activities much more than my work. **(r)**
8. To me my work is just a way of making money. **(r)**

SCALE NAME: Motivation to Work Harder

SCALE DESCRIPTION:

A two-item, seven-point Likert-like summated ratings scale measuring the degree to which a salesperson expects to make a change in the *quantity* of effort put into his/her future selling because of a recent failure to make a sale. This is in contrast to changing the manner (quality) in which sales are made.

SCALE ORIGIN:

The measure was developed by Sujan (1986).

SAMPLES:

Sujan sent letters to 880 sales managers working for large national manufacturing firms representing a wide variety of industries. The 191 who responded indicated a total of 4038 salespeople in their companies who would serve as respondents. Questionnaires were then sent to them and **1283** usable responses were received from salespeople in 123 firms.

RELIABILITY:

An alpha of **.88** was reported for the scale.

VALIDITY:

No specific examination of scale validity was reported.

ADMINISTRATION:

The scale was self-administered by respondents in a mail survey format. Higher scores on the scale indicate that salespeople expect to work harder on their future sales because of a recent failure to make a sale whereas lower scores suggest that they do not think they will expend any more effort in their future selling activity.

MAJOR FINDINGS:

The purpose of the study by Sujan was to use the attributional theory of motivation to understand salespeople's desire to "work smarter." The findings indicated that attributing failure to a lack of effort had a significant positive impact on salespeople's **motivation to work harder** on their future sales.

REFERENCE:

Sujan, Harish (1986), "Smarter Versus Harder: An Exploratory Attributional Analysis of Salespeople's Motivation," *JMR*, 23 (February), 41-49.

SCALE ITEMS: MOTIVATION TO WORK HARDER

Think about what you did in the last twelve months in the instances in which you failed to obtain an order from a customer. In similar instances in the coming year, to avoid failure, do you plan to make a change from last year or stay the same in each of the following.

the same as
last year   ____ : ____ : ____ : ____ : ____ : ____ : ____   a great deal of change from last year
                         1   2   3   4   5   6   7

1. How many hours per week you will work.
2. How hard you will work during these hours.

SCALE NAME: Motivation to Work Smarter

SCALE DESCRIPTION:

A two-item, seven-point Likert-like summated ratings scale measuring the degree to which a salesperson expects to make a change in his/her sales *methods* because of a recent failure to make a sale. This is in contrast to changing the amount of effort (quantity) invested in future selling.

SCALE ORIGIN:

The measure was developed by Sujan (1986).

SAMPLES:

Sujan sent letters to 880 sales managers working for large national manufacturing firms representing a wide variety of industries. The 191 who responded indicated a total of 4038 salespeople in their companies who would serve as respondents. Questionnaires were then sent to them and **1283** usable responses were received from salespeople in 123 firms.

RELIABILITY:

An alpha of **.80** was reported for the scale.

VALIDITY:

No specific examination of scale validity was reported.

ADMINISTRATION:

The scale was self-administered by respondents in a mail survey format. Higher scores on the scale indicate that salespeople expect to change sales tactics in the future because of a recent failure to make a sale whereas lower scores suggest that they do not think they will make any changes in their approaches to selling.

MAJOR FINDINGS:

The purpose of the study by Sujan was to use the attributional theory of motivation to understand salespeople's desire to "work smarter." As expected, attributing failure to poor strategy had a significant positive impact on salespeople's **motivation to work smarter.** Somewhat unexpectedly, attributing past failure to lack of effort had a significant negative effect on **motivation to work smarter** in the future.

REFERENCE:

Sujan, Harish (1986), "Smarter Versus Harder: An Exploratory Attributional Analysis of Salespeople's Motivation," *JMR*, 23 (February), 41-49.

SCALE ITEMS: MOTIVATION TO WORK SMARTER

Think about what you did in the last twelve months in the instances in which you failed to obtain an order from a customer. In similar instances in the coming year, to avoid failure, do you plan to make a change from last year or stay the same in each of the following.

the same as
last year   ____ : ____ : ____ : ____ : ____ : ____ : ____   a great deal of change from last
              1   2   3   4   5   6   7   year

1. The ways in which you approach your customers.
2. How many different approaches you will use with your customers.

SCALE NAME: Munificence (Car Dealer)

SCALE DESCRIPTION:

A five-item, five-point Likert-like summated ratings scale measuring a car dealer's perception of market opportunities for growth and profit.

SCALE ORIGIN:

The scale is original to Dwyer and Oh (1987).

SAMPLES:

Dwyer and Oh gathered data from car dealers in 10 different SMSAs: five areas with high growth characteristics and five markets with low growth characteristics. Ultimately, **167** usable responses were received, which represented a 69% response rate.

RELIABILITY:

An alpha of **.75** was reported for the four-item version of the scale, which was ultimately used in the data analysis.

VALIDITY:

The scale was checked for face validity by four dealers as well as four faculty colleagues. Data from a pretest were used to check for item convergence in a restricted one-factor model. In addition, item correlations and residual analysis were used to check for convergence and consistency.

ADMINISTRATION:

Respondents self-administered the scale along with many other measures. Higher scores on the scale suggest that car dealers think their opportunities for growth and profitability in their markets will be high whereas lower scores indicate that car dealers think their business environments will be very "lean."

MAJOR FINDINGS:

Dwyer and Oh used LISREL to analyze the effects of resource availability on constraints and opportunities in the car dealers' environment. **Munificence** was found to have a significant negative effect on formalization and centralization, but had an insignificant impact on participation in decision making.

COMMENTS:

Item 1 below must be adjusted to make it more contemporary. Further, the scale appears to be amenable for use in other product categories with some minor changes in phrasing.

REFERENCE:

Dwyer, F. Robert and Sejo Oh (1987), "Output Sector Munificence Effects on the Internal Political Economy of Marketing Channels," *JMR*, 24 (November), 347-358.

SCALE ITEMS: MUNIFICENCE (CAR DEALER)

The questions below seek your view of the competitive situation, business climate, and market opportunities for profitability and growth in your metropolitan area. (Please circle the letter preceding your answer.)

1. A recent automotive trade paper article anticipated an average sales gain of 16% in 1985 for new car dealers. Compared to this national average, would you rate your metro market's growth performance . . .
   a. Much higher than average
   b. Slightly higher than average
   c. About average
   d. Slightly below average
   e. Far below the average

2. Thinking about the business climate in general, how would you rate the metropolitan area overall in profit and growth opportunities for new car dealers?
   a. Outstanding opportunities for profits and growth
   b. Good opportunities for profits and growth
   c. Average opportunities for profits and growth
   d. Below average opportunities for profits and growth
   e. Neglible opportunities for profits and growth

3. In the last three years, my own trade area has shown a slowdown in real income, employment, and household formation. **(r)**
   a. Strongly agree
   b. Agree
   c. Neither agree nor disagree
   d. Disagree
   e. Strongly disagree

4. In the next three years, my trade area will show a strong increase in real income, employment, and new residents.
   a. Strongly agree
   b. Agree
   c. Neither agree nor disagree
   d. Disagree
   e. Strongly disagree

5. Five years from now, will your metropolitan market be served by more or fewer new car dealers?
   a. Several additional (net) dealers
   b. A small increase in the number of dealers
   c. About the same number of dealers
   d. A small decline in number of new car dealers
   e. A large decrease in new car dealers

SCALE NAME: Negotiation Skill

SCALE DESCRIPTION:

A 15-item, seven-point Likert-like summated ratings scale measuring a purchasing agent's perceived ability to negotiate.

SCALE ORIGIN:

Banting and Dion (1988) give credit to Raiffa (1982) for the items in the scale, but he in turn cited earlier sources. Apparently, the scale was adapted and used first as a multi-item measure by Dion and Banting (1987). Analysis in their study was based on 302 respondents to a questionnaire mailed to 683 members of the National Association of Purchasing Management. The purpose was to investigate some human variables that affect purchasing performance. Banting and Dion (1988) report the alpha for the scale in this initial study to have been .87.

SAMPLES:

A questionnaire was sent to a random sample of 1424 members of the Purchasing Management Association of Canada. A 32% response rate yielded **460** usable survey forms. There appeared to be no significant differences between the sample and the general membership of the Association. The typical respondent had a mean age of 39 years, income of $35,740, and 12.7 years in purchasing. Respondents worked for firms with an average of 1164 employees and a growth rate between 4% and 6%.

RELIABILITY:

An alpha of **.92** was reported for the scale by Banting and Dion.

VALIDITY:

The validity of the scale was not reported as being assessed.

ADMINISTRATION:

The scale was self-administered by respondents as part of a survey instrument they received in the mail. Lower scores on the scale indicate that respondents view themselves as skillful negotiators whereas higher scores imply that they are pessimistic about their ability to negotiate.

MAJOR FINDINGS:

The study examined the association between negotiation performance, personal characteristics, and aptitudes. **Negotiation skill** was among the best predictors of several measures of overall job performance.

REFERENCES:

Banting, Peter M. and Paul A. Dion (1988), ''The Purchasing Agent: Friend or Foe to the Salesperson?'' *JAMS*, 16 (Fall), 16-22.

Dion, Paul A. and Peter M. Banting (1987), ''Effective Buyers: Are They Cunning or Cooperative?'' *Journal of Purchasing and Materials Management*, 23 (Winter), 26-31.

Raiffa, Howard (1982), *The Art and Science of Negotiation*. Cambridge, Mass.: Harvard University Press.

SCALE ITEMS: NEGOTIATION SKILL

Strongly Agree	Moderately Agree	Slightly Agree	Neither Agree Nor Disagree	Slightly Disagree	Moderately Disagree	Strongly Disagree
1	2	3	4	5	6	7

1. I am usually as well as or better prepared for negotiations than other purchasing agents.
2. I perform well under the pressure of negotiation.
3. I can express myself well in negotiation sessions.
4. I am persuasive in negotiation sessions.
5. I am patient in negotiation sessions.
6. I am decisive in negotiation sessions.
7. During negotiation sessions I am in control of my emotions so that they are not visible to others unless I wish them to be.
8. I can gauge others' feelings in negotiation sessions.
9. I am able to perceive and use power to achieve a negotiation objective.
10. I am aware of the needs and reactions of both my own organization and my opponent's organization in negotiation sessions.
11. I am a competitive person.
12. I am good at debate.
13. I am willing to be disliked by my opponent negotiator to achieve my bargaining goals.
14. I am good at nonverbal communications, such as signs, gestures and silence.
15. I am willing to take business risks.

SCALE NAME: Opportunism (Dealer With Manufacturer)

SCALE DESCRIPTION:

A five-item, five-point Likert-type summated ratings scale measuring the degree to which a retailer/dealer reports that it shirks obligations, distorts information, and engages in opportunistic behavior in its relationship with a manufacturer.

SCALE ORIGIN:

The scale used by Dwyer and Oh (1987) drew heavily on the scale used by John (1984).

SAMPLES:

Dwyer and Oh gathered data from car dealers in 10 different SMSAs: five areas with high growth characteristics and five markets with low growth characteristics. Ultimately, **167** usable responses were received, which represented a 69% response rate.

RELIABILITY:

An alpha of **.79** was reported by Dwyer and Oh for their five-item version of the scale, which was ultimately used in the data analysis.

VALIDITY:

The scale was checked for face validity by four dealers as well as four faculty colleagues. Data from a pretest were used to check for item convergence in a restricted one factor model. In addition, item correlations and residual analysis were used to check for convergence and consistency.

ADMINISTRATION:

Respondents self-administered the scale along with many other measures. Lower scores on the scale suggest that respondents think the relationship they have with their manufacturers involves little opportunistic behavior on their part whereas higher scores indicate that they feel their relationship involves a lot of opportunism.

MAJOR FINDINGS:

Dwyer and Oh used LISREL to analyze the effects of resource availability on constraints and opportunities in the car dealers' environment. Formalization and participation decision-making characteristics had significant positive impacts, and centralization had a negative impact, on quality of the relationship with the manufacturer of which **opportunism** was one component.

COMMENTS:

See also the apparently similar scale used by John (1984).

REFERENCES:

Dwyer, F. Robert and Sejo Oh (1987), "Output Sector Munificence Effects on the Internal Political Economy of Marketing Channels," *JMR*, 24 (November), 347-358.

John, George (1984), "An Empirical Investigation of Some Antecedents of Opportunism in a Marketing Channel," *JMR*, 21 (August), 278-289.

SCALE ITEMS: OPPORTUNISM (DEALER WITH MANUFACTURER)

The statements below assess the quality of your relationship with the manufacturer. Based upon your experience, what do you expect will characterize your dealings with the manufacturer in the coming year?

Strongly Agree	Agree	Neutral	Disagree	Strongly Disagree
5———————	—4———————	—3———————	—2———————	—1

1. There will be some things I will do only if my supplier checks up and insists upon it.
2. At times I may have to overstate my difficulties in order to get manufacturer assistances.
3. I may promise the manufacturer to do some things without actually doing them later.
4. Sometimes, I will have to alter the facts slightly in order to get what I need from the manufacturer.
5. Occasionally I will shirk certain contractual obligations when I see profit opportunities for doing so.

SCALE NAME: Order Processing Activity (Salesperson)

SCALE DESCRIPTION:

A five-item, seven-point Likert-like summated ratings scale measuring the frequency with which a person engages in activities directly related to working with customer orders.

SCALE ORIGIN:

The scale is original to a study by Moncrief (1986). Several scales were developed for use in the study from a review of the literature and from personal interviews and focus groups with salespeople. A total of 121 selling-related activities were identified and included on the survey questionnaire.

SAMPLES:

Using stratified sampling, Moncrief sent survey forms to 800 firms representing 20 SIC codes (#20-#39). Fifty-one firms ultimately participated and sent copies of the questionnaire to their salespeople. Of the total 2322 sales employees working for these firms, 1393 returned usable forms but the factor analysis was based on responses from **1291**.

RELIABILITY:

An alpha of **.80** was reported for the scale.

VALIDITY:

Though scale validity was not specifically addressed in the study, a factor analysis of 121 items indicated that the items below all had loadings greater than .50 on the same factor and loadings less than .40 on other factors. These findings provide some evidence of the convergent and discriminant validity of the scale.

ADMINISTRATION:

The scale was self-administered by respondents along with many other measures in a mail survey format. Higher scores on the scale indicate that respondents frequently work with orders whereas lower scores suggest that they primarily perform activities other than those directly related to order processing.

MAJOR FINDINGS:

The purpose of the study by Moncrief was to develop a comprehensive list of selling-related activities and the taxonomies created from them. A cluster analysis was performed of the salespeople in the sample and six clusters were found. A group called trade servicer, representing 18% of the sample, had the highest mean on the **order processing activity** scale. This cluster had the highest mean of any of the sales groups on seven of 10 sales activity areas examined in the study and it had the second highest mean on the other three activity areas.

REFERENCE:

Moncrief, William C., III (1986), ''Selling Activity and Sales Position Taxonomies for Industrial Salesforces,'' *JMR*, 23 (August), 261-270.

SCALE ITEMS: ORDER PROCESSING ACTIVITY (SALESPERSON)+

Using the following scale, please indicate how frequently you engage in each of the activities listed below. If you do not perform the activity, please code your response as a zero.

Infrequently   ____ : ____ : ____ : ____ : ____ : ____ : ____   Frequently

            1   2   3   4   5   6   7

1. Expedite orders
2. Handle back orders
3. Handle shipment problems
4. Find lost orders
5. Write up orders

+ The actual directions and items were not stated in the article, but are reconstructed here on the basis of information provided.

SCALE NAME: Participation (Buying Group Structure)

SCALE DESCRIPTION:

A five-item, five-point Likert-like summated ratings scale measuring the proportion of time members of a buying group participate (or are encouraged to participate) in making source selection decisions.

SCALE ORIGIN:

Several, though not all, of the items used by McCabe (1987) were adapted from those developed by Duncan (1971).

SAMPLES:

The data in McCabe's study came from buying centers in either the airline or corrugated shipping container industry. In the former, **15** buying centers were involved with the decision to buy aircraft and **13** were involved with the decision to buy jet fuel. In the latter, **14** buying centers were concerned with the purchase of printing inks and **13** were concerned with buying printing presses and other capital equipment. Data were collected just from individuals involved in source selection. There was an average of 1.7 people per buying unit.

RELIABILITY:

An alpha of .**77** was reported for the scale.

VALIDITY:

A factor analysis of several items all related to buying group structure indicated that the five items compng this scale aoaded on the same factor.

ADMINISTRATION:

Though interviews of some sort were conducted with buying group members, the measures in the questionnaire are assumed to have been self-administered. Higher scores on the scale indicate that respondents report that members of their buying groups frequently participate in making source selection decisions.

MAJOR FINDINGS:

McCabe examined opposing views of the relation between buying group structure and environmental uncertainty. The findings indicated that a higher degree of **participation** was associated with lower levels of product complexity and task uncertainty.

REFERENCES:

Duncan, Robert Bannerman (1971), ''The Effects of Perceived Environmental Uncertainty on Organizational Decision Unit Structure: A Cybernetic Model,'' unpublished doctoral dissertation, Yale University.

McCabe, Donald L. (1987), ''Buying Group Structure: Constriction at the Top,'' *JM*, 51 (October), 89-98.

SCALE ITEMS: PARTICIPATION (BUYING GROUP STRUCTURE)

Instructions: The following questions ask about the buying center which makes the source selection decision for printing inks in your organization. They ask what percent of the time members of this group perform various activities in the source selection process. Circle any one of the five nubers for each qtion. The meaning of these numbers is as follows:

1 = Never or seldom (0 to 20% of the time)
2 = Occasionally (21 to 40% of the time)
3 = Half the time (41 to 60% of the time)
4 = Frequently (61 to 80% of the time)
5 = Usually or always (81 to 100% of the time)

1. How often are you encouraged to make suggestions concerning the source selection process?
2. How often do you take an active part in decisions that concern your role as a member of this buying task group?
3. How often does a high ranking member of this buying group make source related decisions without consulting you? (r)
4. How frequently are you asked to participate in decisions that involve your role as a member of this buying group?
5. How frequently are decisions related to your buying role and responsibilities made without your involvement? (r)

SCALE NAME: Participation (Channel Relationship)

SCALE DESCRIPTION:

A three-item, five-point Likert-like summated ratings scale measuring the degree to which a channel member reports that the channel leader solicits and seriously considers member inputs about channel-related decisions. In the study by Schul, Pride, and Little (1983), the scale specifically related to the channel relationships between franchisors and franchisees.

SCALE ORIGIN:

This scale and the study reported in the article by Schul and his coauthors came from the dissertation research by Schul (1980). He reported that a review of the literature and interviews with 50 franchisees helped to generate 19 items for measuring three types of leadership: participative, supportive, and directive. From results of a pilot study with data from 31 franchisees, the list was reduced to just nine items (three items per leadership type). Schul's is the only known use of the scale.

SALES:

The main study involved an eight-page questionnaire that was mailed to 1052 franchised real estate brokers with six different franchise affiliations. After two waves of mailings, a total of **349** usable survey forms were received. There was no evidence of nonresponse bias.

RELIABILITY:

An alpha of **.86** was calculated for the scale.

VALIDITY:

Evidence of content validity came from the pretest interviews. With data from the main study, a factor analysis with oblique rotation was performed on the nine scale items representing the three leadership styles. The three items for each scale loaded together and had low loadings on the other factors. However, the interfactor correlations were rather high, particularly between the participative and supportive leadership factors ($r = .523$). In fact, in a later study in which a varimax rotation was used, items for those two scales loaded on the same factor.

ADMINISTRATION:

The scale was self-administered by respondents along with many other measures in a mail survey format. Higher scores on the scale indicate that channel members report that their channel leaders solicit and seriously consider member inputs about channel-related decisions.

MAJOR FINDINGS:

The purpose of the study by Schul and his coauthors was to investigate the influence of different channel leadership types on channel members' perceptions of intrachannel conflict. The data indicated that **participative leadership** had a significant negative relationship to channel member perception of conflict.

COMMENTS:

Schul (1987) has also used the items composing this scale with several others to measure Channel Leadership (Considerate).

REFERENCES:

Schul, Patrick L. (1980), "An Empirical Investigation of the Conflict Behavior Process in Franchise Channels of Distribution," unpublished doctoral dissertation, Texas A&M University.

_____ (1987), "An Investigation of Path-Goal Leadership Theory and Its Impact on Intrachannel Conflict and Satisfaction," *JAMS*, 15 (Winter), 42-52.

_____, William M. Pride, and Taylor L. Little (1983), "The Impact of Channel Leadership Behavior on Intrachannel Conflict," *JM*, 47 (Summer), 21-34.

SCALE ITEMS: PARTICIPATION (CHANNEL RELATIONSHIP)

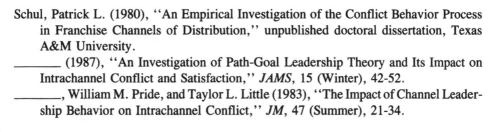

Strongly Disagree	Disagree	Neither	Agree	Strongly Agree
1	2	3	4	5

In my franchise agreement:
1. Franchisees have major influence in the determination of policies and standards for this franchise organization.
2. Good ideas from franchisees often do not get passed along to franchise management. **(r)**
3. Franchisees are not allowed to provide input into the determination of standards and promotional allowances. **(r)**

SCALE NAME: Participation (Channel Relationship)

SCALE DESCRIPTION:

A three-item, five-point Likert-like summated ratings scale measuring the degree to which a channel member such as a retailer reports that its relationship with suppliers is characterized by participation in the decisions made.

SCALE ORIGIN:

Dwyer and Welsh (1985) indicate that items for their scale were adapted from the work of Spekman and Stern (1979), who in turn adapted their items from Duncan (1971).

SAMPLES:

Dwyer and Welsh mailed questionnaires to 7254 retailers in 10 industries whose addresses had been provided by a list broker. Envelopes were simply addressed to "Manager" in each case. After a second wave to 10% of the original sample, a total of **457** responses were used in the analysis. Because of such a low response rate, the authors provided rather detailed information about response rates and characteristics by industry.

RELIABILITY:

An alpha of **.53** was reported by Dwyer and Welsh for their three-item version of the scale, which was ultimately used in the data analysis.

VALIDITY:

Five items adapted from Spekman and Stern were originally used by Dwyer and Welsh, but one item was eliminated because of low item-total correlation and another item was dropped to improve a LISREL restricted factor analysis.

ADMINISTRATION:

Respondents self-administered the scale along with many other measures in the study by Dwyer and Welsh. Higher scores on the scale suggest that respondents think the relationship they have with their suppliers allows a lot of participation in the decision making whereas lower scores indicate that they feel decisions are mostly made without their being consulted.

MAJOR FINDINGS:

Dwyer and Welsh investigated environmental effects on channel structure and processes in a political economy framework. Among their many findings was that direct-to-retailer and three-level channel configurations had significantly more **participation** in decision making than corporate and multiple-wholesaler systems, retailers served by multiple wholesalers in heterogeneous environments were more likely to **participate** in decision making than those in homogeneous environments, and retailers with multiple wholesalers had greater **participation** with more variability in the output sector.

REFERENCES:

Duncan, Robert Bannerman (1971), "The Effects of Perceived Environmental Uncertainty on Organizational Decision Unit Structure: A Cybernetic Model," unpublished doctoral dissertation, Yale University.

Dwyer, F. Robert and M. Ann Welsh (1985), "Environmental Relationships of the Internal Political Economy of Marketing Channels," *JMR*, 22 (November), 397-414.

Spekman, Robert E. and Louis W. Stern (1979), "Environmental Uncertainty and Buying Group Structure: An Empirical Investigation," *JM*, (Spring), 54-64.

SCALE ITEMS: PARTICIPATION (CHANNEL RELATIONSHIP)

Think about the relationship you have with your supplier(s) of this line. There are probably a number of facets involved in marketing the line, e.g., display, mix of assortment, return, etc. Please use the scale below to describe the different aspects of decision making in that relationship.

Never	Seldom	Occasionally	Rather Often	Nearly All The Time
1————	——2————	——3————	——4————	——5

Thinking about your relationship with suppliers, would you say . . .

1. you play an active part in decision making.
2. suggestions from you are encouraged.
3. supplier(s') decisions are made without consulting you. **(r)**

SCALE NAME: Participation (Channel Relationship)

SCALE DESCRIPTION:

A five-item, five-point Likert-like summated ratings scale measuring the degree to which a retailer/dealer reports that its relationship with another channel member is characterized by participation in the decisions made. The version of the scale used by Dwyer and Oh (1988) had an additional two items.

SCALE ORIGIN:

Dwyer and Oh (1987, 1988) imply that they developed their scale on the basis of similar measures used in several other studies in marketing, one of the earliest of which was by Spekman and Stern (1979), who in turn developed their scale by adapting items used by Duncan (1971).

SAMPLES:

Dwyer and Oh (1987) gathered data from car dealers in 10 different SMSAs: five areas with high growth characteristics and five markets with low growth characteristics. Ultimately, **167** usable responses were received, which represented a 69% response rate.

Subsequently, Dwyer and Oh (1988) gathered data through mail surveys of hardware store managers. Addresses of stores were initially taken from yellow pages for 10 cities representing a variety of geographic areas in the United States. Questionnaires were eventually sent to 186 dealers, of whom **133** responded with usable data.

RELIABILITY:

An alpha of **.84** was reported (1987) for the five-item version of the scale, which was ultimately used in the data analysis; **.79** was reported (1988) for the seven-item version.

VALIDITY:

Dwyer and Oh (1987) checked the scale for face validity with four dealers as well as four faculty colleagues. Data from a pretest were used to check for item convergence in a restricted one-factor model. In addition, item correlations and residual analysis were used to check for convergence and consistency.

Dwyer and Oh (1988) used a LISREL chi-square three-factor measurement model to test the items for this scale along with those for two other scales (formalization and centralization). The significance of the measurement model and other data indicated that items for the participation scale showed evidence of discriminate and convergent validity.

ADMINISTRATION:

Respondents self-administered the scale along with many other measures in the studies by Dwyer and Oh. Higher scores on the scale suggest that respondents think the relationship they have with a channel member allows a lot of participation in the decision making whereas lower scores indicate that they feel decisions are mostly made without their being consulted.

MAJOR FINDINGS:

Dwyer and Oh (1987) used LISREL to analyze the effects of resource availability on constraints and opportunities in the car dealers' environment. The availability and abundance of critical resources (profit opportunities, growth potential, competition) were not found to have a significant effect on **participation** in decision making, but **participation** had a significant positive impact on quality of the relationship with the manufacturer.

The purpose of the second study by Dwyer and Oh (1988) was to investigate differences between three types of contractually integrated channel systems and decision-making processes within the channel, as well as their competitive strategies. No significant difference was found in **participation** decision-making style between any of the three channel systems (retailer cooperatives, wholesaler voluntaries, and independents and their respective primary wholesalers).

REFERENCES:

Duncan, Robert Bannerman (1971), "The Effects of Perceived Environmental Uncertainty on Organizational Decision Unit Structure: A Cybernetic Model," unpublished doctoral dissertation, Yale University.

Dwyer, F. Robert and Sejo Oh (1987), "Output Sector Munificence Effects on the Internal Political Economy of Marketing Channels," *JMR*, 24 (November), 347-358.

_____ and _____ (1988), "A Transaction Cost Perspective on Vertical Contractual Structure and Interchannel Competitive Strategies," *JM*, 52 (April), 21-34.

Spekman, Robert E. and Louis W. Stern (1979), "Environmental Uncertainty and Buying Group Structure: An Empirical Investigation," *JM*, 43 (Spring), 54-64.

SCALE ITEMS: PARTICIPATION (CHANNEL RELATIONSHIP) +

To various degrees, each _____ or dealer depends on the other for: 1) product or market access, 2) promotion or sales support, and 3) distribution or inventory efficiency through coordination. How do you and your _____ coordinate your relationship? Is it characterized by standard routines? Joint problem solving? Authority? Please indicate the extent to which you agree or disagree with each statement below.

Strongly Agree	Agree	Neutral	Disagree	Strongly Disagree
5————————	4————————	3————————	2————————	1

1. Policy and procedural changes by my _____ usually receive my input and opinion before implementation.
2. My ideas for ordering, selling and servicing are welcomed by my _____.
3. I play an active part in decision-making when it comes to planning distribution and sales programs with my _____.
4. My _____ encourages suggestions from me for improving distribution and marketing programs.
5. My _____ rarely consults me when formulating distribution and marketing programs. **(r)**
6. Many of my _____ distribution and sales programs seem to reflect very little input and appreciation of my concerns. **(r)**

7. I am not involved in the distribution and marketing decisions of my _____. **(r)**

+ Items 1 through 5 were used in two studies by Dwyer and Oh (1987, 1988). Items 6 and 7 were just used in the latter study. Also, in the former study the blanks were filled with "the manufacturer" whereas in the latter study the items referred to "my primary wholesaler."

SCALE NAME: Participation (Leadership Style)

SCALE DESCRIPTION:

A four-item, five-point Likert-like summated ratings scale measuring the degree to which a salesperson reports that a supervisor allows the salesperson to influence and determine his/her own work responsibilities.

SCALE ORIGIN:

The items used by Teas (1980) were adapted for the sales situation from items developed by Vroom (1960), whose data came from 108 supervisors working fa large delivery company. The test-retest stability was .63 over a seven-month period for 77 supervisors who did not change positions or superiors during the period.

SAMPLES:

Teas use intracompany mail distribution to reach 184 salesmen of a midwestern company's industrial salesforce. Analysis was based on responses from **127** salespeople.

RELIABILITY:

An alpha of **.817** was reported for the scale by Teas.

VALIDITY:

No specific examination of scale validity was reported.

ADMINISTRATION:

The scale was self-administered along with several other measures. Higher scores on the scale indicate that salespeople believe their respective supervisors are willing to let salespeople influence and determine their job responsibilities whereas low scores imply that they feel their supervisors allow them little say about what goes on in their jobs.

MAJOR FINDINGS:

Teas used path analysis to examine simultaneously some causes and results of salesperson perceptions of role ambiguity. **Participative leadership** was found to have a direct effect on role ambiguity (negative) and intrinsic job satisfaction (positive), but only an indirect effect on extrinsic job satisfaction via role ambiguity.

REFERENCES:

Teas, R. Kenneth (1980), "An Empirical Test of Linkages Proposed in the Walker, Churchill, and Ford Model of Salesforce Motivation and Performance," *JAMS*, 8 (Winter), 58-72.

Vroom, Victor H. (1960), *Some Personality Determinants of the Effects of Participation.* Engelwood Cliffs, N.J.: Prentice-Hall, Inc.

SCALE ITEMS: PARTICIPATION (LEADERSHIP STYLE)

```
Very                                                                      Very
Little                                                                    Much
     1——————————2——————————3——————————4——————————5
```

1. The amount of influence I have in what goes on in my sales territory.
2. The degree to which I can influence the decisions of my immediate superior regarding things over which I am concerned.
3. The frequency with which my superior asks my opinion when a problem comes up that involves my work.
4. The feeling that it is easy to get my job improvement ideas across to my superior.

SCALE NAME: Participation (Leadership Style)

SCALE DESCRIPTION:

A four-item, five-point summated ratings scale measuring the degree to which a salesperson perceives that his/her supervisor gives serious consideration to what subordinates have to say before making decisions.

SCALE ORIGIN:

This scale is a slightly modified version of a measure developed by House and Dessler (1974). Their five item scale was reported to have reliability (KR-20) of .67 (n = 129) and .68 (n = 75) for a wide range of employees of two electronics firms.

SAMPLES:

Teas (1981) collected data from **171** salespeople in group interviews during sales meetings. The salespeople represented 74% of the industrial salesforces of three midwestern companies. The typical salesperson was 36 years of age and had spent 6.5 years with his company.

Subsequently, Teas (1983) based his analysis on data collected from two midwestern U.S. firms' salesforces. In both cases, the salespeople were sent survey forms via intracompany mail and were asked to return the completed forms by mail to the researcher at his university address. Usable questionnaires were returned by **116** salespeople, which was described as representing a 55% response rate.

RELIABILITY:

Alpha values of **.822** (1981), and **.743** (1983) were reported for the scale by Teas.

VALIDITY:

Teas (1981) performed a factor analysis on five items thought to measure the construct. Four of the items were found to have loadings greater than .50 on the same factor. He reported no specific examination of scale validity in 1983.

ADMINISTRATION:

In Teas' 1981 study the scale was apparently self-administered by salespeople in "group interviews" during sales meetings, whereas in Teas' 1983 study the scale was apparently self-administered at the salesperson's convenience in a more private setting as described above. Higher scores on this scale indicate that salespeople believe their respective supervisors have leadership styles that consider subordinates' opinions before decisons are made whereas lower scores suggest that they perceive supervisors to allow little participation by subordinates in decision making.

MAJOR FINDINGS:

Teas (1981) investigated the impact of several personality characteristics and job-related perceptions on work motivation. The results indicated that a **supervisor's participatory**

leadership style was a significant positive predictor of performance expectations and job instrumentalities.

Teas (1983) used causal modeling to investigate the relationship between style of sales supervision and salesperson role stress. A **participatory leadership style** was found to be a significant negative predictor of role conflict and ambiguity and a very important positive predictor of job satisfaction.

COMMENTS:

The actual items Teas used in 1983 were not specified, but were implied to be the same as those used in 1981. See another use of the scale by Teas and Horrell (1981).

REFERENCES:

House, Robert J. and Gary Dessler (1974), ''The Path-Goal Theory of Leadership: Some Post-Hoc and A Priori Tests,'' in *Contingency Approaches to Leadership*, James G. Hunt and Lars L. Larson, eds. Carbondale, Ill.: Southern Illinois University Press.

Teas, R. Kenneth (1981), ''An Empirical Test of Models of Salespersons' Job Expectancy and Instrumentality Perceptions,'' *JMR*, 18 (May), 209-226.

———— (1983), ''Supervisory Behavior, Role Stress, and the Job Satisfaction of Industrial Salespeople,'' *JMR*, 20 (February), 84-91.

———— and James F. Horrell (1981), ''Salespeople's Satisfaction and Performance Feedback,'' *Industrial Marketing Management*, 10 (February), 49-57.

SCALE ITEMS: PARTICIPATION (LEADERSHIP STYLE)

Very False		Very True
1————————2————————3————————4————————5		

1. Before making decisions, my supervisor gives serious consideration to what his subordinates have to say.
2. Before taking action, my supervisor gives serious consideration to what his subordinates say.
3. My supervisor asks his subordinates for their suggestions concerning how to carry out job assignments.
4. My supervisor asks his subordinates for their suggestions on what job assignments should be made.

SCALE NAME: Participation in Decision-Making Unit

SCALE DESCRIPTION:

A three-item, five-point Likert-like summated ratings scale measuring the amount of information offered to other members of an industrial decision-making unit for use in making a purchase evaluation and decision.

SCALE ORIGIN:

McQuiston (1989) indicated that he used a measure by Speckman and Stern (1979), but the items were altered enough so that even though the two scales may measure the same or similar constructs they are still distinctly different measures.

SAMPLES:

McQuiston mailed survey instruments to customers of a large manufacturer of capital equipment that had purchased one of three different models of a product line within the 18 months preceding the study. A key informant in each company was contacted with the purpose of obtaining names of others in the organization who had provided input to the purchase decision. Those others were then contacted and, if willing to participate, were sent questionnaires. Of the 273 forms mailed, **182** usable returns were received from employees of 82 different companies.

RELIABILITY:

An alpha of **.892** was reported for the scale.

VALIDITY:

The validity of the scale was not examined.

ADMINISTRATION:

The scale used by McQuiston was self-administered along with several other measures in a mail questionnaire. Higher scores suggest that respondents perceive another person has offered a great amount of information to others in a decision-making unit whereas lower scores imply that they believe a person participated little.

MAJOR FINDINGS:

The purpose of the study by McQuiston was to examine some attributes of the industrial purchase situation and their influence on the purchase decision. Among other findings, **participation** was found to have a significant positive relationship with the influence a person's communication has on the actions of others in the decision-making unit.

REFERENCES:

McQuiston, Daniel H. (1989), ''Novelty, Complexity, and Importance as Causal Determinants of Industrial Buyer Behavior,'' *JM*, 53 (April), 66-79.

Spekman, Robert and Louis Stern (1979), ''Environmental Uncertainty and Buying Group Structure: An Empirical Investigation,'' *JM*, 43 (Spring), 54-64.

SCALE ITEMS: PARTICIPATION IN DECISION MAKING UNIT

Little or none	Some	Quite a lot	A great deal	A very great deal
1————	——2————	——3————	——4————	——5

1. Amount of communication offered to others for consideration during alternative evaluation stage.
2. Amount of communication offered to others for consideration during the choice stage.
3. The total amount of communication offered to others for consideration during the entire process.

SCALE NAME: Performance Control Sensitivity (Branch Manager)

SCALE DESCRIPTION:

> An eight-item, seven-point Likert-type summated ratings scale measuring the presence of company control mechanisms intended to motivate a manager to maximize performance in his/her branch.

SCALE ORIGIN:

> There is no information to indicate that the scale is not original to the study by Phillips (1982).

SAMPLES:

> The data used by Phillips came from a convenience sample of U.S. manufacturers operating sales branch distribution systems. The key informant method was used and no branch was included in the analysis unless responses were received from the headquarters informant, the branch manager informant, and at least two branch personnel other than the manager. Of the 80 branches contacted (two per company), usable information was provided by **70** branch managers. The average (mean) branch participating in the survey had been in operation for 19 years, had 32 employees, a salesforce of 12, and annual net sales for the previous year of $9.8 million. This scale was apparently administered only to branch manager informants.

RELIABILITY:

> Using a monomethod level of analysis, Phillips calculated a composite reliability of **.84.**

VALIDITY:

> A LISREL chi-square goodness-of-fit test provided evidence of convergent validity. When two items were removed from the original 10-item measure, unidimensionality was achieved.

ADMINISTRATION:

> The scale was self-administered along with several other measures in a mail survey format. Higher scores on the scale indicate that respondents believe the control system used by the company strongly encourages branch managers to improve their performances whereas lower scores suggest that they feel evaluation of their performance is not thorough.

MAJOR FINDINGS:

> The purpose of the study by Phillips was to test a theory of control losses in vertically integrated channels as a function of organizational design variables. In a causal model, **branch manager performance control sensitivity** was found to have a significant negative impact on control losses (unjustified travel and entertainment expenses) in sales branch operations.

REFERENCES:

Phillips, Lynn W. (1982), ''Explaining Control Losses in Corporate Marketing Channels: An Organizational Analysis,'' *JMR*, 19 (November), 525-549.

SCALE ITEMS: PERFORMANCE CONTROL SENSITIVITY (BRANCH MANAGER)

The following statements may or may not describe how the company goes about monitoring and evaluating the performance of your sales branch. Using the following scale please indicate how much do you agree or disagree with each statement.

Strongly Disagree	Disagree	Slightly Disagree	Neutral	Slightly Agree	Agree	Strongly Agree
1	2	3	4	5	6	7

1. The persons in the company responsible for overseeing branch operations are not very familiar with the overall level of performance achieved by this branch. **(r)**
2. The performance reports submitted by our branch to the company are not examined very carefully by company personnel. **(r)**
3. The control system used by the company for monitoring branch performance is not a very thorough one. **(r)**
4. Our branch would have to be performing very badly before company management would take corrective action. **(r)**
5. The expense reports submitted by our branch to the company do not undergo a careful and close review by company personnel. **(r)**
6. In its evaluation by the branch, the company takes into account all of those things that influence branch performance.
7. Branch managers have a great deal of incentive to try to improve the performance of their operations.
8. Company audits of records kept by this branch are not very thorough. **(r)**

SCALE NAME: Performance Control Sensitivity (Salesforce)

SCALE DESCRIPTION:

A nine-item, seven-point Likert-like summated ratings scale measuring the presence of control mechanisms intended to motivate a branch sales manager to evaluate and maximize performance in his/her salesforce.

SCALE ORIGIN:

There is no information to indicate that the scale is not original to the study by Phillips (1982).

SAMPLES:

The data used by Phillips came from a convenience sample of U.S. manufacturers operating sales branch distribution systems. The key informant method was used and no branch was included in the analysis unless responses were received from the headquarters informant, the branch manager informant, and at least two branch personnel other than the manager. Of the 80 branches contacted (two per company), usable information was provided by **70** branch managers. The average (mean) branch participating in the survey had been in operation for 19 years, had 32 employees, a salesforce of 12, and annual net sales for the previous year of $9.8 million.

RELIABILITY:

As part of validity testing, the sample was split in half with branch manager informants being deliberately grouped into split-half 1. Using a monomethod level of analysis, Phillips calculated composite reliability **.81** and **.83** for split-halves 1 and 2, respectively.

VALIDITY:

A LISREL chi-square goodness-of-fit test provided evidence of convergent validity. Unidimensionality was achieved for split-half 1 but was initially rejected for split-half 2. A second model hypothesizing three correlated errors among the nine items showed evidence of convergent validity.

ADMINISTRATION:

The scale was self-administered by Phillips along with several other measures in a mail survey format. Higher scores on the scale indicate that respondents believe the control system used by the branch manager strongly encourages salespeople to improve their performances whereas lower scores suggest that they feel evaluation of salesforce performance is not thorough.

MAJOR FINDINGS:

The purpose of the study by Phillips was to test a theory of control losses in vertically integrated channels as a function of organizational design variables. In a causal model,

salesforce performance control sensitivity had a significant negative impact on control losses (travel and entertainment expenses) that were not justified on the basis of necessity, but did not have a significant effect on control loses that exceeded corporate norms.

COMMENTS:

Some attention should be given to the awkward wording of several of the scale items due to the mixing of singular and plural relationships as well as a bias toward a male salesforce.

REFERENCE:

Phillips, Lynn W. (1982), ''Explaining Control Losses in Corporate Marketing Channels: An Organizational Analysis,'' *JMR*, 19 (November), 525-549.

SCALE ITEMS: PERFORMANCE CONTROL SENSITIVITY (SALESFORCE)

The following statements may or may not describe how branch management goes about monitoring and evaluating the performance of your salesforce. Using the following scale please indicate how much do you agree or disagree with each statement.

Strongly Disagree	Disagree	Slightly Disagree	Neutral	Slightly Agree	Agree	Strongly Agree
1	2	3	4	5	6	7

1. The persons in the branch responsible for sales management are not very familiar with the on-the-job performance of the branch salesmen. **(r)**
2. In this branch, salesmee a great deal ncentive to try to do better.
3. The branch closely monitors salesmen's performance according to written records, e.g., records about his sales volume, selling costs.
4. Salesmen are often checked upon by supervisors to see what the salesman is doing on the job.
5. Management is quick to take steps to correct unsatisfactory performance by a salesman in this branch.
6. Supervisors inspect salesmen's work very closely to see that it measures up to standards.
7. Even if a salesman violates a rule pertaining to his job, penalties are rarely imposed. **(r)**
8. In evaluating the performance of a salesman, management takes into account all of the factors that influence a salesman's performance.
9. For the salesman in this branch, there is a very close relationship between the excellence of their job performance and the rewards they receive.

SCALE NAME: Performance Documentation

SCALE DESCRIPTION:

A two-item, five-point Likert-like summated ratings scale measuring the degree to which an employee perceives that available forms of assessment in an organization can document his/her performance.

SCALE ORIGIN:

The scale was apparently developed by Jaworski and MacInnis (1989). The scale and other aspects of the survey instrument were refined through a series of interviews and a pretest of marketing managers.

SAMPLES:

A national sample of marketing mangers was drawn randomly from the American Marketing Association's list of members. Of the 479 managers who appear to have received questionnaires, **379** returned usable forms.

RELIABILITY:

The two items in the scale used by Jaworski and MacInnis had a correlation of .**76**.

VALIDITY:

The validity of the scale was not specifically examined.

ADMINISTRATION:

The scale was self-administered along with many other measures in a mail survey format. Higher scores on the scale indicate that employees strongly believe that present documentation can be used to evaluate their work whereas lower scores suggest that they think their work cannot be adequately assessed with present documentation.

MAJOR FINDINGS:

Among the many purposes of the study by Jawors and MacInnis was to examine the simultaneous use of several types of managerial controls in the context of marketing management. Using structural equations, the authors found that **performance documentation** had a significant positive impact on the use of output, professional, and self control.

REFERENCE:

Jaworski, Bernard J. and Deborah J. MacInnis (1989), ''Marketing Jobs and Management Controls: Toward a Framework,'' *JMR*, 26 (November), 406-419.

SCALE ITEMS: PERFORMANCE DOCUMENTATION

Strongly Disagree	Disagree	Neutral	Agree	Strongly Agree
1—————————	—2—————————	—3—————————	—4—————————	—5

1. Documents exist to measure my performance after activities are complete.
2. My performance can be adequately assessed using existing documents.

SCALE NAME: Performance Evaluation (Ease of Assessment)

SCALE DESCRIPTION:

A six-item, seven-point Likert-like summated ratings scale measuring the difficulty of supervising and evaluating the performance of a company's salespeople.

SCALE ORIGIN:

John and Weitz give no indication that this scale originated elsewhere than in their study.

SAMPLES:

John and Weitz collected data in a two-stage sampling procedure. Personalized requests were mailed to 750 sales managers or sales vice presidents of manufacturing firms with annual sales of at least $50 million. The 266 respondents were then sent a questionnaire and of that group **161** returned usable survey instruments. The sample appeared to be different from the population in some respects but very similar in others.

RELIABILITY:

An alpha of **.70** was reported for the scale. Item-total correlations ranged from .25 to .61.

VALIDITY:

No specific examination of scale validity was made.

ADMINISTRATION:

The scale was self-administered by respondents along with many other measures in a mail questionnaire format. Higher scores on the scale suggest that respondents believe their respective companies have difficulty assessing the performance of their salespeople whereas lower scores indicate that they think it is easy to supervise and evaluate them.

MAJOR FINDINGS:

The purpose of the study by John and Weitz was to examine the role of salary in sales compensation plans by using a transaction cost analysis framework. The difficulty of **salesperson assessment** had its most significant correlation (positive) with the transaction asset specificity between the firm and its salespeople.

REFERENCE:

John, George and Barton Weitz (1989), "Salesforce Compensation: An Empirical Investigation of Factors Related to Use of Salary Versus Incentive Compensation," *JMR*, 26 (February), 1-14.

SCALE ITEMS: PERFORMANCE EVALUATION (EASE OF ASSESSMENT)

Strongly Disagree	Disagree	Slightly Disagree	Neutral	Slightly Agree	Agree	Strongly Agree
1———	———2———	———3———	———4———	———5———	———6———	———7

1. It is just not possible to supervise these salespeople closely.
2. It is difficult to evaluate how much effort any individual in this group really puts into his job.
3. We have accurate activity reports for each of these salespeople. **(r)**
4. It is easy for these salespeople to turn in falsified sales call reports if they want to.
5. Our evaluation of each salesperson in this group is based on quite accurate information. **(r)**
6. These salespeople travel so much that close supervision is impossible.

SCALE NAME: Performance Evaluation (Retailer With Wholesaler)

SCALE DESCRIPTION:

A four-item, eight-point Likert-like summated ratings scale measuring the level of approval a retailer reports having with the performance by a specified wholesaler of certain distribution-related services. It was referred to by John and Reve (1982) as Evaluation of Accomplishment.

SCALE ORIGIN:

Though not specified in the article by John and Reve, it is apparent that their data came from the latter's dissertation (Reve 1980). His initial scale had nine items and the final version had four. As different alpha values were reported for the scales and the items used by John and Reve were not reported, it is not known what else is different about the scales.

SAMPLES:

The data analyzed by John and Reve came from the dissertation research by Reve. Initially, 753 wholesalers in Norway were asked to identify their three largest retail customers. One retailer was selected at random from each of those suggested by the 238 responding wholesalers. Those retailers were contacted and 140 provided usable responses. Finally, the 140 wholesalers identified by the retailers were recontacted for further information. Data were ultimately collected from **99** retailer/wholesaler dyads.

RELIABILITY:

The alpha for the version of the scale used by John and Reve was reported to be .**77**. Items with low item-total correlations were said to have been deleted.

VALIDITY:

John and Reve eliminated items with low loadings on a factor. Further, they used the multitrait, multimethod approach as well as a structural equations model to assess convergent and discriminant validity. These methods indicated poor convergent and discriminant validity.

ADMINISTRATION:

The scale was self-administered by respondents along with many other measures in a mail survey format. High scores on the scale indicate that retailers report a great amount of satisfaction with the performance of distribution-related services by specified wholesalers.

MAJOR FINDINGS:

The purpose of the study by John and Reve was to examine the validity of several measures of channel relationships by using information from wholesaler/retailer dyads. The authors concluded that the "sentiments" variables, including **performance evaluation**, did not show adequate convergent or discriminant validity. For example, the correlation between the retailers' and wholesalers' perceptions of the amount of **performance evaluation** in their dyadic relationships was only .197. Given this finding, the authors wondered if it was not possible that "real" differences existed between dyadic members in their perceptions of this variable.

COMMENTS:

The scale was administered in Norwegian, so it is not known how its psychometric properties might be different if it were used in English as shown below. Further, the scale's current psychometric quality is so low that significant modifications are necessary before it is used further, particularly in English.

REFERENCES:

John, George and Torger Reve (1982), "The Reliability and Validity of Key Informant Data From Dyadic Relationships in Marketing Channels," *JMR*, 19 (November), 517-524.

Reve, Torger (1980), "Interorganizational Relations in Distribution Channels: An Empirical Study of Norwegian Distribution Channel Dyads," unpublished doctoral dissertation, Northwestern University.

SCALE ITEMS: PERFORMANCE EVALUATION (RETAILER WITH WHOLESALER)

Below is listed a number of statements which describe various means of coordination with the supplier level. Please indicate on the following scale to what degree each statement represents a good or poor description of the relationship between your firm and the specified supplier.

Not relevant = 0
Erroneous description = 1
Very poor description = 2
Poor description = 3
Neither poor nor good description = 4
Good description = 5
Very good description = 6
Completely correct description = 7

1. The supplier performs his delivery tasks to our full satisfaction.
2. The sales representatives or consultants are very competent in their work.
3. The supplier's credit terms are very satisfactory from our perspective.
4. The supplier offers us a very satisfactory discount and bonus program.

SCALE NAME: Performance Evaluation (Wholesaler With Retailer)

SCALE DESCRIPTION:

A four-item, eight-point Likert-like summated ratings scale measuring the level of approval a wholesaler reports having with the performance by a specified retailer of certain distribution-related services. The scale also appears to measure some sense of the wholesaler's understanding that its own performance is satisfactory to the retailer. It was referred to by John and Reve (1982) as Evaluation of Accomplishment.

SCALE ORIGIN:

Though not specified in the article by John and Reve, it is apparent that their data came from the latter's dissertation (Reve 1980). His initial scale had nine items. The final version had seven items and an alpha of .768. The scale used by John and Reve had three items less than the final version reported by Reve. As the items used by the former were not reported, it is not known which items below were eliminated.

SAMPLES:

The data analyzed by John and Reve came from the dissertation research by Reve. Initially, 753 wholesalers in Norway were asked to identify their three largest retail customers. One retailer was selected at random from each of those suggested by the 238 responding wholesalers. Those retailers were contacted and 140 provided usable responses. Finally, the 140 wholesalers identified by the retailers were recontacted for further information. Data were ultimately collected from **99** retailer/wholesaler dyads.

RELIABILITY:

The alpha for the version of the scale used by John and Reve was reported to be **.71**. Items with low item-total correlations were said to have been deleted.

VALIDITY:

John and Reve eliminated items with low loadings on a factor. Further, they used the multitrait, multimethod approach as well as a structural equations model to assess convergent and discriminant validity. These methods indicated poor convergent and discriminant validity.

ADMINISTRATION:

The scale was self-administered by respondents along with many other measures in a mail survey format. High scores on the scale indicate that wholesalers report a great amount of mutual satisfaction with the performance of distribution-related services by themselves and specified retailers.

MAJOR FINDINGS:

The purpose of the study by John and Reve was to examine the validity of several measures of channel relationships by using information from wholesaler/retailer dyads. The authors concluded that the "sentiments" variables, including **performance evaluation**, did not show adequate convergent or discriminant validity. For example, the correlation between the retailers' and wholesalers' perceptions of the amount of **performance evaluation** in their dyadic relationships was only .197. Given this finding, the authors wondered if it was not possible that "real" differences existed between dyadic members in their perceptions of this variable.

COMMENTS:

The scale was administered in Norwegian, so it is not known how its psychometric properties might be different if it were used in English as shown below. Further, the scale's current psychometric quality is so low that significant modifications are necessary before it is used further, particularly in English.

REFERENCES:

John, George and Torger Reve (1982), "The Reliability and Validity of Key Informant Data From Dyadic Relationships in Marketing Channels," *JMR*, 19 (November), 517-524.

Reve, Torger (1980), "Interorganizational Relations in Distribution Channels: An Empirical Study of Norwegian Distribution Channel Dyads," unpublished doctoral dissertation, Northwestern University.

SCALE ITEMS: PERFORMANCE EVALUATION (WHOLESALER WITH RETAILER) +

Below is listed a number of statements which describe various means of coordination with the retailing level. Please indicate on the following scale to what degree each statement represents a good or poor description of the relationship between your firm and the specified retail customer.

Not relevant = 0
Erroneous description = 1
Very poor description = 2
Poor description = 3
Neither poor nor good description = 4
Good description = 5
Very good description = 6
Completely correct description = 7

1. We have the impression that the retailer is fully satisfied with our delivery tasks.
2. We think we have good knowledge of the special needs and wants of the final consumers.
3. There are seldom delays in our deliveries to the retailer.
4. The retailer's personnel are very competent in their work.
5. We always try to inform the retailer early about out of stock items or discontinuation of items.

6. We also have the impression that our discount and bonus program is perceived to be very satisfactory by the retailer.
7. There are seldom errors in our deliveries to this retailer.

+ The scale reported in the article by John and Reve (1982) apparently used only four of these items. According to the information provided by Reve (1980, p. 183), item 4 had a much smaller factor loading than the rest and appears to be a good candidate for elimination. Items 2 and 5 had the next smallest loadings.

SCALE NAME: Performance Expectations (Salesperson)

SCALE DESCRIPTION:

A three-item, seven-point Likert-like summated ratings scale measuring the expectations an employee has about the results of putting a lot of effort into his/her work.

SCALE ORIGIN:

The scale was apparently developed by Kohli (1985).

SAMPLES:

The analysis by Kohli (1985) was based on data from **114** salespeople. The sample was obtained from three companies manufacturing and selling industrial products. An overall response rate of 89.8% was reported.

RELIABILITY:

An alpha of **.88** was reported for the scale.

VALIDITY:

Though the specific results were not reported for this scale, Kohli implied that a factor analysis of this and other scales was used to eliminate items with weak loadings on their hypothesized factors. Also, the correlation between this measure and another scale to measure the same construct was .61, which provides some evidence of tthe scale's concurrent validity.

ADMINISTRATION:

The scale was self-administered along with many other measures. High scores on this scale indicate that respondents believe strongly that if they work hard they will be productive and do their jobs well.

MAJOR FINDINGS:

Kohli examined several previously unstudied supervisory behaviors toward salespeople. Two measures of task-specific self-esteem were found to be positively related to **performance expectations**. Specifically, the higher a salesperson's self-esteem related to his/her job, the higher his/her expectations about hard work and high performance.

REFERENCE:

Kohli, Ajay K. (1985), ''Some Unexplored Supervisory Behaviors and Their Influence on Salespeople's Role Clarity, Specific Self-Esteem, Job Satisfaction, and Motivation,'' *JMR*, 22 (November), 424-433.

SCALE ITEMS: PERFORMANCE EXPECTATIONS (SALESPERSON)

Using the scale provided, indicate the degree to which the following statements describe conditions that exist for you in your job.

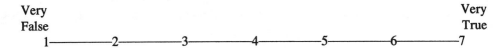

Very False

Very True

1———2———3———4———5———6———7

1. Working hard leads to high productivity.
2. Working hard leads to doing my job well.
3. Working hard leads to good job performance.

SCALE NAME: Performance Expectations (Salesperson)

SCALE DESCRIPTION:

A four-item, five-point Likert-like summated ratings scale measuring the level of expectations an employee has for the results of putting a lot of effort into his/her work. An extra three items were used by Teas (1981).

SCALE ORIGIN:

The first set of items below is a subset of items from previous work (House and Dessler 1973; Sims, Szilagyi, and McKemey 1976). Teas (1981) modified these four items and combined them with three other items that had formed another measure of expectancy. He reports that because the two measures had correlations of .80, he combined the items into one summated ratings scale.

SAMPLES:

The data used by Teas were collected from **171** salespeople in group interviews during sales meetings. The salespeople represented 74% of the industrial salesforces of three midwestern companies. The typical salesperson was 36 years of age and had spent 6.5 years with his company.

The analysis by Kohli (1985) was based on data from **114** salespeople. The sample was obtained from three companies manufacturing and selling industrial products. An overall response rate of 89.8% was reported.

RELIABILITY:

Alpha values of **.792** and **.68** were reported for the scale by Teas and Kohli, respectively.

VALIDITY:

No specific examination of scale validity was reported by Teas, though the two parts of his scale were highly correlated, as noted above. Though the specific results were not reported for this scale by Kohli (1985), he implied that a factor analysis of this and other scales was used to eliminate items with weak loadings on their hypothesized factors.

ADMINISTRATION:

The scale was self-administered along with many other measures in both the Teas and Kohli studies. High scores on this scale indicate that respondents believe strongly that if they work hard they will get done on time and produce high sales volume.

MAJOR FINDINGS:

Teas investigated the impact of several personality characteristics and job-related perceptions on work motivation. The results indicated that task-specific self-esteem and a supervisor's participatory leadership style were positive influencers of **salespeoples' job expectations** whereas perceptions of selling constraints were negative influencers.

Kohli examined several previously unstudied supervisory behaviors toward salespeople. Two measures of task- specific self-esteem were found to be positively related to **performance expectations**. Specifically, the higher a salesperson's self-esteem related to his/her job, the higher his/her expectations about hard work and high performance.

REFERENCES:

House, Robert J. and Gary Dessler (1974), "The Path-Goal Theory of Leadership: Some Post-Hoc and A Priori Tests," in *Contingency Approaches to Leadership*, James G. Hunt and Lars L. Larson, eds. Carbondale, Ill.: Southern Illinois University Press.

Kohli, Ajay K. (1985), "Some Unexplored Supervisory Behaviors and Their Influence on Salespeople's Role Clarity, Specific Self-Esteem, Job Satisfaction, and Motivation," *JMR*, 22 (November), 424-433.

Sims, Henry P., Jr., Andrew D. Szilagyi, and Dale R. McKemey (1976), "Antecedents of Work Related Expectancies," *Academy of Management Journal*, 19 (December), 547-559.

Teas, R. Kenneth (1981), "An Empirical Test of Models of Salespersons' Job Expectancy and Instrumentality Perceptions," *JMR*, 18 (May), 209-226.

SCALE ITEMS: PERFORMANCE EXPECTATIONS (SALESPERSON) +

Using the scale provided, indicate the degree to which the following statements describe conditions that exist for you in your job.

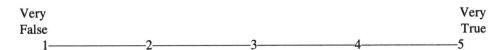

Very False				Very True
1—————	—2—————	—3—————	—4—————	—5

1. Doing things as well as I am capable results in high sales volume.
2. Doing things as well as I am capable results in completing my work on time.
3. Putting forth as much energy as possible would result in high sales volume.
4. Putting forth as much energy as possible would result in completing my work on time.

Using the scale provided, answer the following questions.

No chance	Low probability	50-50 chance	High probability	Certain to occur
1—————	—2—————	—3—————	—4—————	—5

1. What is the likelihood that increasing your selling efforts by 10% would result in increasing your sales by 10%?
2. What is the likelihood that increasing the time you spend trying to obtain new accounts by 10% would result in increasing the number of new accounts you obtain by 10%?
3. What is the likelihood that increasing the time you spend on selling activities by 10% would result in increasing your sales by 10%?

+ Teas (1981) used all of the items as a summated measure whereas Kohli (1985) just used the first set of four items.

SCALE NAME: Performance Sensitivity (Job)

SCALE DESCRIPTION:

A six-item, seven-point Likert-like scale assessing the degree to which an employee's emotions are influenced by the quality of work he/she performs. The scale was called Work Motivation by Dubinsky and Hartley (1986) as well as Hampton, Dubinsky, and Skinner (1986). The short form of the scale with four items was used by Dubinsky et al. (1986) and was referred to as Internal Work Motivation.

SCALE ORIGIN:

The scale used by Dubinsky et al. (1986) was apparently the short version of the Internal Work Motivation scale developed by Hackman and Oldham (1974, 1975). No specific psychometric information was provided for the four-item version, but the six-item version was indicated to be reasonably reliable and valid. Specifically, the internal consistency of the scale was reported to be .76. Evidence of convergent validity was that the scale had high positive correlations with several other related but conceptually different measures such as job satisfaction, growth satisfaction, and work meaningfulness.

SAMPLES:

Analysis by Dubinsky et al. (1986) was based on data collected from **189** salespeople. Letters were sent to a national sample of 2000 senior-level executives asking them to have their least experienced salesperson complete the questionnaire. The respondents represented 189 different companies that marketed 50 different product categories. The sample had a median age of 30.5 years, had spent 1.4 years (median) in their present positions, and were mostly male (86%).

Dubinsky and Hartley (1986) based their analysis on completed questionnaires returned by **120** respondents. Questionnaires were sent to 467 agents who sold lines of a large multi-insurance company. No nonresponse bias was apparent. The sample had a mean age of 39.1 years, had spent 6.6 years (mean) in their present positions, were mostly male (91%), and over half were college graduates (56%).

The sample used by Hampton, Dubinksy, and Skinner (1986) was based on **116** usable responses from a census of 121 retail salespeople who worked in one of five outlets of a department store chain. The sample had a median age of 23.2 years, had spent 1.4 years (median) in their present positions and 1.1 years (median) with their current supervisors, were mostly female (78%), and 66% had some college education.

RELIABILITY:

A LISREL estimate of reliability was **.54** (Dubinsky et al. 1986) and alpha values of **.60** and **.81** were reported by Dubinsky and Hartley and by Hampton and his coauthors, respectively.

VALIDITY:

No examination of scale validity was reported in any of the marketing studies.

ADMINISTRATION:

The scale was self-administered by respondents along with many other measures in a mail survey format in the studies by Dubinsky and his coauthors. Hampton and his coauthors distributed the survey instrument to respondents in a conference room in each store, where they were self-administered. Higher scores on the scale indicate that respondents are very sensitive to the quality of the work they perform in their jobs whereas lower scores suggest that their emotions are not significantly influenced by the performance of their jobs.

MAJOR FINDINGS:

Dubinsky et al. (1986) examined a model of salesforce assimilation. Acceptance by co-workers was the main variable found to have a significant positive impact on **job performance sensitivity.**

The purpose of the study by Dubinsky and Hartley (1986) was to investigate several predictors of salesperson performance and the relationships among those predictors. A path analysis indicated that **job performance sensitivity** had a positive effect on job performance (prior year's commissions). In turn, the former was most significantly affected (positively) by job involvement.

A causal model of retail sales supervisor leadership behavior was studied by Hampton, Dubinsky, and Skinner (1986). The results indicated that job satisfaction had a strong positive effect on **job performance sensitivity.**

COMMENTS:

The internal consistency of the short version of the scale is low and the slightly longer version should be used because of its apparently better reliability.

REFERENCES:

Dubinsky, Alan J. and Steven W. Hartley (1986), "A Path-Analytic Study of a Model of Salesperson Performance," *JAMS*, 14 (Spring), 36-46.

_____, Roy D. Howell, Thomas N. Ingram, and Danny Bellenger (1986), "Salesforce Socialization," *JM*, 50 (October), 192-207.

Hackman, J. Richard and Greg R. Oldham (1974), *The Job Diagnostic Survey: An Instrument for the Diagnosis of Jobs and the Evaluation of Job Redesign Projects*, Technical Report #4, Department of Administrative Sciences, Yale University.

_____ and _____ (1975), "Development of the Job Diagnostic Survey," *Journal of Applied Psychology*, 60 (2), 159-170.

Hampton, Ron, Alan J. Dubinsky, and Steven J. Skinner (1986), "A Model of Sales Supervisor Leadership Behavior and Retail Salespeople's Job-Related Outcomes," *JAMS*, 14 (Fall), 33-43.

SCALE ITEMS: PERFORMANCE SENSITIVITY (JOB) +

Strongly Disagree	Disagree	Slightly Disagree	Neutral	Slightly Agree	Agree	Strongly Agree
1	2	3	4	5	6	7

1. My opinion of myself goes up when I do this job well.
2. I feel a great sense of personal satisfaction when I do this job well.
3. I feel bad and unhappy when I discover that I have performed poorly on this job.
4. My own feelings are generally *not* affected much one way or the other by how well I do on this job. **(r)**
5. Most people on this job feel a great sense of personal satisfaction when they do the job well.
6. Most people on this job feel bad or unhappy when they find that they have performed the work poorly.

+ Items 1 through 4 compose the short form of the scale and are the ones used by Dubinsky et al. (1986).

SCALE NAME: Political Meetings Frequency (Bank)

SCALE DESCRIPTION:

> A three-item, four-point Likert-like summated ratings scale measuring the frequency with which a bank officer reports that a member of the bank's top management meets with political officials.

SCALE ORIGIN:

> McKee, Varadarajan, and Pride (1989) report that they constructed the scales but selected items on the basis of a review of relevant literature and comments by industry executives. Theirs is the only known use of the scale.

SAMPLES:

> The study focused on banks operating in 50 SMSAs of seven states that have unit banking laws. CEOs of the 560 banks in the sample frame were sent questionnaires. A total of **333** usable responses were received and an analysis of asset sizes indicated that respondents' banks were not significantly different from nonrespondents' banks.

RELIABILITY:

> An alpha of **.72** was reported for the scale.

VALIDITY:

> A factor analysis of all items used in the study revealed that items belonging to this scale loaded together on one factor and not on other factors.

ADMINISTRATION:

> The scale was self-administered along with many other measures in a mail questionnaire format. Higher scores on the scale indicate that top management of the respondents' banks engage in frequent meetings with political officials.

MAJOR FINDINGS:

> The purpose of the study was to investigate the relationship between strategic orientation and dynamics of the market. Significant differences were found between organization strategy types in terms of several marketing tactics used. Specifically, the **frequency of political meetings** was significantly greater for ''prospectors'' (those with the highest adaptive capability) than it was for the other three strategic styles.

COMMENTS:

> Though the scale was developed for use with the banking industry, with minor adjustments it could be used in other contexts.

REFERENCE:

McKee, Daryl O., P. Rajan Varadarajan, and William M. Pride (1989), ''Strategic Adaptability and Firm Performance: A Market Contingent Perspective,'' *JM*, 53 (July), 21-35.

SCALE ITEMS: POLITICAL MEETINGS FREQUENCY (BANK)

How frequently does a member of your bank's top management team meet with the following:

Very frequently = two or more times a month
frequently = every month or two
not frequently = less often than every two months

Very Frequently	Frequently	Not Frequently	Never
1	2	3	4

1. State legislators
2. State regulatory personnel
3. City councilmen

SCALE NAME: Power (Coercive)

SCALE DESCRIPTION:

A five-item, seven-point Likert-like scale used to measure the sources of coercive power in a sales manager/sales representative relationship (a sales representative's perceptions of the coercive power sources of his/her sales manager).

SCALE ORIGIN:

The original basis for the perception of coercive power scale can be found in the sources of social power taxonomy defined by French and Raven (1959). In this original taxonomy, coercive power is described as the perception of B that A has the ability to mediate punishments for B. The other forms of power described by French and Raven are reward, expert, referent, and legitimate power. Hunt and Nevin (1974) used a dichotomous classification scheme, coercive and noncoercive, to assess franchisor power. The scales described here measure the *perception* of a coercive power source, as originally suggested by French and Raven.

SAMPLES:

Comer (1984) used **207** sales representatives employed by three companies (two industrial companies, one consumer food products company). A response rate of 62.2% was obtained from an original sample of 333.

RELIABILITY:

Cronbach's alpha was reported to be **.74** (Comer 1984).

VALIDITY:

Comer found that the multi-item measure of coercive power source used was not significantly correlated ($r = .09$) with a single-item measure of the same construct. Additionally, the validity coefficient for the multi-item measure should be greater than the correlations with single-item measures, but this was the case in only eight of 20 comparisons. A factor analysis of the items used in the API scale indicated five items loading at .5 or greater on a factor considered to be coercive power. The coerceive scale was found to have nomological validity, as the relationship between the construct and another (satisfaction) was found to be within the predicted range and of the predicted magnitude.

ADMINISTRATION:

A pencil-and-paper instrument was administered through a mail survey.

MAJOR FINDINGS:

Comer examined the quality of Holzbach's (1974) multi-item attributed power index (API) in comparison with Busch's (1980) single-item power scales. He concluded that the Holzbach API scale for reward, expert, referent, and **coercive power** had high levels of reliability and dimensional measurement. The measurement of the legitimate power base by the API scale, however, was found to be less reliable and to have a bidimensional factor structure.

REFERENCES:

Busch, Paul (1980), ''The Sales Manager's Bases of Social Power and Influence Upon the Sales Force,'' *JM,* 44 (Summer), 91-101.

Comer, James M. (1984), ''A Psychometric Assessment of a Measure of Sales Representatives' Power Perceptions,'' *JMR,* 21 (May), 221-225.

French, John R. P. and Bertram Raven (1959), ''The Bases of Social Power,'' in *Studies in Social Power*, Dorwin Cartwright, ed. Ann Arbor, Mich.: University of Michigan Press.

Holzbach, Robert Lawrence Jr. (1974), ''An Investigation of a Model for Managerial Effectiveness: The Effects of Leadership Style and Leader Attributed Social Power on Subordinate Job Performance,'' unpublished doctoral dissertation, Carnegie-Mellon University.

Hunt, Shelby D. and John R. Nevin (1974), ''Power in a Channel of Distribution: Sources and Consequences,'' *JMR,* 11 (May), 186-193.

SCALE ITEMS: POWER (COERCIVE)

The following adjectives or phrases identify qualities your sales manager may have, actions he/she may take, or your personal feelings toward him/her. How accurate are these adjectives or phrases in describing your boss? Please circle the appropriate response code after each item:

1 = Extremely inaccurate
2 = Very inaccurate
3 = Inaccurate
4 = Don't know or can't decide
5 = Accurate
6 = Very accurate
7 = Extremely accurate

1. Rules by might
2. Retaliative
3. Overly critical
4. Disciplinarian
5. Strict

SCALE NAME: Power (Coercive)

SCALE DESCRIPTION:

A six-item, five-point Likert-like scale used to measure the sources of coercive power in a channel setting (a dealer's perceptions of the coercive power sources of his/her supplier).

SCALE ORIGIN:

The original basis for the perception of coercive power scale can be found in the sources of social power taxonomy defined by French and Raven (1959). In this original taxonomy, coercive power is described as the perception of B that A has the ability to mediate punishments for B. The other forms of power described by French and Raven are reward, expert, referent, and legitimate power. Hunt and Nevin (1974) used a dichotomous classification scheme, coercive and noncoercive, to assess franchisor power. The scale described here measures the *perception* of a coercive power source, as originally suggested by French and Raven. A modified version of the coercive power sources scale used by Gaski and Nevin (1985) was used by Gaski (1986), who altered the scale presented here to measure the exercise (rather than perception) of coercive power in channel relationships.

SAMPLES:

Gaski and Nevin used **238** U.S. and Canadian dealers for a specific manufacturer of heavy industrial machinery. A response rate of 37.5% was obtained from the original population of 634 dealers.

RELIABILITY:

Cronbach's alpha was reported to be **.689** (Gaski and Nevin 1985).

VALIDITY:

Face, content, and discriminant validity measures were used by and Gaski and Nevin. Content validity was achieved through the use of an initial inventory of items taken from the channels literature (Hunt and Nevin 1974; Lusch 1976, 1977) and modified by input from suppliers (i.e., a pretest of survey respondents). Discriminant validity was also asserted, as in no case were the correlations between constructs measured in the study as high as the Cronbach's alpha coefficient (.689) for coercive power source. The correlations between coercive power source and other constructs were: reward power source (r = .267), exercised reward power source (r = −.162), and exercised coercive power source (r = .243).

ADMINISTRATION:

A pencil-and-paper instrument was administered through a mail survey. It was accompanied by a cover letter indicating company permission for suppliers to complete the survey.

MAJOR FINDINGS:

Gaski and Nevin found a relatively weak and negative relationship (p = .083) between **coercive power sources** and satisfaction. They also found that though the correlation between coercive power source and exercised coercive power was significant (r = .243, p = .0002), suppliers possessing a greater amount of a power source were less likely to invoke reward or punishment. Gaski and Nevin interpreted this finding as indicating that when a supplier has great power over a dealer, the exercise of coercive power (imposing punishments) may not be necessary. However, when the relative power of the supplier is less, such punishments may be necessary.

REFERENCES:

French, John R. P. and Bertram Raven (1959), ''The Bases of Social Power'' in *Studies in Social Power*, Dorwin Cartwright, ed. Ann Arbor, Mich.: University of Michigan Press.

Gaski, John F. (1986), ''Interrelations Among a Channel Entity's Power Sources: Impact of the Exercise of Reward and Coercion on Expert, Referent, and Legitimate Power Sources,'' *JMR*, 23 (February), 62-76.

_____ and John R. Nevin (1985), ''The Differential Effects of Exercised and Unexercised Power Sources in a Marketing Channel,'' *JMR*, 22 (May), 130-142.

Hunt, Shelby D. and John R. Nevin (1974), ''Power in a Channel of Distribution: Sources and Consequences,'' *JMR*, 11 (May), 186-193.

Lusch, Robert F. (1976), ''Sources of Power: Their Impact on Intrachannel Conflict,'' *JMR*, 13 (November), 382-390.

_____ (1977), ''Franchise Satisfaction: Causes and Consequences,'' *International Journal of Physical Distribution*, 7, 128-140.

SCALE ITEMS: POWER (COERCIVE)

Please check (X) the appropriate space to indicate how much capability (the supplier) has to take each of the following kinds of action in their dealings with your organization.

No capability ____ : ____ : ____ : ____ : ____ Very much capability
      0   1   2   3   4

1. Delay delivery
2. Delay warranty claims
3. Take legal action against you
4. Refuse to sell
5. Charge high prices
6. Deliver unwanted products

SCALE NAME: Power (Departmental)

SCALE DESCRIPTION:

A four-item, five-point Likert-like scale intended to measure the relative importance of a department to an organization. The basis for the scale and its connection to other power constructs is the belief that power in an organization is due in part to the ability of each department to obtain resources critical to the organization. Departments that are able to obtain more critical resources are considered to be more important and, in turn, more powerful. Accordingly, individuals in such departments should have relatively greater influence in organizational buying decisions than individuals in departments with low power. It is important to note that the power of a department is regarded in the scale as relative to that of other departments. Accordingly, departmental power is assessed by comparing departments with one another on particular aspects of influence.

SCALE ORIGIN:

The scale appears to have been developed in the researched cited herein. The basis for the construct of departmental power can be found in the work of Perrow (1970) and Stagner (1969), who are cited by Kohli (1989) as suggesting that an individual's influence in a purchase committee situation is related to the power of the individual's department in the organization.

SAMPLES:

Kohli used **251** members of the National Association of Purchasing Management as subjects. A response rate of 54.8% was obtained from the original sample of 458.

RELIABILITY:

Cronbach's alpha was reported to be .**88** (Kohli 1989).

VALIDITY:

Kohli used factor analysis to assess convergent and discriminant validity. In the initial factor analysis, four of the five scale items used in the departmental power scale loaded between .61 and .87 on a single factor. The fifth item did not load at .3 or greater on any factor and was subsequently discarded. A second factor analysis was completed with the four remaining scale items. These four items loaded at .62 to .86 on a single factor in the second factor analysis.

ADMINISTRATION:

A pencil-and-paper instrument was administered through a mail survey. Each member of the sample was sent a one dollar bill as a token of appreciation for his/her cooperation. In exchange for completing the survey, participants were offered a copy of the study findings.

MAJOR FINDINGS:

Kohli examined intervening variables that moderate an individual's influence in a buying center. **Departmental power** was found to have no significant effect ($p \geq .05$) on manifest influence under conditions of size, familiarity, risk, time pressure, or influence attempts. Departmental power, along with expert power and reinforcement power, was significantly related ($p \leq .05$) to manifest influence only under conditions of low viscidity. Kohli concluded by stating that though expert and reinforcement power appeared to be related to manifest influence under numerous conditions, departmental power, referent power, informal legitimate power, and information power had little effect on manifest influence except under very specific circumstances.

REFERENCES:

Kohli, Ajay (1989), "Determinants of Influence in Organizational Buying: A Contingency Approach," *JM*, 53 (July), 50-65.

Perrow, Charles (1970), "Departmental Power and Perspectives in Industrial Firms," in *Power in Organizations*, Mayer N. Zald, ed. Nashville, Tenn.: Vanderbilt University Press, 59-89.

Stagner, Ross (1969), "Corporate Decision Making: An Empirical Study," *Journal of Applied Psychology*, 53 (February), 1-13.

SCALE ITEMS: POWER (DEPARTMENTAL)

Subjects were asked to think of a specific joint purchase decision with which they were very familiar. Subjects were asked to select a decision in which no purchase operation was so superior as to be the obvious choice of buying center members. The subject was then asked to rate the power, influence, etc. of a specific committee member (excluding him/herself) and the buying center and situational characteristics.

Strongly Disagree   ___ : ___ : ___ : ___ : ___   Strongly Agree
                                 1   2   3   4   5

1. The functions performed by this department are generally considered to be more critical than others.
2. Top management considers this department to be more important than others.
3. It is easier to recruit employees for this department as compared to others. +
4. This department tends to dominate others in the affairs of the organization.
5. This department is generally regarded as being more influential than others.

+ In the initial factor analysis, this item did not load at .30 or greater on a any factor and hence was not used in the final departmental power scale.

SCALE NAME: Power (Exercised Coercive)

SCALE DESCRIPTION:

A six-item, four-point scale is used to measure a manufacturer's exercise of coercive power on a dealer in a channel setting. A modified version of this scale for the measurement of perceived coercive power sources was reported by Gaski and Nevin (1985).

SCALE ORIGIN:

The original basis for the exercise of coercive power scale can be found in the sources of power taxonomy defined by French and Raven (1959) In this original taxonomy, coercive power is described as the perception of B that A has the ability to mediate punishments for B. The other forms of power described by French and Raven are reward, expert, referent, and legitimate power. Subsequent research efforts have attempted to dichotomize power sources into categories such as coercive/noncoercive (Hunt and Nevin 1974) and economic/noneconomic (Etgar 1978). Gaski (1986) suggested a different dichotomy of quality (referent, legitimate, and expert power) and capability (reward and coercive). The scale discussed here is an extension of French and Raven's and Hunt and Nevin's work. It is important to note that the scale is not intended to measure the perception of a coercive power source, as suggested by French and Raven, but rather measures the *exercise* of coercive power, which is conceptually described as being the result of power (the ability to alter a subject's behavior) **and** an influence attempt.

SAMPLES:

Gaski (1986) and Gaski and Nevin (1985) used **238** U.S. and Canadian dealers for a specific manufacturer of heavy industrial machinery. A response rate of 37.5% was obtained from the original population of 634 dealers.

RELIABILITY:

Cronbach's alpha was **.619** (Gaski 1986; Gaski and Nevin 1985).

VALIDITY:

Face, content, and discriminant validity measures were used in both studies. Content validity was achieved through the use of an initial inventory of items taken from the channels literature (Hunt and Nevin 1974; Lusch 1976, 1977) and modified by input from suppliers. Discriminant validity was also asserted, as in no case were the correlations between constructs measured in the study as high as the Cronbach's alpha coefficient (.619). The correlations between use of coercion and other constructs were: use of reward ($r = -.166$), expert power source ($r = -.424$), referent power source ($r = -.372$), legitimate power source ($r = -.243$), power ($r = .140$), and satisfaction ($r = -.305$).

ADMINISTRATION:

A pencil-and-paper instrument was administered through a mail survey. It was accompanied by a cover letter indicating company permission for suppliers to complete the survey.

MAJOR FINDINGS:

Using LISREL, Gaski found a relationship between the five forms of power as originally described by French and Raven. Specifically, Gaski found that a supplier's use of reward had a positive effect on the perceptions of the supplier's expert, referent, and legitimate power sources, while the **use of coercion** has a negative effect on the perception of the supplier's expert, referent, and legitimate power sources.

Gaski and Nevin found that the **exercise of coercive power** had a stronger negative effect on satisfaction that did the presence of a perceived coercive power source. The exercise of coercive power was also found to have a statistically significant ($p \leq .005$) and positive effect on conflict. The exercise of coercive power and the perception of coercive power sources were found to be significantly correlated ($r = .243$, $p = .0002$). Results suggested that as a greater amount of a power source is possessed by a supplier, a smaller portion of it is actually invoked (Gaski and Nevin 1985, p. 138).

COMMENTS:

Caution about the Gaski findings is advised because of the effect a low Cronbach's alpha coefficient can have on the results achieved through LISREL. Additionally, Gaski reported that the structural models did not meet the absolute goodness-of-fit standard of $p \geq .05$. Finally, the normed fit indices of the models were .87 to .89, slightly below the recommended level of .90.

REFERENCES:

Etgar, Michael (1978), ''Intrachannel Conflict and Use of Power,'' *JMR*, 15 (May), 273-274.

French, John R. P. and Bertram Raven (1959), ''The Bases of Social Power,'' in *Studies in Social Power*, Dorwin Cartwright, ed. Ann Arbor, Mich.: University of Michigan Press.

Gaski, John F. (1986), ''Interrelations Among a Channel Entity's Power Sources: Impact of the Exercise of Reward and Coercion on Expert, Referent, and Legitimate Power Sources,'' *JMR*, 23 (February), 62-76.

_____ and John R. Nevin (1985), ''The Differential Effects of Exercised and Unexercised Power Sources in a Marketing Channel,'' *JMR*, 22 (May), 130-142.

Hunt, Shelby D. and John R. Nevin (1974), ''Power in a Channel of Distribution: Sources and Consequences,'' *JMR*, 11 (May), 186-193.

Lusch, Robert F. (1976), ''Sources of Power: Their Impact on Intrachannel Conflict,'' *JMR*, 13 (November), 382-390.

_____ (1977), ''Franchisee Satisfaction: Causes and Consequences,'' *International Journal of Physical Distribution*, 7, 128-140.

SCALE ITEMS: POWER (EXERCISED COERCIVE)

Please indicate how often (the supplier) takes each of the following kinds of action with your organization.

Never   ___ : ___ : ___ : ___   Often
            0   1   2   3

1. Delay delivery
2. Delay warranty claims
3. Take legal action against you
4. Refuse to sell
5. Charge high prices
6. Deliver unwanted products

#485 Power (Exercised Reward)

SCALE NAME: Power (Exercised Reward)

SCALE DESCRIPTION:

A 15-item, four-point Likert-like scale used to measure the exercise of reward power (i.e., the granting of rewards) by a manufacturer over a dealer in a channel setting.

SCALE ORIGIN:

The original basis for the exercise of reward power scale can be found in the sources of power taxonomy defined by French and Raven (1959) In this original taxonomy, reward power is described as the perception of B that A has the ability to mediate rewards for B. The other forms of power described by French and Raven are coercive, expert, referent, and legitimate power. Hunt and Nevin (1974) used a dichotomous classification scheme, coercive and noncoercive, to assess franchisor power. The scale reported here is an extension from these two earlier works, and uses a quality/capability dichotomy to separate expert, referent, and legitimate power sources (quality) from reward and coercive power sources (capability). An additional distinction from these previous works is that the scale does not measure the perception of a reward power source, as suggested by French and Raven, but rather measures the exercise of reward power, which is conceptually described as being the result of power (the ability to alter a subject's behavior) **and** an influence attempt.

SAMPLES:

Gaski (1986) and Gaski and Nevin (1985) shared the same data and used **238** U.S. and Canadian dealers for a specific manufacturer of heavy industrial machinery. A response rate of 37.5% was obtained from the original population of 634 dealers.

RELIABILITY:

Cronbach's alpha was reported to be **.832** (Gaski 1986; Gaski and Nevin 1985).

VALIDITY:

Face, content, and discriminant validity measures were used in both studies. Content validity was achieved through the use of an initial inventory of items taken from the channels literature (Hunt and Nevin 1974; Lusch 1976, 1977) and modified by input from suppliers. Discriminant validity was also asserted, as in no case were the correlations between constructs measured in the study as high as the Cronbach's alpha coefficient (.832) for use of reward. The correlations between use of reward and other constructs were: use of coercion ($r = -.166$), expert power source ($r = .465$), referent power source ($r = .467$), legitimate power source ($r = .228$), power ($r = .240$), and satisfaction ($r = .351$).

ADMINISTRATION:

A pencil-and-paper instrument was administered through a mail survey. It was accompanied by a cover letter indicating company permission for suppliers to complete the survey.

MAJOR FINDINGS:

Through LISREL, Gaski found that a supplier's **use of reward** had a significant and positive effect ($p \leq .001$) on dealers' perceptions of the supplier's expert, referent, and legitimate power sources, whereas the use of punishment had a negative effect on perceptions of these same three power source. Gaski stated that the implications of his findings were that the use of reward may have a "compound impact" on one's power, as the use of rewards by an entity will have a direct and positive impact on its power level.

Gaski and Nevin found that the **exercise of reward power** had a stronger positive relationship with power than did the presence of a reward power source ($p \leq .10$). For predicting the variable of satisfaction, the standardized regression coefficients for reward power source ($b = .316$) and exercised reward power source ($b = .351$) were not significantly different ($p \leq .10$). The authors conclude that "the potential for reward may be as satisfying as the realization of that potential" (p. 137). Though the correlation between a reward power source and its exercise ($r = .565$) was found to be statistically significant ($p = .0001$), Gaski and Nevin indicated that the greater the amount of a power source (punishment or reward) possessed by a supplier, the smaller the amount of that power actually exercised.

COMMENTS:

Caution about the Gaski findings is advised, because of the effect a low Cronbach's alpha coefficient on another construct can have on the results achieved through LISREL. Additionally, Gaski reported that the structural models did not meet the absolute goodness-of-fit standard of $p \leq .05$. Finally, the normed fit indices of the models were .87 to .89, slightly below the recommended level of .90.

REFERENCES:

French, John R. P. and Bertram Raven (1959), "The Bases of Social Power," in *Studies in Social Power*, Dorwin Cartwright, ed. Ann Arbor, Mich.: University of Michigan Press.

Gaski, John F. (1986), "Interrelations Among a Channel Entity's Power Sources: Impact of the Exercise of Reward and Coercion on Expert, Referent, and Legitimate Power Sources," *JMR*, 23 (February), 62-76.

_____ and John R. Nevin (1985), "The Differential Effects of Exercised and Unexercised Power Sources in a Marketing Channel," *JMR*, 22 (May), 130-142.

Hunt, Shelby D. and John R. Nevin (1974), "Power in a Channel of Distribution: Sources and Consequences," *JMR*, 11 (May), 186-193.

Lusch, Robert F. (1976), "Sources of Power: Their Impact on Intrachannel Conflict," *JMR*, 13 (November), 382-390.

_____ (1977), "Franchisee Satisfaction: Causes and Consequences," *International Journal of Physical Distribution*, 7, 128-140.

SCALE ITEMS: POWER (EXERCISED REWARD)

Please indicate how often (the supplier) takes each of the following kinds of action with your organization.

Never   ____ : ____ : ____ : ____   Often

     0   1   2   3

1. Provide advertising support
2. Give trade allowances/incentives
3. Train personnel
4. Provide sales promotion materials
5. Grant favors (golf, lunches, etc.)
6. Give inventory rebates
7. Provide financing/credit
8. Furnish supplies
9. Give business advice
10. Provide service
11. Give pricing assistance
12. Give free samples
13. Provide ordering assistance
14. Provide inventory management assistance
15. Demonstrate products

SCALE NAME: Power (Expert)

SCALE DESCRIPTION:

A four-item, five-point scale intended to measure ''a target's faith in a source's knowledge-ability'' (Kohli 1989, p. 54). The scale assesses the degree to which an individual in a buying center is perceived to have expert power by asking other members of the buying center their opinions.

SCALE ORIGIN:

The origin for the expert power scale can be found in the original taxonomy of social power as developed by French and Raven (1959). In this taxonomy, expert power is indicated to be one of five sources of social power, along with coercive, reward, referent, and legitimate power. Subsequent research efforts have attempted to dichotomize power sources into categories such as coercive/noncoercive (Hunt and Nevin 1974), economic/noneconomic (Etgar 1976), and quality/capability (Gaski 1986). The expert power scale reported here is intended to measure **perceptions** of the expert power of others (as opposed to measuring the actual expert power of others). The use of such perceived measures in channels power literature has been cited as being a common practice (Michie and Sibley 1985).

SAMPLES:

Kohli used **251** members of the National Association of Purchasing Management as subjects. A response rate of 54.8% was obtained from the original sample of 458.

RELIABILITY:

Cronbach's alpha was reported to be .**85** (Kohli 1989).

VALIDITY:

Kohli used factor analysis with varimax rotation as a check of convergent and discriminant validity. The items in the expert power sources scale loaded on a single factor at .62 to .77, with only one item loading at .3 or greater on any other factor (.34, referent power).

ADMINISTRATION:

A pencil-and-paper instrument was administered through a mail survey

MAJOR FINDINGS:

Kohli investigated the factors that affect an individual's influence in a buying center. **Expert power** was found to be a significant influence ($p \leq .01$ or less) on organizational decision making for both large and small buying centers, low and high familiarity among buying center members, low and high viscidity groups, low and high risk buying situations, low and high time pressure situations, and low influence attempts. Expert power was not found to be significantly related to high influence attempts. In sum, expert power was the most important determinant of manifest influence of those studied.

REFERENCES:

Etgar, Michael (1976), ''Channel Domination and Countervailing Power in Distributive Channels,'' *JMR*, 13 (August), 254- 262.

French, John R. P. and Bertram Raven (1959), ''The Bases of Social Power,'' in *Studies in Social Power*, Dorwin Cartwright, ed. Ann Arbor, Mich.: University of Michigan Press.

Gaski, John F. (1986), ''Interrelations Among a Channel Entity's Power Sources: Impact of the Exercise of Reward and Coercion on Expert, Referent, and Legitimate Power Sources,'' *JMR*, 23 (February), 62-76.

Hunt, Shelby D. and John R. Nevin (1974), ''Power in a Channel of Distribution: Sources and Consequences,'' *JMR*, 11 (May), 186-193.

Kohli, Ajay (1989), ''Determinants of Influence in Organizational Buying: A Contingency Approach,'' *JM*, 53 (July), 50-65.

Michie, Donald A. and Stanley D. Sibley (1983), ''Channel Member Satisfaction: Controversy Resolved,'' *JAMS*, 13 (Spring), 188-205.

SCALE ITEMS: POWER (EXPERT)

Subjects were asked to think of a specific joint purchase decision with which they were very familiar. Subjects were asked to select a decision in which no purchase operation was so superior as to be the obvious choice of buying center members. The subject was then asked to rate the power, influence, etc. of a specific committee member (excluding him/herself) and the buying center and situational characteristics.

None   ____ : ____ : ____ : ____ : ____   All

        1   2   3   4   5

1. They thought he knew a lot about the various suppliers. +
2. They felt he was knowledgeable about the organization's needs with respect to the product.
3. They thought he was competent to make an assessment of the various options.
4. They felt he knew exactly how the product would be used.
5. They felt he had the expertise to make the best decision.

+ This item was eliminated through factor analysis. The remaining four items composed the final scale.

SCALE NAME: Power (Expert)

SCALE DESCRIPTION:

A five-item, five-point scale intended to measure the degree to which a supplier is perceived to have expert power by asking a dealer his/her perceptions of the expert power source of the supplier.

SCALE ORIGIN:

The origin for the expert power scale can be found in the original taxonomy of social power as developed by French and Raven (1959). In this taxonomy, expert power is indicated to be one of five sources of social power, along with coercive, reward, referent, and legitimate power. Subsequent research efforts have attempted to dichotomize power sources into categories such as coercive/noncoercive (Hunt and Nevin 1974), economic/noneconomic (Etgar 1976), and quality/capability (Gaski 1986). The expert power scale reported here is intended to measure the **perceptions** of a supplier's expert power over a dealer (as opposed to measuring the actual expert power of others).

SAMPLES:

Gaski used **238** U.S. and Canadian dealers for a specific manufacturer of heavy industrial machinery. A response rate of 37.5% was obtained from the original population of 634 dealers.

RELIABILITY:

Cronbach's alpha was reported to be **.770** (Gaski 1986).

VALIDITY:

Gaski indicated that the expert power sources scale had face validity as well as internal consistency through Cronbach's alpha. In addition, discriminant validity was asserted as in no case were the correlation coefficients between the expert power construct and the other constructs measured in the study greater than the Cronbach's alpha for the construct (expert power). The correlations between expert power source and other constructs were: use of reward ($r = .465$), use of coercion ($r = -.424$), referent power source ($r = .688$), legitimate power source ($r = .409$), power ($r = .249$), and satisfaction ($r = .551$).

ADMINISTRATION:

A pencil-and-paper instrument was administered through a mail survey. It was accompanied by a cover letter indicating company permission for suppliers to complete the survey.

MAJOR FINDINGS:

Using LISREL, Gaski found that a supplier's use of reward had a significant and positive effect ($p \leq .001$) on dealers' perceptions of the supplier's legitimate, referent, and **expert power sources**, whereas the use of punishment had a negative effect. The author stated that the implications of his findings were that the use of rewards and punishments may result in a "compound impact" on a supplier's power, because the use of rewards and punishments by a supplier will have an impact on the other three French and Raven sources of power: expert, referent, and legitimate.

COMMENTS:

Caution about the Gaski findings is advised, because of the effect a low Cronbach's alpha coefficient in other constructs can have on the results achieved through EL. Additionally, Gaski reted that the stural models did not meet the absolute goodness-of-fit standard of $p \geq .05$. Finally, the normed fit indices of the models were .87 to .89, slightly below the recommended level of .90.

REFERENCES:

Etgar, Michael (1976), "Channel Domination and Countervailing Power in Distributive Channels," *JMR,* 13 (August), 254-262.

French, John R. P. and Bertram Raven (1959), "The Bases of Social Power," in *Studies in Social Power*, Dorwin Cartwright, ed. Ann Arbor, Mich.: University of Michigan Press.

Gaski, John F. (1986), "InterrelationAmong a Channel Entity's Power Sources: Impact of the Exercise of Reward and Coercion on Expert, Referent, and Legitimate Power Sources," *JMR,* 23 (February), 62-76.

Hunt, Shelby D. and John R. Nevin (1974), "Power in a Channel of Distribution: Sources and Consequences," *JMR,* 11 (May), 186-193.

SCALE ITEMS: POWER (EXPERT) +

Please indicate how strongly you agree or disagree with each of the following statements:

Strongly Disagree _____ : _____ : _____ : _____ : _____ Strongly Agree
                        0   1   2   3   4

1. _____ is an expert in its field.
2. I respect the judgement of _____ representatives.
3. The people from _____ don't know what they are doing.
4. I get good advice from _____.
5. Since the _____ people are familiar with their product, I accept what they tell me.

+ Put name of the supplier in the blanks.

SCALE NAME: Power (Expert)

SCALE DESCRIPTION:

A five-item, seven-point scale intended to measure the degree to which a sales manager is perceived to have expert power by asking a sales representative familiar with the manager.

SCALE ORIGIN:

The origin for the expert power scale can be found in the original taxonomy of social power as developed by French and Raven (1959). In this taxonomy, expert power is indicated to be one of five sources of social power, along with coercive, reward, referent, and legitimate power. Subsequent research efforts have attempted to dichotomize power sources into categories such as coercive/noncoercive (Hunt and Nevin 1974), economic/noneconomic (Etgar 1976), and quality/capability (Gaski 1986). The expert power scale reported here is intended to measure the **perceptions** of the expert power of others (as opposed to measuring the actual expert power of others). The particular scale used by Comer (1984) is from the earlier work of Holzbach (1974), who developed a series of scales to measure the French and Raven power taxonomy on an interpersonal level in an organizational environment.

SAMPLES:

Comer used **207** sales representatives employed by three companies (two industrial companies, one consumer food products company). A response rate of 62.2% was obtained from an original sample of 333.

RELIABILITY:

Cronbach's alpha was reported to be **.89** (Comer 1984).

VALIDITY:

Comer indicated convergent validity for the API expert power measure (r = .71 between a single-item and a multi-item measure). Additionally, the validity coefficient of .71 for the expert power measure was greater than the interitem correlations of single-item measures for 19 of 20 correlations. A factor analysis with varimax rotation yielded five items loading on the expert power factor (loadings = .63 to .85), with none of the items loading more than .37 on any additional factor. Nomological validity was also asserted by Comer from the correlation of the perceptions of expert power with job satisfaction (r = .74, p ≤ .0001), which is simlar to results found elsewhere (e.g., Hunt and Nevin 1974).

ADMINISTRATION:

A pencil-and-paper instrument was administered through a mail survey.

MAJOR FINDINGS:

Comer examined the quality of the Holzbach Attributed Power Index (API) scale as a measurement of power bases, using the single-item power scales of Busch (1980) as a basis. He concluded that the Holzbach API scale for reward, coercive, referent, and **expert power** has high levels of reliay and dimensional measurement. The measurement of the legitimate power base by the API scale was found to be less reliable and to have a bidimensional factor structure.

REFERENCES:

Busch, Paul (1980), "The Sales Manager's Bases of Social Power and Influence Upon the Sales Force," *JM*, 44 (Summer), 91-101.

Comer, James M. (1984), "A Psychometric Assessment of a Measure of Sales Representatives' Power Perceptions," *JMR*, 21 (May), 221-225.

Etgar, Michael (1976), "Channel Domination and Countervailing Power in Distributive Channels," *JMR*, 13 (August), 254-262.

French, John R. P. and Bertram Raven (1959), "The Bases of Social Power," in *Studies in Social Power*, Dorwin Cartwright, ed. Ann Arbor, Mich.: University of Michigan Press.

Gaski, John F. (1986), "Interrelations Among a Channel Entity's Power Sources: Impact of the Exercise of Reward and Coercion on Expert, Referent, and Legitimate Power Sources," *JMR*, 23 (February), 62-76.

Holzbach, Robert Lawrence, Jr. (1974), "An Investigation of a Model for Managerial Effectiveness: The Effects of Leadship Style and Leader Attributed Social Power on Subordinate Job Performance," unpublished doctoral dissertation, Carnegie-Mellon University.

Hunt, Shelby D. and John R. Nevin (1974), "Power in a Channel of Distribution: Sources and Consequences," *JMR*, 11 (May), 186-193.

SCALE ITEMS: POWER (EXPERT)

The following adjectives or phrases identify qualities your sales manager may have, actions he/she may take, or your personal feelings toward him/her. How accurate are these adjectives or phrases in describing your boss? Please circle the appropriate response code after each item:

1 = Extremely inaccurate
2 = Very inaccurate
3 = Inaccurate
4 = Don't know or can't decide
5 = Accurate
6 = Very accurate
7 = Extremely accurate

1. Skilled
2. Knowledgeable
3. Experienced
4. Proficient
5. Qualified

SCALE NAME: Power (Informal Legitimate)

SCALE DESCRIPTION:

A two-item, five-point scale intended to measure the degree to which an individual is perceived to have informal legitimate power by another individual or organization. Kohli (1989) drew a distinction between formal and informal legitimate power. Formal legitimate power was described as a situation in which "others feel they ought to comply with an individual in deference to his or her formal position" (p. 52), whereas informal legitimate power was described as being the result of "generally accepted (informal) norms of behavior (e.g., complying with an individual because he or she will be most affected by the decision)". The scale presented here purports to measure the degree to which an individual (A) is perceived to have informal legitimate power by asking another individual (B) to indicate the extent to which B agrees or disagrees with two statements about his/her perception of the informal legitimate power base of A.

SCALE ORIGIN:

The items used in this scale appear to have been developed for the research by Kohli (1989). The origin for the informal legitimate power scale can be found in the original taxonomy of social power as developed by French and Raven (1959). In this taxonomy, five sources of social power are identified: legitimate, expert, referent, coercive, and reward. The informal legitimate power construct reported here, when combined with the construct of formal legitimate power, appears to comprise the original French and Raven category of legitimate power source. Kohli stated that what separates informal from formal legitimate power is whether compliance in the actions of an individual is based on the formal or informal obligation to conform. The use of perceived measures in channels power literature, such as those used in this scale, has been cited as being a common practice (Michie and Sibley 1985).

SAMPLES:

Kohli used **251** members of the National Association of Purchasing Management as subjects. A response rate of 54.8% was obtained from the original sample of 458.

RELIABILITY:

Cronbach's alpha was reported to be **.80** (Kohli 1989).

VALIDITY:

Kohli used factor analysis to assess convergent and discriminant validity. In the initial factor analysis, five scale items used in a legitimate power scale loaded between .38 and .76 on a total of four separate factors. Two of the five scale items pertained to informal legitimate power and loaded highly (.72 and .76) on a separate factor. A second factor analysis was completed with only the two scale items pertaining to informal legitimate power retained. These two items loaded at .77 and .73 on the same factor in the second factor analysis.

ADMINISTRATION:

A pencil-and-paper instrument was administered through a mail survey. Each member of the sample was sent a one dollar bill as a token of appreciation for his/her cooperation. In exchange for completing the survey, participants were offered a copy of the study findings.

MAJOR FINDINGS:

Kohli examined intervening variables that moderate the influence of an individual in a buying center. **Informal legitimate power** was found to have no significant effect ($p \geq .05$) on manifest influence under conditions of size, familiarity, viscidity, risk, or time pressure. Informal legitimate power, along with expert power, was found to be significantly related ($p \leq .05$) to manifest influence under conditions of low influence attempts, whereas reinforcement power had a strong effect ($p \leq .001$) on manifest influence under conditions of high influence attempts. Kohli concluded that powers that induce voluntary cooperation, such as informal legitimate power, diminish when joined by high influence attempts.

REFERENCES:

French, John R. P. and Bertram Raven (1959), "The Bases of Social Power," in *Studies in Social Power*, Dorwin Cartwright, ed. Ann Arbor, Mich.: University of Michigan Press.

Kohli, Ajay (1989), "Determinants of Influence in Organizational Buying: A Contingency Approach," *JM*, 53 (July), 50-65.

Michie, Donald A. and Stanley D. Sibley (1985), "Channel Member Satisfaction: Controversy Resolved," *JAMS*, 13 (Spring), 188-205.

SCALE ITEMS: POWER (INFORMAL LEGITIMATE)

Subjects were asked to think of a specific joint purchase decision with which they were very familiar. Subjects were asked to select a decision in which no purchase operation was so superior as to be thious choice of ng center members. The subject was then asked to rate the power, influence, etc. of a specific committee member (excluding him/herself) and the buying center and situational characteristics.

None   ____ : ____ : ____ : ____ : ____   All
      1   2   3   4   5

1. They felt the purchase decision should reflect his preferences because he had more at stake than others.
2. They felt they ought to comply with him because the purchase decision would affect him more than others.

SCALE NAME: Power (Information)

SCALE DESCRIPTION:

A four-item, five-point Likert-type scale intended to assess an individual's access to and control over information. The scale was used to measure an individual's information power on decision making in an organizational buying center. The information power construct is believed to be related to, though distinct from, expert power. Information power is described as a gatekeeping ability of a buying center member, involving the control of the flow of information to targeted others.

SCALE ORIGIN:

The scale appears to have been developed in the research cited herein. The basis for the information power scale can be found in the original taxonomy of social power sources as developed by French and Raven (1959). In this taxonomy, five sources of power are delineated: referent, legitimate, reward, coercive, and expert. Expert power is typically defined as the perception of B that A has some special knowledge or expertise. In the research reported here, expert power is given a more narrow focus and is used to refer specifically to a source's expertise, whereas information power refers to influencing the actions of a target by providing or withholding information. Thus, the present construct appears to be a subset of the original French and Raven expert power construct.

SAMPLES:

Kohli (1989) used **251** members of the National Association of Purchasing Management as subjects. A response rate of 54.8% was obtained from the original sample of 458.

RELIABILITY:

Cronbach's alpha was reported to be **.90** (Kohli 1989).

VALIDITY:

Kohli used factor analysis to assess convergent and discriminant validity. In the initial factor analysis, four of the five scale items used in the information power scale loaded between .75 and .86 on a single factor. The fifth item did not load at .3 or greater on any factor and was subsequently discarded. A second factor analysis was completed with the four remaining scale items. These four items loaded at .75 to .86 on a single factor in the second factor analysis.

ADMINISTRATION:

A pencil-and-paper instrument was administered through a mail survey. Each member of the sample was sent a one dollar bill as a token of appreciation for his/her cooperation. In exchange for completing the survey, participants were offered a copy of the study findings.

MAJOR FINDINGS:

Kohli examined intervening variables that moderate the influence of an individual in a buying center. **Information power** was found to have no significant effect ($p \geq .05$) on manifest influence under conditions of size, familiarity, risk, time pressure, or influence attempts. Information power, along with expert power, was significantly related ($p \leq .05$) to manifest influence only under conditions of high viscidity. Kohli concluded by stating that though expert and reinforcement power appeared to be related to manifest influence under numerous conditions, departmental power, referent power, informal legitimate power, and information power little effect manifest influence except under very specific circumstances.

REFERENCES:

French, John R. P., Jr. and Bertram H. Raven (1959), "The Bases of Social Power," in *Studies in Social Power*, Dorwin Cartwright, ed. Ann Arbor, Mich.: University of Michigan Press.

Kohli, Ajay (1989), "Determinants of Influence in Organizational Buying: A Contingency Approach," *JM*, 53 (July), 50-65.

SCALE ITEMS: POWER (INFORMATION)

Subjects were asked to think of a specific joint purchase decision with which they were very familiar. Subjects were asked to select a decision in which no purchase operation was so superior as to be the obvious choice of buying center members. The subject was then asked to rate the power, influence, etc. of a specific committee member (excluding him/herself) and the buying center and situational characteristics.

Strongly Disagree   ____ : ____ : ____ : ____ : ____   Strongly Agree
                        1   2   3   4   5

1. He served as a communication link between the suppliers and the committee members.
2. He was in direct contact with the suppliers.
3. He was in a position to screen information from the information other committee members received. +
4. He was responsible for obtaing information asuppliers for the committee members.
5. He held independent discussions with the various suppliers on behalf of the purchase committee.

+ In an initial factor analysis, this item did not load at .30 or greater on a any factor and hence was not used in the final information power scale.

SCALE NAME: Power (Legitimate)

SCALE DESCRIPTION:

A five-item, five-point scale intended to measure the degree to which a supplier is perceived to have legitimate power by a dealer. The scale measures the degree to which a supplier (A) is perceived to have legitimate power by asking a dealer (B) to indicate the extent to which B agrees or disagrees with a series of statements about the perception of the legitimate power base of A. A variation of the Gaski (1986) scale was used by Gaski and Nevin (1985), who modified the scale to measure the extent to which legitimate power is exercised, as opposed to using **perceived** measures of legitimate power.

SCALE ORIGIN:

The origin for the legitimate power scale can be found in the original taxonomy of social power as developed by French and Raven (1959). In this taxonomy, legitimate power is indicated to be one of five sources of social power, along with coercive, reward, expert and referent power. Subsequent research efforts have attempted to dichotomize power sources into categories such as coercive/noncoercive (Hunt and Nevin 1974), economic/noneconomic (Etgar 1976), and quality/capability (Gaski 1986). The legitimate power scale reported here is intended to measure the **perceptions** a dealer has about the right of a supplier to prescribe behavior for the dealer. The use of such perceived measures in channels power literature has been cited as being a common practice (Michie and Sibley 1985).

SAMPLES:

Gaski used **238** U.S. and Canadian dealers for a specific manufacturer of heavy industrial machinery. A response rate of 37.5% was obtained from the original population of 634 dealers.

RELIABILITY:

Cronbach's alpha was reported to be **.653** (Gaski 1986).

VALIDITY:

Gaski indicated that the legitimate power sources scale had face validity as well as internal consistency through Cronbach's alpha. In addition, discriminant validity was asserted, as in no case were the correlation coefficients between the legitimate power construct and the other constructs measured in the study greater than the Cronbach's alpha for the construct (legitimate power). The correlations between "legitimate power source" and other constructs were: use of reward ($r = .228$), use of coercion ($r = -.243$), expert power source ($r = .409$), referent power source ($r = .489$), power ($r = .271$), and satisfaction ($r = .295$).

ADMINISTRATION:

A pencil-and-paper instrument was administered through a mail survey. It was accompanied by a cover letter indicating company permission for suppliers to complete the survey.

MAJOR FINDINGS:

Gaski found that a supplier's use of reward had a significant and positive effect ($p \leq .001$) on dealers' perceptions of the supplier's expert, referent, and **legitimate power sources**, whereas the use of punishment had a negative effect. The author stated that the implications of his findings were that the use of rewards and punishments may result in a "compound impact" on a supplier's power, because the use of rewards and punishments by a supplier will have an impact on the other three French and Raven sources of power: expert, referent, and legitimate. Gaski proposed a quality/capability dichotomy of power sources, where legitimate, expert, and referent power are classified as relating to intrinsic qualities of the power holder and reward and coercive power are classified as reflecting the capabilities of a power holder for action.

COMMENTS:

Caution about the Gaski (1986) findings is advised, because of the effect a low Cronbach's alpha coefficient can have on the results achieved through LISREL. Additionally, Gaski reported that the structural models did not meet the absolute goodness-of-fit standard of $p \geq .05$. Finally, the normed fit indices of the models were .87 to .89, slightly below the recommended level of .90.

REFERENCES:

Etgar, Michael (1976), "Channel Domination and Countervailing Power in Distributive Channels," *JMR*, 13 (August), 254-262.

French, John R. P. and Bertram Raven (1959), "Bases of Social Power," in *Studies in Social Power*, Dorwin Cartwright, ed. Ann Ar, Mich.: University of Michigan Press.

Gaski, John F. (1986), "Interrelations Among a Channel Entity's Power Sources: Impact of the Exercise of Reward and Coercion on Expert, Referent, and Legitimate Power Sources," *JMR*, 23 (February), 62-76.

———— and John R. Nevin (1985), "The Differential Effects of Exercised and Unexercised Power Sources in a Marketing Channel," *JMR*, 22 (May), 130-142.

Hunt, Shelby D. and John R. Nevin (197), "Power in a Channel of Distribution: Sources and Consequences," *JMR*, 11 (May), 186-193.

Michie, Donald A. and Stanley D. Sibley (1985), "Channel Member Satisfaction: Controversy Resolved," *JAMS*, 13 (Spring), 188-205.

SCALE ITEMS: POWER (LEGITIMATE)

Please indicate how strongly you agree or disagree with each of the following statements:

Strongly Disagree ____ : ____ : ____ : ____ : ____ Strongly Agree
   0   1   2   3   4

1. _____ has the right to expect my cooperation.
2. _____ should stay out of my business. **(r)**

3. _____ has no right to tell me what to do. **(r)**
4. Since _____ is my supplier, I should accept their recommendations.
5. Suppliers have a right to expect delares to follow instructions.

+ The supplier's name should be typed in the blanks.

SCALE NAME: Power (Legitimate)

SCALE DESCRIPTION:

A five-item,-seven point scale intended to measure the degree to which a sales manager is perceived to have legitimate power by a sales representative. The scale measures the degree of legitimate power by asking a sales representative to indicate the extent to which he/she agrees with a series of statements about perception of the legitimate power base of a sales manager.

SCALE ORIGIN:

The origin for the legitimate power scale can be found in the original taxonomy of social power as developed by French and Raven (1959). In this taxonomy, legitimate power is indicated to be one of five sources of social power, along with coercive, reward, expert, and referent power. Subsequent research efforts have attempted to dichotomize power sources into categories such as coercive/noncoercive (Hunt and Nevin 1974), economic/noneconomic (Etgar 1976), and quality/capability (Gaski 1986). The legitimate power scale reported here is intended to measure the **perceptions** that a sales representative has about the right of his/her sales manager to prescribe behavior for the sales representative. The use of such perceived measures in power literature has been cited as being a common practice (Michie and Sibley 1985). The scale discussed here (Comer 1984) is from the earlier work of Holzbach (1974), who developed a series of scales to measure the French and Raven power taxonomy on an interpersonal level in an organizational environment.

SAMPLES:

Comer used **207** sales representatives employed by three companies (two industrial companies, one consumer food products company). A response rate of 62.2% was obtained from an original sample of 333.

RELIABILITY:

Cronbach's alpha was reported to be .**68** (Comer 1984).

VALIDITY:

Comer indicated convergent validity (r = .33 between a single-item and a multi-item measure). This validity coefficient of .33, however, was greater than the correlations with single-item measures in only eight of 20 cases. A factor analysis of the five items used in the legitimate power scale indicated that they did not produce a single factor, but rather a bidimensional factor structure. Two of the items loaded on one factor, two loaded on another factor, and a fifth item did not load on any factor. Nomological validity was established by correlating the legitimate power construct with sales representative satisfaction and comparing the correlation with established construct relationships from previous research (e.g., Hunt and Nevin 1974).

ADMINISTRATION:

A pencil-and-paper instrument was administered through a mail survey.

MAJOR FINDINGS:

Comer examined the quality of the Holzbach Attributed Power Index (API) scale as a measurement of power bases, using the single-item power scales of Busch (1980) as a basis. He concluded that the Holzbach API scale for reward, coercive, referent, and expert power had high levels of reliability and dimensional measurement. The measurement of the **legitimate power base** by the API scale was found to be less reliable and to have a bidimensional factor structure.

REFERENCES:

Busch, Paul (1980), "The Sales Manager's Bases of Social Power and Influence Upon the Sales Force," *JMR*, 44 (Summer), 91-101.

Comer, James M. (1984), "A Psychometric Assessment of a Measure of Sales Representatives' Power Perceptions," *JMR*, 21 (May), 221-225.

Etgar, Michael (1976), "Channel Domination and Countervailing Power in Distributive Channels," *JMR*, 13 (August), 254-262.

French, John R. P. and Bertram Raven (1959), "The Bases of Social Power," in *Studies in Social Power*, Dorwin Cartwright, ed. Ann Arbor, Mich.: University of Michigan Press.

Gaski, John F. (1986), "Interrelations Among a Channel Entity's Power Sources: Impact of the Exercise of Reward and Coercion on Expert, Referent, and Legitimate Power Sources," *JMR*, 23 (February), 62-76.

Holzbach, Robert Lawrence, Jr. (1974), "An Investigation of a Model for Managerial Effectiveness: The Effects of Leadership Style and Leader Attributed Social Power on Subordinate Job Performance," unpublished doctoral dissertation, Carnegie-Mellon University.

Hunt, Shelby D. and John R. Nevin (1974), "Power in a Channel of Distribution: Sources and Consequences," *JMR*, 11 (May), 186-193.

Michie, Donald A. and Stanley D. Sibley (1985), "Channel Member Satisfaction: Controversy Resolved," *JAMS*, 13 (Spring), 188-205.

SCALE ITEMS: POWER (LEGITIMATE) +

The following adjectives or phrases identify qualities your sales manager may have, actions he/she may take, or your personal feelings toward him/her. How accurate are these adjectives or phrases in describing your boss? Please circle the appropriate response code after each item:

1 = Extremely inaccurate
2 = Very inaccurate
3 = Inaccurate
4 = Don't know or can't decide
5 = Accurate
6 = Very accurate
7 = Extremely accurate

1. Have an obligation to accept his orders
2. Duty bound to obey him
3. Has authority
4. Entitled to direct my actions on the job
5. Authorized to command

+ Items 1 and 2 loaded in the factor analysis on one factor and items 4 and 5 loaded on another factor. Item 3 did not load at .50 or greater on any factor.

SCALE NAME: Power (Referent)

SCALE DESCRIPTION:

A five-item, five-point Likert-type scale intended to measure the degree to which a supplier is perceived to have referent power by a dealer. The scale measures the degree of referent power by asking the supplier's dealers for their perceptions of the extent of the referent power source of the supplier.

SCALE ORIGIN:

The origin for the referent power scale can be found in the original taxonomy of social power as developed by French and Raven (1959). In this taxonomy, referent power is indicated to be one of five sources of social power, along with coercive, reward, expert and legitimate power. Subsequent research efforts have attempted to dichotomize power sources into categories such as coercive/noncoercive (Hunt and Nevin 1974), economic/noneconomic (Etgar 1976), and quality/capability (Gaski 1986). The referent power scale reported here is intended to measure the **perceptions** of the extent to which a dealer seeks to identify with a supplier. The use of such perceived measures in channels power literature has been cited as being a common practice (Michie and Sibley 1985).

SAMPLES:

Gaski used **238** U.S. and Canadian dealers for a specific manufacturer of heavy industrial machinery. A response rate of 37.5% was obtained from the original population of 634 dealers.

RELIABILITY:

Cronbach's alpha was reported to be **.808** (Gaski 1986).

VALIDITY:

Gaski indicated that the referent power sources scale possess face validity as well as internal consistency through Cronbach's alpha. In addition, discriminant validity was asserted, as in no case were the correlation coefficients between the referent power construct and the other constructs measured in the study greater than the Cronbach's alpha for the construct (referent power). The correlations between referent power source and other constructs were: use of reward ($r = .467$), use of coercion ($r = -.372$), expert power source ($r = .688$), legitimate power source ($r = .489$), power ($r = .281$), and satisfaction ($r = .569$).

ADMINISTRATION:

A pencil-and-paper instrument was administered through a mail survey. It was accompanied by a cover letter indicating company permission for suppliers to complete the survey.

MAJOR FINDINGS:

Gaski found that a supplier's use of reward had a significant and positive effect ($p \leq .001$) on dealers' perceptions of the supplier's expert, legitimate, and **referent power sources**, whereas the use of punishment had a negative effect. The author stated that the implications of his findings were that the use of rewards and punishments may result in a "compound impact" on a supplier's power, because the use of rewards and punishments by a supplier will have an impact on the other three French and Raven sources of power: expert, referent, and legitimate.

COMMENTS:

Caution about the Gaski findings is advised, because of the effect a low Cronbach's alpha coefficient on another construct can have on the results achieved through LISREL. Additionally, Gaski reported that the structural models did not meet the absolute goodness-of-fit standard of $p \geq .05$. Finally, the normed fit indices of the models were .87 to .89, slightly below the recommended level of .90.

REFERENCES:

Etgar, Michael (1976), "Channel Domination and Countervailing Power in Distributive Channels," *JMR,* 13 (August), 254-262.

French, John R. P. and Bertram Raven (1959), "The Bases of Social Power," in *Studies in Social Power*, Dorwin Cartwright, ed. Ann Arbor, Mich.: University of Michigan Press.

Gaski, John F. (1986), "Interrelations Among a Channel Entity's Power Sources: Impact of the Exercise of Reward and Coercion on Expert, Referent, and Legitimate Power Sources," *JMR*, 23 (February), 62-76.

Hunt, Shelby D. and John R. Nevin (1974), "Power in a Channel of Distribution: Sources and Consequences," *JMR,* 11 (May), 186-193.

Michie, Donald A. and Stanley D. Sibley (1985), "Channel Member Satisfaction: Controversy Resolved," *JAMS,* 13 (Spring), 188-205.

SCALE ITEMS: POWER (REFERENT)

Please indicate how strongly you agree or disagree with each of the following statements:

Strongly Agree   ____ : ____ : ____ : ____ : ____   Strongly Disagree

                4   3   2   1   0

1. I like the (supplier's) people I deal with.
2. I couldn't care less what (the supplier) thinks of me. **(r)**
3. I consider (the supplier) an ideal company.
4. I admire (the supplier) and I want to act in a way to merit the respect of the people there.
5. The approval of the (supplier's) people means a lot to me.

SCALE NAME: Power (Referent)

SCALE DESCRIPTION:

A five-item, five-point scale intended to measure the degree to which an individual in a buying center is perceived to have referent power by another individual in the buying center. In this scale, referent power is defined as "a target's regard for and identification with a source" (Kohli 1989, p. 54). The scale measures the degree to which an individual or organization (A), such as a supplier or a sales manager, is perceived to have referent power by asking another individual or organization (B), such as a dealer or sales representative.

SCALE ORIGIN:

The origin for the referent power scale can be found in the original taxonomy of social power as developed by French and Raven (1959). In this taxonomy, referent power is indicated to be one of five sources of social power, along with coercive, reward, expert, and legitimate power. Subsequent research efforts have attempted to dichotomize power sources into categories such as coercive/noncoercive (Hunt and Nevin 1974), economic/noneconomic (Etgar 1976), and quality/capability (Gaski 1986). The referent power scale reported here is intended to measure the **perceptions** of the extent to which one individual seeks to identify with another individual or organization. The use of such perceived measures in channels power literature has been cited as being a common practice (Michie and Sibley 1985).

SAMPLES:

Kohli used **251** members of the National Association of Purchasing Management as subjects. A response rate of 54.8% was obtained from the original sample of 458.

RELIABILITY:

Cronbach's alpha was reported to be **.86** (Kohli 1989).

VALIDITY:

Kohli used factor analysis as a check of convergent and discriminant validity. The five items in the referent power sources scale loaded on a single factor at between .59 and .86, with only one scale item loading at .30 or greater on any additional factor (.30, expert power).

ADMINISTRATION:

A pencil-and-paper instrument was administered through a mail survey.

MAJOR FINDINGS:

Kohli investigated the factors that affect an individual's influence in a buying center. Under conditions of high time pressure, **referent power** was found to have a negative and statistically significant ($p \leq .05$) relationship with manifest influence. This negative relationship was unexpected by the author, who suggested that personal regard for the opinion of others may be less important when time pressure is high. Referent power was also found to be negatively and significantly ($p \leq .05$) related to buying situations of low interpersonal familiarity among members of the buying center and in high risk buying situations.

REFERENCES:

Etgar, Michael (1976), "Channel Domination and Countervailing Power in Distributive Channels," *JMR*, 13 (August), 254-262.

French, John R. P. and Bertram Raven (1959), "The Bases of Social Power," in *Studies in Social Power*, Dorwin Cartwright, ed. Ann Arbor, Mich.: University of Michigan Press.

Gaski, John F. (1986), "Interrelations Among a Channel Entity's Power Sources: Impact of the Exercise of Reward and Coercion on Expert, Referent, and Legitimate Power Sources," *JMR*, 23 (February), 62-76.

Hunt, Shelby D. and John R. Nevin (1974), "Power in a Channel of Distribution: Sources and Consequences," *JMR*, 11 (May), 186-193.

Kohli, Ajay (1989), "Determinants of Influence in Organizational Buying: A Contingency Approach," *JM*, 53 (July), 50-65.

Michie, Donald A. and Stanley D. Sibley (1985), "Channel Member Satisfaction: Controversy Resolved," *JAMS*, 13 (Spring), 188-205.

SCALE ITEMS: POWER (REFERENT)

Subjects (purchasing agents) were asked to think of a specific joint purchase decision with which they were very familiar. Subjects were asked to select a decision in which no purchase option was so superior as to be the obvious choice of buying center members. The subject was then asked to rate the power, influence, etc. of a specific committee member (excluding him/herself) and the buying center and situational characteristics.

```
None  _____ : _____ : _____ : _____ : _____   All
         1       2       3       4       5
```

1. They disliked him as a person.
2. They thought highly of his personality.
3. They shared his personal values.
4. They identified with him as a person.
5. They had high regard for his personal qualities.

SCALE NAME: Power (Referent)

SCALE DESCRIPTION:

A five-item, seven-point scale intended to measure the degree to which a sales manager is perceived to have referent power by a sales representative. The scale measures the degree of referent power by asking a sales representative to indicate the perceived extent of the sales manager's referent power source.

SCALE ORIGIN:

The origin for the referent power scale can be found in the original taxonomy of social power as developed by French and Raven (1959). In this taxonomy, referent power is indicated to be one of five sources of social power, along with coercive, reward, expert, and legitimate power. Subsequent research efforts have attempted to dichotomize power sources into categories such as coercive/noncoercive (Hunt and Nevin 1974), economic/noneconomic (Etgar 1976), and quality/capability (Gaski 1986). The referent power scale reported here is intended to measure the **perceptions** of the extent to which one individual seeks to identify with another individual or organization. The use of such perceived measures in channels power literature has been cited as being a common practice (Michie and Sibley 1985). The scale used by Comer (1984) is from the earlier work of Holzbach (1974), who developed a series of scales to measure the French and Raven power taxonomy on an interpersonal level in an organizational environment.

SAMPLES:

Comer used **207** sales representatives employed by three companies (two industrial companies, one consumer food products company). A response rate of 62.2% was obtained from an original sample of 333.

RELIABILITY:

Cronbach's alpha was reported to be **.87** (Comer 1984).

VALIDITY:

Comer indicated convergent validity for the API referent power measure ($r = .71$ between a single-item and a multi-item measure). Additionally, the validity coefficient of .71 for the referent power measure was greater than the interitem correlations of single-item measures for 19 of 20 correlations. A factor analysis with varimax rotation yielded five items loading on the referent power factor (loadings = .56 to .81), with none of the items loading more than .40 on any additional factor. Nomological validity was also asserted by the author from the correlation of the perceptions of referent power with job satisfaction ($r = .70$, $p < .0001$), which is simlar to results found elsewhere (e.g., Hunt and Nevin 1974).

ADMINISTRATION:

A pencil-and-paper instrument was administered through a mail survey.

MAJOR FINDINGS:

Comer examined the quality of the Holzbach Attributed Power Index (API) scale as a measurement of power bases, using the single-item power scales of Busch (1980) as a basis. He concluded that the Holzbach API scale for reward, coercive, expert, and **referent power** had high levels of reliability and dimensional measurement. The measurement of the legitimate power base by the API scale was found to be less reliable and to have a bidimensional factor structure.

REFERENCES:

Busch, Paul (1980), "The Sales Manager's Bases of Social Power and Influence Upon the Sales Force," *JM*, 44 (Summer), 91-101.

Comer, James M. (1984), "A Psychometric Assessment of a Measure of Sales Representatives' Power Perceptions," *JMR*, 21 (May), 221-225.

Etgar, Michael (1976), "Channel Domination and Countervailing Power in Distributive Channels," *JMR* 13 (August), 254-262.

French, John R. P. and Bertram Raven (1959), "The Bases of Social Power," in *Studies in Social Power*, Dorwin Cartwright, ed. Ann Arbor, Mich.: University of Michigan Press.

Gaski, John F. (1986), "Interrelations Among a Channel Entity's Power Sources: Impact of the Exercise of Reward and Coercion on Expert, Referent, and Legitimate Power Sources," *JMR*, 23 (February), 62-76.

Holzbach, Robert Lawrence, Jr. (1974), "An Investigation of a Model for Managerial Effectiveness: The Effects of Leadership Style and Leader Attributed Social Power on Subordinate Job Performance," unpublished doctoral dissertation, Carnegie-Mellon University.

Hunt, Shelby D. and John R. Nevin (1974), "Power in a Channel of Distribution: Sources and Consequences," *JMR*, 11 (May), 186-193.

Michie, Donald A. and Stanley D. Sibley (1985), "Channel Member Satisfaction: Controversy Resolved," *JAMS*, 13 (Spring), 188-205.

SCALE ITEMS: POWER (REFERENT)

The following adjectives or phrases identify qualities your sales manager may have, actions he/she may take, or your personal feelings toward him/her. How accurate are these adjectives or phrases in describing your boss? Please circle the appropriate response code after each item:

1 = Extremely inaccurate
2 = Very inaccurate
3 = Inaccurate
4 = Don't know or can't decide
5 = Accurate
6 = Very accurate
7 = Extremely accurate

1. Admire him
2. Identify with him
3. Respect him as a person
4. Likeable
5. Friendly

SCALE NAME: Power (Reinforcement)

SCALE DESCRIPTION:

An 11-item, five-point Likert-like agree-disagree scale used to measure the perception by one individual of the reinforcement power of another individual. Reinforcement power is described as the ability to mediate positive and negative reinforcements (rewards and punishments). The scale is essentially a combination of two previously developed scales intended to measure reward power and coercive power. It consists of six items intended to measure the perception of an individual that another has the ability to mediate rewards for a target, plus five items intended to measure the perception of an individual that another has the ability to mediate punishments for a target.

SCALE ORIGIN:

The items used in this scale appear to have been developed by Kohli (1989). The origin for the reinforcement power scale can be found in the original taxonomy of social power as developed by French and Raven (1959). In this taxonomy, five sources of social power are identified: legitimate, expert, referent, coercive, and reward. The reinforcement scale reported here is a combination of the original French and Raven categories of coercive and reward power sources. Kohli stated that making a distinction between a reward and a punishment can be difficult, as when an individual is punished by the withholding of a reward. Kohli suggested that reward and coercive power actually represent a single dimension: the ability to mediate positive and negative reinforcements. Thus, the reinforcement power scale is intended to measure the **perceptions** that an individual has the ability to prescribe reinforcements for a target. The use of such perceived measures in channels power literature has been cited as being a common practice (Michie and Sibley 1985).

SAMPLES:

Kohli used **251** members of the National Association of Purchasing Management as subjects. A response rate of 54.8% was obtained from the original sample of 458.

RELIABILITY:

A Cronbach's alpha of .**95** was reported (Kohli 1989).

VALIDITY:

Kohli used factor analysis to assess convergent and discriminant validity. All 11 scale items loaded between .63 and .92, with only one item loading above .30 on any other item.

ADMINISTRATION:

A pencil-and-paper instrument was administered through a mail survey. Each member of the sample was sent a one dollar bill as a token of appreciation for his/her cooperation. In exchange for completing the survey, participants were offered a copy of the study findings.

MAJOR FINDINGS:

Kohli examined intervening variables that moderate the influence of an individual in a buying center. **Reinforcement power** was found to relate more strongly to manifest influence in small groups ($p \le .001$) than in large groups ($p \le .01$). Reinforcement power was also found to be related to manifest influence in conditions of high time pressure ($p \le .001$), but not in conditions of low time pressure ($p \ge .05$). Finally, reinforcement power was found to have a significant impact ($p \le .001$) when accompanied by strong influence attempts, but little impact when accompanied by weak influence attempts ($p \ge .05$). This is in direct contrast to expert power and informal legitimate power, which are related significantly to manifest influence only under conditions of weak influence attempts.

REFERENCES:

French, John R. P. and Bertram Raven (1959), ''The Bases of Social Power,'' in *Studies in Social Power*, Dorwin Cartwright, ed. Ann Arbor, Mich.: University of Michigan Press.

Kohli, Ajay (1989), Determinants of Influence in Organizational Buying: A Contingency Approach *JM,* 53 (July), 50-65.

Michie, Donald A. and Stanley D. Sibley (1985), ''Channel Member Satisfaction: Controversy Resolved,'' *JAMS,* 13 (Spring), 188-205.

SCALE ITEMS: POWER (REINFORCEMENT)

Subjects were asked to think of a specific joint purchase decision with which they were very familiar. Subjects were asked to select a decision in which no purchase operation was so superior as to be the obvious choice of buying center members. The subject was then asked to rate the power, influence, etc. of a specific committee member (excluding him/herself) and the buying center and situational characteristics.

None   ____ : ____ : ____ : ____ : ____   All

       1   2   3   4   5

Reward Power Items
1. They believed he was capable of getting them pay raises.
2. They believed he could help improve their standing in the organization.
3. They felt it was desireable to be approved of by him.
4. They felt valued receiving recognition from him.
5. They believed he could arrange desireable assignments for them.
6. They believed he was capable of getting them promoted.

Coercive Power Items
7. They believed he was capable of interfering with their promotions.
8. They felt he could take them to task.
9. They felt he could make life difficult for them.
10. They thought he could block their salary increases.
11. They believed he could arrange for them to be assigned to unpleaant tasks.

SCALE NAME: Power (Reward)

SCALE DESCRIPTION:

A five-item, seven-point Likert-like scale used to measure a sales representative's perception of a sales manager's reward power (i.e., the ability to grant rewards).

SCALE ORIGIN:

The original basis for the perception of reward power source can be found in the sources of power taxonomy defined by French and Raven (1959). In this original taxonomy, reward power is described as the perception of B that A has the ability to mediate rewards for B. The other forms of power described by French and Raven are coercive, expert, referent, and legitimate power. Hunt and Nevin (1974) used a dichotomous classification scheme, coercive and noncoercive, to assess franchisor power. Gaski and Nevin (1985) extended these two earlier works by developing a quality/capability dichotomy to separate expert, referent, and legitimate power sources (quality) from reward and coercive power sources (capability). The scale reported here is consistent with the work of French and Raven and others (e.g., Michie and Sibley 1985), who suggest that it is the **perception** of a power source, rather than the exercise of power, that affects action.

SAMPLES:

Comer (1984) used **207** sales representatives employed by three companies (two industrial companies, one consumer food products company). A response rate of 62.2% was obtained from an original sample of 333.

RELIABILITY:

Cronbach's alpha was reported to be **.88** (Comer 1984).

VALIDITY:

Comer indicated that though the correlation between the a single-item measure of reward power source and the API reward power measure was statistically significant ($r = .26$), he failed to establish discriminant validity. A factor analysis yielded five items loading on the reward power factor, with four of the items loading at .76 to .80. The other item loaded only at .32, and actually loaded at a higher level (.43) on the referent power source scale. This item is footnoted in the Scale Items section. Nomological validity was also asserted by the author for the API multi-item measure of reward power from the correlation of the measure with job satisfaction ($r = .68$, .76, and .85 for each of three companies used in Comer's study, $p \leq .0001$). These correlations were indicated to be similar to results found elsewhere in research measuring correlations between the same two constructs (e.g., Burke and Wilcox 1971).

ADMINISTRATION:

A pencil-and-paper instrument was administered through a mail survey.

MAJOR FINDINGS:

Comer examined the quality of Holzbach's (1974) multi-item attributed power index (API) in comparison with Busch's (1980) single-item power scales. He concluded that the Holzbach API scale for coercive, expert, referent, and **reward power** had high levels of reliability and dimensional measurement. The measurement of the legitimate power base by the API scale, however, was found to be less reliable and to have a bidimensional factor structure.

REFERENCES:

Burke, Ronald J. and Douglas S. Wilcox (1971), ''Bases of Supervisory Power and Subordinate Job Satisfaction,'' *Canadian Journal of Behavioral Science*, 3, 182-193.

Busch, Paul (1980), ''The Sales Manager's Bases of Social Power and Influence on the Sales Force,'' *JM*, 44 (Summer), 91-101.

Comer, James M. (1984), ''A Psychometric Assessment of a Measure of Sales Representatives' Power Perceptions,'' *JMR*, 21 (May) 221-225.

French, John R. P. and Bertram Raven (1959), ''The Bases of Social Power,'' in *Studies in Social Power*, Dorwin Cartwright, ed. Ann Arbor, Mich.: University of Michigan Press.

Gaski, John F. and John R. Nevin (1985), ''The Differential Effects of Exercised and Unexercised Power Sources in a Marketing Channel,'' *JMR*, 22 (May), 130-142.

Holzbach, Robert Lawrence Jr., (1974), ''An Investigation of a Model of Managerial Effectiveness: The Effects of Leadership Style and Leader Attributed Social Power on Subordinate Job Performance,'' unpublished doctoral dissertation, Carnegie-Mellon University.

Hunt, Shelby D. and John R. Nevin (1974), ''Power in a Channel of Distribution: Sources and Consequences,'' *JMR*, 11 (May), 186-193.

Michie, Donald A. and Stanley D. Sibley (1985), ''Channel Member Satisfaction: Controversy Solved,'' *JAMS*, 13 (Spring) 188-205.

SCALE ITEMS: POWER (REWARD)

The following adjectives or phrases identify qualities your sales manager may have, actions he/she may take, or your personal feelings toward him/her. How accurate are these adjectives or phrases in describing your boss? Please circle the appropriate response code after each item:

1 = Extremely inaccurate
2 = Very inaccurate
3 = Inaccurate
4 = Don't know or can't decide
5 = Accurate
6 = Very accurate
7 = Extremely accurate

1. Gives credit where credit is due
2. Recognizes achievement
3. Willingness to promote others
4. Rewards good work
5. Offers inducement+

+ This item had a loading of .32 on the reward power scale and a loading of .43 on the referent power scale. It was included by Comer (1984) in the reward power scale, but not in the referent power scale.

SCALE NAME: Power (Reward)

SCALE DESCRIPTION:

A 15-item, five-point Likert-like scale used to measure a dealer's perception of a supplier's reward power (i.e., the ability to grant rewards) in a channel setting.

SCALE ORIGIN:

The original basis for the perception of reward power source can be found in the sources of power taxonomy defined by French and Raven (1959). In this original taxonomy, reward power is described as th perception of B thathas the ability to mediate rewards for B. The other forms of power scribed by French and Ravenare coercive, expert, referent, egitimate power. Hunt and Nevin (1974)ed a dichotomous claation scheme, ce and noncoercive, to assess franchisor power. The scale reported here is an extension from these two earlier works, and uses a quality/capability dichotomy to separate expert, refrent, and legitimate ower sources (quality) from reward and coercive power sources (capability). The scale is consistent with the work of French and Raven and others (e.g., Michie and Sibley 1985), who suggest that it is the **perception** of a power source, rather than the exercise of power, that affects action.

SAMPLES:

Gaski and Nevin (1985) used **238** U.S. and Canadian dealers for a specific manufacturer of heavy industrial machinery. A response rate of 37.5% was obtained from the original population of 634 dealers. Their work was based on the same data collection instrument used later by Gaski (1986).

RELIABILITY:

Cronbach's alpha was reported to be **.866** (Gaski and Nevin 1985).

VALIDITY:

Face, content, and discriminant validity measures were used by Gaski and Nevin. Content validity was achieved through the use of an initial inventory of items taken from the channels literature (Hunt and Nevin 1974; Lusch 1976, 1977) and modified by input from suppliers (i.e., a pretest of survey respondents). Discriminant validity was also asserted, as in no case were the correlations between constructs measured in the study as high as the Cronbach's alpha coefficient (.866) for "reward power source." The correlations between reward power source" and other constructs were: coercive power source (r = .267), exercised reward power source (r = .565), and exercised coercive power source (r = -.258).

ADMINISTRATION:

A pencil-and-paper instrument was administered through a mail survey. It was accompanied by a cover letter indicating company permission for suppliers to complete the survey.

MAJOR FINDINGS:

Gaski and Nevin found that the perception of a **reward power source** had a weaker relationship with power than did the exercise of reward power ($p \leq .10$). For predicting the variable of satisfaction, the standardized regression coefficients for reward power source ($b = .316$) and exercised reward power source ($b = .351$) were not significantly different ($p \geq .10$). The authors concluded that "the potential for reward may be as satisfying as the realization of that potential" (p. 137). Though the correlation between a reward power source and its exercise ($r = .565$) was found to be highly significant ($p = .0001$), Gaski and Nevin indicated that the greater the amount of a power source (punishment or reward) possessed by a supplier, the smaller the amount of that power actually exercised.

REFERENCES:

French, John R. P. and Bertram Raven (1959), "The Bases of Social Power," in *Studies in Social Power*, Dorwin Cartwright, ed. Ann Arbor, Mich.: University of Michigan Press.

Gaski, John F. (1986), "Interrelations Among a Channel Entity's Power Sources: Impact of the Exercise of Reward and Coercion on Expert, Referent, and Legitimate Power Sources," *JMR*, 23 (February), 62-76.

———— and John R. Nevin (1985), "The Differential Effects of Exercised and Unexercised Power Sources in a Marketing Channel," *JMR*, 22 (May), 130-142.

Hunt, Shelby D. and John R. Nevin (1974), "Power in a Channel of Distribution: Sources and Consequences," *JMR*, 11 (May), 186-193.

Michie, Donald A. and Stanley D. Sibley (1985), "Channel Member Satisfaction: Controversy Solved," *JAMS*, 13 (Spring), 188-205.

SCALE ITEMS: POWER (REWARD)

Please check (X) the appropriate space to indicate how much capability (the supplier) has to take each of the following kinds of action with your organization.

No capability ____ : ____ : ____ : ____ : ____ Very much capability
              0   1   2   3   4

1. Provide advertising support
2. Give trade allowances/incentives
3. Train personnel
4. Provide sales promotion materials
5. Grant favors (golf, lunches, etc.)
6. Give inventory rebates
7. Provide financing/credit
8. Furnish supplies
9. Give business advice
10. Provide service

11. Give pricing assistance
12. Give free samples
13. Provide ordering assistance
14. Provide inventory management assistance
15. Demonstrate products

SCALE NAME: Power of Distributor (Exercised)

SCALE DESCRIPTION:

A 17-item, five-point Likert-like scale measuring the exercised power of a distributor over a supplier. Distributor power is defined as "the extent of the distributor's freedom to make marketing decisions about the manufacturer's product" (Butaney and Wortzel 1988). For each of the 17 marketing decisions/activities listed, respondents are asked to indicate who (manufacturer or distributor) has the greatest responsibility. Each of the five points on the scale is anchored, ranging from "complete responsibility" to "no responsibility." It is important to note that the scale measures **exercised distributor power**, as opposed to perceived distributor power. Finally, because some of the 17 items were likely to be more important than others, items were ranked according to importance on an 11-point scale. This ranking was used to create an additional measure, weighted channel member power.

SCALE ORIGIN:

The theoretical background for the scale can be traced to the work of El-Ansary and Stern (1972), who viewed power as a function of the degree to which channel members depend on each other for satitfaction of goals and the relative power sources of each channel member. The exercised distributor power scale was developed by Butaney and Wortzel (1988). Using a panel of expert judges, they developed an original measure of 27 items. Each judge then used a five-point Likert-type scale to indicate whether he/she believed each item to be a likely target of manufacturer-distributor interface. After this review, the measure was shortened to 22 items. A subsequent factor analysis and the removal of items that did not load at .40 or greater on the primary factor of interest resulted in the final 17 item scale.

SAMPLES:

Butaney and Wortzel used **83** distributors in the electronic components industry as a sample. Two product lines, semiconductors and resistors, were studied to provide a range of customer and manufacturer power conditions.

RELIABILITY:

Cronbach's alpha was reported to be **.76** (raw scores) and .85 (weighted scores).

VALIDITY:

A factor analysis was performed on the original 22 item scale. Five items with loadings below .40 on the distributor power factor were dropped. Additionally, both the raw and weighted scores from the scale were correlated with a single item measuring the distributor's bargaining power with the manufacturer. The raw score measure was not significantly correlated with the single-item measure ($r = .04$, $p = .35$), but the weighted measure was ($r = .24$, $p = .01$), thereby suggesting convergent validity for the weighted power measure.

ADMINISTRATION:

A structured questionaire was administered personally to a single individual (a key informant) who was responsible for marketing policy decisions in each distributor firm.

MAJOR FINDINGS:

Butaney and Wortzel examined the effects of customer market power and manufacturer market power on the construct of distributor power. They found support for the hypothesis that distributor power and manufacturer market power are negatively related (adjusted R2 = 11.9%, p ≤ .004). Overall, they found that manufacturer market power alone explained 11% of the variance in distributor power, whereas customer power alone explained 6%. Together, manufacturer and customer market power explained 18.4% of the variance in distributor power (p ≤ .006).

REFERENCES:

Butaney, Gul and Lawrence H. Wortzel (1988), "Distributor Power Versus Manufacturer Power: The Customer Role," *JM,* 52 (January), 52-63.

El-Ansary, Adel and Louis W. Stern (1972), "Power Measurement in the Distribution Channel," *JMR,* 9 (February), 47-52.

SCALE ITEMS: POWER OF DISTRIBUTOR (EXERCISED)

To market and distribute a product, several marketing decisions have to be made. In making these decisions, a distributor may have almost complete responsibility, or freedom to make a decision may be shared with the manufacturer or the manufacturer may have complete responsibility. For each of the marketing decisions and activities listed below, please indicate the level of freedom or responsibility you have as compared to the selected manufacturer (in marketing the manufacturer's brand). Please check the most appropriate category.

1 = I have almost complete responsibility.
2 = I have more responsibility than the manufacturer.
3 = Manufacturer and I share equal responsibility.
4 = Manufacturer has more responsibility than myself.
5 = The manufacturer has almost complete responsibility.

Marketing Decisions and Activities:
1. Choosing geographic territories to sell in
2. Setting sales targets or goals
3. Setting selling prices to customers
4. Determining distribution policies to customers (e.g., delivery time)
5. Determining the training program for your sales force to sell the product
6. Keeping the manufacturer from selling direct in your territory
7. Product-return related issues
8. Choosing customers to sell to
9. Determining pricing policies (e.g., quantity discounts to customers)
10. Deciding to join in cooperative advertising with the manufacturer

11. Keeping the manufacturer's other distributors from selling in your territory
12. Accomodating customers' requests for product modification
13. Margins allowed by the manufacturer
14. Providing presale customer services (e.g., product information)
15. Attending sales meetings organized by the manufacturer
16. Resolving customers' product-related technical problems
17. Determining sales strategies/policies (e.g., frequency of sales calls to customers)

SCALE NAME: Power of Manufacturer

SCALE DESCRIPTION:

A six-item, 11-point scale measuring the relative power of a manufacturer and its boundary personnel by asking dealers to compare their manufacturer's performance with perceived average performance across a specific industry. Respondents are asked to rate the relative power of the manufacturer by responding to six items designed to assess the manufacturers' performance at two broad levels, the corporate strategic center level and the boundary personnel tactical center. The 11-point scale is anchored by -5 (very poor), 0 (average performance), and +5 (very good). Additionally, each of the six individual items is weighted by respondents according to the relative importance of the item to the respondent's firm's goal attainment. Finally, it should be noted that the manufacturer power scale measures **perceptions** of manufacturer power, as opposed to exercised manufacturer power.

SCALE ORIGIN:

The measure was developed in accordance with a dependence theory of Emerson (1962), which suggests that "the basis for one party's possession of power in a dyadic relationship is the other party's dependence therein" (Frazier and Summers 1986). The construct, manufacturer power, is believed by Frazier and Summers to have two levels, the corporate strategic center level and the boundary personnel tactical center level. The scale was originally developed and used by Frazier (1983).

SAMPLES:

Frazier and Summers used **435** new car dealers in Illinois, Indiana, and Ohio as respondents. Questionaires were directed to the "dealer principal" in each dealership. An overall response rate of 46.1% was achieved.

RELIABILITY:

Cronbach's alpha was reported to be .81 and **.83** for the boundary personnel tactical center for weighted and raw scores, respectively, and was .66 and **.70** for the corporate center for weighted and raw scores, respectively.

VALIDITY:

Several validity measures were used by Frazier and Summers. Content validity was shown through a series of pretest measures with car dealers to assure that question content measured the actual construct. Face validity was shown by comparing mean ratings of each item for each manufacturer with available industry data. Discriminant validity was assessed through the use of factor analysis. Two scale items (manufacturer-generated demand and interfirm assistances) loaded on one factor believed to be strategic, whereas the remaining four items loaded on one factor believed to be tactical/boundary spanning. Convergent validity was established by comparing the results for the relationship between dependency and switching to another manufacturer with those reported by Thibaut and Kelley (1959).

ADMINISTRATION:

A pencil-and-paper instrument was administered through a mail survey.

MAJOR FINDINGS:

Frazier and Summers found a negative and statistically significant ($p \leq .01$) relationship between **manufacturer power** and three coercive influence strategies tested (threats, legalistic pleas, and promises). The relationship was significant at both the level of boundary personnel and the corporate level. Three noncoercive strategies (recommendations, requests, and information exchange) were also significantly related to manufacturer power as it relates to boundary personnel ($p \leq .01$), though the relationship with recommendations was negative ($r = -.14$, $p \leq .001$). Of the noncoercive strategies, only information exchange ($r = .20$, $p \leq .001$) was significantly related to role performance at the corporate center level.

REFERENCES:

Emerson, Richard (1962), "Power-Dependence Relations," *American Sociological Review*, 27 (February), 31-41.

Frazier, Gary L. (1983), "On the Measurement of Interfirm Power in Channels of Distribution," *JMR*, 20 (May), 158- 166.

———— and John O. Summers (1986), "Perceptions of Interfirm Power and Its Use Within a Franchise Channel of Distribution," *JMR*, 23 (May), 169-176.

Thibaut, J. W. and H. Kelley (1959), *The Sociology of Groups*. New York, N.Y.: John Wiley & Sons, Inc.

SCALE ITEMS: POWER OF MANUFACTURER +

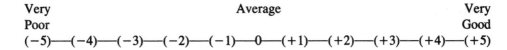

Very Poor					Average					Very Good
(−5)	(−4)	(−3)	(−2)	(−1)	0	(+1)	(+2)	(+3)	(+4)	(+5)

Each dealer indicated how well the manufacturer or its boundary personnel perform in comparison with industry average performance on each of the following role elements:
1. Manufacturer-generated demand for the make (of automobile)
2. Cooperativeness of the manufacturer reps on interfirm issues
3. Car allocation and delivery
4. Interfirm assistances
5. Quality of advice from the manufacturer reps
6. Reimbursement for warranty claims and vehicle preparation

+ Items 1 and 2 apply to the manufacturer's role performance at the corporate strategic center level. Items 3 through 6 apply to the manufacturer's role performance at the boundary personnel tactical center level.

SCALE NAME: Power of Supplier

SCALE DESCRIPTION:

A 10-item, four-point, Likert-like scale intended to measure a supplier's ability to get a dealer to do what he/she would not have otherwise done. The scale is intended to measure the potential influence of a supplier/manufacturer over a dealer's business in eight different areas of potential influence: price, order quantity, product line, advertising and sales promotion, customer service, inventory, customer credit, and display. Price and order quantity (two items each) are weighted more heavily than the other areas (one item each). The scale measures the perception of supplier power as reported by dealers (as opposed to the exercise of power).

SCALE ORIGIN:

The original use of the scale was by Gaski and Nevin (1985), who defined power as "the supplier's ability to get the dealer to do what he would not have done otherwise" (p. 135). The measure appears to be a summary measure of perceived manufacturer/supplier power, as opposed to the more specific five sources of perceived social power originally indicated by French and Raven (1959) or any of the subsequent dichotomies of power, such as coercive/noncoercive (Hunt and Nevin 1974).

SAMPLES:

Gaski (1986) and Gaski and Nevin (1985) used **238** U.S. and Canadian dealers for a specific manufacturer of heavy industrial machinery. A response rate of 37.5% was obtained from the original population of 634 dealers.

RELIABILITY:

Cronbach's alpha was **.865** (Gaski 1986; Gaski and Nevin 1985).

VALIDITY:

Face, content and discriminant validity measures were used in both studies. Content validity was achieved through the use of an initial inventory of items taken from the channels literature (Hunt and Nevin 1974; Lusch 1976, 1977) and modified by input from suppliers. Discriminant validity was also asserted, as in no case were the correlations between constructs measured in the study as high as the Cronbach's alpha coefficient (.865) for power. The correlations between power and other constructs were: use of reward ($r = .240$), use of coercion ($r = -.140$), expert power source ($r = .249$), referent power source ($r = .281$), legitimate power source ($r = .271$), and satisfaction ($r = .269$).

ADMINISTRATION:

A pencil-and-paper instrument was administered through a mail survey. It was accompanied by a cover letter indicating company permission for suppliers to complete the survey.

MAJOR FINDINGS:

Using LISREL, Gaski found that the use of reward and the use of punishment (together) had a positive but nonsignificant direct effect on the **power** of a supplier. When the effects of qualitative power sources (expert, legitimate, and referent power sources) were included, however, the total effects of reward and punishment were significant.

Gaski and Nevin found that the exercise of reward power had a stronger positive relationship with **power** than did the presence of a reward power source ($p \leq .10$). However, there was no significant difference ($p \geq .10$) between the relationship of power with the exercise of coercive power and a coercive power source. Gaski and Nevin concluded that when a supplier has considerable power over a dealer, the supplier may not need to exercise his/her coercive power. However, when the supplier has less relative power, the supplier may need to use coercive power.

COMMENTS:

Caution about the Gaski findings is advised, because of the effect a low Cronbach's alpha coefficient on another construct can have on the results achieved through LISREL. Additionally, Gaski reported that the structural models did not meet the absolute goodness-of-fit standard of $p \geq .05$. Finally, the normed fit indices of the models were .87 to .89, slightly below the recommended level of .90.

REFERENCES:

French, John R.P. and Bertram Raven (195(0, "The Bases of Social Power," in *Studies in Social Power*, Dorwin Cartwright, ed. Ann Arbor, Mich.: University of Michigan Press.

Gaski, John F. (1986), "Interrelations Among a Channel Entity's Power Sources: Impact of the Exercise of Reward and Coercion on Expert, Referent, and Legitimate Power Sources," *JMR*, 23 (February), 62-76.

_____ and John R. Nevin (1985), "The Differential Effects of Exercised and Unexercised Power Sources in a Marketing Channel," *JMR*, 22 (May), 130-142.

Hunt, Shelby D. and John R. Nevin (1974), "Power in a Channel of Distribution: Sources and Consequences," *JMR* , 11 (May), 186-193.

Lusch, Robert F. (1976), "Sources of Power: Their Impact on Intrachannel Conflict," *JMR*, 13 (November), 382-390.

_____ (1977), "Franchisee Satisfaction: Causes and Consequences," *International Journal of Physical Distribution*, 7, 128-140.

SCALE ITEMS: POWER OF SUPPLIER

Please indicate (X) your response to each of the following:

Not at all	Slightly	Moderately	As much as they wanted
0————————————1————————————2————————————3			

1. If (the supplier) wanted you to *raise the prices* you charge for their products, what is the *maximum amount* you would raise prices?

2. If (the supplier) wanted you to *lower the prices* you charge for their products, what is the *maximum amount* you would lower prices?

3. If (the supplier) wanted you to *increase the quantity* of their products you order, what is the *maximum amount* you would increase order quantity?

4. If (the supplier) wanted you to *decrease the quantity* of their products you order, what is the *maximum amount* you would decrease order quantity?

5. If (the supplier) wanted you to change the composition of your *product line*, what is the *maximum amount* you would change your product line?

6. If (the supplier) wanted you to change the type of *advertising and sales promotion* you do for their products, what is the *maximum amount* you would change your advertising and sales promotion?

7. If (the supplier) wanted you to change your *customer service* policy, what is the maximum amount you would change your customer service?

8. If (the supplier) wanted you to change your *inventory* procedures, what is the *maximum amount* you would change your inventory procedures?

9. If (the supplier) wanted you to change your *customer credit* policy, what is the *maximum amount* you would change your customer credit?

10. If (the supplier) wanted you to change the way you *display* their products, what is the *maximum amount* you would change your display of their products?

SCALE NAME: Pricing Analysis Frequency (Bank)

SCALE DESCRIPTION:

> A three-item, four-point Likert-like summated ratings scale measuring the frequency with which a bank officer reports that his/her bank evaluates its own pricing of services as well as those of competitors.

SCALE ORIGIN:

> McKee, Varadarajan, and Pride (1989) reported that they constructed the scales but selected items on the basis of a review of relevant literature and comments by industry executives. Theirs appears to be the only known use of the scale.

SAMPLES:

> The study focused on banks operating in 50 SMSAs of seven states that have unit banking laws. CEOs of the 560 banks in the sample frame were sent questionnaires. A total of **333** usable responses were received and an analysis of asset sizes indicated that respondents' banks were not significantly different from nonrespondents' banks.

RELIABILITY:

> An alpha of .**72** was reported for the scale.

VALIDITY:

> A factor analysis of all items used in the study revealed that items belonging to this scale loaded together on one factor and noother factors.

ADMINISTRATION:

> The scale was self-administered along with many other measures in a mail questionnaire format. Higher scores on the scale indicate that respondents' banks evaluate their own and competitors' services pricing very frequently.

MAJOR FINDINGS:

> The purpose of the study was to investigate the relationship between strategic orientation and dynamics of the market. Significant differences were found between organization strategy types in terms of several marketing tactics used. Specifically, the **frequency of pricing analysis** activities differed between some of the organization strategy types such that "prospectors" (those with the highest adaptive capability) engaged in it most and "reactors" (those with the lowest adaptive capability) engaged in it least.

REFERENCE:

> McKee, Daryl O., P. Rajan Varadarajan, and William M. Pride (1989), "Strategic Adaptability and Firm Performance: A Market Contingent Perspective," *JM*, 53 (July), 21-35.

SCALE ITEMS: PRICING ANALYSIS FREQUENCY (BANK)

For each statement, please check the response that best represents how often your bank conducts these activities.

Very often = two or more times a year
Often = once every year or two
Seldom = less than every two years

Very Often   Often   Seldom   Never
4————————————3————————————2————————————1

How often does your bank:
1. Re-evaluate pricing on deposit service charges.
2. Re-evaluate pricing on ''extra'' services (like safe deposit boxes).
3. Collect information about competitor pricing.

SCALE NAME: Procedural Knowledge

SCALE DESCRIPTION:

A two-item, five-point Likert-type summated ratings scale measuring the degree to which an employee can clearly specify the activities that must be performed to achieve desired outcomes.

SCALE ORIGIN:

The scale was apparently developed by Jaworski and MacInnis (1989). The scale along with other aspects of the survey instrument were refined through a series of interviews and a pretest of marketing managers.

SAMPLES:

A national sample of marketing mangers was drawn randomly from the American Marketing Association's list of members. Of the 479 managers who appear to have received questionnaires, **379** returned usable forms.

RELIABILITY:

The two items in the scale had a correlation of .50.

VALIDITY:

The validity of the scale was not specifically examined.

ADMINISTRATION:

The scale was self-administered along with many other measures in a mail survey format. Higher scores on the scale indicate that employees strongly believe that information and rules are available to guide their work whereas lower scores suggest that they have few formal procedures to help them in approaching their work.

MAJOR FINDINGS:

Among the many purposes of the study by Jaworski and MacInnis was to examine the simultaneous use of several types of managerial controls in the context of marketing management. Using structural equations, they found that **procedural knowledge** had a significant positive impact on the extent of reliance on process controls but was not significantly related to the use of professional or self control.

COMMENTS:

The reliability of the scale might be improved by the addition of a few appropriate items.

REFERENCE:

Jaworski, Bernard J. and Deborah J. MacInnis (1989), "Marketing Jobs and Management Controls: Toward a Framework," *JMR*, 26 (November), 406-419.

SCALE ITEMS: PROCEDURAL KNOWLEDGE

Strongly Disagree	Disagree	Neutral	Agree	Strongly Agree
1————————	—2————————	—3————————	—4————————	—5

1. There exists a clearly defined body of knowledge subject matter that can guide me in doing my work.
2. It is possible to rely upon existing procedures and practices to do my work.

SCALE NAME: Product Complexity

SCALE DESCRIPTION:

A four-item, six-point Likert-type summated ratings scale measuring the perceived complexity of a company's product introduction and the degree of learning necessary by customers. It was referred to as Consumer Learning by Eliashberg and Robertson (1988).

SCALE ORIGIN:

The scale appears to be original to Eliashberg and Robertson and was used only in their study.

SAMPLES:

The sample consisted of 75 business executives who attended a series of executive education seminars at a major university. They were employed by different firms representing a variety of industries. Apparently the executives either held positions that were connected with preannouncement decisions or made those decisions themselves.

RELIABILITY:

An alpha of .70 was reported for the scale.

VALIDITY:

No direct examination of scale validity was reported but results of a factor analysis indicated that the items were part of the same factor.

ADMINISTRATION:

The scale was self-administered along with other parts of a survey instrument. Respondents with higher scores perceive a product to be very complex and to require more time for customers to appreciate its advantages than do those with lower scores.

MAJOR FINDINGS:

The purpose of the study was to identify the conditions associated with the preannouncement of new product introductions. The perceived **product complexity** was not found to be a significant predictor of preannouncing firms.

REFERENCE:

Eliashberg, Jehoshua and Thomas S. Robertson (1988), ''New Product Preannouncing Behavior: A Market Signaling Study,'' *JMR*, 25 (August), 282-292.

SCALE ITEMS: PRODUCT COMPLEXITY

Strongly Disagree	Disagree	Slightly Disagree	Slightly Agree	Agree	Strongly Agree
1	2	3	4	5	6

1. The last new product/service we introduced required a major learning experience by the customer.
2. It takes time until the customers can really understand the full advantages of our new product/service.
3. The last new product we introduced represented a major discontinuity in our product/service line offering.
4. The last new product we introduced is more complex than the other products/services we have offered in the past.

SCALE NAME: Product Complexity

SCALE DESCRIPTION:

A five-item, five-point semantic differential summated ratings scale measuring the perceived complexity of a product.

SCALE ORIGIN:

The scale used by McCabe (1987) was composed of items based on factors identified by Hill (1972, 1973) as important product characteristics to consider when performing buying-related research.

SAMPLES:

McCabe's data came from buying centers in either the airline or corrugated shipping container industry. In the former, **15** buying centers were involved with the decision to buy aircraft and **13** were involved with the decision to buy jet fuel. In the latter, **14** buying centers were concerned with the purchase of printing inks and **13** were concerned with buying printing presses and other capital equipment. Data were collected just from individuals involved in source selection. There was an average of 1.7 people per buying unit.

RELIABILITY:

An alpha of **.80** was reported for the scale.

VALIDITY:

A factor analysis of 10 items related to buying group decisions indicated that the five items composing this scale all loaded on the same factor.

ADMINISTRATION:

Though interviews of some sort were conducted with buying group members, the measures in the questionnaire are assumed to have been self-administered. Higher scores on the scale indicate that respondents believe some specified generic product (such as printing inks) is very complex whereas lower scores suggest that respondents think a product is standardized and/or technically simple.

MAJOR FINDINGS:

McCabe examined opposing views of the relation between buying group structure and environmental uncertainty. The findings indicated that **product complexity** was a significant predictor of centralization and participation issues in buying group decision making, but was not a significant predictor of formalization.

REFERENCES:

Hill, Roy W. (1972), ''The Nature of Industrial Buying Decisions,'' *Industrial Marketing Management*, 2 (October), 45-55.

———— (1973), *Marketing Technological Products to Industry*. Oxford, England: Pergamon Press Ltd.

McCabe, Donald L. (1987), "Buying Group Structure: Constriction at the Top," *JM*, 51 (October), 89-98.

SCALE ITEMS: PRODUCT COMPLEXITY

Instructions: Using the rating scale shown below, please circle one number for each set of factors listed. The numbers have no specific values and are only designed to represent a continuous scale between the high and low definitions provided for each factor. Circle the number which reflects your opinion of where printing inks fall on such a continuum.

Standardized product	____ :	____ :	____ :	____ :	____	Differentiated product
	1	2	3	4	5	
Technically simple	____ :	____ :	____ :	____ :	____	Technically complex
	1	2	3	4	5	
Easy to install/use	____ :	____ :	____ :	____ :	____	Specialized installation/use
	1	2	3	4	5	
No after sales service	____ :	____ :	____ :	____ :	____	Technical after sales service
	1	2	3	4	5	
No consequential adjustment	____ :	____ :	____ :	____ :	____	Large consequential adjustment
	1	2	3	4	5	

SCALE NAME: Product/Component Uniqueness

SCALE DESCRIPTION:

A four-item, seven-point Likert-like scale that measures the uniqueness of the specifications for a product/component one company is buying from another company (e.g., is the product custom-made for the buyer's specific needs or is basically "off-the-shelf?").

SCALE ORIGIN:

The scale was apparently developed by Perdue (1989).

SAMPLES:

The data were collected in a mail survey of purchasing managers drawn from a list from the National Association of Purchasing Management. Managers were sent several copies of the questionnaire; they were asked to fill out one and to have the others completed by eligible purchasing agent(s). Those filling out the questionnaires were asked to answer for a purchase in which they had led the negotiations. Usable forms were received from at least one agent in 240 different firms. The total number of usable instruments was **335**. In general, there was no evidence of response bias with the possible exception of education level.

RELIABILITY:

An alpha of **.78** was reported for the scale. In a subsequent study of the same dataset, item-total correlations ranged from .39 to .72 (Perdue and Summers 1991).

VALIDITY:

Several tests of validity were conducted (Perdue 1989; Perdue and Summers 1991). Factor analyses were conducted on two pretest samples as well as the main survey sample. Confirmatory factor analysis also was conducted. Though the results for this particular scale were not reported individually, the implication is that the findings indicated the items to be unidimensional with evidence of convergent and discriminate validity.

ADMINISTRATION:

The scale was administered along with several other measures included in a mail survey format. Higher scores on the scale mean that purchasing agents indicate that purchases in which they led the negotiations were for very unique components whereas lower scores mean that the components they were negotiating to buy were quite common.

MAJOR FINDINGS:

The purpose of the study by Perdue was to examine the size and composition of the negotiation team in the rebuy of a component part. The findings indicated that engineering and quality control personnel were significantly more likely to participate in the purchase decision when the firm's component specifications were more **unique**.

#506 *Product/Component Uniqueness*

REFERENCES:

Perdue, Barbara C. (1989), ''The Size and Composition of the Buying Firm's Negotiation Team in Rebuys of Component Parts,'' *JAMS*, 17 (Spring), 121-128.

———— and John O. Summers (1991), ''Purchasing Agents' Use of Negotiation Strategies,'' *JMR*, 28 (May), 175-189.

SCALE ITEMS: PRODUCT/COMPONENT UNIQUENESS +

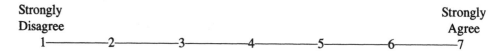

1. This component was very much custom-built for my firm.
2. The specifications for this component were substantially different from those of any other product that this selling firm makes.
3. This selling firm makes basically the same component for many of its other customers. **(r)**
4. This component was very much of an ''off-the-shelf'' item. **(r)**

+ The verbal anchors for this scale were not specified but are likely to have been of the disagree-agree type.

SCALE NAME: Product Line Sophistication (Industrial Buying)

SCALE DESCRIPTION:

A seven-item, seven-point semantic differential summated ratings scale measuring the degree to which a sales manager reports his/her product line to be technically sophisticated.

SCALE ORIGIN:

Items were generated by Anderson, Chu, and Weitz (1987) on the basis of a review of academic and trade literature. Pretesting was performed sequentially with 12 sales managers over several months, which allowed the questionnaire to be revised after each stage. This is the only known use of the scale.

SAMPLES:

The scale was analyzed with data collected from **169** sales managers representing 16 electronic component manufacturers.

RELIABILITY:

An alpha of **.88** was reported for the scale.

VALIDITY:

No specific examination of scale validity was reported.

ADMINISTRATION:

The scale was filled out by respondents as part of a self-administered mail survey. Higher scores on the scale suggest that respondents (sales managers) report their product lines to be technically sophisticated.

MAJOR FINDINGS:

The purpose of the study was to validate the Robinson, Faris, and Wind (1967) framework of industrial buying behavior, with particular focus on straight rebuy and new task situations. The findings indicated that the relationship between buyer behavior and buyclass was not greatly influenced by the **technical sophistication of the product lines**.

REFERENCES:

Anderson, Erin, Wujin Chu, and Barton Weitz (1987), "Industrial Purchasing: An Empirical Exploration of the Buyclass Framework," *JM*, 51 (July), 71-86.
Robinson, Patrick J., Charles W. Faris, Yoram Wind (1967), *Industrial Buying and Creative Marketing*. Boston, Mass.: Allyn and Bacon.

SCALE ITEMS: PRODUCT LINE SOPHISTICATION (INDUSTRIAL BUYING)

On each scale below, please circle the most appropriate rating for your product line taken as a whole.

1. Technical ____ : ____ : ____ : ____ : ____ : ____ : ____ Nontechnical **(r)**
                     1   2   3   4   5   6   7

2. Low engineering content ____ : ____ : ____ : ____ : ____ : ____ : ____ High engineering content
                     1   2   3   4   5   6   7

3. Fast changing ____ : ____ : ____ : ____ : ____ : ____ : ____ Slowly changing **(r)**
                     1   2   3   4   5   6   7

4. Unsophisticated ____ : ____ : ____ : ____ : ____ : ____ : ____ Sophisticated
                     1   2   3   4   5   6   7

5. Commodity ____ : ____ : ____ : ____ : ____ : ____ : ____ Customized
                     1   2   3   4   5   6   7

6. Unique ____ : ____ : ____ : ____ : ____ : ____ : ____ Common **(r)**
                     1   2   3   4   5   6   7

7. Complex ____ : ____ : ____ : ____ : ____ : ____ : ____ Simple **(r)**
                     1   2   3   4   5   6   7

SCALE NAME: Product Preannouncement (Cannibalization Concerns)

SCALE DESCRIPTION:

A five-item, six-point Likert-like summated ratings scale measuring the degree to which a person perceives that preannouncing a new product introduction hurts the sales of other products in a company's line.

SCALE ORIGIN:

The scale appears to be original to Eliashberg and Robertson (1988) and was used only in their study.

SAMPLES:

The sample consisted of 75 business executives who attended a series of executive education seminars at a major university. They were employed by different firms representing a variety of industries. Apparently the executives either held positions connected with preannouncement decisions or made those decisions themselves.

RELIABILITY:

An alpha of .92 was reported for the scale.

VALIDITY:

No direct examination of scale validity was reported but results of a factor analysis indicated that the items were part of the same factor.

ADMINISTRATION:

The scale was self-administered along with other parts of a survey instrument. Respondents with higher scores are much more concerned than those with lower scores that preannouncement of a new product will hurt the sales of their companies' other products.

MAJOR FINDINGS:

The purpose of the study was to identify the conditions associated with the preannouncement of new product introductions. Among respondents in the sample whose companies had not recently preannounced a new product introduction, **cannibalization concerns** were stressed as a reason.

REFERENCE:

Eliashberg, Jehoshua and Thomas S. Robertson (1988), "New Product Preannouncing Behavior: A Market Signaling Study," *JMR*, 25 (August), 282-292.

SCALE ITEMS: PRODUCT PREANNOUNCEMENT (CANNIBALIZATION CONCERNS)

Definitely a reason	____ : ____ : ____ : ____ : ____ : ____	Definitely not a reason
	1　2　3　4　5　6	

Why was the last new product or service that you introduced (not) preannounced? +
1. Preannouncing frequently cannibalizes the sales of the present product in the line.
2. Preannouncing delays customer purchases of the present products in our line.
3. Preannouncing confuses customers who then don't know what to buy.
4. Preannouncing hurts our other products' sales.
5. Preannouncing frequently lowers the sales of other products in our line.

+ Executives of companies that had not recently preannounced the introduction of a product were asked the negative form of the question.

SCALE NAME: Product Preannouncement (Competitive Concerns)

SCALE DESCRIPTION:

A four-item, six-point Likert-like summated ratings scale measuring the degree to which a person perceives that preannouncing a new product introduction helps the competition more than it does the company.

SCALE ORIGIN:

The scale appears to be original to Eliashberg and Robertson (1988) and was used only in their study.

SAMPLES:

The sample consisted of **75** business executives who attended a series of executive education seminars at a major university. They were employed by different firms representing a variety of industries. Apparently the executives either held positions connected with preannouncement decisions or made those decisions themselves.

RELIABILITY:

An alpha of **.87** was reported for the scale.

VALIDITY:

No direct examination of scale validity was reported but results of a factor analysis indicated that the items were part of the same factor.

ADMINISTRATION:

The scale was self-administered along with other parts of a survey instrument. Respondents with higher scores are much more concerned than those with lower scores that preannouncement of a new product will benefit their competitors.

MAJOR FINDINGS:

The purpose of the study was to identify the conditions associated with the preannouncement of new product introductions. Among respondents in the sample whose companies had not recently preannounced a new product introduction, **competitive concerns** were stressed as a reason.

REFERENCE:

Eliashberg, Jehoshua and Thomas S. Robertson (1988), "New Product Preannouncing Behavior: A Market Signaling Study," *JMR*, 25 (August), 282-292.

SCALE ITEMS: PRODUCT PREANNOUNCEMENT (COMPETITIVE CONCERNS)

Definitely							Definitely not
a reason	___ :	___ :	___ :	___ :	___ :	___	a reason
	1	2	3	4	5	6	

Why was the last new product or service that you introduced (not) preannounced? +

1. The benefits of preannouncing are much smaller than the drawbacks of telling our customers what we are up to.
2. If we preannounce, this simply encourages competitors to get to the market sooner.
3. Preannouncing leads to greater competitive reactions.
4. Preannouncing benefits competitors more than it benefits us.

+ Executives of companies that had not recently preannounced the introduction of a product were asked the negative form of the question.

SCALE NAME: Product Preannouncement (Distribution Reasons)

SCALE DESCRIPTION:

A three-item, six-point Likert-like summated ratings scale measuring the degree to which a person perceives that preannouncing a new product introduction is done to gain better distributor support for the product.

SCALE ORIGIN:

The scale appears to be original to Eliashberg and Robertson (1988) and was used only in their study.

SAMPLES:

The sample consisted of **75** business executives who attended a series of executive education seminars at a major university. They were employed by different firms representing a variety of industries. Apparently the executives either held positions connected with preannouncement decisions or made those decisions themselves.

RELIABILITY:

An alpha of **.80** was reported for the scale.

VALIDITY:

No direct examination of scale validity was reported but results of a factor analysis indicated that the items were part of the same factor.

ADMINISTRATION:

The scale was self-administered along with other parts of a survey instrument. Respondents with higher scores are much more likely than those with lower scores to perceive that their companies preannounced their last new product introduction to gain distributor cooperation and support.

MAJOR FINDINGS:

The purpose of the study was to identify the conditions associated with the preannouncement of new product introductions. Among respondents in the sample whose companies had recently preannounced a new product introduction, **distribution reasons** for the announcement were stressed.

REFERENCE:

Eliashberg, Jehoshua and Thomas S. Robertson (1988), "New Product Preannouncing Behavior: A Market Signaling Study," *JMR*, 25 (August), 282-292.

SCALE ITEMS: PRODUCT PREANNOUNCEMENT (DISTRIBUTION REASONS)

Definitely
a reason   ____ : ____ : ____ : ____ : ____ : ____   Definitely not
a reason
            1   2   3   4   5   6

Why was the last new product or service that you introduced (not) preannounced? +
1. To help distributors clean up their inventories.
2. To build advance distributor support.
3. To gain better distributor cooperation.

+ Executives of companies that had not recently preannounced the introduction of a product were asked the negative form of the question.

SCALE NAME: Product Preannouncement (Image Reasons)

SCALE DESCRIPTION:

A four-item, six-point Likert-like summated ratings scale measuring the degree to which a person perceives that preannouncing a new product introduction is done to improve its image among shareholders and others.

SCALE ORIGIN:

The scale appears to be original to Eliashberg and Robertson (1988) and was used only in their study.

SAMPLES:

The sample consisted of **75** business executives who attended a series of executive education seminars at a major university. They were employed by different firms representing a variety of industries. Apparently the executives either held positions connected with preannouncement decisions or made those decisions themselves.

RELIABILITY:

An alpha of **.81** was reported for the scale.

VALIDITY:

No direct examination of scale validity was reported but results of a factor analysis indicated that the items were part of the same factor.

ADMINISTRATION:

The scale was self-administered along with other parts of a survey instrument. Respondents with higher scores are much more likely than those with lower scores to perceive that their companies preannounced their last new product introduction to enhance company image.

MAJOR FINDINGS:

The purpose of the study was to identify the conditions associated with the preannouncement of new product introductions. Among respondents in the sample whose companies had recently preannounced a new product introduction, **image reasons** for the announcement were stressed.

REFERENCE:

Eliashberg, Jehoshua and Thomas S. Robertson (1988), ''New Product Preannouncing Behavior: A Market Signaling Study,'' *JMR*, 25 (August), 282-292.

SCALE ITEMS: PRODUCT PREANNOUNCEMENT (IMAGE REASONS)

Definitely
a reason   ___ : ___ : ___ : ___ : ___ : ___   Definitely not
a reason
           1   2   3   4   5   6

Why was the last new product or service that you introduced (not) preannounced? +
1. To enhance the company's image and reputation.
2. To impress the shareholders and potential shareholders.
3. To build an innovative company image.
4. To build a high-growth company image.

+ Executives of companies that had not recently preannounced the introduction of a product were asked the negative form of the question.

SCALE NAME: Product Preannouncement (Legal Concerns)

SCALE DESCRIPTION:

> A three-item, six-point Likert-like summated ratings scale measuring the degree to which a person perceives that preannouncing a new product introduction could bring charges of unfair competition and prompt legal action.

SCALE ORIGIN:

> The scale appears to be original to Eliashberg and Robertson (1988) and was used only in their study.

SAMPLES:

> The sample consisted of **75** business executives who attended a series of executive education seminars at a major university. They were employed by different firms representing a variety of industries. Apparently the executives either held positions connected with preannouncement decisions or made those decisions themselves.

RELIABILITY:

> An alpha of **.91** was reported for the scale.

VALIDITY:

> No direct examination of scale validity was reported but results of a factor analysis indicated that the items were part of the same factor.

ADMINISTRATION:

> The scale was self-administered along with other parts of a survey instrument. Respondents with higher scores are much more concerned than those with lower scores that preannouncement of a new product is legally risky.

MAJOR FINDINGS:

> The purpose of the study was to identify the conditions associated with the preannouncement of new product introductions. Among respondents in the sample whose companies had not recently preannounced a new product introduction, **legal concerns** were stressed as a reason.

REFERENCE:

> Eliashberg, Jehoshua and Thomas S. Robertson (1988), ''New Product Preannouncing Behavior: A Market Signaling Study,'' *JMR*, 25 (August), 282-292.

SCALE ITEMS: PRODUCT PREANNOUNCEMENT (LEGAL CONCERNS)

Definitely							Definitely not
a reason	____ : ____ : ____ : ____ : ____ : ____						a reason
	1	2	3	4	5	6	

Why was the last new product or service that you introduced (not) preannounced? +

1. Preannouncing can lead to antitrust problems by "overhanging" the market.
2. Preannouncing may encourage legal action by competitors if the preannouncement is considered preemptive.
3. It is difficult to preannounce without charges of unfair competition.

+ Executives of companies that had not recently preannounced the introduction of a product were asked the negative form of the question.

SCALE NAME: Product Preannouncement (Promotional Reasons)

SCALE DESCRIPTION:

A five-item, six-point Likert-like summated ratings scale measuring the degree to which a person perceives that preannouncing a new product introduction is done to improve its promotional and sales impact. This scale was referred to as Demand Stimulation by Eliashberg and Robertson (1988).

SCALE ORIGIN:

The scale appears to be original to Eliashberg and Robertson and was used only in their study.

SAMPLES:

The sample consisted of **75** business executives who attended a series of executive education seminars at a major university. They were employed by different firms representing a variety of industries. Apparently the executives either held positions connected with preannouncement decisions or made those decisions themselves.

RELIABILITY:

An alpha of **.74** was reported for the scale.

VALIDITY:

No direct examination of scale validity was reported but results of a factor analysis indicated that the items were part of the same factor.

ADMINISTRATION:

The scale was self-administered along with other parts of a survey instrument. Respondents with higher scores are much more likely than those with lower scores to perceive that their companies preannounced their last new product introduction to enhance the effectiveness of their promotion and sales.

MAJOR FINDINGS:

The purpose of the study was to identify the conditions associated with the preannouncement of new product introductions. Among respondents in the sample whose companies had recently preannounced a new product introduction, **promotional reasons** for the announcement were stressed.

REFERENCE:

Eliashberg, Jehoshua and Thomas S. Robertson (1988), "New Product Preannouncing Behavior: A Market Signaling Study," *JMR*, 25 (August), 282-292.

SCALE ITEMS: PRODUCT PREANNOUNCEMENT (PROMOTIONAL REASONS)

Definitely							Definitely not
a reason	____ :	____ :	____ :	____ :	____ :	____	a reason
	1	2	3	4	5	6	

Why was the last new product or service that you introduced (not) preannounced? +
1. To identify new customers.
2. To begin building customer awareness.
3. To encourage word-of-mouth advertising among potential customers.
4. To start building advertising impact.
5. To make sales take off more rapidly when we introduce it.

+ Executives of companies that had not recently preannounced the introduction of a product were asked the negative form of the question.

SCALE NAME: Product Preannouncement (Risks)

SCALE DESCRIPTION:

A three-item, six-point Likert-like summated ratings scale measuring the degree to which a person perceives that preannouncing a new product introduction is risky because of the problems of bringing a product to market exactly as announced. It was referred to as Inability to Deliver by Eliashberg and Robertson (1988).

SCALE ORIGIN:

The scale appears to be original to Eliashberg and Robertson and was used only in their study.

SAMPLES:

The sample consisted of 75 business executives who attended a series of executive education seminars at a major university. They were employed by different firms representing a variety of industries. Apparently the executives either held positions connected with preannouncement decisions or made those decisions themselves.

RELIABILITY:

An alpha of .80 was reported for the scale.

VALIDITY:

No direct examination of scale validity was reported but results of a factor analysis indicated that the items were part of the same factor.

ADMINISTRATION:

The scale was self-administered along with other parts of a survey instrument. Respondents with higher scores are much more concerned than those with lower scores that preannouncement of a new product will be risky because of inability to deliver it as promised.

MAJOR FINDINGS:

The purpose of the study was to identify the conditions associated with the preannouncement of new product introductions. Among respondents in the sample whose companies had not recently preannounced a new product introduction, **risks** were stressed as a reason.

REFERENCE:

Eliashberg, Jehoshua and Thomas S. Robertson (1988), ''New Product Preannouncing Behavior: A Market Signaling Study,'' *JMR*, 25 (August), 282-292.

SCALE ITEMS: PRODUCT PREANNOUNCEMENT (RISKS)

Definitely
a reason   ____ : ____ : ____ : ____ : ____ : ____   Definitely not
a reason

       1   2   3   4   5   6

Why was the last new product or service that you introduced (not) preannounced? +

1. Preannouncing is risky business because we may not be able to deliver at the time promised.
2. Preannouncing is risky because the product specifications might change before actual market introduction.
3. Preannouncing may lead to credibility problems because preannouncements are sometimes overly ambitious.

+ Executives of companies that had not recently preannounced the introduction of a product were asked the negative form of the question.

SCALE NAME: Product Service Activity (Salesperson)

SCALE DESCRIPTION:

A nine-item, seven-point Likert-like summated ratings scale measuring the frequency with which a person engages in activities related to servicing the product, with an emphasis on the use of technical skills.

SCALE ORIGIN:

The scale is original to a study by Moncrief (1986). Several scales were developed for use in the study from a review of the literature and from personal interviews and focus groups with salespeople. A total of 121 selling-related activities were identified and included on the survey questionnaire.

SAMPLES:

Using stratified sampling, Moncrief sent survey forms to 800 firms representing 20 SIC codes (#20-#39). Fifty-one firms ultimately participated and sent copies of the questionnaire to their salespeople. Of the total 2322 sales employees working for these firms, 1393 returned usable forms but the factor analysis was based on responses from **1291**.

RELIABILITY:

An alpha of **.81** is reported for the scale.

VALIDITY:

Though scale validity was not specifically addressed, a factor analysis of 121 items indicated that the items below all had loadings greater than .50 on the same factor and loadings less than .40 other factors. These findings proviome evidence of the convergent and discriminant validity of the scale.

ADMINISTRATION:

The scale was self-administered along with many other measures in a mail survey format. Higher scores on the scale indicate that respondents frequently engage in product service activities whereas lower scores suggest that they primarily perform activities other than those directly related to servicing products.

MAJOR FINDINGS:

The purpose of the study by Moncrief was to develop a comprehensive list of selling-related activities and the taxonomies created from them. A cluster analysis was performed of the salespeople in the sample and six clusters were found. A group called trade servicer, representing 18% of the sample, had the highest mean on the **product service activity**. This cluster had the highest mean of any of the sales groups on seven of 10 sales activity areas examined in the study and had the second highest mean on the other three activity areas.

REFERENCE:

Moncrief, William C., III (1986), ''Selling Activity and Sales Position Taxonomies for Industrial Salesforces,'' *JMR*, 23 (August), 261-270.

SCALE ITEMS: PRODUCT SERVICE ACTIVITY (SALESPERSON) +

Using the following scale, please indicate how frequently you engage in each of the activities listed below. If you do not perform the activity, please code your response as a zero.

Infrequently   ____ : ____ : ____ : ____ : ____ : ____ : ____   Frequently
                1   2   3   4   5   6   7

1. Present during repairs
2. Test product
3. Supervise installation
4. Perform maintenance
5. Make deliveries
6. Teach safety instructions
7. Train customers to use products
8. Order accessories
9. Learn about product

+ The actual directions and items were not stated in the article but are reconstructed here on the basis of information provided.

SCALE NAME: Product Understanding

SCALE DESCRIPTION:

A three-item, six-point Likert-type summated ratings scale measuring the perceived degree of customer time and effort required to appreciate a company's product introduction. It was referred to as Product Trial Tendency by Eliashberg and Robertson (1988).

SCALE ORIGIN:

The scale appears to be original to Eliashberg and Robertson and was used only in their study.

SAMPLES:

The sample consisted of **75** business executives who attended a series of executive education seminars at a major university. They were employed by different firms representing a variety of industries. Apparently the executives either held positions connected with preannouncement decisions or made those decisions themselves.

RELIABILITY:

An alpha of **.66** was reported for the scale.

VALIDITY:

No direct examination of scale validity was reported but results of a factor analysis indicated that the items were part of the same factor.

ADMINISTRATION:

The scale was self-administered along with other parts of a survey instrument. Respondents with higher scores perceive a product to require more time and effort for customers to appreciate its advantages than do those with lower scores.

MAJOR FINDINGS:

The purpose of the study was to identify the conditions associated with the preannouncement of new product introductions. The perceived **product understanding** was not found to be a significant predictor of preannouncing firms.

COMMENTS:

The low internal consistency of this scale suggests that it should be used cautiously until more items can be tested and added to improve its reliability.

REFERENCE:

Eliashberg, Jehoshua and Thomas S. Robertson (1988), ''New Product Preannouncing Behavior: A Market Signaling Study,'' *JMR*, 25 (August), 282-292.

SCALE ITEMS: PRODUCT UNDERSTANDING

Strongly Disagree	Disagree	Slightly Disagree	Slightly Agree	Agree	Strongly Agree
1	2	3	4	5	6

1. Customers must try the new product/service before they can really appreciate its benefits.
2. It takes time until the customers can really understand the full advantages of our new product/service.
3. Customers could readily engage in a product/service trial before buying our new product/service. **(r)**

SCALE NAME: Professionalism (Autonomy)

SCALE DESCRIPTION:

A four-item, seven-point Likert-type summated ratings scale measuring the degree to which a person in a professional-type job believes that he/she should be relatively free to make decisions about the means and goals of work without interference from others.

SCALE ORIGIN:

Bullard and Snizek (1988) used a scale by Bartol (1979). The latter indicated that her scale was inspired by the Hall (1968) scale and took into account the suggestions made by Snizek (1972) and others. A corrected split-half reliability of .82 was reported for the scale.

SAMPLES:

Bullard and Snizek selected 900 lawyers, dentists, and CPAs at random from the yellow pages of three metropolitan areas. After two mailings, usable responses were received from **391** professionals. There was no evidence of response bias.

RELIABILITY:

An alpha of **.64** was reported.

VALIDITY:

No specific examination of scale validity was reported.

ADMINISTRATION:

The scale was self-administered along with several other measures in a mail survey format. Higher scores on the scale suggest that respondents expect a great sense of autonomy in their work whereas lower scores indicate that they do not feel they should be free to have much control over their work.

MAJOR FINDINGS:

The purpose of the study by Bullard and Snizek was to investigate the acceptability of various ads by professionals and the influence of professionalism on respondents' willingness to use those ads in promoting their own services. The data did *not* indicate a significant correlation between a desire for **professional autonomy** and willingness to use advertising.

COMMENTS:

The full 20-item professionalism scale used by Bullard and Snizek was reported to have an alpha of .72.

REFERENCES:

Bartol, Kathryn M. (1979), "Professionalism as a Predictor of Organizational Commitment, Role Stress, and Turnover: A Multidimensional Approach," *Academy of Management Journal*, 22 (4), 815-821.

Bullard, Jerri Hayes and William E. Snizek (1988), "Factors Affecting the Acceptability of Advertisements Among Professionals," *JAMS*, 16 (Summer), 57-63.

Hall, Richard H. (1968), "Professionalism and Bureaucratization," *American Sociological Review*, 33 (February), 92-104.

Snizek, William E. (1972), "Hall's Professionalism Scale: An Empirical Reassessment," *American Sociological Review*, 37 (February), 109-114.

SCALE ITEMS: PROFESSIONALISM (AUTONOMY)

Listed below are a number of statements which involve possible feelings about working in one's profession or field of expertise. With respect to your own feelings about the field of expertise in which you now work, please use the following scale to indicate the extent of your agreement or disagreement. There are no right or wrong answers.

Strongly Disagree	Disagree	Slightly Disagree	Neutral	Slightly Agree	Agree	Strongly Agree
1	2	3	4	5	6	7

1. I feel that I should have a lot to say about which projects I work on.
2. People should just tell me about a problem and then leave me to solve it.
3. I should be given considerable latitude to pursue work goals I feel are important.
4. For all practical purposes, I should be allowed to be my own boss.

SCALE NAME: Professionalism (Autonomy)

SCALE DESCRIPTION:

A five-item, five-point Likert-like summated ratings scale measuring the degree to which a person in a professional-type job believes that he/she is relatively free to make decisions about work without interference from other people or organizations.

SCALE ORIGIN:

The original five-dimension index was developed by Hall (1968) and contained 10 items per dimension of professionalism. Snizek (1972) tested the inventory of items, noted problems, and identified the best five items per dimension. The five-item Autonomy scale had reliability (KR-20) of .760 and .738 for the samples used by Hall and Snizek, respectively.

SAMPLES:

A mail survey of 300 attorneys practicing in Virginia was made by Snizek and Crocker (1985). Usable questionnaires were returned by **109**. Nearly half of the respondents were in partnerships and only the responses of practicing attorneys were used. No evidence of response bias was found.

RELIABILITY:

An alpha of **.654** was reported by Snizek and Crocker.

VALIDITY:

No specific examination of scale validity was reported.

ADMINISTRATION:

The scale was self-administered along with several other measures in a mail survey format. Higher scores on the scale suggest that respondents have a great sense of autonomy in their work whereas lower scores indicate that they do not feel very free to make decisions about their work.

MAJOR FINDINGS:

The purpose of the study by Snizek and Crocker was to investigate lawyers' attitudes toward legal services advertising and to determine the influence of professionalism on those attitudes. The data did not indicate a significant correlation between **autonomy** and attitudes toward the advertising.

REFERENCES:

Hall, Richard H. (1968), ''Professionalm and Bureaucratization,'' *American Sociological Review*, 33 (February), 92-104.

Snizek, William E. (1972), "Hall's Professionalism Scale: An Empirical Reassessment," *American Sociological Review*, 37 (February), 109-114.

_____ and Kenneth E. Crocker (1985), "Professionalism and Attorney Attitudes Toward Legal Service Advertising," *JAMS*, 13 (Fall), 101-118.

SCALE ITEMS: PROFESSIONALISM (AUTONOMY)

The following questions are an attempt to measure certain aspects of what is commonly called "professionalism." The referent in the questions is your own profession. Each item then, should be answered in light of the way you yourself both feel and behave as a member of your particular profession.

There are five possible responses to each item. If the item corresponds **VERY WELL** (VW) to your own attitudes and/or behavior, circle that response. If it corresponds **WELL** (W), **POORLY** (P), or **VERY POORLY** (VP), mark the appropriate response. The middle category (**?**) is designed to indicate an essentially neutral opinion about the item. Please answer ALL items in one fashion or another, making sure that you have NO MORE THAN ONE RESPONSE FOR EACH ITEM.

VW	W	?	P	VP
1	2	3	4	5

1. I make my own decisions in regard to what is to be done in my work.
2. I don't have much opportunity to exercise my own judgment. **(r)**
3. My own decisions are subject to review. **(r)**
4. I am my own boss in almost every work-related situation.
5. I know that my own judgment on most matters is the *final* judgment.

SCALE NAME: Professionalism (Client-Orientation)

SCALE DESCRIPTION:

A five-item, seven-point Likert-type summated ratings scale measuring the degree to which a professional reports that he/she should put the client's needs before his/her own needs and provide the best service possible. The scale was referred to as Ethics by Bartol (1979) as well as Bullard and Snizek (1988).

SCALE ORIGIN:

Bullard and Snizek used a scale by Bartol. The latter indicated that her scale was inspired by the Hall (1968) scale and took into account the suggestions made by Snizek (1972) and others. A corrected split-half reliability of .79 was reported for the scale.

SAMPLES:

Bullard and Snizek selected 900 lawyers, dentists, and CPAs at random from the yellow pages of three metropolitan areas. After two mailings, usable responses were received from **391** professionals. There was no evidence of response bias.

RELIABILITY:

An alpha of **.66** was reported.

VALIDITY:

No specific examination of scale validity was reported.

ADMINISTRATION:

The scale was self-administered along with several other measures in a mail survey format. Higher scores on the scale suggest that respondents strongly believe they should put their clients' interests above their own in providing services whereas lower scores suggest that they think their own personal concerns must take priority.

MAJOR FINDINGS:

The purpose of the study by Bullard and Snizek was to investigate the acceptability of various ads by professionals and the influence of professionalism on respondents' willingness to use those ads in promoting their own services. The data indicated a significant positive relationship between belief in a **client-orientation** and willingness to use advertising.

COMMENTS:

The full 20-item professionalism scale used by Bullard and Snizek was reported to have an alpha of .72.

REFERENCES:

Bartol, Kathryn M. (1979), "Professionalism as a Predictor of Organizational Commitment, Role Stress, and Turnover: A Multidimensional Approach," *Academy of Management Journal*, 22 (4), 815-821.

Bullard, Jerri Hayes and William E. Snizek (1988), "Factors Affecting the Acceptability of Advertisements Among Professionals," *JAMS*, 16 (Summer), 57-63.

Hall, Richard H. (1968), "Professionalism and Bureaucratization," *American Sociological Review*, 33 (February), 92-104.

Snizek, William E. (1972), "Hall's Professionalism Scale: An Empirical Reassessment," *American Sociological Review*, 37 (February), 109-114.

SCALE ITEMS: PROFESSIONALISM (CLIENT-ORIENTATION)

Listed below are a number of statements which involve possible feelings about working in one's profession or field of expertise. With respect to your own feelings about the field of expertise in which you now work, please use the following scale to indicate the extent of your agreement or disagreement. There are no right or wrong answers.

Strongly Disagree	Disagree	Slightly Disagree	Neutral	Slightly Agree	Agree	Strongly Agree
1	2	3	4	5	6	7

1. I feel that I should not allow my own self interests to interfere with providing the best possible professional service.
2. I feel I should not let personal feelings get in the way of doing the best job possible.
3. Service to the people who utilize my expertise is my most important priority.
4. I don't care what quality work other people in this field do as long as it doesn't interfere directly with me. **(r)**
5. My own personal career concerns deserve attention ahead of the interests of clients and users. **(r)**

SCALE NAME: Professionalism (Collegial Maintenance)

SCALE DESCRIPTION:

A three-item, seven-point Likert-type summated ratings scale measuring the degree to which a person in a professional-type job believes that his/her work should be evaluated by fellow professionals.

SCALE ORIGIN:

Bullard and Snizek (1988) used a scale by Bartol (1979). The latter indicated that her scale was inspired by the Hall (1968) scale and took into account the suggestions made by Snizek (1972) and others. A corrected split-half reliability of .82 was reported for the scale.

SAMPLES:

Bullard and Snizek selected 900 lawyers, dentists, and CPAs at random from the yellow pages of three metropolitan areas. After two mailings, usable responses were received from **391** professionals. There was no evidence of response bias.

RELIABILITY:

An alpha of **.71** was reported.

VALIDITY:

No specific examination of scale validity was reported.

ADMINISTRATION:

The scale was self-administered along with several other measures in a mail survey format. Higher scores on the scale suggest that respondents strongly believe their work as professionals should be judged by professional colleagues.

MAJOR FINDINGS:

The purpose of the study by Bullard and Snizek was to investigate the acceptability of various ads by professionals and the influence of professionalism on respondents' willingness to use those ads in promoting their own services. The data indicated a significant inverse relationship between belief in **collegial maintenance of professional work** and willingness to use advertising.

COMMENTS:

The full 20-item professionalism scale used by Bullard and Snizek was reported to have an alpha of .72.

#520 *Professionalism (Collegial Maintenance)*

REFERENCES:

Bartol, Kathryn M. (1979),ofessionalism aredictor of Organizational itment, Role Stress, and Turnover: A Multidimensional Approach,'' *Academy of Management Journal*, 22 (4), 815-821.

Bullard, Jerri Hayes and William E. Snizek (1988), ''Factors Affecting the Acceptability of Advertisements Among Professionals,'' *JAMS*, 16 (Summer), 57-63.

Hall, Richard H. (1968), ''Professionalism and Bureaucratization,'' *American Sociological Review*, 33 (February), 92-104.

Snizek, William E. (1972), ''Hall's Professionalism Scale: An Empirical Reassessment,'' *American Sociological Review*, 37 (February), 109-114.

SCALE ITEMS: PROFESSIONALISM (COLLEGIAL MAINTENANCE)

Listed below are a number of statements which involve possible feelings about working in one's profession or field of expertise. With respect to your own feelings about the field of expertise in which you now work, please use the following scale to indicate the extent of your agreement or disagreement. There are no right or wrong answers.

Strongly Disagree	Disagree	Slightly Disagree	Neutral	Slightly Agree	Agree	Strongly Agree
1	2	3	4	5	6	7

1. My work in this field should be evaluated mainly by my peers.
2. The judgement of people above me in the hierarchy should count most heavily in evaluating my performance in this field. **(r)**
3. My fellow professionals are in the best position o judge my competence.

SCALE NAME: Professionalism (Commitment)

SCALE DESCRIPTION:

A three-item, seven-point Likert-type summated ratings scale measuring the degree to which a person in a professional-type job has a strong sense of dedication to the field regardless of the money involved.

SCALE ORIGIN:

Bullard and Snizek (1988) used a scale by Bartol (1979). The latter indicated that her scale was inspired by the Hall (1968) scale and took into account the suggestions made by Snizek (1972) and others. A corrected split-half reliability of .75 was reported for the scale.

SAMPLES:

The study by Bullard and Snizek selected 900 lawyers, dentists, and CPAs at random from the yellow pages of three metropolitan areas. After two mailings, usable responses were received from **391** professionals. There was no evidence of response bias.

RELIABILITY:

An alpha of **.63** was reported.

VALIDITY:

No specific examination of scale validity was reported.

ADMINISTRATION:

The scale was self-administered along with several other measures in a mail survey format. Higher scores on the scale suggest that respondents have a great sense of dedication to their professions whereas lower scores indicate that they have little commitment to their work.

MAJOR FINDINGS:

The purpose of the study by Bullard and Snizek was to investigate the acceptability of various ads by professionals and the influence of professionalism on respondents' willingness to use those ads in promoting their own services. The data did *not* indicate a significant correlation between a desire for **professional commitment** and willingness to use advetising.

COMMENTS:

The full 20-item professionalism scale used by Bullard and Snizek was reported to have an alpha of .72.

REFERENCES:

Bartol, Kathryn M. (1979), ''Professionalism as a Predictor of Organizational Commitment, Role Stress, and Turnover: A Multidimensional Approach,'' *Academy of Management Journal*, 22 (4), 815-821.

Bullard, Jerri Hayes and William E. Snizek (1988), ''Factors Affecting the Acceptability of Advertisements Among Professionals,'' *JAMS*, 16 (Summer), 57-63.

Hall, Richard H. (1968), ''Professionalism and Bureaucratization,'' *American Sociological Review*, 33 (February), 92-104.

Snizek, William E. (1972), ''Hall's Professionalism Scale: An Empirical Reassessment,'' *American Sociological Review*, 37 (February), 109-114.

SCALE ITEMS: PROFESSIONALISM (COMMITMENT)

Listed below are a number of statements which involve possible feelings about working in one's profession or field of expertise. With respect to your own feelings about the field of expertise in which you now work, please use the following scale to indicate the extent of your agreement or disagreement. There are no right or wrong answers.

Strongly Disagree	Disagree	Slightly Disagree	Neutral	Slightly Agree	Agree	Strongly Agree
1	2	3	4	5	6	7

1. I would stay in this profession even if I made a lot less money.
2. The major satisfaction in my life comes from doing a good job in my area of specialty.
3. If I were offered a much higher paying job in another line of work, I'd be inclined to take it. (r)

SCALE NAME: Professionalism (Identification)

SCALE DESCRIPTION:

A five-item, Likert-like summated ratings scale measuring the degree to which a person in a professional-type job relates to the field by reading professional journals, belonging to professional organizations, and attending professional meetings. The versions used by Snizek and Crocker (1985) and Bullard and Snizek (1988) shared four items in common and had five-point and seven-point Likert-type scales, respectively.

SCALE ORIGIN:

The original five-dimension index was developed by Hall (1968) and contained 10 items per dimension of professionalism. Snizek (1972) tested the inventory of items, noted problems, and identified the best five items per dimension. The five-item Organization as Major Referent scale had reliability (KR-20) of .686 and .621 for the samples used by Hall and Shizek, respectively. Bullard and Snizek used a slightly different version of the scale modified by Bartol (1979). She indicated that her scale was inspired by the Hall scale and took into account the suggestions made by Snizek and others. A corrected split-half reliability of .85 was reported for the scale.

SAMPLES:

A mail survey of 300 attorneys practicing in Virginia was made by Snizek and Crocker. Usable questionnaires were returned by **109**. Nearly half of the respondents were in partnerships and only the responses of practicing attorneys were used. No evidence of response bias was found.

Bullard and Snizek selected 900 lawyers, dentists, and CPAs at random from the yellow pages of three metropolitan areas. After two mailings, usable responses were received from **391** professionals. There was no evidence of response bias.

RELIABILITY:

Alpha values of **.698** and **.67** were reported by Snizek and Crocker and by Bullard and Snizek, respectively.

VALIDITY:

No specific examination of scale validity was reported either by Snizek and Crocker or by Bullard and Snizek.

ADMINISTRATION:

In both studies the scale was self-administered along with several other measures in a mail survey format. Higher scores on the scale suggest that respondents are very involved in their professions by engaging in such activities as belonging to professional organizations, attending their meetings, and reading their journals.

MAJOR FINDINGS:

The purpose of the study by Snizek and Crocker was to investigate lawyers' attitudes toward legal services advertising and to determine the influence of professionalism on those attitudes. The data did not indicate a significant correlation between **identifying** with the **profession** and attitudes toward the advertising.

The study by Bullard and Snizek had a similar purpose. However, they found a significant inverse relationship between **identification with a profession** and willingness to use advertising.

COMMENTS:

The full 20-item professionalism scale used by Bullard and Snizek was reported to have an alpha of .72.

REFERENCES:

Bartol, Kathryn M. (1979), "Professionalism as a Predictor of Organizational Commitment, Role Stress, and Turnover: A Multidimensional Approach," *Academy of Management Journal*, 22 (4), 815-821.

Bullard, Jerri Hayes and William E. Snizek (1988), "Factors Affecting the Acceptability of Advertisements Among Professionals," *JAMS*, 16 (Summer), 57-63.

Hall, Richard H. (1968), "Professionalism and Bureaucratization," *American Sociological Review*, 33 (February), 92-104.

Snizek, William E. (1972), "Hall's Professionalism Scale: An Empirical Reassessment," *American Sociological Review*, 37 (February), 109-114.

_____ and Kenneth E. Crocker (1985), "Professionalism and Attorney Attitudes Toward Legal Service Advertising," *JAMS*, 13 (Fall), 101-118.

SCALE ITEMS: PROFESSIONALISM (IDENTIFICATION) +

The following questions are an attempt to measure certain aspects of what is commonly called "professionalism." The referent in the questions is your own profession. Each item then, should be answered in light of the way you yourself both feel and behave as a member of your particular profession.

There are five possible responses to each item. If the item corresponds **VERY WELL** (VW) to your own attitudes and/or behavior, circle that response. If it corresponds **WELL** (W), **POORLY** (P), or **VERY POORLY** (VP), mark the appropriate response. The middle category (**?**) is designed to indicate an essentially neutral opinion about the item. Please answer ALL items in one fashion or another, making sure that you have NO MORE THAN ONE RESPONSE FOR EACH ITEM.

VW	W	?	P	VP
1————	——2————	————3————	————4————	————5

1. I systematically read the professional journals.
2. I regularly attend professional meetings at the local level.
3. I believe that the professional organization(s) should be supported.
4. The professional organization doesn't really do too much for the average member. (r)

5. Although I would like to, I really don't read the journals too often. **(r)**
6. I regularly attend meetings at the national level.

+ This version of the scale is most indicative of the way Snizek and Crocker used it, except that they did not use item 6. Bullard and Snizek used items 1, 2, 3, 6, and a slightly different wording of 4. Also, their instructions were different and a seven-point, agree-disagree response scale was used.

SCALE NAME: Professionalism (Sense of Calling to the Field)

SCALE DESCRIPTION:

A five-item, five-point Likert-like summated ratings scale measuring the degree to which a person in a professional-type job has a strong sense of dedication to the field.

SCALE ORIGIN:

The original five-dimension index was developed by Hall (1968) and contained 10 items per dimension of professionalism. Snizek (1972) tested the inventory of items, noted problems, and identified the best five items per dimension. The five-item Sense of Calling to the Field scale had reliability (KR-20) of .703 and .583 for the samples used by Hall and Snizek, respectively.

SAMPLES:

A mail survey of 300 attorneys practicing in Virginia was made by Snizek and Crocker (1985). Usable questionnaires were returned by **109**. Nearly half of the respondents were in partnerships and only the responses of practicing attorneys were used. No evidence of response bias was found.

RELIABILITY:

An alpha of **.766** was reported by Snizek and Crocker.

VALIDITY:

No specific examination of scale validity was report

ADMINISTRATION:

The scale was self-administered along with several other measures mail survey format. Higher scores on the scale suggest that respondents have a strong sense of calling to the field whereas lower scores indicate that they are not very dedicated.

MAJOR FINDINGS:

The purpose of the study by Snizek and Crocker was to investigate lawyers' attitudes toward legal services advertising and to determine the influence of professionalism on those attitudes. The data did not indicate a significant correlation between **a sense of calling to the profession** and attitudes toward the advertising.

REFERENCES:

Hall, Richard H. (1968), "Professionalism and Bureaucratization," *American Sociological Review*, 33 (February), 92-104.
Snizek, William E. (1972), "Hall's Professionalism Scale: An Empirical Reassessment," *American Sociological Review*, 37 (February), 109-114.

_____ and Kenneth E. Crocker (1985), "Professionalism and Attorney Attitudes Toward Legal Service Advertising," *JAMS*, 13 (Fall), 101-118.

SCALE ITEMS: PROFESSIONALISM (SENSE OF CALLING TO THE FIELD)

The following questions are an attempt to measure certain aspects of what is commonly called "professionalism." The referent in the questions is your own profession. Each item then, should be answered in light of the way you yourself both feel and behave as a member of your particular profession.

There are five possible responses to each item. If the item corresponds **VERY WELL** (VW) to your own attitudes and/or behavior, circle that response. If it corresponds **WELL** (W), **POORLY** (P), or **VERY POORLY** (VP), mark the appropriate response. The middle category (?) is designed to indicate an essentially neutral opinion about the item. Please answer ALL items in one fashion or another, making sure that you have NO MORE THAN ONE RESPONSE FOR EACH ITEM.

VW	W	?	P	VP
1——	—2——	—3——	—4——	—5

1. People in this profession have a real "calling" for their work.
2. The dedication of people in this field is most gratifying.
3. It is encouraging to see the high level of idealism which is maintained by people in this field.
4. Most people would stay in the profession even if their incomes were reduced.
5. There are very few practioners who really believe in their work. **(r)**

SCALE NAME: Professionalism (Self-Regulation)

SCALE DESCRIPTION:

A five-item, five-point Likert-like summated ratings scale measuring the degree to which a person in a professional-type job believes that his/her profession is "self-regulated" because members know what others are doing and are able to judge their competency.

SCALE ORIGIN:

The original five-dimension index was developed by Hall (1968) and contained 10 items per dimension of professionalism. Snizek (1972) tested the inventory of items, noted problems, and identified the best five items per dimension. The five-item Self-Regulation scale had reliability (KR-20) of .731 and .699 for the samples used by Hall and Snizek, respectively.

SAMPLES:

A mail survey of 300 attorneys practicing in Virginia was made by Snizek and Crocker (1985). Usable questionnaires were returned by **109**. Nearly half of the respondents were in partnerships and only the responses of practicing attorneys were used. No evidence of response bias was found.

RELIABILITY:

An alpha of **.641** was reported by Snizek and Crocker.

VALIDITY:

No specific examination of scale validity was reported.

ADMINISTRATION:

The scale was self-administered along with several other measures in a mail survey format. Higher scores on the scale suggest that respondents strongly believe their professions are self-regulated because members are able to judge other members' competency.

MAJOR FINDINGS:

The purpose of the study by Snizek and Crocker was to investigate lawyers' attitudes toward legal services advertising and to determine the influence of professionalism on those attitudes. The only dimension of professionalism that had a significant correlation with attitudes toward the advertising was **belief in self-regulation**. Specifically, the more respondents believed in self-regulation of their profession the less they favored advertising.

REFERENCES:

Hall, Richard H. (1968), "Professionalism and Bureaucratization," *American Sociological Review*, 33 (February), 92-104.

Snizek, William E. (1972), "Hall's Professionalism Scale: An Empirical Reassessment," *American Sociological Review*, 37 (February), 109-114.

———— and Kenneth E. Crocker (1985), "Professionalism and Attorney Attitudes Toward Legal Service Advertising," *JAMS*, 13 (Fall), 101-118.

SCALE ITEMS: PROFESSIONALISM (BELIEF IN SELF-REGULATION)

The following questions are an attempt to measure certain aspects of what is commonly called "professionalism." The referent in the questions is your own profession. Each item then, should be answered in light of the way you yourself both feel and behave as a member of your particular profession.

There are five possible responses to each item. If the item corresponds **VERY WELL** (VW) to your own attitudes and/or behavior, circle that response. If it corresponds **WELL** (W), **POORLY** (P), or **VERY POORLY** (VP), mark the appropriate response. The middle category (?) is designed to indicate an essentially neutral opinion about the item. Please answer ALL items in one fashion or another, making sure that you have NO MORE THAN ONE RESPONSE FOR EACH ITEM.

```
VW            W            ?            P            VP
1————————————2————————————3————————————4————————————5
```

1. My fellow professionals have a pretty good idea about each other's competence.
2. A problem in this profession is that no one really knows what his colleagues are doing. **(r)**
3. We really have no way of judging each other's competence. **(r)**
4. There is not much opportunity to judge how another person does his work. **(r)**
5. My colleagues pretty well know how well we all do in our work.

SCALE NAME: Professionalism (Service to the Public)

SCALE DESCRIPTION:

A five-item, five-point Likert-like summated ratings scale measuring the degree to which a person in a professional-type job believes that his/her profession is more important to society than other professions.

SCALE ORIGIN:

The original five-dimension index was developed by Hall (1968) and contained 10 items per dimension of professionalism. Snizek (1972) tested the inventory of items, noted problems, and identified the best five items per dimension. The five-item Service to the Public scale had reliability (KR-20) of .742 and .640 for the samples used by Hall and Snizek, respectively.

SAMPLES:

A mail survey of 300 attorneys practicing in Virginia was made by Snizek and Crocker (1985). Usable questionnaires were returned by **109**. Nearly half of the respondents were in partnerships and only the responses of practicing attorneys were used. No evidence of response bias was found.

RELIABILITY:

An alpha of **.715** was reported by Snizek and Crocker.

VALIDITY:

No specific examination of scale validity was reported.

ADMINISTRATION:

The scale was self-administered along with several other measures in a mail survey format. Higher scores on the scale suggest that respondents believe their professions are very important to society whereas lower scores indicate that they admit their professions are not as important to society as others are.

MAJOR FINDINGS:

The purpose of the study by Snizek and Crocker was to investigate lawyers' attitudes toward legal services advertising and to determine the influence of professionalism on those attitudes. The data did not indicate a significant correlation between believing that the **profession is important to society** and attitudes toward the advertising.

REFERENCES:

Hall, Richard H. (1968), "Professionalism and Bureaucratization," *American Sociological Review*, 33 (February), 92-104.

Snizek, William E. (1972), ''Hall's Professionalism Scale: An Empirical Reassessment,'' *American Sociological Review*, 37 (February), 109-114.

———— and Kenneth E. Crocker (1985), ''Professionalism and Attorney Attitudes Toward Legal Service Advertising,'' *JAMS*, 13 (Fall), 101-118.

SCALE ITEMS: PROFESSIONALISM (SERVICE TO THE PUBLIC)

The following questions are an attempt to measure certain aspects of what is commonly called professionalism.'' The referent in the questions is your own profession. Each item then, should be answered in light of the way you yourself both feel and behave as a member of your particular profession.

There are five possible responses to each item. If the item corresponds VERY WELL (VW) to your own attitudes and/or behavior, circle that response. If it corresponds WELL (W), POORLY (P), or VERY POORLY (VP), mark the appropriate response. The middle category (?) is designed to indicate an essentially neutral opinion about the item. Please answer ALL items in one fashion or another, making sure that you have NO MORE THAN ONE RESPONSE FOR EACH ITEM.

VW	W	?	P	VP
1———	—2———	—3———	—4———	—5

1. Other professions are actually more vital to society than mine. **(r)**
2. I think that my profession, more than any other, is essential for society.
3. The importance of my profession is sometimes over stressed. **(r)**
4. Some other occupations are actually more important to society than is mine. **(r)**
5. If ever an occupation is indispensable, it is this one.

SCALE NAME: Purchase Complexity

SCALE DESCRIPTION:

A three-item, five-point Likert-type summated ratings scale measuring the extent to which a product's complexity led to an increase in the people and/or information involved in a purchase decision. McQuiston (1989) referred to this measure as Complexity Indicators.

SCALE ORIGIN:

The scale is original to McQuiston. A tentative set of items was generated after a literature review and a focus group with management personnel. These items were pretested on 10 actual purchasers of the product. After elimination of some items, the list was pretested on another set of five actual purchasers. Data from these 15 respondents were ultimately included in the survey sample discussed below.

SAMPLES:

Survey instruments were mailed to customers of a large manufacturer of capital equipment that had purchased one of three different models of a product line within the 18 months preceding the study. A key informant in each company was contacted to obtain names of others in the organization who had provided input to the purchase decision. Those others were then contacted and, if willing to participate, were sent questionnaires. Of the 273 forms mailed, **182** usable returns were received from employees of 82 different companies.

RELIABILITY:

An alpha of **.712** was reported for the scale.

VALIDITY:

Except for some evidence of content validity from the pretests (mentioned above), the validity of the scale was not specifically examined in the study. A factor analysis indicated that all three items loaded highest on another factor, purchase inexperience. The scale formed from that factor had a correlation of .463 with purchase complexity.

ADMINISTRATION:

The scale was self-administered along with several other measures in a mail questionnaire. Higher scores suggest that respondents believe the purchase of a certain product required more people and/or information than normal whereas lower scores imply that they believe a purchase decision was not particularly complex.

MAJOR FINDINGS:

The purpose of the study was to examine some attributes of the industrial purchase situation and their influence on the purchase decision. Contrary to hypotheses, **purchase complexity** (1) was not found to have a significant relationship with the amount of information offered for consideration by members of the decision-making unit and (2) had only a marginally significant relationship with the impact of a person's communication on the actions of others in the decision-making unit.

COMMENTS:

The poor pattern of factor loadings reported for the items in this scale suggests that its validity be examined closely if it is to be used again.

REFERENCE:

McQuiston, Daniel H. (1989), ''Novelty, Complexity, and Importance as Causal Determinants of Industrial Buyer Behavior,'' *JM*, 53 (April), 66-79.

SCALE ITEMS: PURCHASE COMPLEXITY

Strongly Disagree | Disagree | Neutral | Agree | Strongly Agree
1————————2————————3————————4————————5

1. Because of the complex nature of this product, we had to involve more people than we usually do for capital equipment purchases.
2. The purchase of this product required a change in our office procedures.
3. We had to gather more information before purchasing this product than we usually do for capital equipment purchases.

SCALE NAME: Purchase Importance

SCALE DESCRIPTION:

A three-item, five-point Likert-type summated ratings scale measuring the perceived effect of a purchase on an organization's profitability and productivity. McQuiston (1989) referred to this measure as Importance Indicators.

SCALE ORIGIN:

The scale is original to McQuiston. A tentative set of items was generated after a literature review and a focus group with management personnel. These items were pretested on 10 actual purchasers of the product. After elimination of some items, the list was pretested on another set of five actual purchasers. Data from these 15 respondents were ultimately included in the survey sample discussed below.

SAMPLES:

Survey instruments were mailed to customers of a large manufacturer of capital equipment that had purchased one of three different models of a product line within the 18 months preceding the study. A key informant in each company was contacted to obtain names of others in the organization who had provided input to the purchase decision. Those others were then contacted and, if willing to participate, were sent questionnaires. Of the 273 forms mailed, **182** usable returns were received from employees of 82 different companies.

RELIABILITY:

An alpha of .65 was reported for the scale.

VALIDITY:

Except for some evidence of content validity from the pretests (mentioned above), the validity of the scale was not specifically examined in the study. A factor analysis indicated that the items loaded together, though they each had loadings above .35 on another factor also.

ADMINISTRATION:

The scale was self-administered along with several other measures in a mail questionnaire. Higher scores suggest that respondents perceive a purchase will have a great impact on their organization's profitability whereas lower scores imply that they believe the purchase is not very important.

MAJOR FINDINGS:

The purpose of the study was to examine some attributes of the industrial purchase situation and their influence on the purchase decision. As hypothesized, **purchase importance** was found to have a significant positive relationship with both the amount of information offered for consideration by members of the decision-making unit and the impact of a person's communication on the actions of others in the decision-making unit.

COMMENTS:

The low internal consistency and pattern of factor loadings reported for the items in this scale suggest that its psychometric characteristics be examined closely if it is to be used again.

REFERENCE:

McQuiston, Daniel H. (1989), "Novelty, Complexity, and Importance as Causal Determinants of Industrial Buyer Behavior," *JM*, 53 (April), 66-79.

SCALE ITEMS: PURCHASE IMPORTANCE

Strongly Disagree	Disagree	Neutral	Agree	Strongly Agree
1—————	—2—————	—3—————	—4—————	—5

1. The purchase was necessary to better monitor the weight of inbound and outbound shipments.
2. We anticipated this purchase would make a significant improvement in our operations.
3. This purchase was important to our overall profitability.

SCALE NAME: Purchase Importance

SCALE DESCRIPTION:

A four-item, five-point semantic differential summated ratings scale measuring the importance of a purchase decision involving a specified product category (such as printing inks). McCabe (1987) referred to this scale as Commercial Uncertainty.

SCALE ORIGIN:

The scale used by McCabe was composed of items based on factors identified by Hill (1972, 1973) as important product characteristics to consider when performing buying-related research.

SAMPLES:

McCabe's data came from buying centers in either the airline or corrugated shipping container industry. In the former, **15** buying centers were involved with the decision to buy aircraft and **13** were involved with the decision to buy jet fuel. In the latter, **14** buying centers were concerned with the purchase of printing inks and **13** were concerned with buying printing presses and other capital equipment. Data were collected just from individuals involved in source selection. There was an average of 1.7 people per buying unit.

RELIABILITY:

An alpha of **.76** was reported for the scale.

VALIDITY:

A factor analysis of 10 items related to buying group decisions indicated that the four items composing this scale all loaded on the same factor.

ADMINISTRATION:

Though interviews of some sort were conducted with buying group members, the measures in the questionnaire are assumed to have been self-administered. Higher scores on the scale indicate that the purchase of some specified generic product (such as printing inks) is a very important decision because of the size of the order and/or the commitment being made.

MAJOR FINDINGS:

McCabe examined opposing views of the relation between buying group structure and environmental uncertainty. The findings indicated that **purchase importance** was a somewhat significant predictor of centralization in buying group decision making but was not a significant predictor of formalization or participation.

REFERENCES:

Hill, Roy W. (1972), "The Nature of Industrial Buying Decisions," *Industrial Marketing Management*, 2 (October), 45-55.

_____ (1973), *Marketing Technological Products to Industry*. Oxford, England: Pergamon Press Ltd.

McCabe, Donald L. (1987), "Buying Group Structure: Constriction at the Top," *JM*, 51 (October), 89-98.

SCALE ITEMS: PURCHASE IMPORTANCE

Instructions: Using the rating scale shown below, please circle one number for each set of factors listed. The numbers have no specific values and are only designed to represent a continuous scale between the high and low definitions provided for each factor. Circle the number which reflects your opinion of where printing inks fall on such a continuum.

Little investment	____ : ____ : ____ : ____ : ____	High investment
	1 2 3 4 5	

Small order	____ : ____ : ____ : ____ : ____	Large order
	1 2 3 4 5	

Short-term commitment	____ : ____ : ____ : ____ : ____	Long-term commitment
	1 2 3 4 5	

Small potential effect on profitability	____ : ____ : ____ : ____ : ____	Large potential effect on profitability
	1 2 3 4 5	

SCALE NAME: Purchase Inexperience

SCALE DESCRIPTION:

A three-item, five-point Likert-type summated ratings scale measuring the extent to which relevant individuals in an organization are perceived to lack experience with similar purchase situations. McQuiston (1989) referred to this measure as Novelty Indicators.

SCALE ORIGIN:

The scale is original to McQuiston. A tentative set of items was generated after a literature review and a focus group with management personnel. These items were pretested on 10 actual purchasers of the product. After elimination of some items, the list was pretested on another set of five actual purchasers. Data from these 15 respondents were ultimately included in the survey sample discussed below.

SAMPLES:

Survey instruments were mailed to customers of a large manufacturer of capital equipment that had purchased one of three different models of a product line within the 18 months preceding the study. A key informant in each company was contacted to obtain names of others in the organization who had provided input to the purchase decision. Those others were then contacted and, if willing to participate, were sent questionnaires. Of the 273 forms mailed, **182** usable returns were received from employees of 82 different companies.

RELIABILITY:

An alpha of .**791** was reported for the scale.

VALIDITY:

Except for some evidence of content validity from the pretests (mentioned above), the validity of the scale was not specifically examined in the study. A factor analysis indicated that the items loaded together.

ADMINISTRATION:

The scale was self-administered along with several other measures in a mail questionnaire. Higher scores suggest that respondents do not believe people in their organizations are experienced with purchasing a certain type of product. Lower scores imply that they believe company employees are familiar with buying a product.

MAJOR FINDINGS:

The purpose of the study was to examine some attributes of the industrial purchase situation and their influence on the purchase decision. As hypothesized, **inexperience with the purchase of a product line** was found to have a significant positive relationship with the amount of information offered for consideration by members of the decision-making unit.

REFERENCE:

McQuiston, Daniel H. (1989), ''Novelty, Complexity, and Importance as Causal Determinants of Industrial Buyer Behavior,'' *JM*, 53 (April), 66-79.

SCALE ITEMS: PURCHASE INEXPERIENCE

Strongly Disagree	Disagree	Neutral	Agree	Strongly Agree
1	2	3	4	5

1. Before the purchase, some people in the organization had experience in purchasing this product line. **(r)**
2. We did not have much information from past purchases when we were defining the specifications for this product.
3. Few people in this organization had much technical knowledge about this type of product before we purchased this one.

SCALE NAME: Purchase Task Familiarity (Industrial Buying)

SCALE DESCRIPTION:

One version is a 10-item, seven-point Likert-like scale measuring the percentage of situations a sales manager estimates his salespeople face in which a product new to an account and a lot of information is required. The scale was called Newness + Info by Anderson, Chu, and Weitz (1987) and they also reported a seven-item modification of the scale. Two of the items composed a scale called Information by John and Weitz (1989).

SCALE ORIGIN:

Items were generated by Anderson and her coauthors on the basis of a review of academic and trade literature. Pretesting was performed sequentially with 12 sales managers over several months, which allowed the questionnaire to be revised after each stage.

SAMPLES:

The 10-item scale used by Anderson and her coauthors was analyzed with data collected from **169** sales managers representing 16 electronic component manufacturers. The seven-item version of the scale was used in a survey aimed at sales managers of a broad range of manufacturing firms with sales over $50 million a year. Usable survey instruments were returned by **158** respondents.

John and Weitz collected data in a two-stage sampling procedure. Personalized requests were mailed to 750 sales managers or sales vice presidents of manufacturing firms with annual sales of at least $50 million. The 266 respondents were then sent a questionnaire and **161** returned usable survey instruments. The sample appeared to be different from the population in some respects but very similar in others.

RELIABILTY:

Alphas for the 10-item and seven-item versions of the scale were **.73** and **.71**, respectively (Anderson, Chu, and Weitz 1987). The two-item version of the scale had an alpha of **.74** and item-total correlations of .52 and .60 (John and Weitz 1989).

VALIDITY:

Anderson and her coauthors reported that the two versions of the scale showed evidence of face and nomological validity. In factor analyses, however, both versions of the scale had multiple items with loadings below .40 and/or loadings above .30 with another factor, which raise some doubt about their validity. No specific examination of scale validity was reported by John and Weitz.

ADMINISTRATION:

In the two studies reported by Anderson and her coauthors, the scales were filled out by respondents as part of a self-administered mail survey. Higher scores on the scale suggest that respondents (sales managers) report their salespeople as frequently encountering sales situations in which the account has little if any experience purchasing such a product and therefore requires a great amount of information.

MAJOR FINDINGS:

The purpose of the studies by Anderson and her coauthors was to validate the Robinson, Faris, and Wind (1967) framework of industrial buying behavior, with particular focus on straight rebuy and new task situations. The findings of the two studies indicated that salesforces that frequently encountered buying centers facing an **unfamiliar purchase task** reported those accounts to be slow to decide, uncertain about their needs, more concerned about finding the right solution to the problem than getting the lowest price, and less satisfied with their present suppliers.

The purpose of the study by John and Weitz was to examine the role of salary in sales compensation plans by using a transaction cost analysis framework. **Purchase task familiarity** was most highly correlated with complexity of the sales task (.51).

REFERENCES:

Anderson, Erin, Wujin Chu, and Barton Weitz (1987), "Industrial Purchasing: An Empirical Exploration of the Buyclass Framework," *JM*, 51 (July), 71-86.

John, George and Barton Weitz (1989), "Salesforce Compensation: An Empirical Investigation of Factors Related to Use of Salary Versus Incentive Compensation," *JMR*, 26 (February), 1-14.

Robinson, Patrick J., Charles W. Faris, and Yoram Wind (1967), *Industrial Buying and Creative Marketing*, Boston, Mass.: Allyn and Bacon.

SCALE ITEMS: PURCAHSE TASK FAMILIARITY (INDUSTRIAL BUYING) +

The following statements describe circumstances which might exist when one of your salespeople is trying to make a sale. Please indicate how frequently the salesperson would face the situation described in the statement. This can icated by circling ther that most accurately indicates the percentage of sales situations that the statement. Each question is independent: your answers do not need to add to 100% or any other number.

EXAMPLE: It is hard to get an appointment to see the account.

Percentage of Situations

| 0% | 10% | **30%** | 50% | 70% | 90% | 100% |

This manager indicates that in 30% of selling situations, the salesperson has difficulty getting an appointment. Notice that "account" means customer or prospect. Those 30% of selling situations that are difficult could be cold calls, follow-ups with a regular customer, or some combination of prospects and customers.

1. The account seldom purchases this type of product.
2. The product is the first purchase of its kind for the account.
3. The account has not dealt with this product class or requirement before.
4. This is still a rather new purchase for the account.
5. The account's requirements have changed since the product was purchased last.

6. The customer has routinized the purchase decision so that it no longer requires a lot of attention. **(r)**
7. The customer considers the purchase decision to be routine. **(r)**
8. The customer needs a lot of information before making a purchase decision.
9. The account has complete knowledge about what product characteristics are needed to solve the problem. **(r)**
10. The account knows exactly what is needed. **(r)**
11. The purchase decision demands a lot of information.
12. The account is willing to gather and consider a lot of information before deciding.
13. The account is willing to consider new information in making a decision.

+ Items 1 through 5 and 9 through 13 composed the 10-item scale and items 1, 3, and 5 through 9 made up the seven-item version of the scale (Anderson, Chu, and Weitz 1987). Items 1 and 3 composed the scale used by John and Weitz (1989). Also, the items in the two shorter scales used the word "customer" rather than "account."

SCALE NAME: Recruiting/Training Activity (Salesperson)

SCALE DESCRIPTION:

> A four-item, seven-point Likert-like summated ratings scale measuring the frequency with which a person engages in activities involving new sales reps, such as training and recruitment.

SCALE ORIGIN:

> The scale is original to a study by Moncrief (1986). Several scales were developed for use in the study from a review of the literature and from personal interviews and focus groups with salespeople. A total of 121 selling-related activities were identified and included on the survey questionnair.

SAMPLES:

> Using stratified sampling, Moncrief sent survey forms to 800 firms representing 20 SIC codes (#20-#39). Fifty-one firms ultimately participated and sent copies of the questionnaire to their salespeople. Of the total 2322 sales employees working for these firms, 1393 returned usable forms but the factor analysis was based on responses from **1291**.

RELIABILITY:

> An alpha of **.56** was reported for the scale.

VALIDITY:

> Though scale validity was not specifically addressed, a factor analysis of 121 items indicated that the items below all had loadings greater than .50 on the same factor and loadings less than .40 other factors. These findings provide some evidence of the convergent and discriminant validity of the scale.

ADMINISTRATION:

> The scale was self-administered along with many other measures in a mail survey format. Higher scores on the scale indicate that respondents frequently engage in activities involving new sales reps whereas lower scores suggest that they primarily perform other activities.

MAJOR FINDINGS:

> The purpose of the study by Moncrief was to develop a comprehensive list of selling-related activities and taxonomies created from them. A cluster analysis was performed of the salespeople in the sample and six clusters were found. A group called trade servicer, representing 18% the sample, had the highest mean on the **recruiting/training activity** scale. This cluster had the highest mean of any of the sales groups on seven of 10 sales activity areas examined in the study and it had the second highest mean on the other three activity areas.

COMMENTS:

The low alpha indicates that the reliability should be improved before this scale is used further.

REFERENCE:

Moncrief, William C., III (1986), ''Selling Activity and Sales Position Taxonomies for Industrial Salesforces,'' *JMR*, 23 (August), 261-270.

SCALE ITEMS: RECRUITING/TRAINING ACTIVITY (SALESPERSON) +

Using the following scale, please indicate how frequently you engage in each of the activities listed below. If you do not perform the activity, please code your response as a zero.

Infrequently   ___ : ___ : ___ : ___ : ___ : ___ : ___   Frequently

                       1   2   3   4   5   6   7

1. Look for new sales reps
2. Train new salespeople
3. Travel with trainees
4. Help management design sales plan

+ The actual directions and items were not stated in the article but are reconstructed e on the basis information provided.

SCALE NAME: Replaceability of Income From Principal (Agency)

SCALE DESCRIPTION:

A six-item, multipoint Likert-type summated ratings scale measuring the degree to which an agency reports that it can replace the commission income it currently receives from selling a principal's products.

SCALE ORIGIN:

Some of the items in the scale may have been adapted from previous research (e.g., Anderson 1985), but the scale itself is original to Heide and John (1988). This version of the scale is only known to have been used in their study, to which the information below relates.

SAMPLES:

A systematic sample of 400 agencies was made for each of two industries from a manufacturers' agent directory. The survey instrument was mailed to the owner/manager listed in the directory. A total of **199** usable responses were received and nonresponse bias did not appear to be a problem.

RELIABILITY:

An alpha of **.72** was reported for the scale.

VALIDITY:

Evidence supporting the convergent and discriminant validity of the scale was presented.

ADMINISTRATION:

The scale was self-administered along with many other measures in a mail survey format. Higher scores on the scale indicate that respondents believe their agencies could easily replace the commission income currently generated from selling their principals' products.

MAJOR FINDINGS:

The authors extended of the basic transaction cost analysis model by incorporating aspects of dependence theory. Offsetting investments were examined to see whether they were used by small channel members as a means of protecting assets at risk in the agency-principal dyad. Among the many findings was that **replaceability** was positively associated with agency investments in customer relationships but negatively associated with investments in relationships with principals.

REFERENCES:

Anderson, Erin (1985), "The Salesperson as Outside Agent or Employee: A Transaction Cost Analysis," *Marketing Science*, 4 (Summer), 234-254.

Heide, Jan B. and George John (1988), ''The Role of Dependence Balancing in in Safeguarding Transaction-Specific Assets in Conventional Channels,'' *JM*, 52 (January), 20-35.

SCALE ITEMS: REPLACEABILITY OF INCOME FROM PRINCIPAL (AGENCY) +

1. If we no longer represented this principal, the loss of the line would hurt sales of other related product lines. **(r)**
2. If we no longer represented this principal, we would easily compensate for it by switching our efforts to the other lines we carry.
3. If we no longer represented this principal, we could easily replace their product line with a similar line from another principal.
4. It would be relatively easy for our agency to diversify into selling new products.
5. If our relationship with this principal were eliminated, we could suffer a significant loss in income, despite our best efforts to replace the lost income. **(r)**
6. Many principals in this industry would like to have us as their agent.

+ The number of points on the response scale and their verbal anchors were not given in the article (Heide and John 1988), but the scale is likely to be of the five- or seven-point agree-disagree type.

SCALE NAME: Replaceability of Salespeople

SCALE DESCRIPTION:

A two-item, seven-point Likert-type summated ratings scale measuring the degree to which a company has difficulty finding and hiring good salespeople.

SCALE ORIGIN:

John and Weitz (1989) give no indication that this scale originated elsewhere than in their study.

SAMPLES:

John and Weitz collected data in a two-stage sampling procedure. Personalized requests were mailed to 750 sales managers or sales vice presidents of manufacturing firms with annual sales of at least $50 million. The 266 respondents were then sent a questionnaire and **161** returned usable survey instruments. The sample appeared to be different from the population in some respects but very similar in others.

RELIABILITY:

An alpha of **.79** was reported for the scale. Item-total correlations were .62 and .58.

VALIDITY:

No specific examination of scale validity was made.

ADMINISTRATION:

The scale was self-administered by respondents along with many other measures in a mail questionnaire format. Higher scores on the scale suggest that respondents believe their respective companies have difficulty finding and hiring good salespeople whereas lower scores indicate that they think it is easy to replace salespeople when necessary.

MAJOR FINDINGS:

The purpose of the study by John and Weitz was to examine the role of salary in sales compensation plans by using a transaction cost analysis framework. The difficulty of **salesperson replaceability** had its most significant correlations (positive) with environmental uncertainty and need for coordination with other company employees.

REFERENCE:

John, George and Barton Weitz (1989), "Salesforce Compensation: An Empirical Investigation of Factors Related to Use of Salary Versus Incentive Compensation," *JMR*, 26 (February), 1-14.

SCALE ITEMS: REPLACEABILITY OF SALESPEOPLE

Strongly Disagree	Disagree	Slightly Disagree	Neutral	Slightly Agree	Agree	Strongly Agree
1————	——2————	——3————	——4————	——5————	——6————	——7

1. When a salesperson quits, we can easily hire a good replacement. **(r)**
2. We have a difficult time hiring good salespeople.

SCALE NAME: Role Ambiguity (Salesperson & Product Manager)

SCALE DESCRIPTION:

A six-item, seven-point Likert-like summated scale ranging from very false to very true purporting to measure the degree of perceived role ambiguity by noting the reported amount of certainty a salesperson has about his/her responsibilities.

SCALE ORIGIN:

The scale was originally developed by Rizzo, House, and Lirtzman (1970). It was found to have internal consistency reliability exceeding .70 along with high concurrent validity (Schuler, Aldag, and Brief 1977).

SAMPLES:

Teas (1980) used a questionnaire mailed in 1978 to a midwestern corporation's industrial salesforce. A cover letter sent with the questionnaire requested a prompt response and promised anonymity. Additionally, a letter from the firm's vice president of sales was included, indicating support for the survey. Usable responses were obtained from **127** of 184 salesmen surveyed (response rate was 69%).

Subsequently, Teas (1983) obtained data by a mail survey of two midwestern corporations' salesforces. Included with the questionnaires were cover letters from the researcher and the vice president of sales promising confidentiality and indicating company support for the survey. Usable responses were obtained from **116** salespersons, 49 and 67 salespersons in the two companies, respectively (response rate was 55%).

Lysonski (1985) obtained data from questionnaires mailed to 449 product managers in consumer package goods industries. A second mailing to nonrespondents yielded a final return rate of 55%, or 224 completed questionnaires, of which 54 were unusable. The final sample for analysis was **170**.

Dubinsky and Hartley (1986) obtained data from questionnaires mailed to insurance agents located throughout the United States. Included with each questionnaire was a cover letter from the company's divisional vice president indicating support for the project and a cover letter from the researchers promising confidentiality. A total of 467 questionnaires were sent. Usable questionnaires were returned by **120** agents (response rate 25.7%). Ninety-one percent of the respondents were male, the mean age was 39.1 years, approximately 56% had earned at least a bachelor's degree, and mean job tenure was 6.6 years.

Hampton, Dubinsky, and Skinner (1986) obtained data from a census (n = 121) of retail salespeople employed in a department store chain (five outlets). Usable questionnaires were obtained from **116** of the salespeople (response rate of 95.9%). Ninety-one of the respondents were women and 25 wer men. Median age was 23.2 years, approximately 66% had at least some college education, median job tenure was 1.4 years, and median time spent working with the current sales supervisor was 1.1 years.

Fry et al. (1986) obtained data by a mail survey of a national pharmaceutical manufacturer's salesforce. Questionnaires were returned by **216** of 347 salesmen surveyed (response rate 62%). The data analyzed were from men only. Data on age, income, tenure, and education were not specified.

Michaels et al. (1986) obtained data by self-administered questionnaires distributed to 255 full-line salespeople of an industrial building materials manufacturer. Usable questionnaires were returned by 215 salespeople (response rate 84.3%). Mean respondent age was 43.9 years, mean job tenure 12.9 years, mean organization tenure 15.2 years, and mean sales experience 18.1 years. Data were also collected from a sample of industrial buyers. A randomly selected sample of 554 members of the National Association of Purchasing Management constituted the industrial buyer sample. Data were collected by self-administered mail questionnaire. Of the 335 questionnaires returned, **330** were usable (59.6%). Mean respondent age was 42.2 years, mean job tenure 5.7 years, mean organization tenure 10.6 years, and mean purchasing experience 12.5 years.

Cummings, Jackson, and Ostrom (1989) obtained data by self-administered questionnaires distributed by mail to firms selected from the American Marketing Association Membership Directory. The 156 firms that agreed to participate in the study provided a potential sample of 624 product managers, from which a total of 1 useable questionnaire returned.

RELIABILITY:

The folloing Cronbach's alpha values were reported for the scale: **.797**, Teas (1980); **.824**, Teas (1983); **.85**, Lysonski (1985); **.76**, Dubinsky and Hartley (1986); **.74**, Hampton, Dubinsky, and Skinner (1986); **.90**, Fry et al. (1986); **.85**, Michaels et al. (1988); and **.813**, Cummings, Jackson, and Ostrom (1989).

VALIDITY:

Dubinsky and Hartley (1986) noted that the scale had discriminant and predictive validity (Rizzo, House, and Lirtzman 1970) and construct and concurrent validity (Schuler, Aldag, and Brief 1977); in addition, it was shown to be free of semantic confusion (House, Schuler, Levanoni 1983).

ADMINISTRATION:

The scale was self-administered in most of the studies along with several other measures in mail questionnaires. Hampton, Dubinsky, Skinner (1986) used a different approach by administering the questionnaires to the respondents in a conference room at each store, where the questionnaires were completed. Accompanying the questionnaires were a cover letter from the chain's president indicating company support for the project and a cover letter from the researchers promising confidentiality. The scores from each item of the scale are summated. The possible score range is 6 to 42. A low score (lowest possible score is 6) indicates a high degree of perceived role ambiguity.

MAJOR FINDINGS:

Teas' (1980) results indicated that participation and closeness of supervision were significantly ($p \leq .05$) related to role ambiguity. However, the hypothesis that experience is negatively related to role ambiguity was not supported by the results. Role ambiguity was found to be related to job satisfaction ($p \leq .05$).

Teas (1983) found that leader consideration and salesforce participation were negatively related to the salesperson's perception of both role conflict ($p \leq .001$ and $p \leq .05$, respectively) and role ambiguity ($p \leq .005$). Feedback was also negatively related to role ambiguity ($p \leq .025$). Role ambiguity was not a significant predictor of salesforce job satisfaction. Additionally, role ambiguity and role conflict had a high correlation (r = .515).

Lysonski's (1985) results indicated that perceived uncertainty was associated with role conflict and ambiguity (p ≤ .001). Role ambiguity was not associated with boundary spanning except for internal organizational boundary spanning (p ≤ .05). Role autonomy influenced only the role ambiguity-satisfaction relationship (F = 9.38, p ≤ .001). Need for affiliation had a definite moderating influence; it lowered the role conflict-perceived performance relationship (F = 7.02, p ≤ .001), increased the role ambiguity-job related tension relationship (F = 5.83, p ≤ .01), and lowered the role ambiguity-perceived performance relationship (F = 3.83, p ≤ .05). Education reduced the role conflict-job satisfaction relationship (F = 6.04, p ≤ .01) and role ambiguity-job tension relationship (F = 7.25, p ≤ .001). Additionally, experience as a product manager increased the role conflict-job tension relationship (F = 7.42, p ≤ .001) and lowered the role ambiguity-perceived performance relationship (F = 4.85, p. ≤ .05). However, experience with the present product as a product manager increased the role conflict-job tension (F = 6.50, p ≤ .01) and role ambiguity-job tension relationships (F = 6.20, p ≤ .001). Dubinsky and Hartley (1986) found that role ambiguity explained 18% of the variance in job satisfaction. Self-monitoring did not appear to be related to role conflict or role ambiguity. Additionally, role ambiguity was negatively related to job performance (p ≤ .01).

Hampton, Dubinnd Skinner (1986) foun that both initiating structure (p ≤ .03) and consideration ≤ .04) were inversely related to role ambiguity.

Fry et al. (1986) found that role ambiguity (p ≤ .05) had a negative influence on satisfaction with job, company policy and support, and customers. Michaels et al. (1988) found that higher levels of organizational formalization were associated with lower levels of role ambiguity among salespeople (p ≤ .001) and buyers (p ≤ .001). Higher levels of role conflict (p ≤ .001) and ambiguity (p ≤ .001) were associated with lower levels of organizational commitment. Also, higher levels of role ambiguity were associated with higher levels of work alienation (p ≤ .01). This pattern of results was identical in the two samples (salespersons and industrial buyers).

Cummings, Jackson, and Ostrom (1989) did not find a significant relationship between role ambiguity and job structure or job performance. However, role ambiguity was inversely related to job satisfaction (p ≤ .0001).

COMMENTS:

See also Futrell (1980) for another apparent use of this or a similar scale.

REFERENCES:

Cummings, W. Theodore, Donald Jackson, and Lonnie L. Ostrom (1989), ''Examining Product Managers' Job Satisfaction and Performance Using Selected Organizational Behavior Variables,'' *JAMS*, 17 (2), 147- 156.

Dubinsky, Alan J. and Steven W. Hartley (1986), ''A Path-Analytic Study of a Model of Salesperson Performance,'' *JAMS*, 14 (Spring), 36-46.

Fry, Louis W., Charles M. Futrell, A. Parasuraman, and Margaret A. Chmielewski (1986), ''An Analysis of Alternative Causal Models of Salesperson Role Perceptions and Work-Related Attitudes,'' *JM*, 23 (May), 153-163.

Futrell, Charles M. (1980), ''Salesmen and Saleswomen Job Satisfaction,'' *Industrial Marketing Management*, 9, 27-30.

Hampton, Ron, Alan J. Dubinsky, and Steven J. Skinner (1986), "A Model of Sales Supervisor Leadership Behavior and Retail Salespeople's Job-Related Outcomes," *JAMS*, 14 (Fall), 33-43.

House, R. L., R. S. Schuler, and E. Levanoni (1983), "Role Conflict and Ambiguity Scales: Reality on Artifact?" *Journal of Applied Psychology*, 68 (May), 334-337.

Lysonski, Steven (1985), "A Boundary Theory Investigation of the Product Manager's Role," *JM*, 49 (Winter), 26-40.

Michaels, Ronald E., William L. Cron, Alan J. Dubinsky, and Erich A. Joachimsthaler (1988), "Influence of Formalization on the Organizational Commitment and Work Alienation of Salespeople and Industrial Buyers," *JMR*, 25 (November), 376-383.

Rizzo, John R., Robert J. House, and Sidney I. Lirtzman (1970), "Role Conflict and Ambiguity in Complex Organizations," *Administrative Science Quarterly*, 15 (June), 150-163.

Schuler, R. S., R. J. Aldag, and A. P. Brief (1977), Conflict and Ambiguity: A Scale Analysis," *Organizational Behavior and Human Performance*, 20 (October), 111-128.

Teas, R. Kenneth (1980), "An Empirical Test of Linkages Proposed in the Walker, Churchill, and Ford Model of Salesforce Motivation and Performance," *JAMS*, 8 (Winter), 58-72.

————— (1983), "Supervisory Behavior, Role Stress, and the Job Satisfaction of Industrial Salespeople," *JMR*, 20 (February), 84-91.

SCALE ITEMS: ROLE AMBIGUITY (SALESPERSON & PRODUCT MANAGER) +

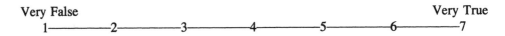

Very False   Very True

1————2————3————4————5————6————7

1. I feel certain about how much authority I have in my selling position.
2. I have clear, planned goals and objectives for my selling position.
3. I know that I have divided my time properly while performing the tasks connected with my selling.
4. I know my responsibilities are in my selling position.
5. I know exactly what is expected of me in my selling position.
6. I receive clear explanations of what has to be done in my selling position.

+ Michaels et al. (1988) used a modified version of Rizzo, House, and Lirtzman's (1970) original scale. The modified version consisted of a nine-item, seven-point Likert-type summated scale, where 7 = high and 1 = low. No specific information was given as to the actual scale items used. Similarly, Cummings, Jackson, and Ostrom (1989) used a modified version of Rizzo, House, and Lirtzman's (1970) original scale. The modified version consisted of a four-item, five-point Likert-type summated scale. No specific information was given as to the actual scale items used.

SCALE NAME: Role Autonomy (Job-Related)

SCALE DESCRIPTION:

A four-item, four-point Likert-like scale ranging from "a lot" to "not at all" purporting to measure role autonomy. The scale was used to measure the degree to which the job provides opportunities for a product manager to exercise freedom of choice in decision making.

SCALE ORIGIN:

The scale was originally developed by Quinn and Shepard (1974), but the only known use of the scale in the domain of marketing literature reviewed was by Lysonski (1985).

SAMPLES:

Lysonski obtained data from questionnaires mailed to 449 product managers in consumer package goods industries. A second mailing to nonrespondents yielded a final return rate of 55%, or 224 completed questionnaires, of which 54 were unusable. The final sample for analysis was **170**.

RELIABILITY:

A Cronbach alpha of **.80** was reported for the scale.

VALIDITY:

No examination of scale validity was reported.

ADMINISTRATION:

The scale was self-administered along with several other measures included in a mail questionnaire format. The scores from each of the items are summed, with a possible score range of 4 to 16. A low score (4 being the lowest possible score) represents a low perceived role autonomy.

MAJOR FINDINGS:

The results indicated that role autonomy moderated the role ambiguity-satisfaction relationship ($F = 9.38$, $p \leq .001$; increased satisfaction).

COMMENTS:

Lysonski stated that he used a six-item scale from Quinn and Shepard, who appear to have used only four items. As Lysonski did not provide the items he used, the discrepancy in the number and nature of items in his scale remains unresolved.

REFERENCES:

Lysonski, Steven (1985), ''A Boundary Theory Investigation of the Product Manager's Role,'' *JM*, Vol. 49, (Winter), 26- 40.

Quinn, R. P. and L. J. Shepard (1974), ''The 1972-1973 Quality of Employment Survey: Descriptive Statistics with Comparison Data From the 1969-1970 Survey of Working Conditions.'' Ann Arbor, Mich.: The Institute for Social Research.

SCALE ITEMS: ROLE AUTONOMY (JOB-RELATED) +

A lot	Somewhat	A little	Not at all
4———————————	——————3——————	——————2——————	——————1

1. How much freedom does your job allow you as to how you do your work?
2. How much does your job allow you to make a lot of decisions on your own?
3. How much does your job allow you to take part in making decisions that affect you?
4. How much in your job is where you have a lot to say over what happens on your job?

+ This is the Quinn and Shepard version of the scale rather than the Lysonski version, as explained in the Comments section.

SCALE NAME: Role Clarity (Salesperson)

SCALE DESCRIPTION:

A five-item, five-point summated ratings scale measuring a salesperson's perceived role clarity. The scale has also been referred to as the Role Clarity Index.

SCALE ORIGIN:

There is no information indicating that the scale originated elsewhere than in the study by Busch (1980). His is the only known use of the scale in the marketing literature reviewed here.

SAMPLES:

Analysis was based on data in **477** usable questionnaires collected from the salespeople of three pharmaceutical companies. The overall response rate was 53.8%. The data base consisted of 436 male respondents and 39 female respondents.

RELIABILITY:

A Cronbach's alpha of **.81** was reported for the scale.

VALIDITY:

No examination of scale validity was reported.

ADMINISTRATION:

The scale was self-administered along with several other measures included in the mail questionnaire. No information was available as to the actual scoring to be used for the scale items. If 1 represents the "not at all clear" anchor and 5 represents the "perfectly clear" anchor, the possible summated scores could range from 5 to 25. A low score (5 being the lowest possible score) would represent a low degree of perceived role clarity.

MAJOR FINDINGS:

The results indicated that expert power was positively related to **role clarity** in all three firms (firm 1, $p \leq .001$; firm 3, $p \leq .002$). Referent power was positively related to role clarity within all three firms. Additionally, two male-female differences were found for the relationship between role clarity and the sales managers' power bases: expert power (male, $r = .33$, $p \leq .05$; female, $r = -.05$) and legitimate power (male, $r = .12$; female, $r = -.15$).

REFERENCE:

Busch, Paul (1980), "The Sales Manager's Bases of Social Power and Influence Upon the Sales Force," *JM*, 44 (Summer), 91-101.

SCALE ITEMS: ROLE CLARITY (SALESPERSON)

Please read the following questions. After carefully reading the questions, CHECK THE SPACE BELOW THE QUESTION WHICH MOST ACCURATELY REFLECTS YOUR FEELINGS. Remember that there are no right or wrong answers to the questions. The main interest is in your own personal feelings. Place a check in one of the spaces after each question.

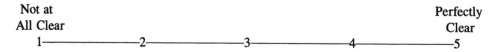

Not at   Perfectly

All Clear   Clear

1————————2————————3————————4————————5

1. How clear are you about the limits of your authority in your present job?
2. Do you feel you are always as clear as you would like to be about what you have to do on your job?
3. Do you feel you are always as clear as you would like to be about how you are supposed to do things on your job?
4. In general, how clearly defined are the policies and the various rules, procedures, and regulations of the company that affect your job?
5. In general, how clearly defined are the rules, policies, and procedures of your department that affect your job?

SCALE NAME: Role Clarity (Salesperson)

SCALE DESCRIPTION:

A five-item, five-point Likert-like scale ranging from very false to very true purporting to measure the clarity with which a salesperson understands what is expected of him/her at work.

SCALE ORIGIN:

The original scale was developed by Schriesheim (1978), but the only known use of the scale in the domain of marketing literature reviewed was by Fry et al. (1986).

SAMPLES:

Fry and his coauthors obtained data from a mail survey of a national pharmaceutical manufacturer's salesforce. Questionnaires were returned by **216** of 347 salesman surveyed (response rate of 62%).

RELIABILITY:

A Cronbach's alpha of **.93** was reported for the scale.

VALIDITY:

The two measures of supervisors' leadership used, role clarity and consideration, were proposed specically for use in research grounded in path-goal theory (House and Baetz 1979). No other examination of scale validity was reported or available.

ADMINISTRATION:

The scale was self-administered along with several other measures included in the mail questionnaire. The possible score range is 5 to 25. A low score represents a low degree of perceived role clarity.

MAJOR FINDINGS:

A supervisor's role clarity was found to negatively influence both role perception variables (role conflict and role ambiguity) and to have an indirect influence on satisfaction through its influence on role conflict except in the case of satisfaction with supervisor.

REFERENCES:

Fry, Louis W., Charles M. Futrell, A. Parasuraman, and Margaret A. Chmielewshi (1986), "An Analysis of Alternative Causal Models of Salesperson Role Perceptions and Work-Related Attitudes," *JMR*, 23 (May), 153-163.

House, Robert J. and Mary L. Baetz (1979), "Leadership: Some Empirical Generalizations and New Research Directions," in *Research in Organizational Behavior*, Barry M. Staw, ed. Greenwich, Conn.: JAI Press, Inc., 341-423.

Schriesheim, C. A. (1978), ''Development, Validation and Application of New Leadership Behavior and Expectancy Research Instruments,'' unpublished doctoral dissertation, The Ohio State University.

SCALE ITEMS: ROLE CLARITY (SALESPERSON)

Directions: First, **Read** each item carefully, Then **Think** about **how true** each item is. Next, **Decide** whether the item is **(1) Very false, (2) False, (3) Neither true nor false, (4) True,** or **(5) Very true.** Finally, write the number you have picked for your answer in the space to the **left** of each statement. For example, write a 1 if the statement is **Very false**.

MY IMMEDIATE SUPERVISOR . . .

1. ＿＿ Gives vague explanations of what is expected of me on my job. **(r)**
2. ＿＿ Gives me unclear goals to reach on my job. **(r)**
3. ＿＿ Explains the level of performance that is expected of me.
4. ＿＿ Explains the quality of work that is expected of me.
5. ＿＿ Explains what is expected of me on my job.

SCALE NAME: Role Clarity (Salesperson)

SCALE DESCRIPTION:

It is a five-item, seven-point Likert-like summated ratings scale purporting to measure salespeoples' perceptions of role clarity.

SCALE ORIGIN:

The scale was originally constructed and used by Rizzo, House, and Lirtzman (1970). On the basis of research by Kahn et al. (1964), they designed it to measure role conflict and role ambiguity. The instrument was sent to 280 central office, plant, and engineering employees of a manufacturing organization. The scale was found to have internal consistency reliability exceeding .70 along with high concurrent validity (Schuler, Aldag, and Brief 1977).

The scale was slightly modified for a selling situation by Teas, Wacker, and Hughes (1979) and reported an alpha of .775. They conducted a discriminant validity analysis using a multitrait-multimethod matrix. The results indicated high discriminant validity among the following concepts: feedback, role clarity, security, social, esteem, autonomy, and self-actualization. Predictive validity was demonstrated by path analysis.

SAMPLES:

Kohli (1985) used a total of **114** responses from salespeople in three companies manufacturing and selling products (response rate 89.9%).

RELIABILITY:

Kohli reported a Cronbach's alpha of **.85** for the scale.

VALIDITY:

Kohli conducted a factor analysis with varimax rotation. The analysis indicated high convergent and discriminant validity.

ADMINISTRATION:

The scale was self-administered along with several other measures included in a mail questionnaire.

MAJOR FINDINGS:

Kohli found that a salesperson's role clarity is positively related to self-esteem as well as intrinsic, extrinsic, and overall job satisfaction and extrinsic instrumentalities. Contingent approving behavior, upward influencing behavior, and achievement-oriented behavior were positively related to role clarity. Additionally, role clarity was not related to intrinsic or overall instrumentalities, or to arbitrary and punitive behavior.

#538 *Role Clarity (Salesperson)*

REFERENCES:

Kahn, R. L., P. M. Wolfe, R. P. Quinn, J. D. Snoek, and R. H. Rosenthal (1964), *Organizational Stress*. New York, N.Y.: John Wiley & Sons, Inc.

Kohli, Ajay K. (1985), "Some Unexplored Supervisory Behaviors and Their Influnce on Salespeople's Role Clarity, Specific Self-Esteem, Job Satisfaction, and Motivation," *JMR*, 22 (November), 424-433.

Rizzo, John R., Robert J. House, and Sidney I. Lirtzman (1970), "Role Conflict and Ambiguity in Complex Organizations," *Administration Science Quarterly*, 15 (June), 150-63.

Schuler, Randall S., Ramon J. Aldag, and Arthur P. Brief (1977), "Role Conflict and Ambiguity: A Scale Analysis," *Organizational Behavior and Human Performance*, 20 (January), 111-128.

Teas, R. Kenneth, John G. Wacker, and R. Eugene Hughes (1979), "A Path Analysis of Causes and Consequences of Salespeople's Perceptions of Role Clarity," *JMR*, 16 (August), 355-369.

SCALE ITEMS: ROLE CLARITY (SALESPERSON)

Each respondent rated the following items on a seven-point scale (1 = minimum amount to 7 = maximum amount) to indicate the extent to which he/she had each perception. Only five of the items were apparently used to calculate the scale score but which item was ultimately eliminated is unknown.

1. The feeling of certainty about how much authority I have in my selling position.
2. Clear, planned goals and objectives for my selling position.
3. The feeling that I have divided my time properly while performing the tasks connected with my selling.
4. The feeling of certainty about what my responsibilities are in my selling position.
5. The knowledge of exactly what is expected of me in my selling position.
6. Receiving, in my selling position, clear explanations of what has to be done.

SCALE NAME: Role Conflict (Salesperson & Product Manager)

SCALE DESCRIPTION:

An eight-item, seven-point Likert-like summated ratings scale ranging from very true to very false purporting to measuring a person's perceived role conflict.

SCALE ORIGIN:

The scale was orginally developed by Rizzo, House, and Lirtzman (1970).

SAMPLES:

Teas (1983) obtained data by a mail survey of two midwestern corporations' salesforces. Included with the questionnaires were cover letters from the researcher and the vice president of sales promising confidentiality and indicating company support for the survey. Usable responses were obtained from **116** salespersons, 49 and 67 salespersons from the two companies, respectively (response rate 55%).

Lysonski (1985) obtained data from questionnaires mailed to 449 product managers in consumer package goods industries. A second mailing to nonrespondents yielded a final return rate of 55%, or 224 completed questionnaires, of which 54 were unusable. The final sample for analysis was **170**.

Dubinsky and Hartley (1986) collected data from questionnaires mailed to insurance agents located throughout the United States. Included with each questionnaire was a cover letter from the company's divisional Vice President indicating support for the project and a cover letter from the researchers promising confidentiality. A total of 467 questionnaires were sent. Usable questionnaires were returned by **120** agents (response rate 25.7%). Ninety-one percent of the respondents were male, mean age was 39.1 years, approximately 56% had earned at least a bachelor's degree, and mean job tenure was 6.6 years.

Fry et al. (1986) obtained data by a mail survey of a national pharmaceutical manufacturer's salesforce. Questionnaires were returned by **216** of 347 salesmen surveyed (response rate 62%). The data analyzed were from men only. Data on age, income, tenure, and education were not specified.

Hampton, Dubinsky, and Skinner (1986) obtained data from a census (n = 121) of retail salespeople employed in a department store chain (five outlets). Usable questionnaires were obtained from **116** of the salespeople (response rate 95.9%). Ninety-one of the respondents were women and 25 were men. Median age was 23.2 years, approximately 66% had at least some college education, median job tenure was 1.4 years, and median time spent working with the current sales supervisor was 1.1 years.

Michaels et al. (1988) obtained data by self-administered questionnaires distributed to 255 full-line salespeople of an industrial building materials manufacturer. Usable questionnaires were returned by **215** salespeople (response rate 84.3%). Mean respondent age was 43.9 years, mean job tenure 12.9 years, mean organization tenure 15.2 years, and mean sales experience 18.1 years. Data were also collected from a sample of industrial buyers. A randomly selected sample of 554 members of the National Association of Purchasing Management constituted the industrial buyer sample. Data were collected by self-administered mail questionnaire. Of the 355 questionnaires returned, 330 were usable (59.6%). Mean respondent age was 42.2 years, mean job tenure 5.7 years, mean organization tenure 10.6 years, and mean purchasing experience 12.5 years.

Cummings, Jackson, and Ostrom (1989) obtained data by self-administered questionnaires distributed by mail to firms selected from the American Marketing Association Membership Directory. The 156 firms that agreed to participate in the study provided a potential sample of 624 product managers, of whom **201** returned usable questionnaires.

RELIABILITY:

The following Cronbach alpha values were reported for the scale: **.881**, Teas (1983); **.84**, Lysonski (1985); Dubinsky and Hartley (1986); **.86**, Fry et al. (1986); **.78**, Hampton, Dubinsky, and Skinner (1986); **.85**, Michaels et al. (1988); and **.791**, Cummings, Jackson, and Ostrom (1989).

VALIDITY:

Dubinsky and Hartley (1986) noted that the scale had discriminant and predictive validity (Rizzo, House, and Lirtzman 1970), and construct and concurrent validity (Schuler, Aldag, and Brief 1977); in addition, it was shown to be free of semantic confusion (House, Schuler, Levanoni 1983).

ADMINISTRATION:

The scale was self-administered along with several other measures included in the mail questionnaire in most of the studies. Hampton, Dubinsky, and Skinner (1986) used a different approach by administering the questionnaires to the respondents in a conference room at each store, where the questionnaires were completed. Accompanying the questionnaires were a cover letter from the chain's president indicating company support for the project and a cover letter from the researchers promising confidentiality.

The scores from each item are summated. The possible score range is 8 to 56. A low score (8 being the lowest possible score) represents high perceived role conflict.

MAJOR FINDINGS:

Teas' (1983) results indicated that the following predictor variables were related to a salesperson's perception of role conflict: consideration, negatively related ($p \leq .001$); initiation of structure, positively related ($p \leq .05$); participation, negatively related ($p \leq .05$); and experience, negatively related ($p \leq .01$). Additionally, the salesperson's perceived role conflict was significantly negatively related ($p \leq .001$) to a salesperson's job satisfaction.

Lysonski's (1985) results indicated that the correlations between role pressures and personal outcome states were significantly correlated in nearly every case. Role conflict and role ambiguity were negatively associated with job satisfaction and perceived performance.

Dubinsky and Hartley (1986) found that self-monitoring and work motivation did not to appear to be related to role conflict or role ambiguity (they were found not to be significant). Additionally, role conflict was not related to job satisfaction. However, role conflict was associated with job performance ($p \leq .01$).

Fry et al. (1986) found that role conflict and ambiguity had a direct negative impact on satisfaction ($p \leq .05$). Role conflict was positively related to job anxiety ($p \leq .05$). Also, a supervisor's consideration affected role conflict ($p \leq .05$). Role conflict had a negative effect ($p \leq .05$) on all job satisfaction dimensions (e.g., job, fellow workers, supervisor pay, promotion and development, and company policy and support) except satisfaction with customer.

Hampton, Dubinsky and Skinner (1986) found that initiating structure did not affect role conflict (was not significant), which supports the findings of Szilagyi and Keller (1976) and Walker, Churchill, and Ford (1975). Consideration was inversely related to role conflict ($p \leq .05$). Additionally, role conflict had a strong inverse relationship with overall job satisfaction ($p \leq .0001$).

Michaels et al. (1988) found that higher levels of role conflict and ambiguity were associated with lower levels of organizational commitment ($p \leq .001$). Additionally, in both samples (industrial buyer sample and salesperson sample), the relationship between formalization and role conflict was negative ($p \leq .001$).

Cummings, Jackson, and Ostrom (1989) found a direct relationship between job structure and role conflict ($p \leq .007$). However, job structure explained only 5% of the variance in role conflict. Role conflict was not significantly related to job satisfaction or job performance.

COMMENTS:

Also see Futrell (1980) for an apparent use of the scale in a study pertaining to job satisfaction.

REFERENCES:

Cummings, W. Theodore, Donald W. Jackson, and Lonnie L. Ostrom (1989), "Examining Product Managers' Job Satisfaction and Performance Using Selected Organizational Behavior Variables, " *JAMS*, 17 (2), 147- 156.

Dubinsky, Alan J. and Steven W. Hartley (1986), "A Path-Analytic Study of a Model of Salesperson Performance," *JAMS*, 14 (Spring), 36-46.

Fry, Louis W., Charles M. Futrell, A. Parasuraman, and Margaret A. Chmielewski (1986), "An Analysis of Alternative Causal Models of Salesperson Role Perceptions and Work-Related Attitudes," *JMR*, 23 (May), 153-163.

Futrell, Charles M. (1980), "Salesmen and Saleswomen Job Satisfaction," *Industrial Marketing Management*, 9, 27-30.

Hampton, Ron, Alan J. Dubinsky, and Steven J. Skinner (1986), "A Model of Sales Supervisor Leadership Behavior and Retail Salespeople's Job-Related Outcomes," *JAMS*, 14 (Fall), 33-43.

House, R. L., R. S. Schuler, and E. Levanoni (1983), "Role Conflict and Ambiguity Scales: Reality on Artifacts?" *Journal of Applied Psychology*, 68 (May), 334-337.

Lirtzman (1970), "Role Conflict and Ambiguity in Complex Organizations," *Administrative Science Quarterly*, 15 (June), 150-163.

Lysonski, Steven (1985), "A Boundary Theory Investigation of the Product Manager's Role," *JM*, 49 (Winter), 26-40.

Michaels, Ronald E., William L. Cron, Alan J. Dubinsky, and Erich A. Joachimsthaler (1988), "Influence of Formalizatio on the Organizational Commitment and Work Alienation of Salespeople and Industrial Buyers," *JMR*, 25 (November), 376-383.

Rizzo, J., R. J. House, and S. I. Schuler, Randall S., Ramon J. Aldag, and Arthur P. Brief (1977), "Role Conflict and Ambiguity: A Scale Analysis," *Organizational Behavior and Human Performance*, 16, 111-128.

Schuler, R. S., R. J. Aldag, and A. P. Brief (1977), "Conflict and Ambiguity: A Scale

Analysis," *Organizational Behavior and Human Performance,* 20 (October), 111-128.

Szilagyi, A. D. and R. T. Keller (1976), "A Comparative Investigation of the Supervisory Behavior Description Questionnaire (SBDQ) and the Revised Leader Behavior Description Questionnaire (LBDQ-Form XII)," *Academy of Management Journal,* 19 (December), 642-649.

Teas, R. Kenneth (1983), "Supervisory Behavior, Role Stress, and the Job Satisfaction of Industrial Salespeople," *JMR,* 20 (February), 84-91.

Walker, Orville C., Gilbert A. Churchill and Neil M. Ford (1975), "Organizational Determinants of the industrial Salesman's Role Conflict and Ambiguity," *JM,* 39 (January), 32-39.

SCALE ITEMS: ROLE CONFLICT (SALESPERSON & PRODUCT MANAGER) +

The following is Rizzo, House, and Lirtzman's (1970) original scale used to measure role conflict (1 = very true; 7 = very false).

1. I have to do things that should be done differently.
2. I receive an assignment without the manpower to complete it.
3. I have to buck a rule or policy in order to carry out an assignment.
4. I work with two or more groups who operate quite differently.
5. I receive incompatible requests from two or more people.
6. I do things that are apt to be accepted by one and not accepted by others.
7. I receive an assignment without adequate resources and materials to execute it.
8. I work on unnecessary things.

+ Teas (1983) used a five-point scale instead of the seven-point scale. Lysonski (1985) used a 10-item version of the scale, but gave no description of the number of points or the actual items used. Michaels et al. (1988) used a nine-item, seven-point version of the scale, but gave no description of the actual items used. Cummings, Jackson, and Ostrom (1989) used a modified version of Rizzo, House, and Lirtzman's (1970) original scale. The modified version was a six-item, five-point Likert-type summated type scale. No information was available as to the actual anchors used.

SCALE NAME: Role Conflict (Work-Nonwork)

SCALE DESCRIPTION:

A two-item, seven-point Likert-type scale assessing the degree to which a salesperson reports having conflicts between his/her work and nonwork roles or at least the degree to which such conflicts are resolved. Dubinsky et al. (1986) referred to this measure as Resolution of Outside Life Conflicts.

SCALE ORIGIN:

The items for the scale were slightly modified from those developed by Feldman (1976). His study was based on data from **118** hospital employees. Scale scores were not only calculated on responses to questionnaire items, but also included a rating based on interviews with each subject. The Spearman-Brown reliability coefficient (corrected for attenuation) was reported as .40. Role conflict was found to have significant positive correlations with resolution of conflicts at work as well as general job satisfaction.

SAMPLES:

Dubinsky and his coauthors collected data from **189** salespeople. Letters were sent to a national sample of 2000 senior-level executives asking them to have their least experienced salesperson complete the questionnaire. The respondents represented 189 different companies that marketed 50 different product categories. The sample had a median age of 30.5 years, had spent 1.4 years (median) in their present positions, and were mostly male (86%).

RELIABILITY:

A LISREL estimate of reliability was **.31** (Dubinsky et al. 1986).

VALIDITY:

No examination of scale validity was reported.

ADMINISTRATION:

The scale was self-administered by respondents along with many other measures in a mail survey format. Higher scores on the scale indicate that respondents have few conflicts between their work and their nonwork roles or at least have resolved the conflicts that did occur.

MAJOR FINDINGS:

Dubinsky and his coauthors examined a model of salesforce assimilation. Work confidence was found to have significant positive impact on **role conflict.**

COMMENTS:

The reliability of the measure is so low that the scale is unreliable and should not be used until its psychometric properties can be substantially improved.

#540 *Role Conflict (Work-Nonwork)*

REFERENCES:

Dubinsky, Alan J., Roy D. Howell, Thomas N. Ingram, and Danny Bellenger (1986), "Salesforce Socialization," *JM*, 50 (October), 192-207.

Feldman, Daniel C. (1976), "A Contingency Theory of Socialization," *Administrative Science Quarterly*, 21 (September), 433-452.

SCALE ITEMS: ROLE CONFLICTS (WORK-NONWORK)

Strongly Disagree	Disagree	Slightly Disagree	Neutral	Slightly Agree	Agree	Strongly Agree
1	2	3	4	5	6	7

1. My job schedule interferes with my life outside work. **(r)**
2. The people I see outside the company don't like to hear about what goes on at my job. **(r)**

SCALE NAME: Role Definition (Salesperson)

SCALE DESCRIPTION:

A three-item, seven-point Likert-type scale ranging from disagree strongly to agree strongly purporting to measure role definition.

SCALE ORIGIN:

The scale used by Dubinsky et al. (1986) was originally developed by Feldman (1976a), but theirs is the only known use of the scale in the domain of marketing literature reviewed. Feldman (1976b) reported a Spearman-Brown reliability coefficient of .775.

SAMPLES:

The data were obtained by a questionnaire sent to a national sample of 2000 senior-level executives throughout the United States. A cover letter requested that the sales executives select their least experienced salesperson to complete the questionnaire. Questionnaires were returned by 189 salespersons in different companies representing 50 different product categories. The median age of the respondents was 30.5 years and the median length of time in present position 1.4 years. Eighty six percent of the respondents were men.

RELIABILITY:

Dubinsky and his coauthors reported two reliability coefficients (.57 and .58), slightly different because of the different models being analyzed.

VALIDITY:

No examination of scale validity was reported.

ADMINISTRATION:

The scale was self-administered along with several other measures included in the mail questionnaire. The possible score range is 3 to 21. A low score represents a high degree of perceived role definition.

MAJOR FINDINGS:

The results were similar to those of Feldman (1976b) in that realism related only to role definition (p = .52) and resolution of conflicting demands at work (p = .70), with congruence being the more important anticipatory stage variable. Greater realism on the part of the salesperson led to greater job satisfaction. The impact of realism on job satisfaction came from better role definition (p = .77), which in turn provided better resolution of conflicting demands (p = .56).

REFERENCES:

Dubinsky, Alan J., Roy D. Howell, Thomas N. Ingram, and Danny N. Bellenger (1986), "Salesforce Socialization," *JM*, 50 (October), 192-207.

Feldman, D.C. (1976a), "A Contingency Theory of Socialization," unpublished doctoral dissertation, Yale University.

———— (1976b), "A Contingency Theory of Socialization," *Administrative Science Quarterly*, 21 (September), 433-450.

SCALE ITEMS: ROLE DEFINITION (SALESPERSON)

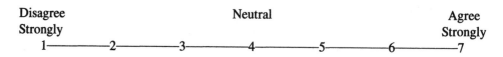

Disagree Strongly			Neutral			Agree Strongly
1——2——3——4——5——6——7						

1. I feel my job description is accurate. **(r)**
2. I frequently wonder why I get assigned some of the jobs I do.
3. Some things I continually have to do at work should really be part of someone else's job.

SCALE NAME: Role Performance

SCALE DESCRIPTION:

A six-item, 11-point Likert-like scale ranging from very poor to very good purporting to measure role performance of manufacturers or boundary personnel from the dealer's perspective.

SCALE ORIGIN:

The scale was developed by Frazier (1983) and his is the only known use of the scale in the domain of literature reviewed. The scale was constructed on the basis of a review of previous literature and unstructured personal interviews with approximately 40 new car dealers. A series of pretests of the questionnaire were conducted with dealers to ensure that the items were appropriate and worded properly.

SAMPLES:

The data were collected by a questionnaire sent to 944 dealers. A followup questionnaire was sent two weeks later to those who had not responded. The final response rate was 46.1%. Only 12 of the returned questionnaires were not usable. Of the 423 usable questionnaires, 92 were produced from the second wave.

RELIABILITY:

Cronbach's alpha was .81 for the weighted measure of role performance at the boundary personnel center and .83 for the unweighted measure. Additionally, in terms of the two items used to reflect role performance at the corporate center, the split-half reliability coefficient after full scale adjustment was .66 for the weighted measure and .70 for the unweighted one.

VALIDITY:

To assess the content and face validity of the scale, the means on the performance and importance ratings were calculated. The means were found to be significantly different across manufacturers' makes ($p \leq .001$ for all but one, which was significant at the $p \leq .025$ level).

A test of the measures' discriminant validity was conducted. The resulting factors explained 67.4% of the variance in the original six performance elements when weighted by the importance ratings and 70.8% of the variance when unweighted. Additionally, converent validity was assessed. The correlation coefficients between chances of switching and role performance were -.55 and -.40 for the corporate and boundary personnel, respectively, for the weighted measures. For the unweighted performance measures, the correlations were slightly lower at -.53 and -.39, respectively. Each correlation was significant at beyond the $p \leq .001$ level. Because the coefficients were of moderate strength, they were interpreted to demonstrate adequate levels of convergent validity for the dependence measures. A nomological validity assessment was also conducted. The analysis indicated that each coefficient was in the expected direction (positive), significant at the $p \leq .001$ level or beyond, and at a moderate level. No conclusive claims about the nomological validity of these measures can be made until the theoretical basis underlying these relationships becomes better established.

ADMINISTRATION:

The scale was self-administered in a mail questionnaire. The scores from each item are summated. The possible score range is -30 to 30. A low score (-30 being the lowest possible score) represents a low level of perceived role performance of manufacturers or boundary personnel from the dealer's perspective.

MAJOR FINDINGS:

The role performance measures appear to be adequate in terms of internal consistency, content and face validity, and discriminant validity. Additionally, promising levels of convergent and nomological validity were demonstrated for these measures. Role performance ($p \leq .001$) at the corporate center was related strongly to dealer "chances of switching" relationships whereas role performance ($p \leq .001$) at the boundary personnel center was related more strongly to dealer satisfaction, manufacturer interest, and agreement on decision strategy variables.

REFERENCE:

Frazier, Gary L. (1983), "On the Measurement of Interfirm Power in Channels of Distribution," *JMR*, 20 (May), 158-166.

SCALE ITEMS: ROLE PERFORMANCE

Dealers were asked to indicate how well their manufacturer or its boundary personnel performed in comparison with industry average performance on each of the following role elements. The respondents used a 11-point scale ranging from -5 (very poor), through 0 (average performance), to 5 (very good) to indicate their responses.

1. manufacturer-generated demand for the make
2. cooperativeness of the manufacturer reps on interfirm issues
3. car allocation and delivery
4. interfirm assistances
5. quality of advice from manufacturer reps
6. reimbursement for warranty claims and vehicle preparation.

SCALE NAME: Sales Constraints

SCALE DESCRIPTION:

A three-item, five-point Likert-like summated ratings scale measuring a salesperson's perception of a set of environmental limitations characteristic of the products sold by his/her company such as product quality, product demand, and sales volume.

SCALE ORIGIN:

The scale appears to have been constructed by Teas (1981).

SAMPLES:

Teas collected data from **171** salespeople in group interviews during sales meetings. The salespeople represented 74% of the industrial salesforces of three midwestern companies. The typical salesperson was 36 years of age and had spent 6.5 years with his company.

RELIABILITY:

An alpha of **.623** was reported for the scale.

VALIDITY:

Teas performed a factor analysis of the items composing many of the scales used in his study and these three items were found to have loadings greater than .40 on the same factor.

ADMINISTRATION:

The scale was self-administered along with many other measures. Higher scores indicate that salespeople have selling constraints such that the products they sell are of low quality, have weak demand, or the company has low sales volume.

MAJOR FINDINGS:

Teas investigated the impact of several personality characteristics and job-related perceptions on work motivation. The results indicated that salespersons' perceptions of **constraints on their sales potential** were significant negative influencers of their job expectations.

REFERENCE:

Teas, R. Kenneth (1981), "An Empirical Test of Models of Salespersons' Job Expectancy and Instrumentality Perceptions," *JMR*, 18 (May), 209-226.

SCALE ITEMS: ENVIRONMENTAL CONSTRAINTS OF COMPANY

```
Very                                                                    Very
False                                                                   True
  1————————2————————3————————4————————5
```

1. Currently, the economic conditions in this country are very favorable in that there is strong demand for the products I sell.
2. When compared to other companies with which my company competes, my company is below average in size of sales volume. **(r)**
3. When compared to other companies with which my company competes, my company is above average in product quality.

SCALE NAME: Sample Representativeness Evaluation

SCALE DESCRIPTION:

A two-item, seven-point Likert-like summated ratings scale measuring the degree to which a sample is considered to be typical or representative of some population.

SCALE ORIGIN:

The scale appears to be original to the study by Lee, Acito, and Day (1987).

SAMPLES:

Data were collected from **170** MBA students enrolled at a large state university. The sample was limited to those who had completed one course in the program and had taken at least one statistics course. A majority of the respondents had some business experience in their background. No significant differences were found between those with formal business experience and those without.

RELIABILITY:

An alpha of **.77** was reported for the scale.

VALIDITY:

Though scale validity was not specifically examined by Lee and his coauthors, some evidence of convergent and discriminant validity comes from the factor analysis they performed. For the four scales they used, each item was reported to have loaded on a single factor above .60 and items were grouped on the expected factors. Cross-loadings were less than .25.

ADMINISTRATION:

The scale was self-administered along with other measures as part of an experiment in a ''laboratory'' setting. Higher scores on the scale indicate that respondents strongly believe a sample used in a study is representative of some targeted population whereas lower scores suggest that they strongly think a sample is not typical of some target population.

MAJOR FINDINGS:

The purpose of the study by Lee and his coauthors was to determine how the perceived quality of marketing research is integrated with prior opinions in making decisions. When results of a study were consistent with prior opinions, the **evaluation of the study's sample** was significantly higher.

REFERENCE:

Lee, Hanjoon, Frank Acito, and Ralph L. Day (1987), ''Evaluation and Use of Marketing Research by Decision Makers: A Behavioral Simulation,'' *JMR*, 24 (May), 187-196.

SCALE ITEMS: SAMPLE REPRESENTATIVENESS EVALUATION

1. Are the sample subjects sufficiently typical for the findings to be useful?

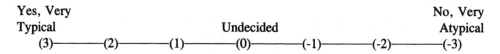

2. How well does the sample of subjects represent the targeted population?

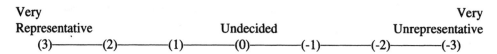

SCALE NAME: Sample Size Evaluation

SCALE DESCRIPTION:

A two-item, seven-point Likert-like summated ratings scale measuring the degree to which a sample size is considered to be useful and appropriate for a study.

SCALE ORIGIN:

The scale appears to be original to the study by Lee, Acito, and Day (1987).

SAMPLES:

Data were collected from **170** MBA students enrolled at a large state university. The sample was limited to those who had completed one course in the program and had taken at least one statistics course. A majority of the respondents had some business experience in their background. No significant differences were found between those with formal business experience and those without.

RELIABILITY:

An alpha of **.93** was reported for the scale.

VALIDITY:

Though scale validity was not specifically examined by Lee and his coauthors, some evidence of convergent and discriminant validity comes from the factor analysis they performed. For the four scales they used, each item was reported to have loaded on a single factor above .60 and items were grouped on the expected factors. Cross-loadings were less than .25.

ADMINISTRATION:

The scale was self-administered along with other measures as part of an experiment in a "laboratory" setting. Higher scores on the scale indicate that respondents strongly believe a sample used in a study is large enough to be useful whereas lower scores suggest that they strongly think a sample is so small that any conclusions drawn from its use will be invalid.

MAJOR FINDINGS:

The purpose of the study by Lee and his coauthors was to determine how the perceived quality of marketing research is integrated with prior opinions in making decisions. When results of a study were consistent with prior opinions, the **evaluation of the study's sample size** was significantly higher. Further, a large survey (n = 600) was evaluated more highly than a small survey (n = 100).

REFERENCE:

Lee, Hanjoon, Frank Acito, and Ralph L. Day (1987), "Evaluation and Use of Marketing Research by Decision Makers: A Behavioral Simulation," *JMR*, 24 (May), 187-196.

SCALE ITEMS: SAMPLE SIZE EVALUATION

1. Is the sample size large enough for the findings to be useful to you?

Definitely Need More Subjects			Undecided			Definitely Do Not Need More Subjects
(3)———	(2)———	(1)———	(0)———	(-1)———	(-2)———	(-3)

2. Does the research ask enough people in order to draw a valid conclusion?

Definitely Need More Subjects			Undecided			Definitely Do Not Need More Subjects
(3)———	(2)———	(1)———	(0)———	(-1)———	(-2)———	(-3)

SCALE NAME: Satisfaction (Dealer With Manufacturer)

SCALE DESCRIPTION:

A four-item, five-point Likert-type summated ratings scale measuring the degree to which a retailer/dealer reports that it is satisfied with its relationship with a manufacturer.

SCALE ORIGIN:

Dwyer and Oh (1987) indicated that they drew heavily on the satisfaction scale reported by Gaski (1986) in developing their measure. Though the two versions of the scale have a couple of items that are very similar, they have enough differences to be treated here as distinct measures.

SAMPLES:

Dwyer and Oh gathered data from car dealers in 10 different SMSAs: five areas with high growth characteristics and five markets with low growth characteristics. Ultimately, **167** usable responses were received, which represented a 69% response rate.

RELIABILITY:

An alpha of **.91** was reported by Dwyer and Oh for their four-item version of the scale, which was ultimately used in the data analysis.

VALIDITY:

The scale was checked for face validity by four dealers as well as four faculty colleagues. Data from a pretest were used to check for item convergence in a restricted one-factor model. In addition, item correlations and residual analysis were used to check for convergence and consistency.

ADMINISTRATION:

Respondents self-administered the scale along with many other measures. Higher scores on the scale suggest that respondents think the relationship they have with their manufacturers is satisfying whereas lower scores indicate that they feel their relationships are not good, are unfair, and/or do not benefit their dealerships.

MAJOR FINDINGS:

Dwyer and Oh used LISREL to analyze the effects of resource availability on constraints and opportunities in the car dealers' environment. Formalization and participation decision-making characteristics had significant positive impacts, and centralization had a negative impact, on quality of the relationship with the manufacturer, of which **satisfaction** was one component.

REFERENCES:

Dwyer, F. Robert and Sejo Oh (1987), ''Output Sector Munificence Effects on the Internal Political Economy of Marketing Channels,'' *JMR*, 24 (November), 347-358.

Gaski, John F. (1986), ''Interrelations Among a Channel Entity's Power Sources: Impact of the Exercise of Reward and Coercion on Expert, Referent, and Legitimate Power Sources,'' *JMR*, 23 (February), 62-77.

SCALE ITEMS: SATISFACTION (DEALER WITH MANUFACTURER)

The statements below assess the quality of your relationship with the manufacturer. Based upon your experience, what do you expect will characterize your dealings with the manufacturer in the coming year?

Strongly Disagree	Disagree	Neutral	Agree	Strongly Agree
1	2	3	4	5

1. In general, I am pretty satisfied with my relationship with the manufacturer.
2. Overall, the manufacturer is a good company to do business with.
3. All in all, the manufacturer has been very fair with me.
4. Overall, the manufacturer's policies and programs benefit my dealership.

SCALE NAME: Satisfaction (Dealer With Manufacturer)

SCALE DESCRIPTION:

A five-item, five-point Likert-type summated ratings scale measuring the degree to which a retailer/dealer reports that it is satisfied with its relationship with a manufacturer.

SCALE ORIGIN:

There is no indication that the scale was not original to Gaski (1986; Gaski and Nevin 1985).

SAMPLES:

Data used in the two studies were based on the same sample consisting of dealers of a manufacturer and distributor of heavy industrial machinery (the Melroe Division of Clarke Equipment). Mail questionnaires were sent to all 634 dealers in the U.S. and Canada. A total of **238** usable responses were eventually received. Several tests were conducted that showed no significant evidence of nonresponse bias.

RELIABILITY:

An alpha of **.764** was reported for the scale.

VALIDITY:

Some weak evidence of discriminant validity was provided, as the correlations between the scale and other variables in the study were not nearly as great as the alpha coefficient calculated for the scale.

ADMINISTRATION:

The scale was self-administered along with several other measures in a mail survey format in both studies. Higher scores on the scale indicate that dealers have a high amount of satisfaction with a manufacturer whereas lower scores suggest that the dealers are not happy doing business with a manufacturer.

MAJOR FINDINGS:

The purpose of the study by Gaski and Nevin was to examine the differential effects of exercised versus unexercised power on several variables of interest to channel managers. Coercive power, exercised coercive power, reward power, and exercised reward power were all significantly associated with **dealer satisfaction**, the first two relationships being negative and the last two being positive. Further, the *exercise* of coercive power did seem to have a significantly greater negative impact on **satisfaction** than just the *potential use* of coercive power.

Similarly, Gaski investigated aspects of power in channel relationships. Specifically, he used causal modeling to study the effects of reward and coercive power on expert, referent, and legitimate power. Reward and coercive power were not found to have significant direct effects on **satisfaction** but did have significant effects on "qualitative power" (a composite of expert, referent, and legitimate power), which in turn had a significant impact on **satisfaction**. Unexpectedly, therefore, the indirect effects of reward and coercive power on **satisfaction** were significant whereas the direct effects were not.

REFERENCES:

Gaski, John F. (1986), "Interrelations Among a Channel Entity's Power Sources: Impact of the Exercise of Reward and Coercion on Expert, Referent, and Legitimate Power Sources," *JMR*, 23 (February), 62-77.

_____ and John R. Nevin (1985), "The Differential Effects of Exercised and Unexercised Power Sources in a Marketing Channel," *JMR*, 22 (May), 130-142.

SCALE ITEMS: SATISFACTION (DEALER WITH MANUFACTURER) +

Strongly Disagree	Disagree	Neutral	Agree	Strongly Agree
1	2	3	4	5

1. In general, I am pretty happy with my dealings with _____.
2. I would discontinue selling _____ products if I could. **(r)**
3. _____ is a good company to do business with.
4. If I had it to do over again, I would not do business with _____. **(r)**
5. I am satisfied with the products and services I get from _____.

+ The blanks are filled with the name of the channel member (e.g., manufacturer) of interest in the study.

SCALE NAME: Satisfaction (Franchisee)

SCALE DESCRIPTION:

A 22-item, five-point Likert-type summated ratings scale measuring the degree to which a franchisee is satisfied with the relationship and arrangements with a franchisor.

SCALE ORIGIN:

This scale and the study reported in the article by Schul (1987) came from his dissertation research (Schul 1980). He reported in a previous article (Schul, Little, and Pride 1983) that a review of the literature, interviews with franchisees, and a pilot study helped to generate and test items. His is the only known use of this scale.

SAMPLES:

The main study involved an eight-page questionnaire mailed to 1052 franchised real estate brokers with six different franchise affiliations. After two waves of mailings, a total of **349** usable survey forms were received. There was no evidence of nonresponse bias.

RELIABILITY:

A Spearman-Brown split-half reliability coefficient of **.71** was reported for the scale.

VALIDITY:

The items composing this scale were factor analyzed and found to represent four factors (Schul, Little, and Pride 1983). No examination of the validity of this combined index was reported.

ADMINISTRATION:

The scale was self-administered by respondents along with many other measures in a mail survey format. Higher scores on the scale indicate that franchisees report a high level of satisfaction with their respective franchisors and arrangements.

MAJOR FINDINGS:

The purpose of the study by Schul (1987) was to investigate the influence of different channel leadership behaviors on channel members' conflict and satisfaction. A path analysis indicated that two types of leadership behavior had significant, direct, and positive effects on **franchisee satisfaction**. Two types of channel conflict had significant, direct, and negative effects on **franchisee** satisfaction.

COMMENTS:

With some modification of the items, this scale might also be a measure of channel member satisfaction.

REFERENCES:

Schul, Patrick L. (1980), ''An Empirical Investigation of the Conflict Behavior Process in Franchise Channels of Distribution,'' unpublished doctoral dissertation, Texas A&M University.

———— (1987), ''An Investigation of Path-Goal Leadership Theory and Its Impact on Intrachannel Conflict and Satisfaction,'' *JAMS*, 15 (Winter), 42-52.

————, Taylor L. Little, and William M. Pride (1983), ''Channel Climate: Its Impact on Channel Members' Satisfaction,'' *JR*, 61 (Summer), 9-38.

SCALE ITEMS: SATISFACTION (FRANCHISEE)

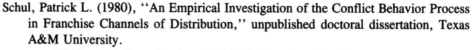

Strongly Disagree	Disagree	Neither	Agree	Strongly Agree
1———	———2———	———3———	———4———	———5

1. My regional director makes every effort to make me feel like I am a valuable member of this franchise organization.
2. My regional director provides me with substantial guidance and assistance in setting up new marketing programs.
3. This franchise organization does not provide me with adequate marketing, financial, and/or management support. **(r)**
4. The various training programs provided by my franchise organization are timely, up-to-date, and informative.
5. Franchise management ignores my suggestions and complaints. **(r)**
6. In my opinion, the monthly service and/or advertising fees charged by my franchise organization are more than reasonable in comparison to those fees charged by other franchise organizations.
7. The initial franchise fee assessed by my franchise organization for obtaining a new franchise is too high in comparison to those fees charged by other franchise organizations. **(r)**
8. My regional director has always been fair and honest in dealings with me.
9. My status in the real estate community has increased considerably since becoming a member of this franchise organization.
10. I am proud to be a member of this franchise organization.
11. My regional director asks for my opinions and suggestions and tries to use them.
12. The recognition/award programs used in this franchise organization do not give the franchise much incentive to increase his/her agency's sales performance. **(r)**
13. The benefits I derive directly from being a member of this franchise organization are more than adequate to justify the costs of franchise membership.
14. I have confidence in the fairness and honesty of the management of this franchise organization.
15. My regional director demonstrates a genuine interest in my agency's brokerage operations.
16. The financial benefits I receive from being a member of this franchise organization are substantial in comparison to those received by franchisees affiliated with other franchise organizations.
17. My franchise organization has assumed a leadership role in the industry with regards to developing the most competitive array of brokerage services.

18. The overall franchise fee structure within my franchise arrangement is more than fair when compared with that of other franchise organizations.
19. My franchise organization is an excellent source for new, creative marketing ideas that I am able to use in my brokerage operations.
20. My regional director does a good job of helping me develop my agency's sales potential.
21. My regional director communicates with me often by telephone, mail, or in face-to face meetings.
22. Franchise management keeps the franchisee in the dark about things he/she ought to know. **(r)**

SCALE NAME: Satisfaction With Job (Composite Index)

SCALE DESCRIPTION:

A 14-item, seven-point Likert-type summated ratings scale measuring the degree to which a person expresses satisfaction with several aspects of his/her work such as feedback from superiors, variety in the job, opportunity to complete the work started, and pay. Each of these aspects was used as a separate scale as well as together in an overall index by Hunt and Chonko (1984).

SCALE ORIGIN:

Hunt and Chonko indicated that they took seven items from the work of Sims, Szilagyi, and Keller (1976) and generated seven more themselves.

SAMPLES:

A questionnaire was mailed to a systematic sample of 4282 members of the American Marketing Association. Usable responses were received from **1076**. Among many other sample characteristics, the typical respondent was male (70%), married (72%), and had a master's degree (53%). A little less than half of the sample worked for firms with over 1000 employees (44%), were in marketing research jobs (41%), and were between the ages of 30 and 39 years (40%).

RELIABILITY:

An alpha of **.89** was reported for the scale (Hunt and Chonko 1984).

VALIDITY:

No examination of the scale's validity was reported.

ADMINISTRATION:

The scale was self-administered along with many other measures in a mail survey format. Higher scores on the scale suggest that employees are very satisfied with their jobs whereas lower scores indicate that several aspects of their jobs are not acceptable and pleasing.

MAJOR FINDINGS:

The purpose of the study by Hunt and Chonko was to determine whether marketers were more Machiavellian than other members of society. Among the findings was that marketers who were high in Machiavellianism were less **satisfied with their jobs**.

COMMENTS:

The scale can be broken down into four subscales which Hunt and Chonko referred to as satisfaction with information, satisfaction with variety, satisfaction with closure, and satisfaction with pay. These subscales were reported to have alpha values of .93, .88, .80, and .56, respectively.

REFERENCES:

Hunt, Shelby D. and Lawrence B. Chonko (1984), "Marketing and Machiavellianism," *JM*, 48 (Summer), 30-42.

Sims, Henry P., Jr., Andrew D. Szilagyi, and Robert T. Keller (1976), "The Measurement of Job Characteristics," *Academy of Management Journal*, 19 (June), 195-212.

SCALE ITEMS: SATISFACTION WITH JOB (COMPOSIT INDEX)

Strongly Disagree	Disagree	Slightly Disagree	Neutral	Slightly Agree	Agree	Strongly Agree
1	2	3	4	5	6	7

Satisfaction with Information
1. I am satisfied with the information I receive from my superior about my job performance.
2. I receive enough information from my supervisor about my job performance.
3. I receive enough feedback from my supervisor on how well I'm doing.
4. There is enough opportunity in my job to find out how I am doing.

Satisfaction with Variety
5. I am satisfied with the variety of activities my job offers.
6. I am satisfied with the freedom I have to do what I want on my job.
7. I am satisfied with the opportunities my job provides me to interact with others.
8. There is enough variety in my job.
9. I have enough freedom to do what I want in my job.
10. My job has enough opportunity for independent thought and action.

Satisfaction with Closure
11. I am satisfied with the opportunities my job gives me to complete tasks from beginning to end.
12. My job has enough opportunity to complete the work I start.

Satisfaction with Pay
13. I am satisfied with the pay I receive for my job.
14. I am satisfied with the security my job provides me.

SCALE NAME: Satisfaction With Job (Extrinsic)

SCALE DESCRIPTION:

A three-item, seven-point Likert-like summated ratings scale measuring the degree to which a salesperson reports security and social needs to be met by his/her work. Teas, Wacker, and Hughes (1979) referred to it as Lower Order Need Fulfillment whereas Teas (1980) called it Extrinsic Satisfaction.

SCALE ORIGIN:

Though the items for this scale are among those developed by Porter and Lawler (1968), use of this particular subset, which is modified for the sales situation, appears to be original to Teas and his coauthors.

SAMPLES:

Intracompany mail distribution was used by Teas (1980) to reach 184 salesmen of a midwestern company's industrial salesforce. Analysis was based on responses from **127** salespeople.

The analysis by Kohli (1985) was based on data from **114** salespeople. The sample was obtained from three companies manufacturing and selling industrial products. An overall response rate of 89.8% was reported.

RELIABILITY:

Alpha values of **.630** and **.72** were reported for the scale by Teas and Kohli, respectively.

VALIDITY:

No specific examination of scale validity was reported by Teas. Though the specific results were not reported for this scale by Kohli, he implied that a factor analysis of this and other scales was used to eliminate items with weak loadings on their hypothesized factors. From this factor analysis and the information in Table 1 (p. 428), the final version of this scale appears to have had five items. As the version used by Teas (1980, p. 368) had only three items, Kohli's factor analysis seems to have resulted in the inclusion of two extra items, most likely from the "instrinsic job needs" scale. Therefore, it is not clear which construct a few of the 13 items in Teas' intrinsic and extrinsic job needs scales most appropriately measure.

ADMINISTRATION:

The scale was self-administered in the Teas study along with several other measures. Higher scores on the scale indicate that salespeople report their jobs as meeting their lower level needs whereas lower scores suggest that they feel their security and social needs are unsatisfied by their work.

MAJOR FINDINGS:

Teas used path analysis to examine simultaneously some causes and results of salesperson perceptions of role ambiguity. Closeness of supervision (initiation of structure leadership style) and a salesperson's role ambiguity were found to have positive and negative direct effects, respectively, on **extrinsic job satisfaction**.

Kohli examined several previously unstudied supervisory behaviors toward salespeople. Role clarity and, to a lesser extent, contingent approving supervisory behavior were found to be positively related to **extrinsic job satisfaction**.

COMMENTS:

As noted in relation to validity, it is not clear from the information provided by Kohli what additional items were included in the final analysis of the scale. Further, he combined the five items he used from this scale and the seven items he retained from a scale of higher level need job satisfaction to have an overall measure of job satisfaction. It was reported to have an alpha of .88.

REFERENCES:

Kohli, Ajay K. (1985), "Some Unexplored Supervisory Behaviors and Their Influence on Salespeople's Role Clarity, Specific Self-Esteem, Job Satisfaction, and Motivation," *JMR*, 22 (November), 424-433.

Porter, Lyman W. and Edward E. Lawler III (1968), *Managerial Attitudes and Performance*. Homewood, Ill.: Richard D. Irwin, Inc.

Teas, R. Kenneth (1980), "An Empirical Test of Linkages Proposed in the Walker, Churchill, and Ford Model of Salesforce Motivation and Performance," *JAMS*, 8 (Winter), 58-72.

_____, John G. Wacker, and R. Eugene Hughes (1979), "A Path Analysis of Causes and Consequences of Salespeople's Perceptions of Role Clarity," *JMR*, 16 (August), 355-369.

SCALE ITEMS: SATISFACTION WITH JOB (EXTRINSIC)

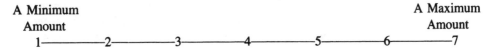

A Minimum
  Amount
1————2————3————4————5————6————7

A Maximum
  Amount

1. The feeling of security in my selling position.
2. The opportunity in my selling position of giving help to others.
3. The opportunity of developing close friendships in my selling position.

SCALE NAME: Satisfaction With Job (Extrinsic)

SCALE DESCRIPTION:

A three-item, seven-point Likert-type summated ratings scale measuring the degree to which an employee reports that his/her sales job is satisfying because of the material rewards it can bring. The measure focuses on *extrinsic* aspects of a job that lead to satisfaction rather than the work itself being inherently satisfying.

SCALE ORIGIN:

The measure was developed by Sujan (1986) and was referred to as a measure of a salesperson's extrinsic reward orientation.

SAMPLES:

Sujan sent letters to 880 sales managers working for large national manufacturing firms representing a wide variety of industries. The 191 who responded indicated a total of 4038 salespeople in their companies who would serve as respondents. Questionnaires were then sent to them and **1283** usable responses were received from salespeople in 123 firms.

RELIABILITY:

An alpha of **.79** was reported for the scale.

VALIDITY:

No specific examination of scale validity was reported.

ADMINISTRATION:

The scale was self-administered by respondents in a mail survey format. Higher scores on the scale indicate that salespeople find a lot of satisfaction from the tangible rewards their jobs can bring whereas lower scores suggest that they do not think much extrinsic satisfaction is associated with their jobs.

MAJOR FINDINGS:

The purpose of the study by Sujan was to use the attributional theory of motivation to understand salespeople's desire to ''work smarter.'' As expected, **extrinsic job satisfaction** had a significant positive impact on attributing failure to a lack of effort.

COMMENTS:

The addition of a few other appropriate items would improve the internal consistency of the scale.

REFERENCE:

Sujan, Harish (1986), ''Smarter Versus Harder: An Exploratory Attributional Analysis of Salespeople's Motivation,'' *JMR*, 23 (February), 41-49.

SCALE ITEMS: SATISFACTION WITH JOB (EXTRINSIC)

Strongly disagree = 1
Moderately disagree = 2
Slightly disagree = 3
Neutral = 4
Slightly agree = 5
Moderately agree = 6
Strongly agree = 7

1. For you, selling is basically a means to get the good things in life.
2. Essentially, you work at your job for the material rewards you get.
3. You work primarily for money and other tangible rewards.

SCALE NAME: Satisfaction With Job (Extrinsic)

SCALE DESCRIPTION:

A seven-item, three-point Likert-like summated ratings scale measuring the degree to which an employee reports being satisfied with the earnings, benefits, and status related to his/her job. The measure focuses on extrinsic aspects of a job that affect satisfaction rather than what is inherently satisfying about the work.

SCALE ORIGIN:

Lucas et al. (1987) reported that the items for the scale were adapted from the Job Dimensions Scale by Schletzer (1965). Theirs is th only known use of the scale in the published marketing literature included here.

SAMPLES:

The dataset used in the study was made available to the researchers by a major national insurance firm. Data had been collected by the company (not the researchers) from its agents in two different time periods: DS1 (1972), DS2 (1976), and DS3 (1976). DS1 consisted of 2357 responses, but only **1412** provided employee identification numbers. DS2 was composed of 2314 usable responses, **1045** of which provided identification numbers. DS3 was aimed at **282** agents who had provided identification numbers and usable responses in both DS1 and DS2. Evidence indicated that the samples were biased in favor of agents who had longer tenure, greater length of service prior to quitting, and higher satisfaction levels than agents not included in the study.

RELIABILITY:

Alpha values of **.617** and **.643** were reported for the scale as used in DS1 and DS2, respectively.

VALIDITY:

No specific examination of scale validity was made.

ADMINISTRATION:

The scale was self-administed by respondents along with other measures. Higher scores on the scale indicate that employees report greater satisfaction with extrinsic aspects of their jobs whereas lower scores suggest that they are not satisfied with such aspects as job earnings, benefits, and status.

MAJOR FINDINGS:

The purpose of the study by Lucas and his coauthors was to make a longitudinal investigation of the effects of demographic and job attitude characteristics on employee turnover. Some evidence was found relating **extrinsic job satisfaction** and length of time spent with the company; however, it was limited to DS2 and DS3 in a discriminant analysis. The results were insignificant in the MANOVA and multiple-descriminant analysis as well as for DS1 in all analyses.

COMMENTS:

The wording of the items should be modified slightly if the measure is used in contexts other than insurance sales.

REFERENCES:

Lucas Jr., George H., A. Parasuraman, Robert A. Davis, and Ben M. Enis (1987), ''An Empirical Study of Salesforce Turnover,'' *JM*, 51 (July), 34-59.

Schletzer, V. (1965), ''A Study of the Predictive Effectiveness of the Strong Vocational Interest Blank for Job Satisfaction,'' unpublished doctoral dissertation, University of Minnesota.''

SCALE ITEMS: SATISFACTION WITH JOB (EXTRINSIC)

Dissatisfied	Neutral	Satisfied
1—————————————————	—2————————————————	————————3

1. The compensation plan underwhich you work
2. Your earnings as an agent
3. Fairness of your earnings in relation to efforts expended
4. Your probable future earnings in the life insurance business
5. The attitude of the public toward _____. +
6. Your benefit plan in general
7. The attitude of the public toward life insurance agents

+ The name of the company goes in this blank.

SCALE NAME: Satisfaction With Job (Generalized)

SCALE DESCRIPTION:

A five-item, seven-point Likert-type scale assessing the degree to which an employee is generally satisfied with the kind of work he/she does. The scale is "general" in the sense that the items do not reflect specific issues such as pay, supervision, coworkers, et cetera. A short form of the scale with three items was used by Dubinsky et al. (1986).

SCALE ORIGIN:

The scale used by Dubinsky and his coauthors was apparently the short version of the job satisfaction scale developed by Hackman and Oldham (1974, 1975). No specific psychometric information was provided about the three-item version but the five-item version was indicated to be reasonably reliable and valid. Specifically, the internal consistency of the scale was reported to be .76. As evidence of convergent validity, the scale had high positive correlations with several other related but conceptually different measures such as social satisfaction, supervisory satisfaction, growth satisfaction, and work meaningfulness.

SAMPLES:

Dubinsky and his coauthors collected data from **189** salespeople. Letters were sent to a national sample of 2000 senior-level executives asking them to have their least experienced salesperson complete the questionnaire. The respondents represented 189 different companies that marketed 50 different product categories. The sample had a median age of 30.5 years, had spent 1.4 years (median) in their present positions, and were mostly male (86%).

Dubinsky and Hartley (1986) based their analysis on completed questionnaires returned by **120** respondents. Questionnaires were sent to 467 agents who sold lines of a large multi-insurance company. No nonresponse bias was apparent. The sample had a mean age of 39.1 years, had spent 6.6 years (mean) in their present positions, were mostly male (91%), and over half were college graduates (56%).

The sample used by Hampton, Dubinsky, and Skinner (1986) was based on **116** usable responses from a census of 121 retail salespeople who worked in one of five outlets of a department store chain. The sample had a median age of 23.2 years, had spent 1.4 years (median) in their present positions and 1.1 years (median) with their current supervisors, were mostly female (78%), and 66% had some college education.

RELIABILITY:

A LISREL estimate of reliability was .83 (Dubinsky et al. 1986) and alpha values of .73 and .81 were reported by Dubinsky and Hartley and by Hampton and his coauthors, respectively.

VALIDITY:

No examination of scale validity was reported in any of the marketing studies.

ADMINISTRATION:

The scale was self-administered by respondents in the studies by Dubinsky and his coauthors along with many other measures in a mail survey format. Hampton and his coauthors distributed the survey instrument to respondents in a conference room in each store, where they were self-administered. Higher scores on the scale indicate that respondents have a high level of general satisfaction with the work they perform in their jobs whereas lower scores indicate that they are very dissatisfied with their jobs.

MAJOR FINDINGS:

Dubinsky and his coauthors examined a model of salesforce assimilation. Job suitability and dealing with conflicts at work were both found to have significant positive impacts on general **job satisfaction**.

The purpose of the study by Dubinsky and Hartley was to investigate several predictors of salesperson performance and the relationships among those predictors. A path analysis indicated that though **job satisfaction** had some effect on job involvement, it had a stronger (positive) effect on organizational commitment. In turn, it was most significantly impacted (negatively) by role ambiguity.

A causal model of retail sales supervisor leadership behavior was studied by Hampton and his coauthors. The results indicated that **job satisfaction** had strong positive effects on organizational commitment and "work motivation." In turn, role conflict had a strong negative impact on **job satisfaction**.

REFERENCES:

Dubinsky, Alan J. and Steven W. Hartley (1986), "A Path- Analytic Study of a Model of Salesperson Performance," *JAMS*, 14 (Spring), 36-46.

_____, Roy D. Howell, Thomas N. Ingram, and Danny Bellenger (1986), "Salesforce Socialization," *JM*, 50 (October), 192-207.

Hackman, J. Richard and Greg R. Oldham (1974), *The Job Diagnostic Survey: An Instrument for the Diagnosis of Jobs and the Evaluation of Job Redesign Projects*, Technical Report #4, Department of Administrative Sciences, Yale University.

_____ and _____ (1975), "Development of the Job Diagnostic Survey," *Journal of Applied Psychology*, 60 (2), 159-170.

Hampton, Ron, Alan J. Dubinsky, and Steven J. Skinner (1986), "A Model of Sales Supervisor Leadership Behavior and Retail Salespeople's Job-Related Outcomes," *JAMS*, 14 (Fall), 33-43.

SCALE ITEMS: SATISFACTION WITH JOB (GENERALIZED) +

Strongly Disagree	Disagree	Slightly Disagree	Neutral	Slightly Agree	Agree	Strongly Agree
1	2	3	4	5	6	7

1. Generally speaking, I am very satisfied with this job.
2. I frequently think of quitting this job. **(r)**

3. I am generally satisfied with the kind of work I do in this job.
4. Most people on this job are very satisfied with the job.
5. People on this job often think of quitting. **(r)**

+ Items 1 through 3 compose the short form of the scale and are the ones used by Dubinsky et al. (1986).

SCALE NAME: Satisfaction With Job (Generalized)

SCALE DESCRIPTION:

An eight-item, six-point Likert-like summated ratings scale measuring the degree of satisfaction a salesperson expresses having with his/her work.

SCALE ORIGIN:

The first four items of the scale originate from the work of Pruden and Reese (1972) and the last four were designed for the specific sales situation studied in the disseration by Bagozzi (1976).

SAMPLES:

The analysis by Bagozzi (1980) was based on **122** completed questionnaires from industrial salespeople assigned to exclusive geographic territories.

RELIABILITY:

An alpha of **.78** was reported for the scale (Bagozzi 1980).

VALIDITY:

No specific examination of scale validity was reported.

ADMINISTRATION:

The scale was apparently self-administered in an unspecified setting as part of a larger survey instrument. Higher scores on the scale suggest that salespeople are very satisfied with several aspects of their jobs whereas lower scores indicate that they are very dissatisfied with their work.

MAJOR FINDINGS:

Bagozzi used causal modeling to investigate the relationship between performance and satisfaction for an industrial salesforce. The results indicated that **job satisfaction** was influenced to a significant degree by motivation to work and sales performance.

COMMENTS:

See also a reanalysis of Bagozzi's data by Joreskog and Sorbom (1982).

REFERENCES:

Bagozzi, Richard P. (1976), "Toward a General Theory for the Explanation of the Performance of Salespeople," unpublished doctoral dissertation, Northwestern University.

_____ (1980), "Performance and Satisfaction in an Industrial Salesforce: An Examination of Their Antecedents and Simultaneity," *JM*, 44 (Spring), 65-77.

Joreskog, Karl G. and Dag Sorbom (1982), "Recent Developments in Structural Equation Modeling," *JMR*, 19 (November), 404-416.

Pruden, Henry O. and Richard M. Reese (1972), "Interorganization Role-set Relations and the Performance and Satisfaction of Industrial Salesmen," *Administrative Science Quarterly*, 17 (December), 601-609.

SCALE ITEMS: SATISFACTION WITH JOB (GENERALIZED)

Use the following scale to response to the first six items.

Definitely Yes	Probably Yes	Maybe Yes	Maybe No	Probably No	Definitely No
6	5	4	3	2	1

1. Do you feel promotion opportunities are wider in jobs other than yours?
2. Do you feel it is as easy to demonstrate ability and initiative in your job as in others?
3. Would you advise a friend looking for a new job to take one similar to yours?
4. Do you think that there is as much a feeling of security in your job as in others?
5. Do you feel your pay is as high in comparison with what others get for similar work in other companies?
6. How satisfied are you with your general work situation?
7. Do you find your work challenging, exciting, and giving you a sense of accomplishment? (Respond on the following scale.)
   Extremely satisfied = 6
   Moderately satisfied = 5
   Somewhat satisfied = 4
   Somewhat dissatisfied = 3
   Moderately dissatisfied = 2
   Extremely dissatisfied = 1
8. How much control do you feel you have over your work activities such as number of calls required in a week, etc.?

No Control	Very Little Control	Slight Amount of Control	Moderate Amount of Control	Very Much Control	Total Control
1	2	3	4	5	6

SCALE NAME: Satisfaction With Job (Intrinsic)

SCALE DESCRIPTION:

A three-item, seven-point Likert-type summated ratings scale measuring the degree to which an employee reports that his/her sales job is inherently satisfying. The measure focuses on intrinsic aspects of a job that lead to satisfaction rather than extrinsic aspects that can also affect satisfaction.

SCALE ORIGIN:

The measure was developed by Sujan (1986) and was referred to as a measure of a salesperson's intrinsic reward orientation.

SAMPLES:

Sujan sent letters to 880 sales managers working for large national manufacturing firms representing a wide variety of industries. The 191 who responded indicated a total of 4038 salespeople in their companies who would serve as respondents. Questionnaires were then sent to them and **1283** usable responses were received from salespeople in 123 firms.

RELIABILITY:

An alpha of **.63** was reported for the scale.

VALIDITY:

No specific examination of scale validity was reported.

ADMINISTRATION:

The scale was self-administered by respondents in a mail survey format. Higher scores on the scale indicate that salespeople find a lot of intrinsic satisfaction in their jobs whereas lower scores suggest that they do not think selling is inherently enjoyable.

MAJOR FINDINGS:

The purpose of the study by Sujan was to use the attributional theory of motivation to understand salespeople's desire to ''work smarter.'' In contrast to expectations, **intrinsic job satisfaction** had significant negative impacts on attributing failure to both a lack of effort and poor sales strategy.

COMMENTS:

The addition of a few other appropriate items would improve the internal consistency of the scale.

REFERENCE:

Sujan, Harish (1986), "Smarter Versus Harder: An Exploratory Attributional Analysis of Salespeople's Motivation," *JMR*, 23 (February), 41-49.

SCALE ITEMS: SATISFACTION WITH JOB (INTRINSIC)

Strongly disagree = 1
Moderately disagree = 2
Slightly disagree = 3
Neutral = 4
Slightly agree = 5
Moderately agree = 6
Strongly agree = 7

1. You get a lot of satisfaction and reward out of just doing your job.
2. Selling is not much fun. **(r)**
3. If you could start over, you would still choose to do the kind of work that you are doing now.

SCALE NAME: Satisfaction With Job (Intrinsic)

SCALE DESCRIPTION:

A four-item, five-point Likert-type summated ratings scale measuring the degree to which an employee reports that his/her job satisfies such needs as personal growth and a sense of accomplishment. The measure focuses on inherent aspects of a job that lead to satisfaction rather than extrinsic aspects that can also affect satisfaction.

SCALE ORIGIN:

Lucas et al. (1987) reported that the items for the scale were adapted from the Job Dimensions Scale by Schletzer (1965). Theirs is the only known use of the scale in the published marketing literature and reported here.

SAMPLES:

The dataset used in the study was made available to the researchers by a major national insurance firm. Data had been collected by the company (not the researchers) from its agents in two different time periods: DS1 (1972), DS2 (1976), and DS3 (1976). DS1 consisted of 2357 responses, but only **1412** provided employee identification numbers. DS2 was composed of 2314 usable responses, **1045** of which provided identification numbers. DS3 was aimed at **282** agents who had provided identification numbers and usable responses in both DS1 and DS2. Evidence indicated that the samples were biased in favor of agents who had longer tenure, greater length of service prior to quitting, and higher satisfaction levels than agents not included in the study.

RELIABILITY:

Alpha values of **.612** and **.835** were reported for the scale as used in DS1 and DS2, respectively.

VALIDITY:

No specific examination of scale validity was made.

ADMINISTRATION:

The scale was self-administered by respondents along with other measures. Higher scores on the scale indicate that employees report that their jobs are inherently satisfying whereas lower scores suggest that they get little if any enjoyment from their work.

MAJOR FINDINGS:

The purpose of the study by Lucas and his coauthors was to make a longitudinal investigation of the effects of demographic and job attitude characteristics on employee turnover. Only in DS1 was a significant relationship found between **intrinsic job satisfaction** and length of time spent with the company.

COMMENTS:

The wording of the items should be modified slightly if the measure is used in contexts other than insurance sales.

REFERENCES:

Lucas Jr., George H., A. Parasuraman, Robert A. Davis, and Ben M. Enis (1987), ''An Empirical Study of Salesforce Turnover,'' *JM*, 51 (July), 34-59.

Schletzer, V. (1965), ''A Study of the Predictive Effectiveness of the Strong Vocational Interest Blank for Job Satisfaction,'' unpublished doctoral dissertation, University of Minnesota.

SCALE ITEMS: SATISFACTION WITH JOB (INTRINSIC)

Strongly Disagree	Disagree	Neutral	Agree	Strongly Agree
1————————	2————————	3————————	4————————	5

1. Our agency does a good job at encouraging professional growth.
2. I get a feeling of accomplishment from the work I am doing.
3. My job is an interesting one.
4. My firm offers opportunities for growth as a career underwriter.

SCALE NAME: Satisfaction With Job (Intrinsic)

SCALE DESCRIPTION:

A 10-item, seven-point Likert-like summated ratings scale measuring the degree to which a salesperson reports esteem, autonomy, and self-actualization needs are met by his/her work. Teas, Wacker, and Hughes (1979) referred to this as Higher Order Need Fulfillment whereas Teas (1980) called it Intrinsic Satisfaction.

SCALE ORIGIN:

The items for this scale were among those developed by Porter and Lawler (1968), but use of this particular subset, which was modified for the sales situation, appears to be original to Teas and his coauthors.

SAMPLES:

Teas (1980) used intracompany mail distribution to reach 184 salesmen of a midwestern company's industrial salesforce. Analysis was based on responses from **127** salespeople.

The analysis by Kohli (1985) was based on data from **114** salespeople. The sample was obtained from three companies manufacturing and selling industrial products. An overall response rate of 89.8% was reported.

RELIABILITY:

Alpha values of **.851** and **.85** were reported for the scale by Teas and Kohli, respectively.

VALIDITY:

No specific examination of scale validity was reported by Teas. Though the specific results were not reported for this scale by Kohli, he implied that a factor analysis of this and other scales was used to eliminate items with weak loadings on their hypothesized factors. From this factor analysis and the information provided in Table 1 (p. 428), it appears that the final version of this scale had seven items. As the version used by Teas (1980, p. 368) had 10 items, Kohli's factor analysis seems to have resulted in fewer items included; most likely items were lost to the "extrinsic job needs" scale. Therefore, it is not clear for a few of the total of 13 items in Teas' intrinsic and extrinsic job needs scales which construct they most appropriately measure.

ADMINISTRATION:

The scale was self-administered in the Teas and Kohli studies along with several other measures. Higher scores on the scale indicate that salespeople report their jobs as meeting their higher level needs whereas lower scores suggest that they feel that their esteem, automony, and self-actualization needs are unsatisfied by their work.

MAJOR FINDINGS:

Teas used path analysis to examine simultaneously some causes and results of salesperson perceptions of role ambiguity. A supervisor's participative leadership style and a salesperson's role ambiguity were found to have positive and negative direct effects, respectively, on **intrinsic job satisfaction.**

Kohli examined several previously unstudied supervisory behaviors toward salespeople. Role clarity and, to a lesser extent, contingent approving supervisory behavior were found to be positively related to **intrinsic job satisfaction.**

COMMENTS:

As noted above in relation to validity, it is not clear from the information provided by Kohli which items below were not included in the final analysis of the scale. Further, he combined the seven items from this scale and the five items he retained from a scale of lower level need satisfaction to have an overall measure of job satisfaction. It was reported to have an alpha of .88.

REFERENCES:

Kohli, Ajay K. (1985), "Some Unexplored Supervisory Behaviors and Their Influence on Salespeople's Role Clarity, Specific Self-Esteem, Job Satisfaction, and Motivation," *JMR*, 22 (November), 424-433.

Porter, Lyman W. and Edward E. Lawler III (1968), *Managerial Attitudes and Performance.* Homewood, Ill.: Richard D. Irwin, Inc.

Teas, R. Kenneth (1979), "An Empirical Test of Linkages Proposed in the Walker, Churchill, and Ford Model of Salesforce Motivation and Performance," *JAMS*, 8 (Winter), 58-72.

————, John G. Wacker, and R. Eugene Hughes (1979), "A Path Analysis of Causes and Consequences of Salespeople's Perceptions of Role Clarity," *JMR*, 16 (August), 355-369.

SCALE ITEMS: SATISFACTION WITH JOB (INTRINSIC)

A Minimum Amount ... A Maximum Amount

1————2————3————4————5————6————7

1. The feeling of self-esteem a person gets from being in my selling position.
2. The prestige of my position inside the company (that is, the regard received from others in the company).
3. The prestige of my selling position outside the company (that is, the regard received from others not in the company).
4. The authority connected with my selling position.
5. The opportunity for independent thought and action in my selling position.
6. The opportunity in my selling position for participating in the setting of goals.
7. The opportunity in my selling position for participating in the determination of methods and procedures.

8. The opportunity for personal growth and development in my selling position.
9. The feeling of self-fulfillment a person gets from being in my selling position (that is, the feeling of being able to use one's own unique capabilities, realize one's own potentialities).
10. The feeling of worthwhile accomplishment in my selling position.

SCALE NAME: Satisfaction With Supervisor

SCALE DESCRIPTION:

A three-item, seven-point Likert-type scale assessing the degree to which an employee is satisfied with the treatment, respect, and guidance received from a supervisor at work.

SCALE ORIGIN:

The scale was developed by Hackman and Oldham (1974, 1975) and was indicated to be reasonably reliable and valid. Specifically, the internal consistency of the scale was reported to be .79. Evidence of convergent validity was that the scale had moderate positive correlations with several other related but conceptually different measures such as general job satisfaction, social satisfaction, and growth satisfaction.

SAMPLES:

The sample used by Hampton, Dubinsky, and Skinner (1986) was based on **116** usable responses from a census of 121 retail salespeople who worked in one of five outlets of a department store chain. The sample had a median age of 23.2 years, had spent 1.4 years (median) in their present positions and 1.1 years (median) with their current supervisors, were mostly female (78%), and 66% had some college education.

RELIABILITY:

An alpha of **.81** was reported by Hampton and his coauthors.

VALIDITY:

No examination of scale validity was reported.

ADMINISTRATION:

Hampton and his coauthors distributed the survey instruments to respondents in a conference room in each store, where they were self-administered. Higher scores on the scale indicate that respondents have a high level of satisfaction with the supervision they receive in their jobs whereas lower scores indicate that they are very dissatisfied with their supervisors.

MAJOR FINDINGS:

A causal model of retail sales supervisor leadership behavior was studied by Hampton and his coauthors. The strongest model found in the study involved **satisfaction with supervision**; its greatest predictor was the sales supervisor being perceived to have a "considerate" leadership style.

REFERENCES:

Hackman, J. Richard and Greg R. Oldham (1974), *The Job Diagnostic Survey: An Instrument for the Diagnosis of Jobs and the Evaluation of Job Redesign Projects*, Technical Report #4, Department of Administrative Sciences, Yale University.

_____ and _____ (1975), "Development of the Job Diagnostic Survey," *Journal of Applied Psychology*, 60 (2), 159-170.

Hampton, Ron, Alan J. Dubinsky, and Steven J. Skinner (1986), "A Model of Sales Supervisor Leadership Behavior and Retail Salespeople's Job-Related Outcomes," *JAMS*, 14 (Fall), 33-43.

SCALE ITEMS: SATISFACTION WITH SUPERVISOR

Strongly Disagree	Disagree	Slightly Disagree	Neutral	Slightly Agree	Agree	Strongly Agree
1	2	3	4	5	6	7

1. I am satisfied with the degree of respect and fair treatment I receive from my immediate supervisor.
2. I am satisfied with the amount of support and guidance I receive from my immediate supervisor.
3. I am very satisfied with the overall quality of supervision I receive from my immediate supervisor.

SCALE NAME: Self-Esteem (Task-Specific for Salesperson)

SCALE DESCRIPTION:

A six-item summated ratings scale measuring how well a salesperson evaluates the quantity and quality of his/her work performance in comparison with all other salespeople in his/her company. As noted below, responses to five of the items are made on a nine-point "percentage" scale representing the top to bottom performers in a company. Responses to one item are made on a five-point likelihood scale ranging from "very slim" to "very strong." Bagozzi (1976) also used a five-point scale for the last item, but used 11-point scales for the first five items. Teas (1981) used five items, modified them slightly, and put them all on seven-point scales. Kohli (1985) also appears to have used just five items in the final analysis of his data.

SCALE ORIGIN:

The items for the scale came from work in the dissertation by Bagozzi (1976) reported in at least two published articles (1978, 1980). The analysis was based on two samples. One consisted of 122 completed questionnaires from industrial salespeople assigned to exclusive geographic territories. The second sample was composed of 38 usable responses from salespeople who sold products similar to those in the first sample but were asssigned to a small number of large accounts. The salespeople were generally older and more experienced than those in the first sample. For both samples, alpha was reported to be .77. Beyond face validity, no details about validity testing were provided. Among the many findings was that task-specific self-esteem was a significant positive predictor of sales performance.

SAMPLES:

Teas collected data from **171** salespeople in group interviews during sales meetings. The salespeople represented 74% of the industrial salesforces of three midwestern companies. The typical salesperson was 36 years of age and had spent 6.5 years with his company.

The analysis by Kohli was based on data from **114** salespeople. The sample was obtained from three companies manufacturing and selling industrial products. An overall response rate of 89.8% was reported.

Hart, Moncrief, and Parasurman (1989) mailed questionnaires to 149 salespeople who worked for 25 independent brokers representing a major food producer. After two followup mailings, usable responses were received from **84** sales representatives.

RELIABILITY:

Alpha values of **.517**, **.77** and **.88** were reported for the scale by Teas, Kohli, and Hart and her coauthors, respectively. Teas noted that item analysis led him to drop one item from the scale, similar to item 4 below.

VALIDITY:

No specific examination of validity was conducted by Teas or Hart and her coauthors. Though the specific results were not reported for this scale by Kohli, he implied that a factor analysis of this and other scales was used to eliminate items with weak loadings on their hypothesized factors. From this factor analysis and the information provided in Table 1 (p. 428), it appears that the final version of this scale had only five items. The particular item that was dropped was not specified.

ADMINISTRATION:

The scale was self-administered by respondents in the form of "group interviews" by Teas, in a mail survey questionnaire by Hart and her coauthors, and in an unspecified context by Kohli. Higher scores on the scale indicate that employees have high self-esteem due to the quality and quantity of their work whereas lower scores mean that they admit performing poorly in comparison with other salespeople in their respective firms. Whether or not the numerical response to item 6 (below) was weighted the same as the responses to other items in the scale was not specified by any of the authors.

MAJOR FINDINGS:

Teas investigated the impact of several personality characteristics and job-related perceptions on work motivation. The results indicated that **task-specific self-esteem** was a significant predictor of job performance expectations.

Kohli examined several previously unstudied supervisory behaviors toward salespeople. **Task-specific self-esteem** was found to be positively related to two measures of salespeople's job "expectancy." Specifically, the higher a salesperson's self-esteem about his/her job, the higher his/her expectations about hard work and high performance.

The purpose of the study by Hart and her coauthors was to investigate goal theory as it relates to sales contests. When used as a moderator variable, the results provided evidence that for persons with high **self-esteem,** goal acceptance was positively related to work performance. For persons with low **self-esteem,** goal acceptance was positively related to work effort and use of a customer-oriented selling method.

COMMENTS:

The Teas version of the scale appears to be easiest to administer because of its use of the same response scale for each item. However, because of its very low reliability, more development and testing are needed before it is used further. See also Joreskog and Sorbom (1982) for a reanalysis of the Bagozzi (1980) data.

REFERENCES:

Bagozzi, Richard P. (1976), "Toward a General Theory for the Explanation of the Performance of Salespeople," unpublished doctoral dissertation, Northwestern University.

_____ (1978), "Salesforce Performance and Satisfaction as a Function of Individual Difference, Interpersonal, and Situational Factors," *JMR*, 15 (November), 517-531.

_____ (1980), "Performance and Satisfaction in an Industrial Salesforce: An Examination of Their Antecedents and Simultaneity," *JM*, 44 (Spring), 65-77.

Hart, Sandra Hile, William C. Moncrief, and A. Parasuraman (1989), "An Empirical Investigation of Salespeople's Performance, Effort and Selling Method During a Sales Contest," *JAMS*, 17 (Winter), 29-39.

Joreskog, Karl G. and Dag Sorbom (1982), "Recent Developments in Structural Equation Modeling," *JMR*, 19 (November), 404-416.

Kohli, Ajay K. (1985), "Some Unexplored Supervisory Behaviors and Their Influence on Salespeople's Role Clarity, Specific Self-Esteem, Job Satisfaction, and Motivation," *JMR*, 22 (November), 424-433.

Teas, R. Kenneth (1981), "An Empirical Test of Models of Salespersons' Job Expectancy and Instrumentality Perceptions," *JMR*, 18 (May), 209-226.

SCALE ITEMS: SELF-ESTEEM (TASK-SPECIFIC FOR SALESPERSON)

A sales representative's quantity and quality of performance is measured in many ways—sales volume, profits, number of new accounts, etc. Comparing yourself to all other salespeople in your company doing work similar to yours, please circle the number representing the preferred answer.

Top %				Middle %				Bottom %
10———	—20———	—30———	—40———	—50———	—40———	—30———	—20———	—10

1. How do you rate yourself in terms of the quantity or volume of sales you achieve? (Circle one of the %.)
2. How do you rate yourself in terms of your ability to reach your quota?
3. How do you rate yourself in terms of the quality of your performance in regard to customer relations?
4. How do you rate yourself in terms of quality of your performance in regard to management of time, planning, ability, and management of expenses?
5. How do you rate yourself in terms of quality of your performance in regard to knowledge of your products, company, competitor's products, and customer's needs?
6. How do you rate yourself in terms of the potential you have for reaching the top 10% in sales volume for all sales representatives in your company? (Circle the appropriate number below.)

Very Slim	Slim	Moderate	Very Strong	Strong
1———	———2———	———3———	———4———	———5

SCALE NAME: Self-Monitoring

SCALE DESCRIPTION:

A 25-item, seven-point Likert-type summated ratings scale measuring the degree to which a person observes and manages the image he/she presents to others, guided by situational-specific cues.

SCALE ORIGIN:

The scale was constructed by Snyder (1974). As he used it, the measure was originally 41 true-false statements. Testing of the items was done on 192 undergraduates. On the basis of an item analysis, the list was reduced to a set of 25 items, which maximized internal consistency. The reliability was calculated as being .70 (KR-20) with a one-month test-retest stability of .83. From a sample of 146 undergraduates at another university, an internal consistency of .63 was noted. A variety of studies reported in the article provide support for the validity of the scale.

SAMPLES:

Dubinsky and Hartley (1986) based their analysis on completed questionnaires returned by **120** respondents. Questionnaires were sent to 467 agents who sold lines of a large multi-insurance company. No nonresponse bias was apparent The sample had a mean age of 39.1 years, had spent 6.6 years (mean) in their present positions, were mostly male (91%), and over half were college graduates (56%).

RELIABILITY:

An alpha of **.72** was reported for the scale (Dubinsky and Hartley 1986).

VALIDITY:

No examination of scale validity was reported.

ADMINISTRATION:

The scale was self-administered by respondents along with many other measures in a mail survey format. Higher scores on the scale indicate that respondents engage in a high level of self-monitoring whereas lower scores suggest that they are not sensitive to social cues and do not readily adapt their behavior to different situations.

MAJOR FINDINGS:

The purpose of the study by Dubinsky and Hartley was to investigate several predictors of salesperson performance and the relationships among those predictors. Unexpectedly, a path analysis indicated that **self-monitoring** had no significant effect on job satisfaction, role conflict, or organizational commitment.

REFERENCES:

Dubinsky, Alan J. and Steven W. Hartley (1986), "A Path-Analytic Study of a Model of Salesperson Performance," *JAMS*, 14 (Spring), 36-46.

Snyder, Mark (1974), "Self-Monitoring of Expressive Behavior," *Journal of Personality and Social Psychology*, 30 (October), 526-537.

SCALE ITEMS: SELF-MONITORING

Instructions: Below is a list of statements that may describe your personal reactions to a number of different situations. No two statements are exactly alike, so please consider each statement carefully before answering. Please indicate how much you agree or disagree with each of the following statements concerning your personal reactions. (Please circle the number that most accurately represents your beliefs about each statement.)

Strongly Disagree	Disagree	Slightly Disagree	Neutral	Slightly Agree	Agree	Strongly Agree
1	2	3	4	5	6	7

1. I find it hard to imitate the behavior of other people. **(r)**
2. My behavior is usually an expression of my true inner feelings, attitudes, and beliefs. **(r)**
3. At parties and social gatherings, I do not attempt to do or say things that others will like. **(r)**
4. I can only argue for ideas which I already believe. **(r)**
5. I can make impromptu speeches even on topics about which I have almost no information.
6. I guess I put on a show to impress or entertain people.
7. When I am uncertain how to act in a social situation, I look to the behavior of others for cues.
8. I would probably make a good actor.
9. I rarely need the advice of my friends to choose movies, books, or music. **(r)**
10. I sometimes appear to others to be experiencing deeper emotions than I actually am.
11. I laugh more when I watch a comedy with others than when alone.
12. In a group of people I am rarely the center of attention. **(r)**
13. In different situations and with different people, I often act like very different persons.
14. I am not particularly good at making other people like me. **(r)**
15. Even if I am not enjoying myself, I often pretend to be having a good time.
16. I'm not always the person I appear to be.
17. I would not change my opinions (or the way I do things) in order to please someone or win their favor. **(r)**
18. I have considered being an entertainer.
19. In order to get along and be liked, I tend to be what people expect me to be rather than anything else.
20. I have never been good at games like charades or improvisational acting. **(r)**
21. I have trouble changing my behavior to suit different people and different situations. **(r)**

22. At a party I let others keep the jokes and stories going. **(r)**
23. I feel a bit awkward in company and do not show up quite so well as I should. **(r)**
24. I can look anyone in the eye and tell a lie with a straight face (if for the right end).
25. I may deceive people by being friendly when I really dislike them.

SCALE NAME: Self-Orientation of Customer (Salesperson's Perception)

SCALE DESCRIPTION:

A four-item, five-point Likert-type summated ratings scale measuring the degree to which a salesperson perceived a customer to have been more interested in him/herself than in the product or what the salesperson had to say. Williams and Spiro (1985) viewed this scale as measuring the self-oriented dimension of customer communication style, which stresses preoccupation with self and lack of concern about the other party to the transaction.

SCALE ORIGIN:

The items were developed from work by Bass (1960) on orientation motivation. On the basis of previous work by others, he suggested that members of groups are motivated to remain in the groups for different reasons. He developed measures of three motivations: the task orientation, the interaction orientation, and the self orientation (Bass 1977). Williams and Spiro adapted these measures for their studies in two ways: their measures were more specific to the sales context and were perceptions of other's behaviors, not self-perceptions.

SAMPLES:

Williams and Spiro collected data from all 13 sporting goods stores in a major southeastern U.S. city. Customers were approached just after leaving the stores. If they agreed to fill out a questionnaire, their respective salespeople were asked to fill out a survey instrument as well. A total of **251** dyadic interactions were captured, with the responses coming from 64 different salespeople and 251 different customers. All salespeople in the stores participated, as did 90% of the customers who were approached.

RELIABILITY:

An alpha of **.63** was reported for the scale and item-total correlations were all above .55.

VALIDITY:

A factor analysis indicated that the items loaded higher on this factor than any other.

ADMINISTRATION:

As implied above, the customer completed a self-administered survey form that included several measures. The authors computed scale scores by averaging numerical responses to the items. Higher scores on the scale suggest that salespersons perceive that the customers with whom they have just interacted were overly interested in themselves and not attentive to what the salesperson said whereas lower scores imply that they feelheir respective customers were interested in the product and what the salesperson had to say.

MAJOR FINDINGS:

The study examined the use of communication styles in dyadic sales situations and their effect on sales outcomes. The findings indicated that though the communication styles of the two parties to the transaction played a role in the outcome, it was the customer's orientation that had the greatest impact. With respect to **customer's self orientation**, it did not appear to have a significant impact of sales.

REFERENCES:

Bass, Bernard M. (1960), *Leadership, Psychology, and Organizational Behavior*. New York, N.Y.: Harper Brothers.

_____ (1977), *ORI-Manual for the Orientation Inventory*. Palo Alto, Calif.: Consulting Psychologists Press, Inc.

Williams, Kaylene C. and Rosann L. Spiro (1985), "Communication Style in the Salesperson-Customer Dyad," *JMR*, 12 (November), 434-442.

SCALE ITEMS: SELF-ORIENTATION OF CUSTOMER (SALESPERSON'S PERCEPTION)

Strongly Disagree	Disagree	Neutral	Agree	Strongly Agree
1	2	3	4	5

1. This customer seemed more interested in himself than in the product or what I had to say.
2. This customer was primarily interested in what he had to say and not in what I had to say.
3. This customer tried to dominate the conversation.
4. This customer tried to impress me with himself.

SCALE NAME: Selling Activity

SCALE DESCRIPTION:

A 12-item, seven-point Likert-like summated ratings scale measuring the frequency with which a person engages in sales activities such as calling on accounts, making presentations, overcoming objections, etc.

SCALE ORIGIN:

The scale is original to a study by Moncrief (1986). Several scales were developed for use in the study from a review of the literature and from personal interviews and focus groups with salespeople. A total of 121 selling- related activities were identified and included on the survey questionnaire.

SAMPLES:

Using stratified sampling, Moncrief sent survey forms to 800 firms representing 20 SIC codes (#20-#39). Fifty-one firms ultimately participated and sent copies of the question- naire to their salespeople. Of the total 2322 sales employees working for these firms, 1393 returned usable forms but the factor analysis was based on responses from **1291**.

RELIABILITY:

An alpha of **.82** is reported for the scale.

VALIDITY:

Though scale validity was not specifically addressed, a factor analysis of 121 items indi- cated that the items below all had loadings greater than .50 on the same factor and loadings less than .40 other factors. These findings provide some evidence of the convergent and discriminant validity of the scale.

ADMINISTRATION:

The scale was self-administered by respondents along with many other measures in a mail survey format. Higher scores on the scale indicate that respondents frequently engage in selling activities whereas lower scores suggest that they primarily perform activities other than those directly related to selling.

MAJOR FINDINGS:

The purpose of the study by Moncrief was to develop a comprehensive list of selling-related activities and the taxonomies created from them. A cluster analysis was performed of the salespeople in the sample and six clusters were found. A group called trade servicer, representing 18% of the sample, had the highest mean on the **selling activity** scale. This cluster had the highest mean of any of the sales groups on seven of 10 sales activity areas examined in the study and it had the second highest mean on the other three activity areas.

REFERENCE:

> Moncrief, William C., III (1986), "Selling Activity and Sales Position Taxonomies for Industrial Salesforces," *JMR*, 23 (August), 261-270.

SCALE ITEMS: SELLING ACTIVITY +

> Using the following scale, please indicate how frequently you engage in each of the activities listed below. If you do not perform the activity, please code your response as a zero.

Infrequently   ____ : ____ : ____ : ____ : ____ : ____ : ____   Frequently
                         1   2   3   4   5   6   7

1. Make a sales presentation
2. Prepare a sales presentation
3. Overcome objections
4. Call on potential accounts
5. Identify person in charge of decision making
6. Plan selling activities
7. Search out leads for prospects
8. Call on new accounts
9. Select products to take on call
10. Prepare presentation "aides"
11. Introduce new products
12. Help clients plan

+ The actual directions and items were not stated in the article, but are reconstructed here on the basis of information provided.

SCALE NAME: Selling Task Complexity (Industrial Selling)

SCAE DESCRIPTION:

A five-item, seven-point summated ratings scale measuring the proportion of purchase decisions encountered by a salesforce that are considered to be complex and are not made quickly. The seven anchors on the graphic scale ranged from 0% to 100%.

SCALE ORIGIN:

John and Weitz (1989) give no indication that this scale originated elsewhere than in their study.

SAMPLES:

John and Weitz collected data in a two-stage sampling procedure. Personalized requests were mailed to 750 sales managers or sales vice presidents of manufacturing firms with annual sales of at least $50 million. The 266 respondents were then sent a questionnaire and of that group **161** returned usable survey instruments. The sample appeared to be different from the population in some respects but very similar in others.

RELIABILITY:

An alpha of **.86** was reported for the scale. Item-total correlations ranged from .61 to .79.

VALIDITY:

No specific examination of scale validity was made.

ADMINISTRATION:

The scale was self-administered by respondents along with many other measures in a mail questionnaire format. Higher scores on the scale suggest that respondents believe their respective salesforces frequently encounter purchase decisions that are complex and slow to close.

MAJOR FINDINGS:

The purpose of the study by John and Weitz was to examine the role of salary in sales compensation plans by using a transaction cost analysis framework. The **complexity of the selling task** was one of the most significant variables in the study. It was the most significant predictor variable in models of salesperson replaceability, time for a salesperson to become familiar with a company's products and customers, the transaction asset specificity between a firm and its salespeople, and the difficulty of assessing salesperson performance.

REFERENCE:

John, George and Barton Weitz (1989), ''Salesforce Compensation: An Empirical Investigation of Factors Related to Use of Salary Versus Incentive Compensation,'' *JMR*, 26 (February), 1-14.

SCALE ITEMS: SELLING TASK COMPLEXITY (INDUSTRIAL SELLING)

The following statements describe circumstances which might exist when one of your salespeople is trying to make a sale. Please indicate how frequently the salesperson would face the situation described in the statement. This can be indicated by circling the number that most accurately indicates the percentage of sales situations that fit the statement. Each question is independent: your answers do not need to add to 100% or any other number. +

Percentage of Situations

0%	10%	30%	50%	70%	90%	100%

1. The purchase decision is made quite quickly. **(r)**
2. A number of people are involved in the purchase decision.
3. The customer needs a lot of information before making a purchase decision. **(r)**
4. The customer considers the purchase decision to be routine.
5. The purchase decision evolves over a long time period. **(r)**

+ The instructions were not included in the article, but are assumed to be something like this.

SCALE NAME: Specialization (Channel Relationship)

SCALE DESCRIPTION:

A two-item, five-point Likert-like summated ratings scale measuring the degree to which a channel member such as a retailer reports that its relationship with suppliers is characterized by decisions that are repetitive and similar over time.

SCALE ORIGIN:

Dwyer and Welsh indicated that items for their scale were adapted from the work of Spekman and Stern (1979), who in turn adapted their items from Duncan (1971).

SAMPLES:

Dwyer and Welsh mailed questionnaires to 7254 retailers in 10 industries whose addresses had been provided by a list broker. Envelopes were simply addressed to ''Manager'' in each case. After a second wave to 10% of the original sample, a total of **457** responses were used in the analysis. Because of such a low response rate, the authors provided rather detailed information about response rates and characteristics by industry.

RELIABILITY:

An alpha of .57 was reported.

VALIDITY:

The two items for this scale adapted from Spekman and Stern were part of a test using a LISREL restricted factor model made by Dwyer and Welsh. Apparently, the items composed an orthogonal factor with salient loadings.

ADMINISTRATION:

Respondents self-administered the scale along with many other measures. Higher scores on the scale suggest that respondents think the decision-making relationship they have with their suppliers is characterized by a lot of repetition whereas lower scores indicate that they feel decisions are rarely the same over time.

MAJOR FINDINGS:

Dwyer and Welsh investigated environmental effects on channel structure and processes in a political economy framework. Among their many findings was that **specialization** was not significantly related to the heterogeneity of the environment or the variability in the output sector.

COMMENTS:

The simple addition of a few appropriate items may raise the internal consistency of this measure.

REFERENCES:

Duncan, Robert Bannerman (1971), "The Effects of Perceived Environmental Uncertainty on Organizational Decision Unit Structure: A Cybernetic Model," unpublished doctoral dissertation, Yale University.

Dwyer, F. Robert and M. Ann Welsh (1985), "Environmental Relationships of the Internal Political Economy of Marketing Channels," *JMR*, 22 (November), 397-414.

Spekman, Robert E. and Louis W. Stern (1979), "Environmental Uncertainty and Buying Group Structure: An Empirical Investigation," *JM*, (Spring), 54-64.

SCALE ITEMS: SPECIALIZATION (CHANNEL RELATIONSHIP)

Think about the relationship you have with your supplier(s) of this line. There are probably a number of facets involved in marketing the line, e.g., display, mix of assortment, return, etc. Please use the scale below to describe the different aspects of decision making in that relationship.

Never	Seldom	Occasionally	Rather Often	Nearly All The Time
1————	——2————	——3————	——4————	——5

Thinking about your relationship with suppliers, would you say . . .
1. the merchandising decisions you make are on the same issues.
2. your responsibilities are repetitive in nature.

SCALE NAME: Study Quality Evaluation

SCALE DESCRIPTION:

> A three-item, seven-point Likert-like summated ratings scale measuring the degree to which a study is considered to provide evidence that will be strongly considered in making a marketing-related decision.

SCALE ORIGIN:

> The scale appears to be original to the study by Lee, Acito, and Day (1987). Two scales were used, with slight differences in wording for survey studies and depth-interview studies.

SAMPLES:

> Data were collected from **170** MBA students enrolled at a large state university. The sample was limited to those who had completed one course in the program and had taken at least one statistics course. A majority of the respondents had some business experience in their background. No significant differences were found between those with formal business experience and those without.

RELIABILITY:

> Alpha values of **.81** and **.83** were reported for the scale for measuring the quality of a depth-interview study and a survey study, respectively.

VALIDITY:

> Though scale validity was not specifically examined, some evidence of convergent and discriminant validity came from the factor analysis. For the four scales, each item was reported to have loaded on a single factor above .60 and items were grouped on the expected factors. Cross-loadings were less than .25.

ADMINISTRATION:

> The two versions of the scale were self-administered along with other measures as part of an experiment in a "laboratory" setting. Higher scores on the scale indicate that respondents strongly believe a study provides evidence of a quality level that justifies its use in shaping a commercial selection decision.

MAJOR FINDINGS:

> The purpose of the study by Lee and his coauthors was to determine how the perceived quality of marketing research is integrated with prior opinions in making decisions. When results of a depth-interview or survey study were consistent with prior opinions, the overall **evaluation of the quality** of that study was significantly higher.

REFERENCE:

> Lee, Hanjoon, Frank Acito, and Ralph L. Day (1987), "Evaluatioand Use of Marketing Research by Decision Makers: A Behavioral Simulation," *JMR*, 24 (May), 187-196.

SCALE ITEMS: STUDY QUALITY EVALUATION+

1. How convincing does the _____ study seem as evidence for proving that one commercial is better than the other?

Completely Convincing			So-So			Completely Unconvincing
(3)	(2)	(1)	(0)	(-1)	(-2)	(-3)

2. How well or poorly has the _____ study been conducted?

Very Well Done			So-So			Very Poorly Done
(3)	(2)	(1)	(0)	(-1)	(-2)	(-3)

3. Are the findings of the _____ study valid enough to be considered for your final decision?

Strongly Agree That It Is Valid			Undecided			Strongly Disagree That It Is Valid
(3)	(2)	(1)	(0)	(-1)	(-2)	(-3)

+ The blanks were filled with either "survey" or "depth-interview."

SCALE NAME: Supportive (Channel Relationship)

SCALE DESCRIPTION:

A three-item, five-point Likert-type summated ratings scale measuring the degree to which a channel member reports that the channel leader exhibits concern for member needs and well-being. In the study by Schul, Pride, and Little (1983), the scale specifically related to the channel relationships between franchisors and franchisees.

SCALE ORIGIN:

This scale and the study reported in the article by Schul and his coauthors (1983) came from the dissertation research by Schul (1980). He reported that a review of the literature and interviews with 50 franchisees helped to generate 19 items for measuring three types of leadership: participative, supportive, and directive. On the basis of results of a pilot study with data from 31 franchisees, the list was reduced to just nine items (three items per leadership type). Schul's is the only known use of the scale.

SAMPLES:

The main study involved an eight-page questionnaire that was mailed to 1052 franchised real estate brokers with six different franchise affiliations. After two waves of mailings, a total of **349** usable survey forms were received. There was no evidence of nonresponse bias.

RELIABILITY:

An alpha of **.92** was calculated for the scale.

VALIDITY:

Evidence of content validity came from the pretest interviews. With data from the main study, a factor analysis with oblique rotation was performed on the nine scale items representing the three leadership styles. The three items for each scale loaded together and had low loadings on the other factors. However, the interfactor correlations were rather high, particularly between the participative and supportive leadership factors (r = .523). In fact, in a subsequent study in which a varimax rotation was used, items for those two scales loaded on the same factor.

ADMINISTRATION:

The scale was self-administered by respondents along with many other measures in a mail survey format. Higher scores on the scale indicate that channel members report that their channel leaders exhibit sincere concern for member welfare.

MAJOR FINDINGS:

The purpose of the study by Schul and his coauthors was to investigate the influence of different channel leadership types on channel members' perceptions of intrachannel conflict. The data indicated that **supportive leadership** had a significant negative relationship to channel member perception of conflict.

COMMENTS:

The items composing this scale have also been used with several others to measure Channel Leadership (Considerate) (Schul 1987).

REFERENCES:

Schul, Patrick L. (1980), "An Empirical Investigation of the Conflict Behavior Process in Franchise Channels of Distribution," unpublished doctoral dissertation, Texas A&M University.

_____ (1987), "An Investigation of Path-Goal Leadership Theory and Its Impact on Intrachannel Conflict and Satisfaction," *JAMS*, 15 (Winter), 42-52.

_____, William M. Pride, and Taylor L. Little (1983), "The Impact of Channel Leadership Behavior on Intrachannel Conflict," *JM*, 47 (Summer), 21-34.

SCALE ITEMS: SUPPORTIVE (CHANNEL RELATIONSHIP)

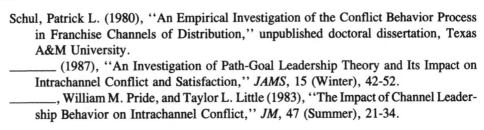

Strongly Disagree	Disagree	Neither	Agree	Strongly Agree
1	2	3	4	5

In my franchise agreement:
1. There is a definite lack of support, coaching and feedback and confidence. **(r)**
2. Once they've sold you the franchise, they forget all about you . . . except when your fees are due again. **(r)**
3. This franchise organization is highly interested in the welfare of its franchises.

SCALE NAME: Task Completion

SCALE DESCRIPTION:

A four-item, five-point Likert-like scale measuring the degree to which an employee is able to complete work that he/she starts. This scale was called Task Identity by Sims, Szilagyi, and Keller (1976) and Task Identification by Cummings, Jackson, and Ostrum (1989).

SCALE ORIGIN:

The scale was developed as part of the Job Characteristics Inventory by Sims and his coauthors though they indicated that they borrowed many items from previous work (Hackman and Lawler 1971). The inventory was tested on a sample of 192 male employees of a large manufacturing firm. The alpha for the task completion portion of the inventory was calculated to be .83. A variety of evidence was presented attesting to the scale's convergent and discriminant validity.

SAMPLES:

The analysis by Cummings and his coauthors was based on data from **201** product managers in firms that had annual sales in the range of $8 million to $35 billion.

RELIABILITY:

An alpha of **.804** was reported for the scale by Cummings.

VALIDITY:

No examination of scale validity was reported.

ADMINISTRATION:

The scale was self-administered along with many other measures in a mail survey format. Higher scores on the scale indicate that employees think they have great opportunity to finish jobs they begin whereas lower scores suggest that they feel they have little freedom to complete tasks. Cummings and his coauthors added each respondent's score on this scale with those on three other dimensions of the JCI to obtain an overall ''job scope'' score.

MAJOR FINDINGS:

The purpose of the study by Cummings and his coauthors was to investigate several aspects of organizational behavior and their impact on the job satisfaction and performance of product managers. **Task completion** was not examined *per se* but was incorporated into the ''job scope'' measure. Path analysis results indicated that the only variable to have a significant effect (negative) on job scope was centralization of decision making.

COMMENTS:

See also a modification of this scale used by Hunt and Chonko (1984).

REFERENCES:

Cummings, W. Theodore, Donald W. Jackson, and Lonnie L. Ostrom (1989), ''Examining Product Managers' Job Satisfaction and Performance Using Selected Organizational Behavior Variables,'' *JAMS*, 17 (Spring), 147-156.

Hackman, J. R. and E. E. Lawler, III (1971), ''Employee Reactions to Job Characteristics,'' *Journal of Applied Psychology*, Monograph 55, 259-268.

Hunt, Shelby D. and Lawrence B. Chonko (1984), ''Marketing and Machiavellianism,'' *JM*, 48 (Summer), 30-42.

Sims, Henry P., Jr., Andrew D. Szilagyi, Robert T. Keller (1976), ''The Measurement of Job Characteristics,'' *Academy of Management Journal*, 19 (June), 195-212.

SCALE ITEMS: TASK COMPLETION +

1. How often do you see projects or jobs through to completion?
2. The degree to which the work I'm involved with is handled from beginning to end by myself.
3. The opportunity to complete work I start.
4. The opportunity to do a job from the beginning to the end (i.e., the chance to do a whole job).

+ The following scale was used for the first item:

Very little		A moderate amount		Very much
1	2	3	4	5

The following scale was used for the last three items:

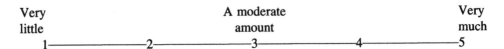

A minimum amount		A moderate amount		A maximum amount
1	2	3	4	5

SCALE NAME: Task-Orientation of Customer (Salesperson's Perception)

SCALE DESCRIPTION:

A five-item, five-point Likert-type summated ratings scale measuring the degree to which a salesperson perceived a customer to have been diligently attempting to complete a particular sales transaction. Williams and Spiro (1985) viewed this scale as measuring the task-oriented dimension of customer communication style that is goal directed and purposeful.

SCALE ORIGIN:

The items were developed from work performed by Bass (1960) on orientation motivation. On the basis of previous work by others, he suggested that members of groups are motivated to remain in the groups for different reasons. He developed measures of three motivations: the task orientation, the interaction orientation, and the self orientation (Bass 1977). Williams and Spiro adapted these measures for their studies in two ways: their measures were more specific to the sales context and were perceptions of others' behaviors, not self-perceptions.

SAMPLES:

Williams and Spiro collected data from all 13 sporting goods stores in a major southeastern U.S. city. Customers were approached just after leaving the stores. If they agreed to fill out a questionnaire, their respective salespeople were asked to fill out a survey instrument as well. A total of **251** dyadic interactions were captured, with the responses coming from 64 different salespeople and 251 different customers. All salespeople in the stores participated, as did 90% of the customers who were approached.

RELIABILITY:

An alpha of **.86** was reported for the scale by Williams and Spiro (1985) and item-total correlations were all above .70.

VALIDITY:

A factor analysis indicated that the items loaded higher on this factor than any other (Williams and Spiro 1985).

ADMINISTRATION:

As implied above, the customer completed a self-administered survey form that included several measures (Williams and Spiro (1985). The authors computed scale scores by averaging numerical responses to the items. Higher scores on the scale suggest that salespersons perceive the customers with whom they have just interacted were very interested in completing the sale whereas lower scores imply that they feel their respective customers were not interested, motivated, and/or persistent enough in completing the sale.

MAJOR FINDINGS:

Williams and Spiro's study examined the use of communication styles in dyadic sales situations and their effect on sales outcomes. The findings indicated that though the communication styles of the two parties in the transaction played a role in the outcome, the customer's orientation had the greatest impact. **Customer's task orientation** appeared to have the greatest effect on sales of all salesperson and customer orientations examined.

REFERENCES:

Bass, Bernard M. (1960), *Leadership, Psychology, and Organizational Behavior.* New York, N.Y.: Harper Brothers.

_____ (1977), *ORI-Manual for the Orientation Inventory.* Palo Alto, Calif.: Consulting Psychologists Press, Inc.

Williams, Kaylene C. and Rosann L. Spiro (1985), "Communication Style in the Salesperson-Customer Dyad," *JMR*, 12 (November), 434-442.

SCALE ITEMS: TASK-ORIENTATION OF CUSTOMER (SALESPERSON'S PERCEPTION)

Strongly Disagree	Disagree	Neutral	Agree	Strongly Agree
1	2	3	4	5

1. This customer tried hard to complete the shopping task.
2. This customer wanted to finish the shopping task.
3. This customer's primary concern was to make the purchase.
4. This customer's main concern was to finish his shopping.
5. This customer wanted to complete his shopping as effectively as possible.

SCALE NAME: Task Significance/Autonomy

SCALE DESCRIPTION:

A six-item, five-point summated ratings scale measuring the degree to which an employee perceives that his/her job has an impact on the lives and well-being of others. This version of the scale also measures the extent of autonomy an employee perceives having in a job. Teas (1981) measured one item on a seven-point scale (see Scale Items section).

SCALE ORIGIN:

The scale is composed of items from three scales used by Hackman and Oldham (1975). Three of the items came from their task significance scale, two from their autonomy scale, and one from their task variety scale.

SAMPLES:

The data used by Teas were collected from **171** salespeople in group interviews during sales meetings. The salespeople represented 74% of the indstrial salesforces of three midwestern companies. The typical salesperson was 36 years of age and had spent 6.5 years with his company.

RELIABILITY:

An alpha of **.856** was reported for the scale.

VALIDITY:

Teas performed a factor analysis of the items composing many of the scales used in his study. Though these six items were not expected to measure the same construct, they were found to have loadings greater than .40 on the same factor.

ADMINISTRATION:

The scale was self-administered along with many other measures. Higher scores on this scale indicate that salespeople believe that their jobs are important in terms of their impact on others and that they have a high amount of independence in their work.

MAJOR FINDINGS:

Teas investigated the impact of several personality characteristics and job-related perceptions on work motivation. The results indicated that though **task significance/autonomy** was not a significant predictor of job expectancies, it was a significant predictor of several job instrumentalities.

COMMENTS:

The factor analysis of 38 items in the Teas study showed these items loading together, but the set has dubious face validity, especially because it does not agree with the considerable work performed by Hackman and Oldham. Though the set of items appears to have strong reliability, it is not clear what the scale truly measures.

REFERENCES:

Hackman, J. Richard and Greg R. Oldham (1974), *The Job Diagnostic Survey: An Instrument for the Diagnosis of Jobs and the Evaluation of Job Redesign Projects*, Technical Report #4, Department of Administrative Sciences, Yale University.

Teas, R. Kenneth (1981), "An Empirical Test of Models of Salespersons' Job Expectancy and Instrumentality Perceptions," *JMR*, 18 (May), 209-226.

SCALE ITEMS: TASK SIGNIFICANCE/AUTONOMY +

```
Very                                                      Very
False                                                     True
  1————————2————————3————————4————————5
```

Significance:
1. My job is one where a lot of other people can be affected by how well my work gets done.
2. My job itself is not very significant or important in the broader scheme of things. (r)
3. In general, how significant or important is your job? That is, are the results of your work likely to significantly affect the lives or well being of other people?

```
A minimum                                            A maximum
 amount                                                amount
  1————————2————————3————————4————————5————————6————————7
```

Autonomy:
4. My job denies me any chance to use personal initiative or discretion in carrying out the work. (r)
5. My job gives considerable opportunity for independence and freedom in my work.

Variety:
6. My job is simple and repetitive. (r)

+ All of the items were responded to using a five-point scale except for item three, which used a seven-point scale.

SCALE NAME: Time Pressure (Buying Center Members)

SCALE DESCRIPTION:

A three-item, five-point Likert-like summated ratings scale measuring the degree to which the members of a buying center are perceived by a member to have been rushed to make a particular decision.

SCALE ORIGIN:

The measure was developed by Kohli (1989) along with other aspects of the survey instrument by reviewing previous measures and pretesting it in 14 personal interviews.

SAMPLES:

A survey instrument was mailed to 500 members of the National Association of Purchasing Management. Usable responses were received from **251** members. No response bias was evident for theoretical variables germane to the study. Respondents provided information about purchases of products in a range of $1000 to $150 million, with an average purchase value of $3.5 million.

RELIABILITY:

An alpha of **.76** was reported for this scale.

VALIDITY:

Though some assessment of validity was made for other scales used in the study, no evaluation of this scale's validity was discussed.

ADMINISTRATION:

The scale was self-administered by respondents along with many other scales in a mail survey format. Higher scores on the scale indicate that the buying center members are perceived by one of the center's members to have been in a rush to make a particular purchase decision.

MAJOR FINDINGS:

The purpose of the study by Kohli was to examine some factors that affect a person's influence in a buying center. When **time pressure** was high among buying center members, reinforcement power had a significant positive effect on manifest influence whereas referent power's effect was unexpectedly negative. Expert power had significant effects on manifest influence when **time pressure** was both high and low, but had the greater effect in the latter condition.

REFERENCE:

Kohli, Ajay (1989), ''Determinants of Influence in Organizational Buying: A Contingency Approach,'' *JM*, 53 (July), 50-65.

SCALE ITEMS: TIME PRESSURE (BUYING CENTER MEMBERS) +

None   ____ : ____ : ____ : ____ : ____   All
            1   2   3   4   5

1. They felt pressured to reach a decision quickly.
2. They felt the decision-making process was rushed.
3. They felt they had ample time to consider the various options carefully. **(r)**

+ Though the directions were not provided in the article, the discussion indicated that respondents were instructed to think of a specific joint purchase decision when answering the questions.

SCALE NAME: Trade Show Performance (Nonselling)

SCALE DESCRIPTION:

A four-item, seven-point Likert-like summated scale measuring the degree to which a person thinks a company performs well at trade shows on certain non-sales-related aspects.

SCALE ORIGIN:

Kerin and Cron (1987) developed the scale after conducting 10 in-depth interviews with executives responsible for their companies' trade show activities.

SAMPLES:

Kerin and Cron surveyed 274 firms drawn randomly from the Trade Show Bureau list. Questionnaires were sent to both the trade show exhibit manager and the senior marketing executive in each company. The authors analyzed the data from 121 completed and matched sets of surveys. However, the scale discussed here was administered just to the marketing executives. The responding firms represented 15 different industries, had average annual sales of $94.7 million, and devoted an average of 19% of their advertising/sales promotion budgets to trade shows.

RELIABILITY:

An alpha of .65 was reported for the scale.

VALIDITY:

No specific examination of scale validity was reported for the scale, but a factor analysis of eight aspects of trade show performance showed that the three items for this scale had loadings greater than .60 on this factor and less than .25 on the other factor.

ADMINISTRATION:

The scale was self-administered by respondents along with other measures in a mail survey format. Higher scores on the scale indicate that respondents think their companies perform very well on non-sales-related aspects of trade show performance whereas lower scores suggest that they believe their firms have very poor nonselling performance at trade shows.

MAJOR FINDINGS:

The purpose of the study by Kerin and Cron was to examine the selling and nonselling roles of trade shows. The results of a t-test indicated that marketing executives thought their companies performed significantly better on the **nonselling** dimension than on the selling dimension of trade shows. However, a cluster anlaysis indicated that they tended to view their companies as either performing well on both dimensions or poorly on both.

COMMENTS:

It is not clear from the information provided in the article whether the items below are as they were presented in the survey instrument or whether they were merely abbreviated phrases.

REFERENCE:

Kerin, Roger A. and William L. Cron (1987), "Assessing Trade Show Functions and Performance: An Exploratory Study," *JM*, 51 (July), 87-94.

SCALE ITEMS: TRADE SHOW PERFORMANCE (NONSELLING)

Very Poor ___ : ___ : ___ : ___ : ___ : ___ : ___ Very Good
         1   2   3   4   5   6   7

1. Identifying new prospects
2. Servicing current customers
3. Enhancing corporate image
4. Gathering competitive information

SCALE NAME: Trade Show Performance (Selling)

SCALE DESCRIPTION:

A three-item, seven-point Likert-like summated scale measuring the degree to which a person thinks a company performs well at trade shows on certain product- and sales-related activities.

SCALE ORIGIN:

Kerin and Cron (1987) developed the scale after conducting 10 in-depth interviews with executives responsible for their companies' trade shows activities.

SAMPLES:

Kerin and Cron surveyed 274 firms drawn randomly from the Trade Show Bureau list. Questionnaires were sent to both the trade show exhibit manager and the senior marketing executive in each company. The authors analyzed the data from 121 completed and matched sets of surveys. However, the scale discussed here was administered just to the marketing executives. The responding firms represented 15 different industries, had average annual sales of $94.7 million, and devoted an average of 19% of their advertising/sales promotion budgets for trade shows.

RELIABILITY:

An alpha of .74 was reported for the scale.

VALIDITY:

No specific examination of scale validity was reported for the scale, but a factor analysis of eight aspects of trade show performance showed that the three items for this scale had loadings greater than .60 on this factor and less than .20 on the other factor.

ADMINISTRATION:

The scale was self-administered by respondents along with other measures in a mail survey format. Higher scores on the scale indicate that respondents think their companies perform very well on sales-related aspects of trade show performance whereas lower scores suggest that they believe their firms have very poor sales performance at trade shows.

MAJOR FINDINGS:

The purpose of the study by Kerin and Cron was to examine the selling and nonselling roles of trade shows. The results of a t-test indicated that marketing executives thought their companies performed significantly better on the nonselling dimension than on the **selling** dimension of trade shows. However, a cluster analysis indicated that they tended to view their companies as either performing well on both dimensions or poorly on both.

COMMENTS:

It is not clear from the information provided in the article whether the items below are as they were presented in the survey instrument or whether they were merely abbreviated phrases.

REFERENCE:

Kerin, Roger A. and William L. Cron (1987), "Assessing Trade Show Functions and Performance: An Exploratory Study," *JM*, 51 (July), 87-94.

SCALE ITEMS: TRADE SHOW PERFORMANCE (SELLING)

Very Poor ____ : ____ : ____ : ____ : ____ : ____ : ____ Very Good
              1   2   3   4   5   6   7

1. Introducing new products
2. Selling at the show
3. New product testing

SCALE NAME: Transaction Asset Specificity (Agency With Accounts)

SCALE DESCRIPTION:

A seven-item, Likert-type summated ratings scale measuring the degree to which an agency has put a lot of time and effort into enhancing its relationship with its accounts for the principal's products. It was referred to as Offsetting Investments by Heide and John (1988).

SCALE ORIGIN:

Some of the items in the scale may have been adapted from the work of Anderson (1985) and John and Weitz (1989), but others were apparently original to the study by Heide and John. This version of the scale is only known to have been used by Heide and John and the information below relates to their study.

SAMPLES:

A systematic sample of 400 agencies was made for each of two industries from a manufacturers' agent directory. The survey instrument was mailed to the owner/manager listed in the directory. A total of **199** usable responses were received and nonresponse bias did not appear to be a problem.

RELIABILITY:

An alpha of .**77** was reported for the scale.

VALIDITY:

Evidence supporting the discriminant validity of the scale is presented.

ADMINISTRATION:

The scale was self-administered along with many other measures in a mail survey format. Higher scores on the scale indicate that agencies have made great investments in the relationships with their accounts.

MAJOR FINDINGS:

Heide and John extended the basic transaction cost analysis model by incorporating aspects of dependence theory. Offsetting investments were examined to see whether they were used by small channel members as a means of protecting assets at risk in the agency-principal dyad. Among the many findings was that greater agency-principal investment was positively related to offsetting agency-account investment; i.e., the **transaction asset specificity** between the agency and its customers was higher.

REFERENCES:

Anderson, Erin (1985), "The Salesperson as Outside Agent or Employee: A Transaction Cost Analysis," *Marketing Science*, 4 (Summer), 234-254.

Heide, Jan B. and George John (1988), ''The Role of Dependence Balancing in Safe-guarding Transaction-Specific Assets in Conventional Channels,'' *JM*, 52 (January), 20-35.

John, George and Barton Weitz (1989), ''Salesforce Compensation: An Empirical Investigation of Factors Related to Use of Salary Versus Incentive Compensation,'' *JMR*, 26 (February), 1-14.

SCALE ITEMS: TRANSACTION ASSET SPECIFICITY (AGENCY WITH ACCOUNTS) +

1. We spend a lot of time with our accounts for this principal's product line to learn to be effective.
2. Our accounts for this principal's product lines don't really care if they buy from us or from other agents. **(r)**
3. We don't just sell products, we build up a relationship with our accounts for this product line.
4. The personal relationships between our salespeople and our accounts for this principal's product lines have a big effect on sales.
5. Our accounts for this product line have a lot of unusual needs which can be met only if you have dealt with them for some time.
6. To be successful with this product line, the most important task is to be responsive to our accounts' needs.
7. Often we try to build more value into this product line by providing special services to our key accounts.

+ The number of points on the response scale and their verbal anchors were not provided in the article (Heide and John 1988), but the scale is likely to have been of the five- or seven-point agree-disagree type.

SCALE NAME: Transaction Asset Specificity (Agency With Principal)

SCALE DESCRIPTION:

A four-item, Likert-type summated ratings scale measuring the degree to which an agency has invested in specific assets that could enhance its relationship with the principal.

SCALE ORIGIN:

Some of the items in the scale were taken from the work of Anderson (1985) and John and Weitz (1989), others were original to the study by Heide and John (1988). This version of the scale is only known to have been used by Heide and John and the information below relates to their study.

SAMPLES:

A systematic sample of 400 agencies was made for each of two industries from a manufacturers' agent directory. The survey instrument was mailed to the owner/manager listed in the directory. A total of **199** usable responses were received and nonresponse bias did not appear to be a problem.

RELIABILITY:

An alpha of .**70** was reported for the scale.

VALIDITY:

Evidence supporting the convergent and discriminant validity of the scale is presented.

ADMINISTRATION:

The scale was self-administered along with many other measures in a mail survey format. Higher scores on the scale indicate that agencies have made great investments in the relationships with their principals.

MAJOR FINDINGS:

Heide and John extended the basic transaction cost analysis model by incorporating aspects of dependence theory. Offsetting investments were examined to see whether they were used by small channel members as a means of protecting assets at risk in the agency-principal dyad. Among the many findings was that agencies with high **transaction asset specificity** attempted to bond themselves more closely to their customers to protect those assets.

REFERENCES:

Anderson, Erin (1985), "The Salesperson as Outside Agent or Employee: A Transaction Cost Analysis," *Marketing Science*, 4 (Summer), 234-254.
Heide, Jan B. and George John (1988), "The Role of Dependence Balancing in in Safe-

guarding Transaction-Specific Assets in Conventional Channels,'' *JM*, 52 (January), 20-35.

John, George and Barton Weitz (1989), ''Salesforce Compensation: An Empirical Investigation of Factors Related to Use of Salary Versus Incentive Compensation,'' *JMR*, 26 (February), 1-14.

SCALE ITEMS: TRANSACTION ASSET SPECIFICITY (AGENCY WITH PRINCIPAL) +

1. It has taken us a lot of time and effort to learn the ins and outs of this principal's organization that we need to know to be effective.
2. Our salespeople have spent a lot of time and effort learning the special selling techniques used by this principal.
3. A lot of the tasks we perform for this principal require close coordination with their people.
4. Our agency has spent a lot of time and effort to develop the sales territory for this principal's lines.

+ The number of points on the response scale and their verbal anchors were not provided in the article (Heide and John 1988), but the scale is likely to have been of the five- or seven-point agree-disagree type.

SCALE NAME: Transaction Asset Specificity (Firm With Salesperson)

SCALE DESCRIPTION:

A seven-item summated ratings scale measuring the degree to which it is difficult for a new salesperson to learn the unique operations and procedures of a company. Four items were semantic differentials and the other three were Likert-type statements.

SCALE ORIGIN:

Six of the items were taken from or similar to items in a scale reported by Anderson (1984, 1985) called Transaction-Specific Assets: Company Nature. It had 10 items and was calculated to have an alpha of .78. The sample used was composed of 159 district sales managers in several companies.

SAMPLES:

John and Weitz (1989) collected data in a two-stage sampling procedure. Personalized requests were mailed to 750 sales managers or sales vice presidents of manufacturing firms with annual sales of at least $50 million. The 266 respondents were then sent a questionnaire and **161** returned usable survey instruments. The sample appeared to be different from the population in some respects but very similar in others.

RELIABILITY:

An alpha of **.71** was reported for the scale by John and Weitz. Item-total correlations ranged from .23 to .58.

VALIDITY:

No specific examination of scale validity was made by John and Weitz.

ADMINISTRATION:

The scale was self-administered by respondents along with many other measures in a mail questionnaire format. Higher scores on the scale suggest that respondents believe their respective company procedures are difficult for new salespeople to learn whereas lower scores indicate that they think new salespeople could learn their systems and be effective soon after being hired.

MAJOR FINDINGS:

The purpose of the study by John and Weitz was to examine the role of salary in sales compensation plans by using a transaction cost analysis framework. **Transaction asset specificity** was found to have its most significant correlation (positive) with environmental uncertainty.

REFERENCES:

Anderson, Erin (1984), *The Salesperson as Outside Agent or Employee: A Transaction Cost Analysis*. Cambridge, Mass.: Marketing Science Institute, Report No. 84-107.

——— (1985), "The Salesperson as Outside Agent or Employee: A Transaction Cost Analysis," *Marketing Science*, 4 (Summer), 234-254.

John, George and Barton Weitz (1989), "Salesforce Compensation: An Empirical Investigation of Factors Related to Use of Salary Versus Incentive Compensation," *JMR*, 26 (February), 1-14.

SCALE ITEMS: TRANSACTION ASSET SPECIFICITY (FIRM WITH SALESPERSON)

Company procedures compared to other companies are:

1. Simple	___ : ___ : ___ : ___ : ___		Complex
	1　　2　　3　　4　　5		
2. Fast	___ : ___ : ___ : ___ : ___		Slow
	1　　2　　3　　4　　5		
3. Standardized	___ : ___ : ___ : ___ : ___		Unstandardized
	1　　2　　3　　4　　5		
4. Informal	___ : ___ : ___ : ___ : ___		Bureaucratic (r)
	1　　2　　3　　4　　5		

Use the following scale to record responses to the next three items:

Strongly Disagree	Disagree	Slightly Disagree	Neutral	Slightly Agree	Agree	Strongly Agree
1	2	3	4	5	6	7

5. It's hard for a new salesperson in this company to get something done for an account (i.e., expediting shipment, handling claims, etc.)

6. In our company, it helps tremendously if a salesperson has been with us for a while; to know who to see to get something done.

7. It takes time for a newcomer to our firm to learn all the ins and outs of our company that a salesperson needs to know to be effective.

SCALE NAME Transaction Asset Specificity (Generalized)

SCALE DESCRIPTION:

A six-item, seven-point Likert-type summated ratings scale measuring the degree to which a person reports that a product requires special knowledge, experience, and/or facilities to market. As noted below, the persons responding to the scale in the Klein (1989) study were exporters.

SCALE ORIGIN:

Klein reported that the items in his scale were adapted from among the many items composing the seven "transaction specificity of assets" scales constructed by Anderson (1985).

SAMPLES:

A mail survey of persons whose names were taken from a Canadian directory of exporters yielded **477** responses with some usable data. Only the **338** fully completely surveys were the basis for testing the model in the study. Evaluation of the constructs was based on all cases for which data were available.

RELIABILITY:

An alpha of **.65** was calculated for the scale by Klein (personal correspondence). As evidence of the scale's reliability, the author pointed out that the items composed a single factor that explained 37% of the variance.

VALIDITY:

No specific analysis of this scale's validity was reported, though the results of a factor analysis provide some evidence of the items' convergent and discriminant validity.

ADMINISTRATION:

The scale was self-administered as part of larger mail survey questionnaire. Higher scores on the scale indicate that respondents report that their product lines require a great amount of experience, knowledge, and/or facilities to market.

MAJOR FINDINGS:

The purpose of the study by Klein was to use a model based on transaction cost analysis to explain vertical control decisions. A regression analysis provided support for the model. The effects of all independent variables were significant and as hypothesized. Degree of vertical control was positively related to channel volume, transaction frequency, **asset specificity**, and complexity of the environment. It was negatively related to the rate at which changes occur in the environment.

REFERENCES:

Anderson, Erin (1985), "The Salesperson as Outside Agent or Employee: A Transaction Cost Analysis," *Marketing Science*, 4 (Summer), 234-254.

Klein, Saul (1989), "A Transaction Cost Explanation of Vertical Control in International Markets," *JAMS*, 17 (Summer), 253-260.

SCALE ITEMS: TRANSACTION ASSET SPECIFICITY (GENERALIZED)

Strongly Disagree	Disagree	Slightly Disagree	Neutral	Slightly Agree	Agree	Strongly Agree
1	2	3	4	5	6	7

1. It is difficult for an outsider to learn our ways of doing things.
2. To be effective, a salesperson has to take a lot of time to get to know the customers.
3. It takes a long time for a salesperson to learn about this product thoroughly.
4. A salesperson's inside information of our procedures would be very helpful to our competitors.
5. Specialized facilities are needed to market this product.
6. A large investment in equipment and facilities is needed to market this product.

SCALE NAME: Travel Activity (Salesperson)

SCALE DESCRIPTION:

A two-item, seven-point Likert-like summated ratings scale measuring the frequency with which a person engages in sales activities that require travel out of town and spending nights on the road away from home.

SCALE ORIGIN:

The scale is original to a study by Moncrief (1986). Several scales were developed for use in the study from a review of the literature and from personal interviews and focus groups with salespeople. A total of 121 selling-related activities were identified and included on the survey questionnaire.

SAMPLES:

Using stratified sampling, Moncrief sent survey forms to 800 firms representing 20 SIC codes (#20-#39). Fifty-one firms ultimately participated and sent copies of the question-naire to their salespeople. Of the total 2322 sales employees working for these firms, 1393 returned usable forms but the factor analysis was based on responses from **1291**.

RELIABILITY:

An alpha of **.74** is reported for the scale.

VALIDITY:

Though scale validity was not specifically addressed, a factor analysis of 121 items indicated that the items below all had loadings greater than .50 on the same factor and loadings less than .40 other factors. These findings provide some evidence of the convergent and discriminant validity of the scale.

ADMINISTRATION:

The scale was self-administered by respondents along with many other measures in a mail survey format. Higher scores on the scale indicate that respondents frequently travel out of town over night whereas lower scores suggest that they primarily perform activities that enable them to spend nights at home.

MAJOR FINDINGS:

The purpose of the study by Moncrief was to develop a comprehensive list of selling-related activities and the taxonomies created from them. A cluster analysis was performed of the salespeople in the sample and six clusters were found. A group called missionary salesper-son, representing 29% of the sample, had the highest mean on the **travel activity** scale. This cluster ranked below most of the other sales groups on all of the other sales activity areas examined in the study, particularly working with orders and servicing products.

REFERENCE:

> Moncrief, William C., III (1986), ''Selling Activity and Sales Position Taxonomies for Industrial Salesforces,'' *JMR*, 23 (August), 261-270.

SCALE ITEMS: TRAVEL ACTIVITY (SALESPERSON) +

> Using the following scale, please indicate how frequently you engage in each of the activities listed below. If you do not perform the activity, please code your response as a zero.

Infrequently   ____ : ____ : ____ : ____ : ____ : ____ : ____   Frequently

         1   2   3   4   5   6   7

1. Spend night on the road
2. Travel out of town

+ The actual directions and items were not stated in the article, but are reconstructed here on the basis of information provided.

SCALE NAME: Trust (Dealer With Manufactuer)

SCALE DESCRIPTION:

A four-item, five-point Likert-type summated ratings scale measuring the degree to which a retailer/dealer reports that it can count on and has faith in a manufacturer with which it does business.

SCALE ORIGIN:

The items used by Dwyer and Oh (1987) are a modified subset reportedly taken from an 11-item measure used by Sullivan et al. (1981), who in turn reported using a modified subset of items from a scale by Rotter (1967).

SAMPLES:

Dwyer and Oh gathered data from car dealers in 10 different SMSAs: five areas with high growth characteristics and five markets with low growth characteristics. Ultimately, **167** usable responses were received, which represented a 69% response rate.

RELIABILITY:

An alpha of **.79** was reported by Dwyer and Oh for their four-item version of the scale, which was ultimately used in the data analysis.

VALIDITY:

The scale was checked for face validity by four dealers as well as four faculty colleagues. Data from a pretest were used to check for item convergence in a restricted one-factor model. In addition, item correlations and residual analysis were used to check for convergence and consistency. Several items were deleted to maintain a unidimensional structure.

ADMINISTRATION:

Respondents self-administered the scale along with many other measures. Higher scores on the scale suggest that respondents think the relationship they have with their manufacturers is characterized by a great amount of trust whereas lower scores imply that they are cautious and suspicious in dealings with their manufacturers.

MAJOR FINDINGS:

Dwyer and Oh used LISREL to analyze the effects of resource availability on constraints and opportunities in the car dealers' environment. Formalization and participation decision-making characteristics had significant positive impacts, and centralization had a negative impact, on quality of the relationship with the manufacturer, of which **trust** was one component.

REFERENCES:

Dwyer, F. Robert and Sejo Oh (1987), "Output Sector Munificence Effects on the Internal Political Economy of Marketing Channels," *JMR*, 24 (November), 347-358.

Rotter, J. (1967), "A New Scale for the Measurement of Interpersonal Trust," *Journal of Personality*, 35 (December), 651-665.

Sullivan, Jeremiah, Richard B. Peterson, Naoki Kameda, and Justin Shimada (1981), "The Relationship Between Conflict Resolution Approaches and Trust—A Cross Cultural Study," *Academy of Management Journal*, 24 (December), 803-815.

SCALE ITEMS: TRUST (DEALER WITH MANUFACTURER)

The statements below assess the quality of your relationship with the manufacturer. Based upon your experience, what do you expect will characterize your dealings with the manufacturer in the coming year?

Strongly Agree	Agree	Neutral	Disagree	Strongly Disagree
5	4	3	2	1

1. I can count on the manufacturer to be *sincere*.
2. I will have to be *cautious* in my dealings with the manufacturer. **(r)**
3. I will be *suspicious* of the manufacturer's recommendations. **(r)**
4. The manufacturer and I will work together as *equals* when it comes to building business in this market.

SCALE NAME: Trust (Retailer With Wholesaler)

SCALE DESCRIPTION:

A four-item, eight-point Likert-type summated ratings scale measuring a retailer's confidence that its dyadic relationship with a specific wholesaler is characterized by adherence to agreed-upon decisions. It was referred to by John and Reve (1982) as Norms of Exchange.

SCALE ORIGIN:

Though not specified in the article by John and Reve, it is apparent that their data came from the latter's dissertation (Reve 1980). His initial scale had nine items and the final version had four. As different alpha values were reported for the scales and the items used by John and Reve were not reported, it is not known what else is different about the scales.

SAMPLES:

The data analyzed by John and Reve came from the dissertation research by Reve. Initially, 753 wholesalers in Norway were askdentify their three largest retail customers. One retailer was selected at random from each of those suggested by the 238 responding wholesalers. Those retailers were contacted and 140 provided usable responses. Finally, the 140 wholesalers identified by the retailers were recontacted for further information. Data were ultimately collected from **99** retailer/wholesaler dyads.

RELIABILITY:

The alpha for the version of the scale used by John and Reve was reported to be .**71**. Items with low item-total correlations were said to have been deleted.

VALIDITY:

John and Reve eliminated items with low loadings on a factor. Further, they used the multitrait, multimethod approach as well as a structural equations model to assess convergent and discriminant validity. These methods indicated poor convergent and discriminant validity.

ADMINISTRATION:

The scale was self-administered by respondents along with many other measures in a mail survey format. High scores on the scale indicate that retailers report a great amount of mutual trust between themselves and specified wholesalers about adherence to agreements and decisions.

MAJOR FINDINGS:

The purpose of the study by John and Reve was to examine the validity of several measures of channel relationships with information from wholesaler/retailer dyads. The authors concluded that the ''sentiments'' variables, including **trust,** did not show adequate convergent or discriminant validity. For example, the correlation between the retailers' and wholesalers' perceptions of the amount of **trust** in their dyadic relationships was only .166. Given this finding, the authors wondered if it was not possible that "real" differences existed between dyadic members in their perceptions of this variable.

COMMENTS:

The scale was administered in Norwegian so it is not known how its psychometric properties might be different if it were used in English as shown below. Further, the scale's current psychometric quality is so low that significant modifications are necessary before it is used further, particularly in English.

REFERENCES:

John, George and Torger Reve (1982), "The Reliability and Validity of Key Informant Data From Dyadic Relationships in Marketing Channels," *JMR*, 19 (November), 517-524.

Reve, Torger (1980), "Interorganizational Relations in Distribution Channels: An Empirical Study of Norwegian Distribution Channel Dyads," unpublished doctoral dissertation, Northwestern University.

SCALE ITEMS: TRUST (RETAILER WITH WHOLESALER)

Not relevant = 0
Very strongly disagree = 1
Strongly disagree = 2
Disagree = 3
Neither agree nor disagree = 4
Agree = 5
Strongly agree = 6
Very strongly agree = 7

1. Informal agreements between the supplier and our firm are as good as written contracts.
2. When an agreement is made, we can always rely that the supplier fulfills all the requirements.
3. In our relationship with this supplier there have never been instances where we have had the feeling of being deceived.
4. We have the feeling that the supplier sometimes hides important information from us. **(r)**

SCALE NAME: Trust (Wholesaler With Retailer)

SCALE DESCRIPTION:

A six-item, eight-point Likert-type summated ratings scale measuring a wholesaler's confidence that its dyadic relationship with a specific retailer is characterized by adherence to agreed upon decisions. It was referred to by John and Reve (1982) as Norms of Exchange.

SCALE ORIGIN:

Though not specified in the article by John and Reve, it is apparent that their data came from the latter's dissertation (Reve 1980). His initial scale had nine items. The final version had six items and an alpha of .794. The scale used by John and Reve had two items less than the final version reported by Reve. As the items used by the former were not reported, it is not known which items below were eliminated.

SAMPLES:

The data analyzed by John and Reve came from the dissertation research by Reve. Initially, 753 wholesalers in Norway were asked to identify their three largest retail customers. One retailer was selected at random from each of those suggested by the 238 responding wholesalers. Those retailers were contacted and 140 provided usable responses. Finally, the 140 wholesalers identified by the retailers were recontacted for further information. Data were ultimately collected from **99** retailer/wholesaler dyads.

RELIABILITY:

The alpha for the version of the scale used by John and Reve was reported to be .**78**. Items with low item-total correlations were said to have been deleted.

VALIDITY:

John and Reve eliminated items with low loadings on a factor. Further, they used the multitrait, multimethod approach as well as a structural equations model to assess convergent and discriminant validity. These methods indicated poor convergent and discriminant validity.

ADMINISTRATION:

The scale was self-administered by respondents along with many other measures in a mail survey format. High scores on the scale indicate that wholesalers report a great amount of mutual trust between themselves and specified retailers about adherence to agreements and decisions.

MAJOR FINDINGS:

The purpose of the study by John and Reve was to examine the validity of several measures of channel relationships with information from wholesaler/retailer dyads. The authors concluded that the "sentiments" variables, including **trust,** did not show adequate convergent or discriminant validity. For example, the correlation between the retailers' and wholesalers' perceptions of the amount of **trust** in their dyadic relationships was only .166. Given this finding, the authors wondered if it was not possible that "real" differences existed between dyadic members in their perceptions of this variable.

COMMENTS:

The scale was administered in Norwegian so it is not known how its psychometric properties might be different if it were used in English as shown below. Further, the scale's current psychometric quality is so low that significant modifications are necessary before it is used further, particularly in English.

REFERENCES:

John, George and Torger Reve (1982), "The Reliability and Validity of Key Informant Data From Dyadic Relationships in Marketing Channels," *JMR*, 19 (November), 517-524.

Reve, Torger (1980), "Interorganizational Relations in Distribution Channels: An Empirical Study of Norwegian Distribution Channel Dyads," unpublished doctoral dissertation, Northwestern University.

SCALE ITEMS: TRUST (WHOLESALER WITH RETAILER)+

Not relevant = 0
Very strongly disagree = 1
Strongly disagree = 2
Disagree = 3
Neither agree nor disagree = 4
Agree = 5
Strongly agree = 6
Very strongly agree = 7

1. Informal agreements between the retailer and our firm are as good as written contracts.
2. When an agreement is made, we can always rely that the retailer fulfills all the requirements.
3. In our relationship with this retailer there have never been instances where we have had the feeling of being deceived.
4. Bargaining is necessary in order to obtain orders from this retailer. **(r)**
5. We have the feeling that the retailer sometimes hides important information from us. **(r)**
6. The building of reciprocal confidence is a key element in our relationship with the retailer.

+ The scale reported by John and Reve (1982) apparently used only four of these items. According to the information provided by Reve (1980, p. 184), items 4 and 6 had much smaller factor loadings than the rest and appear to be good candidates for elimination.

SCALE NAME: Upward-Influencing Supervisory Behavior

SCALE DESCRIPTION:

A five-item, seven-point Likert-like summated ratings scale measuring the degree to which an employee perceives that his/her supervisor has good relations with and influence on others who are higher in the organization's hierarchy.

SCALE ORIGIN:

Though the items for this scale were apparently not original to Kohli (1985), he appears to have been the first to publish them. The items themselves are taken from a scale developed by Ralph M. Stogdill, who passed them on to Fulk and Wendler (1982) in personal correspondence. The latter did not report the items themselves but used them in their study.

SAMPLES:

The analysis by Kohli was based on data from **114** salespeople. The sample was obtained from three companies manufacturing and selling industrial products. An overall response rate of 89.8% was reported.

RELIABILITY:

An alpha of **.90** was reported for the scale.

VALIDITY:

Though the specific results were not reported for this scale by Kohli, he implied that a factor analysis of this and other scales was used to eliminate items with weak loadings on their hypothesized factors.

ADMINISTRATION:

The scale was self-administered along with many other measures in an unspecified context. Higher scores on this scale indicate that respondents view their supervisors as having a very good relationship with upper management whereas lower scores suggest that the employees perceive their supervisors as having little influence over persons higher in the organization.

MAJOR FINDINGS:

Kohli examined several previously unstudied supervisory behaviors toward salespeople. **Upward-influencing supervisory behavior** was found to be positively related only to intrinsic instrumentalities.

COMMENTS:

Instead of "he" and "his," a more neutral descriptor such as "my supervisor" would make the items more generic and applicable to situations involving female supervisors.

REFERENCES:

Fulk, Janet and Eric R. Wendler (1982), "Dimensionality of Leader-Subordinate Interactions: A Path-Goal Investigation," *Organizational Behavior and Human Performance*, 30, 241-64.

Kohli, Ajay K. (1985), "Some Unexplored Supervisory Behaviors and Their Influence on Salespeople's Role Clarity, Specific Self-Esteem, Job Satisfaction, and Motivation," *JMR*, 22 (November), 424-433.

SCALE ITEMS: UPWARD-INFLUENCING SUPERVISORY BEHAVIOR

```
Very                                                          Very
False                                                         True
    1————————2————————3————————4————————5————————6————————7
```

1. He gets along well with people above him.
2. His superiors act favorably on most of his suggestions.
3. His word carries weight with his superiors.
4. He gets what he asks from his superiors.
5. He maintains cordial relations with his superiors.

SCALE NAME: Work Controls (Output)

SCALE DESCRIPTION:

A five-item, five-point Likert-like summated ratings scale measuring the frequency in which an employee perceives that he/she is given work goals, performance is assessed, feedback is provided, and rewards are affected. The emphasis in this measure is on evaluating the output of the work rather than the procedures used to produce the results.

SCALE ORIGIN:

The scale was apparently developed by Jaworski and MacInnis (1989). The scale and other aspects of the survey instrument were refined through a series of interviews and a pretest of marketing managers.

SAMPLES:

A national sample of marketing managers was drawn randomly from the American Marketing Association's list of members. Of the 479 managers who appear to have received questionnaires, **379** returned usable forms.

RELIABILITY:

An alpha of **.88** was reported for the scale.

VALIDITY:

The validity of the scale was not specifically examined.

ADMINISTRATION:

The scale was self-administered along with many other measures in a mail survey format. Higher scores on the scale indicate that employees strongly believe their performance is monitored and their rewards are affected whereas lower scores suggest that they think goals are not set for their work and performance does not affect rewards.

MAJOR FINDINGS:

Among the many purposes of the study by Jaworski and MacInnis was to examine the simultaneous use of several types of managerial controls in the context of marketing management. Using structural equations, the authors found that performance documentation had a significant positive impact on **output controls,** which in turn had a significant negative effect on a subordinate's greater knowledge of a job (relative to superiors).

REFERENCE:

Jaworski, Bernard J. and Deborah J. MacInnis (1989), "Marketing Jobs and Management Controls: Toward a Framework," *JMR*, 26 (November), 406-419.

SCALE ITEMS: WORK CONTROLS (OUTPUT)

Never   Always
5————————————4————————————3————————————2————————————1

1. Specific performance goals are established for my job.
2. My immediate boss monitors the extent to which I attain my performance goals.
3. If my performance goals were not met, I would be required to explain why.
4. I receive feedback from my immediate superior concerning the extent to which I achieve my goals.
5. My pay increases are based upon how my performance compares with my goals.

SCALE NAME: Work Controls (Procedures)

SCALE DESCRIPTION:

A six-item, six-point Likert-type summated ratings scale measuring the degree to which an employee perceives that the procedures used to accomplish his/her assigned work are assessed periodically and violations may be penalized. The emphasis in this measure is on the procedures used to do the work rather than the results of the work.

SCALE ORIGIN:

The scale is very similar to one developed by John (1984).

SAMPLES:

Using a systematic sample, Ferrell and Skinner (1988) mailed questionnaires to 1500 people who were listed as members of the Marketing Research Association or were categorized as researchers in the American Marketing Association. Ultimately, **550** completed forms were received. Thirty percent of the respondents were data subcontractors, 45% were employees of research firms, and the rest worked in corporate research departments. Similar proportions of men and women responded for the last two groups whereas the first group was mostly female (86%).

RELIABILITY:

An alpha of **.72** was reported for the scale by Ferrell and Skinner.

VALIDITY:

Though assessment of scale validity was not the purpose of the study, Ferrell and Skinner did perform a confirmatory factor analysis. The results of a t-test showed all items in the scale to be significant indicators. The factor loadings ranged from .34 to .81.

ADMINISTRATION:

The scale was self-administered by respondents along with other measures in a mail survey format. Lower scores on the scale indicate that employees report their companies inspect their work for procedural violations whereas higher scores suggest that their organizations do not assess work procedures very closely.

MAJOR FINDINGS:

The purpose of the study by Ferrell and Skinner was to investigate the association between organizational structure and ethical behavior in firms involved with marketing research activity. **Work controls** had a no significant relationship with the ethical behavior reported by employees of any of the three different research-related organizations studied.

COMMENTS:

Item 4 below could be easily modified to make it appropriate for firms in other industries. See also the apparently similar scale used by John.

REFERENCES:

Ferrell, O. C. and Steven J. Skinner (1988), ''Ethical Behavior and Bureaucratic Structure in Marketing Research Organizations,'' *JMR*, 25 (February), 103-109.
John, George (1984), ''An Empirical Investigation of Some Antecedents of Opportunism in a Marketing Channel,'' *JMR*, 21 (August), 278-289.

SCALE ITEMS: WORK CONTROLS (PROCEDURES)

Definitely Agree   ____ : ____ : ____ : ____ : ____ : ____   Definitely Disagree
                  1   2   3   4   5   6

1. There are strong penalties for violating my company's procedures.
2. Even if I am found in violation of some procedure, my company rarely imposes penalties. **(r)**
3. Generally, my company is only concerned with results and not how I actually do my work or spend my time and effort. **(r)**
4. I feel that I am watched to be sure that I follow all the rules of doing research for this company.
5. My company's reps inspect my work closely to be sure that it satisfies their standards.
6. I feel this company's reps are always checking me for violations of their procedures.

SCALE NAME: Work Controls (Process)

SCALE DESCRIPTION:

A four-item, five-point Likert-like summated ratings scale measuring the frequency with which an employee perceives that the procedures used to accomplish his/her assigned work are assessed by an immediate supervisor. The emphasis in this measure is on the process used to produce the work rather than the results of the work.

SCALE ORIGIN:

The scale was apparently developed by Jaworski and MacInnis (1989). The scale and other aspects of the survey instrument were refined through a series of interviews and a pretest of marketing managers.

SAMPLES:

A national sample of marketing managers was drawn randomly from the American Marketing Association's list of members. Of the 479 managers who appear to have received questionnaires, **379** returned usable forms.

RELIABILITY:

An alpha of **.82** was reported for the scale.

VALIDITY:

The validity of the scale was not specifically examined.

ADMINISTRATION:

The scale was self-administered along with many other measures in a mail survey format. Higher scores on the scale indicate that employees strongly believe the procedures they use are monitored whereas lower scores suggest that they think their immediate bosses do not closely watch how tasks are accomplished.

MAJOR FINDINGS:

Among the many purposes of the study by Jaworski and MacInnis was to examine the simultaneous use of several types of managerial controls in the context of marketing management. Using structural equations, the authors found that procedural knowledge had a significant positive impact on **process control,** which in turn had a significant negative effect on a subordinate's greater knowledge of a job (relative to superiors).

REFERENCE:

Jaworski, Bernard J. and Deborah J. MacInnis (1989), "Marketing Jobs and Management Controls: Toward a Framework," *JMR*, 26 (November), 406-419.

SCALE ITEMS: WORK CONTROLS (PROCESS)

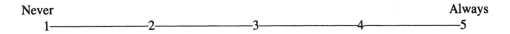

Never   Always
1————————2————————3————————4————————5

1. My immediate boss monitors the extent to which I follow established procedures.
2. My immediate boss evaluates the procedures I use to accomplish a given task.
3. My immediate boss modifies my procedures when desired results are not obtained.
4. I receive feedback on *how* I accomplish my performance goals.

SCALE NAME: Work Controls (Professional)

SCALE DESCRIPTION:

A five-item, five-point Likert-type summated ratings scale measuring the degree to which an employee reports that the division he/she works for encourages interaction and cooperation among marketing professionals on their work activities. The scale focuses on the professional colleagues' positive influence on performance rather than the negative effect they may also have.

SCALE ORIGIN:

The scale was apparently developed by Jaworski and MacInnis (1989). The scale and other aspects of the survey instrument were refined through a series of interviews and a pretest of marketing managers.

SAMPLES:

A national sample of marketing managers was drawn randomly from the American Marketing Association's list of members. Of the 479 managers who appear to have received questionnaires, **379** returned usable forms.

RELIABILITY:

An alpha of **.89** was reported for the scale.

VALIDITY:

The validity of the scale was not specifically examined.

ADMINISTRATION:

The scale was self-administered along with many other measures in a mail survey format. Higher scores on the scale indicate that employees strongly believe the divisions they work for encourage cooperation among marketing professionals in their work whereas lower scores suggest that employees are discouraged from interacting with peers in their divisions.

MAJOR FINDINGS:

Among the many purposes of the study by Jaworski and MacInnis was to examine the simultaneous use of several types of managerial controls in the context of marketing management. Using structural equations, they found that performance control had a significant positive impact on the use of **professional work controls**.

REFERENCE:

Jaworski, Bernard J. and Deborah J. MacInnis (1989), ''Marketing Jobs and Management Controls: Toward a Framework,'' *JMR*, 26 (November), 406-419.

SCALE ITEMS: WORK CONTROLS (PROFESSIONAL)

Strongly Disagree	Disagree	Neutral	Agree	Strongly Agree
1	2	3	4	5

1. The division encourages cooperation between marketing professionals.
2. Most of the marketing professionals in my division are familiar with each other's productivity.
3. The division fosters an environment where marketing professionals respect each other's work.
4. The division encourages job-related discussions between marketing professionals.
5. Most marketing professionals in my division are able to provide accurate appraisals of each other's work.

SCALE NAME: Work Controls (Self)

SCALE DESCRIPTION:

> A three-item, five-point Likert-type summated ratings scale measuring the degree to which an employee reports a commitment to his/her work and a willingness to take responsibility for his/her performance.

SCALE ORIGIN:

> The scale was apparently developed by Jaworski and MacInnis (1989). The scale and other aspects of the survey instrument were refined through a series of interviews and a pretest of marketing managers.

SAMPLES:

> A national sample of marketing managers was drawn randomly from the American Marketing Association's list of members. Of the 479 managers who appear to have received questionnaires, **379** returned usable forms.

RELIABILITY:

> An alpha of **.60** was reported for the scale.

VALIDITY:

> The validity of the scale was not specifically examined.

ADMINISTRATION:

> The scale was self-administered along with many other measures in a mail survey format. Higher scores on the scale indicate that employees are strongly committed to their work whereas lower scores suggest that they have a low amount of interest in their work and do not want to take responsibility for their performance.

MAJOR FINDINGS:

> Among the many purposes of the study by Jaworski and MacInnis was to examine the simultaneous use of several types of managerial controls in the context of marketing management. Using structural equations, the authors found that performance documentation had a significant positive impact on the use of **work-related self-control**, which in turn had a significant negative effect on employee dysfunctional behavior.

COMMENTS:

> Some effort should be made to add a few more items to the scale and increase its reliability, and also to discriminate scores on the scale from those on job satisfaction scales. On the face of it, the present scale has more to do with job satisfaction than to taking responsibility for work effort and results.

REFERENCE:

Jaworski, Bernard J. and Deborah J. MacInnis (1989), ''Marketing Jobs and Management Controls: Toward a Framework,'' *JMR*, 26 (November), 406-419.

SCALE ITEMS: WORK CONTROLS (SELF)

Strongly Disagree	Disagree	Neutral	Agree	Strongly Agree
1—————————	————2————	———3————	————4————	———5

1. The major satisfactions in my life come from my job.
2. The work I do on this job is very meaningful to me.
3. I feel that I should take credit or blame for the results of my work.

SCALE NAME: Work Effort

SCALE DESCRIPTION:

A four-item, seven-point Likert-like summated ratings scale measuring how often an employee expends effort to increase the quantity and/or quality of work performed.

SCALE ORIGIN:

The items for the scale were adapted from work by Ivancevich and McMahon (1977), who used two items to measure effort toward quantity and two items to measure effort toward quality. Hart, Moncrief, and Parasuraman (1989) combined and modified these statements to make one measure of work effort. The results of the Ivancevich and McMahon study indicated that effort toward quantity was related only to feedback from superiors and effort toward quality was related to feedback as well as goal acceptance.

SAMPLES:

Hart and her coauthors mailed questionnaires to 149 salespeople who worked for 25 independent brokers representing a major food producer. After two followup mailings, usable responses were received from **84** sales representatives.

RELIABILITY:

An alpha of **.80** was reported for the scale by Hart and her coauthors.

VALIDITY:

No specific examination of validity was conducted.

ADMINISTRATION:

The scale was self-administered by respondents in the form of a mail survey questionnaire. Higher scores on the scale indicate that employees expend much effort to produce high quantity and quality of work whereas lower scores suggest that they are not concerned about working hard at their jobs.

MAJOR FINDINGS:

The purpose of the study by Hart and her coauthors was to investigate goal theory as it relates to sales contests. The results provided evidence that goal acceptance and difficulty were very much related to **work effort**.

REFERENCES:

Hart, Sandra Hile, William C. Moncrief, and A. Parasuraman (1989), "An Empirical Investigation of Salespeople's Performance, Effort and Selling Method During a Sales Contest," *JAMS*, 17 (Winter), 29-39.

Ivancevich, John M. and J. Timothy McMahon (1977), "A Study of Task-Goal Attributes,

Higher Order Need Strength, and Performance," *Academy of Management Journal*, 20 (December), 552-563.

SCALE ITEMS: WORK EFFORT

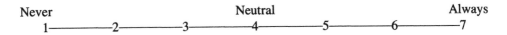

Never   Neutral   Always
1————2————3————4————5————6————7

1. How often do you work hard to do a lot of work?
2. How often do you increase your work pace?
3. How often do you perform the most professional job you are capable of performing?
4. How often do you make sure that your work is considered top quality by those who depend on you?

SCALE NAME: Work Evaluation Congruence

SCALE DESCRIPTION:

A two-item, seven-point Likert-type scale assessing the degree to which a salesperson reports being in agreement with work evaluations by superiors.

SCALE ORIGIN:

The items for the scale were slightly modified from those developed by Feldman (1976). His study was based on data from **118** hospital employees. Scale scores were not only calculated on responses to questionnaire items, but also included a rating based on interviews with each subject. The Spearman-Brown reliability coefficient (corrected for attenuation) was reported as **.743**. Work evaluation congruence had its strongest positive correlation with degree of control over the way work is carried out by persons in the unit.

SAMPLES:

Dubinsky et al. (1986) collected data from **189** salespeople. Letters were sent to a national sample of 2000 senior-level executives asking them to have their least experienced salesperson complete the questionnaire. The respondents represented 189 different companies that marketed 50 different product categories. The sample had a median age of 30.5 years, had spent 1.4 years (median) in their present positions, and were mostly male (86%).

RELIABILITY:

A LISREL estimate of reliability was **.63** (Dubinsky et al. 1986).

VALIDITY:

No examination of scale validity was reported.

ADMINISTRATION:

The scale was self-administered by respondents along with many other measures in a mail survey format. Higher scores on the scale indicate that respondents strongly agree with evaluations made about their performance by superiors whereas lower scores suggest that they believe there is a low congruence between what they have done and what the evaluations have indicated.

MAJOR FINDINGS:

Dubinsky and his coauthors examined a model of salesforce assimilation. Among many other salient results, job suitability was found to have a significant positive impact on **work evaluation congruence**.

REFERENCES:

Dubinsky, Alan J., Roy D. Howell, Thomas N. Ingram, and Danny Bellenger (1986), ''Salesforce Socialization,'' *JM*, 50 (October), 192-207.

Feldman, Daniel C. (1976), "A Contingency Theory of Socialization," *Administrative Science Quarterly*, 21 (September), 433-452.

SCALE ITEMS: JOB EVALUATION CONGRUENCE

Strongly Disagree	Disagree	Slightly Disagree	Neutral	Slightly Agree	Agree	Strongly Agree
1	2	3	4	5	6	7

1. People around here rarely tell you how good they think your work is. **(r)**
2. I think I may be doing better in my job than my supervisors give me credit for. **(r)**

Reading List For
Scale Development and Use
. . . .

Anderson, James C. and David W. Gerbing (1988), "Structural Equation Modeling in Practice: A Review and Recommended Two-Step Approach," *Psychological Bulletin*, 103 (3), 411-423.

Bagozzi, Richard P. and Youjae Yi (1991), "Multitrait-Multimethod Matrices in Consumer Research," *JCR*, 17 (March), 426-439.

Campbell, Donald T. and Donald W. Fiske (1959), "Convergent Validity and Discriminant Validity by the Multitrait-Multimethod Matrix," *Psychological Bulletin*, 56 (March), 81-105.

Carmines, Edward G. and Richard A. Zeller (1979), *Reliability and Validity Assessment.* Newbury Park, Calif.: Sage Publications, Inc.

Churchill, Gilbert A., Jr. (1979), "A Paradign for Developing Better Measures of Marketing Constructs," *JMR*, 16 (February), 64-73.

_____ (1992), "Better Measurement Practices are Critical to Better Understanding of Sales Management Issues," *Journal of Personal Selling & Sales Management*, 12 (Spring), 73-80.

_____ and J. Paul Peter (1984), "Research Design Effects on the Reliabiity of Rating Scales: A Meta-Analysis," *JMR*, 21 (November), 360-375.

Cox, Eli P., III (1980), "The Optimal Number of Response Alternatives for a Scale: A Review," *JMR*, 17 (November), 407-422.

Cronbach, Lee J. (1951), "Coefficient Alpha and the Internal Structure of Tests," *Psychometrika*, 16 (September), 297-334.

Crowne, Douglas P. and David Marlowe (1960), "A New Scale of Social Desirability Independent of Psychopathology," *Journal of Consulting Psychology*, 24 (August), 349-354.

DeVellis, Robert F. (1991), *Scale Development: Theory and Applications.* Newbury Park, Calif.: Sage Publications, Inc.

Didow, Nicholas M., Jr., Kevin Lane Keller, Hiram C. Barksdale, Jr., and George R. Franke (1985), "Improving Measure Quality by Alternating Least Squares Optimal Scaling," *JMR*, 22 (February), 30-40.

Edris, Thabet A. and A. Meidan (1990), "On the Reliability of Psychographic Research: Encouraging Signs for Measurement Accuracy and Methodology in Consumer Research," *European Journal of Marketing*, 24 (3), 23-41.

Gerbing, David W. and James C. Anderson (1988), "An Updated Paradigm for Scale Development Incorporating Unidimensionality and Its Assessment," *JMR*, 25 (May), 186-192.

Givon, Moshe M. and Zur Shapira (1984), "Response to Rating Scales: A Theoretical Model and Its Application to the Number of Categories Problem," *JMR*, 21 (November), 410-419.

Heeler, Roger M. and Michael L. Ray (1972), "Measure Validation in Marketing," *JMR*, 9 (November), 361-370.

Hensel, Paul J. and Gordon C. Bruner II (1992), "Multi-Item Scaled Measures in Sales-Related Research," *Journal of Personal Selling & Sales Management*, 12 (Summer), 77-82.

Jacoby, Jacob (1978), "Consumer Research: A State of the Art Review," *JM*, 42 (April), 87-96.

John, George and Deborah L. Roedder (1981), "Reliability Assessment: Coeficients Alpha and Beta," *AMA Educators' Proceedings*, 354-357.

Nunnally, Jum C. (1979), *Psychometric Theory*. New York, N.Y.: McGraw-Hill Publications.

Peter, J. Paul (1979), "Reliability: A Review of Psychometric Basics and Recent Marketing Practices," *JMR*, 16 (February), 6-17.

_____ (1981), "Construct Validity: A Review of Basic Issues and Marketing Practices," *JMR*, 18 (May), 133-145.

_____ and Gilbert A. Churchill, Jr. (1986), "Relationships Among Research Design Choices and Psychometric Properties of Rating Scales: A Meta-Analysis," *JMR*, 23 (February), 1-10.

Revelle, William (1979), "Hierarchial Cluster Analysis and the Internal Structure of Tests," *Multivariate Behavioral Research*, 14 (January), 57-74.

Singh, Jagdip, Roy D. Howell, and Gary K. Rhoads (1990), "Adaptive Designs for Likert-Type Data: An Approach for Implementing Marketing Surveys," *JMR*, 27 (August), 304-321.

Spector, Paul E. (1992), *Summated Ratings Scale Construction*. Newbury Park, Calif.: Sage Publications, Inc.

Strahan, Robert and Kathleen C. Gerbasi (1972), "Short, Homogeneous Versions of the Marlowe-Crowne Social Desirability Scale," *Journal of Clinical Psychology*, 28 (April), 191-193.

AUTHOR INDEX

· ·

The numbers following the author name refer to the *scale number* located at the top of each page.

Note: Alphabetically listed by first author for multiple authored references.

SUBJECT INDEX

• •

The numbers following the key word refer to the *scale number* located at the top of each page.